The Cambridge Handbook of Computing Education Research

This handbook describes the extent and shape of computing education research today. Over 50 leading researchers from academia and industry (including Google and Microsoft) have contributed chapters that together define and expand the evidence base.

The foundational chapters set the field in context, articulate expertise from key disciplines, and form a practical guide for new researchers. They address what can be learned empirically, methodologically, and theoretically from each area. The topic chapters explore issues that are of current interest, why they matter, and what is already known. They include discussion of motivational context, implications for practice, and open questions that might suggest avenues of future research.

The authors provide an authoritative introduction to the field that is essential reading for policy makers, as well as both new and established researchers.

SALLY A. FINCHER is Professor of Computing Education in the School of Computing at the University of Kent, UK, where she leads the Computing Education Research Group. She is also an Association for Computing Machinery Distinguished Scientist, a UK National Teaching Fellow, a Senior Fellow of the UK Higher Education Academy, and a Fellow of the Royal Society of Arts.

ANTHONY V. ROBINS is Professor of Computer Science at the University of Otago, New Zealand. He is also Associate Journal Editor of *Computer Science Education* and has co-organized multinational research studies. He has worked for the Ministry of Education, New Zealand, on new programming assessment standards and related instructional materials for secondary schools.

The Cambridge Handbook of Computing Education Research

Edited by

Sally A. Fincher
University of Kent

Anthony V. Robins
University of Otago

CAMBRIDGE
UNIVERSITY PRESS

CAMBRIDGE
UNIVERSITY PRESS

University Printing House, Cambridge CB2 8BS, United Kingdom

One Liberty Plaza, 20th Floor, New York, NY 10006, USA

477 Williamstown Road, Port Melbourne, VIC 3207, Australia

314-321, 3rd Floor, Plot 3, Splendor Forum, Jasola District Centre, New Delhi - 110025, India

79 Anson Road, #06-04/06, Singapore 079906

Cambridge University Press is part of the University of Cambridge.

It furthers the University's mission by disseminating knowledge in the pursuit of education, learning and research at the highest international levels of excellence.

www.cambridge.org
Information on this title: www.cambridge.org/9781108496735
DOI: 10.1017/ 9781108654555

© Cambridge University Press 2019

First published 2019

A catalogue record for this publication is available from the British Library

Library of Congress Cataloging in Publication data
Names: Fincher, Sally, 1959– editor. | Robins, Anthony (Anthony V.) editor.
Title: The Cambridge handbook of computing education research /
edited by Sally A. Fincher, University of Kent, Anthony V. Robins,
University of Otago.
Other titles: Handbook of computing education research
Description: New York, NY: Cambridge University Press, 2019. |
Includes bibliographical references and index.
Identifiers: LCCN 2018039947 | ISBN 9781108496735 (hardback) |
ISBN 9781108721899 (paperback)
Subjects: LCSH: Computer science – Study and teaching – Handbooks, manuals, etc.
Classification: LCC QA76.27.C355 2019 | DDC 004.071–dc23
LC record available at https://lccn.loc.gov/2018039947

ISBN 978-1-108-49673-5 Hardback
ISBN 978-1-108-72189-9 Paperback

To our parents, present and passed. A hardy generation – they should build battleships out of them.

Contents

List of Figures   *page* x
List of Tables   xii
List of Contributors   xiii
Acknowledgments   xv

0 An Important and Timely Field   1
   SALLY A. FINCHER AND ANTHONY V. ROBINS

   Part I Background   9

1 The History of Computing Education Research   11
   MARK GUZDIAL AND BENEDICT DU BOULAY

2 Computing Education Research Today   40
   SALLY A. FINCHER, JOSH TENENBERG, BRIAN DORN,
   CHRISTOPHER HUNDHAUSEN, ROBERT MCCARTNEY,
   AND LAURIE MURPHY

3 Computing Education: Literature Review and
   Voices from the Field   56
   PAULO BLIKSTEIN AND SEPI HEJAZI MOGHADAM

   Part II Foundations   79

4 A Study Design Process   81
   ANDREW J. KO AND SALLY A. FINCHER

5 Descriptive Statistics   102
   PATRICIA HADEN

6 Inferential Statistics   133
   PATRICIA HADEN

7 Qualitative Methods for Computing Education   173
   JOSH TENENBERG

8 Learning Sciences for Computing Education   208
   LAUREN E. MARGULIEUX, BRIAN DORN, AND KRISTIN A. SEARLE

9   Cognitive Sciences for Computing Education   231
    ANTHONY V. ROBINS, LAUREN E. MARGULIEUX,
    AND BRIANA B. MORRISON

10 Higher Education Pedagogy   276
    KERRY SHEPHARD

11 Engineering Education Research   292
    MICHAEL C. LOUI AND MAURA BORREGO

    Part III   Topics   323

    Systemic Issues   325

12 Novice Programmers and Introductory Programming   327
    ANTHONY V. ROBINS

13 Programming Paradigms and Beyond   377
    SHRIRAM KRISHNAMURTHI AND KATHI FISLER

14 Assessment and Plagiarism   414
    THOMAS LANCASTER, ANTHONY V. ROBINS,
    AND SALLY A. FINCHER

15 Pedagogic Approaches   445
    KATRINA FALKNER AND JUDY SHEARD

16 Equity and Diversity   481
    COLLEEN M. LEWIS, NIRAL SHAH, AND KATRINA FALKNER

    New Milieux   511

17 Computational Thinking   513
    PAUL CURZON, TIM BELL, JANE WAITE, AND MARK DORLING

18 Schools (K–12)   547
    JAN VAHRENHOLD, QUINTIN CUTTS, AND KATRINA FALKNER

19 Computing for Other Disciplines   584
    MARK GUZDIAL

20 New Programming Paradigms   606
    R. BENJAMIN SHAPIRO AND MIKE TISSENBAUM

    Systems Software and Technology   637

21 Tools and Environments   639
    LAURI MALMI, IAN UTTING, AND ANDREW J. KO

22 Tangible Computing   663
    MICHAEL HORN AND MARINA BERS

23 Leveraging the Integrated Development Environment
    for Learning Analytics   679
    ADAM CARTER, CHRISTOPHER HUNDHAUSEN, AND DANIEL OLIVARES

    Teacher and Student Knowledge   707

24 Teacher Knowledge for Inclusive Computing Learning   709
    JOANNA GOODE AND JEAN J. RYOO

25 Teacher Learning and Professional Development   727
    SALLY A. FINCHER, YIFAT BEN-DAVID KOLIKANT,
    AND KATRINA FALKNER

26 Learning Outside the Classroom   749
    ANDREW BEGEL AND ANDREW J. KO

27 Student Knowledge and Misconceptions   773
    COLLEEN M. LEWIS, MICHAEL J. CLANCY, AND JAN VAHRENHOLD

28 Motivation, Attitudes, and Dispositions   801
    ALEX LISHINSKI AND AMAN YADAV

29 Students As Teachers and Communicators   827
    BETH SIMON, CHRISTOPHER HUNDHAUSEN, CHARLIE MCDOWELL,
    LINDA WERNER, HELEN HU, AND CLIF KUSSMAUL

    Case Studies   859

30 A Case Study of Peer Instruction: From University
    of California, San Diego to the Computer
    Science Community   861
    LEO PORTER AND BETH SIMON

31 A Case Study of Qualitative Methods   875
    COLLEEN M. LEWIS

    Index   895

Figures

4.1	A study design process spanning four iterative phases that come before executing a study	*page* 82
5.1	PI, OD, and DV	105
5.2	Generic FD	108
5.3	Comparing FDs	108
5.4	FDs with positive and negative skew	110
5.5	Positive skew in time to solve a homework problem	111
5.6	Bimodal FD	111
5.7	Factorial plot	112
5.8	Histogram-style factorial plot	113
5.9	Small, medium, and large standard deviations	116
5.10	Comparing scores from different distributions	117
5.11	Hypothetical scatter plots for height and weight, age and visual acuity, and height and IQ	120
5.12	Strong and weak positive correlations	120
5.13	Scatter plots of data sets	122
5.14	The influence of outliers on r	124
5.15	Possible experimental design	127
6.1	Population frequency distributions showing no effect and a real effect of the independent variable	137
6.2	The hypothesis testing decision matrix	142
6.3	Distribution of values of t for a given sample size and population variability when H_0 is true	148
6.4	Crossover interaction	152
6.5	Moderate interaction	152
6.6	No interaction	153
6.7	Generic one-way ANOVA table in SPSS 24	154
6.8	Factorial plot for computing interest study (hypothetical)	155
6.9	SPSS 24 output for two-way ANOVA	156
6.10	CI for a population mean	157
6.11	SPSS 24 output for a significant Pearson product moment correlation	160
6.12	Salary by years employed (hypothetical)	161
6.13	Outcome of a regression study predicting CS1 mark from math mark (hypothetical)	163
6.14	Linear regression (hypothetical data) with line of best fit in Excel	164

6.15	Output of linear regression analysis in SPSS 24	165
6.16	A poor predictor	165
6.17	Line of best fit for a poor predictor	166
6.18	Linear regression analysis for a poor predictor in SPSS 24	166
9.1	Levels of analysis and their application to an example system	233
15.1	The combination of student-centered learning activity and teacher-centered instruction as adopted within blended learning	457
15.2	Memory visualization exploring primitive data types and the correspondence between variable name and value	466
15.3	Memory visualization of a C++ program facilitating understanding of memory addressing, allocation, and deallocation	467
17.1	Agreement and disagreement around two views of what computational thinking should be	515
20.1	A neural network with hidden layers	611
20.2	FitBit for dogs	621
20.3	Dog collar beacon program	626
22.1	A prototype tangible programming language based on computer vision technology	669
22.2	KIBO robot and its blocks	669
23.1	Process model for IDE-based learning analytics in computing education	685
23.2	Programming process data that can be automatically collected through a standard IDE	688
23.3	Data that can be automatically collected through an IDE augmented with additional features and functionality	689
23.4	Taxonomy of design dimensions for IDE-based interventions	696
24.1	Teacher knowledge	713
29.1	Reduction in course fail rates by course	838
29.2	Reduction in course fail rates for instructors teaching the same course with and without PI	839
29.3	Two locations of isomorphic, multiple-choice questions to test learning gain (q2) and retention (q3)	840
31.1	Completed drawing of a brick wall in Scratch	881

Tables

0.1	Frequently discussed topics and the chapters they occur in	*page* 7
5.1	Strength of positive correlations (apply symmetrically for negative correlations)	123
7.1	Data collection methods	184
7.2	Data analysis strategies	194
12.1	A programming framework	335
15.1	Pedagogic approaches and relevant pedagogic practices	450
23.1	Comparison of five IDEs used in computing education based on the data they collect for the programming category	691
23.2	Comparison of five IDEs used in computing education based on the data they collect for the social, testing, survey/quiz, and physiological categories	692
23.3	A taxonomy of useful information derivable from IDE data	693
25.1	Knowledge in the TPACK model	734
27.1	Truth table for modus ponens, $P \rightarrow Q$	782
27.2	Overlap between logical operators AND, if-then, and if-and-only-if	784
29.1	Key findings of a study of PCRs	845

Contributors

ANDREW BEGEL, Microsoft, USA

TIM BELL, University of Canterbury, New Zealand

MARINA BERS, Tufts University, USA

PAULO BLIKSTEIN, Stanford University, USA

MAURA BORREGO, University of Texas, USA

ADAM CARTER, Humboldt State University, USA

MICHAEL J. CLANCY, University of California Berkeley, USA

PAUL CURZON, Queen Mary University of London, UK

QUINTIN CUTTS, University of Glasgow, UK

MARK DORLING, Queen Mary University of London, UK

BRIAN DORN, University of Nebraska at Omaha, USA

BENEDICT DU BOULAY, University of Sussex, UK

KATRINA FALKNER, University of Adelaide, Australia

SALLY A. FINCHER, University of Kent, UK

KATHI FISLER, Brown University, USA

JOANNA GOODE, University of Oregon, USA

MARK GUZDIAL, Georgia Institute of Technology, USA

PATRICIA HADEN, University of Otago, New Zealand

MICHAEL HORN, Northwestern University, USA

HELEN HU, Westminster College, USA

CHRISTOPHER HUNDHAUSEN, Washington State University, USA

ANDREW J. KO, University of Washington, Seattle USA

YIFAT BEN-DAVID KOLIKANT, Hebrew University of Jerusalem, Israel

SHRIRAM KRISHNAMURTHI, Brown University, USA

CLIF KUSSMAUL, Muhlenberg College, USA

THOMAS LANCASTER, Imperial College London, UK

COLLEEN M. LEWIS, Harvey Mudd College, USA

ALEX LISHINSKI, Michigan State University, USA

MICHAEL C. LOUI, Purdue University, USA

LAURI MALMI, Aalto University, Finland

LAUREN E. MARGULIEUX, Georgia State University, USA

ROBERT MCCARTNEY, University of Connecticut, USA

CHARLIE MCDOWELL, University of California Santa Cruz, USA

SEPI HEJAZI MOGHADAM, Google, USA

BRIANA B. MORRISON, University of Nebraska at Omaha, USA

LAURIE MURPHY, Pacific Lutheran University, USA

DANIEL OLIVARES, Washington State University, USA

LEO PORTER, University of California San Diego, USA

ANTHONY V. ROBINS, University of Otago, New Zealand

JEAN J. RYOO, University of California Los Angeles, USA

KRISTIN A. SEARLE, Utah State University, USA

NIRAL SHAH, Michigan State University, USA

R. BENJAMIN SHAPIRO, University of Colorado, USA

JUDY SHEARD, Monash University, Australia

KERRY SHEPHARD, University of Otago, New Zealand

BETH SIMON, University of California San Diego, USA

JOSH TENENBERG, University of Washington Tacoma, USA

MIKE TISSENBAUM, University of Illinois at Urbana Champaign, USA

IAN UTTING, University of Kent, UK

JAN VAHRENHOLD, Westfälische Wilhelms-Universität Münster, Germany

JANE WAITE, Queen Mary University of London, UK

LINDA WERNER, University of California Santa Cruz, USA

AMAN YADAV, Michigan State University, USA

Acknowledgments

We would like to acknowledge and thank everyone listed as an author for their contributions to the open reviewing culture within which this book was written. Many of them also took part in the systematic reviewing process.

Other reviewers or advisors (who are not also authors) were Mordechai (Moti) Ben-Ari, Neil Brown, Paul Carins, Sebastian Dziallas, Christopher Hoadley, Yasmin Kafai, Raymond Lister, and Elizabeth Patitsas. Our thanks to them for taking the time to help us improve the work.

Shriram Krishnamurthi and Kathi Fisler at Brown University organized the reviewing of most chapters by students in a graduate computing education course. Thanks to those participants: Natasha Danas, Nicholas DeMarinis, Justin Pombrio, Sorawee Porncharoenwase, Sam Saarinen, Preston Tunnell Wilson, and John Wrenn. You helped a lot!

Thanks also to our editor David Repetto, content manager Adam Hooper, and editorial assistant Emily Watton at Cambridge University Press, and project manager Céline Durassier at Newgen Publishing UK, who provided us excellent support and allowed us the flexibility that we needed.

Finally, of course, we have to extend enormous thanks to our families for their patience and support.

0 An Important and Timely Field

Sally A. Fincher and Anthony V. Robins

Computing education (CEd) is important, everyone agrees. President Obama committed hundreds of millions of dollars to "Computer Science for All" (White House, 2016); governments have developed curricula and made computing a school subject across the world (see Chapter 18); online providers compete to teach coding (such as Code Academy, code.org, the Hour of Code, Khan Academy and Coursera); and tech giants put money into supporting CEd projects (CISCO supports the BlueJ and Scratch initial programming environments and Google funds substantial professional development programs and has produced a series of CEd research reports – one of which forms the basis for Chapter 3).

With all of the effort and resources going into CEd, it would be comforting to think that we know what we are doing – that the problems of teaching and learning computing topics are well understood, that the solutions are known, and that best practice is widely shared. But this ideal picture is very much a work in progress. We still don't know enough about how students learn computing subjects, what effects different teaching approaches have, or how to equally engage people of all races and genders in the field. CEd research (CEdR) is how we work to understand and improve this. In order to make the most of the resources currently going into CEd efforts around the world, CEdR is an important and timely field.

0.1 Why It's Important

The sudden interest and investment in CEd are no accidents. Computing technology is reshaping the world around us at an ever-increasing pace, changing the way that we work (or don't work), communicate, consume, learn, create, entertain ourselves, and more. At the time of writing, some of the major computing-driven issues being widely debated include: the rise of artificial intelligence applications (automation of work, digital assistants, self-driving vehicles); the use and abuse of social media and personal data; and the advent of disruptive cryptocurrencies.

In this context, there are many rationales as to why CEd and therefore CEdR are important. Blikstein and Moghadam (Chapter 3 of this handbook, summarizing their Google report into the current state of CEd) outline four of them. *The labor market rationale*: computing skills are explicitly required for an increasingly large number of jobs and will be generally useful for very many more. *The computational thinking rationale*: computational ways of thinking (e.g., algorithms, heuristics, problem-solving skills) are all useful and transferable. In practical terms, the belief that they are good preparation for later specialist topics (e.g., learning to program) has helped to drive the widespread introduction of computational thinking in schools (these and related issues are focuses of Chapters 17–20). *The computational literacy rationale*: general familiarity with programming and other computing skills is sometimes equated with mathematical or textual literacy (Chapters 18 and 19). Some further argue that computational literacy goes beyond computational thinking to enable new types of mental operations, knowledge representations, and modes of expression (see Chapter 3). *The equity of participation rationale*: computing knowledge will be increasingly required for the best jobs, for civic participation, and even for understanding the functioning of the society around us. As is readily apparent, current participation in CEd has a long way to go to achieve anything like equity of participation in terms of race or gender (see Chapters 16 and 24).

0.2 Why It's Timely

In 2004, when *Computer Science Education Research* (Fincher & Petre, 2004) was written, CEd researchers were essentially all academics teaching in university computer science departments. Almost universally they had strong disciplinary computing backgrounds and their loci of research were their interests, which meant (almost universally) tertiary-level CEd. In the intervening 15 years, times have changed. Researchers in schools of education are becoming interested in the field, there are many agencies funding research, and there are increasing numbers of specialist academics with PhDs in CEd. The locus of research has expanded to include adult "returners" and children in K–12 education (which adds the complexity of cognitive development to the mix). And the subject itself has expanded beyond its academic disciplinary construction in university computing departments, bursting through the classroom walls into everyday life and "computational thinking."

One of the ways in which these changes are reflected is in our decision, as editors, to use the inclusive phrases "computing" education (CEd) and "computing" education research (CEdR), which the reader will find in widespread use in this handbook, instead of the previously common "computer science" phrasing.

As interest in the subject explodes, and as teaching and learning of computing happen in ever more diverse ways in ever more diverse environments, so CEdR must keep pace. This handbook is a contribution to the widening discourse – in it, we capture what is already known, look out to what is known in other fields, and examine what we might be moving toward as computing technologies continue to evolve and our knowledge of CEd develops.

0.3 How This Book Is Organized

All of the chapters are new and have been written explicitly for this handbook (Chapters 3 and 23 draw on previous sources). However, we wanted this to be more than just a collection of writings from a collection of interesting authors. We solicited chapters in three **parts**. The purpose of the **Background** part is to briefly orient the reader within the field of CEdR, its history, and its current status. The substantive Foundations and Topics parts each have a specific purpose and a different set of shared **themes** running "vertically" through their chapters.

The **Foundations** part serves a "textbook" function. It is intended to set our field in context and to be a practical guide for new researchers. In 2005, the Association for Computing Machinery's Special Interest Group in Computer Science Education (SIGCSE) held a panel discussion on challenges to CEdR. Panelists commented on the "isolation" of our discipline, that "Too much of the research in computing education ignores the hundreds of years of education, cognitive science, and learning sciences research that have gone before us." They reflected on "the challenge of diversifying the research methods we employ" and on the need to understand our methods and seek rigor (Almstrum et al., 2005). Looking back on these challenges more than ten years later, although there has been progress, we think it is fair to say that every one of them remains relevant today. This handbook works to address those concerns, to provide an overview of CEdR work and methods, and to show how they fit with other intellectual traditions.

Some of the chapters in this part are broadly concerned with "methods," both quantitative and qualitative (Chapters 4–7). Although a reader might expect to find similar chapters – certainly similarly titled chapters – in many books, our authors have closely contextualized these within CEdR work. Note that there are two extensive chapters on statistical methods. In our opinion (frequently reinforced while reviewing in various contexts), the need for an improved level of statistical rigor is a particular priority within our field.

CEdR (like education research more broadly) borrows techniques (and terminology and methods) from other disciplines in a "trading zone" activity. The idea of an intellectual "trading zone" was first proposed by Peter Galison in his work on physics:

> I intend the term "trading zone" to be taken seriously, as a social, material, and intellectual mortar binding together the disunified traditions of experimenting, theorizing, and instrument building [in subcultures of physics]. Anthropologists are familiar with different cultures encountering one another through trade, even when the significance of the objects traded – and of the trade itself – may be utterly different for the two sides.
> (Galison, 1997)

It is one of the goals of this handbook to situate CEdR with related fields, our "intellectual trading partners," from whom we have much to learn, and to whom we have much to offer: Chapters 8–11 in the Foundations part seek to do just that. They each articulate expertise from key partner disciplines and explore their boundaries and our common edges. Over time, of course, the nature of the trading zones and their borders shift. These chapters focus on historical CEd trading zones where researchers trained as computer scientists encountered unfamiliar epistemologies and methods. As computing becomes a school subject and becomes an integrated part of other disciplines (such as bioinformatics), new and important trading partners will emerge.

The authors of chapters in the Foundations part were asked to addresses three particular themes: what can we learn **empirically**, **methodologically**, and **theoretically** from their distinctive, separate foundational fields. Themes are signaled in different ways in various chapters, sometimes as section headings, sometimes as bold keywords in relevant places in the text.

The **Topics** part contains chapters that explore the "state of the art." We have chosen topics that are of current and abiding interest in CEdR to illustrate the kinds of problems that we are trying to address and why they matter to us. Very often in this part, chapters draw on a considerable body of existing work, which should help orient new researchers. The themes of this part were **motivational context** (why we care about this issue), **implications for practice**, and **open questions**/suggestions for future research. Once again, these themes will be reflected in various ways in the chapters.

CEdR is essentially applied research, and there is no point in doing this kind of research if you are not interested in affecting practice and making CEd better in some way, perhaps more effective or more equitable. So "implications for practice" was chosen as a theme for this part, as a reminder both to researchers and practitioners that our work is meant to be useful.

The chapters in this part are grouped into four subsections. *Systematic Issues* (Chapters 12–16) are the "bread and butter" areas that continually offer questions and often attract the interest of new researchers. Chapters in the *New Milieux* section (Chapters 17–20) consider more recent issues that have arisen with the spread of computing beyond the "traditional" university setting, situated in a formal classroom within a department of computing. The *Systems and Software Technology* section (Chapters 21–23) recognizes a disciplinary advantage that CEd researchers have, in that we can build computational tools both in support of CEd and to provide new lenses for CEdR. The *Teacher and Student Knowledge* section (Chapters 26–29) investigates issues concerned with the production and acquisition of computing knowledge.

0.3.1 Case Studies

We conclude the Topics part with two case studies. They are written from a different viewpoint and serve a different purpose to other chapters. Chapter 30, *A Case Study of Peer Instruction*, covers the life cycle of an intervention, demonstrating how results from CEdR may be directly applied to practice. Chapter 31, *A Case Study of Qualitative Methods*, details the progress of a paper from inception to publication. This is an uncommon view, and a valuable one. Many CEd researchers come from computing backgrounds, with a grounding in analytic knowledge. Seeing how qualitative research "plays out" in a study, and in presentation, broadens understanding.

0.4 How This Book Was Written

Although talked about in a desultory fashion for a period of time, a definite point marked the genesis of this handbook. A fortuitous period of study leave following Dagsthul seminar 16072 (Assessing Learning in Introductory Computer Science) allowed the prospective editors to be in the same place for an extended time.

We met frequently over a period of weeks to write the proposal, mapping out an initial list of chapters and identifying a pool of possible contributors (many of whom we had already talked with at Dagsthul and other community venues, such as the annual International Computing Education Research conference). Once the proposal had been reviewed and accepted, we formally invited contributors, directing them to a Google document indexing the proposal, our provisional chapter list, and other relevant resources. Over the first few weeks, building on feedback from both reviewers and contributors, the chapter list was modified and extended, and prospective authors "voted" for the topics and chapters they were interested in contributing to. From this, a lead author was identified for each chapter and writing teams were organized. An initial deadline for chapter completion was set.

Every chapter was written as a Google document, viewable and editable by all contributors to the handbook. We established the convention that only the authors writing a particular chapter were expected to edit the main text, with other contributors suggesting changes, leaving marginal comments, or adding notes in preface pages specifically designated for that purpose. This totally open model was designed to encourage a high level of peer review and discussion, and in that it was moderately successful. Collectively, the contributors left 2,070 comments on their own and each other's chapters, and many more extended notes in the preface pages. Most chapters benefited significantly from this communal sharing of knowledge.

This was a high-trust model from the outset, and we were alert to a number of infringements that would be possible. We were worried that the model might risk authors making unauthorized changes to another person's text; that there might be public and unresolvable disputes between authors; that text might be "borrowed" and published elsewhere; and, in good open source style, that someone (or some group) might decide to disrupt the project. None of that happened.

There were minor abuses, which are common to all models of collective action (Ostrom, 1990). There was some *free-riding* (where contributors took their share of the benefits, but did not make an equal contribution) and some *rule-breaking* (authors not delivering on time, or at all; authors extending their authorial invitation to others), but these could have equally occurred in less trustful forms of engagement. A more significant issue – and not obvious to us at the outset – was that some chapters went in different (sometimes very different) directions from what we expected. This was sometimes a good thing, where our initial expectations were poorly informed, but occasionally led to more mixed outcomes.

Our initial deadline came and went (as deadlines will do) with many chapters incomplete. As experienced academics, we had anticipated and allowed for this, and so put the second deadline in place. During this period, we began a systematic review, where every chapter was read and commented on by a group made up of both the editors, other handbook contributors with relevant expertise, and, on occasion, additional subject experts. Each week, a review group met with chapter authors (as time zones allowed) via Skype to discuss reviewers' feedback.

In parallel, a second, independent, and rather unusual review process was taking place. Contributors Shriram Krishnamurthi and Kathi Fisler were teaching a graduate course in CEd at Brown University and suggested their class might read and review the chapters. As graduate students with an interest in the field, they represented one of the key intended audiences for the handbook; this was a great opportunity that we enthusiastically accepted. The class subsequently reviewed almost every chapter (a huge achievement!), and contributors benefited from the additional, external, targeted feedback resulting from this process. At the end of these review processes, authorial teams responded to feedback (some chapters changed markedly in this process) and finalized chapters.

0.5 Accessible Structure

As already mentioned, one of our goals for the Handbook was to present a well-organized body of work, where the structure is made evident and accessible to the reader. This goal drove the organization into parts, and the "vertical themes" running through Parts II and III. We also encouraged authors to make explicit cross-references to other chapters where applicable. This resulted in more than 120 internal references to other chapters to help the reader find related information all over the book (a result that would not have been possible without the open writing process).

As a final effort in this regard, Table 0.1 lists topics that receive substantial attention across several chapters. It is a mix of broad theoretical frameworks (constructivism, cognitivism, behaviorism) and topics specific to our field (learning to program, the notional machine, the McCracken study of novice programmers). We were surprised by some of the entries (Logo commands a lot of attention!). Many other topics are discussed, in varying levels of detail, in more than one chapter. We regard this overlap as a feature, not a bug – from the multiple perspectives of multiple authors, the reader should get a sense of the scope and richness of these topics.

Table 0.1 *Frequently discussed topics and the chapters they occur in.*

Topic	Chapters
Logo (Papert)	1, 3, 8, 17, 19, 20, 22, 27
Constructivism (Vygotsky, Bruner)	1, 8, 9, 10, 11, 15, 24, 29
Teaching methods	1, 8, 10, 12, 15, 24, 27
Learning to program	1, 3, 12, 13, 21, 27
The notional machine	1, 12, 13, 15, 21, 27
Cognitivism	1, 9, 10, 11, 15
Behaviorism	1, 9, 10, 11, 15
Assessment	10, 11, 14, 18, 21
Motivation/efficacy	3, 11, 17, 24, 28
McCracken study	1, 4, 12, 13, 14
Computational thinking	3, 17, 18, 20, 24
Equity/diversity	11, 15, 16, 24

0.6 Looking Back

Our process was "loosely specified." In retrospect, we might have made life easier for ourselves if we had implemented a more formal process. We could have asked authors to submit outlines and drafts of chapters for approval, or we could have asked more people to take on editorial oversight. Such measures would have likely made chapters more consistent and may have led to there being less overlap in some topic areas, with authors "carving up the territory" and claiming the right to reference certain topics exclusively.

What we gained through our process, however, is a collection of strong contributions, with every authorial team working on topics they cared deeply about. Our trade-off is a plurality of views on some topics and idiosyncratic presentation in some chapters.

It is unlikely that this is the first work that has been produced in such an open and collaborative fashion, but it is almost impossible to conceive of such a process being possible in earlier times without the infrastructure of the twenty-first century internet.

0.7 Looking Forward

The handbook is finished, but the work is not. Given the technological, social, and educational changes currently in progress, there is every reason to expect a new wave of interest and participation in CEdR. We hope that the handbook will serve as a useful resource for some time to come as instruction for the novice, a guide for the curious, and a companion for the experienced.

References

Almstrum, V. L., Hazzan, O., Guzdial, M., & Petre, M. (2005). Challenges to computer science education research. In *Proceedings of the 36th SIGCSE Technical Symposium on Computer Science Education* (pp. 191–192). New York: ACM.

Fincher, S., & Petre, M. (2004). *Computer Science Education Research*. London: RoutledgeFalmer.

Galison, P. (1997). *Image and Logic: A Material Culture of Microphysics*. Chicago, IL: University of Chicago Press.

Ostrom, E. (1990). *Governing the Commons: The Evolution of Institutions for Collective Action*. Cambridge: Cambridge University Press.

White House (2016). Computer Science for All. Retrieved from https://obamawhitehouse.archives.gov/blog/2016/01/30/computer-science-all

PART I

Background

1 The History of Computing Education Research

Mark Guzdial and Benedict du Boulay

1.1 The Scope of Computing Education Research

Teachers have been educating students about computing for many years. For almost as many years, computing education researchers have been studying, in particular, how students learn programming and how to improve that process. Programming languages such as Fortran (1957) and COBOL (1959) were originally invented to be easier than assembler and other early notations so that programming could be made available to a wider range of programmers. Programming languages such as BASIC (1964) and Pascal (1970) were invented explicitly to ease learning how to program. In the late 1960s, researchers started gathering data and studying how learners were learning programming, when they did not, and how they experienced programming.

We are limiting the scope of this chapter in three ways. The *content focus* of this chapter on the history of computing education research is very specifically on research into how students come to understand programming rather than other aspects of computing such as databases, networks, theory of computation, and so on. The *time focus* of this chapter is from the first efforts to observe students learning programming (1967) up to the first offering of the International Computing Education Research (ICER) Conference in 2005. We consider the "modern era" of computing education research to be post-2005.

Finally, we have filtered the historical events to focus on those that inform today's current work in computing education research. Computing education researchers have explored many paths over the last 50 years, and not all have been fruitful. We focus on the historical events that have the clearest connection to today's computing education research. As we review these events, we use three lenses:

- **Tools**: Educators in science, engineering, and mathematics may use computing technology, but computing education is necessarily tied to technology. Just as chemists cannot directly touch individual atoms and physicists cannot touch velocity, the bits and processes of programs cannot be directly sensed and manipulated by learners. Instead, we create tools that provide views on the program and its execution at different levels of granularity and from different viewpoints, so making computing more malleable. What tools do we use, what have we used, and how do we design tools to serve our educational needs?

- **Objectives**: Why are we teaching students about computing? The answer has varied over the previous five decades, from preparing future programmers, to influencing how learners view their world, to being a necessary part of general education like mathematics or history.
- **Research Methods**: How do we evaluate the effectiveness of computing education research or answer our questions about how students learn? The earliest researchers applied the empirical methods they knew, but as our tools, objectives, and strategies have changed, we have also changed our research methods. We have even invented methods unique to computing education research.

The 1970s saw the emergence of many of the tools, objectives, and research methods that underpinned work in later decades. Section 1.2 of this chapter looks at the computing education research conducted in the 1970s. It was an era when the programming technology available was fairly primitive, notably in terms of limited input and output devices. Section 1.3 explores the rapid developments in computing technology in the 1980s, particularly in interface capabilities, and how these affected computing education research.

Various claims had been made for the benefits of learning programming as a vehicle for developing various thinking skills, notably by Papert. While there had been some experimental work in the 1970s to test these claims, it was in the 1980s that educational researchers brought longitudinal research methods to bear on these issues. This was also the time when cognitive science research started to burgeon, and this had an effect on the way that programming was conceptualized via cognitive models of the processes of programming, such as debugging. Section 1.4 explores the impacts of these two disciplines on computing education research.

We then shift our focus in Section 1.5 to the organization of computing education research activity over these decades, and in Section 1.6 we draw the threads together in anticipation of the next chapter in this book, looking at the current state of computing education research.

Given the breadth of coverage in this Handbook, there is a certain amount of overlap between this chapter and others. In addition to the next chapter on computing education today and tomorrow, we draw the reader's attention particularly to Chapter 12 on introductory programming and Chapter 13 on programming paradigms. This latter chapter extends the discussion in this chapter on notional machines, on the problems faced by novices, and on programming paradigms that go beyond the procedural that is presented below. This chapter says a certain amount about teaching methods, but Chapters 10 and 15 extend the discussion much further. For a review of research on teaching methods for introductory programming, see Pears et al. (2007).

1.2 Early Studies in Computing Education Research

The late 1960s and early 1970s were already periods of dynamic activity in computing education research. There were two partially interacting streams of activity based on different objectives. The objective of the first stream was to understand the psychology around the activity of programming. The first stream was centered on the theoretical and empirical study of programming as a human skill, including issues of learning, as exemplified by the work of Green and his colleagues (see, for example, Sime, Arblaster, & Green, 1977b) and the publication of the first book on the psychology of computer programming (Weinberg, 1971). One driver of this stream was industry's need for programmers and their use of aptitude tests to identify them (see Chapter 12, Section 12.2.1). The second stream was centered more specifically on the learning of programming in educational settings as exemplified by the work of Papert and his colleagues (Papert, 1980) and the publication of the first paper on the Logo programming language (Feurzeig, Papert, Bloom, Grant, & Solomon, 1969). The objective of this second stream was to understand the cognitive benefits of programming to the student programmer.

1.2.1 Learning Programming in General

Weinberg's book on the psychology of computer programming was quite short on the empirical results of both learning of programming and exercising the skill of programming, but heralded an energetic decade of such work. Many of the research methods that survive into today's research emerged then, such as comparing novices and experts across different aspects of programming skill and analyzing the ease of use and ease of learning of different representations of code. A review of the early work on the empirical studies of programming can be found in du Boulay and O'Shea (1981). This section of the chapter draws heavily from that review, characterizing the kinds of empirical work that were undertaken at that time. Note that the research predated personal computers, mice, and much of the screen-based interaction we take for granted today. We return to this issue in Section 1.3 and show how the changes in hardware and software changed the focus of computing education research.

Two related areas of work were of special interest in this period: novices' difficulties with programming and language design for novices. Learning to program was already known to be difficult, so attempts were made to understand the specific nature of those difficulties as well as to explore how the design of programming languages and programming environments might mitigate those difficulties.

Novices' difficulties with programming were reported using observational research methods and small-scale laboratory-based studies of the skills and understanding of planning, coding, and debugging. Two kinds of planning difficulty emerged: one concerned with the translation of a problem expressed in everyday terms into a formulation suitable for coding; the other concerned the degree of generality with which a problem was tackled (i.e., the requirement that a program would normally have to work with a range of possible data values, rather than a specific set). For example, concerning the issue of translation, Miller (1974) studied how novices approached the problem of developing algorithms for simple sorting tasks and found that disjunctions of properties caused more problems than conjunctions. He also reported that novices found it hard to turn everyday qualification statements (such as "PUT RED THINGS IN BOX 1") into the kind of conditional format (such as "IF THING IS RED PUT IN BOX 1") required by many programming languages (Miller, 1975). Concerning generality, Hoc (1977) studied programmers developing an algorithm for a change-giving machine and found that beginners tended to deal with specific instances of the problem rather than the general case.

In terms of coding, several researchers analyzed the errors in novices' programs in various languages. For example, Youngs (1974) observed both novices and experts programming in a variety of languages (ALGOL, BASIC, COBOL, FORTRAN, PL/1). He categorized their errors into "syntactic," "semantic," "logical," or "clerical" and found that, for novices, semantic errors predominated, and that they found these the hardest to debug. By contrast, experts' errors were more evenly distributed across the categories. Gannon (1978) found that novices' errors were clustered around specific language constructs. When the overall relative frequency of use of different constructs was taken into account, Youngs (1974) and Friend (1975), working on AID, a language similar to BASIC, found that conditional constructs were a common cause of errors. Friend also found that many syntax errors arose from novices overgeneralizing the syntactic rules of the language.

There were several studies of debugging, mostly among experts, but some among novices (Gould & Drongowski, 1974; Miller, 1974; Youngs, 1974). One conclusion that has stood the test of time is that there was great variability even among experts in terms of their debugging skill and speed (Gould, 1975). Eason (1976) found that novices' attitude to learning programming affected the degree to which they were willing to engage in the hard task of learning debugging, as well as the mastery of the tools needed (e.g., an interactive development environment) and their command languages.

The work cited above mostly used observational methods to characterize different aspects of novice and expert programming behavior. A newer research methodology also started to emerge in terms of building models of programmer cognition. For example, Brooks (1977) developed a model of the cognitive processes in computer programming based on the Newell and Simon (1972) theory of problem-solving and the role of short-term memory. Brooks used think-aloud methods and protocol analysis to uncover some of the implicit planning rules that programmers used to develop code. These issues are explored later in this chapter in Sections 1.4 and 1.6.

Language Design for Novices. In terms of high-level language design considerations, Weinberg (1971) argued for uniformity, compactness, and locality, while Barron (1977) argued for economy of concepts, uniformity, and orthogonality – each of them anticipating later work on cognitive dimensions (Green & Petre, 1996). One important line of experimental work concentrated on comparing, in laboratory settings, different ways of representing the code for flow of control and specifically conditionals. For example, Sime, Green, and others conducted several studies on both the coding and comprehensibility of different ways of specifying conditional flow of control in tiny programs consisting only of conditionals (Sime, Arblaster, & Green, 1977a; Sime, Arblaster, & Green, 1977b; Sime, Green, & Guest, 1977). They introduced the important distinction between "sequence information," which describes what a program will do under a given set of conditions, and "taxon information," which describes what set of conditions would cause a program to reach a given point. The experiments showed that a certain amount of redundancy in the notation reduced novices' errors and improved debugging success. In one notable study, the introduction of an **else** clause led to an enormous decrease in novice ability to solve taxon information problems.

Again using laboratory-based research methodologies, both Love (1977) and Shneiderman (1977a) conducted experiments on the ability of novices and experts to memorize short programs, either in different forms (Love), or scrambled (not working) vs. working (Shneiderman). Both sets of experiments showed that novices attended to the surface form of the code, whereas more expert programmers paid attention to its deeper-level structure, just as cognitive scientists had noted among novices and experts solving physics problems (Larkin et al., 1980).

1.2.2 Learning Programming in Educational Settings

One of the issues emerging in the 1970s centered on the design of the tools to be used by novices. A central issue was the choice of the novice's programming language and the programming environment in terms of their capability to make the workings of the underlying *notional machine* (the user-understandable semantics of the language) implied by the language both more explicit and more visible (du Boulay, O'Shea, & Monk, 1981). For example, Logo and its use of a Turtle to trace out a drawing constituted a good way of reifying the flow of control as a program executed and of relating procedures to sub-procedures. Similar notions were also applied in BASIC where, for pedagogical purposes, Mayer (1979) characterized the behavior of a BASIC program in terms of a sequence of "transactions," and Barr, Beard, and Atkinson (1976) built the BIP system for teaching BASIC that highlighted each BASIC statement on the display as it was executed. Similar execution tracing systems were built for other languages such as Pascal (Nievergelt et al., 1978) and FORTRAN (Shapiro & Witmer, 1974). Note the further discussion of notional machines in Chapter 13 on programming paradigms.

The next two subsections explore work undertaken in two areas. The first is on learning topics through learning programming, such as thinking skills and cognitive science. The second concentrates on learning programming for its own sake.

Learning through Programming. Logo (Feurzeig et al., 1969) was a language derived from LISP (1958) and championed by Papert with the objective of teaching mathematics and problem-solving through programming rather than teaching programming per se (Papert, 1972, 1980a). On the back of attempts to see whether Papert's goals could be achieved (see Section 1.4 of this chapter), there were several detailed investigations of novices (both children and adults) learning Logo. For example, Cannara (1976) documented the difficulties that children had in learning Logo. These difficulties turned out to be both in terms of the language itself, such as the recursion/iteration distinction and the binding of argument values, but also in terms of more general aspects of programming, such as the need for complete precision in coding (rather than assuming that the computer would figure out what they had meant to say) and the ability to break down complex problems into simpler parts. Similar difficulties were observed by Statz (1973) in her work with children, by Austin (1976) in work teaching student teachers, and by du Boulay (1978) also working with student teachers. So irrespective of the bigger issue of teaching mathematics through Logo programming, Logo as a first programming language produced its own share of difficulties for the learner. These arose for three reasons. First, the focus was much more on what programs could do rather than on the form of the programming language itself. Second, the language was developed by experts without input from learners. Third, the language was designed at the end of the 1960s when the psychology of programming was in its infancy.

Toward the end of the decade, Eisenstadt (1979) developed the declarative language Solo at the Open University (UK), designed with the objective of teaching topics in cognitive science. This language was semantically similar to Prolog, but was designed to have an easier syntax and a specialized editor that helped reduce syntax errors by including a predictive text facility. For example, if the user typed the "if" part of a conditional, the "then" and "else" branches were automatically provided to be filled in. This kind of facility was crucial, as students at the Open University often worked remotely without the benefit of a tutor nearby to help sort out programming difficulties. Students learning Solo were studied by Kahney (1982), who explored their different, and often incorrect, understandings of the notion of recursion, and by Hasemer (1983), who looked at their debugging behavior and built a tool to support debugging based on those observations.

Learning Programming in Its Own Right. While the developers of Logo and Solo had objectives beyond simply teaching programming, other languages were studied whose aims were more to teach computing. We have already referred to the work of Friend (1975) on AID (similar to BASIC). Like Youngs (1974), she cataloged the errors that students made and also found that the required number of conditions, loops, and subroutines was a good measure of how difficult beginners would find a problem.

Pascal (1970) was designed for novices and widely used in computer science departments as a vehicle for undergraduates to learn programming. Pascal was the language of the first Advanced Placement Computer Science exam in 1984.

There were various critiques of its problems, which had little impact on its popularity (Habermann, 1973; Lecarme & Desjardins, 1975; Welsh, Sneeringer, & Hoare, 1977). Ripley and Druseikis (1978) studied computer science students' errors and found that about 60 percent of the errors concerned punctuation, mostly the use of the semicolon, and that variable declarations were another problematic area. A study by Pugh and Simpson (1979) came to similar conclusions about the use of the semicolon. We see comparable results today in analyses of Java error messages, and with the worldwide scale of current data collection efforts (Altadmri & Brown, 2015), we know that these problems are common and not just local to a particular study.

A pervading problem for learners of Pascal as well as other languages was misunderstanding the capability of the computer. A study by Sleeman, Putnam, Baxter, and Kuspa (1986) of Pascal learners noted that students attributed "to the computer the reasoning power of an average person," which Pea named the "superbug" problem (Pea, 1986). This was an issue already identified by Cannara (1976) in relation to Logo.

1.2.3 Research on Teaching Methods

Chapters 10 and 15 in this Handbook focus on pedagogic methods more broadly. Here, we concentrate on issues specifically associated with early computing education research. One of the questions emerging in this period was "What is the best programming language for novices?" (Tagg, 1974), though we might now disagree that such a question is useful in its most general form. An interesting variation on this question was whether one should start with a low-level language (e.g., assembler) or a high-level language (e.g., BASIC). Weyer and Cannara (1975) compared teaching Logo and then SIMPER (a low-level language) versus SIMPER and then Logo versus teaching Logo and SIMPER at the same time. They found that the joint approach worked best in that the differences and similarities between the languages helped with understanding, despite some novices exhibiting a certain amount of muddling up of commands between the languages.

Various experiments were conducted on characterizing the notional machine, as we have indicated above. For example, Mayer (1975, 1976) showed that providing a simplified model of the FORTRAN notional machine was helpful in both coding and comprehension, and this was most pronounced where the programming problems were more difficult. Mayer (1975) found only a limited positive effect in learning FORTRAN. Shneiderman, Mayer, McKay, and Heller (1977) found no effect in learning FORTRAN. Researchers also examined the utility of using flowcharts as a learning aid. Brooks (1978) found that a variable dictionary (an annotated listing of variables in a program) provided more effective assistance than a flowchart for students working in FORTRAN.

The issue of learning in pairs or groups was also explored. Lemos (1978, 1979) found that students who debugged COBOL programs in small groups were more favorably disposed toward programming and came to understand the language better. Likewise, Cheney (1977) found that students who worked on their programming assignments in pairs learned more effectively – an interesting foretaste of much later research on pair-programming (Bryant, Romero, & du Boulay, 2008). Bork (1971) explored the best order for introducing programming concepts, contrasting top-down ("whole program") with bottom-up ("grammatical"). Lemos (1975) found no difference between the two approaches for FORTRAN, but Shneiderman (1977b) argued for a "spiral approach" that amalgamated both methods.

The main outcome arising from the work in the 1970s was greater clarity about the difficulties that novices faced in learning to program. These difficulties included learners understanding (i) what programming was for, (ii) how they should reconceptualize a problem in terms of the kinds of structures and mechanisms available in the programming language being used, and (iii) how those structures and mechanisms functioned when a program was executed. There were also advances in the tools, notably in language design and in programming environment design that helped to mitigate these issues.

1.3 Redesigning the Learner's Interface for Computing Education

As mentioned earlier, the nature of computing education research was strongly influenced by the hardware and systems software available at the time. Papert's Logo and the rest of the programming languages discussed above from the 1960s and 1970s were designed to be a predominantly text-based experience. Logo was originally programmed using a teletype. The first uses of Logo by children were to manipulate text, such as a program to make poems or play games (Papert, 1972; Papert & Solomon, 1971). The turtle came shortly thereafter, but was still controlled from a text-based interface. Starting in the 1970s, researchers explored how the interface might be changed so that the tool might better fit the objectives.

1.3.1 Smalltalk

Alan Kay visited Seymour Papert during the early Logo experiments and saw the potential learning benefits of computers (Kay, 1972). He reconceived the challenge of building a programming language for students as the challenge of building computational media for learners, where programming was part of an authorial or creative process. Where Papert had an objective of providing the computer as an object to think with (Papert, 1980), Kay saw the computer as a tool for expression and communication, as well as reflection and problem-solving (Kay, 1993).

Kay designed Smalltalk, the first language explicitly called "object-oriented." The earliest version of Smalltalk, Smalltalk-72, had a syntax similar to Logo (Goldberg & Kay, 1976). The later versions of Smalltalk (through the middle of the 1970s) were often used by children (Kay & Goldberg, 1977), but the focus of Smalltalk development shifted to support professional developers. By the time Smalltalk was released in 1981, it had evolved into a tool that was much more challenging for children to use (Goldberg & Robson, 1983).

When Kay and his group were designing Smalltalk, they wanted learners to be able to use the environment as a creative medium. They wanted students to be able to draw and use their drawings as part of animations that were programmed by computer. They wanted students to be able to play music and write programs that would make music. They developed the desktop user interface, with overlapping windows containing multiple fonts and styles, pop-up menus, icons, and a mouse pointer (Kay & Goldberg, 1977). Computer icons were first invented in Smalltalk-72 (Smith, 1975). The user interface that we use daily today was designed in order to achieve Kay's vision of the computer as a creative medium, where programming was one of the ways in which learners would express and communicate in this medium.

The research that Kay and his group did with Smalltalk was observation-based. Students would visit their lab at the Xerox PARC to test the feasibility of students working with the medium they were inventing. Smalltalk was used in a Palo Alto school for a while as a classroom-based experiment (Kay, 1993). In those studies, the team documented some of the challenges that students had with object-oriented programming, such as class-instance differences and finding functionality in a large class hierarchy.

1.3.2 Boxer and Programmable Toys

Of those first programming languages designed for learners (e.g., Logo, SOLO, Pascal), Smalltalk has arguably had the largest impact on computing today, because of the user interface inventions it advanced. Other early computer education research groups recognized the importance of using the advancing user interface technologies in order to go beyond simple text to provide a rich computational environment for learning. There are two threads of this work that have had impact on today's work. One is Boxer, which has given us theory for how students come to understand computing. The second are the interactions between toys and programming that have had an influence on today's blocks-based programming languages.

diSessa and Abelson developed Boxer as a successor to Logo (diSessa 1985; diSessa & Abelson, 1986). Like Kay, their goal was to use more advanced user interface techniques to improve the learning experience. Unlike any previous effort, Boxer gave semantic meaning to these user interface elements. Everything in Boxer was in a graphical box on the screen, both data and procedures. References to variables and binding to arguments (mentioned earlier as a challenge in Logo) become references to concrete named boxes with visible values on the screen. Boxer was developed with a similar objective to Smalltalk, which was to serve as a medium for computational literacy (diSessa, 2001). The idea of using graphical elements as semantically meaningful parts of a beginner's programming language started in Boxer and has led us to the blocks-based languages that are developed and studied today.

The earliest Logo turtle was a physical robotic device, which made the user's experience of programming more than just text from the beginning. In the 1970s, physical programming of the turtle was made possible through Radia Perlman's buttons and slots, which moved away from text or graphics for the learner's programming interface (McNerney, 2004). In McNerney's (2004) review of physical programming environments, he draws a direct line from Perlman's buttons and slots to the development of a variety of connections between Logo and Lego building sets (Resnick, Martin, Sargent, & Silverman, 1996), including MultiLogo (Resnick, 1990). Allison Druin built physical programming environments where students built physical, interactive spaces for story-telling, a different objective than previous programming activities (Druin et al., 2011; Sherman et al., 2001). Resnick's work on developing programming languages that were more accessible for children programming intelligent Lego bricks led to some of the early blocks-based languages, including Scratch, the most well-known blocks-based programming language today (Maloney et al., 2004; Maloney, Peppler, Kafai, Resnick, & Rusk, 2008).

The main outcome of the work described in this section was the emergence of the components of computer interfaces that we now take for granted, including windows, icons, pointers, and mice. This outcome has certainly influenced the design of development environments. Specifically for computing education research, a second but important theme is consideration of non-textual elements (including physical devices) in supporting student learning and programming.

1.4 Enter the Education Researchers

Two related disciplines started to impact on computing education research. One was education research, bringing with it an emphasis on research using large cohorts over extended periods of time. The other was cognitive science, which emerged in the 1970s/1980s, and its research methodology based on modeling human cognition. The involvement of these researchers broadened computer education research. Cognitive researchers modeled the user, not just the language or the interface. Both in general and in educational settings, the cognitively informed researchers who then started exploring computing considered cognitive outcomes and transfer, as well as the learning process.

1.4.1 The Impact of Education Researchers

Earlier work had already shown that Logo as a programming language had its own share of difficulties for novices (see, for example, Cannara, 1976). It was a series of studies by Pea, Kurland, and their colleagues that now examined whether learning Logo had the benefits claimed for it in terms of increased problem-solving ability and other thinking skills (Papert, 1980). Taking a developmental and cognitive perspective, Pea and Kurland (1984) undertook a theoretical analysis and review of how learning to program might, in principle, impact on children's ability "to plan effectively, to think procedurally, or to view their flawed problem solutions as 'fixable' rather than 'wrong'." Now the research methodology shifted away from small-scale laboratory-based methods to longer-term evaluative studies in authentic educational settings. In an empirical study of 8–10-year-old children learning Logo over a year, Pea, Kurland, and their colleagues found that these children were no better at a planning task at the end of the year than children who had not learned Logo (Pea, Kurland, & Hawkins, 1985). In a much larger study involving 15–17-year-old students learning a range of languages over a year, including Logo over 9 weeks within that year, they found similar results as well as misunderstandings of the Logo language and how it worked (Kurland, Pea, Clement, & Mawby, 1986). Likewise, Kurland and Pea (1985) found in a small study with children that they developed various incorrect mental models of how recursion worked, similar to those reported in other studies of the understanding of recursion.

Papert and Pea famously debated these studies in 1987. Papert argued that Pea was exhibiting "technocentric thinking" by studying the technology as opposed to studying the educational culture that could be created with tools like Logo (Papert, 1987). Papert argued that we were too early in the development of the new kinds of educational culture that computers might facilitate to evaluate it in a treatment model. Pea argued in response that we must study what we build, and that we can too easily fool ourselves into believing that our interventions work without careful study (Pea, 1987). The Pea and Papert position papers highlight the sharp contrast between computing and educational research in terms of both their objectives and their research methods. Is the goal of teaching programming to improve the classroom or to remake it into something new that cannot be studied in the same way? Should we use the traditional methods of educational research, or do we need new methods?

These rather negative findings regarding Logo's influence on the development of thinking skills were underlined in a wide-ranging review of the literature covering Logo, BASIC, and Pascal (Palumbo, 1990). However, Palumbo criticized much of the research he reviewed for not paying proper attention to "five critical issues concerning this area of research: (a) sufficient attention to problem solving theory, (b) issues related to the programming treatment, (c) the programming language selected and the method of instruction, (d) system-related issues, and (e) the selection of an appropriate sample."

Following this, Palumbo and Reed (1991) attempted to deal with these critical issues and compared a group of students learning BASIC with a group learning computer literacy, which focused on basic skills involved in computer operations, and they did find evidence of improved problem-solving in the group who had learned BASIC. In a similar fashion, Carver found that the skill of debugging could be learned by 8–11-year-olds through experience with Logo programming (Carver, 1986). Carver's critical insight was that transfer occurred only when that transferable skill was made an explicit part of the Logo curriculum, rather than hoping it might be learned simply in passing (Carver, 1986).

1.4.2 The Impact of Cognitive Science

Brooks' work, mentioned earlier, continued into the 1980s with a theory of the comprehension of programs that tried to explain the great variability in skill among both experts and novices (Brooks, 1983). In a parallel vein, Soloway and Ehrlich (1984) empirically explored questions around programmers' knowledge of "programming plans – stereotypic action sequences," and of the "rules of programming discourse … which govern the composition of plans into programs." They used both fill-in-the-blank methods and recall methods to demonstrate the effects of these two kinds of programming knowledge. Likewise, Wiedenbeck (1986) introduced the notion of beacons – "lines of code which serve as typical indicators of a particular structure or operation" – that assisted experts better than novices to recall programs that they had studied. This work on plans and beacons reflected the interest in mental models and schemata in the cognitive science of the time (see, for example, Johnson-Laird, 1983).

With the emphasis on problem-solving emerging from cognitive science, it was not surprising that work on understanding the nature of debugging was undertaken. Lukey (1980) built a system, PUDSY, to embody and model his theory of how programmers debug (Pascal) programs. His system made use of rules to segment programs, a description of the flow of control, the recognition of debugging clues, and simple data flow analysis, but as far as we know there was no empirical work based on the system. In a series of empirical studies, Katz and Anderson (1987) observed and analyzed students' debugging strategies in detail as applied to LISP programs. Among other results, they identified a range of students' bugs in LISP programs, in a similar fashion to Soloway and his colleagues' analysis of bugs in student Pascal programs (Johnson, Soloway, Cutler, & Draper, 1983; Spohrer et al., 1985). These kinds of analyses provided evidence about which aspects of these languages required extra tutorial support, as well as providing the basis for progress on automated tutors and debugging systems.

There was also interest in novices learning Prolog (Taylor & du Boulay, 1987). This is a declarative language with a complex internal reasoning mechanism that novices find difficult to comprehend, even when (and sometimes especially when) the "trace mechanism" is switched on to show the internal reasoning steps. In effect, the work on trace mechanisms was an attempt to provide the programmer with a Prolog notional machine (Eisenstadt & Brayshaw, 1990) – very different, of course, from the Logo notional machine mentioned earlier. The work on programming plans and beacons applicable to procedural languages morphed into understanding Prolog programmers' knowledge in terms of Prolog schemata. These were stereotypical, slightly abstracted chunks of Prolog code (Gegg-Harrison, 1991). A useful guide to this work on Prolog can be found in Brna, du Boulay, and Pain (1999).

New kinds of tool for novices were also emerging in the form of tutors, error diagnosis systems and support environments for learning programming, including tutors for learning Prolog (see du Boulay & Sothcott, 1987, for a review). A notable example emerged from cognitive science: Anderson and Reiser (1985) developed a tutor for LISP, arising both out Anderson's cognitive science learning theory, "Adaptive Character of Thought" (ACT), and his analysis of students learning to program, which was mentioned above. The strategy in this work was to exploit a cognitive science view of how a tutor might support a student's declarative understanding of programming ("what it is") as it developed into procedural skill ("how to do it"). This tutor was the forerunner of a large family of tutors that modeled the skills of a domain – in this case, programming in LISP – based on a production-rule representation and were able to guide students step by step through problem-solving (Anderson, Corbett, Koedinger, & Pelletier, 1995). Empirical evaluations of the tutor largely showed that it helped learners to master simple programming more quickly than other methods (e.g., lectures and textbooks), but that it did not necessarily provide deeper understanding than the other methods. This was not the only tool developed at that time to assist computer science students that took a cognitive science stance toward learning programming. We have already referred to Soloway and his colleagues' analysis of programming knowledge in terms of "plans" (Soloway & Ehrlich, 1984). In addition, Johnson and Soloway (1987) developed an error diagnosis system for student Pascal programs, PROUST, based on these ideas.

1.4.3 Phenomenographic Research

Cognitive science, with its notion of mental models, was not the only perspective on computing education research. By contrast, the phenomenographic perspective studied students in authentic settings to capture a sense of their personal experience of learning computer science (Marton, 1981). Phenomenography entered computing education research through educational psychologist Ference Marton and his student, Shirley Booth. For a brief guide to several approaches for research in computer science education, including cognitive science and phenomenography, see Ben-Ari, Berglund, Booth, and Holmboe (2004).

Phenomenography emphasized the individual quality of the learning experience of each student in relation to the context in which it was learned.

> Fundamental to an understanding of the phenomenographic approach is to realise that its epistemological stance is *not* "psychological," treating man and his behaviour as separable from the world in which he moves and lives. *Nor* is it "mentalist," treating cognition and cognitive acts as isolated to the mind and separable from the one who lives through them. The phenomenographic epistemological stance is that man is in relation to his world, and that cognition is such a relation …
> (Booth, 1992, p. 52)

An interesting example of the approach was the thesis work of Booth on undergraduates learning computer science. In addition to teasing out the learner's ways of understanding concepts such as recursion, she used an interview technique asking oblique questions to gain a sense of what they thought it meant and what they believed it took to learn to program (Booth, 1993). The phenomenographic approach was later linked with Activity Theory to study how the learning situation for students doing a distributed course in computer systems influenced their learning (Berglund, 2002). The phenomenographic approach was also used to explore the learning of advanced network concepts in a distributed course (Berglund & Pears, 2003).

There were three main outcomes of the work described in this section. First was the use of large cohorts and longitudinal studies to study learning programming in classrooms rather than in laboratories. The second was the emergence of cognitive science to enable more detailed understanding of novice and expert programming skills, runnable models of human programming activity, and tools to support that activity to be built. The third was the use of phenomenographic methods to capture the individuality of the experience of students learning programming and other computing concepts.

1.5 Computing Education Emerges as a Research Discipline

This section looks at the emergence of organizations for computing education research rather than at the content of the research itself as we have done in the previous sections.

Two international groups were formed in the 1980s to promote and support computer education research. One was the Psychology of Programming Interest Group (PPIG), formed in the UK in 1987 and holding its first workshop in 1989. The other was the Empirical Studies of Programmers (ESP), formed in the USA and holding its first workshop in 1986 (Soloway & Iyengar, 1986). Both groups ran a series of workshops and conferences: ESP until 1997, but with PPIG still doing so to the present day. A brief history of ESP can be found on the PPIG website as follows:

> The ESP series was managed by the USA-based Empirical Studies of Programmers Foundation. The last published list of the Board of Directors of that Foundation (in 1997) was Deborah Boehm-Davis, Wayne Gray, Thomas Moher, Jean Scholtz and James Spohrer.
>
> There were seven ESP conferences, all held in the USA. The research coverage of the series was very similar to the European (UK-based) PPIG series, which is the host organisation for this newsletter. Many people considered ESP and PPIG to be sister organisations. All ESP conferences except ESP 3 published formal proceedings volumes. Until ESP 6, the publisher of those proceedings was Ablex. The proceedings of ESP 7 in 1997 was published by the ACM Press. An attempt was made to convene an ESP 8 meeting that would have been held in 1999, although insufficient submissions were received for the meeting to be viable. The papers received

were instead published as a special issue of the International Journal of Human-Computer Studies (Volume 54, Number 2, published February 2001). (Alan Blackwell, PPIG website, www.ppig.org/news/2006-06-01/whatever-happened-empirical-studies-programmers)

Over the years, both groups were concerned with general issues in computer education research as well as studies of expert programmers. To give an idea of the flavor of ESP work, their first workshop included papers on novice/expert differences in debugging and in specifying procedures, cognitive processes in program comprehension, novice debugging in LISP, bugs in novice programs in Pascal, novice problems in coding BASIC, and a plea that expert professional programmers should also be studied. This range of papers suggest differences in objectives among these researchers. For the early Logo researchers, the goal of teaching programming was to change thinking. For some of the first ESP researchers, the goal of teaching programming was to get students to exhibit expert behavior, so it was important to study expert professional programmers and to contrast novice/expert differences. A useful account of what was known about the psychology of programming at this time can be found in Hoc, Green, Samurcay, and Gilmore (1990).

The Association for Computing Machinery (ACM) Special Interest Group in Computer Science Education (SIGCSE) was one of the first organizations focused on computer science education. Their annual symposium was started in 1970 and continues to attract over 1,000 attendees annually. The SIGCSE Symposium was initially focused on providing a forum for teachers of computing education to share their best practices, but research results were often presented at the symposia. ACM SIGCSE's non-US conference, Innovation and Technology in Computer Science Education (ITiCSE), started in 1996. ITiCSE has been particularly important for its "working groups" that served as fertile ground for developing computing education research. Other conferences, such as the Institute of Electrical and Electronics Engineers (IEEE) Symposium on Visual Languages and Human-Centric Computing (started in 1984), also often included computing education research results.

In 2001, the McCracken Working Group invented a research method for computing education research, the Multi-Institutional Multi-National (MIMN) study (McCracken et al., 2001). McCracken and his colleagues recognized that the validity of any study at one institution was subject to criticism because of experimental variables that might be unique to that institution or in common with only a subset of institutions. These threats to validity made it difficult to make progress in computing education research. The McCracken Working Group used a common task across five different institutions in four different countries in order to avoid the limitations of single-institution studies. The results were convincing to the computing education research community, and the surprisingly poor performance was a clarion call to make change in how we teach (Lister, 2011). Soon, other MIMN studies were conducted (e.g., Lister, Box, Morrison, Tenenberg, & Westbrook, 2004), and MIMN studies were generalized and defined as a research method (Fincher et al., 2005).

Some years later, the McCracken Working Group study was replicated. The results were not better, but were no longer surprising (Utting et al., 2013). It is a measure of progress in computing education research that we now better understand computing education and the challenges in that field.

In the USA, there was growing recognition that more computing education research was needed. Tenenberg, Fincher, and Petre began the Bootstrapping project, which helped develop computer science educators who wanted to become researchers. The success of Bootstrapping led to another project in the USA (Scaffolding) and more capacity-building projects around the world (Fincher & Tenenberg, 2006). Today, most computing education researchers in the USA were part of one of the capacity-building projects in the early 2000s or are a student of someone who was.

Because of the capacity-building efforts, there were more active computing education researchers than ever before. The community needed its own conference. While the ACM SIGCSE technical symposium had been around since the late 1960s, the focus there was on supporting practitioners, not on advancing research. Fincher, Anderson, and Guzdial were the first organizers of the ACM SIGCSE International Computing Education Research (ICER) conference in 2005 (Anderson, Fincher, & Guzdial, 2005). ICER became the best known and most respected computing education research venue globally. ICER continues to grow, attracting 150 participants in 2017. ICER papers are wide-ranging and cover tools, objectives, and research methods.

1.6 Research Questions in Computing Education Research

The list of research questions that have been explored in the approximately five decades of computing education research could already fill a book. For an excellent overview of the first four decades of this field, see Robins, Rountree, and Rountree (2003). In this section, we consider three that are often revisited and connect across these decades.

1.6.1 Developing a Notion of Programming

One of the most significant problems in learning to program is developing a mental model of what the computer is doing when it executes a program. The problem was first identified by du Boulay in 1986, wherein he coined the term "notional machine" to describe a model of how the computer interprets and executes a program (du Boulay, 1986). The first step in the process is recognizing that the computer does not contain a homunculus that is trying to understand the program. The belief that the computer contains a kind of human inside it is called "the superbug" by Pea (1986). Resnick identified the challenge that the computer is an external agent, and a robot being programmed is yet another agent (Resnick, 1990). Children growing up rarely face the challenge of giving detailed process instructions to another agent, let alone the complexity of instructing a non-human agent who does not share a common language.

Some researchers in the 1960s believed that eventually computers would understand humans and natural language so that the task of programming would go away (Greenberger, 1962). Perlis argued in 1961 that we would never reach that stage, that there would always be "friction" because of the mismatch between humans and computers. "Procedural literacy" is what Mateas (2008) called the knowledge and skills needed to overcome that mismatch. The challenge of developing a mental model of the notional machine is one that researchers have revisited every decade since the question was first defined (Sorva, 2013).

A similar problem to developing a mental model of the notional machine is developing a mental model of the programming process (Garner, Haden, & Robins, 2005; Joni & Soloway, 1986). Setting aside the complexity of syntax and semantics, students struggle with the notion of the interpreter or compiler, the act of debugging, and how the output or result of a program might be found (Sleeman, 1986). A decade after Sleeman first identified these issues, Clancy and Linn reported that students struggled to understand how all the different aspects of programming fit together (Clancy & Linn, 1992). A further decade later, researchers described the puzzling debugging strategies of students (Murphy et al., 2008). Graphical user interfaces and physical programming may have increased the complexity for students trying to understand the process of creating software and answering questions like, "Where is the program that's causing this behavior?" For example, students did not understand what their programs did when they were run (Hundhausen & Brown, 2007), nor where their programs were stored (Resnick, 1990). More positively, the advent of the Internet may allow us to explore recording student process information while programming, and studying that may give us new insights into the development of models of how students develop software and what they think is going on (Hundhausen, Olivares, & Carter, 2017).

1.6.2 Programming as a Notation for Thinking

Human languages, especially literacy in written language, have had a dramatic impact on society (McLuhan, 1962, 1964), and even on individual readers' brains (Wolf, 2007). The early computing education researchers expected that programming and computational literacy would have a similar impact (Kay, 1993), but they recognized that the design of the language would be critical for broad social and individual impact (diSessa 1985).

Like Papert, diSessa and his students argued that programming would lead to different kinds of understanding in mathematics from traditional pen-and-paper-based forms. Turtles allow students to explore issues as complicated as differentials and general relativity through programs that can be more accessible than the equivalent equations (Abelson & DiSessa, 1986). Programming can be used by students to invent new kinds of graphical notations to represent variables of interest and their relations (diSessa, Hammer, Sherin, & Kolpakowski, 1991).

In physics, equations better represent balance, but programs can be better for representing causal and temporal relationships (Sherin, 2001).

The form of the programming language has been studied since the development of graphical user interfaces. Green, Petre, and colleagues studied a variety of graphical notations (such as LabView and Petri nets) and found that textual programming interfaces led to better performance by programmers (Green & Petre, 1992; Green & Petre, 1996; Green, Petre, & Bellamy, 1991). They suggest that the superiority of textual languages was likely not inherent, but learned. We have much more experience with textual notations than with visual notations (Petre, 1995).

The trade-off between graphical and textual languages may be different for beginners. Hundhausen, Farley, and Brown (2006) found that a visual, direct-manipulation language led to students writing programs sooner than another group of students using a textual language. Weintrop and Wilensky found that some of the conditionals and iteration errors that students make with text-based languages are much less common when students use graphical blocks-based languages (Weintrop & Wilensky, 2015). Several studies have shown that students learning blocks-based languages can transfer their knowledge to more traditional text-based languages (e.g., Weintrop & Wilensky, 2015). The future of computational literacy will likely be of mixed modality. Students will use different kinds of programming languages at different stages (e.g., blocks-based languages as beginners, text-based languages if they become computing professionals, and perhaps domain-specific languages with graphical or textual forms for end-user programmers).

1.6.3 Representing Execution

In 1987, Brown introduced the idea of animating algorithms in order to make them accessible to students and professional programmers (Brown, 1987). For decades, we have been asking if animated representations of program execution do help with understanding, when they might, and how they should best be designed. A challenge in this research is deciding the objective of the animation. Is the objective to improve learning of the algorithm, to provide new insights when the programmer already understands the program, or to support debugging? Sorva's (2012) dissertation is an excellent starting point for understanding program visualization.

In general, there is little evidence that viewing algorithm animations leads to improved learning about the animations (Hundhausen, Douglas, & Stasko, 2002). However, we can use algorithm animations as part of other learning goals and develop successful learning activities beyond just viewing. For example, Stasko found that students learned from building the animations, rather than just viewing them (Stasko, 1997a, 1997b), and from answering questions about static representations after viewing a dynamic animation (Byrne, Catrambone, & Stasko, 1999). While animations themselves may have limited impact on learning, they are motivating and can engage students to achieve greater time on task and thus greater learning (Kehoe, Stasko, & Taylor, 2001). Sorva has suggested a different role for program execution visualizations – to teach a mental model of the notional machine, rather than to teach the particular algorithm being taught (Sorva, 2012; Sorva & Sirkiä, 2010).

1.7 Conclusion: Future Research Questions in a Historical Context

We started this chapter by mentioning the tools, objectives, and research methods of computing education research.

The computational power and interface capability of the tools available to learners have increased greatly since the early days of computing education research (Good, 2011), as has the ubiquity of devices to learn with and on, including smartphones, tablets, tangible computing, and a range of cheap hardware kits such as the Arduino. The kinds of problem that a beginner programmer can tackle are richer and more varied, and no longer restricted to printing "Hello World" or printing out the Fibonacci sequence, not least because the range of input and output devices has also developed dramatically since turtles first crawled the floor. Indeed, programming novices may even use their own bodies as input devices for coding up dance and other movement sequences (Romero, du Boulay, Robertson, Good, & Howland, 2009). We see that the hardware and systems software available to students and teachers influence what students were taught and how they were taught. The advent of more computational materials suggests the need to explore how these new media influence student learning.

The objectives argued about in the Papert vs. Pea debate mentioned earlier have now reemerged in two new ways. First, around the world there is interest in introducing school pupils to programming at an early age (e.g., see www .computingatschool.org.uk and www.csforall.org). This has happened in response to the increased importance of computing in our everyday lives and the expectation that informed citizens should have at least some understanding of programming to be able to function effectively, or possibly choose a career in computing. This has reawakened many of the questions around how novices can come to understand programs and programming as a process that we have sketched earlier. Even the word "algorithm" has now entered everyday vocabulary, though perhaps with different meanings from what was meant when Perlis and Snow talked about teaching algorithms to all undergraduates in (Greenberger, 1962). However, children are now so surrounded by computers of many kinds that the issue of understanding in principle what a computer and a program might be used for may be less problematic than in the early days (du Boulay, 1986). The ubiquity and invisibility of programs might make developing understanding of how programs work even harder. It is hard to learn about something one cannot see.

International interest in making computing education accessible to all puts the computing education literature in a new light. The studies we have reviewed here do not always tell us who was doing the learning. Papert's studies were mostly with children, but we do not have data about class or socioeconomic status. Most of the studies in computing education that we have reviewed here have been undertaken with computer science students in higher education, which is a privileged subset of students (Margolis & Fisher, 2002). Many studies published in venues like ACM SIGCSE do not tell us the gender of the participants. There are very few studies of students with learning disabilities or below-average intelligence (Ladner & Israel, 2016). Indeed, we now have a whole new cohort of the population who need to learn to program their smart devices and their homes (see, for example, Blackwell, Rode, & Toye, 2009). We need to revisit past studies and consider if the results might have been different with a broader sample of study participants.

The second echo of the Papert vs. Pea debate centers on the notion of computational thinking (Wing, 2006). This develops some of Papert's ideas about how programming offers a model of how to think effectively, solve problems and manage complex situations that can be applied in other areas of life. Today school pupils and college students are offered computational thinking courses that help them practice some of the thinking skills that programmers apply, without necessarily learning to program. The echo of Pea's paper can still be heard as the field struggles to measure computational thinking (Roman-Gonzalez, Perez-Gonzalez, & Jimenez-Fernandez, 2016).

In terms of research methods, we now see a wide variety of methods derived from educational research including long- and short-term evaluations, data-driven and at-scale methods (Moreno-León, Robles, & Román-González, 2017), design-based research from learning sciences (Ericson, Guzdial, & Morrison, 2015), action-based research by teachers (Ni, Tew, Guzdial, & McKlin, 2011), and learner-centered design methods for building programming environments for novices (Good, 2011; Guzdial, 2015; Howland, Good, & du Boulay, 2013). From psychology and cognitive science, we see both qualitative and quantitative analyses of programming processes involving a range of data-capture technologies such as eye-tracking (Bednarik & Tukiainen, 2006), think-aloud protocols (Bryant et al., 2008), as well as modeling. We also see measures of cognitive load applied to learning programming, from validated instruments (Morrison, Dorn, & Guzdial, 2014) to setting a background task to be undertaken in parallel (Abdul-Rahman & du Boulay, 2014).

We are limited in our research methods by who comes to our research enterprise today. In the early years, computing education research occurred across campus (e.g., Perlis described research in business and economics departments in Greenberger, 1962). Section 1.4 described the education researchers entering into computing education research. Today, most authors publishing at ICER are computer scientists or have a strong computing background. We have too few education researchers (or learning scientists, or psychologists), which means that we have too few people bringing new research methods into the community. We need that rich interdisciplinary background that our field used to enjoy in the past.

Back in the 1960s, the two most prominent objectives for starting computing education were (1) to prepare future programmers (see Sackman, 1968, cited in Ensmenger, 2010) and (2) to use computing as a tool for thinking and problem-solving (Greenberger, 1962). The former focused on industry-standard programming tools, while the latter encouraged the development of new learner-focused programming tools. Computing education research started when scientists began asking whether these efforts worked. The research methods selected have always been inextricably tangled with the objectives. As we define new roles for computing in people's lives, we will be defining new objectives, creating new tools, and applying a variety of research methods as we try to understand what happens when humans learn to control machines and to measure how successful the humans are at the task.

References

Abdul-Rahman, S. S., & du Boulay, B. (2014). Learning programming via worked-examples: Relation of learning styles to cognitive load. *Computers in Human Behavior, 30*, 286–298.

Abelson, H., & DiSessa, A. (1986). *Turtle Geometry: The Computer as a Medium for Exploring Mathematics*. Cambridge, MA: MIT Press.

Altadmri, A., & Brown, N. C. (2015). 37 million compilations: Investigating novice programming mistakes in large-scale student data. In *Proceedings of the 46th ACM Technical Symposium on Computer Science Education* (pp. 522–527). New York: ACM.

Anderson, J. R., Corbett, A. T., Koedinger, K. R., & Pelletier, R. (1995). Cognitive tutors: Lessons learned. *The Journal of the Learning Sciences, 4*(2), 167–207.

Anderson, J. R., & Reiser, B. J. (1985). The LISP tutor. *BYTE, 10*(4), 159–175.

Anderson, R., Fincher, S. A., & Guzdial, M. (2005). *Proceedings of the 1st International Computing Education Research Workshop, ICER 2005*. New York: ACM.

Austin, H. (1976). *Teaching Teachers Logo: The Lesley Experiments*. Retrieved from http://hdl.handle.net/1721.1/6237

Barr, A., Beard, M., & Atkinson, R. C. (1976). The computer as a tutorial laboratory: The Stanford BIP project. *International Journal of Man–Machine Studies, 8*(5), 567–582.

Barron, D. W. (1977). *An Introduction to the Study of Programming Languages*. Cambridge: Cambridge University Press.

Bednarik, R., & Tukiainen, M. (2006). *An Eye-tracking Methodology for Characterizing Program Comprehension Processes*. Paper presented at the Proceedings of the 2006 Symposium on Eye Tracking Research & Applications (ETRA '06), San Diego, CA.

Ben-Ari, M., Berglund, A., Booth, S., & Holmboe, C. (2004). What do we mean by theoretically sound research in computer science education? *ACM SIGCSE Bulletin, 36*, 230–231.

Berglund, A. (2002). Learning computer systems in a distributed course: Problematizing content and context. *European Association for Research on Learning and Instruction (EARLI), SIG, 10*, 1–22.

Berglund, A., & Pears, A. (2003). *Students' Understanding of Computer Networks in an Internationally Distributed Course.* Paper presented at the 3rd IEEE International Conference on Advanced Learning Technologies (ICALT'03), Athens, Greece.

Blackwell, A. F., Rode, J. A., & Toye, E. F. (2009). How do we program the home? Gender, attention investment, and the psychology of programming at home. *International Journal of Human-Computer Studies,* 67(4), 324–341.

Booth, S. (1992). *Learning to Program: A Phenomenographic Perspective* (PhD thesis), University of Gothenburg.

Booth, S. (1993). A study of learning to program from an experiential perspective. *Computers in Human Behavior,* 9(2–3), 185–202.

Bork, A. M. (1971). *"Learning to Program for the Science Student." Technical Report. University of California, Irvine. Physics Computer Science Project.* Washington, DC: National Science Foundation.

Brna, P., du Boulay, B., & Pain, H. (Eds.). (1999). *Learning to Build and Comprehend Complex Information Structures: Prolog as a Case Study.* Stamford, CT: Ablex Publishing Corporation.

Brooks, R. (1977). Towards a theory of the cognitive processes in computer programming. *International Journal of Man-Machine Studies,* 9(6), 737–751.

Brooks, R. (1978). Using a behavioral theory of program comprehension in software engineering. In *Proceedings of the 3rd International Conference on Software Engineering* (pp. 196–201). Hoboken, NJ: IEEE Press.

Brooks, R. (1983). Towards a theory of the comprehension of computer programs. *International Journal Man–Machine Studies,* 18(6), 543–554.

Brown, M. H. (1987). *Algorithm Animation.* Providence, RI: Brown University.

Bryant, S., Romero, P., & du Boulay, B. (2008). Pair programming and the mysterious role of the navigator. *International Journal of Human–Computer Studies,* 66(7), 519–529.

Byrne, M. D., Catrambone, R., & Stasko, J. T. (1999). Evaluating animations as student aids in learning computer algorithms. *Computers & Education,* 33(4), 253–278.

Cannara, A. B. (1976). *Experiments in Teaching Children Computer Programming* (doctoral dissertation), School of Education, Stanford University.

Carver, S. M. (1986). *Transfer of Logo Debugging Skill: Analysis, Instruction, and Assessment* (PhD thesis), Carnegie-Mellon University.

Cheney, P. H. (1977). Teaching computer programming in an environment where collaboration is required. *Journal of the Association for Educational Data Systems,* 11(1), 1–5.

Clancy, M. J., & Linn, M. (1992). *Designing Pascal Solutions: A Case Study Approach.* New York: W.H. Freeman & Company.

diSessa, A. (2001). *Changing Minds.* Cambridge, MA: MIT Press.

diSessa, A. A. (1985). A principled design for an integrated computational environment. *Human-Computer Interaction,* 1(1), 1–47.

diSessa, A. A., & Abelson, H. (1986). Boxer: A reconstructible computational medium. *Communications of the ACM,* 29(9), 859–868.

diSessa, A. A., Hammer, D., Sherin, B. L., & Kolpakowski, T. (1991). Inventing graphing: Meta-representational expertise in children. *Journal of Mathematical Behavior,* 2, 117–160.

Druin, A., Knell, G., Soloway, E., Russell, D., Mynatt, E., & Rogers, Y. (2011). The future of child–computer interaction In *CHI EA '11: CHI '11*

Extended Abstracts on Human Factors in Computing Systems (pp. 693–696). New York: ACM.

du Boulay, B. (1986). Some difficulties of learning to program. *Journal of Educational Computing Research, 2*(1), 57–73.

du Boulay, B., & O'Shea, T. (1981). Teaching novices programming. In M. J. Coombs & J. L. Alty (Eds.), *Computing Skills and the User Interface* (pp. 147–200). Cambridge, MA: Academic Press.

du Boulay, B., O'Shea, T., & Monk, J. (1981). The black box inside the glass box: presenting computing concepts to novices. *International Journal of Man–Machine Studies, 14*(3), 237–249.

du Boulay, B., & Sothcott, C. (1987). Computers teaching programming: An introductory survey of the field. In R. W. Lawler & M. Yazdani (Eds.), *Artificial Intelligence and Education* (Vol. 1, pp. 345–372). Norwood, NJ: Ablex.

du Boulay, J. B. H. (1978). *Learning Primary Mathematics through Computer Programming* (PhD thesis), University of Edinburgh.

Eason, K. D. (1976). Understanding the naive computer user. *The Computer Journal, 19*(1), 3–7.

Eisenstadt, M. (1979). A friendly software environment for psychology students. In *AISB Quarterly*, 34, 589–593.

Eisenstadt, M., & Brayshaw, M. (1990). A fine-grained account of Prolog execution for teaching and debugging. *Instructional Science, 19*(4–5), 407–436.

Ensmenger, N. L. (2010). *The Computer Boys Take Over: Computers, Programmers, and the Politics of Technical Expertise*. Cambridge, MA: MIT Press.

Ericson, B. J., Guzdial, M. J., & Morrison, B. B. (2015). *Analysis of Interactive Features Designed to Enhance Learning in an Ebook*. Paper presented at the Proceedings of the 11th Annual International Conference on International Computing Education Research, Omaha, NE, USA.

Feurzeig, W., Papert, S., Bloom, M., Grant, R., & Solomon, C. (1969). Programming-Languages as a Conceptual Framework for Teaching Mathematics. Final Report on the First Fifteen Months of the Logo Project. Retrieved from https://eric.ed.gov/?id=ED038034

Fincher, S., Lister, R., Clear, T., Robins, A., Tenenberg, J., & Petre, M. (2005). Multi-institutional, multi-national studies in CSEd Research: some design considerations and trade-offs. In *ICER '05: Proceedings of the First International Workshop on Computing Education Research* (pp. 111–121). New York: ACM.

Fincher, S., & Tenenberg, J. (2006). Using theory to inform capacity-building: Bootstrapping communities of practice in computer science education research. *Journal of Engineering Education, 95*(4), 265–277.

Friend, J. (1975). *Programs Students Write*. Retrieved from https://eric.ed.gov/?id=ED112861

Gannon, J. D. (1978). *Characteristic Errors in Programming Languages*. Paper presented at ACM '78, Washington, DC, USA.

Garner, S., Haden, P., & Robins, A. (2005). *My Program is Correct but it Doesn't Run: a Preliminary Investigation of Novice Programmers' Problems*. Paper presented at the 7th Australasian Conference on Computing Education–Newcastle, New South Wales, Australia.

Gegg-Harrison, T. S. (1991). Learning Prolog in a schema-based environment. *Instructional Science, 20*(2–3), 173–192.

Goldberg, A., & Kay, A. (1976). *Smalltalk-72: Instruction Manual.* Palo Alto, CA: Xerox Corporation.

Goldberg, A., & Robson, D. (1983). *Smalltalk-80: The Language and Its Implementation.* Boston, MA: Addison-Wesley Longman Publishing Co., Inc.

Good, J. (2011). Learners at the wheel: Novice programming environments come of age. *International Journal of People-Oriented Programming (IJPOP),* 1(1), 1–24.

Gould, J. D. (1975). Some psychological evidence on how people debug computer programs. *International Journal Man–Machine Studies,* 7(2), 171–182.

Gould, J. D., & Drongowski, P. (1974). An exploratory study of computer program debugging. *Human Factors,* 16(3), 258–277.

Green, T. R. G., & Petre, M. (1992). When visual programs are harder to read than textual programs. In G. C. van der Veer, M. J. Tauber, S. Bagnarola, & M. Antavolits (Eds.), *Human–Computer Interaction: Tasks and Organisation, Proceedings EECE-6 (6th European Conference on Cognitive Ergonomics)* (pp. 167–180). Rome, Italy: CUD.

Green, T. R. G., & Petre, M. (1996). Usability analysis of visual programming environments: a "cognitive dimensions" framework. *Journal of Visual Languages & Computing,* 7(2), 131–174.

Green, T. R. G., Petre, M., & Bellamy, R. K. E. (1991). Comprehensibility of visual and textual programs: A test of "superlativism" against the "match–mismatch" conjecture. In J. Koenemann-Belliveau, T. Moher, & S. Robertson (Eds.), *Empirical Studies of Programmers: Fourth Workshop* (pp. 121–146). Norwood, NJ: Ablex.

Greenberger, M. (1962). *Computers and the World of the Future.* Cambridge, MA: MIT Press.

Guzdial, M. (2015). *Learner-Centered Design of Computing Education: Research on Computing for Everyone.* San Rafael, CA: Morgan & Claypool Publishers.

Habermann, A. N. (1973). Critical comments on the programming language Pascal. *Acta Informatica,* 3(1), 47–57.

Hasemer, T. (1983). *An Empirically-based Debugging System for Novice Programmers* (Open University Technical Report No. 6) (PhD thesis). The Open University.

Hoc, J.-M. (1977). Role of mental representation in learning a programming language. *International Journal Man–Machine Studies,* 9(1), 87–105.

Hoc, J.-M., Green, T. R. G., Samurcay, R., & Gilmore, D. J. (1990). *Psychology of Programming.* Cambridge, MA: Academic Press.

Howland, K., Good, J., & du Boulay, B. (2013). Narrative threads: A tool to support young people in creating their own narrative-based computer games. In Z. Pan, A. D. Cheok, W. Müller, I. Iurgel, P. Petta, & B. Urban (Eds.), *Transactions on Edutainment X* (pp. 122–145). Berlin, Germany: Springer Berlin Heidelberg.

Hundhausen, C. D., & Brown, J. L. (2007). An experimental study of the impact of visual semantic feedback on novice programming. *Journal of Visual Languages and Computing,* 18(6), 537–559.

Hundhausen, C. D., Douglas, S. H., & Stasko, J. T. (2002). A meta-study of algorithm visualization effectiveness. *Journal of Visual Languages and Computing,* 13, 259–290.

Hundhausen, C. D., Farley, S., & Brown, J. L. (2006). *Can Direct Manipulation Lower the Barriers to Programming and Promote Positive Transfer to Textual Programming? An Experimental Study.* Paper presented at the Proceedings of the Visual Languages and Human-Centric Computing.

Hundhausen, C. D., Olivares, D. M., & Carter, A. S. (2017). IDE-based learning analytics for computing education: A process model, critical review, and research agenda. *Transactions of Computing Education,* 17(3), 1–26.

Johnson, W. L., & Soloway, E. (1987). Proust: An automatic debugger for Pascal programs. In G. P. Kearsley (Ed.), *Artificial Intelligence & Instruction: Applications and Methods* (pp. 49–67). Reading, MA: Addison-Wesley Publishing.

Johnson, W. L., Soloway, E., Cutler, B., & Draper, S. (1983). *Bug Catalogue 1 (286). Technical Report.* New Haven, CT: Yale University.

Johnson-Laird, P. N. (1983). *Mental Models: Towards a Cognitive Science of Language, Inference and Consciousness.* Cambridge, MA: Harbard University Press.

Joni, S.-N. A., & Soloway, E. (1986). But my program runs! Discourse rules for novice programmers. *Journal of Educational Computing Research,* 2(1), 95–125.

Kahney, H. (1982). *An In-Depth Study of the Cognitive Behaviour of Novice Programmers (Technical Report No. 5).* Milton Keynes, UK: The Open University.

Katz, I. R., & Anderson, J. R. (1987). Debugging: An analysis of bug-location strategies. *Human–Computer Interaction,* 3(4), 351–399.

Kay, A., & Goldberg, A. (1977). Personal dynamic media. In *IEEE Computer* (pp. 31–41). Hoboken, NJ: IEEE Press.

Kay, A. C. (1972). *A Personal Computer for Children of All Ages.* Paper presented at the ACM Annual Conference, 1972. Boston, MA, USA.

Kay, A. C. (1993). The early history of Smalltalk. In *The Second ACM SIGPLAN Conference on History of Programming Languages* (pp. 69–95). New York: ACM.

Kehoe, C., Stasko, J., & Taylor, A. (2001). Rethinking the evaluation of algorithm animations as learning aids. *International Journal of Human–Computer Studies,* 54(2), 265–284.

Kurland, D. M., & Pea, R. D. (1985). Children's mental models of recursive Logo programs. *Journal of Educational Computing Research,* 1(2), 235–243.

Kurland, D. M., Pea, R. D., Clement, C., & Mawby, R. (1986). A study of the development of programming ability and thinking skills in high school students. *Journal of Educational Computing Research,* 2(4), 429–458.

Ladner, R. E., & Israel, M. (2016). "For all" in "computer science for all". *Communications of the ACM,* 59(9), 26–28.

Larkin, J., McDermott, J., Simon, D. P., & Simon, H. A. (1980). Expert and novice performance in solving physics problems. *Science,* 208(4450), 1335–1342.

Lecarme, O., & Desjardins, P. (1975). More comments on the programming language Pascal. *Acta Informatica,* 4(3), 231–243.

Lemos, R. S. (1975). FORTRAN programming: An analysis of pedagogical alternatives. *Journal of Educational Data Processing,* 12(3), 21–29.

Lemos, R. S. (1978). Students' attitudes towards programming: The effects of structured walk-throughs. *Computers & Education,* 2(4), 301–306.

Lemos, R. S. (1979). Teaching programming languages: A survey of approaches. *ACM SIGCSE Bulletin – Proceedings of the 10th SIGCSE Symposium on Computer Science,* 11(1), 174–181.

Lister, R. (2011). Ten years after the McCracken Working Group. *ACM Inroads,* 2(4), 18–19.

Lister, R., Box, I., Morrison, B., Tenenberg, J., & Westbrook, D. S. (2004). The dimensions of variation in the teaching of data structures. *SIGCSE Bulletin,* 36(3), 92–96.

Love, T. (1977). *An Experimental Investigation of the Effect of Program Structure on Program Understanding*. Paper presented at the ACM Conference on Language Design for Reliable Software, Raleigh, NC, USA.

Lukey, F. J. (1980). Understanding and debugging programs. *International Journal of Man–Machine Studies*, 12(2), 189–202.

Maloney, J., Burd, L., Kafai, Y., Rusk, N., Silverman, B., & Resnick, M. (2004). Scratch: a sneak preview. In *C5 '04: Proceedings of the Second International Conference on Creating, Connecting and Collaborating through Computing* (pp. 104–109). Washington, DC: IEEE Computer Society.

Maloney, J. H., Peppler, K., Kafai, Y., Resnick, M., & Rusk, N. (2008). *Programming by Choice: Urban Youth Learning Programming with Scratch*. Paper presented at SIGCSE '08: The 39th SIGCSE Technical Symposium on Computer Science Education, New York, NY, USA.

Margolis, J., & Fisher, A. (2002). *Unlocking the Clubhouse: Women in Computing*. Cambridge, MA: MIT Press.

Marton, F. (1981). Phenomenography – Describing conceptions of the world around us. *Instructional Science*, 10(2), 177–200.

Mateas, M. (2008). Procedural literacy: Educating the new media practitioner. In D. Drew (Ed.), *Beyond Fun* (pp. 67–83). Pittsburgh, PA: Carnegie Mellon University: ETC Press.

Mayer, R. E. (1975). Different problem-solving competencies established in learning computer programming with and without meaningful models. *Journal of Educational Psychology,* 67(6), 725–734.

Mayer, R. E. (1976). Comprehension as affected by structure of problem representation. *Memory and Cognition,* 4(3), 249–255.

Mayer, R. E. (1979). A psychology of learning BASIC. *Communications of the ACM,* 22(11), 589–593.

McCracken, M., Almstrum, V., Diaz, D., Guzdial, M., Hagan, D., Kolikant, Y. B.-D., … Wilusz, T. (2001). A multi-national, multi-institutional study of assessment of programming skills of first-year CS students. *ACM SIGCSE Bulletin,* 33(4), 125–140.

McLuhan, M. H. (1962). *The Gutenberg Galaxy: The Making of Typographic Man.* Toronto, CA: University of Toronto Press.

McLuhan, M. H. (1964). *Understanding Media: The Extensions of Man.* Cambridge, MA: MIT Press.

McNerney, T. S. (2004). From turtles to tangible programming bricks: explorations in physical language design. *Personal and Ubiquitous Computing,* 8(5), 326–337.

Miller, L. A. (1974). Programming by non-programmers. *International Journal of Man–Machine Studies,* 6(2), 237–260.

Miller, L. A. (1975). *Naive Programmer Problems with Specification of Transfer-of-control*. Paper presented at the AFIPS '75 National Computer Conference, Anaheim, CA, USA.

Moreno-León, J., Robles, G., & Román-González, M. (2017). Towards data-driven learning paths to develop computational thinking with Scratch. *IEEE Transactions on Emerging Topics in Computing*, 99, 1.

Morrison, B. B., Dorn, B., & Guzdial, M. (2014). *Measuring Cognitive Load in Introductory CS: Adaptation of an Instrument*. Paper presented at the 10th Annual Conference on International Computing Education Research, Glasgow, UK.

Murphy, L., Lewandowski, G., McCauley, R., Simon, B., Thomas, L., & Zander, C. (2008). Debugging: The good, the bad, and the quirky – A qualitative analysis of novices' strategies. *ACM SIGCSE Bulletin*, 40(1), 163–167.

Newell, A., & Simon, H. A. (1972). *Human Problem Solving*. Upper Saddle River, NJ: Prentice-Hall.

Ni, L., Tew, A. E., Guzdial, M. J., & McKlin, T. (2011). *A Regional Professional Development Program for Computing Teachers: The Disciplinary Commons for Computing Educators*. Paper presented at the 2011 Annual Meeting of the American Educational Research Association, New Orleans, LA, USA.

Nievergelt, J., Frei, H. P., Burkhart, H., Jacobi, C., Pattner, B., Sugaya, H., Weibel, B., & Weydert, J. (1978). XS-0: A self-explanatory school computer. *ACM SIGCSE Bulletin*, 10(4), 66–69.

Palumbo, D. J. (1990). Programming language/problem-solving research: A review of relevant issues. *Review of Educational Research*, 60(1), 65–89.

Palumbo, D. J., & Reed, M. W. (1991). The effect of basic programming language instruction on high school students' problem solving and computer anxiety. *Journal of Research on Computing in Education*, 23(3), 343–372.

Papert, S. (1972). Teaching children to be mathematicians versus teaching about mathematics. *International Journal of Mathematical Education in Science and Technology*, 3(3), 249–262.

Papert, S. (1980). *Mindstorms: Children, Computers, and Powerful Ideas*. New York: Basic Books.

Papert, S. (1987). Information technology and education: Computer criticism vs. technocentric thinking. *Educational Researcher*, 16(1), 22–30.

Papert, S. A., & Solomon, C. (1971). *Twenty Things to do With a Computer*. Retrieved from https://dspace.mit.edu/handle/1721.1/5836

Pea, R. D. (1986). Language-independent conceptual "bugs" in novice programming. *Journal of Educational Computing Research*, 2(1), 25–36.

Pea, R. D. (1987). The aims of software criticism: Reply to professor papert. *Educational Researcher*, 16(5), 4–8.

Pea, R. D., & Kurland, D. M. (1984). On the cognitive effects of learning computer programming. *New Ideas in Psychology*, 2(2), 137–168.

Pea, R. D., Kurland, D. M., & Hawkins, J. (1985). Logo and the development of thinking skills. In M. Chen & W. Paisley (Eds.), *Children and Microcomputers: Research on the Newest Medium* (pp. 193–317). Thousand Oaks, CA: SAGE.

Pears, A., Seidman, S., Malmi, L., Mannila, L., Adams, E., Bennedsen, J., & Paterson, J. (2007). A survey of literature on the teaching of introductory programming. *ACM SIGCSE Bulletin*, 39(4), 204–223.

Petre, M. (1995). Why looking isn't always seeing: Readership skills and graphical programming. *Communications of the ACM*, 38(6), 33–44.

Pugh, J., & Simpson, D. (1979). Pascal errors – Empirical evidence. *Computer Bulletin*, 2, 26–28.

Resnick, M. (1990). MultiLogo: A study of children and concurrent programming. *Interactive Learning Environments*, 1(3), 153–170.

Resnick, M., Martin, F., Sargent, R., & Silverman, B. (1996). Programmable bricks: Toys to think with. *IBM Systems Journal*, 35(3–4), 443–452.

Ripley, G. D., & Druseikis, F. C. (1978). A statistical analysis of syntax errors. *Computer Languages*, 3(4), 227–240.

Robins, A., Rountree, J., & Rountree, N. (2003). Learning and teaching programming: A review and discussion. *Computer Science Education,* 13(2), 137–172.

Roman-Gonzalez, M., Perez-Gonzalez, J.-C., & Jimenez-Fernandez, C. (2016). Which cognitive abilities underlie computational thinking? Criterion validity of the Computational Thinking Test. *Computers in Human Behavior,* 72, 678–691.

Romero, P., du Boulay, B., Robertson, J., Good, J., & Howland, K. (2009). Is Embodied Interaction Beneficial When Learning Programming? In *VMR '09 Proceedings of the 3rd International Conference on Virtual and Mixed Reality: Held as Part of HCI International 2009* (pp. 97–105). Berlin, Germany: Springer-Verlag.

Sackman, H. (1968). Conference on Personnel Research. *Datamation,* 14(7), 74–76.

Shapiro, S. C., & Witmer, D. P. (1974). Interactive visual simulators for beginning programming students. *ACM SIGCSE Bulletin – Proceedings of the 4th SIGCSE Symposium on Computer Science Education,* 6(1), 11–14.

Sherin, B. L. (2001). A comparison of programming languages and algebraic notation as expressive languages for physics. *International Journal of Computers for Mathematical Learning,* 6, 1–61.

Sherman, L., Druin, A., Montemayor, J., Farber, A., Platner, M., Simms, S., Porteous, J., Alborzi, H., Best, J., Hammer, J., & Kruskal, A. (2001). StoryKit: Tools for children to build room-sized interactive experiences. In *CHI'01 Extended Abstracts on Human Factors in Computing Systems* (pp. 197–198). New York: ACM.

Shneiderman, B. (1977a). Measuring computer program quality and comprehension. *International Journal Man-Machine Studies,* 9(4), 465–478.

Shneiderman, B. (1977b). Teaching programming: A spiral approach to syntax and semantics. *Computers and Education,* 1(4), 193–197.

Shneiderman, B., Mayer, R. E., McKay, D., & Heller, P. (1977). Experimental investigations of the utility of detailed flowcharts in programming. *Communications of the ACM,* 20(6), 373–381.

Sime, M. E., Arblaster, A. T., & Green, T. R. G. (1977a). Reducing programming errors in nested conditionals by prescribing a writing procedure. *International Journal Man–Machine Studies,* 9(1), 119–126.

Sime, M. E., Arblaster, A. T., & Green, T. R. G. (1977b). Structuring the programmer's task. *Journal of Occupational Psychology,* 50(3), 205–216.

Sime, M. E., Green, T. R. G., & Guest, D. J. (1977). Scope marking in computer conditionals – A psychological evaluation. *International Journal Man-Machine Studies,* 9(1), 107–118.

Sleeman, D. (1986). The challenges of teaching computer programming. *Communications of the ACM,* 29(9), 840–841.

Sleeman, D., Putnam, R. T., Baxter, J., & Kuspa, L. (1986). Pascal and high school students: A study of errors. *Journal of Educational Computing Research,* 2(1), 5–23.

Smith, D. C. (1975). *PYGMALION: A Creative Programming Environment* (PhD thesis), Stanford University.

Soloway, E., & Ehrlich, K. (1984). Empirical studies of programming knowledge. *IEEE Transactions on Software Engineering, SE-10,* 5(5), 595–609.

Soloway, E., & Iyengar, S. (Eds.) (1986). *Empirical Studies of Programmers: Papers Presented at the First Workshop on Empirical Studies of Programmers.* Norwood, NJ: Ablex.

Sorva, J. (2012). *Visual Program Simulation in Introductory Programming Education* (Doctor of Science in Technology thesis), Aalto University School of Science.

Sorva, J. (2013). Notional machines and introductory programming education. *Transactions in Computing Education,* 13(2), 8:1–8:31.

Sorva, J., & Sirkiä, T. (2010). *UUhistle: A Software Tool for Visual Program Simulation.* In *Proceedings of the 10th Koli Calling International Conference on Computing Education Research* (pp. 49–54). New York: ACM.

Spohrer, J. C., Pope, E., Lipman, M., Sack, W., Freiman, S., Littman, D., & Soloway, E. (1985). *Bug Catalogue: II, III, IV* (Technical Report 386). New Haven, CT: Yale University Press.

Stasko, J. T. (1997a). *Supporting Student-built Algorithm Animation as a Pedagogical Tool.* Paper presented at the CHI '97 Extended Abstracts on Human Factors in Computing Systems, Atlanta, GA, USA.

Stasko, J. T. (1997b). *Using Student-built Algorithm Animations as Learning Aids.* Paper presented at the 28th SIGCSE Technical Symposium on Computer Science Education, San Jose, CA, USA.

Statz, J. A. (1973). *The Development of Computer Programming Concepts and Problem-solving Abilities Among Ten-year-olds Learning Logo* (PhD thesis), Syracuse University.

Tagg, W. (1974). Programming languages for school use. *Computer Education,* 16, 11–22.

Taylor, J., & du Boulay, B. (1987). Why novices may find programming in Prolog hard. In J. C. Rutkowska & C. Crook (Eds.), *Computers, Cognition and Development: Issues for Psychology and Education* (pp. 153–176). New York: Wiley.

Utting, I., Tew, A. E., McCracken, M., Thomas, L., Bouvier, D., Frye, R., & Wilusz, T. (2013). A fresh look at novice programmers' performance and their teachers' expectations. In *Proceedings of the ITiCSE Working Group Reports Conference on Innovation and Technology in Computer Science Education-working Group Reports* (pp. 15–32). New York: ACM.

Weinberg, G. M. (1971). *The Psychology of Computer Programming.* New York: Van Nostrand/Reinhold.

Weintrop, D., & Wilensky, U. (2015). *Using Commutative Assessments to Compare Conceptual Understanding in Blocks-based and Text-based Programs.* Paper presented at the 11th Annual International Conference on International Computing Education Research, Omaha, NE, USA.

Welsh, J., Sneeringer, W. J., & Hoare, C. A. R. (1977). Ambiguities and insecurities in Pascal. *Software: Practice and Experience,* 7(6), 685–696.

Weyer, S. A., & Cannara, A. B. (1975). *Children Learning Computer Programming: Experiments with Languages, Curricula and Programmable Devices* (Technical Report 250). Stanford, CA: Institute for Mathematical Studies in Social Science.

Wiedenbeck, S. (1986). Beacons in computer program comprehension. *International Journal of Man–Machine Studies,* 25(6), 697–709.

Wing, J. (2006). Computational thinking. *Communications of the ACM,* 49(3), 33–35.

Wolf, M. (2007). *Proust and the Squid: The Story and Science of the Reading Brain.* New York: Harper Collins.

Youngs, E. A. (1974). Human errors in programming. *International Journal of Man–Machine Studies,* 6(3), 361–376.

2 Computing Education Research Today

Sally A. Fincher, Josh Tenenberg, Brian Dorn,
Christopher Hundhausen, Robert McCartney,
and Laurie Murphy

This chapter is based around conversations held at the 11th International Computing Education Research (ICER) conference in Tacoma, Washington, on August 18–20, 2017. The conversations were between the current (and immediately past) editors of two premier publication venues for computing education research, the journal *Computer Science Education* (CSE) and the ACM *Transactions on Computing Education* (TOCE). As well as editorial experience, four of the six participants had also served as ICER chairs or co-chairs.

Broadly, then, this group of people represent community "gatekeepers," those that establish and maintain standards for submission and reviewing, for what gets published and what gets rejected, and for what – at this time – represents good work in the field. These conversations also give a chance for the reader to be exposed to rationale and discourse that doesn't usually appear in the literature.

Conversationalists:

- Sally Fincher – CSE Editor 2000–2016; Founding ICER Co-Chair 2004–2006
- Laurie Murphy – CSE Editor 2007–2017
- Brian Dorn – CSE Editor 2016–present; ICER Co-Chair 2014–2016
- Josh Tenenberg – Founding TOCE Editor 2010–2015; ICER Co-Chair 2016–2017
- Robert McCartney – Founding TOCE Editor 2010–2015; ICER Program Co-Chair 2018–2019
- Chris Hundhausen – TOCE Editor 2015–present

Question: So what are the topic areas you're seeing? We know there are more K–12 and teacher preparation papers, but what is staying the same? What topics are the bread-and-butter subjects that you see?

[JT]:	We would see a lot of things with tools, various software tools. Visualization tools, animation tools, things like that.
[CH]:	That's gone down. That went down last year: down to 6 percent at TOCE.
[BD]:	I get the impression from reviewers sometimes that they're tooled out. It's *yet another* environment to work with novice programmers, or something.
[RM]:	And those papers generally don't review well.
[LM]:	They don't review well. Well, a lot of the time the assessment piece is just not there.
[RM]:	Which you can sort of understand when you read the papers. They built a computer system: it's really cool!

[LM]:	It's a *cool* tool …
[RM]:	… here's the architecture … here are my design rationales …
[LM]:	… and then they did a survey!
[JT]:	And as I remember, those papers were often the ones from people most closely identified with the discipline of computing. And so were less familiar with the kinds of social and behavioral ways in which you collect empirical data, and so their papers were also estranged from any theoretical rationale. They stepped aside from trying to understand how people think, or learn, or things like that, and instead said, "This is a cool idea, and of course its contribution is obvious."
[BD]:	Yes, you're right. In effect they just say, "Here's the architecture of the system," which ultimately doesn't matter. What we care about is: Is it effective? And: What is the evidence for that?
	I think the bread-and-butter submissions are still located within introductory programming, within CS1. It might not be as much pair programming, or other styles of group work that were more common, what, ten years ago, but there are still people trying out a new thing – peer instruction – or whatever it might be this week.
[LM]:	And that's almost always in CS1 or maybe CS2. We rarely get anything higher division.
[BD]:	I think we have had only a couple of papers in the last year for CSE that were both undergraduate and outside of CS1.
[LM]:	We're not seeing the range of the discipline, from upper-level topics, for instance. We used to see more of that, I think.
[JT]:	And when you do get them, those are the ones where you often get tools papers as well, because you get the specialized compiler, visualizer, or this upper-level architecture thing.
[LM]:	There have been a handful trying to pull higher-level topics down into CS1. "We're going to do parallelization," or, "We're going to do security." Or string matching. "We're going to do something that you would normally consider to be a higher-level topic … *but in CS1.*"

Question: What about theory and methods? Are you seeing the community moving, are you seeing different theories, different kinds of theory, being drawn on?

[RM]:	You mean educational theory?
[JT]:	Any kind. Whatever theory might be brought to bear. Or methods of inquiry.
[CH]:	Rarely as a paper in and of itself, but you see theory and methods in the service of something else.
[JT]:	Are you seeing changes in those also?
[CH]:	Well, we now have explicit author criteria. Our criteria [on the author page] say you ought to have a theory.
[SF]:	Does it help?
[RM]:	Do the authors understand what you mean?
[CH]:	I hope so. It's in the *Tips from the Editor in Chief* section, and I try to make it pretty simple. [Make ties to learning theory explicit. Paper authors are strongly encouraged to frame their research in terms of one or more learning theories. This can be accomplished, for example, by motivating research questions or hypotheses with the help of learning theory, or by interpreting results in terms of learning theory.]

[BD]:	I think, methodologically, what I've seen in ICER, certainly over the last five years, is increasing sophistication of method, particularly quantitative methods. So, multi-level modeling, more advanced regression analyses, path analysis, SEM [structural equation modeling]. They require a little bit more hardware to do, and I think it's probably good to see maturity there. But it does make it difficult when you haven't read a lot of that, and the reviewers are not as familiar with some of these methods. It makes it hard for authors, I think, to explain what they're doing, and they have to do that sometimes.
[RM]:	It's important, because often we would get a review back from somebody that says, "Well, I don't really understand the stats."
[BD]:	"But I liked it!"
[RM]:	Yes, "I like the paper, but I can't really comment on the applicability of these statistics." Or actually, for any upper-level computing course you might get the same thing. "I haven't really kept up with operating systems, but this seems pretty good."
[BD]:	And it cuts both ways, too. So you see, "I'm attracted by the conclusion of the paper, and I'm really interested in that, and want to be able to cite this, but I'm not sure about the method. But I'm so attracted to this conclusion that I'm just going to give it a six." The danger in that, of course, is that if something is wrong in the chain of reasoning, and the numbers don't quite add up, and you haven't exposed that to rigorous inspection, then you are citing something for which there isn't a valid chain of reasoning. We've had this situation at times, where papers get bifurcated reviews.
[LM]:	Yes. The stats people say, "This is a mess."
[BD]:	There are wider problems with these more sophisticated quantitative methods, because in some sense we're clicking buttons in SPSS as a community, and maybe we don't always realize what that means.

Question: How much is it a dialogic activity, do you think?

[JT]:	I don't think we're at the place, if we ever will be, where we could take the *PLoS* model, which says if it syntactically meets some minimal standards, it's just going to get published. One of the people who works here was one of their Associate Editors, and she said they get, like, 1,000 articles a week. It was some insane number. They just check method, and looking very little at significance or anything like that, they just say, "Let the community decide what's important."
[RM]:	Well, of course, we could never do that. We always had a page budget, right?
[JT]:	Yes, but even more so, there's the sense that we play a real filtering role. That we, and the reviewers, are setting some kind of standard, and the paper has to meet that.
[BD]:	Right, and that's thinking about building a set of reviewers that are bringing different things to the table, and if they don't all agree, well, that's not really the point, because when you pick them you intend for them to give you different perspectives. You know a priori at least why you've asked someone.

Question: How much are reviewers part of the dialogue?

[RM]:	Some reviewers will do a really cursory job, and what we tried to do was to send them back and say, "Not good enough, do it again." But outside

of that bottom few percent, it's a range. Some reviewers are very, very careful. They clearly put in a lot of work, and do a lot of work: they find citations for everything. Which probably means they get more papers to review! Sad for them.

[CH]: I think the trick is finding reviewers who are excited about the work, and who are experts. Or who have expertise in that field. That's a challenge. For TOCE, I think a lot of that work goes down to our Associate Editors and their networks, finding the people who are good matches with paper topics. You can see that reflected in the reviews. If they've nailed it, you often get three really strong reviews. But if it's an esoteric topic, or if I had to assign it to an Associate Editor who wasn't quite the best match in the first place, they're going to then have trouble finding people.

[RM]: That's true, but there are also the pragmatics of the situation. When we were at TOCE, we had a great set of Associate Editors, but they didn't span every bit of computer science. We would get papers for which no one would admit to having expertise – and neither of us did either, really. Sometimes you have to work with what you have, and if they're not experts in an area, chances are they won't know any experts either, and so the reviewers they get may not be as good.

[BD]: The other thing is, I think we're afraid to go outside of computer science at times. For instance, if we have a paper about a concept inventory, we should not be scared to send it to a concept inventory expert in chemistry, because if it's about the development and validation of an instrument, the subject matter, the topic, doesn't matter so much. But cold-calling an expert from some other domain can be daunting as an Associate Editor: it probably needs to be taken on by the Editors.

[CH]: And if you do, I think it's important to articulate why you're asking them in the email you send them. Then they can draw that connection and maybe get excited about it a little more than they would otherwise.

[RM] If you want to have people review papers, you have to take them seriously. That being said, they're not making the decision. They're providing input, same with the Associate Editors. They suggest a decision. Often, usually, as Editor you'll go along with it; sometimes you don't.

[JT]: The nice thing, a thing I really liked in TOCE, was dialogue. Of course, we pushed back a bit to the Associate Editors, but they also pushed us. It was really a dialogue, where we were collectively figuring out, "Well, what is this publication? Where do we stand on this?" So at times, when Robert and I might have thought "No," someone may have been pushing back on that. That dialogue then causes us to go, "OK, yes. OK, we see what you're saying. We see that."

I felt it was very much a dialogue, and I think we were trying to encourage our Associate Editors to have that with the reviewers as well, and so we always made sure that reviewers could see the review, the decision, and the letters that got returned to the authors.

And sometimes it's a dialogue with authors. I remember one in particular: it was a tools paper. There wasn't anything empirical in it, but it was a radical and interesting idea. We turned it down. Then we got a very eloquent rebuttal, which made the case that, "You don't want to let all these good ideas go just because we have no empirical evidence." So we talked about it and we decided to let the paper through – but on the condition that the author joined the Editorial Board, so when we got papers like that in the future, we just gave them to them.

[BD]:   In terms of the back-and-forth with reviewers, some reviewers, I think, are very amenable to that, and they'll let you know as soon as they submit a review, and they'll send you a personal email about the rationale. It expands even more, and they're very open to that dialogue, but then other reviewers just submit it and you never hear from them even if you reach out. So it really varies, I think. It can be really helpful, though. Like the discussion period during ICER review. In some cases, it really is helpful, and adds extra information for an Associate Chair. Of course, in other cases it doesn't add much to the conversation.

[CH]:   The reviewer decisions I usually question are the ones that come back "reject" where I don't see the rationale as being crystal clear, and so I have a dialogue with the Associate Editor, with a few back-and-forth emails. I say, "Either accept the paper with major revisions, or if you're going to reject it, please write a better rationale." And we might have to iterate on that a bit. Usually what happens there is that the Associate Editor will say, "Yes, I think I was too harsh." So, the decision flips.

[JT]   Another thing is, in a journal rather than a conference situation, you've got time. So with rejections, for instance, you can often have an email exchange with the Associate Editors, saying, "Do you know, usually, with this kind of paper that's come back three times now, they're not actually making very much progress? And although we all like the direction they're going, it's not clear this process is ever going to end. So what we usually do here is just call it a day." We've had that kind of conversation a lot.

[CH]:   We've got an explicit policy at TOCE now that says you only get one shot at a major review. So we send it out for peer review twice only. If it doesn't get improved from major review to minor, it's out. That's the new rule, and I think that's the way forward.

Question: Do all papers go out to review?

[CH]:   Exactly half the papers submitted last year I desk rejected. For various reasons. Some of them are just …

[LM]:   "What *is* this?"

[BD]:   Completely out of scope, yes.

[CH]:   And then there are some tough decisions where I don't think they meet the review criteria, and I don't want to overburden the Editorial Board, because they're a precious resource.

[BD]:   I think the ones we get like that are the "experience report" papers. Where an author has legitimately crafted this thing that is telling a story about what they did in their classroom, right? It's the classic experience report from a SIGCSE Symposium-style publication. And those are not quite ready to go out for review in a lot of cases because they lack the empirical rigor that we would expect. For those, you have to write back and suggest perhaps a more preliminary conference venue would be a better starting point for what they have, or that they work to find additional data. Because you just can't overburden the Editorial Boards and the reviewers for things that you know aren't going to meet a standard.

[LM]:   That just aren't going to get in.

[RM]:   Right, and we would see papers like this as well. Usually, there was no real evaluation. Whatever they're planning. It was obvious that if you sent that paper out for review, it would come back at least as a major revision, because the evaluation was not good enough. So why send it to the reviewers? Send it back to the author and say, "Look, without good evaluation, this paper will not be accepted. So work on the evaluation," and sometimes you suggest things. You suggest possibilities.

[BD]: Yes, and I think that's one of the difficult things. When, in a smallish community, your role not only is disseminating high-quality work, but also to some degree helping inform and raise awareness of what standards are. That developmental sort of role that the review process leads to, I think, can take a ton of time, and sometimes we don't have enough time to do that thing.

[JT]: I felt the same way, and what happened was I got to the point where, "Oh, it's clearly time for me to step down, because I simply don't have the patience or energy for this."

[LM]: I feel like maybe we get fewer of those than we used to, yes. Yes, just like you see more research papers at the SIGCSE Symposium than you used to. I think there are fewer. You still get them, of course. Where they've done something, but it's not good enough.

[SF]: I always crudely categorized them as the, "Oh, it's a 'and the students seem to like it' paper." Where they think they've got to do something empirical, and the reflex response is, "Oh, I'll ask them. I'll do a quick survey."

[LM]: Right, right. "I'll do a survey." Of my 28 students.

[BD]: Actually, it's "a qualitative study" … that just has a list of quotes.

[LM]: Right, quotes.

[BD]: Four pages of quotes. No analysis.

[LM]: Or just a table of notes.

[RM]: Survey results!

[CH]: It's true. We saw so many of those that it's explicit in our review criteria now. It can't just be an end-of-semester survey. That's disallowed. It's in our review criteria now, and so I just refer them to that. [Generally speaking, evaluations of computing education interventions published in TOCE must go beyond the analysis of end-of-course student evaluation surveys. While such qualitative data can be informative, additional data should be collected and analyzed (e.g., video data, log data, interview data, and/or student artifacts) in order to gain deeper insight into the teaching and learning of computing.]

[JT]: I do remember that something we started seeing was people doing something empirical, but it had nothing to do with their research question. It's like, you've asked them if they're happy, but your research question was about how well they were learning.

[LM]: Or if they felt that they learned something. "Do you *think* this helped you learn?"

[JT]: Yes, yes.

Question: Do you have a feeling after reading some number of years' worth of papers for what is reasonable empirical evidence? Or what is reasonable evidence for claims?

[CH]: I think one of the most difficult decisions I face, as an editor, is whether a paper has a sufficient enough contribution and whether their claims can be believed.

We could, perhaps, be more explicit about what standard of evidence we will accept, and maybe even how it's reported. JEE [*Journal of Engineering Education*, see Chapter 11] has gone to some length in that regard. If we could do that, we think it could raise the quality of the journal while at the same time making it more accessible. This has been led by a member of the Editorial Board whose research is strongly empirical. And I've had discussions with the Editorial Board where there has been some pushback, with others saying, "Well, you don't want to go so far that you then exclude papers and research that is actually of interest and relevance to our community." So, we have to find this line, this balance, between raising the level of rigor while also reporting and publishing on things that are relevant and interesting.

[RM]:   In a sense, we're trying to teach people how to evidence their work.

[BD]:   "Guidance to Authors" about the expectations and the genre norms of a journal can play a role in that. There's a signaling piece that comes with these documents that tells some authors, "You're welcome here," or, "No you're not."

The challenge, of course, is in being appropriately explicit. Because we have such a varied set of methodological and philosophical traditions in the research that is done, how do you write a set of policies that are sufficiently detailed but also reasonably broad enough to cover that?

In writing something that provides evidence standards for quasi-experimental work, or highly experimental work, how do you not alienate the phenomenology-style work? Or the grounded theory-style work?

[RM]:   Or even coming up with the appropriate reviewers, because if you have qualitative work and somebody from a more quantitative tradition looks at it, they may say, "Well, I'm sorry, the n is too small," or "What's the p-value?" Clearly, they don't understand the methodology that's being used. And it may be that the author sometimes doesn't either. It may be that the author has only a vague idea of how a grounded theory works. Sort of by the fingernails.

[BD]:   I think this goes back to the front matter of the CSEd Research Book [Fincher & Petre, 2004]. "What is the claim you're trying to make from the data that you have and what are the limits of that?" What we want are contributions that are sound within the parameters of what they have set up. The expectations of what makes a sound contribution in case study-style work are different from the level of data that is presented. It's not to say that there is more data here or less data here, it's that the analysis is different and the nature of the claim that is made is different, and the generalizability and all those things.

[RM]:   I think it puts a little bit more on the authors, though. Given that there's a broad variety of methods, it's up to the author to some degree to explain what's the case study, what's the data case study, and what's the generalizability. They have to explain more of the underlying theory than they might if they were writing in a more established discipline where everybody basically gets it. Where everyone knows what a case study is. You don't have to tell the reviewers.

[SF]:   *"The Journal of Case Study Research."*

[RM]:   Right.

[SF]:   You wouldn't have to explain that.

[BD]:   And what do you do with the theoretical, analytical pieces that are looking at the field and drawing up understandings of those things? Perhaps as a meta-review article that has empiricism to it. Or as a more broad kind of literature review. What do you do with those? Not to say "think piece," but is there a place for those? I think they do play a valuable role in helping shape our understanding of the field.

[RM]:   I think certainly that it's useful that people reflect on the field of what's going on and what the research is.

[BD]:   But then how do you set an evidence standard for that?

Question: OK. So what sort of papers do you really like? What are the joys? What are the really good ones?

[CH]:   I like papers that try to organize the field, to set the stage for future research, I like review papers a lot, and I'd like to see more of them. If they do it well, organize, do a nice review of the literature, and try to identify areas for future research, they really set a research agenda. That's my own personal preference.

[JT]:   I like papers when people bring in theory and methods from other fields.

[LM]:   I like something novel that I haven't seen before, yes.

[BD]:   I think just using theory and leveraging it to underpin methodological decisions and study design and being very deliberate about that chain of reasoning. You read these papers every now and then, and they're just a joy. They can be qualitative, they can be quantitative, but they're shining examples, and you read them once and go, "That's really clever. I had never thought of something before, and that makes total sense. And, yes, we ought to be doing that," and it happens so rarely.

[RM]:   Yes, I really like papers where people are very careful, and they're very careful about explaining exactly what they do, whether they tie it to a theory or not. If someone can present evidence in a clear enough way to convince me that it's reasonable, that's a paper that I like. And that's even if what they're claiming may be a little bit "out there": if they can convince me that painting everyone's fingernails green actually has a good effect, well, OK!

[SF]:   I like that. I like that tightness, that care, that coherence. I like a paper that's all of a piece, a paper where every part has been thought about.

[BD]:   I think that the thing that always drives me crazy are the data-dump papers. Those that are, "We collected tons and tons of survey data … and this … and that … because we could," and it's a sort of CYA ["cover your ass"]. You collect a little bit of extra stuff because you can, to explore alternative hypotheses should what you're looking for not actually work out. In case something bad happens, you can fall back on some other data you have. But then – they just choose to present it all! Rather than knowing when to say no.

[SF]:   As a reviewer – I think as a reviewer particularly – but also as an editor, I hate the opposite. I hate salami-sliced papers. I absolutely hate them. As a reviewer, I hate them because sometimes you don't know – because they've anonymized their own publications. So you can't go back and look, and find the tiny little change they've made that makes this a separate contribution. I really dislike those.

[BD]:   As an editor, I don't like those LPU [least publishable unit] papers either. But as an author, I've had the regret where you submit a paper and you then think, "Oh, I should have broken that in two."

[LM]:   That could have been two papers.

[BD]:   "That could have been two, what was I doing? That was two studies. I know why I wrote it the way I did, but that was two papers. Oh well." So you do take on a different perspective on your own work sometimes.

[SF]:   Ah, yes.

[BD]:   Well, and how much is enough? What size of contribution is needed? I think reviewers don't agree, necessarily. And what differentiates a journal paper from a conference paper? I'm not sure as a field we have any kind of cohesive sense for that yet.

[RM]: It's the review process is what. It's the chance, it's revision after review, and I think that really does make a difference. I think the quality is better. You see a big improvement between the first submission and what actually gets published, and you don't so much in conferences.

[JT] That reminds me, though, of something that Robert and I saw a ton of, which I couldn't believe, was we saw a huge percentage of the papers that got major revision. Papers where the decision on the first review cycle was major: most of those, we never saw again. And those that did come back usually went to minor revision on the next review cycle, so if people did put in the additional energy, it paid off. I didn't understand why – for some reason – authors thought it wasn't worthwhile for them to keep going.

What I finally thought was that authors thought it would be an easy publication. That our authors maybe don't get high value for an education paper in their disciplinary department, and the reward of publication wasn't worth the effort of revision.

[RM]: It's hard to say. If you're not – and I think most of our authors are not – in an education department, a major journal and a minor journal are equal. To the Dean. Perhaps.

[LM]: Yes, there are some that just, sort of, go in a black hole, and you just never hear from them again. We ping them a couple of times, but if they were being asked to go back and get more data, or change the method of analysis, or do something like that, then yes, they might not come back.

[JT]: Yes. Those are the ones. We'd only see a small percentage of those again. A small percentage.

[SF]: Which is strange, because of course that's what you get with a journal over a conference; you get that opportunity to revise and resubmit.

[JT]: Well, that was the other thing. I remember when I started, I used to approach authors who had papers in the SIGCSE Symposium and ICER and similar venues and say, "Hi, have you thought about extending …"

[LM]: "Hi, I really liked your paper …"

[JT]: Yes, "I liked your paper, have you thought about extending it?" And a huge percentage of them wouldn't even respond to my email. I just stopped doing that, because it takes huge amounts of time.

Question: Well, that brings on to another question: Who is the audience for our journals that we publish? Who are we trying to influence, to do what?

[JT]: I actually think that's a really good point. I think that's changing. Because originally we were thinking of practitioners, largely, as being the audience. I think we would have loved to publish some of the sorts of papers you're outlining here, but if we'd gone down that route we'd have said, "We might as well close the doors now." Right?

[RM]: Right, we won't get any papers, and we won't have any readers.

[JT]: But we may be talking to a very different audience. Which is more of an audience of researchers.

[BD]: Which is the audience for this Handbook, right? So, 15 years ago, there wasn't a cohort of PhD students in the wings, waiting for resources like this. Or junior faculty that needed places to publish and things to read. I don't think that community was mature enough 15 years ago. We're maybe not quite there yet, but there are certainly places hiring CSEd people, and programs that are advertising CSEd research postdocs and PhD focus areas in CSEd.

So I think maybe we'll move toward a more traditional audience of folks that are active researchers in the space. As opposed to researchers-slash-practitioners: wearing that double hat always makes it a bit harder.

Question: So will they no longer have the CS background? Are we looking at psychologists, and people from education?

[BD]: I think we're already seeing some of that. I think we are seeing authors that are coming from disciplinary training and background, and colleges of education that have some formal connection to computing. With, say, undergraduate training, or as a coauthor. They are interested in different questions. They will bring new things to the table, and I think that's probably good, because if you look at JEE, there's some of that. Or in any discipline-based education research community.

[RM]: But in some sense, don't we want to affect practice? We're doing research for a reason, right? It's not just to convince the other researchers that we have good ideas.

[BD]: So there is a really interesting ... There was a Facebook feed conversation after the ICER reviews came out this year, and one of the comments said, "One of the reviewers liked my paper because it was immediately applicable, and clearly they don't know what ICER is for," and I pushed back. I said, "Well, wait a second. Translational characteristics of research are not necessarily a dirty thing." Some research, I agree, should have clear implications in direct practice, and have a short timetable to making and influencing change, but basic research is also of interest. We might not know what the payoff timeline is, and it may not be clear yet.

[RM]: Right, but the hope is at some point there's a payoff.

[BD]: Yes, but it might not happen in 10 or 15 years. Certainly, I think that in the portfolio of things that are published in journals, there should be a collection of things that are directly applicable tomorrow, and others where you say, "Huh, we know something now that we didn't know before about computing education. We're not quite sure what to do with it yet, or where it comes into play, but it's solid work, and we're convinced it's a thing."

[RM]: So, who do you want to read the journal? Who should read the journal, then?

[CH]: Both researchers and practitioners, ideally.

[RM]: I mean, part of the difficulty of increasing the formalism on the educational side is that you lose the practitioner, because they don't have the background to understand socio-whatever theory.

[BD]: Maybe we could look to forms of discourse that mean you have to be able to break it down for another audience. Maybe attach an executive summary to articles. I'm not sure that's the right way to go, but I'm sure in other discipline-based education research venues they've done things like this. "What is the practical significance of the thing that you've done for practitioners?"

[RM]: When we started TOCE, or before we started TOCE, we were looking at JEE as a model, because they became much more formal.

[SF]: Quite deliberately.

[RM]: That's absolutely right. It was deliberate, "We are going to be a formal education journal, and we're going to have standards of professionalism."

And they lost part of their audience. Do you need somebody to translate between the really formal research results and the things that people want to do in the classroom? Those papers won't get published, the ones that tell you, "OK, here's a lesson plan."

[BD]:   Really, does this have implications beyond your local context? Does it have some sort of broader connection to theory? Is it trying to be something that helps us understand the known knowns? Or is it about program improvement, is it about effective best practices in the classroom?

[SF]:   Even the very best action research papers, and those are few and far between, I found difficult to publish because they are necessarily so tied to their context.

[RM]:   Right, but shouldn't there be a venue? Should there not be a venue?

[SF]:   Yes. I think, yes.

[BD]:   Sally's been arguing for this for years.

[SF]:   Yes I have.

[BD]:   Right, but the output of action research does not generally take the form of scholarly articles.

[SF]:   Exactly right.

Question: Let's finish by looking forward. What are the papers that you don't see but wish you did? What are the ones that the community is *not* producing?

[CH]:   Well, based on my analysis of the 2016 submissions to TOCE, we got only 6 percent teacher training. Which seems low, given all of the initiatives that are out there. So, I'd like to see more.

[RM]:   We would see that – with a lag – we would see upticks in certain kinds of papers, depending on what had been funded, because two years into the grant, they need papers. So we would get a flood of that sort, and most of them weren't particularly good. The evaluation was what was expected by the funding agency, but not really up to research standard. Sort of shallow.

[BD]:   I'd like to see theory-building papers. We so rarely have a paper that attempts to develop theories that are unique to computing. If there's theory, it's usually borrowed in, and an application to an area. As opposed to looking at the extent to which those theories hold up, and developing new theories about particular learning. So I think some of that would be interesting. I think the notion of learning progressions, there's a lot of talk about it, but I don't know that we've seen any convincing articles on that yet.

[CH]:   Innovations in evaluation would be another thing. Evaluation instruments and methodologies specific for computing education, for getting at stuff that we care about. I'd like to see a lot of those papers.

[JT]:   I don't see papers that are using some of what I see as advances in cognitive science. Embodied cognition, gesture studies, and deeper uses of various sociocultural theories that I think have had real purchase in math and science education. I read really different kinds of literature there. So that's one. The other is, and it surprises me, is we've had few really deep ethnographic studies. Like fieldwork, like serious fieldwork, where we have anthropologists with a deep sense of the discipline, or who come to develop a deep sense of the discipline. There are some classic and beautiful ethnographies in education, but I don't think we've seen them in computing education. I think work like that could really be quite amazing.

I've wanted to see those. And if I were to start over, I'd want to do those. But I'm not going to start over.

[BD]: I'd like to see papers on learning that's happening outside the auspices of formal education. There's a little bit with after-school clubs, elementary schools. But not the adults that are just mucking about, and the things that happen when you're in the workplace. Even the lifelong learning that happens in computing ... and maybe I'm biased a little bit, because I work in this area.

[RM]: I got excited about this too, but I could never get anybody with money to be excited. And, in fact, I couldn't engage most of the people in the community. They just basically said, "I'm not interested. I don't care about what happens outside the classroom, I'm interested in what happens in the classroom."

[BD]: But I think now we have this push of code camps, or boot camps, or whatever they're calling them, and you have start-up companies where the majority of their developers are folks who picked up a little bit of Ruby on Rails in six weeks and are now building websites for clients. What are the shortcomings in those kinds of experiences? And what are the benefits or advantages of those kinds of experiences? How does this apprentice-style learning on the job play out?

How do we develop communities within a workplace? So, I was talking with some staff at a local employer, and all of their staff (except the CEO) are from code schools. So they have developed these processes for code review to ensure that there are other people looking over their shoulders. Because they recognize that they don't have the formal knowledge to prevent security holes in particular, like SQL injection attacks. One of them was telling this seemingly hilarious story to them, but it sounded like a huge security hole to me. Happy ending – it got caught in one of these review processes.

So, what is the on-the-job experience that mitigates these things? I think there's a really rich, and perhaps ethnographic, story to tell about that sort of learning that happens. And maybe it doesn't happen because that sort of work isn't funded.

[RM]: Well, maybe, but it's also true that it would be really interesting, and I think we hear, essentially, nothing. We don't hear about on-the-job stuff pretty much at all.

[BD]: With the exception of Andy Begel's and Beth Simon's work [Begel & Simon, 2008a, 2008b].

[RM]: With all these things like code camps, where people are coming from non-traditional backgrounds and being put into traditional computing jobs, it would be really interesting to find out about – What do they do?

[LM]: Right, what do they do? How do they learn?

[RM]: Do they make it work? What happens to them in three years, when technology changes, are they able to keep current enough to keep that job?

[SF]: Yes, and what happens when they move jobs?

[JT]: What I've been wondering is sort of an update on the kind of study that Sylvia Scribner did [Scribner, 1984] on the practical arithmetic of workers in a dairy distribution plant. She went to some of these dairy men and looked at their practice, at how they packed crates, and how they used material structures and their affordances in order to actually do some of their mathematical calculations. Jean Lave did similar ones with grocery shopping, and how people do everyday mathematics [Lave, 1988]. And we have so much more computation. They looked at everyday cognition, and everyday mathematics, and you know, we have much more everyday computation where people are having to deal with these computational artifacts. I would love to see the ways in which people are learning, appropriating, and using the material in order to be part of some computational thing. I don't think we yet have that kind of study.

[BD]:   You know the other study I was thinking about recently is a serious literature review meta-analysis about the lies we tell, and the advocacy push for computing for all, right? All of the claims, it improves problem-solving ...

[RM]:   It might.

[LM]:   It could.

[SF]:   Maybe.

[BD]:   ... Special Issues on, for example, let's take five of these claims and do a deep dive and say, "What evidence to we have that this claim is real, or not, or we don't know?" It's back to the Logo, marketing push, and there were all these unsubstantiated claims back in the '70s and '80s. I think we're rushing headfirst into implementation in schools, and if three, four years from now we find that, "You know, it turns out it was really expensive and not much happened, because we weren't attuned to what we needed to be looking for." What are the variables that matter?

In the code.org ACM framework, the research chapter [K–12 Computer Science Framework, 2016], we had a lot of conversations along the lines of, "You can't say that. We don't have evidence for that, you can't make a statement that's not true. You can't cite that paper in that way, it doesn't say that. It says this, more narrowly scoped, thing," I think, as the research community, we owe it to policy-makers and the deciders in school systems to be very open and honest and say, "Here's what we know, and here's what we don't know."

Closing

In the opening paragraphs, we noted that this sort of conversation is something that is not usually reported in the literature. This raises the question that, if this is a form that is not usually "in the literature," why is it included in this Handbook? The first response is that it is an appropriate way in which to capture and present the state of computing education research "today." The second response exposes some underlying epistemologies of research practice that it is appropriate to explore in this venue.

There are other ways we could have examined contemporary practice. For example, there is a modest tradition of classifying computing education research by examining the artifacts that are produced; that is, the papers that are published. David Valentine (2004) and Justus Randolph were early proponents (Randolph, 2007; Randolph et al., 2007; Randolph, 2008; Randolph et al., 2009). The most well-known strand of this tradition has been undertaken by Simon, often with Lauri Malmi, and other colleagues (Malmi et al., 2010, 2014; Pears et al., 2005; Simon et al., 2008a, 2008b; Simon, 2016). In undertaking this work, these researchers treat manuscripts as if they were unproblematized natural objects, like pieces of wood or rock, and they have worked with them as objects through close examination, characterizing their structures or composition, and sorting them into categories; that is, by taxonomizing them.

There are advantages to such a decontextualized, descriptive approach. It permits comparison of work that is, on the surface, profoundly dissimilar and it allows quantitative claims to be made, perhaps that there is more of a certain type of paper over another, or that one type of paper is more prevalent at different times (e.g., in the same conference in another year) or in different venues, or that different venues are similar in given ways. Researchers who take this positivist stance want to abstract away from detail of expression to make "objective" claims about the construction and development of the field of computing education research as a whole, and to gain an understanding of how it is situated in relation to other discipline-based educational research areas.

However, what this approach sacrifices is any understanding of the context of production. It cannot capture *why* a given piece of work was undertaken, or what the authors considered to be important when designing the research, or when thinking it worth publishing, or when they put it into a form that would be interesting and useful to others when "writing up" their work. Nor does it consider any other processes (such as authorial choices of where to submit their work and editorial choices such as processes of peer review and selection) that must have been engaged for it to be published at all.

Neither does this approach take historicity into account, but rather it treats each paper as equal to each other paper, no matter when it was produced. They take these papers as data, as "decontextualized, disembodied authorless forms of neutral information that fall ready made out of the sky" (Vansledright, 2010, p. 116). We all live – and research and write papers – within our time, and what we research and write will be influenced by many things happening in the contemporaneous world. Some obvious influences are changes in demographics and funding of university education, national curricula efforts to introduce (and strengthen) the study of computing in primary and secondary schools, funding priorities by national and multinational research agencies, high-stakes evaluative exercises in various countries in which "research productivity" is measured within and across institutions of higher education and then used as a basis for funding allocations (as well as other political–economic uses), and undoubtedly many other things.

This chapter, and the rationale for presenting it in this way, takes a situated and contextual standpoint and considers these influences to be important. Rather than see "research" to be a simple progression of papers, it considers that computing education research may be examined as something that has been reflexively constituted by the people who participate in it (that is, sociologically). Taking this view, it is not only in the artifacts – in the published papers – that research is manifest, but it also importantly lies in the engagements that produce them. Here, "research" exists in conference program committee meetings, in dialogue between journal editors and reviewers. It is made visible when new review criteria are established for a conference or journal, and it lives in conversations such as the one represented in this chapter. It is in these engagements that we can see the "work" involved in its construction.

In humanistic traditions, progress occurs not through a blind, evolutionary process similar to the pressures that act on the biological world (that is, papers become more rigorous because weaker papers die out), but because people, like those who speak in this chapter, get together and try to work things out – to ask: "What's next?", "What do we need as a community?" – and then take deliberate action as a result, such as start a new journal, start a new conference, or collaborate to write a Handbook. In this framing, it is through the self-conscious and deliberate efforts of actors that the field is developed and the quality and status of what constitutes computing education research is formed.

Thus, this chapter provides both an "insider" view of the state of the field at the present time and also an illustration of how the question "What constitutes a research field?" may be addressed from a qualitative stance.

The following chapter, in reporting "voices from the field," takes a similar approach in that it places high value on discovering and reporting the authentic views of "key players." It is different in that there the method used is to separately interview participants to a common (albeit loose) script. Then, in reporting, the researcher filters and interprets the respondents' voices, in pursuit of synthesizing a coherent (if not a 100-percent consensus) view on specific topics of interest. Taken together, both of these chapters illustrate a configuration of the role of the knower (the researcher) with what can be known (the object of our investigation) that is similar to each other and distinct from an "objective" positivist position. They take the stance that investigating human endeavor requires methods that embrace the complexity of human agency rather than working to eliminate it.

Endnote: How the Work Was Conducted

A broad set of questions was circulated in advance. The conversation was professionally transcribed and then edited by Sally Fincher, who also wrote the framing. The edited version was then sent to all conversationalists for comment. Josh Tenenberg contributed to the conclusion.

References

Begel, A., & Simon, B. (2008a). Novice software developers, all over again. In *Proceedings of the Fourth International Workshop on Computing Education Research* (pp. 3–14). New York: ACM.

Begel, A., & Simon, B. (2008b). Struggles of new college graduates in their first software development job. In *Proceedings of the 39th SIGCSE Technical Symposium on Computer Science Education* (pp. 226–230). New York: ACM.

Fincher, S., & Petre, M. (2004). *Computer Science Education Research*. Abingdon, UK: Routledge.

K–12 computer science framework (2016). Retrieved from www.k12cs.org

Lave, J. (1988). *Cognition in Practice: Mind, Mathematics and Culture in Everyday Life.* Cambridge, UK: Cambridge University Press.

Malmi, L., Sheard, J., Simon, Bednarik, R., Helminen, J., Kinnunen, P., Korhonen, A., Myller, N., Sorva, J., & Taherkhani, A. (2014). Theoretical underpinnings of computing education research: What is the evidence? In *Proceedings of the Tenth Annual Conference on International Computing Education Research* (pp. 27–34). New York: ACM.

Malmi, L., Sheard, J., Simon, Bednarik, R., Helminen, J., Korhonen, A., Myller, N., Sorva, J., & Taherkhani, A. (2010). Characterizing research in computing education: A preliminary analysis of the literature. In *Proceedings of the Sixth International Workshop on Computing Education Research* (pp. 3–12). New York: ACM.

Pears, A., Seidman, S., Eney, C., Kinnunen, P., & Malmi, L. (2005). Constructing a core literature for computing education research. *SIGCSE Bulletin, 37*(4), 152–161.

Randolph, J. J. (2007). Findings from a methodological review of the computer science education research: 2000–2005. *SIGCSE Bulletin, 39*(4), 130.

Randolph, J. J. (2008). A methodological review of computer science education research. *Journal of Information Technology Education, 7,* 135–162.

Randolph, J. J., Julnes, G., Bednarik, R., & Sutinen, E. (2007). A comparison of the methodological quality of articles in computer science education journals and conference proceedings. *Computer Science Education, 17*(4), 263–274.

Randolph, J. J., Julnes, G. & Sutinen, E. (2009). Trends, tribes, and territories in computer science education research. *Journal for Computing Teachers, 1*(1), 1–19.

Scribner, S. (1984). Studying working intelligence. In B. Rogoff & J. Lave (Eds.), *Everyday Cognition: Its Development in Social Context* (pp. 9–44). Cambridge, MA: Harvard University Press.

Simon (2016). A picture of the growing ICER community. In *Proceedings of the 2016 ACM Conference on International Computing Education Research* (pp. 153–159). New York: ACM.

Simon, Carbone, A., de Raadt, M., Lister, R., Hamilton, M., & Sheard, J. (2008a). Classifying computing education papers: Process and results. In *Proceedings of the Fourth International Workshop on Computing Education Research* (pp. 61–172). New York: ACM.

Simon, Sheard, J., Carbone, A., de Raadt, M., Hamilton, M., Lister, R., & Thompson, E. (2008). Eight years of computing education papers at NACCQ. In *21st Annual Conference of the National Advisory Committee on Computing Qualifications (NACCQ 2008)* (pp. 101–107). Auckland, New Zealand: National Advisory Committee on Computing Qualifications.

Valentine, D. W. (2004). CS educational research: A meta-analysis of SIGCSE technical symposium proceedings. In *Proceedings of the 35th SIGCSE Technical Symposium on Computer Science Education* (pp. 255–259). New York: ACM.

Vansledright, B. (2010). What does it mean to think historically and how do you teach it? In W. Parker (Ed.), *Social Studies Today: Research and Practice* (pp. 113–120). New York: Routledge.

3 Computing Education

Literature Review and Voices from the Field

Paulo Blikstein and Sepi Hejazi Moghadam

Dedicated to Francisco Walter Durán Segarra (in memoriam), Ecuadorian polymath, professor, and educational researcher, an ahead-of-his-time mind who never gave up the fight for a more emancipatory, meaningful, and democratic education.

3.1 Introduction

In 1967, Seymour Papert, Cynthia Solomon, and Wally Feurzeig created the Logo computer language, the first designed for children (Papert, 1980) – an event widely considered as the beginning of computing education (CEd).[1] In a time when computers cost millions of dollars and occupied entire rooms, teaching computing to children, while visionary, was a hard sell for school systems and policy-makers. From the mid-1970s to the early 1990s, CEd slowly penetrated schools worldwide. Despite a decade of popularity in the 1980s, it never reached as deeply into the educational mainstream as Papert and his colleagues wished. Since the mid-2000s, however, there has been a pronounced shift in the focus on science, technology, engineering, and mathematics (STEM) education, and CEd is at the forefront of this process (National Research Council, 2012). As computational technologies have become inexpensive and pervasive in our lives, the demand for an educated and technologically literate labor force has continued to increase (Noonan, 2017; US Department of Labor, 2007). This is not merely about the labor force, but also about citizenship. The need for children to become future producers of technology – fluent in the medium of our time, instead of merely consumers – has become a major focus for policy-makers and researchers. Today, educators and CEd advocates are pushing ahead with plans to add computing to the list of topics that all students should study (K–12 Computer Science Framework Steering Committee, 2016).

Other catalysts driving the mainstream acceptance of CEd include the launch of the Scratch, Blockly, NetLogo, and Alice programming environments; the launch of organizations such as the Computer Science Teachers Association (CSTA; an international body founded by the Association for Computing Machinery [ACM]), the rise of the maker movement and fablabs (Blikstein, 2013, 2018); the creation of organizations providing CS learning opportunities

---

1 John Kemeny and Thomas Kurtz (Dartmouth College) created the BASIC programming language in 1964, but Logo is used as a landmark because of its comprehensive focus on all segments and age levels of education, especially children.

such as Code.org, Black Girls Code, Girls Who Code, and others[2]; and the rollout of national programs such as CS4All in the USA. As a result, there is an almost overwhelming demand from school systems worldwide for research and implementation guidelines, one that the relatively small CEd research community is simply not able to meet (Guzdial, 2017). The newness of the discipline is also an important factor. For example, while the US National Council of Teachers of Mathematics (NCTM) was founded in 1920, and its science counterpart, the National Science Teachers Association (NSTA), was formed in 1944, CSTA was not launched until 2004. When NCTM and NSTA were formed, school infrastructure was already in place for these disciplines, thousands of mathematics and science teachers were teaching in schools across the USA, and teacher colleges supported a strong pipeline for more. *CEd does not have those advantages today.* The current focus on CEd has also generated much discourse regarding its purpose. Is the rationale for CEd to fulfill job market needs, promote personal empowerment, teach children to code, develop students' fluency in a new literacy, address historical educational inequalities, or some combination of all of the above?

The goal of this chapter (which is based on a longer report originally commissioned by Google[3,4]) is to better understand the state of CEd by using a methodological innovation. Instead of only examining the published literature, we also interviewed some of the main voices in the field, inquiring about two topics in particular: the multiple rationales for teaching computing and the obstacles for sustainable implementation. With these goals in mind, this chapter summarizes interviews conducted with several leading researchers and practitioners, in addition to providing an examination of literature reviews and articles.

3.2 Methods

We utilized three main data sources for this chapter: interviews, literature reviews, and analysis of papers recommended by the interviewees. For the interviews, we selected leaders in the field from various universities, institutions, and organizations, trying to balance intellectual traditions, academic backgrounds, and expertise. The selection focused mostly on the USA, not because it is representative of what happens in other countries, but mostly to have a more complete picture of CEd in one country. The final group of interviewees consisted of 14 people: Matthew Berland (University of Wisconsin-Madison), Leah Buechley (Rural Digital), Michael Clancy (University of California,

---

2 There is a large number of such organizations, many focusing on underserved populations: Black Girls Code, Girls Who Code, Girls Code it, CoderDojo, Technovation, and Yes We Code.
3 Available at https://services.google.com/fh/files/misc/pre-college-computer-science-education-report.pdf
4 Stanford University has strict rules to avoid conflicts of interest or bias in reports written for private entities. The original report was created following those rules.

Berkeley), Andrea "Andy" diSessa (University of California, Berkeley), Sally Fincher (University of Kent), Shuchi Grover (formerly SRI International), Mark Guzdial (Georgia Institute of Technology), Mike Horn (Northwestern University), Jane Margolis (University of California, Los Angeles), Mitchel Resnick (Massachusetts Institute of Technology), Sue Sentance (King's College, London), Ben Shapiro (University of Colorado, Boulder), David Weintrop (University of Maryland), and Pat Yongpradit (Code.org).

All invited interviewees accepted to be interviewed, except one professor, who nominated another scholar in his own department (Michael Clancy, University of California, Berkeley), and Andrea diSessa, who preferred to send an in-preparation paper instead (the paper is used in this chapter in lieu of an interview and is listed in the references). All participants were given the option of anonymity and none opted for it. After the first complete draft was finished, all 14 interviewees were given the opportunity to fully review the text and suggest further changes, which were individually considered for the final version.

We used a semi-structured protocol for the interviews that included questions about the relevance and importance of teaching computing, the main research findings in the field, and research, policy, and implementation agendas for years to come. The interviews were conducted remotely by the first author via videoconference, audio recorded, transcribed in their entirety, and analyzed using a grounded coding approach. The principal themes extracted from the initial coding were: (a) teacher preparation; (b) policy and scale-up; (c) curriculum development; (d) cultural, diversity, and equity issues; (e) pedagogy; and (f) historical aspects of CEd. These categories informed a further refining of the coding, so the data were recoded for more fine-grained topics, resulting in approximately 1,000 excerpts grouped into 130 sub-codes. Those were then recategorized in terms of the six initial themes and informed the structure of the analysis. For the purposes of this chapter, we will focus mostly on two of those six main clusters of: the rationales for teaching computing and CEd implementation.

The literature was selected using a combination of recommendations from the interviewees, well-established policy documents such as the CSTA K–12 Computer Science Standards (Seehorn et al., 2011) and the K–12 Computer Science Framework (K–12 Computer Science Framework Steering Committee, 2016), foundational works in the field, and existing literature reviews. We used the literature to add a layer of peer-reviewed research to the topics extracted from the interviews, and triangulated research findings across interviews and the literature.

We chose this hybrid format (interviews and reviews) to simultaneously capture well-established facts and findings, but also novel information that has not yet made it to the publication venues in the field. Also, some of the important challenges and issues in CEd often do not show up in peer-reviewed publications because many active members of the community are also tool developers instead of researchers – so their work could not be entirely captured in a traditional literature review. This combined use of interviews and literature offered a more comprehensive view of the state of the very young and dynamic field of CEd.

We will reference the interviews using the conventional reference format for personal communication (it might help readers to keep in mind that most references from 2017 are, in fact, the interviews).

3.3 Findings: Rationales for Justifying CS Education

The first theme emerging from the interviews and literature, and one of the main topics of this chapter, was the differing reasons for teaching CS and their considerable consequences for CS implementation programs. Similar to a recent study by Vogel, Santo, and Ching (2017), we found that the interdisciplinary nature of CS brings together very different stakeholders and views. CEd includes professionals from different academic cultures and professional allegiances: university professors, K–12 educators, CEOs of technology companies, entrepreneurs, government officials, and diversity and equity advocates. Not surprisingly, the data from the interviews and literature revealed many different justifications for why CS should be taught in public education systems (e.g., diSessa, 2000; Wing, 2006). These rationales can be expressed as four distinct positions:

- *The labor market rationale:* Labor market changes and the need to sustain a competitive economy are the main driving forces for this rationale. Some consider that CS knowledge will be useful not only for professional programmers but also in a variety of twenty-first-century non-technical jobs, thus universally valuable for all professions.
- *The computational thinking rationale:* The argument for "computational thinking" is that computer scientists' ways of thinking, heuristics, and problem-solving strategies are universally important, and would transfer to a variety of knowledge domains and everyday problems. It would also support the development of students' higher-order thinking skills.
- *The computational literacy rationale:* Computational literacy is not a new skill or a class of problem-solving strategies, but a set of material, cognitive, and social elements that generate new ways of thinking and learning. It enables new types of mental operations and knowledge representations, creates new kinds of "literatures," makes it possible for people to express themselves in new ways, changing how people accomplish cognitive tasks.
- *The equity of participation rationale:* CS knowledge will be required for the best and most creative jobs, for civic participation, and for understanding the impact of computation on society. Additionally, since our cognitive capabilities will be limited by our ability to utilize computation, equity of participation in CEd becomes the central concern, and is one of the most significant gaps in research and implementation.

Making these four rationales explicit is important because they drive the way we write curricula, train teachers, and implement CEd in schools. Interviewees pointed out that the public's lack of awareness about these different viewpoints – and the ways they are similar, dissimilar, complementary, and compatible – must be addressed (e.g., Buechley, 2017; Resnick, 2017).

3.3.1 The Labor Market Rationale

Changes in the global labor market have been a major driver of the efforts to teach CS in schools. This rationale is primarily related to the demands for more workers with new skill sets and is frequently championed by industry leaders and policy-makers. The labor market argument comes in two chief forms. The first cites the hundreds of thousands of open jobs in CS (Google LLC & Gallup Inc., 2016; Grover & Pea, 2013) and notes that this number will increase in years to come, with data science and artificial intelligence becoming mainstream fields relevant across many industries. Similarly, it is argued that the economic productivity or contributions of a country will be determined by its capacity to generate more scientists and engineers. CEd can presumably contribute to this vision by fixing the "leaky" STEM pipeline and driving more students to pursue CS careers. However, Grover and Horn point out that in grades K–8 especially, this concern with jobs might be misplaced:

> In elementary school, students and teachers are definitely not thinking about jobs. It is about what are the foundational knowledge and skills that children should have? At the middle school level, even though it is not a jobs argument, I think there is an identity argument there. This is especially relevant to computing because there are so many stereotypes associated with it. (Grover, 2017)

> We have gone a little too far on the commercial end of the spectrum, we have become preoccupied with training the next generation of engineers, these economic motivations are outweighing the computational literacy ideas. (Horn, 2017)

The second form the labor market argument takes is a subtler one. It argues for more CS knowledge embedded in all careers, instead of simply training more programmers. Several of the interviewees mentioned that while professional programmers will be necessary, the need could be restricted to a relatively small number of positions that are highly specialized (Guzdial, 2017; Resnick, 2017; Shapiro, 2017). Some reports suggest that only about 6 percent of the workforce will need to do coding with the scope and specialization of professional programmers (Noonan, 2017). The greatest demand would not be for professional programmers, but for other professionals who will have to use CS and programming for automating spreadsheets, programming queries, accessing online databases, using data-mining software tools, and operating physical computing devices in interactive art or home automation.

3.3.2 The Computational Thinking Rationale

The second argument for teaching CS derives from the concept of "computational thinking" (CT), as put forth in a position paper written by Jeanette Wing (2006). Wing proposed that computer scientists' ways of thinking, heuristics, and problem-solving strategies are universally important both for applying computing ideas to do work in other disciplines and for applying computing ideas in everyday life. Examples are the ability to use abstractions and pattern recognition to represent problems in new ways, to break down problems into smaller parts, and to employ algorithmic thinking. With 3,500 citations (according to Google Scholar as of April 2018), the position put forward by Wing has played a critical role in shaping the world of CEd. Her paper and her influential position as a National Science Foundation (NSF) officer helped reinvigorate the field. Some researchers, however, are skeptical about how well students transfer CS knowledge to everyday life and general problem-solving. diSessa (2018) mentions that there have been several attempts over the last 100 years to teach children transferable problem-solving or higher-order thinking skills (HOTS) using mathematics, Latin, or Greek, but these endeavors often failed. Guzdial (2017) mentions several studies on the transfer of CEd knowledge and points out that generally "students fail to apply even simple computing ideas to fairly simple problems." Yongpradit further notes that:

> CEd is not immune to the misconceptions about high-level transfer. I know that there are advocates ... saying that computing can improve general critical thinking skills. That's not supported by research. It will not magically improve your math scores.
> (Yongpradit, 2017)

Because Wing's original ideas are still influential in the field, the need for more empirical evidence and the absence of a more definitive unpacking of the term CT are considered to be major issues in CEd – after all, would the "ways of thinking" of computer scientists transfer to other domains and contexts?

However, the definition of CT has been evolving over the last few years, and steering away from the original one put forth by Wing, as Grover notes:

> The definition of CT has been evolving since Wing, and in its evolution it has broadened to encompass aspects of CT concepts, practices, as well as learners' dispositions and perspectives, perhaps fueled by a genuine desire to broaden participation, thus including aspects such as creativity, collaboration, and communication in practices of CT.
> (Grover, 2017)

CT is further discussed in Chapters 17–20 of this Handbook.

3.3.3 The Computational Literacy Rationale

With more than 1,100 citations (according to Google Scholar as of April 2018), Andrea diSessa's book *Changing Minds* is the most established account of the idea of "computational literacy" (diSessa, 2000). In the book, and in recent publications (diSessa, 2018), he explains how different computational literacy is from the original definition of CT (a similar discussion appears in Wilensky & Papert, 2010).

> Learning to use a new medium takes effort. The printing press was a huge leap in human history, but that leap did not happen until many more people became literate. A printing press is not of much use unless authors know how to write and your audience knows how to read. Achieving computational literacy in society means that people can read and write with computation, which includes an ability to read and write computer programs.
> (diSessa, 2000)

> I view computation as, potentially, providing a new, deep, and profoundly influential literacy – computational literacy – that will impact all STEM disciplines at their very core, but most especially in terms of learning.
> (diSessa, 2018)

diSessa claims that computational literacy is not simply a new job skill or generic CS-inspired problem-solving strategy, but a set of material, cognitive, and social elements that generate a new way of knowing, thinking, learning, and representing knowledge. A new literacy makes new types of mental operations and knowledge representations possible, creates new kinds of previously non-existent "literatures," and changes how people interact with each other and use digital devices when they are accomplishing cognitive tasks. He also mentions that there is a semantic confusion between computational literacy versus terms like digital literacy, computer literacy, or information communication and technology (ICT) literacy. These latter terms refer to the competent use of different computational devices and technologies. Computational literacy, conversely, is concerned with how computational media can change the way we know, learn, and think (in contrast with the focus on problem-solving or HOTS).

diSessa also argues that concepts in science and mathematics can be made simpler using computational representations. For example, velocity and acceleration are simple to understand algorithmically, but unnecessarily complex to learn using traditional algebraic representations. Chemical processes such as diffusion, given their probabilistic nature, are convoluted when represented in algebraic terms, but very simple to learn using computational tools such as agent-based models (e.g., NetLogo; Wilensky, 1999), in which students can program the behavior of individual atoms. The argument for computational literacy extends beyond the need for teaching programming languages. It makes the claim that several disciplines could be fundamentally transformed if taught using computational tools, in the same way that text literacy changed the teaching of so many disciplines centuries ago.[5] Sentance, Resnick, and Horn also stress that computational literacy is multi-faceted, and more than just learning CT or programming concepts:

> I think computational thinking skills exist ... I think we just have to be careful about thinking that computing is only computational thinking. CS ... involves

5 Text literacy fundamentally changed how we accomplish cognitive operations – for example, it acts as external memory, it is shareable, and it is permanent. diSessa and others claim that computational literacy could have the same revolutionary consequences.

modeling and design and creativity, more than just the cognitive elemental thinking skills. That is what we need to teach in K–8. We need to teach the whole subject and be cautious of being too narrow in what we are offering in the curriculum in school.
(Sentance, 2017)

Gaining a literacy is a matter of developing your thinking, your voice, and your identity … The reason for learning to write is not just for doing practical things but being able to express your ideas to others. Computation is a new way of expressing ourselves and it's important for everyone to learn … If you want to feel like a full participant in the culture, you need to be a contributor with the media of the times.
(Resnick, 2017)

It is about supporting computation in many different genres or niches. As a poet, the way you use computation might be very different than a journalist, a researcher, or somebody who works in government. Just like we have different forms of literacy, we might have different forms of computational literacy.
(Horn, 2017)

However, as diSessa states, discussions about the role and importance of CEd are far from over, and these views should all be earnestly considered with their implicit contradictions:

The labor market view and the computational thinking view contain at least implicit criticisms of the computational literacy view. The former might think that immediate and practical economic effects are more important, and the latter suggests that computational literacy is diffuse, hard to implement, and might insist that high-order thinking skills do exist, so these perspectives should not be ignored.
(diSessa, 2018)

Some interviewees pointed out that the boundaries between CT and computational literacy are not well-defined. While Grover (2017) states that new definitions of CT have been evolving to include, for example, creativity and collaboration, formerly mostly associated with computational literacy, Guzdial (2017) worries that these new CT definitions "are going too broad," and Resnick notes that the definition of CT "out in the field" is still very much connected to the original one as stated in Wing's (2006) paper. Computational literacy is further discussed in Chapters 18 and 19.

3.3.4 The Equity of Participation Rationale

Several interviewees mentioned equity as their central concern in CEd, arguing that it has traditionally been a side issue in the field and one of the most significant gaps in research and implementation. There are two main issues related to the topic:

- Understanding the impact of computation on society, and
- Ensuring equity and diversity in participation.

The K–12 Computer Science Framework (K–12 Computer Science Framework Steering Committee, 2016) also recognized equity and broadening participation as core issues in CEd. Students excluded from CEd may struggle to fully participate in twenty-first-century society along multiple dimensions. Not only will the best and most creative jobs require CS knowledge, but our cognitive capabilities to solve problems will be limited by our inability to utilize computation fully. Even traditional forms of civic participation will require an understanding of Computing. As Buechley stated:

> We live in a computationally mediated world, and it is important for people to have an understanding of how computational systems work and the role that they play in those systems, how those systems impact their lives, our democracy, the economy, and the way we socialize and interact with people. (Buechley, 2017)

Several interviewees gave examples of how computing will become increasingly crucial for civic participation and informed decision-making. These examples include knowing what algorithms are, how computational tools can manipulate social media, how to participate in a social discourse mediated by algorithms, and how to make sense of job displacement due to automation. It is also important to be aware of the presence and consequences of technologies such as machine learning (ML) and artificial intelligence (AI) in a number of everyday devices and experiences, understanding how much information we divulge (sometimes unknowingly) about ourselves, and being aware of the ways in which bias can get built into technologies that influence critical decisions such as prison sentencing, mortgage allocation, and the deployment of neighborhood policing resources (O'Neil, 2016; Shapiro, 2017). The comprehension of the rapidly evolving landscape of devices and tools that are key for active participation in modern society is also central to this argument. Students who do not fully understand these issues risk being more easily manipulated as consumers, voters, and citizens, and more vulnerable to cybercrime. They also are less likely to have access to leadership positions and high-status jobs and are more likely to be on the sidelines of future societal change.

The interviewees also noted that Computing drives innovation across many disciplines and industries and that the resulting changes have had both an economic and a sociological impact. Some also said that allowing students to explore their social and cultural concerns using computing helps motivate and engage them and makes Computing relevant to their lives, especially in diverse populations (Margolis, 2017). Buechley (2017) adds that when you put computing in contexts that can be compelling and exciting to different groups of people, "you get diverse populations to show up and participate," and stresses the importance of making conscious, deliberate space for that to happen. Many interviewees noted that private and more affluent schools will most certainly be able to offer CEd programs with high complexity, while less affluent or public school systems will only offer very simplified versions:

> Private schools do not do just generic education. They have kids working on portfolios. They have children doing internships. They have kids doing projects and making it relevant to them … Standardized education which has no connection to kids' lives is what is often given to poor kids.
> (Margolis, 2017)

> [I was] working first in informal settings and then in recent years, I have moved more in the formal space. I saw it as being more relevant because that is now seen as a way to level the playing field and make sure that all children get it, not just those that happen to be fortunate to get it through after-school experiences.
> (Grover, 2017)

Grover noted that the Obama administration's naming of the national CEd effort as "Computer Science for All" when it was announced in January 2016 supported this equity-oriented perspective:

> This of course came as a result of notions the community grew to accept over the previous 5 years … CSForAll is now a well-used term that captures this "equity of participation" notion.
> (Grover, 2017)

Sentance (2017) stresses the importance of making CS mandatory in all schools, for all students, not as mere "exposure," but as a way to avoid self-selection. The interviewees also noted that the lack of a diverse CS workforce results in the design of products and services that cater to a very narrow range of people and problems, thus perpetuating inequality. Researchers concerned with the equity argument also posit that we could see a much more perverse version of the "digital divide" in the years to come if immediate and intentional actions are not taken to address these inequities while we are still in early design stages of CEd. Equity issues are further discussed in Chapters 16 and 24.

3.4 Sustainable Implementation and Systemic Obstacles

The second cluster of findings stemming from the interviews and the literature relates to key components needed across the CEd system to support wider and more effective implementation. The "system" we define includes the various interrelated institutions and mechanisms that shape and support CEd teaching and learning in the classroom.

The six key components of CEd implementations reviewed in this section are equity, scaling, quality of implementation, pluralism, curriculum, and teacher development. It is difficult to focus on any particular component without considering how it is influenced by – and how it in turn influences – the other components. For example, what students learn is clearly related to what they are taught, which itself depends on many elements: the instructional materials available in the market; the curriculum adopted locally; teachers' content and pedagogical knowledge; how teachers elect to use the curriculum; the kinds of resources, time, and space that teachers have for their practice; what the community values regarding student learning; and how local, state, and national standards and assessments influence instructional practice.

I am not attempting to provide a full discussion of all possible influences on CEd; rather, I focus on the themes that emerged from the data and how they might contribute to a more coherent and inclusive implementation of CEd.

3.4.1 Equity and Broadening Participation

Several interviewees mentioned broadening participation in and changing perceptions of CS as perhaps the most important challenges for our community. Berland, Buechley, Margolis, Sentance, and others stressed the striking contrast between what happens in Computing classrooms in affluent schools and in less affluent schools. Almost all of the interviewees expressed concern with the unequal presence of programming in public schools, the quality of instruction, and the unconscious bias of some educators and counselors regarding who is "suited" to take the Computing classes. They also noted that while affluent schools are more likely to offer comprehensive Computing programs for their students, most public districts are ill-equipped to offer anything more than very brief, standardized experiences, which they fear could give school administrators and teachers an incorrect metric for CEd adoption and distract them from implementing more robust programs in their schools. The interviewees also worry that the numbers of children reached as advertised by nonprofits and industry providers give the impression that the "mission has been accomplished," whereas most agree that we are still very far from providing CEd to all students. At least three researchers also noted that funding currently provided to large national organizations would be better directed to research institutions or smaller, more local nonprofits. But Yongpradit (2017) noted that national organizations can be a channel for funding to smaller organizations.

Regarding broadening participation, most interviewees favored programs that make learning Computing more attractive by focusing on personal expression and creativity, especially at the K–8 level. They also agreed on the importance of culturally relevant curricula that support diverse ways of approaching CEd and diverse ways of expressing one's knowledge. Buechley (2017), for example, mentioned that computer scientists and engineers tend to discount culture and cultural relevance as key factors in learning and in tool design. In her work, she instead focuses on creating *new types of clubhouses* and computing cultures that speak to these diverse practices. Michael Clancy also advocated for CEd that incentivizes meaningful engagement:

> Students will be more motivated to work if the assignments allow creativity, and allow the student to relate to his or her experience. Part of that would be more flexible tools that allow a student to make better use of his or her experience. What I would like to see is some way to have a broader scope and interest of activities.
> (Clancy, 2017)

Some identified the need to make CEd mandatory for all students as a means of ensuring equitable participation. Sentance (2017), for example, argued that "if we don't make computing mandatory, we know from previous experience that self-selecting groups of people will choose computing … so we have a responsibility to offer that to all children and to reach everybody." Yongpradit (2017) stated that schools should at least be required to offer CEd, and that we should make CEd courses available permanently for students in public schools. Guzdial (2017) expressed concern that some states are trying to implement "CS4All" without an explicit focus on underserved groups. He points out that affluent schools will be able to move quickly to provide Computing for their students, while less affluent schools will struggle with financial limitations, further exacerbating the "coding divide." Margolis also noted that, while the "CS for California" campaign has an equity agenda:

> The rush to scale and the pressure to put curriculum and teacher professional development (PD) online will possibly have dangerous unintended consequences for the issue of equity … The learning partnership of teachers and of researchers needs to become part of a dynamic iterative cycle for continuous improvement … For programs to sustain themselves, to change the culture of the schools so that teachers are supported to have active, engaged, inclusive classrooms, for programs to be fully embraced by the districts themselves. It is the slow work of relationship building and learning together that is required. For this to happen there also needs to be a holistic awareness of all the educational issues in schools that continue to threaten equity. CS in schools does not exist on isolated islands. All of the large issues impacting education, such as the move for privatization, de-professionalizing teachers, and school tracking will affect our broadening participation in the computing mission.
> (Margolis, 2017)

3.4.2 Scaling and Assessment

Buechley, Shapiro, Berland, and other interviewees expressed concern about traditional forms of school reform taking over the implementation of CEd. Specifically, they noted that fixed curricula, standardized assessments, and inflexible teacher training programs do not foster real scientific or mathematical thinking in students (National Research Council, 2006, 2012) and have a questionable track record for motivating students to pursue STEM careers (Maltese & Tai, 2011). For Buechley (2017), one dominant narrative around CEd is that "we need to figure out the concepts, and teach them in the right way in a fixed curriculum." She disagreed with this narrative, however, and instead advocated for a perspective in which motivation, engagement, personally relevant projects, and culturally aware curriculum design take precedence. According to Buechley, CEd lends itself especially well to projects and interdisciplinary work that connect programming to art, design, biology, or mathematics:

> Connecting computation and computing to different practices, which sometimes coincide with really different ways of approaching and making sense of the world, is the most powerful way that you can engage different kinds of people in computing … As one example, I have been connecting computation to textile crafts, textile design, and fashion design, and I have found that through doing that, you can dramatically change the gender participation ratios. You

can get lots of young women to engage enthusiastically with computing in a way that they just do not do in more traditional computing contexts.

Computer science is a fundamentally creative discipline. You construct things when you write a computer program. And in that sense, it's really distinct from mathematics or science. That is a distinction that is not fully appreciated and made sense of, but is very powerful and important.
(Buechley, 2017)

Berland expressed a similar concern:

There are very few subjects in which students feel like they can make a change in the world and they can express their independent selves. I think their ability to make their own games, make their own art, make them in ways that are shareable with code, is really powerful. [Instead of giving students the right answer] it is better to create safe spaces to fail, to play, to tinker … This is where you get the bang for the buck. That's where the learning happens. Another truism of education is that things are driven by the ways that they are assessed. If you assess people for knowing this or that keyword in C++,[6] then that's what you're going to get and that's not particularly valuable, but if you assess people on their ability to teach each other complex concepts, that's what you're going to get.
(Berland, 2017)

Fincher (2017) cited the UK's Project Quantum[7] as an example of an explicitly research-based project that combines scholarly work, practical utility, curriculum scaffolds, and teacher PD.

3.4.3 Reliance on Surface-Level, Low-Quality Solutions

Another topic that was mentioned by many interviewees as a systemic obstacle was related to the pace and depth of many of the current CEd implementations, pointing to the fact that many seem to be superficial and overly simplified, especially in public education. Margolis expressed concerns about the speed at which they are being developed and put into classrooms, and argued that this approach has unintended educational consequences, especially for members of underrepresented groups:

[The idea of many programs is] ship it out. Get it out there and we will see if there are bugs in it, right? That has some real potential dangers in education because you put something online and the school district says, "Okay, we're going to do computing online," and then all of a sudden the girls and a lot of the students of color don't do well, and then the principal says, "See? Our kids are not up for computing. They didn't do well. They're not interested." In fact, they just experienced horrible instruction, and so they get turned off, but in their minds they're not cut out for it, and in the minds of the principals they're not cut out for it.
(Margolis, 2017)

Grover voiced a similar concern. She has been observing and researching citywide implementations in the USA and examining the quality and depth of the projects.

6 C++ is a very popular professional programming language.
7 http://community.computingatschool.org.uk/resources/4382/single

She noted the simplicity of the projects she observed and the need to more deeply engage groups that have been historically underrepresented in Computing:

> Almost no one uses Boolean logic. They use variables but just as a count or a score. You barely ever see expressions with variables being used or you will rarely see a loop with a terminating condition that is controlled by a Boolean expression with variables. Also, I read this paper from Yasmin Kafai and Deborah Fields where they analyzed the Scratch community projects [in 2012].[8] Most children stayed at the shallow end, they used the simplest constructs.
> (Grover, 2017)

Shapiro (2017) voiced concerns about the concentration of resources in just a few CEd organizations, which could lead to "very homogeneous curricula/ programs which would move us in the opposite direction" from many of the progressive approaches discussed in the CEd community. Similar concerns have been voiced by many prominent educators in light of large-scale implementations in many US cities. As those implementations roll out, the quality of instruction has often been criticized as superficial, stifled, and insufficient to create fluency. Gary Stager observed:

> I wish I had 1 cent for every educator who has told me that her students "do a little Scratch." I always want to respond, "Call me when your students have done a lot of Scratch." The epistemological benefit of programming computers comes from long intense thinking. Fluency should be the goal.
> (Stager, 2017)

One of the paths to address these issues is the creation of partnerships between researchers and governments, since government officials need support in scaling efforts in order to go beyond oversimplified solutions. Guzdial (2017) is currently helping many states conduct landscape surveys[9] to determine the state of CEd in different parts of the country. He contends that policy decisions and coordination between different stakeholders would be much easier if landscape surveys were standard operating practice, as they allow states to gauge the growth of CEd offerings, PD programs, and enrollments. Yongpradit (2017) also noted that federal and state-level organizations urgently need technical assistance around creating certifications, growing the CEd teacher pipeline, and implementing curricula. Because CEd is such a new field, there are too few trained professionals and specialized organizations that can offer those services, leading to simplified and superficial implementations. But the issue of superficiality is also related to funding: Yongpradit expressed concern with current funding levels, noting that CEd requires more PD, standards development, and support for task forces to create implementation plans.

---

8 The paper examined data from a subset of about 5,000 users in January 2012 (Fields, Giant, & Kafai, 2013).

9 http://ecepalliance.org/resources/landscape-reports

3.4.4 Pluralism in CEd: Exploring New Domains and Tools

Another systemic issue raised by many interviewees and the literature was the importance of allowing for different ways of doing Computing, in terms of tools, programming languages, developmental levels, and approaches to organizing one's practice. In 1990, Sherry Turkle and Seymour Papert published an influential paper on *epistemological pluralism*, in which they described a study where children engaged in programming in a variety of non-canonical ways that were all ultimately successful (Turkle & Papert, 1990). Even though some children were violating traditional programming practice (the "bricoleurs"), they were doing so in a personally meaningful way that allowed them to create a strong connection with programming. Echoes of this influential paper were heard in almost all the interviews, and the principle of epistemological pluralism appears to have taken hold in CEd at the K–8 level. Grover (2017), however, pointed out that the epistemological pluralism approach needs to be combined with the teaching of some agreed-upon concepts and programming practices. When Resnick (2017) pointed out the need to keep pushing for epistemological pluralism, he noted that some systems only reward students for standard ways of doing coding (i.e., the smallest number of blocks when solving a puzzle), and some automated assessment programs still grade students solely based on the number and types of programming blocks they use. The interviewees also expressed the belief that traditional professional or college-level practices should not be automatically used in K–8 environments, since nontraditional approaches to programming (such as bricolage) may make sense only for younger students, even if advanced programmers might sometimes make use of these techniques as well (Berland, Martin, & Benton, 2013; Blikstein, 2011; Blikstein et al., 2014; Brennan, 2013; Graham, 2004).

3.4.5 Curriculum and Instructional Materials

The production of a quality curriculum and curricular materials is, for many interviewees, a key component for successful CEd implementations at scale. The interviewees noted that this is an area of significant and ongoing challenge despite efforts such as the K–12 CS Framework (K–12 Computer Science Framework Steering Committee, 2016):

> No one yet has written out a full, coherent K–12 curriculum built around a foundational framework. The K–12 CS Framework and the CSTA standards have laid out concepts, practices, and performance expectations but how do these things get manifested in curriculum and activities and experiences in K–12? That is a huge problem in computing right now that directly affects implementation.
> (Yongpradit, 2017)

Creating comprehensive curriculum materials is especially challenging because there is a natural tension between uniformity and the potential for customization to the learners' interests. Many interviewees noted the need to design culturally and personally relevant curricula that would cater to diverse populations (Buechley, 2017; Margolis, 2017; Resnick, 2017; Shapiro, 2017):

> The most important challenge is relating computing to [students'] culture and their identity. If you can get someone excited about something and engaged, they are incredibly motivated to learn.
> (Buechley, 2017)

Another important principle for curriculum design in CEd is the pedagogical approach in terms of how students will come into contact with the programming language. Pears et al.'s (2007) review of the literature found three major approaches: (a) focus on generic problem-solving; (b) focus on learning a particular programming language; and (c) focus on code production, or project-oriented CEd courses. As we discussed previously, the focus on higher-order problem-solving skills is problematic. Palumbo's (1990) review examined transfer between learning to program and problem-solving and concluded that more advanced forms of transfer (far or generalized transfer) should not be expected in introductory courses, since typically there is no time to develop such skills. In other words, if curricula aim for the transfer of problem-solving skills to other domains, explicit time and effort should be put into it. Scholarship has shown that positive results in problem-solving require a high involvement from teachers and well-developed theoretical foundations (Clements, 1990; De Corte & Verschaffel, 1989), as well as a considerable time investment. In one study, 150 hours of experience were needed to generate positive learning gains in problem-solving (Liu, 1997). Guzdial noted that this issue of programming and transfer is far from resolved, especially when the affinities and the unity of content and computation are not clear:

> Most people don't teach programming for transfer, and if they did, they would not be able to cover as much of programming. I think it is a zero-sum game: teach for programming fluency or teach for transferable problem-solving skills. You cannot get both in the same time.
> (Guzdial, 2017)

The second approach – focus on learning a particular programming language – is by far the most common. Textbooks, lesson plans, and assessments are designed based on the constructs of a programming language. This focus, common in introductory college courses and Advanced Placement (AP) classes in the USA, has been criticized by several interviewees as being too limited and too vocational. Buechley, for example, praised new initiatives (such as the new Advanced Placement Computer Science Principles course) that are moving AP classes away from the "one-language" model:

> So [Computer Science Principles] is a class that provides a different model of engaging with computing than the traditional computer science AP class did. And a model that is much more focused on foundational concepts and big ideas as opposed to the nuts and bolts of programming in a particular

language. And because of that, it has the potential to provide more accessible pathways to more diverse kids, which is really important.
(Buechley, 2017)

The third approach is code production or project-oriented learning. Instead of small assignments and tasks based on language constructs, or more general problem-solving training, students learn to create more complex systems to accomplish a task through projects. Even though this approach is harder to structure and assess, it seems to be more aligned with the approaches advocated by most interviewees. Resnick, for example, advocated for a project-oriented approach rather than small puzzles or language-based activities:

> There are a lot of schools where they do something with coding but it is done very superficially, just learning a few tricks of how to put some blocks together … but not really connecting in a deep way. [CEd should not be] just puzzles for kids learning to solve a problem, but a platform for expressing yourself.
> (Resnick, 2017)

Another common type implementation of code production or project-oriented approaches has been to make use of Computer Science-inspired mathematics and science practices. Science and mathematics as professional practices have been deeply transformed by computation, both in terms of the core disciplines themselves and the creation of entirely new fields such as bioinformatics, computational statistics, chemometrics, and neuroinformatics. Efforts to improve and modernize the teaching of science and mathematics should include computation as a core curricular component. Skills that can be developed through CS-infused science and mathematics include the ability to deal with open-ended problems, the creation of abstractions, recognizing and addressing ambiguity in algorithms, manipulating and analyzing data, and creating models and simulations (Weintrop et al., 2016).

Most of the interviewees identified infusing mathematics and science curricula with computation as a productive way to bring Computing to classrooms. diSessa (2018) highlighted that "there are people deeply enmeshed in non-CS disciplines, yet sufficiently expert with CS ideas and practices, to really get this agenda accomplished now." And Grover stated:

> It is very synergistic … computation makes the science and the math more real, authentic, and engaging. Students see aspects of the discipline that they would not see in the static form of learning from a textbook. Conversely, computation becomes alive because of the context in which it is used.
> (Grover, 2017)

Some interviewees expressed skepticism as to whether there are a sufficient number of available CEd teachers and whether it is possible to carve out space in the busy K–8 curriculum for a brand-new discipline. As a result, the interviewees noted that retraining science and mathematics teachers to add Computing to their teaching and generating new accompanying CS-infused lesson plans might be a more sustainable approach. Yongpradit (2017) also suggested that enabling teachers to receive dual certification in mathematics (or science) and Computing might be a positive alternative approach for addressing the current teacher shortage.

3.4.6 Teacher Development

One last (and crucial) systemic obstacle for large CEd implementations is the preparation of teachers. Ultimately, it is the interactions between teachers and students in classrooms that will determine whether students learn successfully. Thus, it is not surprising that the interviewees expressed the belief that teachers are the linchpin in any effort to implement or change CEd. The preparation, effective development, and retention of CEd teachers will need to be prioritized.

Teacher development was a central concern for most interviewees. Clancy (2017), Margolis (2017), and Yongpradit (2017) highlighted the challenges in building the CEd teacher workforce, and noted the need for teacher certification, training programs based on these certifications, and incentives for teachers to seek these qualifications. Guzdial (2017) highlighted the importance of preservice teacher development as the most viable way to achieve sustainability.

The need for equity in teacher development was also highlighted, since more affluent schools are more capable of offering high-quality programs. Interviewees noted that it is not enough to expose teachers to Computing content. Teachers need time to practice inclusive CEd, and these pedagogies should be interwoven into the entire teacher preparation program. Margolis (2017) also raised the need to educate teachers regarding bias, so that they can reflect on belief systems and perceptions about which students can excel in computing and how these beliefs would impact their relationships with students.

In general, there was concern about the rapid scaling of several initiatives and the capacity to prepare thousands of teachers adequately in a very short time. The interviewees argued that scaling too quickly disproportionately impacts underserved communities and populations that are historically excluded from STEM.

Margolis was particularly concerned with making equity a core tenet in teacher development, mentioning that, in her research, she encountered significant variability among teachers in their capacity for guiding deeper cognitive thinking. She found that teaching was particularly productive when teachers identified the specific Computing concepts for the students while they were learning them and discussed how they could relate the concepts to other areas of knowledge. The capacity to competently guide students in this way was found to be a predictor of student learning, but it varied considerably among teachers. Not surprisingly, teachers in less affluent areas were found to be the least prepared to enact these strategies in the classroom, in part because their districts had less funding for teacher PD. Margolis adds:

> Not only do teachers need to be introduced to the CS content, but they need to have time practicing pedagogies that are aimed at creating an inclusive

CS learning environment, building on the assets, interests, and motivations of traditionally underrepresented students. Also, CS teacher PD must have equity and inclusion woven throughout everything that happens in PD, not just isolating this issue to a discrete one-hour discussion. For instance, as teachers are experiencing teaching lessons during PD, the other teachers who are in the roles as students or observers should be reflecting on their own experiences of inclusion (or not), thinking about their own students in their classrooms, and what works (or does not) to ignite the interest of all students. Also, teachers need time, and a safe learning environment, to reflect on all the biased belief systems associated with which students can and cannot excel in computing, to reflect on their own belief systems, and how belief systems impact their relationships with the students in their classrooms. Traditionally CS education has not been a place where these types of discussions or reflections have taken place, but they must if we are to broaden participation in computing.
(Margolis, 2017)

Teacher development is further discussed in Chapter 25.

3.5 Conclusion

The year 2017 marked the 50th anniversary of the Logo programming language. In just five decades, an entirely new domain of knowledge has evolved from an idea in the minds of a few visionaries to national public policy. And while CEd is a relatively new discipline with a less substantial research base, there is much reason for optimism. Ensuring that we continue this progress, however, requires the commitment, work, and flexibility of a large number of stakeholders. We are now facing the growing pains intrinsic to progressing from pilot projects to large-scale implementations, and we must look and work beyond these growing pains to ensure that CEd fulfills its educational promise in sustainable and equitable ways.

Despite these challenges, CEd offers many advantages and the potential to transform learning environments and school work. Computing includes algorithms, design, data, making, creativity, and personal expression. CEd also facilitates productive collaboration in the classroom, connects to personally meaningful aspects of the lives of students, allows for new types of knowledge and assessments to be valued in schools, boosts the potential of project-based learning approaches, and opens possibilities of innovative ways to organize learning environments (e.g., Berland et al., 2013; Blikstein et al., 2014; Brennan, 2013; Buechley & Eisenberg, 2008; diSessa, 2000; Sherin, 2001; Turkle & Papert, 1990). Addressing and harnessing these advantages is important as our world becomes more technological and digital, and equitable participation requires computational fluency. This makes CEd necessary in K-8 not just as an elective subject, but as a mandatory topic. There is no question anymore about the importance of CEd and its place and need in public education, but there are differing opinions on why and how it should be done. Among the most prominent rationales for increasing access to CEd is that it can serve as a foundational literacy upon which other knowledge/activities can be built, and as a powerful context for profound, authentic, and interdisciplinary learning in other subjects. CEd can serve as an expressive, creative medium to allow young learners to express ideas in ways that are socially and culturally relevant, and it can also be a valuable tool for civic and political participation.

Given the importance of CEd, many of the interviewees believe that national rollouts of robust programs will require massive investment in the creation of state-level standards and curricula, teacher preparation and certification, software/hardware infrastructure, and research. It is not clear if all stakeholders are aware of the depth of the effort, but many feel that partial rollouts have the potential to increase social disparities and educational inequalities, privileging more affluent or well-resourced schools and districts. Additionally, although large-scale "CS exposure" programs are reaching millions of children, there is concern that they do not guarantee sustained engagement, particularly for underserved youth. Addressing these concerns requires better metrics, arms-length evaluation of programs, and more consensus on what constitutes success. In addition, exposure programs could benefit from follow-up activities, curricula, and sufficient resources to support deeper learning and stronger outcomes. And despite the growing demand for large-scale rollouts and the temptation of the adoption of one single implementation model, researchers advocate for a repertoire of well-studied and well-rationalized models that are sufficiently flexible to be adapted to multiple local contexts.

With an eye toward stronger outcomes, a reliance on high-quality curricula and assessments alone is not a guarantee of effective implementation. Education is always instantiated by teachers, so attention to pedagogy, teacher support, and the complex dynamics of adopting new curricula is crucial. Specifically, we found that teacher development is a key factor in the success of CEd, both preservice and in-service. In addition, the understanding of equity, inclusiveness, and unconscious biases about CS success are viewed as necessary to teacher development programs.

In sum, the time is ripe for thoughtfully targeted and comprehensive action to advance the CEd community. A large and diverse body of perspectives indicates that we must address the social, economic, and cultural barriers surrounding computing. If access and inclusiveness are addressed effectively, we can meet current and future workforce and citizenship demands. And we can do so in ways that equitably drive technological and social progress and give youth new avenues for personal expression and empowerment. Above all, we should avoid the trivialization and the oversimplification of computing knowledge, making it another missed opportunity to bring an exciting new set of practices, content, and cognitive tools to students.

This effort requires the cooperation and coordination of interdisciplinary, inter-sector teams that thoughtfully design, implement, evaluate, and learn from CEd initiatives. Only in this way can we achieve the hoped-for scale and sustainability and realize the ultimate vision of generations of researchers, practitioners, and policy-makers that have been trying, for the last 50 years, to bring computing to all students.

3.6 Acknowledgments

The authors wish to thank the 14 interviewees for their willingness to share a few centuries of accumulated knowledge about CEd, as well as their invaluable insight and vision for the future: Matthew Berland (University of Wisconsin – Madison), Leah Buechley (Rural Digital), Michael Clancy (University of California, Berkeley), Andrea "Andy" diSessa (University of California, Berkeley), Sally Fincher (University of Kent), Shuchi Grover (formerly SRI International), Mark Guzdial (Georgia Institute of Technology), Mike Horn (Northwestern University), Jane Margolis (University of California, Los Angeles), Mitchel Resnick (Massachusetts Institute of Technology), Sue Sentance (King's College London), Ben Shapiro (University of Colorado, Boulder), David Weintrop (University of Maryland), and Pat Yongpradit (Code.org).

References

Berland, M. (2017). Phone interview with Paulo Blikstein.

Berland, M., Martin, T., & Benton, T. (2013). Using learning analytics to understand the learning pathways of novice programmers. *Journal of the Learning Sciences,* 22(4), 564–599.

Blikstein, P. (2011). Using learning analytics to assess students' behavior in open-ended programming tasks. In *Proceedings of the 1st International Conference on Learning Analytics and Knowledge – LAK 2011* (pp. 110–116). New York: ACM.

Blikstein, P., Worsley, M., Piech, C., Sahami, M., Cooper, S., & Koller, D. (2014). Programming pluralism: Using learning analytics to detect patterns in novices' learning of computer programming. *Journal of the Learning Sciences,* 23(4), 561–599.

Blikstein, P. (2013). Digital Fabrication and 'Making' in Education: The Democratization of Invention. In J. Walter-Herrmann & C. Büching (Eds.). *FabLabs: Of Machines, Makers and Inventors* (pp. 203–221). Bielefeld: Transcript Publishers.

Blikstein, P. (2018). *Pre-College Computer Science Education: A Survey of the Field.* Mountain View, CA: Google LLC. Retrieved on 1 November 2018 from https://goo.gl/gmS1Vm

Brennan, K. (2013). Learning computing through creating and connecting. *Computer,* 46(9), 52–59.

Buechley, L. (2017). Phone interview with Paulo Blikstein.

Buechley, L., & Eisenberg, M. (2008). The LilyPad Arduino: Toward wearable engineering for everyone. *IEEE Pervasive Computing,* 7(2), 12–15.

Clancy, M. (2017). Phone interview with Paulo Blikstein.

Clements, D. H. (1990). Metacomponential development in a LOGO programming environment. *Journal of Educational Psychology,* 82(1), 141.

De Corte, E., & Verschaffel, L. (1989). Logo: A vehicle for thinking. In B. Greer & G. Mulhern (Eds.), *New Directions in Mathematics Education* (pp. 63–81). London/New York: Routledge.

diSessa, A. (2000). *Changing Minds: Computers, Learning, and Literacy.* Cambridge, MA: MIT Press.

diSessa, A. (2018). Computational literacy and "the big picture" concerning computers in mathematics education. *Mathematical Thinking and Learning,* 20(1), 3–31.

Fincher, S. (2017). Phone interview with Paulo Blikstein.

Google LLC. & Gallup Inc. (2016). Diversity gaps in computer science: Exploring the underrepresentation of girls, Blacks and Hispanics. Retrieved from http://goo.gl/PG34aH

Graham, P. (2004). *Hackers & Painters: Big Ideas from the Computer Age.* Sebastopol, CA: O'Reilly Media.

Grover, S. (2017). Phone interview with Paulo Blikstein.

Grover, S., & Pea, R. (2013). Computational thinking in K–12: A review of the state of the field. *Educational Researcher,* 42(1), 38–43.

Guzdial, M. (2017). Phone interview with Paulo Blikstein.

Horn, M. (2017). Phone interview with Paulo Blikstein.

K–12 Computer Science Framework Steering Committee (2016). *K–12 Computer Science Framework* (978-1-4503-5278-9). Retrieved from http://k12cs.org/wp-content/uploads/2016/09/K%E2%80%9312-Computer-Science-Framework.pdf

Liu, M. (1997). The effects of HyperCard programming on teacher education students' problem-solving ability and computer anxiety. *Journal of Research on Computing in Education,* 29(3), 248–262.

Maltese, A., & Tai, R. (2011). Pipeline persistence: Examining the association of educational experiences with earned degrees in STEM among US students. *Science Education,* 95(5), 877–907.

Margolis, J. (2017). Phone interview with Paulo Blikstein.

National Research Council (2006). *America's Lab Report: Investigations in High School Science.* Washington, DC: National Academies Press.

National Research Council (2012). *A Framework for K–12 Science Education: Practices, Crosscutting Concepts, and Core Ideas.* Washington, DC: National Academies Press.

Noonan, R. (2017). *STEM Jobs: 2017 Update (ESA Issue Brief # 02-17).* Retrieved from www.esa.gov/reports/stem-jobs-2017-update

O'Neil, C. (2016). *Weapons of Math Destruction.* New York: Crown Publishing Group.

Palumbo, D. (1990). Programming language/problem-solving research: A review of relevant issues. *Review of Educational Research,* 60(1), 65–89.

Papert, S. (1980). *Mindstorms: Children, Computers and Powerful Ideas.* New York: Basic Books.

Pears, A., Seidman, S., Malmi, L., Mannila, L., Adams, E., Bennedsen, J., & Paterson, J. (2007). A survey of literature on the teaching of introductory programming. *ACM SIGCSE Bulletin,* 39(4), 204–223.

Resnick, M. (2017). Phone interview with Paulo Blikstein.

Seehorn, D., Carey, S., Fuschetto, B., Lee, I., Moix, D., O'Grady-Cunniff, D., ..., Verno, A. (2011). *CSTA K–12 Computer Science Standards: Revised 2017.* Retrieved from www.csteachers.org/page/standards

Sentance, S. (2017). Phone interview with Paulo Blikstein.

Shapiro, B. (2017). Phone interview with Paulo Blikstein.

Sherin, B. L. (2001). A comparison of programming languages and algebraic notation as expressive languages for physics. *International Journal of Computers for Mathematical Learning, 6*(1), 1–61.

Stager, G. (2017). *A Modest Proposal.* Retrieved from http://stager.tv/blog/?p=4153

Turkle, S., & Papert, S. (1990). Epistemological pluralism: Styles and voices within the computer culture. *Signs: Journal of Women in Culture and Society, 16*(1), 128–157.

US Department of Labor (2007). The STEM workforce challenge: The role of the public workforce system in a national solution for a competitive science, technology, engineering, and mathematics (STEM) workforce. Retrieved from https://digitalcommons.ilr.cornell.edu/key_workplace/637/

Vogel, S., Santo, R., & Ching, D. (2017). Visions of computer science education: Unpacking arguments for and projected impacts of CS4All initiatives. In *Proceedings of the 48th ACM Technical Symposium on Computer Science Education – SIGCSE 2017* (pp. 609–614). New York: ACM.

Weintrop, D., Beheshti, E., Horn, M., Orton, K., Jona, K., Trouille, L., & Wilensky, U. (2016). Defining computational thinking for mathematics and science classrooms. *Journal of Science Education and Technology, 25*(1), 127–147.

Wilensky, U. (1999, updated 2006, 2017). NetLogo [Computer software] (Version 6). Evanston, IL: Center for Connected Learning and Computer-Based Modeling. Retrieved from http://ccl.northwestern.edu/netlogo

Wilensky, U., & Papert, S. (2010). Restructurations: Reformulating knowledge disciplines through new representational forms. In *Proceedings of Constructionism 2010 Paris* (p. 15). Paris, France: American University of Paris.

Wing, J. M. (2006). Computational thinking. *Communications of the ACM, 49*(3), 33–35.

Yongpradit, P. (2017). Phone interview with Paulo Blikstein.

PART II

Foundations

4 A Study Design Process

Andrew J. Ko and Sally A. Fincher

Chapters in this Handbook provide foundations for conducting research, ranging from theories of learning and knowledge to methodological tools common to computing education research. In this chapter, we discuss the research process itself. We deconstruct one skill, focusing on *study design*, a critical start to many kinds of computing education research.

Sadly, a book chapter is inherently inadequate for actually learning to design studies. Becoming expert at anything, study design included, requires extensive deliberate practice, and this chapter cannot give you that practice. Instead, this chapter gives a framework to *structure* your deliberate practice, helping you to more effectively select what you practice, how you practice it, and how you seek feedback on it. This chapter is therefore scaffolding for skills that will take years to develop.

Our approach to structuring your practice is to frame study design as a *process*, and in particular, a *design* process (Lawson, 2006), involving iteration, feedback, and prototyping, including divergent generation of new ideas and convergent refinement and selection of ideas. As is common with all design activities, the experience of designing studies is one that almost always begins with immense ambiguity and ends with clarity (in the case of study design, in the form of data collection instruments, procedures, and analysis plans).

Note that **empirically**, **methodologically**, and **theoretically**, study design processes are not inherently different from the numerous other fields from which computing education research borrows its theories, methodologies, and empirical epistemologies. What *is* different is the knowledge and strategies researchers must use to design a successful study. For example, one way that study design is hard is that *what* you are designing is mostly invisible. Unlike designing cars, clothing, or devices, "studies" are not inherently visible or tangible. Therefore, a critical part of effective study design is making studies *visible*, by prototyping them in forms you can apprehend, critique, and refine. This is true of studies of anything, but in the design of studies about the learning and teaching of computing, the prototypes of studies we make are all domain-specific. Therefore, knowledge of the structure of computing education studies, and how to make these types of studies successful, is domain-specific.

In this chapter, we will mostly talk about studies devised and executed by a single researcher (or small team). However, one type of study often found in

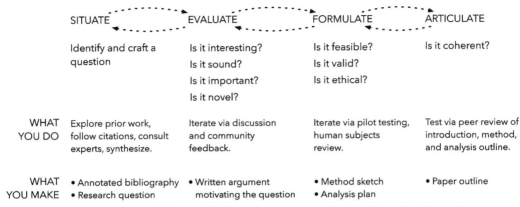

Figure 4.1 *A study design process spanning four iterative phases that come before executing a study.*

computing education is the multinational, multi-institutional (MNMI) study, where data are gathered in many countries and many institutions, to investigate questions across different cultures and different teaching practices. The best-known example is "the McCracken study" (McCracken et al., 2001), which was replicated in 2013 (Utting et al., 2013), but many groups, especially those associated with the Association for Computing Machinery (ACM) Innovation and Technology in Computer Science Education (ITiCSE) conference use the model. Fincher et al. (2005) provide an overview.

Finally, before embarking on a tour through the elements of the study design process, Figure 4.1 presents a map of the process we will discuss. This process includes key activities and questions to answer about the output of those activities and a checklist to guide study design practice from an initial idea to completion and report. The outcome of each step in the map is an artifact that will contribute to the overall design. After step 1, you should have the components of a literature review (perhaps written as an annotated bibliography). After step 2, you should have an argument motivating the question. After step 3, you should have a method sketch and pilot of your analysis. After step 4, you should have a paper outline that allows you to execute your plan.

Although we have presented this sequentially, be aware that study design is hardly ever an orderly process – don't be deceived by a neat representation. Good study design is an inherently iterative activity and you can expect to loop through stages, revisiting and refining, often many times. With practice, some parts may be collapsed and taken together, and with different kinds of study (as in software engineering methodologies), sometimes a different order makes better sense than others.

This necessary iteration, combined with the significant effort required to answer the questions, is why high-quality study design can take so long. Throughout this chapter, we will discuss strategies for streamlining all of these activities.

4.1 Situate: Identify a Research Question

As portrayed in Figure 4.1, the first critical aspect of a study design process is identifying a research question by situating your thinking in prior work. And although it is often called "finding a question," as with any design process, the initial stage is largely about exploring and framing a problem. Before you can formulate a question, you have to have an *idea* for a question. This is an inherently *generative* activity, and like anything creative, can require inspiration from unexpected and diverse places.

Research – of any kind – is not a solitary activity, but is constructed within a community. Therefore, ideas for questions can come from numerous places, people, and concepts. For example, you may find yourself observing someone try to solve a programming problem in a class through brute force, compelling you to ask why they've chosen that strategy over another. This might lead to you theorizing about strategy, which then leads you to dive into the literature about strategy.

Novice study designers in computing education often begin with an idea for a *solution* to a problem. While this is usually premature, from solutions, one can derive questions, and even theories that underlie those questions. For example, imagine you were trying to teach basic ideas behind supervised machine learning with decision trees. Your first instinct might be to come up with an explanation for information gain and use a study to test whether that explanation is effective. Instead of leaping from a solution to a study design, first ask, "What is hard about the concept of information gain and what about the explanation would make it easier?" The answer to *that* question is a theory that explains why your explanation of information gain might work, which is a more rigorous way to devise predictions about the explanation's effects and ultimately test them. This is critical to understanding the causes underlying problems and to designing a good study.

You can also find research questions in the "future work" discussion of a recent publication, a dissertation, or an interesting blog post about the learning or teaching of computing that poses, but does not answer, a question. Many research questions come from conversations with other researchers, such as those with colleagues, advisors, or other researchers, in PhD meetings, at conferences, or online. Whatever the source, ideas for research questions are unlikely to come purely from your own mind, but from the richness of the writing, people, and phenomena you surround yourself with.

To illustrate some of these circuitous paths to questions, here are two brief origin stories. In 2009, the first author of this chapter added a line to the list of interests on his faculty website that said something like, "Designing playful interactions with code." A prospective doctoral student, Michael Lee, saw that statement, decided to apply, and ultimately joined the first author's lab. Now, the first author was not doing any work on "play," and he did not at that time have a vision for what that might mean, but he was curious to find out. When Mike arrived, he had numerous conversations with the first author, which generated hundreds of different ideas for research questions. After dozens of discussions, reading hundreds of papers, and extensively refining his thoughts, Michael eventually converged on the question, "What is the effect of framing a compiler as a collaborator rather than an authority?" That triggered a design process that ultimately led to Gidget (Lee et al., 2014) and, eventually, numerous published studies.

Another story: in 2003, the second author replied encouragingly to an email from a prospective PhD student. Matt Jadud started his doctoral studies later that year. At first, there was no clear direction to the work. Matt was interested in classroom interactions and had many hours of video, which we initially thought to analyze. Over the next few months, in many meetings and many discussions on many walks, the work moved away from focusing on what teachers were doing to support students – or what students were saying to each other to support their programming practice – to the *invisible interactions* they were having with the compiler. This led to Matt instrumenting the BlueJ environment and writing some of the very first papers that quantitatively identify novice students' compilation behaviors (Jadud, 2006).

There are three things to notice about these stories: one is that these were not activities conducted in isolation; we all brought a lot "into the room," in the form of observations, literature, and discussions between ourselves and with others. The second is that the process of identifying a research question was not systematic: it was highly social, highly iterative, and highly unpredictable. Third, the exploration in these stories was not random or haphazard, it was *informed* – by prior research, by the expertise of advisors and collaborators, and by the broader community in which these students were learning. This stage of research can be frustrating and feel fruitless (and it sometimes is), but informed, collaborative exploration is a necessary part of study design.

Research questions *can* be derived more mechanistically, most notably from theories. For example, one theory often cited in the computing education research literature is Cognitive Load Theory (Sweller et al., 2011), which presents the concept of "extraneous cognitive load." Cognitive Load Theory claims that people have a fixed capacity for cognition, and if a task contains too much extraneous load, it is poorly learned as it leaves no room for acquiring the intrinsic and germane elements. By simply interrogating the *words* in these ideas, we can mechanically extract several potential research questions:

- Is the claim about extraneous load true?
- What is "load?"
- What counts as "extraneous" load?
- What determines a task's "capacity" for promoting learning?
- How can one measure "extraneous" load?
- How can we distinguish extraneous load from other types of load?
- How does extraneous load interact with prior knowledge?

New theories can also be a source of questions. Computing education research, as a distinct research area, needs to define domain-specific theories about how people learn computing, what it means to know programming languages and how to program, and what constitutes programming and software engineering expertise. All of these are important research questions. Questions may also arise from features of disciplinary practice – and computing is particularly rich in this regard. The development and deployment of new tools and computing environments and the compilation of ever-larger datasets in computing research are all rich sources of investigation. For example, what does it mean to understand machine learning sufficiently to build software that leverages machine learning? Theorizing about this knowledge, developing instruments to assess this knowledge, and designing new ways of helping people acquire this knowledge are fruitful areas for computing education research.

4.2 Evaluate: Is It Any Good?

As we portrayed in Figure 4.1, identifying an idea and formulating a research question are just parts of a longer process. Not all questions are equal – some cannot be researched adequately, some are too broad, others too narrow, and some are beyond your skill or resources to answer. So, when you have a question, the next step is evaluative: Is it any good?

4.2.1 Is It Interesting?

One of the first things to evaluate is whether a question is interesting *to you*. This might seem like an odd criterion, but it's actually quite important: if you are not interested, why should anyone else care? If you're not interested, what is going to motivate you to do all of the remaining work that the research will require? Curiosity is the fuel of research, and so regardless of how important, timely, or novel the work is, it's really not worth *you* doing it if you don't really care about the answer.

Of course, interest and curiosity are not always so easy to judge. Perhaps you have multiple diverse interests. What if you might *become* interested in a question after further reading? Perhaps your interest is driven not by the content of a question, but more in the process of answering it or engaging with the community of people who might be interested in the answer. Because of these nuances, judging interest, and selecting one question over another, is often a very personal endeavor that requires reading, reflection, discussion with mentors and advisors, and engagement with research communities.

If it's interesting to you, is it interesting to anyone else? Research is never a private activity – it lives in interaction with a community, building on other's work and making itself available for use by others. When thinking about study design as a *design* process, it is instructive to think of the product: who is the audience for your work? It might be a supervisor, attendees of a particular conference, or readers of a particular journal. Each of these will have a different focus. Working out why they might be interested in your work – in what you have to say – is part of the design.

While we cannot prescribe a process for gauging interest, we can make some general statements about the arc of judging interest: reflect, ponder, and ruminate about your chosen area, and make sure to talk to potential audiences about what they find interesting about the question. Without some feedback, and the necessary iteration on a question, you risk the question being uninteresting to anyone. If that happens, no matter how rigorously you answer it, you risk no one caring about what you have discovered.

Do not iterate on this step – or any other – forever. As we discuss in the following sections, there are many other factors to consider, and they may force you to abandon a question that is interesting to you or others.

4.2.2 Is It Theoretically Sound?

Suppose you have found a question that's interesting. The next step is to reflect on whether your question is *theoretically sound*. Soundness is fundamentally about whether the ideas in the question rationally leverage everything we already know about learning, education, and computing.

To illustrate, let's consider a simple research question: "Do debugging tools help students learn to code better?" One process for critiquing a question's soundness is to deconstruct the ideas in its words. For example, the question starts with "Do tools help?" and implies that the answer is either a "Yes" or a "No." We know from prior work on learning that the answer is rarely binary, but rather, "It depends." Similarly, consider the phrase "help students." What kind of help? There's a difference between learning, finishing an assignment, fixing a bug but not understanding the fix, etc. This question mostly ignores these factors, which means it ignores prior work, making it theoretically unsound.

Because theoretical soundness concerns how consistent a question is in respect to prior work, judging soundness means *knowing* prior work: the more you read, the more you'll be able to judge. What can make this difficult in computing education research is that the number of sources for knowledge is vast. We have few dedicated research conferences, handfuls of practitioner conferences, and multiple journals. But there are dozens of venues in education research and learning science, all of which are also important to the theoretical soundness of our work. Many other areas of computer science are also adding "education tracks" to their conferences. Judging soundness therefore requires monitoring many sources for new evidence, as well as mining many sources for existing evidence.

4.2.3 Is It Important?

Another consideration is the extent to which your question is *important*.

Importance can be judged by many different stakeholders along many dimensions. For example, at the smallest level, is it important to you, your advisor, and your collaborators? It might be important because of the funding tied to answering it, because of some personally important goal, or it may be of strategic importance to the lab or institution you are part of. There may be a mismatch between student and advisor goals: because doctoral students depend on the advice, attention, and resources of their advisors, a supervisor's judgment of the importance of your question can matter a great deal in getting the resources you need to answer it. This can be more acute in computing education research, since there is less basic research funding for broad exploration and much more funding for the specific implementation of educational interventions, which can constrain what resources are available.

At a broader level, research communities judge importance against their values. For example, submitting a research paper to the ACM International Computing Education Research (ICER) conference is different from submitting it to the International Conference on Learning Sciences: the former values work specifically about the learning and teaching of computing, while the latter values foundational theories of learning, largely agnostic to domain. Your question might be important to one community but not the other.

Communities also judge research questions against their impact on knowledge in a research community. For example, a research question about how to effectively leverage a rarely used feature of a rarely used learning technology that is on the brink of becoming obsolete may be judged as far less important than a MNMI study of a widely used, promising new pedagogy.

Finally, there are stakeholders of questions beyond academia. Would teachers, students, parents, policy-makers, employers, or other groups find the questions important? Some questions that are important to researchers may be viewed as quite irrelevant to those in practice, and vice versa. That does not mean that you shouldn't follow your interests, but that you should know whether your question's importance lies in basic or applied research. Knowing *who* you're trying to impact can clarify how you report and disseminate your discoveries in that it helps you empathize with your audience's interests.

4.2.4 Is It Novel?

A good research question is *novel* when we do not yet have a robust answer to it, although there may be parts of answers. To evaluate novelty, you need to understand the body of evidence that already exists to answer it. We believe this is best done before thinking about study methods, data collection, or other matters we will discuss later, since prior work is full of good ideas about how to tackle a question, but you can also start with an idea for a study first and verify its novelty later. Either way, this process will be iterative, reshaping your questions and whatever study ideas you've generated.

In the general case, understanding a body of evidence means reading everything you can find that provides some evidence for the answer. Because of the way research papers are written and archived, this is often a messy process: authors use different words for the same concepts, they publish in multiple different journals, conferences, and books, and scholarly search engines are not particularly good at organizing this mess.

Perhaps the fastest approach to understanding what we know about a question is to find an expert who's already read the work relevant to the question. This might be a highly cited scholar or a fresh PhD student who performed a literature review on the topic recently. If you don't know which expert to ask, approach scholars who might know, negotiating the social network of experts until you find someone who does know. Make sure your approach is specific and polite, and you'll often get a reply. If you don't, move on; don't become a persistent pest. If no one knows of work that answers your question, it's probably novel! More likely, they will know of works that are loosely related to your question, which also reveals something about the novelty of your question. (Note that discussing research opportunities with others poses inherent risks of being scooped, but it can also lead to fruitful collaborations and replication, and so should not be feared).

In the absence of an expert, another good strategy is to find a survey, review, or "systematic literature review" article (hint: this book is full of them). These papers synthesize a large body of work for the purpose of conveying what we know and do not know with confidence about some phenomenon. If you're lucky, someone will have written one that shows you all of the work related to your question. More often, it will describe *much* of the work, but you will still have to do some searching and synthesizing of your own to characterize what is known about your question.

If you can't find an expert or a review article, you may need to do a literature search of your own, searching digital libraries for every possible relevant prior work. Think of all of the terms that might be relevant, all of the journals and conferences that might be relevant, and query a digital library search engine for relevant papers. Once you find a few related works, find papers that those papers cite and especially what papers cite that paper, traversing the citation graph for all of the relevant work you can find. You'll know you're done when you stop finding new research.

While you're searching, you'll want to read the relevant work in detail to understand and extract the evidence that exists, along with any additional terminology that will help you in your search. If after this reading you still do not see an answer to your research question, or the evidence is sparse, uncertain, or partial, so that we need more evidence, then your research question is novel. On the other hand, if the evidence is robust, perhaps your time is better spent investigating something else. Sometimes researchers undertake replication studies to strengthen poorly supported answers to research questions. But if the evidence is strong enough that your question will only add a negligible amount of increased confidence or knowledge, it may be worth abandoning it in favor of something that will contribute more to our body of knowledge.

One final consideration of novelty is whether all possible outcomes of a study would be novel, or just some of them. For example, imagine you designed a controlled experiment to evaluate the impact of some new learning intervention: if the study shows that it causes increases in learning, then that may be a novel contribution, but what happens if the study does *not* show that increase? What if it shows a decrease? What if nothing changes? You could run the study and take the risk; you could try and formulate secondary questions that result in discovery, no matter the outcome; you could also reframe the question so that, no matter the outcome, the study reveals something we do not know with high confidence. For example, gathering data about what caused (or failed to cause) a difference would allow you instead to investigate the mechanisms of the learning intervention in addition to its downstream effects. Of course, replications can also be novel if they bolster our certainty about something.

By the time you have considered all of these points, you should have a good grasp of the space that your question will inhabit. You should make sure your notes are collated as an annotated bibliography or the like, which will form the basis of the "related work" section of an eventual report.

4.2.5 Prototyping Research Questions

As you iterate on research questions, it is critical to continually express your research question in a form that allows you to observe, critique, and refine it. So far, we've mostly just listed the question ideas. However, the *form* that a research question ultimately takes is an *argument*, beginning with the state of the world and our knowledge and ending with the question. Outlining these arguments is the best form of prototype to integrate all of the evidence about novelty, soundness, and importance that you have iteratively developed.

Let's look at an example of one such argument and then dissect it. We'll extract the argument from the paper that won the "Chairs" award[1] at ICER 2016, titled "Learning to Program: Gender Differences and Interactive Effects of Students' Motivation, Goals, and Self-Efficacy on Performance," authored by Alex Lishinski et al. (2016). The argument in their introduction is as follows:

1. Measures of self-regulated learning (SRL) predict students' academic outcomes.
2. Previous research in computer science (CS) education has examined motivation and subcomponents of SRL as possible predictors of success in introductory programming courses.
3. Previous research has also suggested that there are gender differences with respect to self-efficacy that may affect course outcomes.
4. However, previous studies have focused on examining the relationships between individual SRL and self-efficacy constructs and course outcomes, rather than investigating how multiple components of SRL (e.g., goal orientation and metacognitive strategies) and self-efficacy interact over time as students learn to program.

---

1 This award is given by the program committee chairs as a signal of rigor and excellence.

5. Research question: What are the relationships between self-efficacy, goal orientation, metacognitive strategies, and course outcomes in introductory programming students?

These four claims and question together represent an argument that substantiates all non-personal qualities of research questions we have discussed thus far. For *novelty*, claim 4 clearly states a gap in prior work, crisply stating that constructs have been studied in isolation rather than together. For *importance*, claim 1 states that self-regulated learning is an important indicator of student outcomes, implying we should understand it more deeply. For *soundness*, the references cited in the paper for all claims 1–4 substantiate each statement and tie the concepts used to theory. The research question itself uses the same concepts in the cited theory, further establishing soundness.

Arguments like the above are a powerful genre for capturing and evaluating a research question's quality – its motivation, theoretical grounding, and relevant prior work. The benefit to this form is that it's *low-fidelity*: it's much easier to discard a few sentences than an entire draft. Moreover, it's faster to iterate, because there is less text. It's also easier to get feedback on it from collaborators, because they can quickly evaluate the merits of your argument.

4.3 Formulate: Can You Research It?

Congratulations, you have a novel, theoretically sound, important, interesting question! This is no small feat: evaluating each of those criteria is challenging and slow. Unfortunately, you still need a way to ensure that your question is researchable. Methods are how we generate evidence to answer questions, and so you must devise a feasible method.

As Figure 4.1 shows, formulating a method is a creative, iterative, and often social process. However, research questions often imply requirements about the methods that are appropriate to use in addressing them. If you are comparing samples, or populations, then you will need to be able to make quantitative, statistical claims – which will affect your study design. If you are investigating the sense that students make of their education ten years after they graduate, then you will need to talk to them: that will affect your study design. Method choice is also often informed by the repertoire of methods that a researcher is comfortable with executing, that they've used before, and know will provide evidence that satisfies them. For instance, it is unusual for someone who habitually does controlled studies that provide quantitative answers to take on a phenomenographic enquiry (or vice versa). This is not necessarily a negative limitation: the more you use a method, the more you understand the nuance of its application and so, in turn, are able to design better studies.

To illustrate, let's consider the research question: "What barriers exist to higher-education faculty adopting alternative pedagogical methods in large CS1 courses?" Let's deconstruct the requirements implied by this question:

- We know we're looking for a set of "barriers."
- We know we're going to focus on CS1 courses in higher education with a large number of students.
- We know that we're focused on pedagogy, and not other aspects of instruction.
- Our unit of analysis is faculty and not departments or universities.

From these four facts about the question, many methods are ruled out. For example, there's no comparison, so we're not running a controlled experiment. The type of data we're seeking is inherently qualitative (we're not looking for *how many* barriers exist, but rather characterizations of them, and characterizations are qualitative). And because we're looking for a *set* of barriers, the question implies that we'd like a *complete* set of those barriers, not a biased, partial set with unknown barriers unaccounted for. This suggests that we may want to do some kind of survey, interview, or observation of a diverse population of higher-education faculty focused on the various moments in which faculty are devising pedagogy to teach a course. We may consider a diary study, or longitudinal sampling. Whichever type of method we choose, the question also implies that we need to somehow access the decisions of faculty, since the barriers that exist are affecting those adoption decisions.

Generating ideas for methods partly requires knowing what types of methods exist, but also requires creativity. Taking a good social science research methods course can provide a basic foundation for this. You can also read one of countless books about research methods (Babbie, 2013; Baxter & Jack, 2008; Bordens & Abbott, 2002; Creswell & Clark, 2007; Coolican, 2017; McMillan & Schumacher, 2014). But this foundational knowledge isn't enough. You need to ideate, brainstorm, and generate method ideas, and that requires having seen many examples of methods. Having a large set of examples in your head will help you devise a particular method for your study.

One way to capture your method ideas is to *sketch* the set of facts we would normally report in a "Methods" section of a research paper. To help us illustrate how to critique and refine a method, let's sketch a method for the research question above (not the only possible one, of course):

- **Population**. All higher CS education faculty in the world.
- **Sampling**. We will obtain the faculty mailing lists of all CS departments in the world.
- **Recruiting**. We will write a message to all mailing lists explaining our research goals, asking for volunteers to participate in a 15-minute phone call, scheduling calls for all who reply.
- **Procedure**. Before starting the interview, we will explain the study to the faculty and obtain their consent to participate. During the interview, we will first ask the faculty member about their current pedagogical practices and where they learned them. Then, we will ask about their awareness of alternative pedagogies and experiences they have in considering the adoption of them. If they have considered new pedagogies, we will ask about their decisions of whether to adopt those pedagogies.

- **Data collection**. We will audio record all interviews and then have them transcribed.
- **Data analysis**. We will analyze each transcript for barriers to adoption of new pedagogy techniques, creating a set of barriers across the sample.

Let us put aside for the moment the content of the method and focus on its role as a *sketch*. Note that it is concise, it has structure, and, most importantly, it describes what you and your research team would do to answer the question. As a sketch, it is not complete, but it allows us to see what is missing, what is ambiguous, what is invalid, etc. By prototyping the idea, we can now critique it and improve it.

Just as research questions have many criteria for quality, study designs must be feasible, reproducible, internally valid, externally valid, construct-valid, and ethical. In the rest of this section, we discuss how to use a sketch of a method to evaluate these criteria.

4.3.1 Is It Feasible?

Unfortunately, the world is full of good research questions that we simply cannot answer. We may not have access to all the CS departments in the world, we may not know how to tell if populations are equivalent, or we may not be skilled in the analysis that the question requires. Assessing feasibility is therefore key.

There are many aspects of feasibility to consider:

- Is there a method that will give the right sort of data to allow you to address the question?
- Do you have the skills to carry it out?
- Do you have the time it will take?
- Do you have the resources (money, people, materials, etc.) it will take?

Let's consider the method sketch we just completed above. There's definitely a method we can use to answer the question, but feasibility issues lurk. For example, to get the faculty mailing lists of all of the CS departments in the world, we need to know who to contact to get those lists, and then we need rights to post to each list. We may not be able to get these for all departments. Worse yet, even if we could get access to the lists, faculty may be so disinterested in helping that we would get too few replies for us to get a reasonable sample. None of these is guaranteed to be an issue, but they are risks to assess and mitigate. For example, mitigation strategies might be to target a small, representative sample of faculty, writing personal email requests to each rather than broadcasting to mailing lists. This might take more work upfront, but may lead to a higher response rate overall.

What skills does this method require? Because it's an interview, it requires interviewing skills. But the sampling and recruiting also require coordination, scheduling, and organizational skills. The analysis will require substantial experience in building categories from qualitative data. The trade-offs in this are numerous. Perhaps you have these skills already, in which case risk is low. Or perhaps you want to learn them, in which case risk of poorly executing the method is higher, but the reward may also be greater, since you will acquire new research skills. One way to mitigate this risk might be to find a collaborator with good planning and organizational skills and delegate planning to them. You might still learn the skills through their mentorship, while mitigating risk.

Is there time to execute the method? There are many CS faculties, so if the response rate is high, then that could be hundreds of hours of interviews. Perhaps a doctoral student focused on data gathering for months would be able to do this. If the key individual contributor is an undergraduate working five hours a week during full-time classes, it's probably not feasible. Mitigating these risks might involve using a different data collection method, such as a survey, which scales data collection and eliminates interviewing time, but this would be at the expense of the richness and depth of the data.

And finally, do you have the resources to do the study? There has to be money to pay for researchers' time and to pay for the transcription of the audio, and there may need to be some financial incentives to get faculty to reply. If there is no money, you might subsidize the work with your time or choose methods that take less time and require fewer resources. For example, perhaps instead of paying faculty to reply, there is a way of motivating them through altruism (recruiting colleagues that you and your collaborators have personal relationships with). This will bias the sample in several ways, but it will likely require fewer resources and lead to a higher response rate. Bias of some form is rarely escapable, and so this might be a worthy trade-off if future studies can overcome the bias with a different method.

Most research methods are hard in some way. When there are too many hard or high-risk things, it may be worth considering a different method, or possibly a different question altogether. That said, conservatism around the feasibility of methods is also one of the most significant barriers to progress in research: methods are simply tools for building knowledge, and if we only ever use the same tools, we will only ever build the same kinds of knowledge. Taking risks and learning new methods that a research community has not yet used could result in new knowledge.

One example we know of this is from psephology, the study and analysis of voting and elections. Among those who conduct exit polls, there is one team of researchers in the UK led by Professor John Curtice from the University of Strathclyde, who regularly produce the most accurate predictions (BBC, 2017). One of the reasons for this is their use of method. Like all such researchers, they carefully sample and carefully control their sample so that it is representative of the nation. However, this team does not *ask* people how they voted, which is a sensitive subject and may invite voters to given an expected answer rather than a truthful one. Neither do they question nor do they interview voters. Instead, "Participants are provided with a mock ballot paper that mimics almost exactly the one they have just completed, and are invited to place it in a mock ballot box, thereby ensuring that they do not have to reveal to the interviewer how they have just voted" (Curtice et al., 2017). By using a new method, they get more accurate predictions than self-report.

4.3.2 Is It (Sufficiently) Construct-Valid?

Even if a method is feasible, it may not be valid. There are several aspects to validity that you will need to consider (Messick, 1995). One of the first kinds of validity to consider – construct validity – ensures that the way you are collecting data, including the measures and instruments you are using, actually represents a genuine phenomenon and faithfully reflects how it exists in the world.

Take, for example, the notion of a "barrier" to pedagogy adoption. Are there really such things as barriers in faculty's heads that faculty figuratively "bump into" and cannot overcome? Or is it a problem of risk, where faculty encounter some alternative way of teaching, but they see a high risk for failure? Or perhaps it's not risk, but rather a complete oversight of the existence of other ways of teaching? Will any of the interview questions posed in this study successfully access whatever forms of factors affect faculty adoption of new pedagogies? Without a strong alignment between the theorized existence of "barriers" and a carefully designed way of observing them, our study design is not valid.

In computing education research, nowhere is this more important than in measures of *engagement* and *learning*. Without strong theoretical grounding of what we believe engagement or learning to be, and strong measures of those phenomena grounded in those theories, we cannot make valid claims about either. For example, is engagement best conceived of as a measure of sustained attention over time, or as a proxy for intrinsic motivation to learn? Or, is learning to code best conceived of as learning a well-defined systematic process for solving problems or as an art, shaped and informed by a community of practice? We don't have these theories yet. Instead, we have partially validated measures with rudimentary notions of learning like the Foundational CS1 (Tew & Guzdial, 2011) or Secondary CS1 (Parker et al., 2016). These allow us to make some progress, but to continue to make progress, we need to build, validate, and use instruments across a community and over time, while we also develop the theories that support their validation.

4.3.3 Is It (Sufficiently) Internally Valid?

Another validity consideration for a study method is its internal validity, which concerns the capacity for the design to relate cause and effect with some certainty. While this validity issue is most relevant to randomized controlled trials (also known as controlled experiments), it is actually an issue anytime a study design attempts to infer causality.

To illustrate, let's return to our faculty interview study. We wanted to understand what prevents faculty from adopting novel pedagogy. Prevention is about causality, and so our study is inherently about studying cause and effect. But can our interview study actually observe cause and effect? Not really: the only way to do that would be somehow to access the decision-making process a faculty member goes through in their mind (assuming it's a conscious process) and observe the factor that is preventing adoption. Unfortunately, we don't have direct access to people's minds, so we have to be assured that our instruments gather what they're thinking. Most research on decision-making shows that most naturalistic decision-making is first emotional and then post-rationalized (Lerher, 2010). Our interview study is much more likely to capture the rationalizations of non-adoption, rather than the emotional contexts that actually prevented adoption.

In general, research methods are carefully evolved instruments for ensuring internal validity. Therefore, the easiest way to increase the internal validity of your study is to follow the best practices of a method. Those best practices might be expressed in textbooks, exemplary research papers, or occasionally in papers describing how to execute a particular method.

Internal validity is also quite challenging in computing education research, as many of the phenomena we hope to observe (such as learning, interest, identity, attitudes, and engagement) are not overtly visible in the world, but hidden inside learners' and teachers' minds.

4.3.4 Is It (Sufficiently) Externally Valid?

Most study designs narrowly focus on a tiny fraction of a much larger population of people, places, or things. *External validity* (also known as "generalizability") is the extent to which the conclusions we draw about these tiny samples might generalize to other people, places, or things. Methods with high internal validity tend to have low external validity, and vice versa; this is because gaining certainty about causality usually requires one to look closely and in a controlled setting, with the trade-off that you cannot account for the other contexts not being observed. Similarly, the more diverse the contexts you observe, the less control you have. One can overcome some of these trade-offs at scale; for example, a randomized controlled experiment with 15,000 participants testing a new drug can account for a lot of variation. The variation in social context learning and the variation in individual learning are harder to control and measure. Moreover, there are fewer resources in education than in health sciences to run large-scale studies. This makes this trade-off hard to overcome.

The external validity of our hypothetical interview study depends very much on how many faculty participate in interviews and *who* participates in those interviews. If just 10 of 10,000 faculty reply, it seems unlikely that the set of barriers those 10 teachers report would reflect the set of barriers present in the broader population. Worse yet, if the 10 that replied were all from the same CS department, the external validity would drop even further. We can try to control external validity in this case by increasing the chances that we get a large, diverse sample. Or we can try to measure external validity by comparing the sample we *did* get with the overall sample, showing that they are similar to each other; for example, by showing that we recruited faculty from most colleges and universities, from most research areas, and from most academic trainings.

External validity in computing education research is particularly challenging because learning and education are so strongly affected by culture and learners' prior knowledge. Moreover, controlling for these is hard since we have few valid measures of either. Thus, once again, we aim for *sufficient* external validity, in the hopes that our methods of characterizing external validity improve and that others replicate our work.

4.3.5 Is It Ethical?

Another criterion is ensuring your study design is ethical. For most academic research, there are legal protections for human participants against a wide range of harms, certainly including physical harm, but also emotional and psychological harms, including stress that can come from challenging tasks or distress that can come from deception.

In computing education research, there are many settings in which these harms can arise, and in unexpected ways. Take stress, for example – when the first author was an undergraduate, he conducted a study of the learnability of three different integrated development environments for statistical hypothesis testing. One environment was particularly notorious for its steep learning curve, and the tasks the participants were asked to do only exacerbated the challenges that curve imposed. While the study had been approved by the university's institutional review board (IRB), and the first author had already engaged 50 participants, the 51st had a particularly negative emotional experience with the tasks, as she had just failed a class in which she had to demonstrate similar competence. Having to relive that failure and be reminded of its effects on her delayed graduation were so traumatizing that she complained to the IRB and the study was halted for further review. Neither of these outcomes – the trauma to the student or the delays to the first author's research – was desirable. In the best case, IRB ethics reviews can help to prevent these sort of things from happening through some upfront investment in careful ethical reflection on your study design.

Ethical considerations are often especially complex in MNMI studies, where approval for the study has to be obtained at every location where data are collected. Sometimes it is enough that approval has been granted at the lead institution. However, just as often, multiple approvals have to be sought, and sometimes in quite complex ways. In one study, a 17-site consortium had four "lead institutions," as that was the only way approval could be obtained from four of the sites. When designing MNMI studies, you should certainly build in extra time for this step.

4.3.6 Pilot to Analysis

A key strategy for successful study design is to find a way to pilot as many elements as possible – even if only with one person. This can greatly improve your procedures, data collection, and data quality.

Many people pilot data gathering (be it interview protocols or testing survey designs), but it is important not to stop the piloting effort too soon. Gathering data is not the last step: analysis is. A key part of prototyping a study design is describing and implementing the actual procedures you will follow to clean, process, and analyze the data you gather. What steps will you follow? What scripts do you need to write? What statistics will you compute? Failing to plan for analysis can have a range of consequences. For example, a year-long diary study conducted by the second author failed to adequately consider analysis: the quantity of data received was so large that even reading it in a sensible time allowance was forbidding. So the data stays, sitting in a database, unused and unanalyzed. In contrast, the first author ran a survey study with two students, omitted the analysis planning, and only realized after gathering data from over 4,000 people that the survey didn't ask a key question of every respondent.

Piloting to analysis is especially important in two situations: one when you are unfamiliar with the methods, and the other in MNMI studies. A colleague tells the story of taking data to a statistician after they were collected only to be told that the design was flawed for quantitative analysis (for various reasons) and couldn't support the claim they were trying to make. "Had you consulted me earlier," said the statistician with a sad smile, "you could have got it right." In MNMI studies, data are always gathered from multiple sites by multiple researchers, and often analyzed collectively. It is imperative that you are quite certain the main pieces of analysis are achievable.

Preventing these problems is all about verifying that the elaborate plans you've made for data collection can actually answer the question you posed.

As with research questions, an excellent approach to capturing, evaluating, and refining study designs is to prototype them into an articulation of the method and analysis plan as you might publish in the "Methods" section of a research paper. Here's why:

- Having detailed documentation on the study plan can help you and others execute the plan consistently and reliably.
- If you wait to write it later, you may forget crucial details about the design that need to be captured to support reproducibility.
- In writing the full detail of a design, you'll inevitably find more flaws, ambiguities, and details to determine before running the study.
- By detailing exactly how you plan to analyze the data, you'll verify that you will have the data you need to answer the question, and that the types of analyses you have planned are appropriate for the data you're collecting.

4.4 Articulate: Is It Coherent?

By the time you are ready to actually execute your study, there should be minimal uncertainty about what you are going to do and what you expect to happen. This doesn't guarantee that you will get the results you want – this is research, after all, and if we knew the result in advance, we wouldn't need to do the study. But you should know that your question is interesting, sound, important, and novel, and you should have a detailed description of method and piloted analysis that you know will answer this question. Judging a study's overall *coherence* is therefore a key final step before proceeding.

You can think of coherence as a thread of logic running through the entire chain of reasoning, from the first claim of the argument, to the research question, all the way through the data collection procedures and data analysis plan. Throughout this entire line of logical reasoning, every claim made should be substantiated, every question sound, every step of a method valid, every statistic consistent with its assumptions, and every interpretation congruous with the evidence gathered. This is ultimately a holistic judgment, and the same judgment made by other researchers during peer review, so doing this *before* you execute a study is a critical way to further eliminate flaws.

Let's consider one example study and discuss its coherence. We will focus on the ICER 2017 paper by Danielsiek et al. (2017), who sought to build a validated instrument for measuring self-efficacy in introductory programming courses. Below is a set of claims that run through their paper; try judging the coherence of the claims:

- Introduction
  - Self-efficacy is the personal belief of one's ability to succeed in a situation or task.
  - How a teacher teaches can influence self-efficacy.
  - Knowing the impact of teaching on self-efficacy requires measurement.
  - There is no measure of self-efficacy in introductory algorithms courses.
  - What is a conceptually valid measure of self-efficacy in algorithms courses?
- Method
  - We partnered with four institutions to measure self-efficacy.
  - We adapted a previously designed instrument to an algorithms course context.
  - We administered the adapted instrument in four classes, obtaining 130 responses.
- Results
  - We verified the data had sufficient sphericity to be factorizable.
  - We performed a factor analysis, finding four factors that explained 66 percent of the variance.
  - The factors were consistent with the instrument's intended measurements, indicating construct validity.
  - Cronbach's alpha was 0.938, suggesting reliability.
  - The instrument did not correlate with measures of self-regulation, suggesting divergent validity.
  - The instrument did correlate with measures of personality traits, suggesting nomological validity.
- Conclusion

- Therefore, the instrument we designed is a conceptually valid measure of self-efficacy in introductory algorithms courses.

Note how each of the claims in this overarching argument are *all* in support of the final conclusion statement, achieving coherence. Viewing a study design from this perspective allows you also to assess the final conclusion based on the claims that support it. For example, one could quibble about whether the amount of evidence to support divergent validity is enough to claim that the measure is valid. Or one could point out (as the authors do) that because this was the first study to instrument self-efficacy in this context, there is no evidence to support convergent validity. This threatens the final claim that the instrument is valid, as it cannot be tested until more studies are conducted in the same area.

In the first author's lab, students are expected to write arguments like the above to support such assessments. The best form of this task is to actually write the skeleton of the research paper reporting the results *before* running a study. That means writing an introduction with a series of claims leading to a question, all of the related work necessary to substantiate its soundness, importance, and novelty, a method description of the information needed to execute the study, and an analysis plan that has been verified for feasibility and its ability to answer the question. Also writing a "Limitations" or "Threats to Validity" section *before* executing the study will help brainstorm all of the flaws in the study that you might be able to eliminate before gathering data. With a skeleton of the paper, assessing coherence is then a matter of evaluating it as it will be assessed in peer review, but without actual results or a discussion of implications. This is not only great practice for reviewing, but also the best way to verify that your research plan is a quality one.

4.5 Execute

Once you're ready to execute a study, data collection and analysis should be straightforward, at least to the extent that you have sufficiently planned it. Of course, rarely (actually, never) does everything we have described in this chapter go perfectly. Time and resource limitations can lead to satisficing; lack of skills can lead to a wide range of mistakes and errors, some of which can be catastrophic to a study. The key is to learn the foundations in this book and get as much feedback as possible before you gather data.

Treating study design as a design process furnishes you with a number of artifacts along the way:

- A literature review of the prior literature about your question;
- A series of claims that establish the importance, soundness, and novelty of a research question, refined through feedback and further literature review;
- A sketch of your method and analysis plan, refined through piloting into a paper outline.

With these in hand *before* you execute your study plan, if execution and analysis goes well, all that is left is writing the results, adding a discussion of implications, and then sharing your discoveries with the community.

In this chapter, we have presented a series of heuristics for considering study design as a design process. Like all heuristics, they offer "[a] process that may solve a given problem, but offers no guarantees of doing so" (Newell et al., 1957). Using them should give a better result than not using them, but achieving power and elegance in design, in this as in other fields, rests with the skill of the practitioner.

References

Babbie, E. R. (2013). *The Basics of Social Research*, 13th edn. Boston, MA: Cengage Learning.

Baxter, P., & Jack, S. (2008). Qualitative case study methodology: Study design and implementation for novice researchers. *The Qualitative Report*, 13(4), 544–559.

BBC (2017). Election 2017: Methodology. Retrieved from www.bbc.co.uk/news/election-2017-40104373

Bordens, K. S., & Abbott, B. B. (2002). *Research Design and Methods: A Process Approach*. New York: McGraw-Hill.

Coolican, H. (2017). *Research Methods and Statistics in Psychology*. Hove, UK: Psychology Press.

Creswell, J. W., & Clark, V. L. P. (2007). *Designing and Conducting Mixed Methods Research*. Thousand Oaks, CA: Sage Publications.

Curtice, J., Fisher, S., Kuha, J., & Mellon, J. (2017). On the 2017 exit poll – Another surprise, another success. *Discover Society, Focus*, Issue 46. Retrieved from https://discoversociety.org/2017/07/05/focus-on-the-2017-exit-poll-another-surprise-another-success/

Danielsiek, H., Toma, L., & Vahrenhold, J. (2017). An instrument to assess self-efficacy in introductory algorithms courses. In *ACM International Computing Education Research Conference* (pp. 217–225). New York: ACM.

Fincher, S., Lister, R., Clear, T., Robins, A., Tenenberg, J., & Petre, M. (2005). Multi-institutional, multi-national studies in CSEd research: Some design considerations and trade-offs. In *Proceedings of the First International Conference on Computing Education Research* (pp. 111–121). New York: ACM.

Jadud, M. C. (2006). *An Exploration of Novice Compilation Behaviour in BlueJ* (doctoral dissertation). University of Kent.

Lawson, B. (2006). *How Designers Think: The Design Process Demystified*. New York: Routledge.

Lee, M. J., Bahmani, F., Kwan, I., LaFerte, J., Charters, P., Horvath, A., Luor, F., Cao, J., Law, C., Beswetherick, M., Long, S., Burnett, M. M., & Ko, A. J. (2014). Principles of a debugging-first puzzle game for computing education. In *IEEE Symposium on Visual Languages and Human-Centric Computing (VL/HCC)* (pp. 57–64). New York: IEEE.

Lehrer, J. (2010). *How We Decide*. Boston, MA: Houghton Mifflin Harcourt.

Lishinski, A., Yadav, A., Good, J., & Enbody, R. J. (2016). Learning to program: Gender differences and interactive effects of students' motivation, goals, and self-efficacy on performance. In *ACM International Computing Education Research Conference* (pp. 211–220). New York: ACM.

McCracken, M., Almstrum, V., Diaz, D., Guzdial, M., Hagan, D., Kolikant, Y. B., Laxer, C., Thomas, L., Utting, I., & Wilusz, T. (2001). A multi-national, multi-institutional study of assessment of programming skills of first-year CS students. In *ITiCSE Working Group Reports* (pp. 125–180). New York: ACM.

McMillan, J. H., & Schumacher, S. (2014). *Research in Education: Evidence-based Inquiry*, 7th edn. London, UK: Pearson Higher Education.

Messick, S. (1995). Validity of psychological assessment: Validation of inferences from persons' responses and performances as scientific inquiry into score meaning. *American Psychologist*, 50, 741–749.

Newell. A., Shaw, J. C., & Simon, H. A. (1957). Empirical explorations with the logic theory machine. In *Proceedings of the Western Joint Computer Conference, Vol. 15* (pp. 218–239). New York: ACM.

Parker, M. C., Guzdial, M., & Engleman, S. (2016). Replication, validation, and use of a language independent CS1 knowledge assessment. In *ACM International Computing Education Research Conference* (pp. 93–101). New York: ACM.

Sweller, J., Ayres, P., & Kalyuga, S. (2011). *Cognitive Load Theory* (Vol. 1). Berlin, Germany: Springer.

Tew, A. E., & Guzdial, M. (2011). The FCS1: A language independent assessment of CS1 knowledge. In *ACM Technical Symposium on Computer Science Education* (pp. 111–116). New York: ACM.

Utting, I., Tew, A. E., McCracken, M., Thomas, L., Bouvier, D., Frye, R., Paterson, J., Caspersen, M. Kolikant, Y. B.-D., Sorva, J., & Wilusz, T. (2013). A fresh look at novice programmers' performance and their teachers' expectations. In *ITiCSE Working Group Reports* (pp. 15–32). New York: ACM.

5 Descriptive Statistics

Patricia Haden

5.1 Introduction

Computing pedagogy can be guided and informed to some extent by the traditional education research literature. However, computing education has unique demands and features (e.g., its scaffolded nature; cf. Robins, 2010) that are likely to require specially tailored approaches, and current formal research in the area is addressing a wide range of pertinent questions. For example, at Special Interest Group on Computer Science Education (SIGCSE) 2017[1] (a large computing education conference in the USA), researchers presented work exploring all of the following topics (among many others):

- How to measure students' understanding of programming constructs like variables and loops.
- The impact of small group work embedded into large computer science lecture classes.
- Computing course design for students with numeracy challenges.
- Ease of marking for a new style of programming exam question.
- The impact of compiler error message content on debugging performance.
- Children's stereotypes of computer science.
- The use of algorithmic visualizations as a teaching tool.
- The impact of collaborative formative examination on learning programming.
- How self-reported feelings about computing classes differ between the genders.
- How computing students use online discussion forums.
- How to identify the incidence and impact of plagiarism in coding assignments.
- The use of massive open online courses to train primary school computing teachers.

Although computing education research may be situated in a unique computing context, it relies on the core methodological and statistical principles that underlie all education research (and to an extent, empirical research in general).

In this chapter and the next, we present the fundamental material you need in order to be an informed consumer of the quantitative computing education literature and to design and develop your own research programs. It is not our

---

1 Conference proceedings at https://dl.acm.org/citation.cfm?id=3017680

intention to present exhaustively the theoretical and applied mathematics that underpins quantitative methodology and analysis. That would fill a whole book (multiple books, in fact), not just a couple of chapters. Also, such detail is not always necessary in this age of powerful statistical software, which does the algebraic heavy lifting for us. Rather, in these chapters, we will discuss the underlying logical principles that drive good experimental design and data analysis and constrain the inferences we can draw from both basic and advanced analysis techniques. By being aware of these principles, you can avoid common mistakes. You can design studies whose data will give you real insight into your research questions. You can select appropriate analysis techniques to extract knowledge from your raw data. You can avoid drawing conclusions that go beyond the logical limits of your study. And you can recognize those situations that are sufficiently complicated that you need to get some expert statistical advice.

Almost all quantitative research follows a traditional scientific paradigm: decide what you are interested in, set up an empirical study, collect your data, analyze your data, and see what you have learned. Within this basic structure, there are thousands of special cases, nuances, and esoteric things one might need to be concerned about. A professional statistician needs to know about all of these things. Everyone else can, fortunately, largely ignore these rare situations. The majority of quantitative studies share a small number of common components. These components each have a small number of attributes or properties that you need to get right in order to be able to learn things from your data. Understanding these basic principles will be sufficient 99 percent of the time.[2]

In this chapter, we will look at the heart of any research process – the data. We will learn how to get good-quality data and we will consider various statistical techniques for describing and summarizing our data, which is the first step in discovering what they can tell us about our research questions. As we do this, we will acquire a common vocabulary that we can use when talking about statistical issues. (Many statistical terms are common words that, when used in a statistical context, have very different meanings from when they are used colloquially.) In the next chapter, we will explore the theory and practice of statistical techniques that allow us to draw confident conclusions that go beyond what we are able to explicitly observe. When appropriate, we will situate these discussions in computing education, but some examples will come from contexts where the principles are easier to illustrate. In either case, the underlying logic is the same.

5.2 Dependent Variables – Defining Your Data

Every research study is performed because an experimenter is interested in something about his or her subjects[3]: how tall or how old they are, how well

---

2 That's a completely made-up statistic, but it sounds authoritative, doesn't it? Watch out for this.
3 In educational research, those being studied are often called "participants." We will use the terms "subject" and "participant" interchangeably.

they perform some task, how much money they make, how self-confident they are, whether they are healthy, etc. This thing – what the researcher wants to learn about – is called, in statistics, the **property of interest** (PI).

The goal of any research study is to measure the property of interest under particular conditions in order to learn something about it. This measure must, in quantitative research, be some value that can be written down or typed into a spreadsheet. This measure is called the **dependent variable** (DV).

Some PIs are easy to measure. That is, there is a direct, obvious DV. For example, if someone is studying baby birth weight, they simply put the baby onto a scale and see how many kilograms he or she weighs. The PI is weight and the DV is kilograms as reported by the scale.

Some PIs, however, are not easy to measure. For example, one might be studying happiness, or creativity, or student engagement. There is no scale to put one's subjects on that will give a direct and precise measure of how happy they are, or how creative they are, or how engaged they are in their studies. In these cases, the DV must be an indirect measure of the PI. That is, the researchers must define some observable, recordable measure that they believe accurately reflects the PI. This is called the **operational definition** (OD) of the PI. The relationship between the PI, the OD, and the dependent variable DV is shown in Figure 5.1.

Note that there is potentially an infinite number of possible ODs (and hence possible DVs) for a given PI. There can be both good and bad ODs. A bad OD leads to a DV that doesn't really measure your PI. We'll talk about this formally in a moment, but first, let's consider an example of the process of operationally defining a property of interest in order to obtain a quantitative DV.

Many computing educators are exploring ways to introduce computing principles to primary school children (see, e.g., DeWitt et al., 2017; Ericson & McKlin, 2012). These projects aim not only to increase computational skills, but also to engender positive attitudes toward computer science and information technology. Thus, there are two properties of interest – computing skill and how much the children like computing. Consider, for this discussion, the latter. There is no tape measure or bathroom scale for "liking," so an indirect approach – an OD – is required. The OD must specify a measurable and recordable DV. In many studies in this area, researchers use self-report. That is, they present a statement such as "I like computing" and record the participant's response on a scale from 1 (strongly disagree) to 5 (strongly agree).[4] In evaluating any conclusions that are derived from such data, we must first evaluate the quality of the DV. Specifically, does the DV (response on a 1–5 scale) measure attitude toward computing in the same sense that, for example, "centimeters tall" measures height?

There are some formal criteria for judging the quality of a DV, which we will discuss in a moment, but you can start by thinking about how an accurate

---

4 This is a Likert scale. This simple measure is extremely common in many fields of research, including computing education, but there is a surprising amount of controversy surrounding its correct use. We will revisit the Likert scale several times in this chapter.

Figure 5.1 *PI, OD, and DV.*

measure can be interpreted. If this DV for "liking" is accurate, the answer to all the following questions should be "yes":

- If person A and person B give the same response to the statement "I like computing" (i.e., the same value on the 1–5 scale), are they guaranteed to like computing exactly the same amount?
- If person A gives a higher answer than person B, does person A definitely like computing more than person B does?
- If person A says 4 and person B says 2, does person A like computing exactly twice as much as person B does?
- If person A says 3 today, will she say 3 again if you ask her next week?

With centimeters as a measure of height, you could say "yes" to all of the comparable questions. With the self-report OD (and resultant DV) for liking, you would be reluctant to do so. Therefore, this is not a perfect OD, and thus not a perfect DV. Sometimes there is no perfect OD/DV for a complex PI. This doesn't mean one shouldn't study it, it just means that when doing so, or when evaluating someone else's research, you need to watch for potential problems resulting from an imperfect OD.

5.2.1 Formal Properties of a Good DV

A DV (and hence the underlying OD) is good or bad in specific ways in statistics. There are, again, many nuances and special cases, but these are three critical criteria:

Valid: A DV is Valid If It Measures What It Is Supposed to Measure. For example, you might want to study physical fitness. You could create an OD/DV that involved blood pressure, cardio recovery time, upper body strength, etc. This would probably be fairly valid – that is, it would actually be measuring physical fitness. Alternatively, you could operationally define physical fitness as "number of cute exercise outfits in closet." This might even be an accurate measure in some cases, in that someone with lots of exercise outfits might work out a lot and so be fit, but most of the time, this DV does not measure fitness. It is not valid. (What might it actually be measuring, if not fitness?)

Reliable: A DV Is Reliable If It Gives the Same Result When the Measurement Is Repeated in the Same Situation. As an example, self-report DVs are notoriously unreliable. For example, if I operationally define marriage satisfaction as a self-reported value on a scale from 1 to 10, I might get very different responses the day before and the day after a subject has a big argument with his or her spouse.

Unbiased: A DV Is Unbiased If It Is Not Consistently Wrong in One Direction (i.e., Consistently Too High or Consistently Too Low). Anything that is not directly measurable will have some error, will not be perfectly exact – this is unavoidable. Statistical techniques are designed to cope with this. But they cannot cope with systematic error. For example, measuring alcohol consumption by asking people how much they drink is biased – people are much more likely to underreport than to overreport.

In addition to these three primary qualities, there are other pragmatic concerns around DVs. For example, one must avoid **floor and ceiling effects**. A DV suffers from a floor effect if all subjects produce very low scores (scores near the minimum possible) on the measure. A DV suffers from a ceiling effect if all subjects produce very high scores (near the maximum possible) on the measure. For example, imagine that you are comparing the efficacy of two teaching methodologies using score on an exam as your DV. If the exam is so easy that nearly all students earn more than 90 percent, you have a ceiling effect. If the exam is so difficult that nearly all students earn less than 10 percent, you have a floor effect. In either case, it will be very difficult to detect any difference between the two methodologies you are comparing. Floor and ceiling effects squash all subjects at one end of the possible data distribution, masking differences between subjects on the PI. Problems with DVs can also arise due to cost, difficulty of administration, and ethical concerns.

5.2.2 Data Scales

Each DV belongs to one of these four classes of data (called data scales):

- Ratio: regular numeric data (e.g., grade point average, number of compile events, household income).
- Interval: evenly spaced numeric data that do not have a meaningful, fixed null/zero value (e.g., calendar year).
- Ordinal: named or numbered categories with a true order, but no presumption of even spacing (e.g., military rank).
- Categorical: categories with no order (e.g., eye color, gender). This class is sometimes called "nominal."

It can sometimes be surprisingly difficult to figure out what the data scale of a DV is. For example, is a Likert response scale (i.e., those very common questions where you answer between 1 and 5 from something like "strongly disagree" to "strongly agree") interval data or ordinal data? Although many people treat it as interval (because it is a number), others maintain that is more accurately considered ordinal (because the distances between adjacent responses aren't necessarily identical; see Carifio & Perla, 2007, for a review of these arguments).

It is very important to know what kind of data you have because, as we will see below, certain kinds of statistical analyses can only accurately be done on certain kinds of data. Having the wrong kind of data can lead to nonsense results that look convincing, but are actually false.

5.3 Descriptive Statistics – Getting to Know Your Data

After collecting our data, we have a big pile of numbers that, on their own, aren't much use. We must apply our statistical techniques to this big pile. If we do it right, we can begin to answer our research questions. This is a process of discovery and can be both fun and exciting.

There are two general classes of statistical technique: **descriptive** statistics summarize and describe the data you have *observed*. They do not tell you anything directly about whether the same results would be seen in other subjects in other contexts. **Inferential** statistics allow you make inferences beyond the people you have actually tested and measured. It is common to apply descriptive techniques first to get a picture of the patterns occurring *in your specific sample*. These analyses can then inform the application of inferential techniques. We discuss inferential statistical techniques in the next chapter.

5.3.1 Graphical Descriptives

Since the purpose of descriptive analysis is to obtain a picture of our observed data, it is not surprising that some of the most useful techniques are those that produce – literally – pictures. These data-graphing techniques provide a quick and informative first analytical step.

The three most common graphs are frequency distributions, factorial plots, and correlation scatter plots. All of these can be generated by statistical software or in spreadsheet programs such as Excel.

5.3.1.1 Frequency Distributions

The x-axis of a frequency distribution (FD) takes values (or value ranges) of the DV. The y-axis takes the count (the frequency) or the proportion (relative frequency) at each x value (Figure 5.2).

The FD is a very common and very simple type of graph, and yet it illustrates one of the most important properties of a data set – how those data are **distributed**. The FD answers questions like "What is a typical score in this data set?" and "Do the scores tend to all be similar, or are people quite different on this measure?" Without any math at all, an FD can give you important insight into your data. For example, consider the two FDs shown in Figure 5.3.

The left-hand FD depicts a data set where people are quite variable. There are some relatively common values in the middle and relatively rare ones at the tails, but there are a good number of people at most of the values on the x-axis.

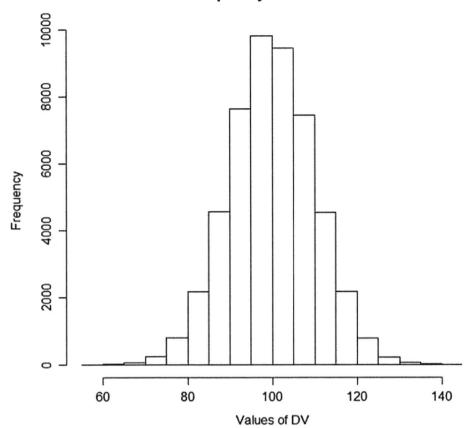

Figure 5.2 *Generic FD.*

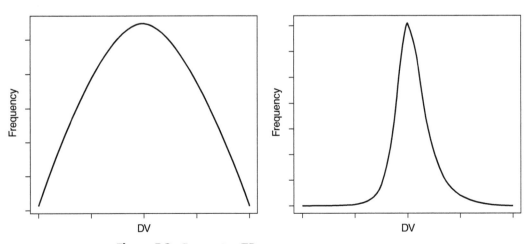

Figure 5.3 *Comparing FDs.*

If you measured the *heights* of all students in a large CS1 course, it might look something like this. The data illustrated in the right-hand FD measure something where people tend to all be quite similar. Values are bunched in the middle of the x-axis, with very few instances of the extreme high and low values. If you measured the *ages* of all students in a large CS1 course, it might look something like this.[5]

An FD will also reveal **skew** – the presence of rare scores at one extreme of the DV's range of values (Figure 5.4). Variables such as income tend to be distributed in this way, with most people earning values in the middle, but a few very wealthy people at the extreme high end. Skew can occur in either direction – that is, the long "tail" of the distribution can point either toward the high end (positive skew; top image in Figure 5.4) or the low end (negative skew; bottom image in Figure 5.4) of the DV value range.

The presence of skew can indicate some sort of extreme feature or behavior in the sample. For example, Edgecomb et al. (2017) measured the amount of time that CS1 students spend working on homework problems. Figure 5.5 shows the distribution of minutes spent working on a specific problem. While most students spent only two or three minutes on the problem, some spent more than ten minutes. In this case, the skewed distribution shows that a small proportion of students are taking an unusually long time to solve this problem, perhaps indicating students who are at risk.

In addition to giving an overall picture of a data set,[6] a frequency distribution often makes it easy to identify common, frequently occurring scores. Often, but not always, there is a single "peak" in the distribution (as in all of the previous figures) at the most common, most typical score. Sometimes, however, an FD has multiple distinct peaks (Figure 5.6). This pattern may indicate the presence of multiple groups hidden within your sample. Distributions of CS1 grades are often **bimodal**; that is, they have two distinct peaks – a group of students who perform very well and a group of students who fail (cf. Robins, 2010). See Chapter 12 for a discussion of possible causes of this pattern. Many common statistical treatments are not appropriate for use with bimodal data (see Section 5.3.2.1 for an example).

5.3.1.2 Factorial Plots

This second common type of graph is used when a study compares different groups. Grouping factors are formally called **independent variables**, and are discussed in detail in Section 5.4. Factorial plots show group averages (see Section 5.3.2.1 for computational details). An example factorial plot is shown in Figure 5.7 for a hypothetical study of the utility of three different programming

---

5 These shapes have formal names: the shape on the left is platykurtic, while the shape on the right is leptokurtic.

6 This assumes a sufficiently large sample size. With small sample sizes, many values or value ranges may have frequencies of 0. In these cases, FDs may not present a clear picture of the data.

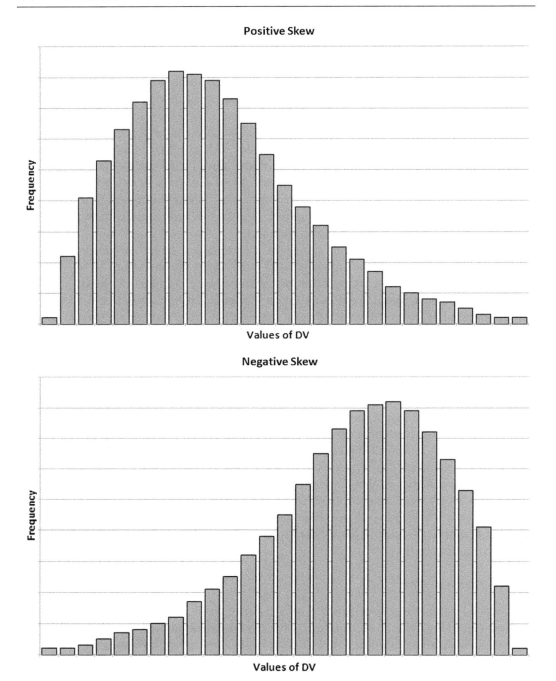

Figure 5.4 *FDs with positive and negative skew.*

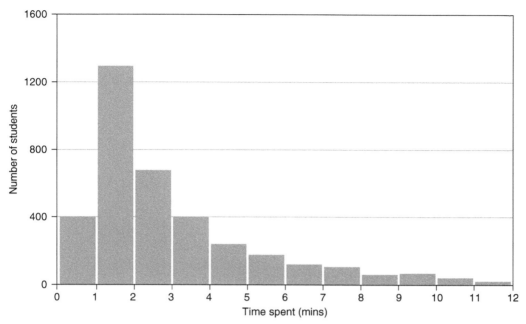

Figure 5.5 *Positive skew in time to solve a homework problem. Reproduced with permission from Edgecombe et al. (2017).*

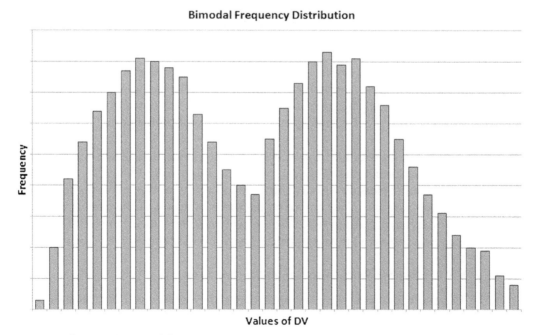

Figure 5.6 *Bimodal FD.*

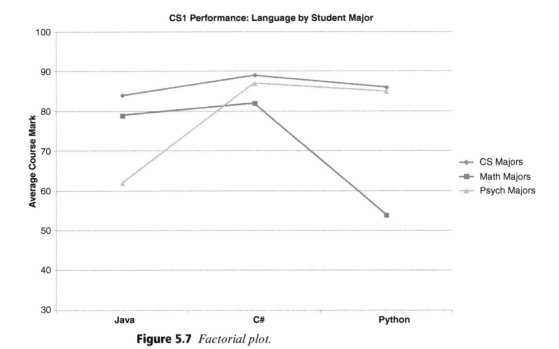

Figure 5.7 *Factorial plot.*

languages (Java, C#, and Python) for students from three different majors (CS, Math, and Psychology). The DV (course mark) is on the y-axis. One grouping factor (programming language) is on the x-axis. A separate line is plotted for each value of the second grouping factor (major). Each data point is the average score on the DV, across all participants in the indicated group.

Factorial plots are extremely revealing. The plot in Figure 5.7, for example, would show simply by inspection that Math majors in the study were confounded by Python, while Psychology majors coped well with Python, but struggled with Java.

Factorial plots can be drawn as histograms rather than as line graphs. In this alternative format, the above data would be shown as in Figure 5.8. Histogram-style factorial plots may seem to better reflect reality, as they make explicit the discontinuous nature of the groups on the x-axis. However, as the number of groups increases, the histogram style becomes cluttered and difficult to read. The job of the researcher is to provide graphical descriptives that present the data clearly.

5.3.1.3 Scatter Plots (Also Called Scattergrams)

This third common type of graph is used when we have two DVs. We discuss this type of graphical representation in Section 5.3.4 when we consider this experimental design variation.

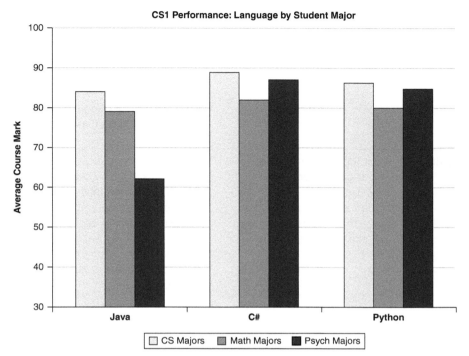

Figure 5.8 *Histogram-style factorial plot.*

5.3.2 Numerical Descriptives

In our discussion of graphical techniques, we noted that FDs can illustrate clearly the typical or common score(s) in a data set and the extent to which the elements of that data set are generally similar to, or different from, each other. While these concepts are intuitively tractable, it is possible to obtain very precise numerical measures of them. These values are informative in their own right, and are also essential components of the computations used in inferential statistics (discussed in the next chapter).

5.3.2.1 Measures of Central Tendency

For the majority of DVs, some scores are common and some are not. For example, if we are measuring height of adults, 170 cm (5'7") is common and 220 cm (7'3") is not. This notion is quite intuitive. Although we accept that not everyone is exactly 170 cm tall, we are comfortable with identifying it as a normal, typical sort of height. This summarization of a complete data set with a single value allows us to give sensible answers to questions such as, "The pass rate for my CS1 paper is 72 percent. Is that reasonable for CS1, or do I have a problem?" The formal numerical measures of this typicality are called measures of central tendency (MCTs). There are three common MCTs:

Measure	Definition	When to use
Mean	The arithmetic average Symbolized as $\bar{x}$ (pronounced "x-bar")	For interval or ratio data whose distribution is not extremely skewed and has a single "peak" value Unless you have a good reason not to (see some good reasons not to below)
Median	The middle score when all your data values are sorted by size If you have an even number of values, take the average of the two center scores	When your interval or ratio data are very skewed. Extreme scores in skewed data sets have a disproportionate impact on the arithmetic average; the mean is generally not a truly representative value for these data sets. Use the median With ordinal data
Mode	The value in the data set with the highest frequency (i.e., the most common score) If you have ties (or near ties) for "highest frequency," you have multiple modes	When your FD has multiple distinct peaks. Both the mean and the median can actually be low-frequency (obviously not typical) scores in a multi-modal data set. Use the mode With categorical data

As statistical concepts go, few seem as simple as the MCTs. Nonetheless, errors are often made in their application and interpretation. For example, it is extremely common to see the mean used as an MCT for Likert scale data. Mathematically, this is not entirely correct. An arithmetic average assumes that the distances between adjacent values on the scale being used are equal (i.e., you have ratio or interval data). For a measure like centimeters, this assumption holds true: the difference in length between 100 cm and 101 cm is exactly the same as the difference between 434 cm and 435 cm; something that is 4 cm long is exactly half as long as something that is 8 cm long. For Likert scales (as also discussed in Section 5.2), this is not necessarily the case. A typical Likert scale assigns numerical values to a conceptual range, for example:

1	2	3	4	5
Strongly disagree	Tend to disagree	Don't care	Tend to agree	Strongly agree

There is unfortunately no guarantee in this case that the difference between a respondent who chooses 1 and a respondent who chooses 2 is exactly the same as the difference between a choice of 2 and of 3. A person who selects "tend to agree" isn't showing exactly twice as much agreement as a person who choose "tend to disagree." Two scores of 2 certainly don't "add up" to the same as a single score of 4 – and so on. From a purely mathematical perspective, therefore, it is not correct to compute the mean of a set of Likert scale responses. The median or mode are mathematically more accurate (and a frequency distribution gives the most complete illustration of the data set). Nonetheless, averaging of Likert scores is common practice (cf. Robertson, 2011). The cautious consumer of data will want to be aware that this can be occasionally misleading. When in doubt, insist on seeing the complete FD.

5.3.2.2 Measures of Variability

A frequency distribution allows us to see if our subjects all tended to produce similar values (the FD is "bunched up" around its typical score) or dissimilar values (the FD is "spread out"). This property of a data set is called its **variability**. Unlike the MCTs, there is little choice to be made when measuring variability: in almost all cases, one uses the **standard deviation,** symbolized as *s.* The formula for the standard deviation is[7]:

$$s = \sqrt{\frac{\sum_{i=1}^{N}(x_i - \bar{x})^2}{N}}$$

Mathematically, the standard deviation is *almost* the average distance from the mean of all the scores in your data set. When interpreting your data, it is quite sensible to conceptualize it in that way. If all your scores are bunched around the mean, their average distance is small, so *s* is small; if your scores tend to spread widely, many scores will be far from their mean, and *s* will be large (shown schematically in Figure 5.9).

Statistics students often ask why we don't use as our preferred measure of variability the actual average distance from the mean. We could obtain this by simply using the absolute value of $x - \bar{x}$ rather than the square. The reason has to do with the special mathematical relationship between the standard deviation (with its squared distances) and an extremely important, specific, bell-shaped frequency distribution known as the **normal distribution**. Many naturally occurring measures are distributed normally, or nearly normally. The normal distribution, the standard deviation, and the relationship between them underpin a vast portion of statistical analyses, including several of the most common inferential techniques. The exact mathematics is beyond the scope of this discussion, but we will see a simple example below.

5.3.3 Individuals and Distributions (Normalization)

With a measure of central tendency, a measure of variability, and a general sense of the shape of a distribution, you can get an informative picture of a data

---

7 N is the number of values in the data set. In some complex situations, the denominator of the fraction is $N - 1$, but the interpretation is the same.

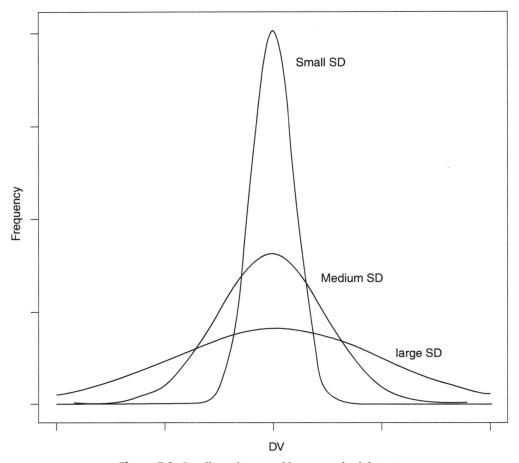

Figure 5.9 *Small, medium, and large standard deviations.*

set as a whole. In addition, you can learn a lot about the nature of an individual score relative to the data set in which it is contained. This is helpful when you need to compare multiple DVs.

For example, the traditional high attrition and failure rates in computing education (especially in CS1) have motivated many to search for the underlying skills and abilities that determine CS1 success. One early hypothesis was that programming requires the same sort of symbolic manipulation skills that math requires, and many studies have looked for relationships between math skill and programming skill.[8] Imagine that you had the final marks for your CS1 class, and had also obtained the mark for every student in a math class taken in the same semester. You noted that the highest-scoring CS1 student had earned a mark of 92 percent, but she had earned only 52 percent in her math paper.

8 Note that the research in totality shows no single, clear relationship between math ability and programming ability – we are simplifying the argument here to illustrate the relevant statistical concepts.

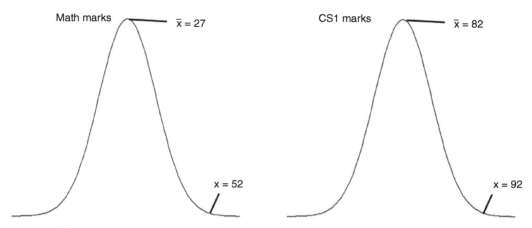

Figure 5.10 *Comparing scores from different distributions.*

You might feel this argued against the "math and programming have a lot in common" hypothesis – until you discovered that the mean mark for her math paper had been 27 percent, and your student's 52 percent had actually been the highest rewarded mark.

The critical feature of this situation is that, when comparing the math mark and the CS1 mark, you are comparing scores from *different distributions*. Often, comparing *raw* scores from different distributions is not meaningful. The two distributions might look as shown in Figure 5.10.

Although the two raw scores, 52 and 92, are very different, they are both the highest values *in their own distributions*. Since their relative positions in their own distributions are the same, there is a sense in which they are equivalent, and we would conclude that the student's performance in her math and CS1 papers was, in fact, consistent.

To precisely quantify the notion of "a score's position in its own distribution" and to allow comparison of scores from different distributions, we use a measure called a **z-score** or **normal score**. The formula for the z-score is:

$$z_i = \frac{x_i - \overline{x}}{s}$$

The z-score expresses the distance an individual score is from its own mean, in units of its own standard deviation. We can convert any individual score into its z-score, and we can compare directly and sensibly z-scores from different distributions. Two data values that have a z-score of, for example, –1, are exactly one standard deviation below the mean *in their own distributions*. Regardless of their raw values, they share this identical position. Whenever you wish to compare scores from different distributions, and those distributions are approximately normal, you should consider converting raw scores to their corresponding normal scores.

For example, Haden et al. (2017) used an online survey tool to gather student feedback on practical lab tasks in CS1. Students rated each lab along a number of continua including Boring to Interesting, Difficult to Easy, and Unfamiliar to Familiar.

Each response was given on a scale from –10 to 10. However, the distributions of responses (specifically the central tendencies) differed markedly between the continua. For example, most labs were judged to be at least somewhat interesting, so the mean "Interest" rating was positive. Most labs were also judged to be somewhat difficult, so the mean "Difficulty" rating was negative. Thus, a score of 0, for example, would be comparatively low on the Boring–Interesting scale, but comparatively high on the Difficult–Easy scale. To allow sensible comparisons between the response scales, one can simply convert all scores to their respective z-scores. A raw Interest score of 0, being below its own mean, will have a negative z-score, indicating that the lab was found to be less interesting than most. A raw Difficulty score of 0, being above its own mean, will have a positive z-score, indicating that the lab was found to be easier than most. It is then meaningful to compare two z-scores, because each reflects the position of the raw value in the distribution in which it occurs.

The use of z-scores also allows us to draw very precise conclusions about the positions of individual scores when those scores come from normal, or approximately normal (i.e., bell-shaped), distributions.[9] The involved techniques are used to compute the familiar **percentile rank** metric often used with very large data sets like national exam results. This use of z-scores, although interesting, is less relevant than normalization in CS education research, where sample sizes are often small, so we will not discuss it here. However, the interested reader will find presentations of the technique in most general statistics texts (see, e.g., Gravetter & Wallnau, 2012, Chapter 6).

5.3.4 Correlation – Descriptive Techniques for Two DVs

In the previous section, we explored using z-scores to compare two different DVs. Often, when we have two measures on each subject, we want to do more than compare them – we want to explore, in detail, the *relationship* between them. Specifically, we wish to ask: As one measure goes up, does the other measure also tend to go up? Does it tend to go down? Do neither of these patterns apply?

For example, if you measure height and weight for a group of subjects, you will find that, as height goes up, weight also *tends* to go up. This relationship will not be perfect – it is quite possible for Person A to be taller than Person B but to also weigh less – but there will be a general tendency for taller people to weigh more. Similarly, if you measure age and visual acuity for a group of subjects, you will find that as age goes up, visual acuity tends to go down (sadly). Finally,

---

9 These analyses are fairly robust (i.e., remaining pretty close to accurate) in the face of small to moderate violations of normality.

if you measure height and IQ, you will probably not find any consistent change in IQ corresponding to change in height.

Statistically, these types of relationships are called **correlations**. Descriptive analysis of correlation involves both graphical and numerical techniques.

5.3.4.1 Displaying Correlation Graphically

Correlations between two dependent variables are graphed on **scatter plots**. One DV goes on the x-axis, the other goes on the y-axis. A point is placed on the graph at the intersection of the DV_1 and DV_2 values for each subject. For the three example DV pairs described above, the scatter plots might look something like the examples in Figure 5.11.

If two variables are correlated, the data points on their scatter plot will form an approximate line (sometimes a wide and messy line). The nature of the correlation – either going up together or moving in opposition – is reflected in the slope of this line. The direction of the slope is used to describe the correlation. If as DV_1 increases DV_2 also tends to increase (e.g., height and weight), the scatter plot "line" has a positive slope; this is a positive correlation. If as DV_1 increases DV_2 tends to decrease (e.g., age and visual acuity), the scatter plot "line" has a negative slope; this is a negative correlation. If there is no correlation between the two DVs (e.g., height and IQ), the scatter plot tends to look round – there is no distinct line, so there is no slope.

The stronger the relationship between the two variables, the closer the points of the scatterplot will be to a perfect line. (In the extreme case – e.g., if you measure height in centimeters and height in inches – all the points will lie exactly on a single line.) Figure 5.12 shows two positive correlations. The points in the first scatter plot are clustered more tightly around a straight line than are those in the second; the correlation in the first plot is stronger. With a strong correlation, you will have few points that defy the rule that a large score on DV_1 is associated with a large score on DV_2 and a small score on DV_1 is associated with a small score on DV_2.

5.3.4.2 Representing Correlation Numerically

Scatter plots are easy to make and very informative – they illustrate, at a glance, both the direction and the strength of the relationship between two DVs. However, we usually need a more precise measure of the correlation. To obtain this (assuming we have ratio or interval data), we compute the Pearson product moment correlation, commonly denoted as *r*.

The value of *r* is always between –1 and 1 (this is a property of the formula for *r*). The sign of *r* (negative or positive) indicates the direction of the correlation. The size (absolute value) of *r* indicates the strength of the correlation. If your two DVs produce a perfect line (as with height in centimeters and height in inches), they will have an *r* of 1 (if the slope of the line is positive) or –1 (if the slope of the line is negative). An *r* of 0 usually corresponds to a "round" scatter plot – no relationship between the two DVs. However, *r* will also be 0 if one of

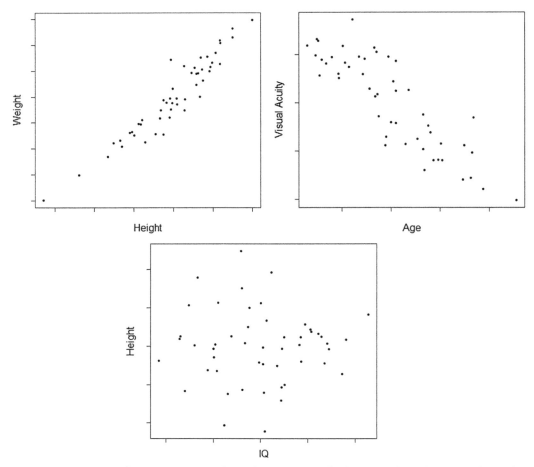

Figure 5.11 *Hypothetical scatter plots for height and weight, age and visual acuity, and height and IQ.*

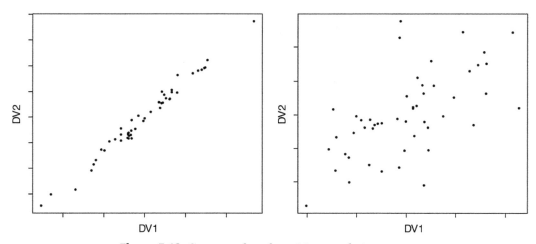

Figure 5.12 *Strong and weak positive correlations.*

the DVs is a constant (the scatterplot is a horizontal or vertical line) or if there is a non-linear relationship between the two variables (e.g., if the relationship is quadratic). Figure 5.13 shows some real data sets with their corresponding values of r.

The mathematical computation of r is laborious, but all modern software packages and spreadsheets will compute the Pearson correlation for two sets of values.

The largest value of r, and hence the strongest correlation that can exist, is 1 (or equivalently –1), indicating a perfect relationship between two variables. The weakest correlation produces an r of zero. But at what point between 0 and 1 (or equivalently –1) does a correlation become large enough to be interesting? Recalling that our original imaginary research question (a long time ago now) was based on deciding whether math marks were related to CS1 marks, we would like to know how big r would have to be before we could say: yes, math skill is relevant to CS1 success. Or, more specifically, math skill is *predictive* of CS1 success. In part, this is a question that can only be answered by inferential techniques, and we discuss it in the next chapter in that context. However, it is only common sense to argue that a correlation of 0.01 is not as predictive as a correlation of 0.95. There are various rules of thumb that are used to categorize strength of correlation based on the value of r; however, most approaches are close to that shown in Table 5.1 (e.g., Martella et al., 2013; Rumsey, 2016).

5.3.4.3 The Impact of Outliers

The Pearson r is sensitive to the presence of **outliers** – data points that do not fit the general pattern of the data set. For example, the two data sets in Figure 5.14 appear, by inspection, to illustrate very different relationships between the pairs of DVs. Intuitively, the bottom data set seems to have much the stronger correlation. However, the Pearson r for both data sets is 0.63. The bottom data set contains three outliers (the points with circular markers) that exert a strong downward influence on r. A complete descriptive analysis of correlation should, therefore, include both r and a scatter plot.

5.3.4.4 Correlation and Causality

Statistical techniques are various, clever, and mathematically beautiful, but in the end, they only produce numbers and pictures. Extracting knowledge from data requires interpretation of those outputs. Correlation analysis is notoriously susceptible to errors of interpretation – it is easy to draw conclusions from r that are logically unsound.

The problem is that it often seems clear that if Measure Y goes up when Measure X goes up, the change in Y must be *caused by* the change in X. For example, some researchers have found that hours studying and exam marks are positively correlated (Krohn & O'Connor, 2005). Students who study more tend to get higher exam scores. It may seem obvious that more study is *causing* the improvement in exam performance. Therefore, if you can convince a student

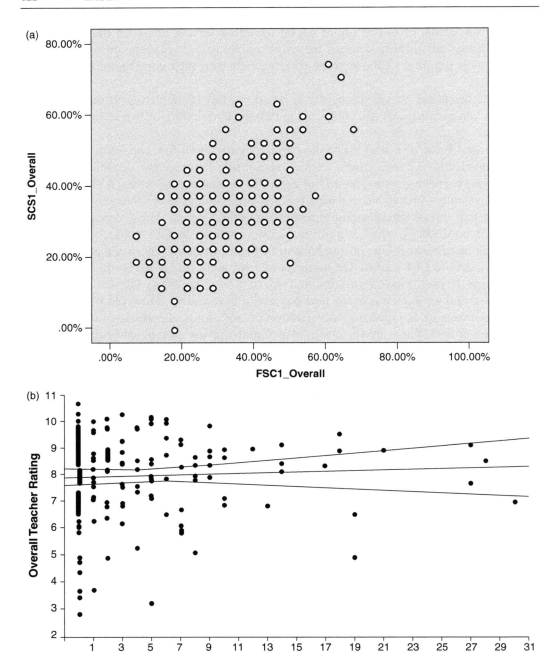

Figure 5.13 *Scatter plots of data sets. (a) r = 0.566 (reproduced with permission from Parker et al., 2016). (b) r = 0.03 and 95 percent confidence interval (reproduced with permission from Marsh & Hattie, 2002). (c) r = –0.79 (reproduced with permission from Murray, 2013).*

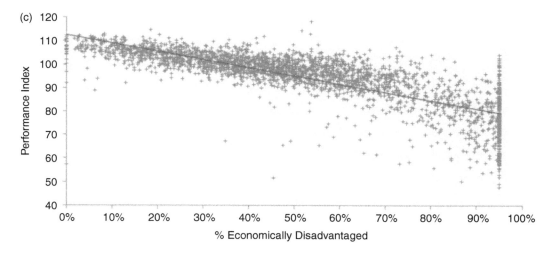

Figure 5.13 (*Cont.*)

Table 5.1 *Strength of positive correlations (apply symmetrically for negative correlations).*

Absolute value of r	Strength of relationship
0–0.1	Very weak
0.1–0.3	Weak
0.3–0.6	Moderate
0.6–0.9	Strong
0.9–1	Very strong

to study more, you are likely to see an improvement in his or her exam scores. Similarly, maternal nutrition and baby birth weight are positively correlated (Amosu & Degun, 2014). Again, it seems obvious that this is causal – better maternal nutrition *causes* increased birth weight. Thus, if you can improve maternal nutrition in a community, you will see an increase in average birth weight. Common sense tells us that these explanations and predictions are probably true. However, they are not *mathematically* sound. The existence of correlation, even strong correlation, does not *necessarily* imply causation. There are other forces that can cause correlation.

A correlation between two measures X and Y can actually be caused by a third factor Z, which is simultaneously controlling the behavior of both X and Y. X and Y can themselves be essentially independent. A favorite example in statistics classes is that in Australia, ice cream consumption and the frequency of shark attacks are positively correlated. That is, as people tend to eat more ice cream, there tend to be more shark attacks. To assume causality would be

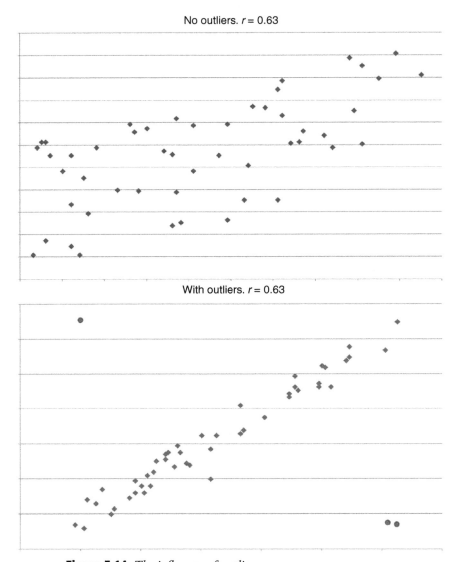

Figure 5.14 *The influence of outliers on r.*

to conclude that somehow the consumption of ice cream is directly responsible for the increase in shark attacks. Possibly consuming ice cream makes people too full to swim rapidly enough to escape sharks. Or perhaps people who have become sticky from ice cream are more tasty. (Statisticians take great amusement from coming up with such explanations.) In both of these explanations, ice cream consumption is *causing* the increase in shark attacks and, therefore, eliminating ice cream would reduce the frequency with which people get bitten by sharks. This is, of course, absurd. It is much more likely that the high outdoor temperature of summer causes an increase in both ice cream consumption and the number of people swimming in the ocean where the sharks are. Factor Z (temperature) causes X (ice cream consumption) and Y (shark attacks) to rise together, while X and Y are essentially independent. And of course, since there is no causal relationship, controlling ice cream consumption will have no impact on shark attack rates.[10]

The preceding example may seem frivolous, but it actually applies equally well to both of the "obvious" examples we presented earlier. Increased study hours may not be causing improved exam scores at all. It may be that a little increased study time helps students to sleep better, and it is being more rested that improves exams scores. If students increase study time at the expense of sleeping, their exams scores will actually fall. Maternal nutrition may not be improving baby birth weight directly. It may be that in affluent communities with good maternal nutrition, expectant mothers work fewer hours each day, and that is what causes improved infant birth weight. If women's nutrition is improved but their physical workload remains too high, infant birth weight will not increase.

Even when a correlational relationship is actually causal, one can err when explaining the *direction* of that causality. For example, a well-known study found that elderly people who rated higher on a measure of "positive attitude toward aging" also scored higher on hearing and physical fitness tests (Levy, 2003). That is, there was a positive correlation between attitude toward aging and physical wellness. Some popular media interpreted this as showing that maintaining a positive attitude would improve wellness in the elderly. That is, they concluded that the correlation was observed because a subject's attitude *caused* the subject's wellness. Improving attitude therefore would improve wellness. Unfortunately, a more compelling (and equally mathematically valid) explanation is that the causality works in the opposite direction. That is, elderly subjects who have good hearing and fitness feel more positive about aging. If this is the actual mechanism underlying the correlation, any "increased positivity" one might be able to produce would have absolutely no impact on physical wellness.

This complexity is captured in the statistician's motto: "correlation does not imply causation." Correlations, no matter how numerically strong, do not prove that the changes on one DV are *causing* the changes on the other. They show only a tendency of the measures to move together (either in concert or in opposition) and the strength of that tendency. Explanations for why the two measures move together require non-correlational data.

5.4 Independent Variables – Comparing Groups

Most empirical studies have some sort of manipulation or treatment that participants experience. The purpose of the study is to observe the effect(s) of the manipulation on the DV and hence on the property of interest. This

---

10 For further examples, see www.tylervigen.com/spurious-correlations

treatment is called the **independent variable** (IV). The different treatment conditions or groups are called the **levels** of the IV. For example:

- Comparing males vs. females: IV = gender; levels = male/female
- Comparing Java vs. Python vs. Scratch for a first programming language: IV = language; levels = Java/Python/Scratch
- Comparing middle-school girls' attitudes toward CS before and after coding summer camp: IV = camp attendance history; levels = before/after

The last example shows that the IV is sometimes hard to name elegantly, but it is usually very easy to identify. It is that which defines your comparison groups.

5.4.1 Properties of IVs

5.4.1.1 Within vs. Between Subjects

For a **within-subjects** IV, each subject is tested in every level of the IV. For a **between-subjects** IV, each subject is tested in only one level of the IV.

For example, if a researcher is comparing problem-solving performance under conditions of sleep deprivation and normal rest, the IV is "sleep condition," and the levels are "sleep deprived" and "normal." To use this IV in a within-subjects design, each subject would be tested twice – once when they are sleep deprived and once when they are rested. To use this IV in a between-subjects design, there would be two separate groups of subjects. Members of one group would be tested only when sleep-deprived; members of the other group would be tested only when rested.

As we will see in the next chapter, different analysis techniques are required for within- and between-subjects IVs.

5.4.1.2 Counterbalancing

When using within-subjects IVs, we often need to consider the order in which we test the participants in the different levels. Imagine, for example, that you are looking at two methods for teaching debugging skills to novice programmers – a text-based method and an interactive online method. The IV is teaching method, with two levels, text-based and online. Assume you have a good DV. You use the design illustrated in Figure 5.15 for all your participants.

After collecting and analyzing your data, you find that the improvement between skills test #2 and skills test #3 is always larger than the improvement between skills test #1 and skills test #2. That is, subjects show a larger improvement in debugging skill after online training than they do after text-based training. Can you conclude that online training improves debugging skill more than text-based training does?

No. It might be that having had the text-based training first made the students better able to benefit from the online training. Simply having the online training alone might not work nearly so well. This is called an **order effect** – where the order in which experimental treatments are applied affects the outcome.

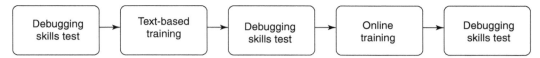

Figure 5.15 *Possible experimental design.*

To eliminate the order effect, you should give half your subjects text-based training first and give the other half online training first. Any order effects will essentially cancel each other out. This arrangement of treatment conditions is called **counterbalancing.** For studies with large numbers of IVs and levels, accurate counterbalancing becomes very complicated (see, e.g., Shuttleworth, 2009).

There is actually another possible design that would eliminate the order effect: you could make your IV between-subjects. That is, each student receives only one teaching method, *either* text-based or online training, but not both. This eliminates the order effect, but may increase the noise in the data, because you can now observe only overall group performance, not individual improvement. This can mask any impact of the independent variable.

5.4.1.3 True Experiment vs. Quasi-Experiment

Assume that you have a between-subjects IV. That is, each subject will participate in only one level of the IV. There are two different ways in which subjects may be assigned to levels:

- Under experimenter control
- Not under experimenter control

For example, if a medical research study is comparing a medicine and a placebo, the experimenter can directly assign subjects to conditions. In the simplest case, this is done randomly. (The reasons for this are mathematical and quite beautiful, but beyond the scope of this discussion.) However, in a research study comparing men to women, smokers to non-smokers, adults to children, etc., the experimenter cannot assign subjects to levels of the IV. They come preassigned.

Studies of these two types have different formal names:

- If the experimenter assigns subjects to levels, it is a **true experiment**.
- If the experimenter does not assign subjects to levels, it is a **quasi-experiment**.

Although researchers are often casual and call everything an experiment, technically, if the researcher doesn't control assignment, the study is a quasi-experiment. It is very important to be aware of whether data are from a true experiment or from a quasi-experiment, because the kinds of conclusions you can legitimately draw from the two types of study are different. In a true experiment, with random assignment of subjects to conditions, you can claim that any experimental effect you observe *is caused by* the experimental manipulation. In a quasi-experiment, you cannot. This is because, if participants are not randomly assigned to conditions, there may be differences between experimental groups *other than* the IV. The logic is similar to that which prevents us from drawing causal conclusions from observed correlations. We discuss this issue further in Section 5.4.3.

5.4.1.4 Control Groups

In many studies, there is a special level of the IV in which no treatment is given – a sort of "do nothing" condition. This is called a **control group** or **comparison group**. Without an appropriate control group, it may be impossible to make correct inferences from your data. For example, imagine that a medical researcher wants to know if taking echinacea helps people recover from colds. She recruits several people with colds, gives them echinacea and carefully measures their recovery time. Can she tell if the echinacea helped? No, she can't, because she doesn't know how long it would have taken the subjects to recover *without* the echinacea.

In situations like this, we need a comparison group that does not receive the experimental manipulation/treatment to serve as a **baseline**. When analyzing our data, we compare the results of the control group(s) to the results of the treatment group(s) to see if there is a difference.

In a computing education context, we often measure classroom interventions. In this case, the control group would be composed of students who do not receive the intervention (but for whom the rest of the educational content is the same). This can be difficult to manage in a classroom setting and/or can raise ethical questions. Specifically, if you really believe a particular educational intervention is beneficial, you cannot withhold it from some students, potentially adversely affecting their learning (and their marks), but not others. Such issues are complex in education research, and are discussed further in Chapter 4.

5.4.2 Multiple IVs

In many studies, the researcher is interested in more than one thing. For example, one might want to compare two different teaching languages (e.g., Java and Python) and simultaneously compare the efficacy of those languages for male and for female students. This study would have two IVs[11]:

- IV1 = language; levels = Java and Python
- IV2 = gender; levels = male and female

Most commonly, when we have multiple IVs, we want to test all possible combinations of all the levels. For this example, there would be four combinations: men doing Java, men doing Python, women doing Java, and women doing Python. This is called a **factorial design**. We will see in the next chapter

---

11 Note that this is the type of design illustrated in the factorial plot in Section 5.3.1.2.

that some statistical techniques are specifically structured to work with factorial designs.

5.4.3 Confounding Variables

We have looked at two critical components of an empirical study – the DV and the IV(s). There is a third type of variable we need to be aware of, *which is not part of the experimental design*. It is a bad thing that lurks around our experiment, ruining our ability to find truth in our data. This is the **confounding variable.** A confounding variable is something *other than* the IV(s) that causes a *pattern* in the DV.

For example, imagine you are (again) comparing Java and Python as a first language in CS1. You must use a between-subjects design, because a person can only have one "first" programming language. You need students from two programming courses – one that is taught in Java and one that is taught in Python. Assume that Lecturer Bob teaches using Java and Lecturer Charlotte teaches using Python. You discover that students in the Python class score much better on a standardized programming exam than do students in the Java class. Have you learned that Python is better than Java for CS1? Not necessarily. You may have only learned that Charlotte is a better teacher than Bob. Here, "lecturer" is a confounding variable – something *other than the IV* that could be causing the observed difference between our groups.

In this case, we could modify our experimental design to eliminate the confound. For example, we could have the same lecturer teach both classes, or we could have each lecturer teach one semester with each language and combine all the student results. However, sometimes this is not possible. The design most affected by confounds is a quasi-experimental study, where assignment to levels of the IV cannot be controlled by the experimenter. When subjects come "preassigned" to conditions, it is extremely likely that the experimental groups will differ for reasons other than the IV. For example, if a study compares vegetarians to non-vegetarians, these two groups may differ not only in their diets, but also in their ages, genders, socioeconomic backgrounds, physical activity levels, etc. If a difference is observed between groups, you can't tell which of these factors is actually responsible for that effect.

There are some rather tortuous techniques for reducing the impact of confounds. For example, if you are concerned that age might be a confounding variable in the above study, you can try to select all your subjects in pairs – one vegetarian and one non-vegetarian – of the same age. However, in the absence of random assignment of subject to condition (i.e., a true experiment), it is impossible to definitively prove that you have eliminated all potential confounds. This is why one can only draw *causal* conclusions in true experiments, not in quasi-experiments.

Confounds are very common and they are sneaky. Many "statistical lies" are due to unrecognized (or unmentioned) confounding variables. See Campbell

(1974) for an entertaining and instructive discussion of the dangers of confounding variables.

5.4.4 Quantifying Effect Size

In empirical studies with groups (i.e., where there are IVs), the researcher intends to compare the performance of the different groups on the DV to gain insight into the effect of the IV. For example, we spoke above of comparing exam scores for students who used Java against exam scores for students who used Python. This comparison is usually made on the means of the groups – if we find that the average score of Java students exceeds the average score of Python students, we conclude that Java was more effective. From a practical perspective, it is often useful to know not only which group is better, but *how much better* that group is. One would not, for example want to completely migrate a class from Python to Java if the expected benefit was very small. Statistical techniques that quantify this notion of "how much" are called **measures of effect size**.

Intuitively, one might feel that, for our two-group example, simply looking at the difference between the two group means would be a sufficient measure of effect size. If your Java students perform, on average, 30 points better than your Python students, then that is more impressive than if the gain is only three points. Unfortunately, simply comparing means neglects both units of measurement and variability (e.g., a 15-point difference between two means is a large difference if the DV is age, but a small difference if the DV is income in dollars). Fortunately, both measurement units and variability are accurately represented by the standard deviation (see Section 5.3.2.2). Hence, accurate measures of effect size for two groups incorporate both the difference between the group means and the standard deviation of the data.

A common measure of effect size for two groups is **Cohen's d** (Cohen, 1988), which is conceptually:

$$d = \frac{\text{Difference between the group means}}{\text{Pooled measure of variability}}$$

The pooled measure of variability combines the standard deviations of the two groups, weighted by the size of each group. It is computed as follows (n_i is the sample size of group i and s_i is the standard deviation of group i):

$$\sqrt{\frac{(n_1 - 1)s_1^2 + (n_2 - 1)s_2^2}{n_1 + n_2 - 2}}$$

Thus, Cohen's d is the ratio of the size of your observed effect to the variability in your data. The numerator is how much difference you observed between your groups, and the denominator is a measure of how much difference you might expect to see *simply by chance* due to the nature of your DV. This ratio is conceptually very important in statistics, and we will encounter it again in our discussion of inferential techniques in the next chapter.

The formula for Cohen's *d* eliminates the original units of your DV, so it is necessary to have a scale for interpreting *d* (i.e., deciding how big your effect is). Cohen (1988) suggests that a value of *d* up to 0.2 is a small effect, 0.5 is a medium effect, and 0.8 is a large effect. A more fine-grained scale has been proposed by Sawilowsky (2009).

Cohen's *d* is one of many, many effect size measures. It is important to choose a measure that is appropriate to your research context. It must also be noted that there is some controversy in the statistical literature about exactly what conclusions should be drawn from such measures. For a discussion of the range of techniques and issues associated with their use, see Coe (2002) and Dankel et al. (2017).

5.5 Limitations of Descriptive Statistical Techniques

The concepts and techniques discussed in this chapter show us how to design a robust experiment and how to make useful summaries, both graphical and numerical, of the data we obtain. It is important to remember, however, that these techniques only address the data we observed for our particular participants in our particular experiment. If we want to extrapolate from our observed data to the world at large, we must use inferential statistics. These techniques, for a computing education context, are discussed in the next chapter.

References

Amosu, A. M., & Degun, A. M. (2014). Impact of maternal nutrition on birth weight of babies. *Biomedical Research*, 25(1), 75–78.

Campbell, S. (1974). *Flaws and Fallacies in Statistical Thinking*. Upper Saddle River, NJ: Prentice-Hall.

Carifio, J., & Perla, R. J. (2007). Ten common misunderstandings, misconceptions, persistent myths and urban legends about Likert scales and Likert response formats and their antidotes. *Journal of Social Sciences*, 3(3), 106–116.

Coe, R. (2002). It's the effect size, stupid. What effect size is and why it is important. In *Annual Conference of the British Educational Research Association* (pp. 12–14). London, UK: British Educational Research Association.

Cohen, J. (1988). *Statistical Power Analysis for the Behavioral Sciences*. New York: Routledge.

Dankel S. J., Mouser J. G., Mattocks K. T., Counts B. R., Jessee M. B., Buckner S. L., Loprinzi P. D., & Loenneke J. P. (2017). The widespread misuse of effect sizes. *Journal of Science and Medicine in Sport*, 20(5), 446–450.

DeWitt, A., Fay, J., Goldman, M., Nicolson, E., Oyolu, L., Resch, L., Martinez Saldaña, J., Sounalath, S., Williams, T., Yetter, K., Zak, E., Brown, N., & Rebelsky, S. A. (2017). Arts coding for social good: A pilot project for middle-school outreach. In *Proceedings of the 48th ACM Technical Symposium on Computer Science Education (SIGCSE '17)* (pp. 159–164). New York: ACM.

Edgcomb, A., Vaihd, F., Lyseckky, R., & Lysecky, S. (2017). Getting students to earnestly do reading, studying, and homework in an introductory programming class. In *Proceedings of the 2017 ACM SIGCSE Technical Symposium on Computer Science Education (SIGCSE '17)* (pp. 171–176). New York: ACM.

Ericson, B., & McKlin, T. (2012). Effective and sustainable computing summer camps. In *Proceedings of the 43rd ACM Technical Symposium on Computer Science Education* (pp. 289–294). New York: ACM.

Gravetter, F., & Wallnau, W. B. (2012). *Essentials of Statistics for the Behavioral Sciences*, 8th edn. Boston, MA: Wadsworth Publishing.

Haden, P., Parsons, D., Wood, K., & Gasson, J. (2017). Student affect in CS1: Insights from an easy data collection tool. In *Proceedings of the 17th Koli Calling International Conference on Computing Education Research, Koli Calling '17* (pp. 40–49). New York: ACM.

Krohn, G. A., & O'Conner, C. M. (2005). Student effort and performance over the semester. *Journal of Economic Education*, 36(1), 3–29.

Levy, B. R. (2003). Mind matters: Cognitive and physical effects of aging self-stereotypes. *Journal of Gerontology: Psychological Sciences*, 58, 203–211.

Marsh, H. W., & Hattie, J. (2002). The relation between research productivity and teaching. effectiveness: Complementary, antagonistic, or independent constructs? *The Journal of Higher Education*, 73(5), 603–641.

Martella, R. C., Nelson, R., Morgan, R. L., & Marchand-Martella, N. E. (2013). *Understanding and Interpreting Educational Research*. New York: Guilford Press.

Murray, J. (2013). Ohio Gadfly Daily. Retrieved from https://edexcellence.net/links-and-broken-links-on-the-relationship-between-proficiency-progress-and-poverty

Parker, M. C., Guzdial, M., & Engleman, S. (2016). Replication, validation and use of a language independent CS1 knowledge assessment. In *Proceedings of the 2016 ACM Conference on International Computing Education Research ICER '16* (pp. 93–101). New York: ACM.

Robertson, J. (2011). Stats: We're Doing It Wrong. Retrieved from https://cacm.acm.org/blogs/blog-cacm/107125-stats-were-doing-it-wrong/fulltext

Robins, A. (2010). Learning edge momentum: A new account of outcomes in CS1. *Computer Science Education*, 20, 37–71.

Rumsey, D. J. (2016). How to interpret a correlation coefficient r. Retrieved from www.dummies.com/education/math/statistics/how-to-interpret-a-correlation-coefficient-r/

Sawilowsky, S. S. (2009). New effect size rules of thumb. *Journal of Modern Applied Statistical Methods*, 8(2), 597–599.

Shuttleworth, M. (2009). Counterbalanced Measures Design. Retrieved from https://explorable.com/counterbalanced-measures-design

6 Inferential Statistics

Patricia Haden

6.1 Introduction

Descriptive statistical techniques (see Chapter 5) provide succinct and illuminating pictures of the data we record *from our own subjects*. They do not, on their own, tell us if we could expect to see similar patterns were we to apply our experimental manipulations to any other people. To make that logical leap – from our specific subjects to the larger world – we need a second group of statistical techniques, called **inferential statistics**. The inferential techniques allow us to make inferences beyond our particular **sample** to large (possibly infinite) **populations**. For example, we may find that our classroom of students learn complex algorithms more quickly when shown an animation. Inferential statistics will tell us if other instructors, working with different groups of students, should expect to see the same benefit.

The theory underlying inferential statistics is huge and complex. Obviously, we are only going to be able to cover a very small portion of that material in this chapter. Our focus will be on those elements that are essential for understanding and interpreting the existing literature and for supporting our own research practice. We will skip anything that is not essential to that focus. Most noticeably, we are going to ignore quite a lot of the elegant mathematics that underlie inferential statistical techniques. However, if you are interested in learning more about the (quite beautiful) math behind it all, see Gravetter and Wallnau (2012, chapters 7 and 8) and Miller and Haden (2006).

In this chapter, we present a specific inferential approach, called null hypothesis significance testing (NHST; Pearce, 1992). In the computing education literature, NHST is by far the most common inferential paradigm. However, you should be aware that there are other approaches to making inferences from samples to populations. Some authors, for example, advocate an alternative called **Bayesian analysis.** Simplifying greatly, NHST methods assume a single inferential hypothesis and determine, to some degree of certainty, whether the evidence is sufficient to falsify it. Bayesian methods assume multiple inferential hypotheses and determine the relative credibility of each. Details of Bayesian techniques can be found in, for example, Edwards, Lindman, and Savage (1963), Van de Shoot et al. (2014), and Wagenmakers (2007). For guidance on when to use each inferential framework, see Francis (2017). For an overview of the sometimes spirited arguments surrounding these different approaches, see Nickerson (2000).

6.2 Inference

Statistical inference is the process of using what you can observe to make an educated guess about something you cannot observe. This type of inference is something we do all the time. For example, when you look out of the window in the morning to decide whether it's safe to hang out the laundry, you are making an inference. Specifically, you are using the appearance of the sky in the morning (what you can observe) to make an educated guess (an inference) about whether it will rain in the afternoon (something you cannot observe at the moment).

In research, we need to be able to infer beyond what we can see, because it is not possible to observe directly every person we are interested in. For example, imagine that a medical researcher is interested in comparing two treatments for asthma – one that is entirely medical and one that uses breath training, yoga, and other physical/behavioral interventions. She can give two groups of people these treatments and measure each subject's peak flow before and after treatment. She can compute the group means and see which treatment, on average, improves peak flow most. She will have learned which treatment is better, but only for those specific people. Of course, the researcher is not interested in just those people she has measured; she is interested in finding out which treatment works better for asthma patients in general – all asthma patients, all over the world. In fact, since a good asthma treatment will be used for years, she is interested in assessing the effectiveness of each treatment for patients who haven't even been diagnosed yet – for patients *who haven't even been born yet*. Obviously, one can never test all of those people directly.

Thus, in an experimental situation, there are actually two sets of people: The **sample** – the people we take measurements on – and the **population**, this infinite, unknowable, unmeasurable set of people that we want to learn something about. What inferential statistics lets us do is look at our sample, and make inferences about how our experimental manipulations would work on the population, if we were able to test everyone. And, as we shall see, we can make these inferences in a very precise way.

6.3 Hypothesis Testing

6.3.1 The Logic of Hypothesis Testing

The inferential statistical tests covered in this chapter all use the same pattern of inference. This technique is called **hypothesis testing.** When we talk about hypothesis testing in its formal, statistical context, it can seem confusing, but as with predicting the weather from the morning sky, it is a chain of reasoning that we frequently follow in real life. Let's look first at a real-life example, and then see how it equates to the formal process used in a quantitative statistical analysis.

Meeting for Coffee

Imagine that your friend, Bob, was supposed to meet you for coffee at Starbucks at 10.00. It is now 10.20 and Bob has not arrived. Should you be worried? This is an inferential question. You are going to use something you know to make an inference about something you don't know.
What you know:

> Bob is 20 minutes late

What you want to infer:

> Is Bob just running late and will soon arrive, or has something happened to Bob that will prevent him from showing up?

To make this decision, you start with information you have about Bob. Specifically, how does Bob usually behave? Is Bob often late, or is he usually right on time? If Bob is often late, you will probably assume nothing unusual has happened and just continue to wait. But if Bob is usually on time, being 20 minutes late today is very unusual, and you might be concerned about Bob. This chain of reasoning is the basis of all inferential statistics. We can summarize the process as:

Observed data	Bob is 20 minutes late
Desired inference	Is everything normal, or has something unusual happened to Bob?
Required information	How punctual is Bob ordinarily, when nothing unusual has happened?
Decision	If being 20 minutes late is fairly typical for Bob, infer that probably nothing unusual has happened to Bob
	If being 20 minutes is late is not typical for Bob, infer that probably something unusual has happened to Bob

To see the logic even more clearly, imagine that Bob is always late and Zoe is always on time. If you have to wait 20 minutes for Bob, you wouldn't worry. You'd just say, "That Bob, he's never on time". But if Zoe was 20 minutes late, you would be concerned, and you would be texting her to find out if she was sick, had a flat battery in her car, etc. In each case, you are making an inference from what you know to what you don't know, based on *what is typical*.

The General Case

We can extend our "What's up with Bob?" pattern to any similar problem. In a quantitative study, the logic of an inferential hypothesis looks like this:

Observed data	What you know happened; the data you collected from your sample
Desired inference	Is something going on here? Specifically, is your treatment having an effect?
Required information	What would your data look like *if nothing was going on*? That is, what would you expect to observe if your treatment has no effect?
Decision	If your data look like what you would expect if nothing is going on, decide that nothing is going on
	If your data do not look like what you would expect if nothing is going on, decide that something is up

What Kind of Inference Can We Make?

Before we try to apply this logical pattern to a data analysis situation, we must first look at exactly what kinds of inferences the techniques allow us to draw.

In hypothesis testing situations, we make inferences about population averages.[1] When we say "men are taller than women," we really mean that the population average height of men is larger than the population average height of women. When we say "smoking causes cancer," we really mean that, on average, smoking raises the risk of getting cancer. When we say "the use of a visual programming language (VPL) improves CS1 retention rates," we really mean that the average retention rate for classes that use a VPL is higher than the average retention rate for classes that do not. This is the best you can do, and all inferential statistics deals with aggregated behavior.

Imagine that you wish to study the value of using pair programming (PP) with CS1 students. You wish to compare programming skill after completion of a CS1 course when PP is used to that when it is not. For your dependent variable (DV) you decide to use a standardized CS1 final exam. You want to answer the question: "Do students score better on the exam if they have been taught using PP?" What you are asking statistically is, "Is the *population average* score on the exam when PP is used greater than the *population average* score when it is not?"

We can illustrate the situation we are exploring as follows. Imagine that you were somehow magically able to test every student in the infinite, unknowable population of CS1 students, both with PP and without (and because this is magic, you don't have to worry about order effects). You could plot the two frequency distributions – one for scores with PP and one for scores without.[2] The result would look like one of the two examples in Figure 6.1.[3]

---

1 Note there are also inferential tests to look at population proportions, correlations, etc., but the logic is the same, and it is easiest to start by concentrating on averages. The important thing is that we can only make inferences about population *summaries*, not about *individuals*.
2 For simplicity, we will assume that the shape (i.e., variability and frequency) of the population distributions is the same. The major statistical tests are robust in the face of moderate violations of this assumption.
3 Technically, there is a third option – students who use PP could actually do worse on the exam than those who do not. Inferential techniques work correctly in this case as well. To simplify this discussion, we will omit that possibility.

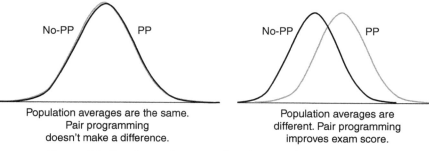

Population averages are the same. Pair programming doesn't make a difference.

Population averages are different. Pair programming improves exam score.

Figure 6.1 *Population frequency distributions showing no effect and a real effect of the independent variable.*

Reality can look one of these two ways: if using PP really doesn't make any difference, student performance will be the same with or without it, and the two distributions will lie on top of each other, as shown on the left. If using PP really does enhance learning, students will score better on the exam when PP is used, and the distributions will be separated, as shown on the right. The distance that the two distributions are separated is how much PP helps. When we do a hypothesis test, we are using our sample data to try to infer which of the two pictures represents the true state of the infinite, unknowable populations.

The Logic of Hypothesis Testing in an Experiment

We apply the same logic that helped us decide whether we needed to call Bob to the question of comparing these two population averages.

Observed data	Difference between average exam scores for PP and no-PP students, observed for our sample
Desired inference	Are the population averages really equal, or really different?
Required information	What would your data look like if nothing was going on? That is, PP had no impact and therefore the population averages were really equal (the image on the left in Figure 6.1)
Decision	If our observed average difference is something that *could easily happen* (due to sampling error) even if the population averages are equal, decide that the population averages probably are equal – or, more correctly, that you have no reason to assume otherwise
	If our observed average difference is something that *would be rare* when the population averages are really equal, decide that the population averages are probably not equal

Inferential statistical tests quantify very precisely those notions of "could easily happen" and "would be rare."

"Could Easily Happen" or "Would be Rare?"

To understand how inferential tests quantify the likelihood of our observed data, consider the following:

Assume that we have performed our PP vs. no-PP study using a between-subjects design (i.e., two separate groups of students; two separate CS1 classes). We have computed the average exam score for each of the two groups. Compare these two possible outcome scenarios:

Scenario 1:

Average no-PP exam score = 64
Average PP exam score = 65

Scenario 2:

Average no-PP exam score = 64
Average PP exam score = 83

In both scenarios, the observed sample means are different, and the mean score for students who used PP is higher. But which scenario would convince you, intuitively, that there is a real advantage to using PP? Presumably, Scenario 2, with its 19-point observed difference. In Scenario 1, the PP students did do better overall on the exam, but only by a very small amount. It is easy to imagine that, even if the population averages are truly equal (i.e., PP has no impact), you might observe a one-point difference between your group averages simply by chance. Your PP sample might have just contained a few more high-scoring students than did your non-PP sample. But a 19-point difference, as in the second scenario, seems much less likely to have occurred unless the population averages truly are different. Mathematically, the 19-point difference would be possible if PP had no effect and you just happened to have the bad luck to get two very non-representative samples, but you certainly wouldn't expect it to happen very often.

Inferential statistical tests use math to quantify this intuition exactly. They compute, to a very high degree of accuracy, how likely your observed average difference would be, *if the population averages were the same.*

The computation uses your observed means, your observed standard deviation, and your sample size. It determines the frequency distribution of all possible observed mean differences when the population means are really equal. It then computes the exact probability of a difference at least as large as your observed one in this distribution. If that probability is small (i.e., it wouldn't happen very often if the population means were equal), you will assume the population means are not equal. Conventionally in scientific disciplines, "small" is defined as 5 percent.[4] That is, if your observed data would occur 5 percent of

---

4 Although it is still extremely common, there is a growing controversy around the rigid use of "5 percent = a small chance" in inferential tests. Many of the arguments are mathematically very complex, but a tractable overview of the issues can be found at www.nature.com/news/scientific-method-statistical-errors-1.14700

the time (or less) when the population averages are equal, you can assume that they are not.

Meeting for Coffee, Again

Now that we have considered the formalisms of hypothesis testing, let us once again see how it equates to our problem with Bob. We should be able to see that, while the context has become more complex, the important components are the same.

Hypothesis Testing Context	Meeting for Coffee Context
The frequency distribution of all possible observed mean differences when the population means are really equal	How late is Bob usually (i.e., what is his distribution of arrival times)?
The exact probability of a difference as large as your observed one in this frequency distribution	Exactly how often is Bob at least 20 minutes late?
If that probability is small, assume the population means are not equal	"Even Bob is rarely as much as 20 minutes late. I better call and make sure he's OK"

The Two Hypotheses

In both our PP study and the meeting-for-coffee scenario, there are two competing hypotheses, and we try to use our observed data to decide which hypothesis is correct. When waiting for Bob, the two hypotheses are (1) "Something has happened to Bob, and he is not going to show up," and (2) "Bob's just running late as usual, he'll be here soon." In the PP study, the two hypotheses are (1) "Use of PP in CS1 facilitates learning," and (2) "Use of PP in CS1 has no impact." In hypothesis testing, there are always two hypotheses. Informally, one hypothesis says "something interesting is going on here" and the other hypothesis says "nothing interesting is going on here." The "something interesting" is usually an effect of our independent variable (IV; i.e., the population means are different). The "nothing interesting" hypothesis states that our IV has no effect (i.e., the population means are not different). The "something interesting" hypothesis is called the **experimental hypothesis** and is denoted H_1. The "nothing interesting" hypothesis is called the **null hypothesis** and is denoted H_0.

H_1	H_0
The experimental hypothesis	The null hypothesis
The population means are different	The population means are not different
The population average exam score is higher with PP than without	The population average exam score is the same with PP as without

In the examples above, we asked ourselves, "How likely is it that our observed data would occur if nothing bad has happened to Bob?" and, "How likely is it that our observed data would occur if the PP and no-PP groups are really the same?" That is, in both cases, we asked ourselves, "How likely are our observed data *if the null hypothesis is true*?" This is the pattern for all inferential tests.[5] Based on the probability our test computes for us, we consider whether there is evidence that the null hypothesis is true. If we decide it is not (because our observed data would happen rarely when H_0 was true), we say that we **reject the null hypothesis**. Otherwise, we say that we **fail to reject the null hypothesis**.

There is a subtle, yet very important detail in the two conclusions above: when our observed means are very different, we conclude that H_0 is false. But, note very carefully that when our observed means are close to each other, *we do not conclude that H_0 is true*. (To do so is known as "accepting the null hypothesis," and it is a serious statistical faux pas.) We may only *fail to conclude that it is false*. More specifically, we would say that "we have no evidence that H_0 is false." We must take this conservative position because of sampling error. The population means could actually be different (i.e., H_0 could be false) and our observed means might have been close together simply because of the particular samples we drew. If we repeated the experiment, we might obtain very different results, with observed means that were far apart. Thus, we can only say that, based on our current data, we cannot reject the null hypothesis.

Often, we can think of H_0 as the opposite of H_1. If H_1 is "two conditions are different," H_0 will be "two conditions are not different." We must be careful, however, as null hypotheses are a special kind of opposite. They always describe the situation where nothing is happening. Consider the following examples, with special attention to the last two:

If H_1 is …	… then H_0 is …
The population means are different	The population means are the same
The population correlation is different from 0 (i.e., the two DVs are correlated)	The population correlation is 0 (i.e., the two DVs are not correlated)
In the population, Group A occurs more frequently than Group B	In the population, Groups A and B have equal frequency *NOT "Group B occurs more frequently than Group A."* H_0 always says "nothing is happening" – no difference, no effect
The population mean for Condition 1 is larger than the population mean for Condition 2	The population means are the same *NOT "The population mean for Condition 1 is smaller than the population mean for Condition 2."* H_0 always says "nothing is happening" – no difference, no effect

5 More specifically, it is the pattern for all inferential tests under the NHST paradigm.

6.3.2 The Hypothesis Testing Procedure

With all the elements now defined, we can consider the formal description of a hypothesis testing situation:

1. State H_1 and H_0.
2. Collect your data.
3. Let your test determine how likely it is that you would have gotten your observed data if H_0 were true.
4. If it is very unlikely (usually defined as occurring 5 percent or less of the time), infer that H_0 is not true. Reject the null hypothesis. Otherwise, fail to reject the null hypothesis.

Then What Happens ...?

If You Reject H_0:

1. Your result is "statistically significant." Note that this is a formal statistical term that means only that your observed data would occur less than 5 percent of the time when H_0 is true. It *does not mean* that your result is important or interesting or any of the other meanings we give to the word "significant" in colloquial usage.
2. You say you reject H_0 "with 95 percent confidence" or "at the 95 percent confidence level" (see below for further explanation).
3. Since H_1 is the (special) opposite of H_0, if you reject H_0, you may infer that H_1 is true.[6]

If You Fail to Reject H_0:

1. Your result is not statistically significant.
2. Do not infer that H_0 is false. As discussed above, also *do not infer that H_0 is true*. Failing to reject H_0 simply means that you did not find evidence that H_0 was false. H_0 could still be false, and you didn't find it because of flaws in your experiment, unfortunate sampling error, a small population effect that is difficult to detect, or any of a number of other possible reasons. If you fail to reject H_0, *conclude only that there is not sufficient evidence to make any inference.*

6.3.3 The Big Problem with Hypothesis Testing

There is one serious problem with hypothesis testing: you could be wrong.

Recall that the logic is: If your observed result would occur less than 5 percent of the time when H_0 is true, infer that H_0 is false. This means:

1. Five percent of the observed outcomes that occur when H_0 is true will be identified as "unlikely."
2. When one of those outcomes occurs, H_0 will be rejected *even though it is true.*

---

6 *Probably* true – technically, you have found evidence in support of H_1. See further discussion below.

Out in the world...

		H_0 is true	H_0 is false
Based on your test you...	**Reject H_0**	WRONG!! False Alarm Type I error	Correct rejection
	Fail to reject H_0	Correct failure to reject	WRONG!! Miss Type II error

Figure 6.2 *The hypothesis testing decision matrix.*

3. Therefore, 5 percent of the occasions when a true H_0 is tested, it will be rejected, and the wrong decision will have been made.

In fact, there are two ways that you can be wrong when you do a hypothesis test. Let's consider all the possible outcomes:

- In the real world, H_0 is either true or false.
- Based on the results of your hypothesis test, you will either reject H_0 or fail to reject H_0.
- Two of these decisions are correct, and two are incorrect, as shown in Figure 6.2.

This uncertainty is unavoidable. It is a consequence of not being able to measure everyone in the population. To understand the scientific literature as a whole, it is critical that you understand that there is always a chance of landing in one of the error boxes, so a proportion of published results are actually wrong. For some of the four possible outcomes shown in Figure 6.2, we can determine the odds very precisely; for others, we must estimate, but that is usually adequate to understand the results.

Consider the left-hand column of the matrix in Figure 6.2, which shows the two possibilities when H_0 is true. We know that we reject when we obtain a result that occurs no more than 5 percent of the time when H_0 is true. Therefore, decisions to reject will be wrong exactly 5 percent of the time (when the researcher happens to get one of those extreme rare scores that occur exactly 5 percent of the time). This error (rejecting when H_0 is true) is formally called a **Type I** error.[7] Informally it is called a **false alarm** because it causes the researcher to claim an effect of the IV when no such effect actually exists. This is an important thing

---

7 This outcome is also called a **false positive**, but some people initially find this nomenclature confusing, in that you are claiming a *positive* outcome when you have *rejected*, which seems like a negative sort of thing to do.

to think about. For example, in the 1970s, there were hundreds of experiments performed looking for evidence of extrasensory perception (ESP). About 5 percent of them found such evidence (i.e., they rejected the null hypothesis "H_0: ESP does not exist"; they concluded that ESP does, in fact, exist). Those were the 5 percent of rare extreme observed scores that occur even when H_0 is true.

The probability of a Type I error (5 percent in our discussion so far) is also called **alpha**. Therefore, when you reject at 5 percent, you can say any of the following:

- Your data are significant at alpha = 0.05.
- Your Type I error probability is 5 percent.
- Your alpha is 5 percent.
- You have rejected with 95 percent certainty.
- Etc.

Next, consider the right-hand column of the matrix, where H_0 is really false out in the world. Failing to reject H_0 when it is actually false is formally called a **Type II** error.[8] Informally, it is called a **miss**, because there really is an effect of the IV, and your study missed it. The probability of a Type II error – formally known as **beta** – is complicated to compute, and depends on the sample size, the population variabilities, and the true population effect size. If you have very few subjects, you are more likely to miss a difference between population means; if your data are very noisy, you are more likely to miss any effect due to increased sampling error; if the effect of a treatment is small, you're more likely to miss it. The probability of a Type II error (beta) can also depend on the experimental setup. For example, if you use an insensitive instrument, you are more likely to miss a false H_0. The ability to detect an effect when present is called **power**. You will sometimes hear experiments criticized for having "insufficient power." This means that they have a low chance of correctly detecting a false H_0. Calculations can be done before you begin collecting data to estimate how much power your study will have. These computations, and their interpretation, are best done with the support of a statistician. For an overview, see Gravetter and Wallnau (2012, chapter 8).

The important thing to remember is that, after you do an inferential test, you can never tell with 100 percent certainty whether you have made an error or not. You can only know (or estimate) the probabilities. Understanding this will help you to be an informed statistical consumer and to interpret accurately the results of your own research.

6.4 Hypothesis Tests In Action

6.4.1 Basics

6.4.1.1 Which Test to Use?

There are literally hundreds of different inferential tests, and there are new ones being developed all the time for new experimental situations. It is extremely

---

8 Also called a **false negative**.

important that the correct test is used for each inferential analysis. Later in this chapter, we will look in detail at the tests you are most likely to use and encounter in computer science education research.

6.4.1.2 Reporting Results Numerically

In a scientific paper, inferential test outcomes are generally described with two elements: the computed test result and the **p-value.** Some examples are:

$$t = 6.5; \quad p < 0.05$$
$$F_{3,11} = 18.6; \quad p < 0.001$$
$$\chi^2 = 1.2; \quad p > 0.05$$
$$r = 0.86; \quad p < 0.01$$

Each test has its own name or symbol. The four results shown above are, respectively, a t-test, an analysis of variance (ANOVA; these tests both compare group means), a chi-squared (a test for population frequencies), and a test for correlation. We will discuss each of these techniques below.

In each case, the computed statistic (e.g., $t = 6.5$) is given first. Unless you have done a lot of statistics, these numbers are somewhat meaningless, as their interpretation depends on the test, the number of levels of the IV, and the sample size. However, the second value, the **p-value**, is extremely informative. The p-value for any inferential result tells you *exactly how frequently the observed data would occur if H_0 were true.* As discussed above, in much of the scientific literature, the cutoff for "rare enough to reject" is conventionally 5 percent. Thus, if the p-value is less than or equal to 5 percent, the computed statistic is considered unlikely to occur when H_0 is true and thus constitutes evidence that H_0 is not true. If $p < 0.05$, reject H_0. For the four results shown above, the t-test, the ANOVA, and the correlation test results are significant; the chi-squared is not.

6.4.1.3 Knowing the H_0 Distribution

Recall that all inferential tests follow the same logical pattern:

1. Collect your observed data.
2. Figure out how likely your observed data are, if H_0 is true.
3. If they are sufficiently unlikely, reject H_0.

The mathematical key to inferential testing is step 2 – being able to figure out how likely various outcomes are when H_0 is true. The distribution of all possible outcomes when H_0 is true must be calculable (by statisticians). Your statistical software looks at where your particular observed score falls in this distribution to determine the p-value.

For some inferential tests, this "distribution when H_0 is true" can be calculated exactly using the formula for the normal distribution and some fancy math. An alternative technique in modern statistics is to generate the H_0 distribution by computer simulation, running millions of artificial trials where values are sampled from the distribution described by H_0.

The different inferential tests have different computational formulae and therefore have different H_0 distributions. For example,[9] when performing a t-test, 4.00 would be a fairly large observed result, but when performing a multi-factor χ^2 test, 4.00 would be a fairly small result. It is not the absolute size of the computed statistic that matters; it is how likely it would be to occur, for the test you are doing, when H_0 is true.

Conveniently, when performing an inferential test for data analysis purposes, you don't need to worry about the whole H_0 distribution. Modern statistical analysis software will give you the p-value, which is the probability of your observed score in the H_0 distribution. (More formally, it is the proportion of the H_0 distribution composed of scores equal to, or more extreme than, your observed result.) If that probability is less than 5 percent, you reject. Thus, we can understand the output of the common inferential tests without having to worry about the derivations of their H_0 distributions.

6.4.2 The Common Inferential Tests

Although there are dozens of different inferential tests, you rarely see most of them in practice. In typical research studies in education, you are most likely to see one of the following:

Test	Symbol for computed statistic	Used for ...	H_0
Two-sample t-test	t	Comparing exactly two groups with a between-subjects IV	The population means[10] are the same ($\mu_1 = \mu_2$)
Paired t-test (sometimes called the repeated measures t-test)	t	Testing difference scores (e.g., in a pre-test/post-test design). Used when you have a single, within-subjects IV with exactly two levels	The average population difference is 0 ($\mu_{\text{difference}} = 0$)
ANOVA[11]	F	Testing designs with more than two groups. This can be a single IV with three or more levels or multiple IVs in a factorial design	For each IV, the population averages for all levels are equal For all combinations of IVs, there are no interaction effects (see below for an explanation of interaction effects)

(*continued*)

9 We will look at these computations in detail in just a minute.
10 μ, the Greek letter "mu," is the symbol for a population mean. It is pronounced "myoo."
11 The symbol F is used in honor of the inventor of ANOVA, Sir Ronald Fisher.

Test	Symbol for computed statistic	Used for ...	H_0
Tests for correlation	r	Testing the correlation between two DVs For interval or ratio data, compute the Pearson product moment correlation. For ranks, compute the Spearman rank-order correlation	The population correlation[12] is 0 ($\rho = 0$)
Linear regression	F	Testing whether an outcome variable can be predicted from one or more measurement variables	The accuracy of the prediction is no better than chance
Chi-squared[13]	χ^2	Test for frequency (proportion) data	Proportions in the different conditions are equal and/or independent (discussed in detail below)

Note that in each case, H_0 says "there is no effect in the population." H_1, as we know, says that there is an effect. In each case, if you reject H_0, you can conclude, with known confidence, that H_1 is correct. For example, if you reject H_0 in a two-sample t-test, you have evidence that the population means of your two conditions are different. If you reject H_0 in a multiple regression experiment, you have evidence that the accuracy of a prediction made from your measurement variables is better than chance. If you reject H_0 in a correlation study, you have evidence that your two DVs really have some non-zero correlation in the population – and so on.

In the following sections, we will discuss each of these tests in detail. We will not focus on the underlying mathematics, which these days is handled by statistical software. Instead, we will concentrate on (1) understanding for which research context each test should be used and (2) how to interpret the results of each test. Throughout the discussion, note that although the different tests appear computationally very disparate, they all rest on the common logical framework of hypothesis testing described above.

12 ρ, the Greek letter "rho," is the symbol for a population correlation. It is pronounced "row" – rhymes with "know."
13 χ, the Greek letter "chi," in the name of this test is pronounced "kie" – rhymes with "pie."

6.4.3 Inferential Tests for Means

6.4.3.1 Comparing Groups

In this section, we will look in detail at the two t-tests and the ANOVA. These tests all make inferences about population means. They are all very common in the scientific literature. We will discuss how to choose which test is appropriate for your data set, how they are computed conceptually, and how the computed values are used to make precise decisions about H_0. As discussed above, these logical principles are essentially identical for all hypothesis tests. If you understand them in the context of the t-tests (where they are comparatively straightforward), you understand the fundamental concepts of all inferential analyses.

t-tests

The t-tests are used when you have *exactly* two groups or conditions – that is, one IV with two levels. Statistical software will accept the raw data values from the two groups and compute a t-observed and associated p-value. The t-observed is, essentially, the ratio of the difference between your groups to the total variability in the data.[14] It thus compares the difference you observed to the difference that could be expected by chance.[15] If that ratio is large, the difference between your groups is unlikely to be caused simply by data noise – it is more likely to reflect a difference in the underlying population means.

When you have a single *between-subjects* IV with exactly two levels, you should perform a **two-sample t-test**. This test compares the two group means. However, when you have a single *within-subjects* IV with exactly two levels, you should perform a **paired t-test**. When using a within-subjects IV, each subject is tested in both levels of the DV, so you can observe the effect of your manipulation by considering not the absolute performance at each level, but the difference between the two levels for each subject. In a paired t-test, the computation of t-observed is based on the subjects' difference scores. By using difference scores, you reduce, to a degree, the noise introduced into your data by variation from one subject to the next.

The H_0 Decision

Modern statistical analysis software such as SPSS will perform both types of t-test, as will mathematical scripting languages/environments such as R and MATLAB. It is only necessary then to determine if your computed *t* is "large." More formally, under the logic of hypothesis testing, we wish to determine *the probability that our observed t would have occurred if the population means are equal.* As discussed above, if that probability is small (usually under 5 percent), we reject H_0, the null hypothesis that states there is no difference between

---

14   This should remind you of Cohen's *d*, and the two techniques are, in fact, closely related.
15   For full computational details, see any introductory statistics text or the many available online resources, such as www.statisticshowto.com/probability-and-statistics/t-test/

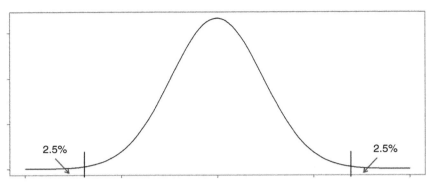

Figure 6.3 *Distribution of values of t for a given sample size and population variability when H₀ is true.*

population means, and we conclude, with 95 percent confidence, that the difference observed between our two sample groups is present in the population.

It is possible, using elegant mathematics, to determine the exact distribution of t-values that would be obtained when two population means are equal, for a specified sample size and population standard deviation. As discussed above, this distribution is used to determine exactly how big a t-value is needed to reject H_0. That value, known as **t-critical**, is the value that would be exceeded only 5 percent of the time when H_0 is true. This is illustrated in Figure 6.3, where the mean is 0 and the vertical lines indicate the locations of t-critical, both positive and negative. Values more extreme than t-critical occur only a total of 5 percent of the time.

Before analysis software became common, to determine whether a t-test was significant, you had to look up the t-critical value for your given sample size in a large table included in the back of every statistics textbook. If your t-observed exceeded[16] the value in the table, you rejected; if it did not, you failed to reject. Modern analysis software typically gives us more precise information than whether our observed *t* has exceeded t-critical. It usually tells us the exact p-value, the probability that our observed group difference would occur when H_0 is true. If, for example, we do a two-sample t-test and we see "$p = 0$ .172," this means that our observed group difference would occur 17.2 percent of the time when the two population means are actually equal. We cannot be 95 percent confident that the population means are not equal (we can only be 82.8 percent confident), so we fail to reject H_0. If we see "$p < 0.01$," this means that our observed group mean difference would occur less than 1 percent of the time were the population means actually equal. We thus conclude that they are not the same. We conclude that the difference we observed in our samples would also be found if we were able to test every member of the infinite and unknowable population. We reject H_0 and we do so, in this case, with 99 percent confidence. Note that, in published papers, the *t* and *F* statistics are often

---

16 "Exceeded" in this context means "is more extreme than." That is, it refers to the absolute value of your observed *t*.

given with numbers in round brackets. For example, you might see "$t(26) = 1.03$; $p = 0.312$" or "$F(1,34) = 8.53$; $p < 0.01$." The numbers in the brackets are related to the sample size and numbers of levels in the IVs. If you were doing the tests by hand, you would need those values to look up your p-values in the tables.

One-Tailed vs. Two-Tailed Tests

In Figure 6.3, we identify t-critical as the value which "cuts off" 5 percent of the t-distribution when H_0 is true. This 5 percent is accumulated by cutting off 2.5 percent from each end of the distribution. If, for a given sample size, t-critical is 1.98, that means that 2.5 percent of the t-values obtained when H_0 is true are greater than 1.98 and 2.5 percent are less than -1.98. If you obtain a t-observed of either 3.5 or -3.5, you reject. This makes sense if your experimental hypothesis H_1 is that there is *some difference* between the population means, but does not specify the direction of that difference. However, often H_1 is implicitly **directional**. For example, if you have introduced a classroom intervention that you anticipate will improve scores on the final exam, you expect the treatment group's mean to be higher than the control group's mean if the intervention works and to be no different from the control group's mean if the intervention is not effective. You have no theoretical motivation to expect that the treatment group's mean might be *worse* than the control group's. In the case of such a directional hypothesis, you want the t-test to compute the difference between your groups as *treatment group mean – control group mean*, and you are only interested in positive values of t. You might argue that your t-critical should, therefore, be the value that cuts 5 percent off the *positive* end of the t-distribution. This value will always be smaller than the t-critical that cuts 2.5 percent off each end, making it "easier" to reject. This procedure is called a **one-tailed test** and it is, in fact, a legitimate protocol in some cases. However, it is possible to get results that are significant by a one-tailed test and *not significant* by a two-tailed test (when your observed t is more extreme than the 5 percent cutoff value, but less extreme than the 2.5 percent cutoff value), which leads one-tailed tests to be viewed with some suspicion. For a one-tailed test to be mathematically and logically appropriate, a number of specific conditions must be met. Before deciding to do one-tailed tests, you may wish to seek statistical advice.

Interpretation

Modern analysis software has relieved us of the need to perform manual computations in most data analysis situations, but it is still our responsibility to correctly interpret the values the software gives us. As discussed above, if your observed t exceeds t-critical (or, equivalently, if your observed p-value is less than 0.05), you reject H_0. That is, you conclude with 95 percent confidence that the two population means are not equal. It is acceptable to assume that the direction of that difference (i.e., which population mean is the larger of the two) corresponds to the direction seen in your observed data. If your observed t is less extreme than t-critical (or, equivalently, your p-value is greater than 0.05), you fail to reject H_0. You do not, of course, conclude that H_0 is true. You simply conclude that, in this particular situation, you have not found sufficient evidence to assume that the two population means are different.

ANOVA

ANOVA is one of the most common, and arguably the most important, of the inferential statistical techniques. It can be used to make inferences about population means for any number of groups and any number of IVs. It is also mathematically extremely complex. There are many college and university courses where one can spend an entire semester learning how to understand and perform the different kinds of ANOVA. We will concentrate on basic interpretation of the results of an ANOVA – identifying the null hypotheses and determining whether they can be rejected.

One IV: The One-Way ANOVA

When there is only one IV, the test performed is called a **one-way ANOVA**. If you have one IV and only two levels, you may perform a t-test, as above. However, if you have three or more levels, you *must* use the ANOVA. In the one-way ANOVA, the null hypothesis is that *the population averages for all levels of the IV are the same*. If you reject this null hypothesis, you can infer only that there is some difference somewhere between the population averages. Further tests are required to formally compare specific pairs of conditions (see Gravetter & Wallnau, 2012, Chapter 6). However, in practice, it is common to assume that the pattern observed in the sample would also occur in the population, unless the observed effects are very small.

Multiple IVs: The Multi-Way ANOVA

Recall from the previous chapter that when we have multiple IVs, we usually test subjects in all possible combinations of levels, in a **factorial design**. In this situation, you must use an ANOVA – a t-test will not work. If you have two IVs, you perform a two-way ANOVA; if you have three IVs, you perform a three-way ANOVA, and so on.

A multi-way ANOVA simultaneously tests *multiple null hypotheses*. First, it tests for the effect of each IV (i.e., H_0: the population means of all levels are equal) on its own, collapsing across all levels of any other IVs. Imagine that you wish to determine the relative efficacy of lecture-based and laboratory practical-based instructions in CS1. You might also be interested in whether male and female students were differentially affected by this pedagogical difference. One approach would be a factorial design, as shown below, with a number of students in each of the four cells of the table. For each student, you could measure course grade or other appropriate performance metrics.

	Lecture-based course	Practical-based course
Women		
Men		

Because you have more than one IV and more than two groups (you have four), you must not use a t-test (or multiple t-tests[17]) on these data. You should perform an ANOVA. Because it has two IVs, this is a two-way ANOVA. The ANOVA tests multiple null hypotheses simultaneously while maintaining the correct overall probability of Type I error.

The two-way ANOVA for this design would test for a difference between pedagogies, collapsed across gender. It would also test for a difference between men and women, collapsed across pedagogy. These two null hypotheses would be formally stated as:

$$H_0: \mu_{Lecture} = \mu_{Practical}$$
$$H_0: \mu_{Women} = \mu_{Men}$$

Imagine that you were able to reject $H_0: \mu_{Lecture} = \mu_{Practical}$ (we will see in a moment how you decide when to reject). This would mean that you had evidence that the two teaching methods were different, *ignoring the effect of gender.* This would be logically equivalent to having simply compared the two teaching methods and not kept track of gender at all.

Imagine that, at the same time, you *failed* to reject $H_0: \mu_{Women} = \mu_{Men}$. This would mean that you found no evidence of a difference in the population averages for men and women *ignoring the effect of teaching method.* This would be logically equivalent to having compared men and women and not kept track of which pedagogical method they had experienced. These tests that consider a single IV while ignoring the other IV are called tests for **main effects**. If the results were as described above, you would say that you found a main effect of pedagogy, but no main effect of gender.

In addition, the two-way ANOVA tests for a new kind of effect called an **interaction**. An interaction is present when the effect of one IV is different for the different levels of the other IV. Continuing with our imaginary CS1 teaching experiment, we could collect our data and make a **factorial plot** – a graph showing the average performance for each of the four groups in the design (men in lectures, men in practicals, women in lectures, and women in practicals). The graph might look like that shown in Figure 6.4.

Figure 6.4 shows us that (in our sample) lectures are more effective for men while practicals are more effective for women. That is, the effect of the pedagogy IV is different for the different levels of the gender IV. This is an interaction.

Figure 6.5 shows another, more subtle possibility.

Figure 6.5 shows us that, for our participants, practical-based teaching is better than lecture-based teaching for both men and women, but the difference between the two treatments is much larger for women. For the men, it hardly matters which treatment you use; for the women, it matters a great deal. Again, the effect of the pedagogy IV is different for the different levels of the gender IV. There is an interaction.

---

17 See the Section 6.5 for a discussion of why you must not do multiple t-tests.

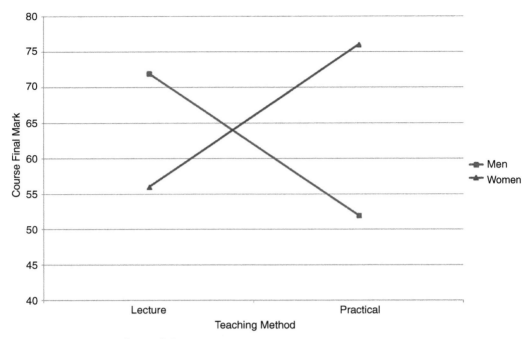

Figure 6.4 *Crossover interaction.*

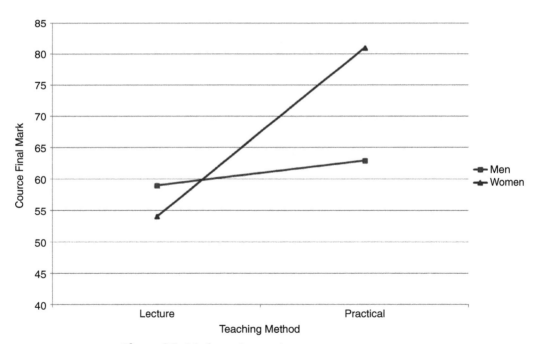

Figure 6.5 *Moderate interaction.*

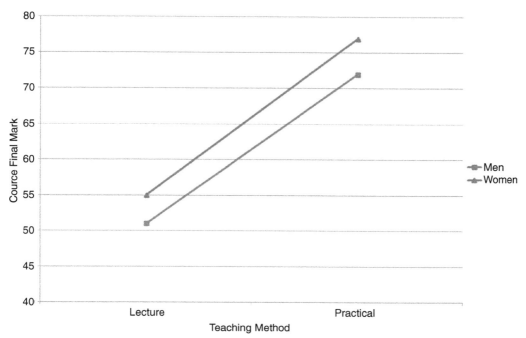

Figure 6.6 *No interaction.*

Finally, the factorial plot might have looked like Figure 6.6.

In this case, the mean for practical-based teaching is approximately 20 units larger than the mean for lecture-based teaching for both men and women. That is, the size and direction of the effect of the pedagogy IV is the same for both levels of the gender IV. There is therefore no interaction.

Comparing the three graphs, you can see that the more the two lines of a factorial plot deviate from parallel, the more extreme is the interaction. This makes it easy to get a sense of the presence of an interaction in your data simply by visual inspection of the factorial plot. But, as always, we need to do an inferential test to establish whether we would expect the pattern in our observed data to also be present in the population. When testing for interactions, the null hypothesis is "H_0: there is no interaction in the population." If we reject, we infer that there is an interaction in the population, and the pattern in the population is the same as the pattern seen in the observed group means.

With a two-way ANOVA, you test for two main effects and one interaction. By extension, if you have three IVs in a factorial design, you test for three main effects (IV_1, IV_2, and IV_3), three two-way interactions (each pairwise interaction of IV_1 by IV_2, IV_1 by IV_3, and IV_2 by IV_3, collapsed across the other IV), and a single three-way interaction that tests to see if all of the two-way interactions are the same at all levels of the third IV – and so on, for as many IVs as you have in your design. Unfortunately, these higher-order interactions are very delicate to interpret. So, while the ANOVA is quite happy to take dozens of IVs and test

Tests of Between-Subjects Effects

Dependent Variable: Dependent_Variable

Source	Type III Sum of Squares	df	Mean Square	F	Sig.
Corrected Model	194.600[a]	2	97.300	3.796	.035
Intercept	15732.300	1	15732.300	613.744	.000
Independent_Variable	194.600	2	97.300	3.796	.035
Error	692.100	27	25.633		
Total	16619.000	30			
Corrected Total	886.700	29			

a. R Squared = .219 (Adjusted R Squared = .162)

Figure 6.7 *Generic one-way ANOVA table in SPSS 24.*

hundreds of simultaneous interactions, in practice, one rarely sees more than three IVs and a three-way ANOVA.

The ANOVA Table

To compute an ANOVA, you need special statistical software. (As of this writing, Excel can only do simple ANOVAs without a special statistics plug-in module.) The output of an ANOVA is not a single value as with a t-test, but a table of values. Different lines in the table correspond to different null hypotheses. As with the t-test, all you have to do is find the p-value for each null hypothesis to decide whether you can reject.

The One-Way ANOVA Table

The results of a one-way ANOVA will look something like Figure 6.7 (this is output from SPSS 24).[18]

The numbers of interest in this table are the *F* of 3.796 and the Sig. of 0.035 in the row headed "Independent_Variable." These are, respectively, the computed statistic *F* and the p-value for the main effect of your IV. Since the p-value is less than 0.05, you would reject the null hypothesis that the population means of all your levels are equal. You can look at your sample means to get an idea of which conditions are different, but as stated above, additional tests are required to make precise inferences about pairwise comparisons. The ANOVA formally only tells you that there is some difference somewhere.

The Two-Way ANOVA Table

A two-way ANOVA tests three null hypotheses simultaneously (the two main effects and the interaction). Therefore, the two-way ANOVA table has more rows – one row for each null hypothesis.

Consider the following (made-up) experiment: a researcher wishes to know if a person's interest in computer science depends on gender and current

18 In an actual analysis, the name "Independent_Variable" would be changed to something descriptive.

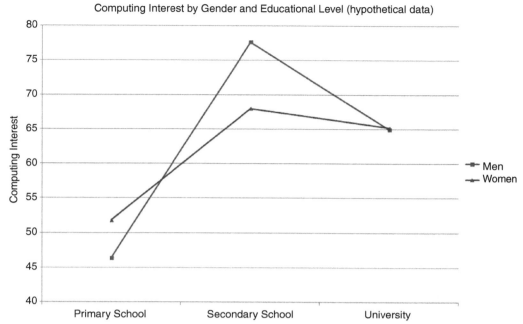

Figure 6.8 *Factorial plot for computing interest study (hypothetical).*

educational level. The study has two IVs: gender (levels = male and female) and educational level (levels = primary school, secondary school, and university). In a factorial design, there are thus six groups of subjects: male–primary, male–secondary, male–university, female–primary, female–secondary, and female–university. Assume that you have some good DV for measuring interest in computer science. Data are collected in all six groups and the group means are as shown in Figure 6.8.

In our observed data, it appears that interest in computing rises between primary and secondary school and then falls in university. This effect appears to be more extreme for men than for women. As always, however, we need to use inferential statistics to tell us how likely it is that we would observe such a pattern just by chance. Since we have two IVs, we perform a two-way ANOVA. The output from a recent version of SPSS for this data set is shown in Figure 6.9.

As with the one-way ANOVA, we can ignore much of this table, and simply look for the *F* and p-values for each null hypothesis. We see here one line for each of the three null hypotheses we test: the two main effects and the interaction.

The *F* for the main effect of EducationLevel is 337.3. The p-value is 0.000 (for $p < 0.0001$, SPSS gives up and calls it zero). Thus, we reject H_0: *the population mean computing interest scores for all education levels are the same.* We infer that interest in computer science is different for primary school, secondary school, and university students. We make this inference at very high confidence (99.999 percent). Informally, we can conclude that the pattern in the population

Tests of Between-Subjects Effects

Dependent Variable: ComputingInterest

Source	Type III Sum of Squares	df	Mean Square	F	Sig.
Corrected Model	3226.667[a]	5	645.333	148.923	.000
Intercept	116563.333	1	116563.333	26899.231	.000
EducationLevel	2923.267	2	1461.633	337.300	.000
Gender	13.333	1	13.333	3.077	.092
EducationLevel * Gender	290.067	2	145.033	33.469	.000
Error	104.000	24	4.333		
Total	119894.000	30			
Corrected Total	3330.667	29			

a. R Squared = .969 (Adjusted R Squared = .962)

Figure 6.9 *SPSS 24 output for two-way ANOVA.*

means is the same as the pattern in our sample means – interest rises from primary to secondary school, and then dips in university.

The *F* for the main effect of Gender is 3.077. The p-value is 0.092. Since this is greater than 0.05, we fail to reject H_0: *the population means for men and women are equal.* We have not found evidence that interest in computer science is different, on average, for men and women. This result is, at first glance, surprising. Statistically, we have concluded that there is no difference between males and females, even though it is obvious just by inspection that the line for males and the line for females in the factorial plot are different. In this situation, it is essential to remember that the null hypothesis for a main effect *collapses across all levels of other IVs.* To get a more complete picture, one must consider the role of the interaction.

The *F* for the interaction (EducationLevel × Gender) is 33.469. The p-value is 0.000 (i.e., $p < 0.001$). Thus, we reject H_0: *the effect of educational level on interest in computing is the same for men and for women.* Looking at the means, we can informally conclude that the jump in interest between primary school and secondary school is more extreme for men than it is for women. Or, considering the whole pattern, we could say that, in primary school, girls are more interested in computing than boys, this effect is reversed in secondary school, and by university, the interest levels of both genders are, on average, about the same. Note that, had we simply lumped all our subjects of all ages together and looked only at the effect of gender, we would have concluded there was no difference between males and females on this measure. The extended experimental design (taking education level into account) and analysis that includes the statistical interaction provide a much more nuanced, and more informative, insight into our research question.

Note that while we could probably have made these interpretations informally just by looking at the factorial plot, the ANOVA tells us that we can be confident that this pattern is not simply an accident in our sample, is not just

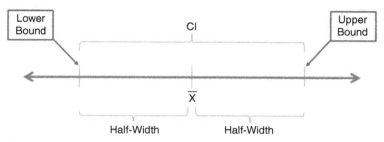

Figure 6.10 *CI for a population mean.*

due to random data variability, but would most likely be found if we could test everyone in the infinite, unknowable population.

6.4.3.2 Inference via Parameter Estimation – Confidence Interval for μ

The t-tests and ANOVA allow us to make inferences about population means based on observed data from samples, each a subset of their population. When making these inferences, we are distinguishing between a measure (in this case, an average) taken from a sample and the same measure taken from an infinite population. The former is formally called a *statistic*; the latter is called a *parameter*. The t-tests and ANOVA allow us to explore differences between population group means (parameters). There is also an alternative approach – the **confidence interval** (CI) – that allows us to estimate the value of a population parameter directly. CI analyses produce a range of values into which you can be 95 percent certain (assuming alpha is set to 0.05) the true population parameter value falls. A CI is centered around your observed sample statistic and extends symmetrically above and below that value, as shown in Figure 6.10.

The logic is that your sample statistic is your best single-value estimate of the true population parameter, and you then need to give yourself some room on either side of that estimate. The formula for the half-width of the CI incorporates the variability and size of your sample and the confidence level you wish to achieve. CIs are simple to compute[19] and can be performed in most statistical software.

CIs offer a useful descriptive analysis on their own, but they can also be used for formal hypothesis testing. Assume that you are implementing a nationalized computing exam for high school seniors and that your education department states that such exams must take, on average, no more than 60 minutes to complete. You fear that the exam you have written will take longer than that. You have $H_1: \mu > 60$ and $H_0: \mu = 60$ (or equivalently $\mu \le 60$). If you give the exam to a large sample of high school seniors, you can record their completion times and compute a CI for μ. Assume that the resulting CI is (65, 71). You can therefore

---

19 CIs are so easy you can compute them by hand, if necessary. See http://onlinestatbook.com/2/estimation/mean.html for an example.

be 95 percent confident that the true population mean (i.e., what you would get if you could test all of the high school seniors in your educational system) is between 65 and 71. Hence, you are 95 percent certain that it is *above* 60. You reject H_0 and conclude with 95 percent confidence that the exam is too long.

6.4.4 An Inferential Test for Frequencies

The two-sample t, the paired t, the ANOVA, and the CI for μ all allow inferences about population means. All are concerned with numerical data sets, where we compute group averages as measures of central tendency and make inferences from the observed group means to the corresponding population means. But not all quantitative research is interested in measures of central tendency – often we are interested in **frequency**. That is, we wish to know how often (or what proportion of the time) some particular condition or response occurs in our data. In these cases, we wish to infer not a population average, but a *population frequency*. We wish to infer how often (or what proportion of the time) a condition or response would occur in our infinite, unknowable population.

6.4.4.1 The Frequency Fallacy

Caution must be used when interpreting frequencies, as it is easy to make misleading, yet accurate, statistical statements. For example, it is well known that more people die each year from beestings than from skydiving accidents. Certain people (primarily skydivers) cite this fact as evidence that going skydiving is safer than being stung by a bee. But while the bare statistical fact is true (it is – if you just count them up, more people die each year from beestings), the interpretation is not. The problem is that the *total number of beestings that occur each year is much higher than the total number of skydives*. Thus, even if an individual beesting and an individual skydive are equally risky, you will get a larger number of beesting deaths, simply because there are more beestings overall. In fact, you can get a larger number of beesting deaths even if skydiving is actually more dangerous per event, as long as there are sufficiently more beestings.

As another example, if you look at combat injuries among military personnel, there are invariably more men injured than women. Does this mean that men are more foolhardy and take greater risks? No, it simply reflects the fact that there are more men in combat, so naturally more men are injured. To quantify this, assume that among the military personnel you are studying, there are 90 percent men and 10 percent women. If you observe 100 injuries, how many women would you expect to be injured and how many men, assuming that men and women actually have the same chance of getting hurt? Because you have 90 percent men, you would expect 90 percent of your injuries to be men (i.e., 90 out of 100) and 10 percent of your injuries to be women (i.e., 10 out of 100). In absolute frequencies, you have many more injuries to men than to women (90 vs. 10), but that pattern is exactly what you would expect by chance when the real injury risk for men and women is the same.

Assume that your actual distribution of injuries was 80 men and 20 women. You still have many more injured men in absolute terms, but now it appears that it is actually women who are at greater risk of injury than men, because you have many more injured women (20) than you would expect by chance (10). You can see that it takes some statistical nous to be able to explain why, in this case, *20 is actually larger than 80.*

To avoid this confusion, frequency data are usually presented as percentages or proportions, rather than as absolute counts.[20] In our combat injury example above, 10 percent of our sample were women, but 20 percent of our injuries were to women. This causes us to suspect some relationship between risk and gender. As always, our next step is to determine whether this observed pattern in our sample is due to chance or if it would be found in the unmeasured population of all military personnel.

6.4.4.2 Inferential Test for Frequency Dependence – χ^2

If there is no patterned relationship between two factors (like injury risk and gender in our combat example), they are said to be **independent**. To make an inference about dependency from sample frequency data, you use a test called the **chi-squared**,[21] symbolized as χ^2, available in most statistical software. The χ^2 computes a measure based on the total difference between your expected frequencies and your observed frequencies. In the combat injuries example, since we have 90 percent men and 10 percent women in our sample, we *expect* 90 percent of the injuries to be to men and 10 percent to be to women. If we actually had 80 injuries to men and 20 to women, our observed frequencies (80 and 20 percent) would be different from our expected frequencies (90 and 10 percent), and the computed χ^2 would be greater than 0. Like all inferential tests, χ^2 gives us a p-value that tells us how likely our observed data are to occur when H_0 is true – that is, if our categories are truly independent in the population. If our data are unlikely to occur when H_0 is true ($p < 0.05$), we reject, and infer that the categories are not independent.

6.4.5 Inferential Tests for Correlation

In the previous chapter on descriptive statistics, we described the use of Pearson product moment correlations to quantify the relationship between two DVs. As with means and frequencies, we can use hypothesis testing to make inferences from our observed correlation r to the population correlation ρ. In a correlational context, the null hypothesis is that the two variables are uncorrelated, H_0: $\rho = 0$. Symmetrically, the experimental hypothesis is H_1: $\rho \neq 0$ (i.e., there is, in the population, some non-zero correlation between the two DVs). Following

---

20 This assumes sufficiently large sample sizes. With small numbers of participants, percentages can be misleading. For clarity, authors may wish to present both absolute counts and percentages.
21 Alternatively, "chi-square." Both are acceptable.

Correlations

		Difficulty	Familiarity
Difficulty	Pearson Correlation	1	-.305[**]
	Sig. (2-tailed)		.009
	N	72	72
Familiarity	Pearson Correlation	-.305[**]	1
	Sig. (2-tailed)	.009	
	N	72	72

[**]. Correlation is significant at the 0.01 level (2-tailed).

Figure 6.11 *SPSS 24 output for a significant Pearson product moment correlation.*

the now familiar logic of hypothesis testing, we need to determine the probability of obtaining our observed sample correlation r when H_0 is true. If that probability is small (once again, less than 0.05), we reject H_0 and conclude that we have evidence in support of H_1. When hypothesis testing for r, there is no additional value to compute (like a t or an F) – you just need r-critical, the value that cuts off 5 percent of the r distribution for your sample size when H_0 is true. You can obtain r-critical from tables in statistics books, and modern analysis software usually provides a p-value when you compute a sample correlation. An example from SPSS is shown in Figure 6.11, where the p-value is 0.009, as given in the row labeled "Sig. (2-tailed)." If the provided p is less than 0.05, you may reject the null hypothesis that your two DVs are uncorrelated in the population.

6.4.6 Inferential Tests for Prediction

We have looked at various inferential tests for differences between groups. We can use these techniques to see how a particular teaching method works *on average*. However, in some situations, we may want to know not only how a method works on average, but *for whom it will work best*.

Imagine that you had found a teaching technique that improved performance on average, but there was a great deal of variability in outcome. That is, it worked for some students, but not for others. Studies have found, for example, that PP raises lab completion rates for some students, but lowers them for others (e.g., Wood et al., 2013). You would like to know exactly what properties of the students or their situation determined whether the technique had worked for them. You could then use this knowledge to decide in advance if the method was likely to work for a given student. Especially if the method was costly or difficult to use, you would like to be able to *predict the outcome* based on your knowledge of individual students.

To allow prediction, we use a multivariable experimental methodology. As always, we have a primary outcome measure – our DV – whose behavior

Figure 6.12 *Salary by years employed (hypothetical).*

we wish to understand. But instead of grouping our subjects according to a categorical IV, we take one or more other measures for each subject (as when exploring the correlation between two DVs). These measures are things that we have reason to believe may be related to how well our experimental treatment works. They are called **predictor variables**. We then use statistical techniques to try to predict, from the values of the predictors, the value of the outcome variable. The statistical techniques compute an equation we can use in the future. We measure the predictor variables on a new subject, plug the values into our equation, and compute an expected value on our primary outcome measure.

This predictive statistical technique is called **regression**. There are various flavors of regression for different data situations, but they all work to predict an outcome variable from a set of one or more predictor variables. The most common form of regression is **linear regression**, in which outcome values are predicted to fall approximately on a line. We will first consider this notion of "falling on a line," then we will look at how to use linear regression.

Imagine that you have taken a job teaching programming at a local polytechnic. At this school, teachers earn a starting annual salary of $40,000. They get a raise of $2,000 for each year they are employed. Thus, after one year, you would be earning $42,000, after two years, $44,000, after 5 years, $50,000, and so on. We could make a graph showing the relationship between salary and years employed. It would look like Figure 6.12.

We would describe the way salary is determined as "$40,000 plus $2,000 for every year you have been employed." If we wrote this in mathematical notation, it would be:

Salary = $40,000 + ($2,000 × Years Employed)

The above expression is an example of the algebraic formula for a straight line $y = a + bx$. The simplest linear regression, where you use one numeric predictor variable to predict one numeric outcome variable, produces an equation of this form; x is the predictor, y is the variable to be predicted, and a and b are the intercept and slope of the line, respectively. The slope and intercept values define the single line *that best fits our observed data*. We give the analysis program all of our x and y pairs and it produces the values for a and b. This equation is called a **regression model** because it describes (models) the mathematical relationship between predictor and predicted.

6.4.6.1 Simple Linear Regression

In the example above, we could predict total salary *exactly* knowing only the number of years of employment. Life is rarely ever this tidy. Usually, predictor and predicted show a trend, not a perfect straight-line relationship. Linear regression uses math to find the straight line that is closest to our real data. It also tells us how close our data are to that line. When we use the equation to make a prediction, we can then gain a sense of how accurate the prediction is likely to be.

In the previous chapter, in the context of normal scores, we discussed the need to discover determinants (predictors) of eventual success in programming courses. This type of research situation – where you wish to predict one DV from another – is an appropriate problem for a regression approach. Imagine you were continuing to explore the relationship between math ability and programming ability. One approach would be to collect, from a number of students, their final mark in a math course (your predictor variable) and their final mark in CS1 (what you wish to be able to predict). Since you have two scores for each subject (math mark and CS1 mark), you can make a scatterplot. Your results might look like those shown in Figure 6.13.

While the data points don't all lie perfectly on a straight line, you can see that there is a definite trend in the upward direction (i.e., a positive correlation). Students who performed well in math tended to perform well in CS1. A linear regression on these data (which can be done in SPSS, MATLAB, etc.) would give you the following linear formula:

Predicted CS1 Mark = 11.16 + (0.86 × Math Mark)

Thus, for a student who got a mark of 57 in math, the predicted CS1 mark is $11.16 + (0.86 × 57) = 60.12$. For a student with a math mark of 94, the predicted CS1 mark is $11.16 + (0.86 × 94) = 91.9$. You could compute the predicted CS1 for any student for whom you had a math mark simply by plugging that value into the equation.

The linear model (the equation) produced by simple linear regression is known as the **line of best fit**. It describes the linear set of points for which the difference

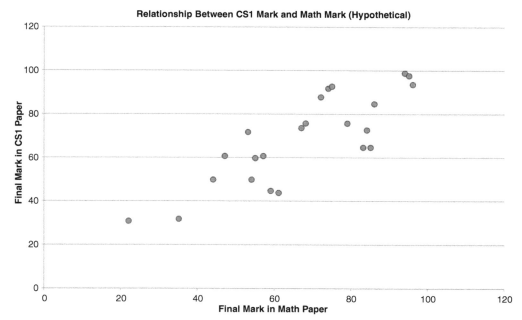

Figure 6.13 *Outcome of a regression study predicting CS1 mark from math mark (hypothetical).*

between the actual dependent scores in our data set (the variable we are trying to predict) and those values produced by the equation is minimized. Most analysis programs can display the line of best fit on the scatter plot. For our hypothetical data set, Figure 6.14 shows the line of best fit as produced in Excel.

The real data points don't fall exactly on the line, but the line does run through the center of the points. The math behind regression ensures that this is precisely the line that is closest *to all of the points as a group.* It is thus the most accurate linear formula to use for prediction.

6.4.6.2 Regression and Inference

The regression equation is computed based on your observed data – the predictor and predicted values you have collected. As such, like any descriptive statistic, it can tell you only about the predictive relationship *in your sample.* Fortunately, regression analysis also performs an inferential test and computes a p-value. The null hypothesis is that the true slope of the regression line (if you could gather x and y values from every member of the population) is 0. A slope of 0 would mean that the line of best fit was flat, indicating that changes on the x-axis (the predictor variable) had no consistent relationship (either increasing or decreasing) with changes on the y-axis. Intuitively, you can view H_0 for regression as stating that "this equation predicts the outcome variable no better than chance" (i.e., random guessing). If your p-value allows you to

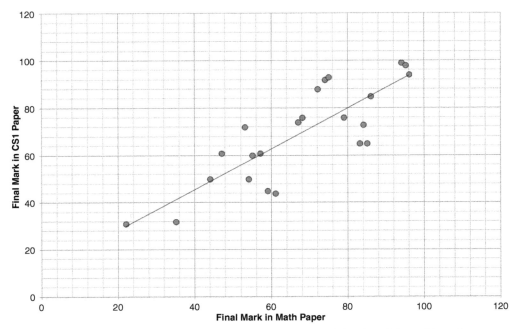

Figure 6.14 *Linear regression (hypothetical data) with line of best fit in Excel.*

reject H_0 (i.e., it is less than 0.05), you can assume that your regression equation predicts better than chance. You can get a sense of how accurate your prediction is likely to be by looking at the scatter plot. Roughly, the closer your data points are to the line of best fit, the more accurate your prediction. For more precision, a regression analysis will return a value R^2, the **explained variance**. The underlying mathematical logic is complex, but intuitively, R^2 measures the extent to which the differences between subjects' outcome measure scores can be explained by looking at their predictor variable scores. Values range between 0 and 1, and the larger R^2 is, the more accurate are your regression equation's predictions.

Figure 6.15 shows the output of linear regression for the hypothetical "maths predicting CS1" data set shown above using SPSS 24.

The upper table in Figure 6.15 shows R^2 as discussed. The lower table shows the intercept (column B, row Constant) and slope (column B, row Math) of the regression equation. The "Sig." column displays the p-values. The p-value for the Math predictor variable is shown as 0 (it is, of course, not really 0, but it is a value that is too small to be displayed in SPSS's three significant digits), allowing us to reject H_0. We can thus conclude that math mark predicts CS1 mark better than chance.

Naturally, not all measures are useful predictors. Imagine that our math and CS1 scores were as shown in Figure 6.16 (the CS1 scores are the same as in the earlier dataset; the math scores have been changed).

Model Summary

Model	R	R Square	Adjusted R Square	Std. Error of the Estimate
1	.828[a]	.685	.670	11.74971

a. Predictors: (Constant), Math

Coefficients[a]

Model		Unstandardized Coefficients B	Unstandardized Coefficients Std. Error	Standardized Coefficients Beta	t	Sig.
1	(Constant)	11.157	8.879		1.257	.223
	Math	.859	.127	.828	6.762	.000

a. Dependent Variable: CS1

Figure 6.15 *Output of linear regression analysis in SPSS 24.*

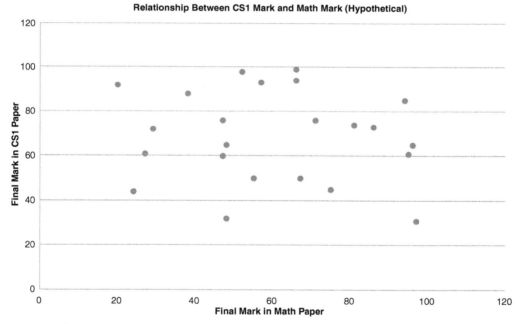

Figure 6.16 *A poor predictor.*

By eye, the relationship certainly looks less predictive than it did before. This intuition is supported by inspecting the Pearson correlations of the two versions (0.828 for the first example data set and –0.103 for the second). It is also easy to see that the slope of the line of best fit (in Figure 6.17) is much closer to 0 (i.e., a flat line) for the second set of values than it was for the first.

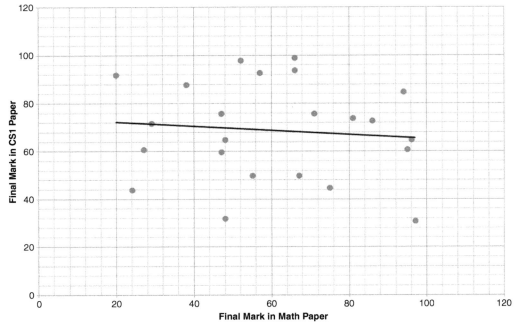

Figure 6.17 *Line of best fit for a poor predictor.*

Model Summary

Model	R	R Square	Adjusted R Square	Std. Error of the Estimate
1	.103[a]	.011	−.036	20.833

a. Predictors: (Constant), Math

Coefficients[a]

Model		Unstandardized Coefficients		Standardized Coefficients	t	Sig.
		B	Std. Error	Beta		
1	(Constant)	74.151	11.924		6.219	.000
	Math	−.088	.184	−.103	−.476	.639

a. Dependent Variable: CS1

Figure 6.18 *Linear regression analysis for a poor predictor in SPSS 24.*

The output of the linear regression analysis for this second data set is shown in Figure 6.18.

The R^2 is small (0.011), indicating that the values predicted by the best linear model for these data are not close to the actual data values. The p-value is large (0.639), so we fail to reject H_0. Logically, we have no evidence from these data to conclude that math mark can be used to accurately predict CS1 mark.

6.4.6.3 Other Kinds of Regression

There are three common variations on the simple linear regression discussed above.

Multiple Linear Regression

It is possible to collect multiple predictor variables and use them simultaneously to predict your outcome measure. For example, in our math and CS1 mark example above, you might also have measured each subject's verbal skill, problem-solving skill, age, etc. All of these predictors are submitted to the statistical test, and you get a single equation of the form:

$$y = a + b_1x_1 + b_2x_2 + \cdots + b_nx_n$$

The x_i are your different predictor variables; y is the outcome variable you wish to predict. The equation contains a coefficient (the corresponding b_i) for each predictor. If you have a new student, you can measure all of the predictors (math mark, verbal skill mark, problem-solving skill, etc.) and plug them into the equation to get a predicted CS1 mark. Multiple regression analysis usually gives a p-value for each individual predictor and a p-value for the best possible (most accurate) model that can be constructed from all the predictors you provide. The mathematics behind multiple regression is very beautiful (see Miller & Haden, 2006, for details). Not surprisingly, a multiple regression equation is often more accurate than a simple regression equation with only one predictor variable.

Logistic Regression

It is also possible to predict outcome measures that are categorical rather than numerical. For example, you might want to use math mark to predict whether students pass or fail CS1. Linear regression can only be used to predict numerical DVs, not categorical ones like pass/fail. The technique for predicting categorical outcomes is called logistic regression. Logistic regression analyses allow you to predict not a numerical value, but the *likelihood* that an individual, based on the values of his or her predictor variable(s), will end up in each category of the outcome measure. The interpretation of a linear regression analysis involves principles of mathematical probability and is quite subtle. It is easy to make technical errors when interpreting logistic regression. It is recommended, therefore, that if you choose to use logistic regression, you consult a statistician for assistance.

Hierarchical Linear Modeling

In simple linear regression, all data points are treated as independent of each other. This makes it impossible to capture the impact of natural nestings and groupings in the data, such as "all the students in the same classroom" or "all the colleges in the same country." To perform regression that maintains such structures, one can use hierarchical linear modeling. Again, it is best to consult a statistician in this case.

6.4.7 Parametric vs. Nonparametric Tests

When you are reading the scientific literature, you will often see χ^2 described as a "nonparametric" test. There are two general classes of statistical test – parametric and nonparametric. The parametric tests are those that operate accurately only on ratio or interval, approximately normally distributed data.[22] If you use them on data that do not fulfill these criteria, they don't work correctly (specifically, your Type I error probability won't be accurate). The t-tests and ANOVA are parametric tests – they require numeric, approximately normally distributed data. Tests that are designed for use on categorical data, frequency data, non-normal data, etc., are called nonparametric. There are many nonparametric tests, each specific to a particular kind of non-numeric or non-normal analysis situation. There is no sense in which either category of test – parametric or nonparametric – is superior to the other; it is simply important to always use a test that is appropriate for your data set. For a detailed discussion of non-parametric methods commonly used in education and the social sciences, see Corder and Foreman (2014).

6.5 Common Mistakes (and How to Avoid Them)

Statistical analysis, especially if you own a copy of SPSS or Excel, is deceptively easy to do. Fling in a bunch of numbers, click a few menus, get a p-value. Unfortunately, the statistical process is filled with snares and traps for the unwary. Statistical errors can occur in all aspects of design, presentation, analysis, and interpretation. Detailing all of the ways that stats can be misused (both inadvertently and maliciously) is beyond the scope of this chapter. Interested readers are directed to Campbell (1974), a classic text on the subject, which is both informative and entertaining, or to Smith (2012) for a more technical presentation.

We have already discussed some of these errors. There are errors of design: choosing invalid, unreliable, or biased DVs dooms your search for knowledge from the start; omitting a control group obscures true effect sizes; failing to counterbalance can introduce subtle order effects. There are errors of logic: accepting the null hypothesis and inappropriate causal inference can both cause a researcher to draw conclusions from his or her data that are not logically sound. There are formal mechanical errors: for example, using a parametric test on extremely non-normal data. In this section, we discuss a few slightly more complex, yet common mistakes that researchers, and readers, should watch out for.

6.5.1 Alpha Bloat

Recall that when we do a hypothesis test, we choose a confidence/significance level (alpha), typically of 5 percent. We reject when $p < 0.05$; we are 95 percent certain

---

22 There are formal tests for normality, but they are beyond the scope of this discussion. If your frequency distribution looks distinctly non-normal, consult a statistician to see if you need to use a nonparametric test.

that our decision to reject is correct, and so on. The underlying mathematics of the tests ensures that these probabilistic statements are true, and this certainty allows us to judge accurately the complete body of literature in our scientific area.

But there is a problem. When you do a single test on your data, and reject, you have a 5 percent chance of being wrong. If you do a second test *on those same data* and reject, you have *another* 5 percent chance of being wrong. If you do a third test and reject, you have *yet another* 5 percent chance of being wrong. Because of the complexity of probabilities, these 5 percent chances don't necessarily simply add up, but they do accumulate. If you do multiple tests on the same set of data, your overall alpha (your Type I error probability) is not really 5 percent; it is something larger (much larger, if you do a lot of tests) than 5 percent. Thus, we say that your alpha is "bloated."

Unfortunately, we often want to do multiple inferential tests on a single set of data. We have multiple DVs and we want to test all the pairwise correlations between them. We have multiple questions on a survey and we want to compare group means on each one to see on which questions our groups differ – and so on. Our goal is to be able to perform all of these inferential tests while maintaining a *total* Type I error probability, across all our tests, of 5 percent. To do this, we must reduce the critical p-value for each *individual* test. That is, we must require a smaller p-value (and hence a larger observed effect size) to reject any individual null hypothesis. The most straightforward technique for determining what this "smaller" critical value for p should be is the Bonferroni correction (McDonald, 2015). The Bonferroni correction says that, if you want alpha = a and you want to do n tests, you can only reject p-values smaller than a / n. For example, if you are doing ten tests on the same data set, and you want to maintain a total Type I error probability of 5 percent, your critical p-value for each individual test is 0.05 / 10 = 0.005. That is, you can only reject H_0 for tests that return a p-value less than or equal to 0.005. Obviously, you will need much larger observed effect sizes in order to reject. Equally obviously, making rejection more difficult will increase the chances of missing a genuine significant effect (i.e., making a Type II error).

The arguments about which type of error (a false alarm or a miss) is worse are complex and philosophical and depend on the research context, but simplifying greatly, Type I errors lead people to say "we know this to be true," while Type II errors only lead people to say "we didn't learn anything from this experiment," so Type I errors are probably more dangerous. We should avoid alpha bloat. The Bonferroni correction is very easy to do, but it is somewhat over-conservative (your total alpha sometimes actually falls short of 5 percent). There are other, more complicated but more elegant correction methods. See Simes (1986) for a popular alternative.

6.5.2 The File Drawer Problem

Throughout our discussion of inferential analysis, we concentrated on when we could reject H_0. Recall that we conceptualize H_0 as the "nothing is happening" hypothesis. Naturally, it is satisfying to be able to reject it and conclude that something is, after all, happening. It is, in fact, common for researchers to prefer to publish only those studies where H_0 was rejected and H_1 was supported. Why, after all, would you want to publicize the fact that your research hypothesis was, quite possibly, wrong? It is also often claimed that it is more *difficult* to publish null results. Journals and conferences are less interested in studies that "didn't work." This pattern is known as the **file drawer problem** (Rosenthal, 1979). We publish our results when we reject H_0, but stick the rest into the file drawer.[23]

The file drawer problem is dangerous in a number of ways. First, it suppresses results that may be of practical value. For example, Maxwell and Taylor (2017) compared student performance (using grades) in two CS2 courses, one with a visual media focus and one with a scientific computation focus. They found no significant difference between the two courses. Rather than tossing this study in the file drawer, the authors used it as an opportunity to consider the extent to which CS material can be embedded into a variety of non-CS contexts.

Second, we must remember that, in NHST, there is a 5 percent (assuming alpha = 5 percent) probability that a decision to reject H_0 is *wrong*. When there is a bias toward publishing significant results, these studies, although they are wrong, actually have an extra chance of being published. In the worst case, for a given false research hypothesis (i.e., when H_0 is true and H_1 is false), the 5 percent of studies that incorrectly support it will be published, and the 95 percent of studies that correctly fail to support it will not be published, leading to a completely inaccurate picture across the literature.

There is no simple answer to the file drawer problem, unfortunately. A cultural change on the part of readers, authors, and journal editors might be required to eliminate it. Recently, there have even been suggestions that all raw research data should simply be made openly accessible on the Internet, so that the "file drawer" becomes publicly available (Yarkoni, 2011).

6.5.3 p-Hacking

The file drawer problem is one consequence of the fact that it's easier to get significant results published than non-significant ones. This **publication bias** means that researchers are under pressure to find significant results. Ideally, we would all increase our chances of getting significant results only through careful experimental design and data collection. Unfortunately, there are other ways to do it that are, essentially, cheating. For example, you could simply exclude any data that don't support your H_1. If you have multiple DVs, you can simply suppress any that don't produce significant results. You can leverage alpha bloat and keep running more and more tests until you find something significant (ignoring the fact that it may well be a Type I error). Such manipulations are collectively termed **p-hacking.** They are methods for manipulating your data

---

23 Rosenthal coined this term back when people still used paper and kept it in file cabinets. A more modern digital equivalent is probably needed.

until you get p-values that you like, and they are bad statistics. If sufficient p-hacking occurs in a research area, it leads to publication of many false claims and conclusions. In some fields, there is evidence that many published results cannot be replicated, indicating a high incidence of Type I errors, possibly due to systematic p-hacking (Ioannidis, 2005).

The best protection against p-hacking is to decide exactly what data you are going to collect and exactly how you are going to analyze them *before you begin your study.* Do not give in to any later temptations to tweak or fiddle with your data in order to get significant results. There are now online repositories[24] that allow you to pre-register your research plan in advance in order to provide publicly verifiable evidence that your results are free of p-hacks.

6.5.4 Skimping on the Results Section

We have described some of the abundant opportunities to make mechanical, logical, and even philosophical errors in statistical analysis and interpretation. It is every author's responsibility to provide evidence that he or she has avoided these pitfalls by explicating all necessary statistical detail in every manuscript. It is, for example, never sufficient to offer a p-value without saying what inferential test was run to generate it.[25] How can the reader judge whether the correct test was chosen if the test is not identified? It is not sufficient to claim a difference between groups without providing actual data values (group means and, when appropriate, a measure of effect size). How can the reader judge if an effect is of practical value without knowing how large it is? It is not sufficient to omit details of who the participants were, exactly what was measured, how the data were collected, and whether any data values were excluded from the analyses. Without such information, how can the reader assess the validity, reliability, and potential bias of the DV? Assuming that your design and analysis have been performed correctly, providing full details to the reader will give him or her confidence in the conclusions you draw.

6.6 Conclusion

Most computing educators are not statisticians. It is hard enough to be both a teacher and a computer scientist – there's not necessarily time left over to become an expert in statistics. However, to do effective computing education research, we need to follow the correct statistical path. By observing the general principles and techniques described in this chapter, you can successfully find the knowledge buried in your data in the majority of cases. And you will be able to recognize those tricky situations where you need an expert statistical hand to guide you.

---

24 See, for example, https://osf.io/
25 This actually happens quite frequently in published manuscripts.

References

Campbell, S. (1974). *Flaws and Fallacies in Statistical Thinking*. Upper Saddle River, NJ: Prentice Hall.

Corder, G. W., & Foreman, D. L. (2014). *Nonparametric Statistics: A Step-by-Step Approach*, 2nd edn. Hoboken, NJ: Wiley.

Edwards, W., Lindman, H., & Savage, L. J. (1963). Bayesian statistical inference for psychological research. *Psychological Review*, 70(3), 193–242.

Francis, G. (2017). Equivalent statistics and data interpretation. *Behavior Research Methods*, 49, 1524–1538

Gravetter, F., & Wallnau, W. B. (2012). *Essentials of Statistics for the Behavioral Sciences*, 8th edn. Boston, MA: Wadsworth Publishing.

Ioannidis, J. P. (2005). Why most published research findings are false. *PLoS Medicine*, 2, e124.

Maxwell, B. A., & Taylor, S. R. (2017). Comparing outcomes across different contexts in CS1. In *Proceedings of the 48th ACM Technical Symposium on Computer Science Education (SIGCSE '17)* (pp. 399–403). New York: ACM.

McDonald, J. H (2015). *Handbook of Biological Statistics (online edition)*. Retrieved from www.biostathandbook.com/multiplecomparisons.html

Miller, J., & Haden, P. (2006). *Statistical Analysis with the General Linear Model*. Retrieved from www.otago.ac.nz/psychology/otago039309.pdf

Nickerson, R. S. (2000). Null hypothesis significance testing: A review of an old and continuing controversy. *Psychological Methods*, 5(2), 241–301.

Pearce, S. C. (1992). Introduction to Fisher (1925): Statistical methods for research workers. In S. Kotz & N. L. Johnson (Eds.), *Breakthroughs in Statistics: Volume 2: Methodology and Distributions* (pp. 59–65). New York: Springer-Verlag.

Rosenthal, R. (1979). The file drawer problem and tolerance for null results. *Psychological Bulletin*, 86(3), 638–641.

Simes, R. J. (1986). An improved Bonferroni procedure for multiple tests of significance. *Biometrika*, 73(3), 751–754.

Smith, M. (2012) *Common ~~Misteaks~~ Mistakes in Using Statistics: Spotting and Avoiding Them*. Retrieved from www.ma.utexas.edu/users/mks/statmistakes/StatisticsMistakes.html

Van de Schoot, R., Kaplan, D., Denissen, J., Asendorpf, J. B., Neyer, F. J., & van Aken, M. A. G. (2014). A gentle introduction to Bayesian analysis: Applications to developmental research. *Child Development*, 85, 842–860.

Wagenmakers, E. J. (2007). A practical solution to the pervasive problems of p values. *Psychonomic Bulletin & Review*, 14, 779–804.

Wood, K., Parsons, D., Gasson, J., & Haden, P. (2013). It's never too early: Pair programming in CS1. In *Proceedings of the Fifteenth Australasian Computing Education Conference* (pp.13–21). Darlinghurst, Australia: Australian Computer Society.

Yarkoni, T. (2011). *Solving the file drawer problem by making the internet the drawer*. Retrieved from www.talyarkoni.org/blog/2009/11/26/solving-the-file-drawer-problem-by-making-the-internet-the-drawer/

7 Qualitative Methods for Computing Education

Josh Tenenberg

7.1 Qualitative Methods: A Broad Church

Curiosities that arise when we want to improve teaching are often of the form, "If I do this new thing instead of what I've always done, will learning outcomes improve?" Having asked this question, if we are keen to get an answer, we carry out an experiment whereby we divide our students into two groups, one receiving the new teaching intervention (the "treatment" condition) and one receiving the status quo teaching (the "control" condition). To some extent, the question in its very phrasing will lead us down this experimental research design path. And it is such research questions and the methods that give purchase on these that are discussed in the chapters in this Handbook on statistical methods.

But there are many other research questions that arise that are not so amenable to investigation through these experimental methods. For instance, we might wonder: how do students understand class diagrams, given their ubiquity in teaching software design? Or how does a teacher experienced in teaching procedural programming go about learning and teaching object-oriented programming, a common enough occurrence? Or how do novice programmers conceive of computer science (CS) concepts that they encounter in learning to program, such as *class* and *object*? Study designs that compare intervention X to Y in order to measure Z are not going to be much help in providing insight into *these* research questions. And it is just these questions for which the *qualitative research methods* are most appropriate. In fact, each of these questions has already been investigated using qualitative methods and published in the computing education (CEd) research literature – Boustedt (2012), Liberman, Ben-David Kolikant, and Beeri (2009), and Eckerdal and Thuné (2005), respectively.

We typically employ qualitative methods when our research inquiries lead us into areas where our present understandings of the phenomena of interest do not permit the kinds of categorization, counting, and experimental manipulation associated with quantitative research methods. It is into this space of uncertainty, where we may not fully understand a phenomenon – or even what the important phenomena are in a situation – that qualitative research methods are particularly appropriate.

Qualitative research methods have developed over several decades within the *human sciences*, those disciplines in which human thinking, being, consciousness, and sociality are the objects of study. These disciplines include but are not limited to Sociology, Anthropology, Cognitive Science, Psychology, Education, Philosophy, History, Economics, and Political Science. In using these methods, researchers in CEd thus borrow not only forms of data collection, analysis, and reporting, but also the **theoretical, empirical, and methodological** foundations that are the historical precipitate of these human sciences and embedded in their forms of research.

Qualitative research methods include "in-depth interviews, focus group discussions, observation, content analysis, visual methods, and life histories" (Hennink, Hutter, & Bailey, 2011, p. 9), among dozens (if not hundreds) of others. This vast space of **borrowed methods from across the human sciences** has been described in aggregate as a "broad church" (Harreveld, Danaker, Lawson, Knight, & Busch, 2016, p. 2), an apt metaphor, since different practitioners often pursue their investigations – and discuss their allegiances to these methods – with religious fervor. These methods span "a bewildering profusion of similarity with elusive differences often requiring years of immersion to understanding its scholarship" (Harreveld, Danaker, Lawson, Knight, & Busch, 2016, p. 2).

Given the breadth of this church, how have I written this chapter so as to orient a newcomer, someone who might not yet be a congregant, but who wants to know something of the forms of worship? One way is to provide a broad overview, describing the different parts common to qualitative research studies. Second, in order to better see how these parts function together, I discuss in detail a single illustrative example of a qualitative research study drawn from the CEd literature. This discussion is sequenced in the same order as the structure of the study's research report: its title, the research questions asked, the data collected, the forms of analysis and reporting, and the discussion of the results. I interweave the particulars of this study with a discussion of this same topic more broadly so as to situate these particulars within the larger space of methodological possibility available to a qualitative researcher. Third, I mirror in my form of report the data-analytic strategies that I explicate below, producing examples of each of the identified methods of analysis and reporting in different parts of this chapter. The purpose is to engender within the reader the experience of reading and undertaking a qualitative research study.

7.2 Reading *Boys' Needlework*: A Case of Qualitative Research

The paper that serves as the focus of discussion is by Kristen Searle and Yasmin Kafai, entitled "Boys' Needlework: Understanding Gendered and Indigenous Perspectives on Computing and Crafting with Electronic Textiles," presented at the Association for Computing Machinery (ACM)/Special Interest Group on Computer Science Education (SIGCSE) International Conference on Computing Education (ICER) in 2015 (Searle & Kafai, 2015). To simplify, I refer to this paper as *Boys' Needlework*. Although I encourage the reading of the Searle and Kafai paper alongside this one, I do not assume that the reader does so in the exposition that follows. I distinguish the discussion of

Boys' Needlework from the discussion of methodological generalities by pla-cing each in its own subsection ("in *Boys' Needlework*" versus "in General") of the methodological topic of focus. In addition, I provide a brief **recapitulation** of prior discussion of *Boys' Needlework*, signaled explicitly as such, so that the connections between the sections and overall coherence of *Boys' Needlework* are not lost.

I have chosen this paper for four reasons. First, the paper received the John Henry Award from the participants of the ICER 2015 conference, given to the paper that "pushes the upper limits of our pedagogy." Second, the paper uses multiple forms of (qualitative) data requiring multiple methods of data collection and analysis. Third, it clearly identifies the theory on which it builds, which is particularly important for qualitative studies. And fourth, it ventures into territory that goes beyond the strictly technical aspects of learning how to "think" computationally, and in doing so suggests that these technical aspects of learning can never be fully cleaved from the culture, identity, and social setting of the people learning and doing the computation. Qualitative methods are par-ticularly well suited for this kind of theorizing, so this paper provides a basis for discussing how and why this is so.

7.2.1 Title

7.2.1.1 *Title in* Boys' Needlework

In reading the noun phrase that starts the title, *boys' needlework*, I am moment-arily unbalanced. The cause is the noun modifier *boys'* that precedes *needlework*, an incongruity because *needlework* is not an activity commonly associated with *boys*. Boys in many parts of the USA (and perhaps in many other parts of the world) do not learn and practice sewing, knitting, crocheting, and other such "craft" activities often associated with the domestic sphere. In creating this incongruity, Searle and Kafai are pointing out that there is a problem with the status quo concerning the "gendering" of labor (i.e., that there are social norms associated with the kinds of work appropriate for people of different genders to carry out). The title, then, *Boys' Needlework*, suggests that the gendering of labor will receive scrutiny in the research to follow. And it is from the subtitle ("Understanding Gendered and Indigenous Perspectives on Computing and Crafting with Electronic Textiles") that a reader comes to understand that it is not needlework that is at issue, but *computation*. The authors thus set themselves up for what follows in the rest of the paper: an account, developed through a qualitative research study, of boys' needlework with e-textiles that makes visible and challenges the status quo conception of the gendering (and social stratifica-tion) of computational labor.

7.2.1.2 *Title in General*

The reader's first encounter with a research report is the title. Creating an incon-gruity in the title of a paper to problematize accepted ways of viewing the world is a common practice among practitioners in the human sciences who carry out qualitative research. This is because qualitative research is particularly well suited for highlighting, challenging, and reworking a conceptual landscape in relation to what is commonly taken for granted and treated as "normal." As examples, consider the following titles, all drawn from the qualitative research literature in human science disciplines:

- "Death without Weeping" (Scheper-Hughes, 1992), Anthropology
- "The Acquisition of a Child By a Learning Disability" (McDermott, 1993), Education
- "The Making of Blind Men" (Scott, 1969), Sociology

In each case, a status quo assumption about the world is problematized through the juxtaposition of terms that, in their incongruity, make the "normal" visible: death is normally accompanied by weeping; children sometimes acquire disabilities (not the reverse); blind men are born blind or become blind through illness or accident. Stating the incongruity, the researcher implies that the study to follow will interrogate the incongruity: *How is it that the incongruity referenced in the title can come to be "normal?"* How is it that death can come *without* weeping? How can blind men be *made*? And in answering this question – an answer provided by a qualitative research study – a challenge is made to "normal" ways of viewing the world. Often, this challenge is made because of the persistence of hidden injustices that are so taken for granted that they are no longer visible, and in this way sustained.

7.2.2 Problem Formulation and Research Questions

7.2.2.1 Problem Formulation and Research Questions in Boys' Needlework

Boys' Needlework begins: "Most of the conversations about broadening participation in computing have focused on gendered differences in participation ... Much less attention has been paid to the equally important but far more complicated intersections of gender with race and ethnicity." The general topic of the paper is immediately introduced: *broadening participation in computing.* A gap in the research literature is indicated in the second sentence, concerning "intersections of gender with race and ethnicity." What is then elaborated in the rest of the paragraph is that treating gender as a unitary category (e.g., that all boys and men will experience computing similarly) has the effect of "erasing the experiences of males from non-dominant racial and ethnic groups." This attention to the fact that the lives and experiences of individuals at the intersection of social categories, particularly of gender, race, and ethnicity, may be quite different from those represented in universalized statements of fact about a single, broad social category. These statements concerning "intersections" of social categories have historical roots in the research by critical race theorists and feminist scholars starting in the 1960s, and are generally referenced by the term *intersectionality* (Cole, 2009; Samuels & Ross-Sheriff, 2008). Though not specifically mentioning this term, the authors index it using "intersection" and elaborate its principles in the context of "broadening participation in computing."

These two sentences reveal an important aspect of the discourse in a research study and how it is shaped *for* a specific audience, for this is what determines what needs to be said and what can "go without saying." The authors begin by stating the general area in which this paper's contribution will be made: broadening participation in computing. Yet no more is said about broadening participation *in general* before moving to the second sentence. The paper thus takes it that "we (the audience that is being addressed) all know" about the underrepresentation of people from different social categories (gender, race, ethnicity) in the computing field. Were this paper addressed to a different audience, such as critical race or feminist scholars, this underrepresentation of people from different social groups *in computing* might need more elaboration and evidencing. Similarly, the concept of intersectionality that would need no more than passing reference for critical race and feminist theorists requires elaboration here for the CEd research audience.

In terms of how these two sentences function, the authors carry out considerable rhetorical work that might not at first be apparent. First, the authors set the general topic of the paper: the underrepresentation in computing of people from particular social groups. Second, in doing so, the audience is reminded that the problem (of underrepresentation) *persists*, which implies that prior attempts to deal with it have not yet succeeded – it is ongoing. Third, the authors reference that the *standard* orientation to this problem – dealing with it as a matter of gender as a unitary social category – might not be sufficiently nuanced. In making this particular conceptualization of the problem salient, there is the suggestion that this conceptualization of underrepresentation in computing in terms of broad categories may account, at least partly, for why solutions based on it may not have been fully successful. Fourth, they introduce the theoretical concept of intersectionality as a way to better understand *who* participates in computing. In doing so, fifth, they set themselves up for the research study to come that will explicate *how* an intersectional perspective provides a deeper understanding of the problem of representation, with the implication that an avenue for broadening participation will be in designing interventions that takes account of how each person is situated at the intersection of gender, race, and ethnicity.

In the paragraphs of the Introduction that follow, we see how intersectionality is relevant for computing. The authors identify a group of "American Indian boys (12–14 years)" (note the intersectionality) who learn computing during a "three-week e-textiles unit" in a Native Studies course, working with Arduino-based e-textile construction kits. The authors indicate that *for these boys* this activity links to a craft tradition and "heritage cultural practices" from the American Indian community in which the boys are a part. In other words, they suggest that *boys' needlework* (i.e., the actual work with e-textiles that these boys do) has positive significance for these particular boys in a way that might be different than the significance of these activities for other boys not similarly situated, since working with e-textiles has the potential to link to forms of craft-work that have constituted the cultural matrix in which the boys under investigation have lived.

Having provided a conceptual framework for understanding the problem and a language that references it, the authors are now in a position to state their research questions: "(1) How did boys initially engage with e-textiles materials? (2) How did boys' computational perspectives develop through the process of making and programming their own e-textiles artifacts?" In the second question, the term "computational perspective" is given special status by the authors. They define this term in the Background section of the paper as "learners' perceptions of computing, where they see applications for computing, and how they see themselves within the field and future careers." The authors identify Brennan and Resnick's tripartite taxonomy of computational perspectives, termed *expressing, connecting,* and *questioning* (Brennan & Resnick, 2012). "Expressing refers to the ability to create something that allows for self-expression through computation. Connecting emphasizes the value of making something computationally in collaboration with others and for an authentic audience (as opposed to just a teacher who will evaluate the assignment). Questioning highlights learners' abilities to ask questions of and with technology."

To summarize, the research study to be described is focused on developing insight into what the boys' *did* with these materials and how their perspectives in relation to computing change over time. Note that the linkage to a topic of frequent discourse in CEd, the problematizing of the status quo approaches to broadening participation, and the conceptual framework of intersectionality answer *for the reader* a set of questions that Ko and Fincher (Chapter 4) indicate are the internalized questions that a researcher needs to ask themselves in designing an empirical study: Is the research question interesting, sound, important, and novel?

7.2.2.2 Problem Formulation and Research Questions in General

Research questions drive a qualitative research study, just as they do any other kind of research. A research question is generally asked to address a lacuna in the literature that is problematic along one or more dimensions for the audience addressed. In a qualitative study, it is common to spend considerable text in laying out a conceptual landscape – usually embedded in specialized language – as a means to situate the research within a larger context. It is sometimes the case that a research question cannot be asked or understood until a conceptual framework has been presented, since this framework is what provides the language and the analytic lens through which the research study will be viewed. Because of the importance of the theoretical ideas that are being challenged and/ or illuminated in a qualitative study, authors typically take considerable care in setting the terms of discussion at the outset so that readers can thereby link the empirical study to be described to the prevailing and historical discourse within the community that is being addressed. In short, the authors not only establish the significance of the research questions that they are asking (i.e., answering the implicit question "so what?" that is ever present for any research report), but also provide the reader with an orientation as to how the authors will answer the questions that they are asking. And often this orientation is very different from what a naive reading might provide.

When the theoretical frameworks of a study are taken for granted and left unstated, this is what Kuhn (1962) labels *paradigmatic* research. Science advances within a paradigm because each researcher working within it does not need to establish de novo in each new study the theoretical foundations on which they build. In other words, *whatever question a researcher asks presupposes some existing theoretical framework*, whether explicitly stated or left implicit. Qualitative research is well suited for making explicit the anomalies, problems, and contradictions of the taken-for-granted paradigm as a means to present a new theoretical understanding to the community.

7.2.3 Context and Sampling

7.2.3.1 Context and Sampling in Boys' Needlework

Recapitulation. *Boys' Needlework* is concerned with broadening participation in computing and approaches this topic from an intersectional perspective. The study inquires into how a group of American Indian boys engaged with e-textiles and how their computational perspectives changed over a three-week learning unit.

The authors identify the site at which data were collected, describing its characteristics and the individuals from whom data were collected. The research participants were "ten eighth grade American Indian boys (12–14 years) who attended a charter school on tribal lands located just outside of Phoenix, Arizona." The boys were enrolled in "an elective, gender-segregated Native Studies class" in a school whose population "was almost entirely American Indian (99%), with slightly less than half of the students (46%) eligible for free or reduced lunch." The students "had little sense of what computing entailed and who could or could not do it."

This description of the field setting, though not further elaborated in *Boys' Needlework*, makes reference to terms ("charter school," "tribal lands," "free or reduced lunch") that have a particular meaning as a result of historical conditions in the USA. In not elaborating on these terms, the authors presuppose that these meanings are held in common with their reader, which may not be the case for the reader of this chapter. I elaborate on these meanings here because they are important for understanding how this research study *in its specifics* seeks to interrogate concerns of underrepresentation in computing and intersectionality. It is only in knowing the situated particulars of a qualitative research study that we can consider how far the results might generalize.

As in many other regions of the world colonized by Europeans, there is a lengthy (500-year) history of genocide and oppression of indigenous populations in the Americas, well documented in contemporary scholarship (Madley, 2016; Stannard, 1992), whose effects continue to be felt. American Indians, who make up less than 2 percent of the US population, have a higher rate of poverty than any other self-identified single-race group in the USA, double the rate of the US population as a whole (United States Census Bureau, 2016). "Free or reduced lunch" signifies the federally funded National School Lunch Program of the US Department of Agriculture, where a lunch that meets "Federal meal pattern requirements" is available free to students from families "with incomes at or below 130 percent of the Federal poverty level" and at a reduced cost to students from families "with incomes between 130 and 185 percent of the Federal poverty level" (United States Department of Agriculture, n.d.). The percentage of students in a school participating in this lunch program is often taken as a proxy for the income level of the community from which the students are drawn. A high proportion (one in three) of American Indians live on "tribal lands" (Pew Research Center, 2014), which are geographically contiguous regions within the USA that retain a measure of American Indian self-governance and sovereignty (US Department of the Interior Indian Affairs, n.d.). Because of how public schools in the USA are funded, there is considerable variance in the kind and quality of instruction available from one area to another, sometimes within the same city, with funding available for instruction significantly determined by the economic level of the taxpayers within a local area. Areas with high rates of poverty (and therefore low tax bases) are less likely to provide access to instruction in a number of areas, CS among these (Margolis, 2008). In addition, there is considerable evidence that the socially stratified instruction available in public education in the USA as a result of its funding structure continues to reproduce these very inequalities of socioeconomic status (Bowles & Gintis, 2011).

7.2.3.2 Context and Sampling in General

For a number of reasons, *sampling* in qualitative research studies is viewed and understood quite differently from in statistical forms of research (see Chapters 5 and 6). It is often impossible in qualitative research studies for sampling to be random, nor even to use quasi-experimental designs where statistical methods control for non-randomness between a treatment and non-treatment group. In many cases, the commitment required over a long period of time by organizations from which research participants are recruited and data collected often severely limits the possible research sites. In addition, only some sites have the characteristics or display the phenomenon of interest that researchers are interested in studying; that is, not just any site will do. There are times as well when the sheer volume of data that will be collected in any individual site is so great that data collection and analysis *across* sites, between a treatment and control group, or with more research participants are infeasible. Further, ethical standards constrain researchers to collecting and analyzing data from those individuals who voluntarily consent to participate in the research, thus introducing some amount of selection bias. And in the case of qualitative research methods that include the use of video and audio, the intrusiveness is greater than in other forms of research, such as filling out a closed-question survey. This is complicated in the case of children, where it is generally the case that not only the child, but also the parent or guardian has to consent for the child to participate. In *Boys' Needlework*, the authors do not state their method of sampling, either for the site or for the individuals. But the reasons just articulated concerning sampling are sufficiently known by qualitative researchers that a reader can presuppose, in the absence of commentary by the authors, that most if not all were operative for this study.

7.2.4 Data Collection

7.2.4.1 Data Collection in Boys' Needlework

Searle and Kafai spend considerable text describing the teaching intervention that structured the activities around which data were collected. They summarize this by stating "The e-textile design activity described here focused on making 'human sensor' sweatshirts … using the LilyPad Arduino construction kit." The authors provide technical details associated with the materials, including that "[s]tudents were asked to design and make e-textile patches comprised of a culturally-relevant aesthetic design, a LilyPad Arduino, at least two LED lights, and two metal snaps attached to the negative ground and an analog port respectively." The authors also describe the pedagogy, its organization, use of the materials, and forms of instruction. We learn that the teaching intervention occurred over a three-week period, that students in sequence "chose a design from one of ten templates," "drew a circuitry blueprint" for placement of the LilyPad and LED lights, sewed with conductive thread, and coded the behavior of the e-textiles.

Searle and Kafai describe the data that they collect for analysis in the Data Collection and Analysis section of *Boys' Needlework*. These include "[d]aily field notes [that] documented what happened in the [one-hour] class each day, focusing on what students were learning and what they were struggling with in designing and crafting with e-textiles. We also collected students' circuitry blueprints, daily photographs of students' design progress, and code screenshots. Most classroom sessions were video recorded (depending on the permission of the classroom teacher and students)." In addition, "[s]ix [of ten] students also participated in final reflective interviews, which were video recorded and lasted around twenty minutes. Topics included where students saw connections between the cultural content of Native Studies and the e-textiles unit, what aspects of their projects they were most proud of, what aspects of their projects were the most challenging, and how other individuals (family and friends) responded to their projects." Additional data subjected to analysis that are mentioned include "photographs of … in-process and completed project[s]."

7.2.4.2 Data Collection in General

There are three basic kinds of phenomena produced by the people who are being studied: *activities*, *accounts*, and *artifacts*. By *activities*, I refer to the actions that human beings take in the world with one another, which often involve the use of tools and materials: writing computer programs, conducting classroom sessions, working in a computer laboratory, to name just a few of the infinite variety. Activities are concerned with what people *do*. As embodied, lived, and therefore ephemeral phenomena, the data collected in order to study human activity require *instrumentation* so as to record features of the activity for later analysis. What is available for analysis depends crucially on the instrumentation, and this changes as technology changes. For example, 100 years ago, the most common form of data collection was *field notes*, contemporaneous handwritten notes and drawings from researchers who participated in the setting; little else was available for capturing activity. Though field notes are still common, additional forms of instrumentation have greatly expanded the type and amount of data that can be recorded in a setting, including audio-visual recording and time-lapse photography. And with these new forms of data collection, analysis can be undertaken by researchers who have never physically been in the setting in which data were collected.

Although having access to video records can give the impression of having "objective data" about the situation under investigation, such records are always taken from a perspective in terms of where the camera is pointed, its resolution and arc of capture (how much of the 360° visual field is recorded, which also implies what is left out of the capture), from which location in the setting (e.g., from a ceiling-mounted camera versus a camera mounted at eye level), and similar (Pink, 2013). In addition, the more audio-visual data that are captured, the more the data files proliferate and the larger amount of time the researcher needs to spend in developing and maintaining an audit trail that tracks the specifics of each recording (i.e., which recordings are made on which days at which locations with which participants). This also complicates the analysis considerably when a researcher wants to analyze the same or similar events from different perspectives provided by the different audio and visual recording devices (Socha et al., 2016). Additional forms of data collected from human activity include audio recordings without video, still photographic images, and traces left from the instrumentation of the tools and/or materials used by the actors in the setting. This latter includes such things as the logged keystrokes, mouse movements, and screen captures from people working at computers, as well as eye-tracking and other biometric data such as galvanic skin response and functional magnetic resonance imaging (fMRI) of neural activity. However, because some of this instrumentation results in very large amounts of data (tens to hundreds of terabytes, depending on the project's scope), much of it is not amenable to qualitative analysis.

An important ethical issue that is raised in the recording of activity concerns the extent to which research participants are identifiable in the data, due to the particularities of a setting that might be captured, including the speech within it and the images of the participants that might be represented. In addition, it is often infeasible to anonymize participant identities in the data, such as in audio-visual recordings, nor is this often practicable or desirable during analysis. We see these ethical concerns manifest in *Boys' Needlework* in the reporting that "[m]ost classroom sessions were video recorded (depending on the permission of the classroom teacher and students)."

Accounts refers specifically to the use of language in human activity to carry it out (e.g., in coordinating human actions between people) or to describe human activity either as it is ongoing or in retrospect. By *account*, I also refer to speaking and writing, often in response to researcher prompts in interview situations, which are typically treated as externalizations of beliefs, goals, desires, plans, intentions, and similar. Audio recordings from research participants are most often used for collecting spoken accounts, while written texts, such as diaries or typed answers to researcher prompts, are another common form for collecting accounts. Common types of accounts are conversations, narratives, biographies, oral histories (frequently elicited by researchers in one-on-one interviews), focus group discussions, and diaries.

By *artifacts*, I refer to objects intentionally produced by research participants (as opposed to researchers) that have a persistent manifestation in the world, typically involving the use of one or more tools for their production. These are the kinds of objects of study such as pottery sherds and stone tools familiar from archaeological research seeking the material traces of past cultures. I include the word "intentional" in the definition to distinguish artifacts from the uninten-tional traces of human activity that are sometimes left behind as a consequence of activity and/or instrumentation, such as wet footprints or garbage (sometimes studied as a form of data related to *activity*, above). By "persistent manifestation," I mean to distinguish ephemeral phenomena such as human speech (discussed in *accounts* above) and performances of various kinds such as dancing or carrying out a class session (discussed in *activities* above) from material and digital objects that can be examined and reexamined during analysis. I take the set of human artifacts to effectively be infinite, and include among them textbooks, computer programs, diagrams, sketches, and mathematical proofs, to name just a few.

Some data collection methods involve the combination of two or all three of these types of human phenomena. For instance, *verbal protocols* ("think-alouds") collect accounts contemporaneously with the activities for which the account is given. Specifically, a verbal protocol is collected by asking research participants to do "concurrent verbalization of thinking" while carrying out an activity, usually problem-solving tasks (Ericsson & Simon, 1993). Another common combination is the use of artifacts, documents, and similar to "stimu-late recall" during interviews (Cherrington & Loveridge, 2014), when particular events may be difficult to recall without such stimulation.

In Table 7.1, for each of the three types of phenomena, I summarize common forms of data collection using the names by which these data collection methods are often referenced in the literature. In the middle column, I include citations

Table 7.1 *Data collection methods.*

Data collection method	Methodology	Examples of use
Activity		
Observation/field notes	Emerson, Fretz, & Shaw, 2011, Spradley, 1980	Barker et al., 2002, Marwick, 2010
Videos	Goldman, Pea, Barron, & Derry, 2007, Heath, 2010	Lewis, 2012
Time-lapse photography		Whyte, 1980
Still photographs	Harper, 2002	Harper, 1987
Eye-tracking	Duchowski, 2007	Busjahn et al., 2014
fMRI		Greene, 2013, Lieberman, 2013
Accounts		
Interviews	Kvale, 1996, Spradley, 1979	Bonar & Soloway, 1983, Boustedt, 2012
Focus group discussions	Stewart, Shamdasani, & Rook, 2007	Hitchens & Lister, 2009, Scanniello, Romano, Fucci, Turhan, & Juristo, 2016
Narratives	Mishler, 1986, Mitchell, 1980, Riessman, 2008	Dziallas & Fincher, 2016, Schulte & Knobelsdorf, 2007
Artifacts		
Program designs		Socha & Tenenberg, 2013, Tenenberg et al., 2005
Program code		Spohrer & Soloway, 1989
Combinations		
Verbal protocols	Ericsson & Simon, 1993	Bonar & Soloway, 1985
Talk-in-interaction	Goodwin, 2000	Tenenberg et al., 2018

to methodological overviews of these methods from the human sciences, and in the rightmost column, I provide an example of a study that uses the data collection method, either from CEd or from one of the human sciences in which the method has been developed.

When multiple forms of data are collected in a study, this is generally called *triangulation*, a term that highlights how different data can provide different perspectives on the same phenomenon of interest (some researchers call this *mixed-methods*, though I find this confusing since others only consider a study to be mixed-method when it combines qualitative with quantitative forms of analysis). We see triangulation with the data that Searle and Kafai describe: field notes and classroom recordings represent activity, interviews provide accounts, and blueprints, design photos, code, and projects under development are artifacts.

A fundamental choice that researchers must make, regardless of type of phenomenon to be studied, is about the site at which data will be collected. At the coarsest level, this choice concerns whether researchers collect data *in situ* or *in the lab*. *In situ* (sometimes called "in the field" or simply "field-work") refers to collecting data in the setting in which it normally occurs: in classrooms, computer labs, workplaces, homes, street corners. Capturing in situ data presents considerable challenges for the researcher that go beyond the straightforward (though sometimes daunting) problems associated with where to place the cameras and other instrumentation. Among other things, these challenges include the fact that any instrumentation of a setting to record human activity affects how participants go about their activities as a result of being observed – the so-called *Hawthorne effect* (McCambridge, Witton, & Elbourne, 2014). This not only affects the validity of the results, in that participants might alter what they "normally" do, but also has the potential to harm participants either as a result of this alteration or due to breaches of confidentiality. At the least, in situ data collection may distract or reduce the motivations of the participants to engage in the activity, who are presumably undertaking it for purposes other than to be observed for researcher benefit. It also has the potential to make what are often private or semi-private performances more widely viewable by those who are normally excluded from access to them, especially if the researcher does not take sufficient care in securing confidentiality and access to the data. Despite these disadvantages, a considerable advantage of in situ data collection is that there are often materials, resources, people, and other affordances for activity in a "natural" setting that are difficult if not impossible to reproduce in the lab. This is what is often referred to as high *ecological validity*.

Capturing data "in the lab," on the other hand, involves creating a simulacrum of what the researcher takes to be the salient characteristics of the setting and/or activity, recruiting research participants to come to the location at which this simulacrum is set up ("the lab"), and recording participant activity within the simulated environment. A distinct advantage of using such lab studies is the fine-grained researcher control over virtually all characteristics of the simulated environment – a key reason why lab studies are so often used in experimental designs. In addition, in the lab, researchers are often able to carry out much more extensive instrumentation and recording of the activities than is normally feasible in situ, such as the use of fMRI, eye-tracking, and screen capture, to name a few. The main cost is that ecological validity can be significantly reduced – that is, the extent to which what is observed in the lab bears a correspondence to what actually occurs in the natural setting – and it is often difficult for the researcher to know if this is (or will be) the case (Henrich et al., 2005). What Anne Brown (1992, p. 152) notes about the classroom is true of other settings in which learning also occurs: "The classroom is not the natural habitat of many experimental psychologists, and our methods did not evolve to capture learning in situ." In addition, lab studies can severely limit the demographics of research participants to only those who are able to travel to the lab where the study will be undertaken, thereby reducing the generalizability of the results to other study populations (Henrich, Heine, & Norenzayan, 2010).

7.2.5 Data Analysis

7.2.5.1 Data Analysis in Boys' Needlework

Recapitulation. *Boys' Needlework* is concerned with broadening participation in computing, and approaches this topic from an intersectional perspective. It inquires into how a group of ten eighth-grade American Indian boys from a charter school on tribal lands in the southwestern USA engaged with e-textiles in a three-week Native Studies learning unit and how their computational perspectives changed over this time. Data collected for analysis include video recordings and field notes from daily class sessions, students' circuitry blueprints, photographs of students' designs, and project code. Six students participated in reflective interviews at the end of the three weeks.

Searle and Kafai begin their exposition of their analytic activity by referencing a theoretical orientation that guided their analysis: "We used a multi-faceted identity lens … to understand how the heritage craft element of e-textiles might be leveraged to attract boys from non-dominant backgrounds to learn computing and to address the identity gap." This statement makes visible how these researchers build on existing social theory for making sense of the data that they are analyzing. The term "lens" signals that the data are viewed "through" or in relation to a particular theoretical concept ("multi-faceted identity"). By "identity," this suggests a well-explored construct in the social-psychological and educational literature that references the social categories into which people place themselves (Stets & Burke, 2000) and/or the social categories by which an individual is recognized (placed into) by others (Gee, 2000).

The authors then describe how they undertook their analysis with the collected materials, and which materials provided insight into what aspects of the research questions they interrogate:

> Analysis of boys' e-textiles artifacts and field notes allowed us to better understand their practices and participation in the classroom community. A portfolio was created for each student that combined his initial circuitry blueprint, photographs of his in-process and completed project, and any available iterations of the code for his project. Field notes and interview transcripts were initially coded using a two-step open coding process … allowing themes to emerge from the data and then be refined. Salient codes included the gendered nature of craft and boys' uncertainty about participating in craft practices, design agency, and the importance of a culturally-connected assignment. This analysis of field notes helped us to better understand boys' practices during the Native Studies e-textiles unit and analysis of interviews allowed us to better understand boys' perspectives on learning computing through e-textiles activities.

7.2.5.2 Data Analysis in General

Data analysis refers to the activities that researchers undertake to link collected data to *claims*, "any sentence that asserts something that may be true or false and so needs support" (Booth, Colomb, & Williams, 2008, p. 116). Claims are generally about the individuals studied and/or about a group of individuals larger than, but including, those studied. Within experimental research, the term *validity* is generally used in discussing the strength of the inferences that link empirical data to conclusions, whereas the term *trustworthiness* is typically used in referencing the strength of these inferences in qualitative research (Lincoln & Guba, 1985). The difference between these terms signifies epistemological differences that, when understood, can help researchers distinguish between these different traditions of analytic research. The purpose of distinguishing the qualitative from the quantitative perspectives on research is not to set up binary opposites between which a researcher must choose, but rather to illuminate the ends of a spectrum of methods of investigation available to any researcher.

One of the key features that frequently distinguishes quantitative from qualitative research concerns the degree of experimental control available to the researcher. As the statistical methods chapters of this Handbook illuminate (Chapters 5 and 6), in a simple experimental design, the researcher randomly divides a population in two, identifies the important, measurable independent variables within a setting, defines a *treatment* designed for its causal effect that will manifest in a measured outcome variable of interest, applies the treatment to one group but not the other, and then compares variance on the outcome variable between the two groups. What allows for making strong inferences in experimental design is what is often referred to as the *ceterus parabus* ("all other things being equal") condition (i.e., that as many of the variables as can be are held equal between the two populations). That is, since it is only the treatment condition that varies, the measured effect can be attributed to the treatment and not to some extraneous factor, which permits the elimination of *rival hypotheses* that could account for the measured changes. The experimental design is an accomplishment of human ingenuity and is responsible for profound advancements in human knowledge.

Given this powerful form of reasoning, what is a primary motivation for undertaking a *qualitative* research study? The most important reason in my view is to *make visible particular characteristics of the unknown world*. What do I mean by this odd turn of phrase, "characteristics of the unknown world?" Looking again at quantitative research approaches, they depend upon numerical relationships between particular *variables* or *properties* that characterize the phenomena of interest. In the Searle and Kafai paper examined here, had the authors pursued a quantitative study, these variables might have been *gender*, *race/ethnicity*, and *perspective on computing*, among others. But in order to count particular values of variables as they manifest in the units that are being counted (in this case, the American Indian boys), it would be necessary to have a *well-understood and fully articulated ontology of the variables of interest*. In the research described in *Boys' Needlework*, this would mean that (among other things) "perspective on computing" has to be sufficiently well understood that the different "perspectives" can be placed into categories and named. And "gender" has to be placed into an ontology, an ontology currently undergoing considerable debate not only among academics, but in the larger social world (Budgeon, 2013; Drescher, 2007). Further, as the statistics chapters explain, these perspectives have to be precisely measurable in their having empirical features of the situation that can be validly and reliably "read off" or inferred from the actual data collected by independent observers. In short, we can say that the quantitative methods are suited for research questions seeking the relationship between properties of a *known world*, one in which the object and relation ontologies are taken to be well understood. This is not a *completely* known world, else there would be no reason to investigate it in any form. But quantitative research presupposes that what it is in the world and what is measurable are already taken as fact by the research community in which this research is being carried out and reported. For the physical sciences and many areas of research in the human sciences, we are accustomed to measuring and seeking relationships between properties of just this kind of known world. Yet we recognize that, historically, the taxonomies and understandings of the known world by scientific communities have undergone change, at times "revolutionary" (Kuhn, 1962).

But what about aspects of the world that are less well known in the sense discussed here? These are the cases where there may be little other than intuition or taken-for-granted presuppositions for creating the ontologies that will be counted and related were a quantitative study to be undertaken. Or where there is no shared agreement of the phenomenon of interest among the interested community of researchers, since it is in flux or new to the community of researchers. Or it might be that the world is experienced and hence known differently by different people who inhabit it, and not all of these subjective positions are well understood in the research community in which the research is to be reported. There may be as yet no language (at least among researchers) for expressing such a worldview.

What are taken to be "objective" features of the human world depend crucially on one's presuppositions about how the world operates. This is true for researchers just as it is for "American Indian boys," all of whose worldviews have been shaped by the cultural worlds through which they have traversed; we are all, researcher and researched alike, conditioned by the language, theories, beliefs, and cultures shared in the communities and situations that constitute our personal and collective histories. Qualitative research offers the possibility of interrogating the taken for granted and accepted (e.g., gendered perspectives on computing) and replacing it with a different and more subtle understanding (e.g., an intersectional perspective on computing). In one of his pedagogical papers about sociological method, Bourdieu remarks that "the power of a mode of thinking never manifests itself more clearly than in its capacity to constitute socially insignificant objects into scientific objects ... or, what amounts to the same thing, to approach a major socially significant object from an unexpected angle" (Bourdieu, 1992, p. 221).

This discussion of the known and unknown, of interrogating the taken for granted, may appear abstract and theoretical, and in this way distant from the everyday concerns of the empirical researcher. An example of what I am trying to define may help.

Imagine a scientist who is testing adult research participants on how they carry out mundane categorization tasks. In the research protocol, the investigator shows subjects pictures of four everyday objects with which the subjects are familiar and asks each subject to group the three that are similar and to leave out of the group the one that is dissimilar. The following discussion ensues when the research subject is shown drawings of *glass–saucepan–spectacles–bottle*.

Subject: These three go together, but why you've put the spectacles here, I don't know. Then again, they also fit in. If a person doesn't see too good, he has to put them on to eat dinner.

Researcher: *But one fellow told me one of these things didn't belong in this group.*

Subject: Probably that kind of thinking runs in his blood. But I say they all belong here. You can't cook in the glass, you have to fill it. For cooking, you need the saucepan, and to see better, you need the spectacles. We need all four of these things, that's why they were put here.

This example comes from Luria (1976), based on studies that he and colleagues carried out in the Soviet Union in the 1930s when the state was collectivizing work and introducing formal schooling in parts of the country where the population previously had little to no formal schooling nor collective forms of labor. The researchers wanted to exploit this "natural experiment" that was currently happening (and would soon disappear) in which they could compare the performance of people from different populations (i.e., those with different social relations of labor and different amounts of formal schooling). The researchers' overall goal was to test Vygotsky's theorizing about how individuals internalize within their own cognitive mechanisms what they previously experienced as external social relations (Vygotsky, 1978, 1981). What Luria and colleagues found was confirmation of Vygotsky's *genetic law of cultural development*, in that the kind of categorization in which abstract categories (such as "tool") form the basis of reasoning only begin to appear as individuals encounter formal education, where such abstract forms of reasoning are encountered and taught. The kind of reasoning displayed in the excerpt above, of an "illiterate peasant" from a rural district who had never traveled outside the few miles of his district and never been to any urban centers, is what Luria describes as "practical," where objects are organized "according to their role in a practical situation."

On first encounter, I found this dialogue quite strange, to say the least. I saw categorization of everyday objects along abstract dimensions (e.g., "tool") as so obvious that I was stunned that not only would someone do categorization differently, but that they would similarly take as common sense *their* organizational principles for categorization, so different from my own. Had I (or another researcher) entered the research site with a predetermined view of how people categorize, assuming that it was universal, I could easily conclude that the subjects studied were mentally deficient, or at least very poor at categorizing, using standard measures of categorization.

As researchers, then, we face a profound paradox. While we might like to undertake quantitative studies to exploit the power of *ceterus parabus* and experimental control to make strong inferences about causality, such experiments do not construct themselves out of the natural materials of the world. Rather, they are the human product of the current ontologies and beliefs of the researchers who undertake them, and these very beliefs are conditioned by the particulars of any researcher's culture and history.

How, then, are we to undertake qualitative studies with sufficient inferential strength and rigor so that we and others can trust the results that so often challenge and seek to redefine existing conceptual frameworks? What I enumerate here are four ways that qualitative researchers address this paradox, four primary *analytic strategies*. I term these *thick description, inductive categorization, ethnographic adequacy*, and *case comparison*. I claim neither that these are exhaustive of all forms of qualitative analysis, nor that others would group the space of strategies similarly. Rather, I believe this to be a useful taxonomy for understanding a great deal of qualitative analytic work.

Thick Description. This term comes from Geertz (1973), who wrote trenchantly about the essential work of cultural anthropologists. Cultural anthropologists spend considerable time "in the field," living with and participating in the lives of the people whom they study. Toward what end? For Geertz, it was in order to gain an understanding of the coherences of the form of life under investigation, where this coherence is what links human action to meaning-in-context. Explaining the coherences of meaning to an audience, then, is what Geertz calls *thick description*. It is easy to misinterpret "thick" to mean "large quantity," or "detailed," but this is to miss Geertz's point. Thickness has to do with understanding and making visible to others the specific ways that a person or culture constructs and shares meaning. Thick description provides an account for what might otherwise seem strange to the outsider, but "normal" to an insider, such as why and how boys' needlework is or can become a normative male practice. In making visible what is significant to the people who are studied, thick description uncovers the *teleological coherence*, the chains of in-order-to motives (Schutz, 1967) by which human activity is rendered intelligible.

What are the research questions for which thick descriptions constitute answers? Thickly descriptive work is undertaken when a researcher seeks to understand what actions take place by which individuals within a particular context given its unique history, tools, resources, and language and what are the meanings and motives of these actions as understood by those who produce them. Thick description is necessarily situated and case oriented: "by putting forth, *in situation*, precepts applied directly to the *particular case* at hand" (Bourdieu, 1992, p. 221, emphasis in original). In being case-oriented, researchers "treat cases as whole entities and not as collections of parts ... Thus, the relations between the parts of a whole are understood within the context of the whole" (Ragin, 1987, p. x). In CEd, one might undertake a thickly descriptive study to answer, "What communication patterns are used in the CEd classroom, and how do these contribute to the social aspect of these classrooms?" as did Barker, Garvin-Doxas, and Jackson (2002). Or one might ask, "How do individuals in a hackerspace maintain their community and relate to one another?" as did Toombs, Bardzell, and Bardzell (2015)

Inductive Categorization. Pace the categorical reasoning illustrated by Luria above, the use of named categories for grouping things (actions, events, and phenomena more generally) is ubiquitous in human language and reasoning, and for good reason: when similar instances are placed into a group, general principles can be learned and applied to all members of the group, avoiding the need to deal idiosyncratically with each group element sui generis. Rosch (1978, p. 3) summarizes this rationale for categorical reasoning with two principles that she names *cognitive economy* and *perceived world structure*: "the task of category systems is to provide maximum information with the least cognitive effort ... the perceived world comes as structured information rather than as arbitrary or unpredictable attributes."

Given the importance of making visible, challenging, and reconceptualizing current ontologies for reasoning about the world, such as "gender," it should come as no surprise that qualitative researchers often spend considerable time in developing these ontologies from their empirical materials. The method is inductive and iterative. The researcher first determines the primitive semantic unit. For example, a *concept* is taken as the primitive semantic unit in *grounded theory*, one of the most well-known forms of inductive categorization (Corbin & Strauss, 1990). The researcher then completely divides the data into these units, "reads" through the data unit by unit, and places each unit into a category using the existing set of categories. If no existing category is appropriate, a new category is added to the ontology and the unit is placed in this new category. Developing categories and placing units into categories often goes under the term *coding*, while a *code* refers to a category name or descriptor. When all units are categorized (i.e., coded), the categories are compared, merged, or split as deemed appropriate, and often ordered in some fashion, such as set/subset or before/after. The process is not substantially different if the researcher starts the analysis with a predetermined set of categories rather than with no categories, though there are some who believe that starting with a predefined set biases the researcher too strongly so that features of the world immanent in the data will be overlooked (Strauss & Corbin, 1990). When there is more than one researcher carrying out the coding activity, researchers often develop a written "coding manual" that describes each category in a way so that the group of researchers can come to a high level of agreement (sometimes formally measured and termed "inter-rater reliability") about how the categorization is to be done. The categorization thus provides a parsimonious representation of the data (cognitive economy) and makes visible the perceived structure of the research subjects' world.

The research questions for which inductive categorization is appropriate are generally focused on understanding what are the kinds or types that subdivide the object of study, such as a domain concept, an experience, or an artifact. In CEd, Booth (1992) uses inductive categorization for answering, "What are the different ways in which students conceive of programming and learning to program?" Eckerdal and Thuné (2005) investigate "What are conceptions of 'class' and 'object' held by novice Java programmers?" And Knobelsdorf (2011) interrogates the computing experiences of CEd students beginning tertiary education within the personal biographies that they report.

Ethnographic Adequacy. At the risk of confusion with the first category that is so often used when writing ethnographies, I borrow this term from McDermott et al. (1978, p. 247): "We can use the ways members [to a situation] have of making clear to each other and to themselves what is going on to locate to our own satisfaction an account of what it is that they are doing with each other." That is, whatever it is that the parties to a situation rely upon for making their actions intelligible to one another or themselves so that they can keep it going is, if recorded by a researcher, available for analysis.

Methodologically, language use-in-interaction within specific settings is taken as the most common data to be analyzed. It is also common to include for analysis additional sign-related aspects of a situation that people create and make use of in their interactions, including gestures, gaze and body orientation, and symbolic inscriptions (external representations) such as text on a whiteboard, drawings on a piece of paper, or code on a computer display (Goodwin, 2000). The philosophical rationale that underlies much of this research is that language not only *expresses* or *communicates* meaning, but more importantly carries out *work between people in the social realm* (Wittgenstein, 2009). Language, under this view, is *functional*. It is the role of the analyst to uncover just what the purpose and function of the language used within a particular setting carries out.

The research questions most commonly pursued with this analytic strategy are *how* questions with respect to the phenomenon under investigation, so as to uncover how it is that this situation is organized and sustained. Lewis (2012) (see Chapter 31 in this Handbook) provides an ethnographically adequate account of *how an individual undertakes a debugging task* using audio-visual recordings of his verbalized self-talk while engaged in debugging and the corresponding displays on the computer about which he talks. Tenenberg et al. (2018) provide an ethnographically adequate account for *how a teacher and students write code together in the CEd classroom* using audio-visual recordings, gaze orientation, bodily configuration of the actors, and inscriptions on the blackboard, all of which are simultaneously employed by the actors in the setting during a single class session.

Case Comparison. Case comparison is used to compare *across* cases. Each case in the comparison is analyzed as a separate and coherent whole, either as part of the current study or prior to it. Multiple cases are placed in juxtaposition for two primary purposes. One is to determine the range of variation of the same or a similar phenomenon, such as the different ways in which the programming concept "class" is understood by novice students (Eckerdal & Thuné, 2005) or how childbirth is carried out in different human cultures (Jordan, 1993). In juxtaposition, differences become salient. The other purpose for case comparison is to determine those properties that are *invariant* across all cases. In noting the similarities and differences across cases, the case-comparative method is an approximate and qualitative version of *ceterus parabus* reasoning discussed above, where the world presents multiple, "natural" experiments that constitute the separate cases (Ragin, 1987). What is often the most difficult part of case comparison is determining the dimensions along which each case should be compared, because these are often unknown until each case is understood in depth and viewed in relation to the others.

The philosophical rationale that underlies case comparison is one that acknowledges that, both for individual cognition and social interaction, there are few generalizations that apply to all contexts and situations. Rather, the researcher is often concerned with determining *under what conditions the phenomenon under investigation is likely to occur*, what are often called *conditional generalizations* (Stern, Dietz, Dolšak, Ostrom, & Stonich, 2002). Case comparison is particularly well suited to answering these kinds of questions. Case comparison can also be used for answering variations (or constituents) of these conditional questions, such as, "What conditions account for similarities and/or differences in outcomes between cases of a phenomenon?" In CEd, Margolis (2008) investigates the factors that account for significantly fewer African American and Latino/a high school students studying CS in the USA in comparison to their representation in the US population. This is carried out using a comparison of three high schools in Los Angeles, California. One high school is "an extremely overcrowded facility in East Los Angeles with an almost entirely Latino/a student population," a second is "an aerospace mathematics science magnet in mid-Los Angeles with a predominantly African American population," and the third is "a neighborhood school surrounded by mansions overlooking the Pacific Ocean ... located in a white and wealthy community [where] two-thirds of the school population are students of color" (p. 4).

I summarize these different data analytic strategies in Table 7.2, listing for each its common variants, a canonical methodological reference to the analytic strategy, and references to one or more studies in CEd or one of the human sciences that use this strategy.

There is one additional point that it is important to note here, since it cuts across all forms of data analysis. This concerns the researchers' choice of unit of analysis. The term *unit of analysis* (sometimes called *unit of study*) refers to that unit of an empirical phenomenon about which the researcher is making general claims (Patton, 2002). To elaborate, the point of undertaking a study is not simply to understand something about particular people, talk, activities, and/or artifacts at a particular time and place as if these phenomena have no bearing on any other people, talk, etc., at *some other* time and place. Yet any reader of a study will ultimately want to know why the study results *matter*. Of what consequence are they for this

Table 7.2 *Data analysis strategies.*

Data analysis strategy	Methodology	Examples of use
Thick description		
Ethnography	Atkinson & Hammerseley, 1994, Spradley, 1980	Barker et al., 2002, Basso, 1996
Single-case study	Yin, 2003	Lewis, 2012, Shinohara & Tenenberg, 2009
Oral history	Ritchie, 2015	Computer History Museum, n.d.
Inductive categorization		
Phenomenography	Marton, 1981	Booth, 1992, Boustedt, 2012, Eckerdal & Thuné, 2005
Grounded theory	Strauss & Corbin, 1990	Schulte & Knobelsdorf, 2007
Ethnographic adequacy		
Discourse analysis	Gee, 2018	Gee, 2004, Tannen, 1989
Conversation analysis	Goodwin & Heritage, 1990	Pomerantz, 1984, Sacks et al., 1974
Multimodal analysis	Mondada, 2016	Murphy, Ivarsson, & Lymer, 2012, Tenenberg et al., 2018
Ethnomethodology	Garfinkel, 1967, Roth, 2013	McDermott, 1993, Mehan, 1979, Suchman, 1987
Case comparison		
Multiple-case study	Ragin, 1987, Yin, 2003	Margolis, 2008, Ostrom, 1990

research community in understanding the studied phenomenon more generally? The unit of analysis is a choice that the researcher makes, and arguably the most important one, since it becomes embedded in all aspects of the study, from research question, to population and site of empirical data collection, to the specifics of the data collected, to the method of analysis and reporting of results. Common units of analysis are the *individual person*, particularly in cognitively oriented research, and the *social group*, particularly in socioculturally oriented research.

7.2.6 Reporting Results

7.2.6.1 *Reporting Results in* Boys' Needlework

Recapitulation. *Boys' Needlework* is concerned with broadening participation in computing, and it approaches this topic from an intersectional perspective. It inquires into how a group of ten eighth-grade American Indian boys from a charter school on tribal lands in the southwestern USA engaged with e-textiles in a three-week Native Studies learning unit, and how their computational perspectives changed over this time. Data collected for analysis included video recordings and field notes from daily class sessions, students' circuitry blueprints, photographs of students' designs, and project code. Six students also participated in reflective interviews at the end of the three weeks. Artifacts and field notes were analyzed to provide insight into the boys' participation in the practices of the classroom community, while field notes and interviews were coded into themes. Interviews were also analyzed to understand the boys' computational perspectives.

In reporting their findings, Searle and Kafai remark that the codes that they developed through their inductive categorization "closely mirrored Brennan and Resnick's ... conceptualization of computational frameworks" (of *expressing, connecting*, and *questioning*) that they introduced in the Background section. These three categories serve as the main structural basis for reporting their results, in that three case studies are discussed in detail, where each case focuses on a single student and one of the computational perspectives. From their analysis, the authors note that *each* student interviewed (six of ten) exhibited *each* of these computational perspectives. Further, each student's perspective changed as they engaged in the activities of the three-week unit. The case studies are illustrative (i.e., thickly descriptive) of each of the thematic categories that had already been systematically derived. I describe one of these cases (*expressing*) in more detail to give a sense for all three.

This case is told as a narrative about a single individual's experience chronologically from the start of the learning unit to its completion. A variety of data are drawn upon and explicitly referenced in evidencing many of the claims. For example, at the outset of the case, the authors report: "Sammy [the student pseudonym] also returned to school after learning about the project and reported that his mom had said sewing was for ladies. When asked what he thought in response, he replied, 'I think it doesn't matter.'" This quote illustrates that *this* boy's upcoming needlework challenged gender norms within some part of his community, though the authors do not comment upon this in their case description. Sammy, we are told, chooses a lightning bolt for his design based on its connection to comic book superheroes, his second choice after another student has already taken Sammy's preferred choice of "one of the community's sacred mountains." Sammy's "pace of working" and "dedication" are noted. The project develops through a process of visual design (e.g., number and color of elements that will compose the design), interaction design (placement of sensors and lights), coding, and sewing. Throughout the discussion, the authors highlight the *personal meaning and significance* of the evolving design, largely centered on the emergent e-textile garment as an expression of Sammy's aesthetic sensibilities. The authors complete the case in noting that the "e-textiles project as a means of personal expression was a theme in all of the interviews we conducted." The other two cases are reported similarly.

After all three cases are presented, the Discussion section returns to the general themes of broadening participation in computing and intersectionality that motivated the study, discussing these in light of the *expressing*, *connecting*, and *questioning* themes identified in the analysis. The authors note that the design of the instructional intervention – the use of e-textiles – can "both reify and challenge existing gendered and cultural norms around who can engage in craft practices and who can engage in computing." The authors attribute the "culturally responsive aspect of the assignment" and its appropriation by the boys for personal expression as causal in moving their conceptions beyond what for some had been a view of "craft, circuitry, and computing as gendered." Through their work with e-textiles, the students strengthened their connections to others within their valued communities, both family members (such as a grandmother who "always sews") and students in other classes in the high school. Finally, the authors discuss how students developed "abilities to question with and through computation," as they reflexively began to "push back against the dominant narratives" of technology as defined in Western science, learning about the long history of appropriation and shaping of technology from within their American Indian communities. The authors conclude their paper in remarking that as computing disseminates through increasingly diverse populations, "the incorporation of novel, hybrid materials and heritage craft practices" can provide an avenue for developing the computational perspectives described within their study. "[I]t is important that educators not only engage the variety of perspectives, experiences, and cultural backgrounds that students bring with them but also recognize that computing must make a contribution back to the community to be valued, whether through developing language learning software or encouraging youth to take up heritage cultural practices."

What should be clear from the exposition above is that *Boys' Needlework* uses several forms of data analysis and reporting of results. *Inductive categorization* results in the identification of a three-part taxonomy of computational perspectives, mirroring that in Brennan and Resnick (2012). *Thick description* is used in making visible the way in which each of the three categories manifests and has coherence within the systems of meaning of the boys who were studied. Examples drawn from the collected data are used to evidence many of the assertions made within the narrative case of each student. Finally, *case comparison* is used as a reporting strategy to both highlight the differences in the identified categories and to argue for their universality among all of the students interviewed.

7.2.6.2 Reporting Results in General

Each of the four forms of analysis presented in the prior section is associated with common forms of reporting the results. The division of text between the "methods" section dealing with how an analysis is undertaken, the "results" (often called "findings") section, and the "discussion" section is not fixed. This is because understanding how an analysis is undertaken in many cases only becomes apparent in the reporting of the results and discussing its significance in relation to the research questions under investigation. In addition, without understanding the relationship between analysis, results, and discussion, it is all too easy to dismiss reports that involve relatively small units of data as mere "anecdotes" and "non-representative samples" when they are anything but.

Thick Description. To carry out thick description usually requires an analytic process that I will call *living-with*, whereby the researcher comes to learn about the world of their informants with sufficient depth so as to make it legible for others – an apprenticeship in someone else's form of life. It is, as Ingold (2013, p. 2) describes, "a protracted masterclass in which the novice gradually learns to see things, and to hear and feel them too, in the ways his or her mentors [informants] do."

One of the most skilled practitioners of thick description and *living-with* is Keith Basso, who studied the Western Apache (American Indians of the US southwest) for several decades. To get a better sense of how thick description is reported, I provide a precis from one of his essays, "Wisdom Sits in Places" (Basso, 1996). For the Western Apache, according to Basso, narrative, location within a physical world, and moral instruction become so intertwined that they cannot be separated, a form of life unfamiliar to the majority of Westerners living a mobile, urban existence. It is only in its specific and culturally bound features – its thick description – that such an understanding can be made visible. He describes an event to which he is witness, in which three horsemen are cooling themselves in a grove of junipers after having spent ten hours earlier in the day "sorting steers and branding calves" (p. 58). Another rider joins the group, a man "who is highly regarded as an accomplished roper and a fearless rider in pursuit of bolting cattle" (p. 59). But recently, following the collapse of a love affair, this man, who is "normally restrained," has "lost control of himself" through "prodigious drinking of beer" and obnoxious behavior (p. 59). "In a soft and halting voice he reports that he has been sober for three days and would like to return to work. He adds that he is eager to get away from the village because people there have been gossiping about him" (p. 59). A brief dialogue then ensues. "A grinning Dudley speaks first [only the English translation is provided]: 'So! You've returned from Trail Goes Down Between Two Hills!' Followed by a brightly animated Charles: 'So! You got tired walking back and forth!' followed by Sam, on the verge of laughter: 'So! You've smelled enough burning piss!' followed by Talbert, who is smiling now himself: 'For a while I couldn't see!' Followed once more by Dudley: 'It's true. Trail Goes Down Between Two Hills will make you wise. We'll work together tomorrow'" (p. 60).

Basso leaves this encounter utterly confused about what he has just witnessed. He then describes how he comes to understand this dialogue from a sequence of conversations with the parties to the witnessed dialogue. From one conversation, his informant tells Basso "that there were several reasons for dealing with Talbert as they did. To have criticized Talbert explicitly – to have told him in so many words that his recent behavior was foolish, insensitive, and disruptive – would have been insulting and condescending. As judged from Talbert's apologetic demeanor, he had reached these conclusions himself, and to inform him openly of what he already knew would be to treat him like a child. In addition, because Talbert was unrelated by ties of kinship to either Dudley or Sam, and because he was related only distantly to Charles, none of them possessed the requisite authority to instruct him directly on matters pertaining to his personal life; this was the proper responsibility of his older matrilineal kin" (p. 64). And from several other conversations, Basso slowly learns about a number of culturally shared stories that constitute an important locus of moral instruction, where each such story occurs in a particular physical location that is part of the known Apache landscape. By referencing one of these stories in stating its location (Trail Goes Down Between Two Hills), the men draw a parallel between the moral instruction provided in the story and its application to the concrete conditions of Dudley's recent experience of being out of control but coming back into himself.

While the dialogue that is analyzed might thus be seen as merely "anecdotal," being "cherry-picked" and therefore unrepresentative (and hence to be discounted), it takes on a completely different significance in a study analyzed through thick description. This dialogue, in its very specificity, represents a general phenomenon that links moral instruction, language, behavior, and geographic location characteristic of Western Apache life.

Inductive Categorization. Reports of inductive categorization discuss the categories developed and describe what each category represents. As an example, Boustedt (2012) undertakes an inductive categorization strategy, *phenomenography* (Marton, 1981), in his study of how university computing students understand unified modeling language (UML) class diagrams. He asks three research questions: what students take to be the purpose and use of class diagrams, how they are conceived in general, and how two similar syntactic elements ("black and white diamond symbols") are distinguished and understood (p. 31). As Boutstedt (p. 33) summarizes, "phenomenographic research aims to find and show the differences and variations in the way phenomena in the world are 'understood' (described) by people." Boustedt reports on his phenomenographic analysis of interviews of 20 students drawn from four Swedish universities who were completing their degrees in CS or Computer Engineering. "A phenomenographic approach was used to analyze the interviews, which means that the transcribed interviews were examined to find expressions of 'meaning' of various phenomena related to class diagrams. For each research question, the goal was to establish an 'outcome space'; a set of categories that expressed distinct ways of experiencing the 'phenomenon' in question, on a collective level" (p. 34).

Boustedt analyzes this material by first transcribing it and reading all transcripts and, while doing so, "all text sections relating to the specific phenomenon, e.g., class diagrams were marked" (p. 36). He collected all such sections and then entered these into *Atlas.ti*, a software tool that facilitates the inductive categorization (coding) of the text. He explains: "[t]he tool made it possible to browse through the text, to add comments, and to mark those quotes that in some sense ascribed a meaning to the phenomenon in question. One or more labels were added, identifying interpretations of each marked quote" (p. 36). Finally, "[t]he various codes of meaning were then analyzed to find qualitative similarities and differences between them, and hence, different clusters of meanings were condensed" (p. 36).

I describe his reporting of the results only related to his first research question concerning conceptions of the purpose and use of UML class diagrams, since he does similarly with his other two research questions and this is typical of reporting inductive categorization analyses more generally. Boustedt's analysis results in an outcome space of three categories, named and described as follows (p. 37): *Code*: "class diagrams are used as a documentation of existing program code"; *Design*: "Class diagrams are used as a way to develop software designs"; and *Dialogue*: "Class diagrams are used as a way to design software and are used as a means for a dialogue with team members in a dynamic design process that will end up in program code." In reporting this analysis, Boustedt elaborates on each of these categories, provides his summative interpretation across his research informants, and illustrates each with several verbatim quotations from his transcripts. For example, for the category of "Code," one of the transcript quotations is "… due to the fact that the experience I have from UML is almost exclusively in relation to writing code, so by old habit, I see it as code" (p. 38).

Here again, the reporting of specific quotations may seem anecdotal and non-representative to a reader unfamiliar with inductive categorization. But such quotations simply provide a "prototypical" semantic unit that illustrates, concretizes, and in this way represents the entire category, where the space of categories is developed through a systematic and complete process of coding *all* of the data whose structure is distilled in the set of categories and their descriptors.

Ethnographic Adequacy. In ethnographically adequate reporting, specific instances of a social phenomenon are chosen from a larger corpus to provide the basis for making claims about the phenomenon more generally. As an example, Goodwin (2000) provides an ethnographically adequate description of two girls playing hopscotch to argue for the variety and necessity of a range of *semiotic resources* ("sign systems with alternative properties") that are employed in everyday talk. It is only by virtue of these semiotic resources, Goodwin argues, that "the constitution of particular kinds of action being invoked through talk" (p. 1489) is made possible. That is, Goodwin is engaging in a discourse with other researchers who use talk (*accounts*, as I call them in this chapter) as a primary form of data under analysis, stating that the words alone may be insufficient to uncover the social meaning of the communication. The data that are analyzed, in significant detail, are less than one minute in duration, consisting of 11 turns at talk (i.e., places where the speaker changes) (Sacks, Schegloff, & Jefferson, 1974). Rather than seeking "semantics" or conceptual meaning as immanent in the words of each separate speaker (presupposed in carrying out many forms of inductive categorization), Goodwin demonstrates how the intelligibility of the situation to its participants comes from not just the words, but the way in which they are spoken (i.e., their "prosodic" properties of rhythm, tone, pitch, volume, and similar). Meaning is also built from the gestures (of hands and feet) that are interleaved with the words, along with body movements, gaze orientation, and the hopscotch grid itself that is drawn on the ground over which the two girls play. To give a feel for his analysis, I provide a small example. He analyzes a point in their action when the two hopscotch players are having a heated dispute. "The dispute being examined here begins when Diana stands at the top of the hop-scotch grid ... throws her beanbag into a particular square, and starts to hop through the grid. Right after the beanbag lands (in what will be argued to be the wrong square) and as Diana starts to jump, Carla walks into the grid, physically stops Diana from continuing, and then argues that Diana has made an illegal move by throwing her beanbag onto the fifth square instead of the fourth" (p. 1493). He continues with a moment-by-moment analysis of how all of the semiotic resources in the situation are employed, concluding that "the action that occurs here is built through the visible, public deployment of multiple semiotic fields that mutually elaborate each other" (p. 1494).

Again, one unfamiliar with the ethnographically adequate analytic strategy might view a single dialogue as mere anecdote, unrepresentative of anything else. Yet here, through a careful analysis that unpacks the work that the participants carry out in employing a variety of sign systems, work that is so mundane that its features are easily overlooked and therefore "hiding in plain sight," Goodwin makes an argument about the multimodality of face-to-face communication more generally.

Case Comparison. In case comparison studies, each case is summarized, showing the relations between the elements internal to the case, followed by a discussion of similarities and differences between the cases, often leading to generalizations derived therefrom.

A trenchant example of comparative case analysis is by Elinor Ostrom (1990) on the community governance of shared natural resource systems (what she calls a *commons*) that led to her receipt of the Nobel Prize in Economics in 2009. Ostrom motivates her case comparison strategy by noting that Garret Hardin, in his famous paper "Tragedy of the Commons," "posited that all users of a commons were helplessly trapped in a causal process leading to overuse, if not destruction, of the very resources on which they were dependent." As a result, Hardin states that only two governance options are possible for preventing this tragedy: coercive centralized government control or dividing the commons into privately owned pieces.

Ostrom provides analyses of six cases of where communities collectively self-governed (without external coersion) natural resources with considerable success (i.e., they were not subject to the tragedy of the commons, thereby refuting Hardin's assertion). She then asks, "What forms of governance predict or account for those situations when tragedy does or does not occur?" She answers this by seeking invariants across the cases (i.e., properties of the governance regimes common to each) that appeared determinative of successful outcomes for the natural resource system that was collectively governed. Eight such properties are found, which she terms "institutional design principles." These principles are expressed as Boolean-valued assertions, such as, "Most individuals affected by the operational rules can participate in modifying the operational rules," and, "The rights of appropriators to devise their own institutions are not challenged by external governmental authorities" (Ostrom, 1990, p. 90). To further test the causal validity of these principles, she presents eight additional cases, similar to the six successful cases, but where the common resource system had either failed (in five cases) or was "fragile" (in three cases; i.e., at considerable risk of failing). In the five failed cases, at least five of the eight institutional design principles were not satisfied, and in the three fragile cases, at least three of the eight institutional design principles were not satisfied.

7.3 Conclusion

Qualitative research methods provide the basis for interrogating existing and taken-for-granted conceptions of the world. They allow asking questions about the meaning and motives of individual and social action from the actors' point of view, the ontologies of actors within a setting, the ways in which individual and social action are carried out and organized, and the conditions under which particular outcomes are likely to come about.

A variety of qualitative research methods already exist, borrowed from the human sciences. Three forms of empirical phenomena are identified about which qualitative researchers collect data: activities, accounts, and artifacts. These data are usually analyzed using one or more of four inference strategies that link data to claims: thick description, inductive categorization, ethnographic adequacy, and case comparison. Reflexively, I have used all four forms of these data analysis methods and reporting in presenting this chapter. First, and most obviously, I use thick description of a single case in making visible the coherence and intelligibility of *Boys' Needlework* as a whole, placing it within the larger context of a discussion of qualitative research generally. In discussing the title, context, and research questions, I provide an ethnographically adequate description of the authors' precise use of language, unpacking in considerable detail what is coded within, "hiding in plain sight." Inductive categorization is undertaken in the data collection and analysis ontologies presented. Finally, case comparison is carried out in discussing the four analytic methods. In comparative juxtaposition, this range of methods in aggregate delineates a large space of analytic possibility, highlights differences between methods, and shows how each must nonetheless as an invariant property carry the weight of making trustworthy connections between the data that are collected and the answers developed to the research questions that motivate a study.

Qualitative methods continue to evolve in response to the changing priorities of a number of research communities, who raise new questions and provide new perspectives for answering them. In addition, new instrumentation (some of which computers enable) makes possible new forms of data collection and analysis. Qualitative research will continue to be an essential part of CEd research into the future.

References

Atkinson, P., & Hammerseley, M. (1994). Ethnography and participant observation. In N. Denzin & Y. Lincoln (Eds.), *Handbook of Qualitative Research* (pp. 248–261). Thousand Oaks, CA: Sage.

Barker, L., Garvin-Doxas, K., & Jackson, M. (2002). Defensive climate in the computer science classroom. In *Proceedings of the 33rd SIGCSE Technical Symposium on Computer Science Education* (pp. 43–47). New York: ACM.

Basso, K. H. (1996). *Wisdom Sits in Places: Landscape and Language Among the Western Apache*. Albuquerque, NM: University of New Mexico Press.

Bonar, J., & Soloway, E. (1983). Uncovering principles of novice programming. In *Proceedings of the 10th ACM SIGACT-SIGPLAN Symposium on Principles of Programming Languages (POPL '83)* (pp. 10–13). New York: ACM.

Bonar, J., & Soloway, E. (1985). Preprogramming knowledge: A major source of misconceptions in novice programmers. *Human–Computer Interaction*, 1, 133–161.

Booth, S. A. (1992). *Learning to Program: A Phenomenographic Perspective* (doctoral thesis). Acta Universitatis Gothobergensis.

Booth, W. C., Colomb, G. G., & Williams, J. M. (2008). *The Craft of Research*, 3rd edn. Chicago, IL: University of Chicago Press.

Bourdieu, P. (1992). The practice of reflexive sociology (the Paris Workshop). In P. Bourdieu & L. J. D. Wacquant (Eds.), *An Invitation to Reflexive Sociology* (pp. 216–260). Chicago, IL: Chicago University Press.

Boustedt, J. (2012). Students' different understandings of class diagrams. *Computer Science Education*, 22(1), 29–62.

Bowles, S., & Gintis, H. (2011). *Schooling in Capitalist America: Educational Reform and the Contradictions of Economic Life*. Chicago, IL: Haymarket Books.

Brennan, K., & Resnick, M. (2012). New frameworks for studying and assessing the development of computational thinking. In *Annual Meeting of the American Educational Research Association* (pp 1–25). Washington, DC: American Educational Research Association.

Brown, A. (1992). Design experiments: Theoretical and methodological challenges in creating complex interventions in classroom settings. *Journal of the Learning Sciences*, 2(2), 141–178.

Budgeon, S. (2013). The dynamics of gender hegemony: Femininities, masculinities and social change. *Sociology*, 48(2), 317–334.

Busjahn, T., Schulte, C., Sharif, B., Simon, Begel, A., Hansen, M., … Antropova, M. (2014). Eye tracking in computing education. In *Proceedings of the Tenth Annual Conference on International Computing Education Research (ICER '14)* (pp. 3–10). New York: ACM.

Cherrington, S., & Loveridge, J. (2014). Using video to promote early childhood teachers' thinking and reflection. *Teaching and Teacher Education*, 41, 42–51.

Cole, E. R. (2009). Intersectionality and research in psychology. *American Psychologist*, 64, 170–180.

Computer History Museum (n.d.). Oral History Collection. Retrieved from www .computerhistory.org/collections/oralhistories/

Corbin, J., & Strauss, A. (1990). Grounded theory research: Procedures, canons and evaluative criteria. *Zeitschrift Für Soziologie*, 19(6), 418–427.

Drescher, J. (2007). From bisexuality to intersexuality: Rethinking gender categories. *Contemporary Psychoanalysis*, 43(1), 204–228.

Duchowski, A. (2007). *Eye Tracking Methodology: Theory and Practice*, 2nd edn. London, UK: Springer-Verlag London Ltd.

Dziallas, S., & Fincher, S. (2016). Aspects of graduateness in computing students' narratives. In *Proceedings of the 2016 ACM Conference on International Computing Education Research (ICER '16)* (pp. 181–190). New York: ACM.

Eckerdal, A., & Thuné, M. (2005). Novice Java progammers' conceptions of "object" and "class", and variation theory. *SIGCSE Bulletin*, 37(3), 89–93.

Emerson, R. M., Fretz, R. I., & Shaw, L. L. (2011). *Writing Ethnographic Fieldnotes*, 2nd edn. Chicago, IL: University of Chicago Press.

Ericsson, K. A., & Simon, H. A. (1993). *Protocol Analysis: Verbal Reports as Data* (Revised edn.). Cambridge, MA: MIT Press.

Garfinkel, H. (1967). *Studies in Ethnomethodology*. Englewood Cliffs, NJ: Prentice Hall.

Gee, J. P. (2000). Identity as an analytic lens for research in education. *Review of Research in Education*, 25, 99–125.

Gee, J. P. (2004). *Situated Language and Learning: A Critique of Traditional Schooling*. Abingdon, UK: Routledge.

Gee, J. P. (2018). *Introducing Discourse Analysis: From Grammar to Society*. Abingdon, UK: Routledge.

Geertz, C. (1973). *The Interpretation of Culture*. New York: Basic Books.

Goldman, R., Pea, R., Barron, B., & Derry, S. J. (Eds.) (2007). *Video Research in the Learning Sciences*. Mahwah, NJ: Erlbaum.

Goodwin, C. (2000). Action and embodiment within situated human interaction. *Journal of Pragmatics*, 32, 1489–1522.

Goodwin, C., & Heritage, J. (1990). Conversation analysis. *Annual Review of Anthropology*, 19, 283–307.

Greene, J. (2013). *Moral Tribes: Emotion, Reason, and the Gap Between Us and Them*. New York, NY: Penguin Press.

Harper, D. A. (1987). *Working Knowledge: Skill and Community in a Small Shop*. Berkeley, CA: University of California Press.

Harper, D. A. (2002). Talking about pictures: A case for photo elicitation. *Visual Studies*, 17(1), 13–26.

Harreveld, B., Danaker, M., Lawson, C., Knight, B. A., & Busch, G. (Eds.) (2016). *Constructing Methodology for Qualitative Research*. London, UK: Palgrave MacMillan.

Heath, C. (2010). *Video in Qualitative Research: Analysing Social Interaction in Everyday Life*. Los Angeles, CA: SAGE.

Hennink, M., Hutter, I., & Bailey, A. (2011). *Qualitative Research Methods*. Thousand Oaks, CA: SAGE Publications, Inc.

Henrich, J., Boyd, R., Bowles, S., Camerer, C., Fehr, E., Gintis, H., … Tracer, D. (2005). "Economic man" in cross-cultural perspective: Behavioral experiments in 15 small-scale societies. *Behavioral and Brain Sciences*, 28, 795–855.

Henrich, J., Heine, S. J., & Norenzayan, A. (2010). The weirdest people in the world? *Behavioral and Brain Sciences*, 33, 61–135.

Hitchens, M., & Lister, R. (2009). A focus group study of student attitudes to lectures. In *Proceedings of the Eleventh Australasian Conference on Computing Education (ACE '09)* (pp. 93–100). Darlinghurst, Australia: Australian Computer Society.

Ingold, T. (2013). *Making: Anthropology, Archaeology, Art and Architecture*. London, UK: Routledge.

Jordan, B. (1993). *Birth in Four Cultures: A Crosscultural Investigation of Childbirth in Yucatan, Holland, Sweden, and the United States*, 4th edn. Long Grove, IL: Waveland Press, Inc.

Knobelsdorf, M. (2011). *Biographische Lern- und Bildungsprozesse im Handlungskontext der Computernutzung (Biographical Learning and Educational Processes in the Context of Computer Experiences)* (PhD thesis). Freie Universität Berlin.

Kuhn, T. S. (1962). *The Structure of Scientific Revolutions*. Chicago, IL: University of Chicago Press.

Kvale, S. (1996). *InterViews: An Introduction to Qualitative Research Interviewing*. Thousand Oaks, CA: SAGE Publications, Inc.

Lewis, C. (2012). The importance of students' attention to program state: A case study of debugging behavior. In *Proceedings of the Ninth Annual International Conference on International Computing Education Research (ICER '12)* (pp. 127–134). New York: ACM.

Liberman, N., Ben-David Kolikant, Y., & Beeri, C. (2009). In-service teachers learning of a new paradigm: A case study. In *Proceedings of the Fifth International Workshop on Computing Education Research Workshop (ICER '09)* (pp. 43–50). New York: ACM.

Lieberman, M. D. (2013). *Social: Why Our Brains Are Wired to Connect*. New York: Crown Publishers.

Lincoln, Y. S., & Guba, E. G. (1985). *Naturalistic Inquiry*. Newbury Park, CA: SAGE Publications, Inc.

Luria, A. L. (1976). *Cognitive Development: Its Cultural and Social Foundations*. Cambridge, MA: Harvard University Press.

Madley, B. (2016). *American Genocide: The United States and the California Indian Catastrophe*. New Haven, CT: Yale University Press.

Margolis, J. (2008). *Stuck in the Shallow End: Education, Race, and Computing*. Cambridge, MA: MIT Press.

Marton, F. (1981). Phenomenography – Describing conceptions of the world around us. *Instructional Science*, 10, 177–200.

Marwick, A. E. (2010). *Status Update: Celebrity, Publicity and Self-branding in Web 2.0* (PhD thesis). New York University.

McCambridge, J., Witton, J., & Elbourne, D. R. (2014). Systematic review of the Hawthorne effect: New concepts are needed to study research participation effects. *Journal of Clinical Epidemiology*, 67(3), 267–277.

McDermott, R. P. (1993). The acquisition of a child by a learning disability. In S. Chaiklin & J. Lave (Eds.), *Understanding Practice: Perspectives on Activity and Context* (pp. 60–70). Cambridge, UK: Cambridge University Press.

McDermott, R. P., Gospodinoff, K., & Aron, J. (1978). Criteria for an ethnographically adequate description of concerted activities and their contexts. *Semiotica*, 24(3/4), 245–275.

Mehan, H. (1979). *Learning Lessons: Social Organization in the Classroom*. Cambridge, MA: Harvard University Press.

Mishler, E. G. (1986). *Research Interviewing: Context and Narrative*. Cambridge, MA: Harvard University Press.

Mitchell, W. J. T. (Ed.) (1980). *On Narrative*. Chicago, IL: University of Chicago Press.

Mondada, L. (2016). Challenges of multimodality: Language and the body in social interaction. *Journal of Sociolinguistics*, 20(3), 336–366.

Murphy, K. M., Ivarsson, J., & Lymer, G. (2012). Embodied reasoning in architectural critique. *Design Studies*, 33, 530–556.

Ostrom, E. (1990). *Governing the Commons: The Evolution of Institutions for Collective Action*. Cambridge, UK: Cambridge University Press.

Patton, M. Q. (2002). *Qualitative Evaluation and Research Methods*, 3rd edn. Newbury Park, CA: SAGE.

Pew Research Center (2014). One-in-four Native Americans and Alaska Natives are living in poverty. Retrieved from www.pewresearch.org/fact-tank/2014/06/13/1-in-4-native-americans-and-alaska-natives-are-living-in-poverty/

Pink, S. (2013). *Doing Visual Ethnography*, 3rd edn. London, UK: SAGE.

Pomerantz, A. (1984). Agreeing and disagreeing with assessments: Some features of preferred/dispreferred turn shapes. In J. M. Atkinson & J. Heritage (Eds.), *Structures of Social Action: Studies in Conversation Analysis* (pp. 57–101). Cambridge, UK: Cambridge University Press.

Ragin, C. C. (1987). *The Comparative Method*. Berkeley, CA: University of California Press.

Riessman, C. K. (2008). *Narrative Methods for the Human Sciences*. Thousand Oaks, CA: SAGE Publications, Inc.

Ritchie, D. A. (2015). *Doing Oral History*, 3rd edn. Oxford, UK: Oxford University Press.

Rosch, E. (1978). Principles of categorization. In E. Rosch & B. B. Lloyd (Eds.), *Cognition and Categorization* (pp. 27–48). Hillsdale, NJ: Lawrence Erlbaum Associates.

Roth, W.-M. (2013). *What More in/for Science Education: An Ethnomethodological Perspective*. Rotterdam/Boston/Taipei: Sense Publishers.

Sacks, H., Schegloff, E., & Jefferson, G. (1974). A simplest systematics for the organization of turn-taking for conversation. *Language*, 50(4), 696–735.

Samuels, G. M., & Ross-Sheriff, F. (2008). Identity, oppression, and power. *Affilia: Journal of Women and Social Work*, 23(1), 5–9.

Scanniello, G., Romano, S., Fucci, D., Turhan, B., & Juristo, N. (2016). Students' and professionals' perceptions of test-driven development: A focus group study. In *Proceedings of the 31st Annual ACM Symposium on Applied Computing* (pp. 1422–1427). New York: ACM.

Scheper-Hughes, N. (1992). *Death without Weeping: The Violence of Everyday Life in Brazil*. Berkeley, CA: University of California Press.

Schulte, C., & Knobelsdorf, M. (2007). Attitudes towards computer science–computing experiences as a starting point and barrier to computer science. In *Proceedings of the Third International Workshop on Computing Education Research (ICER '07)* (pp. 27–38). New York: ACM.

Schutz, A. (1967). *Phenomenology of the Social World*. Evanston, IL: Northwestern University Press.

Scott, R. A. (1969). *The Making of Blind Men: A Study of Adult Socialization.* New York: Russell Sage Foundation.

Searle, K. A., & Kafai, Y. B. (2015). Boys' needlework: Understanding gendered and indigenous perspectives on computing and crafting with electronic textiles. In *Proceedings of the Eleventh Annual International Conference on International Computing Education Research (ICER '15)* (pp. 31–39). New York: ACM.

Shinohara, K., & Tenenberg, J. (2009). A blind person's interactions with technology. *Communications of the ACM*, 52(8), 58–66.

Socha, D., Adams, R., Franznick, K., Roth, W.-M., Sullivan, K., Tenenberg, J., & Walter, S. (2016). Wide-field ethnography: Studying software engineering in 2025 and beyond. In *Proceedings of the 38th International Conference on Software Engineering Companion (ICSE '16)* (pp. 797–802). New York: ACM.

Socha, D., & Tenenberg, J. (2013). Sketching software in the wild. In *Proceedings of the 35th International Conference on Software Engineering (ICSE 2013)* (pp. 1237–1240). New York: IEEE.

Spohrer, J. C., & Soloway, E. (1989). Novice mistakes: Are the folk wisdoms correct? In J. C. Spohrer & E. Soloway (Eds.), *Studying the Novice Programmer* (pp. 401–416). Hillsdale, NJ: Lawrence Erlbaum.

Spradley, J. P. (1979). *The Ethnographic Interview.* Belmont, CA: Wadsworth Cengage Learning.

Spradley, J. P. (1980). *Participant Observation.* Belmont, CA: Wadsworth Cengage Learning.

Stannard, D. E. (1992). *American Holocaust.* New York, NY: Oxford University Press.

Stern, P. C., Dietz, T., Dolšak, N., Ostrom, E., & Stonich, S. (2002). Knowledge and questions after 15 years of research. In E. Ostrom, T. Dietz, N. Dolšak, P. C. Stern, S. Stonich, & E. U. Weber (Eds.), *The Drama of the Commons* (pp. 445–489). Washington, DC: National Academy Press.

Stets, J. E., & Burke, P. J. (2000). Identity theory and social identity theory. *Social Psychology Quarterly*, 63(3), 224–237.

Stewart, D. W., Shamdasani, P. N., & Rook, D. W. (2007). *Focus Groups: Theory and Practice*, 2nd edn. Thousand Oaks, CA: SAGE Publications, Inc.

Strauss, A., & Corbin, J. (1990). *Basics of Qualitative Research: Grounded Theory Procedures and Techniques.* Thousand Oaks, CA: SAGE Publications, Inc.

Suchman, L. (1987). *Plans and Situated Actions: The Problem of Human–Machine Communication.* Cambridge, MA: Cambridge University Press.

Tannen, D. (1989). *Talking Voices: Repetition, Dialogue, and Imagery in Conversational Discourse.* Cambridge, UK: Cambridge University Press.

Tenenberg, J., Fincher, S., Blaha, K., Bouvier, D. J., Chen, T.-Y., Chinn, D., … VanDeGrift, T. (2005). Students designing software: A multi-national, multi-institutional study. *Informatics in Education*, 4(1), 143–162.

Tenenberg, J., Roth, W.-M., Chinn, D., Jornet, A., Socha, D., & Walter, S. (2018). More than the code: Learning rules of rejection in writing programs. *Communications of the ACM*, 61(5), 66–71.

Toombs, A. L., Bardzell, S., & Bardzell, J. (2015). The proper care and feeding of hackerspaces: Care ethics and cultures of making. In *Proceedings of the 33rd Annual ACM Conference on Human Factors in Computing Systems (CHI '15)* (pp. 629–638). New York: ACM.

United States Census Bureau (2016). Facts for Features: American Indian and Alaska Native Heritage Month: November 2016. Retrieved from www.census.gov/newsroom/facts-for-features/2016/cb16-ff22.html

United States Department of Agriculture (n.d.). National School Lunch Program. Retrieved from www.fns.usda.gov/sites/default/files/cn/NSLPFactSheet.pdf

US Department of the Interior Indian Affairs (n.d.). Frequently Asked Questions. Retrieved from www.bia.gov/frequently-asked-questions

Vygotsky, L., edited by Cole M., John-Steiner, V., Scribner, S., & Souberman, E. (1978). *Mind in Society: The Development of Higher Psychological Processes*. Cambridge, MA: Harvard University Press.

Vygotsky, L. (1981). The genesis of higher mental functions. In J. Wertsch (Ed.), *The Concept of Activity in Soviet Psychology* (pp. 144–188). Armonk, NY: Sharpe.

Whyte, W. H. (1980). *The Social Life of Small Urban Spaces*. New York, NY: Project for Public Spaces.

Wittgenstein, L., edited by Hacker P., & Schulte J. (2009). *Philosophical Investigations, 4th edition*. (translated by Anscombe G., Hacker P., & Schulte J.) Malden, MA: Wiley-Blackwell.

Yin, R. K. (2003). *Case Study Research: Design and Methods*, 3rd edn. Thousand Oaks, CA: SAGE Publications, Inc.

8 Learning Sciences for Computing Education

Lauren E. Margulieux, Brian Dorn, and Kristin A. Searle

8.1 Introduction

The learning sciences are an amalgamation of fields that study learning and learning environments. When learning sciences emerged in the 1990s, learning scientists were people who had been training in other disciplinary fields and wanted to apply their skills in multidisciplinary teams to improve learning environments. Some of the fields under the purview of the learning sciences are education, psychology, computer science, educational technology, linguistics, and data analytics. At the time that this book was published, learning scientists were still primarily trained in one of these component disciplines (Yoon & Hmelo-Silver, 2017), though many universities now offer learning-sciences-oriented programs, and some even offer a Masters or PhD in Learning Sciences (Sommerhoff et al., 2018). This shift in training represents a shift in infrastructure for learning sciences work. Many universities have centers for learning sciences in which researchers from various fields can find resources to work together. The professional society, the International Society of the Learning Sciences, was founded in 2002 and organizes annual conferences and supports high-quality publications. Most importantly, learning scientists have developed relationships with places of learning (e.g., K–12 schools, colleges, and museums) so that we can study learning in authentic environments while simultaneously improving the experience of learners right now.

One of the first things that learning scientists discovered when they started working together is that they all have different definitions of learning (Alexander, Schallert, & Reynolds, 2009). Those from cognitive psychology and neuropsychology tend to define learning as a change in the brain – a development of neural architecture and synapses. Those from computer science and educational technology tend to define learning as mastery of a sequence of concepts – a list of rules that build upon each other to allow the learner to understand. Those from education and linguistics tend to define learning as a change in experience – a change in what learners can accomplish and their attitudes about topics or situations, especially as they relate to a sociocultural context. All of these perspectives are considered equal in the learning sciences, and learning scientists intentionally attend to each perspective. For example, a computer scientist might build educational software based on a sequence of concepts that needs to be learned. If the computer scientist was also a learning scientist, they would design the learning experience around how these concepts connect to the existing cognitive architecture that the learner has and the identity, motivations, and experiences of the learner. Taking a learning sciences perspective would mean that to evaluate the software, we need to not only measure how learners progressed through the sequence, but also what they thought as they progressed and how they applied their knowledge outside of the system.

Among various definitions of learning and among various fields that contribute to the learning sciences, there are a few common tenets that define learning science research. Learning sciences research has the following components (derived from Nathan, Rummel, & Hay, 2016, and Nathan & Sawyer, 2014):

- Design of learning environments and practices based on learning theories (see Section 8.2 on theoretical foundations);
- Application-focused basic research, typically involving mixed methods and design-based research (see Section 8.3 on methodology);
- Authentic practices and settings to test hypotheses and build upon learning theories (see Section 8.3 on methodology);
- An engineering ethos to design and develop new practices and resources (see Section 8.4 on project stages).

These tenets emerged from several central, field-building movements. These movements demonstrated the importance of authenticity and interdisciplinarity (Kolodner, 2004), design-based research (Brown, 1992), computer-supported collaborative learning (Stahl, 2005), technology-enhanced learning environments (Pea, 1994), a broad definition of learning (Yoon & Hmelo-Silver, 2017), and accepting only evidence-based findings to build learning theories (Nathan & Sawyer, 2014). From these tenets and movements, some general research foci that learning scientists share include anchoring learning in prior knowledge, the role of expert knowledge in instruction, learning through social interaction, designing to scaffold levels of understanding, and designing technological supports for knowledge building (Sawyer, 2014).

8.1.1 Learning Sciences and Computing Education: Twins Separated at Birth

The learning sciences and computing education can trace their roots back to a related field: cognitive science. Cognitive science emerged in the 1960s from a combination of fields (see Chapter 9). The two that are relevant here are cognitive psychology and computer science. As these fields grew together, they forged a connection between how humans learn and how machines learn. Herb Simon's group was among the first groups of researchers to model human cognition using computers by making analogies between the human brain and computing processes (Newell & Simon, 1972). By the early 1990s, the field had made great progress in understanding how humans and machines learned, creating learning theories and the foundations of artificial intelligence.

Around this time, a group led by Roger Schank and then Janet Kolodner started to become disillusioned with the epistemology followed in cognitive science. For example, during the late 1980s and early 1990s, John Anderson developed a cognitive tutor to teach LISP and ultimately proposed the ACT-R theory (seen also in Chapter 9), concluding that human problem-solving boiled down to the mastery and aggregation of problem-solving rules. Anderson (1996) stated that learning to solve problems was simply the sum of its parts, but there were a lot of parts. The first learning scientists, in contrast, argued that this view of learning and the research in cognitive science were too sterile to be applied to authentic learning. Authentic learning includes not only cognitive factors, but also the environment, the instructor, fellow learners, personal attitudes and beliefs, and use of technology (Kolodner, 2004). Therefore, the learning sciences broke from the traditions in cognitive science of highly controlled experiments in lab settings to embrace new practices of application-minded design experiments that are less controlled (and less scientifically rigorous), but more generalizable to authentic learning environments (Hoadley, 2004).

The balance in the learning sciences between the scientific study of learning and the design of environments to support learning is similar to the balance that computing education has embraced since the late 1960s (see Chapter 1). Some computing education researchers from then until now would be considered learning scientists, whether they would describe themselves that way or not. Computer scientists in computing education bring a valuable skill set to the learning sciences – the skills to design and develop learning technologies and environments to support learning. For example, Papert (1980) used Logo, a programming language that allows users to draw with a turtle and makes it easier for the learner to map between the written program and the output, as a technological tool to teach math and problem-solving skills. His work expanded our knowledge of how children learn using an authentic environment that still echoes in how we teach children programming today. Many introductory programming experiences still use drawing with a turtle (e.g., Code.org and PencilCode), and Logo informed the development of Scratch (Maloney et al., 2004; Resnick & Ocko, 1990), the most widely used and researched programming environment for children in primary school (e.g., Kafai & Burke, 2014). The aspect of Papert's work that qualifies it as learning sciences work is that it drew attention to the multitude of epistemological approaches to programming (Turkle & Papert, 1990), emphasizing the importance of social context, including culture, and personal attitudes toward learning a discipline.

Despite overlapping values and some overlapping researchers between computing education and the learning sciences, the two fields have not been as integrated as would be beneficial (Almstrum et al., 2005; Robins, 2015). Computing education researchers tend to focus primarily on developing and evaluating the instruction and tools used in computing education without emphasizing the context of learning (e.g., social factors or personal beliefs) or making connections to more general theories of learning. Of course, there are exceptions (e.g., Ben-David Kolikant & Ben-Ari, 2008; Guzdial & Tew, 2006), but this focus limits the generalizability of computing education research. Without examining the context of learning, educators who want to implement the instruction or tools in their own learning environments have very little information about how to be successful. In contrast, learning scientists focus more broadly on the design of the learning environment and emphasize development of knowledge about mechanisms and theories of learning, sometimes while contributing only shallowly to discipline-specific education knowledge. These differences play to each group's skills, but both sets of skills are valuable in both fields.

In recent decades, computing education and the learning sciences have made significant steps toward integration. Computing education research has more diligently incorporated learning theory, use of mixed methods, and testing with rigorous statistical analyses (Lishinski et al., 2016; Malmi et al., 2014), which are all common in learning sciences research. In turn, computing education, especially around computational thinking, has become present in learning sciences conferences and journals more regularly (e.g., Margulieux et al., 2016; Orton et al., 2016). Both fields are taking on issues related to equity and bias, particularly concerning learners who are of color, female, from low socioeconomic status families, or with limited access to resources (see Chapter 16 on equity and diversity). This reciprocal relationship benefits both fields and should continue to grow. This chapter provides an introduction to the theories, methods, and practices of the learning sciences, particularly as they relate to computing education, to help those who are unfamiliar with the learning sciences discover the connections between these fields.

8.2 Theoretical Foundations

In this section, we introduce some of the underlying **theoretical** foundations of the learning sciences to discuss what the computing education research community can learn about theory from the learning sciences. The four theories discussed here have long histories of empirical work and represent major components of learning and learning environments. Constructivism addresses how learners cognitively build knowledge; cognitive apprenticeship addresses how instruction scaffolds learners' emerging skills and knowledge; sociocultural theory addresses the social and environmental aspects of learning environments; and expectancy-value theory addresses the role of motivation in learning. Of course, these components do not exist in isolation in the learning environment, and similarly, these theories interact with each other. We will discuss these interactions at the end of this section.

8.2.1 Constructivism

Constructivism is a commonly used theory, both inside and outside of computing education (see Chapters 11 and 15), about how people cognitively acquire knowledge. In essence, constructivism states that people learn best when they construct knowledge for themselves rather than being told explicitly what to know and how to learn it (Tobias & Duffy, 2009). There is a lot to unpack in that definition. "Construct knowledge for themselves" means that learners are making sense of new information through reasoning and invoking their prior knowledge rather than being told how to interpret and organize new information, as is common in more direct instruction (i.e., instruction in which the instructor explicitly tells the students everything that they need to know). It also means that students are learning concepts and skills through exploration that is guided by an instructor but not prescribed by an instructor, as it would be in more direct instruction. The instructor can still have learning objectives, but there are multiple paths to achieve them. In the definition, "learn best" has several different meanings. It means that constructivist approaches help learners perform better on tasks and tests by increasing their depth of thought and connections to prior knowledge, resulting in better retention and transfer of knowledge (Bruner, 1973; see more about transfer in Chapter 9). It also means improving motivation and emotion by increasing student agency in learning and helping them connect knowledge to their lives (Searle & Kafai, 2015).

The theory of constructivism stems from Piaget's work in cognitive development (as described in Chapter 9). Constructivism became refined, popularized, and applied to instructional strategy in Vygotsky's and Bruner's work starting in the 1960s (as stated in Chapter 10). Unlike the author of Chapter 10, who believes that current work on constructivist pedagogy is nonscientific, the authors of this chapter would call this work scientific even though it does not meet the standards of control found in the hard sciences. We are hardly the first group of people to disagree on this topic. The debate between constructivist and direct instructionist pedagogies reached its peak in the 2000s when Kirschner, Sweller, and Clark (2006) published a paper arguing that all types of minimally guided and unguided learning, which roughly equates to approaches that are fundamentally aligned with constructivism, have not been as effective as direct instruction. Hmelo-Silver, Duncan, and Chinn (2007) and Schmidt, Loyens, van Gog, and Paas (2007) published papers in response to make counterarguments that constructivist learning methods are effective when sufficient guidance is provided by the instructor to the student. In turn, Sweller, Kirschner, and Clark (2007) responded with criticisms of the scientific validity of their evidence, leading to a book edited by Tobias and Duffy (2009) that includes authors from both sides of the debate and allowed them to criticize and respond to the arguments in each other's chapters.

At the center of this debate is a fundamental difference in the definition of learning. The direct instructionists view learning as a change in the brain caused by the storage of new information, and they therefore argue that direct instruction is the most efficient and easiest method for learning. The constructivists view learning as a change in knowledge that is not worth much without a concomitant change in professional skills (e.g., solving authentic problems) and soft skills (e.g., working collaboratively). The latter is much harder to study in true experiments than the former, leading to criticism of scientific rigor by the direct instructionists. Constructivists argued, however, that scientific rigor is not worth research that is conducted in sterile environments (i.e., labs) that are fundamentally different from the authentic environments (e.g., classrooms) in which the research will be applied (discussed further in Section 8.3.1 on design-based research; Brown, 1992). As with most debates, many researchers and educators fall in the middle, recognizing the contributions of both types of instruction and treating them as two ends of a spectrum. Therefore, instruction can be more direct or more constructive depending on the needs of the learner and what is most appropriate. For example, when novice programmers are first introduced to Java, they will likely learn more efficiently by being told exactly how to write an assignment statement than they will from being asked to come up with their own ideas about how to write an assignment statement. This type of instruction will likely lead to more shallow learning than a less direct approach, but the balance between depth of knowledge and learning efficiency must be considered. If the Java learners were already experienced with Python, though, using less direct instruction and a constructivist activity to scaffold the connection between new Java knowledge to prior Python knowledge will likely help them to learn Java more deeply without significantly impacting efficacy. A core question in the research on constructivism – and learning sciences more generally – is how much guidance is optimal to support learning.

This section only scratches the surface of constructivism as a theory and the instructional strategies that are based upon it, but there are many other places in this book to learn more, especially in the context of computing education.

- Chapter 1 discusses Papert's work on constructionism. Constructionism and constructivism are related, but they are not the same and should not be used interchangeably. Constructionism is based upon constructivism, but it stipulates that the learner should externally construct artifacts to aid the internal construction of knowledge structures.
- Chapter 9 discusses some of the cognitive science theories that relate to constructivism.
- Chapters 24 and 29 discuss the critical social aspects of constructivist pedagogies.

8.2.2 Cognitive Apprenticeship

Early work in the learning sciences drew inspiration from a variety of places, including non-school environments where successful learning has been taking place for centuries. Collins, Brown, and Newman (1989) noted that the vast majority of learning throughout history was structured as a relationship between a master, who is an expert in the domain knowledge and skills to be learned, and an apprentice, who aspires to become a master. The apprentice learns through observation and deliberate practice under the guidance of the master. Tasks are sequenced to gradually increase in complexity in line with the apprentice's emerging skills. Traditional apprenticeships are often associated with trades like carpentry or midwifery, but many academic private tutoring models share similar properties.

There are two primary challenges with apprenticeship-style learning when viewed in a modern school context (Collins & Kapur, 2014; Lave & Wenger, 1991). First, traditional apprenticeships rely on a small student–teacher ratio with one master supervising at most a handful of apprentices at any one time. This level of individualized attention is impractical in a typical classroom setting, and thus it is easy to see how schools evolved direct instruction pedagogies to address the scale of universal education. Secondly, the knowledge and skills acquired in a traditional apprenticeship are narrowly scoped to one specific work domain. The goal of developing generalizable knowledge and skills that is central to modern education seems, at first glance, incompatible with apprentice-style pedagogy (for more information about knowledge transfer, see the transfer section of Chapter 9).

Cognitive apprenticeship was proposed as a means to integrate the successful practices of traditional apprenticeships with the more general knowledge and cognitive skills sought by traditional school settings (Collins, Brown, & Newman, 1989). This approach to orchestrating a learning environment holistically considers four unique components: content, method, sequence, and sociology (Collins & Kapur, 2014). *Content* in this sense is concerned not only with domain knowledge, but also with the heuristic strategies used by experts within the domain to solve problems, the metacognitive control strategies used to monitor one's progress while completing a task, and the more general strategies to learn new things.

A myopic focus on domain knowledge in a learning environment often leaves tacit these strategic components of content, and cognitive apprenticeships seek to avoid this by externalizing both novice and expert strategies explicitly in the learning environment. A hallmark of a cognitive apprenticeship is employing a variety of pedagogical *methods* to synergistically achieve this goal. Expert modeling is used by a teacher to demonstrate a particular task while voicing one's inner thought process for direct observation by the learners. While modeling often precedes the learner's attempt at a task, learning sciences researchers continue to research when and how to model tasks for maximum impact (see Section 8.2.2.1 on productive failure). A variety of coaching techniques are employed by the instructor as students carry out tasks, and the instructor provides scaffolding (Wood, Bruner, & Ross, 1976) artifacts to aid learners along the way. Also central to cognitive apprenticeships is that learners engage in deliberately articulating their knowledge and reasoning, and they have multiple opportunities to reflect on how their approaches compare to those of the experts and other learners. Lastly, learners are encouraged to engage in independent exploration of the problem space. It is important to distinguish this exploration from the type of completely unstructured inquiry criticized by Kirschner, Sweller, and Clark (2006), as described in the previous section. The other strategies must be used carefully in concert to help guide the learning and mitigate demands on a learner's working memory during exploration (Hmelo-Silver, Duncan, & Chinn, 2007).

Consistent with Vygotsky's constructivist Zone of Proximal Development (1978), cognitive apprenticeship learning environments consider the careful *sequencing* of learning activities to increase the task complexity and diversity of skill learners develop alongside their growing abilities. Additionally, considering global skills (rather than local skills) first helps orient the learner toward the big-picture tasks to be addressed (Collins & Kapur, 2014). Scaffolding can be provided to abstract away the local skills early on, and learners gradually see more detail as they progress.

Lastly, these learning environments embrace the *socially embedded* and cooperative nature of learning seen in traditional apprenticeship environments. Content is situated in real-world contexts and explored by communities of learners (see Section 8.2.3 of this chapter) while fostering learners' intrinsic motivation (see Chapter 28 of this volume).

At a high level, the elements of cognitive apprenticeship outlined here stake out the multifaceted and holistic research endeavor that is the learning sciences. Each component, like instructor modeling and coaching techniques, learner self-explanation/reflection, and social influences on learning, carries with it a rich body of knowledge and a set of ongoing open research questions to be explored empirically. Indeed, many of these ideas are only just now finding their way into the computer science education researcher literature (see, e.g., Morrison, Decker, & Margulieux, 2016, and Section 8.4 of this chapter), but adopting the systems-level viewpoint that cognitive apprenticeship suggests may both strengthen the theoretical soundness and practical impacts of our work. In the sub-sections to follow, we explore additional theories that underpin some of the practices of cognitive apprenticeship described here.

8.2.2.1 Productive Failure

Productive failure is a learning design that formalizes the process of learning from one's mistakes. Most productive failure research has been carried out in math and science contexts in which many problems have canonical solutions, but a growing body of literature examines how to design for productive failure in less-structured contexts, including computing and engineering tasks, such as debugging. Productive failure has four central mechanisms: activating learners' prior knowledge and experience; drawing attention to critical features of the concept; elaborating on critical features; and integrating critical features into a unified understanding of the targeted concept (http://manukapur.com/productive-failure/). These four interrelated mechanisms are embedded in two phases: a generation phase and a consolidation phase (Kapur, 2015; Kapur & Bielaczyc, 2012). Learners first work in small groups to generate and explore multiple representations and solution methods (RSMs) to an ill-structured problem that is beyond their current problem-solving abilities. Thus, prior knowledge is activated, but failure is encountered because the problem is beyond learners' current problem-solving abilities. In the second phase, the RSMs generated by the learners are compared and contrasted with canonical RSMs and learners consolidate knowledge, integrating the solutions they generated with the targeted concepts. Ultimately, learners who initially experienced failure when faced with an ill-structured problem are better equipped to solve a well-structured problem as well as subsequent ill-structured problems (Kapur, 2008). Further, the more solutions generated in the first generation and exploration phase, the more knowledge gained, in what Kapur (2015) has called the solution generation effect. Over a series of studies, Kapur and colleagues (2008, 2012, 2014, 2015) have shown similar levels of procedural fluency to direct instruction, in addition to significantly better gains in terms of conceptual knowledge and knowledge transfer (Collins & Kapur, 2014).

8.2.3 Sociocultural Theory

In addition to many theoretical approaches embraced by learning scientists that focus on individual-level cognitive factors, sociocultural theories of learning take a situative perspective on learning. They emphasize learning as an activity that is embedded within social, cultural, and historical context and occurs in interaction with others and with available tools and resources. Sociocultural theory is not a single theory, but rather a group of theories largely growing out of the work by Russian psychologists, including Vygotsky, Luria, and Leont'ev (Sannino, Daniels, & Gutierrez, 2009). Sociocultural theories emphasize the importance of studying learning in real-world contexts rather than laboratories and are uniquely suited to addressing issues of power and equity in learning environments (Esmonde, 2017). Due to space constraints, here we address situated learning (Lave & Wenger, 1991) and activity theory (Engeström, 1987; Greeno & Engeström, 2014).

Exploring professional communities in tailoring, butchering, midwifery, and other trades, Lave and Wenger (1991) argued that learning occurs as an individual moves from being on the edges of a community (legitimate peripheral participation) to more full participation in a community of practice. A community of practice can be understood as a group of people who have in common some form of "practice" such as a type of work or a hobby (Wenger, 1998). As learners move from legitimate peripheral participation to fuller participation in the community, they begin to act like a member of that community, understanding what constitutes community membership, what members of the community do, and how members of the community talk and interact with others, both inside and outside of the community. In other words, learners begin to identify with that community. In such a view, learning *is* identity construction. As learners become full-fledged participants in a community of practice (an academic discipline), they take up new habits and practices associated with that group of people.

In computing education, ideas of legitimate peripheral participation and communities of practice matter in terms of both recognizing the social, cultural, and historical contexts in which computing is situated (Margolis & Fisher, 2002; Margolis et al., 2008) and providing opportunities for learners to take on the identity of a computer scientist (see Chapter 16). For instance, there is a body of work that examines scaffolding computing education for novices by providing a context for doing computing (Cooper & Cunningham, 2010; Guzdial, 2003, 2010) and fostering opportunities for learners to work together (Porter et al., 2013). Another significant strand of computing education research focuses on addressing the "identity gaps" that exist for women and non-dominant individuals entering into computer science (Tan et al., 2013) and finding ways to mitigate those through more approachable introductions to programming, such as storytelling (Kelleher, Pausch, & Kiesler, 2007), game design (Kafai, 1995), and fashion (Kafai et al., 2014).

Like situated learning, activity theory emphasizes the study of learning at the level of activity systems (e.g., a small group of students working together or an individual learner interacting with tools and materials to make something). Activity systems are composed of interactions between a subject (or group of subjects), an object or overarching goal, and the available tools and resources (Vygotsky, 1978). Further, "tools are created and transformed during the development of the activity itself and carry with them a particular culture – the historical evidence of their development" (Kaptelinin & Nardi, 2006). In this way, tools represent an accumulation of social knowledge and its transmission. For example, if we look at laptop computers or tools for teaching computing to young children, the tools themselves represent an accumulation of knowledge about where, when, and how the tool is used in an activity. Individuals or groups of individuals learn at least some of this knowledge through interaction with the tool.

Engeström's (1987) cultural-historical activity theory (CHAT) further elaborated Vygotsky's model of an activity system to include subject, object, instruments, rules, community, and division of labor. Learning within an activity system is not about individual identity shifts, as is the case in a situated learning perspective, but rather about how the practices of the system as a whole change as a result of a conflict within the system and how that change was accomplished. Further, effective change, according to Engeström, requires an expanded understanding of the object that takes into account both temporal (taking a long view) and socio-spatial elements (Engeström & Sannino, 2010). Activity theory is particularly prevalent in human–computer interaction (Kaptelinin & Nardi, 2006) as a way to understand the role of technology within meaningful activities.

8.2.4 Expectancy-Value Theory

Related to sociocultural theory, much research in learning sciences includes motivational factors, such as learner experience, attitude, values, dispositions, mindsets, and identity. Much more about these factors can be found in Chapter 28. In this section, which is intended to give high-level overviews of theory, we will describe one popular theory of motivation: expectancy-value theory.

Expectancy-value theory is a motivation theory to explain choice, persistence, and performance. Originally developed outside of an education context, it expanded into education in the 1980s with work by Eccles (1983, 1987). It continues to be a prominent theory for motivation in education today (Wigfield, Tonks, & Klauda, 2009). Expectancy-value theory is primarily applied in K–12 education, but no research suggests that age or developmental stage impacts the predictive value of the theory (Wigfield & Eccles, 2000).

The two components of expectancy-value theory, unsurprisingly, are a learner's expectancy and subjective task value. Expectancy is a learner's belief about whether they can produce a successful outcome for a task. Task value is a learner's subjective assessment of the value of the success or failure of a task's outcome. Task value has four components: attainment value or importance (i.e., importance for self, identity, or community), intrinsic value (i.e., interest and enjoyment), utility value (i.e., usefulness), and cost (i.e., time to achieve, effort to achieve, emotional and physical toll, and trade-off with other valued alternatives; e.g., spending nights at college courses or with family) (Wigfield, 1994).

Expectancy and value interact with each other to predict motivation. When expectancy and value are both high, the learner is highly motivated to successfully complete the task. When expectancy and value are both low, the learner is unmotivated to complete the task. When expectancy and value do not match, they can interact with each other in interesting ways to affect motivation.

- When expectancy is high but task value is low, motivation will generally be low unless task value increases. In some cases, high expectancy can increase the task value, especially for intrinsic value, which is related to enjoyment and interest.
- When task value is high but expectancy is low, motivation will generally be low unless task value is extremely high or expectancy increases. In some cases, low expectancy can decrease the task value by changing subjective evaluation of any of the four components of value (e.g., decrease intrinsic interest or decrease perceived usefulness).

Most interventions related to expectancy-value theory aim to increase motivation, and ultimately achievement, by increasing expectancy or increasing task value, especially by decreasing cost and increasing utility by connecting learning to students' lives (Blackwell, 2002; Blackwell, Trzesniewski, & Dweck, 2007; Hulleman & Harackiewicz, 2009; Wigfield & Eccles, 2000). Though expectancy-value theory seems highly relevant to computing education, it has largely not been used to predict motivation in computing education. More about motivation in computing education can be found in Chapter 28.

8.2.5 Summary

In this section, we have introduced four theories that are part of the foundation of learning sciences work. It is not uncommon to find one or more of these theories discussed in a learning sciences paper, even if the main contribution of the paper does not expand upon them. These theories, and others like them, feed into each other. For example, constructivism is a theory about the nature of knowledge and how learners build knowledge, and it influences how instruction and learning are implemented in cognitive apprenticeship. Both theories aim to predict the types of scaffolding that help students learn and perform well. Sociocultural theories consider this cognitive development of knowledge and skill as one aspect of the learning environment and examine the impact of social, cultural, and historical context on performance and other critical components of learning, such as a change in identity or experience. Cognitive, social, cultural, and historical components of learning both impact and are impacted by expectancy and value – the parts of expectancy-value theory – and contribute to motivation. Therefore, learning sciences research considers these interwoven connections among theories to design learning environments and the methods used to evaluate them.

8.3 Methodology

In this section, we explore common **methodology** used in the learning sciences to discuss what computing education research can learn about methods from the learning sciences. The methods used in learning sciences research are as diverse as the fields that contribute to it. Much like in computing education research, it is common in conferences and journals to find all kinds of research designs (see Chapter 4) that are analyzed with both qualitative (see Chapter 7) and quantitative (see Chapters 5 and 6) approaches. The most frequently used methods in the learning sciences reflect the origins of the field. This means that researchers pay attention to different definitions of learning and measure both the process of learning (i.e., the experience during and the steps of learning) and the product of learning (i.e., the change in knowledge or experience caused by learning). Research methods and measurements in the learning sciences also make sure to capture the learning environment and its effects. The environment includes features of the immediate surroundings, such as teachers, peers, technology, room, and time, in addition to the more abstract context, such as culture, identity, and family and friend relationships. Not every learning sciences study measures all of these environmental factors, but they do recognize and consider the potential impact that environment might have on the results.

8.3.1 Design-Based Research

A particularly common research method that is used to capture the complexities in learning sciences research is design-based research (DBR). DBR is an evolving research methodology with origins in design experiments (Brown, 1992; Collins, 1992) that is well suited and increasingly used in computing education research (Kelly et al., in press; Shapiro et al., 2017). Using a DBR protocol, a team of researchers will identify a learning problem and potential solution. The learning problem could be a social problem, such as underrepresentation of certain groups in computing; a motivation problem, such as students dropping out of certain types of classes; a knowledge problem, such as students performing poorly on assignments; a cultural problem, such as students (or their teachers) not identifying as someone who could do well in computing; and much more. The team will then identify a group of learners, such as a classroom of students, who are representative of the population that experiences the learning problem. The team will then develop an intervention to address the problem that is specifically designed for the selected group of learners. If the intervention does not work as intended at first, the team will adjust it and iterate as needed. Once the intervention has successfully addressed the learning problem for the first group of learners, the team will identify a new group of learners and adapt and iterate the intervention until it works for the next group. Through several iterations, the team eventually develops an intervention that addresses the learning problem for the entire population of interest.

DBR is based on several ontological viewpoints. First, DBR is rooted in the premise that cognition is inseparable from context, and therefore it is used to design new kinds of learning environments and to research their implementation in the complexity of real-world settings. Second, it is based on the stance that to understand the effect of a variable, that variable must be manipulated while the effects are measured. Therefore, DBR is explicitly interventionist. As a result of these two viewpoints, DBR interventions are studied in design experiments that are positioned to balance the internal validity of experiments, in which researchers attribute differences among groups to the intervention, and the ecological validity of naturalistic settings, in which the manipulated intervention might not be implemented as planned, but the context represents a real learning environment. By working within this balance, DBR is particularly useful for helping researchers to develop theories that explain why something is happening, the conditions under which a particular type of learning or interaction can take place, and the ways in which an individual's mind interacts with the environment and available tools. As a result, DBR sees interventions that change features of environments, activities, or tools as part of the process to be studied.

Studying the process of design experiments in crucial because DBR is both *prospective* and *reflective*. Designs are initially implemented based upon some hypothesized learning trajectory and means of supporting it through a particular design or design feature. However, as the design is implemented, new features of the environment emerge as salient, and both design and implementation may be refined. As a result, iteration is necessary in design to allow designers and researchers to deal with multiple aspects of a learning ecology (Brown, 1992; Collins, 1992). Both design and research take place through cycles of design, implementation, analysis, redesign, re-implementation, and analysis. Therefore, methods and measurements must be able to document all of these phases in order to adequately capture the dynamics of the learning ecology (Cobb et al., 2003).

To capture these dynamic components, DBR uses a collection of methodological approaches that share some common features (Barab & Squire, 2004; Cobb et al., 2003; Design-Based Research Collective, 2003; Edelson, 2002).

DBR has two goals that are intertwined: the design of learning environments and the development of pedagogical theories. This means that theories are often mid-level and populations are typically more narrow than in psychological research. For example, instead of attempting to create a theory-based intervention that would work for all novice programmers, as psychological research would, DBR would focus on ninth- or tenth-grade novice programmers in a particular region or using a particular curriculum. As Cobb et al. (2003) elaborate, "Rather than grand theories of learning that may be difficult to project into particular circumstances, design experiments tend to emphasize an intermediate theoretical scope (DiSessa, 1991) that is located between a narrow account of a specific system (e.g., a particular school district, a particular classroom) and a broad account that does not orient design to particular contingencies" (p. 11). Theories developed through DBR must do real work in the world, facilitating sharing with practitioners and other designers while improving educational outcomes for participants. As Hermes, Bang, and Marin (2012) articulate in thinking through an Ojibwe language revitalization project, "DBR ... has the affordance of engaging educational researchers in developing immediate solutions for critical, timely, and practical problems in education" (p. 384).

By focusing on design, DBR positions itself to focus on innovation. Edelson (2002) argues that one of the main benefits of DBR is that it puts researchers in real learning situations with a somewhat open-ended focus on improvement, opening the door to learn unique lessons and developing original interventions. In other words, much DBR demands a break from business as usual in classrooms, schools, and other educational contexts. For this reason, DBR research must have buy-in from everyone who is invested in the educational context. DBR is typically carried out by teams of researchers working in partnership with administrators, teachers, students, parents, and other community members. It also demands active, engaged participation from the team of researchers to refine theories and measurement as the work progresses.

If creating real change within educational contexts in a relatively rapid time period is one of DBR's greatest strengths, it is also one of its greatest weaknesses. The theories and designs generated through DBR are often critiqued as being too formative in nature, the timescale too condensed (Barab, 2014). Further, in spite of its focus on situating learning in context, DBR has been relatively silent about the roles that culture and sociohistorical context play in schooling and design more generally. Ironically, "the lessons involved in DBR often uncover the sociohistoric foundations in which learning, education, and language are deeply entrenched" (Hermes et al., 2012, p. 384). In other words, while DBR has not historically focused on issues of culture and power, these sociohistoric issues are uncovered as a result of DBR.

8.3.2 Lessons to Learn from DBR for Computing Education Research

DBR is very relevant to computing education research, and computing education research is well suited to using DBR (see Section 8.4). Aligned with the goals of DBR, computing education research often focuses on innovation. With a relatively short history, learning environments in computing are open to changes in instruction and tools. Moreover, researchers in computing education often have interdisciplinary backgrounds and form teams to aggregate expertise around a research question. Perhaps the most important shared feature between DBR and computing education research in general is that it is conducted in authentic learning environments with students who are learning computing.

Given that computing education research is conducted in authentic learning environments, often computing courses, it is important that the community recognize the difference between DBR and Scholarship of Teaching and Learning (SOTL). SOTL is the practice of integrating teaching with research about teaching (Hutchings & Schulman, 1999). In SOTL, the instructor of a course will test instructional design, tools, and activities within their own courses and collect data on their efficacy. Though this evidence-based approach is reminiscent of DBR, SOTL focuses on advancing the practice of teaching (Bender & Gray, 1999), while DBR balances advancing the practice of teaching with building learning theory.

DBR, therefore, is in the middle of the spectrum between methods that focus on improving practice, such as SOTL, and methods that focus on building theory, such as psychological research. It maintains this balance by employing experimental methodology, but only as far as it fits within the authentic learning environment. In addition, the research team might include the instructor, but the instructor is not the sole researcher in DBR. In DBR, outside perspectives of the learning environment, especially as an intervention is tested in multiple environments, help to distinguish between generalizable features of the intervention and context-specific features. A larger research team also helps implement multiple methods of collecting and analyzing data. A mixed-methods approach (i.e., using both qualitative and quantitative methods and analyses) is common in DBR because it captures multiple aspects of learning and the environment, which is a central feature of learning sciences work.

DBR is a good neutral point for researchers in computing education who are developing the methods for a study. It will not be the best approach for every research question, but its basic tenets are valuable across many types of projects. Of course, research that is more practically driven or more theoretically driven will be more appropriate for some studies, depending on the goals or the strengths of the research team. In any case, though, DBR is a good starting point that will push the community to think about both the rigor and impact of our research.

8.4 Stages of Learning Sciences Projects

We have introduced the learning sciences as a field that embraces constructivist pedagogies, values holistic exploration of learning environments, and engages in design innovation in systematic ways to understand and coevolve educational interventions. This often means that **empirical** projects in the learning sciences are made up of four stages: (1) conducting studies to better understand a learning context and its learners; (2) designing initial interventions based on these findings; (3) iterating on the designs based on lessons learned during empirical trials; and (4) scaling up a well-tested intervention beyond the local context in which it was refined to contribute to theory. In this section, we will highlight three recent research projects that are comfortably situated between the learning sciences and computing education communities while also exemplifying these core stages.

Stage 1: Prior to designing something, learning scientists engage in studies that aim to inform the intervention, regardless of whether that intervention is a piece of educational software, a set of classroom activities, or an entire informal learning environment. In addition to a thorough literature search, this exploration includes qualitative and/or quantitative studies that uncover details about the targeted content, the attitudes and dispositions of learners, and other sociotechnical elements in the learning environment. These studies are often motivated by observable opportunities in the world, but might also be theoretically driven.

DiSalvo's early work on the Glitch project illustrates many of these elements. Her work initially sought to explore the relationship between videogame play and participation in undergraduate computing majors, with a particular eye toward differences connected to learners' race and gender (DiSalvo & Bruckman, 2009). This early work identified a curious pattern that young black and Hispanic men were the most frequent game players, despite being traditionally underrepresented in computing fields. Additional studies (DiSalvo & Bruckman, 2010; DiSalvo, Crowley, & Norwood, 2008; DiSalvo, Yardi, & Bruckman, 2011) about the unique gaming attitudes, play practices, and cultural values of young African American men directly shaped the initial Glitch Game Tester program. The intervention competitively engaged participants as beta-testers for forthcoming games related to their passions while learning about programming so that they could provide more actionable bug reports to the professional developers (DiSalvo et al., 2013). The extensive formative work to understand the important variables and opportunities for the learners was a crucial element in ensuring the experience was both effective and perceived as authentic.

Stage 2: Having distilled insights about the design space from prior literature and formative studies, the learning scientist then seeks to reify these observations in a way that will positively impact one or more aspects of the learning environment. Consistent with DBR practices, initial interventions are often collaboratively devised by teams of researchers and teachers with the intent of being deployed in a particular educational context. Generalizability is not of great concern at this stage, but rather the goal is to pilot a proof of concept for the intervention and explore the pros and cons of its affordances for learning.

The work of Shapiro and colleagues on BlockyTalky provides a helpful example of this second stage. Their initial explorations around learning environments involving creative engineering tasks raised questions about what and how we assess student learning in these settings (Deitrick, O'Connell, & Shapiro, 2014). They then created a programming environment and physical computing platform called BlockyTalky, which provide a rich toolkit for the creation of projects using distributed computational elements while also abstracting away technical details like network protocols and explicit data transfer between computational nodes. The initial version was piloted in a computer music summer camp experience in which middle school students designed and built novel musical instruments (Deitrick et al., 2015; Shapiro et al., 2017). These early deployments of BlockyTalky sought to explore both the affordances of the technical system and also the rich creative and social learning environment in which it was used. For example, distributed cognition theory (Deitrick et al., 2015) was used as a lens to understand how knowledge is shared, offloaded, and transformed in the classroom.

Stage 3: As indicated in the discussion of DBR, learning scientists regularly engage in the iterative refinement of an intervention in order to "get it right" in the desired context. Rarely (if ever) do initial deployments meet all of the design objectives, and both empirical data and formative feedback from project stakeholders are vital in making improvements. At this stage, the context of the investigation might still be quite limited, focusing on a single teacher's class or a single institution. Alternatively, researchers might explore deployment in a handful of carefully selected contexts. The overarching goal is to carefully hone the intervention over time while collecting evidence about its effectiveness in particular contexts. Some efforts also engage in initial theory-building work at this stage so as to begin rising above a particular context.

Continuing the prior example, work on BlockyTalky demonstrates how the research team has iterated to expand the system's capabilities and its applicability to a much wider range of making tasks beyond musical computing. Subsequent iterations explored its use in more general makerspace classrooms while also refining the pedagogical practices and classroom routines employed while students create their projects (Deitrick, Shapiro, & Gravel, 2016; Kelly et al., in press). Formative feedback from learners and facilitators highlighted important and unexpected downsides of abstracting network communication, and new versions of BlockyTalky feature language structures that are more explicit about the flow of control between decentralized components to help learners better understand where and when their code is executing (Kelly et al., in press). At the same time, the researchers have identified opportunities to provide BlockyTalky integration with the rich set of computational tools that were also being used by their partner teachers and students, thus spurring ongoing development work.

Stage 4: Once learning scientists have found an effective intervention, they turn their attention to generalization. Generalization can take many forms, such as scaling up in similar learning contexts or replicating results with new populations, content, or learning environments. This stage is critical to building theory, but it is often overlooked in learning sciences and computing education research. Many times we do a great job with the first three stages, building a great tool or designing an effective learning environment, but then we move on to the next project before we test the boundaries. This last stage, however, is crucial to the science of learning sciences.

Margulieux and Morrison's work on subgoal labels illustrates one way to approach generalization. Margulieux started exploring the efficacy of subgoal-labeled worked examples in undergraduate programming education in a lab, not a classroom, in order to carefully control the learning environment and learners' prior knowledge (i.e., stage 3) (Margulieux, Guzdial, & Catrambone, 2012). Because participants in the lab would not know anything about programming, she used a block-based programming language and gave participants 30 minutes of instruction at a time, neither of which are typical in undergraduate programming education. When the results of these lab studies were positive, Morrison recommended that they try out subgoal-labeled worked examples in a more authentic environment with real introduction to programming students (Morrison, Margulieux, & Guzdial, 2015). They then went on to replicate their results at three universities, each with unique characteristics, to ensure that their findings would replicate with new populations (Margulieux et al., 2016; Morrison, Decker, & Margulieux, 2016). Morrison, Decker, and Margulieux are continuing their work at the time of writing this chapter to develop subgoal-labeled worked examples for an entire introduction to programming curriculum and to evaluate their efficacy in universities across the USA. By doing so, they are contributing to theory on subgoal learning, cognitive load, and development of problem-solving skills.

8.5 Conclusion

Learning sciences and computing education research have a lot in common, yet the two communities can still learn from each other and benefit from a closer relationship. Computing education researchers should draw from the rich literature, general learning theories, and methodologies that the learning sciences offers to guide our research, increasing the rigor within our community and contributing to education outside of computing. In turn, computing education research can inform big challenges in education, such as cognitive development of skill in other technical and complex disciplines, sociocultural development of identity in disciplines with underrepresentation issues, integration of computing and computational thinking throughout other disciplines, and much more. Perhaps the most pressing problem right now is that computing is becoming ubiquitous, but computing education is not. More connections between computing education researchers and learning scientists would contribute to the integration of computing into the education of other disciplines. Integration with other disciplines not only increases the impact of our work, but also serves to increase computing literacy for everyone.

References

Alexander, P. A., Schallert, D. L., & Reynolds, R. E. (2009). What is learning anyway? A topographical perspective considered. *Educational Psychologist*, 44(3), 176–192.

Almstrum, V. L., Hazzan, O., Guzdial, M., & Petre, M. (2005). Challenges to computer science education research. In *Proceedings of the 36th SIGCSE Technical Symposium on Computer Science Education* (pp. 191–192). New York: ACM.

Anderson, J. R. (1996). ACT: A simple theory of complex cognition. *American Psychologist*, 51(4), 355.

Barab, S. (2014). Design-based research: A methodological toolkit for engineering change. In R. Keith Sawyer (Ed.), *The Cambridge Handbook of the Learning Sciences,* 2nd edn. (pp. 151–170). Cambridge, UK: Cambridge University Press.

Barab, S., & Squire, K. (2004). Design-based research: Putting a stake in the ground. *The Journal of the Learning Sciences*, 13(1), 1–14.

Ben-David Kolikant, Y., & Ben-Ari, M. (2008). Fertile zones of cultural encounter in computer science education. *The Journal of the Learning Sciences*, 17(1), 1–32.

Bender, E., & Gray, D. (1999). The scholarship of teaching. *Research and Creative Activity,* 12(1). Retrieved from www.indiana.edu/~rcapub/v22n1/p03.html

Blackwell, A. F. (2002). First steps in programming: A rationale for attention investment models. In *Human Centric Computing Languages and Environments* (pp. 2–10). Piscataway, NJ: IEEE.

Blackwell, L. S., Trzesniewski, K. H., & Dweck, C. S. (2007). Implicit theories of intelligence predict achievement across an adolescent transition: A longitudinal study and an intervention. *Child Development,* 78(1), 246–263.

Brown, A. L. (1992). Design experiments: Theoretical and methodological challenges in creating complex interventions in classroom settings. *The Journal of the Learning Sciences*, 2(2), 141–178.

Bruner, J. S. (1973). Beyond the information given. In J. M. Anglin (Ed.), *Beyond the Information Given: Studies in the Psychology of Knowing* (pp. 143–175). New York: W.W. Norton & Company.

Cobb, P., Confrey, J., DiSessa, A., Lehrer, R., & Schauble, L. (2003). Design experiments in educational research. *Educational Researcher*, 32(1), 9–13.

Collins, A. (1992). Toward a design science of education. In *New directions in Educational Technology* (pp. 15–22). Berlin, Germany: Springer.

Collins, A., Brown, J. S., & Newman, S. E. (1989). Cognitive apprenticeship: Teaching the crafts of reading, writing, and mathematics. *Knowing, Learning, and Instruction: Essays in Honor of Robert Glaser*, 18, 32–42.

Collins, A., & Kapur, M. (2014). Cognitive apprenticeship. In R. Keith Sawyer (Ed.), *The Cambridge Handbook of the Learning Sciences,* 2nd edn. (pp. 109–127). Cambridge, UK: Cambridge University Press.

Cooper, S., & Cunningham, S. (2010). Teaching computer science in context. *ACM Inroads*, 1(1), 5–8.

Design-Based Research Collective (2003). Design-based research: An emerging paradigm for educational inquiry. *Educational Researcher*, 32(1), 5–8.

Deitrick, E., O'Connell, B., & Shapiro, R. B. (2014). The discourse of creative problem solving in childhood engineering education. In *Proceedings of the International Conference of the Learning Sciences* (pp. 591–598). Boulder, CO: ISLS.

Deitrick, E., Shapiro, R. B., Ahrens, M. P., Fiebrink, R., Lehrman, P. D., & Farooq, S. (2015). Using distributed cognition theory to analyze collaborative computer science learning. In *Proceedings of the Eleventh Annual Conference on International Computing Education Research* (pp. 51–60). New York: ACM.

Deitrick, E., Shapiro, R. B., & Gravel, B. (2016). How do we assess equity in programming pairs? Singapore. In *Proceedings of the International Conference of the Learning Sciences* (pp. 370–7). Singapore: ISLS.

DiSessa, A. A. (1991). Local sciences: Viewing the design of human–computer systems as cognitive science. In J. M. Carroll (Ed.), *Designing Interaction: psychology at the human-computer interface* (pp. 162–202). Cambridge, UK: Cambridge University Press.

DiSalvo, B. J., & Bruckman, A. (2009). Questioning video games' influence on CS interest. In *Proceedings of the 4th International Conference on Foundations of Digital Games* (pp. 272–278). New York: ACM.

DiSalvo, B., & Bruckman, A. (2010). Race and gender in play practices: Young African American males. In *Proceedings of the Fifth International Conference on the Foundations of Digital Games* (pp. 56–63). New York: ACM.

DiSalvo, B. J., Crowley, K., & Norwood, R. (2008). Learning in context: Digital games and young black men. *Games and Culture,* 3(2), 131–141.

DiSalvo, B., Guzdial, M., Meadows, C., Perry, K., McKlin, T., & Bruckman, A. (2013). Workifying games: Successfully engaging African American gamers with computer science. In *Proceedings of the 44th ACM Technical Symposium on Computer Science Education* (pp. 317–322). New York: ACM.

DiSalvo, B., Yardi, S., Guzdial, M., McKlin, T., Meadows, C., Perry, K., & Bruckman, A. (2011). African American men constructing computing identity. In *Proceedings of the SIGCHI Conference on Human Factors in Computing Systems* (pp. 2967–2970). New York: ACM.

Eccles, J. S. (1983). Expectancies, values, and academic behaviors. In J. T. Spence (Ed.), *Achievement and Achievement Motives* (pp. 75–146). San Francisco, CA: Freeman.

Eccles, J. S. (1987). Gender roles and women's achievement-related decisions. *Psychology of Women Quarterly*, 11(2), 135–172.

Edelson, D. C. (2002). Design research: What we learn when we engage in design. *The Journal of the Learning Sciences,* 11(1), 105–21.

Engeström, Y. (1987). *Learning by Expanding*. Cambridge, UK: Cambridge University Press.

Engeström, Y., & Sannino, A. (2010). Studies of expansive learning: Foundations, findings and future challenges. *Educational Research Review*, 5(1), 1–24.

Esmonde, I. (2017). Power and sociocultural theories of learning. In I. Esmonde & A. Booker (Eds.), *Power and Privilege in the Learning Sciences: Critical and Sociocultural Theories of Learning* (p. 6). New York: Routledge.

Greeno, J. G., & Engeström, Y. (2014). Learning in activity. In R. Keith Sawyer (Ed.), *The Cambridge Handbook of the Learning Sciences*, 2nd edn. (pp. 128–150). Cambridge, UK: Cambridge University Press.

Guzdial, M. (2003). A media computation course for non-majors. *ACM SIGCSE Bulletin*, 35(3), 104–108.

Guzdial, M. (2010). Does contextualized computing education help? *ACM Inroads*, 1(4), 4–6.

Guzdial, M., & Tew, A. E. (2006). Imagineering inauthentic legitimate peripheral participation: An instructional design approach for motivating computing education.

In *Proceedings of the Second International Workshop on Computing Education Research* (pp. 51–58). New York: ACM.

Hermes, M., Bang, M., & Marin, A. (2012). Designing Indigenous language revitalization. *Harvard Educational Review*, 82(3), 381–402.

Hmelo-Silver, C. E., Duncan, R. G., & Chinn, C. A. (2007). Scaffolding and achievement in problem-based and inquiry learning: A response to Kirschner, Sweller, and Clark. *Educational Psychologist*, 42(2), 99–107.

Hoadley, C. M. (2004). Methodological alignment in design-based research. *Educational Psychologist*, 39(4), 203–212.

Hulleman, C. S., & Harackiewicz, J. M. (2009). Promoting interest and performance in high school science classes. *Science*, 326, 1410–1412.

Hutchings, P., & Shulman, L. S. (1999). The scholarship of teaching: New elaborations, new developments. *Change: The Magazine of Higher Learning*, 31(5), 10–15.

Kafai, Y. B. (1995). *Minds in Play*. Hillsdale, NJ: Lawrence Erlbaum Associates.

Kafai, Y. B., & Burke, Q. (2014). *Connected Code: Why Children Need to Learn Programming*. Cambridge, MA: MIT Press.

Kafai, Y. B., Lee, E., Searle, K., Fields, D., Kaplan, E., & Lui, D. (2014). A crafts-oriented approach to computing in high school: Introducing computational concepts, practices, and perspectives with electronic textiles. *ACM Transactions on Computing Education (TOCE)*, 14, 1.

Kaptelinin, V., & Nardi, B. A. (2006). *Acting with Technology: Activity Theory and Interaction Design*. Cambridge, MA: MIT Press.

Kapur, M. (2008). Productive failure. *Cognition and Instruction*, 26(3), 379–424.

Kapur, M. (2014). Productive failure in learning math. *Cognitive Science,* 38(5), 1008–1022.

Kapur, M. (2015). The preparatory effects of problem solving versus problem posing on learning from instruction. *Learning and Instruction*, 39, 23–31.

Kapur, M., & Bielaczyc, K. (2012). Designing for productive failure. *Journal of the Learning Sciences*, 21(1), 45–83.

Kelleher, C., Pausch, R., & Kiesler, S. (2007). Storytelling Alice motivates middle school girls to learn computer programming. In *Proceedings of the SIGCHI Conference on Human Factors in Computing Systems* (pp. 1455–1464). New York: ACM.

Kelly, A., Finch, L., Bolles, M., & Shapiro, R.B. (2018). BlockyTalky: New programmable tools to enable students learning networks. *International Journal of Child-Computer Interaction*, 18, 8–18.

Kirschner, P. A., Sweller, J., & Clark, R. E. (2006). Why minimal guidance during instruction does not work: An analysis of the failure of constructivist, discovery, problem-based, experiential, and inquiry-based teaching. *Educational Psychologist*, 41(2), 75–86.

Kolodner, J. L. (2004). The learning sciences: Past, present, and future. *Educational Technology: The Magazine for Managers of Change in Education,* 44(3), 37–42.

Lave, J., & Wenger, E. (1991). *Situated Learning: Legitimate Peripheral Participation*. Cambridge, UK: Cambridge University Press.

Lishinski, A., Good, J., Sands, P., & Yadav, A. (2016). Methodological rigor and theoretical foundations of CS education research. In *Proceedings of the 2016 ACM Conference on International Computing Education Research* (pp. 161–169). New York: ACM.

Malmi, L., Sheard, J., Bednarik, R., Helminen, J., Kinnunen, P., Korhonen, A., … Taherkhani, A. (2014). Theoretical underpinnings of computing education research: what is the evidence? In *Proceedings of the Tenth Annual Conference on International Computing Education Research* (pp. 27–34). New York: ACM.

Maloney, J., Burd, L., Kafai, Y., Rusk, N., Silverman, B., & Resnick, M. (2004). Scratch: A sneak preview [education]. In *Creating, Connecting and Collaborating through Computing.* (pp. 104–109). Piscataway, NJ: IEEE.

Margolis, J., & Fisher, A. (2002). *Unlocking the Clubhouse.* Cambridge, MA: MIT Press.

Margolis, J., Estella, R., Goode, J., Holme, J., & Nao, K. 2008. *Stuck in the Shallow End: Education, Race, and Computing.* Cambridge, MA: MIT Press.

Margulieux, L. E., Guzdial, M., & Catrambone, R. (2012). Subgoal-labeled instructional material improves performance and transfer in learning to develop mobile applications. In *Proceedings of the Ninth Annual International Conference on International Computing Education Research* (pp. 71–78). New York: ACM.

Margulieux, L., Morrison, B. B., Guzdial, M., & Catrambone, R. (2016). Training learners to self-explain: Designing instructions and examples to improve problem solving. In *Proceedings of the International Conference of the Learning Sciences* (pp. 98–105). Singapore: ISLS.

Morrison, B. B., Decker, A., & Margulieux, L. E. (2016). Learning loops: A replication study illuminates impact of HS courses. In *Proceedings of the Twelfth Annual International Conference on International Computing Education Research* (pp. 221–330). New York: ACM.

Morrison, B. B., Margulieux, L. E., & Guzdial, M. (2015). Subgoals, context, and worked examples in learning computing problem solving. In *Proceedings of the Eleventh Annual International Conference on International Computing Education Research* (pp. 21–29). New York: ACM.

Nathan, M. J., Rummel, N., & Hay, K. E. (2016). Growing the learning sciences: Brand or big tent? Implications for graduate education. In M. A. Evans, M. J. Packer, & R. K. Sawyer (Eds.), *Reflections on the Learning Sciences* (pp. 191–209). Cambridge, UK: Cambridge University Press.

Nathan, M. J., & Sawyer, R. K. (2014). Foundations of the learning sciences. In R. Keith Sawyer (Ed.), *The Cambridge Handbook of the Learning Sciences*, 2nd edn. (pp. 21–43). Cambridge, UK: Cambridge University Press.

Newell, A., & Simon, H. A. (1972). *Human Problem Solving.* Englewood Cliffs, NJ: Prentice-Hall.

Orton, K., Weintrop, D., Beheshti, E., Horn, M., Jona, K., & Wilensky, U. (2016). Bringing computational thinking into high school mathematics and science classrooms. In *Proceeding of the International Conference of the Learning Sciences* (pp. 705–712). Singapore: ISLS.

Papert, S. (1980). *Mindstorms: Children, Computers, and Powerful Ideas.* New York: Basic Books, Inc.

Pea, R. D. (1994). Seeing what we build together: Distributed multimedia learning environments for transformative communications. *The Journal of the Learning Sciences*, 3(3), 285–299.

Porter, L., Guzdial, M., McDowell, C., & Simon, B. (2013). Success in introductory programming: What works? *Communications of the ACM,* 56(8), 34–36.

Resnick, M., & Ocko, S. (1990). *LEGO/LOGO – Learning through and about Design.* Cambridge, MA: Epistemology and Learning Group, MIT Media Laboratory.

Robins, A. (2015). The ongoing challenges of computer science education research. *Computer Science Education,* 25(2), 115–119.

Sannino, A., Daniels, H., & Gutiérrez, K. (Eds.) (2009). *Learning and Expanding with Activity Theory*. Cambridge, UK: Cambridge University Press.

Sawyer, R. K. (2014). The future of learning: Grounding educational innovation in the learning science. In R. Keith Sawyer (Ed.), *The Cambridge Handbook of the Learning Sciences,* 2nd edn. (pp. 1–19). Cambridge, UK: Cambridge University Press.

Schmidt, H. G., Loyens, S. M., Van Gog, T., & Paas, F. (2007). Problem-based learning is compatible with human cognitive architecture: Commentary on Kirschner, Sweller, and Clark. *Educational Psychologist*, 42(2), 91–97.

Searle, K. A., & Kafai, Y. B. (2015). Boys' needlework: Understanding gendered and indigenous perspectives on computing and crafting with electronic textiles. In *Proceedings of the Eleventh Annual Conference on International Computing Education Research* (pp. 31–39). New York: ACM.

Shapiro, R. B., Kelly, A., Ahrens, M., Johnson, B., Politi, H., & Fiebrink, R. (2017) Tangible distributed computer music for youth. *The Computer Music Journal*, 41(2), 52–68.

Sommerhoff, D., Szameitat, A., Vogel, F., Chernikova, O., Loderer, K., & Fischer, F. (2018). What do we teach when we teach the learning sciences? A document analysis of 75 graduate programs. *Journal of the Learning Sciences*, 27(2), 319–351.

Stahl, G. (2005). Group cognition in computer-assisted collaborative learning. *Journal of Computer Assisted Learning*, 21(2), 79–90.

Sweller, J., Kirschner, P. A., & Clark, R. E. (2007). Why minimally guided teaching techniques do not work: A reply to commentaries. *Educational Psychologist*, 42(2), 115–121.

Tan, E., Kang, H. O'Neill, T., & Calabrese Barton, A. (2013). Desiring a career in STEM-related fields: How middle school girls articulate and negotiate between their narrated and embodied identities in considering a STEM trajectory. *Journal of Research in Science Teaching,* 50(10), 1143–1179.

Tobias, S., & Duffy, T. M. (Eds.) (2009). *Constructivist Instruction: Success or Failure?* Abingdon, UK: Routledge.

Turkle, S., & Papert, S. (1990). Epistemological pluralism: Styles and voices within the computer culture. *Signs: Journal of Women in Culture and Society*, 16(1), 128–157.

Vygotsky, L. S. (1978). *Mind in Society*. Cambridge, MA: Harvard University Press.

Wenger, E. (1998). *Communities of Practice: Learning, Meaning, and Identity*. Cambridge, UK: Cambridge University Press.

Wigfield, A. (1994). Expectancy-value theory of achievement motivation: A developmental perspective. *Educational Psychology Review*, 6(1), 49–78.

Wigfield, A., & Eccles, J. S. (2000). Expectancy-value theory of achievement motivation. *Contemporary Educational Psychology*, 25(1), 68–81.

Wigfield, A., Tonks, S., & Klauda, S. L. (2009). Expectancy-value theory. In K. Wentzel & D. Miele (Eds.), *Handbook of Motivation at School* (pp. 55–75). New York: Routledge.

Wood, D., Bruner, J. S., & Ross, G. (1976). The role of tutoring in problem solving. *Journal of Child Psychology and Psychiatry*, 17(2), 89–100.

Yoon, S. A., & Hmelo-Silver, C. E. (2017). What do learning scientists do? A survey of the ISLS membership. *The Journal of the Learning Sciences*, 26(2), 167–183.

9 Cognitive Sciences for Computing Education

Anthony V. Robins, Lauren E. Margulieux, and Briana B. Morrison

9.1 Introduction

Cognitive science is typically defined as the interdisciplinary study of the mind and its processes. The field emerged in the 1950s, driven largely by progress in cognitive psychology and artificial intelligence; see Gardner (1985) for a history. The disciplines usually included within its scope are philosophy, neuroscience, psychology, anthropology, linguistics, and artificial intelligence.

The field of computing education research (CEdR)[1] is an example of discipline-based education research (Singer, Nielsen, & Schweingruber, 2012). It has developed within the context of, and been shaped by, cognitive science and education. **Methodologically**, CEdR shares the tools and methods of enquiry employed within these disciplines (see Chapters 4, 5, 6, and 7). **Empirically**, CEdR has been guided and influenced by what we know about human cognition and learning. During the 1970s through to the 1980s, the emerging CEdR field was characterized by a focus on "the psychology of programming," and it adopted findings such as the limitations of working memory and the importance of the knowledge structures of schemata/plans (see Chapters 1 and 12). **Theoretically**, CEdR adopted paradigms such as cognitivism and (later) constructivism (see Chapters 8, 10, and 15). In recent decades, it has continued adopting and exploring theoretical frameworks like developmental stages, mental models, and cognitive load (Chapter 12).

Arguably, however, research within CEdR would benefit from further and ongoing exploration of foundational cognitive science. In 2005, the Special Interest Group in Computer Science Education (SIGCSE) held a panel discussion on Challenges to Computer Science Education Research. Panelists commented on the "isolation" of CEdR, and that "Too much of the research in computing education ignores the hundreds of years of education, cognitive science, and learning sciences research that have gone before us" (Almstrum et al., 2005). Despite progress since 2005, this criticism remains relevant today. This chapter is intended to be a contribution toward addressing it by summarizing some of the findings of these "hundreds of years" of research as they pertain to human cognition and learning, and by drawing out the implications for CEdR. This is not an easy task, and readers familiar with particular topics

---

1 Frequently used acronyms are listed at the end of the chapter.

will see that we have summarized heavily. We aim to provide an introduction to foundational concepts with a roadmap to the broader literature (Sections 9.2–9.5) and to highlight two areas of particular interest (Sections 9.6 and 9.7).

9.2 Brains, Computers, and Levels of Analysis

In the most general sense, both the brain and the computer process information. In the brain, various patterns of neural activation give rise to emergent phenomena that we experience and describe as sensations, thoughts, memories, and the like. Our memories are made up of overlapping patterns that are approximately recreated in the process of recall, and our reasoning is determined by heuristics, expectations, and mental models of real or imagined worlds. In the computer, a central processor reads and writes binary patterns that we interpret as symbols from and to specified locations in a passive memory. Various sequences of symbolic manipulation give rise to emergent phenomena that we describe as computations, processes, and other forms of output behavior.

Cognitive science generally shares the methods and frameworks of its component disciplines. There is, however, one **theoretical** insight that arose within the field that we should draw attention to: Marr's concept of "levels of analysis" (Marr, 1982; Marr & Poggio, 1976). Marr proposes that explanations of the functioning of information processing systems should consider three distinct but complementary levels: computational, algorithmic, and implementational. The *computational level* describes what the system does, its purpose, and the tasks that it performs. The *algorithmic level* describes the representations and algorithms that the system uses to perform its tasks. The *implementational level* describes how the system is physically implemented. Marr's levels have been variously reinterpreted as semantic, syntactic, and physical, or content, form, and medium (McClamrock, 1991). Figure 9.1 shows the three levels of analysis applied to an example information processing system: a simple calculator.[2]

Without necessarily committing to any particular formulation, the idea of different levels of analysis/description is both general and powerful. A lot of scientific explanation is reductive, accounting for phenomena at one level (e.g., learning) by providing a description at a "lower" level (e.g., storage in long-term memory). Conversely, some of the most interesting phenomena are emergent, where factors at one level (e.g., the behavior of individual students) give rise to interesting properties at a "higher" level (e.g., the complex structures and behaviors of a classroom). Each level of explanation has its uses and each affords a language and a set of concepts that are distinct from, and difficult or impossible to rephrase in, the others. Each level is self-contained but incomplete; in combination, they provide a more thorough understanding. These ideas may come naturally to computing educators given that many of the complex systems

---

2 The CORDIC algorithm(s) used by most calculators were initially developed by Volder (1959).

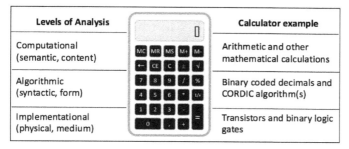

Levels of Analysis		Calculator example
Computational (semantic, content)		Arithmetic and other mathematical calculations
Algorithmic (syntactic, form)		Binary coded decimals and CORDIC algorithm(s)
Implementational (physical, medium)		Transistors and binary logic gates

Figure 9.1 *Levels of analysis and their application to an example system.*

that we use – programming languages, operating systems, applications – make extensive use of multiple layers of abstraction (as discussed in Chapter 17).

CEdR has not in general been explicit about different levels of analysis. Consider two examples of how they might apply. First, a hypothetical student appears to have learned a fact one day, but not the next. A low-level explanation might be the weakening of certain synapses within a hippocampal circuit. A mid-level explanation might identify a failure of recall due to insufficient consolidation of the encoded knowledge during sleep. A high-level explanation might note that the student was highly anxious and not sleeping well. Absent a magic pill for selectively strengthening synapses, the mid- and high-level explanations suggest different kinds of intervention, from explicit consolidation of material, to sleep management techniques, to addressing the underlying anxiety.

For a second example, it is frequently observed in introductory programming courses (when compared to other courses) that a larger-than-usual percentage of the class fails and a larger-than-usual percentage achieves high grades (this is discussed at length in Chapter 12). Historically, one explanation for this phenomenon has been that some individuals simply have an aptitude for programming and some do not – that programmers are "born and not made." The appeal to an innate capacity ("nature" over "nurture") sets this explanation in the high-level framework of evolution. Consideration at this level makes clear the claim's implausibility, as the idea that evolutionary forces can possibly have selected for programming (or some adaptive programming-like analogue) is highly problematic at best. An alternative account attempts to explain the pattern of outcomes using the widely accepted educational observation that we learn "at the edges of what we know." If programming language concepts have unusually structured and interconnected "edges," then early success or failure of learning will lead to momentum toward successful or unsuccessful outcomes over all. Recognizing that this explanation is framed in specific lower-level mechanisms of human learning leads to hypotheses about the nature of the process and testable predictions about programming languages as a domain of knowledge and the crucial importance of the early stages of learning to program (see Robins, 2010, summarized in Chapter 12).

In short, recognizing and making more explicit use of different levels of analysis may be of some benefit to CEdR. The remaining sections of this chapter attempt to summarize research pertaining to human cognition and learning. If at times the material seems to be too "low level" to be of educational use, consider both the popularity of reductive explanations and that we do not know at what level of analysis the most interesting or effective account of a given phenomenon might be found.

9.3 Perception and Attention

Perception is the process by which we as cognitive agents receive, register, and process stimuli from the external world (and from our own bodies). We begin with this low-level process to inform the higher-level process of attention. In perception, the physical or chemical stimulation of sense organs is translated into patterns of neural firing that are conducted by the nervous system to the brain. The classical senses are vision, hearing, touch, taste, and smell. We have far more than five senses, though, including proprioception (our sense of the positions of parts of our body), temperature, balance, vibration, different internal chemoreceptors, and pain.

Each of the senses is a field of study in itself; for overviews, see, for example, Mather (2016) or Goldstein and Brockmole (2016). In educational terms, they suggest a focus on good ergonomics (Smith, 2007) and human–computer interface design, and attention to the obvious issues raised by dealing with sensory impairment and equity of access. While the working of individual senses has generally been regarded as too early a stage of processing to be of significant interest in the educational literature, there has been some focus on "multisensory learning" (e.g., Shams & Seitz, 2008); see Kátai, Juhász, and Adorjáni (2008) for a CEd example.

Sensory processes are not a passive, "bottom-up" delivery of inputs; they are active processes incorporating "top-down" information from higher-level systems. These top-down influences are evident in the kinds of artifacts of processing that cause sensory illusions (particularly visual illusions), in perceptual effects such as grouping and continuity ("Gestalt laws"), in the influence of existing knowledge or current state (e.g., motivation or expectation) on what is perceived, in the use of attention (including consciously mediated attentional focus) to select specific stimuli, and in the subjective experience of a consistent external world that emerges from complex and ever-changing inputs. Top-down effects are discussed in, for example, Gregory (1997), Engel, Fries, and Singer (2001), and Gilbert and Sigman (2007); see also the interesting debate presented in Firestone and Scholl (2016) and the subsequent commentary. An example in CEdR can be found in Hansen, Lumsdaine, and Goldstone (2013), who manipulated the white space (e.g., blank lines) in coding examples, which caused confusion for both experts and novices.

Attention is the ability to select particular information from the vast and continuous array of sensory inputs. The term encompasses a range of complex phenomena, from the preconscious selection of specific stimuli, to overt or covert conscious selection, to the intentional direction of high-level processing ("trains of thought"). The extent to which these are aspects of the same or different underlying cognitive mechanisms is not yet clear. Historically, a central question in research was whether sensory inputs are selected and then interpreted for meaning (called "early selection") or whether they are all interpreted before selection (called "late selection"). In practice, experimental evidence questions either model individually, and some form of compromise appears to be the case (Pashler, 2016, p. 5); see, for example, the influential "feature-integration theory" (Treisman & Gelade, 1980). Attention has been variously conceptualized as: a "spotlight," a visually based model where the spotlight consists of a focus, a margin, and a fringe (e.g., Posner, Snyder, & Davidson, 1980); a "zoom lens," which can trade off the size of the focus and the efficiency of processing (e.g., Eriksen & James, 1986); or the allocation of limited resources such as working memory. One tool used to study attention that has been employed in CEdR is eye-tracking (e.g., Busjahn et al., 2014; Klaus-Dieter, 2018).

In educational terms, the concepts of attention, working memory, and cognitive load are closely related, and all are discussed further below. Beyond the perceptual and core cognitive mechanisms summarized here, "attention" also has a behavioral and clinical interpretation in the guise of attention deficit disorders. These have significant educational and practical impacts (e.g., see Morris, Begel, & Wiedermann, 2015, on challenges within the technical workforce), but are beyond the scope of this review.

9.4 Memory and Learning

Our memories are central to how we understand both the world and ourselves as individuals. Popularly, a memory is some item of information that we are able to recall to mind, but within cognitive science, memory is a general term for a variety of mechanisms, including the *encoding*, *storage*, and *retrieval* of information. The foundations of current views in memory were set out by Atkinson and Shiffrin (1968), who proposed a distinction between different kinds of memory: a "sensory register" (now called sensory memory), a "short-term store" (short-term or working memory), and a long-term store (long-term memory).

The material presented in this section is widely agreed upon, and rather than referencing each claim, the reader is referred to some of the classic and contemporary sources, such as Norman (1970), Baddeley (1999), Tulving and Craik (2000), Baddeley, Eysenck, and Anderson (2015), or Radvansky (2016).

9.4.1 Sensory, Short-Term, and Working Memory

Sensory memory (SM) refers to the automatic and brief retention of sensory phenomena after the stimulus itself is gone. It is usually studied in the visual modality (iconic memory), but also includes hearing (echoic memory) and touch (haptic memory). In typical experiments, humans are able, for a short time after exposure, to recall some details after an image is briefly seen (for less than one second) and then removed. As far as we are aware, SM has not been explored in the context of CEdR.

Short-term memory (STM) refers to the capacity to actively hold a small amount of information in conscious focus for a short period of time (Revlin, 2012, suggests up to 18 seconds). The retention period can be extended with active strategies such as conscious rehearsal.

A "small amount" of information is generally held to be 4 ± 1 items (Cowan, 2001), refining the original famous estimate of 7 ± 2 items by Miller (1956) ("Miller's Law" or the "magical number" of memory). However, this estimate is somewhat complicated by "chunking" – the fact that an item can contain other items. For example, humans are generally able to recall a list of four single-digit numbers (e.g., 3, 7, 2, 9), but they can also recall four multi-digit numbers (72, 123, 18, 446), which between them contain many more digits. The judicious use of chunking (grouping individual pieces of information into a meaningful whole) is central to the efficient use of STM, and it is a strategy that can be taught and learned (see Chapter 27 for further discussion of chunking).

The term *working memory* has been, and often still is, used as a synonym for STM. However, most researchers accept the distinction proposed by Baddeley and Hitch (1974) that STM involves the simple retention of information, while working memory involves additional systems for manipulating this information so as to perform such activities as comprehension, problem-solving, reasoning, and learning. (The systems proposed by Baddeley and Hitch include a central executive, a phonological loop, an episodic buffer, and a visuospatial sketchpad.)

The capacity of working memory is of significant interest – why can we only concentrate on a few things at a time? Suggestions include limitations that arise from the competition for some underlying cognitive resource such as attention, or that active memory items decay or interfere with each other. It is widely accepted that the concepts of attention (the ability to selectively process information) and working memory (the ability to retain information in a useable state) are separate but closely linked (Fougnie, 2008), and that mechanisms such as attentional capture (implicitly or explicitly attending to a specific stimulus) provide inputs to working memory. Deco and Rolls (2005) describe a unifying theory of attention, STM, and action selection.

Programming tasks generally involve working with a lot of information relating to the current state of the data represented and the processes being executed, the overall design and goals of the program, and also the language and tools being used. In order to accomplish this with a limited working memory, programmers must make extensive use of chunking and organizing knowledge structures such as schemata/plans (see below), and they must hold only parts of the overall task/program design in working memory at any given time. We know very little about how this is accomplished, or what individual variations in capacity or strategy exist. Also relevant in this context is the concept of *cognitive load* discussed below.

9.4.2 Long-Term Memory

Both SM and STM have a limited capacity and duration. *Long-term memory* (LTM) is the encoding, storage, and retrieval of large amounts of information for significant periods of time – up to years or a lifetime. At a low level of analysis, learning is the formation of memories through the processes of encoding, storage, and retrieval of information.

The *encoding* of a memory is the process by which the brain alters its structure so as to create a lasting representation of some currently perceived or attended to stimulus or item of information. Different brain regions are involved in the initial stages of encoding for different senses, but creating representations of different kinds of information (in concrete terms, some pattern of neural activation) appears to depend on a common mechanism (changes to the strengths of the synaptic connections between neurons). While the hippocampus and associated structures are involved in the encoding process, the resulting representations are not (in most cases) strongly tied to any particular location in the brain (Tonegawa et al., 2015).

The basic mechanism of encoding was first recognized by Hebb (1949), who proposed that a synaptic connection between two neurons is strengthened when the neurons are active at the same time. While the details are complex (depending on issues of timing and recent activity), Hebb was essentially correct – synaptic plasticity is recognized as the fundamental neural process underlying memory formation (Takeuchi, Duszkiewicz, & Morris, 2014). The resulting physical trace of a memory is called an engram: "If the inputs to a system cause the same pattern of activity to occur repeatedly, the set of active elements constituting that pattern will become increasingly strongly interassociated ... We may call a learned (auto-associated) pattern an engram" (Allport, 1985, p. 44).

Many issues can affect the success or failure of memory encoding. These include environmental factors (distractors, stressors, context), cognitive and emotional state, and the "predicted reward" associated with the stimulus. Significant events, especially those involving emotional content, appear to be strongly encoded. Encoding typically omits much of the richness of a stimulus/sensory experience and appears to primarily represent semantic content (meaning) (Baddeley, 1966). Consistent with this observation, one of the most reliable results in the memory research literature is that encoding can be improved by "elaboration": interacting with the stimulus at the time of encoding, processing it in meaningful ways, and in particular relating it to already existing long-term memories. This finding has had a huge impact on education, where much of teaching practice is about timing and scaffolding the introduction of content appropriately and engaging learners actively with the new material.

Consolidation is a mechanism (variously considered either separate from or part of either encoding or storage) by which initial encoding of a memory is strengthened. Processes that occur during sleep are important to consolidation (Stickgold, 2005). These appear to involve the reactivation of recently learned information and (particularly for novel semantic information) a transfer from initial storage in the hippocampus (and associated structures) to the cortex, over periods ranging from days to years. Good sleep is important to good learning.

If some memory (pattern of activation) has been encoded and sometime later can be retrieved, then in between these times the memory is in some sense stored. Note that what is stored is not the pattern itself, but changes to synaptic connection strengths that allow the pattern to be recreated. By analogy, the process of remembering a piece of music is more akin to creating a musical score than it is to making a recording.

The *storage* of memories is not a passive or a perfect system. The synaptic encoding of memories can degrade over time or change as a result of new experiences or new memory formation. It is not currently clear exactly what mechanisms are involved in the maintenance (of the encodings) of memories, but once again processes that occur during sleep appear to play a role, particularly in protecting existing memories during new learning (Robins, 1996). One mechanism known to be important is reconsolidation. Every time a memory is retrieved, it appears to be (to a certain extent) re-encoded. Significant experimental evidence shows that memories can change over time, often in accordance with various desires, expectations, or schemata (as discussed below), and the drift that occurs with multiple reconsolidations appears to be part of this process. Our memories change over time.

The *retrieval* of a memory is the recreation of the pattern of activation (or similar) that encoded the original stimulus/item. It is an active process, reconstructing the pattern from other inputs ("cues") and the encoding synapses. Two kinds of retrieval are distinguished: *recognition*, where the original stimulus is present again (and thus in effect serves as its own cue); and *recall*, in which the original stimulus is absent (other factors serve as cues). Recognition appears to be automatic – if a stimulus matches a stored memory, we experience a sense of familiarity/"match." Recall can take different forms (free or explicitly cued) and appears to be a more complex process, which can involve retrieving different candidate memories and evaluating their match to the cues. Recall is improved if the context in which it is attempted (environmental, emotional, or physiological) is similar to the context in which it was encoded (Tulving & Thomson, 1973). For example, information learned in a specific room will be better recalled in the same room, and information learned while under the influence of alcohol will be better recalled in the same state. This is relevant to the discussion of transfer below.

At a level of analysis above these underlying mechanisms, learning can be seen as a process of forming associations between stimuli and/or behaviors. *Associationism* featured heavily in early animal learning research, such as Thorndike's "Law of Effect" (Thorndike, 1911), and it underlies the behaviorist theories of learning described below. But associationism has developed as a broad and flexible framework that contributes at different levels to various theories of thought and learning (Mandelbaum, 2017), including the learning algorithms of artificial neural networks (Hinton & Anderson, 1989).

Evidence suggests that more information is stored in the brain than can be successfully recalled, and that the phenomenon of forgetting is largely a failure of recall (Tulving, 1974). This has led to the exploration of techniques (such as hypnotism) to assist recall and to a popular focus on "recovered memories," which has unfortunately proved to be of very mixed validity (yes, it is possible to assist recall, but it is also possible to "lead" it). Much of what we think we recall is inaccurate, especially as the time since the original encoding increases, and especially because recall is a reconstructive process that incorporates current cues. This is well known in a legal context, where the reliability of eyewitness testimony is higher for statements taken soon after an event, and where witnesses can be "led" by the phrasing of questions.

To relate these mechanisms to a CEd context, consider, for example, two concerning phenomena observed in novice programmers: firstly, the prevalence of "fragile" knowledge (i.e., knowledge that appears to be missing [forgotten], inert [learned but not used], or misplaced [learned but used inappropriately]); and secondly, student performance that is significantly worse than expected after completion of a course. (Both of these issues are discussed in Chapter 12.) We would respond to these issues in different ways if they were shown to arise from partial or complete failures of attention vs. failures of encoding vs. failures of recall.

9.4.3 Kinds of LTM

Many different kinds of information are represented in LTM. *Declarative* (or *explicit*) memory is memory for facts or events that can be consciously recalled/ "declared." It is sometimes described as "knowing that" (e.g., knowing that the capital of France is Paris or knowing the syntax for a specific statement in a specific programming language). *Procedural* (or *implicit*) memory is memory for skills or motor tasks (movements) that are not consciously recalled but can be performed. It is sometimes described as "knowing how" (e.g., knowing how to ride a bike or how to debug a program). Declarative memories are based on information that is consciously experienced and can be formed after a single exposure, whereas procedural memories typically require repetition/practice.

Declarative memory can be subdivided into episodic and semantic memory. *Episodic* memory is memory for events, such as a recent holiday. It is personal and roughly serial – we can locate specific episodes within the sequence of personal experiences that make up our lives. Episodic memory, and in particular *spatial* memory (relating to spatial positioning), depends on the hippocampus and appears to be consolidated and transferred to the neocortex during sleep. In CEdR, an example of episodic memory may be when you first learned how to compile a program, and spatial memory can apply to where in a program a specific piece of code exists.

In contrast, *semantic* memory is memory for meanings, concepts, or facts, such as the two times table. Semantic memory must be derived from specific learning episodes, but it is abstract and can be independent of direct personal experience (e.g., we can learn by being told, by reading, or from other indirect sources). An example of semantic memory in programming may be the behavior of specific programming statements.

Our episodic memories generally transition to semantic memories over time, losing detail and becoming more abstract. (Most of us have things that we can "remember" about our childhood as facts, but no longer as personal experiences). Both episodic and semantic memories are subject to error and mismatch. Episodic memories are necessarily subjective (two people may remember the same event differently) and can change over time as described above. Semantic information must be somewhat common between people, but people also construct the world differently (we can all agree on the spelling of "politician," but not on whether a particular politician is good or bad).

While most memory is necessarily retrospective, *prospective* memory is "remembering to remember"/planning for future action ("I must remember to pick up some chocolate on the way home"). Schacter, Addis, and Buckner (2007) suggest the concept of the "prospective brain" – that we can recombine elements of retrospective memories to imagine/predict/simulate future events and that humans can thereby engage in "mental time travel" (Tulving, 1985). Memory, planning, and mental models of future action are all closely related.

Programming must involve a considerable demand on both memory and prospective memory. The programmer must "remember to remember" to close structures at multiple levels, from local constructs such as loops, to the functionality of organizing structures such as classes, to overall program designs/ patterns. In general terms, planning and problem-solving require both retrospective and prospective memory, as possible solutions to goals and subgoals are explored and discarded or adopted.

9.4.4 Memory Structures and Representations

How is information organized in memory? These issues are explored in the context of a higher level of analysis, but are assumed to rest on the lower mechanisms just described.

The most fundamental structure is the *category*, a collection of items that we recognize as being instances of the "same thing," such as a chair, a tree, or a person. "There is nothing more basic to thought and language than our sense of similarity; our sorting of things into kinds" (Quine, 1969, p. 116). There is strong evidence that there exist "basic-level categories" characterized by obvious similarities that humans learn first and react to most strongly (Rosch et al., 1976). For example, "dog" is a basic-level category, with superordinate categories (such as "animal") and subordinate categories (such as "Labrador") emerging later in development. The hierarchical organization of categories is sometimes described as a *type hierarchy*, with instances of a type being *tokens*.

The question of how categories are represented in the brain is a matter of very active debate. The *probabilistic* approach suggests that categories are represented by some measure of the central tendencies of instances, such as a set of characteristic features or dimensions, or an instance-like "prototype." The prototypical dog doesn't exist, but we all know a lot about it. The *exemplar* approach proposes that categories are encoded not by a single representation, but by the separate representations of salient instances. Individual instances may be more significant than an abstract average; for example, our earth is a very influential instance of the category "planet." Both of these approaches can account for graded category membership (a sparrow is a better example of a bird than a penguin) and fuzzy category boundaries (when does a stream become a river?). Experimental evidence supports both approaches, suggesting that we use a mixture of strategies (Hampton, 2016; Medin, Altom, & Murphy, 1984; Minda & Smith, 2002).

One construct that is problematic for standard models of categorization is the "ad hoc" category (Barsalou, 1983). These are the "categories" that can be created by an arbitrary specification. For example, consider the category of "things you would rescue if your house was burning down." It has a similar structure to traditional categories, including graded membership (good and bad instances) and prototypical members (rescue other people!), but it appears to emerge from an active process, which is difficult to account for in terms of the structure of LTM.

Speculatively, it may be interesting to explore the relationship between programming constructs and cognitive categories. Data types define categories of data that can be treated in the same way – we have understandings and expectations about both the type/category and specific tokens/examples. Given that object-oriented programming was developed as a tool to give us "natural" ways of thinking about tasks, it is not surprising that object types are hierarchical and can be prototype based. Where new data types/classes are created, these could be seen as examples of ad hoc categories.

More specialized kinds of memory structures have been described, within cognitive psychology and artificial intelligence, by the related terms schema, frame, script, or plan (Schank & Abelson, 1975, 2013; Whitney, 2001). A *schema* is a unit of declarative knowledge that organizes items of information and the semantic relationships between them. Examples include schemata for objects such as "triangle" or "horse," for scientific constructs such as a specific logic or the periodic table, for archetypes/social roles such as "teacher" or "parent," or for belief systems such as a religion or "worldview." They are "generic representations" of "preconceived knowledge" that structure our perception and cognition both individually and collectively (a particularly salient example being social schemata such as racial or political stereotypes). Schemata also influence memories over time, as "typical" information not present at the time of encoding is added during episodes of recall and reconsolidation. A *frame* is a structure consisting of "slots" and "fillers" (e.g., the "teacher" frame might consist of slots representing subject and school level, with default values such as "math" and "secondary"). A *script* or a *plan* is an "action-oriented" schema for some sequence of actions or events (e.g., a birthday party script or a restaurant script). These can be shown to influence the recall of descriptions by adding common/script details (e.g., adding birthday presents) that were not present in the memorized material.

Schemata/plans were adopted by the CEdR community during the 1970s through to the 1990s, and featured heavily in research on the "psychology of programming" that was popular at the time. Expert programmers are characterized by a large library of useful schemata/plans that chunk and organize significant amounts of information in a form that reduces cognitive load. Many of the difficulties experienced by novice programmers arise from their lack of such organizing knowledge structures. These issues are discussed in some detail in Chapter 12.

9.4.5 Memory in Practice

Much of what is known about practically improving memory, such as actively engaging with and elaborating new material, has been incorporated into standard pedagogical practice and typical "study skills" advice to learners (Dunlosky et al., 2013). Active strategies for remembering date back to the Greek use of the "method of loci" (in the context of rhetoric), which draws on well-practiced spatial memory to organize and help remember other material at need. Today, there are many proven mnemonic techniques and many popular books, websites, and other resources that explain and promote their use (e.g., Foer, 2012). We are not aware of any specific exploration of study skills or application of mnemonic techniques in CEd.

Similarly, there are many general issues that impact on learning and memory, such as health, age, diet, stress, exercise, and sleep, which are well known in clinical contexts and widely discussed in popular sources. Various physical and cognitive disorders affect memory, including amnesias, agnosias, the effects of brain injury, and conditions associated with aging such as Alzheimer's disease or dementia. It is not likely that any of these effects would be specific to our field.

9.5 Topics in Cognition

In this section, we give very brief overviews of some of the important topics in cognition. In the remaining sections of the chapter, we explore in more detail two topics of particularly practical significance to educators: the transfer of learning and cognitive load.

9.5.1 Cognitive Development and Language Acquisition

Humans acquire knowledge, skills, and capabilities on different timescales and as a result of different processes of physical, neurological, and cognitive maturation/development and learning. The field of cognitive development has fundamentally shaped educational theory and practice. It is also of increasing relevance to CEd as computing makes its way into many early school curricula.

Jean Piaget was the first to formalize the observation that growing children pass through roughly predictable stages, effectively founding the field of cognitive development with his *developmental stage theory* (Piaget, 1964, 1971a, 1971b). Piaget's early stages introduced such concepts as object permanence and conservation (of volume, number, or mass). The later stages are defined largely in terms of the acquisition of logical capacities such as transitive inference. The fundamental unit of knowledge in the theory is the *schema*, a cohesive, repeatable "action sequence" organized around a "core meaning" (Piaget, 1952). Learning is seen as involving *assimilation*, the integration of new information into schemata, and *accommodation*, the process of adjusting schemata (when existing ones do not suffice). In a large-scale meta-analysis of factors influencing educational outcomes (Hattie, 2009, 2012), "Piagetian level" of development was identified as one of the "super-effects" – the higher a student's assessed level, the better their outcomes (Killian, 2016).

Piaget's framework had a huge impact on curriculum design and educational practice internationally. It introduced concepts that are now taken for granted, such as the active engagement of the child with learning, and it was one of the major influences on the now dominant educational philosophy of *constructivism*. His impact on education and the field of cognitive development is difficult to overstate (Flavell, 1996; Scholnick et al., 1999).

Aspects of Piaget's original theory, however, were problematic, particularly the observed variation between individuals and the lack of explanation for the "miraculous" transition between stages (Feldman, 2004). It is not clear what the relationship is between individual differences in development and individual differences in IQ, and what exactly is measured by the different tests for these attributes (Cianciolo & Sternberg, 2004; Sternberg, 1982). Attempts to address such problems led to various "neo-Piagetian" theories; these are discussed in the context of novice programmers in Chapter 12.

Other influential ideas in development arose from the work of early psychologist, Lev Vygotsky; for an overview, see Rieber and Robinson (2004). Vygotsky noted that there was a distance between children's developmental level as determined by their independent performance and their potential level when assisted by a teacher or in a social context. Vygotsky called this space, within which children are capable of learning and making progress, the *Zone of Proximal Development* (ZPD), suggesting that this was the most effective level at which to target instruction and assistance. The ZPD has become a standard and influential concept in both cognitive development and education; see, for example, Wertsch (1984) and Chaikin (2003), and the discussions in Chapters 8 and 24.

The term *scaffolding* (Wood, Bruner, & Ross, 1976) refers to the support given to the learner within their ZPD. Such support includes direct instruction or advice, resources, modeling, and well-designed tasks, and it is reduced/

withdrawn as the learner becomes more independent (see Chapter 8). In contrast, *bootstrapping* (Bereiter, 1985) describes the process of learners progressing independently, without the assistance of others (Bereiter explores ten possible mechanisms that might support this). For overviews of further topics in cognitive development and links with other disciplines, see, for example, Fischer (1980), Wertsh and Tulviste (1990), Flavell (1992), and Bandura (1993).

One major interdisciplinary topic spanning development, linguistics, and education is the acquisition of language (McNeill, 1970). It is widely claimed that there are maturational constraints on language learning (Newport, 1990), that there are critical periods in the process (Lenneberg, 1967; Singleton & Ryan, 2004), and that children learn languages easily based on procedural memory, while adults learn via a more explicit process based on declarative memory (Ferman & Karni, 2012). While we are not aware of any suggestion that children learn programming languages more easily than adults, the recent addition of computing into the school curriculum highlights the need to explore children's learning processes and the ways they may differ from adults in this domain.

An examination of the vast field of language is beyond the scope of this chapter; for an overview, see Crystal (2010). In the context of CEd, Bonar and Soloway (1989) explore preconceptions based on natural language as a source of misconceptions about programming (for more, see Chapter 27), and there has been some discussion of parallels between learning a programming language and the acquisition of a second (human) language (Baldwin & Macredie, 1999; Pandža, 2016). Ullman (2001, 2004) proposed a model of language learning where lexical forms (words) are stored in declarative "rote memory" and grammar is a set of rule-like mental operations that is dependent upon procedural memory. Do the lexical elements of programming languages and the knowledge of how to combine and use them exhibit a similar dichotomy?

9.5.2 Behaviorist Accounts of Learning

Behaviorism was the dominant school of thought within psychology during the first half of the twentieth century. *Methodological behaviorism* (Watson, 1913, 1930) holds that the only scientifically valid object of study is observable behavior; any consideration of subjective, phenomenological, or mental states or processes is excluded. Behavior in this framework is seen to arise as a result of environmental stimuli interacting with an individual's history of reinforcement or punishment and/or current drives (e.g., hunger). *Radical behaviorism* (Skinner, 1938, 1953) acknowledges the existence and valid study of "private events" (e.g., thoughts, feelings, mental states), but holds that environmental factors control these just as they control observable behaviors. Internal states cannot explain behavior (such attempts circularly presuppose their own explanation); instead, they should be understood and translated into behavioral terms.

Behaviorism was rooted in earlier work on animal learning, which it developed and applied to animals and humans in two main theoretical and practical directions. *Classical conditioning* involves the association of innate reflexes with new stimuli (the famous example being Pavlov's dog being taught to salivate at the sound of a bell). *Operant conditioning* is the modification of behavior using *reward* (stimuli that increase its frequency) or *punishment* (stimuli that decrease its frequency). Reward or punishment may be *positive* (added to the environment) or *negative* (removed from the environment). Complex behaviors may be *shaped* by the careful rewarding of sequences of antecedent or partial behaviors. Rewards or punishments on various *schedules* can result in behavior with mixed patterns of frequency and robustness. For a review and modern synthesis, see Bouton (2016).

Despite the fact that the underlying theory fell out of favor, behaviorism achieved major and practical insights into both animal and human learning that are still widely employed today. Classical conditioning led to what are now called behavioral therapies (such as aversion therapy, systematic desensitization, and flooding). Similarly, operant conditioning led to applied behavior analysis ("behavior modification"), the practical modification of behavior in fields such as behavioral interventions for children, criminology, animal training, addiction and dependence, health and exercise, and more. Reinforcement (applied under various schedules) is also widely used in the gambling and gaming industries, including video and online games – it is no accident that they are "addictive." Reinforcement-based management of behavior in general is also important in economics, workplace and business management, and education (McSweeney & Murphy, 2014), and has made its way into popular culture with the understanding that we should "reinforce good behavior." Concepts from this tradition have also influenced reinforcement learning, a major topic in the context of machine learning/artificial intelligence (Sutton & Barto, 1998).

In the context of education, *behavior analysis* is a field of interest (Cooper, 1982; Twyman, 2014), and behavioral tools are an important aspect of classroom management (Emmer & Stough, 2001; Woollard, 2010). We are not aware of any significant exploration of behavior-based methods in CEd or CEdR so far, but suggest that there are two emerging topics where they could be relevant. The first of these is the "gamification" of learning (Kapp, 2012), especially as this might be applied to the teaching and learning of programming and computing topics. An understanding of reinforcement schedules and behavioral techniques will help to maximize the efficacy of game-based teaching and learning.

A second area of potential application is suggested by the field of behavior informatics/behavior computing (Cao, 2010; Cao & Philip, 2012). This field encompasses the extraction of information about patterns of behavior from large volumes of data (e.g., financial transactions, system use, social media) and its use for understanding, modeling, and predicting future behavior (e.g., risk analysis, marketing design, load prediction). As CEd is now adopting the use of learning analytics (Chapter 23) and large bodies of data collected from instrumented compilers (Chapter 21), there is an opportunity to explore these related tools and ideas. What do our data sets tell us about events that make certain behaviors more or less probable? Can we add reinforcement to our tools to shape appropriate behaviors?

9.5.3 Cognitivist Accounts of Learning

Arising from the late 1950s "cognitive revolution" and superseding behaviorism as the dominant paradigm within psychology, cognitivism invited the study of internal/mental states and processes (see further discussion in Chapter 10). The underlying assumptions view the brain as a processor of information and thought as a form of computation (Glass, Holyoak, & Santa, 1979; Lindsay & Norman, 1977).

The account of memory and learning set out in Section 9.4 is cognitivist. It describes functional organization and internal processes such as attention, working memory and LTM. It describes learning/memory formation (at a low level of analysis) and (at a higher level) knowledge structures such as cognitive categories and schemata. It explores aspects of internal representation such as the prototype vs. exemplar accounts of categories. This is the context within with CEdR has developed, particularly with the focus in the 1970s through to the 1990s on the "psychology of programming." Aspects of learning theory that have been particularly influential within CEdR include the central importance of organized knowledge structures such as schemata/plans and the application of various learning taxonomies, such as the Bloom (Bloom et al., 1956) and SOLO (Biggs & Collis, 1982) taxonomies, as described in Chapter 12.

Work within the cognitivist tradition has explored a range of specific forms of knowledge representation and/or processing, such as semantic networks, frames, decision trees, production rules, blackboard models, and more (Brachman & Levesque, 1985; Sowa, 2000). From the many formal models of cognitive process, two particularly ambitious examples stand out. The Adaptive Control of Thought (ACT/ACT-R) model (in various iterations) of John Anderson (Anderson, 1976, 1982) was based on an associative network model of LTM and production rules representing procedural memory. It encompassed problem-solving and a model of learning as the compilation of declarative into procedural representations. The Soar Cognitive Architecture (in various iterations) of Rosenbloom, Laird, Newell, and colleagues (Laird & Rosenbloom, 1996; Rosenbloom et al., 1991) is based on representations of search spaces and the operators that can be applied to them. It encompasses different kinds of memory and representation, problem-solving, and learning as a process of reinforcement and the chunking/organization of the rules that trigger operators. Soar remains an ongoing research program (Soar, 2018).

In the CEdR literature, Rist (1995) proposes an example of a comprehensive formal model of a complex topic, the process of program generation. Knowledge is represented using indexed nodes (encoding actions) in memory (working, episodic, and semantic). A program is built by starting with a search cue such as <find, average, rainfall> and retrieving and expanding any matching nodes. Outputs are called plans, and common/useful plans are assumed to be stored as schema–like knowledge structures. Experts can retrieve relevant plans from memory, but novices must typically create plans through a process of "focal expansion."

In an exploration of novice programmers, Robins (2010) appeals to the educational principle that new learning builds on existing knowledge – we learn at the edges of what we know (e.g., the concepts of the ZPD, scaffolding, and bootstrapping discussed above). For some knowledge representations, learning can be described as, for example, "a series of local repairs of a knowledge structure" involving mechanisms such as adding and adjusting links (Chi & Ohlsson, 2005). Robins suggests that different domains of knowledge have edges and interconnections of different complexities, and that in the case of densely connected domains (such as programming languages), success or failure in the integration of new knowledge can have a compounding "momentum" that significantly affects learning outcomes.

To sum up, of the two major learning frameworks to succeed behaviorism, cognitivism, as discussed above, grew out of psychology and artificial intelligence. Constructivism (as widely discussed elsewhere in the Handbook; see Chapters 1, 8, 10, 11, 15, 24, and 29) grew out of education and child development. See Ertmer and Newby (1993) and Cooper (1993) for reviews and comparisons of all three frameworks.

9.5.4 Reasoning and Problem-Solving

Reasoning has been variously defined as including thinking, understanding, deciding, making sense, evaluating, problem-solving, changing beliefs, and other abstract (high-level) descriptions of aspects of cognitive function. For an overview of this broad topic, see Holyoak and Morrison (2005).

Early attempts to formalize reasoning gave rise to logic – rules and principles for drawing valid conclusions. *Propositional* logic (propositions that can be true or false, logical operators) was set out by George Boole (1815–1864, now immortalized as a data type). From this foundation, a succession of theorists developed further logical systems, and formalized concepts such as syntax, semantics, proof, and forms of reasoning such as deduction and induction (e.g., see Enderton, 2001). Logic underlies the theory and practice of computation, early work in artificial intelligence, approaches to design and verification, forms of economic modeling, and more.

Humans can use logic. It defines some kind of ideal, but human reasoning does not strictly adhere to logic. We are prone to formal fallacies (e.g., affirming a disjunct, denying the antecedent, base rate fallacy, etc.), practical fallacies (e.g., gambler's fallacy, circular reasoning, false equivalence, etc.), and a bewildering array of cognitive biases (e.g., confirmation bias, framing bias, stereotyping, etc.); see Pohl (2004) for an overview. Further exploring the impact of known fallacies or biases in the context of specific computing topics seems like a productive area for future research. Fallacies so far observed within CEd (mostly relating to programming) have been termed misconceptions, as described in Chapter 27.

If not logic, what? *Human Problem Solving* (Newell & Simon, 1972) sparked a wave of cognitivist research into reasoning. The authors explore problem-solving within the constraints imposed by the "human information processing system" (serial processing, a small STM, a large LTM with fast retrieval but slow storage) and stress the importance of "simple schemes of heuristic search." The topic of heuristics was further developed by Tversky and Kahneman (1974). Noting that most reasoning takes place in the context of incomplete/uncertain information, the authors review and present evidence relating to three heuristics that pervasively influence human cognition: availability (the ease with which relevant information can be recalled), representativeness (the impact of similarity and prototypes), and anchoring (the impact of initially stated information). A subsequent program of research by these and other authors identified and categorized further heuristics. These do not appear to have received much attention in CEdR. Is novice reasoning about programming influenced by common cognitive heuristics? If so, how? And how do we take account of this as educators?

Another framework used to explore reasoning is mental models (Gentner, 2002; Gentner & Stevens, 1983; Johnson-Laird, 1983). These are internal models of how some aspect of the world works, an iconic representation of selected aspects of external objects and systems. Mental models have predictive power – they can be used to understand the observed behavior of the world and reason about future behavior. The use of mental models generally, and of a particular kind of mental model (the "notional machine"), has been widely adopted in the CEdR literature, as described in Chapter 12.

Problem-solving is a pervasive and practical version of the topic of reasoning, discussed in contexts from solving mathematical puzzles, to managing businesses, to interpersonal relationships. The range of formalized problem-solving strategies includes, for example, divide and conquer (breaking a problem down into smaller, solvable problems), analogy (adapting the solution to a structurally similar problem), and means–ends analysis (choosing an action at each step to move toward the goal). Within the cognitivist framework, problem-solving is usually construed as a process of search within some representation of the problem space. For more on this, and for a range of perspectives on problem-solving, see Schoenfeld (1985), Novice and Bassok (2005), Wang and Chiew (2010), and Robertson (2016).

Individuals vary in their capacity to solve problems and perform tasks, which is one of the topics explored under the general heading of intelligence, as formalized in various IQ measures. The literature relating to intelligence is diverse, with debate as to whether it should be thought of as single general factor "g," a few major factors (such as verbal and spatial intelligence), or multiple factors (such as the logical, linguistic, spatial, musical, kinesthetic, naturalist, intrapersonal, and interpersonal intelligences proposed by Gardner, 1993). One of the most general results, however, is that performance on one standard psychometric test is highly predictive of performance on other such tests, a phenomenon known as "the positive manifold" (Jensen, 1998) and sometimes used as an argument for the existence of g. The importance of intelligence in programming and CEd is discussed by Pea and Kurland (1984) and reviewed in Robins (2010).

In CEd practice, problem-solving is usually introduced, along with algorithms, in a first programming course ("CS1"). Courses vary in the prominence they give the topic and its order in the curriculum, but many CS1 courses are explicitly "problem-solving based," as described in the Association for Computing Machinery (ACM) curriculum guidelines (ACM/IEEE-CS, 2013). An increasing focus on problem-solving in CEd was noted by Caspersen and Bennedsen (2007), with most (but not all) studies suggesting improved outcomes. Hazzan, Lapidot, and Ragonis (2014) set out practical guidelines for teaching problem-solving. Many studies relating to problem-solving in the CEdR literature are reviewed in Chapter 12.

One of the most important lessons from the study of problem-solving is that it can be a highly contextual process. A widely discussed illustration of this effect is the reported ability of children to perform mathematical operations in the context of purchases (e.g., "making change"), but performing significantly worse on the same calculations when presented as "math problems." The classic study on "street math" is Carraher, Carraher, and Schliemann (1985); the many follow-up studies include current work in India by Banerjee et al. (2017). Further important examples of the contextualization of problem-solving are discussed in Chapter 28. This is the issue underlying the importance of the topic of transfer in teaching and learning, as discussed in the next section.

9.6 Transfer

Because of its practical significance to educators, we have chosen to focus in some detail on the topic of transfer, which is a major theme within the learning literature. This section will illustrate how some of the lower-level processes, such as attention and memory, are applied to higher-level phenomena, such as problem-solving and learning.

9.6.1 What Is Transfer?

For the purposes of CEd, we define transfer as a student's ability to transfer the knowledge that they've learned and apply it to solving new problems. For example, if a student learns to write a program to find the average of a waiter's tips, then they should be able to write a program that finds the average score on a test. Instructors and content creators tend to think that transfer will come naturally to learners, but in reality, learners, especially those who have little knowledge of the domain, struggle to apply what they (tenuously) know to novel problems. Trouble with transfer is best documented in computing by performance on Soloway's Rainfall Problem. Soloway's Rainfall Problem has been given to students at the end of introductory programming courses to test their knowledge on several concepts. Students commonly perform poorly on this problem, even though their instructors think that it is a straightforward application of the concepts they have learned throughout the semester (Guzdial, 2015).

Before we discuss what makes transfer so difficult for learners and how to promote it in our students, let's consider the various types of transfer. The type of transfer that we want to enable is spontaneous transfer. In spontaneous transfer, the student recognizes the similarities between what they already know and the knowledge required to solve the new problem without help or guidance (Bassok & Holyoak, 1989). When spontaneous transfer doesn't occur, students can often be guided to transfer by pointing out the similarities between old and new problems or asking the student to find similarities (Gick & Holyoak, 1980). Because instructors will not always be around to provide guidance, spontaneous transfer is our ultimate goal. Spontaneous transfer is related to transfer distance.

9.6.1.1 Types of Transfer

Barnett and Ceci (2002) provide a comprehensive taxonomy for transfer distance. They created the taxonomy to identify dimensions that can be used to describe different types of transfer in a more sophisticated manner than only "near" or "far," which is how it had been commonly described in the literature. The first dimension of transfer that Barnett and Ceci discuss, which is by far the most common dimension that people explore, is the knowledge domain. For this reason, it is discussed in more depth than the others.

1. *Knowledge domain transfer* is transfer within or between different disciplines.
   - Near transfer – transfer within a discipline:
     - Isomorphic transfer – the problem-solving context (i.e., cover story) between problems is the same and only the values in the problem are different. The term *isomorphic* comes from the math field (Bassok, 1990), but it has been applied (transferred, if you will) to similar scenarios in other fields (e.g., Morrison, Margulieux, & Guzdial, 2015).
     - Contextual transfer – the problem-solving procedure between problems is the same and the contexts of the problem are different. For example, transferring knowledge from writing a program to find the average value of a waiter's tips to writing a program to find the average rainfall is contextual transfer. The context difference might cause slight variations in the problem solution, but the general steps of the procedure are the same.
     - Procedural transfer – the type of problem is the same and the problem-solving procedures are different. For example, transferring knowledge from writing a while loop to find the sum of values to writing a while loop to find the average of values is procedural transfer. The steps of the procedure differ based on the components of the problem (summing or averaging), but the type of problem (using a while loop) is the same.
   - Far transfer – transfer between disciplines:
     - Several shared elements – the domains share several elements that make general problem-solving procedures applicable to both. For example, learning to create algorithms in math can be applied to creating algorithms in computing, and the general problem-solving strategies used to achieve both are similar.

- Few shared elements – the domains do not share many elements, making transfer possible at only an analogical level. For example, writing about a sequence of events in English is conceptually similar to writing a program for a sequence of events, but the procedures and knowledge required to complete each are very different.

2. *Physical context transfer* is transfer among spaces (e.g., classroom, dorm room, kitchen table at parents' house). Because information is encoded with the physical context in which it was learned, location can affect transfer.

3. *Temporal context transfer* is transfer across time (e.g., weeks, months, semesters). Because synaptic connections fade over time (i.e., ability to recall information decays), the time between solving problems can affect transfer. Time transfer is also commonly called **retention**.

4. *Functional context transfer* is transfer among purposes (e.g., authentic web development problems, academic exercises to learn concepts used in web development).

5. *Social context transfer* is transfer among group compositions (e.g., solving problems individually, solving problems in teams).

6. *Modality transfer* is transfer between medium of instruction and application at the macro-level (e.g., auditory instructions vs. written assignment) or micro-level (e.g., instructing based on tracing, reading, or writing code vs. testing based on tracing, reading, or writing code).

9.6.1.2 Why Is Transfer So Hard?

Reviewing these six dimensions should give you an idea of how contexts can change between learning to solve a problem and solving a novel problem. Any contextual differences that make it difficult for the learner to recognize similarities between problems will hinder transfer (Gick & Holyoak, 1980). The more abstract instruction is, the more easily students can transfer knowledge spontaneously (Day & Goldstone, 2012). Abstract instructions, however, are very difficult for novices to grasp because they do not have enough knowledge about the domain to connect abstract information to their existing cognitive architecture (i.e., connect to prior knowledge), making it difficult to retrieve (Jonassen, 2000). Therefore, providing surface details (i.e., cover stories) for problems is essential to teaching novices, even though those surface details can promote ineffective problem-solving schemata and mental models (Eiriksdottir & Catrambone, 2011).

Surface details promote ineffective knowledge structures in LTM because novices have difficulty seeing past surface details to identify structural parts of problem-solving procedures that apply to all similar problems (Bransford, Brown, & Cocking, 1999). Instead of mentally organizing information around structural details, they create knowledge structures around surface details (Chi, Feltovich, & Glaser, 1981). For example, novice programmers are more likely to organize information around an application type, whereas more advanced programmers will organize information around an underlying algorithm (Weiser

& Shertz, 1983). Therefore, novices' mental organizations of information often suppress spontaneous transfer. To fix these issues, we need to help learners identify structural parts of problem-solving procedures and enable them to connect them to a variety of problems.

9.6.2 How to Promote Transfer within a Domain

The best way to help students transfer their knowledge is to teach them how to transfer their knowledge. Cognitively speaking, learning content is not the same as learning how to transfer content (Bransford et al., 1999; van Merriënboer, Clark, & de Croock, 2002). Too often instructors will assume that if students see enough examples and understand the content, transfer will come automatically. Instead, instructors should tell students how to recognize similarities between novel problems and problems that they know how to solve, and they should give students practice and feedback on novel problem-solving (Singley & Anderson, 1989).

9.6.2.1 Frameworks for Helping Students to See Past Surface Details

One of the biggest problems that keeps students from successfully transferring their knowledge is that they don't recognize similarities between problems that they know how to solve and new problems, called the inert knowledge problem (Reed, Ernst, & Banerji, 1974). In one of the classic transfer studies, Gick and Holyoak (1980) showed participants a problem in which a general was attempting to take a town, but his army was too big and vulnerable to attack to march into the town on the main road. The solution was to split the army up and converge on the town from multiple directions at once. After Gick and Holyoak taught participants to solve this problem, they asked participants to solve Duncker's radiation problem, a problem in which a doctor is attempting to treat a patient with a tumor. The tumor can be destroyed with a laser ray, but if the laser is at a high enough intensity to destroy the tumor, it will also destroy all of the healthy tissue in the laser's path. The solution is the same as the army problem: align several low-intensity lasers to converge on the tumor so that the tumor is destroyed and the healthy tissue is not. Despite the similarities in problems and solutions, only 20 percent of participants were able to solve Duncker's radiation problem, even though they had just learned the solution to the army problem. When participants were told to find analogies between problems or given hints about similarities between problems, 92 percent of participants successfully solved it. The takeaway from this and related studies is that students need to be guided or told how problems are similar until they have developed a generalized mental model or schema for problem-solving that can recognize structural similarities between problems.

Helping students to identify structural similarities between problems is important in computing education because we typically rely on worked examples to help teach computing concepts. A worked example is a problem with a worked-out solution that students can study before they are able to solve problems independently (Renkl, 2017). We have strong evidence that asking students to study worked examples is more effective in the early stages of learning than asking them to solve problems from abstract instructions (Renkl, 2017; Sweller, 2010). The problem with worked examples is that they show learners how to solve only one problem because examples have to include a cover story. Just like in Gick and Holyoak's (1980) army problem, students who study worked examples are able to solve novel problems better when they are guided to see past the surface details.

The subgoal learning framework has been used to help students see past the surface details of worked examples. Subgoals are functional pieces that are inherent in problem-solving processes (e.g., initiating a loop is a subgoal in a problem that uses loops). The worked example is visually broken down into subgoal components, then each subgoal is meaningfully labeled (Margulieux, Guzdial, & Catrambone, 2012; Morrison, Margulieux, & Guzdial, 2015). The subgoal label, a short instructional explanation of the purpose of the subgoal, is abstract and does not contain any of the surface details of the problem, meaning that it can be applied to any similar problem. In the subgoal learning framework, students are given multiple examples, each with different surface features but with the same subgoal labels, so that they can compare and contrast the problem-solving steps that achieve the same subgoals across multiple examples (Margulieux et al., 2012). For example, in a while loop worked example, one of the subgoal labels could be "determine initial values," in which you would specify values before the loop begins (Morrison et al., 2015). Explaining the purpose of steps in a worked example at this low level helps novices to transfer their knowledge to solving novel problems and retain the problem-solving process for longer (Margulieux et al., 2012; Morrison et al., 2015).

Analogical encoding is another strategy that is used to help students recognize the common structure between examples (Ferguson, 1994). It is based on analogical reasoning, in which people create analogies between fundamentally similar concepts (Gick & Holyoak, 1983). Creating analogies helps students to recognize when two examples share the same problem-solving procedure, promoting development of schemata (see more about schema instruction below; Kurtz, Miao, & Gentner, 2001). When students are encouraged to create analogies, their transfer to novel problems improves, whether they receive guidance on the similarities or not (Gentner, Loewenstein, & Thompson, 2003). Please note that analogical encoding is different from using analogies in instruction. In analogical encoding, students are the creators of analogies and the analogies are between two examples of the same problem-solving process. When an instructor gives students an analogy, the student is not creating the analogy and the analogy is typically between two disparate examples of similar concepts: the concept that they are learning and a concept that they already know (e.g., electricity is like flowing water; Gentner, 1983).

In contrast to analogical encoding, which helps students to build schemata for themselves, schema instruction is a method of explicitly training students on schemata in a field to jump-start their problem-solving potential before they have enough experience to develop schemata themselves. As discussed earlier, a schema is a framework for solving a class of problems (Marshall, 1995), like an abstract recipe. There are two types of schema instruction (Powell, 2011). The first is schema-based instruction, in which instructors teach students a schema or set of schemata and also teach students to classify problems to match a problem to the appropriate schema. Examples of schema-based instruction in programming education can be found in *How to Design Programs: An Introduction to Programming and Computing* by Felleisen et al. (2001). The second is schema-broadening instruction, which is more focused on transfer. In schema-broadening instruction, instructors help students to match problems that have new features (e.g., a different problem structure) to an existing schema (Powell, 2011).

While all of these approaches to improving transfer are very similar, they have some differences. They differ in the amount of direct instruction that students receive about underlying problem-solving structures (e.g., subgoal labels explicitly describe the structure, whereas analogical encoding asks students to identify the structure). They also differ in the source of schemata (e.g., schema instruction provides schemata and analogical encoding asks students to create them). Though the approaches have never been empirically compared, their efficacy likely depends on the content being taught, the prior knowledge of the student, and the style of the instructor. For reasons that will be discussed in the next section, more complex content or students with less prior knowledge will probably benefit from more direct instruction approaches, such as subgoal labels and schema instruction. For content with less novel information or students with significant prior knowledge, more student-driven approaches, such as analogical encoding, would probably be more effective.

9.6.2.2 Helping Students to Retain Knowledge

Recognizing structural similarities between problems is likely the biggest barrier to transfer, but transfer also suffers when neural connections to relevant prior knowledge decays over time, causing a lack of retention, or time transfer. A common retention problem occurs in classes that have prerequisites. Instructors often complain that their students do not have the prior knowledge that they should have from previous classes. Assuming that students did learn what they needed to in previous classes, however, they would have a hard time activating it if their neural connections have sufficiently decayed. The good news is that it is much faster to relearn material (i.e., restrengthen neural connections) than it is to learn it for the first time (Hansen, Umeda, & McKinney, 2002). To promote retention, instructors should focus on learning and teaching strategies that will develop strong neural connections that will take a long time to decay.

A major factor in retention is how students learn knowledge. The default teaching style in higher education is direct instruction, meaning that an instructor tells students what they need to know. Many argue that this method is more effective and less taxing on learners than constructive methods, in which students build knowledge for themselves by exploring the problem-solving space (Kirschner, Sweller, & Clark, 2006). Constructed knowledge, however, often leads to better retention in the long run, when it is successful (Tobias & Duffy, 2009). Learning constructively by exploring problem spaces benefits from the generation effect. The *generation effect* states that learners are more likely to remember information when they generate it for themselves than when they are told it because the cues that they encounter while encoding information are similar to the cues that they encounter when they solve problems (de Winstanley, Bjork, & Bjork, 1996; Jacoby, 1978). Therefore, learners are more likely to activate relevant prior knowledge to solve problems if they constructed that knowledge while working on problems. Constructive learning, however, is not appropriate for all learning situations (e.g., when learners have little prior knowledge) and should be carefully conceptualized and planned before it is used (Tobias & Duffy, 2009).

When learning constructively is not a good option, consider how learners are practicing using the information that they have been told. A large body of research supports the notion that spaced practice, in which learners solve problems across several sessions, results in better retention than massed practice, in which learners solve problems in one sitting (Donovan & Radosevich, 1999). Massed practice can be good while students are building schemata and learning to recognize similarities between different examples, but spaced practice requires that learners devote attention to other tasks and then refocus on the problem-solving procedure, resulting in better long-term retention (Donovan & Radosevich, 1999). Most spaced practice studies have intervals from minutes to weeks, but spaced practice also explains why students who take cumulative final exams retain knowledge better (though students expecting a final exam also spend more time integrating information; Szpunar, McDermott, & Roediger, 2007). In related research, Trafton and Reiser (1993) found that interleaving studying examples and solving problems improves retention. In their paradigm, students studied examples and then applied what they had learned to solving a problem before studying a new example. This interleaved approach was more effective than studying all examples at once and then solving all problems at once (Trafton & Reiser, 1993).

The last technique to improve retention that we will discuss is the timing of feedback on problem-solving practice. In some cases, immediate feedback is the most effective type of feedback. Especially in language learning, which is related to syntax learning in programming, immediate feedback to fix errors is most beneficial (Kulik & Kulik, 1988). In more conceptually focused problem-solving, however, slightly delaying feedback can allow learners to recognize when they have made a mistake and fix it for themselves, improving retention (Mathan & Koedinger, 2003). Related to the spaced practice effect, delaying feedback by a significant amount of time (i.e., enough time to switch tasks) gives the learner another opportunity to encode information about correctly implementing the problem-solving process (called the delay-retention effect; Smith & Kimball, 2010).

9.6.3 Can We Promote Transfer between Domains?

Sometimes problem-solving strategies can be applied in multiple domains. For example, students' knowledge of algorithms should transfer to support problem-solving in math and science. The difficulty with cross-domain transfer, however, is that it becomes very difficult for learners to recognize commonalities among problem-solving contexts (Barnett & Ceci, 2002). Spontaneous transfer within a domain is already difficult; therefore, some cognitive scientists believe that spontaneous transfer across domains is very rare, at least for novices (Anderson, Reder, & Simon, 1996; Brown, 1992; Feldon, 2007; Singley & Anderson, 1989). They argue that knowledge is embedded in the context in which it was learned (e.g., in a classroom, with an example about averaging a waiter's tips in LISP; Anderson et al., 1996; Singley & Anderson, 1989). Therefore, if you want to promote transfer across domains, then you have to include contexts from all domains in the learning of knowledge (Brown, 1992). Including multiple domain-specific sets of information, however, places unreasonable demands on learners' cognitive resources and/or time (Feldon, 2007; Guzdial, 2015).

While some evidence suggests that novices cannot spontaneously transfer their knowledge to new domains, some people have had success. For example, Bassok (1990) explored methods of highlighting similarities between algebra and physics problems to promote spontaneous transfer between those fields. Stieff and Uttal (2015) have had success training students in spatial reasoning to improve their performance in science, technology, engineering, and mathematics (STEM) fields. In the computing domain, Klahr and Carver (1988) found that teaching elementary school children to debug Logo programs over several months helped them to complete a number of tasks in various domains, including allocating resources, following a route on a map, and correcting instructions. Computational thinking work has presented some evidence that teaching students computing concepts can improve their performance in other domains, like science (Basawapatna et al., 2011; Koh et al., 2010) and math (Schanzer et al., 2015; Schanzer, Fisler, & Krishnamurthi, 2018).

There are many more studies exploring transfer across disciplines, but the research is not conclusive and the arguments are too complex to succinctly describe in a section meant to introduce the transfer literature. In this section, we highlighted some of the foundational work from cognitive science for improving transfer with some examples of how it is applied to CEd. Much more work is needed, though, to explore various methods of promoting transfer and the conditions in which they are most successful.

9.7 Cognitive Load

Within an educational setting, we wish to focus the student's attention on the material to be learned. Learning occurs when the information from sensory input is attended to, processed within working memory, and then committed to LTM in the form of schemata or plans. One interesting theoretical framework that aids the design of effective instructional material is called *cognitive load*. This framework draws together many aspects of cognition. We focus in some detail on it and its practical implications for educators. See also Chapter 12 for a discussion of cognitive load in programming.

9.7.1 What Is Cognitive Load?

Cognitive load is the amount of work imposed on a learner's working memory while learning a specific task (van Gog & Paas, 2012). Cognitive Load Theory (CLT) is based on the architecture of the human brain, with the brain having both working memory and LTM. Working memory is limited in both capacity and duration (Cowan, 2010; Peterson & Peterson, 1959). Learning occurs when new information is related to knowledge already stored and organized in LTM, yielding a new, more elaborate, and extensive knowledge base (Sweller, 1988). The central problem identified by CLT is that learning is impaired when the total amount of processing requirements exceeds the limited capacity of working memory (Plass et al., 2010). Learning is reliant upon the degree of complexity of the new information to be processed and the way in which that information is presented. Using CLT, instructors attempt to design instructional material in a manner that will not overload working memory, so as to maximize learning.

As originally defined, CLT was the sum of three individual components: (1) *extraneous* load, the effort used to process information that is not fundamental to the concept or process that is being learned; (2) *intrinsic* load, the innate difficulty of the material being learned combined with the learner's characteristics (Leppink et al., 2013); and (3) *germane* load, the effort used to learn the actual material or concept. Recently, however, several researchers have questioned whether germane load is a separate component or is actually a piece of the intrinsic load (Kalyuga, 2011). The overall goal behind CLT is to reduce extraneous and intrinsic load, so as not to overload the cognitive process of working memory and impair learning.

Extraneous cognitive load is any information presented to the learner that is not strictly necessary for learning the material or concept. Having redundant information presented both textually and auditorily would be extraneous cognitive load. Extraneous load becomes a problem only when intrinsic load is high (Sweller, 1994). If there is minimal demand on cognitive resources, there is ample working memory to handle any extraneous load and learning can still occur. Worked examples, for instance, contain extraneous information, but if presented correctly, they can aid overall learning.

A topic is considered to have a high intrinsic load if the material being learned is interconnected; that is, learning requires processing several elements simultaneously to understand their relations and interactions (Sweller & Chandler, 1994). In CEd, simply learning the reserved words of a programming language represents very low interactivity (each is a separate, memorizable token), as opposed to understanding all of the elements in a program, where all of the tokens may potentially interact with each other (high interactivity).

Because intrinsic load is essential for comprehending the material and constructing knowledge structures, the instructional material must provide all of the components necessary to accommodate this load without exceeding the limits of working memory. Intrinsic load can also vary with the domain expertise and previous knowledge of the learner (Sweller et al., 2011), in that learners with a higher level of previous knowledge may chunk the material differently from novices (Bransford, 2000), allowing them to hold more information in working memory. Thus, the intrinsic load can change based on the learner. An element or a chunk of information for a learner and specific task is determined by the organized knowledge structures or *schemata* in that learner's LTM. With the development of expertise, the size of a person's chunks increases, and many interacting elements for a novice become encapsulated into a single element for an expert. The magnitude of the intrinsic cognitive load experienced by a learner is determined by the degree of interactivity of the essential elements relative to the level of learner expertise within the domain (Kalyuga, 2011). This begins to explain the difference between novice and expert programmers.

Sweller now defines germane load in terms of the working memory resources devoted to dealing with intrinsic cognitive load (Sweller, 2018). If, in the material to be learned, the interacting elements are intrinsic to the information being processed, then an intrinsic load is imposed. If multiple elements interact because of an instructional design choice, then extraneous cognitive load is imposed. Germane load is defined in terms of the resources of working memory that are devoted to dealing with the intrinsic load. The more resources that are devoted to intrinsic load, the fewer resources are available for extraneous factors, and higher germane load results. Using this definition, germane cognitive load is dependent on the relationship between the intrinsic and extraneous loads, and is not an independent source of load.

9.7.2 Empirical Evidence

Research findings supporting CLT principles come from four distinct types of measures:

(1) Indirect measures of cognitive load through task performance or accuracy (Ayres, 2001; Cooper & Sweller, 1987) or the time needed for task performance (Chandler & Sweller, 1991, 1992);
(2) Dual-task performance measures (Brünken et al., 2002, 2004);
(3) Direct physiological measures such as functional magnetic resonance imaging (Whelan, 2007) or electroencephalographic (Antonenko et al., 2010) or eye-tracking variables (van Gog & Scheiter, 2010);
(4) Subjective measurement rating scales (Leppink et al., 2013, 2014; Paas, 1992).

For a thorough treatise on measuring cognitive load, see Zheng (2018).

The implications of CLT have led to the understanding of several different known "effects" that a learner can experience during the learning process.

Empirical studies have found that by altering the instructional design materials, learning can be facilitated or impeded. These changes in learning are known as effects. All known effects can be explained using the CLT framework. For a full list and explanation of the effects attributed to cognitive load, see Sweller et al. (2011).

Found effects that have implications in CEd include:

- Worked example (problem completion) effect – students produce fewer errors and take less time to complete problems when they study expert solutions, or worked-out solutions, than when they solve the same problems from scratch with no sample solution to follow (Cooper & Sweller, 1987). The same is true for partially solved problems (problem completion) (Paas & van Merriënboer, 1994).
- Split-attention effect – information should be presented in a way that is as integrated as possible, both spatially and temporally (Sweller et al., 1990). Examples should imbed explanations rather than separate them into their own text.
- Modality effect – this occurs when multiple sources of information that cannot be understood in isolation are needed to be processed simultaneously, usually presented using spoken rather than written text (Tindall-Ford et al., 1997).
- Redundancy effect – this is when unnecessary, additional information is presented to the learner (Chandler & Sweller, 1991). This can occur when duplicate information is presented both textually and verbally.
- Expertise reversal effect – occurs when learning material gets in the way of learning for those with prior knowledge (Kalyuga et al., 2003).
- Guidance fading effect – states that novices should be provided with many worked examples, followed by completion problems and then full problems (Renkl & Atkinson, 2003; Renkl et al., 2004).
- Self-explanation effect – requiring the learner to self-explain new procedures or concepts to enhance learning (Chi et al., 1989; Renkl, 1997).
- Element interactivity effect – if intrinsic cognitive load is low, other cognitive load effects cannot be observed; however, if elements are highly interactive, variations in element interactivity can have profound effects on other load effects dependent on extraneous load (Sweller & Chandler, 1994; Tindall-Ford et al., 1997).

9.7.3 Cognitive Load in Computing

Incorporating CLT into computing education research occurs in the following forms: (1) use of worked examples; (2) use of subgoals; (3) Parsons' problems (a specific question format); and (4) attempts to measure cognitive load. The first three of these are all intended to reduce load.

9.7.3.1 Worked Examples

The first research involving cognitive load in computing used worked examples (Pirolli & Recker, 1994; Recker & Pirolli, 1995) for LISP. In a series of studies designed for implementing and testing a cognitive tutor, researchers used forms of worked examples to test student knowledge and learning capabilities. The result of the studies showed that students who studied the worked examples, especially with self-explanation skills, performed better than those who simply solved problems or had poor self-explanation skills.

The first extensive study on using a worked example completion format was conducted by van Merriënboer, using introductory computer programming problems (van Merriënboer & Krammer, 1990). A follow-up study (van Merriënboer & De Croock, 1992) examined students who generated programs from scratch compared to those who completed partially constructed programs. For students in the completion group, the presentation of new information and programming practice were linked to incomplete programs, and learners were only required to complete the partial solutions. In the generation group, both model programs and generation assignments were presented, with the model programs serving as the worked example; however, the students were not required to study the model program before beginning generation. The completion group had better post-performance.

Casperson and Bennedsen (2007) present a case for using worked examples in computing, but provide no empirical evidence validating their use. Skudder and Luxton-Reilly (2014) present sample worked examples that might be used in an introductory programming class with reasoning on why they might be beneficial, but no empirical evidence on their use within an actual class. Gray et al. (2007) present a detailed set of suggestions for implementing faded worked examples (similar to program completion) for an introductory programming course in C++. They decompose the task of programming into components whose cognitive load can be adequately handled by the students. The decomposition is based on abstract algorithmic dimensions and associated concrete programming constructs. The authors provide fully worked examples for all design–construct and implementation–construct pairs. However, once again, no empirical evidence exists on using the examples with students in either a laboratory- or a classroom-based study.

Finally, Garner (2002) designed and implemented a code restructuring tool to implement code completion tasks based on CLT and worked examples. The tool was designed to teach the Visual Basic programming language. A quasi-experimental study showed that students receiving the intervention spent less time solving problems, but had no learning gains over the control group.

9.7.3.2 Subgoals

Another way CEd researchers have attempted to lower the cognitive load of learners is through the use of subgoal labels (see Section 9.6.2.1). The first known work using subgoals in computing is Margulieux et al. (2012). This work used subgoal labels to teach learners how to develop a mobile application using MIT's Android AppInventor. Participants were shown a video using subgoal labels as callouts to provide structure to the solution process. The subgoal group attempted and completed successfully more subgoal steps of the assessment tasks, in addition to completing the tasks more quickly than the control group. The subgoal group also successfully completed more tasks on a retention task tested one week later. In a second study involving a think-aloud protocol while completing the app-building task, the subgoal group outperformed the control group. In addition, Margulieux et al. found that the student vocabulary included the subgoals.

Morrison et al. (2015) expanded the use of subgoals to learning with a text programming language using loops. The findings indicated that students who learned using subgoals performed better than those who learned without subgoals.

9.7.3.3 Parsons' Problems

One interesting approach to the teaching and assessment of programming is Parsons' problems (Parsons & Haden, 2006), in which correct code is broken into code fragments that have to be put in the correct order with the correct indentation. There are several variants, such as including unnecessary code as distractors (Denny et al., 2008). (See Chapter 15 for additional information on Parsons' problems.)

Work in this area has found that Parsons' problem scores correlate significantly with code-writing scores. Parsons' problems are simpler than writing code, in particular because students cannot get syntax errors, which lowers cognitive load. Students are more able to focus on issues like meaning and sequencing within problem-solving. This means that Parsons' problems might be a more efficient way to engage with programming than traditional code-writing tasks (Morrison et al., 2016).

9.7.4 Measuring Cognitive Load

Initial work in this area within CEd was done by Mason et al. (2012) and Mason and Cooper (2012). In this work, Mason and colleagues surveyed students in introductory programming courses offered by Australian universities and asked them about mental effort. Participants were asked to rate their own levels of mental effort on each of the three components of cognitive load using a nine-point Likert scale. They were also asked to estimate the levels of mental effort on each component experienced by an average student in their introductory programming course and that experienced by a student in the "bottom 10 percent of performance" in their course; however, the survey questions were never published or validated.

In Morrison et al. (2014), the authors adapted an existing cognitive load measurement (Leppink et al., 2013) to computing. They attempted to measure cognitive load components (intrinsic, extraneous, and germane) of learners in a computing environment. The instrument had good internal reliability, but has yet to be replicated.

9.8 Discussion

This chapter has briefly summarized a range of important topics from cognitive science, noting links with the CEdR literature and speculating about further avenues for research where possible. Apart from the inevitable conclusion that more work is needed, we will return to the concept of levels of analysis (Section 9.2) and recommend a general framework for describing CEdR.

Pedagogical: This level describes the aims, methods, subject matter, and theory of CEd in the abstract. Questions that fall into this level include: What are we trying to achieve? What is known about how individuals, groups, and communities construct knowledge? What is the current curriculum and the intended learning outcomes and what pedagogical methods will best deliver them? What target knowledge, skills, and mental models do learners need to be successful? What social and cultural factors affect learning outcomes? What educational concepts and frameworks usefully apply? Research relevant to this level will be being conducted in many disciplines and contexts, but may include specific disciplinary (CEd) topics.

Functional: This level describes the application and interaction of pedagogical and cognitive factors in practical CEd contexts (i.e., as they occur in real classrooms, institutions, or other learning environments). Are we achieving our goals? How are learners constructing and sharing their knowledge? Are they making progress with the intended curriculum and outcomes? Are they developing sound mental models? Are techniques for promoting transfer and reducing cognitive load working? What range of variation exists within a given group/population, why, and how can we influence it? How does the particular subject matter and tools of our field impact on teaching and learning? How do institutional context and policy settings affect outcomes? Research relevant to this level is specific to CEd. It is guided, shaped, and constrained by both of the pedagogical cognitive levels.

Cognitive: This level describes phenomena relating to the cognition and behavior of individuals. How do individuals represent and acquire knowledge and skills and how do they develop correct (and incorrect) mental models? What constraints arise from the nature of our learning and memory systems? How do attitudes, motivation, and specific behaviors affect learning outcomes? What factors promote transfer and reduce cognitive load? What is the range of variation and how (and how much) can individuals change or improve? Research relevant to this level will be being conducted generally in the cognitive sciences, but may include specific topics suggested by work at the functional level.

The functional level is the main and characteristic level of our field, but it is informed and constrained by both higher-level pedagogical and lower-level cognitive factors. When exploring a particular research topic within CEd, we suggest that all levels should be considered. Relevant factors, insights, or mechanisms might be found at any level.

Acronyms

CEd	Computing Education
CEdR	Computing Education Research
CLT	Cognitive Load Theory
LTM	Long-Term Memory
SM	Sensory Memory
STM	Short-Term Memory

References

ACM/IEEE-CS Joint Task Force on Computing Curricula (2013). *Computer Science Curricula 2013*. New York: ACM Press and IEEE Computer Society Press.

Allport, D. A. (1985). Distributed memory, modular systems and dysphasia. In S. K. Newman & R. J. Epstein (Eds.), *Current Perspectives in Dysphasia* (pp. 32–60). London, UK: Churchill Livingstone.

Almstrum, V. L., Hazzan, O., Guzdial, M., & Petre, M. (2005). Challenges to computer science education research. In *Proceedings of the 36th SIGCSE Technical Symposium on Computer Science Education (SIGCSE '05)* (pp. 191–192). New York: ACM.

Anderson, J. R. (1976). *Language, Memory, and Thought*. Hillsdale, NJ: Lawrence Erlbaum.

Anderson, J. R. (1982). Acquisition of cognitive skill. *Psychological Review*, 89, 369–406.

Anderson, J. R., Reder, L. M., & Simon, H. A. (1996). Situated learning and education. *Educational Researcher*, 25(4), 5–11.

Antonenko, P., Paas, F., Grabner, R., & Van Gog, T. (2010). Using electroencephalography to measure cognitive load. *Educational Psychology Review*, 22, 425–438.

Atkinson, R. C., & Shiffrin, R. M. (1968). Human memory: A proposed system and its control processes. In K. W. Spence & J. T. Spence (Eds.), *Psychology of Learning and Motivation* (pp. 89–195). New York: Academic Press.

Ayres, P.L. (2001). Systematic mathematical errors and cognitive load. *Contemporary Educational Psychology*, 26, 227–248.

Baddeley, A. D. (1966). The influence of acoustic and semantic similarity on long-term memory for word sequences. *The Quarterly Journal of Experimental Psychology*, 18(4), 302–309.

Baddeley, A. D. (1999). *Essentials of Human Memory*. Hove, UK: Psychology Press.

Baddeley, A. D., Eysenck, M. W., & Anderson, M. C. (2015). *Memory*, 2nd edn. London and New York: Psychology Press, Taylor and Francis.

Baddeley, A. D., & Hitch, G. (1974). Working memory. In G. H. Bower (Ed.), *The Psychology of Learning and Motivation* (pp. 47–89). New York: Academic Press.

Baldwin, L. P., & Macredie, R. D. (1999). Beginners and programming: Insights from second language learning and teaching. *Education and Information Technologies*, 4(2), 167–179.

Bandura, A. (1993). Perceived self-efficacy in cognitive development and functioning. *Educational Psychologist*, 28(2), 117–148.

Banerjee, A. V., Bhattacharjee, S., Chattopadhyay, R., & Alejandro, J. G. (2017). The Untapped Math Skills of Working Children in India: Evidence, Possible Explanations, and Implications. Retrieved from www.alejandroganimian.com/s/Banerjee-et-al-2017-2017-08-17.pdf

Barnett, S. M., & Ceci, S. J. (2002). When and where do we apply what we learn?: A taxonomy for far transfer. *Psychological Bulletin*, 128(4), 612–637.

Barsalou, L. W. (1983). Ad hoc categories. *Memory & Cognition*, 11(3), 211–227.

Basawapatna, A., Koh, K. H., Repenning, A., Webb, D. C., & Marshall, K. S. (2011). Recognizing computational thinking patterns. In *Proceedings of the 42nd ACM Technical Symposium on Computer Science Education* (pp. 245–250). New York: ACM.

Bassok, M. (1990). Transfer of domain-specific problem-solving procedures. *Journal of Experimental Psychology: Learning, Memory, and Cognition*, 16(3), 522–533.

Bassok, M., & Holyoak, K. J. (1989). Interdomain transfer between isomorphic topics in algebra and physics. *Journal of Experimental Psychology: Learning, Memory, and Cognition*, 15(1), 153–166.

Bereiter, C. (1985). Toward a solution of the learning paradox. *Review of Educational Research*, 55, 201–226.

Biggs, J., & Collis, K. (1989). Towards a model of school-based curriculum development and assessment using the SOLO taxonomy. *Australian Journal of Education*, 33(2), 151–163.

Bloom, B., Englehart, M. D., Furst, E. J., Hill, W. H., & Krathwohl, D. (1956). *Taxonomy of Educational Objectives: Handbook I: Cognitive Domain*. New York: Longmans.

Bonar, J., & Soloway, E. (1989). Preprogramming knowledge: A major source of misconceptions in novice programmers. In E. Soloway & J. C. Spohrer (Eds.), *Studying the Novice Programmer* (pp. 324–353). Hillsdale NJ: Lawrence Erlbaum.

Bouton, M. E. (2016). *Learning and Behavior: A Contemporary Synthesis*, 2nd edn. Sunderland, MA: Sinauer Associates.

Brachman, R. J. & Levesque, H. J. (Eds.) (1985). *Readings in Knowledge Representation*. San Francisco, CA: Morgan Kaufmann Publishers, Inc.

Bransford, J. (2000). *How People Learn: Brain, Mind, Experience, and School*. Washington, DC: National Academies Press.

Bransford, J. D., Brown, A., & Cocking, R. (1999). *How People Learn: Mind, Brain, Experience, and School*. Washington, DC: National Research Council.

Brown, A. L. (1992). Design experiments: Theoretical and methodological challenges in creating complex interventions in classroom settings. *The Journal of the Learning Sciences*, 2(2), 141–178.

Brünken, R., Plass, J. L., & Leutner, D. (2004). Assessment of cognitive load in multimedia learning with dual-task methodology: Auditory load and modality effects. *Instructional Science*, 32, 115–132.

Brünken, R., Steinbacher, S., Plass, J. L., & Leutner, D. (2002). Assessment of cognitive load in multimedia learning using dual-task methodology. *Experimental Psychology*, 49, 109–119.

Busjahn, T., Schulte, C., Sharif, B., Begel, A., Hansen, M., Bednarik, R., Orlov, P., Ihantola, P., Shchekotova, G., & Antropova, M. (2014). Eye tracking in computing education. In *Proceedings of the Tenth Annual Conference on International Computing Education Research* (pp. 3–10). New York: ACM.

Cao, L. (2010). In-depth behavior understanding and use: The behavior informatics approach. *Information Sciences*, 180(17), 3067–3085.

Cao, L., & Philip, S. Y. (Eds.) (2012). *Behavior Computing: Modeling, Analysis, Mining and Decision*. London, UK: Springer Verlag.

Carraher, T. N., Carraher, D. W., & Schliemann, A. D. (1985). Mathematics in the streets and in schools. *British Journal of Developmental Psychology*, 3(1), 21–29.

Caspersen, M. E., & Bennedsen, J. (2007). Instructional design of a programming course: a learning theoretic approach. In *Proceedings of the Third International Workshop on Computing Education Research* (pp. 111–122). New York, NY: ACM.

Chaiklin, S. (2003). The zone of proximal development in Vygotsky's analysis of learning and instruction. In A. Kozulin, B. Gindis, V. Ageyev, & S Miller (Eds.), *Vygotsky's Educational Theory in Cultural Context* (pp. 39–64). Cambridge, UK: Cambridge University Press.

Chandler, P., & Sweller, J. (1991). Cognitive load theory and the format of instruction. *Cognition and instruction,* 8, 293–332.

Chandler, P., & Sweller, J. (1992). The split-attention effect as a factor in the design of instruction. *British Journal of Educational Psychology,* 62, 233–246.

Chi, M. T., Bassok, M., Lewis, M. W., Reimann, P., & Glaser, R. (1989). Self-explanations: How students study and use examples in learning to solve problems. *Cognitive Science*, 13(2), 145–182.

Chi, M. T., Feltovich, P. J., & Glaser, R. (1981). Categorization and representation of physics problems by experts and novices. *Cognitive Science*, 5(2), 121–152.

Chi, M. T. H., & Ohlsson, S. (2005). Complex declarative learning. In K. J. Holyoak & R. G. Morrison (Eds.), *Cambridge Handbook of Thinking and Reasoning* (pp. 371–399). Cambridge, UK: Cambridge University Press.

Cianciolo, A. T., & Sternberg, R. J. (2004). *Intelligence: A Brief History*. Oxford, UK: Blackwell Publishing.

Cooper, G., & Sweller, J. (1987). Effects of schema acquisition and rule automation on mathematical problem-solving transfer. *Journal of Educational Psychology*, 79, 347–362.

Cooper, J. O. (1982). Applied behavior analysis in education. *Theory into Practice,* 21(2), 114–118.

Cooper, P. A. (1993). Paradigm shifts in designed instruction: From behaviorism to cognitivism to constructivism. *Educational Technology*, 33(5), 12–19.

Cowan, N. (2001). The magical number 4 in short-term memory: A reconsideration of mental storage capacity. *Behavioral and Brain Sciences*, 24, 87–185.

Cowan, N. (2010). The magical mystery four: How is working memory capacity limited, and why? *Current Directions in Psychological Science*, 19, 51–57.

Crystal, D. (2010) *The Cambridge Encyclopedia of Language*, 3rd edn. Cambridge, UK: Cambridge University Press.

Day, S. B., & Goldstone, R. L. (2012). The import of knowledge export: Connecting findings and theories of transfer of learning. *Educational Psychologist*, 47(3), 153–176.

Deco, G., & Rolls, E. T. (2005). Attention, short-term memory, and action selection: A unifying theory. *Progress in Neurobiology*, 76, 236–256.

Denny, P., Luxton-Reilly, A., & Simon, B. (2008). Evaluating a new exam question: Parsons problems. In *Proceedings of the Fourth International Workshop on Computing Education Research* (pp. 113–124). New York: ACM.

de Winstanley, P. A., Bjork, E. L., & Bjork, R. A. (1996). Generation effects and the lack thereof: The role of transfer-appropriate processing. *Memory*, 4, 31–48.

Donovan, J. J., & Radosevich, D. J. (1999). A meta-analytic review of the distribution of practice effect: Now you see it, now you don't. *Journal of Applied Psychology,* 84(5), 795–805.

Dunlosky, J., Rawson, K. A., Marsh, E. J., Nathan, M. J., & Willingham, D. T. (2013). Improving students' learning with effective learning techniques: Promising directions from cognitive and educational psychology. *Psychological Science in the Public Interest,* 14(1), 4–58.

Eiriksdottir, E., & Catrambone, R. (2011). Procedural instructions, principles, and examples: how to structure instructions for procedural tasks to enhance performance, learning, and transfer. *Human Factors,* 53(6), 749–770.

Emmer, E. T., & Stough, L. M. (2001). Classroom management: A critical part of educational psychology, with implications for teacher education. *Educational Psychologist,* 36(2), 103–112.

Enderton, H. B. (2001). *A Mathematical Introduction to Logic,* 2nd edn. San Diego, CA: Academic Press.

Engel, A. K., Fries, P., & Singer, W. (2001). Dynamic predictions: Oscillations and synchrony in top-down processing. *Nature Reviews Neuroscience,* 2(10), 704–716.

Eriksen, C. W., & James, J. D. S. (1986). Visual attention within and around the field of focal attention: A zoom lens model. *Perception & Psychophysics,* 40(4), 225–240.

Ertmer, P. A., & Newby, T. J. (1993). Behaviorism, cognitivism, constructivism: Comparing critical features from an instructional design perspective. *Performance Improvement Quarterly,* 6(4), 50–72.

Feldman, D. H. (2004). Piaget's stages: The unfinished symphony of cognitive development. *New Ideas in Psychology,* 22, 175–231.

Feldon, D. F. (2007). The implications of research on expertise for curriculum and pedagogy. *Educational Psychology Review,* 19(2), 91–110.

Felleisen, M., Findler, R. B., Flatt, M., & Krishnamurthi, S. (2001). *How to Design Programs: An Introduction to Programming and Computing.* Cambridge, MA: MIT Press.

Ferguson, R. W. (1994). MAGI: Analogy-based encoding using regularity and symmetry. In *Proceedings of the 16th Annual Conference of the Cognitive Science Society* (pp. 283–288). London, UK: Psychology Press, Cognitive Science Society.

Ferman, S., & Karni, A. (2012). Procedural and declarative memory in the acquisition of morphological knowledge: A model for second language acquisition in adults. In M. Leikin, M. Schwartz, & Y. Tobin (Eds.), *Current Issues in Bilingualism. Literacy Studies (Perspectives from Cognitive Neurosciences, Linguistics, Psychology and Education),* Vol. 5 (pp. 201–216). Dordrecht, The Netherlands: Springer.

Firestone, C., & Scholl, B. J. (2016). Cognition does not affect perception: Evaluating the evidence for "top-down" effects. *Behavioral and Brain Sciences,* 20, 1–77.

Fischer, K. W. (1980). A theory of cognitive development: The control and construction of hierarchies of skills. *Psychological Review,* 87(6), 477–531.

Flavell, J. H. (1992). Cognitive development: Past, present, and future. *Developmental Psychology,* 28(6), 998–1005.

Flavell, J. H. (1996). Piaget's legacy. *Psychological Science,* 7(4), 200–203.

Foer, J. (2012). *Moonwalking with Einstein: The Art and Science of Remembering Everything.* London, UK: Penguin.

Fougnie, D. (2008). The relationship between attention and working memory. In N. B. Johansen (Ed.), *New Research on Short-Term Memory* (pp. 1–45). Hauppauge, NY: Nova Science Publishers.

Gardner, H. (1985). *The Mind's New Science: A History of the Cognitive Revolution.* New York: Basic Books.

Gardner, H. (1993). *Frames of Mind: The Theory of Multiple Intelligences.* New York: Basic Books.

Garner, S. (2002). Reducing the cognitive load on novice programmers. In P. Barker & S. Rebelsky (Eds.), *Proceedings of ED-MEDIA 2002 – World Conference on Educational Multimedia, Hypermedia & Telecommunications* (pp. 578–583). Denver, CO: Association for the Advancement of Computing in Education (AACE).

Gentner, D. (1983). Structure-mapping: A theoretical framework for analogy. *Cognitive Science*, 7(2), 155–170.

Gentner, D. (2002). Mental models, psychology of. In N. Smelser & P. B. Bates (Eds.), *International Encyclopedia of the Social and Behavioral Sciences* (pp. 9683–9687). Amsterdam, The Netherlands: Elsevier Science.

Gentner, D., Loewenstein, J., & Thompson, L. (2003). Learning and transfer: A general role for analogical encoding. *Journal of Educational Psychology*, 95(2), 393–408.

Gentner, D. & Stevens, A. L. (Eds.) (1983). *Mental Models.* Hillsdale, NJ: Erlbaum.

Gick, M. L., & Holyoak, K. J. (1980). Analogical problem solving. *Cognitive Psychology*, 12(3), 306–355.

Gick, M. L., & Holyoak, K. J. (1983). Schema induction and analogical transfer. *Cognitive Psychology*, 15(1), 1–38.

Gilbert, C. D., & Sigman, M. (2007). Brain states: Top-down influences in sensory processing. *Neuron*, 54(5), 677–696.

Glass, A. L., Holyoak, K. J., & Santa, J. L. (1979). *Cognition.* Reading, MA: Addison-Wesley.

Goldstein, E. B., & Brockmole, J. (2016). *Sensation and Perception*, 10th edn. Belmont, CA: Wadsworth Cengage Learning.

Gray, S., St Clair, C., James, R., & Mead, J. (2007). Suggestions for graduated exposure to programming concepts using fading worked examples. In *Proceedings of the Third International Workshop on Computing Education Research* (pp. 99–110). New York: ACM.

Gregory, R. (1997). *Eye and Brain: The Psychology of Seeing*, 5th edn. Oxford, UK: Oxford University Press.

Guzdial, M. (2015). Learner-centered design of computing education: Research on computing for everyone. *Synthesis Lectures on Human-Centered Informatics*, 8(6), 1–165.

Hampton, J. A. (2016). Categories, prototypes and exemplars. In N. Riemer (Ed.), *The Routledge Handbook of Semantics* (pp. 125–141). New York: Routledge.

Hansen, L., Umeda, Y., & McKinney, M. (2002). Savings in the relearning of second language vocabulary: The effects of time and proficiency. *Language Learning*, 52(4), 653–678.

Hansen, M. E., Lumsdaine, A., & Goldstone, R. L. (2013). An experiment on the cognitive complexity of code. In *Proceedings of the Thirty-Fifth Annual Conference of the Cognitive Science Society*. London, UK: Psychology Press,

Cognitive Science Society. Retrieved from www.indiana.edu/~pcl/papers/hansencode2013.pdf

Hattie, J. A. (2009). *Visible Learning: A Synthesis of 800+ Meta-Analyses on Achievement*. Abingdon, UK: Routledge.

Hattie, J. (2012). *Visible Learning for Teachers: Maximizing Impact on Learning*. Abingdon, UK: Routledge.

Hazzan, O., Lapidot, T., & Ragonis, N. (2014). Problem-solving strategies. In O. Hazzan, T. Lapidot, & N. Ragonis (Eds.), *Guide to Teaching Computer Science* (pp. 75–93). London, UK: Springer.

Hebb, D. O. (1949). *The Organization of Behavior: A Neuropsychological Theory*. New York: John Wiley & Sons.

Hinton, G. E., & Anderson, J. A. (1989). *Parallel Models of Associative Memory*. Hillsdale, NJ: Lawrence Erlbaum Associates, Inc.

Holyoak, K. J., & Morrison, R. G. (Eds.) (2005). *The Cambridge Handbook of Thinking and Reasoning*. Cambridge, UK: Cambridge University Press.

Jacoby, L. L. (1978). On interpreting the effects of repetition: Solving a problem versus remembering a solution. *Journal of Verbal Learning and Verbal Behavior*, 17(6), 649–667.

Jonassen, D. H. (2000). Toward a design theory of problem solving. *Educational Technology Research and Development*, 48(4), 63–85.

Jensen, A. R. (1998). *The g Factor*. Westport, CT: Praeger.

Johnson-Laird, P. N. (1983). *Mental Models: Towards a Cognitive Science of Language, Inference, and Consciousness*. Cambridge, MA: Harvard University Press.

Kalyuga, S. (2011). Cognitive load theory: How many types of load does it really need? *Educational Psychology Review*, 23, 1–19.

Kalyuga, S., Ayres, P., Chandler, P., & Sweller, J. (2003). The expertise reversal effect. *Educational Psychologist*, 38, 23–31.

Kapp, K. M. (2012). *The Gamification of Learning and Instruction: Game-Based Methods and Strategies for Training and Education*. San Francisco, CA: John Wiley & Sons.

Kátai, Z., Juhász, K., & Adorjáni, A. K. (2008). On the role of senses in education. *Computers & Education*, 51(4), 1707–1717.

Killian, S. (2016). Hattie Effect Size 2016 Update. Retrieved from www.evidencebasedteaching.org.au/hattie-effect-size-2016-update/. Reproduced in Lubelfeld, M., Polyak, N., & Caposey, P. J. (2018). *Student Voice: From Invisible to Invaluable* (p. 3). Lanham, MD: Rowman & Littlefield.

Kirschner, P. A., Sweller, J., & Clark, R. E. (2006). Why minimal guidance during instruction does not work: An analysis of the failure of constructivist, discovery, problem-based, experiential, and inquiry-based teaching. *Educational Psychologist*, 41(2), 75–86.

Klahr, D., & Carver, S. M. (1988). Cognitive objectives in a LOGO debugging curriculum: Instruction, learning, and transfer. *Cognitive Psychology*, 20(3), 362–404.

Klaus-Dieter, G. (2018). Eye Movements in Programming Education Workshops. Retrieved from www.mi.fu-berlin.de/en/inf/groups/ag-ddi/Gaze_Workshop/index.html

Koh, K. H., Basawapatna, A., Bennett, V., & Repenning, A. (2010). Towards the automatic recognition of computational thinking for adaptive visual language learning. In *Visual Languages and Human-Centric Computing (VL/HCC)* (pp. 59–66). New York: IEEE.

Kulik, J. A., & Kulik, C. L. C. (1988). Timing of feedback and verbal learning. *Review of Educational Research*, 58(1), 79–97.

Kurtz, K. J., Miao, C. H., & Gentner, D. (2001). Learning by analogical bootstrapping. *The Journal of the Learning Sciences*, 10(4), 417–446.

Laird, J. E., & Rosenbloom, P. (1996). The evolution of the Soar cognitive architecture. In D. M. Steier & T. M. Mitchell (Eds.), *Mind Matters: A tribute to Allen Newell* (pp. 1–50). Mahwah, NJ: Lawrence Erlbaum Associates.

Lenneberg, E. H. (1967). The biological foundations of language. *Hospital Practice*, 2(12), 59–67.

Leppink, J., Paas, F., Van der Vleuten, C. P., Van Gog, T., & van Merriënboer, J. J. (2013). Development of an instrument for measuring different types of cognitive load. *Behavior Research Methods*, 45, 1058–1072.

Leppink, J., Paas, F., van Gog, T., van der Vleuten, C. P. & van Merriënboer, J. J. (2014). Effects of pairs of problems and examples on task performance and different types of cognitive load. *Learning and Instruction*, 30, 32–42.

Lindsay, P. H., & Norman, D. A. (1977). *Human Information Processing: An Introduction to Psychology*, 2nd edn. London, UK: Academic Press.

Mandelbaum, E. (2017). Associationist Theories of Thought. *The Stanford Encyclopedia of Philosophy (Summer 2017 Edition)*, E. N. Zalta, ed. Retrieved from https://plato.stanford.edu/archives/sum2017/entries/associationist-thought/

Margulieux, L. E., Guzdial, M., & Catrambone, R. (2012). Subgoal-labeled instructional material improves performance and transfer in learning to develop mobile applications. In *Proceedings of the Ninth Annual International Conference on International Computing Education Research* (pp. 71–78). New York: ACM.

Marr, D. (1982). *Vision: A Computational Investigation into the Human Representation and Processing of Visual Information*. New York: Freeman.

Marr, D., & Poggio, T. (1976). *From Understanding Computation to Understanding Neural Circuitry. A.I. Memo 357*. Cambridge, MA: Massachusetts Institute of Technology.

Marshall, S. P. (1995). *Schemas in Problem Solving*. Cambridge, UK: Cambridge University Press.

Mason, R., & Cooper, G. (2012). Why the bottom 10% just can't do it: Mental effort measures and implication for introductory programming courses. In *Proceedings of the Fourteenth Australasian Computing Education Conference*, Vol. 123 (pp. 187–196). Sydney, Australia: Australian Computer Society.

Mason, R., Cooper, G., & de Raadt, M. (2012). Trends in introductory programming courses in Australian universities: languages, environments and pedagogy. In *Proceedings of the Fourteenth Australasian Computing Education Conference*, Vol. 123 (pp. 33–42). Sydney, Australia: Australian Computer Society.

Mathan, S., & Koedinger, K. R. (2003). Recasting the feedback debate: Benefits of tutoring error detection and correction skills. In *Proceedings of the International Conference on Artificial Intelligence in Education* (pp. 13–20). Amsterdam, The Netherlands: IOS Press.

Mather, G. (2016). *Foundations of Sensation and Perception*, 3rd edn. London & New York: Routledge.

McClamrock, R. (1991). Marr's three levels: A re-evaluation. *Minds and Machines*, 1(2), 185–196.

McNeill, D. (1970). *The Acquisition of Language: The Study of Developmental Psycholinguistics*. New York & London: Harper and Row.

McSweeney, F. K., & Murphy, E. S. (Eds.) (2014). *The Wiley Blackwell Handbook of Operant and Classical Conditioning*. Madden, MA: John Wiley & Sons.

Medin, D. L., Altom, M. W., & Murphy, T. D. (1984). Given versus induced category representations: Use of prototype and exemplar information in classification. *Journal of Experimental Psychology: Learning, Memory, and Cognition*, 10(3), 333–352.

Miller, G. A. (1956). The magical number seven, plus or minus two: Some limits on our capacity for processing information. *Psychological Review*, 63, 81–97.

Minda, J. P., & Smith, J. D. (2002). Comparing prototype-based and exemplar-based accounts of category learning and attentional allocation. *Journal of Experimental Psychology: Learning, Memory, and Cognition*, 28(2), 275–292.

Morris, M. R., Begel, A., & Wiedermann, B. (2015). Understanding the challenges faced by neurodiverse software engineering employees: Towards a more inclusive and productive technical workforce. In *Proceedings of the 17th International ACM SIGACCESS Conference on Computers & Accessibility* (pp. 173–184). New York: ACM.

Morrison, B. B., Dorn, B., & Guzdial, M. (2014). Measuring cognitive load in introductory CS: Adaptation of an instrument. In *Proceedings of the Tenth Annual Conference on International Computing Education Research (ICER '14)* (pp. 131–138). New York: ACM.

Morrison, B. B., Margulieux, L. E., & Guzdial, M. (2015). Subgoals, context, and worked examples in learning computing problem solving. In *Proceedings of the Eleventh Annual International Conference on International Computing Education Research* (pp. 21–29). New York: ACM.

Morrison, B. B., Margulieux, L. E., Ericson, B., & Guzdial, M. (2016). Subgoals help students solve Parsons problems. In *Proceedings of the 47th ACM Technical Symposium on Computing Science Education (SIGCSE '16)* (pp. 42–47). New York: ACM.

Newell, A., & Simon, H. A. (1972). *Human Problem Solving*. Englewood Cliffs, NJ: Prentice-Hall.

Newport, E. L. (1990). Maturational constraints on language learning. *Cognitive Science,* 14(1), 11–28.

Norman, D. A. (Ed.) (1970). *Models of Human Memory*. New York & London: Academic Press.

Novick, L. R., & Bassok, M. (2005). Problem solving. In K. J. Holyoak & R. G. Morrison (Eds.), *Cambridge Handbook of Thinking and Reasoning* (pp. 321–349). Cambridge, UK: Cambridge University Press.

Paas, F. G. (1992). Training strategies for attaining transfer of problem-solving skill in statistics: A cognitive-load approach. *Journal of Educational Psychology,* 84, 429–434.

Paas, F. G., & van Merriënboer J. J. (1994). Variability of worked examples and transfer of geometrical problem-solving skills: A cognitive-load approach. *Journal of Educational Psychology*, 86(1), 122–133.

Pandža, N. B. (2016) Computer programming as a second language. In D. Nicholson (Ed.), *Advances in Human Factors in Cybersecurity. Advances in Intelligent Systems and Computing*, Vol. 501 (pp. 439–445). Cham, Switzerland: Springer.

Parsons, D., & Haden, P. (2006). Parson's programming puzzles: A fun and effective learning tool for first programming courses. In *Proceedings of the 8th*

Australasian Conference on Computing Education – Volume 52 (ACE '06) (pp. 157–163). Darlinghurst, Australia: Australian Computer Society.

Pashler, H. (Ed.) (2016). *Attention*. New York: Psychology Press.

Pea, R. D., & Kurland, D. M. (1984). *On the Cognitive Prerequisites of Learning Computer Programming. Technical Report No. 18.* New York: Bank Street College of Education.

Peterson, L., & Peterson, M. J. (1959). Short-term retention of individual verbal items. *Journal of Experimental Psychology*, 58, 193–198.

Piaget, J. (1952). *The Origins of Intelligence in Children*. New York: International Universities Press.

Piaget, J. (1964). Part I: Cognitive development in children: Piaget development and learning. *Journal of Research in Science Teaching*, 2(3), 176–186.

Piaget, J. (1971a). The theory of stages in cognitive development. In D. R. Green, M. P. Ford, & G. B. Flamer (Eds.), *Measurement and Piaget* (pp. 1–11). New York: McGraw-Hill.

Piaget, J. (1971b). Developmental stages and developmental processes. In D. R. Green, M. P. Ford, & G. B. Flamer (Eds.), *Measurement and Piaget* (pp. 172–188). New York: McGraw-Hill.

Pirolli, P., & Recker, M. (1994). Learning strategies and transfer in the domain of programming. *Cognition and Instruction,* 12, 235–275.

Plass, J. L., Moreno, R., & Brünken, R. (2010). *Cognitive Load Theory*. Cambridge, UK: Cambridge University Press.

Pohl, R. (Ed.) (2004). *Cognitive Illusions: A Handbook on Fallacies and Biases in Thinking, Judgement and Memory*. Hove, UK: Psychology Press.

Posner, M. I., Snyder, C. R., & Davidson, B. J. (1980). Attention and the detection of signals. *Journal of Experimental Psychology: General*, 109(2), 160–174.

Powell, S. R. (2011). Solving word problems using schemas: A review of the literature. *Learning Disabilities Research & Practice*, 26(2), 94–108.

Quine, W. V. (1969). Natural kinds. In C. G. Hempel, D. Davidson, & N. Rescher (Eds.), *Essays in Honor of Carl G. Hempel* (pp. 5–23). Dordrecht, The Netherlands: Springer.

Radvansky, G. (2016). *Human Memory*, 2nd edn. New York: Routledge.

Recker, M., & Pirolli, P. (1995). Modeling individual differences in students' learning strategies. *The Journal of the Learning Sciences*, 4, 1–38.

Reed, S. K., Ernst, G. W., & Banerji, R. (1974). The role of analogy in transfer between similar problem states. *Cognitive Psychology*, 6(3), 436–450.

Renkl, A. (2017). Learning from worked-examples in mathematics: Students relate procedures to principles. *ZDM Mathematics Education*, 49(4), 571–584.

Renkl, A., Atkinson, R., & Grosse, C. (2004). How fading worked solution steps works – A cognitive load perspective. *Instructional Science*, 32, 59–82.

Renkl, A., & Atkinson, R. (2003). Structuring the transition from example study to problem solving in cognitive skill acquisition: A cognitive load perspective. *Educational Psychologist*, 38(1), 15–22.

Renkl, A. (1997). Learning from worked-out examples: A study on individual differences. *Cognitive Science*, 21, 1–29.

Revlin, R. (2012). *Cognition: Theory and Practice*. New York: Worth Publishers.

Rieber, R. W., & Robinson, D. K. (Eds.) (2004). *The Essential Vygotsky*. New York: Kluwer Academic/Plenum Publishers.

Rist, R. S. (1995). Program structure and design. *Cognitive Science, 19,* 507–562.

Robertson, S. I. (2016). *Problem Solving: Perspectives From Cognition and Neuroscience.* New York: Rutledge.

Robins, A. (1996). Consolidation in neural networks and in the sleeping brain. *Connection Science*, 8(2), 259–276.

Robins, A. (2010). Learning edge momentum: A new account of outcomes in CS1. *Computer Science Education*, 20, 37–71.

Rosch, E., Mervis, C. B., Gray, W. D., Johnson, D. M., & Boyes-Braem, P. (1976). Basic objects in natural categories. *Cognitive Psychology*, 8(3), 382–439.

Rosenbloom, P. S., Laird, J. E., Newell, A., & McCarl, R. (1991). A preliminary analysis of the Soar architecture as a basis for general intelligence. *Artificial Intelligence*, 47(1–3), 289–325.

Schacter, D. L., Addis, D. R., & Buckner, R. L. (2007). Remembering the past to imagine the future: the prospective brain. *Nature Reviews Neuroscience*, 8(9), 657–661.

Schank, R. C., & Abelson, R. P. (1975). Scripts, plans, and knowledge. In *Proceedings of the 4th International Joint Conference on Artificial Intelligence (IJCAI'75) – Volume 1* (pp. 151–157). San Francisco, CA: Morgan Kaufmann Publishers.

Schank, R. C., & Abelson, R. P. (2013). *Scripts, Plans, Goals, and Understanding: An Inquiry into Human Knowledge Structures.* New York: Psychology Press.

Schanzer, E., Fisler, K., & Krishnamurthi, S. (2018). Assessing bootstrap: Algebra students on scaffolded and unscaffolded word problems. In *Proceedings of the 49th ACM Technical Symposium on Computer Science Education (SIGCSE '18)* (pp. 8–13). New York: ACM.

Schanzer, E., Fisler, K., Krishnamurthi, S., & Felleisen, M. (2015). Transferring skills at solving word problems from computing to algebra through bootstrap. In *Proceedings of the 46th ACM Technical Symposium on Computer Science Education* (pp. 616–621). New York: ACM.

Schoenfeld, A. H. (1985). *Mathematical Problem Solving.* London, UK: Academic Press.

Scholnick, E. K., Nelson, K., Gelman, S. A., & Miller, P. H. (Eds.) (1999). *Conceptual Development: Piaget's Legacy.* New York: Psychology Press.

Shams, L., & Seitz, A. R. (2008). Benefits of multisensory learning. *Trends in Cognitive Sciences*, 12(11), 411–417.

Singer, S. R., Nielsen, N. R., & Schweingruber, H. A. (Eds.) (2012). *Discipline-Based Education Research: Understanding and Improving Learning in Undergraduate Science and Engineering.* Washington, DC: National Academies Press.

Singleton, D. M., & Ryan, L. (2004). *Language Acquisition: The Age Factor.* Clevendon, UK: Multilingual Matters.

Singley, M. K., & Anderson, J. R. (1989). *The Transfer of Cognitive Skill* (No. 9). Cambridge, MA: Harvard University Press.

Skinner, B. F. (1938). *The Behavior of Organisms: An Experimental Analysis.* Oxford, UK: Appleton-Century.

Skinner, B. F. (1953). *Science and Human Behavior.* New York: Macmillan.

Skudder, B., & Luxton-Reilly, A. (2014). Worked examples in computer science. In *Proceedings of the Sixteenth Australasian Computing Education Conference-Volume 148* (pp. 59–64). Sydney, Australia: Australian Computer Society.

Smith, T. J. (2007). The ergonomics of learning: Educational design and learning performance. *Ergonomics*, 50(10), 1530–1546.

Smith, T. A., & Kimball, D. R. (2010). Learning from feedback: Spacing and the delay–retention effect. *Journal of Experimental Psychology: Learning, Memory, and Cognition*, 36(1), 80–95.

Soar (2018). Soar Home. Retrieved from https://soar.eecs.umich.edu/

Sowa, J. F. (2000). *Knowledge Representation: Logical, Philosophical, and Computational Foundations.* Pacific Grove, CA: Brooks/Cole.

Sternberg, R. J. (Ed.) (1982). *Handbook of Human Intelligence.* New York: Cambridge University Press.

Stickgold, R. (2005). Sleep-dependent memory consolidation. *Nature*, 437(7063), 1272–1278.

Stieff, M., & Uttal, D. (2015). How much can spatial training improve STEM achievement? *Educational Psychology Review*, 27(4), 607–615.

Sutton, R. S., & Barto, A. G. (1998). *Reinforcement Learning: An Introduction* (Vol. 1, No. 1). Cambridge, MA: MIT Press.

Sweller, J. (1994). Cognitive load theory, learning difficulty, and instructional design. *Learning and Instruction,* 4, 295–312.

Sweller, J. (1988). Cognitive load during problem solving: Effects on learning. *Cognitive Science,* 12, 257–285.

Sweller, J. (2010). Element interactivity and intrinsic, extraneous, and germane cognitive load. *Educational Psychology Review*, 22(2), 123–138.

Sweller, J. (2018). The role of independent measures of load in cognitive load theory. In R. Z. Zheng (Ed.), *Cognitive Load Measurement and Application* (pp. 17–22). New York: Routledge.

Sweller, J., Ayres, P., & Kalyuga, S. (2011). *Cognitive Load Theory.* New York: Springer.

Sweller, J., & Chandler, P. (1994). Why some material is difficult to learn. *Cognition and Instruction,* 12, 185–233.

Sweller, J., Chandler, P., Tierney, P., & Cooper, M. (1990). Cognitive load as a factor in the structuring of technical material. *Journal of Experimental Psychology: General*, 119, 176–192.

Szpunar, K. K., McDermott, K. B., & Roediger, H. L. (2007). Expectation of a final cumulative test enhances long-term retention. *Memory & Cognition*, 35(5), 1007–1013.

Takeuchi, T., Duszkiewicz, A. J., & Morris, R. G. (2014). The synaptic plasticity and memory hypothesis: Encoding, storage and persistence. *The Philosophical Transactions of the Royal Society B*, 369(1633), 20130288.

Thorndike, E. (1911). *Animal Intelligence: Experimental Studies.* New York: Macmillan.

Tindall-Ford, S., Chandler, P., & Sweller, J. (1997). When two sensory modes are better than one. *Journal of Experimental Psychology: Applied*, 3(4), 257–287.

Tobias, S., & Duffy, T. M. (Eds.) (2009). *Constructivist Instruction: Success or Failure?* New York: Routledge.

Tonegawa, S., Pignatelli, M., Roy, D. S., & Ryan, T. J. (2015). Memory engram storage and retrieval. *Current Opinion in Neurobiology*, 35, 101–109.

Trafton, J. G., & Reiser, B. J. (1993). Studying examples and solving problems: Contributions to skill acquisition. In *Proceedings of the 15th conference of the Cognitive Science Society* (pp. 1017–1022). London, UK: Psychology Press, Cognitive Science Society.

Treisman, A. M., & Gelade, G. (1980). A feature-integration theory of attention. *Cognitive Psychology*, 12(1), 97–136.

Tulving, E. (1985). *Elements of Episodic Memory*. Oxford, UK: Clarendon Press.

Tulving, E., & Craik, F. I. (Eds.) (2005). *The Oxford Handbook of Memory*. New York: Oxford University Press.

Tulving, E., & Thomson, D. M. (1973). Encoding specificity and retrieval processes in episodic memory. *Psychological Review*, 80(5), 352–373.

Tulving, E. (1974). Cue-dependent forgetting: When we forget something we once knew, it does not necessarily mean that the memory trace has been lost; it may only be inaccessible. *American Scientist*, 62(1), 74–82.

Tversky, A., & Kahneman, D. (1974). Judgment under uncertainty: Heuristics and biases. *Science*, 185(4157), 1124–1131.

Twyman, J. S. (2014). Behaviour analysis in education. In F. K. McSweeney & E. S. Murphy (Eds.), *The Wiley Blackwell Handbook of Operant and Classical Conditioning* (pp. 553–558). Madden, MA: John Wiley & Sons.

Ullman, M. T. (2001). A neurocognitive perspective on language: The declarative/procedural model. *Nature Review Neuroscience*, 2, 717–726.

Ullman, M. T. (2004). Contribution of memory circuits to language: The declarative/procedural model. *Cognition*, 92, 231–270.

van Gog, T., & Paas, F. (2012). Cognitive load measurement. In N. M. Seel (Ed.), *Encyclopedia of the Sciences of Learning* (pp. 599–601). New York: Springer.

van Gog, T., & Scheiter, K. (2010). Eye tracking as a tool to study and enhance multimedia learning. *Learning and Instruction,* 20, 95–99.

van Merriënboer, J. J., & Krammer, H. P. (1990). The "completion strategy" in programming instruction: Theoretical and empirical support. In S. Dijkstra, B. H. A. M. van Hout Wolters, & P. C. van der Sijde (Eds.), *Research on Instruction: Design and Effects* (pp. 45–61). Englewood Cliffs, NJ: Educational Technology Publications.

van Merriënboer, J. J., & De Croock, M. B. (1992). Strategies for computer-based programming instruction: Program completion vs. program generation. *Journal of Educational Computing Research,* 8, 365–394.

van Merriënboer, J. J., Clark, R. E., & De Croock, M. B. (2002). Blueprints for complex learning: The 4C/ID-model. *Educational Technology Research and Development*, 50(2), 39–61.

Volder, J. E. (1959). The CORDIC trigonometric computing technique. *IRE Transactions on Electronic Computers*, 3, 330–334.

Wang, Y., & Chiew, V. (2010). On the cognitive process of human problem solving. *Cognitive Systems Research*, 11(1), 81–92.

Watson, J. B. (1913). Psychology as the behaviorist views it. *Psychological Review*, 20, 158–177.

Watson, J. B. (1930). *Behaviorism*. New York: Norton.

Weiser, M., & Shertz, J. (1983). Programming problem representation in novice and expert programmers. *International Journal of Man–Machine Studies*, 19(4), 391–398.

Wertsch, J. V. (1984). The zone of proximal development: Some conceptual issues. *New Directions for Child and Adolescent Development,* 23, 7–18.

Wertsh, J. V., & Tulviste, P. (1990). Apprenticeship in thinking: Cognitive development in social context. *Science*, 249(4969), 684–686.

Whelan, R. R. (2007). Neuroimaging of cognitive load in instructional multimedia. *Educational Research Review*, 2, 1–12.

Whitney, P. (2001). Schemas, frames, and scripts in cognitive psychology. In N. J. Smelser & P. B. Baltes (Eds.), *International Encyclopedia of the Social & Behavioral Sciences* (pp. 13522–13526). Amsterdam, The Netherlands: Elsevier.

Wood, D., Bruner, J. S., & Ross, G. (1976). The role of tutoring in problem solving. *Journal of Child Psychology and Psychiatry*, 17(2), 89–100.

Woollard, J. (2010). *Psychology for the Classroom: Behaviourism*. New York: Routledge.

Zheng, R. Z. (2018). *Cognitive Load Measurement and Application: A Theoretical Framework for Meaningful Research and Practice*. New York: Routledge.

10 Higher Education Pedagogy

Kerry Shephard

10.1 Introduction

Three things have dominated my thinking in the context of this chapter. The first relates to the advice given to me by one of the commissioning editors: that the chapter should address what "someone with no prior background who is thinking of getting into some educational research (e.g., a computing teacher) [should] know before they start." The resulting conundrum is how to summarize effectively and usefully several centuries of educational research and thinking into one quite short chapter. The way that I have tried to do this is to encourage readers to consider the nature of learning in higher education as comprising "what we know," "what skills we have to put our knowledge into effect," and "what we choose to do with the knowledge and skills at our disposal." This division has certainly helped me to articulate what I know about this topic and to provide computing education (CEd) researchers with some key questions to punctuate their reading. The approach may even stimulate a research agenda for CEd researchers.

The second addresses the nature of educational research, with particular reference to researching educational practices from within a discipline. Boyer is credited with reminding the academic world that academic tasks need to be undertaken in a scholarly manner. Boyer went on to provide some ideas about what scholarship actually entails and how we might, as a profession of scholarly teachers, undertake its evaluation or assessment. Boyer published his important work on academic scholarship in 1990 and followed it in 1996 with some observations on assessing scholarship (Boyer, 1990, 1996). Boyer identified four broad categorizations of scholarship (discovery, essentially research; integration, emphasizing multidisciplinary approaches; application, generally referred to nowadays as engagement; and teaching) and conceptualized these as interacting with one another as a university professor goes about his or her everyday work. Some might suggest that the focus of Boyer's papers was to address an increasing disconnect between university research, which by and large was scholarly, and teaching, which was often less scholarly. For each of his scholarships, Boyer suggested six standards: clear goals, adequate preparation/appropriate procedures, appropriate methods, significant results, effective presentation, and reflective critique. Boyer went on to identify four approaches that should in general terms be used to evaluate the quality of the scholarship involved: self-review, peer review, review of clients, and review by students. Boyer envisaged, I think, the general principle that the sources of evaluative evidence should be broadly based and systematic. Why is this important and relevant to CEd researchers reading this chapter? Fundamentally, and from the perspective of the scholarship of teaching and learning, this discourse describes a system where professional higher education teachers also, and to a degree, research their own teaching practice. Several authors have since taken Boyer's proposals and simplified them. Shulman, in particular, emphasized that scholarship in the context of teaching requires that the work: must be made public; must be available for peer review and critique according to accepted standards; and must be able to be reproduced and built on by other scholars (e.g., see Hutchings & Shulman, 1999). Naturally, and in line with Boyer's original standards, the scholar involved also needs to build his or her practice on what has come before. The development is therefore not simply in the practice of an individual, but in that of the profession. From Boyer's perspective, the construct of CEd research is potentially problematic, as research into computer science education should be something that all scholarly computer science teachers should be doing as a matter of course. Nevertheless, if higher education teachers of computer science do research their teaching practice, they are obliged to undertake this in essentially the same way, and with the same level of scholarly integrity, as they undertake their disciplinary computer science research.

The third is described here not, as it may seem at first glance, as obsequious or flattering toward the discipline of computer science, but rather as an expression of concern. Not all higher education disciplines have well-developed, pedagogically focused research networks. I've often wondered if computer science does because it needs to more than most. I have no doubt that with pedagogical knowledge comes pedagogical power. If we are not smart about the way that we teach our historians, our scientists, or our politicians, we trouble the world with inadequate intellectuals. Our computer science graduates, on the other hand, perhaps more now than ever before, enter a world where one bright idea could change the world forever.

10.2 Learning Theories and Some Big Educational Ideas

Many teachers have heard, or have, opinions along the lines of, "Learning theories? I've been teaching in universities for years now and I got on perfectly well without theories, other than my own, of course. And those fine scholars who taught me all those years ago didn't appear to me to have great insights into learning theories!" And what about jargon, or "education speak?" Do we really need to know about active learning, lifelong learning, and pedagogy, or even epistemology, ontology, and epistemic shifts, to teach nowadays?

Fair enough – why make teaching more complicated than it need be? On the other hand, learning and teaching in higher education are probably substantially different from what they were in years gone by. Classes are generally larger and generally drawn from wider socioeconomic backgrounds. Expectations are different, and in particular, nowadays a range of evaluative processes make life difficult for higher education teachers who, in the opinion of students, are not particularly good higher education teachers. And, in all probability, most readers of this chapter will have some personal experience of being taught by one or more teachers who not only had little educational theory to draw on, but who also persisted in simply telling students what they needed to know to pass the exams. Most readers of this chapter will wish to be better than those teachers were. On balance, I think it is worth progressing with the idea that knowledge about learning theories, and about new ideas in higher education learning and teaching, will not necessarily do harm to those who teach.

We should start with a broad categorization of learning theories. When we encounter a new term or idea, we should at least be able to understand where it fits within the broad range of educational ideas. I think it is fair to say that most of the terms that new higher education teachers encounter while learning to teach in higher education fit within the broad category of constructivism. The essence of constructivism is that learners develop their own mental models of the world around them and new information is subjectively interpreted by them, based on their prior personal experience. The consequence of thinking of learning in a constructivist way is that knowledge is not necessarily uniform, but varies from person to person. No matter what the teacher thinks he or she is teaching, the learner may be learning something very different. Many of the modern paradigms of learning and teaching in higher education have developed from constructivist ways of thinking. These include problem-based learning, enquiry-based learning, and the broad area of social learning.

Constructivism is highly fashionable in modern learning and teaching discourse and, in a historical sense, is situated within a relativist epistemology and subjective ontology, and a long way from science. Its leading theorists include Bruner and Vygotsky. It is especially important to mention Vygotsky because so much of learning and teaching in higher education nowadays is considered to be a social phenomenon. Social constructivism suggests that learning isn't an individual process, but involves social networks, with "culture" providing mediating influences. In some respects, and as emphasized by Vygotsky, the interaction between a teacher and the learner is itself a social interaction, and the differential impact on learning that the teacher has is undoubtedly an important concept. Readers who wish to know more about these ideas might usefully consult Lave and Wenger (1991) in exploration of social learning and communities of practice.

Often seen as "the alternative" to constructivism, behaviorism is firmly rooted within positivism and objectivism and is distinctly unfashionable in many teaching and learning circles. Those with a grudge against behaviorism tend to suggest that it involves simple transfer of information from teacher to learner. More enlightened advocates of behaviorist ways of doing things tend to emphasize that, in at least some circumstances, teachers do quite like to identify what it is that the student is supposed to be learning and use this "intended learning outcome" as a means to consider the most appropriate forms of teaching activity that may enable the learner to achieve these outcomes. Similarly, if learners are told what it is they are expected to learn, they may in some circumstances be more self-motivated in achieving these learning outcomes. Behaviorism also does contribute quite substantially to traditional ways of identifying the roles and operation of feedback to students on the basis of what they've learned so far and what they may need in order to do better in future. Most of us have some experience of the personal benefits of positive reinforcement – likely one of the most important features of behaviorism as applied to teaching. Readers of this chapter will understand that personally I find behaviorist ways of thinking about learning to be very useful in some situations. Leading theorists include Skinner, and some would identify Bloom and Krathwohl's work on cognitive (knowledge and skills) and affective (values and attitudes) learning domains to be derived from behaviorist ways of thinking about learning (e.g., see Bloom, Hastings, & Madaus, 1971, as a useful introduction to this way of thinking).

Our third category, cognitivism, somewhat pragmatically attempts to straddle the gulf between these epistemological and ontological extremes. The leading theorist for pragmatic ways of thinking about learning was Dewey, but Gagne is thought to have contributed significantly to our current interpretations of this category. Cognitivist interpretations of learning tend to focus on the cognitive processes that contribute to the processing of information from experience through to memory. An important contribution to this category was work in the 1960s by psychologists in identifying concepts, processes, or structures, such as short-term memory, working memory, and long-term memory. Some cognitivist theorists in this area hypothesize close comparisons between the way that the human brain works and the way that a computer works, although not being an expert in either, I'm not convinced. Driscoll (2005) is credited with many of the ideas that encourage teachers to facilitate learning in relation to cognitive processing theory.

One problem in education nowadays stems from the multiplicity of its theoretical building blocks. The ideas and concepts that are widely used and coexist in education nowadays do come from quite divergent theoretical backgrounds. And as they work together, they evolve and merge, and sometimes it is difficult to identify precisely the journey that they've undertaken. Many educators and educational researchers nowadays are pragmatic about these matters. And being a very pragmatic person myself, I am inclined to take aspects of these learning theories that make sense to me and use them where I think they will be helpful to me for understanding the nature of the teaching that I'm doing and of the learning that I'm facilitating. Readers with this mind-set would do well to consult Biggs and Tang (2007).

It does seem to me that CEd researchers reading this chapter would benefit by reflecting on their use of educational theory and the links that they find between these theories and the concepts that they make use of in their CEd research. Research on learning and teaching that is not, at its heart, based on theory may not find the same acceptance outside of the particular discipline as research that is.

So what's that about big educational ideas?

10.2.1 Intended Learning Outcomes and Constructive Alignment

I doubt that it will be possible to identify the real origins of the ideas behind constructive alignment, but the term itself was developed by John Biggs and is in essence the theme that provides structure to Biggs' textbooks on teaching for learning at university (Biggs & Tang, 2007). Constructive alignment developed from a substantial twentieth-century educational movement that nowadays is identified as outcomes-based education (OBE) or outcomes-based teaching and learning. In essence, the movement suggests that educators and education work best when the educator concerned considers what, precisely, learners will be able to do after they've been taught that they couldn't do before they were taught.

Central to OBE is the intended learning outcome (ILO), and it is probably fair to say that the adoption of ILOs has contributed more angst and frustration to higher education teachers than has any other development in recent times. Before OBE and ILOs, higher education teachers in most disciplines generally described their teaching in terms of what the teacher does and what the teacher will do, with a focus on the topics that will be lectured on or discussed in the university course. Those who adopt OBE and ILOs do need to focus on the learning that the students achieve and the processes that the students go through in order to achieve this learning. Higher education teachers who have embraced OBE and ILOs have needed either to learn this afresh or to transform the way that they think about their teaching. In this process of transformation, higher education teachers will inevitably need to think about the best approach that teachers can adopt to encourage student learning and the best approach that students can adopt to achieve this learning. These approaches are described as teaching and learning approaches (TLAs). Then almost inevitably, higher education teachers with this mind-set think about the best way to assure themselves, their students, and other stakeholders in the system of the extent to which the learners have learned the ILOs. And there we have constructive alignment – constructive because the ideas focus on what the students do and learn, rather than on what the teacher does; and alignment because there needs to be some sort of alignment between the intended learning (or ILO), the teaching and learning activity (or TLA), and the assessment that confirms that the students have learned. For those who appreciate it, constructive alignment has provided a great way to think about their teaching.

But not everyone appreciates the ILO and its contribution to constructive alignment (Havnes & Prøitz, 2016). Reasons for objecting to an almost universal use of ILOs in some educational systems are quite diverse, but often are based on analyses that deny the constructivist origins of these ideas and emphasize the ILO's behaviorist links. Many educators doubt, for example, that it is possible to define and to measure outcomes clearly enough for the ideas behind constructive alignment to be useful. Certainly, many higher education teachers have experiences where the teacher hopes that the students will learn something, but the complexity of the teaching and learning environment that they are working in means that it is challenging to define what that something is and to develop an assessment to ensure its learning. Constructive alignment can be aspirational rather than obligatory.

It does seem to me that CEd researchers reading this chapter would benefit by reflecting on their own assumptions about ILOs and OBE in their teaching and CEd research, and to think deeply about the kinds of outcomes that they anticipate or hope for. Sometimes this process results in constructively aligned anticipation of what students will know and can do, but sometimes also earnest hopes that are only tenuously related to what and how teaching is envisioned.

10.2.2 Phenomenography and Deep Approaches to Learning

Although substantial research into university teaching occurred throughout the latter half of the twentieth century, higher education teachers began to feel the force of this in the 1980s. A key contributor was undoubtedly phenomenography. This developed initially as a research approach, essentially getting to grips with the diversity of ways that teachers and learners conceptualized their activities (Entwistle, 1997; Trigwell, 2006). A founding question related to the ways in which students approached and conceptualized their learning as either a deep approach or a surface approach. More recently, researchers in this domain identified that some students in some situations take a strategic approach. Phenomenography opened the way to a great deal of research that identified that students approach learning tasks in different ways and that the ways that teachers teach have some influence on the ways that students learn. Deeper approaches to learning probably are better in some contexts than surface approaches to learning, and teachers who teach in a way that encourages deeper approaches to learning may, in some contexts, be better teachers.

10.2.3 Student-Centered Teaching

One good idea may well lead to another, and the next big educational idea that we should consider attempts to put much late-twentieth-century educational research into one easily managed concept. Teachers whose teaching encourages students to take deep approaches to their learning by and large tend to emphasize a particular range of teaching approaches. They may, as examples, involve students in the design of their curriculum and frequently ask students for feedback on their teaching approaches. No doubt the teaching will be outcome-oriented and constructively aligned, and it will encourage learning activities that relate directly to the nature of the desired learning. Rather than students listening in lectures to what the teacher tells them they should be doing, they will spend most time actually doing these things. Teachers who put the students at the center of learning rather than themselves tend to think about what students are expected to learn in the course, rather than what teachers hope to teach. The teaching becomes student-centered rather than teacher-centered. O'Neill and McMahon (2005) reviewed much of the relevant literature in this area.

Biggs (1999) describes two interacting variables that influence the effectiveness of learning. The first variable is the level of engagement adopted by learners. At one level, they may be simply trying to memorize what is taught; a relatively lowly cognitive process. At a higher cognitive level, they may be involved in theorizing, reflecting, and abstracting about what has been taught. The second variable is the extent to which the teaching method obliges learners to be actively involved. Problem-based learning, for example, requires activity by learners, whereas a standard instructional lecture may not. It is then possible to describe how individual learners approach their learning in relation to these two variables. Some will require very little teacher-induced activity to be highly engaged with the task, while others will only engage when required to, such as by the imposition of a required learning activity. Biggs maintains that "good teaching is getting most students to use the higher cognitive level processes that the more academic students use spontaneously" (Biggs, 1999, p. 4). The variable that teachers have some control over is their teaching method, and many of the teaching approaches that can be adopted to encourage learners to use higher-cognitive-level processes fall into the category of learner-centered approaches to teaching. Naturally, there is another complication, in that the teaching methods likely to work best depend to a large extent on the circumstances.

10.2.4 Academic Development

Academic development units developed substantially within higher education institutions throughout the 1970s and 1980s. Units were supported by educational researchers and academic development specialists who had transferred from education departments (which had previously had a focus on school-based education with strong links to teacher training). Units also included some with an increasing focus on technologies in education (arguably starting with the overhead projector, but rapidly developing into the learning technologies). Land (2001) described a range of different orientations to academic development that substantially describe the varying nature of higher education development nowadays. Strong links are nowadays made between academic development for new teachers (often involving compulsory courses in higher education), changes in educational practice (fewer lectures, more focus on student activity, clearly identified learning outcomes, diverse assessments, much more formative assessment, more group work, and some link to general educational outcomes or graduate attributes). Research that ties this together includes that by Gibbs and Coffey (2004), who explored the extent to which the application of these ideas actually improved student learning.

There are also strong links between educational ideas and ideas about lifelong learning and learning in less formal situations. CEd researchers and computer science teachers reading this chapter may wish to ask themselves if their teaching approaches will encourage learners to take responsibility for their own learning, and therefore be most likely to extend beyond the constraints of the course, or degree, both temporally and spatially, as well as to ask what forms of learning will be most valued by their students. In the long term, will students most value the knowledge and skills that they are learning, or might students be simultaneously learning and valuing opportunities to consider what they might wish to do with this knowledge and these skills?

10.3 How Will You Teach? The Power of Feedback

There appears little doubt that a major predictor of both good teaching and good learning is good feedback. Feedback is one of the most researched aspects of education, and yet probably is one of the most challenging aspects of higher education teaching in any discipline nowadays. Large group sizes, highly diverse student groups, and heavy academic workloads tend to go against the good intentions that many higher education teachers have to provide good feedback to their students. Feedback as a topic within educational research has also changed significantly in recent years. Books on higher education teaching in the last century may not have even mentioned feedback as a separate topic, including it rather as an element of assessment with a focus on formative assessment, and likely from a behaviorist theoretical standpoint, with an emphasis on correcting aberrant learning. Nowadays, feedback is a topic in its own right, and its importance reflects the extent to which it has been researched in recent years. In some respects, how a university teacher conceptualizes the process of providing feedback to learners is likely a defining characteristic of how that teacher conceptualizes both teaching and learning and their theoretical standpoint on how students learn. Constructivism has had a significant impact on the nature of feedback and research into feedback in recent years.

It may seem disrespectful to so much research by so many researchers who came before, but it was Hattie and Timperley (2007) who developed a framework for effective feedback, based on literally hundreds of meta-reviews of that research, and so they have dominated thinking about feedback in education most recently. Hattie and Timperley identified four levels of feedback: *task level*, essentially how well tasks have been completed; *process level*, the extent to which learners have understood the tasks to be completed; *self-regulation level*, the extent to which learners have conceptualized their own learning; and *self level*, feedback directed at the learners' appreciation of themselves or their generalized self-efficacy. These researchers went on to identify three major questions that those who provide feedback and those who receive it could or perhaps should be asking ("Where am I going?" in relation to the goals of learning; "How am I doing?" in relation to, usually, some established standard or success criterion; and "Where to next?" in relation to ongoing challenges). This framework provides a highly focused resource for higher education teachers to help them identify the nature of the feedback that they usually provide to students and also the changes that they may make in the future.

As with other frameworks, however, it obscures, or takes for granted, so much that CEd researchers may be interested in. For example, implicit within the framework is the idea that goals, perhaps specified as ILOs, are referenced as criteria that all learners may be capable of achieving (albeit to varied standards). Much of higher education, however, either openly or in some unthinking way, still proceeds on the basis that not all students can possibly gain A+ grades and that some unwritten regulation demands that only the best in any given cohort can get the best grade. Questions like these demand that higher education teachers, and those who research university teaching, reflect on their own points of view about the nature of higher education and of higher education teaching. The feedback that we actually provide to our students does not necessarily fit the Hattie and Timperley framework. Similarly, there is an implicit assumption in much of this research that students actually engage with the feedback that higher education teachers provide them, but research by Price, Handley, and Millar (2011) confirms that student engagement with feedback can be limited at several key stages.

Feedback has been reviewed in detail recently (Ott, Robins, & Shephard, 2016) with a particular focus on CEd and on feedback at the self-regulation level.

10.4 Assessment, Evaluation, and Assurance of Learning

The terms "assessment" and "evaluation" have simple, everyday meanings, and in some ways this everyday use downplays the complexity and importance of assessment and evaluation in higher education. In addition, the terms mean different things in different countries in a higher education sense. In New Zealand and in much of Europe, assessment is what teachers do to individual students to discover if they've learned what the teachers think they ought to have learned. Assessments often involve examinations in which named individuals participate. Evaluation, on the other hand, in these settings is a broadbrush approach ideally (from my perspective) applied by the teacher concerned to discover if the learning and teaching processes worked as they were supposed to. In general, if students are asked to contribute to an evaluation, they are anonymous in the process. These terms are reversed in some other countries, making comparisons difficult at times. I'm increasingly using the term "assurance of learning" because in some ways this combines both approaches. Teachers need to assure themselves and others that the teaching that they've been doing has been good enough to achieve the learning that was intended. They also need to assure themselves that individual students have learned and earned the academic credits that they expect.

10.4.1 Assessment

When it comes to assessment, those who appreciate the benefits of constructive alignment, outcome-based assessment, and the ILO do have a substantial advantage over other educators who do not. Advocates for constructive alignment and its logical consequential processes will have on their mind the nature of the intended learning outcome involved when they design their assessment. They will, for example, find it easier to describe learning outcomes in the cognitive domain than in the affective domain, and similarly, find it far easier to describe lower-order cognitive learning (such as remembering and understanding) than higher-order cognitive learning (such as application, synthesis, and evaluation). This ease of describing outcomes translates directly into ease of designing assessments that explore the attainment of these outcomes. Formal, traditional written examinations are likely unsurpassed as tools to assess what students have remembered or can explain. Practical examinations involving computers are likely good tools to assess what students can actually do with the computer. Neither are necessarily ideal tools to allow students to demonstrate their higher-order cognitive skills such as creativity and the ability to evaluate the worth of their knowledge. Nor are they necessarily tools to enable students to demonstrate a range of outcomes involving both cognitive and affective learning, such as teamwork or behaving ethically. Supervised project work may provide better tools for these purposes.

The same framework helps teachers to address a range of other pedagogical questions. Assessment theory demands that assessments are both valid (in that they actually assess what it is that the students are supposed to have learned and not something else) and reliable (in that a given student with a given level of learning would likely achieve similarly in a different but similar assessment). By constructively aligning the assessment with the ILO, teachers will find it relatively straightforward to ensure validity (by ensuring that the assessment provides learners with an opportunity to demonstrate their attainment of the learning outcome) and reliability (by designing a range of assessments, all of which will adequately assess the intended outcome). Alternative approaches do exist, of course, and no doubt some higher education teachers do design their assessments in the context of "let's keep the field open and see what students produce."

Higher education teachers often ask – sometimes in the context of the idea that "assessment somehow drives learning" (rather than perhaps what we would prefer as "learners' interests drive learning" or "motivating teachers drives learning") – if all of the intended outcomes do need to be assessed, or just some of them. For a course with many detailed intended outcomes, such an approach could place substantial assessment burdens on both the teacher and student. There is no doubt that higher education assessment nowadays is a more substantial enterprise than it was when I was a student. In days gone by, assessment was addressed in end-of-year exams, whereas nowadays assessments in some universities, some subject areas, and some departments appear to occur every week with assessed essays and assignments and project reports, as well as end-of-year exams. The scenario plays out differently in different topics, but in general terms, such a question brings into consideration additional assessment topics.

- Many intended outcomes are consequential on others and therefore appear in nested arrangements. Formal assessments can focus on the major intended outcomes and in so doing can address the minor, more basic outcomes.

- Although the process of designing a complex set of ILOs may be a great asset to a university teacher as they design their teaching and their assessments, too much complexity will almost certainly detract from the authenticity of the learning and teaching situation and of the assessment. Authenticity in this context refers to the nature of the task that a professional might engage in. Often this is in the form of a complex report or the creation of a product, rather than the detail of a particular action. Teachers will need to assure themselves that the students are capable of undertaking the particular actions, but they may do this best by designing their assessment to be as authentic, to the professional, as possible. Biggs and Tang provide extensive advice on teaching and assessing "functional knowledge" that, at its heart, needs to be authentic (Biggs & Tang, 2007).
- Arguably, the majority of assessment in higher education ought to be formative in nature rather than summative. Formative assessment enables teachers to provide feedback to students in a way that does not jeopardize their final grade for any particular course. This feedback enables students to reassess their mental models of whatever is being taught and to actually benefit from the interaction that they are having with their teacher. In many cases, a summative assessment provides little opportunity for constructive feedback, and there is substantial evidence that many students fail to engage with the feedback that comes with summative assessments (Price et al., 2011).
- How can we know that the individual asking for academic credit has created the work being assessed? Personally, I think that this increasingly provides higher education's greatest challenge (Löfström et al., 2015).

10.4.2 Evaluation

For me, the obligation to evaluate my teaching is not part of a neoliberal plot to commodify my contribution to higher education, nor a managerial process imposed on me to demonstrate my effectiveness, although for others it may be these things. For me, the evaluation of my teaching and of the consequences of my teaching is a part of being a professional and is closely allied to my commitment to scholarship. I'm interested in how well I do what I do and how to improve what I do. A great deal of research has been undertaken on how best to evaluate teaching in higher education, but in general, most researchers come to the conclusion that the evaluation process should make use of a diverse range of indicators. In my preferred order of importance, these are the following:

Self-evaluation: This category owes much to the work of Schön in developing the idea of the reflective practitioner (Schön, 1983). Reflective practitioners think deeply about what they're doing and what they've done. This deep thinking provides higher education teachers with a great deal of insight into how they're teaching and how effectively this is converted into learning. Many professions require their professionals to keep portfolios, and for many of us, the teaching portfolio is an important tool to help us gather evidence of what we've done and how well we have done it, as well as the vehicle within which an evidence-based reflective commentary can be situated. If our teaching isn't effective, we should be the first to know about it.

Peer evaluation: Teaching in higher education should ideally not be a lonely pursuit. Most of us work in teams to support our students, and most of us encourage teamwork in our teaching. Peer review, or peer evaluation, is not always an easy option, but if done well, it can greatly contribute to an effective evaluation of teaching. Peers do not have to attend our lectures. They can comment on our course designs or on the feedback that we give to our students. They can second-mark our assessments or meet with our students to discuss any concerns they may have.

Outcome measures: No matter how wonderful the teaching may or may not appear to be, if all of the students fail their exams, then surely something is amiss. Learning outcomes are, in my view, an essential element of an evaluative process. But as with other contributors to evaluation, there do need to be some checks and balances. No matter how well-intentioned, if the same university teacher designs the course, teaches the course, and assesses the course, they may not be able to maintain the level of objectivity necessary for a fair evaluation. On the other hand, in some higher education situations nowadays, higher education teachers are under a great deal of pressure to maintain class numbers and to boost retention figures. It does appear to me that some form of external oversight is an essential element of evaluative contributions based on outcome measures. External oversight may be in the form of an external assessor, external examiner, or a regular contribution from a peer.

Feedback from students: In my own institution, it often appears as if the only data relevant to the evaluation of teaching are from student feedback. Students are routinely asked to comment on how well organized the teacher was, how well they stimulated interest, and a myriad of other concerns that may or may not be relevant to an evaluation of teaching. As well as contributing to the teachers' reflection on teaching, they also contribute in a quite direct way to promotion applications. I offer the opinion that they are divisive and incorrectly applied in this way. Nevertheless, student feedback on their experiences is no doubt an important element of an evaluation of teaching, and most teachers are pleased to hear student opinions on many facets of the learning and teaching environment. By and large, I suggest that students' opinions on how well organized the teacher was are more valuable than our students' opinions on, as examples, the content of the course or the academic level of this content. There is, of course, a danger that too much power in the hands of groups of students, who are not as committed to the discipline being studied as the teachers are, will contribute to softening or even dumbing down of the teaching. In these situations, there needs to be something else that balances this effect.

And, let us be clear: evaluation is not the end of a process. If anything, it is simply a step on the way to scholarly teaching and an essential element of the CEd researcher's data set.

10.4.3 Assurance of Learning

For me, this is a relatively new but exciting concept. It certainly helps us to overcome some of the tragic confusion that exists around the use of the terms "assessment" and "evaluation" in different parts of the world, hence allowing us to research these concepts on an international basis. It also forces us to identify the relationships that exist between assessment and evaluation, teachers and learners, teaching and learning, and to articulate the responsibilities that each of the stakeholders has within these dualities. Personally, I think it's quite reasonable for those who pay the fees, be they taxpayers or students, and those who employ the graduates to ask the overriding question, "What have students learned (to know, to do, or to be) that they didn't know, couldn't do, or wouldn't be before?" and to expect some relatively jargon-free answers.

Personally, I need to know more than the fact that 80 percent of the students passed the course, of which 30 percent scored very highly, alongside a list of topics taught in the curriculum. Such information would certainly not assure me that the students have learned what they're supposed to have learned. On the way, I would like particular information that assures me that students have not achieved a pass on the basis of good learning in some areas that compensates for poor learning in others areas; and if this is the case, I do need the details. For example, if the course or the program identifies good communication skills as an outcome alongside skills in computer programming, I would like to be assured that our excellent computer programmer also has reasonable communication skills; and if not, please do tell me just how bad they are at communicating. Assurance of learning as a concept implies some degree of transparency on behalf of the student, the teacher, and the institution.

10.5 Dispositions and Graduate Attributes

It has become fashionable nowadays for institutions to claim that their teaching will foster learning that not only is directly relevant to a particular discipline, but also is relevant to graduateness and citizenship. Our teaching will encourage graduates to be honest, to have integrity, and to be socially and environmentally responsible and globally competent. Our teaching will also contribute to overcoming racial and gender biases in our societies. There are in many cases clear links between what the institution expects of its graduates and what professional bodies expect of their professionals, often described in the form of professional values.

Within the world of science education, however, there are serious concerns about the extent to which science education not only ignores these contributions, but also deliberately or inadvertently discourages learners to consider, for example, the social implications of their newfound knowledge (Cech, 2014). Given the nature of computing and its development within our societies, it is not unreasonable to suggest that these concerns may be particularly relevant to computer science, to computer science teachers, and to CEd researchers.

For some teachers in higher education, the teaching should be as far removed from values as is possible. Others identify upfront the values that they think they exemplify and the absurdity of trying to teach in a values-free way (e.g., see Shephard & Furnari, 2013). Others identify the hidden curriculum as an inevitable feature of any teaching that tries to obscure its values base. There is an expanding literature on values education in higher education and on the roles of role models in teaching and learning.

One area that fascinates me, and that may help CEd researchers to grapple with learning and teaching in the affective domain, relates to critical thinking. Critical thinking is often included in institutional lists of graduate attributes as an all-round good thing. Critical thinking is often included within departmental or discipline-specific curricula. Many higher education teachers describe their teaching as encouraging critical thinking, as opposed to transmitting disciplinary knowledge. But we would be unlikely to discover a generally accepted definition of critical thinking or a clearly articulated and proven approach to teaching critical thinking. The work of Facione is particularly relevant here (Facione, 1990, 2000). This researcher asked expert educators to reach a consensus on the skills involved in critical thinking (these include interpretation, analysis, inference, evaluation, explanation, and self-regulation, several of which also appear as key elements of other categorizations of learning). Facione's research went on to describe the dispositions that students need to possess in order to effectively make use of the thinking skills that they are learning.

A key point for me is that the task for the teacher intent on teaching critical thinking skills involves far more than simply teaching skills. In order to think critically, learners need to learn a range of dispositions in order to think critically. These dispositions include being inquisitive, open-minded, analytical, self-confident, systematic, and truth-seeking – all outcomes firmly situated within the affective domain – alongside a willingness to work in teams, to behave in a culturally sensitive manner, to do the "right thing," and to say no to the "wrong thing." As higher education teachers, we either will or will not conceptualize these dispositions as something to do with us, but as CEd researchers, we may not have this luxury. Our research data may well be impacted by such considerations.

Such dispositions are elements of long-standing models of learning and teaching. Krathwohl, Bloom, and Masia's (1988) affective domain of learning includes an ability to listen, to respond in interactions with others, to demonstrate attitudes or values appropriate to particular situations, to demonstrate balance and consideration, and, at the highest level, to display a commitment to principled practice on a day-to-day basis, alongside a willingness to revise judgment and change behavior in the light of new evidence.

It does seem to me that CEd researchers reading this chapter would benefit by reflecting on their own assumptions about critical thinking and its related dispositions and about their role in developing them. Do you think, as examples, that computer science teachers should be teaching their students not only the skills involved in truth-seeking, but also the obligation to seek the truth? Are you open-minded about such matters and happy to teach your students to be open-minded? Will you do this openly, or will it be hidden within your approach to computer science, to research, to teaching, or to life?

References

Biggs, J. (1999). What the student does: Teaching for enhanced learning. *Higher Education Research & Development*, 18(1), 57–75.

Biggs, J., & Tang, C. (2007). *Teaching for Quality Learning at University*, 3rd edn. Maidenhead, UK: Society for Research into Higher Education and Open University Press.

Bloom, B. S., Hastings, J. T., & Madaus, G. F. (1971). *Handbook on the Formative and Summative Rvaluation of Student Learning*. New York: McGraw-Hill.

Boyer, E. L. (1990). *Scholarship Reconsidered: Priorities of the Professoriate*. Princeton, NJ: Carnegie Foundation for the Advancement of Teaching.

Boyer, E. L. (1996). From the scholarship reconsidered to scholarship assessed. *Quest*, 48(2), 129–139.

Cech, E. A. (2014). Education: Embed social awareness in science curricula. *Nature*, 505(7484), 477–478.

Driscoll, M. P. (2005). *Psychology of Learning for Instruction*. Boston, MA: Allyn and Bacon.

Entwistle, N. (1997). Introduction: Phenomenography in higher education. *Higher Education Research & Development*, 16(2), 127–134.

Facione, P. A. (1990). *Critical Thinking: A Statement of Expert Consensus for Purposes of Educational Assessment and Instruction*. Millbrae, CA: The California Academic Press.

Facione, P. A. (2000). The disposition toward critical thinking: Its character, measurement, and relation to critical thinking skill. *Informal Logic*, 20(1), 61–84.

Gibbs, G., & Coffey, M. (2004). The impact of training of higher-education teachers on their teaching skills, their approach to teaching and the approach to learning of their students. *Active Learning in Higher Education*, 5(1), 87–100.

Hattie, J., & Timperley, H. (2007). The power of feedback. *Review of Educational Research*, 77(1), 81–112.

Havnes, A., & Prøitz, T. S. (2016). Why use learning outcomes in higher education? Exploring the grounds for academic resistance and reclaiming the value of unexpected learning. *Educational Assessment, Evaluation and Accountability*, 28(3), 205–223.

Hutchings, P., & Shulman, L. (1999). The scholarship of teaching: New elaborations, new developments. *Change*, 31(5), 10–15.

Krathwohl, D., Bloom, B., & Masia, B. (1988). *Taxonomy of Educational Objectives, Handbook II: The Affective Domain*. New York: David McKay Co.

Land, R. (2001). Agency, context and change in academic development. *International Journal for Academic Development*, 6(1), 4–20.

Lave, J., & Wenger, E. (1991). *Situated Learning: Legitimate Peripheral Participation.* Cambridge, UK: Cambridge University Press.

Löfström, E., Trotman, T., Furnari, M., & Shephard, K. (2015). Who teaches academic integrity and how do they teach it? *Higher Education*, 69(3), 435–448.

O'Neill, G., & McMahon, T. (2005). Student centred learning: What does it mean for students and lecturers? In G. O'Neill, S. Moore, & B. McMullin (Eds.), *Emerging Issues in the Practice of University Learning and Teaching* (pp. 27–36). Dublin, Ireland: AISHE.

Ott, C., Robins, A., & Shephard, K. (2016). Translating principles of effective feedback for students into the CS1 context. *ACM Transactions on Computing Education (TOCE)*, 16(1), 1–27.

Price, M., Handley, K., & Millar, J. (2011). Feedback: Focusing attention on engagement. *Studies in Higher Education*, 36(8), 879–896.

Schön, D. (1983). *The Reflective Practitioner: How Professionals Think in Action.* London, UK: Temple Smith.

Shephard, K., & Furnari, M. (2013). Exploring what higher-education teachers think about education for sustainability. *Studies in Higher Education*, 38(10), 1577–1590.

Trigwell, K. (2006). Phenomenography: An approach to research into geography education. *Journal of Geography in Higher Education*, 30(2), 367–372.

11 Engineering Education Research

Michael C. Loui and Maura Borrego

11.1 Introduction

In the **Foundations** part of this book, we review the history, infrastructure, **theories**, **methodologies**, and key **empirical findings** from engineering education research. This chapter could benefit computing education researchers because computing and engineering have many similarities. Undergraduate programs in computing and engineering prepare professionals to apply mathematics and science to solve practical problems by designing artifacts such as software and skyscrapers. Both computing and engineering programs have difficulty recruiting and retaining diverse groups of students. Instruction in both computing and engineering is growing in K–12 (precollege) education in both formal and informal settings, especially through integration with instruction in mathematics and science. Both computing and engineering have incorporated discipline-based education research (DBER) activities, similar to physics education research, biology education research, and others.

Computing education researchers may be particularly interested in the strategies and policies that have enabled the growth of engineering education research. Although the American Society for Engineering Education (ASEE) was founded more than 100 years ago, modern engineering education research began to coalesce around 2003, when the *Journal of Engineering Education* changed its mission to focus exclusively on research, and when engineering education departments and doctoral programs emerged at multiple universities in the USA. These changes resulted from a shift to outcomes-based criteria for engineering accreditation that had begun in 1997. The emphasis on assessment of outcomes prompted engineering faculty members in the USA to identify course learning objectives and to gather evidence of student learning. During this period, the US National Science Foundation funded several engineering education coalitions, each with a group of universities. Some coalitions focused on assessment, which laid the foundation for increasingly scholarly investigations of engineering student learning and retention (Froyd & Borrego, 2014).

Research projects in engineering education require expertise both in engineering and in social sciences. Since the inception of engineering education research, these projects have been conducted through interdisciplinary collaborations of researchers with different areas of expertise (Borrego & Newswander, 2008). As a consequence, engineering education research has borrowed theories and research methods from social science fields such as education, psychology, sociology, and management rather than developing its own theories and methods. Today, engineering education researchers are trained through formal courses and degree programs in which students learn these theories and methods. Although projects are still pursued through collaborations between engineers and social scientists, other projects are conducted by researchers who are trained in engineering education.

Currently, engineering education research is supported by professional societies, annual conferences, and scholarly journals. The societies, conferences, and journals in engineering education parallel and overlap those in computing education. The Association for Computing Machinery (ACM) supports education and research in computing, and the ASEE and other engineering education societies around the world support education and research in engineering. The ACM publishes the *ACM Transactions on Computing Education* journal, and the ASEE publishes the *Journal of Engineering Education*. The Institute of Electrical and Electronics Engineers (IEEE) publishes the *IEEE Transactions on Education*, which includes research articles in both computing education and electrical engineering education. The annual Frontiers in Education Conference covers both computing education and engineering education research.

11.2 Engineering Education as a Scholarly Field

Formal education in engineering began in France with the establishment of the École Polytechnique in 1794. In the USA, the US Military Academy at West Point began offering engineering programs in the early 1800s. The four-year curriculum at West Point was based on the École's (Davis, 1998, pp. 18–19). Engineering education expanded greatly with the passage of the Morrill Act in 1862, which led to the founding of land-grant colleges and universities to teach agriculture and engineering. By the end of the nineteenth century, a group of academic engineering leaders founded the Society for the Promotion of Engineering Education (SPEE) in 1893. This organization is now known as the ASEE (Froyd & Lohmann, 2014). Other organizations devoted to engineering education were established in the twentieth century: the Internationale Gesellschaft für Ingenieurpädagogik in 1972, the Société Européenne pour la Formation des Ingénieurs in 1973, and the Australasian Association of Engineering Education in 1989 (Froyd & Lohmann, 2014). Today, many nations have engineering education associations, and they belong to the International Federation of Engineering Education Societies (www.ifees.net). Although engineering education is a worldwide endeavor, this chapter focuses on scholarship in engineering education in the USA, because it is the setting with which we are most familiar.

In 1910, SPEE began publishing the first periodical devoted to engineering education. Originally titled the *Bulletin of the Society for the Promotion of Engineering Education*, and later simply *Engineering Education*, this magazine published opinion pieces, reports on engineering enrollments, and descriptions of pedagogical practices in classrooms and laboratories. By the 1980s, *Engineering Education* regularly published research studies in the "Findings" section. A few of the more scholarly articles in *Engineering Education* became highly influential (e.g., Stice, 1976, 1987). Scholarly papers on classroom innovations were presented at ASEE Annual Conferences and at the annual Frontiers in Education Conference, which began in 1971 (http://fie-conference.org).

In 1986, a report of the US National Science Board called for the application of scholarship to strengthen undergraduate education in science, engineering, and mathematics. This report prompted the US National Science Foundation to allocate substantial funding for grants to improve education programs in all fields of science and engineering (Froyd & Lohmann, 2014). To obtain these grants, proposals required "serious assessment planning" (Wankat et al., 2002).

The assessment of student outcomes was incorporated into the guidelines for accreditation of engineering programs. Because engineering is a profession, engineering programs in colleges and universities seek formal accreditation as a certification of their quality. To obtain a professional license, an engineer must have earned a baccalaureate degree from an accredited program. After the US Department of Education (1988) began requiring that accreditation agencies ask institutions for assessments of educational quality, the Accreditation Board for Engineering and Technology (now simply "ABET") adopted new criteria and procedures in 1997. Called Engineering Criteria 2000 (EC 2000), these criteria required programs to assess their own effectiveness in achieving student outcomes (Prados, Peterson, & Lattuca, 2005). These outcomes included both technical skills, such as design and problem-solving, and professional skills (sometimes called "soft skills"), such as communication and teamwork. At about the same time, Engineers Australia, the accrediting agency for Australia, also adopted outcomes-based accreditation criteria (Godfrey & Hadgraft, 2009). The USA, Australia, and other countries are signatories to the Washington Accord, which recognizes the substantial equivalence of the accredited engineering programs in the signatory countries. The Washington Accord defines attributes of engineering graduates that are generally consistent with the outcomes defined by ABET (Passow & Passow, 2017). These outcome-based accreditation requirements prompted engineering faculty members to gather assessment data about student learning. These data could also be used to demonstrate the effectiveness of instructional innovations. The focus on assessment and evidence, coupled with an infusion of funding from the National Science Foundation at this time, accelerated research activity in engineering education (Borrego, 2007).

In 1993, the magazine *Engineering Education* was replaced by two periodicals: a magazine titled *ASEE Prism* and a "scholarly professional journal" titled the *Journal of Engineering Education* (JEE). During the 1990s, articles published in JEE primarily reported the results of scholarship of teaching and learning (SoTL) studies. These studies aimed to improve student learning in classrooms and instructional laboratories. SoTL studies in engineering typically used surveys of students, end-of-course ratings, and grades as assessment data (Wankat et al., 2002).

In 2003, JEE changed its mission "to serve as an archival record of scholarly research in engineering education" (Lohmann, 2003). In 2005, the first of four Engineering Education Research Colloquies was held. By 2006, researchers began calling for "rigorous research" in engineering education (Streveler & Smith, 2006). This research would aim not to improve teaching and learning in individual classrooms, which was the goal of SoTL studies, but instead to build general knowledge that addressed fundamental questions about how students learn. This research would be grounded in an appropriate theory, and it would be conducted using rigorous methods (Streveler & Smith, 2006). In 2008, ASEE created a new journal, *Advances in Engineering Education*, to publish applications of engineering education research and SoTL studies, which would no longer be published in JEE (Shuman, Besterfield-Sacre, & Litzinger, 2013).

The change in the mission of JEE marked a milestone in the development of engineering education research as a species of DBER, along with physics education research and chemistry education research. DBER addresses fundamental questions about education in particular academic disciplines, typically at the undergraduate level. DBER draws on more general research in the learning sciences, but is grounded in the epistemology, priorities, and culture of a particular discipline (Singer, Nielsen, & Schweingruber, 2012, p. 9). As a consequence, DBER projects require deep expertise in the target discipline.

Engineering education research examines both undergraduate education and precollege (K–12) education. While teachers in elementary and secondary schools have always used engineering and technology as contexts for lessons in mathematics and science (Sneider & Purzer, 2014), precollege curricula have been developed specifically to teach engineering concepts and skills, with an emphasis on engineering design. Two of the largest curricular efforts are Engineering is Elementary for students in elementary schools and Project Lead the Way for students in middle and high schools (Brophy et al., 2008). Since the 1990s, national standards for science education in the USA have increased the attention given to incorporating engineering and technology. In 2013, the Next Generation Science Standards called explicitly for integrated instruction in science, technology, engineering, and mathematics (STEM) (Sneider & Purzer, 2014). A consensus report of the National Academy of Engineering and the National Research Council emphasized the need for research on the potential benefits of an integrated approach to STEM instruction (Katehi, Pearson, & Feder, 2009).

11.3 The Structure of Engineering Education Research Today

Research in engineering education is supported through the same structures as research in older academic disciplines: university departments, doctoral programs, research centers, academic journals, specialized conferences, and groups within professional societies (Borrego & Bernhard, 2011). In this section, we describe each of these structures.

The first two departments of engineering education were established at US universities in 2004 (Benson et al., 2010). As of 2017, there are six such departments in the USA. All six arose from academic units that had previously been responsible for teaching engineering programs for first-year undergraduates, but then expanded their missions to include research and doctoral programs. A few other US universities without engineering education departments now offer PhD degrees in engineering education. Outside the USA, there are doctoral programs in engineering education in Sweden, Denmark, and Malaysia. In fact, in Europe, PhD degrees in engineering education have been awarded as early as 1929 (Borrego & Bernhard, 2011). Several universities around the world offer doctoral programs in STEM education, usually within a college of education rather than a college of engineering, but in collaboration with engineering faculty members (Engineering Education Community Resource, 2017). At universities without doctoral programs in engineering education, engineering education research is also conducted at teaching and learning centers (Litzinger, 2010), in research centers (Benson et al., 2010; Borrego & Bernhard, 2011), and by individuals in traditional engineering departments.

Engineering education researchers publish articles in peer-reviewed academic journals. Journals that focus on specific engineering disciplines include the following:

- *Chemical Engineering Education*
- *IEEE Transactions on Education* (electrical and computer engineering)
- *International Journal of Electrical Engineering Education*
- *International Journal of Mechanical Engineering Education*
- *Journal of Professional Issues in Engineering Education and Practice* (civil engineering)

Journals that cover all engineering disciplines include the following:

- *Advances in Engineering Education*
- *Australasian Journal of Engineering Education*
- *European Journal of Engineering Education*
- *International Journal of Engineering Education*
- *Journal of Engineering Education*
- *Journal of Pre-College Engineering Education Research*
- *Online Journal for Global Engineering Education*

Engineering education research also appears in journals devoted to all of STEM education (Borrego & Bernhard, 2011).

Some journals are published by professional societies. These societies also sponsor annual conferences. The ASEE and the Société Européenne pour la Formation des Ingénieurs (SEFI; European Society for Engineering Education) each hold an annual conference. The proceedings of the ASEE Annual Conference are available via open access at the website http://peer.asee.org.

The IEEE Education Society, the IEEE Computer Society, and the ASEE Educational Research and Methods Division jointly sponsor the annual Frontiers in Education Conference (http://fie-conference.org). The proceedings of this conference are available through the IEEE Xplore Digital Library (http://ieeexplore.ieee.org). The International Federation of Engineering Education Societies holds the World Engineering Education Forum each year in a different country. The Research in Engineering Education Symposium is a biennial international conference that also travels to different countries.

As the field of engineering education research has grown in diverse ways in different countries, drawing on ideas from multiple disciplines, it is sometimes difficult for researchers to locate related work. To help researchers communicate with each other, a taxonomy for engineering education research has been developed (Finelli, Borrego, & Rasoulifar, 2015). This taxonomy is currently maintained at the University of Michigan, and a small group of volunteers is dedicated to maintaining and updating the taxonomy. The JEE and the *IEEE Transactions on Education* now require authors to use at least some keywords from the taxonomy to describe their articles.

11.4 Theories in Engineering Education Research

In education research, theories can inform the design of empirical studies and the interpretation of the collected data. Theories can explain observed phenomena and predict future events. Tying education research to a theory helps establish the generalizability or transferability of studies conducted in one specific setting. Engineering education research borrows theories of learning, motivation, and identity development from other academic disciplines, notably cognitive science, education, learning sciences, psychology, and sociology. These theories were introduced to engineering education researchers by Svinicki (2010) in her primer, *Guidebook on Conceptual Frameworks for Research in Engineering Education*. The *Guidebook*, in turn, was based on an earlier book by Svinicki (2004) and the *How People Learn* framework (National Research Council, 2000). Occasionally, engineering education research uses theories from other DBER areas. For instance, the Lesh translational model was developed by mathematics education researchers and used in an engineering education study (Moore et al., 2013).

11.4.1 Identity and Professional Formation

Identity is a popular lens for studying the persistence of students in several STEM fields, including engineering (Tonso, 2007, 2014). Students who identify with engineering, or who view their own identities as consistent with engineering, are more likely to select engineering as a career and to persist through engineering programs (Matusovich, Streveler, & Miller, 2010; Patrick & Borrego, 2016).

In a seminal qualitative study, Carlone and Johnson (2007) found that science identity depends on performance, recognition, and competence. Subsequent quantitative studies of mathematics and physics identities among high school and undergraduate students have identified performance/competence, interest, and recognition as separate constructs that can be used to predict identity and major choices as outcomes (e.g., Hazari, 2010). This work has been extended to explore engineering identity (Godwin et al., 2016; Prybutok et al., 2016).

In general, students choose to major in engineering because they intend to pursue professional careers as engineers. Social cognitive career theory (SCCT) is a popular theory that describes the primary influences on students as they choose careers. According to SCCT, students' decisions about careers are influenced by their personal attributes and by contextual factors that might support or hinder them from achieving their career goals. Personal attributes include self-efficacy beliefs, outcome expectations, interests, and goals. (Self-efficacy is described in Section 11.4.3.) Contextual factors include the availability of role models, encouragement from family members, and funding for college expenses. Atadero, Rambo-Hernandez, and Balgopal (2015) used SCCT to analyze outcomes from introducing design projects in one section of a statics course. They found that, as predicted by SCCT, students in the projects section connected their engineering self-efficacy and their positive outcome expectations with their goal of becoming an engineer.

11.4.2 Cognition

Engineering education research borrows theories of learning from psychology (Newstetter & Svinicki, 2014). Two major kinds of learning theories are behavioral and cognitive. Whereas the behavioral approach to learning emphasizes only the observed behaviors of students, the cognitive approach focuses on the internal workings of students' minds. The most prevalent cognitive theory in engineering education is *constructivism*, which states that students create their own mental models of concepts and phenomena based on their prior experiences. According to constructivism, instructors should help students modify these initial mental models so that they align better with accepted scientific conceptions. Research on students' mental models of concepts in engineering thermodynamics revealed several misconceptions. In particular, students have difficulty distinguishing equilibrium from steady-state (Streveler et al., 2014).

A specific cognitive theory, *cognitive load theory* (Sweller, van Merrienboer, & Paas, 1998), categorizes the kinds of difficulties that students experience in learning a subject. In this theory, *intrinsic cognitive load* refers to difficulties that are inherent to the subject, *extraneous cognitive load* refers to difficulties that are induced by the instructional presentation, and *germane cognitive load* refers to the effort required to construct a *schema*, which is the mental model that organizes the student's knowledge about the topic. Good instructional design can minimize extraneous cognitive load and increase germane cognitive load (Sweller, van Merrienboer, & Paas, 1998). Cognitive load theory has been used to explain how students' levels of prior knowledge affect their learning in a multimedia presentation on electric circuits (Johnson et al., 2013).

Engineering education researchers have studied cognitive differences between experts and novices, particularly in studies of design. Researchers have found that experts organize knowledge differently from novices. This organization enables experts to recall information, recognize patterns, and solve problems more efficiently than novices. Researchers have examined differences between experts and novices in unstructured design activities (Atman et al., 2007) and in solving textbook problems (Chi, Feltovich, & Glaser, 1981; Larkin et al., 1980). To explain expert–novice differences in engineering design, researchers have used the theory of *adaptive expertise* (McKenna, 2014). This theory posits two dimensions of expertise: *efficiency* and *innovation*. Efficiency refers to the ability to apply domain-specific knowledge with speed and accuracy. Innovation refers to the ability to identify problems and to generate ideas to achieve ambitious goals. In this theory, *novices* exhibit low efficiency and low innovation, *routine experts* exhibit high efficiency and low innovation, and *adaptive experts* exhibit high efficiency and high innovation.

11.4.3 Self-Beliefs and Motivation

Engineering education researchers have used theories of motivation, previously developed by psychologists, to investigate the role of student motivation in engineering education. Motivation theories explain the reasons that individuals initiate and sustain behaviors. In the context of engineering education, these theories can explain students' behaviors with academic tasks and their persistence through an engineering program. In this section, we review popular motivation theories in engineering education research: self-efficacy, expectancy-value theory (EVT), self-determination theory (SDT), mindsets, and goal orientation theory. This section is particularly long as a reflection of the emphasis on motivation and persistence in engineering education research.

Defined by Bandura (1977), *self-efficacy* is an individual's belief in their ability to complete a task in order to achieve a desired goal. Self-efficacy combines confidence – an emotion – with a justification for that confidence. Self-efficacy is context-dependent. Bandura (1977) identified four sources of self-efficacy: mastery experience, vicarious experience, verbal persuasion, and physiological states. Students have a *mastery experience* when they perceive success or failure in their efforts to achieve a learning objective. Students have a *vicarious experience* when they see other students succeed or fail. *Verbal persuasion* consists of feedback from peers and teachers such as praise or criticism. *Physiological states* are the emotions that students feel: emotions such as joy and anxiety can affect students' self-efficacy beliefs. Hutchison-Green, Follman, and Bodner (2008) showed that the self-efficacy of first-year engineering students is strongly influenced by comparisons of their academic performance with other students, a form of vicarious experience. Mamaril et al. (2016) developed an instrument to measure the self-efficacy of students in academic engineering tasks.

EVT was developed by Wigfield and Eccles (2000) and their colleagues to understand the motivations for students' academic behaviors. This theory posits that an individual's motivation for a task is determined by their competence beliefs and value beliefs about the task. *Competence* beliefs, which resemble self-efficacy, comprise the individual's expectations of success in completing the task. *Value beliefs* comprise the individual's beliefs about how well the task matches their desires and goals. EVT specifies four categories of values. *Attainment* value is the perception of the importance of the task for the individual's self-concept. *Intrinsic or interest* value is the individual's interest in the task itself. *Utility* value is the perception of how the task might help the individual achieve some goal other than the task. *Cost* value is the perception of the time, effort, and psychological impact required by the task. Using EVT, Peters and Daly (2013) identified the costs considered by engineering students who pursued doctoral degrees after five or more years of work outside the academy. Matusovich, Streveler, and Miller (2010) used EVT to understand students' motivations to enroll in and persist through undergraduate engineering programs.

Intrinsic motivation has been the focus of other studies in engineering education that used SDT. Developed by Ryan and Deci (2000), SDT states that an individual's intrinsic motivation is driven by three basic psychological needs: competence, autonomy, and relatedness. *Competence* is the desire to master a skill or to be effective in achieving a goal. *Autonomy* is the condition of having control to make decisions. *Relatedness* is the urge to connect with other people. Besides defining three elements of intrinsic motivation, SDT also specifies a range of extrinsic motivations. Trenshaw et al. (2016) used SDT to examine the outcomes of a core engineering course that was redesigned to promote intrinsic motivation. Kajfez and Matusovich (2017) studied the factors that affected the competence, autonomy, and relatedness of graduate teaching assistants who taught first-year engineering courses at five different universities.

Student motivation can be affected by students' beliefs about intelligence. Dweck (1999) and her collaborators studied the differences in the beliefs of students when they faced difficult academic challenges, specifically mathematical problems. They classified students into two groups – incremental self-theorists and entity self-theorists – based on their beliefs about intelligence. Students with the *incremental* theory (now called the *growth mindset*) believe that intelligence can improve with effort. Students with the *entity* theory (now called the *fixed mindset*) believe that intelligence cannot be changed: they believe in innate talents – you have it or you don't. When faced with difficult mathematical problems, incremental theorists believe that they can solve the problems with more knowledge or effort, whereas entity theorists attribute difficulty to a lack of intelligence in themselves. Further, students with a growth mindset adopt *mastery goal orientations*, in which they strive to master an academic subject, but students with a fixed mindset adopt *performance goal orientations*, in which they aim only to earn a grade or to perform better than peers. Stump, Husman, and Corby (2014) showed that engineering students with incremental beliefs (i.e., a growth mindset) tended to report that they engaged in collaborative learning and knowledge-building behaviors, such as connecting new ideas with previous knowledge and constructing personal understandings of new material. By contrast, engineering students who held entity beliefs were less likely to engage in knowledge-building behaviors. Reid and Ferguson (2011) found that engineering students drifted from incremental beliefs toward entity beliefs during the first year of undergraduate studies. Reid and Ferguson presented no data beyond one year, however.

11.4.4 Summary

In this section, we have highlighted some of the theories that engineering education researchers have borrowed from other disciplines. The research practices in adopting and applying these theories have evolved since the beginning of the "rigorous research" movement around 2006. Initially, researchers merely named and cited the theories that guided their studies. Nowadays, researchers are expected to justify their choices of theories, to explain why they rejected alternative theories, and to integrate the chosen theories into the design of their studies and the interpretation of their results. Some contemporary researchers in engineering education have begun to develop theoretical and conceptual frameworks specifically for engineering. For example, Canney and Bielefeldt (2015) created the Professional Social Responsibility Development Model as a conceptual framework for describing how engineers develop their understandings of the social responsibilities of professionals. As another example, Walther, Miller, and Sochacka (2017) drew on intellectual traditions in social work to propose a theoretical model of empathy in engineering as a teachable skill, a practice orientation, and a professional way of being. We expect the trend toward sophistication in the use and development of theories to continue.

11.5 Methodologies in Engineering Education Research

In engineering education research, empirical studies predominate over theoretical studies, particularly in the USA. To conduct empirical studies, engineering education researchers now use a wide range of quantitative methods, qualitative methods, mixed methods, and synthesis methodologies (Borrego, Douglas, & Amelink, 2009).

In the USA, quantitative methods are historically the most popular. Quantitative studies primarily involve survey research. To argue for the validity and reliability of their surveys, researchers often cite the article by Douglas and Purzer (2015) on validity and the article by Allen et al. (2008) on coefficient alpha.

Some researchers develop survey instruments – see Section 11.6.5. Quantitative researchers also conduct experimental and quasi-experimental studies to compare the effectiveness of different pedagogies. Some researchers have conducted single-institution correlational studies of student transcript data, but for the most part, engineering education researchers have not taken advantage of national databases such as the Integrated Postsecondary Education Data System (IPEDS) maintained by the US Department of Education. One notable exception is the stream of research that uses the Multiple-Institution Database for Investigating Engineering Longitudinal Development (MIDFIELD), which now includes transcript data from engineering students at 113 institutions (Ohland et al., 2016).

While qualitative methods have been popular in engineering education research in Europe and Australia, they have recently become widespread in the USA, too. Case and Light (2011) used studies in engineering education to illustrate different approaches to qualitative research: action research, case study, discourse analysis, ethnography, grounded theory, narrative analysis, and phenomenography. Bernhard and Baillie (2016) provided an extensive review of research quality criteria in engineering education and other DBER disciplines. This review included the popular Q^3 framework developed by Walther and his colleagues (Walther & Sochacka, 2014; Walther, Sochacka, & Kellam, 2013).

In mixed-methods research, quantitative and qualitative approaches are thoughtfully and logically integrated (Creswell & Plano Clark, 2007). Borrego, Douglas, and Amelink (2009) discussed how quality criteria and study designs apply in engineering education using examples of studies previously published in JEE. Crede and Borrego (2010) expanded this analysis to include seven different journals, and analyzed how 16 studies had applied mixed methods to engineering education research.

Another category of research approaches that is rapidly gaining popularity in engineering education research is *systematic literature reviews*, which synthesize what is known in a particular research area using primary studies. Unlike narrative reviews, which are the most common kind of literature reviews, systematic reviews adopt detailed procedures for collecting and analyzing primary studies. Unlike meta-analyses, which use only quantitative methods to synthesize only quantitative studies, systematic reviews may use quantitative, qualitative, or mixed methods to synthesize quantitative, qualitative, and mixed-methods studies (Borrego, Foster, & Froyd, 2014). Borrego, Foster, and Froyd (2015) reviewed systematic reviews of interest to STEM educators.

11.6 Some Empirical Results in Engineering Education Research

In this section, we describe a selection of key empirical results in engineering education research. Although early research in engineering education focused on the effectiveness of classroom pedagogies to teach design and problem-solving skills, research today considers a much broader variety of research questions. Engineering education research can be divided into five categories (Adams et al., 2006):

Engineering epistemologies. In this category are research questions on how students and instructors think about concepts, theories, and principles. For example, how do students interpret diagrams and representations of physical situations? How do engineering instructors understand the purpose and use of mathematical models?

Engineering learning mechanisms. In this category are research questions on how and why different methods of teaching can foster student learning in classrooms and laboratories. For instance, for what reasons does cooperative learning promote problem-solving skills?

Engineering learning systems. In this category are research questions about larger issues beyond classrooms. For example, what factors influence engineering instructors to adopt new pedagogies? How do institutional cultures and policies affect systemic changes in engineering education?

Engineering diversity and inclusiveness. In this category are questions about students. For instance, what factors affect the retention of women and minority students in engineering programs? How do engineering students develop self-efficacy and professional identities?

Engineering assessment. To determine how well a teaching method works, we need valid, reliable assessment instruments. This category includes efforts to develop "concept inventories" for common engineering subjects such as statics, dynamics, circuits, and thermodynamics. Instruments have also been developed to assess the development of professional skills such as teamwork and ethical reasoning.

These five categories define the overall organization of the *Cambridge Handbook of Engineering Education Research* (Johri & Olds, 2014), which provides a comprehensive overview of the field.

11.6.1 Engineering Epistemologies

Engineers and engineering students model physical situations with a variety of representations, including mathematical formulae, abstract sketches, and computational simulations. These simulations enable students to visualize dynamic physical processes. Students must continually translate between these representations as they apply conceptual knowledge to solve engineering problems. For example, Moore et al. (2013) studied the role of representational fluency in conceptual understanding. Nelson et al. (2017) examined how computational simulations can induce student misconceptions.

A robust stream of research has investigated how students learn concepts and change their conceptual understandings; some concepts such as thermodynamic equilibrium seem difficult to learn (Streveler et al., 2014). For many difficult concepts, students' understandings are fragmentary and incoherent (Herman, Zilles, & Loui, 2014). Researchers have also described the general epistemological beliefs of engineering students (Gainsburg, 2015) and engineering faculty members (Montfort, Brown, & Shinew, 2014).

At the precollege level, researchers have studied the perceptions, beliefs, and attitudes of both students and teachers about engineers and engineering. For example, Capobianco et al. (2011) used the Draw an Engineer Test to investigate how children in grades 1 through 5 understand engineers and engineering. Their most common conceptions were a mechanic who fixes engines or drives vehicles, a laborer who constructs buildings or roads, and a technician who repairs electronics or computers. Rarely did students draw someone who designs technologies. Few boys drew female engineers. Besides students, teachers are an important group to study because almost none have backgrounds in engineering or in engineering education (Hynes et al., 2017). As an example of research on teachers, Hynes (2012) documented the levels of teachers' understandings of different stages of the engineering design process.

11.6.2 Learning Mechanisms

Across science and engineering disciplines, many DBER studies have compared the effectiveness of different instructional methods (Singer, Nielsen, & Schweingruber, 2012). In particular, DBER researchers have examined the impact of introducing student activities into lectures, which are still the predominant instructional method in science and engineering. Both a literature review by Prince (2004) and an extensive meta-analysis by Freeman et al. (2014) have concluded that active learning is superior to didactic lectures in fostering student understanding across science and engineering. One way to accommodate active learning is through a *flipped classroom* approach, which provides lecture material or other resources as assignments to free up class time for active engagement in learning. Flipped classrooms have been gaining in popularity in engineering since 2012, as documented in recent reviews (Karabulut-Ilgu, Jaramillo Cherrez, & Jahren, 2017; Kerr, 2015).

Active learning often occurs in the instructional laboratory. As in science education, the laboratory has been considered an essential component of engineering education since the nineteenth century (Feisel & Rosa, 2005). Despite its importance, there has been little research on the instructional laboratory in engineering (Singer, Nielsen, & Schweingruber, 2012, p. 134).

Among active learning pedagogies, collaborative learning strategies have been investigated extensively in engineering because they provide opportunities for students to learn teamwork skills, which are essential in professional practice. Cooperative learning is a particular form of collaborative learning that requires common goals, positive interdependence between group members, and individual accountability. In a watershed study published in five parts, Felder, Felder, and Dietz (1998) provided some of the first evidence about the effectiveness of active learning for engineering students. A cohort of students who took a series of five courses that used cooperative learning earned higher grades and graduated at higher rates than a comparison cohort who took the same courses that used traditional teaching methods (Felder, Felder, & Dietz, 1998). Menekse et al. (2013) found that interactive pedagogies that involve student collaboration are more powerful than other kinds of active learning pedagogies in promoting student learning. Team design projects are also very common in engineering education. Borrego et al. (2013) reviewed how teams have been used in engineering education, including prior studies of team formation and functioning. Loughry, Ohland, and Woehr (2014) and Willey and Gardner (2010) developed robust tools for managing peer assessment in team projects.

A popular form of active learning in engineering is problem-based learning (PBL) (Kolmos & de Graaff, 2014). In PBL, an instructor starts with an actual or realistic problem. The problem is structured to motivate students to learn fundamental concepts and principles in engineering. For example, if the problem is to improve the efficiency of a heating and ventilation system for an office building, then students must learn and apply relevant principles of thermodynamics and heat transfer. PBL focuses on the process of learning rather than on developing and prototyping a product. Studies show that PBL increases student motivation, enhances the long-term retention of knowledge, and improves the development of transferable process skills such as communication, teamwork, and project management (Kolmos & de Graaff, 2014, pp. 153–154).

Some problems for PBL are design problems, in which students must design a device, process, or system to meet a specification. All undergraduate engineering programs include instruction in design, both to meet accreditation requirements and to prepare students for professional practice. In the USA, design courses are prevalent in the first and last years of undergraduate education (Froyd, 2005). Researchers have used a variety of methods to investigate instruction in engineering design in a variety of settings, including first-year and capstone courses (Atman et al., 2014). For instance, using verbal protocol analysis, Atman et al. (2007) found that, in solving a design problem, experts spent more time than novices on scoping the problem and gathering relevant information. Crismond and Adams (2012) similarly distinguished between beginning designers and informed designers in their synthesis of the literature on teaching and learning engineering design.

In precollege settings, design is the primary goal of engineering literacy: students should gain the ability to apply the engineering design process to solve problems and to achieve human goals (Snider & Purzer, 2014). In addition, design problems can provide a context for science instruction. Wendell and Rogers (2013) showed that, in elementary schools, design problems can improve students' understandings of science concepts. Chao et al. (2017) investigated the role of design tools in the development of students' science knowledge.

11.6.3 Learning Systems

The category of "learning systems" includes research on institutional change. As in other DBER fields, in engineering education, there is growing interest in examining instructional change; specifically, what motivates engineering instructors to adopt evidence-based instructional practices to support student learning. Although the effectiveness of these practices, such as active learning, has been confirmed by decades of research (Freeman et al., 2014; Prince, 2004), only a minority of faculty have adopted these practices (Froyd et al., 2013). While there is a long history of research on engineering faculty development (Felder & Brent, 2010), only recently has engineering education research focused on quantifying and increasing the adoption rates of evidence-based instructional practices. Early change initiatives focused on developing course-based interventions and using assessment evidence to convince others to adopt the interventions (Clark et al., 2004). More recent studies have focused on academic policies and reward systems that may encourage or inhibit the adoption of evidence-based practices.

In April 2014, a special issue of JEE (vol. 103, no. 2) focused on "The Complexities of Transforming Engineering Higher Education." Most articles in this issue used a model developed by physics education and institutional change researchers (Henderson, Beach, & Finkelstein, 2011). This model categorizes change strategies along two dimensions. One dimension, *intended outcome*, ranges from *prescribed* to *emergent*. The other dimension, *aspects of the system to be changed*, ranges from *individuals* to *environments and structures*. Consequently, the model defines four quadrants: prescribed for individuals; emergent for individuals; prescribed for environments; and emergent for environments.

The special issue had six regular articles. Borrego and Henderson (2014) provided specific examples of theories that might guide a change initiative in each quadrant of the model. Besterfield-Sacre et al. (2014) used the model to categorize survey responses in a project sponsored by ASEE that focused on instructional change. Jamison, Kolmos, and Holgaard (2014) used a historical analysis to develop a model to help educators transform engineering education in today's complex settings. Matusovich et al. (2014) and Finelli, Daly, and Richardson (2014) applied the expectancy value theory of motivation to understand the attitudes of engineering faculty toward instructional change. Holloway et al. (2014) described a statistical analysis that revealed a significant gender bias in the engineering admissions process, which they traced to a policy on the use of standardized test scores in admissions decisions. After this policy was changed, the representation of women among engineering students increased significantly.

These studies have shown that institutional change is complex and that effective change requires a scholarly approach. In the next few years, we expect more publications on learning systems and institutional change in engineering education, resulting from projects funded by the National Science Foundation in the Revolutionizing Engineering and Computer Science Departments program (National Science Foundation, 2015). More generally, the Accelerating Systemic Change in STEM Higher Education Network connects individuals and resources in its mission to build knowledge about STEM change (http://ascnhighered.org).

11.6.4 Understanding Students

Engineering education was once characterized as a "leaky pipeline." At the undergraduate level in the USA, most students who do not finish engineering degrees leave during the first or second year. Overall, data from the MIDFIELD indicate that among those who start as first-year students in engineering, only 57 percent persist in engineering to the eighth semester (Ohland et al., 2008); nearly all of these students earn engineering degrees within six years of entry (Ohland et al., 2012). Within the MIDFIELD data set, the persistence rates vary by institution from 37 to 66 percent (Ohland et al., 2008). These persistence rates for engineering are similar to other majors, but one important difference is that few students transfer into engineering to augment the number of graduates (Ohland et al., 2008). Students are discouraged from transferring into engineering from other majors because most engineering programs require long sequences of technical courses, each a prerequisite for the next.

MIDFIELD data have also helped demonstrate that many students who choose to leave engineering have grade point averages as high as students who stay (Ohland et al., 2004; Tseng, Chen, & Sheppard, 2011). Numerous studies have identified reasons for attrition from undergraduate engineering programs, such as excessive coursework and diminished interest (Seymour & Hewitt, 1997), poor teaching and advising (Marra et al., 2012), and lack of confidence in mathematics and science skills (Eris et al., 2010).

Many research studies have documented cultural barriers to the recruitment of women and minorities to engineering and to the retention of these underrepresented groups in engineering programs (Lichtenstein et al., 2014, p. 321). For example, through the story of a female, multi-minority engineering student with a low socioeconomic status background, Foor, Walden, and Trytten (2007) elicited the ways in which the student felt unwelcome in her engineering program. More recent research in this area, particularly on racial/ethnic minorities, focuses on the assets that students bring to classrooms, rather than treating students or their backgrounds as deficits to be overcome (e.g., Martin, Simmons, & Yu, 2013; Samuelson & Litzler, 2016; Wilson-Lopez et al., 2016).

Since engineering is a profession, academic engineering programs seek not only to teach students engineering knowledge, but also to acculturate students into the profession. In other words, through engineering programs, successful students become engineers themselves. Numerous studies have investigated how this sense of professional identity develops (Stevens et al., 2008; Tonso, 2014). For example, using expectancy value theory, Matusovich, Streveler, and Miller (2010) determined that attainment values played a crucial role in students' decisions to enter engineering. As a consequence, if engineering programs emphasize attainment values, students will more closely identify with engineering, and they will be more likely to complete engineering degrees.

The development of engineering identity provides a source of motivation for students. Other sources of motivation were identified by the Academic Pathways of People Learning Engineering Survey (APPLES) project (Sheppard et al.,

2014). In this study, the researchers used the metaphor of a "pathway" rather than a "pipeline" to characterize students' journeys into engineering. Based on 2,143 responses from students at 21 diverse institutions, the APPLES study found two important sources of motivation: intrinsic psychological motivation and financial motivation (Sheppard et al., 2014). Self-efficacy also plays an important role in engineering student motivation (Hutchison-Green, Follman, & Bodner, 2008).

11.6.5 Assessment

To determine whether students have achieved intended learning objectives, both instructors and researchers need assessment instruments that measure students' knowledge accurately. As a consequence, to support both instruction and research, discipline-based education researchers have devoted considerable effort to developing and validating assessment instruments for fundamental disciplinary knowledge.

Physics education researchers developed the Force Concept Inventory (FCI) instrument (Hestenes, Wells, & Swackhamer, 1992), which measures students' understanding of the force concept, as taught in a high school physics course and in a first-year college physics course. The FCI comprises multiple-choice questions that require no calculation to answer. Each incorrect choice reflects a common student misconception about force. Using the FCI, Hake (1998) showed that interactive engagement pedagogies are superior to traditional pedagogies in fostering students' conceptual understanding of force.

Inspired by the success of the FCI, engineering education researchers have developed concept inventory instruments for the following core engineering subjects: statics (Steif & Dantzler, 2005), dynamics (Gray et al., 2005), thermal and transport processes (Streveler et al., 2011), thermodynamics (Firetto et al., 2016), materials engineering (Krause, Decker, & Griffin, 2003), and digital logic (Herman, Zilles, & Loui, 2014), among other subjects. To illustrate these efforts, we summarize the development and validation of the Digital Logic Concept Inventory (DLCI). First, the researchers identified the most important and difficult concepts in a first course in digital logic through a Delphi process, which seeks consensus by a panel of subject matter experts through multiple rounds of polling. For the DLCI, the researchers asked a panel of experts on teaching digital logic to propose core concepts and to rate the importance and difficulty of each concept (Goldman et al., 2010). Second, the researchers selected digital logic problems that highlighted the most important, difficult concepts, and they asked students to verbalize their thoughts as they solved these problems. These "think-aloud" interviews enabled the researchers to identify common student misconceptions. Third, the researchers created multiple-choice questions and incorrect answers that reflected these misconceptions. They tested the resulting DLCI with hundreds of students at multiple institutions and analyzed the results (Herman, Zilles, & Loui, 2014).

While strong conceptual knowledge provides a basis for technical skills, such as design and problem-solving, ABET's EC 2000 accreditation criteria state clearly that engineering programs must develop not only students' technical skills, but also their professional skills, such as communication and teamwork. To compare the effectiveness of different methods for teaching professional skills, researchers need valid and reliable assessment instruments for them. Engineering education researchers have thus developed instruments to assess skills in teamwork (Ohland et al., 2012), leadership (Ahn et al., 2014), entrepreneurship (Duval-Couetil, Reed-Rhoads, & Haghighi, 2010), ethical reasoning (Borenstein et al., 2010; Zhu et al., 2014), and many others (Douglas et al., 2016). Engineering education researchers also use more general instruments developed for undergraduate students in any major, including the Collegiate Learning Assessment (Klein et al., 2007), which measures analytical reasoning and critical thinking, the Motivated Strategies for Learning Questionnaire (Pintrich et al., 1993), which measures student motivation and learning strategies, and the National Survey of Student Engagement (Kuh, 2009).

In many situations, qualitative or mixed-methods approaches to assessment may be appropriate as well. For example, researchers may not yet know enough about a new or emergent phenomenon to develop survey items. Qualitative methods are particularly helpful for investigating "how" and "why" research questions, in contrast to "what" questions best addressed through quantitative approaches (Borrego, Douglas, & Amelink, 2009). Leydens, Moskal, and Pavelich (2004) described several qualitative assessment methods, including interviews, focus groups, and observations, and how they can be used in undergraduate engineering education settings.

In summary, computing education researchers who require assessments could use or adapt the assessment instruments that were previously developed for engineering education. To identify appropriate extant instruments that measure a construct such as self-efficacy and to determine whether those instruments are valid for a specific setting in computing education, researchers can work with an expert in educational measurement. Checking the validity of an instrument on a new population could be a valuable example of replication research (Benson & Borrego, 2015).

11.7 A Comparison of Computing Education Research with Engineering Education Research

In this section, we compare computing education research with engineering education research. Their similarities and differences reflect the differences between computing and engineering as academic fields. On the surface, both computing and engineering are technical fields in which teams of practitioners apply mathematical and scientific knowledge to design technologies that meet human needs. Undergraduate programs in both computing and engineering have chains of prerequisite courses, from fundamental mathematics, to required disciplinary courses, to advanced technical electives. Whereas programs in engineering are offered at about 400 colleges and universities in the USA, programs in computing are offered at more than 1,000 tertiary institutions (Tims, Zweben, & Timanovsky, 2017). So although some computer science departments are located within colleges of engineering at universities, the majority are not affiliated with engineering. Furthermore, in the USA, only 284 bachelor's degree programs in computer science, 34 in information technology, and 25 in software engineering are accredited by ABET (as of September 30, 2017). By comparison, 343 bachelor's degree programs in mechanical engineering, 331 in electrical engineering, and 259 in civil engineering are accredited by ABET (as of September 30, 2017). Because few computing programs are accredited, computing has not had the expectation for regular, ongoing assessment of student learning outcomes that has been characteristic of engineering since the 1990s. The emphasis on outcomes assessment for accreditation has strongly influenced engineering education research (e.g., Passow & Passow, 2017).

As we have noted earlier, engineering education research in the USA is conducted within academic departments of engineering education. These departments, and other universities without such departments, offer doctoral programs in engineering education – a structural feature that makes engineering education PhDs more visible than some other DBER fields. As of this writing, there are no comparable departments of computing education and no doctoral programs specifically in computing education. Nevertheless, doctoral students in computer science and in education do complete dissertations in computing education research, such as within PhD programs in computer science, informatics, education, and human-centered computing.

Computing education researchers present their work at the annual Special Interest Group on Computer Science Education (SIGCSE) Technical Symposium, the annual Conference on Innovation and Technology in Computer Science Education (ITiCSE), and the annual International Computing Education Research (ICER) conference, which are sponsored by the SIGCSE within the Association for Computing Machinery. These conferences resemble the annual Frontiers in Education Conference sponsored by the IEEE Education Society, the IEEE Computer Society, and the Educational Research and Methods Division of the ASEE; the ASEE Annual Conference; and the Annual Conference of the SEFI. All of these conferences require peer review of submitted papers, and they produce proceedings. ICER accepts only research studies with strong theoretical and empirical bases, whereas the other five conferences accept a broader range of papers, including research studies, SoTL studies, and reports of promising practices. In addition to these six major conferences, researchers in both computing education and engineering education present papers at smaller, regional conferences.

Despite the similarities in conference publication practices, computing and engineering education researchers differ in their journal publication practices. Following the practices of technical researchers in computer science, computing education researchers publish mostly in conferences, rather than in journals. By contrast, engineering education researchers often present preliminary work at conferences and then polish their manuscripts for subsequent publication in peer-reviewed journals.

Computing education researchers historically favored quantitative methods such as surveys, (quasi-)experiments, and correlational studies. Qualitative research in computing education is gaining in popularity, however (see Chapter 7). Although engineering education research in the USA previously favored quantitative methods too (Borrego, Froyd, & Knight, 2007), engineering education researchers today embrace qualitative and mixed methods as well (Loui, 2017).

Engineering education research is still struggling to become an internationally integrated field, as publication venues are primarily segregated by region. While US engineering education researchers have conducted large-scale, multi-institutional studies such as APPLES (Sheppard et al., 2014) and MIDFIELD (Ohland et al., 2016), there are few international collaborations, particularly involving US researchers. In contrast, computing education researchers have developed a range of multi-institutional, multinational research methodologies that aim for both high statistical power and attention to cultural influences on the results (Fincher et al., 2005). Conferences and collaborations alike frequently combine data, perspectives, and researchers from multiple countries.

Like engineering education researchers, computing education researchers borrow theoretical and conceptual frameworks from the learning sciences and educational psychology (see Chapters 8 and 9). Both computing and engineering education researchers investigate the effectiveness of active and cooperative learning pedagogies and the barriers to participation by students from underrepresented groups. Just as engineering education researchers study the development of engineering thinking by precollege students and their teachers, computing education researchers study the development of computational thinking by precollege students. To assess the effectiveness of computing instruction in high schools in the USA, computing education researchers have used the Advanced Placement Computer Science Test. By contrast, there is no Advanced Placement test in engineering. The development of such a test has been stymied by disagreements over how and whether to assess design as a central characteristic of engineering. Computing education has a shorter history of developing assessment instruments for college-level instruction than engineering education.

Whereas precollege engineering education promotes engineering literacy, analogous to scientific and mathematical literacy (Snider & Purzer, 2014), undergraduate engineering education prepares students to become professional engineers. As a consequence, engineering education researchers have studied how engineering students develop professional identities. In contrast, there is little research on student identity development in computing.

Many computing education studies have investigated introductory courses in computer science (CS1). Similarly, engineering education research has devoted significant attention to first-year programs for undergraduates in engineering. This attention follows naturally from the responsibility of engineering education departments to deliver first-year engineering courses.

For computing educators just getting started in computer science education, there are several ways to learn more. Reading this Handbook (and its citations of particular interest) is a good start. It may help to discuss the readings with others, such as by organizing a local or virtual reading group. Courses in education or in psychology offered by colleges and universities would provide a directed reading and discussion structure to computing faculty who audit the course. Presenting one's work at campus teaching and learning events and at computing education conferences and talking to other authors and speakers are other ways to learn more. Teaching and learning centers, STEM centers, learning technology centers, and assessment and evaluation centers are other good places to start on college campuses. It also helps to know you aren't alone in struggling with the differences between disciplinary research and DBER (Borrego, 2007). Computing educators may eventually want to seek out collaborators. Local collaborators might be found in social science departments. It is also possible to recruit collaborators from among the authors of specific prior studies. These potential collaborators may be interested in expanding their data collection to additional students and institutional settings. Some people will be too busy. But many successful collaborations are born of both casual local interactions and cold calls to researchers at other institutions (Borrego & Newswander, 2008).

11.8 Conclusion

In 2009, Godfrey and Hadgraft declared that engineering education research was "coming of age." That is, it was reaching a state of maturity. Similarly, with the publication of this Handbook, we authors declare that computing education research is coming of age. Just as engineering education researchers have drawn inspiration from other DBER fields such as physics education research and chemistry education research, computing education researchers could adopt ideas and practices from other DBER fields, including engineering education research. Conversely, computing education research has contributed models and methods that could benefit other DBER fields. In summary, as suggested by Henderson et al. (2017), interdisciplinary collaborations between researchers from different DBER communities could facilitate exchanges of ideas and thereby advance the development of education research in every discipline.

Acknowledgments

Monica Cardella recommended articles on precollege engineering education. Robin Adams and Şenay Purzer recommended articles on engineering design education. Cynthia Taylor helped us compare engineering education research with computing education research. Benjamin Ahn, Zahra Atiq, Natasha Danas, Colin Flavin, Jane Folliard, Mark Guzdial, Shriram Krishnamurthi,

Colleen Lewis, Jacqueline McNeil, Justin Pombrio, Sorawee Porncharoenwase, Paul Reckamp, Preston Tunnell Wilson, and John Wrenn offered constructive suggestions on drafts of this chapter. This work was supported in part by the National Science Foundation under grants 1504883 and 1626287.

References

Adams, R., Aldridge, D., Atman, C., Barker, L., Besterfield-Sacre, M., Bjorklund, S., & Young, M. (2006). The research agenda for the new discipline of engineering education. *Journal of Engineering Education*, 95(4), 259–261.

Ahn, B., Cox, M. F., London, J., Cekic, O., & Zhu, J. (2014). Creating an instrument to measure leadership, change, and synthesis in engineering undergraduates. *Journal of Engineering Education*, 103(1), 115–136.

Allen, K., Reed-Rhoads, T., Terry, R. A., Murphy, T. J., & Stone, A. D. (2008). Coefficient alpha: An engineer's interpretation of test reliability. *Journal of Engineering Education*, 97(1), 87–94.

Atadero, R. A., Rambo-Hernandez, K. E., & Balgopal, M. M. (2015). Using Social Cognitive Career Theory to assess student outcomes of group design projects in statics. *Journal of Engineering Education*, 104(1), 55–73.

Atman, C. J., Adams, R. S., Cardella, M. E., Turns, J., Mosborg, S., & Saleem, J. (2007). Engineering design processes: A comparison of students and expert practitioners. *Journal of Engineering Education*, 96(4), 359–379.

Atman, C. J., Eris, O., McDonnell, J., Cardella, M. E., & Borgford-Parnell, J. L. (2014). Engineering design education: Research, practice, and examples that link the two. In A. Johri & B. M. Olds (Eds.), *Cambridge Handbook of Engineering Education Research* (pp. 201–225). New York: Cambridge University Press.

Bandura, A. (1977). Self-efficacy: Toward a unifying theory of behavioral change. *Psychological Review*, 84(2), 191–215.

Benson, L. C., Becker, K., Cooper, M. M., Griffin, O. H., & Smith, K. A. (2010). Engineering education: Departments, degrees and directions. *International Journal of Engineering Education*, 26(5), 1042–1048.

Benson, L., & Borrego, M. (2015). The role of replication in engineering education research. *Journal of Engineering Education*, 104(4), 388–392.

Bernhard, J., & Baillie, C. (2016). Standards for quality of research in engineering education. *International Journal of Engineering Education*, 32(6), 2378–2394.

Besterfield-Sacre, M., Cox, M. F., Borrego, M., Beddoes, K., & Zhu, J. (2014). Changing engineering education: Views of U.S. faculty, chairs, and deans. *Journal of Engineering Education*, 103(2), 193–219.

Borenstein, J., Drake, M. J., Kirkman, R., & Swann, J. L. (2010). The Engineering and Science Issues Test (ESIT): A discipline-specific approach to assessing moral judgment. *Science and Engineering Ethics*, 16(2), 387–407.

Borrego, M. (2007). Development of engineering education as a rigorous discipline: A study of the publication patterns of four coalitions. *Journal of Engineering Education*, 96(1), 5–18.

Borrego, M., & Bernhard, J. (2011). The emergence of engineering education research as an internationally connected field of inquiry. *Journal of Engineering Education*, 100(1), 14–47.

Borrego, M., Douglas, E. P., & Amelink, C. T. (2009). Quantitative, qualitative, and mixed research methods in engineering education. *Journal of Engineering Education*, 98(1), 53–66.

Borrego, M., Foster, M. J., & Froyd, J. E. (2014). Systematic literature reviews in engineering education and other developing interdisciplinary fields. *Journal of Engineering Education*, 103(1), 45–76.

Borrego, M., Foster, M. J., & Froyd, J. E. (2015). What is the state of the art of systematic review in engineering education? *Journal of Engineering Education*, 104(2), 212–242.

Borrego, M., Froyd, J., & Knight, D. (2007). Accelerating emergence of engineering education via the International Conference on Research in Engineering Education (ICREE). *Journal of Engineering Education*, 96(4), 281–282.

Borrego, M., & Henderson, C. (2014). Increasing the use of evidence-based teaching in STEM higher education: A comparison of eight change strategies. *Journal of Engineering Education*, 103(2), 220–252.

Borrego, M., Karlin, J., McNair, L. D., & Beddoes, K. (2013). Team effectiveness theory from industrial and organizational psychology applied to engineering student project teams: A review. *Journal of Engineering Education*, 102(4), 472–512.

Borrego, M., & Newswander, L. K. (2008). Characteristics of successful cross-disciplinary engineering education collaborations. *Journal of Engineering Education*, 97(2), 123–134.

Brophy, S., Klein, S., Portsmore, M., & Rogers, C. (2008). Advancing engineering education in P–12 classrooms. *Journal of Engineering Education*, 97(3), 369–387.

Capobianco, B. M., Diefes-Dux, H. A., Mena, I., & Weller, J. (2011). What is an engineer? Implications of elementary school student conceptions for engineering education. *Journal of Engineering Education*, 100(2), 304–328.

Canney, N., & Bielefeldt, A. (2015). A framework for the development of social responsibility in engineers. *International Journal of Engineering Education*, 31(1B), 414–424.

Carlone, H. B., & Johnson, A. (2007). Understanding the science experiences of successful women of color: Science identity as an analytic lens. *Journal of Research in Science Teaching*, 44(8), 1187–1218.

Case, J. M., & Light, G. (2011). Emerging research methodologies in engineering education research. *Journal of Engineering Education*, 100(1), 186–210.

Chao, J., Xie, C., Nourian, S., Chen, G., Bailey, S., Goldstein, M. H., Purzer, S., Adams, R. S., & Tutwiler, M. S. (2017). Bridging the design-science gap with tools: Science learning and design behaviors in a simulated environment for engineering design. *Journal of Research in Science Teaching*, 54(8), 1049–1096.

Chi, M. T., Feltovich, P. J., & Glaser, R. (1981). Categorization and representation of physics problems by experts and novices. *Cognitive Science*, 5(2), 121–152.

Clark, M. C., Froyd, J. E., Merton, P., & Richardson, J. (2004). The evolution of curricular change models within the foundation coalition. *Journal of Engineering Education*, 93(1), 37–47.

Crede, E., & Borrego, M. (2010). A content analysis of the use of mixed methods studies in engineering education. In *ASEE Annual Conference* (pp. 15.22.1–5.22.18). Washington, DC: American Society for Engineering Education.

Creswell, J. W., & Plano Clark, V. L. (2007). *Designing and Conducting Mixed Methods Research*. Thousand Oaks, CA: Sage.

Crismond, D. P., & Adams, R. S. (2012). The informed design teaching and learning matrix. *Journal of Engineering Education*, 101(4), 738–797.

Davis, M. (1998). *Thinking Like an Engineer: Studies in the Ethics of a Profession.* New York: Oxford University Press.

Douglas, K. A., & Purzer, S. (2015). Validity: Meaning and relevancy in assessment for engineering education research. *Journal of Engineering Education*, 104(2), 108–118.

Douglas, K. A., Rynearson, A., Purzer, S., & Strobel, J. (2016). Reliability, validity, and fairness: A content analysis of assessment development publications in major engineering education journals. *International Journal of Engineering Education*, 32(5a), 1960–1971.

Duval-Couetil, N., Reed-Rhoads, T., & Haghighi, S. (2010). Development of an assessment instrument to examine outcomes of entrepreneurship education on engineering students. In *Frontiers in Education Conference* (p. T4D-1). New York: IEEE.

Dweck, C. S. (1999). *Self-Theories: Their Role in Motivation, Personality, and Development*. Philadelphia, PA: Psychology Press.

Engineering Education Community Resource (2017). Engineering education departments and programs. Retrieved from http://engineeringeducationlist.pbworks.com/w/page/27610307/Engineering%20Education%20Departments%20and%20Programs%20(Graduate)

Eris, O., Chachra, D., Chen, H. L., Sheppard, S., Ludlow, L., Rosca, C., Bailey, T., & Toye, G. (2010). Outcomes of a longitudinal administration of the persistence in engineering survey. *Journal of Engineering Education*, 99(4), 371–395.

Feisel, L. D., & Rosa, A. J. (2005). The role of the laboratory in undergraduate engineering education. *Journal of Engineering Education*, 94(1), 121–130.

Felder, R. M., & Brent, R. (2010). The National Effective Teaching Institute: Assessment of impact and implications for faculty development. *Journal of Engineering Education*, 99(2), 121–134.

Felder, R. M., Felder, G. N., & Dietz, E. J. (1998). A longitudinal study of engineering student performance and retention. V. Comparisons with traditionally-taught students. *Journal of Engineering Education*, 87(4), 469–480.

Fincher, S., Lister, R., Clear, T., Robins, A., Tenenberg, J., & Petre, M. (2005). Multi-institutional, multi-national studies in CSEd research: Some design considerations and trade-offs. In *Proceedings of the First International Workshop on Computing Education Research* (pp. 111–121). New York: ACM.

Finelli, C. J., Borrego, M., & Rasoulifar, G. (2015). Development of a taxonomy of keywords for engineering education research. *Journal of Engineering Education*, 104(4), 365–387.

Finelli, C. J., Daly, S. R., & Richardson, K. M. (2014). Bridging the research-to-practice gap: Designing an institutional change plan using local evidence. *Journal of Engineering Education*, 103(2), 331–361.

Firetto, C. M., Van Meter, P. N., Turns, S. R., & Litzinger, T. A. (2016). The validation of a conceptual reasoning inventory for introductory thermodynamics. *International Journal of Engineering Education*, 32(6), 2635–2652.

Foor, C. E., Walden, S. E., & Trytten, D. A. (2007). "I wish that I belonged more in this whole engineering group:" Achieving individual diversity. *Journal of Engineering Education*, 96(2), 103–115.

Freeman, S., Eddy, S. L., McDonough, M., Smith, M. K., Okoroafor, N., Jordt, H., & Wenderoth, M. P. (2014). Active learning increases student performance in science, engineering, and mathematics. *Proceedings of the National Academy of Sciences*, 111(23), 8319–8320.

Froyd, J. E. (2005). The Engineering Education Coalitions program. In *Educating the Engineer of 2020: Adapting Engineering Education to the New Century* (pp. 82–97). Washington, DC: National Academies Press.

Froyd, J. E., & Borrego, M. (2014). Leadership insights from the National Science Foundation Engineering Education Coalitions program and other large curriculum initiatives. *Journal of Leadership Studies*, 8(1), 45–50.

Froyd, J. E., Borrego, M., Cutler, S., Henderson, C., & Prince, M. (2013). Estimates of use of research-based instructional strategies in core electrical or computer engineering courses. *IEEE Transactions on Education*, 56(4), 393–399.

Froyd, J. E., & Lohmann, J. R. (2014). Chronological and ontological development of engineering education as a field of scientific inquiry. In A. Johri & B. M. Olds (Eds.), *Cambridge Handbook of Engineering Education Research* (pp. 3–15). New York: Cambridge University Press.

Gainsburg, J. (2015). Engineering students' epistemological views on mathematical methods in engineering. *Journal of Engineering Education*, 104(2), 139–166.

Godfrey, E., & Hadgraft, R. (2009). Engineering education research: Coming of age in Australia and New Zealand. *Journal of Engineering Education*, 98(4), 307–308.

Godwin, A., Potvin, G., Hazari, Z., & Lock, R. (2016). Identity, critical agency, and engineering: An affective model for predicting engineering as a career choice. *Journal of Engineering Education*, 105(2), 312–340.

Goldman, K. J., Gross, P., Heeren, C., Herman, G., Kaczmarczyk, L., Loui, M. C., & Zilles, C. (2010). Setting the scope of concept inventories for introductory computing subjects. *ACM Transactions on Computing Education (TOCE)*, 10(2), 1–29.

Gray, G. L., Costanzo, F., Evans, D., Cornwell, P., Self, B., & Lane, J. L. (2005). The Dynamics Concept Inventory Assessment Test: A progress report and some results. In *ASEE Annual Conference and Exposition* (pp. 4819–4833). Washington, DC: American Society for Engineering Education.

Hake, R. (1998). Interactive-engagement vs. traditional methods: A six-thousand-student survey of mechanics test data for introductory physics courses. *American Journal of Physics*, 66, 64–74.

Hazari, Z., Sonnert, G., Sadler, P. M., & Shanahan, M. C. (2010). Connecting high school physics experiences, outcome expectations, physics identity, and physics career choice: A gender study. *Journal of Research in Science Teaching*, 47(8), 978–1003.

Henderson, C., Beach, A., & Finkelstein, N. (2011). Facilitating change in undergraduate STEM instructional practices: An analytic review of the literature. *Journal of Research in Science Teaching*, 48(8), 952–984.

Henderson, C., Connolly, M., Dolan, E. L., Finkelstein, N., Franklin, S., Malcom, S., Rasmussen, C., Redd, K., & St. John, K. (2017),. Towards the STEM DBER Alliance: Why we need a discipline-based STEM education research community. *Journal of Engineering Education*, 106(3), 349–355.

Herman, G. L., Zilles, C., & Loui, M. C. (2014). A psychometric evaluation of the digital logic concept inventory. *Computer Science Education*, 24(4), 277–303.

Hestenes, D., Wells, M., & Swackhamer, G. (1992). Force concept inventory. *The Physics Teacher*, 30(3), 141–158.

Holloway, B. M., Reed, T., Imbrie, P. K., & Reid, K. (2014). Research-informed policy change: A retrospective on engineering admissions. *Journal of Engineering Education*, 103(2), 274–301.

Hutchison-Green, M. A., Follman, D. K., & Bodner, G. M. (2008). Providing a voice: Qualitative investigation of the impact of a first-year engineering experience on students' efficacy beliefs. *Journal of Engineering Education*, 97(2), 177–190.

Hynes, M. M. (2012). Middle-school teachers' understanding and teaching of the engineering design process: A look at subject matter and pedagogical content knowledge. *International Journal of Technology and Design Education*, 22(3), 345–360.

Hynes, M. M., Mathis, C., Purzer, S., Rynearson, A., & Siverling, E. (2017). Systematic review of research in P–12 engineering education from 2000–2015. *International Journal of Engineering Education*, 33(1B), 453–462.

Jamison, A., Kolmos, A., & Holgaard, J. E. (2014), Hybrid learning: An integrative approach to engineering education. *Journal of Engineering Education*, 103(2), 253–273.

Johnson, A. M., Ozogul, G., Moreno, R., & Reisslein, M. (2013). Pedagogical agent signaling of multiple visual engineering representations: The case of the young female agent. *Journal of Engineering Education*, 102(2), 319–337.

Johri, A., & Olds, B. M. (Eds.) (2014). *Cambridge Handbook of Engineering Education Research*. New York: Cambridge University Press.

Kajfez, R. L., & Matusovich, H. M. (2017). Competence, autonomy, and relatedness as motivators of graduate teaching assistants. *Journal of Engineering Education*, 106(2), 245–272.

Karabulut-Ilgu, A., Jaramillo Cherrez, N., & Jahren, C. T. (2017). A systematic review of research on the flipped learning method in engineering education. *British Journal of Educational Technology*, 49(3), 398–411.

Katehi, L., Pearson, G., & Feder, M. (Eds.) (2009). *Engineering in K–12 Education: Understanding the Status and Improving the Prospects*. Washington, DC: National Academies Press.

Kerr, B. (2015). The flipped classroom in engineering education: A survey of the research. In *International Conference on Interactive Collaborative Learning* (pp. 815–818). New York: IEEE.

Klein, S., Benjamin, R., Shavelson, R., & Bolus, R. (2007). The Collegiate Learning Assessment: Facts and fantasies. *Evaluation Review*, 31(5), 415–439.

Kolmos, A. & de Graaff, E. (2014). Problem-based and project-based learning in engineering education: Merging models. In A. Johri & B. M. Olds (Eds.), *Cambridge Handbook of Engineering Education Research* (pp. 141–160). New York: Cambridge University Press.

Krause, S., Decker, J. C., & Griffin, R. (2003). Using a Materials Concept Inventory to Assess Conceptual Gain in Introductory Materials Engineering Courses. In *Frontiers in Education Conference* (p. T3D-7). New York: IEEE.

Kuh, G. D. (2009). The national survey of student engagement: Conceptual and empirical foundations. *New Directions for Institutional Research*, 141, 5–20.

Larkin, J., McDermott, J., Simon, D. P., & Simon, H. A. (1980). Expert and novice performance in solving physics problems. *Science*, 208(4450), 1335–1342.

Leydens, J. A., Moskal, B. M., & Pavelich, M. J. (2004). Qualitative methods used in the assessment of engineering education. *Journal of Engineering Education*, 93(1), 65–72.

Lichtenstein, G., Chen, H. L., Smith, K. A., & Maldonado, T. A. (2014). Retention and persistence of women and minorities along the engineering pathway in the United States. In A. Johri & B. M. Olds (Eds.), *Cambridge Handbook of Engineering Education Research* (pp. 311–334). New York: Cambridge University Press.

Litzinger, T. A. (2010). Engineering education centers and programs: A critical resource. *Journal of Engineering Education, 99*(1), 3–4.

Lohmann, J. R. (2003). The editor's page: Mission, measures, and ManuscriptCentral™. *Journal of Engineering Education*, 92(1), 1.

Loughry, M. L., Ohland, M. W., & Woehr, D. J. (2014). Assessing teamwork skills for assurance of learning using CATME team tools. *Journal of Marketing Education*, 36(1), 5–19.

Loui, M. C. (2017). Wickenden award, thanks, and farewell. *Journal of Engineering Education*, 106(3), 347–348.

Mamaril, N. A., Usher, E. L., Li, C. R., Economy, D. R., & Kennedy, M. S. (2016). Measuring undergraduate students' engineering self-efficacy: A validation study. *Journal of Engineering Education*, 105(2), 366–395.

Marra, R. M., Rodgers, K. A., Shen, D., & Bogue, B. (2012). Leaving engineering: A multi-year single institution study. *Journal of Engineering Education*, 101(1), 6–27.

Martin, J. P., Simmons, D. R., & Yu, S. L. (2013). The role of social capital in the experiences of Hispanic women engineering majors. *Journal of Engineering Education*, 102(2), 227–243.

Matusovich, H. M., Paretti, M. C., McNair, L. D. & Hixson, C. (2014). Faculty motivation: A gateway to transforming engineering education. *Journal of Engineering Education*, 103(2), 302–330.

Matusovich, H. M., Streveler, R. A., & Miller, R. L. (2010). Why do students choose engineering? A qualitative, longitudinal investigation of students' motivational values. *Journal of Engineering Education*, 99(4), 289–303.

McKenna, A. F. (2014). Adaptive expertise and knowledge fluency in design and innovation. In A. Johri & B. M. Olds (Eds.), *Cambridge Handbook of Engineering Education Research* (pp. 227–242). New York: Cambridge University Press.

Menekse, M., Stump, G. S., Krause, S., & Chi, M. T. H. (2013). Differentiated overt learning activities for effective instruction in engineering classrooms. *Journal of Engineering Education*, 102(3), 346–374.

Montfort, D., Brown, S., & Shinew, D. (2014). The personal epistemologies of civil engineering faculty. *Journal of Engineering Education*, 103(3), 388–416.

Moore, T. J., Miller, R. L., Lesh, R. A., Stohlmann, M. S., & Kim, Y. R. (2013). Modeling in engineering: The role of representational fluency in students' conceptual understanding. *Journal of Engineering Education*, 102(1), 141–178.

National Research Council (2000). *How People Learn: Brain, Mind, Experience, and School*. Washington, DC: National Academies Press.

National Science Foundation (2015). News release #15-066 "NSF awards $12 million to spur an engineering education revolution." Retrieved from www.nsf.gov/news/news_summ.jsp?cntn_id=135379

Nelson, K. G., McKenna, A. F., Brem, S. K., Hilpert, J., Husman, J., & Pettinato, E. (2017). Students' misconceptions about semiconductors and use of knowledge in simulations. *Journal of Engineering Education*, 106(2), 218–244.

Newstetter, W., & Svinicki, M. (2014). Learning theories for engineering education practice and research. In A. Johri & B. Olds (Eds.), *Cambridge Handbook of Engineering Education Research* (pp. 29–46). New York: Cambridge University Press.

Ohland, M. W., Long, R. A., Layton, R. A., Lord, S. M., Orr, M. K., & Brawner, C. E. (2016). Making the Multiple Institution Database for Investigating Engineering Longitudinal Development (MIDFIELD) more accessible to researchers. In *Frontiers in Education Conference* (pp. 1–3). New York: IEEE.

Ohland, M. W., Loughry, M. L., Woehr, D. J., Finelli, C. J., Bullard, L. G., Felder, R. M., Layton, R. A., Pomeranz, H. R., & Schmucker, D. G. (2012). The comprehensive assessment of team member effectiveness: Development of a behaviorally anchored rating scale for self and peer evaluation. *Academy of Management Learning & Education*, 11(4), 609–630.

Ohland, M. W., Sheppard, S. D., Lichtenstein, G., Eris, O., Chachra, D., & Layton, R. A. (2008). Persistence, engagement, and migration in engineering programs. *Journal of Engineering Education*, 97(3), 259–278.

Ohland, M. W., Zhang, G., Thorndyke, B., & Anderson, T. J. (2004). Grade-point average, changes of major, and majors selected by students leaving engineering. In *Frontiers in Education Conference* (p. T1G-12). New York: IEEE.

Passow, H. J., & Passow, C. H. (2017). What competencies should undergraduate engineering programs emphasize? A systematic review. *Journal of Engineering Education*, 106(3), 475–526.

Patrick, A., & Borrego, M. (2016). A review of the literature relevant to engineering identity. In *ASEE Annual Conference* (pp. 26–29). Washington, DC: American Society for Engineering Education.

Peters, D. L., & Daly, S. R. (2013). Returning to graduate school: Expectations of success, values of the degree, and managing the costs. *Journal of Engineering Education*, 102(2), 244–268.

Pintrich, P. R., Smith, D. A., Garcia, T., & McKeachie, W. J. (1993). Reliability and predictive validity of the Motivated Strategies for Learning Questionnaire (MSLQ). *Educational and Psychological Measurement*, 53(3), 801–813.

Prados, J. W., Peterson, G. D., & Lattuca, L. R. (2005). Quality assurance of engineering education through accreditation: The impact of Engineering Criteria 2000 and its global influence. *Journal of Engineering Education*, 94(1), 165–184.

Prince, M. (2004). Does active learning work? A review of the research. *Journal of Engineering Education*, 93(3), 223–231.

Prybutok, A., Patrick, A., Borrego, M., Seepersad, C. C., & Kirisits, M. J. (2016). Cross-sectional survey study of undergraduate engineering identity. In *ASEE Annual Conference*. Washington, DC: American Society for Engineering Education.

Reid, K., & Ferguson, D. M. (2011). Enhancing the entrepreneurial mindset of freshman engineers. In *ASEE Annual Conference and Exposition* (pp. 22.622.1–22.622.10). Washington, DC: American Society for Engineering Education.

Ryan, R. M., & Deci, E. L. (2000). Self-determination theory and the facilitation of intrinsic motivation, social development, and well-being. *American Psychologist*, 55(1), 68–78

Samuelson, C. C., & Litzler, E. (2016). Community cultural wealth: An assets-based approach to persistence of engineering students of color. *Journal of Engineering Education*, 105(1), 93–117.

Seymour, E., & Hewitt, N. M. (1997). *Talking about Leaving: Why Undergraduates Leave the Sciences*. Boulder, CO: Westview Press.

Sheppard, S. D., Antonio, A. L., Brunhaver, S. R., & Gilmartin, S. K. (2014). The early career pathways of engineering students. In A. Johri & B. M. Olds (Eds.), *Cambridge Handbook of Engineering Education Research* (pp. 283–309). New York: Cambridge University Press.

Shuman, L., Besterfield-Sacre, M., & Litzinger, T. (2013). AEE and JEE: Where are the boundaries? Should there be boundaries? Do we need boundaries? *Journal of Engineering Education*, 102(2), 224–226.

Singer, S. R., Nielsen, N. R., & Schweingruber, H. A. (Eds.) (2012). *Discipline-Based Education Research*. Washington, DC: National Academies Press.

Sneider, C., & Purzer, S. (2014). The rising profile of STEM literacy through national standards and assessments. In S. Purzer, J. Strobel, & M. Cardella (Eds.). *Engineering in Pre-College Settings: Synthesizing Research, Policy, and Practices* (pp. 3–19). West Lafayette, IN: Purdue University Press.

Steif, P. S., & Dantzler, J. A. (2005), A statics concept inventory: Development and psychometric analysis. *Journal of Engineering Education*, 94(4), 363–371.

Stevens, R., O'Connor, K., Garrison, L., Jocuns, A., & Amos, D. M. (2008). Becoming an engineer: Toward a three dimensional view of engineering learning. *Journal of Engineering Education*, 97(3), 355–368.

Streveler, R. A., Brown, S., Herman, G. L., & Montfort, D. (2014). Conceptual change and misconceptions in engineering education: Curriculum, measurement, and theory-focused approaches. In A. Johri & B. M. Olds (Eds.), *Cambridge Handbook of Engineering Education Research* (pp. 83–101). New York: Cambridge University Press.

Streveler, R. A., Miller, R. L., Santiago-Román, A. I., Nelson, M. A., Geist, M. R., & Olds, B. M. (2011). Rigorous methodology for concept inventory development: Using the "assessment triangle" to develop and test the Thermal and Transport Science Concept Inventory (TTCI). *International Journal of Engineering Education*, 27(5), 968–974.

Streveler, R. A., & Smith, K. A. (2006). Conducting rigorous research in engineering education. *Journal of Engineering Education*, 95(2), 103–105.

Stice, J. E. (1976). A first step toward improved teaching. *Engineering Education*, 66(5), 394–398.

Stice, J. E. (1987). Using Kolb's learning cycle to improve student learning. *Engineering Education*, 77(5), 291–296.

Stump, G. S. Husman, J., & Corby, M. (2014). Engineering students' intelligence beliefs and learning. *Journal of Engineering Education*, 103(3), 369–387.

Svinicki, M. D. (2004). *Learning and Motivation in the Postsecondary Classroom*. Bolton, MA: Anker Publishing.

Svinicki, M. D. (2010). *A Guidebook on Conceptual Frameworks for Research in Engineering Education*. Retrieved from www.dl.icdst.org/pdfs/files1/af66d923f b150b6c895b32655eb9b5ce.pdf

Sweller, J., van Merrienboer, J. J. G., & Paas, F. G. W. (1998). Cognitive architecture and instructional design. *Educational Psychology Review*, 10(3), 251–296.

Tims, J., Zweben, S., & Timanovsky, Y. (2017). ACM-NDC study 2016–2017: Fifth annual study of non-doctoral-granting departments in computing. *ACM Inroads*, 8(3), 48–61.

Tonso, K. L. (2007). *On the Outskirts of Engineering: Learning Identity, Gender, and Power via Engineering Practice*. Rotterdam, The Netherlands: Sense Publishers.

Tonso, K. L. (2014). Engineering identity. In A. Johri & B. M. Olds (Eds.), *Cambridge Handbook of Engineering Education Research* (pp. 267–282). New York, NY: Cambridge University Press.

Trenshaw, K. F., Revelo, R. A., Earl, K. A., & Herman, G. L. (2016). Using Self Determination Theory principles to promote engineering students' intrinsic motivation to learn. *International Journal of Engineering Education*, 32(3A), 1194–1207.

Tseng, T., Chen, H. L., & Sheppard, S. (2011). Early academic experiences of non-persisting engineering undergraduates. In *ASEE Annual Conference and Exposition* (pp. 22.516.1–22.516.23). Washington, DC: American Society for Engineering Education.

US Department of Education (1988). Secretary's procedures and criteria for recognition of accrediting agencies, 53 Fed. Reg. 25088–25099 (proposed July 1, 1988) (to be codified at 34 CFR § 602–603).

Walther, J., Miller, S. E., & Sochacka, N. W. (2017). A model of empathy in engineering as a core skill, practice orientation, and professional way of being. *Journal of Engineering Education*, 106(1), 123–148.

Walther, J., & Sochacka, N. W. (2014). Qualifying Qualitative Research Quality (The Q3 Project): An interactive discourse around research quality in interpretive approaches to engineering education research. In *Frontiers in Education Conference* (pp. 1–4). New York: IEEE.

Walther, J., Sochacka, N. W., & Kellam, N. N. (2013). Quality in interpretive engineering education research: Reflections on an example study. *Journal of Engineering Education*, 102(4), 626–659.

Wankat, P. C., Felder, R. M., Smith, K. A., & Oreovicz, F. S. (2002). The scholarship of teaching and learning in engineering. In M. T. Huber & S. P. Morreale (Eds.), *Disciplinary Styles in the Scholarship of Teaching and Learning* (pp. 217–237). Washington, DC: American Association for Higher Education.

Wendell, K. B., & Rogers, C. (2013). Engineering design-based science, science content performance, and science attitudes in elementary school. *Journal of Engineering Education*, 102(4), 513–540.

Wigfield, A., & Eccles, J. S. (2000). Expectancy-value theory of achievement motivation. *Contemporary Educational Psychology*, 25(1), 68–81.

Willey, K., & Gardner, A. (2010). Investigating the capacity of self and peer assessment activities to engage students and promote learning. *European Journal of Engineering Education*, 35(4), 429–443.

Wilson-Lopez, A., Mejia, J. A., Hasbún, I. M., & Kasun, G. S. (2016). Latina/o adolescents' funds of knowledge related to engineering. *Journal of Engineering Education*, 105(2), 278–311.

Zhu, Q., Zoltowski, C. B., Feister, M. K., Buzzanell, P. M., Oakes, W. C., & Mead, A. D. (2014). The development of an instrument for assessing individual ethical decisionmaking in project-based design teams: Integrating quantitative and qualitative methods. In *ASEE Annual Conference* (pp. 24.1197.3–24.1197.12). Washington, DC: American Society for Engineering Education.

PART III

Topics

Systemic Issues

12 Novice Programmers and Introductory Programming

Anthony V. Robins

12.1 Introduction

One of the central topics in computing education research (CEdR) is the exploration of how a person learns their first programming language, also described in terms such as understanding "novice programmers," introductory programming, teaching and learning in "CS1" (a first course in computer science), and so on. This chapter explores key issues and surveys some of the important research in this domain.

Programming languages are complex artificial constructs. Like the grammatical rules of natural language, they consist of a relatively small number of elements that can be combined in infinitely many productive ways. The question of how people come to understand and practically apply such a body of knowledge is inherently interesting in the context of disciplines such as psychology and education. There is also a significant practical interest from computing educators. Decades of experience have shown that learning to program is a difficult process for many people. Introductory programming courses typically have high rates of student dropout and failure. This creates significant challenges for educators, who naturally want their students to progress successfully, and sometimes face significant institutional pressures if they do not.

Issues around programming have also been a focus of attention for major IT companies such as IBM and Google and an important focus for the technology sector's main professional and scientific society, the Association for Computing Machinery (ACM). The ACM acknowledges both the challenges facing teachers and the lack of consensus on many topics, and therefore offers little advice on teaching and a range of suggestions on curriculum structure, which is indicative of the wide variety of opinion in the field (ACM/IEEE-CS, 2013). More recently, the question of how best to teach programming has attracted the attention of national teaching organizations and governments, as several countries grapple with how best to deliver technology topics and when to introduce programming in the school curriculum.

In short, the **motivational context** for exploring the teaching and learning of programming includes academic, pedagogical, and practical factors. The field has attracted considerable interest from researchers, teachers, practitioners, industry, and governments alike. There is now a significant body of relevant literature, but many important questions remain open.

The sections of this chapter review the challenge of programming (from various perspectives), literature relating to novice programmers (largely from a cognitive perspective), and recommendations relating to teaching programming (in the context of a typical CS1 course). Although the focus is on CS1, much of this material is relevant to learning programming in any context (e.g., schools).

12.2 The Challenge of Programming

12.2.1 Historical Perspectives

The ACM was founded as a scientific and educational computing society in 1947. Computing developed as a widespread technology and commercial reality during the 1950s and 1960s. Programming rapidly emerged as the central challenge:

> It was generally assumed that coding the computer would be a relatively simple process of translation that could be assigned to low-level clerical personnel. It quickly became apparent that computer programming, as it came to be known, was anything but straightforward and simple. Skilled programmers developed a reputation for creativity and ingenuity, and programming was considered by many to be a uniquely intellectual activity, a black art that relied on individual ability and idiosyncratic style. By the beginning of the 1950s, however, programming had been identified as a key component of any successful computer installation. By the early 1960s, the "problem of programming" had eclipsed all other aspects of commercial computer development.
> (Ensmenger, 2010, p. 29)

The early decades of rapid growth were characterized by a continual shortage of programmers, a state of "chronic crisis" (Gibbs, 1994).

Prior to the development of academic qualifications, most programmers were trained "in house" by their employers. The outcomes were very mixed, with high rates of failure. In 1962, the US Army applied its own tests to 190 trainees in their Automatic Data Processing Programming course "in an attempt to reduce the wasted training time and costs associated with the prevailing high attrition rate" (Bauer, Mehrens, & Vinsonhaler, 1968).

The obvious challenges of programming and the desire to reduce the costs of selecting and training successful programmers led to the development of various screening tests. The most significant of these was the IBM Programmer Aptitude Test (PAT), first released in 1955. By the early 1960s, an estimated 80 percent of businesses employing programmers used aptitude tests, around half of them the PAT (Lawson, 1962). In 1967 alone, the PAT was administered to over 700,000 people (McNamara, 1967). Other popular tests included the Computer Programmer Aptitude Battery and the Wolfe Programming Aptitude Tests, as described, for example, by Pea and Kurland (1984).

Despite their widespread use, it was never clear that early aptitude tests were actually effective:

> Ever since the 1950s, when the [PAT] was developed by IBM to help select programmer trainees, consistently modest correlations (at their best from 0.5 to 0.7, hence accounting for only a quarter to a half of the variance), and in many cases much lower, have existed between an individual's score on such a measure and his or her assessed programming skill.
> (Pea & Kurland, 1984)

Many studies from the 1960s to the 1980s reported that the predictions of programmer aptitude tests with respect to actual job performance were poor, and that tests of this type should not be administered to university students because the results were unreliable (Robins, 2010). More sophisticated tests were subsequently developed, with the Berger Aptitude for Programming Test (B-APT) emerging as the most popular. Several alternatives for predicting success were also explored, including the use of demographic factors, past high school achievement (SAT scores), mathematical ability, and "general cognitive processes" such as problem-solving strategies. No reliable predictor of programming ability was found, however, and even large-scale analysis of multiple factors results in only limited predictive power (Robins, 2010).

Beyond in-house training, a large number of vocational schools sprang up during the mid-1960s. These were "generally profit-oriented enterprises more interested in quantity than quality" (Ensmenger, 2010, p. 75), with correspondingly poor outcomes. Increasing academic involvement was reflected in the foundation of the ACM Special Interest Group in Computer Personnel Research (SIGCPR) in 1962, and its publication of two major journals, *Computer Personnel* and the yearly *Proceedings of the Nth Annual Computer Personnel Research Conference*. The ACM introduced and popularized the idea of "computer science" as a discipline, and an ACM committee developed the first standardized curriculum. For different reasons, both vocational schools (regarded as too lax) and early academic programs (regarded as too stringent) were seen as problematic, and "Neither was believed to be a reliable short-term solution to the burgeoning labor shortage in programming" (Ensmenger, 2010, p. 80).

Two well-received and influential books appeared in the 1970s: *The Psychology of Computer Programming* (Weinberg, 1971) and *The Mythical Man Month* (Brooks, 1975). Weinberg presented the first empirical study of programming as a complex human activity, setting the stage for much that followed in the field of CEdR. Brooks addressed the practical process of software development and the reasons that so many programming-based projects failed, drawing attention to the need for new ideas about how to manage programmers.

One of the most influential claims to emerge from early research was that of huge variability in the productivity of professional programmers. An early IBM study claimed that a good programmer was at least 25 times more efficient than an average one (Sackman, Erickson, & Grant, 1968), with others claiming an even greater disparity. Sackman et al. opined that "When a programmer is good, he is very, very good. But when he is bad, he is horrid."

The stubborn problems in predicting and training successful programmers, combined with the significant variability in their effectiveness, led to a widespread acceptance of the claim that good programmers are "born, not made" (Dauw, 1967; Webster, 1996). Other persistent and widely held beliefs about programming can also be traced back to these early decades. These include claims that programming is an inherently creative or "artistic" process, that it is not amenable to "scientific" analysis or standard managerial methods, and that programmers are typically male and often socially withdrawn. While many would argue today that these are mostly outmoded myths (see Chapter 16), they have influenced both the nature of CEdR and the public perception of programming. Further perspectives on the history of research into programming can be found in Chapter 1 of this Handbook.

12.2.2 The Nature of Learning Outcomes

The opportunity to learn programming today is available in many forms, including a wide range of academic courses, private and commercial training, online resources such as interactive environments, open course materials, and massive open online courses (MOOCs). This chapter focuses on issues that are relevant to a first academic course in programming, often called CS1 (Computer Science 1). Other modes of teaching and learning are addressed elsewhere in the Handbook.

12.2.2.1 High Dropout and Failure Rates

Consistent with the historical issues surrounding programming, CS1 has typically been regarded as difficult for students, with persistent and widespread reports of high student fail and dropout rates; see, for example, Newman, Gatward, and Poppleton (1970), Garcia (1987), Allan and Kolesar (1997), Sheard and Hagan (1998), Guzdial and Soloway (2002), Beaubouef and Mason (2005), Kinnunen and Malmi (2006), Howles (2009), Guzdial (2010), Corney, Teague, and Thomas (2010), Teague (2011), Mendes et al. (2012), and Watson and Li (2014). This issue has been one of the main practical concerns for computing teachers, and one of the main drivers of research in CEd.

In an attempt to quantify the problem, Bennedsen and Caspersen (2007) surveyed 63 institutions internationally, collecting data on numbers of students who *abort* (drop out), *skip* the final exam, or sit and *fail*. They observed an aggregated failure rate that was on average roughly 33 percent and commonly up to 50 percent or more, but with huge institutional variation (as is to be expected with different countries, institutions, courses, and policy settings). In a follow-up study, Watson and Li (2014) surveyed the literature relating to 51 institutions. The results reported were very similar, with the same average fail rate and huge variation. Fail rates varied by different countries, but did not vary over programming language or improve over time.

Both studies found that small class size was correlated with lower fail rates. Both informally conclude that while fail rates in CS1 courses appear to be high, they are not "alarmingly" so. Unfortunately, both studies suffer from failing to compare CS1 courses with other courses at the same institution, making it difficult to separate the effects of institutional variation from the effects of programming as a subject. (Luxton-Reilly, 2016, compares the 67 percent pass rate found in both studies with an 82 percent pass rate "across all degree-level courses" in New Zealand.) The authors also themselves urge caution in the interpretation of their results. The first study is based on a survey of research-active computing teachers with an institutional response rate of just 12.7 percent. The second is based on an analysis of research literature. In both cases, it is highly likely that the data are drawn from engaged and active sources, possibly presenting the upper end of the spectrum of outcomes. Bennedsen and Caspersen (2007) note that "We hypothesize that if we could see the full picture, things would look very different, but we have no data to support this belief."

12.2.2.2 Fragile Learning

Concerns have also been raised about whether all of those who pass CS1 have learned what they should. An early study of students who had completed a single semester of programming (Soloway et al., 1983) found that when asked to write a loop that calculated an average, only 38 percent were able to complete the task correctly (even when syntax errors were ignored). The averaging task, called the "Rainfall Problem," has been something of a benchmark in the literature ever since. A similar study of students with two years of programming instruction (Kurland et al., 1989) concluded that "many students had only a rudimentary understanding of programming." In an overview, Winslow comments that "One wonders ... about teaching sophisticated material to CS1 students when study after study has shown that they do not understand basic loops" (Winslow, 1996).

The most influential work on the limitations of learning in CS1 was the report of a 2001 ITiCSE working group (McCracken et al., 2001). The "McCracken group" consisted of ten authors from eight tertiary institutions in various countries. The group assessed the ability of a combined pool of 216 post-CS1 students using a common set of programming problems selected such that "students in any type of Computer Science programme should be able to solve them" (McCracken et al., 2001). The majority of students performed much worse than their teachers expected, with most failing to finish the problem set. Given the scale and the multinational nature of the collaboration, these results were widely viewed as significant and compelling.

The McCracken study motivated a range of follow-up projects. Utting et al. (2013) revisited the study with improved support for 418 student participants, finding both well- and poorly-performing groups. The Leeds group (Lister et al., 2004) examined the performance of 941 nearly or recently completed CS1 students. The study used multiple-choice questions designed to explore basic programming skills and the ability to trace (follow and reason about) short pieces of code. The results showed that "many students were weak at these tasks," suggesting that "such students have a fragile grasp of skills that are a prerequisite for problem-solving" (Lister et al., 2004).

Unfortunately, such studies suggest that many students are "passing" CS1 courses without a strong grasp of programming basics. This is consistent with ample anecdotal evidence that some students who attempt later programming courses are poorly equipped to do so, contributing to the widespread perception of programming as a difficult topic at all levels.

12.2.2.3 Bimodal Outcomes

Based on the evidence so far reviewed, it is tempting to assume that programming is simply harder than most other topics to learn and to teach. This alone would more than justify the field of CEdR and attempts to find effective methods. A further observation complicates this simple view, however, namely that typical CS1 courses often have an unusually high rate of highly achieving students. It is as if there is a significant subset of students who find programming easy:

> In every introduction to programming course, 20% of the students just get it effortlessly – you could lock them in a dimly lit closet with a reference manual, and they'd still figure out how to program. 20% of the class never seems to get it.
> (Guzdial, 2007)

Similar comments from other teachers refer to "two populations: those who can, and those who cannot" Dehnadi (2006), and that there is a "double hump" in grade distributions that "has been observed in programming courses all over the world, largely independent of geographical or social context, and over a long period of time" (Kölling, 2009).

This paradoxical state of affairs has of course been the focus of considerable attention. The term "bimodal" is often used to describe the resulting grade distributions (with higher than usual rates of both failure and of high grades, there are necessarily fewer students in the mid-range). Bimodal distributions are described as characteristic of CS1 in, for example, Hudak and Anderson (1990), Bornat, Dehnadi, and Simon (2008), Corney, Teague, and Thomas (2010), Robins (2010), Yadin (2013), and Elarde (2016). Student outcomes in the influential McCracken study discussed above have also been described as bimodal (Lister & Leaney, 2003) and exhibiting the "two hump effect" (Guzdial, 2010), with a follow-up study (Utting et al., 2013) observing that "there are clearly two distinct populations within the current study's overall cohort" (low- and high-performing groups). Note that a wide variation in student outcomes is consistent with historical observations of the variation in professional programmer performance.

In a widely circulated and commented-on draft (Dehnadi & Bornat, 2006), the authors claimed to have developed a diagnostic test that could accurately predict which students would or would not succeed at programming. Other researchers were unable to replicate the results (Bornat, Dehnadi, & Simon, 2008; Caspersen, Larsen. & Bennedsen, 2007), and the claim of a predictive test was later withdrawn (Bornat, 2014). Patitsas et al. (2016) claim to present "Evidence that computer science grades are not bimodal," but the claim is problematic. The grade distributions analyzed are all from one institution, and they do not include data for students who withdraw (abort). The "psychology experiment" demonstrates that participants can be cued to report bimodality in a noisy artificial dataset (see the issue of subject bias in research design; e.g., Mitchell & Jolley, 2012), but this does not show that the pattern does not exist in real-world data sets. For more on evidence relating to bimodal outcomes, see Robins (2018).

Despite contributing to the practice (Robins, 2010), I now consider the use of the term "bimodal" to be somewhat unfortunate. It has invited a focus on statistical definitions and tests, often without clarity on the underlying definition or counting of abort or skip outcomes (as stressed by Bennedsen & Caspersen, 2007), and often without recognition that binning grades in various ways leads to different results (as demonstrated by Höök, 2015). Given that there are huge variations in institutional outcomes and reporting practice, I suggest that the more useful questions are broader and more contextual. If a given CS1 course has a higher failure rate than comparable courses (at the same institution), then this is a concern. If it also typically has a higher rate of high grades, then this is of interest. If the grade distribution reflects both of these effects, then it might usefully but informally be described as "bimodal." It is probably too late to attempt to change the term, which is in widespread use in the literature, but it should be used with caution. We return to a discussion of potential reasons for "bimodal" outcomes in Section 12.3.7.

12.2.2.4 Summary

It is certainly not the case that all CS1 courses have bimodal outcomes, though reports of this trend are common. Nor is it the case that they all have high dropout and failure rates, though reports of this are even more common (and further concerns have been raised about the performance of passing students). We suggest that both trends will be more typically seen in large courses with open entry to students (compared to small and selective courses) and note that institutional background and policy settings, and the intended scope and nature of each individual course, can significantly impact outcomes. Both trends are consistent with the historical development of programming as a discipline and are observed and commented on frequently enough to be part of the "received wisdom" of the CEd community.

12.2.3 The Task

Given the historical and current educational complexities around learning to program, it is useful to briefly examine what is involved. Programming is often called "coding," but this is a very limited term for the richness and complexity of the task.

12.2.3.1 Requirements

A good overview (du Boulay, 1989) describes five overlapping domains that must be mastered: (1) general orientation, what programs are for and what can be done with them; (2) the notional machine, a general model of the computer as it relates to executing programs; (3) notation, the syntax and semantics of a particular programming language; (4) structures, the use of schemata/plans as ways of organizing knowledge; and (5) pragmatics, the skills of planning, developing, testing, debugging, and so on. While most explicit programming instruction and attention is focused on the third item, in general, of course, a novice programmer will be dealing with many of these issues at once, compounding the difficulties.

In a broad review of the literature relating to novice programmers, Robins, Rountree, and Rountree (2003) summarized the range of topics explored using the dimensions shown in Table 12.1. The columns describe the attributes that are required to write a program, namely *knowledge* of a programming language and tools, the *strategies* for applying this knowledge appropriately, and the capacity to construct and compare mental *models* of program states. The rows describe the stages of creating a program, namely the processes of *design*, *generation* (writing code), and *evaluation*. The cells of this framework should be thought of as fuzzy rather than absolute divisions, and once again, at any given time, an actual programmer will usually be dealing with several of these requirements at once.

Rogalski and Samurçay (1990) summarize the task of programming as involving "a variety of cognitive activities, and mental representations," the "construction of conceptual knowledge, and the structuring of basic operations … into schemas and plans," and the need for flexible strategies. Emphasizing the active and dynamic nature of programming, Green (1990) suggested that programming is best regarded as an exploratory process where programs are created "opportunistically and incrementally." Similarly, Davies (1993) concluded that "emerging models of programming behavior suggest an incremental problem-solving process where strategy is determined by localized problem-solving episodes and frequent problem re-evaluation." Kim and Lerch (1997) describe programming as a process of scientific discovery, with different representations required in multiple "problem spaces."

12.2.3.2 Perceived Difficulties and Errors

Along with the multiple necessary competencies and the complex and interactive nature of the programming process, it is also worth noting that strict constraints apply to the final product of the programming process. In human languages, shared context and "common sense" fill in many of the gaps, while ambiguity and miscommunications abound. In programming languages, the

Table 12.1 *A programming framework. Adapted from Robins, Rountree, and Rountree (2003).*

	Knowledge	Strategies	Models
Design	Of planning methods, algorithm design, formal methods	For planning, problem-solving, designing algorithms	Of problem domain, notional machine
Generation	Of language, libraries, environment/tools	For implementing algorithms, coding, accessing knowledge	Of desired programs
Evaluation	Of debugging tools and methods	For testing, debugging, tracking/tracing, repair	Of actual program

final product must be, at least to a certain functional level, complete, unambiguous, and error free.

Lahtinen, Ala-Mutka, and Järvinen (2005) surveyed 559 novice programming students (and 34 teachers) at six European universities. Respondents perceived the most difficult aspects of programming to be "understanding how to design a program to solve a certain task," "dividing functionality into procedures," and "finding bugs from their own programs." None of these issues relate to knowledge of the specifics of any programming language, or even of general language constructs – they are issues of developing mental models ("understanding") and strategy (Table 12.1).

A related study explored the problems encountered by novice students attempting laboratory tasks for two populations (containing roughly 220 and 250 individuals) over two successive years (Garner, Haden, & Robins, 2005; Robins, Haden & Garner, 2006). The most frequently recorded problems were understanding the task, issues relating to overall program design and structure, and "basic mechanics" (a general category covering typos, trivial syntax errors, missing semicolons, and the like). Of the many specific language-related problems observed, the most frequent related to loops, arrays, and passing data to/from modules. Like the study discussed above, this suggests that developing an overall program design/algorithm is a more difficult task than deploying any particular programming language construct (although in aggregate there are many language constructs to consider).

McCall and Kölling's (2014) review attempts to use the analysis of compiler error messages to classify the mistakes made by novices, pointing out that different conceptual mistakes can generate the same error message, and conversely that the same conceptual mistake can manifest itself in different error messages. The authors hand-analyze 333 error messages and the associated code produced by 240 students and other anonymous users of the BlueJ Java programming environment. The most common errors are "Variable not declared," "; missing," "Variable name written incorrectly," and "Invalid syntax." This is consistent with the dominance of the "basic mechanics" category in the previous study above.

12.3 Novice Programmers

Many topics relating to novice programming have been explored since the 1960s. During the 1970s through to the 1990s, there was an active and productive focus on the "psychology of programming." This work drew on concepts from cognitive psychology, such as knowledge representation, problem-solving, working memory, and so on (see Chapter 9).

Several key books marked the development of the field. Weinberg (1971) was influential in identifying programming as an area of psychological interest and stimulating research. The collection of papers in *Studying the Novice Programmer* by Soloway and Spohrer (1989) was a significant contribution; similarly, see Hoc et al. (1990). Sheil (1981) is an early review that discusses a range of methodological issues. Other reviews include Robins, Rountree, and Rountree (2003) and Pears et al. (2007). Drawing on these and other sources, this section notes some of the main trends and topics in this area, with a focus on the cognitive properties of novice programmers.

12.3.1 Properties of Novices

One way of exploring the challenges faced by novices in a field is to compare them to experts. Soloway and Spohrer (1989) outline deficits in novice programmers' understanding of various specific language constructs (e.g., variables, loops, arrays, and recursion), note shortcomings in their planning and testing of code, explore general issues relating to the use of program plans, show how prior knowledge can be a source of errors, and more. Similarly, Winslow (1996) notes that novice programmers are limited to surface and superficially organized knowledge, lack detailed schemata/scripts/mental models, fail to apply relevant knowledge, and approach programming "line by line" rather than using meaningful program "chunks" or structures. In short, novices are "very local and concrete in their comprehension of programs" (Wiedenbeck et al., 1999). Winslow (1996) states that it takes around ten years for a novice to become an expert programmer.

During the early stages of teaching and learning, the contrast between novice and expert is less important than that between different kinds of novice. Perkins et al. (1989) distinguish between "stoppers," "movers," and "tinkerers." Stoppers are those who stop and appear to "abandon all hope" when confronted with a problem or a lack of a clear direction to proceed. They are likely to be those who are frustrated by or have a negative emotional reaction to errors. Movers are those who keep trying, experimenting with and modifying their code. They can use feedback about errors effectively to solve problems and progress. Tinkerers are extreme movers who are not able to trace their code and may be making changes more or less at random, with little chance of progress.

Perkins et al.'s categories have proved to be very enduring and are still cited. Note, however, that the term "tinkering" is variously applied in the CEdR literature. Berland et al. (2013) review many other uses, concluding that "tinkering" is commonly defined as an "exploratory activity" and is suggested to play a crucial role in successful learning.

Two simple functional categories are suggested by the tendency to polarized/bimodal outcomes in CS1 courses as discussed above (Robins, Rountree, & Rountree, 2003). Effective novices are those who make progress in learning to program, typically leading to successful outcomes. Ineffective novices are those who do not make progress (or require inordinate effort and personal attention), typically leading to unsuccessful outcomes. Both the historical use of aptitude testing and much of the research reviewed below can be seen as attempting to predict whether given individuals will be effective or ineffective novice programmers and/or to understand the properties of these groups.

12.3.2 Knowledge

Learning to program involves acquiring both declarative knowledge (e.g., being able to state how a "for" loop works) and practical strategies for its application (e.g., using a "for" loop appropriately in a program) (Davies, 1993). Of the two, it is knowledge that receives the most explicit attention in typical textbooks and CS1 courses, which usually focus on presenting knowledge about a particular language. Related domains include knowledge of computers, programming tools and resources, and theory and formal methods.

One kind of knowledge representation that has historically been identified as central to both reading/understanding and writing programs is the structured chunk of related content. This has variously been called a schema or frame, or (if action oriented) a script or plan (Ormerod, 1990). For example, most experienced programmers will have a schema for the design of a class with encapsulated data fields and a public interface, or a plan for finding the average of the values stored in a one-dimensional array. There is considerable evidence that the plan is the basic cognitive unit used in program design and understanding, but what specifically is meant by a plan has varied considerably between authors (Rist, 1995).

Soloway and Ehrlich (1984) present a study supporting their claims that expert programmers use two types of programming knowledge: plans ("generic program fragments that represent stereotypic action sequences") and "rules of programming discourse" (the conventions that govern the composition of the plans into programs). Expert programmers are characterized in part by the large number of schemata/plans that they have internalized, and many studies have emphasized the importance of acquiring these organizing structures. Brooks (1990) introduced a special issue of the *International Journal of Man–Machine Studies* devoted to plans and other knowledge representations used by programmers. Soloway (1986) proposed that novices should be explicitly taught about common plans and "stereotypical solutions," as well as how to combine and use them (see also Clancy & Linn, 1999). Rist (2004) describes learning to program as a process of schema creation, application, combination, and evaluation, and explores "how changes in the form and structure of knowledge lead to the different types of behaviour seen at different levels of expertise." A distinct approach to understanding programming based on the explicit use of "design patterns" has emerged; see, for example, texts such as Gamma et al. (1995) and Freeman et al. (2004).

Two related educational theories regarding particularly important forms of knowledge – fundamental ideas (Bruner, 1960) and threshold concepts (Meyer & Land, 2003, 2006) – have both received attention within CEd. Fundamental ideas are those that have "wide as well as powerful applicability" and apply "at any stage of development" (Bruner, 1960). Discussing fundamental ideas in CEd, Schwill (1994, 1997) suggests the following four criteria: *horizontal* (the idea is relevant across many disciplines or sub-disciplines), *vertical* (the idea pervades all levels from elementary through to highly advanced), *time* (the idea is recognized as important and it endures), and *sense* (the idea has meaning in "everyday life"). Schwill argues that candidate fundamental ideas in computing include *algorithmization*, *structured dissection*, and *language*, with more specific ideas definable under each category (e.g., under language are the ideas of syntax and semantics).

Threshold concepts are those that are key challenges in learning a given knowledge domain; if successfully acquired, they enable a qualitatively different understanding. Meyer and Land (2003, 2006) describe them as likely to be *transformative* (creating a new way of viewing, understanding, or describing), *integrative* (allowing new connections and relationships to be perceived), *irreversible* (causing a fundamental change that cannot be "unlearned"), *troublesome* (being problematic to grasp or difficult to integrate into current understanding), and *boundary markers* (helping define the scope of the knowledge domain).

Threshold concepts attracted considerable attention within CEdR. In 2005, a group of researchers from several institutions across Europe and the USA launched an ongoing effort to identify threshold concepts in computer science, resulting in several publications, as described in Shinners-Kennedy and Fincher (2013). An initial informal survey of 36 instructors from 9 countries identified 33 candidate concepts "with most popular being: levels of abstraction; pointers; the distinction between classes, objects, and instances; recursion and induction; procedural abstraction; and polymorphism." Note that "while some concepts came up again and again, there was no universal consensus" (Boustedt et al., 2007).

A lack of consensus has proved to be a general problem within the literature on threshold concepts, with problems of definition, subjectivity, granularity, and the like being identified by several authors (e.g., O'Donnell, 2009; Rowbottom,

2007). Shinners-Kennedy and Fincher (2013) conclude that researchers have reached a "dead end" in the exploration of threshold concepts in CEd, but work continues in other disciplines. Further ideas on the interaction between fundamental ideas and threshold concepts in CEd are explored in both Sorva (2010) and Rountree, Robins, and Rountree (2013).

12.3.3 Strategies

As discussed above, programming knowledge necessarily goes hand in hand with the strategies/skills that are required to apply it. The latest ACM Curriculum Report for computer science (ACM/IEEE-CS, 2013) lists one of its goals as being to "identify the fundamental skills and knowledge that all computer science graduates should possess," and notes that "graduates need to understand how to apply the knowledge they have gained to solve real problems." The distinction between programming knowledge and strategies echoes fundamental distinctions in human memory and cognition between declarative (or semantic) and procedural knowledge, or the philosophical contrast between "knowing that" and "knowing how." The field of mathematics education has a long-standing and important distinction between "conceptual" and "procedural" knowledge; see, for example, Hiebert and Lefevre (1986).

Strategies are relevant at all stages of the programming process, from design to evaluation/debugging (Table 12.1). Design may involve utilizing problem-solving strategies such as divide-and-conquer or means–ends analysis, the use of patterns and analogies, or evaluating task- or language-specific factors that influence the structure of an appropriate program. Program generation involves strategies for implementing the design/algorithm, accessing knowledge as required and applying it appropriately, and using any relevant coding environment or tools. Program evaluation may involve strategies for tracing/tracking, testing, and debugging code.

Within CEdR, several authors have stressed the importance or preeminence of the strategic aspects of programming to successful learning outcomes (Davies, 1993; Perkins et al., 1989; Robins, Rountree, & Rountree 2003; Soloway, 1986), and similar discussion can be found using related terms such as programming skills, practice, or problem-solving. Many of the factors that distinguish expert from novice programmers relate to strategies (Sheil, 1981; Widowski & Eyferth, 1986). Perkins and Martin (1986) show (relating to the fragile learning discussed in Section 12.2.2.2) that both knowledge and strategies can be missing (forgotten), inert (learned but not used), or misplaced (learned but used inappropriately), and note that novices are often observed to be using generic and inefficient problem-solving strategies. Eckerdal (2009) argues that "concepts and practise are equally important parts of the learning goals, and equally difficult for students to learn," and that "there is a mutual dependency and complex relationship between the two." In concluding their discussion of threshold concepts, Shinners-Kennedy and Fincher (2013) noted that "the [Threshold Concept] group altered direction and started to search not for threshold concepts in computing, but instead posited the existence of threshold skills."

Davies (1993) reviews a range of literature on programming strategies and suggests that research should move beyond attempts to simply characterize strategies and instead focus on why they emerge and how they relate to factors such as the problem domain, the specific task, and the programming language and tools. In particular, research should focus on "exploring the relationship between the development of structured representations of programming knowledge and the adoption of specific forms of strategy" (Davies, 1993).

An excellent example of research fulfilling this specification is developed in a sequence of studies of novice and experienced programmers by Rist (1986, 1989, 1995, 2004), reviewed in Sorva (2012). Rist describes top-down, bottom-up, forward-development, backward-development, breadth-first, and depth-first design/programming strategies and mechanisms for schema expansion and combination. Rist suggests that programmers use top-down, forward-developing, breadth-first strategies whenever they have a suitable schema/plan available. In the absence of suitable schemata (e.g., for unfamiliar or particularly difficult problems), programmers revert to bottom-up, backward-developing, depth-first strategies in order to develop new solutions and new schemata/plans for later use. Programmers can use a mixture of these strategies as they work on familiar or unfamiliar sub-problems. Implicit in this theory is that the availability of relevant knowledge is a major driver of strategy, confirming the widely agreed-upon principle that the most significant difference between novices and experts is the richness of their respective experience/libraries of learned schemata.

Also implicit in Rist's framework is that the key factor separating novices (who all lack rich schemata) into effective and ineffective groups is the relative effectiveness of the strategies that they are employing (Robins, Rountree, & Rountree, 2003), and therefore the speed with which problems can be solved and schemata acquired. The knowledge required to support this process is available from a range of sources, with courses and textbooks designed to introduce it in a structured way. Without the strategies for accessing this knowledge and applying it to the practical task of programming, however, successful progress and therefore the acquisition of effective schema cannot take place. Conversely a novice with the right initial strategies can teach themselves to program by drawing on knowledge sources as needed. We suggest that progress in the successful teaching of programming can be made by exploring the following questions: What are the strategies employed by effective novices? How do they relate to their knowledge and their relevant mental models? Can these strategies be taught to ineffective novices?

12.3.4 Mental Models

The concept of a "mental model" has a long history in CEdR. Like "schema," the term is adopted from the cognitive science literature, where it is widely used and variously defined (Gentner, 2002; Gentner & Stevens, 1983; Johnson-Laird, 1983). Mental models are generally held to be internal models of how some aspect of the world works, an iconic representation of selected aspects of external objects and systems. Mental models have predictive power – they can be used to understand the observed behavior of the world and reason about future behavior.

One important model that novices need to acquire is of the "notional machine," an abstraction of the software and hardware of a computer that characterizes its role as the executor of programs, and that therefore provides a context for understanding the behavior of those programs (Cañas, Bajo, & Gonzalvo, 1994; du Boulay, 1986; du Boulay, O'Shea, & Monk, 1989; Hoc & Nguyen-Xuan, 1990; Mayer, 1989). du Boulay (1986) suggests that "A running program is a kind of mechanism and it takes quite a long time to learn the relation between a program on the page and the mechanism it describes," and likens the task to trying to understand how a car engine works based on a diagram. In the absence of an accurate understanding of a notional machine, novices can develop their own "bizarre theories" about how programs are executed (du Boulay, 1986). Mayer (1989) showed that students supplied with a notional machine model (which he called a "concrete model") were better at solving some kinds of problem than those without the model.

du Boulay, O'Shea, and Monk (1989) suggest that different programming languages afford different features of a notional machine, that they can be used to explain "hidden" actions and side effects of a program's operation, and that they should be should be simple and supported with some kind of concrete tool that allows the machine to be observed (a "glass box" instead of a "black box"). The later requirement is met by Berry and Kölling (2014), who propose an example notional machine and graphical notation for object-oriented programming and introduce an implementation of it within the popular BlueJ programming environment for Java (Kölling et al., 2003). See also the "stepper" in DrScheme for a functional programming example (Findler et al., 2002), and similar examples discussed in Chapter 21.

Sorva (2013) presents an excellent review of the notional machine concept and the misconceptions that can arise from incorrect models, even for topics that most programmers regard as obvious, such as simple assignment. A particular strength of the review is the discussion of notional machines in the context of broader theoretical frameworks such as mental models, constructivism, phenomenography, and threshold concepts. Sorva argues that teachers should "acknowledge the notional machine as an explicit learning objective and address it in teaching," and that in some cases, such as object-oriented languages, teaching "may benefit from using multiple notional machines at different levels of abstraction."

Schulte and Bennedsen (2006) surveyed 457 CS1 teachers on the importance and difficulty of broad categories of programming topics. Among their findings, the authors noted that only 29 percent of respondents explicitly addressed a notional machine in their teaching. While factors relevant to notional machines were rated as important, the topic of notional machines as a whole was rated as relevant but not important. This suggests that the theoretical significance of notional machines has not been successfully communicated to teaching practitioners, or at the very least that there is confusion about the definition. See also Chapters 1, 13, 15, 21, and 27 for other perspectives on the notional machine.

Programming is sometimes described as a particular "way of thinking" (Eckerdal, Thuné, & Berglund, 2005). Beyond the notional machine, writing a program involves holding many details in mind, including the problem domain and target design/algorithm, knowledge of a programming language and tools, the current state of the program, and plans and strategies for proceeding. Many of these requirements have been explored within the framework of mental models.

> Models are crucial to building understanding. Models of control, data
> structures and data representation, program design and problem domain are
> all important. If the instructor omits them, the students will make up their
> own models of dubious quality.
> (Winslow, 1996)

Problem domain models have been explored by, for example, Brooks (1977, 1983), Spohrer, Soloway, and Pope (1989), Davies (1993), and Rist (1995), and the interaction between "domain models" and "program models" by Corritore and Wiedenbeck (1991), Wiedenbeck and Ramalingam (1999), Wiedenbeck et al. (1999), and Burkhardt, Détienne, and Wiedenbeck (1997, 2002). The topic of program models is complicated by the distinction between a program as it was intended and the program as it actually is. Designs can be incorrect, unpredicted interactions can occur, bugs happen, and programmers are frequently faced with the need to understand unexpected program behavior. This requires the ability to trace code in order to build a model of the program and its behavior (which Perkins et al., 1989, call "close tracking" and describe as "taking the computer's point of view") and the capacity to compare this model with the intended model/behavior.

In some situations (e.g., major bug fixes), significant alterations to a desired program model may be necessary. Gray and Anderson (1987) call alterations to program code "change episodes" and suggest that they can be rich in information, helping to reveal the programmer's models, goals, and planning activities. Wiedenbeck, Fix, and Scholtz (1993) described expert mental models of programs as grounded in the use of schemata/patterns that are hierarchical and multilayered, with explicit mappings between layers and being well connected internally and well founded in the program text. Novice representations generally lacked these characteristics, but in some cases were working toward them. Soloway (1986) suggested that "learning to program amounts to learning how to construct mechanisms and how to construct explanations," and "language constructs do not pose major stumbling blocks for novices ... the real problems novices have lie in 'putting the pieces together,' composing and coordinating components of a program."

One of the earliest studies of mental models and programming is also one of the most comprehensive. Mayer (1985) presented a formal analysis of the models underlying BASIC statements, empirical evidence of the utility of the analysis in explaining the way BASIC is learned, comprehended, and used, and an analysis of common misconceptions. Learning the language is more successful when it is based on rich and relevant conceptual knowledge. Mayer suggests that "specific kinds of mental models can be successfully taught and that such training tends to enhance students' ability to solve programming problems." Other empirical studies that explore the problems arising from misconceptions and illustrate the advantages of rich mental models for learning and transfer include Kurland and Pea (1985), Bhuiyan, Greer, and McCalla (1992), Cañas, Bajo, and Gonzalvo (1994), and Shih and Alessi (1993).

Consistent with the fragile learning discussed above, Ma et al. (2007) explore the viability of mental models at the end of a CS1 Java course. The authors found that "approximately one third of students held non-viable mental models of value assignment and only 17% of students held a viable mental model of reference assignment." Unsurprisingly, students with viable mental models performed significantly better than those with non-viable models. Sorva (2013) presents a useful review of the relevant literature and explores the activity of code tracing as an example of the active/predictive nature of mental models. Sorva concludes that the main challenges to the successful running of a program model are "keeping track of program state in working memory, and the difficulty of forming mental models that are robustly founded on context-free run-time semantics of each construct."

As a final observation, the construction of mental models of programs can clearly be supported by a range of tools such as debuggers, software visualization tools, and features of rich programming environments such as BlueJ; see, for example, Storey, Fracchia, and Müller (1999) and Chapter 21.

12.3.5 Cognitive Load

The concept of "cognitive load" has been a more recent addition to the CEdR literature, again adopted from cognitive science. Cognitive load theory is a broad framework for describing the load placed on (or the "effort" expended by) working memory during the execution of a task (Paas, Renal, & Sweller, 2003; Plass, Moreno, & Brünken, 2010; Sweller, 1988, 1994). As originally proposed, the theory described three kinds of load: *intrinsic* (the difficulty or required effort inherent in a specific task or topic), *extraneous* (effort arising from and varying with the way that information is presented), and *germane* (the effort required to integrate new information into permanent schemata). (Subsequent variations are discussed in Chapter 9.) One of the main determinants of intrinsic load is element interactivity – the extent to which the task involves interacting elements that must be held in working memory simultaneously. Many principles of good pedagogy can be construed as attempts to reduce (particularly extraneous) cognitive load for learners or to promote the useful learning resulting from germane load.

It seems obvious that programming tasks typically involve high element inter-activity and therefore high intrinsic load. The most effective way to manage this is to exploit one of the known properties of working memory – our ability to "chunk" elements together into meaningful wholes. The capacity of working memory (number of elements that can be simultaneously "held") is generally taken to be 4 ± 1 (Cowan, 2001). However, what exactly constitutes an "element" is not well defined, and elements can be complex, containing other elements. For example, humans are generally able to recall a list of four single-digit numbers (e.g., 3, 7, 2, 9), but they can also recall four multi-digit numbers (72, 123, 18, 446), which between them contain many more digits. In short, the judicious use of "chunking" is a way to effectively hold many elements in working memory (as parts of more complex elements). This is the reason that structured units of knowledge such as schemata are so important in programming (and cogni-tion generally), where experts are distinguished largely by their learned libraries of useful schemata, and novices experience many difficulties as they work to acquire them.

Cognitive load theory leads to several empirically verified "effects" or "principles" (Plass, Moreno, & Brünken, 2010), some of which are discussed in the context of CEd by Sorva (2012). Whereas learning through problem-solving is a popular technique, the cognitive load for novices (lacking the necessary schemata) is high. The *worked-out-example effect* suggests that extraneous load is reduced by studying worked examples of problems rather than trying to solve the problems from scratch, and similarly the *completion effect* suggests that load is reduced when the learner starts with partial solutions. Other examples include the *guidance-fading effect*, stating that novices need extensive support that can be reduced over time, and the *isolated/interacting elements effect*, stating that tasks with high element interactivity will be learned more successfully if elem-ents are first introduced in isolation before being combined.

Sorva (2012) reviews examples where cognitive load theory has been applied to CS1. van Merriënboer (1990) and van Merriënboer and de Croock (1992) present evidence for the completion effect over two experiments where students who modified and extended existing programs achieved better outcomes than control groups that wrote programs from scratch. Garner (2002) presents a pro-gramming environment that facilitates code completion examples. Linn and Clancy (1992) demonstrated advantages for novices who were supplied with expert worked examples compared to novices who designed and wrote their own programs. "These activities emphasize the pedagogical value of reading code, as opposed to merely designing and writing it" (Sorva, 2012).

Evidence supporting the guidance-fading effect is described in Stachel et al. (2013). Student participants in a Visual Basic for Applications programming course were divided into a control group and an experimental group, the latter being provided with an additional scaffolding tool to support laboratory assignments. In the first phase of the study, the experimental group achieved better laboratory scores and reported lower self-rated cognitive load scores. These advantages persisted during the second phase when the scaffolding tool was withdrawn, and the experimental group also achieved a higher average final score. Gray et al. (2007) suggest combining worked example programs and guidance fading to generate "faded worked examples" (i.e., worked example sequences with fewer code steps explicitly provided as the learner progresses through the sequence).

Caspersen and Bennedsen (2007) combine cognitive load theory with related ideas (cognitive apprenticeship, skill acquisition, and worked examples) to describe a CS1 design that utilizes "worked examples, scaffolding, faded guidance, cognitive apprenticeship, and emphasis of patterns to aid schema creation and improve learning." Similarly, Mead et al. (2006) combine cognitive load theory, fundamental ideas, threshold concepts and standard curriculum designs to propose the ideas of "anchor concepts" and "anchor graphs" as tools for curriculum planning in the CS1/CS2 sequence. Alexandron et al. (2014) suggest that "scenario-based programming" using visual "live sequence charts" encourages abstract thinking and ordering tasks by level of increasing complexity and is an effective way of reducing cognitive load. Morrison, Dorn, and Guzdial (2014) adapted an existing "Cognitive Load Component Survey" to the domain of introductory programming and observed the correlations between different components of load over two lectures, concluding that the results replicated earlier studies in the domain of statistics and that the revised survey would be a useful tool for comparing pedagogical interventions.

While the previous section concluded that learning outcomes are improved by tools that aid program visualization and the construction of accurate mental models, research on cognitive load suggests a competing design imperative – the need to keep novice programming tools as simple as possible so as to reduce extraneous load. In a study of novices using a block-based programming environment, Mason and Cooper (2013) conclude that "having extra options available in the environment – even if they are not used or referenced – hinders learning," crucially that it also "causes the students to perceive programming in both that environment and subsequent environments as more difficult," and overall that "novice students benefited from a simplified first-programming environment." A review is beyond the scope of this chapter, but the desire to reduce complexity underlies the design of novice programming environments such as DrScheme (Findler et al., 2002), BlueJ (Kölling et al., 2003), and Greenfoot (Kölling, 2010), of "teaching languages" such as Pascal and ABC (precursor to the currently popular Python), and of block-based programming languages.

12.3.6 Taxonomies and Measures

Cognitive scientists have developed many tools for classifying and understanding people and the learning process. These include personality inventories, developmental models, measures of attitude and motivation, IQ tests, and more. Many of these have been applied to novice programmers, often in an attempt to explain or predict the patterns of success or failure discussed above.

The most influential of these tools is Bloom's taxonomy of learning objectives, which has been widely used in educational research and practice. The original taxonomy (Bloom et al., 1956) described six levels of increasingly sophisticated objectives for learning within the "cognitive domain," namely: *Remembering, Comprehending, Applying, Analyzing, Synthesizing,* and *Evaluating.* (Similar frameworks were set out for "affective" and "psychomotor" domains.) The Revised Bloom's Taxonomy (RBT) (Anderson et al., 2001; Krathwohl, 2002) proposes a two-dimensional model: the Knowledge Dimension, defined over the categories of Factual, Conceptual, Procedural, and Metacognitive knowledge (the latter two are effectively "strategies" in the language of this chapter), and the Cognitive Process Dimension, defined over the levels of *Remember, Understand, Apply, Analyze, Evaluate,* and *Create.*

Versions of Bloom's taxonomy have been widely applied in computing education and in studies of novice programming. The ACM curriculum guidelines discussion of learning outcomes states that "In defining different levels we drew from other curriculum approaches, especially Bloom's Taxonomy, which has been well explored within computer science" (ACM/IEEE-CS, 2013). The taxonomy has influenced many other curriculum documents, including the CSTA K–12 Computer Science Standards (CSTA, 2017) from the Computer Science Teachers Association. In a useful review, Sorva (2012) notes that there is general agreement that programming involves performance at high (and therefore difficult) levels of the taxonomy. Oliver et al. (2004) used a weighted average of the Bloom levels of assessment items to calculate a "Bloom rating" for a range of computing courses. Their analysis suggested that typical CS1 courses have high Bloom ratings compared to other computing topics.

While there is general agreement that the ability to create a program to solve an unfamiliar problem can be classified at the (original) Synthesizing or (revised) Create level, there is less agreement about more specific tasks. Thompson et al. (2008) note that a task may be classified as Apply if the student has relevant knowledge/experience, but as Create otherwise. Sorva (2012) states that "Code-tracing skills, for instance, have been variously classified within the literature as understand or analyze, and many interpretations have been presented as to how to 'Bloom rate' program-writing assignments of different kinds." Some of the disagreement may relate to varying assumptions about the backgrounds and current levels of varying students. Bloom's original group stressed the role of prior knowledge in determining relevant levels, and this is consistent with the importance of known schemata and cognitive load, reviewed above. Further CEdR studies that employ Bloom's taxonomy are too numerous to review individually; they include Buck and Stucki (2000), Lister (2000), Lister and Leaney (2003a, 2003b), Scott (2003), Johnson and Fuller (2006), Whalley et al. (2006), Thompson et al. (2008), Starr, Manaris, and Stalvey (2008), Lopez et al. (2008), Alaoutinen and Smolander (2010), Meerbaum-Salant, Armoni, and Ben-Ari (2010), Gluga et al. (2012), Sarawagi (2014), and Ginat and Menashe (2015).

Another very influential educational tool is the developmental stage theory of Jean Piaget (Piaget, 1964, 1971a, 1971b). Piaget defined the following four stages of children's development: *sensorimotor* (from birth to the acquisition of language at around 2 years old), *pre-operational* (to 7 years), *concrete operational* (to 11 years), and *formal operational* (to adulthood at between 15 and 20 years). The later stages in particular are defined largely in terms of the acquisition of logical capacities such as transitive inference. Within CEd, it has been suggested (Barker & Unger, 1983) that developmental stages, particularly the transition to the formal operational stage, may have an important impact on computational thinking. In a brief review, White and Sivitanides (2002) conclude that reaching the formal operational stage "is a required cognitive characteristic of people for learning procedural programming," and they claim that "the majority of adults and many college students fail to develop to full formal operational thinking skills." In contrast, Bennedsen and Caspersen (2006) found no correlation between stage of development (particularly "abstraction ability") and final grade in an introductory object-oriented programming course. Further ambiguous results are reviewed by Lister (2011).

Piaget's theory has been criticized, particularly in terms of the observed variation between the capacities of individuals of different ages and the lack of explanation for the "miraculous" transition between stages (Feldman, 2004). Attempts to address such problems have led to various "neo-Piagetian" theories. These typically distinguish stages of development based on "features of the child's information processing system" (such as speed of processing and working memory capacity) rather than logical competence (Morra et al., 2007), and include "domain specificity" (that an individual may display different levels of performance across different domains; for some task types, performance is highly dependent on relevant knowledge).

Lister (2011) summarizes a strong neo-Piagetian position, "that people, regardless of their age, are thought to progress through increasingly abstract forms of reasoning as they gain expertise in a specific problem domain." Lister goes on to explore aspects of programming within neo-Piagetian interpretations of functionally defined (but still classically named) stages, noting that many students do not progress beyond the pre-operational stage, while much instruction is delivered at the formal operational level (see also Corney et al., 2012). Teague (2015) conducted think-aloud studies with novice programmers and found evidence consistent with the neo-Piagetian model. Falkner, Vivian, and Falkner (2013) present an analysis of students' reflections on their software development processes, characterizing the stages in terms of "representative mental models" based on observed behaviors and strategies.

Inspired by Piaget and influential within CEd, the SOLO taxonomy (Biggs & Collis, 1982) is a general educational framework for describing the "Structure of the Observed Learning Outcome" in terms of levels of increasing complexity, from *pre-structural* (displaying no understanding), to *uni-structural, multi-structural, relational,* and *extended abstract* (understanding is abstracted to a high level and may be generalized to other tasks or topics). Brabrand and Dahl (2009) analyzed a range of courses at a Danish university (that consistently uses the SOLO taxonomy to specify course goals), finding that programming-related competencies were typically relational, and that computing courses in general had significantly higher levels than mathematics or other science courses.

A range of studies have found that the taxonomy can be fairly consistently applied to evaluating novice programmers (Clear et al., 2008; Lister et al., 2006; Sheard et al., 2008; Whalley et al., 2006). The BRACElet project (an ITiCSE working group) conducted a multiyear, multinational study of novice programmers that analyzed examination answers for both code reading and writing tasks, and refined and extend earlier SOLO level definitions as applied to programming (Lister et al., 2010). Other applications to programming include Jimoyiannis (2013), Ginat and Menashe (2015), Izu, Weerasinghe, and Pope (2016), and Castro and Fisler (2017).

The Bloom and SOLO taxonomies are complementary, and they are sometimes discussed together in the context of CEdR (e.g., Whalley et al., 2006). Creating a program for an unfamiliar task requires performance at the SOLO relational level/Bloom synthesizing or create level. As noted above, programming-related courses have been rated as more challenging than other courses using both the SOLO (Oliver et al., 2004) and Bloom (Brabrand & Dahl, 2009) taxonomies. Difficulties have been observed for both taxonomies in categorizing performance or tasks reliably and in accounting for the way that prior experience/variation in existing knowledge or skills affects classification level. Fuller et al. (2007) discuss these and other problems for applying generic taxonomies to computing. The authors propose a version of Bloom's revised taxonomy adapted to the requirements of computing tasks, conceived of as a matrix through which different paths are possible. Similarly, Bower (2008) proposed a hierarchy of task types based specifically on programming.

In a fascinating study, Margulieux, Catrambone, and Schaeffer (2018) present a methodology that appears to rank learning domains by complexity for the learner. Students solving problems in one of three domains (programming, chemistry, or statistics) were supplied with relevant subgoal-labeled worked examples and/or subgoal-labeled explanatory text. A different pattern of results was observed in the three domains: "While the subgoal labeled worked example consistently improved performance, the subgoal labeled expository text, which interacted with subgoal labeled worked examples in programming, had an additive effect with subgoal labeled worked examples in chemistry and no effect in statistics" (Margulieux, Catrambone, & Schaeffer, 2018). The results suggest that programming is the most difficult domain (both forms of support material interacted in improving performance), followed by chemistry, then statistics. The authors note that "Differences in patterns of results are believed to be due to complexity of the content to be learned."

A wide range of other tests and instruments have been used to explore novice programmers and the factors that influence their performance. The review presented in Robins (2010) covers the following topics: *demographic factors* – following on from early aptitude tests, a range of subsequent studies have explored the significance of factors such as age, gender, ethnicity, marital status, grade point average, mathematics background, science background, ACT/SAT math scores, ACT composite score, SAT verbal scores, high school rank, previous computing experience, and more. *Cognitive capacity* – aptitude tests and related research have used a range of tasks including letter series, figure analogies, number series, verbal meaning, and tests of accuracy, mathematical reasoning, algorithmic execution, alphanumeric translation, deductive and logical ability, the ability to reason with symbols, the detection of patterns, and reading comprehension (many of these are components of common IQ tests as discussed in the next section). *Cognitive style* – Is there a particular learning style or personality type that contributes to success? Tests that have been used to explore this possibility include the Myers–Briggs Type Indicator and the Kolb Learning Style Inventory. *Attitude and motivation* – Similarly, is attitude/motivation critical? Studies have explored the Biggs revised two-factor Study Process Questionnaire (R-SPQ-2F), students' self-reports, measures of self-efficacy, and factors such as perfectionism, self-esteem, coping tactics, affective states, and optimism. General conclusions are discussed in the next section.

12.3.7 Predicting or Accounting for Novice Outcomes

Given the wealth of research on novice programmers, what factors are most significant in influencing success at learning to program and what, if anything, explains the pattern of polarized/bimodal outcomes that is often observed in CS1? As noted above, frustration at the failure of early attempts to predict aptitude led to the widely held and subsequently enduring belief that programmers are "born and not made" (Dauw, 1967; Webster, 1996) or (tongue in cheek) that there exists a "geek gene" for programming (Lister, 2010): either you have it or you don't. If so, we would expect to have found some evidence, component, or correlate of this innate ability by now. In this section, the strongest potential factors identified in the above review are briefly evaluated and a different kind of possible explanation is discussed.

The early attempts to develop cognitive aptitude tests met with limited success. Building on this experience, a number of subsequent tests and studies of demographic and cognitive factors likewise did not reach strong conclusions (Robins, 2010). The range of studies of multiple factors that find conflicting results or at best modest statistical correlation with programming success (typically as measured by final course grade) include Mayer and Stalnaker (1968), Bateman (1973), Newstead (1975), Wileman, Konvalina, and Stephens (1981), Wileman, Konvalina, and Stephens (1981), Pea and Kurland (1984), Curtis (1984), Werth (1986), Evans and Simkin (1989), Cronan, Embry, and White (1989), Subramanian and Joshi (1996), Wilson and Shrock (2001), Rountree et al. (2004), Woszczynski, Haddad, and Zgambo (2005), Bennedsen and Caspersen (2005), Ventura (2005), Bergin and Reilly (2006), Simon et al. (2006), and Lau and Yuen (2011). The use of behavioral measures to augment such "traditional" factors in predictive models is discussed by Carter, Hundhausen, and Adesope (2017). In short, no factor or combination of factors that clearly predict success in learning a first programming language has been found.

The most widely studied and intuitively appealing potential cognitive factor is mathematical ability. Most (though not all) studies that explore it find that it is one of the better predictors. However, as was noted more than 30 years ago:

> To our knowledge, there is no evidence that any relationship exists between general math ability and computer programming skill, once general ability has been factored out. For example, in some of our own work we found that better Logo programmers were also high math achievers. However, these children also had generally high scores in English, social studies, and their other academic subjects as well. Thus, attributing their high performance in computer programming to their math ability ignores the relationship between math ability and general intelligence.
> (Pea & Kurland, 1984)

As we might expect, a high IQ is also moderately associated with success in programming (Pea & Kurland, 1984), and most of the individual mathematical, verbal, spatial, and logical factors noted above are employed in a range of IQ tests. One of the most pervasive and general results about IQ, however, is that performance on various standard psychometric measures is highly correlated, a phenomenon known as "the positive manifold." This is sometimes used as an argument for the existence of a single general factor of intelligence called "g." Thus, the various cognitive factors that are weak to moderate predictors of success in programming may have no explanatory power that is independent of IQ. Furthermore, given that intelligence is at least roughly normally distributed in the population, it is not at all obvious how variations in IQ can simply account for any bimodal distribution of outcomes.

Affective factors such as motivation, constructive attitudes to learning, positive expectations, and high self-efficacy or effort are also usually found to be correlated with success in programming (see Chapter 28). However, the same proviso applies. These factors are moderate predictors of success in many domains, and thus are not likely to account for any particular properties or pattern of outcomes in programming.

Developmental factors appear to offer a strong potential explanation for programming outcomes. For example, White and Sivitanides (2002) suggest that in cases of bimodal grade distributions, "The low mode may indicate Piaget's concrete operation stage" and "The high mode may indicate Piaget's formal operation stage." While this is intuitively appealing for students in the critical age range (15–20 years), it does not work for younger or older learners, who are just as likely to exhibit polarized outcomes. This is an example of the kind of problem with Piaget's original theory that motivated the neo-Piagetian and SOLO frameworks, replacing the reliance on chronological age with levels that are complex, contextual, and dependent on individual factors such as prior knowledge. Note that these frameworks are therefore descriptive rather than predictive: the range of studies reviewed above describe observed behaviors (or artifacts) as exhibiting performance at different levels. But to then use that level as an "explanation" of success at programming seems rather circular – learners who are observed to perform well at programming are observed to perform well at programming.

The failure of more than 40 years of research to find a factor or factors that strongly and reliably (let alone uniquely) predict success or failure suggests that we may be looking in the wrong place for an explanation of programming outcomes. Maybe there is no "geek gene"/innate capacity or combination of cognitive or other factors that predicts or accounts for success or failure at programming, any more or less than for other domains of learning. Robins (2010) proposed a different kind of possible explanation for programming outcomes: the Learning Edge Momentum (LEM) hypothesis.

The theoretical foundation for LEM is the principle that we learn "at the edges" of what we already know by adding to existing knowledge. The more that new information is given a meaningful interpretation (i.e., the richer and more elaborate the links between new and old knowledge), the more effective learning appears to be (e.g., see the topics of educational scaffolding, transfer in learning, analogy, and the zone of proximal development as discussed in Chapter 9). The hypothesis is simply that, given some target domain of concepts to be learned, successful learning makes it somewhat easier to acquire related concepts, and unsuccessful learning makes it somewhat harder. In other words, the early acquisition (or otherwise) of concepts in a new domain becomes self-reinforcing, creating momentum toward successful or unsuccessful outcomes.

This LEM effect will vary in strength depending on the extent to which the concepts in the target domain are either independent or interdependent. When the domain consists of tightly integrated concepts (strong and well-defined edges), the momentum effect will be strong. Robins (2010) further proposed that a typical programming language is a domain of concepts that are unusually tightly integrated (at one end of the spectrum when compared to other domains). Factors that appear to support this proposal include the formal precision of programming languages (syntax and semantics), the ratings that programming content has received compared to other subjects on both the SOLO and Bloom taxonomies (Brabrand & Dahl, 2009; Oliver et al., 2004), preliminary evidence that programming is more complex than other learning domains (Margulieux, Catrambone, & Schaeffer, 2018), and the lack of agreement among computing educators on the correct order in which to teach programming language concepts.

If we accept these assumptions, then a plausible explanation for polarized/ bimodal distributions of outcomes in CS1 emerges. They occur not because CS1 students are somehow different from others, but because the subject matter is different. The tightly integrated nature of language concepts results in a strong LEM effect. It is not the case that programming is simultaneously both hard and easy to learn for two different populations; rather, programming effectively becomes both harder and easier to learn for two different emerging groups. In short, an inherent systemic bias arising from the interaction between the learner and the learned acts to drive different subsets of the student population toward extreme outcomes. In this context, the historical failure to distinguish special kinds of programming students is entirely understandable. Programming students are much like any others, and they succeed or fail for reasons that are idiosyncratic and complex (although this review has stressed the importance of effective strategies, and as in other subjects, factors such as IQ, attitude, and prior experience are significant).

Studies that have supported predictions of the LEM account of programming outcomes, particularly with respect to the importance of the first one to three weeks of a CS1 course, include Porter and Zingaro (2014), Porter, Zingaro, and Lister (2014), Hola and Andreae (2014), and McCane et al. (2017).

12.3.8 Further Topics

The material in this section has explored the psychology of novice programmers, focusing on their knowledge, strategies, mental models, cognitive load, classification in various learning-related taxonomies, and the nature of possible explanations for the polarized outcomes often observed in typical CS1 courses. Many other topics relevant to novice programming have been explored, from narrow topics such as the relative ease of learning different kinds of programming language, to very broad ones such as issues of equity and diversity in the makeup of CS1 courses. Some of these are major topics explored elsewhere in this Handbook. A very brief pointer to some relevant topics and literature is noted below.

Researchers have debated the merits of teaching different kinds of programming language, such as procedural vs. object-oriented languages (Burkhardt, Détienne, & Wiedenbeck, 2002; Kunkle & Allen, 2016; Rist, 1995; Schulte & Bennedsen, 2006; Wiedenbeck & Ramalingam, 1999; Wiedenbeck et al., 1999) and the recent use of block-based languages as an alternative or supplement to textual languages (Bau et al., 2017; Maloney et al., 2010; Price & Barnes, 2015; Weintrop & Wilensky, 2015; Weintrop, Killen & Franke, 2018). The relationship between the separate but related skills of program code generation/writing and comprehension/reading (also called tracing or tracking) have been widely studied (Brooks 1977, 1983; Busjahn & Schulte, 2013; Corritore & Wiedenbeck, 1991; Davies, 1993; Lister et al., 2004; Lopez et al., 2008; Rist, 1995; Venables, Tan, & Lister, 2009; Whalley et al., 2006; Wiedenbeck et al., 1999). Various methods have been used to explore the specific difficulties experienced by novice programmers (Altadmri & Brown, 2015; Ebrahimi, 1994; Garner, Haden, & Robins, 2005; Jadud, 2006; Lahtinen, Ala-Mutka, & Järvinen, 2005; McCall & Kölling, 2014; Pea, 1986; Soloway & Spohrer, 1989; Spohrer & Soloway, 1989; Winslow, 1996). For further issues relating to programming paradigms, see Chapter 13 of this Handbook. Pedagogical tools such as programming environments are explored in Chapter 21, issues relating to prior knowledge and misconceptions in Chapter 27, attitude and motivation in Chapter 28, the teaching of programming in schools in Chapter 18, and pervasive issues of equity and diversity in Chapter 16.

12.4 Teaching and Learning in CS1

The basics of effective teaching and learning are the same in most subjects. For teachers, they include the provision of clear and relevant course materials, clear learning objectives, assessment that is well aligned with objectives, rich and timely feedback to students, fostering student engagement, pastoral care, competent classroom skills, and more. Educators are increasingly exploring the use of new tools and methods such as online resources and social media, feedback mechanisms, peer assessment, blended learning, flipped classrooms, and the use of naturally occurring performance measures ("learning analytics"). For students, learning outcomes will be influenced by motivation and attitude, forms of engagement, IQ, attitudes to learning, time management skills, personal circumstances, sociocultural factors, and more. The teaching and learning process as a whole is interpreted in the context of underlying educational philosophies or styles, such as cognitivism or constructivism. In general, the goal is to foster deep learning of principles and skills and to create independent, reflective, lifelong learners.

Most of these topics are explored elsewhere in the Handbook. In this section, we focus on issues that are specific to introductory programming as a subject or are particularly significant in this context. Pears et al. (2007) provide an excellent review of relevant literature; see also Robins, Rountree, and Rountree (2003).

12.4.1 A Lack of Agreement

There is unfortunately no agreement on the practical details of the best way to teach programming, or even on fundamentals such as which topics should be taught and what order they should be taught in. The most influential source of curriculum advice, the Joint Task Force on Computing Curricula, begins its chapter on introductory courses as follows:

> Computer science, unlike many technical disciplines, does not have a well-described list of topics that appear in virtually all introductory courses. In considering the changing landscape of introductory courses, we look at the evolution of such courses from CC2001 to CS2013 ... we believe that advances in the field have led to an even more diverse set of approaches in introductory courses than the models set out in CC2001. Moreover, the approaches employed in introductory courses are in a greater state of flux. (ACM/IEEE-CS, 2013)

For perspectives from teachers, see the paper by Bruce (2004) titled "Controversy on how to teach CS 1: A discussion on the SIGCSE-members mailing list." It was suggested above that this lack of agreement arises in part because of the densely connected and interdependent nature of the concepts in the domain of a programming language. There is no one right path through the maze. Despite disagreements on practical specifics, however, there is consensus on many theoretical issues and guidelines arising from the experience of practitioners and from CEd research.

12.4.2 CS1 Design and Pedagogy

Various iterations of the ACM Computing Curricula have presented a range of course options and exemplars that serve as useful reference points for the field.

Beyond such guidelines, however, there are many challenges involved in learning to program, as reviewed in Section 12.3. In this context, the design and delivery of a CS1 course should be realistic in its expectations and systematic in its development. In a significant survey of the literature on teaching programming, Pears et al. (2007) discuss three general approaches based on "the primary emphasis of the instructional setting," namely: "problem solving, learning a particular programming language, and code/system production."

Schneider (1978) presents ten principles that he suggests capture the "essential objectives of an initial programming course," all of which remain relevant for consideration today. The principles (abstracted from the explanatory text) are:

> 1) Students should immediately be taught that a clear, concise problem statement is always the first step in programming. 2) The single most important concept in a programming course is the concept of an algorithm. 3) It is important to introduce the duality of data structures and algorithms in the programming process. 4) Choose a programming language that enhances the learning process. 5) The presentation of a computer language should concentrate on semantics and program characteristics not syntax. 6) The presentation of a computer language must include concerns for programming style from the very beginning. 7) The subject of debugging should be formally presented. 8) The subject of program testing and verification should be formally presented. 9) The subject of documentation should be formally presented. 10) A student should be introduced to realistic programming applications and realistic programming environments.
> (Schneider, 1978)

Linn and Dalbey (1989) set out an ideal "chain of cognitive accomplishments" for teaching and learning programming. The links of the chain are: (1) features of the language being taught; (2) design skills, including knowledge templates/schemata/plans and the procedural skills of planning, testing, and reformulating code; and (3) problem-solving skills, including knowledge, strategies and procedural skills abstracted from the specific language that can be applied to new languages and situations.

Recognizing the importance of problem-solving, many of the ACM course exemplars since 2001 address it before or along with language features (ACM/IEEE-CS, 2013). Some (but not all) studies show improved outcomes for this approach (Davies, 2008; Hill, 2016; Koulouri, Lauria, & Macredie, 2014). Rist (1995) and Winslow (1996), however, suggest that problem-solving is necessary but not sufficient for programming. Winslow notes, for example, that most undergraduates can average a list of numbers, but fewer than half of them can write a loop to do the same operation. A discussion of the issues involved in problem-based learning, a description of various examples, and a three-year longitudinal follow-up of students is described in Kay et al. (2000). The authors observe "a substantial improvement in basic programming competence" (although possible confounding factors are acknowledged). The relationship between problem-solving and programming skills is extensively reviewed by Palumbo (1990).

Fincher (1999) asks, "What are we doing when we teach programming?" and compares the following four conceptual frameworks: "syntax-free," "problem-solving," "literacy," and "computation-as-interaction." Felleisen et al. (2001) argue that programming is for everyone, and that it is best learned by focusing on the design process. The authors provide "a set of explicit design guidelines" (such as data- and test-driven program design and writing examples before code) for developing computational solutions in a step-by-step manner. Other resources produced by the Program by Design group (http://programbydesign. org) include a specialized programming environment for beginners. Fisler (2014) provides evidence of the success of this approach in a study of five CS1 classes at four institutions (using program by design methods and a functional language). Students in this cohort significantly outperformed other reported study results on the classic Rainfall Problem. For a very different perspective that argues in favor of teaching programming based on formal methods such as predicate calculus and proofs of correctness, see Edsger Dijkstra's much-debated "On the cruelty of really teaching computer science" (Dijkstra, 1989).

Underlying much of the debate about the strengths and weaknesses of various approaches to teaching is the issue of transfer in learning. Facts and skills that are learned in one context (e.g., problem-solving) do not necessarily transfer to other contexts (e.g., writing code). Mayer (1992) notes that, in practice, CS1 courses have typically focused on language features, with varying opportunities to learn in ways that promote transfer. Transfer in learning programming is further discussed in Chapter 3, and transfer as a general phenomenon is learning is explored in Chapter 9.

The known difficulties of teaching programming have motivated various special languages and tools, an early example being the Logo language and "turtle graphics" introduced in 1967. du Boulay, O'Shea, and Monk (1989) made a case for the use of simple, specially designed teaching languages. Examples of such languages include Logo (released in 1967), Pascal (in 1970), Eiffel (in 1986), Python (in 1989), and Alice (in 1994), as well as the student languages of Racket (in 2001) and Scratch (in 2003). Pears et al. (2007) discuss factors that influence the choice of language in current courses and trade-offs such as richness vs. complexity. Commercially popular languages such as Java, C, and C++ are dominant for practical reasons (e.g., student demand), but their suitability for teaching has been much debated. The obvious and widespread intuition that syntactic complexity hampers learning has been supported by many studies (e.g., Koulouri, Lauria, & Macredie, 2014; Mannila, Peltomäki, & Salakoski, 2006; Yadin, 2011). One popular approach to exercises for teaching and assessing programming is Parsons' problems (Parsons & Haden, 2006), which present unordered statements that can be correctly ordered into working code. This approach is generally held to reduce cognitive load by providing syntactically correct building blocks.

Soloway and Spohrer (1989) summarize several suggestions relating to the design of programming environments/tools for novices, including the following: the use of "graphical languages" to make control flow explicit; a simple underlying machine model; short, simple, and consistent naming conventions; graphical animation of program states (with no "hidden" actions or states); design principles based on spatial metaphors; and the gradual withdrawal of initial supports and restrictions. Kelleher and Pausch (2005) present a taxonomy and review of languages and environments "designed to make programming more accessible to novice programmers of all ages." Some recent research on visualization tools, programming environments, and block-based programming languages is noted above; see Pears et al. (2007) and Chapter 21 for much broader reviews.

Given that much is now known about novice programmers, it is possible for teachers to anticipate and attempt to support different kinds of learners. Within any large class, there is likely to be a group who are making excellent progress (effective novices), a large group who are struggling (ineffective), and others in between. It is not possible for a typical course to perfectly suit both the effective and ineffective groups – CS1 will almost certainly move too quickly for many students and too slowly for some. This can be partially addressed by trying to set the course at the level of the "average" student and providing both extension work for the high-achieving group and targeted support to those who are struggling. If the strategies of effective novices can be identified, it may be possible to promote effective strategies to all groups. In other words, rather than focusing exclusively on the end product of programming knowledge, teachers could focus at least in part on the enabling step of functioning as an effective novice. Considerations of motivation and self-efficacy (Chapter 28) and gender and diversity (Chapter 16) are also important in this context. Ideally, course design and delivery would motivate all students, engage them in the process, and support them with the tools and strategies needed to become effective learners of programming.

12.4.3 Dimensions of Learning and Practical Examples

Considering CS1 in terms of the three dimensions of knowledge, strategies, and mental models provides a useful framework for course design and delivery. Making these explicit to students may also aid their understanding of the learning process in which they are engaged. Successful learning on all three dimensions is crucially dependent on broad experience of practical programming tasks.

The typical CS1 course focuses on knowledge of the elements of a programming language and practice in their application. As noted in Section 12.2.3.2, however, surveys and studies of novice programmers have shown that the main problems that they experience relate not to individual language constructs, but to overall program design and structure. This is consistent with frequent recommendations in the literature that instruction should emphasize the combination and use of language features and the underlying issue of program design. Spohrer and Soloway suggested "focusing explicitly on specific strategies for carrying out the coordination and integration of the goals and plans that underlie program code," that "students should be made aware of such concepts as goals and plans, and such composition statements as abutment and merging," and that "students be given a whole new vocabulary for learning how to construct programs" (Spohrer & Soloway, 1989). Mayer (1989) suggested that "explicit naming and teaching of basic schemata ... may become part of computer programming curricula." Bearing out this prediction:

> A minor but remarkable collection of programming education research from the past ten to fifteen years concerns a pattern-based approach to instruction which utilize a shift from emphasis on learning the syntactic details of a specific programming language to the development of general problem-solving and program-design skills.
> (Caspersen & Bennedsen, 2007)

(Here, the authors use "pattern" as more or less synonymous with "schema".) The use of full-fledged design patterns (Freeman et al., 2004; Gamma et al., 1995), which is particularly common in an object-oriented context, is widely regarded as too complex for CS1 unless simplified and customized (Hundley, 2008; Lewis et al., 2004; Wick, 2005).

Several authors have noted that the teaching of knowledge structures must be anchored in, and learning may most effectively emerge from, practical experience and examples.

> The acquisition of schemata, such as a general design schema or programming plans, requires mindful abstraction, presupposes the confrontation with a well-chosen range of problems and their solutions (i.e., worked examples), and provides analogies that may guide subsequent behavior in solving unfamiliar aspects of new programming problems.
> (van Merriënboer & Paas, 1990)

Caspersen and Bennedsen (2007) also stress the importance of worked examples, along with "scaffolding, faded guidance, cognitive apprenticeship, and emphasis of patterns to aid schema creation and improve learning."

As noted in Section 12.3.3, many authors have suggested that strategies are the most important factor in determining the success or failure of learning to program. We have similarly proposed (Robins, Rountree, & Rountree, 2003) that it is differences in strategy that most significantly separate ineffective and effective novices. Despite their importance, strategies typically receive less explicit attention in CS1 than knowledge. Furthermore, as Brooks (1990) points out, strategies themselves cannot (in most cases) be deduced from the final "static" form of a program, even though they may have had a strong impact in the design and coding process and thus on the final form. As pedagogical examples, finished programs are rich and accessible sources of information about the language, but the strategies that created those programs are much harder to make explicit.

These factors highlight the importance of actively developing programs and explicitly addressing the strategies involved as part of CS1 design and delivery. While this can be demonstrated in lectures and teaching resources, hands-on experience is obviously the most effective form of learning for students. This highlights again the need for well-designed example tasks and the practical opportunities for students to engage with them. The design, delivery, and assessment (see below) of laboratory/practical sessions may be the most important element of CS1.

The mental models that novices must develop, both with respect to an underlying notional machine and as important aspects of planning, understanding, and debugging programs, are also very important to successful learning outcomes. As noted above, a broad survey (Schulte & Bennedsen, 2006) suggests that teachers regard an explicit notional machine as relevant, but only 29 percent of respondents explicitly addressed it in their teaching. Mental models of specific programs are of course internal, personal, and relative to particular examples, and therefore impossible to "teach," but many aspects of typical CS1 design and pedagogy can implicitly support learners in the process of their acquisition. Example methods include the use of modeling languages such as UML, demonstrating and encouraging the practice of program tracing/tracking, graphical representations of program states and animations of their operations, and the use of tools such as debuggers or programming environments that facilitate the observation of program states.

In summary, programming knowledge, skills, and mental models cannot be effectively acquired in the abstract – they must be anchored in rich practical experience. This highlights the importance of laboratory/practical sessions in the design and delivery of CS1. Programming tasks also have many pedagogically useful features. Each one can form a "case-based" problem-solving session where students can work and learn at their own pace. The feedback supplied by compilers and other tools is immediate, consistent, and (ideally) informative. For teachers, change episodes (where an alteration is made to code) may be rich in information about the students' models, plans, and goals (Gray & Anderson, 1987). For students, the reinforcement and motivation derived from creating a working program can be very powerful (programs with graphical and animated output can be particularly popular). One of the strongest results to emerge from the study of practical programming tasks is the success of collaborative work and "peer learning" (see Chapters 29 and 30).

12.4.4 Effective and Ideal Interventions

One of the most important ways of supporting learning in educational contexts in general is the effective use of formative assessment: "Assessment that is explicitly designed to promote learning is the single most powerful tool we have for raising standards and empowering life-long learning" (Assessment Reform Group, 1999). While this finding is not specific to CEd, there are a number of discipline-specific factors to consider in the assessment of programming, as discussed in Chapter 14. It may well be that understanding and improving our assessment practices is the single most effective intervention we can make. Hattie (2009, 2012) presents a large-scale meta-analysis of a range of factors influencing educational outcomes in general.

The literature reviewed above includes many research-based examples of course design decisions or interventions that are specific to teaching programming and have been shown to have a beneficial effect on learning outcomes. These include: the use of syntactically simple languages and rich (but not overly complex) programming environments and tools; providing and encouraging the use of a notional machine that underlies the language; attention to both reading (tracing/tracking) and writing code; a focus on problem-solving, combining language elements, and program design; explicit attention to programming strategies; facilitating the acquisition of appropriate mental models; the extensive use of well-designed example programs and practical tasks; and (Chapters 29 and 30) the use in this context of pair programming and peer learning methods.

In a very useful review, Vihavainen, Airaksinen, and Watson (2014) attempt to quantify the improvements in learning outcomes that can be attributed to various kinds of intervention. From a broad initial sample, the authors identified 32 articles describing interventions in CS1 courses that included pre- and post-intervention pass rates, sometimes over multiple instances (e.g., semesters), for a total of 60 interventions. Within this sample, the authors collaboratively coded the intervention types. The ten most commonly observed interventions were *collaboration* (encouraging student collaboration), *content change* (updates to teaching material), *contextualization* (alignment toward a specific context; e.g., games or media), *CS0* (the creation of a preliminary course), *game theme* (introduction of a game-themed component), *grading schema* (e.g., increasing the weighting for practical tasks), *group work* (e.g., team-based learning or cooperative learning), *media computation* (programming in the context of digital media), *peer support* (pairs, groups, or peer tutors), and *support* (an umbrella term for increased teacher hours or additional support channels, for example). The most frequent intervention was content change (followed by peer support and collaboration); the least was CS0.

As an overall summary, the average course pass rate prior to an intervention was a mean of 61.4 percent (standard deviation [SD] 1.15 percent) and after an intervention was a mean of 74.4 percent (SD 11.7 percent). The average "realized improvement" (the extent to which the post-intervention pass rate closed the gap between the pre-intervention pass rate and 100 percent) for each of the interventions ranged from media computation (mean 48 percent, SD 16 percent) to game theme (mean 18 percent, SD 23 percent). The authors note that there was considerable variation over individual interventions and combinations of interventions, including 5 (of the 60) cases of pass rates decreasing. They conclude that "the interventions reported in the literature increase introductory programming course pass rates by one third on average," and that "no statistically significant differences between the effectiveness of the teaching interventions were found." However, given that "the results suggest that almost any planned intervention improves the existing state," the source articles need to be evaluated for the extent to which they did (or did not) account for common threats to validity such as experimenter bias or the Hawthorne effect (Mitchell & Jolley, 2012).

Returning to the LEM hypothesis (Section 12.3.7), recall that it suggests that either early success or failure in learning programming become, over time, compounding effects. Once negative momentum is established, it is very hard to overcome; ideally, positive momentum should be established right from the start. This implies that the very early stages of CS1 are critical to outcomes. Everything possible should be done to ensure that the initial student experiences are successful and to facilitate learning during this critical time. Particular attention should be paid to the careful introduction of concepts and the systematic development of the connections between them. Any extra resources or support (e.g., increased access to tutors) should be focused on the early stages. Students showing signs of disengagement (missing labs or tutorials, failing to submit work) should be followed up immediately and actively, as early as in the first week. Students could also be told why the early period of learning is critical, as this "meta-knowledge" may increase engagement and motivation. They should absolutely be encouraged to seek immediate help at the first sign of difficulty – keeping up is vital. Studies that have supported the predictions of the LEM hypothesis, particularly with respect to the importance of the early weeks of a CS1 course, were noted in Section 12.3.7.

Most CS1 courses are constrained by practical considerations of resources, time, and large student populations. In an ideal world, we would like to provide individual and personally designed tuition and support to every student. It may be that breakthroughs in intelligent tutoring systems will one day achieve this ideal. In the meantime, however, the closer we can get to this goal within the practical constraints that we have, the more successful learner outcomes will be.

One suggestion in this context is to address the usual constraint of a single fixed flow (rate and path of progression) through the curriculum. The clear message from the literature is that there is no point in expecting a student to acquire a new layer of complex concepts if the foundation of prerequisite concepts does not exist. This could potentially be addressed by introducing some flexibility into the delivery of the course, so that students are more able to work and learn at their own pace and in ways that allow them to make sustainable progress. For example, CS1 could be offered in multiple streams that progress at different rates or vary in the amount of material covered. Students could select streams, or move between them, possibly as guided by an early diagnostic test. "Recovery streams" could be offered so that students have the option to backtrack and revise. For maximum flexibility, streams (through which students progress at the same rate) could be replaced by self-paced learning, where courses consist of just resource materials and a sequence of exercises to be completed at any time. Mastery models of learning and apprenticeships are common in some teaching contexts and may be interesting to explore as alternative models for the teaching of programming.

12.5 Discussion

There are many reasons why so much of CEdR is directed at the topics of novice programmers and CS1 (this **motivational context** was described in the introduction). From this research, many **implications for practice** have emerged. We know that both the teaching and the learning of programming can be improved, resulting in better learning outcomes. We know a fair bit about specific methods that improve teaching and/or learning, although perhaps we don't know much of this for sure (see below). It is therefore incumbent on us as teachers to familiarize ourselves with this literature, to adopt the methods that will work in our context, and to be the best teachers that we can be. Specific methods that appear to be effective in practice for programming are summarized in Section 12.4.4. These should be seen in the context of the broader issues of pedagogic methods, motivation and affect, tools, assessment, issues of equity and diversity, and other matters that are addressed elsewhere in this Handbook. As always, the most general and important lesson is that by understanding the learner and designing our courses to support the learning process, we can achieve better outcomes as teachers. Much is known about novice programmers as learners, giving teachers much to work with.

There remain many **open questions**. Further investigation and replication within most CEdR topics would be welcome (in a sense, all questions are open). In particular, we can't be sure that we know all of the reasons why programming is so difficult to learn for so many, and we still don't know much about why it appears to be quite easy for some. Most CEdR has been inward looking. Although we think programming has some unique challenges, we still don't know much about how it is similar to or different from other topics for teachers and for learners. We absolutely don't know the best language(s) for learners or the best way to teach any given language, and we have yet to find the most effective ways of supporting learners.

Of the dimensions of knowledge, strategies, and mental models, we know least about the mental models constructed by learners. How are they acquired? How do they vary? How can we facilitate useful ones? How do we intervene and correct false ones? How do we best reduce the cognitive load of programming or learning to program? While we know a fair bit about the differences between experts and novices, we know less about the differences between effective and ineffective novices. What are effective novices doing that works so well? Can it be identified, and can it be used to support currently ineffective novices? Have we found out as much as we can about why some novice programmers succeed and not others? Are the crucial differences cognitive, attitudinal, or behavioral, or impossible to separate? What is best teaching practice as it relates to each of these dimensions? We haven't found one yet, but is there a configuration of circumstances or a diagnostic test that can accurately predict who will or will not be successful at programming? Can we yet rule out the meme of the programmer gene and do away with the idea that programmers are born and not made? Many countries are currently embarking on large-scale educational experiments, but will the move toward teaching computational thinking or elements of programming in schools be successful? How best can it be supported? What are the implications for teaching and learning programming at later levels?

As argued in the introduction to this Handbook, this is an important and exciting time to be engaged in CEdR. A focus on novice programmers and the topics of teaching and learning programming is likely to remain of central importance to the field for the foreseeable future.

References

ACM/IEEE–CS Joint Task Force on Computing Curricula (2013). *Computer Science Curricula 2013*. New York: ACM Press and IEEE Computer Society Press.

Alaoutinen, S., & Smolander, K. (2010). Student self-assessment in a programming course using Bloom's Revised Taxonomy. In *Proceedings of the Fifteenth Annual Conference on Innovation and Technology in Computer Science Education (ITiCSE '10)* (pp. 155–159). New York: ACM.

Alexandron, G., Armoni, M., Gordon, M., & Harel, D. (2014). Scenario-based programming: Reducing the cognitive load, fostering abstract thinking. In *Companion Proceedings of the 36th International Conference on Software Engineering* (pp. 311–320). New York: ACM.

Allan, V. H., & Kolesar, M. V. (1997). Teaching computer science: A problem solving approach that works. *ACM SIGCUE Outlook*, 25(1–2), 2–10.

Altadmri, A., & Brown, N. C. (2015). 37 million compilations: Investigating novice programming mistakes in large-scale student data. In *Proceedings of the 46th ACM Technical Symposium on Computer Science Education* (pp. 522–527). New York: ACM.

Anderson, L. W., Krathwohl, D. R., Airasian, P. W., Cruikshank, K. A., Mayer, R. E., Pintrich, P. R., Raths, J., & Wittrock, M. C. (Eds.) (2001). *A Taxonomy for Learning and Teaching and Assessing: A Revision of Bloom's Taxonomy of Educational Objectives*. New York: Addison Wesley Longman.

Assessment Reform Group (1999). *Assessment for Learning: Beyond the Black Box*. Cambridge, UK: Cambridge University Press.

Barker, R. J., & Unger, E. A. (1983). A predictor for success in an introductory programming class based upon abstract reasoning development. *ACM SIGCSE Bulletin,* 15(1), 154–158.

Bateman, C. R. (1973). Predicting performance in a basic computer course. In *Proceedings of the Fifth Annual Meeting of the American Institute for Decision Sciences* (pp. 130–133). Atlanta, GO: AIDS Press.

Bau, D., Gray, J., Kelleher, C., Sheldon, J., & Turbak, F. (2017). Learnable programming: Blocks and beyond. *Communications of the ACM*, 60(6), 72–80.

Bauer, R., Mehrens, W. A., & Vinsonhaler, J. F. (1968). Predicting performance in a computer programming course. *Educational and Psychological Measurement*, 28, 1159–1164.

Beaubouef, T. B., & Mason, J. (2005). Why the high attrition rate for computer science students: Some thoughts and observations. *Inroads – The SIGCSE Bulletin*, 37(2), 103–106.

Bennedsen, J., & Caspersen, M. E. (2007). Failure rates in introductory programming. *ACM SIGCSE Bulletin*, 39(2), 32–36.

Bennedsen, J., & Caspersen, M. E. (2005). An investigation of potential success factors for an introductory model-driven programming course. In *Proceedings of the*

First International Workshop on Computing Education Research (ICER '05) (pp. 155–163). New York: ACM.

Bennedsen, J., & Caspersen, M. E. (2006). Abstraction ability as an indicator of success for learning object-oriented programming? *SIGCSE Bulletin*, 38(2), 39–43.

Bergin, S., & Reilly, R. (2006). Predicting introductory programming performance: A multi-institutional multivariate study. *Computer Science Education*, 16(4), 303–323.

Berland, M., Martin, T., Benton, T., Petrick Smith, C., & Davis, D. (2013). Using learning analytics to understand the learning pathways of novice programmers. *Journal of the Learning Sciences*, 22(4), 564–599.

Berry, M., & Kölling, M. (2014). The state of play: A notional machine for learning programming. In *Proceedings of the 2014 Conference on Innovation and Technology in Computer Science Education* (pp. 21–26). New York: ACM.

Bhuiyan, S., Greer, J. E., & McCalla, G. I. (1992). Learning recursion through the use of a mental model-based programming environment. In *International Conference on Intelligent Tutoring Systems* (pp. 50–57). Berlin, Germany: Springer.

Biggs, J. B., & Collis, K. F. (1982). *Evaluating the Quality of Learning: The SOLO Taxonomy (Structure of the Observed Learning Outcome)*. New York: Academic Press.

Bloom, B., Englehart, M. D., Furst, E. J., Hill, W. H., & Krathwohl, D. (1956). *Taxonomy of Educational Objectives: Handbook I: Cognitive Domain*. New York: Longmans.

Bornat, R. (2014). Camels and humps: A retraction. Retrieved from: http://eis.sla.mdx.ac.uk/staffpages/r_bornat/papers/camel_hump_retraction.pdf

Bornat, R., Dehnadi, S., & Simon (2008). Mental models, consistency and programming aptitude. In *Proceedings of the Tenth Australasian Computing Education Conference (ACE 2008)* (pp. 53–62). Darlinghurst, Australia: Australian Computer Society.

Boustedt, J., Eckerdal, A., McCartney, R., Moström, J. E., Ratcliffe, M., Sanders, K., & Zander, C. (2007). Threshold concepts in computer science: Do they exist and are they useful? *ACM SIGCSE Bulletin*, 39(1), 504–508.

Bower, M. (2008). A taxonomy of task types in computing. *ACM SIGCSE Bulletin*, 40(3), 281–285.

Brabrand, C., & Dahl, B. (2009). Using the SOLO taxonomy to analyze competence progression of university science curricula. *Higher Education*, 58(4), 531–549.

Brooks, F. P. (1975). *The Mythical Man-Month: Essays on Software Engineering*. New York: Addison-Wesley.

Brooks, R. E. (1977). Towards a theory of the cognitive processes in computer programming. *International Journal of Man–Machine Studies*, 9, 737–751.

Brooks, R. E. (1983). Towards a theory of the comprehension of computer programs. *International Journal of Man–Machine Studies,* 18, 543–554.

Brooks, R. E. (1990). Categories of programming knowledge and their application. *International Journal of Man–Machine Studies,* 33(3), 241–246.

Bruce, K. B. (2004). Controversy on how to teach CS 1: A discussion on the SIGCSE-members mailing list. *ACM SIGCSE Bulletin*, 36(4), 29–34.

Bruner, J. S. (1960). *The Process of Education*. Cambridge, MA: Harvard University Press.

Buck, D., & Stucki, D. J. (2000). Design early considered harmful: Graduated exposure to complexity and structure based on levels of cognitive development. *ACM SIGCSE Bulletin*, 32(1), 75–79.

Burkhardt, J. M., Détienne, F., & Wiedenbeck, S. (2002). Object-oriented program comprehension: Effect of expertise, task and phase. *Empirical Software Engineering*, 7(2), 115–156.

Burkhardt, J. M., Détienne, F., & Wiedenbeck, S. (1997). Mental representations constructed by experts and novices in object-oriented program comprehension. In *Proceedings of the IFIP TC13 International Conference on Human–Computer Interaction (INTERACT '97)* (pp. 339–346). London, UK: Chapman & Hall.

Busjahn, T., & Schulte, C. (2013). The use of code reading in teaching programming. In *Proceedings of the 13th Koli Calling International Conference on Computing Education Research* (pp. 3–11). New York: ACM.

Cañas, J. J., Bajo, M. T., & Gonzalvo, P. (1994). Mental models and computer programming. *International Journal of Human–Computer Studies, 40*(5), 795–811.

Carter, A. S., Hundhausen, C. D., & Adesope, O. (2017). Blending measures of programming and social behavior into predictive models of student achievement in early computing courses. *ACM Transactions on Computing Education (TOCE), 17*(3), 12.

Caspersen, M. E., & Bennedsen, J. (2007). Instructional design of a programming course: a learning theoretic approach. In *Proceedings of the Third International Workshop on Computing Education Research* (pp. 111–122). New York: ACM.

Caspersen, M. E., Larsen, K. D., & Bennedsen, J. (2007). Mental models and programming aptitude. *ACM SIGCSE Bulletin, 39*(3), 206–210.

Castro, F. E. V., & Fisler, K. (2017). Designing a multi-faceted SOLO taxonomy to track program design skills through an entire course. In *Proceedings of the 17th Koli Calling International Conference on Computing Education Research (Koli Calling '17)* (pp. 10–19). New York: ACM.

Clancy, M. J., & Linn, M. C. (1999). Patterns and pedagogy. *ACM SIGCSE Bulletin, 31*(1), 37–42.

Clear, T., Whalley, J., Lister, R. F., Carbone, A., Hu, M., Sheard, J., Simon, B., & Thompson, E. (2008). Reliably classifying novice programmer exam responses using the SOLO taxonomy. In *21st Annual Conference of the National Advisory Committee on Computing Qualifications (NACCQ 2008)* (pp. 23–30). Auckland, New Zealand: National Advisory Committee on Computing Qualifications.

Corney, M., Teague, D., & Thomas, R. N. (2010). Engaging students in programming. In *Proceedings of the Twelfth Australasian Conference on Computing Education Volume 103* (pp. 63–72). Darlinghurst, Australia: Australian Computer Society,

Corney, M., Teague, D., Ahadi, A., & Lister, R. (2012). Some empirical results for neo-Piagetian reasoning in novice programmers and the relationship to code explanation questions. In *Proceedings of the Fourteenth Australasian Computing Education Conference Volume 123* (pp. 77–86). Darlinghurst, Australia: Australian Computer Society.

Corritore, C. L., & Wiedenbeck, S. (1991). What do novices learn during program comprehension? *International Journal of Human–Computer Interaction, 3*, 199–222.

Cowan, N. (2001). The magical number 4 in short-term memory: A reconsideration of mental storage capacity. *Behavioral and Brain Sciences, 24*, 87–185.

Cronan, T. P., Embry, P. R., & White, S. D. (1989). Identifying factors that influence performance of non-computing majors in the business computer information systems course. *Journal of Research on Computing in Education, 21* (4), 431–441.

CSTA (2017). About the CSTA K–12 Computer Science Standards. Retrieved from www.csteachers.org/page/standards

Curtis, B. (1984). Fifteen years of psychology in software engineering: Individual differences and cognitive science. In *Proceedings of the 7th International Conference on Software Engineering* (pp. 97–106). New York: IEEE.

Dauw, D. (1967). Vocational interests of highly creative computer personnel. *Personnel Journal*, 46(10), 653–659.

Davies S. P. (1993). Models and theories of programming strategy. *International Journal of Man–Machine Studies*, 39, 237–267.

Davies, S. P. (2008). The effects of emphasizing computational thinking in an introductory programming course. In *Frontiers in Education Conference (FIE 2008)* (p. T2C-3). New York: IEEE.

Dehnadi, S. (2006). Abstract for Dehnadi & Bornat (2006). Retrieved from www.eis.mdx.ac.uk/research/PhDArea/saeed

Dehnadi, S., & Bornat, R. (2006). The camel has two humps (working title). Retrieved from www.eis.mdx.ac.uk/research/PhDArea/saeed/paper1.pdf

Dijkstra, E. W. (1989). On the cruelty of really teaching computer science. *Communications of the ACM*, 32(12), 1398–1404.

du Boulay, B., O'Shea, T., & Monk, J. (1989). The black box inside the glass box: Presenting computing concepts to novices. In E. Soloway & J. C. Spohrer (Eds.), *Studying the Novice Programmer* (pp. 431–446). Hillsdale, NJ: Lawrence Erlbaum.

du Boulay, B. (1986). Some difficulties of learning to program. *Journal of Educational Computing Research*, 2(1), 57–73.

du Boulay, B. (1989). Some difficulties of learning to program. In E. Soloway & J. C. Spohrer (Eds.), *Studying the Novice Programmer* (pp. 283–299). Hillsdale, NJ: Lawrence Erlbaum.

Ebrahimi, A. (1994). Novice programmer errors: Language constructs and plan composition. *International Journal of Human–Computer Studies*, 41(4), 457–480.

Eckerdal, A. (2009). *Novice Programming Students' Learning of Concepts and Practice* (doctoral dissertation). Acta Universitatis Upsaliensis.

Eckerdal, A., Thuné, M., & Berglund, A. (2005). What does it take to learn "programming thinking"? In *Proceedings of the First International Workshop on Computing Education Research* (pp. 135–142). New York: ACM.

Elarde, J. (2016). Toward improving introductory programming student course success rates: experiences with a modified cohort model to student success sessions. *Journal of Computing Sciences in Colleges*, 32(2), 113–119.

Ensmenger, N. L. (2010). *The Computer Boys Take Over: Computers, Programmers, and the Politics of Technical Expertise*. Cambridge, MA: MIT Press.

Evans, G. E., & Simkin, M. G. (1989). What best predicts computer proficiency? *Communications of the ACM*, 32(11), 1322–1327.

Falkner, K., Vivian, R., & Falkner, N. J. (2013). Neo-Piagetian forms of reasoning in software development process construction. In *Learning and Teaching in Computing and Engineering (LaTiCE)* (pp. 31–38). New York: IEEE.

Feldman, D. H. (2004). Piaget's stages: The unfinished symphony of cognitive development. *New Ideas in Psychology*, 22, 175–231.

Felleisen, M., Findler, R. B., Flatt, M., & Krishnamurthi, S. (2001). *How to Design Programs: An Introduction to Programming and Computing*. Cambridge, MA: MIT Press.

Fincher, S. (1999). What are we doing when we teach programming? In *Frontiers in Education Conference (FIE'99) Volume 1* (pp. 12A4-1–12A4-5). New York: IEEE.

Findler, R. B., Clements, J., Flanagan, C., Flatt, M., Krishnamurthi, S., Steckler, P., & Felleisen, M. (2002). DrScheme: A programming environment for Scheme. *Journal of Functional Programming*, 12(2), 159–182.

Fisler, K. (2014). The recurring Rainfall Problem. In *Proceedings of the Tenth Annual Conference on International Computing Education Research* (pp. 35–42). New York: ACM.

Freeman, E., Robson, E., Bates, B., & Sierra, K. (2004). *Head First Design Patterns: A Brain-Friendly Guide*. Sebastopol, CA: O'Reilly Media.

Fuller, U., Johnson, C. G., Ahoniemi, T., Cukierman, D., Hernán-Losada, I., Jackova, J., Lahtinen, E., Lewis, T. L., Thompson, D. M., Riedesel, C., & Thompson, E. (2007). Developing a computer science-specific learning taxonomy. *ACM SIGCSE Bulletin*, 39(4), 152–170.

Gamma, E., Helm, R., Johnson, R., & Vlissides, J. (1995). *Design Patterns: Elements of Reusable Object-Oriented Software*. New York: Addison-Wesley.

Garcia, R. A. (1987). *Identifying the Academic Factors that Predict the Success of Entering Freshmen in a Beginning Computer Science Course* (doctoral dissertation). Texas Tech University.

Garner, S. (2002). Reducing the cognitive load on novice programmers. In *Proceedings of World Conference on Educational Multimedia, Hypermedia and Telecommunications* (pp. 578–583). Chesapeake, VA: AACE.

Garner, S., Haden, P., & Robins, A. (2005). My program is correct but it doesn't run: A preliminary investigation of novice programmers' problems. In *Proceedings of the Seventh Australasian Computing Education Conference (ACE2005) CRPIT 42* (pp. 173–180). Darlinghurst, Australia: Australian Computer Society.

Gentner, D. (2002). Mental models, psychology of. In N. Smelser & P. B. Bates (Eds.), *International Encyclopedia of the Social and Behavioral Sciences* (pp. 9683–9687). Amsterdam, The Netherlands: Elsevier Science.

Gentner, D., & Stevens, A. L. (Eds.) (1983). *Mental Models*. Hillsdale, NJ: Erlbaum.

Gibbs, W. W. (1994). Software's chronic crisis. *Scientific American*, 271(3), 86–95.

Ginat, D., & Menashe, E. (2015). SOLO taxonomy for assessing novices' algorithmic design. In *Proceedings of the 46th ACM Technical Symposium on Computer Science Education* (pp. 452–457). New York: ACM.

Gluga, R., Kay, J., Lister, R., Kleitman, S., & Lever, T. (2012). Coming to terms with Bloom: an online tutorial for teachers of programming fundamentals. In *Proceedings of the Fourteenth Australasian Computing Education Conference Volume 123* (pp. 147–156). Darlinghurst, Australia: Australian Computer Society,

Gray W. D., & Anderson J. R. (1987). Change-episodes in coding: When and how do programmers change their code? In G. M. Olson, S. Sheppard, & E. Soloway (Eds.), *Empirical Studies of Programmers: Second Workshop* (pp. 185–197). Norwood, NJ: Ablex.

Gray, S., St Clair, C., James, R., & Mead, J. (2007). Suggestions for graduated exposure to programming concepts using fading worked examples. In *Proceedings of the Third International Workshop on Computing Education Research* (pp. 99–110). New York: ACM.

Green T. R. G. (1990). Programming languages as information structures. In J. M. Hoc, T. R. G. Green, R. Samurçay, & D. J. Gillmore (Eds.), *Psychology of Programming* (pp. 117–137). London, UK: Academic Press.

Guzdial, M. (2007) What makes programming so hard? Retrieved from http://home. cc.gatech.edu/csl/uploads/6/Guzdial-blog-pieces-on-what-is-CSEd.pdf

Guzdial, M. (2010). Why is it so hard to learn to program? In A. Oram & G. Wilson (Eds.), *Making Software: What Really Works, and Why We Believe It* (pp. 111–124). Sebastopol, CA: O'Reilly Media.

Guzdial, M., & Soloway, E. (2002). Teaching the Nintendo generation to program. *Communications of the ACM*, 45(4), 17–21.

Hattie, J. A. (2009). *Visible Learning: A Synthesis of 800+ Meta-Analyses on Achievement.* Abingdon, UK: Routledge.

Hattie, J. (2012). *Visible Learning for Teachers: Maximizing Impact on Learning.* Abingdon, UK: Routledge.

Hiebert, J., & Lefevre, P. (1986). Conceptual and procedural knowledge in mathematics: An introductory analysis. In J. Hiebert (Ed.), *Conceptual and Procedural Knowledge: The Case of Mathematics, 2* (pp. 1–27). Hillsdale, NJ: Erlbaum.

Hill, G. J. (2016). Review of a problems-first approach to first year undergraduate programming. In S. Kassel & B. Wu (Eds.), *Software Engineering Education Going Agile* (pp. 73–80). Basel, Switzerland: Springer International Publishing.

Hoc J. M., & Nguyen-Xuan, A. (1990). Language semantics, mental models and analogy. In J. M. Hoc, T. R. G. Green, R. Samurçay, & D. J. Gillmore (Eds.), *Psychology of Programming* (pp. 139–156). London, UK: Academic Press.

Hoda, R., & Andreae, P. (2014). It's not them, it's us! Why computer science fails to impress many first years. In *Proceedings of the Sixteenth Australasian Computing Education Conference Volume 148* (pp. 159–162). Darlinghurst, Australia: Australian Computer Society.

Höök, L. J., & Eckerdal, A. (2015). On the bimodality in an introductory programming course: An analysis of student performance factors. In *Learning and Teaching in Computing and Engineering (LaTiCE 2015)* (pp. 79–86). New York: IEEE.

Howles, T. (2009). A study of attrition and the use of student learning communities in the computer science introductory programming sequence. *Computer Science Education*, 19(1), 1–13.

Hudak, M. A., & Anderson D. E. (1990). Formal operations and learning style predict success in statistics and computer science courses. *Teaching of Psychology*, 17(4), 231–234.

Hundley, J. (2008). A review of using design patterns in CS1. In *Proceedings of the 46th Annual Southeast Regional Conference (ACM SE'08)* (pp. 30–33). New York: ACM.

Izu, C., Weerasinghe, A., & Pope, C. (2016). A study of code design skills in novice programmers using the SOLO taxonomy. In *Proceedings of the 2016 ACM Conference on International Computing Education Research* (pp. 251–259). New York: ACM.

Jadud, M. C. (2006). Methods and tools for exploring novice compilation behaviour. In *Proceedings of the Second International Workshop on Computing Education Research* (pp. 73–84). New York: ACM.

Jimoyiannis, A. (2013). Using SOLO taxonomy to explore students' mental models of the programming variable and the assignment statement. *Themes in Science and Technology Education*, 4(2), 53–74.

Johnson-Laird, P. N. (1983). *Mental Models: Towards a Cognitive Science of Language, Inference, and Consciousness*. Cambridge, MA: Harvard University Press.

Johnson, C. G., & Fuller, U. (2006). Is Bloom's taxonomy appropriate for computer science? In *Proceedings of the 6th Baltic Sea Conference on Computing Education Research, Koli Calling* (pp. 120–123). New York: ACM.

Kay, J., Barg, M., Fekete, A., Greening. T., Hollands, O., Kingston, J., & Crawford, K. (2000). Problem-based learning for foundation computer science courses. *Computer Science Education*, 10, 109–128.

Kelleher, C., & Pausch, R. (2005). Lowering the barriers to programming: A taxonomy of programming environments and languages for novice programmers. *ACM Computing Surveys (CSUR)*, 37(2), 83–137.

Kim, J., & Lerch, F. J. (1997). Why is programming (sometimes) so difficult? Programming as scientific discovery in multiple problem spaces. *Information Systems Research*, 8(1), 25–50.

Kinnunen, P., & Malmi, L. (2006). Why students drop out CS1 course? In *Proceedings of the Second International Workshop on Computing Education Research* (pp. 97–108). New York: ACM.

Kölling, M. (2009). Quality-oriented teaching of programming. Retrieved from: https://blogs.kcl.ac.uk/proged/2009/09/04/quality-oriented-teaching-of-programming

Kölling, M. (2010). The Greenfoot programming environment. *ACM Transactions on Computing Education (TOCE)*, 10(4), 14.

Kölling, M., Quig, B., Patterson, A., & Rosenberg, J. (2003). The BlueJ system and its pedagogy. *Computer Science Education*, 13(4), 249–268.

Koulouri, T., Lauria, S., & Macredie, R. D. (2014). Teaching introductory programming: A quantitative evaluation of different approaches. *ACM Transactions on Computing Education (TOCE)*, 14(4), 26.

Krathwohl, D. R. (2002). A revision of Bloom's taxonomy: An overview. *Theory Into Practice*, 41(4), 212–218.

Kunkle, W. M., & Allen, R. B. (2016). The impact of different teaching approaches and languages on student learning of introductory programming concepts. *ACM Transactions on Computing Education (TOCE)*, 16(1), 3.

Kurland D. M., Pea, R. D., Clement, C., & Mawby, R. (1989). A study of the development of programming ability and thinking skills in high school students. In E. Soloway & J. C. Spohrer (Eds.), *Studying the Novice Programmer* (pp. 83–112). Hillsdale, NJ: Lawrence Erlbaum.

Kurland, D. M., & Pea, R. D. (1985). Children's mental models of recursive LOGO programs. *Journal of Educational Computing Research*, 1(2), 235–243.

Lahtinen, E., Ala-Mutka, K. & Järvinen, H. M. (2005). A study of the difficulties of novice programmers. *ACM SIGCSE Bulletin*, 37(3), 14–18.

Lau, W. W., & Yuen, A. H. (2011). Modelling programming performance: Beyond the influence of learner characteristics. *Computers & Education*, 57(1), 1202–1213.

Lawson, C. (1962). A survey of computer facility management. *Datamation,* 8(7), 29–32.

Lewis, T. L., Rosson, M. B., & Pérez-Quiñones, M. A. (2004). What do the experts say?: Teaching introductory design from an expert's perspective. *ACM SIGCSE Bulletin*, 36(1), 296–300.

Linn, M. C., & Dalbey, J. (1989). Cognitive consequences of programming instruction. In E. Soloway & J. C. Spohrer (Eds.), *Studying the Novice Programmer* (pp. 57–81). Hillsdale, NJ: Lawrence Erlbaum.

Linn, M. C., & Clancy, M. J. (1992). The case for case studies of programming problems. *Communications of the ACM*, 35(3), 121–132.

Lister, R. (2000). On blooming first year programming, and its blooming assessment. In *Proceedings of the Australasian Conference on Computing Education (ACSE '00)* (pp. 158–162). Darlinghurst, Australia: Australian Computer Society.

Lister, R. (2010). Geek genes and bimodal grades. *ACM Inroads*, 1(3), 16–17.

Lister, R. (2011). Concrete and other neo-Piagetian forms of reasoning in the novice programmer. In *Proceedings of the Thirteenth Australasian Computing Education Conference Volume 114* (pp. 9–18). Darlinghurst, Australia: Australian Computer Society.

Lister, R., & Leaney, J. (2003a). Introductory programming, criterion-referencing, and Bloom. *ACM SIGCSE Bulletin*, 35(1), 143–147.

Lister, R., & Leaney, J. (2003b). First year programming: Let all the flowers bloom. In *Proceedings of the Fifth Australasian Computing Education Conference (ACE 2003) Volume 20* (pp. 221–230). Darlinghurst, Australia: Australian Computer Society.

Lister, R., Adams, E. S., Fitzgerald, S., Fone, W., Hamer, J., Lindholm, M., McCartney, R., Moström, J. E., Sanders, K., Seppälä, O., & Simon, B. (2004). A multinational study of reading and tracing skills in novice programmers. *ACM SIGCSE Bulletin*, 36(4), 119–150.

Lister, R., Clear, T., Bouvier, D. J., Carter, P., Eckerdal, A., Jacková, J., Lopez, M., McCartney, R., Robbins, P., Seppälä, O., & Thompson, E. (2010). Naturally occurring data as research instrument: Analyzing examination responses to study the novice programmer. *ACM SIGCSE Bulletin*, 41(4), 156–173.

Lister, R., Simon, B., Thompson, E., Whalley, J. L., & Prasad, C. (2006). Not seeing the forest for the trees: Novice programmers and the SOLO taxonomy. *ACM SIGCSE Bulletin*, 38(3), 118–122.

Lopez, M., Whalley, J., Robbins, P., & Lister, R. (2008). Relationships between reading, tracing and writing skills in introductory programming. In *Proceedings of the Fourth International Workshop on Computing Education Research* (pp. 101–112). New York: ACM.

Luxton-Reilly, A. (2016). Learning to program is easy. In *Proceedings of the 2016 ACM Conference on Innovation and Technology in Computer Science Education* (pp. 284–289). New York: ACM.

Ma, L., Ferguson, J., Roper, M., & Wood, M. (2007). Investigating the viability of mental models held by novice programmers. *ACM SIGCSE Bulletin*, 39(1), 499–503.

Maloney, J., Resnick, M., Rusk, N., Silverman, B., & Eastmond, E. (2010). The scratch programming language and environment. *ACM Transactions on Computing Education (TOCE)*, 10(4), 16.

Mannila, L., Peltomäki, M., & Salakoski, T. (2006). What about a simple language? Analyzing the difficulties in learning to program. *Computer Science Education*, 16(3), 211–227.

Margulieux, L. E., Catrambone, R., & Schaeffer, L. M. (2018). Varying effects of subgoal labeled expository text in programming, chemistry, and statistics. *Instructional Science, 46*(5), 707–722.

Mason, R., & Cooper, G. (2013). Distractions in programming environments. In *Proceedings of the Fifteenth Australasian Computing Education Conference Volume 136* (pp. 23–30). Darlinghurst, Australia: Australian Computer Society.

Mayer R. E. (1989). The psychology of how novices learn computer programming. In E. Soloway & J. C. Spohrer (Eds.), *Studying the Novice Programmer* (pp. 129–159). Hillsdale, NJ: Lawrence Erlbaum.

Mayer, D. B., & Stalnaker, A. W. (1968). Selection and evaluation of computer personnel – The research history of SIG/CPR. In *The Proceedings of the 1968 ACM National Conference (23rd ACM National Conference)* (pp. 657–670). New York: ACM.

Mayer, R. E. (1985). Learning in complex domains: A cognitive analysis of computer programming. *Psychology of Learning and Motivation*, 19, 89–130.

Mayer, R. E. (1992). Teaching for transfer of problem-solving skills to computer programming. In E. De Corte, M. C. Linn, H. Mandl, & L. Verschaffel (Eds.), *Computer-Based Learning Environments and Problem Solving. NATO ASI Series (Series F: Computer and Systems Sciences), Vol. 84* (pp. 193–206). Berlin, Germany: Springer.

McCall, D., & Kölling, M. (2014). Meaningful categorisation of novice programmer errors. In *Frontiers in Education Conference (FIE)* (pp. 1–8). New York: IEEE.

McCane, B., Ott, C., Meek, N., & Robins, A. (2017). Mastery learning in introductory programming. In *Proceedings of the Nineteenth Australasian Computing Education Conference* (pp. 1–10). New York: ACM.

McCracken, M., Almstrum, V., Diaz, D., Guzdial, M., Hagan, D., Kolikant, Y. B., Laxer, C., Thomas, L., Utting, I., & Wilusz, T. (2001). A multi-national, multi-institutional study of assessment of programming skills of first-year CS students. *ACM SIGCSE Bulletin*, 33, 125–180.

McNamara, W. J. (1967). The selection of computer personnel: Past, present, future. In *Proceedings of the Fifth SIGCPR Conference on Computer Personnel Research (SIGCPR '67)* (pp. 52–56). New York: ACM Press.

Mead, J., Gray, S., Hamer, J., James, R., Sorva, J., Clair, C. S., & Thomas, L. (2006). A cognitive approach to identifying measurable milestones for programming skill acquisition. *ACM SIGCSE Bulletin*, 38(4), 182–194.

Meerbaum-Salant, O., Armoni, M., & Ben-Ari, M. (2010). Learning computer science concepts with Scratch. In *Proceedings of the Sixth International Workshop on Computing Education Research (ICER '10)* (pp. 69–76). New York: ACM.

Mendes, A. J., Paquete, L., Cardoso, A., & Gomes, A. (2012). Increasing student commitment in introductory programming learning. In *Frontiers in Education Conference (FIE)* (pp. 1–6). New York: IEEE.

Meyer, J. H., & Land, R. (Eds.) (2006). *Overcoming Barriers to Student Understanding: Threshold Concepts and Troublesome Knowledge*. London, UK: Routledge.

Meyer, J. H. F., & Land, R. (2003). *Threshold Concepts and Troublesome Knowledge: Linkages to Ways of Thinking and Practising within the Disciplines (ETL Project: Occasional Report No. 4)*. Edinburgh, UK: University of Edinburgh Press.

Mitchell, M. L., & Jolley, J. M. (2012). *Research Design Explained*, 8th edn. Wadsworth, CA: Cengage Learning.

Morra, S., Gobbo, C., Marini, Z., & Sheese, R. (2007). *Cognitive Development: Neo-Piagetian Perspectives*. New York: Psychology Press.

Morrison, B. B., Dorn, B., & Guzdial, M. (2014). Measuring cognitive load in introductory CS: Adaptation of an instrument. In *Proceedings of the Tenth Annual Conference on International Computing Education Research* (pp. 131–138). New York: ACM.

Newman, R., Gatward, R., & Poppleton, M. (1970). Paradigms for teaching computer programming in higher education. *WIT Transactions on Information and Communication Technologies*, 7, 299–305.

Newstead, P. R. (1975). Grade and ability predictions in an introductory programming course. *ACM SIGCSE Bulletin*, 7, 87–91.

O'Donnell, R. (2009). Threshold concepts and their relevance to economics. In *14th Annual Australasian Teaching Economics Conference (ATEC 2009)* (pp. 190–200). Brisbane, Australia: School of Economics and Finance, Queensland University of Technology.

Oliver, D., Dobele, T., Greber, M., & Roberts, T. (2004). This course has a Bloom rating of 3.9. In *Proceedings of the Sixth Australasian Conference on Computing Education (ACE '04)* (pp. 227–231). Darlinghurst, Australia: Australian Computer Society.

Ormerod T. (1990). Human cognition and programming. In J. M. Hoc, T. R. G. Green, R. Samurçay, & D. J. Gillmore (Eds.), *Psychology of Programming* (pp. 63–82). London, UK: Academic Press.

Paas, F., Renkl, A., & Sweller, J. (2003). Cognitive load theory and instructional design: Recent developments. *Educational Psychologist*, 38(1), 1–4.

Palumbo, D. (1990). Programming language/problem-solving research: A review of relevant issues. *Review of Educational Research*, 60(1), 65–89.

Parsons, D., & Haden. P. (2006). Parson's programming puzzles: A fun and effective learning tool for first programming courses. In *Proceedings of the 8th Australasian Conference on Computing Education (ACE '06) Volume 52* (pp. 157–163). Darlinghurst, Australia: Australian Computer Society.

Patitsas, E., Berlin, J., Craig, M., & Easterbrook, S. (2016). Evidence that computer science grades are not bimodal. In *Proceedings of the 2016 ACM Conference on International Computing Education Research* (pp. 113–121). New York: ACM.

Pea, R. D. (1986). Language-independent conceptual "bugs" in novice programming. *Journal of Educational Computing Research*, 2(1), 25–36.

Pea, R. D., & Kurland, D. M. (1984). *On the Cognitive Prerequisites of Learning Computer Programming. Technical Report No. 18*. New York: Bank Street College of Education.

Pears, A., Seidman, S., Malmi, L., Mannila, L., Adams, E., Bennedsen, J., Devlin, M., & Paterson, J. (2007). A survey of literature on the teaching of introductory programming. *ACM SIGCSE Bulletin*, 39(4), 204–223.

Perkins, D. N., & Martin, F (1986). Fragile knowledge and neglected strategies in novice programmers. In E. Soloway & S. Iyengar (Eds.), *Empirical Studies of Programmers, First Workshop* (pp. 213–229). Norwood, NJ: Ablex.

Perkins, D. N., Hancock, C., Hobbs, R., Martin, F., & Simmons, R. (1989). Conditions of learning in novice programmers. In E. Soloway & J. C. Spohrer (Eds.), *Studying the Novice Programmer* (pp. 261–279). Hillsdale, NJ: Lawrence Erlbaum.

Piaget, J. (1964). Part I: Cognitive development in children: Piaget development and learning. *Journal of Research in Science Teaching*, 2(3), 176–186.

Piaget, J. (1971a). The theory of stages in cognitive development. In D. R. Green, M. P. Ford, & G. B. Flamer (Eds.), *Measurement and Piaget* (pp. 1–11). New York: McGraw-Hill.

Piaget, J. (1971b). Developmental stages and developmental processes. In D. R. Green, M. P. Ford, & G. B. Flamer (Eds.), *Measurement and Piaget* (pp. 172–188). New York: McGraw-Hill.

Plass, J. L., Moreno, R., & Brünken, R. (Eds.) (2010). *Cognitive Load Theory.* Cambridge, UK: Cambridge University Press.

Porter, L., & Zingaro, D. (2014). Importance of early performance in CS1: Two conflicting assessment stories. In *Proceedings of the 45th ACM Technical Symposium on Computer Science Education* (pp. 295–300). New York: ACM.

Porter, L., Zingaro, D., & Lister, R. (2014). Predicting student success using fine grain clicker data. In *Proceedings of the Tenth Annual Conference on International Computing Education Research* (pp. 51–58). New York: ACM.

Price, T. W., & Barnes, T. (2015). Comparing textual and block interfaces in a novice programming environment. In *Proceedings of the Eleventh Annual International Conference on International Computing Education Research* (pp. 91–99). New York: ACM.

Rist, R. S. (1995). Program structure and design. *Cognitive Science*, 19, 507–562.

Rist, R. S. (1986). Plans in programming: Definition, demonstration, and development. In E. Soloway & S. Iyengar (Eds.), *Empirical Studies of Programmers* (pp. 28–47). Norwood, NJ: Ablex Publishing.

Rist, R. S. (1989). Schema creation in programming. *Cognitive Science*, 13, 389–414.

Rist, R. S. (2004). Learning to program: Schema creation, application, and evaluation. In S. Fincher & M. Petre (Eds.), *Computer Science Education Research* (pp. 175–195). London, UK: Taylor & Francis.

Robins, A. V. (2010). Learning edge momentum: A new account of outcomes in CS1. *Computer Science Education*, 20, 37–71.

Robins, A. V. (2018). Outcomes in introductory programming. *Computer Science Technical Report, OUCS-2018-02,* The University of Otago. Retrieved from www.otago.ac.nz/computer-science/otago685184.pdf

Robins, A. V., Haden, P., & Garner, S. (2006). Problem distributions in a CS1 course. In *Proceedings of the Eighth Australasian Computing Education Conference (ACE2006), CRPIT, 52* (pp. 165–173). Darlinghurst, Australia: Australian Computer Society.

Robins, A. V., Rountree, J., & Rountree, N. (2003). Learning and teaching programming: A review and discussion. *Computer Science Education*, 13(2), 137–172.

Rogalski J., & Samurçay R. (1990). Acquisition of programming knowledge and skills. In J. M. Hoc, T. R. G. Green, R. Samurçay, & D. J. Gillmore (Eds.), *Psychology of Programming* (pp. 157–174). London, UK: Academic Press.

Rountree, J., Robins, A., & Rountree, N. (2013). Elaborating on threshold concepts, *Computer Science Education*, 23(3), 265–289.

Rountree, N., Rountree, J., Robins, A., & Hannah, R. (2004). Interacting factors that predict success and failure in a CS1 course. *ACM SIGCSE Bulletin*, 36(4), 101–104.

Rowbottom, D. P. (2007). Demystifying threshold concepts. *Journal of Philosophy of Education*, 41, 263–270.

Sackman, H., Erickson, W. J., & Grant, E. E. (1968). Exploratory experimental studies comparing online and offline programming performance. *Communications of the ACM*, 11(1), 3–11.

Sarawagi, N. (2014). A flipped CS0 classroom: Applying Bloom's taxonomy to algorithmic thinking. *Journal of Computing Sciences in Colleges*, 29(6), 21–28.

Schneider, G. M. (1978). The introductory programming course in computer science: Ten principles. *ACM SIGCSE Bulletin*, 10(1), 107–114.

Schulte, C., & Bennedsen, J. (2006). What do teachers teach in introductory programming? In *Proceedings of the Second International Workshop on Computing Education Research* (pp. 17–28). New York: ACM.

Schwill, A. (1997). Computer science education based on fundamental ideas. In D. Passey & B. Samways (Eds.), *Information Technology. IFIP Advances in Information and Communication Technology* (pp. 285–291). Boston, MA: Springer.

Schwill, A. (1994). Fundamental ideas of computer science. *EATCS-Bulletin*, 53, 274–295.

Scott, T. (2003). Bloom's Taxonomy applied to testing in computer science classes. *Journal of Computing in Small Colleges*, 19(1), 267–274.

Sheard, J., & Hagan, D. (1998). Our failing students: A study of a repeat group. *ACM SIGCSE Bulletin*, 30(3), 223–227.

Sheard, J., Carbone, A., Lister, R., Simon, B., Thompson, E., & Whalley, J. L. (2008). Going SOLO to assess novice programmers. *ACM SIGCSE Bulletin*, 40(3), 209–213.

Sheil, B. A. (1981). The psychological study of programming. *Computing Surveys*, 13, 101–120.

Shih, Y. F., & Alessi, S. M. (1993). Mental models and transfer of learning in computer programming. *Journal of Research on Computing in Education*, 26(2), 154–175.

Shinners-Kennedy, D., & Fincher, S. A. (2013). Identifying threshold concepts: From dead end to a new direction. In *Proceedings of the Ninth Annual International ACM Conference on International Computing Education Research* (pp. 9–18). New York: ACM.

Simon, Fincher, S., Robins, A., Baker, B., Box, I., Cutts, Q., de Raadt, M., Haden, P., Hamer, J., Hamilton, M., Lister, R., Petre, M., Sutton, K., Tolhurst, D., & Tutty, J. (2006). Predictors of success in a first programming course. In *Proceedings of the 8th Australasian Conference on Computing Education Volume 52* (pp. 189–196). Darlinghurst, Australia: Australian Computer Society,

Soloway, E., Ehrlich, K., Bonar, J., & Greenspan, J. (1983). What do novices know about programming? In B. Shneiderman & A. Badre (Eds.), *Directions in Human–Computer Interactions* (pp. 27–54). Norwood, NJ: Ablex.

Soloway, E. (1986). Learning to program = learning to construct mechanisms and explanations. *Communications of the ACM*, 29(9), 850–858.

Soloway, E., & Ehrlich, K. (1984). Empirical studies of programming knowledge. *IEEE Transactions on Software Engineering*, 5, 595–609.

Soloway, E., & Spohrer, J. C. (Eds.) (1989). *Studying the Novice Programmer*. Hillsdale, NJ: Lawrence Erlbaum.

Sorva, J. (2010). Reflections on threshold concepts in computer programming and beyond. In *Proceedings of the 10th Koli Calling International Conference on Computing Education Research, Koli Calling '10* (pp. 21–30). New York: ACM.

Sorva, J. (2012). *Visual Program Simulation in Introductory Programming Education* (doctoral dissertation 61/2012). Aalto University.

Sorva, J. (2013). Notional machines and introductory programming education. *ACM Transactions on Computing Education (TOCE)*, 13(2), 8.

Spohrer, J. C., & Soloway, E. (1989). Novice mistakes: Are the folk wisdoms correct? In E. Soloway & J. C. Spohrer (Eds.), *Studying the Novice Programmer* (pp. 401–416). Hillsdale, NJ: Lawrence Erlbaum.

Spohrer, J. C., Soloway, E., & Pope, E. (1989). A goal/plan analysis of buggy Pascal programs. In E. Soloway & J. C. Spohrer (Eds.), *Studying the Novice Programmer* (pp. 355–399). Hillsdale, NJ: Lawrence Erlbaum.

Stachel, J., Marghitu, D., Brahim, T. B., Sims, R., Reynolds, L., & Czelusniak, V. (2013). Managing cognitive load in introductory programming courses: A cognitive aware scaffolding tool. *Journal of Integrated Design and Process Science*, 17(1), 37–54.

Starr, C. W., Manaris, B., & Stalvey, R. H. (2008). Bloom's taxonomy revisited: Specifying assessable learning objectives in computer science. *ACM SIGCSE Bulletin*, 40(1), 261–265.

Storey, M. A., Fracchia, F. D., & Müller, H. A. (1999). Cognitive design elements to support the construction of a mental model during software exploration. *Journal of Systems and Software*, 44(3), 171–185.

Subramanian, A., & Joshi, K. (1996). Computer aptitude tests as predictors of novice computer programmer performance. *Journal of Information Technology Management*, 7, 31–41.

Sweller, J. (1988). Cognitive load during problem solving: Effects on learning. *Cognitive Science*, 12(2), 257–285.

Sweller, J. (1994). Cognitive load theory, learning difficulty, and instructional design. *Learning and Instruction*, 4(4), 295–312.

Teague, D. (2015) *Neo-Piagetian Theory and the Novice Programmer* (doctoral thesis). Queensland University of Technology.

Teague, M. M. (2011). *Pedagogy of Introductory Computer Programming: A People-First Approach* (master's thesis). Queensland University of Technology.

Thompson, E., Luxton-Reilly, A., Whalley, J. L., Hu, M., & Robbins, P. (2008). Bloom's taxonomy for CS assessment. In *Proceedings of the Tenth Conference on Australasian Computing Education (ACE '08)* (pp. 155–161). Darlinghurst, Australia: Australian Computer Society.

Utting, I., Tew, A. E., McCracken, M., Thomas, L., Bouvier, D., Frye, R., Paterson, J., Caspersen, M., Kolikant, Y., Sorva, J., & Wilusz, T. (2013). A fresh look at novice programmers' performance and their teachers' expectations. In *Proceedings of the ITICSE Working Group Reports Conference on Innovation and Technology in Computer Science Education* (pp. 15–32). New York: ACM.

van Merriënboer, J. J. G. (1990). Strategies for programming instruction in high school: Program completion vs. program generation. *Journal of Educational Computing Research*, 6(3), 265–285.

van Merriënboer, J. J. G., & de Croock, M. B. M. (1992). Strategies for computer–based programming instruction: Program completion vs. program generation. *Journal of Educational Computing Research*, 8(3), 365–394.

van Merriënboer, J. J., & Paas, F. G. (1990). Automation and schema acquisition in learning elementary computer programming: Implications for the design of practice. *Computers in Human Behavior*, 6(3), 273–289.

Venables, A., Tan, G., & Lister, R. (2009). A closer look at tracing, explaining and code writing skills in the novice programmer. In *Proceedings of the Fifth International Workshop on Computing Education Research* (pp. 117–128). New York: ACM.

Ventura, P. (2005). Identifying predictors of success for an objects-first CS1. *Computer Science Education*, 15(3), 223–243.

Vihavainen, A., Airaksinen, J., & Watson, C. (2014). A systematic review of approaches for teaching introductory programming and their influence on success. In *Proceedings of the Tenth Annual Conference on International Computing Education Research* (pp. 19–26). New York: ACM.

Watson, C., & Li, F. W. (2014). Failure rates in introductory programming revisited. In *Proceedings of the 2014 Conference on Innovation & Technology in Computer Science Education* (pp. 39–44). New York: ACM.

Webster, B. F. (1996). The real software crisis: The shortage of top-notch programmers threatens to become the limiting factor in software development. *Byte Magazine,* 21, 218.

Weinberg, G. M. (1971). *The Psychology of Computer Programming*. New York: Van Nostrand Reinhold.

Weintrop, D., & Wilensky, U. (2015). To block or not to block, that is the question: Students' perceptions of blocks-based programming. In *Proceedings of the 14th International Conference on Interaction Design and Children* (pp. 199–208). New York: ACM.

Weintrop, D., Killen, H., & Franke, B. (2018). Blocks or Text? How Programming Language Modality Makes a Difference in Assessing Underrepresented Populations. In *Proceedings of the 13th International Conference of the Learning Sciences* (ICLS2018) (pp. 328–335). London, UK: International Society of the Learning Sciences.

Werth, L. H. (1986). Predicting student performance in a beginning computer science class. *ACM SIGCSE Bulletin*, 18(1), 138–143.

Whalley, J. L., Lister, R., Thompson, E., Clear, T., Robbins, P., Ajith Kumar, P. K., & Prasad, C. (2006). An Austalasian study of reading and comprehension skills in novice programmers, using the Bloom and SOLO taxonomies. In *Proceedings of the 8th Australian Conference on Computing Education (ACE '06)* (pp. 243–252). Darlinghurst, Australia: Australian Computer Society.

White, G., & Sivitanides, M. (2002). A theory of the relationships between cognitive requirements of computer programming languages and programmers' cognitive characteristics. *Journal of Information Systems Education*, 13(1), 59–66.

Wick, M. R. (2005). Teaching design patterns in CS1: A closed laboratory sequence based on the game of life. *ACM SIGCSE Bulletin*, 37(1), 487–491.

Widowski, D., & Eyferth, K. (1986). Comprehending and recalling computer programs of different structural and semantic complexity by experts and novices. In H. P. Willumeit (Ed.), *Human Decision Making and Manual Control* (pp. 267–275). Amsterdam, The Netherlands: North–Holland, Elsevier.

Wiedenbeck, S., Fix, V., & Scholtz, J. (1993). Characteristics of the mental representations of novice and expert programmers: An empirical study. *International Journal of Man–Machine Studies*, 25, 697–709.

Wiedenbeck, S., & Ramalingam, V. (1999). Novice comprehension of small programs written in the procedural and object-oriented styles. *International Journal of Human–Computer Studies*, 51(1), 71–87.

Wiedenbeck, S., Ramalingam, V., Sarasamma, S., & Corritore, C. L. (1999). A comparison of the comprehension of object-oriented and procedural programs by novice programmers. *Interacting with Computers*, 11(3), 255–282.

Wileman, S. A., Konvalina, J., & Stephens, L. J. (1981). Factors influencing success in beginning computer science courses. *Journal of Educational Research*, 74, 223–226.

Wilson, B. C., & Shrock, S. (2001). Contributing to success in an introductory computer science course: A study of twelve factors. *ACM SIGCSE Bulletin*, 33(1), 184–188.

Winslow, L. E. (1996) Programming pedagogy – A psychological overview. *ACM SIGCSE Bulletin*, 28(3), 17–22.

Woszczynski, A., Haddad, H., & Zgambo, A. (2005). Towards a model of student success in programming courses. In *Proceedings of the 43rd Annual Southeast Regional Conference – Volume 1 (ACM-SE 43)* (pp. 301–302). New York: ACM.

Yadin, A. (2011). Reducing the dropout rate in an introductory programming course. *ACM Inroads*, 2(4), 71–76.

Yadin, A. (2013). Using unique assignments for reducing the bimodal grade distribution. *ACM Inroads*, 4(1), 38–42.

13 Programming Paradigms and Beyond

Shriram Krishnamurthi and Kathi Fisler

13.1 Introduction and Scope

Programming is central to computing. It is both the practical tool that actually puts the power of computing to work and a source of intellectual stimulation and beauty. Therefore, programming education must be central to computing education. In the process, instructors need to make concrete choices about which languages and tools to use, and these will depend on their goals. Some emphasize the view of programming as a vocational skill that students must have to participate in the modern digital economy. Some highlight programming as an exciting, creative medium, comparable to classical media such as natural language, paint, and stone. Irrespective of the motivation for teaching programming, from a professional computing perspective, programs are a common medium for representing and communicating computational processes and algorithms.

Different languages have different affordances. As many people have remarked, programming languages are a human–computer interface. At the same time, programming languages are executed by computers, which work with an unyielding logic that is very different from that of most human-to-human communication. This tension between human comprehension and computer interpretation has manifested in many computing education research (CEdR) studies over the years. Indeed, navigating that tension (and helping students learn to do the same) is one of the great challenges of computing education, and hence CEdR.

Computing educators need a lexicon and criterion through which to make, discuss, and teach choices about programming languages. Historically, much of our vocabulary has centered around a notion of "paradigms" that clusters languages by a combination of programming style and language behavior.[1] However, as programming languages and our technical understanding of them evolve, this notion is harder to maintain. This chapter therefore moves beyond paradigms to more nuanced ways of discussing languages, both among educators and with our students. We examine criteria and models for understanding languages through the lens of prior CEdR, with an eye toward exciting **open problems** (which will be flagged in boldface) that can take the field forward.

---

1 In this chapter, we use the term *behavior* to loosely refer to how a program executes, and *semantics* only to refer to a precise, formal description of behavior.

This chapter is written for aspiring researchers in computing education. It pushes for a deeper understanding of languages than at the level of syntax (though syntactic mistakes, like using = for assignment, deserve their own opprobrium), pointing out that a given syntactic program can behave in several different ways (Section 13.2). Understanding those behaviors – often captured in the concept of a notional machine (Section 13.5) – is essential to making sense of the power and affordances of languages (Section 13.6). The chapter discusses several long-running debates in the design and use of languages (Section 13.7), including several other topics that remain wide open for researchers to investigate (Section 13.8) that impact education. Rather than a single section of open questions, these are peppered throughout the chapter in context.

13.2 Beyond Syntax: Discussing Behavior

A lot of discussion about programming languages inevitably centers around syntax, because this is the most easily visible aspect of the language and the one that programmers primarily manipulate. A major challenge in programming, however, is mapping syntax to behavior, because computer behavior is hard to see and control. Furthermore, the ultimate goal is to create programs that behave in a particular way. Therefore, we will discuss many behavioral aspects of programs in this chapter.

We can make our discussion more concrete if we can refer to example programs. This section distills these into two examples. Consider the following two programs written in a generic syntax. For each one, predict what answer will be printed at the end of program execution:

Program 1:
```
y = 0
x = y + 5
y := 7 // change y
print(x)
```

Program 2:
```
o = {x: 1, y: 12} // o is an "object" with two fields, x and y

procedure p(v):
  v.x:= 5
end

p(o)
print(o.x)
```

Now that you have made your prediction, please revisit each program and ask whether it could reasonably produce a *different* value: What would that value be and how might it come about?

Stop! Did you make your predictions? If not, go back and do so first!

Most readers would expect the first program to print 5 and the second to also print 5, because this is the outcome produced by the corresponding programs in languages like Java and Python. However, here are alternative explanations:

1. In the first program, x is defined to be 5 more than the value of y, *whatever that value might be*. Thus, when y changes to be 7, the value of x automatically updates to 12.

2. In the second program, the modification to the x field is strictly local to p. When computation returns from p, the value of o is left unchanged (most probably, p received and changed a *copy* of o). Thus, the program prints 1.

These alternative behaviors might strike some readers as natural but others as eccentric, so let us discuss them in more depth.

In Program 1, most readers probably find the answer 5 so obvious as to not even consider another possible outcome. Yet, when presented with the same program in a *spreadsheet* – where the variables become cells, = is a reference, and assignment to y becomes an update to its cell – nobody would expect anything but the *other* behavior, where x becomes 12. Yet the spreadsheet behavior of automatically updating references is also found in textual programming languages, such as reactive languages (Bainomugisha et al., 2013). (It's worth noting that some of the odd student expectations mentioned in Pea's [1986] "Superbug" paper can just as well be interpreted as students expecting the language to behave reactively.)

In Program 2, the behavior comes down to a question of *aliasing* (Smaragdakis & Balatsouras, 2015, provide a useful summary): When is a name (here, v) just an alias for another (here, o)? Numerous studies have found that students (and even professional programmers) do not have a clear understanding of aliasing (Fleury, 1991; Ma, 2007; Tunnell Wilson, Fisler, & Krishnamurthi, 2017) and that languages behave in ways that confound their expectations (Miller et al., 2017; Tunnell Wilson, Pombrio, & Krishnamurthi, 2017). Yet aliasing is a crucial issue in programming, and one we will return to later in this chapter (Section 13.6.2).

What these examples show is that *syntax does not inherently determine behavior*, as others have noted in the past (Fitter, 1979; Plum, 1977). Furthermore, though experienced programmers may have been primed to expect certain behaviors, (a) novices are not necessarily so primed (the reactive version of the first program shows that) and (b) even experienced programmers may not all agree (Tunnell Wilson, Pombrio, & Krishnamurthi, 2017) – the aliasing disagreement in the second program shows that. Irreconcilable variation between syntax and behavior is par for the course, independent of efforts to make them align better in particular cases (Stefik & Siebert, 2013). Therefore, we need to investigate language *behavior* as a topic beyond the bounds of syntax.

13.3 Paradigms As a Classical Notion of Classification

To structure the study of languages, many authors have used the notion of the "paradigm." Paradigms are supposedly groups that differentiate one class of similar languages from others in some high-level way, usually focused on features that exhibit common behaviors. Authors conventionally list a few major paradigms: imperative, object-oriented (henceforth "OO"), functional (henceforth "FP"), and logic, and other authors tend to add one or more of scripting, web, database, and/or reactive.

We have already seen an example of reactive programming in the alternative interpretation of Program 1: in reactive languages, the program expresses *dependencies*, but the language handles updating the values of variables in the presence of mutation. Similarly, in logic and database paradigms, programs express logical dependencies between elements of data, but determining answers is done through an algorithm that is hard-coded into the language. (Some authors dub all of these as "declarative" languages and imply that programmers can think only about the logic of problem-solving independent of algorithms, but in reality programs often have to be modified to adjust to the algorithms built into the language – sometimes even to ensure something as basic as termination.)

OO is a widely used term chock-full of ambiguity. At its foundation, OO depends on *objects*, which are values that combine data and procedures. The data are usually hidden ("encapsulated") from the outside world and accessible only to those procedures. These procedures have one special argument, whose hidden data they can access, and are hence called *methods*, which are invoked through *dynamic dispatch*. This much seems to be common to all OO languages, but beyond this they differ widely:

- Most OO languages have one distinguished object that methods depend on, but some instead have *multimethods*, which can dispatch on many objects at a time.
- Some OO languages have a notion of a *class*, which is a template for making objects. In these languages, it is vital for programmers to understand the class–object distinction, and many students struggle with it (Eckerdal & Thune, 2005). However, many languages considered OO do not have classes. The presence or absence of classes leads to very different programming patterns.
- Most OO languages have a notion of *inheritance*, wherein an object can refer to some other entity to provide default behavior. However, there are huge variations in inheritance: Is the other entity a class or another (*prototypical*) object? Can it refer to only one entity (*single-inheritance*) or to many (*multiple-inheritance*), and if the latter, how are ambiguities resolved? Is what it refers to fixed or can it change as the program runs?
- Some OO languages have types, and the role of types in determining program behavior can be subtle and can vary quite a bit across languages.
- Even though many OO aficionados take it as a given that objects should be built atop imperative state, it is not clear that one of the creators of OO, Alan Kay, intended for that: "the small scale [motivation for OOP] was to find a more flexible version of assignment, and then to try to eliminate it altogether"; "[g]enerally, we don't want the programmer to be messing around with state" (Kay, 1993).

In general, all of these variations in behavior tend to get grouped together as OO, even though they lead to significantly different language designs and corresponding behaviors, and are not even exclusive to it (e.g., functional closures also encapsulate data). Thus, a phrase like "objects-first" (Section 13.7.1) can in principle mean dozens of wildly different curricular structures, though in practice it seems to refers to curricula built around objects as found in Java.

Finally, FP also shows up often in the education literature, popularized by the seminal book by Abelson and Sussman (1985). In FP, programmers make little to no use of imperative updates. Instead, programs consume and produce *values*, and programming is viewed as the arrangement of functions to compose and decompose values (some have even dubbed FP as "value-oriented programming"). Due to the lack of mutation (Section 13.5.1), aliasing problems (Section 13.2) are essentially non-existent. FP is characterized by two more traits: the ability to pass functions as values, which creates much higher-level operations than traditional loops (an issue that manifests in plan composition; Section 13.7.3), and tail-calls, which make loop-like recursive solutions just as efficient as loops, thus enabling recursion as a primary, and generalizable, form of looping. The two main variations in FP are whether the language is typed or not and whether computation is eager or lazy, each of which leads to a significant difference in language flavor and programming style.

13.4 Beyond Paradigms

While paradigms have been in use for a long time, it is worth asking what they contribute to our understanding. First of all, should we view paradigms as classifiers that lump languages into exclusive bins? They are certainly interpreted that way by many readers, but two things should give us pause:

- As we saw in Program 1, being imperative does not preclude being reactive. Therefore, these cannot be viewed as independent. Reactivity simply gives an additional interpretation to an imperative update; furthermore, functional reactive languages have reactive behavior without explicitly imperative features, and reactivity can also be added to objects (Bainomugisha et al., 2013, provide a useful survey). Put differently, while OO and FP are statements about program *organization*, reactivity is a statement about program *behavior* on update. These are essentially orthogonal issues, enabling reactivity to be added to existing languages.
- Languages do not organize into hierarchical taxonomies the way plants and animals do; they are artificial entities that can freely be bred across supposed boundaries. Language authors can pick from several different bins when creating languages, and indeed modern mainstream languages are usually a mélange of many of these bins. Even archetypal OO languages like Java now have functional programming features (Gosling et al., 2015).

Furthermore, the paradigm bins sometimes conflate syntax and behavior. For instance, some authors now think of visual, block-based languages as a paradigm; however, blocks are purely a matter of program syntax and construction, whereas the other paradigms are about behavior. Indeed, block interfaces exist for imperative, OO, and FP. Thus, it is unclear whether blocks should even be listed as a paradigm – which further highlights the confusion that this term creates.

Another source of confusion is whether "paradigms" are statements about programming *languages* or about programming *styles*. For instance, one might argue that they are programming in an "FP style" in a language that is not normally thought of as "functional." These claims have a little validity, but must be viewed with some skepticism. For instance, a C programmer who is passing around function pointers is simulating a superficial level of functional programming, but in the absence of automatic closure construction and corresponding garbage collection, this is a weak and often unsatisfying simulation. Similarly, Python's lack of tail-call elimination makes many natural FP patterns unusable in practice. Nevertheless, the possibility of such simulations makes it even harder to understand what paradigms are.

Yet another source of confusion is between the language and the operating environment. In a "batch" program, the program has a well-defined beginning and end. It may periodically pause to accept input, but the program determines when that happens. In contrast, in an event-driven program, it is the operating environment that is in charge; each event (whether a keystroke, a screen touch, a web request, a network packet arrival, or the tick of a clock) causes some part of the program to run in response. After responding to the event, the program (usually) returns to quiescence, and "wakes up" on the next event. Such a program has no well-defined beginning or end, and in principle runs forever. The programmer's challenge is to arrange how state is transferred between the events. This can be done in several ways: imperatively, using objects, functionally, reactively, and so on. Thus, event-driven programming is another cross-cutting notion that is independent of and orthogonal to the *program*'s organization – rather, it is a statement about the program's relationship with its *operating environment*. Lacking a clear definition of "paradigm," it is therefore entirely unclear whether event-driven-ness is one.

Thus, even though paradigms are widely used by authors and in the literature, some authors – especially in the programming languages research community – question or even reject their use (Krishnamurthi, 2008). Our examples and discussion points illustrate why a focus on *behavioral* properties and features provides a more meaningful framing.

13.5 Notional Machines

Whereas a programming languages researcher captures program behavior through semantics, computing education researchers instead use the idea of *notional machines* (du Boulay, 1986; Guzdial, 2015; Sorva, 2013). A notional machine is a crisp, human-friendly abstraction that explains how programs execute in a given language or family of closely related languages (i.e., a model of computation). While notional machines are usually viewed as a tool for learning to write and trace programs, they are also a useful way for us to think about language classification: essentially, the similarity between two languages is the extent to which a notional machine for one gives an accurate account of the behavior of the other. Seen this way, many eager FP languages have very similar notional machines (and may even share implementations); many "scripting" languages have strong similarities in some respects (but notable differences in others); while many OO languages actually have significantly different notional machines (e.g., the semantics of Java [Flatt, Krishnamurthi, & Felleisen, 1998] and of JavaScript [Guha, Saftoiu, & Krishnamurthi, 2010] are vastly different). There can be many notional machines for a given language, reflecting different goals, degrees of sophistication, levels of abstraction, and so forth.

Novice programmers do not infer accurate notional machines just from writing programs, as established from the literature on misconceptions (see Chapter 27). They sometimes see a program just as syntactic instructions, without a clear sense of how the instructions actually control some underlying device (du Boulay, 1986). The idea that a program controls a device, and thus has dynamic behavior, has been identified as an essential concept in learning about programming (Schwill, 1994; Shinners-Kennedy, 2008). Notional machines concretize this idea in a specific behavioral model. This suggests that teaching about notional machines and semantics is important (though some who take an extreme constructivist perspective might disagree [Greening, 1999]). Sorva's (2013) survey article on notional machines covers various theoretical framings for why students need to learn a semantics.

Despite some noticeable treatment in the literature, notional machines do not feature prominently in curricula or texts for computing courses. While execution models are often implicit in visualization and debugging tools (Hundhausen, Douglas, & Stasko, 2002; Kölling, Brown, & Altadmri, 2015; Naps et al., 2003; Sorva, 2012), few papers present notional machines explicitly alongside teaching programming constructs. Research suggests, however, that teaching notional machines early could have significant value. Cognitively, building a new mental model (in this case, of program execution) is significantly easier than updating an existing (flawed) one (Gupta, Hammer, & Redish, 2010; Schumacher & Czerwinski, 1992; Slotta & Chi, 2006). Building accurate and effective models is more likely to occur through activities that engage explicitly with the content (in contrast to passively working with visualizations, for example) (Freeman et al., 2014; Kessel & Wickens, 1982; Savery & Duffy, 2001). Practically, Nelson et al. taught students tracing through a notional machine at the very start of a programming course (Nelson, Xie, & Ko, 2017). These students performed better on the second test of introductory computer science (CS1) knowledge (Parker, Guzdial, & Engleman, 2016) than students who did code-writing tutorials rather than tracing. diSessa and Abelson (1986) leveraged user interface design to convey aspects of the notional machine (such as scoping) with their Boxer system, noting that learning a notional machine is a necessary challenge. They also raised questions about which notional machine to teach to end users who are learning programming in order to control computational media at a small scale compared to those preparing for professional software practice.

Research evidence on which notional machines to teach and when is sorely lacking in the computing education literature. Some work has evaluated specific models while checking for specific student misunderstandings (Ma, 2007; McCauley et al., 2015; Tessler, Beth, & Lin, 2013), but this body of research is not substantial enough to support general conclusions. Furthermore, there is scant attention to how notional machines evolve as students gain sophistication in upper-level computing courses. Sometimes, upper-level students even need to correct inaccurate models that formed in earlier courses (Tunnell Wilson, Krishnamurthi, & Fisler, 2018); finding mechanisms for doing so is an **open problem** that needs attention in CEdR.

13.5.1 The Challenge of Mutation and State

Notional machines are a useful lens through which to explore the complexities of reasoning about state (program behavior in the presence of mutation). Stateful programming has been taken by many as a sine qua non of programming education (e.g., it is virtually never mentioned as an assumption or threat to validity or generalizability). At the same time, numerous studies show that students struggle with this concept (du Boulay, 1986; Goldman et al., 2010; Sirkiä & Sorva, 2012), both as novices and as upper-level students (through interactions between state and other language features) (Tunnell Wilson, Krishnamurthi, & Fisler, 2018), while students working in non-stateful paradigms sometimes perform well on problems that are challenging in stateful contexts (Fisler, Krishnamurthi, & Siegmund, 2016). Taken together, these observations make comparative studies between stateful and non-stateful features one of the most significant **understudied** topics in computing education.

If state is so challenging for students to learn, why is it so popular in introductory contexts? Purely as a language feature (setting aside pedagogy for a moment), state has many benefits:

- It provides cheap communication channels between different parts of a program.
- It trades off persistence for efficiency.
- It appears to have a relatively straightforward notional machine, which lends itself to familiar-looking metaphors (like "boxes").
- It corresponds well to traditional control operations like looping.

However, these benefits of state become far less clear once we broaden our scope beyond very rudimentary programming. For instance:

- State introduces time and ordering (as Program 1 reveals) and forces students to think about them.
- State reveals aliasing (as Program 2 reveals). Aliasing is particularly problematic in the case of parallelism/concurrency, which is increasingly a central feature in programming.

State thus requires a complex notional machine to account for all of these factors. The apparent simplicity of stateful notional machines arises because most computing education literature usually just ignores some of these features (e.g., compound data with references to other compound data). This results in notional machines that are not faithful to program behavior, and hence are either useless or even misleading to students.

Thus, we believe it is worthwhile to revisit our basic assumptions about stateful programming's role in education – perhaps as an *advanced* introductory concept rather than as the most introductory one. State is a powerful tool that must be introduced with responsibilities. In short, while the community continues to have a debate about "objects-first" (Section 13.7.1), it is also worth having a "state-first" debate. Making progress on this issue is an **open challenge** in this field, but it will require educators with deep-seated beliefs to be willing to reexamine them.

It is worth noting that such shifts in conventional wisdom are feasible. For decades, automatic memory management (often called garbage collection) was considered a fringe feature, and most mainstream languages did not offer it. Students were therefore forced to confront memory management operations relatively early in their curriculum. As garbage collection has become widespread and the problems caused by poor manual memory management have become better known, this topic has moved to more advanced courses, where it is hopefully taught with more care. The growing understanding in industrial practice of the problems with unfettered state may therefore similarly result in many more "state-later" curricula.

13.5.2 Notional Machines for Related Disciplines and Transfer

When computing is used or taught in conjunction with another discipline (a model frequently proposed to scale precollege computing education; Stanton et al., 2017), it is important for the computing curricula to align well with the (sometimes implicit) behavioral models used in the other discipline. This seems necessary both to avoid confusing students and to eventually achieve transfer (see Chapter 9). For instance, using programming to teach algebra suggests programming with a notional machine that matches what students see in their math classes: one whose functions pass the "vertical line test" (i.e., they truly are functions), whose function application corresponds to algebraic substitution, whose variables behave like algebraic variables rather than stateful ones, and so on. Similarly, in physics, it is standard to model systems in terms of differential equations, which suggests different models of reactive programming (Felleisen et al., 2009) from traditional imperative event-driven code. In a data science curriculum, it may be important to first acquaint students with query operations before loops. It is therefore not only important to adjust the notional machine of computing to match those of other disciplines in interdisciplinary contexts, it is also worth wondering whether insights about computational models from other disciplines may lead to a less onerous study path for students of computing.

13.6 Human-Factor Issues

Thus far, our discussion of languages has taken a technical perspective, framed largely by semantic behavior. Some debates about paradigms have invoked human-factor issues, such as whether one paradigm provides a more "natural" way to think about programs (Lister et al., 1986; Wiedenbeck et al., 1999) or whether some constructs align better than others with how novices conceive of computations (Miller, 1981). Human-factor questions arise around each of syntax, behavior, and integrated development environments (IDEs) for programming languages, both in isolation and in their interactions (Kelleher & Pausch, 2005). Programming involves many tasks – reading, writing, debugging, and modifying code – and each has its own human-factor nuances. Furthermore, not all programming education has the same end goal: different environments are designed to, for instance, help novices with mainstream languages (e.g., Greenfoot, www.greenfoot.org), prepare students for professional practice (e.g., Eclipse, www.eclipse.org), motivate students to play with computing (e.g., Scratch; Resnick et al., 2009), or help students visualize program behavior dynamically as code is edited (e.g., Learnable Programming; Victor, 2012). A meaningful discussion of programming languages in educational contexts must account for human-factor issues, including the differing goals and abilities of the target student audience.

13.6.1 Interference between Human Language and Behavior

Programming languages use terminology from human languages (such as "if" or "while") that suggest the desired behavior of particular constructs. In practice, programming languages have more precise semantics for these terms than does human language. Many early and recent studies have identified gaps between programming semantics and humans' intuited semantics. For example:

- Pea's classic "Superbug" paper (1986) proposed that students ascribe an intelligent "hidden mind" to program execution that would make programs behave in accordance with human communication patterns.
- Soloway, Bonar, and Erlich (1983) showed differences in how novices interpreted program results based on different structural organizations of repeat loops in Pascal. More recent studies by Stefik and his colleagues show confusion due to keyword choices (Stefik & Gellenbeck, 2011) and leverage

user studies to design constructs to be more intuitive for novices (Stefik & Siebert, 2013). Most of these works identified problems with the specification of control flow in programs.

- Miller's studies of how non-programmers expressed computations (Miller, 1974, 1975) highlighted various ways in which complex control flow raised significant differences between human languages and programming languages: among the issues he cited were the need to specify initialization and exceptional cases in programming (neither of which are common in everyday human communication) and the precision required to bound iteration in programming (where human language often leaves such bounds vague).

Pane's dissertation (2002) provides more extensive coverage of this topic, including survey instruments and details results from multiple user studies (some of which worked with children).

13.6.2 Inferring Mental Models of Notional Machines

Interference between natural language and programming semantics matters because it affects users' construction of mental models of program execution. Ideally, programming education would help users form an accurate model of a notional machine for the language they are using. In practice, programmers often construct mental models of computation that are inconsistent with the actual behavior. This inconsistency seems unavoidable for many reasons. For instance, the mapping from the surface syntax to intended behavior may not be obvious or may have multiple reasonable interpretations (see the programs in Section 13.2). In addition, programmers develop their understanding of languages incrementally (Findler et al., 2002; Section 3.1), and their initial models may clash with some later behavior they have not yet learned. Sorva's detailed review of the literature on notional machines and mental models explains that "a novice's mental model of a notional machine is likely to be – typically of mental models in general – incomplete, unscientific, deficient, lacking in firm boundaries, and liable to change at any time" (Sorva, 2013, p. 10).

Inaccuracies in inferred mental models reflect *misconceptions* about program execution. The computing education literature abounds with evidence and descriptions of misconceptions about program execution, particularly among novice programmers. An entire chapter of this handbook focuses on this topic (Chapter 27). From the perspective of this chapter, misconceptions are interesting because they can manifest differently across programming languages or notional machines for those languages.

Understanding how different notional machines for the same language impact formation of mental models of program execution is a significant **open problem**. The potential implications are even more interesting: If some notional machines prove easier or more robust for students to learn at first, should that affect the order in which we introduce language features, even if it means moving away from the models that currently underlie most introductory curricula?

Different notional machines may also demand different cognitive loads; we are **not aware of any existing research** that contrasts the cognitive loads or demands of different notional machines for different programming-related activities (such as authoring versus debugging). In fact, we **conjecture** that the cognitive loads of different styles of programming may vary by activity: it may be that imperative programming is much easier for writing programs quickly (since state provides convenient communication channels between parts of a program), but these same benefits make subsequent reasoning and debugging much harder; functional programming may have the opposite affordances.

These questions of cognitive load are not just a question for novice programmers: aliasing, for example, has proven difficult to reason about even for professional programmers working with parallel programming (Cooper et al., 1993). Understanding these issues along all these different dimensions should give us a much more nuanced and sophisticated understanding of the impact of paradigms, programming styles, and notional machines than we currently find in the literature (where, for instance, it is very uncommon to find a paper that asks students to explain their own programs six months later and see how well they are able to fare).

Research is also needed well beyond the early curriculum. Student misconceptions about programming concepts can persist into the upper-level curriculum: one recent study found juniors and seniors holding substantial misconceptions about aliasing in Java, despite taking several programming courses (and having other experiences) that used the language (Fisler, Krishnamurthi, & Tunnell Wilson, 2017). As students move beyond the first year or into jobs, they often learn new programming languages. Do students take their old notional machines with them, even if the new languages have different features that contradict the behavior of the notional machine that they knew? How do we teach students to adapt existing models to accommodate new features? How do we migrate students to an entirely new notional machine when needed (such as when moving from non-reactive to reactive programming) or when starting to confront parallelism? There are significant **open problems** and opportunities for research that explore how notional machines and students' informal programming models can and do evolve across languages, features, and complexity of problems.

13.6.3 Visual and Blocks-Based Languages

Blocks-based or visual notations provide a significantly different user interface than textual languages. These notations do not inherently correspond to new language features. Visual notations can, however, have rich interactions with behavior that affect how users interact with or evaluate programs. Early work in visual languages used spatial relationships among syntactic features to convey semantic relationships between concepts and constructs (Haarslev, 1995). Different visual notations were suited to reflecting different semantic relationships. In some languages (Kahn & Saraswat, 1990), program execution was reflected in transformations of the visual notation (similar in spirit to what a substitution model [Felleisen & Hieb, 1992; Plotkin, 1975] allows); in such cases, the program syntax also provided syntax for the state of the notional machine. Sorva's dissertation (2012) provides a detailed discussion of tools and taxonomies for integrating visual representations with behavior or program evaluation in a pedagogical context.

Blocks languages such as Scratch, Alice, Snap!, and Blockly use visual representations to simplify syntax and convey grammatical features, rather than to illustrate behavior or program execution. Blocks syntax for imperative languages, for example, uses different shapes or connectors to distinguish statements (such as assignment operators or control flow) from value-producing expressions. In contrast, blocks syntax for a functional language might use color or shape to distinguish data types, restricting block nesting to cases in which the expected and provided types match up (Code.org, n.d.; Schanzer, Krishnamurthi, & Fisler, 2015; Vasek, 2012). Blocks typically introduce an additional syntactic layer between the programmer and an underlying textual language (used for compilation or interpretation): this provides expressive flexibility for designers of blocks languages to create constructs or keywords from natural-language phrases that may not exist in an underlying textual language (Weintrop & Wilensky, 2015a).

Multiple studies contrast blocks and textual languages and find differences with respect to misconceptions, program comprehension, and learning outcomes. Weintrop and Wilensky (2015b, 2017a) tested high school students on program-tracing questions given in each of Java syntax and Snap!. Students generally performed better with blocks. The reason, however, may be due to issues beyond the mere use of blocks. For example, Snap! labels its repetition block as `repeat`, while Java uses `for`: studies of loop naming in textual languages suggest that `for` is not an intuitive term for repetition among novice programmers (du Boulay, 1986; Stefik & Gellenbeck, 2011). A follow-up study contrasted student work using isomorphic blocks and textual environments; students in the blocks condition performed better on a content assessment than those in the text condition (Weintrop & Wilensky, 2017a). This study identified some concrete affordances of blocks. For example, students were more likely to (correctly) assert that only one branch of an `if/else` expression would be evaluated when working in block syntax. This may be due to the shapes of blocks, in which a multiline statement or expression is part of a single visual element, rather than spread across separate lines of text. Other observations about misconceptions around variables and function calls appear *attributable* to block syntax features (Weintrop & Wilensky, 2015b). Grover and Basu (2017) found misconceptions about variables and loops in their study of block syntax with middle school students. Lewis (2010) contrasted attitudinal and learning outcomes between Scratch and Logo with 10–12-year-old novice programmers. The Scratch students showed improved performance at interpreting the behavior of conditionals, but not at interpreting loops. These studies reinforce the notion that blocks do not inherently address long-standing challenges that students have with comprehending and evaluating core programming constructs.

Students who continue beyond an early blocks-based introduction to computing confront the transition to textual syntax. This transition is multifaceted: while the syntax clearly changes, the notional machine may change as well if the textual language has a richer or different feature set. In addition, the switch to textual syntax often accompanies an increased complexity in programming tasks. The program construction habits that students developed for simple blocks programs may not scale to larger problems, a problem that Meerbaum-Salant et al. (2011) observed with Scratch students. Powers, Ecott, and Hirshfield (2007) tracked issues that arose as tertiary students transitioned from Alice to one of Java or C++. They hypothesized that differences in code organization between the Alice IDE (which uses different panels for different concepts) and textual code might explain the considerable difficulties that students demonstrated in writing and understanding the textual programs. Armoni, Meerbaum-Salant, and Ben-Ari (2015) did not observe such problems when using Scratch as the initial blocks language with middle school students (who later transitioned to C++ or Java). Their data show students performing better on questions about looping when working in Scratch (a result that contradicts that of Lewis, 2010), though measures on other constructs were not statistically significant. These and other studies (Grover & Basu, 2017; Malan & Leitner, 2007) generally show blocks as having positive impact on some combination of performance, motivation, or retention (though not for all students, as authenticity can be a concern, as we discuss momentarily). The main takeaway from these studies is that blocks have many affordances, but also some notable challenges in the larger scope of early computing education.

Several efforts attempt to ease the transition through hybrid environments that allow students to switch between blocks and textual notation: some hybrid tools interleave blocks and textual notation (Bau et al., 2015; Kölling, Brown, & Altadrmi, 2015; Mönig, 2015), while others let students switch their view of the same code between blocks and textual syntax (Bau et al., 2015; Homer & Noble, 2014). Ongoing research into the affordances of each modality considers many criteria, including student learning gains, attitudes, and preferences (Weintrop & Wilensky, 2017b). Evidence suggests that the hybrid tools enable students to construct code more quickly and with fewer errors than in purely textual tools (Price et al., 2016), but each modality appears to support some tasks and goals better than the other (Weintrop & Wilensky, 2017b). In general, careful attention to pedagogy and design is needed to create tools through which students learn to migrate across notations (Dann et al., 2012).

Although much of the research on blocks focuses on students' initial programming experience, some work looks at the longer-term impacts of starting in blocks. Weintrop and Wilensky's (2017a) studies with high school students showed that differences between starting in blocks versus text faded after ten weeks of programming in Java. This suggests that blocks may not be as critical for all student audiences. Another concern arises from a human-factor perspective. Students gain more confidence, and sometimes interest, in programming when they perceive what they are learning as authentic (relative to their perceptions of programming practice) (Lewis et al., 2014). Both DiSalvo's (2012) Glitch Game Testers work and Weintrop and Wilensky's (2015a) studies with high school students reveal that students sometimes view blocks as an inauthentic programming experience. Identifying an appropriate interplay of textual and visual notations in early programming education thus remains an important **open problem** for future research.

13.6.4 Accessibility of Program Authoring and Environments

Discussions about learning languages can easily mask hidden assumptions that all programmers are similarly abled. Programming notations, whether text or blocks, tend to rely on the ability to manipulate code visually. Drag-and-drop programming tools demand fine motor skills. Cognitive loads from debugging could differ dramatically across users who process information differently, simply based on the nature or amount of information that an IDE expects a programmer to remember. A programmer may not know the human language or alphabet from which keywords are taken, thus depriving them of context. Supporting differently abled users obviously depends on interface design for IDEs, but technical decisions regarding syntax and behavior can limit or enhance how interface designers support differently abled users. In keeping with this chapter's focus on behavioral features, we focus this section on the interplay of technical decisions, interface decisions, and user abilities.

Most IDEs require users to leverage sight to navigate through and skim code, to scan a display of options in interfaces that support discoverability, and to validate code while typing. To communicate with visually impaired users, IDEs use auditory information, often delivered through screen readers. Reading code one token at a time, however, provides too much information for high-level navigation and comprehension tasks (Stefik, 2008). Effective auditory tools instead attempt to convey high-level code structure (Baker, Milne, & Ladner, 2015). Abstract syntax trees (ASTs) capture this structure, but ASTs are difficult to create for in-progress or buggy programs that don't properly parse (an issue that can arise with textual but not blocks syntax). So-called bicameral syntax (Krishnamurthi, 2006) – such as the parenthetical structure of Lisp-ish languages or the distinction between well-formedness and validity in XML – splits adherence to the grammar into two phases rather than one. This provides an intermediate level of lexical structure, which can enable navigation of code that satisfies the intermediate syntax even though it does not yet properly parse. Quorum (Stefik, 2008) uses particular keyword orders to direct screen readers to relevant tokens through which to convey code structure (without requiring bicameral syntax). Languages designed to interface with screen readers must consider the representation of program output as well as source code: if a program produces a tree, an image, or a video, for example, the screen reader must be able to explain all of those outputs to a user (Bootstrap, 2017).

Research on instructional design (Mayer & Moreno, 2003) shows that users with full access to both their visual and auditory channels can process information from both channels simultaneously. Some tools (Stefik & Gellenbeck, 2009) provide both verbal and auditory information during program execution, finding that purely auditory tools are less effective for sighted users. Stefik, Hundhausen, and Patterson (2011) found that well-designed auditory cues could enable (sighted) users to approach the effectiveness of programmers working without visual cues. More novel approaches have attempted to create musical renditions to communicate program execution behavior (Vickers & Alty, 2002). How to convey program execution and notional machines for differently abled users is a significant **open question**.

Other substantial other work in IDE design impacts how differently abled users construct (rather than read) programs. These include creating structured editors or simplified spoken-language commands to enable voice-driven code construction (Begel & Graham, 2005), internationalization support to customize menu entries, replacing English keywords with ones in other languages, or writing new languages for speakers of human languages other than English. These efforts are too broad to treat comprehensively in this chapter, but they represent the myriad ways in which designers of languages and tools can accommodate the needs of diverse users.

In short, language design for differently abled users is an **open area**. Accessible interfaces cannot simply be bolted onto existing designs: language design determines what needs to be communicated in the first place, which in turn affects the mechanisms that can be used. Developing programs requires tasks beyond coding – such as tracing, debugging, and navigating documentation – that require tool support (Ko, Myers, & Aung, 2004). Practitioners should consider the needs of users and students when selecting tools. Researchers should assess the abilities being assumed in their tool designs, both theoretically and with user studies. Such studies have value beyond supporting accessibility: tools that accommodate users with severe impairments often benefit significant numbers of users with milder, less visible impairments of the same type, as well as non-impaired users (a user interface design principle called Universal Design; Mace, Hardie, & Place, 1991).

13.7 Long-Running Debates and Questions

Many topics in computing education have been discussed for a long time and at great length, but remain unresolved. Several of these pertain to language features, either directly or indirectly. We briefly discuss a few of these that fit particularly well with the themes of this chapter.

13.7.1 Objects-First Debate

Introductory CS pedagogy largely used procedural languages (such as COBOL, Basic, Pascal, and C) until the late 1990s. As C++ and Java gained hold in industry, both industry partners and parents pressured schools to transition to teaching OO in CS1 (de Raadt, Watson, & Toleman, 2002). Independently, some instructors began questioning whether OO programming could foster better software design skills than procedural programming in CS1 students (Decker & Hirshfield, 1994). The resulting educational interest in OO led to significant discussion of the affordances and limitations of *objects-first* or *objects-early* pedagogies and curricula. Although objects-early pedagogies frequently use Java (which really presents a *class*-oriented view of programming rather than a purely *object*-oriented one), many languages support programming with classes and objects. Different instructors have used the term "objects-early" for at least three different curricular goals: using objects, defining and implementing classes, and using other features of OO (such as inheritance) (Bennedsen & Schulte, 2007).

Proponents of objects-early claim that classes and objects effectively model real-life problems and interactions (Hu, 2004), which should enable introductory courses to motivate and situate content better than with procedural languages. Some researchers have questioned whether OO is indeed a natural way for humans to view systems (Pane, Ratanamahatan, & Myers, 2001). Furthermore, not all data that get modeled through objects have real-world analogues. Skeptics of objects-first argued that focusing on objects early squeezes out time used for basic programming constructs (Reges, 2006) and algorithmic thinking and problem-solving (Lister et al., 2006). Programming with objects can involve both basic imperative constructs as well as defining methods (functions), leading some to question whether OO demands more than either imperative or functional programming would (Cooper, Dann, & Pausch, 2003; Sajaniemi & Kuittinen, 2008). A notional machine that supports objects is more complicated than one supporting only procedures over atomic data (Sajaniemi & Kuittinen, 2008). Different researchers have argued for different notional machines for objects: some based just on message passing, others on conventional models of state (Sorva, 2012). In 2004, a heated debate about objects-first erupted on the Special Interest Group in Computer Science Education (SIGCSE) email list: Bruce (2005) summarized the discussion in an article that touches on teacher preparation, IDEs, order of content, OO learning goals, and other factors that faculty use in considering first programming languages. The summary also called for educational research to study questions about first programming languages more systematically.

Research on the objects-first debate largely attempted to compare objects to procedural programming for introductory students. Wiedenbeck and colleagues showed that students instructed in a procedural pedagogy were better at comprehending (short) programs than students instructed in an objects-early pedagogy, though students instructed in an objects-early pedagogy were better at understanding functions at the individual class level (Wiedenbeck & Ramalingam, 1999; Wiedenbeck et al., 1999). Yet other studies (Ehlert & Schulte, 2009; Vilner, Zur, & Gal-Ezer, 2007) have shown that objects-first versus objects-later leads to similar learning gains. Students in these populations differ only in terms of perceived difficulty of topics. Additionally, the amount of scaffolding

required for teaching objects early is greater than that for a procedural pedagogy (Nordström & Börstler, 2011). Some argue that instructors have to work
harder in order to come up with pedagogically appropriate examples when
starting with objects (Nordström & Börstler, 2011). Ideally, studies would also
examine the cognitive load of starting with objects. One study (with upper-level
software engineering students) has shown that inheritance leads to increased
mental overheads (Cartwright, 1998), but not all objects-first curricula address
inheritance early on.

Objects are sometimes taught with visual environments that illustrate the
behavior of programs. The Alice programming environment (www.alice.
org) teaches programming in the context of microworlds, where each visible
entity in the world corresponds to an object within an OO program. Cooper,
Dann, and Pausch (2003) argue that visualizations and simulations are an
important technique for controlling the complexity that students would otherwise have to confront when working with objects early in their programming
education.

Despite the amount of work published on both sides of the debate, there is
no definitive evidence that objects-early is better than procedural or some other
approach (Bailie et al., 2003; Sajaniemi & Kuittinen, 2008; Tew, McCracken, &
Guzdial, 2005). One key challenge in studying this question arises because an
objects-first curriculum may focus on different skills or styles of programs than
curricula that start with other approaches: these differences can make it hard to
run studies in which students from different approaches are asked to attempt the
same questions. Given that studies have nevertheless compared objects-early to
imperative counterparts, it is unclear why there are few if any studies against the
long-standing tradition of teaching functional programming. Conducting them
remains an **open problem**.

Similar questions about commensurability arose in earlier language choice
debates as well (Brilliant & Wiseman, 1996; Johnson, 1995). Social factors (such
as which languages have currency in industry) may also affect linguistic choices
in some settings. This is a different aspect of the debate that arises as people
discuss the rationale for broad efforts to expose all students to computing
(Guzdial, 2015).

13.7.2 Repetition: Iteration, Recursion, and More

Repetition is a central concept in programming: processing a collection of
data requires some form of repetition. A long-standing debate has been which
forms of repetition to use. Most curricula focus heavily on *iteration*, as manifest in features like loops, while some curricula depend instead on *recursion*,
characterized by procedures that directly or indirectly invoke themselves.
A great deal of literature has been written about the differences between the two
(see Chapter 27). Rather than recapitulate this literature, we instead highlight
important issues that arise from a programming languages perspective, but have
been largely overlooked in existing research.

- The study of recursion has been negatively impacted by inane examples such as Fibonacci and factorial functions, which have little computational value and confuse issues such as performance with the notion of recursion. In contrast, recursion arises naturally in the processing of recursive *data* such as trees or recursively defined lists. Since many introductory curricula do not cover these data, the research literature on this topic is often missing the point of using recursion in the first place.
- Repetition often interacts in interesting ways with mutation. For instance, consider building a calculator application, which displays a panel of ten buttons, pressing each of which prints the corresponding digit. One might write the following loop:

```
for (i = 0; i < 10; i ++):
  buttons[i].set-handler(lambda(): print i)
```

Contrast this to the seemingly equivalent recursive solution:

```
map(lambda(i): buttons[i].set-handler(lambda(): print i),
    [0 .. 9])
```

The latter program works exactly as desired, but the former program, when run in a conventional imperative setting, is buggy: every button will result in the output 10, because of aliasing (Section 13.2). (The reader may find it instructive to consider why these programs behave as they do.)
- Even the study of recursion on recursive data has important distinctions. A *structurally* recursive solution follows the structure of the data precisely – just as a loop does over a linear structure – resulting in simpler code and predictable performance and termination. A *generatively* recursive solution computationally creates new sub-problems on recursive calls and hence lacks the advantages of structural recursion (Felleisen et al., 2001). Therefore, structural recursion is much simpler and a gentler way to introduce students to recursion, while still enabling sophisticated programs. Unfortunately, many popular introductory recursive problems (such as fractals, Euclid's algorithm, Newton–Raphson, etc.) are generative, thereby creating artificial complexity that confuses the outcome of studies.

In addition to iteration and recursion, there are more forms of repetition used widely in programming, but rarely studied in introductory programming. For instance, programmers in languages from Haskell to Python can use *comprehensions*, which are inspired by the mathematical notation of set theory. Big data programmers use abstractions such as MapReduce (Dean & Ghemawat, 2008) that consume high-level descriptions of behavior. The users of these abstractions do not perform explicit iteration, as that is hidden inside the implementation of the abstraction, freeing it up to parallelize and otherwise optimize execution. Similarly, every database programmer using SQL makes extensive use of repetition patterns through queries. To an iterative thinker, a query might look like loops, and to a recursive thinker, they might appear to be higher-order recursive operators, but the query writer does not write any explicit repetition at all. Thus, students exposed to SQL-style interfaces can possibly begin to program repetition – and hence tackle interesting data sets – quickly and with a much higher-level notional machine that does more behind the scenes. (Curricula that use high-level operators before teaching iteration or recursion include Harvey and Wright's [1999] *Simply Scheme* and Bootstrap:Data Science [Bootstrap, 2018], both of which use high-level operators before teaching iteration or recursion.) As computing curricula increasingly embrace big data, the need for alternative and richer notions of repetition will grow in importance.

13.7.3 Plan Composition

Soloway (1986) proposed the Rainfall Problem in the early 1980s in the context of studying how students composed code for the subtasks of a problem into a cohesive program (a process he termed *plan composition*). Roughly, the Rainfall Problem asks for the average of non-negative numbers that occur in the input before some sentinel value (such as –999). Soloway's group introduced a rich vocabulary of *plans*, *goals*, *mechanisms*, and *explanations* (Soloway, 1986). Their finding that students struggled to develop solutions to this problem spawned many subsequent efforts to understand students' successes and failures with so-called *plan composition*, with multiple studies corroborating the initial results (Ebrahimi, 1994; Simon, 2013).

By and large, the first 25 years of research on plan composition did not consider the influence of programming languages on how students structure code. Ebrahimi (1994) considered that language might make a difference and had students trained in different programming languages solve the Rainfall Problem; the results were uniformly weak across languages. However, Ebrahimi's students worked within the imperative model in each language (including Lisp), rather than considering other models such as functional; this limited the potential impact of looking at different languages. In 2014, Fisler (2014) published the first study of the Rainfall Problem with students who were trained in functional programming (with higher-order functions and without assignment statements, using the *How to Design Programs* curriculum; Felleisen et al., 2001). The students in her study performed much better than in prior studies; more interestingly, however, these students produced solutions with very different high-level structures and task clustering than in earlier studies. In particular, whereas students in earlier studies tried to solve the entire problem in a single traversal of the data (using a `for` or `while` loop), Fisler's participants often used built-in or higher-order functions to implement some subtasks. This created solutions that performed multiple passes over the input data, often to clean out unwanted data before computing the average.

Subsequent studies of the Rainfall Problem in diverse programming paradigms (Fisler, Krishnamurthi, & Siegmund, 2016; Seppälä et al., 2015) suggest that languages affect planning in the following two ways: different languages have different idioms and provide different built-ins. FP teaches students to compose short functions for specific tasks; this style often creates intermediate data. With procedural programming, students often learn to create fixed-size arrays. For typical planning programs, the sizes of intermediate arrays are often only determined on the fly; this could steer students away from multi-traversal solutions. Students who know library functions that transform entire lists or strings may use them instead of creating loops to manually traverse these data structures as arrays; in a later study (Fisler, Krishnamurthi, & Siegmund, 2016), students working in Java who knew such library functions produced multi-traversal solutions akin to those in functional programming. Iterators with task-specific or semantically rich names such as `map` and `filter` may suggest different decompositions than generically named constructs such as `for`. Efforts to teach novices named patterns (Muller, Ginat, & Haberman, 2007) and strategies (de Raadt, Watson, & Toleman, 2009) have shown promise in helping students implement multitask programs from the plan composition literature. The potential influence of built-in language constructs that provide these patterns has yet to be studied in detail. All of these points raise hypotheses about languages and planning that **warrant further investigation**. Such studies should also explore potential pitfalls to richer language support, such as the challenges of tracing higher-order control flows.

In summary, fine-grained details of languages and idioms – as well as problems that students have solved previously (Pirolli & Anderson, 1985; Rist, 1991; Spohrer & Soloway, 1989) – all appear to impact how students plan programs. Researchers conducting or reporting studies in this area should include details on the code patterns students were taught, the built-in operators that they had seen, and where the planning problems fit into a course's larger curricular sequence. Merely reporting on the language used for a study does not provide sufficient context.

13.8 Some (Other) Open Questions

Some linguistic topics that are highly pertinent to computing education have not gotten the attention we believe they deserve. We introduce them below as a spur to future research.

13.8.1 Sublanguages and Language Levels

Consider a typical programming textbook. It begins with a small core of a language and gradually expands the size of the language as the student progresses in their learning. Yet most language implementations (compilers, programming environments, etc.) do not mirror this growth. As a result, a student may accidentally – even by means as innocent as a typo – stumble upon parts of the language they have not been taught. This can either result in a program "working" (i.e., producing an answer, which the student has no way of understanding) or resulting in an error that can be baffling. (Similarly, an errant mouse click in an IDE may launch a tool that bewilders the student.)

As an illustrative example, consider this code fragment (taken from a classroom observation by the first author's team): a student early in the semester, tasked with computing a wage, writes the seemingly reasonable

```
wage * hours = salary
```

However, this program is meant to be in C. Not only does this not mean what they expect, in the full C language, it is actually valid to write * on the left side of an assignment, due to pointers – a concept that the student will not confront for many more months. Depending on the compiler, this can result in an error about "lvalues," a concept that may not be introduced until much later in the course, making this error message baffling to students.

We can view this problem through the lens of notional machines. Students (at least implicitly) learn notional machines as they progress through computing, and these grow increasingly sophisticated. Ideally, the language they are using matches the notional machine they have been taught until then. The errors we are discussing here are the result of a mismatch, where the implementation provides a much more complex notional machine.

As a result of such observations, many researchers have recognized (du Boulay, O'Shea, & Monk, 1999, p. 268; Findler et al., 2002; Holt & Wortman, 1974) the need for sublanguages. Some call for it because they feel that almost any programming language that is useful for constructing real systems probably also contains features that would confuse a beginner. Alternatively, they might want to present all of the language but introduce it gradually, growing the language with the student's learning. In either case, they expect the sublanguage to also provide feedback – such as error messages – at a level appropriate to the student's knowledge. In the C example above, for instance, an early language level would not have pointers at all, the grammar of assignment would be restricted, and the compiler would be expected to report that expressions can only go on the right of an assignment. In short, the notional machine provided by the implementation would match that being used in education.

There are many ways to design restricted languages. As the example above shows, it could be based on syntactic complexity or the omission of certain features. One particularly useful design criterion – consistent with the principles of this chapter – is to layer the complexity of the notional machine. In DrRacket (Findler et al., 2002), for instance, progressive student levels correspond to increasingly complex notional machines, with concepts like mutation and aliasing – which require a much more detailed notional machine, one that effectively reveals memory layout – appearing only after students have gained familiarity with basic programming techniques.

13.8.2 Errors and Error Messages

Programming environments present error messages in response to several kinds of errors, including syntax errors, type errors, and run-time errors. (In languages with suitable support, there could also be test failure errors [Felleisen et al., 2014], algorithm errors [Rivers & Koedinger, 2015; Sudol, 2011], and more). Several studies have attempted to catalog the kinds of errors that students make in different languages and curricula (Altradmri & Brown, 2015;; Hristova et al., 2003; Jackson, Cobb, & Carver, 2005; Jadud, 2006; Marceau, Fisler, & Krishnamurthi, 2011; Tirronen, Uusi-Mäkelä, & Isomöttönen, 2015). Each of syntax, semantic, and type errors arise frequently in these studies, with some variation (unsurprisingly) across programming languages (run-time errors are less frequent, as many of these studies worked with only with compilation logs).

Getting students to actually read error messages may be difficult in practice (Denny, Luxton-Reilly, & Carpenter, 2014) (though this is not necessarily true of developers; Barik et al., 2017). Some of the difficulty arguably arises from usability issues with error messages (Barik et al., 2014; Traver, 2010). In languages that support professional-grade programming, for example, error messages default to terminology that experienced programmers understand (such as "lvalue") that may be beyond novices' experience with and understanding of the language – once again reflecting a mismatch between the notional machine of the implementation and that of the education. Some projects attempt to rewrite error messages in beginner-friendly terms (Denny, Luxton-Reilly, & Carpenter, 2014), though such rewrites do not necessarily lead to reduced time to resolve errors (Denny, Luxton-Reilly, & Carpenter, 2014; Pettit, Homer, & Gee, 2017). Other projects have gone further, creating semantically meaningful subsets of languages (Section 13.8.1) that omit constructs or some behaviors of constructs to match what students have learned in various points in a curriculum; these projects produce error messages that are tailored to the language subset and student skill level. These projects use the traditional high-level user interface for error messages: a textual message anchored to a fragment of code through hyperlinks or highlights. Marceau et al. observed that highlights and anchors may have inconsistent meanings across messages within the same language (Marceau, Fisler, & Krishnamurthi, 2011), and proposed guidelines for using multiple highlights as a part of consistent principles for connecting error terminology to code.

Lee and Ko's (2011) Gidget project explores a vastly different interface for error messages, one in which the problem of debugging is framed as helping a character find problems in code. This work suggests that an anthropomorphic compiler increases users' willingness to figure out error messages. Such a tool also proposes an interface for presenting notional machines, which in turn leads to issues in debugging. Debugging is beyond the scope of this chapter, but existing surveys provide overviews of work on debugging in an educational context (Fitzgerald et al., 2008).

Overall, creating error messages that engage and support novice, casual, or end-user programmers remains an **open question** in computing education. There are many possible goals for error messages, from aiding in debugging, to identifying misconceptions, to reinforcing terminology about a language. Such work requires attention to many human-factor issues, including interface design, cognitive alignment, and user motivation; technical issues are also at play, as a user's errors may reveal misunderstandings of parsing or program execution processes that are not explicit in the user's mental model of how programs run.

13.8.3 Cost Models

A *cost model* tells us how many resources a computation will consume. We usually think of resources as time and space, but many others are also relevant, such as energy, network bandwidth, and so on.

Cost models of computation are not routinely covered in the computing education literature. This may be because so much of the literature is devoted to introductory courses, and the cost of computation – such as big-O models – is sometimes not covered at this level. However, there is some evidence that students do form opinions about the cost of computation before they have been instructed to do so and even when they are explicitly instructed to ignore it (Fisler, Krishnamurthi, & Siegmund, 2016).

Cost models are inextricably tied to notional machines, because they depend on the semantics of the language. For instance, consider the *time* cost of evaluating this expression:

```
f(g(x), h(y))
```

In most languages, each of g(x) and h(y) must first reduce to answers, which are then passed to f. Thus, the cost just to start running the body of f is the time to evaluate each of the arguments, and a constant for applying f itself. In contrast, in a *lazy* semantics (used by languages such as Haskell), neither g(x) nor h(y) is evaluated right away; rather, they are turned into closures, which take essentially constant time, before f begins to evaluate. (The full cost model is more involved.) A reactive model can be even more complicated, since it depends not only on which arguments change, but also on whether the change to the argument results in a change to the result.

A study of cost models thus parallels that of notional machines and recapitulates it. Students form their own models based on brief observations as well as commentary they hear from peers and other sources (e.g., about certain languages being "efficient" or otherwise). They sometimes form flawed models because of a simplistic understanding of the mapping of "lines of code" to operations (sometimes missing that a "line" can be complex and hence take non-constant time; Cooper et al., 2013), which in turn can impact the way they write code (Fisler, Krishnamurthi, & Siegmund, 2016). Understanding student cost models and determining how we can improve their understanding remains an **open question**.

13.8.4 Static Types

A source of some debate in programming education is when one should introduce and use static types. There are natural benefits to types: in addition to the common experience of catching errors early (Tichy & Prechelt, 1998), they also provide an alternative and simpler representation of a program's behavior, making it possible to study a program and communicate its meaning at a high level. For instance, it should be fairly clear which compositions of the following functions are valid just from their type signatures, without looking at their implementations (indeed, it may be easier from looking at the types than at the implementations):

```
open  :: () -> InputPort
close :: InputPort -> ()
read  :: InputPort -> String
```

However, types can also be viewed as problematic for a few reasons. At a time when students may already be struggling with one language, they effectively introduce a second one (Tirronen, Uusi-Mäkelä, & Isomöttönen, 2015). This language has its own grammar and its own notional machine (a type-checker traverses a program differently than does a compiler or interpreter; Krishnamurthi, 2006). Furthermore, the checker is essentially invisible except when students make an error – a time when they may already feel nervous or demoralized – and demands to be understood at this fraught time. On the other hand, by catching errors early, it saves significant time and pain later. A thorough study of these trade-offs does not seem to have been done and **remains open**.

Part of the difficulty in having a discussion about types is that it surely hinges on what notion of types is under consideration. Educators of a certain age may remember the weaknesses of Pascal's type system, which at least in some quarters earned it a reputation for inflexibility. As one of the creators of SNAP!, Brian Harvey (1993), wrote, "Pascal is part of the same machinery as hall passes, dress codes, advisors' signatures, single-sex dorms, and so on." Part of its inflexibility was due to a lack of parametric polymorphism. In contrast, parametric polymorphism is a natural part of languages like ML and Haskell. In addition, the support these languages offer for type inference lets a programmer write a function as if it has no types, and yet get the benefit of static typing (but at the cost of even more complicated type errors, a long-standing **open problem** in programming languages; Wand, 1986). Any study of types must therefore take the richness of the type system into account. Studying the use of type inference in education **remains especially open**.

13.8.5 Non-Standard Programming Models

An enormous amount of attention in computing education has focused on traditional CS1 courses. However, the context of computing is changing rapidly: some CS1 courses are evolving and new courses are being created that deserve just as much attention. Earlier, we briefly mentioned the demands of data science (Section 13.5.2). Another important topic is embedded-systems programming, which is relevant to robotics, the Internet of Things, and so on. Embedded programs are very different from traditional ones in a few ways. First, they follow an event-driven structure with inverted control (Myers, 1991). Second, they are largely non-terminating computations, with no "beginning" and "end." Third, their debugging needs are very different from those of conventional programs. In both topics, notice that the programming models may use quite different notional machines from what students are already used to, and these models of computation are far less developed in the literature. Therefore, understanding the needs, difficulties, and misconceptions of students in these courses is **wide open** and an important and pressing task.

Indeed, we will soon need to look even farther, as even the popular press has noticed (Somers, 2017). Program creation techniques such as program generation from specifications and other formal models (broadly, "synthesis"; Green, 1969) have already seen industrial success in mission-critical systems and are now reaching maturity in a variety of areas (Gulwani, Polozov, & Singh, 2017, offer a useful summary of the state of the art), fueled by advances in various computing technologies from SAT solving to machine learning (which introduce entirely new notional machines!). What synthesis techniques consume, however, are not programs in a traditional sense, but rather specifications, which are declarative and require holistic thinking about all possible behaviors of a system – an **open topic** rarely studied in computing education, though there is some knowledge in the broader computing community about the human–computer interaction challenges of these techniques (Dix, 2013). This technological advance, with the potential for wide-ranging impacts on all forms of programmers, thus represents entirely new challenges for CEdR.

13.9 Implications Moving Forward

This chapter argues that the conventional focus on "paradigms" is too limited. Today's programming languages embrace features from across the conventional paradigms, and the problems we observe in education tie more to features and particular kinds of notional machines than to the paradigms themselves.

Just as we should embrace going beyond coarse paradigms, we must also stop presenting courses and research with phrases like, "We taught the course in language X." This description is too broad. We must discuss the *features* we presented, which problems and examples our course taught and assigned, and which explanations (if not notional machines) we used to describe program behavior to students. Knowing that a course was taught in Python, for example, does not convey whether students learned imperative programming, list comprehensions, or an integration of the two, yet these distinctions are critical to understanding what kind of programming students are learning.

If we embrace that students should learn to program in different sets of linguistic features over their education, we should better understand how students do and do not evolve their understanding of notional machines and program semantics over time. There has been some work looking at how students transfer knowledge from one language to another (Scholtz & Wiedenbeck, 1990), but this work only rarely extends into upper-level curricula (Fisler, Krishnamurthi, & Tunnell Wilson, 2017) or looks at how students maintain different mental models of notional machines and language features. This is part of a broader need to extend CEdR beyond first-year courses and novice experiences.

Once we accept that different language features engender different mental models of program evaluation, our studies of how students are learning must try to account for (or at least report) the perspectives that students bring into a new course. For example, a student learning Java after a course in functional programming may well program with different patterns than a student whose prior experience was entirely imperative. Our studies need to consider what programs students had been exposed to previously and the extent to which certain problems arise more naturally with some language features than with others.

Giving up on "language-independent" programming assessments – including those using pseudocode – is another necessary casualty of embracing different models for different sets of language features. Language-"independent" assessments typically depend on a common (subset of a) notional machine, even if the surface syntax changes dramatically; this naturally leaves out all languages that aren't well explained by that machine, thereby undermining any claims of being "independent" of language. Indeed, assessments that accommodate each of imperative, functional, and reactive models after a first computing course can have little common behavior to draw on (beyond perhaps the behavior of a conditional or the interpretation of Boolean operators or a Turing machine). The AP CS Principles framework in the USA (The College Board, n.d.) is an instance of this, boxing curricula into the narrow space of imperative notional machines while claiming to be independent.

The overarching takeaway for researchers is to think more deeply about linguistic assumptions and how they interact with pedagogy of prior and current courses. For teachers, we must remember that we choose not just the syntax and IDE in which we will teach – we also choose the pedagogy, problems, and notional machine through which students experience our chosen language. As computing is applied to more and more domains, more end users become casual programmers, and more languages arise to meet these needs, CEdR gains a wealth of interesting problems to explore that are far more nuanced than that covered by our earlier conception of paradigms.

13.10 Acknowledgments

Members of our research group at Brown and WPI – Francisco Castro, Natasha Danas, Justin Pombrio, Sorawee Porncharoenwase, Preston Tunnell Wilson, and John Wrenn – were invaluable in our writing effort. Wrenn, Castro, Danas, and Tunnell Wilson helped conduct literature reviews. Wrenn, Tunnell Wilson, Danas, Pombrio, and Porncharoenwase read closely and provided numerous remarks that greatly improved the quality of this chapter. Castro, Tunnell Wilson, and Wrenn contributed to research that informed this chapter. All participated in numerous stimulating discussions about programming languages and computing education.

We sought input from research colleagues as we scoped this chapter; thanks to Mark Guzdial, Andy Ko, Andrew Luxton-Reilly, Briana Morrison, Guido Rößling, Simon of Newcastle, and Beth Simon for their thoughts on what readers would want from a chapter on this topic. David Weintrop provided multiple rounds of feedback on the details of Section 13.6.3. Colleen Lewis, Andy Ko, Josh Tenenberg, Anthony Robins, Brian Harvey, and Sally Fincher all provided valuable feedback on drafts of this chapter.

Matthias Felleisen and Dan Friedman have influenced our thinking about languages and semantics for decades.

Our work was partially supported by US National Science Foundation grants.

References

Abelson, H., & Sussman, G. J. (1985). *Structure and Interpretation of Computer Programs*. Cambridge, MA: MIT Press.

Altadmri, A., & Brown, N. C. (2015). 37 million compilations: Investigating novice programming mistakes in large-scale student data. In *Proceedings of the ACM Symposium on Computer Science Education (SIGCSE)* (pp. 522–527). New York: ACM.

Armoni, M., Meerbaum-Salant, O., & Ben-Ari, M. (2015). From Scratch to "real" programming. *Transactions on Computing Education (TOCE)*, 14(4), 25:1–25:15.

Bailie, F., Courtney, M., Murray, K., Schiaffino, R., & Tuohy, S. (2003). Objects first – Does it work? *Journal of Computing Sciences in Small Colleges*, 19(2), 303–305.

Bainomugisha, E., Carreton, A. L., van Cutsem, T., Mostinckx, S., & de Meuter, W. (2013). A survey on reactive programming. *ACM Computing Surveys*, 45(4), 52:1–52:34.

Baker, C. M., Milne, L. R., & Ladner, R. E. (2015). StructJumper: A Tool to Help Blind Programmers Navigate and Understand the Structure of Code. In *Proceedings of the ACM Conference on Human Factors in Computing Systems* (pp. 3043–3052). New York: ACM.

Barik, T., Witschey, J., Johnson, B., & Murphy-Hill, E. (2014). Compiler error notifications revisited: An interaction-first approach for helping developers more effectively comprehend and resolve error notifications. In *Companion Proceedings of the 36th International Conference on Software Engineering (ICSE Companion)* (pp. 536–539). New York: ACM.

Barik, T., Smith, J., Lubick, K., Holmes, E., Feng, J., Murphy-Hill, E., & Parnin, C. (2017). Do developers read compiler error messages? In *International Conference on Software Engineering (ICSE)* (pp. 575–585). New York: IEEE Press.

Bau, D., Bau, D. A., Dawson, M., & Pickens, C. S. (2015). Pencil code: Block code for a text world. In *Proceedings of the International Conference on Interaction Design and Children* (pp. 445–448). New York, NY: ACM.

Begel, A., & Graham, S. L. (2005). Spoken programs. In *IEEE Symposium on Visual Languages and Human-Centric Computing (VLHCC)* (pp. 99–106). New York: IEEE Press.

Bennedsen, J., & Schulte, C. (2007). What does "objects-first" mean?: An international study of teachers' perceptions of objects-first. In *Proceedings of the Koli Calling Conference on Computing Education* (pp. 21–29). Sydney, Australia: Australian Computer Society, Inc.

Bootstrap (2017). The Bootstrap Blog–Accessibility (Part 2): Images. Retrieved from www.bootstrapworld.org/blog/accessibility/Describing-Images-Screenreaders.shtml

Bootstrap (2018). Data Science Curriculum (Spring 2018 edition). Retrieved from www.bootstrapworld.org/materials/spring2018/courses/data-science/english/

Brilliant, S. S., & Wiseman, T. R. (1996). The first programming paradigm and language dilemma. In *Proceedings of the ACM Symposium on Computer Science Education (SIGCSE)* (pp. 338–342). New York: ACM.

Bruce, K. B. (2005). Controversy on how to teach CS 1: A discussion on the SIGCSE-members mailing list. *SIGCSE Bulletin*, 37(2), 111–117.

Cartwright, M. (1998). An empirical view of inheritance. *Information and Software Technology*, 40(14), 795–799.

Code.org (n.d.). Computer Science in Algebra. Retrieved from https://code.org/curriculum/algebra

Cooper, G. H., Guha, A., Krishnamurthi, S., McCarthy, J., & Findler, R. B. (2013). Teaching garbage collection without implementing compilers or interpreters. In *Proceedings of the ACM Symposium on Computer Science Education (SIGCSE)* (pp. 385–390). New York: ACM.

Cooper, K. D., Hall, M. W., Hood, R. T., Kennedy, K., McKinley, K. S., Mellor-Crummey, J. M., Torczon, L., & Warren, S. K. (1993). The ParaScope parallel programming environment. *Proceedings of the IEEE*, 81(2), 244–263.

Cooper, S., Dann, W., & Pausch, R. (2003). Teaching objects-first in introductory computer science. In *Proceedings of the ACM Symposium on Computer Science Education (SIGCSE)* (pp. 191–195). New York: ACM.

Dann, W., Cosgrove, D., Slater, D. Culyba, D., & Cooper, S. (2012). Mediated transfer: Alice 3 to Java. In *Proceedings of the ACM Symposium on Computer Science Education (SIGCSE)* (pp. 141–146). New York: ACM.

de Raadt, M., Watson, R., & Toleman, M. (2002). Language trends in introductory programming courses. In *Proceedings of Informing Science* (pp. 329–337). Santa Rosa, CA: Informing Science Institute.

de Raadt, M., Watson, R., & Toleman, M. (2009). Teaching and assessing programming strategies explicitly. In *Proceedings of the Australasian Computing Education Conference (ACE)* (pp. 45–54). Sydney, Australia: Australian Computer Society, Inc.

Dean, J., & Ghemawat, S. (2008). MapReduce: simplified data processing on large clusters. In *Communications of the ACM*, 51(1), 107–113.

Decker, R., & Hirshfield, S. (1994). The top 10 reasons why object-oriented programming can't be taught in CS 1. In *Proceedings of the ACM Symposium on Computer Science Education (SIGCSE)* (pp. 51–55). New York: ACM.

Denny, P., Luxton-Reilly, A., & Carpenter, D. (2014). Enhancing syntax error messages appears ineffectual. In *Proceedings of the SIGCSE Conference on Innovation and Technology in Computer Science Education (ITiCSE)* (pp. 273–278). New York: ACM.

DiSalvo, B. (2012). *Glitch game testers: the design and study of a learning environment for computational production with young African American males* (PhD thesis). Georgia Institute of Technology.

diSessa, A. A., & Abelson, H. (1986). Boxer: A reconstructible computational medium. *Communications of the ACM*, 29(9), 859–868.

Dix, A. J. (2013). Formal methods. In *The Encyclopedia of Human–Computer Interaction*, 2nd edn. Aarhus, Denmark: The Interaction Design Foundation, Article 29.

du Boulay, B. (1986). Some difficulties of learning to program. *Journal of Educational Computing Research*, 2(1), 57–73.

du Boulay, B., O'Shea, T., & Monk, J. (1999). The black box inside the glass box. *International Journal of Human–Computer Studies*, 51(2), 265–277.

Ebrahimi, A. (1994). Novice programmer errors: language constructs and plan composition. *International Journal of Human–Computer Studies*, 41, 457–480.

Eckerdal, A., & Thune, M. (2005). Novice Java programmers conceptions of object and class, and variation theory. *SIGCSE Bulletin*, 37(3), 89–93.

Ehlert, A., & Schulte, C. (2009). Empirical comparison of objects-first and objects-later. In *Proceedings of the Conference on International Computing Education Research (ICER)* (pp. 15–26). New York: ACM.

Felleisen, M., & Hieb, R. (1992). The revised report on the syntactic theories of sequential control and state. *Theoretical Computer Science*, 102, 235–271.

Felleisen, M., Findler, R. B., Flatt, M., & Krishnamurthi, S. (2001). *How to Design Programs*. Cambridge, MA: MIT Press.

Felleisen, M., Findler, R. B., Flatt, M. & Krishnamurthi, S. (2009). A functional I/O system or, fun for freshman kids. In *Proceedings of the 14th ACM SIGPLAN International Conference on Functional Programming* (ICFP '09) (pp. 47–58). New York, NY: ACM.

Felleisen, M., Findler, R. B., Flatt, M., & Krishnamurthi, S. (2014). *How to Design Programs*, 2nd edn. Cambridge, MA: MIT Press.

Findler, R. B., Clements, J., Flanagan, C., Flatt, M., Krishnamurthi, S., Steckler, P., & Felleisen, M. (2002). DrScheme: A programming environment for Scheme. *Journal of Functional Programming*, 12(2), 159–182.

Fisler, K. (2014). The recurring Rainfall Problem. In *Proceedings of the Conference on International Computing Education Research (ICER)* (pp. 35–42). New York: ACM.

Fisler, K., Krishnamurthi, S., & Siegmund, J. (2016). Modernizing plan-composition studies. In *Proceedings of the ACM Symposium on Computer Science Education (SIGCSE)* (pp. 211–216). New York: ACM.

Fisler, K., Krishnamurthi, S., & Tunnell Wilson, P. (2017). Assessing and teaching scope, mutation, and aliasing in upper-level undergraduates. In *Proceedings of the ACM Symposium on Computer Science Education (SIGCSE)* (pp. 213–218). New York: ACM.

Fitter, M. (1979). Towards more natural interactive systems. *International Journal of Man-Machine Studies*, 11(3), 339–350.

Fitzgerald, S., Lewandowski, G., McCauley, R., Murphy, L., Simon, B., Thomas, L., & Zander, C. (2008). Debugging: finding, fixing and flailing, a multi-institutional study of novice debuggers. *Computer Science Education*, 18(2), 93–116.

Flatt, M., Krishnamurthi, S., & Felleisen, M. (1998). Classes and mixins. In *ACM SIGPLAN-SIGACT Symposium on Principles of Programming Languages* (pp. 171–183). New York: ACM.

Fleury, A. E. (1991). Parameter passing: The rules the students construct. In *Proceedings of the ACM Symposium on Computer Science Education (SIGCSE)* (pp. 283–286). New York: ACM.

Freeman, S., Eddy, S. L., McDonough, M., Smith, M. K., Okoroafor, N., Jordt, H., & Wenderotha, M. P. (2014). Active learning increases student performance in science, engineering, and mathematics. *Proceedings of the National Academy of Sciences of the United States of America*, 111(23), 8410–8415.

Goldman, K., Gross, P., Heeren, C., Herman, G. L., Kaczmarczyk, L., Loui, M. C., & Zilles, C. (2010). Setting the scope of concept inventories for introductory computing subjects. *Transactions on Computing Education (TOCE)*, 10(2), 5:1–5:29.

Gosling, J., Joy, B., Steele, Jr., G. L., Bracha, G., & Buckley, A. (2015). *The Java Language Specification, Java SE 8 Edition*. Redwood Shores, CA: Oracle America, Inc.

Green, C. C. (1969). Application of theorem proving to problem solving. In *International Joint Conference on Artificial Intelligence* (pp. 219–239). San Francisco, CA: Morgan Kaufmann Publishers Inc.

Greening, T. (1999). Emerging constructivist forces in computer science education: Shaping a new future. In T. Greening (Ed.), *Computer Science Education in the 21st Century* (pp. 47–80). Berlin, Germany: Springer.

Grover, S., & Basu, S. (2017). Measuring student learning in introductory block-based programming: Examining misconceptions of loops, variables, and Boolean logic. In *Proceedings of the ACM Symposium on Computer Science Education (SIGCSE)* (pp. 267–272). New York: ACM.

Guha, A., Saftoiu, C., & Krishnamurthi, S. (2010). The essence of JavaScript. In *European Conference on Object-Oriented Programming (ECOOP)* (pp. 126–150). Berlin, Germany: Springer-Verlag.

Gulwani, S., Polozov, O., & Singh, R. (2017). Program synthesis. *Foundations and Trends in Programming Languages*, 4(1–2), 1–119.

Gupta, A., Hammer, D., & Redish, E. F. (2010). The case for dynamic models of learners' ontologies in physics. *Journal of the Learning Sciences*, 19, 285–321.

Guzdial, M. (2015). *Learner-Centered Design of Computing Education: Research on Computing for Everyone*. San Rafael, CA: Morgan and Claypool.

Haarslev, V. (1995). Formal semantics of visual languages using spatial reasoning. In *Proceedings of the IEEE Symposium on Visual Languages* (pp. 156–163). New York: IEEE Press.

Harvey, B. (1993. Discussion forum comment on comp. lang. scheme. Retrieved from https://groups.google.com/forum/#!msg/comp.lang.scheme/zZRSDcZdV2M/MZJLiU6gE64J

Harvey, B., & Wright, M. (1999). *Simply Scheme: Introducing Computer Science*, 2nd edn. Cambridge, MA: MIT Press.

Holt, R. C., & Wortman, D. B. (1974). A sequence of structured subsets of PL/I. *SIGCSE Bulletin*, 6(1), 129–132.

Homer, M., & Noble, J. (2014). Combining tiled and textual views of code. In *IEEE Working Conference on Software Visualization (VISSOFT)* (pp. 1–10). New York: IEEE Press.

Hristova, M., Misra, A., Rutter, M., & Mercuri, R. (2003). Identifying and correcting Java programming errors for introductory computer science students.

In *Proceedings of the ACM Symposium on Computer Science Education (SIGCSE)*. New York: ACM.

Hu, C. (2004). Rethinking of teaching objects-first. *Education and Information Technologies*, 9(3), 209–218.

Hundhausen, C. D., Douglas, S. A., & Stasko, J. T. (2002). A meta-study of algorithm visualization effectiveness. *Journal of Visual Languages and Computing*, 13(3), 259–290.

Jackson, J., Cobb, M., & Carver, C. (2005). Identifying top Java errors for novice programmers. In *Frontiers in Education* (FIE '05) (pp. T4C:24-T4C:27). New York, NY: IEEE.

Jadud, M. C. (2006). Methods and tools for exploring novice compilation behaviour. In *Proceedings of the Conference on International Computing Education Research (ICER)* (pp. 73–84). New York: ACM.

Johnson, L. F. (1995). C in the first course considered harmful. *Communications of the ACM*, 38(5), 99–101.

Kahn, K. M., & Saraswat, V. A. (1990). *Complete Visualizations of Concurrent Programs and Their Executions. Tech. Rept. SSL-90-38 [P90-00099]*. Palo Alto, CA: Xerox Palo Alto Research Center.

Kay, A. C. (1993). The early history of Smalltalk. In *ACM SIGPLAN Conference on History of Programming Languages* (pp. 69–95). New York: ACM.

Kelleher, C., & Pausch, R. (2005). Lowering the barriers to programming: A taxonomy of programming environments and languages for novice programmers. *ACM Computing Surveys*, 37(2), 83–137.

Kessel, C. J., & Wickens, C. D. (1982). The transfer of failure-detection skills between monitoring and controlling dynamic systems. *Human Factors*, 24(1), 49–60.

Ko, A. J., Myers, B. A., & Aung, H. (2004). Six learning barriers in end-user programming systems. In *IEEE Symposium on Visual Languages and Human-Centric Computing (VLHCC)* (pp. 199–206). New York: IEEE Press.

Kölling, M., Brown, N. C. C., & Altadmri, A. (2015). Frame-based editing: Easing the transition from blocks to text-based programming. In *Workshop in Primary and Secondary Computing Education* (pp. 29–38). New York, NY: ACM.

Krishnamurthi, S. (2006). Programming Languages: Application and Interpretation. Retrieved from www.cs.brown.edu/~sk/Publications/Books/ProgLangs/

Krishnamurthi, S. (2008). Teaching programming languages in a post-Linnaean age. In *SIGPLAN Notices*, 43(11), 81–83.

Lee, M. J., & Ko, A. J. (2011). Personifying programming tool feedback improves novice programmers' learning. In *Proceedings of the Conference on International Computing Education Research (ICER)* (pp. 109–116). New York: ACM.

Lewis, C., Esper, S., Bhattacharyya, V., Fa-Kaji, N., Dominguez, N., & Schlesinger, A. (2014). Children's perceptions of what counts as a programming language. *Journal of Computing Sciences in Colleges*, 29(4), 123–133.

Lewis, C. M. (2010). How programming environment shapes perception, learning and goals: Logo vs. Scratch. In *Proceedings of the ACM Symposium on Computer Science Education (SIGCSE)* (pp. 346–350). New York: ACM.

Lister, R., Berglund, A., Clear, T., Bergin, J., Garvin-Doxas, K., Hanks, B., Hitchner, L., Luxton-Reilly, A., Sanders, K., Schulte, C., & Whalley, J. L. (2006). Research perspectives on the objects-early debate. In *Working Group Reports on ITiCSE on Innovation and Technology in Computer Science Education* (pp. 146–165). New York: ACM.

Ma, L. (2007). *Investigating and Improving Novice Programmers Mental Models of Programming Concepts* (PhD thesis). University of Strathclyde, Department of Computer & Information Sciences.

Mace, R. L., Hardie, G. J., & Place, J. P. (1991). Accessible environments: Toward universal design. In W. E. Preiser, J. C. Vischer, & E. T. White (Eds.), *Design Intervention: Toward a More Humane Architecture* (pp. 155–176). Reinhold, NY: Van Nostrand.

Malan, D. J., & Leitner, H. H. (2007). Scratch for budding computer scientists. *SIGCSE Bulletin*, 39(1), 223–227.

Marceau, G., Fisler, K., & Krishnamurthi, S. (2011). Measuring the effectiveness of error messages designed for novice programmers. In *Proceedings of the ACM Symposium on Computer Science Education (SIGCSE)* (pp. 499–504). New York: ACM.

Mayer, R. E., & Moreno, R. (2003). Nine ways to reduce cognitive load in multimedia learning. *Educational Psychologist*, 38(1), 43–52.

McCauley, R., Hanks, B., Fitzgerald, S., & Murphy, L. (2015). Recursion vs. iteration: An empirical study of comprehension revisited. In *Proceedings of the ACM Symposium on Computer Science Education (SIGCSE)* (pp. 350–355). New York: ACM.

Meerbaum-Salant, O., Armoni, M., & Ben-Ari, M. (2011). Habits of programming in Scratch. In *Proceedings of the SIGCSE Conference on Innovation and Technology in Computer Science Education (ITiCSE)* (pp. 168–172). New York: ACM.

Miller, L. A. (1974). Programming by non-programmers. *International Journal of Man Machine Studies*, 6, 237–260.

Miller, L. A. (1975). Naive programmer problems with specification of transfer-of-control. In *Proceedings of the National Computer Conference and Exposition* (pp. 657–663). New York: ACM.

Miller, L. A. (1981). Natural language programming: Styles, strategies, and contrasts. *IBM Systems Journal*, 20, 184–215.

Miller, M. S., Von Dincklage, D., Ercegovac, V., & Chin, B. (2017). Uncanny valleys in declarative language design. In *LIPIcs-Leibniz International Proceedings in Informatics*, Vol. 71 (pp. 9:1–9:12). Wadern, Germany: Schloss Dagstuhl-Leibniz-Zentrum fuer Informatik.

Mönig, J., Ohshima, Y., & Maloney, J. (2015). Blocks at your fingertips: Blurring the line between blocks and text in GP. In *Proceedings of the Blocks and Beyond Workshop* (pp. 51–53). New York, NY: IEEE.

Muller, O., Ginat, D., & Haberman, B. (2007). Pattern-oriented instruction and its inuence on problem decomposition and solution construction. In *Proceedings of the SIGCSE Conference on Innovation and Technology in Computer Science Education (ITiCSE)* (pp. 151–155). New York: ACM.

Myers, B. A. (1991). Separating application code from toolkits: Eliminating the spaghetti of call-backs. In *ACM Symposium on User Interface Software and Technology* (pp. 211–220). New York: ACM.

Naps, T. L., Rössling, G., Almstrum, V., Dann, W., Fleischer, R., Hundhausen, C., Korhonen, A., Malmi, L., McNally, M., Rodger, S., & Velázquez-Iturbide, J. A. (2003). Exploring the role of visualization and engagement in computer science education. *SIGCSE Bulletin*, 35(2), 131–152.

Nelson, G. L., Xie, B., & Ko, A. J. (2017). Comprehension first: Evaluating a novel pedagogy and tutoring system for program tracing in CS1. In *Proceedings of the*

Conference on International Computing Education Research (ICER) (pp. 2–11). New York: ACM.

Nordström, M., & Börstler, J. (2011). Improving OO Example Programs. *IEEE Transactions on Education*, 54(10), 1–5.

Pane, J. F. (2002). *A Programming System for Children That Is Designed for Usability* (PhD thesis). Carnegie Mellon University, Computer Science Department.

Pane, J. F., Ratanamahatana, C., & Myers, B. A. (2001). Studying the language and structure in non-programmers' solutions to programming problems. *International Journal of Human-Computer Studies*, 54(2), 237–264.

Parker, M. C., Guzdial, M., & Engleman, S. (2016). Replication, Validation, and Use of a Language Independent CS1 Knowledge Assessment. In *Proceedings of the 2016 ACM Conference on International Computing Education Research (ICER)* (pp. 93–101). New York: ACM.

Pea, R. D. (1986). Language-independent conceptual "bugs" in novice programming. *Journal of Educational Computing Research*, 2(1), 25–36.

Pettit, R. S., Homer, J., & Gee, R. (2017). Do enhanced compiler error messages help students?: Results inconclusive. In *Proceedings of the ACM Symposium on Computer Science Education (SIGCSE)* (pp. 465–470). New York: ACM.

Pirolli, P. L., & Anderson, J. R. (1985). The role of learning from examples in the acquisition of recursive programming skills. *Canadian Journal of Psychology/Revue Canadienne de Psychologie*, 39(2), 240–272.

Plotkin, G. D. (1975). Call-by-name, call-by-value, and the λ-calculus. *Theoretical Computer Science*, 1(2), 125–159.

Plum, T. (1977). Fooling the user of a programming language. *Software Practice and Experience*, 7, 215–221.

Powers, K., Ecott, S., & Hirshfield, L. M. (2007). Through the looking glass: Teaching CS0 with Alice. *SIGCSE Bulletin*, 39(1), 213–217.

Price, T. W., Brown, N. C. C., Lipovac, D., Barnes, T., & Kölling, M. (2016). Evaluation of a frame-based programming editor. In *Proceedings of the Conference on International Computing Education Research (ICER)* (pp. 32–42). New York: ACM.

Reges, S. (2006). Back to basics in CS1 and CS2. In *Proceedings of the ACM Symposium on Computer Science Education (SIGCSE)* (pp. 293–297). New York: ACM.

Resnick, M., Maloney, J., Monroy-Hernández, A., Rusk, N., Eastmond, E., Brennan, K., Millner, A., Rosenbaum, E., Silver, J., Silverman, B., & Kafai, Y. (2009). Scratch: Programming for all. *Communications of the ACM*, 52(11), 80–87.

Rist, R. S. (1991). Knowledge creation and retrieval in program design: A comparison of novice and intermediate student programmers. *Human–Computer Interaction*, 6(1), 1–46.

Rivers, K., & Koedinger, K. R. (2015). Data-driven hint generation in vast solution spaces: A self-improving Python programming tutor. *International Journal of Artificial Intelligence in Education*, 27(1), 1–28.

Sajaniemi, J., & Kuittinen, M. (2008). From procedures to objects: A research agenda for the psychology of object-oriented programming education. *Human Technology*, 4(1), 75–91.

Savery, J. R., & Duffy, T. M. (2001). *Problem Based Learning: An Instructional Model and Its Constructivist Framework. Tech. Rept. 16-01*. Bloomington, IN: Indiana University Center for Research on Learning and Technology.

Schanzer, E., Krishnamurthi, S., & Fisler, K. (2015). Blocks versus text: Ongoing lessons from Bootstrap. In *Proceedings of the Blocks and Beyond Workshop* (pp. 125–126). New York, NY: IEEE.

Scholtz, J., & Wiedenbeck, S. (1990). Learning second and subsequent programming languages: A problem of transfer. *International Journal of Human-Computer Interaction*, 2(1), 51–72.

Schumacher, R. M., & Czerwinski, M. P. (1992). Mental models and the acquisition of expert knowledge. In R. R. Hoffman (Ed.), *The Psychology of Expertise: Cognitive Research and Empirical AI* (pp. 61–79). Berlin, Germany: Springer.

Schwill, A. (1994). Fundamental ideas of computer science. *Bulletin of the European Association for Theoretical Computer Science*, 53, 274–274.

Seppälä, O., Ihantola, P., Isohanni, E., Sorva, J., & Vihavainen, A. (2015). Do we know how difficult the rainfall problem is? In *Proceedings of the Koli Calling Conference on Computing Education* (pp. 87–96). New York: ACM.

Shinners-Kennedy, D. (2008). The everydayness of threshold concepts: State as an example from computer science. In R. Land & J. H. F. Meyer (Eds.), *Threshold Concepts within the Disciplines* (pp. 119–128). Rotterdam, The Netherlands: Sense Publishers.

Simon (2013). Soloway's Rainfall Problem has become harder. In *LATICE '13 Proceedings of the 2013 Learning and Teaching in Computing and Engineering* (pp. 130–135). Washington, DC: IEEE Computer Society.

Sirkiä, T., & Sorva, J. (2012). Exploring programming misconceptions: An analysis of student mistakes in visual program simulation exercises. In *Proceedings of the Koli Calling Conference on Computing Education* (pp. 19–28). New York: ACM.

Slotta, J. D., & Chi, M. T. H. (2006). The impact of ontology training on conceptual change: Helping students understand the challenging topics in science. *Cognition and Instruction*, 24, 261–289.

Smaragdakis, Y., & Balatsouras, G. (2015). Pointer analysis. *Foundations and Trends in Programming Languages*, 2(1), 1–69.

Soloway, E. (1986). Learning to program = learning to construct mechanisms and explanations. *Communications of the ACM*, 29(9), 850–858.

Soloway, E., Bonar, J., & Ehrlich, K. (1983). Cognitive strategies and looping constructs: An empirical study. *Communications of the ACM*, 26(11), 853–860.

Somers, J. (2017). The coming software apocalypse. *The Atlantic*, Sept. Retrieved from www.theatlantic.com/technology/archive/2017/09/saving-the-world-from-code/540393/

Sorva, J. (2012). *Visual Program Simulation in Introductory Programming Education* (PhD thesis). Aalto University, Department of Computer Science and Engineering.

Sorva, J. (2013). Notional machines and introductory programming education. *Transactions on Computing Education (TOCE)*, 13(2), 8:1–8:31.

Spohrer, J. C., & Soloway, E. (1989). *Simulating Student Programmers* (pp. 543–549). Morgan Kaufmann Publishers, Inc. San Francisco, CA, USA.

Stanton, J., Goldsmith, L., Adrion, W. R., Dunton, S., Hendrickson, K. A., Peterfreund, A., Youngpradit, P., Zarch, R., & Zinth, J. D. (2017). *State of the States Landscape Report: State-Level Policies Supporting Equitable K12 Computer Science Education*. Retrieved from www.edc.org/sites/default/files/uploads/State-States-Landscape-Report.pdf

Stefik, A., & Gellenbeck, E. (2009). Using spoken text to aid debugging: An empirical study. In *IEEE International Conference on Program Comprehension* (pp. 110–119). New York: IEEE Press.

Stefik, A., & Gellenbeck, E. (2011). Empirical studies on programming language stimuli. *Software Quality Journal*, 19(1), 65–99.

Stefik, A., & Siebert, S. (2013). An empirical investigation into programming language syntax. *Transactions on Computing Education (TOCE)*, 13(4), 19:1–19:40.

Stefik, A., Hundhausen, C., & Patterson, R. (2011). An empirical investigation into the design of auditory cues to enhance computer program comprehension. *International Journal of Human–Computer Studies*, 69(12), 820–838.

Stefik, A. M. (2008). *On the Design of Program Execution Environments for Non-Sighted Computer Programmers* (PhD thesis). Washington State University.

Sudol, L. A. (2011). *Deepening Students Understanding of Algorithms: Effects of Problem Context and Feedback Regarding Algorithmic Abstraction* (PhD thesis). Carnegie Mellon University.

Tessler, J., Beth, B., & Lin, C. (2013). Using Cargo-bot to provide contextualized learning of recursion. In *Proceedings of the Conference on International Computing Education Research (ICER)* (pp. 161–168). New York: ACM.

Tew, A. E., McCracken, W. M., & Guzdial, M. (2005). Impact of alternative introductory courses on programming concept understanding. In *Proceedings of the Conference on International Computing Education Research (ICER)* (pp. 25–35). New York: ACM.

The College Board (n.d.). AP Computer Science Principles: Course Overview. Retrieved from https://apstudent.collegeboard.org/apcourse/ap-computer-science-principles

Tichy, W. F., & Prechelt, L. (1998). A controlled experiment to assess the benefits of procedure argument type checking. *IEEE Transactions on Software Engineering*, 24(4), 302–312.

Tirronen, V., Uusi-Mäakelä, S., & Isomöttönen, V. (2015). Understanding beginners' mistakes with Haskell. *Journal of Functional Programming*, 25, e11.

Traver, V. J. (2010). On compiler error messages: What they say and what they mean. *Advances in Human–Computer Interaction*, 2010, 602570.

Tunnell Wilson, P., Pombrio, J., & Krishnamurthi, S. (2017). Can we crowdsource language design? In *Proceedings of SPLASH Onward* (Onward! '17) (17 pages). Vancouver, Canada: Onward.

Tunnell Wilson, P., Fisler, K., & Krishnamurthi, S. (2017). Student understanding of aliasing and procedure calls. In *SPLASH Education Symposium* (SPLASH-E '17) (6 Pages). New York, NY: ACM.

Tunnell Wilson, P., Krishnamurthi, S., & Fisler, K. (2018). Evaluating the tracing of recursion in the substitution notional machine. In *Proceedings of the ACM Symposium on Computer Science Education (SIGCSE)* (pp. 1023–1028). New York: ACM.

Vasek, M. (2012). *Representing Expressive Types in Blocks Programming Languages*. Retrieved from https://repository.wellesley.edu/thesiscollection/24/

Vickers, P., & Alty, J. L. (2002). When bugs sing. *Interacting with Computers*, 14(6), 793–819.

Victor, B. (2012). *Learnable Programming: Designing a Programming System for Understanding Programs*. Retrieved from http://worrydream.com/#!/Learnable Programming

Vilner, T., Zur, E., & Gal-Ezer, J. (2007). Fundamental concepts of CS1: Procedural vs. object oriented paradigm – A case study. *SIGCSE Bulletin*, 39(3), 171–175.

Wand, M. (1986). Finding the source of type errors. In *ACM SIGPLAN-SIGACT Symposium on Principles of Programming Languages* (pp. 38–43). New York: ACM.

Weintrop, D., & Wilensky, U. (2015a). To block or not to block, that is the question: Students perceptions of blocks-based programming. In *Proceedings of the*

International Conference on Interaction Design and Children (pp. 199–208). New York, NY: ACM.

Weintrop, D., & Wilensky, U. (2015b). Using commutative assessments to compare conceptual understanding in blocks-based and text-based programs. In *Proceedings of the Conference on International Computing Education Research (ICER)*. New York: ACM.

Weintrop, D., & Wilensky, U. (2017a). Comparing blocks-based and text-based programming in high school computer science classrooms. *Transactions on Computing Education (TOCE)*, 18(1), 3:1–3:25.

Weintrop, D., & Wilensky, U. (2017b). Between a block and a typeface: Designing and evaluating hybrid programming environments. In *Proceedings of the International Conference on Interaction Design and Children* (pp. 183–192). New York, NY: ACM.

Wiedenbeck, S., & Ramalingam, V. (1999). Novice comprehension of small programs written in the procedural and object-oriented styles. *International Journal of Human–Computer Studies*, 51(1), 71–87.

Wiedenbeck, S., Ramalingam, V., Sarasamma, S., & Corritore, C. L. (1999). A comparison of the comprehension of object-oriented and procedural programs by novice programmers. *Interacting with Computers*, 11(3), 255–282.

14 Assessment and Plagiarism

Thomas Lancaster, Anthony V. Robins,
and Sally A. Fincher

14.1 Motivational Context

14.1.1 Introduction

14.1.1.1 Subject-Specific Importance

The areas of assessment and plagiarism would seem destined to be closely interlinked. For computing students, demonstrating achievement in summative assessments where their academic performance is evaluated is important in the context of formal education. Were such a student found to have committed plagiarism, the achievement they intended to demonstrate would become derailed.

Due perhaps to its importance to students and its crucial role in the education system, a large body of work already exists on assessment, some within computing. A much smaller body of research exists on plagiarism. But despite the apparent links between plagiarism and assessment, there are few academic sources giving meaningful consideration to both topics (Lancaster, 2017). In particular, much of the classic research on student assessment does not discuss plagiarism, or makes only a passing reference to it.

This chapter is intended to provide a more balanced view of both of these topics – assessment and plagiarism – within computing education (CEd). One of the intentions is to demonstrate how assessment design needs to be considered in light of known findings on plagiarism and other forms of academic misconduct.

There are many indicators that the extent of cheating and plagiarism is disproportionally higher in computing than in other disciplines. Fraser (2014) provides a detailed summary of this. One seminal study by Roberts (2002) considered academic misconduct cases seen at Stanford University over a ten-year period. Although students on computing courses only accounted for 7 percent of the student population, they represented 37 percent of all academic misconduct cases. Suggestions for the level of computing undergraduate students who have cheated run as high as 79 percent, as found in a study of 504 students who admitted to at least 1 out of 16 cheating practices (Sheard, Markham, & Dick, 2003).

14.1.1.2 Implications for Researchers and Instructors

For a researcher entering this field or an instructor looking to incorporate best practice, there already exists a confusing world of academic publications and associated recommendations. The field has developed a vast lexicon, much of which is used inconsistently from one group of authors to the next.

For the computing instructor, understanding assessment offers further challenge due to the fast-moving nature of technological advances, the associated terminology, and the need to assess students in skills beyond writing reports and essays. Computing students do still need to write, but this is just one of a number of skills they need to demonstrate. As a subject that is often considered vocational in nature, computing students also need to demonstrate standard skills of employability, which lacks an overall infrastructure (Fincher & Finlay, 2016). Fincher and Finlay also note that the acquisition of "employability skills" is largely dependent on students undertaking industrial experience (a placement or the like), or an equivalent where that is impractical. Some practitioners use assessments to simulate this experience, such as industry-facing final-year projects or the use of "industry fellows" coming into the classroom (Fincher & Knox, 2013).

An additional challenge relates to the nature of computing assessments and whether the use of existing materials, such as code fragments found in online repositories, should be allowable. Such an approach is common in professional circles for students who have proven their ability to program. A detailed discussion of what is acceptable in different situations is beyond the scope of this chapter, as is the discussion of in which circumstances a student should be punished for plagiarizing.

14.1.1.3 Chapter Benefits

This chapter introduces key principles that need to be considered in order to best develop assessments that are fit for purpose, while also considering how to preserve academic integrity throughout this process. These include general principles for assessment design that apply to all disciplines, supported by further refinements that are particularly useful for computing. Practical examples from the literature relating to assessment design are given. The chapter also considers how software tools designed to detect plagiarism can be used during assessment.

This chapter is intended to aid those new to CEd research (CEdR). It is hoped that the discussion will also prove useful for those people who are new to computing teaching and the more experienced educators who are looking for ideas to innovate and review their assessment practice. Many of the ideas given are suitable as the basis for further research, including investigating attitudes toward academic misconduct, the scale of the problem, the utility of the assessment techniques suggested, and the pedagogical benefits of such assessment changes. Every student cohort is different, and in the fast-moving field of computing, further research is always needed. Many research opportunities are also suitable for staff new to research, PhD students, MSc students, and undergraduates, alongside those more established in their academic careers. The chapter concludes by suggesting particular research opportunities within plagiarism and assessment that would benefit from the technical and mathematical skills of computer scientists.

14.1.2 Assessment and Student Learning Outcomes

14.1.2.1 Context

"Assessment" is an overstuffed portmanteau: it is loosely used to mean many things in education, from formative activities (gauging how students are progressing with their learning) to summative (testing their achievement). It is at the summative end of the range that plagiarism is most often looked for (and most often found).

Assessment may be carried out at many scales, from the individual student (ipsative) through to the class, the school (in high-stakes comparison), the nation (in standardized exams), and even the world in multinational tests such as the Programme for International Student Assessment (PISA). Considerable effort goes into developing assessment tools that are both valid and reliable.

For general overviews of assessment, see, for example, Bloom, Hastings, and Madaus (1971), Ebel and Frisbie (1986), or Linn and Gronlund (1995). Educational assessment is part of the broader field of psychometric testing, which includes theoretical frameworks such as classical test theory and item response theory – see Crocker and Algina (1986) for an introduction.

14.1.2.2 Assessment and Learning Outcomes

Whatever we as teachers want our students to learn, their perceptions of what is significant (and therefore where and how to direct their efforts) are strongly shaped by the lens of assessment. Of higher education, Ramsden (2003) writes: "The most important thing to keep in mind is that students adapt to the requirements they perceive teachers to make of them … They do what they think will bring rewards in the systems they work in." In his classic text on assessment, Rowntree (1977) is even blunter: "The spirit and style of student assessment defines the de facto curriculum."

The emerging understanding of the practical significance of assessment drove the promotion and widespread adoption of teaching practices such as constructive alignment and formative assessment (see Chapter 10). Constructive alignment, a term popularized by Biggs and Tang (2007), is the careful design of teaching, learning, and assessment activities so that these reflect and support intended learning outcomes, and therefore support the learner in their construction of meaning. Formative assessment, as originally defined (Scriven, 1967), referred to the collection of information to guide and improve teaching practice. As later adapted and popularized (Bloom, Hastings, & Madaus, 1971), the term has come to variously represent a range of practices that focus on improving learning outcomes rather than assigning grades. It is often described as assessment "of and for learning." Complementing these concepts is a recognition of the importance of rich, relevant, and timely feedback to students, closing the loop of the assessment process (see Chapter 10).

In a comprehensive and influential synthesis, Black and Wiliam (1998) review more than 250 studies of formative assessment, which they define as "all those activities undertaken by teachers, and/or by their students, which provide information to be used as feedback to modify the teaching and learning activities in which they are engaged." Summarizing their findings, they state: "The research reported here shows conclusively that formative assessment does improve learning," and that the gains are "amongst the largest ever reported for educational interventions." As a subsequent summary puts it, "Assessment that is explicitly designed to promote learning is the single most powerful tool we have for raising standards and empowering life-long learning" (Assessment Reform Group, 1999). Further studies that confirmed the practical significance of formative assessment are noted in Earl (2012), and the adoption of "assessment for learning" internationally is summarized by Birenbaum et al. (2015).

14.1.2.3 The Assessment of Programming

The importance of assessment for good learning outcomes begs the question: Are we assessing CEd topics appropriately? Most of the focus has been on the assessment of programming. In this section, we briefly consider just one influential study.

The McCracken group undertook an investigation of programming based on a combined sample of 216 students across four universities (McCracken et al., 2001). The study is mostly cited for its surprising and influential finding that students who had completed one or two courses in computer science performed much more poorly on a trial programming test (developed by the authors) than their teachers expected. But the underlying purpose of the study was to explore the assessment of programming and develop appropriate tools.

McCracken et al. (2001) note the distinction between objective testing (where an answer can be assessed as right or wrong without expert judgment; e.g., multiple-choice questions) and performance-based assessment (which directly tests relevant performance in an authentic way; e.g., creating a specified program). They specify seven criteria for performance-based assessment: "fairness, generalisability, cognitive complexity, content quality (depth) and coverage (breadth), meaningfulness, and cost," and use them to evaluate three common assessment methods. *Take-home programming assignments* are described as fair, generalizable, and meaningful, but the authors note the impact of external time commitments and the risk of plagiarism. *Exams* (short answer) are described as difficult but not impossible to make meaningful or generalizable and as low cost. *Charettes* (short assignments; e.g., lab exercises) are described as "more superficial and less cognitively complex" than take-home assignments, but also as less vulnerable to plagiarism.

Student participants in the McCracken group study were asked to complete a charette consisting of three exercises. Most performed "much more poorly than we expected," with the most obvious difficulty observed being "abstracting the problem to be solved from the exercise description" (this finding is consistent with other research on the difficulties experienced by novice programmers; see Chapter 12). Significantly, the authors note: "In this trial assessment, as in the 'real world', it may be that black-box assessment of students' submissions reinforces students' views of implementation and syntax as the key focus of computer programming." Given the cognitive complexity and multifaceted nature of programming as a task, it is important to ask whether our assessment of programming, as students perceive it, is sending the right messages about where they should direct their efforts.

14.1.2.4 A Lack of Consensus and the Need for Research

While progress has been made in the 17 years since the McCracken study, there is still little consensus on how best to design and employ assessment for computing topics in general, or for programming in particular. This is consistent with the lack of consensus on how to teach programming, as discussed in Chapter 12.

In their (albeit small-scale) survey of how computing educators set exams, for example, Sheard et al. (2013) found "little evidence of explicit references to learning theories or models, indicating that the process is based largely on intuition and experience." Unfortunately, what the evidence does suggest is that our intuitions as educators are highly variable.

For example, in an exploration of introductory programming questions, Petersen, Craig, and Zingaro (2011) had nine experienced teachers analyze questions using both the structure of observed learning outcomes (SOLO) taxonomy, a programming skills taxonomy, and a list of typical programming concepts. (The SOLO taxonomy is used to categorize "observed learning outcomes" in terms of levels of increasing complexity; see Section 14.2.1.2.) The authors note: "Our evaluators had difficulty agreeing on SOLO level, and persuasive arguments could often be made to categorise a question in more than one level," and that "developing a group consensus on skills is just as difficult." While there was reasonable consensus on concepts directly "evaluated" by a question, participants often missed related concepts that were "used."

Similarly, an attempt to develop a classification scheme for programming exams (Sheard et al., 2011) had 12 experienced teachers rate example questions on dimensions including topic areas, necessary skills, explicitness, difficulty, and several kinds of complexity. Participants were surprised by the often poor inter-rater reliability. The authors note, for example, that, "Essentially, there was little or no consensus on whether questions were easy, moderate, or difficult." This is a difficult starting point for building well-targeted assessment!

In summary, our motivations for a focus on assessment are that it has a strong effect on learning outcomes and that there is not yet a widely agreed theory, or even consensus on the practical details, of how to conduct assessment in our field. There are many open questions to be explored.

14.1.3 Plagiarism and Academic Misconduct

14.1.3.1 Context

Definitions of plagiarism within education vary, but in the context of student work, this term generally refers to a student using the words or ideas of another person without acknowledging the source of those words or ideas. Within computing, plagiarism can include copying in text-based assessments, but it can also involve technical assignments, such as programming or database production. A distinction has to be made between acceptable levels of code reuse and plagiarism, although the dividing line between these entities could be considered fuzzy. An associated area to misconduct is students colluding on work without acknowledgment when submitting.

Many commentators, such as Austin and Brown (1999), have attributed a growth in student plagiarism to the widespread availability of information that can be "copied and pasted" from the Internet. Technology is also thought to have increased the ease with which students can plagiarize. This is demonstrated, for example, by a survey of students in Slovenia who said that the ease of finding material to copy from motivated them to cheat (Šprajc et al., 2017). Students also identified pressures of time as their major reason for plagiarizing, as opposed to issues of workload. Studies specific to computing also identified time pressure to be a reason why students plagiarized, as well as fear of failure (Sheard & Dick, 2012; Sheard, Markham, & Dick, 2003). As countering influences, they found that it was necessary to ignite the desire of students to learn and to know what they have learned.

14.1.3.2 Understanding of the Issues

A particular challenge for computing, as well as a motivational factor for writing this chapter, has been the variety of perceptions on plagiarism and collusion identified by both staff and students, including knowing when this is acceptable. As an example, Fraser (2014) defines collusion as a "group activity that is unpermitted" and comparable to the acceptable collaboration, which is "a group of students working together on an assignment."

Several large studies of computing students have consistently reported that students do not understand what constitutes plagiarism and collusion, or agree on what is acceptable. These include Joy et al. (2011) with a sample size of 770, Simon et al. (2014) with a sample size of 486, and Sheard and Dick (2011) with a sample size of 415.

There are recommendations in the literature regarding how code reuse can be approached. For instance, Gibson (2009) recommends introducing a code of practice, requiring reused code to be clearly acknowledged and submitted in a separate file to new code intended for marking. A difference between the acceptable practice expected by industry professionals and computing academics has also been observed (Simon et al., 2016). An alternative approach, used by Baugh et al. (2012), has seen students assessed based on how well they repurpose provided code. Any local analysis of what constitutes plagiarism in a particular setting does have to be considered with the process that has been agreed regarding software reuse in mind.

14.1.3.3 Detecting Plagiarism

Technology has increased the opportunities for student plagiarism, but it has also provided new mechanisms through which students who are plagiarizing can be detected. The earliest plagiarism detection systems were developed to identify students who had colluded on the production of source code assessments (Ottenstein, 1976; Parker & Hamblen, 1989).

Lancaster and Culwin (2004) review the different classifications of systems available to detect plagiarism in student source code submissions. Some notable examples in the field include Sherlock (Joy & Luck, 1999), JPlag (Prechelt et al., 2002), and MOSS (Schleimer et al., 2003), with the latter two systems available over the Internet. A study of the use of source code plagiarism detection software in the UK revealed widespread adoption (Culwin et al., 2001). Source code plagiarism detection systems have also been found to be of value to educators. For instance, MOSS was academically reviewed as a "major innovation" (Bowyer & Hall, 1999).

Plagiarism can also be observed in types of computing assignments other than programming. For instance, Lancaster and Clarke (2015) identify techniques used to find plagiarism in database modules. Singh (2013) presents specific techniques that can be used with MS Access database assignments. Similar studies are available that are specific to other technical fields.

The need to detect plagiarism now also extends to free-text assessments, such as essays and reports. Although free-text similarity detection systems were generally developed after source code plagiarism detection systems, the underlying working of both groups of systems is similar. An early example of how a system to detect plagiarism in text documents could work was CHECK (Si et al., 1997).

Lancaster (2013b) provides a summary of the tools used to identify similar text, their workings, and how they can be used by instructors. Other contributors have provided lists of tools with a comparison of their features (Lukashenko et al., 2007). New tools continue to emerge regularly showing new features and demonstrating incremental improvements on other tools. However, the market-leading tools, such as Turnitin, tend to provide many of the features needed for matching similar text. Tools are not the only solution needed against copy-and-paste plagiarism. For instance, Culwin (2009) demonstrated that tools such as Turnitin could not be relied on to detect all plagiarized work from the Internet, as there were blind spots of websites that had not been indexed.

Gillam, Marinuzzi, and Ioannou (2010) showed that many well-used plagiarism detection systems for text were susceptible to small changes, for instance by a "lazy plagiarist" systematically changing words within a document and replacing them with alternatives.

Students also have access to mechanisms that they can use to bypass plagiarism detection software. Tools exist that allow students to rewrite the content of an essay, either manually or automatically. For example, Rogerson and McCarthy (2017) have discussed the use of online paraphrasing tools, which students can use to highlight words or phrases within an essay and select alternatives.

Other approaches exist that a student can use to automatically convert text into a new version. One mechanism cited in the literature is back translation (Jones & Sheridan, 2015). In its simplest form, this sees a student using automated language translation software to convert text into another language, then back to English, with the new version of text appearing different to the original. An early investigation into this area looked at automatic translation, as well as other essay spinning techniques, such as the automatic replacement of terms with their synonyms (Lancaster & Clarke, 2007). Making changes of these types to essays may not always leave them in a readable form, but this can be addressed by editing. Since these written documents have been substantially changed, it can be difficult to detect plagiarism of this type through traditional automated techniques.

14.1.3.4 Contract Cheating

A subcategory of plagiarism that is of particular concern to computing instructors is contract cheating. Originally observed by Clarke and Lancaster (2006), this describes the behavior where a student outsources, or attempts to outsource, the production of their assessed work to a third party. A wide range of computing assessments can be outsourced, including large numbers of programming assignments, as well as major pieces of work such as final-year projects (Lancaster & Clarke, 2007). O'Malley and Roberts (2012) propose some solutions.

Studies within computing have identified that programming assessments can be outsourced for a low cost (Jenkins & Helmore, 2006). Other studies have shown that students do not need to preplan in order to outsource their assessments (Wallace & Newton, 2014). Original work can be outsourced and returned quickly, often on the same day, and there is an abundance of worker capacity offering to complete these assessments.

Many surveys have asked students if they have indulged in contract cheating. A meta-analysis of these surveys from Curtis and Clare (2017) found that 3.5 percent of all students had used other people to complete their assessments for them. An accompanying result identified that 62.5 percent of this group of students had contract cheated at least twice.

14.1.3.5 Academic Misconduct and Academic Integrity

Plagiarism and contract cheating can be considered to be types of academic misconduct – the group of activities where a student attempts to get an unfair advantage over other students.

It is important to balance the negative concept of academic misconduct with the more positive concept of academic integrity, which can be defined as "a commitment, even in the face of adversity, to six fundamental values: honesty, trust, fairness, respect, responsibility, and courage" (ICAI, 2014). Students can be encouraged to approach their assessments with academic integrity in order to promote a more positive harmony in the classroom.

14.2 Implications for Practice

14.2.1 Assessment Design for Computing

14.2.1.1 Practical Considerations

There is good evidence that undertaking tests (i.e., quizzes or exams) is an effective strategy for improving student learning (Dunlosky, 2013). There is much practical skill in devising and administering such assessments, and this is different at primary and secondary school from university education. At all levels, differentiating between assessment, grading, and feedback is important, and the weights these activities have is different at different levels (see Hendrick & MacPherson, 2017, for an overview of research-informed practice in schools). In this section, we briefly note research relating to practical considerations in assessment.

In a substantial review of the assessment of computing at school and tertiary levels, the Innovation and Technology in Computer Science Education (ITiCSE) working group of Giordano et al. (2015) lists the following best practices:

> de-emphasize syntax; formulate assessments independent from specific programming language by resorting to pseudocodes that avoid any form of ambiguity (Cutts et al., 2014); make use of grading rubrics to make the assessments of projects less subjective and more transparent to students (Vasilevskaya, Broman, & Sandahl, 2014); resort to gamification and competitions to render assessment more engaging (Gouws, Bradshaw, & Wentworth, 2013; Hakulinen, Auvinen, & Korhonen, 2015).

Many authors have explored the makeup and use of typical programming exam questions (e.g., Sheard, 2012; Simon et al., 2012). Lister (2000) argues strongly for the validity of multiple-choice questions and that many of the common criticisms of them are invalid or based on poorly designed examples. He also argues that curricula and assessment should be guided by a mastery approach based on Bloom's taxonomy, "a cognitive model of how students learn." Later studies used the Bloom and SOLO taxonomies (see below) to explore in detail what is being tested by assessment items and programming exams (e.g., Lister et al., 2006; Whalley et al., 2006). Petersen, Craig, and Zingaro (2011) had experienced teachers review introductory programming exams from a variety of North American institutions, finding that "reviewers regularly underestimated the number of CS1 concepts required to answer these questions," and that "in order to succeed, students must internalise a large amount of CS1 content." Similar conclusions about the highly integrated nature of the knowledge required by programming assessments are reached by Luxton-Reilly and Petersen (2017). Fincher, Petre, and Clark (2001, p. ix) explore reasons why computing as an academic discipline often uses projects for assessment, noting their role as both a vehicle for effective learning and a way to demonstrate mastery of a practical domain. Later papers in the volume explore the practicalities of project work at different levels of a computing curriculum. Hahn, Mentz, and Meyer (2009) consider the practicalities of assessment in a pair programming context, comparing peer-, self-, and facilitator-based measures. More work is needed in this area, given that pair programming has emerged as a particularly effective teaching method within CEd (see Chapters 29 and 30).

Various studies have explored alternatives to the status quo of typical assessment types. Parsons and Haden (2006) introduced a new kind of question particular to programming, "Parsons' problems," which are based on the reordering of given lines of code to produce working code fragments. As an alternative to typical tasks based on code reading or writing/completion, these quickly proved to be a popular form of problem for both research and practice (e.g., Denny, Luxton-Reilly, & Simon, 2008). Noting that CEd is still, after decades, struggling with the issues of teaching and learning programming (Chapter 12), Parsons, Wood, and Haden (2015) ask, "What are we doing when we assess programming?" The authors suggest that the problem is "the methods of assessment, which do not reflect the knowledge and skills that a real programmer needs to write real code," and propose an alternative format for assessment based on activity diagrams. Cardell-Oliver (2011) notes that different kinds of typical assessment item can generate different grade distributions and questions the validity of a final single course grade that is based on a combination of disparate measures. She recommends assessment based on the use of software metrics, such as program size, functional correctness, efficiency, program style, and client validation.

14.2.1.2 Theoretical Frameworks

As already noted, assessment in CEd typically takes place without explicit reference to any theoretical framework. Having said that, common practice in the field, and the practitioner intuitions on which it is based, are both clearly shaped by current theory. The broadest educational theories, in the general sense, are constructivism (a philosophy of knowledge and learning) and cognitivism (the dominant paradigm within psychology), both of which are widely explored in this Handbook (e.g., Chapters 1, 8, 9, 10, and 15). Assessment theory, which has developed within this context, has introduced concepts and practices such as constructive alignment, meaningful and engaging tasks, formative assessment, and rich and timely feedback; see summaries in Palomba and Banta (1999), Yorke (2003), and Brown and Knight (2012).

The Bloom and SOLO taxonomies are both theoretical frameworks that have been highly influential within education generally and have contributed to the theory and practice of assessment in our field. Bloom's taxonomy of learning objectives (Bloom et al., 1956) describes six levels of increasingly sophisticated objectives for learning within the "cognitive domain," namely Remembering, Comprehending, Applying, Analyzing, Synthesizing, and Evaluating. (See also the Revised Bloom's Taxonomy; Anderson et al., 2001; Krathwohl, 2002.) The SOLO taxonomy (Biggs & Collis, 1982) describes the "Structure of the Observed Learning Outcome" in terms of levels of increasing complexity, from pre-structural (displaying no understanding), to uni-structural, multi-structural, relational, and extended abstract (understanding is abstracted to a high level and may be generalized to other tasks or topics).

A number of CEd studies have used these taxonomies to try and understand the complexity and/or difficulty of assessment items and/or to design fair and balanced assessment tools. Whalley et al. (2006) and Clear et al. (2008) found that student responses to a code comprehension exam question could be categorized in the SOLO taxonomy as multi-structural or relational. Lister et al. (2006) applied the taxonomy to novice programming students performing small code comprehension tasks, finding it to be "a useful organizing framework for comparing work relevant to the testing of novice programmers via reading problems." Sheard et al. (2008) replicated aspects of Lister et al.'s study and found that students are "relatively consistent" in the SOLO level of sample exam answers, and similarly that their levels on code reading and writing tasks were positively correlated. SOLO was used as an organizing framework in the ITiCSE working group BRACElet project, a multiyear, multinational study of novice programmers. A project summary (Lister et al., 2010) replicated and extended earlier project papers based on analysis of exam answers for both code reading and writing tasks, and this refined and extended earlier SOLO level definitions as applied to programming.

There is general agreement that creating a program for an unfamiliar task requires performance at the SOLO relational/Bloom synthesizing or create level, but there is less agreement about more specific tasks. Sorva (2012) states: "Code-tracing skills, for instance, have been variously classified within the literature as understand or analyze, and many interpretations have been presented as to how to 'Bloom rate' program-writing assignments of different kinds." As noted above, Petersen, Craig, and Zingaro (2011) found that experienced teachers analyzing assessment questions "had difficulty agreeing on SOLO level, and persuasive arguments could often be made to categorise a question in more than one level." Much of the disagreement may relate to different assumptions about the preexisting knowledge and varying capabilities of learners (indeed, Bloom's original group stressed the importance of prior knowledge in determining relevant levels). For example, Thompson et al. (2008) note that a task may be classified as Apply if the student has relevant knowledge/experience, but as Create otherwise.

Fuller et al. (2007) discuss these and other problems for applying general taxonomies to computing and propose a version of Bloom's Revised Taxonomy adapted to the requirements of computing tasks. In investigating novice programmers in Scratch, Meerbaum-Salant et al. (2010) create a novel taxonomy that combines the Uni-structural, Multi-structural, and Relational categories from SOLO with the Understanding, Applying, and Creating levels from Bloom. In devising this hybrid, they address limitations identified by other authors (as above) and create a tool specifically nuanced for CEdR that captures the cognitive characteristics of computing practice.

For higher education, the framework of "assessment literacy" devised by Carol Evans is a step toward articulating assessment practice between staff and students (Evans, 2013, 2016). The framework embeds and expresses a number of research-based principles. For literacy, these are as follows: clarify what constitutes good; clarify how assessment elements fit together; clarify student entitlement; and clarify the requirements of the discipline. Thus, a literate assessment will be designed to deepen a student's understanding of the central concepts of computing so that their achievement feeds into disciplinary competence. A literate assessment will scaffold a student's understanding of what is good performance, ensure that they understand the different pieces, and clarify what support is available and when. A distinctive feature of Evans' framework is that it contains both lecturer and student views. The development of a common understanding in this way moves beyond simply "telling" students what is acceptable practice. It should significantly address understanding of the purpose and products of assessment, and so reduce ambiguity in regard to what constitutes plagiarism and the practice of plagiarism itself.

14.2.1.3 Toward Standardized Tools

The McCracken study (McCracken et al., 2001) and a range of similar evidence (see Chapter 12) raise concerns about the quality of outcomes for students learning programming. Tew and Guzdial (2010) question whether these poor results "are the product of failures of student comprehension or our inability to accurately measure their performance." Such concerns motivate attempts to develop standardized and validated assessment tools.

In some countries, de facto standard assessments are created by national curriculum documents or tests. In the USA, for example, the Advanced Placement (AP) exams offer high school students an opportunity to earn credit for college-level courses. Curricula and exams are developed and validated in each subject by a Test Development Committee, consisting of teachers from colleges/universities and schools, with input from Educational Testing Services (ETS) – see Patterson and Ewing (2013). The "Computer Science A" (CS A) exam (College Board, 2018) is based on a prescribed subset of Java, including object-oriented programming concepts. It consists of a mixture of multiple-choice and free-response questions at a level comparable to a typical CS1 course. The development of the CS A is occasionally discussed in Special Interest Group on Computer Science Education (SIGCSE) panel sessions (Astrachan et al., 2009). While often criticized (e.g., as being too narrowly focused on Java), the CS A is an influential standardized assessment based on considerable practical experience and professional expertise.

One goal for standardized tools is that they can be used across languages and institutional contexts. An influential example within CEd is the "Foundational CS1" (FCS1) instrument (Tew & Guzdial, 2011), which uses pseudo-code and a multiple-choice question format to assess three different dimensions of programming: definition, tracing, and code completion. The development of this instrument was supported by "a large scale empirical study" (952 participants studying Java, MATLAB, or Python), and the authors "established the validity of the assessment using a multi-faceted argument, combining interview data, statistical analysis of results on the assessment, and CS1 exam scores" (Tew & Guzdial, 2011). The case for the FCS1 and other validated tools in CEdR is further advanced in Tew and Dorn (2013).

The FCS1 has been cited in a range of subsequent publications and used in some further studies, notably by an ITiCSE working group (Utting et al., 2013) that compared the performance of students on the FCS1 (as a measure of understanding of programming concepts) and a specific implementation task (as a measure of practical programming skill). The FCS1 has also been replicated in the form of the Secondary CS1 (SCS1) instrument (Parker, Guzdial, & Engleman, 2016).

Concept inventories (CIs) are a popular standardized tool for assessing the learning of core concepts. They are used within some sciences, notably physics, where they have had a significant impact on pedagogy. Taylor et al. (2014) note that there are no widely used, validated CIs for computing, which is "distinctly behind" other science, technology, engineering, and mathematics (STEM) disciplines in this respect. Taylor and colleagues explore the challenges of developing a CI in computing, including the general lack of students' preexisting knowledge in this field, the rapidly changing nature of programming languages and computing technology, the lack of theoretical clarity about the distinction between knowledge and skills, and the practical difficulties of assessment. Despite these difficulties, preliminary work in some areas, such as digital logic and data structures and algorithms, is discussed, and the authors note the FCS1 as related work in the field. Plans for the development of inventories for CS1 are described by Goldman et al. (2010) and Caceffo et al. (2016), and for CS2 by Wittie, Kurdia, and Huggard (2017). Note, however, that some (e.g., Guzdial, 2010) argue that CIs are an inappropriate tool for computing – indeed, for any "science of the artificial" – as the misconceptions they identify are rooted in naive models of the natural world (e.g., that it gets hotter in summer because the earth moves "closer to the fire").

Another approach to standardization and the sharing of best practice is the use of public repositories of assessment items. Sanders et al. (2013) created one such example: 654 multiple-choice questions covering CS1 and CS2 topics, usefully tagged with metadata including difficulty, language, and topic. Like other studies, they found low inter-rater reliability on some fields, including difficulty. The long-running Nifty Assignment repository (Parlante, 2018) covers CS0 to CS2, seeking to provide assignments with a "fun factor," with the aim of being inspirational, thought-provoking, and open-ended. The PeerWise project (Denny et al., 2008) adopts a novel approach, where questions are contributed and evaluated by students. This approach has been successfully applied in computing and other domains. In the UK, the Computing at School (CAS) Project Quantum is working to crowdsource a bank of high-quality multiple-choice questions for assessing computing in schools (Project Quantum, 2016). Buffum et al. (2015) present "a seven-step approach to designing, iteratively refining, and validating knowledge assessment instruments," and describe its use in a three-year game-based learning project for middle school computing. Many other examples are noted in Giordano et al. (2015), who also describe their own prototype collaborative VIVA platform. Fincher et al. (2010) discuss the practical adoption and use of such repositories, noting low awareness and uptake among practitioners and problematic issues such as the control, cataloguing, and maintenance of content.

14.2.1.4 Automated Assessment

Automated assessment is widely used in CEd and is the focus of a considerable body of research. Beyond that which has been successfully captured in the formalization, automation removes the element of human judgment from assessment. Only objective tasks can be used in this way, limiting both the range of task options and the scope of possible feedback that can be returned (a very significant shortcoming). However, the advantages of automation include "speed, availability, consistency and objectivity of assessment" (Ala-Mutka, 2005).

Multiple-choice questions are the canonical task for automated marking and are widely used in many fields, but other types of task can be automatically assessed. In particular, the correctness of a program can be tested (at least at a basic functional level) by matching its output against a specification. Depending on the nature of the task and the supplied resources, the full range of programming knowledge and skills can potentially be assessed in this way (indeed, this is the approach adopted by most programming competitions). Some form of feedback can be supplied based on the use of software metrics (Ala-Mutka, 2005). Arguably, this is a very authentic form of assessment: if we want students to learn to produce complete working programs, then that is exactly what we should assess. Daly and Waldron (2004), for example, state that exercises of this form, which can be conducted under exam conditions (to make plagiarism more difficult to accomplish), are "more accurate assessors of programming ability than traditional methods such as written exams or programming assignments."

A large number of specific automated assessment systems have been reported in the CEdR literature, many more than can be examined in this brief review – see further discussion in Chapter 21 of this Handbook, and also, for example, Ala-Mutka (2005), Amelung, Piotrowski, & Rösner (2006), Ihantola et al. (2010), Koh et al. (2014), and Staubitz et al. (2015). Note also that automated essay scoring systems, some of which include plagiarism detection, represent an active field of research (e.g., Dikli, 2006; McNamara et al., 2015).

14.2.2 Plagiarism Detection and Deterrence

14.2.2.1 Detecting Plagiarism

Much of the literature on plagiarism specific to the computing discipline discusses plagiarism detection software and how this can be used to find students who are cheating.

Although "copy-and-paste" plagiarism is largely a solved problem now, many researchers are still investigating other techniques. These investigations see the treatment of detecting plagiarism as solely a mathematical and technical challenge. With developments such as the growth in translation software being used to aid plagiarism, some techniques designed to identify similar work across multiple languages show promise (Ferrero et al., 2017).

Research publications aimed at addressing new challenges in both source code and free-text plagiarism detection continue to emerge regularly. Papers such as that of Ďuračík, Kršák, and Hrkút (2017) are also beginning to emerge that address the issues the large data sets of student work that now need efficiently checking for plagiarism. Others have addressed the opportunities to apply artificial intelligence techniques to plagiarism detection (Engels et al., 2007). Work on using the contextual information within student submissions as a possible method to detect contract cheating has also been proposed (Lancaster, 2013a; Lancaster & Clarke, 2014).

The techniques used to assess student learning in computing are now moving beyond requiring students to develop simple source code assessments. Students are expected to demonstrate skills of collaboration and software reuse and to use industry-standard version control tools. This raises further challenges in automatically addressing software plagiarism. Some research solutions to this are beginning to emerge, such as methods for finding similar software repositories on Github (Zhang et al., 2017).

14.2.2.2 Detecting Contract Cheating

Although the current research activity aimed at detecting plagiarism is useful, much of this does not also directly address the issue of contract cheating. In practical terms, the outsourcing of student work is very hard to detect using automated techniques. Some systems have attempted to authenticate that the correct person is interacting with the system and that text is not being pasted into a word processor interface, such as by monitoring keystroke patterns. Two such examples are Cadmus (2017) and Doctupus (2017). Neither solution looks to be widely used, perhaps due to the additional constraints these put on students regarding their preferred working patterns.

Other people have investigated stylometrics, considering submitted student work to see if the writing or programming style matches that which would be expected from the student (Grieve & Ross, 2016; Juola, 2017). Such techniques show some promise, but do not yet replicate the knowledge of an educator who knows their students well.

Some studies are beginning to show success at identifying work not done by a student by looking at unusual patterns of marks. Clare, Walker, and Hobson (2017) have demonstrated that such discrepancies can be an indicator of contract cheating. Within computing, an example of this could be where a student performs very well in programming coursework, but cannot complete a simple exercise under exam conditions. There is still work to be done to determine what the best thresholds for identifying possible contract cheating should be, particularly considering the variety of assessment methods and marking styles that are in use.

14.2.2.3 The Benefits of Deterrence

Whether or not technology for identifying academic misconduct during the assessment process is yet completely successful or not, one of the best uses for this has to be for the deterrence of cheating. This provides some motivation for students who do not want to risk getting caught to put the effort in and to complete their own work.

14.2.3 Assessment Design for Plagiarism Prevention

14.2.3.1 General Principles

The literature documents much good practice in how assessments can be designed to maintain academic integrity. These same general recommendations apply also to computing. This section includes some suggestions for assessment design that are intended to make both plagiarism and contract cheating more difficult. Many of these ideas are derived from Lancaster and Clarke (2016).

Instructors are recommended to avoid standard essay-style assessments. These are the "bread-and-butter" assessments that essay mills are ready to prepare for students quickly. Instead, instructors are encouraged to think about alternative types of assessments and to look for methods where the student involvement in the process can be evaluated, rather than just the end result.

Assessments can be taken under controlled conditions. This could involve a traditional written exam or test format, but practical exams also make sense within the computing discipline. Viva voce exams, where a student is asked questions about their understanding of the subject to be answered verbally, also offer an alternative approach.

Students can be asked to work in teams or to collaborate. In theory, this should make academic misconduct more difficult, as this would require buy-in from all team members. In practice, care needs to be taken with the assessment design to ensure that the work cannot be simply split between team members, with all of them independently creating their part of a wider deliverable.

Assessments can be produced that require localized knowledge, which would make them difficult to outsource. For instance, these could involve a student collecting and analyzing data from the local area. This is something that would be difficult for a remotely based hired worker, although instructors would still need to aware of the potential for invented data and research fraud. They could also relate to classroom discussions, although it may be possible for a student to audio record these. Regardless of the care that has been put into the design of an assessment, there are often ways for a student to cheat if they are so inclined.

14.2.3.2 Multiple Activities

It can be useful for student progress to be evaluated using more than one classroom assessment event. The contract cheating literature suggests that these should be in different formats; for instance, unsupervised programming coursework could be accompanied by a practical programming exam

(Lancaster & Clarke, 2016). This would make it harder for a student to cheat in the same way in both of these types of assessment.

The term "authentic assessment" is often associated with discussions of academic integrity. This can be considered to be where instructors "directly examine student performance on worthy intellectual tasks" (Wiggins, 1990). Related to this, Brookhart and Durkin (2003) suggest that assessments need to be structured to make students feel they have ownership of them. This should include tasks that are both achievable and worth putting in effort to obtain results. Within computing, students could develop a portfolio showing the software they've produced on the course. Wider aspects of employability could be considered by getting a student to develop a suitable professional online presence.

Milligan and Kennedy (2017) recommend an alternative approach to assessment design based on students gaining micro-credentials, perhaps in the form of badges. These can use existing systems to ensure the robustness of the badges awarded, such as through advanced massive open online courses (MOOCs). These badges can then be displayed on student profiles. The value of the micro-credentials does depend on the robustness of the approach used to award them. The micro-credentials collected could be used by students to demonstrate that they have met the requirements of university graduate attributes.

14.2.3.3 Acceptable Practice

It has been proposed that computing assessments should be accompanied by learning outcome-linked considerations that are about what constitutes expected academic practice for that assessment (Simon et al., 2016). That would allow students to see a link between the different skills that they are expected to develop at each level. For instance, a first-year programming assignment may restrict allowable support to educators and textbooks. An advanced assessment may simulate industry practice and allow the use of coworkers and asking for support on online forums. A more controversial view is that this advanced assessment may also allow the outsourcing of some of the assessment in a manner that would need to be acknowledged and evaluated.

14.2.4 Course Design

14.2.4.1 Student Support

The design of assessments needs to be considered in conjunction with the construction of a course as a whole.

Brown and Janssen (2017) are among the groups of instructors advocating using activities and open discussions on plagiarism with students. They deliver two-hour workshops and provide practical recommendations about how to explore these issues. Some of the activities they recommend using include working with students to define plagiarism, showing students real cases of plagiarism, and developing agreed codes of integrity with them. They also recommend providing students with access to plagiarism detection software, such as Turnitin, as well as demonstrating to students how to use it correctly.

Running formative student work through a plagiarism detection system can also be of value. It allows educators to put early interventions in place if students are found to be plagiarizing accidentally. Davis and Carroll (2009) found that going through Turnitin reports with students improved their ability to reference and reduced reported plagiarism. Halgamuge (2017) also gives evidence that providing students with access to Turnitin improves their academic writing ability. However, some caution with unrestricted student access to plagiarism detection systems is necessary. Commentators have noted that some students have used this access to find ways to defeat such systems (Attwood, 2008).

The technique of showing students how their work would be seen by a plagiarism detection system has mainly been discussed in the literature in relation to free text. It may be worth exploring if similar systems for source code could also be used to support students who are learning to program.

14.2.4.2 Partnership with Students

Others have looked at ways to engage students in discussions about academic integrity. For instance, Gilliver-Brown and Ballinger (2017) have developed online comics looking at aspects of student plagiarism and cheating. Separate to this development, institutions have held events to discuss academic integrity in students and to discuss what happens when others do not act with integrity. Gaining the support of students in building a culture of academic integrity seems necessary for this to make an impact.

Regardless of how an overall course is designed, measures need to be put in place to ensure that there is evaluation of success of assessments and associated academic integrity techniques. Such an evaluation could take place as part of the normal course review process, such as during an annual monitoring cycle, and can be considered beneficial to those educators who are striving to be reflective practitioners in the classroom.

14.3 Open Questions

14.3.1 Research Opportunities: Assessment

14.3.1.1 Theoretical Opportunities

Any theoretical advance in our understanding of teaching and learning computing topics or how to constructively influence student behavior and learning outcomes would be an opportunity to be explored in the context of assessment. Such contributions may arise from advances in the theory of pedagogy (see Chapters 10 and 15) or from consideration of the underlying cognitive processes of learning, including topics such as transfer and cognitive load (see Chapter 9).

Currently, there is a focus on the "gamification" of learning (Kapp, 2012), including examples within CEd (e.g., Ibáñez, Di-Serio, & Delgado-Kloos, 2014). This is based in part on the understanding and use of reinforcement (Chapter 9). Can these techniques be applied to the design of engaging assessment activities? How can they best be deployed in the context of an automated marking environment or a full-fledged intelligent tutoring system?

Further exploration of existing theoretical frameworks, such as the Bloom and SOLO taxonomies, is also warranted. Their use has helped us to make explicit the cognitive complexity of different kinds of assessment activity and has highlighted inconsistencies in practitioner judgment in this respect. Can these frameworks be further developed and tailored to specific computing topics, such as programming? Can they contribute to attempts to develop standardized and validated forms of assessment in our field?

14.3.1.2 Practical Opportunities

Researchers and practitioners alike are still debating the best ways to assess computing topics, in particular how to validly assess programming. Most large introductory programming courses still use "pen-and-paper" exams – how does this measure compare with practical programming tasks? Are certain kinds of student advantaged or disadvantaged by one or other approach? What kinds of assessment lead to the best learning outcomes?

Given the lack of consensus on what it is that specific assessment items are testing or how difficult they are, it seems likely that there is considerable unintended variation in what exactly is being tested in different courses and how difficult it is to pass or excel. While there have been, as noted above, many attempts to produce collections of standardized assessments, there are issues with the uptake and maintenance of these collections (Fincher et al., 2010). More work is needed in this area: How can we address the barriers to their uptake? What would convince practitioners to use them?

Formative assessment can be used to assess the progress of a group or class, but it can also be analyzed at an individual level. We need to build on existing work to further explore how best to use the results of assessment to understand individual learners. Possible uses for diagnostic information include early intervention when difficulties are detected, personalized instruction or resources to address particular difficulties, and the provision of personalized feedback.

14.3.1.3 Wider Opportunities

The McCracken group authors recommend that future research on the assessment of programming should include a richer analysis of factors such as the quality of source code, and students' own reflections, and that "In general, data analysis using qualitative approaches can provide information to help improve educational processes and refine assessment tools" (McCracken et al., 2001). Qualitative methods are discussed in Chapter 7.

Most work on assessment focuses, naturally, on learners. There has been some work on how CEd teachers create, deploy, and mark assessment items (e.g., Carter et al., 2003; Fitzgerald et al., 2013), but more could be done in this area. Can best practice be identified and supported?

Automated assessment has several advantages, but limitations on the richness of the feedback that can be offered are a concern – see Carter et al. (2003) for a discussion. Can we go beyond software metrics? How will advances in artificial intelligence impact this field?

14.3.2 Research Opportunities: Plagiarism

14.3.2.1 Opportunities within Computing

As part of the literature-guided research into assessment and plagiarism presented in this chapter, opportunities for research have emerged throughout. There are many opportunities to reevaluate previous ideas, to solve technical challenges more elegantly, and to apply techniques to different fields within computing and to different types of students.

This chapter has particularly considered plagiarism, as it relates to written assignments and programming assignments. Other subjects are taught within computing, and there is a need for further development of insight into student cheating in those areas and the methods through which this can be detected. Plagiarism detection can also be extended into other areas, such as graphical work, diagrams, and mathematics.

14.3.2.2 Technical Opportunities

Some technical challenges would also benefit from further investigation. More effort needs to be placed on detecting plagiarism from work that has been deliberately disguised from its source document; for instance, by being manually rewritten or through essay spinning techniques such as back translation. This may require looking for the sequence of ideas within a document or looking for the signatures that translation software leaves behind.

The growth of areas of the web on which answers can be given to a student, but that are outside the Internet crawled by search engines, provides blind spots to plagiarism detection software. Students who are programming have access to vast quantities of sample code and open-source repositories. Students who are contract cheating have original work produced for them. New methods of detection need to be developed that can verify the authorship of documents, whether in whole or in part. The era of "big data" also requires the scalability of such solutions to be considered.

The issue of code reuse, acceptable practices, and assessing to meet industry expectations remains a major challenge. Students are now expected to be familiar with collaborative software development, using version control systems such as Git and refactoring existing components, which may include those found in online open-source repositories. However, academic institutions still have the responsibility of ensuring that students can program and that they do not just reuse existing code. The opportunity is there for continued work on technical solutions to differentiate between acceptable, agreed, and acknowledged reuse from all these sources and unacceptable plagiarism and collusion. Such software needs to be accompanied by clear, consistent, and industry-agreed guidance on what is acceptable for the sector, which takes into account the move of students from novice to more experienced developers.

14.3.2.3 Wider Opportunities

Much of the focus of this chapter has been on the differences between the computing discipline and others, in particular related to plagiarism and assessment. This is also pronounced in how well wider institutional initiatives and policies are fit for the specific needs and purposes of computing. An example of this is illustrated by the work of Riedesel et al. (2012). They found many examples of tertiary institution-level academic integrity policies that were too general to meet the needs of computing. As a result, the computing departments were having to make local decisions regarding the interpretation of these policies, to introduce their own policy extensions, or in some cases to create their own policies to replace the tertiary institution-wide ones.

The opportunity exists to work on suitable plagiarism and assessment policies for computing that also work for wider tertiary institutions as a whole. It may also be possible to address the wider issue of a lack of consistency in these areas across multiple academic institutions, including an inconsistent application of academic misconduct penalties. This would help to ensure that academic integrity is demonstrated at an institutional level.

14.4 Closing Remarks

Academics in the computing discipline need to continue to be alert to student cheating in all of its forms. Within the discipline, Alam (2004) has identified programming assignments as having the highest self-reported rates of cheating by students. With contract cheating providing students with new methods to cheat, instructors need to develop assessments that show robustness while continuing to ensure that they motivate and get the best out of students.

Sheard et al. (2017) provide a useful summary of techniques being used to encourage academic integrity in computing. They interviewed 30 instructors in Australia responsible for first-year tertiary institution teaching, with most teaching programming, from whom they identified strategies designed to reduce cheating that closely mirror many of the recommendations from this chapter.

Key to their results were supporting and empowering students, including providing them with resources concerning academic integrity. They identified the need to make cheating difficult, such as through individualized assessments and by reducing the benefits of cheating (e.g., by making assessment low stakes and coursework marks verified by exam). Their results also recommend discouraging cheating through the use of punishments as well as making student work visible so that students who are cheating can be reported as doing so.

Breaches of academic integrity do have the potential to cause real harm to students and the educational environment. As Dick et al. (2003) spell out, where academic institutions allow such breaches to take place, both the institution and subject face reputational risks. On a larger scale, this can extend to the whole computing profession. Addressing student plagiarism through suitably designed assessment is a starting point.

Despite this, the computing discipline does need to reframe its view of academic misconduct. The academic literature has traditionally looked at plagiarism in computing as offering a challenge whereby cheating students need to be caught and punished. The sector is diverging from considering academic misconduct as a problem. Instead, the movements toward academic integrity being at the forefront of education is one that it is important to embrace. This requires staff and students to work together in partnership. By looking at assessment through this new lens, it should be possible to ensure that the majority of students, who are respectful and engaged, are rewarded for the efforts that they are putting into their studies.

Acknowledgments

Many thanks to Raymond Lister for providing his resources and notes on assessment, which helped to shape this chapter.

References

Ala-Mutka, K. M. (2005). A survey of automated assessment approaches for programming assignments. *Computer Science Education,* 15(2), 83–102.

Alam, L. (2004). Is plagiarism more prevalent in some forms of assessment than others. In *Beyond the Comfort Zone: Proceedings of the 21st ASCILITE Conference* (pp. 48–57). Tugun, Australia: Australasian Society for Computers in Learning in Tertiary Education.

Amelung, M., Piotrowski, M., & Rösner, D. (2006). EduComponents: Experiences in e-assessment in computer science education. In *Proceedings of the 11th Annual SIGCSE Conference on Innovation and Technology in Computer Science Education (ITICSE '06)* (pp. 88–92). New York: ACM.

Anderson, L. W., Krathwohl, D. R., Airasian, P. W., Cruikshank, K. A., Mayer, R. E., Pintrich, P. R., Raths, J. & Wittrock, M. C. (Eds.) (2001). *A Taxonomy for Learning and Teaching and Assessing: A Revision of Bloom's Taxonomy of Educational Objectives.* New York: Addison Wesley Longman.

Assessment Reform Group (1999). *Assessment for Learning: Beyond the Black Box.* Cambridge, UK: Cambridge University Press.

Astrachan, O., Walker, H., Stephenson, C., Diaz, L., & Cuny, J. (2009). Advanced placement computer science: the future of tracking the first year of instruction. *ACM SIGCSE Bulletin,* 41(1), 397–398.

Attwood, R. (2008). Institutions limit access to anti-cheat software. *Times Higher Education,* June 26, 2008. Retrieved from www.timeshighereducation.co.uk/story.asp?sectioncode=26&storycode=402540&c=2

Austin, M., & Brown, L. (1999). Internet plagiarism: Developing strategies to curb student academic dishonesty. *The Internet and Higher Education,* 2(1), 21–33.

Baugh, J., Kovacs, P., & Davis, G. (2012). Does the computer programming student understand what constitutes plagiarism. *Issues in Information Systems*, 13(2), 138–145.

Biggs, J., & Tang, C. (2007). *Teaching for Quality Learning at University*, 3rd edn. Maidenhead, UK: Society for Research into Higher Education and Open University Press.

Biggs, J. B., & Collis, K. F. (1982). *Evaluating the Quality of Learning: The SOLO Taxonomy (Structure of the Observed Learning Outcome)*. New York: Academic Press.

Birenbaum, M., DeLuca, C., Earl, L., Heritage, M., Klenowski, V., Looney, A., Smith, K., Timperley, H., Volant, L., & Wyatt-Smith, C. (2015). International trends in the implementation of assessment for learning: Implications for policy and practice. *Policy Futures in Education*, 13(1), 117–140.

Black, P., & Wiliam, D. (1998). Assessment and classroom learning. *Assessment in Education: Principles, Policy & Practice*, 5(1), 7–74.

Bloom, B. S., Englehart, M. D., Furst, E. J., Hill, W. H., & Krathwohl, D. (1956). *Taxonomy of Educational Objectives: Handbook I: Cognitive Domain.* New York: Longmans.

Bloom, B. S., Hasting, T., & Madaus, G. (1971). *Handbook of Formative and Summative Evaluation of Student Learning.* New York: McGraw-Hill.

Boywer, K., & Hall, L. (1999). Experience using "MOSS" to detect cheating on programming assignments. In *29th ASEE/IEEE Frontiers in Education Conference* (pp. 18–22). New York: IEEE.

Brookhart, S., & Durkin, D. (2003). Classroom assessment, student motivation, and achievement in high school social studies classes. *Applied Measurement in Education*, 16(1), 27–54.

Brown, N., & Janssen, R. (2017). Preventing plagiarism and fostering academic integrity: A practical approach. *Journal of Perspectives in Applied Academic Practice*, 5(3), 102–109.

Brown, S., & Knight, P. (2012). *Assessing Learners in Higher Education.* New York, NY: Routledge.

Buffum, P. S., Lobene, E. V., Frankosky, M. H., Boyer, K. E., Wiebe, E. N., & Lester, J. C. (2015). A practical guide to developing and validating computer science knowledge assessments with application to middle school. In *Proceedings of the 46th ACM Technical Symposium on Computer Science Education (SIGCSE '15)* (pp. 622–627). New York: ACM.

Caceffo, R., Wolfman, S., Booth, K. S., & Azevedo, R. (2016). Developing a computer science concept inventory for introductory programming. In *Proceedings of the 47th ACM Technical Symposium on Computing Science Education (SIGCSE '16)* (pp. 364–369). New York: ACM.

Cadmus (2017). What is Cadmus? Retrieved from http://cadmus.io

Cardell-Oliver, R. (2011). How can software metrics help novice programmers? In *Proceedings of the Thirteenth Australasian Computing Education Conference Volume 114* (pp. 55–62). Darlinghurst, Australia: Australian Computer Society.

Carter, J., Ala-Mutka, K., Fuller, U., Dick, M., English, J., Fone, W., & Sheard, J. (2003). How shall we assess this? *ACM SIGCSE Bulletin*, 35(4), 107–123.

Clare, J., Walker, S., & Hobson, J. (2017). Can we detect contract cheating using existing assessment data? Applying crime prevention theory to an academic integrity issue. *International Journal for Educational Integrity*, 13, 4.

Clarke, R., & Lancaster, T. (2006). Eliminating the successor to plagiarism? Identifying the usage of contract cheating sites. In *2nd Plagiarism: Prevention, Practice and Policy Conference 2006*. Newcastle, UK. Retrieved from www.plagiarism.org/paper/eliminating-the-successor-to-plagiarism

Clear, T., Whalley, J., Lister, R. F., Carbone, A., Hu, M., Sheard, J., Simon, B., & Thompson, E. (2008). Reliably classifying novice programmer exam responses using the SOLO taxonomy. In *21st Annual conference of the National Advisory Committee on Computing Qualifications (NACCQ 2008)* (pp. 23–30). Auckland, New Zealand: National Advisory Committee on Computing Qualifications.

College Board (2018). AP Computer Science A. Retrieved from https://apcentral.collegeboard.org/courses/ap-computer-science-a/course

Crocker, L., & Algina, J. (1986). *Introduction to Classical and Modern Test Theory*. Orlando, FL: Holt, Rinehart and Winston.

Culwin, F. (2009). The efficacy of Turnitin and Google. In *Proceedings of the Tenth Annual Higher Education Academy Conference in Information and Computer Sciences* (pp. 65–69). Newtownabbey, UK: HE Academy Subject Centre for ICS.

Culwin, F., MacLeod, A., & Lancaster, T. (2001). Source code plagiarism in UK HE computing schools. In *2nd Annual Conference of the LTSN Centre for Information and Computer Sciences*. London, UK: LTSN Centre for Information and Computer Sciences.

Curtis, G., & Clare, J. (2017). How prevalent is contract cheating and to what extent are students repeat offenders? *Journal of Academic Ethics*, 15(2), 115–124.

Cutts, Q., Connor, R., Michaelson, G., & Donaldson, P. (2014). Code or (not code). In *Proceedings of the 9th Workshop in Primary and Secondary Computing Education (WiPSCE '14)* (pp. 20–28). New York: ACM.

Daly, C., & Waldron, J. (2004). Assessing the assessment of programming ability. *ACM SIGCSE Bulletin*, 36(1), 210–213.

Davis, M., & Carroll, J. (2009). Formative feedback within plagiarism education: Is there a role for text-matching software? *International Journal for Educational Integrity*, 5(2), 58–70.

Denny, P., Hamer, J., Luxton-Reilly, A., & Purchase, H. (2008). PeerWise: Students sharing their multiple choice questions. In *Proceedings of the Fourth International Workshop on Computing Education Research* (pp. 51–58). New York: ACM.

Denny, P., Luxton-Reilly, A., & Simon, B. (2008). Evaluating a new exam question: Parsons problems. In *Proceedings of the Fourth International Workshop on Computing Education Research (ICER '08)* (pp. 113–124). New York: ACM.

Dick, M., Sheard, J., Bareiss, C., Carter, J., Joyce, D., Harding, T., & Laxer, C. (2003). Addressing student cheating: Definitions and solutions. *ACM SIGCSE Bulletin*, 35(2), 172–184.

Dikli, S. (2006). An overview of automated scoring of essays. *The Journal of Technology, Learning and Assessment*, 5(1), 36 pages.

Doctupus (2017). Contract Cheating Detection. Retrieved from https://angel.co/doctupus

Dunlosky, J. (2013). Strengthening the student toolbox: Study strategies to boost learning. *American Educator*, 37(3), 12–21.

Ďuračík, M., Kršák, E., & Hrkút, P. (2017). Current trends in source code analysis, plagiarism detection and issues of analysis big datasets. *Procedia Engineering*, 192, 136–141.

Earl, L. M. (2012). *Assessment as Learning: Using Classroom Assessment to Maximize Student Learning*. Thousand Oaks, CA: Corwin Press.

Ebel, R., & Frisbie, D. (1986). *Essentials of Educational Measurement*. Englewood Cliffs, NJ: Prentice Hall.

Engels, S., Lakshmanan, V., & Craig, M. (2007). Plagiarism detection using feature-based neural networks. *ACM SIGCSE Bulletin*, 39(1), 34–38.

Evans, C. (2013). Making sense of assessment feedback in higher education. *Review of Educational Research*, 83(1), 70–120.

Evans, C. (2016). Enhancing assessment feedback practice in higher education: The EAT framework. Retrieved from https://eatframework.org.uk/

Ferrero, J., Agnès, F., Besacier, L., & Schwab, D. (2017). Using word embedding for cross-language plagiarism detection. In *Proceedings of the 15th Conference of the European Chapter of the Association for Computational Linguistics: Volume 2, Short Papers* (pp. 415–421). Stroudsburg, PA: Association for Computational Linguistics.

Fincher, S., & Finlay, J. (2016). Computing graduate employability: Sharing practice. Project report. Council of Professors and Heads of Computing, Kent, UK. Retrieved from https://kar.kent.ac.uk/53848/

Fincher, S., & Knox, D. (2013). The porous classroom: Professional practices in the computing curriculum. *Computer*, 9, 44–51.

Fincher, S., Kölling, M., Utting, I., Brown, N., & Stevens, P. (2010). Repositories of teaching material and communities of use: nifty assignments and the greenroom. In *Proceedings of the Sixth International Workshop on Computing Education Research* (pp. 107–114). New York: ACM.

Fincher, S., Petre, M., & Clark, M. (Eds.) (2001). *Computer Science Project Work: Principles and Pragmatics*. London, UK: Springer.

Fitzgerald, S., Hanks, B., McCauley, R., Lister, R., & Murphy, L. (2013). What are we thinking when we grade programs? In *Proceedings of the 44th ACM Technical Symposium on Computer Science Education (SIGCSE '13)* (pp. 471–476). New York: ACM.

Fraser, R. (2014). Collaboration, collusion and plagiarism in computer science coursework. *Informatics in Education – An International Journal*, 13(2), 179–195.

Fuller, U., Johnson, C. G., Ahoniemi, T., Cukierman, D., Hernán-Losada, I., Jackova, J., Lahtinen, E., Lewis, T. L., Thompson, D. M., Riedesel, C., & Thompson, E. (2007). Developing a computer science-specific learning taxonomy. *ACM SIGCSE Bulletin*, 39(4), 152–170.

Gibson, J. (2009). Software reuse and plagiarism: a code of practice. *ACM SIGCSE Bulletin*, 41(3), 55–59.

Gillam, L., Marinuzzi, J., & Ioannou, P. (2010). Turnitoff – Defeating plagiarism detection systems. In *11th Annual Conference of the Subject Centre for Information and Computer Sciences* (pp. 84–88). Heslington, UK: Higher Education Academy.

Gilliver-Brown, K., & Ballinger, D. (2017). The integrity games: Using interactive comics to teach academic integrity concepts. *ATLAANZ Journal*, 2(1), 68–81.

Giordano, D., Maiorana, F., Csizmadia, A. P., Marsden, S., Riedesel, C., Mishra, S., & Vinikienė, L. (2015). New horizons in the assessment of computer science at school and beyond: Leveraging on the viva platform. In *Proceedings of the 2015 ITiCSE on Working Group Reports* (pp. 117–147). New York: ACM.

Goldman, K., Gross, P., Heeren, C., Herman, G. L., Kaczmarczyk, L., Loui, M. C., & Zilles, C. (2010). Setting the scope of concept inventories for introductory computing subjects. *ACM Transactions on Computing Education (TOCE)*, 10(2), 5.

Gouws, L. A., Bradshaw, K., & Wentworth, P. (2013). Computational thinking in educational activities. In *Proceedings of the 18th ACM Conference on Innovation and Technology in Computer Science Education (ITiCSE '13)* (pp. 10–15). New York: ACM.

Grieve, A., & Ross, B. (2016). Plagiarism by contract writing: Insights from forensic linguistics. In *Learning and Teaching Conference*. Melbourne, Australia. Retrieved from www.academia.edu/26115664/Plagiarism_by_contract_writing_Insights_from_forensic_linguistics

Guzdial, M. (2010). How computing and physics learning differ. Retrieved from https://computinged.wordpress.com/2010/04/01/how-computing-and-physics-learning-differ/

Hahn, J. H., Mentz, E., & Meyer, L. (2009). Assessment strategies for pair programming. *Journal of Information Technology Education: Research*, 8, 273–284.

Hakulinen, L., Auvinen, T., & Korhonen, A. (2015). The effect of achievement badges on students' behavior: An empirical study in a university-level computer science course. *International Journal of Emerging Technologies in Learning (iJET)*, 10(1), 18–29.

Halgamuge, M. (2017). The use and analysis of anti-plagiarism software: Turnitin tool for formative assessment and feedback. *Computer Applications in Engineering Education*, 25(6), 895–909.

Hendrick, C., & MacPherson, R. (2017) *What Does This Look Like in the Classroom?: Bridging the Gap between Research and Practice*. Woodbridge, UK: John Catt Educational.

Ibáñez, M. B., Di-Serio, A., & Delgado-Kloos, C. (2014). Gamification for engaging computer science students in learning activities: A case study. *IEEE Transactions on Learning Technologies*, 7(3), 291–301.

ICAI (2014). Fundamental values of academic integrity. Retrieved from https://academicintegrity.org/fundamental-values

Ihantola, P., Ahoniemi, T., Karavirta, V., & Seppälä, O. (2010). Review of recent systems for automatic assessment of programming assignments. In *Proceedings of the 10th Koli Calling International Conference on Computing Education Research* (pp. 86–93). New York: ACM.

Jenkins, T., & Helmore, S. (2006). Coursework for cash: The threat from online plagiarism. In *Proceedings of 7th Annual Higher Education Academy Conference in Information & Computer Sciences* (pp. 121–126). Newtownabbey, UK: HE Academy Subject Centre for ICS.

Jones, M., & Sheridan, L. (2015). Back translation: An emerging sophisticated cyber strategy to subvert advances in "digital age" plagiarism detection and prevention. *Assessment & Evaluation in Higher Education*, 40(5), 712–724.

Joy, M., & Luck, M. (1999). Plagiarism in programming assignments. *IEEE Transactions on Education*, 42(2), 129–133.

Joy, M., Cosma, G., Yau, J., & Sinclair, J. (2011). Source code plagiarism – A student perspective. *IEEE Transactions on Education*, 54(1), 125–132.

Juola, P. (2017). Detecting contract cheating via stylometric methods. In *Plagiarism Across Europe and Beyond 2017* (pp. 187–198). Brno, Czech Republic: European Network for Academic Integrity.

Kapp, K. M. (2012). *The Gamification of Learning and Instruction: Game-Based Methods and Strategies for Training and Education*. San Francisco, CA: John Wiley & Sons.

Koh, K. H., Basawapatna, A., Nickerson, H., & Repenning, A. (2014). Real time assessment of computational thinking. In *Visual Languages and Human-Centric Computing (VL/HCC)* (pp. 49–52). New York: IEEE.

Krathwohl, D. R. (2002). A revision of Bloom's taxonomy: An overview. *Theory Into Practice*, 41(4), 212–218.

Lancaster, T. (2013a). The application of intelligent context-aware systems to the detection of student cheating. In *Complex, Intelligent, and Software Intensive Systems (CISIS)* (pp. 517–522). New York: IEEE.

Lancaster, T. (2013b). The use of text matching tools for the prevention and detection of student plagiarism. In *Plagiarism Phenomenon In Europe: Research Contributes To Prevention* (pp. 37–49). Braga, Portugal: Aletheia – Associação Científica e Cultural da Faculdade de Filosofia da Universidade Católica Portuguesa.

Lancaster, T. (2017). Plagiarism and assessment. Retrieved from http://thomaslancaster.co.uk/blog/plagiarism-and-assessment

Lancaster, T., & Clarke, R. (2007). Assessing contract cheating through auction sites – A computing perspective. In *8th Annual Higher Education Academy Conference in Information and Computer Sciences* (pp. 91–95). Newtownabbey, UK: HE Academy Subject Centre for ICS.

Lancaster, T., & Clarke, R. (2014). An initial analysis of the contextual information available within auction posts on contract cheating agency websites. In *Advanced Information Networking and Applications Workshops (WAINA)* (pp. 548–553). New York: IEEE.

Lancaster, T., & Clarke, R. (2015). The implications of plagiarism and contract cheating for the assessment of database modules. In *13th International Workshop on Teaching, Learning and Assessment of Databases (TLAD 2015)* (pp. 55–66). York, UK: Higher Education Academy.

Lancaster, T., & Clarke, R. (2016). Contract cheating – The outsourcing of assessed student work. In T. Bretag (Ed.), *Handbook of Academic Integrity* (pp. 639–654). Berlin, Germany: Springer.

Lancaster, T., & Culwin, F. (2004). A comparison of source code plagiarism detection engines. *Journal of Computer Science Education*, 14(2), 101–112.

Linn, R., & Gronlund, N. (1995). *Measurement and Assessment in Teaching*. Upper Saddle River, NJ: Prentice Hall.

Lister, R. (2000). On blooming first year programming, and its blooming assessment. In *Proceedings of the Australasian Conference on Computing Education* (pp. 158–162). New York: ACM.

Lister, R., Clear, T., Bouvier, D. J., Carter, P., Eckerdal, A., Jacková, J., Lopez, M., McCartney, R., Robbins, P., Seppälä, O., & Thompson, E. (2010). Naturally occurring data as research instrument: Analyzing examination responses to study the novice programmer. *ACM SIGCSE Bulletin*, 41(4), 156–173.

Lister, R., Simon, B., Thompson, E., Whalley, J. L., & Prasad, C. (2006). Not seeing the forest for the trees: Novice programmers and the SOLO taxonomy. *ACM SIGCSE Bulletin*, 38(3), 118–122.

Lukashenko, R., Graudina, V., & Grundspenkis, J. (2007). Computer-based plagiarism detection methods and tools: an overview. In *Proceedings of the 2007 International Conference on Computer Systems and Technologies* (p. 40). New York: ACM.

Luxton-Reilly, A., & Petersen, A. (2017). The compound nature of novice programming assessments. In *Proceedings of the Nineteenth Australasian Computing Education Conference* (pp. 26–35). New York: ACM.

McCracken, M., Almstrum, V., Diaz, D., Guzdial, M., Hagan, H., Kolikant, Y. B., Laxer, C., Thomas, L., Utting, I., & Wilusz, T. (2001). A multi-national, multi-institutional study of assessment of programming skills of first-year CS students. *SIGCSE Bulletin*, 33(4), 125–180.

McNamara, D. S., Crossley, S. A., Roscoe, R. D., Allen, L. K., & Dai, J. (2015). A hierarchical classification approach to automated essay scoring. *Assessing Writing*, 23, 35–59.

Meerbaum-Salant, O., Armoni, M., & Ben-Ari, M. (2010). Learning computer science concepts with scratch. In *Proceedings of the Sixth International Workshop on Computing Education Research (ICER '10)* (pp. 69–76). New York: ACM.

Milligan, S., & Kennedy, G. (2017). To what degree? Alternative micro-credentialing in a digital age. In R. James, S. French & P. Kelly (Eds.), *Visions for Australian Tertiary Education* (pp. 41–54). Melbourne, Australia: Melbourne Centre for the Study of Higher Education.

O'Malley, M., & Roberts, T. (2012). Plagiarism on the rise? Combating contract cheating in science courses. *International Journal of Innovation in Science & Mathematics Education*, 20(4), 16–24.

Ottenstein, K. (1976). An algorithmic approach to the detection and prevention of plagiarism. *ACM SIGCSE Bulletin*, 8(4), 30–41.

Palomba, C. A., & Banta, T. W. (1999). *Assessment Essentials: Planning, Implementing, and Improving Assessment in Higher Education*. San Francisco, CA: Jossey-Bass.

Parker, A., & Hamblen, J. (1989). Computer algorithms for plagiarism detection. *IEEE Transactions on Education*, 32(2), 94–99.

Parker, M. C., Guzdial, M., & Engleman, S. (2016). Replication, validation, and use of a language independent CS1 knowledge assessment. In *Proceedings of the 2016 ACM Conference on International Computing Education Research* (pp. 93–101). New York: ACM.

Parlante, N. (2018) Nifty Assignments. Retrieved from http://nifty.stanford.edu/

Parsons, D., & Haden, P. (2006). Parson's programming puzzles: a fun and effective learning tool for first programming courses. In *Proceedings of the 8th Australasian*

Conference on Computing Education (pp. 157–163). Darlinghurst, Australia: Australian Computer Society.

Parsons, D., Wood, K., & Haden, P. (2015). What are we doing when we assess programming? In *Proceedings of the 17th Australasian Computing Education Conference, CPIT 160* (pp. 119–127). Sydney, Australia: ACS.

Patterson, B. F., & Ewing, M. (2013). Validating the use of AP exam scores for college course placement. *College Board Research Report 2013-2*. Retrieved from https://files.eric.ed.gov/fulltext/ED558108.pdf

Petersen, A., Craig, M., & Zingaro, D. (2011). Reviewing CS1 exam question content. In *Proceedings of the 42nd ACM Technical Symposium on Computer Science Education (SIGCSE '11)* (pp. 631–636). New York: ACM.

Prechelt, L., Malpohl, G., & Philippsen, M. (2002). Finding plagiarisms among a set of programs with JPlag. *Journal of Universal Computer Science*, 8(11), 1016–1038.

Project Quantum (2016). Project Quantum: Tests worth teaching. Retrieved from http://community.computingatschool.org.uk/resources/4382/single

Ramsden, P. (2003). *Learning to Teach in Higher Education*, 2nd edn. Abingdon, UK: RoutledgeFalmer.

Riedesel, C., Clear, A., Cross, G., Hughes, J., Simon, & Walker, H. (2012). Academic integrity policies in a computing education context. In *Proceedings of the Final Reports on Innovation and Technology in Computer Science Education 2012 Working Groups* (pp. 1–15). New York: ACM.

Roberts, E. (2002). Strategies for promoting academic integrity in CS courses. In *Frontiers in Education (FIE 2002)* (pp. F3G-14–F3G-19). New York: IEEE.

Rogerson, A., & McCarthy, G. (2017). Using Internet based paraphrasing tools: Original work, patchwriting or facilitated plagiarism? *International Journal for Educational Integrity*, 13, 2.

Rowntree, D. (1977). *Assessing Students: How Shall We Know Them*. London, UK: Harper & Row.

Sanders, K., Ahmadzadeh, M., Clear, T., Edwards, S. H., Goldweber, M., Johnson, C., Lister, L., McCartney, R., Patitsas, E., & Spacco, J. (2013). The Canterbury questionbank: Building a repository of multiplechoice CS1 and CS2 questions. In *Proceedings of the 18th Annual Conference on Innovation and Technology in Computer Science Education (ITiCSE) – Working Group Reports* (pp. 33–52). New York: ACM.

Schleimer, S., Wilkerson, D. S., & Aiken, A. (2003). Winnowing: Local algorithms for document fingerprinting. In *Proceedings of the 2003 ACM SIGMOD International Conference on Management of Data* (pp. 76–85). New York: ACM.

Scriven, M. (1967). The methodology of evaluation. In R. E. Stake (Ed.), *Perspectives of Curriculum Evaluation Vol. 1* (pp. 39–55). Chicago, IL: Rand McNally.

Sheard, J. (2012). Exams in computer programming: What do they examine and how complex are they? In *Proceedings of the 23rd Annual Conference of the Australasian Association for Engineering Education* (pp. 283–291). Barton, Australia: Engineers Australia.

Sheard, J., & Dick, M. (2011). Computing student practices of cheating and plagiarism: A decade of change. In *Proceedings of the 2011 Conference on Innovation & Technology in Computer Science Education* (pp. 233–237). New York: ACM.

Sheard, J., & Dick, M. (2012). Directions and dimensions in managing cheating and plagiarism of IT students. In *Proceedings of the 14th Australasian Computing*

Education Conference (pp. 177–185). Darlinghurst, Australia: Australian Computer Society.

Sheard, J., Carbone, A., D'Souza, D. & Hamilton, M. (2013). Assessment of programming: pedagogical foundations of exams. In *Proceedings of the 18th ACM Conference on Innovation and Technology in Computer Science Education* (pp. 141–146). New York: ACM.

Sheard, J., Carbone, A., Lister, R., Simon, B., Thompson, E., & Whalley, J. L. (2008). Going SOLO to assess novice programmers. *ACM SIGCSE Bulletin*, 40(3), 209–213.

Sheard, J., Markham, S., & Dick, M. (2003). Investigating differences in cheating behaviours of IT undergraduate and graduate students: The maturity and motivation factors. *Journal of Higher Education Research and Development*, 22(1), 91–108.

Sheard, J., Simon, Butler, M., Falkner, K., Morgan, M., & Weerasinghe, A. (2017). Strategies for maintaining academic integrity in first-year computing courses. In *Proceedings of the 2017 ACM Conference on Innovation and Technology in Computer Science Education* (pp. 244–249). New York: ACM.

Sheard, J., Simon, Carbone, A., Chinn, D., Laakso, M. J., Clear, T., De Raadt, M., D'Souza, D., Harland, J., Lister, R., Philpott, A., & Warburton, G. (2011). Exploring programming assessment instruments: A classification scheme for examination questions. In *Proceedings of the Seventh International Workshop on Computing Education Research* (pp. 33–38). New York: ACM.

Si, A., Leong, H., & Lau, R. (1997). Check: a document plagiarism detection system. In *Proceedings of the 1997 ACM Symposium on Applied Computing* (pp. 70–77). New York: ACM.

Simon, Cook, B., Sheard, J., Carbone, A., & Johnson, C. (2014). Student perceptions of the acceptability of various code-writing practices. In *Proceedings of the 2014 Conference on Innovation & Technology in Computer Science Education* (pp. 105–110). New York: ACM.

Simon, Sheard, J. Carbone, A., Chinn, D., Laakso, M., Clear, T., de Raadt, M., D'Souza, D., Lister, R., Philpott, A., Skene, A., & Warburton, G. (2012). Introductory programming: Examining the exams. In *Proceedings of the Fourteenth Australasian Computing Education Conference* (pp. 61–70). Darlinghurst, Australia: Australian Computer Society.

Simon, Sheard, J., Morgan, M., Petersen, A., Settle, A., Sinclair, J., Cross, G., & Riedesel, C. (2016). Negotiating the maze of academic integrity in computing education. In *Proceedings of the 2016 ITiCSE Working Group Reports* (pp. 57–80). New York: ACM.

Singh, A. (2013). Detecting plagiarism in MS Access assignments. *Journal of Information Systems Education*, 24(3), 177–180.

Sorva, J. (2012). *Visual Program Simulation in Introductory Programming Education* (doctoral dissertation). Aalto University.

Šprajc, P., Urh, M., Jerebic, J., Trivan, D., & Jereb, E. (2017). Reasons for plagiarism in higher education. *Organizacija*, 50(1), 33–45.

Staubitz, T., Klement, H., Renz, J., Teusner, R., & Meinel, C. (2015). Towards practical programming exercises and automated assessment in Massive Open Online Courses. In *Teaching, Assessment, and Learning for Engineering (TALE 2015)* (pp. 23–30). New York: IEEE.

Taylor, C., Zingaro, D., Porter, L., Webb, K. C., Lee, C. B., & Clancy, M. (2014). Computer science concept inventories: past and future. *Computer Science Education*, 24(4), 253–276.

Tew, A. E., & Dorn, B. (2013). The case for validated tools in computer science education research. *Computer*, 46(9), 60–66.

Tew, A. E., & Guzdial, M. (2010). Developing a validated assessment of fundamental CS1 concepts. In *Proceedings of the 41st ACM Technical Symposium on Computer Science Education* (pp. 97–101). New York: ACM.

Tew, A. E., & Guzdial, M. (2011). The FCS1: A language independent assessment of CS1 knowledge. In *Proceedings of the 42nd ACM Technical Symposium on Computer Science Education* (pp. 111–116). New York: ACM.

Thompson, E., Luxton–Reilly, A., Whalley, J. L., Hu, M., & Robbins, P. (2008). Bloom's taxonomy for CS assessment. In *Proceedings of the Tenth Conference on Australasian Computing Education (ACE '08)* (pp. 155–161). Darlinghurst, Australia: Australian Computer Society.

Utting, I., Tew, A. E., McCracken, M., Thomas, L., Bouvier, D., Frye, R., Paterson, J., Caspersen, M., Kolikant, Y., Sorva, J., & Wilusz, T. (2013). A fresh look at novice programmers' performance and their teachers' expectations. In *Proceedings of the ITICSE Working Group Reports Conference on Innovation and Technology in Computer Science Education* (pp. 15–32). New York: ACM.

Vasilevskaya, M., Broman, D., & Sandahl, K. (2014). An assessment model for large project courses. In *Proceedings of the 45th ACM Technical Symposium on Computer Science Education (SIGCSE '14)* (pp. 253–258). New York: ACM.

Wallace, M., & Newton, P. (2014). Turnaround time and market capacity in contract cheating. *Educational Studies*, 40(2), 233–236.

Whalley, J. L., Lister, R., Thompson, E., Clear, T., Robbins, P., Ajith Kumar, P. K., & Prasad, C. (2006). An Austalasian study of reading and comprehension skills in novice programmers, using the Bloom and SOLO taxonomies. In *Proceedings of the 8th Australian Conference on Computing Education (ACE '06)* (pp. 243–252). Darlinghurst, Australia: Australian Computer Society.

Wiggins, G. (1990). The case for authentic assessment. *Practical Assessment Research and Evaluation*, 2(2), 6.

Wittie, L., Kurdia, A., & Huggard, M. (2017). Developing a concept inventory for computer science 2. In *Frontiers in Education Conference (FIE)* (pp. 1–4). New York: IEEE.

Yorke, M. (2003). Formative assessment in higher education: Moves towards theory and the enhancement of pedagogic practice. *Higher Education*, 45(4), 477–501.

Zhang, Y., Lo, D., Kochhar, P., Xia, X., Li, Q., & Sun, J. (2017). Detecting similar repositories on GitHub. In *IEEE 24th International Conference on Software Analysis, Evolution and Reengineering (SANER)* (pp. 13–23). New York: IEEE.

15 Pedagogic Approaches

Katrina Falkner and Judy Sheard

15.1 Why Is Pedagogy Important?

Over the last couple of decades, there has been a shift in focus in our education systems from teacher-centered to student-centered education and increasing use of technology. These changes have provided impetus for the development and adoption of new and different pedagogic approaches. There are many factors that influence the choice of pedagogy, including contextual and discipline-based factors. These are important to understand as the pedagogic approach has direct and profound implications for student learning and the student learning experience.

Within the computing discipline, pedagogic approaches are of great concern. There are specific learning challenges in computing associated with comprehension of complex concepts, analytical and problem-solving skills, and implementation of a solution in a programming language. As evidence of these challenges is the extensive literature on students' difficulties with learning how to program. As a result, computing programs are often reported, although somewhat contentiously, as having high attrition and high failure rates (Watson & Li, 2014). Another concern related to pedagogic approaches is the lack of diversity within our student cohort, and in particular low numbers of female students.

The rapid evolution of computing poses additional challenges. To address industry needs, student preference, and pedagogic improvement, educators often choose to incorporate constant change in the programming languages, paradigms, platforms, and technologies they use. A recent challenge is the sharp increase in enrollments in many computing courses; at the same time, however, there are signs of decreasing student engagement. Although there has been considerable effort invested into adapting to students' learning needs, there is an apparent mismatch between the pedagogic approaches we use to teach our students and how they want to learn.

There are huge opportunities afforded by technology that can be used to address many teaching and learning issues and bring many benefits to students. Within the computing discipline, we have the knowledge to design, build, and adapt technology for teaching and learning. It is essential, however, to understand how technology can best enable or be effectively incorporated into a pedagogic approach, as the use of technology without clear purpose or adequate pedagogic support can introduce further risk of reducing student engagement (Preston et al., 2010).

With the range of pedagogic approaches we now have available, it is important that we are able to share practices that address the unique challenges of our discipline, increase accessibility and success in the learning of computing, and ensure an engaging and valuable learning experience for our students.

15.2 Background

Pedagogy is the science of how we promote learning and it consists of the learning activities, strategies, and techniques that provide the environment where learning may take place. Pedagogy is a widely applied but complex concept that includes relationships between the teacher, students, activities, and learning context. An important distinction is that pedagogy is about *how* teaching is done, rather than *what* is taught, while noting that one may influence the adoption of the other.

The term "pedagogy" can be applied to the educational approach used in a range of contexts from an individual activity to an entire course or teaching program. For the purposes of this chapter, we will use *pedagogy* when describing a set of activities and strategies that guide the teaching of a course. A pedagogy may define a specific approach (e.g., *blended learning*, a specific approach blending modes of learning) or a broad range of approaches (e.g., *active learning*, describing a number of approaches built around active student participation). We will use *pedagogic practice* when describing a specific activity within a course (e.g., *peer instruction*) (Simon & Cutts, 2012). In some cases, pedagogy will be used as an umbrella term for a set of pedagogic practices (e.g., contributing student pedagogy) (Collis & Moonen, 2005; Hamer et al., 2008).

There are many influences on the development of a pedagogy and how it is applied (Firmin et al., 2012). Some of these influences relate specifically to the discipline in which they are used, and this has led to the concept of *signature* pedagogies (Shulman, 2005). In our discussion, we will focus on pedagogies that are used in the computing discipline, and some of these will be specific to the computing discipline.

The two prominent theoretical positions that have influenced conceptions of learning are derived from *behavioral* and *cognitive* psychology. These provide quite different perspectives from which to understand the nature of learning. Behavioral psychologists view learning as directly observable behavior that can be measured by behavioral responses in the learner. Learning is seen as a process of conditioning by instruction that can guide and shape the learning through sequences of *stimuli, responses, feedback*, and *reinforcement* (Phillips & Soltis, 2015). Behaviorists equate learning with observable behavioral outcomes and do not consider the role of mental operations in the learning process. In contrast, cognitive psychologists focus on the mind as the agent of learning. They are concerned with the internal mental constructions and activities of the learner in preference to their external behavior. Cognitive psychologists stress the importance of learning through a variety of learning strategies that depend on the type of learning outcomes desired, reflecting associated cognitive processes. These strategies include *memorization, drill and practice, deduction,* and *induction* (Atkins, 1993; Jonassen, 1991; Reeves & Reeves, 1997).

Behaviorism and cognitive psychology are often presented as opposing philosophies in their explanations of learning. However, there are similarities in that both seek to effect learning through the design of specific tasks. The main differences are the foci on either external or internal activities of the learner and the epistemologies on which they are based (Jonassen, 1991). The behaviorist position draws on an *objectivist* view of knowledge. The central tenet of *objectivism* is that there exists a reality with a structure that can be assimilated by the learner. The role of the educator is to interpret, model, and present this reality to their students (Jonassen, 1991). From behaviorism and objectivism the *instructivist* approach to teaching and learning has evolved. This approach focuses on the structure and presentation of the learning material rather than the learners who act as recipients of the instruction.

In contrast, cognitive psychology focuses on the cognitive activity of the learner. Cognitive psychology encompasses a broad range of views on the structure of knowledge and the processes involved in learning. These range in a continuum from a view that learning is affected and monitored by external stimuli and mediated by cognitive processes to a view that learning is a cognitive process initiated by the learner. The first view is linked to an objectivist epistemology and the second to a *constructivist* epistemology (Lowyck & Elen, 1993).

Constructivism states that "students construct knowledge rather than merely receive and store knowledge transmitted by the teacher" (Ben-Ari, 1998). From a constructivist perspective, students learn by relating new concepts to existing ones, either by combining new knowledge with existing knowledge to create new cognitive structures or through reflection upon existing knowledge. Duffy and Cunningham (1996) propose that two commonly agreed-upon tenets of constructivism are as follows (p. 171):

- Learning is an active process of constructing rather than acquiring knowledge.
- Instruction is a process of supporting that construction rather than communicating knowledge.

Constructivist pedagogy encourages students to engage with and develop ownership over their learning processes, encouraging reflective and deep learning through supporting critical thinking, transferability, and self-directedness. In its simplest form, a constructivist pedagogy integrates student activities into the classroom (e.g., by incorporating group discussions, quizzes, or silent reflection designed to encourage engagement with learning objectives).

There has been significant research into the application of constructivist learning strategies, in both small and large classes, with the majority of studies identifying significant benefit in learning outcomes (Ben-Ari, 1998; Geer & Rudge, 2002; Prince, 2004). Prince (2004) undertakes a review of constructivist learning studies within Engineering or related courses, identifying that considerable evidence exists for the core elements of these approaches, while noting that results across the numerous studies vary in strength and the difficulty in assessing and measuring complex pedagogic approaches.

Constructivism is often classified into two views providing related but in some respects complementary perspectives (Duffy & Cunningham, 1996). One view is *cognitive constructivism*, an individual view of constructivism where knowledge is not transferred from one person to another, but in contrast, individuals construct knowledge by making connections between new experiences and established ideas (based on the work of Piaget, 1972, and Papert, 1993), and the other view is *sociocultural constructivism*, where knowledge is created through social and cultural activation (Ernest, 1995). Theories of sociocultural constructivism and community-based learning build upon the ideas that students engage more deeply with their learning processes when actively involved and when learning as part of a group.

Vygotsky (1978) elaborates the ideas of sociocultural constructivism through his observations of the *zone of proximal development*: that learning awakens a variety of internal development processes that operate only when one is working with others; that is, learning is achieved within a social context (a pairing or group) and as a direct result of the group activities. He viewed learning as a profoundly social process and emphasized the importance of the learner–instructor and learner–learner dialogue in order to help the learner progress through their zone of proximal development. He maintained that this is more than just exposing the learner to new material through the provision of resources or lectures; it is through dialogue with others that the learner constructs their understanding. The essential point is that learning is a mediated process. Learners are able to challenge their thoughts, beliefs, perceptions, and existing knowledge by collaborating with other students (Ewing, Dowling, & Coutts, 1998). In this model, learning of new concepts and processes is achieved by first establishing mastery as a group, and only then developing mastery as an individual through continued practice and internalization of knowledge.

Wenger (1998) also describes the importance of learning communities through his definition of communities of practice: communities of peers gathering to share and develop knowledge in a common context. In these communities, the roles of teacher and student are not fixed, but move around the group according to the current focus and expertise provided by individuals. This model of community-based learning echoes practice within industry, where cooperation with colleagues is suggested as a key professional skill and is also a key requirement in achieving expertise in software development (Sonnentag, 1998).

Modern pedagogic practice has tended toward constructivist or student-centered approaches over instructivist approaches. Approaches that support constructivist learning are frequently known as *active* learning approaches. Active learning pedagogic practices designed to support *cognitive constructivism* range from small-scale active learning practices that may be integrated into broader learning opportunities, such as minute papers and mind mapping (Phillips & Soltis, 2015), through to problem-based or enquiry-based learning approaches, where learning is driven by student motivation via the problem-solving process.

Sociocultural constructivist perspectives can be supported by a range of active, social pedagogic approaches, including collaborative learning, cooperative learning, contributing student pedagogy, blended learning, and massive open online course (MOOC)-based pedagogic approaches.

15.2.1 The Influence of Technology on Pedagogy

The increased integration of technology within our learning environments has inspired the development of pedagogic practices that take advantage of the affordances of technology. These technology-enabled and technology-enhanced pedagogic practices have had a profound impact on the teaching and learning of computing.

Advances in information, network, and communication technologies have enabled the development of online educational platforms and led to the proliferation of online learning resources. Increasingly, learning material and activities used in face-to-face mode are being made available online. In addition, technology has afforded new forms of resources, leading to innovative pedagogic practices. For example, the use of social media in education has led to new forms of learning activities and assessment (e.g., Vickers et al., 2014; Vozniuk, Holzer, & Gillet, 2014).

The ready availability of computing and communication devices means that students are now able to access learning resources and communicate with teaching staff and other students while off campus and at any time. This has inspired pedagogic approaches that recognize that learning now happens in many situations. Arguably the most widely used example is *blended learning*, where a course is designed with both face-to-face and online learning activities, with the educator selecting the most appropriate mode for each activity to achieve the learning outcomes. A pedagogic practice that draws on this approach is the *flipped classroom* (Bishop & Verleger, 2013).

Other technology innovations have inspired or enhanced pedagogic practices. A prominent example is MOOCs, which have motivated new pedagogic practices associated with blended and online learning. Another example is the use of learning analytics, which have led to pedagogic practices that enable students to monitor and understand their learning progress.

15.3 Implications for Practice within Computing

There exists a wide range of pedagogic approaches within the computing discipline supported, in turn, by a number of associated pedagogic practices. For example, in their recent survey, Sanders et al. (2017) identify 38 different forms of active learning in the computing literature alone, some building on well-established techniques from other disciplines, while others are specific to computing, often building from industry practice. Table 15.1 provides a representation of the key pedagogic approaches we are exploring in this chapter, along with relevant examples of pedagogic practice from the computing literature.

Implementation of pedagogic practice typically occurs within a real-world context, with matters such as physical space availability, technical capabilities,

Table 15.1 *Pedagogic approaches and relevant pedagogic practices.*

Pedagogy	Pedagogic practices	Description
Active learning	E.g., Parson's problems (Parsons & Haden, 2006); in-lecture activities or e-tivities (Salmon, 2004); test-driven development (Beck, 2002); test-first development (Politz, Krishnamurthi, & Fisler, 2014); live coding (Rubin, 2013)	General term to describe a range of practices where students are involved in actively *doing* and *reflecting* to facilitate their learning
Collaborative learning	E.g., peer instruction (Simon & Cutts, 2012); studio-based learning (Hundhausen, Narayanan, & Crosby, 2008)	General term to describe a range of practices where students collaborate in the learning process
Cooperative learning	E.g., Jigsaw (Aronson et al., 1978); pair programming (Williams & Kessler, 2002)	General term to describe a range of practices where students collaborate and have accountability for group learning
Contributing student pedagogy	E.g., content creation; activity creation; peer assessment or review (Earl, 1986)	General term to describe a range of collaborative practices where students produce valued artifacts for the purpose of contributing to other students' learning
Blended learning	E.g., Flipped classroom (Bishop & Verleger, 2013)	General term to describe a range of active instructional practices that blend modes of learning, typically online and face-to-face. Can be either individual or collaborative, but primarily collaborative
MOOC	E.g., xMOOC (Glance, Forsey, & Riley 2013); cMOOC (Siemens, 2005); hybrid models	General term to describe pedagogic approaches built on top of the MOOC format; used in other pedagogic practices

and budgetary or staffing considerations often constraining or influencing adoption and adaptation. It is common for implementations as described in the literature to express variations incurred from these or similar factors, and for characteristics from multiple pedagogic practices to be adopted together in order to meet to needs of the specific environmental context or cohort. An example of this is the work by Pollock and Harvey (2011), which integrates studio-based learning (Hundhausen, Narayanan, & Crosby, 2008), problem-based learning (Barrows, 1986), and active learning practices as a single practice. Another example is a CS1 course where a trio of pedagogic practices – media computation (Rich, Perry, & Guzdial, 2004), pair programming (Williams & Kessler, 2002), and peer instruction (Simon & Cutts, 2012) – were used in order to improve the quality of the course, improve retention, and appeal to a broader cohort of students (Porter & Simon, 2013)

Within our discussion here, we will attempt to provide a general overview of each pedagogic approach and include examples specific to computing, or applied within computing, of relevant pedagogic practices.

15.3.1 Active Learning (Cognitive Constructivist Approaches)

Sanders et al. (2017) identify that "active learning" is a poorly understood but widely used pedagogic term within the computing discipline, encompassing a wide range of pedagogic approaches with variation in their underpinning philosophy. They define active learning as having the following two key elements: students actively undertaking an activity and having an opportunity to think and/or reflect about their learning as part of the process. However, while most examples of active learning are indeed "active," not all encompass opportunities for reflection.

Prince (2004) provides a cross-discipline overview of active learning techniques and their effectiveness, while Hativa (2000) presents a general discussion of active learning activities that are suitable for integration within lectures (both cognitive and sociocultural constructivist).

Active learning practices are often, but not always, social. We draw a distinction between those active learning techniques that are based on a cognitive constructivist approach versus those that integrate elements of social or collaborative learning. Cognitive constructivist approaches to active learning provide opportunities for students to individually apply, test, and reflect on their learning and may vary in context, duration, and complexity.

Kurtz et al. (2014) present an example active learning pedagogic practice that requires students to take part in brief, tablet-based active learning activities during lectures. In this example, students undertake a mixture of *logical microlabs*, which require them to solve an abstract problem, submitted graphically via their tablet, and *code magnet microlabs*, where students are asked to solve the same problem, but this time programmatically. The approach used by Kurtz et al. creates a learning cycle where, after a period of lecture exploring new concepts, students firstly complete a logical microlab to facilitate understanding of the problem space, followed by a worked example *invention* phase where the instructor models the development of algorithmic understanding from the abstract problem, through to concrete implementation in the code magnet microlab. Students are given individual, immediate, high-level feedback via the assessment tools on their tablet.

Ebert and Ring (2016) present a similar pedagogic practice based on structured live-coding activities within lectures, building on a web-based presentation framework that allows sharing of developed software solutions within the lecture session. A similar, less technologically enhanced approach has been explored by Falkner and Palmer (2009).

Parsons and Haden (2006) introduced the idea of *Parsons' problems*, an active learning approach where students solve programming puzzles in which lines of code that represent a correct, well-formed solution to a programming problem must be placed in the correct order. Parsons' problems promote understanding of programming construction while enabling students to focus on program semantics rather than syntax. Parsons' problems constrain the logic choices within the program solution, providing enhanced scaffolding. The inclusion of *distractors* – incorrect lines of code included in the set of possible code segments – helps focus students on common errors while still providing constraint over the overall solution space. Web-based implementations provide automated and immediate feedback. Sirkiä (2016) combines Parsons' problems with algorithmic visualization, demonstrating potential for increased understanding through exposure of the notional machine (du Boulay, 1986; see also Section 15.4.4 and Chapter 12 for further discussion).

Active learning, both individual and collaborative, within the computing discipline can benefit greatly from inspiration from industry practice, adopting and adapting active application models used within industry to facilitate learning, while also exploring and building capacity in industry norms. Test-first development is an active learning pedagogic practice that applies the writing of software tests to guide the software development process (Politz et al., 2014), while test-driven development is a similarly active learning practice with a more formal process and structure for test and associated code development (Beck, 2002). Edwards (2004) argues for the benefits of test-driven development in building self-reflection skills, while Politz et al. (2014) explore the combination of peer review and test-first development through their construction of *in-flow* peer review of tests, identifying a causal impact on student learning improvement. Paul (2016) explores the explicit pedagogic practice of test-driven development activities as a way of exploring and understanding the problem space prior to undertaking the software development process.

15.3.2 Collaborative Learning

Collaborative learning involves students working together to informally facilitate their learning, embodying the sociocultural constructivist perspective. Collaboration in the computing classroom can take the form of the adoption of general collaborative practices such as incorporating activities like *think–pair–share* or scaffolded discussions in classroom settings (Hativa, 2000), technology-assisted collaborative note-taking (Jonas, 2013; Reilly et al., 2014), and computing-specific collaborative activities, including peer instruction (Simon & Cutts, 2012), studio-based learning (Hundhausen, Narayanan, & Crosby, 2008), and peer reviews (Clarke et al., 2014; Hundhausen, Agrawal, & Agarwal, 2013; Politz, Krishnamurthi, & Fisler, 2014).

Peer instruction involves students collaboratively problem-solving, with the aim being for students to engage in the practice of explaining core concepts as they collectively attempt to solve problems. Key aspects of the peer instruction practice include pre-review of content, with a pre-quiz on content knowledge to motivate and prime students with relevant content knowledge, and the development of a suite of problems that require students to demonstrate deep understanding of key concepts in order to approach a correct solution. Peer instruction has been shown to significantly improve student learning outcomes; as a key pedagogic practice within computing, peer instruction is discussed in more detail with a focus on students as teachers in Chapter 29.

Studio-based learning (Hundhausen, Narayanan, & Crosby, 2008) is a collaborative learning approach based on the idea of students working within a shared design space, supported frequently by technology aiding collaboration, discussion and sharing of application experiences. Students are typically presented with a substantial problem or series of related problems and iterate between a number of structured phases. These phases include independent design and development (within the *design studio*) and presentation and collaborative peer review within a design critique phase. Informal collaboration may occur within the independent stages, as needed and instigated by the learners; however, collaboration is critical to the success of the presentation and critique phase.

Studio-based implementations can vary in the degree of scaffolding and structure, however. Hundhausen, Narayanan, and Crosby (2008) identify the following two key elements that are common to all approaches:

- Representation construction, where students define their own visual presentation representations for their work (e.g., code, visualizations or algorithms);
- Representation presentation and discussion, where design critiques are used for presentation and discussion as a collaborative exercise.

Hundhausen, Narayanan, and Crosby (2008) identify that studio-based learning provides benefit through scalability, adaptability, and independence from technology, as students explore their own model of visualization or representation for their work, which may range from the use of art supplies through to sophisticated algorithm visualization technology. In their description, multiple implementation examples are explored, demonstrating the flexibility within the pedagogic practice and the variation in dependence on collaboration.

Carbone and Sheard (2002) describe a studio-based learning approach within a first-year IT context, adopting a studio model where students work across four studio spaces: a design studio dedicated to fundamental skill development, where students work either independently or in small groups; a second design studio dedicated to teamwork and large-scale discussions; a cafe-style informal meeting place facilitating reflection and informal social time; and a meeting room for more structured meetings, presentations, and consultations.

Hundhausen, Agrawal, and Agarwal (2013) extend the studio-based learning practice with the integration of pedagogic code reviews. In this extension, a code review process based on industry-inspired formal code inspection is part of the design critique phase. This extension expands on the opportunity to build communication, collaboration, feedback, and reflection skills available within the design critique phase with industry-based skills specific to the computing discipline.

15.3.3 Cooperative Learning

Cooperative learning (Slavin, 1991) is a sociocultural constructivist approach where students work in small groups or teams to help each other learn and are also responsible for each other's learning (in contrast to collaborative learning). In cooperative learning pedagogic practices, students are encouraged to discuss and debate discipline concepts, with a focus on assisting all students in the team with their learning. Typically, cooperative learning examples incorporate elements of individual accountability toward achieving group goals (i.e., the success of the team depends on individual learning, meaning that it is in each student's interest to facilitate the learning of others). In some cooperative learning approaches, the assessment itself is aligned with cooperative principles, with the group being assigned recognition or assessment grades based on the average academic performance of each member (Slavin & Cooper, 1999).

An important aspect of many cooperative learning implementations is that they embody *equal opportunities for success* (Slavin, 1991). In this approach, individual success is determined by improvement from past assessment exercises, providing each student with the opportunity to succeed. Slavin and Cooper (1999) have explored this aspect of cooperative learning as a means for managing and enhancing academic diversity in the classroom, as each student, regardless of their experience or capability, can contribute to the success of the group, with a reduction in competitiveness and individualism.

Portillo and Campos (2009) describe an implementation of the *jigsaw* cooperative learning technique applied to the creation of analysis class diagrams. The jigsaw technique (Aronson et al., 1978) consists of students working in teams, where each member of the team is assigned a specific task. Across the class, all students assigned the same task, who subsequently have the most knowledge of the class relevant to that task, meet in a so-called *expert group* to discuss and refine their understanding further. Each student then returns to their original group, where they are responsible for teaching their teammates the relevant aspects of their task. In Portillo and Campos's approach, each member of the team is asked to complete an analysis class diagram for a different use case specification, with expert teams being formed around each use case.

Beck and Chizik (2013) describe the use of cooperative learning within an introductory CS1 course using an approach similar to process-oriented guided-inquiry learning (POGIL) (Moog & Spencer, 2008). In this approach, the instructor takes on the role of leader and assists learning by asking questions that prompt deeper thinking or reflection. In Beck and Chizik's approach, there is an emphasis on evaluation, involving the whole class in questioning and discussion during the evaluation phase, to increase learning and aid reflection. Students are assigned roles during each activity, which are rotated in subsequent activities to provide a broad learning experience. Different forms of cooperative learning are applied in this approach, with students working in groups at times and in pairs at others.

Pair programming (Williams & Kessler, 2002) involves students working in pairs, with one member *driving* the cooperation by leading the typing or writing, while the other – the *navigator* – observes the driver, asking questions and making suggestions. These roles are switched at structured points. Williams et al. (2008) have identified a set of key guidelines for implementing pair programming within the classroom based on several years of experience in classroom application. Research has demonstrated that pair programmers are more effective, producing higher-quality outcomes in less time (Williams, 2000). A meta-analysis of 18 pair programming studies in an educational setting with a total sample size of 3,308 students found significant and positive effects on students' grades on programming assignments and exams and on student persistence (pass rates), but there was no significant effect on students' attitudes (Umapathy & Ritzhaupt, 2017). As a key pedagogic practice with students as teachers within the computing discipline, pair programming is explored further in Chapter 29.

15.3.4 Contributing Student Pedagogy

Contributing student pedagogy (CSP) (Collis & Moonen, 2005; Hamer et al., 2008) is a sociocultural constructivist approach that places the student firmly at the center of learning, with an emphasis on students using, and explicitly valuing, the products of other students' learning. Examples of pedagogic approaches supporting a CSP perspective include peer assessment and supplemental instruction.

In Hamer et al. (2008), CSP is defined as "A pedagogy that encourages students to contribute to the learning of others and to value the contribution of others," and this definition was subsequently refined as "A pedagogy that requires students to produce an artifact for the purpose of contributing to other students' learning, and encourages students to value these peer contributions" (Hamer et al., 2011). Key features of this refinement are (Hamer et al., 2011) as follows:

- The instructor is explicitly using a contributing student pedagogic design.
- The pedagogy includes the requirement that students produce artifacts.
- The students are aware that the audience for these artifacts includes other students.
- These artifacts are shared with other students for the purposes of their learning.

Peer assessment (Earl, 1986) involves peers reviewing, assessing, and providing feedback on student contributions and motivates students to engage in critical analysis skills. Purchase (2000) describes a peer assessment where students assess software artifacts (in this case, interface designs) produced by other students. Purchase introduces a training exercise encompassing the requirements and boundaries of peer review, including specific assessment criteria.

Peer review has been extended in several studies to software testing, including Smith et al.'s (2012) study, where a peer testing component is added to programing assignments within an introductory data structures course. Students first produce their own solution, then move to evaluating and testing other students' work, including the production of a testing methodology report, before the final phase of each student reviewing and reflecting on their own experience and the artifacts produced by their peers in the production of a peer testing report evaluating the process as a whole.

Politz, Krishnamurthi, and Fisler (2014) present an example of *in-flow peer review* within an online learning environment that incorporates test review and peer review while the student is developing their solution, rather than afterwards. In their approach, students are required to submit their software implementations and test suites at multiple points within the development process. Initial submissions at each point are then submitted to other students for review, judging both correctness and thoroughness. Students are only able to submit at later points if they have submitted all of their required reviews. With peer review occurring throughout the development process, it is more likely to be considered useful and to be used by peers (Clarke et al., 2014). Students are also able to establish a comparative baseline with others' work and to receive early, detailed feedback on misconceptions or poorly thought-out strategies. A detailed analysis of in-flow peer review and the choices available when implementing this pedagogic practice, including the critical aspect of rubric usage, is provided in Clarke et al. (2014).

Content creation, similar to supplemental instruction (Blanc, DeBuhr, & Martin, 1983), involves students learning through the development of teaching materials. Ching et al. (2005) explore a graduate class where students prepare instructional materials for a tutorial topic, which are then evaluated by their peers. The time required to prepare high-quality materials is recognized by the students involved, as are the benefits resulting from this effort. Nortcliffe (2005) describes an approach where students work collaboratively in designing and developing instructional materials for a web design course. Nortcliffe introduces an assessment function that incorporates individual and group performance and peer and self-assessment.

Further examples of content creation include the collaborative preparation of learning resources, such as glossaries and knowledge bases for discipline topics, frequently supported by online tools such as wikis and blogs (Elgort, Smith, & Toland, 2008; Lutteroth & Luxton-Reilly, 2008), and the development of algorithm visualizations (Crescenzi & Nocentini, 2007).

Activity creation involves students preparing learning activities that other students are expected to undertake, such as the creation of physical sorting games to illustrate the sorting method (Gehringer & Miller, 2009), as well as the learning materials on a core discipline concept, matched with an online

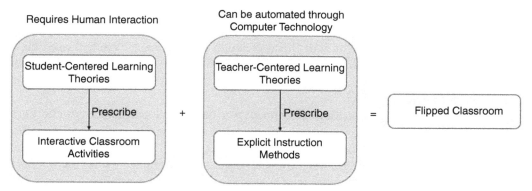

Figure 15.1 *The combination of student-centered learning activity and teacher-centered instruction as adopted within blended learning (adapted from Bishop & Verleger, 2013).*

quiz (Abad, 2008). PeerWise (Denny, Luxton-Reilly, & Hamer, 2008) is an activity creation practice that engages students to create multiple-choice questions as an assessment task, including the definition of multiple alternative answers and an explanation of why the correct answer is correct. Students are able to engage with the system to attempt to answer questions and are given the option of rating the difficulty of the question and providing comments. PeerWise promotes critical analysis, and research has shown that there is a positive correlation between activity within the PeerWise system and learning outcome (Luxton-Reilly et al., 2012). Studysieve (Luxton-Reilly, Plimmer, & Sheehan, 2010) is an extension of this model, supporting questions with free-text answers.

Kaczmarczyk, Boutell, and Last (2007) describe an approach combining content and activity creation within a CS1 course, where students are required to prepare instructional materials in the form of a *capsule* of learning designed to address one of a specific set of topics and including both content and activity design, assessment, and discussion prompts.

15.3.5 Blended Learning

Blended learning, implemented via the flipped classroom pedagogic practice (Bishop & Verleger, 2013), takes advantage of the availability of online or established resources, such as MOOCs, to *flip* the learning model toward an active pedagogic approach. In this model, face-to-face instructional time is focused on active or collaborative learning activities designed to encourage the application of learning, while access to discipline content, provided by existing resources, is undertaken independently, and ideally prior to the opportunities for application.

Figure 15.1 illustrates the relationship between student-centered (constructivist) and teacher-centered (instructivist) approaches within blended learning.

In this perspective, ownership of learning is placed within the student's context, with motivation for learning and engagement with resources being driven by active engagement with the application of knowledge. While flipped classroom pedagogies do not solely rely on the existence of online learning resources, their ease of use when these resources do exist has made this an increasingly prominent approach.

The flipped classroom pedagogy has been used extensively in the computing discipline. In a systematic review of the research on flipped classrooms by Giannakos, Krogstie, and Chrisochoides (2014), almost half of the studies reported (15 out of 32) were from computer science courses. More recent reports provide evidence of widespread uptake in computer science courses. For example Maher et al. (2015) describe strategies for flipped classroom implementations in four different computer science courses.

The terms "flipped" or "inverted" may imply a simple swapping of activities; however, in many cases, the implementation of a flipped classroom results in more complex pedagogic changes, with most involving technology. The review by Giannakos et al. (2014) found a variety of technologies used to flip the classroom. Video lectures were the most frequently used technology, but there were also a number of examples of animated readings and simulations. Online quizzes were used extensively either during or outside classes. Despite the emphasis on technology, a study (n = 284) by Tarimo, Deeb, and Hickey (2015) that compared outcomes from computer-based and pen-and-paper-based interactive classes found that while students preferred in-class engagements and interactions using computers, there were no significant differences in learning outcomes or the students' enjoyment of the material. A smaller study (n = 47) by Lacher and Lewis (2015) on the effectiveness of gate-check video quizzes found no differences in grades between the students who took the quizzes and those who did not.

Many studies have reported positive effects of flipped classrooms. The review by Giannakos et al. (2014) found benefits for students' performance, attitudes, and engagement. An early comparative quasi-experimental study (n = 46) by Day and Foley (2006) of flipped classroom and traditional offerings (control) of an introductory human–computer interaction class found that the students in the flipped classroom gained significantly higher grades and reported stronger positive attitudes about their experiences in contrast to the control group. A larger, more recent comparative study (n = 1901) by Horton et al. (2015) also found that students in the flipped classroom gained significantly higher grades; however, there were no differences in the pass rates and enjoyment of their course between this group and the control group. A smaller quasi-experimental study (n = 65) by Reza and Baig (2015) that investigated the effectiveness of a flipped (inverted) classroom model in a data structures and algorithms course found that students in the flipped classroom had higher levels of programming and problem-solving abilities than students in the traditional classroom, but there was no difference in their theoretical knowledge. Titterton, Lewis, and Clancy (2010), in their study of three blended learning cohorts, identified that increased learning outcomes were not consistent across all forms of assessment, with no significant difference in self-reported procrastination.

A flipped classroom pedagogy can present challenges to instructors and their students. Giannakos et al. (2014) found the main difficulties faced by instructors were that they spend more time in preparation, the students do not always respond well to the flipped classroom model, and there can be a decrease in class attendance. Students have reported negative experiences and impressions of the flipped classroom pedagogy. A flipped classroom typically requires students to prepare before class and be actively engaged in class, which some can find challenging. Lockwood and Esselstein (2013), reporting experiences in a flipped introductory programming class, found that some students struggled with time management and the requirement to attend class regularly. Maher et al. (2015), describing their experiences flipping four different courses, found from student feedback that some students felt that not enough time was spent on in-class teaching.

15.3.6 MOOC-Based Pedagogy

MOOCs have been adopted as a means to deliver content (usually freely) across distributed environments to anyone with an Internet connection and computer, often supported by social media structures that offer opportunities for collaboration and knowledge sharing, despite learner locations. MOOCs offer one means to deliver education at a broad scale to individuals with technological means and Internet access. Although online learning is not new, it has been argued that the difference between online learning and MOOC environments are the combination of teaching approaches course instructors use, the massive levels of participation, and their openness (Glance et al., 2013). Previously, technology-driven education has seen many names applied to describe this mode of learning, such as distance education and e-learning (Rudesta & Schoenholtz-Read, 2010).

Typically, two different types of MOOCs have been identified, one being based on existing university courses that embrace the use of videos to deliver content and online assessment ("xMOOCs") (Glance et al., 2013) and the other courses based around online communities and sociocultural constructivist principles called "cMOOCs" (Siemens, 2005).

At their simplest, xMOOCs, the current dominant model, support an instructivist perspective, with the structure of the MOOC focused on the computer-mediated presentation of learning material, with the majority of opportunities for student engagement through automated activities (Toven-Lindsey, Rhoads, & Lozano, 2015). A survey of a range of MOOC stakeholders (n = 106) by Armellini et al. (2016) found that "MOOCs provide good examples of technological innovation but also of highly debatable approaches to pedagogy" (p. 25).

Automated instruction platforms aim to facilitate learning at scale, and they can be personalized through reaction and modification in response to student activity and assessment results. Many xMOOCs adopt a model akin to this approach, with learners assimilating content in small, incremental steps, with immediate feedback and reinforcement provided through small, automated assessment exercises, such as "missing word" exercises or multiple choice questions. cMOOCs can be seen as the antithesis in many ways, with learners creating content and connecting opportunities for learning as an independent, self-directing community. However, as the development of MOOCs progresses, examples that integrate both cognitive and sociocultural constructivist pedagogic practices with more structured, content-driven learning approaches, forming a *hybrid* MOOC model, have become more common (Bayne & Ross, 2014). Swan, Day, and Bogle (2016) found variation in pedagogic approach in their analysis of 20 MOOCs from across multiple platforms, with increased adoption of collaborative and participatory approaches.

MOOCs provide the potential for the development of new pedagogic approaches within the online learning space, while also facilitating leveraging existing pedagogy for adaptation to the online learning space, particularly when adopted as part of a blended learning approach. There is further opportunity to explore the development of MOOC-specific pedagogy, with MOOCs still tending to adopt traditional distance learning pedagogy (Vassiliadis, Kameas, & Sgouropoulou, 2016).

Falkner et al. (2016) describe the development of a MOOC designed around active and collaborative pedagogic practices, incorporating motivational context through media computation (Rich, Perry, & Guzdial, 2004). They found higher than average participation rates from female learners in comparison to both online and traditionally taught introductory computing courses. While learning outcomes demonstrated effectiveness in building initial skill with fundamental programming concepts in a pattern that repeated through the course, when first designing and using new constructs, students reverted to their more limited usage of previous concepts, indicating a lack of depth of understanding and a need to explore further scaffolding.

Rizzardini and Amado-Salvatierra (2017) describe their MicroMasters MOOC model where the MOOC itself is explicitly positioned as only one of three learning phases, with pre-MOOC and post-MOOC phases designed to facilitate the construction of ongoing learning communities in order to provide opportunities for social learning. Piccioni, Estler, and Meyer (2014) describe their experiences in developing an introductory programming MOOC as a supplementary learning environment for their on-campus course. In this approach, the MOOC was an optional component, with the course retaining its standard approach (i.e., not flipped), with students engaging significantly in both on-campus and MOOC learning activities.

Grover, Pea, and Cooper (2014) present a computational thinking MOOC targeted at middle school, explicitly identifying strategies for promoting active learning within a MOOC environment, including the use of worked examples, code tracing, quizzes, Parsons' problems and hands-on assignment tasks. This approach showed equivalent or slightly better results in learning outcomes compared with previous face-to-face course cohorts. Falkner et al. (2017)

describe the design of a MOOC to support teacher professional development in computing, adopting a sociocultural constructivist perspective, defining active learning through scaffolded, direct application of MOOC content to the professional context, and using a community of practice model of shared repository building.

15.4 Influences on Pedagogic Practices

Within the computing discipline, there are contextual factors that guide and shape the development of pedagogy and influence how it is applied in a particular situation. An important consideration is that there are factors that prevent or constrain application of a pedagogy. For example, changing from a standard lecture or tutorial class to a studio environment may not be possible if there are no suitable teaching spaces available. In some circumstances, the desire to implement a particular pedagogy becomes a strong driver for change. For example, there is evidence to indicate that pedagogy has influenced the design of teaching spaces (and vice versa) (Walker, Brooks, & Baepler, 2011). Some educational development environments developed for learning programming have been designed to facilitate particular pedagogic approaches. For example, Scratch, Alice, and Greenfoot aim to engage and empower students by enabling the development of games, simulations, and stories that can connect to their interests (Utting et al., 2010)

When exploring the pedagogic approach that may be best suited to our purposes, it is important to also understand the context and motivations that most effectively guide learning and the application of pedagogic practice. With the current emphasis on student-centered education, the factors that influence pedagogy are often related to awareness and understanding of students' needs. This places emphasis on practices that address specific learning challenges, attempt to interest and motivate students, and increase access and inclusion.

15.4.1 Addressing Learning Challenges

There are a number of pedagogic approaches that address students' learning challenges specific to the computing discipline. For example, it is understood that explicit awareness of the *notional machine* (du Boulay, 1986) – an abstract representation of the machine that corresponds to program execution in the language being learned – facilitates learning to program and establishing a correct mental model for program execution (this is discussed further below). As another example, we can observe the creation of specific pedagogic practices based around supporting objects-first or objects-last approaches to teaching programming within the object-oriented programming paradigm (e.g., Cooper, Dann, & Pausch, 2003; Kölling & Barnes, 2004; Moritz & Blank, 2005). The desire to prepare students for future work in industry has motivated the adoption and expansion of pedagogic approaches that build communication, collaboration, and cooperation skills, as well as pedagogic practices explicitly derived from industry practice (e.g., test-driven development).

15.4.2 The Importance of Context and Motivation for Pedagogic Practice

Concerns about low student engagement and poor retention rates in computing courses have been an impetus for pedagogic practices that are tailored to students' interests. For example, teaching programming through the context of games, media computation, or creative coding provides a motivational context that can assist in engaging students and increasing retention rates.

Games are used extensively in computing courses and, in particular, there are many reports of game-based pedagogies in introductory programming courses. When used for a learning activity in a programming course, games can be played or they can be designed and built. A review by Batista et al. (2016) identified a number of reports on the use of game-based construction to teach programming. They found that most studies reported an increase in students' motivation and engagement, as well as other benefits. For example, Leutenegger and Edgington (2007) used a "games-first" approach to teaching introductory programming. Using Flash and ActionScript for game development, they found higher retention and increased interest, and this approach positively influenced both men and women. They argue that games-based curricula can entice students to study computer science and games-based assignments can engage and motivate students, potentially leading to increased learning outcomes. Corral et al. (2014) used a game-based approach with tangible user interfaces (TUIs). In an experimental study (n = 30) that compared their innovative approach with a traditional approach, they found that students in the game-based TUI approach showed higher interest and achieved higher grades than students in the traditional course. With all of the changes needed to incorporate games into a course, Batista et al. (2016) argue for the need and propose a framework for an effective game-based pedagogy. While there is extensive evidence to support games as a motivating context, there is a lack of critical research to support increased learning outcomes (Battistella & Gresse von Wangenheim, 2016).

Another game-related pedagogic approach is gamification, where game design elements such as leaderboards, badges, and constant feedback are incorporated into instruction. Pirker, Riffnaller-Schiefer, and Gütl (2014) used gamification in their pedagogic approach in an introductory programming class. An end-of-semester survey (n = 21) showed that students found the course more motivating than other courses they had taken and identified a higher degree of interactivity. While numerous studies exist applying gamification and badges as a motivational approach, there is evidence that these forms of extrinsic motivation may be problematic for long-term learning gain and broader learning motivation

(Falkner & Falkner, 2014). There is a need for further research to isolate the specific benefits of gamification and to ascertain any lasting impact.

Media computation is a pedagogic approach for teaching introductory programming whereby manipulation of media, such as digital images and sounds, is used as a context to teach programming concepts. The purpose of using media computation is to make the learning of programming engaging and relevant to students, resulting in increased retention and learning outcomes. Guzdial (2013), in a review of ten years of running media computation courses, found evidence in support of increases in course retention, but not in learning gains. A particular goal of Guzdial's use of media computation was to increase the engagement and success of female students. From interview studies, Guzdial reports that female students found the content useful and the course more motivating than traditional courses.

Another pedagogic approach designed to interest and motivate is where students learn to program using physical devices. Some education technologies have been developed for this purpose, such as Lego Mindstorms (Lui et al., 2010; Wakeling, 2008). Programming physical devices gives students real, hands-on experience with immediate feedback, creating an engaging learning experience; however, they also pose distinct challenges through the cognitive load of understanding the physical device itself (Desportes et al., 2016). Summet et al. (2009) describe their introductory programming class where each student has their own robot, giving them the freedom to explore these devices both during and out of class. Blank (2006) proposes that giving each student their own robot personalizes the learning experience, helping to attract more students and a diversity of students to computer science.

15.4.3 Accessibility and Inclusivity

Computing programs are characterized by low diversity within the student population. Concerns about equity and diversity issues such as low numbers of female students have inspired pedagogic approaches that are accessible and inclusive. For example, giving students experiences that demonstrate the diversity of computing applications and emphasize their social relevance has been argued to promote the accessibility and inclusivity of a computing course (Buckley, Nordlinger, & Subramanian, 2008; Fisher & Margolis, 2002; Khan & Luxton-Reilly, 2016).

A longitudinal study by Fisher and Margolis (2002) involving over 230 interviews of computer science students found that the stereotypical view of the "geek" computing student led to an alienating culture that reduced confidence, interest, and ultimately success rates, and this negative impact was greater on females and minority groups. To remedy this, Margolis and Fisher proposed a pedagogic approach that puts computing in a social context and shows students that there are multiple ways to be a computer scientist.

Aligned to this view, Pulimood and Wolz (2008) propose that equity in computer science programs can be achieved through changing the classroom pedagogy. They describe their implementations of authentic learning environments where students work in heterogeneous groups solving real problems. They argue that collaborative problem-solving in a gender-neutral, culturally and ethnically diverse, and multidisciplinary groups will make computer science more accessible to females and minority groups. Pulimood and Wolz also claim that this approach better prepares students for the workforce.

Rubio et al. (2015) contend that "if we want to include more women in computing, the pedagogy of introductory programming courses needs to change" (p. 410). They designed and implemented modules using physical computing activities with the Arduino microcontroller board. In an experimental study (n = 38) to determine any differences in the perceptions of learning to program and learning outcomes, they found that, with traditional teaching methods, women perceived programming to be harder than men and they indicated less desire to continue with programming in their study or profession. However, there was no difference with the group that learned to program using the Arduino device.

From a similar motivation of accessibility but with a different approach, Brady et al. (2017) engage students' interest through projects with contexts that illustrate the social and collaborative aspects of computer science. They use physical computing activities and participatory simulations to prepare students for the diverse domain of computing. Brady et al. describe the implementation of this pedagogic approach in a Computational Thinking for Girls (CT4G) project and propose that showing students the social and diverse aspects of computing can be a powerful tool to engage underrepresented groups.

Medel and Pornaghshband (2017) use examples of teaching material from different computer science courses to demonstrate how a pedagogic approach can introduce a gender bias through particular representations of gender, stereotypical imagery, and male-centered language. Medel and Pornaghshband offer suggestions for reducing or eliminating this bias to maximize gender inclusion.

15.4.4 The Notional Machine and Supporting Pedagogic Practices

The act of learning programming involves concurrently developing skill and knowledge in several related areas: planning, design, programming language structure, and also an understanding of how programs are to be executed. Students must learn both how to craft programs to achieve a fixed output as well as comprehending what an existing program will do. Knowledge of the *notional machine*, as defined by du Boulay (1986), consists of "the general properties of the machine that one is learning to control," as defined by the semantics of the programming language in use, and is designed to facilitate learning of programming by making program execution explicit as part of the learning process. The notional machine formed an important concept with a strong influence on pedagogic development within computer science and in informing a significant amount of computer science education research (see Chapter 12 for further description).

Pedagogic practices have been introduced in order to support the notional machine as an abstraction of programming execution designed to expose those elements of the execution process that will aid understanding, such as memory usage and instruction sequencing, without exposing those details that are unnecessary to form the appropriate mental model of programming semantics. The level of detail required in our notional machine varies by the learning context and the depth and detail of the required mental model to be established (Sorva, 2013); similarly, our notional machine will vary depending on the programming language in use. From this perspective, a notional machine is an abstract, idealized representation of aspects of runtime execution for a specific programming language and context that are relevant to supporting the understanding of how a program is executed.

Without an appropriate mental model of a notional machine, it is considered that student knowledge of the programming process and processing languages is "fragile" (Perkins, Schwartz, & Simmons, 1990) and that challenges faced by novices in learning to program are frequently due to their mental model of the notional machine being "inadequate" (Smith & Webb, 1995). Without making the notional machine explicit in our learning processes, we risk students forming incomplete or conflicting mental models that are littered with misconceptions and often informed by guesswork. Indeed, when forming initial mental models, beginners tend to attribute human reasoning to the computer, incorporating assumptions about the semantics implied by natural language analogies of programming language terms (du Boulay, O'Shea, & Monk, 1981), the semantics of variables names, or the positioning of statements within the overall code (Ragonis & Ben-Ari, 2005) (see Chapter 13 for a related discussion).

Research designed to support notional machine mental model construction has introduced both pedagogic approaches (e.g., comprehension-first and design-based pedagogy) as well as instructional approaches, such as the construction of program writing and visualization tools to facilitate exposing the notional machine as part of the learning process.

Visualization in particular has developed as a common instructional device for supporting comprehension-first or comprehension-based pedagogy. Sorva, Karavirta, and Malmi (2013) present a comprehensive review of generic program visualization systems used for introductory programming education, exploring visualization as a technique for establishing a notional machine, as well as more broadly to support the development of conceptions of the dynamic nature of program execution, addressing common misconceptions, and supporting the skill of tracing.

Visualizations, be they manual visualization exercises or sophisticated, automated tools, have long been proposed as a mechanism for establishing a mental model of a notional machine, from early work by Mayer (1975, 1976) through to Cunningham et al.'s (2017) recent replication study of the use of sketching and sketching strategies to illustrate understanding, identifying benefits in distributing cognition and managing cognitive load. A constructivist

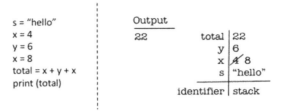

Figure 15.2 *Memory visualization exploring primitive data types and the correspondence between variable name and value (adapted from Dragon & Dickson, 2016).*

perspective encourages students to actively engage with visualizations through active and collaborative learning activities instead of solely observing visualization operation (Hundhausen, Douglas, & Stasko, 2002). There are many examples of visualization activities and tools, and we would advise the reader to review Sorva et al. (2013) and Hundhausen et al. (2002) for more detailed discussions. However, we will present a small number of examples here to highlight the applicability of these approaches and current practice.

Hertz and Jump (2013) and Dragon and Dickson (2016) present hand-drawn approaches to tracing memory usage within programs to help establish a mental model of the notional machine and facilitate understanding of program execution. Both approaches describe interactive student activities where students work through a series of tracing exercises using established templates for memory visualization. Dragon and Dickson present multiple examples, crossing languages and concepts, illustrating the development of the notional machine and its increasing complexity through increasing detail and sophistication of their visualization techniques as students' understanding and experience develop, moving from a simple stack visualization (see Figure 15.2) through to examples supporting visualization of pointers, explicit vs. implicit allocation, and deallocation (see Figure 15.3).

Recent work in the context of visualization tools include Sorva and Sirkiä's (2010) work within the UUhistle environment (a highly interactive visualization environment representing memory as abstract graphics) that introduces the idea of visual program simulation as an explicit active learning activity that requires learners to control the progression of the simulation – in a sense, acting as the "computer." Sirkliä and Sorva (2015) extend their efforts in this domain with more recent work in the development of a new program visualization framework that supports educators in integrating program visualizations into their teaching context, including annotations with text, audio, and interactive activities.

Another recent development is Guo's (2013) web-based Python simulation and visualization environment that allows learners to move backward and forward through an execution, visualizing stack frames and variables, heap object contents, and memory. While earlier work has long provided similar technical support for this degree of program simulation and visualization (Findler et al, 2002), an interesting aspect of this tool is the ability to generate a URL for a

```
#include <iostream>
using namespace std;
int main () {
    int stackX = 5;
    int* stackPtr = &stackX;
    int* heapPtr = new int;
    *stackPtr = 10;
    *heapPtr = 20;
    cout << "\n on stack: " << stackX;
    cout << "\m on heap: " << *heapPtr;
    delete heapPtr;
    heapPtr = nullptr;
    return 0;
}
```

Output
on stack: 10
on heap: 20

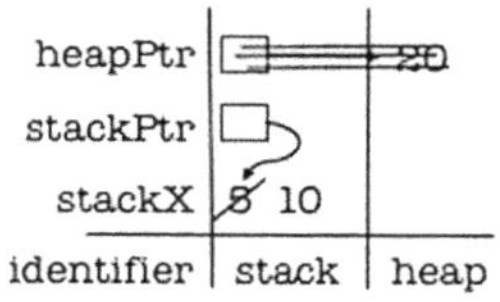

Figure 15.3 *Memory visualization of a C++ program facilitating understanding of memory addressing, allocation, and deallocation (adapted from Dragon & Dickson, 2016).*

specific point in the execution visualization, which can be shared among learners to aid collaboration and discussion.

More recent work has explored the explicit structuring of much of this pedagogic basis in the form of an explicit comprehension-first pedagogy (Nelson, Xie, & Ko, 2017), where programming semantics are taught prior to the learning of how to program. In this example of comprehension-first pedagogy, students learn to trace and understand the execution of a program prior to learning program development and through the execution of a notional machine.

15.5 Challenges and Future Directions

Computing educators have many options for their pedagogic practices, and there is much evidence of innovative teaching techniques, tools, and resources in computing education. Much of the recent effort has been in response to a focus on student-centered and active learning and has been largely facilitated by advancements in computing and information technology. Despite these efforts, however, computing educators face a number of challenges. A fundamental issue is an apparent mismatch between the pedagogy used and the way students choose to learn. This is widely evidenced by changes in the way that students engage with traditional learning resources, including teaching spaces (Kandiko & Mawer, 2013; Morgan et al., 2017). These issues are compounded by changing student populations. As enrollments increase in some areas of the world (Computing Research Association, 2017; CSER, 2017), we are seeing increasing concern over maintaining diversity and quality within our learning environments. The Generation CS report (Computing Research Association, 2017) presents the impact of growth across the USA and Canada, identifying challenges in providing appropriate teaching spaces for preferred pedagogic practices and changes in the pedagogic practices employed. This report also indicates changes in our cohorts, with an increase in non-majors enrolling in computer science courses and variation in representation of minority groups. Patitsas, Craig, and Easterbrook (2016) argue that a number of policy changes made in response to growing enrollments have a direct negative impact on diversity, presenting a worrying trend for our discipline over coming years and a need for further research on the relationship between policy development and pedagogic practice.

There are also opportunities within the computing discipline for creative pedagogies, with technology often an inspiration for change and a key component of a teaching innovation. Sharples et al. (2016), in their Open University Innovation Pedagogy 2016 Report, identify ten emerging innovations that are predicted to cause major changes in pedagogic approach and practice: learning through social media, productive failure, teachback, design thinking, learning from the crowd, learning from video games, formative analytics, learning for the future, translanguaging, and blockchain for the future. These innovations offer a lens through which to view the evolution of computer science pedagogy over the coming years and to motivate future research into the specific impact upon computer science education research and pedagogy.

Learning through social media addresses increased usage of social media platforms (both specific to learning and in general) on promoting different ways of engaging with learners and different conceptualizations of the role of the teacher. Early work within the computer science field includes Vickers et al. (2014) and Vozniuk, Holzer, and Gillet (2014). The increased usage of social media platforms, along with other online learning spaces, presents a challenge for educators and learners in developing pedagogic approaches that support learners in moving seamlessly between environments while maintaining scaffolding and consistency of learning.

Productive failure encourages students to tackle challenging problems with potential for failure prior to receiving direct instruction. While associated in structure with problem-based learning approaches, productive failure has a specific emphasis on the use of failure as a pivotal point in the learning process (Kapur, 2008; Schneider & Blikstein, 2016). Lui et al. (2017) explore the use of productive failure in their work within inclusive pedagogy design using e-textiles; however, this is one of few such works in computer science education research to date.

Teachback, where learners explain back to the teacher what they have learned and what they think they know, helps the learner to reflect on and conceptualize gaps in their learning. Aligned with CSP approaches and building on early pedagogic development (Pask, 1976), teachback has a specific focus on being taught then "teaching back" to deepen knowledge, increase reflection, and increase transparency of learning.

There is an opportunity to exploit artificial intelligence techniques in the creation of new pedagogic practices associated with teachback, particularly in online environments that may support growth and scale requirements. Rudman (2002) constructs an automated approach to analyzing discourse (captured digitally) in order to identify associated resource suggestions. There are further opportunities to expand upon existing work in applying natural language processing techniques in the exploration of automated concept map development (Atapattu, Falkner, & Falkner, 2017), topic modeling, and discourse analysis (Atapattu & Falkner, 2016) to assist learners in visualizing and connecting their explanations and also to assist in contrasting explanations and conceptualizations of learning.

Design thinking is a structured approach to problem-solving that supports episodic phases of creativity and critical thinking, identifying possibilities and constraints before moving on to analysis and construction – the "solving" process itself. While this is a long-standing pedagogic approach (Lawson, 2005), this approach has gained recent interest as a means for building innovation and creativity skills (Koh et al., 2015).

Learning from the crowd uses crowdsourced information and platforms as the basis for learning, establishing pedagogic practices that use and engage with crowdsourcing platforms and approaches to solve problems and gather information. Again, there are opportunities here for computer science education research in terms of exploring learning at scale through crowdsourced participation in educational studies.

Learning through video games builds on an extensive history of games within learning – video game pedagogies that exploit game characteristics that trigger and sustain learning. There has been extensive work exploring the development of video games within computing education (Battistella & Gresse von Wangenheim, 2016), including digital systems (Srinivasan, Butler-Purry, & Pedersen, 2008) and recursion (Lee et al., 2014), but with the majority focused on software engineering education. However, in their systematic literature review, Battistella and Gresse von Wangenheim (2016) identify a lack of integration into the learning context, with a need for further research in establishing connection with increased learning outcomes and designing game contexts that support learning.

Formative analytics expands upon the use of learning analytics to report on learning (the more traditional view of learning analytics) toward the development of analytics directly informing and assisting the learner (Higher Education Commission, 2016). As discussed further below, this represents a valuable area for computer science education research, one that can influence the refinement and development of new pedagogic approaches. Formative analytics that support personalized learning with awareness of stereotype threat and associated equity concerns is one potential strategy to explore here (see Chapter 16 for further discussion).

The growth of learning analytics, online learning, and learning at scale has provided computer science educators with new data sources and experimental techniques to explore how our students learn. The increased availability of detailed learner behavior and interactions in MOOC environments, as well as other large-scale learning platforms, provides a new opportunity to analyze and understand fine-grained learner behavior and the impact of pedagogic changes on learner outcomes (Milligan, 2015; Milligan et al., 2016). There is considerable opportunity for expanded computer science education research in this space, including the identification of relevant data points associated with measuring learning, pedagogic approaches that leverage formative analytics, the establishment of frameworks for analyzing and reporting on learning outcomes, assessment of pedagogy, and the development of analytics frameworks supporting rigorous comparison of pedagogic approaches.

Learning for the future encompasses a range of pedagogic approaches that support autonomy, resourcefulness, critical thinking skills, and interpersonal skills, building on existing pedagogic approaches and practices, including studio-based learning, project-based learning, and personalized learning assisted by learning analytics.

Translanguaging recognizes the global nature of future learning environments and the subsequent need for pedagogic practices and environments that support multi-language development and encourage diversity in language and cultural context (Creese & Blackledge, 2010).

The final innovation, *blockchain for learning*, defines new ways of storing, validating, and trading educational qualifications and evidence for learning. Pedagogic approaches, building on early attempts at gamification, can be established here, providing new opportunities for understanding and exploring the benefits of gamification. Further, these mechanisms provide a means for establishing reputation (as a learner or as a professional) and provide new means for engaging with social media and crowdsourced pedagogies (as described above).

Many of the innovation opportunities identified by Sharples et al. (2016) are driven by increased technology usage, accessibility, and integration with education, whether it be increased pervasiveness of technology platforms, such as social media and blockchain, or increased opportunity to influence and use data on learner behavior and outcomes. Increased technology integration and evolution of our physical teaching spaces also afford opportunities for the evolution of pedagogic practice, seen already through increases in physical computing and studio-based approaches. How we develop pedagogic approaches and practices that negotiate the abundance of online learning spaces, mediated through technology-rich physical environments, remains an important question for future research.

15.6 Conclusion

The variety of pedagogical approaches that are used in computing education take different forms that we have broadly categorized as active learning, collaborative learning, cooperative learning, CSP, blended learning, and MOOCs. Associated with these approaches are many different and creative teaching techniques, often supported by innovative tools and resources. The development of these has been motivated by a range of contextual and external factors.

We foresee that pedagogic approaches will continue to evolve in response to the changing situation in computing programs and their student populations, making this area a fertile ground for future computing education research.

References

Abad, C. L. (2008). Learning through creating learning objects: Experiences with a class project in a distributed systems course. In *13th Annual Conference on Innovation and Technology in Computer Science Education (ITiCSE '08)* (pp. 255–259). New York: ACM.

Armellini, A., & Padilla Rodriguez, B. C. (2016). Are Massive Open Online Courses (MOOCs) pedagogically innovative? In *Journal of Interactive Online Learning*, 14(1), 17–28.

Aronson, E., Blaney, N., Stephen, C., Sikes, J., & Snapp, M. (1978). *The Jigsaw Classroom.* Beverly Hills, CA: Sage.

Atkins, M. J. (1993). Theories of learning and multimedia: An overview. *Research Papers in Education*, 8(2), 251–271.

Atapattu, T., & Falkner, K. (2016). A framework for topic generation and labeling from MOOC discussions. In *3rd ACM Conference on Learning@Scale (L@S'2016)* (pp. 201–204). New York, NY: ACM.

Atapattu, T., Falkner, K., & Falkner, N. (2017). A comprehensive text analysis of lecture slides to generate concept maps. *Computers & Education*, 115, 96–113.

Barrows. H. S. (1986). A taxonomy of problem-based learning methods. *Medical Education*, 20, 481–486.

Batista, A. L. F., Connolly, T., & Angotti, J. A. P. (2016). A framework for games-based construction learning: A text-based programming languages approach. In *European Conference on Games Based Learning* (pp. 815–823). Reading, UK: Academic Conferences International Ltd.

Battistella, P., & Gresse von Wangenheim, C. (2016). Games for teaching computing in higher education – A systematic review. *IEEE Technology and Engineering Education*, 1(3), 8–30.

Bayne, S., & Ross, J. (2014). *The Pedagogy of the Massive Open Online Course: The UK view.* York, UK: The Higher Education Academy.

Beck, K. (2002). *Test-Driven Development: By Example.* Boston, MA: Addison-Wesley.

Beck, L., & Chizhik, A. (2013). Cooperative learning instructional methods for CS1: Design, implementation, and evaluation. *Transactions on Computing Education (TOCE)*, 13(3), 10.

Ben-Ari, M. (1998). Constructivism in computer science education. In D. Joyce, D. & J. Impagliazzo (Eds.), *29th SIGCSE Technical Symposium on Computer Science Education (SIGCSE '98)* (pp. 257–261). New York: ACM.

Bishop, J. L., & Verleger, M. A. (2013). The flipped classroom: A survey of the research. *ASEE National Conference*, 30(9), 1–18.

Blanc, R., DeBuhr, L., & Martin, D. (1983). Breaking the attrition cycle: The effects of supplemental instruction on undergraduate performance and attrition. *The Journal of Higher Education*, 54(1), 80–90.

Blank, D. (2006). Robots make computer science personal. *Communications of the ACM*, 9(12), 5–27.

Brady, C., Orton, K., Weintrop, D., Anton, G., Rodriguez, S., & Wilensky, U. (2017). All roads lead to computing: making, participatory simulations, and social computing as pathways to computer science. *IEEE Transactions on Education*, 60(1), 59–66.

Buckley, M., Nordlinger, J., & Subramanian, D. (2008). Socially relevant computing. In *39th SIGCSE Technical Symposium on Computer Science Education (SIGCSE '08)* (pp. 347–351). New York: ACM.

Buffardi, K., & Edwards, S. H. (2012). Impacts of teaching test-driven development to novice programmers. *International Journal of Information and Computer Science*, 1(6), 135–143.

Carbone, A., & Sheard, J. (2002). A studio-based teaching and learning model in IT: What do first year students think? In *7th Annual Conference on Innovation and Technology in Computer Science Education (ITiCSE '02)* (pp. 213–217) New York: ACM.

Ching, E., Chen, C. T., Chou, C. Y., Deng, Y. C., & Chan, T. W. (2005). A pilot study of computer supported learning by constructing instruction notes and peer expository instruction. In *Conference on Computer Support for Collaborative Learning: Learning 2005: The Next 10 Years! (CSCL)* (pp. 63–67). Taipei, Taiwan: International Society of the Learning Sciences.

Clarke, D., Clear, T., Fisler, K., Hauswirth, M., Krishnamurthi, S., Politz, J. G., Tirronen, V., & Wrigstad, T. (2014). In-flow peer review. In A. Clear & R. Lister (Eds.), *Working Group Reports of the 2014 Innovation & Technology in Computer Science Education Conference (ITiCSE-WGR '14)* (pp. 59–79). New York: ACM.

Collis, B., & Moonen, J. (2005). *An On-Going Journey: Technology as a Learning Workbench*. Enschede, The Netherlands: University of Twente.

Computing Research Association (2017). Generation CS: Computer Science Undergraduate Enrollments Surge Since 2006. Retrieved from https://cra.org/data/Generation-CS/

Cooper, S., Dann, W., & Pausch, R. (2003). Teaching objects-first in introductory computer science. In *34th SIGCSE Technical Symposium on Computer Science Education (SIGCSE '03)* (pp. 191–195). New York: ACM.

Corral, J. M. R., Balcells, A. C., Estévez, A. M., Moreno, G. J., & Ramos, M. J. F. (2014). A game-based approach to the teaching of object-oriented programming languages. *Computers & Education*, 73, 83–92.

Creese, A., & Blackledge, A. (2010). Translanguaging in the bilingual classroom: A pedagogy for learning and teaching? *The Modern Language Journal*, 94(1), 103–115.

Crescenzi, P., & Nocentini, C. (2007). Fully integrating algorithm visualization into a CS2 course: A two-year experience. In *12th Annual SIGCSE Conference on Innovation and Technology in Computer Science Education (ITiCSE '07)* (pp. 296–300). New York: ACM.

CSER (2017). A look at IT and Engineering Enrolments in Australia – Updated. Retrieved from: https://blogs.adelaide.edu.au/cser/2017/02/15/a-look-at-it-and-engineering-enrolments-in-australia-updated/

Cunningham, K., Blanchard, S., Ericson, B., & Guzdial, G. (2017). Using tracing and sketching to solve programming problems: Replicating and extending an analysis of what students draw. In *2017 ACM Conference on International Computing Education Research (ICER '17)* (pp. 164–172). New York: ACM.

Day, J. A., & Foley, J. D. (2006). Evaluating a web lecture intervention in a human–computer interaction course. *IEEE Transactions on Education*, 49(4), 420–431.

Denny, P., Luxton-Reilly, A., & Hamer, J. (2008). The PeerWise system of student contributed assessment questions. In Simon & M. Hamilton (Eds.), *10th conference on Australasian computing education – Volume 78 (ACE '08)*, Vol. 78 (pp. 69–74). Darlinghurst, Australia: Australian Computer Society, Inc.

DesPortes, K., Anupam, A., Pathak, N., & DiSalvo, B. (2016). BitBlox: A redesign of the breadboard. In *15th International Conference on Interaction Design and Children (IDC '16)* (pp. 255–261). New York: ACM.

Dragon, T., & Dickson, P. E. (2016). Memory diagrams: A consistent approach across concepts and languages. In *47th ACM Technical Symposium on Computing Science Education (SIGCSE '16)* (pp. 546–551). New York: ACM.

du Boulay, B. (1986). Some difficulties of learning to program. *Journal of Educational Computing Research*, 2(1), 57–73.

du Boulay, B., O'Shea, T., & Monk, J. (1981). The black box inside the glass box: Presenting computing concepts to novices. *International Journal of Man-Machine Studies*, 14(3), 237–249.

Duffy, T. M., & Cunningham, D. J. (1996). Constructivism: Implications for the design and delivery of instruction. In D. H. Jonassen (Ed.), *Handbook of Research for Educational Communications and Technology* (pp. 170–198). New York: Macmillan.

Earl, S. E. (1986). Staff and peer assessment – Measuring an individual's contribution to group performance. *Assessment & Evaluation in Higher Education*, 11(1), 60–69.

Ebert, M., & Ring, M. (2016). A presentation framework for programming in programing lectures. In *Global Engineering Education Conference* (EDUCON '16) (pp. 369–374). New York, NY: IEEE.

Edwards, S. H. (2004). Using software testing to move students from trial-and-error to reflection-in-action. In *35th SIGCSE Technical Symposium on Computer Science Education (SIGCSE '04)* (pp. 26–30). New York: ACM.

Elgort, I., Smith, A., & Toland, J. (2008). Is Wiki an effective platform for group course work? *Australasian Journal of Educational Technology*, 24(2), 195–210.

Ernest, E. (1995). The one and the many. In L. Steffe & J. Gale (Eds.), *Constructivism in Education* (pp. 459–486). New York: Lawrence Erlbaum.

Ewing, J. M., Dowling, J. D., & Coutts, N. (1998). Learning using the World Wide Web: A collaborative learning event. *Journal of Educational Multimedia and Hypermedia*, 8(1), 3–22.

Falkner, N. J. G., & Falkner, K. (2014). "Whither, badges?" or "wither, badges!": A metastudy of badges in computer science education to clarify effects, significance and influence. In *14th Koli Calling International Conference on Computing Education Research (Koli Calling '14)* (pp. 127–135). New York: ACM.

Falkner, K., Falkner, N., Szabo, C., & Vivian, R. (2016). Applying validated pedagogy to MOOCs: An introductory programming course with media computation. In *2016 ACM Conference on Innovation and Technology in Computer Science Education* (pp. 326–331). New York, NY: ACM.

Falkner, K., & Palmer, E. (2009). Developing authentic problem solving skills in introductory computing classes. In *40th ACM Technical Symposium on Computer Science Education (SIGCSE '09)* (pp. 4–8). New York: ACM.

Falkner, K., Vivian, R., Falkner, N., & Williams, S. (2017). Reflecting on three offerings of a community-centric MOOC for k-6 computer science teachers. In *2017 ACM SIGCSE Technical Symposium on Computer Science Education (SIGCSE '17)* (pp. 195–200). New York: ACM.

Findler, R. B., Clements, J., Flanagan, C., Flatt, M., Krishnamurthi, S., Steckler, P., & Felleisen, M. (2002). DrScheme: A programming environment for Scheme. *Journal of. Functional Programming*, 12(2), 159–182.

Firmin, S., Sheard, J., Carbone, A., & Hurst, J. (2012). An exploration of factors influencing tertiary IT educators' pedagogies. In M. de Raadt & A. Carbone (Eds.), *14th Australasian Computing Education Conference – Volume 123 (ACE '12)*, Vol. 123 (pp. 157–166). Darlinghurst, Australia: Australian Computer Society, Inc.

Fisher, A., & Margolis, J. (2002). Unlocking the clubhouse: The Carnegie Mellon experience. *SIGCSE Bulletin*, 34(2), 79–83.

Geer, U., & Rudge, D. (2002). A review of research on constructivist-based strategies for large lecture science classes. *Electronic Journal of Science Education*, 7(2). Retrieved from www.scholarlyexchange.org/ojs/index.php/EJSE/article/view/7701

Gehringer, E. F., & Miller, C. S. (2009). Student-generated active-learning exercises. In *40th ACM Technical Symposium on Computer Science Education (SIGCSE '09)* (pp. 81–85). New York: ACM.

Giannakos, M. N., Krogstie, J., & Chrisochoides, N. (2014). Reviewing the flipped classroom research: Reflections for computer science education. In E. Barendsen & V. Dagiené (Eds.), *Computer Science Education Research Conference (CSERC '14)* (pp. 23–29). New York: ACM.

Glance D., Forsey M., & Riley M. (2013). The pedagogical foundations of massive open online courses. *First Monday,* 18(5). Retrieved from http://firstmonday.org/ojs/index.php/fm/article/view/4350/3673

Grover, S., Pea, R., & Cooper, S. (2014). Promoting active learning & leveraging dashboards for curriculum assessment in an OpenEdX introductory CS course for middle school. In *1st ACM Conference on Learning @ Scale Conference (L@S '14)* (pp. 205–206). New York: ACM.

Guo, P. J. (2013). Online python tutor: Embeddable web-based program visualization for cs education. In *44th ACM Technical Symposium on Computer Science Education (SIGCSE '13)* (pp. 579–584). New York: ACM.

Guzdial, M. (2013). Exploring hypotheses about media computation. In *9th Annual International ACM Conference on International Computing Education Research (ICER '13)* (pp. 19–26). New York: ACM.

Hamer, J., Cutts, Q., Jackova, J., Luxton-Reilly, A., McCartney, R., Purchase, H., Riedesel, C., Saeli, M., Sanders, K., & Sheard, J. (2008). Contributing student pedagogy. *SIGCSE Bulletin*, 40(4), 194–212.

Hamer, J., Luxton-Reilly, A., Purchase, H. C., & Sheard, J. (2011). Tools for "contributing student learning". *ACM Inroads*, 2(2), 78–91.

Hativa, N. (2000). Active learning during lectures. In *Teaching for Effective Learning in Higher Education* (pp. 87–110). Dordrecht, The Netherlands: Springer.

Hertz, M., & Jump, M. (2013). Trace-based teaching in early programming courses. In *44th ACM Technical Symposium on Computer Science Education (SIGCSE '13)* (pp. 561–566). New York: ACM.

Higher Education Commission (2016). *From Bricks to Clicks: The Potential of Data and Analytics in Higher Education*. London, UK: Higher Education Commission.

Horton, D., & Craig, M. (2015). Drop, fail, pass, continue: Persistence in CS1 and beyond in traditional and inverted delivery. In *46th ACM Technical Symposium on Computer Science Education (SIGCSE '15)* (pp. 235–240). New York: ACM.

Hundhausen, C. D., Agrawal, A., & Agarwal, P. (2013). Talking about code: Integrating pedagogical code reviews into early computing courses. *ACM Transactions on Computing Education (TOCE)*. 13(3), 14.

Hundhausen, C. D., Douglas, S. A., & Stasko, J. T. (2002). A meta-study of algorithm visualization effectiveness. *Journal of Visual Languages & Computing*, 13(3), 259–290.

Hundhausen, C. D., Narayanan, N. H., & Crosby, M. E. (2008). Exploring studio-based instructional models for computing education. In *39th SIGCSE Technical Symposium on Computer Science Education (SIGCSE '08)* (pp. 392–396). New York: ACM.

Jonas, M. (2013). Group note taking in Mediawiki, a collaborative approach. In *14th Annual ACM SIGITE Conference on Information Technology Education (SIGITE '13)* (pp. 131–132). New York: ACM.

Jonassen, D. H. (1991). Objectivism versus constructivism: Do we need a new philosophical paradigm? *Educational Technology Research & Development*, 39(3), 5–14.

Kaczmarczyk, L., Boutell, M., & Last, M. (2007). Challenging the advanced first-year student's learning process through student presentations. In *3rd International Workshop on Computing Education Research (ICER '07)* (pp. 17–26). New York: ACM.

Kandiko, C. B., & Mawer, M. (2013). *Student Expectations and Perceptions of Higher Education*. London, UK: King's Learning Institute.

Kapur, M. (2008). Productive failure. *Cognition and Instruction*, 26(3), 379–424.

Khan, N. Z., & Luxton-Reilly, A. (2016). Is computing for social good the solution to closing the gender gap in computer science? In *Australasian Computer Science Week Multiconference (ACSW '16)* (p. 17). New York: ACM.

Koh, J. H. L., Chai, C. S., Wong, B., & Hong, H.-Y. (2015). *Design Thinking for Education*. Singapore: Springer.

Kölling, M., & Barnes, D. J. (2004). Enhancing apprentice-based learning of Java. In *35th SIGCSE Technical Symposium on Computer Science Education (SIGCSE '04)* (pp. 286–290). New York: ACM.

Kurtz, B. L., Fenwick, J. B., Tashakkori, R., Esmail, A., & Tate, S. R. (2014). Active learning during lecture using tablets. In *45th ACM Technical Symposium on Computer Science Education (SIGCSE '14)* (pp. 121–126). New York: ACM.

Lacher, L. L., & Lewis, M. C. (2015). The effectiveness of video quizzes in a flipped class. In *46th ACM Technical Symposium on Computer Science Education (SIGCSE '15)* (pp. 224–228). New York: ACM.

Lawson, B. (2005). *How Designers Think: The Design Process Demystified*, 4th edn. London, UK: The Architectural Press.

Lee, E., Shan, V., Beth, B., & Lin, C. (2014). A structured approach to teaching recursion using cargo-bot. In *10th Annual Conference on International Computing Education Research (ICER '14)* (pp. 59–66). New York: ACM.

Leutenegger, S., & Edgington, J. (2007). A games first approach to teaching introductory programming. In *38th SIGCSE Technical Symposium on Computer Science Education (SIGCSE '07)* (pp. 115–118). New York: ACM.

Lui, D., Anderson, E., Kafai, Y. B., & Jayathirtha, G. (2017). Learning by fixing and designing problems: A reconstruction kit for debugging e-textiles. In *7th Annual Conference on Creativity and Fabrication in Education (FabLearn '17)* (p. 6). New York: ACM.

Lui, A. K., Ng, S. C., Cheung, Y. H. Y., & Gurung, P. (2010). Facilitating independent learning with Lego Mindstorms robots. *ACM Inroads*, 1(4), 49–53.

Lockwood, K., & Esselstein, R. (2013). The inverted classroom and the CS curriculum. In *44th ACM Technical Symposium on Computer Science Education (SIGCSE '13)* (pp. 113–118). New York: ACM.

Lowyck, J., & Elen, J. (1993). Transitions in the theoretical foundation of instructional design. In T. M. Duffy, J. Lowyck, & D. H. Jonassen (Eds.), *Designing Environments for Constructive Learning* (pp. 213–229). Berlin, Germany: Springer-Verlag.

Lutteroth, C., & Luxton-Reilly, A. (2008). Flexible learning in CS2: A case study. In *21st Annual Conference of the National Advisory Committee on Computing Qualifications* (pp. 77–83). New Zealand: Computing and Information Technology Research and Education New Zealand (CITRENZ).

Luxton-Reilly, A., Bertinshaw, D., Denny, P., Plimmer, B., & Sheehan, R. (2012). The impact of question generation activities on performance. In *43rd ACM Technical Symposium on Computer Science Education (SIGCSE '12)* (pp. 391–396). New York: ACM.

Luxton-Reilly, A., Plimmer, B., & Sheehan, R. (2010). StudySieve: A tool that supports constructive evaluation for free-response questions. In *11th International Conference of the NZ Chapter of the ACM Special Interest Group on Human-Computer Interaction (CHINZ '10)* (pp. 65–68). New York: ACM.

Maher, M. L., Latulipe, C., Lipford, H., & Rorrer, A. (2015). Flipped classroom strategies for CS education. In *46th ACM Technical Symposium on Computer Science Education (SIGCSE '15)* (pp. 218–223). New York: ACM.

Mayer, R. E. (1975). Different problem-solving competencies established in learning computer programming with and without meaningful models. *Journal of Educational Psychology*, 67(6), 725–734.

Mayer, R. E. (1976). Some conditions of meaningful learning for computer programming: Advance organizers and subject control of frame order. *Journal of Educational Psychology*, 68(2), 143–150.

Medel, P., & Pournaghshband, V. (2017). Eliminating gender bias in computer science education materials. In *2017 ACM SIGCSE Technical Symposium on Computer Science Education (SIGCSE '17)* (pp. 411–416). New York: ACM.

Milligan, S. (2015). Crowd-sourced learning in MOOCs: learning analytics meets measurement theory. In *5th International Conference on Learning Analytics & Knowledge (LAK '15)* (pp. 151–155). New York: ACM.

Milligan, S., He, J., Bailey, J., Zhang, R., & Rubinstein, B. I. P. (2016). Validity: A framework for cross-disciplinary collaboration in mining indicators of learning from MOOC forums. In *6th International Conference on Learning Analytics & Knowledge (LAK '16)* (pp. 546–547). New York: ACM.

Moog, R. S. & Spencer, J. N. (Eds.) (2008). *Process-Oriented Guided-Inquiry Learning (POGIL)*. Washington, DC: American Chemical Society.

Morgan, M., Butler, M., Sinclair, J., Cross, G., Fraser, J., Jackova, J., & Thota, N. (2017). Understanding international benchmarks on student engagement: Awareness, research alignment and response from a computer science perspective. In *2017 ACM Conference on Innovation and Technology in Computer Science Education (ITiCSE '17)* (pp. 383–384). New York: ACM.

Moritz, S. H., & Blank, G. D. (2005). A design-first curriculum for teaching Java in a CS1 course. *SIGCSE Bulletin*, 37(2), 89–93.

Nelson, G. L., Xie, B., & Ko, A. J. (2017). Comprehension first: Evaluating a novel pedagogy and tutoring system for program tracing in CS1. In *2017 ACM Conference on International Computing Education Research (ICER '17)* (pp. 2–11). New York: ACM.

Nortcliffe, A. (2005). Student-driven module: promoting independent learning. *International Journal of Electrical Engineering Education*, 42(3), 247–512.

Papert, S. (1993). *Mindstorms: Children, Computers, and Powerful Ideas*. New York: Basic Books.

Parsons, D., & Haden, P. (2006). Parson's programming puzzles: a fun and effective learning tool for first programming courses. In D. Tolhurst & S. Mann (Eds.), *8th Australasian Conference on Computing Education – Volume 52 (ACE '06)* (pp. 157–163). Darlinghurst, Australia: Australian Computer Society, Inc.

Pask, G. (1976). *Conversation Theory, Applications in Education and Epistemology*. Amsterdam, The Netherlands: Elsevier.

Patitsas, E., Craig, M., & Easterbrook, S. (2016). How CS departments are managing the enrolment boom: Troubling implications for diversity. In *Research on Equity and Sustained Participation in Engineering, Computing and Technology (RESPECT)* (pp. 1–2). New York, NY: IEEE.

Paul, J. (2016). Test-driven approach in programming pedagogy. *Journal of Computing Sciences in Colleges*, 32(2), 53–60.

Perkins, D. N., Schwartz, S., & Simmons, R. (1990). Instructional strategies for the problems of novice programmers. In R. E. Meyer (Ed.), *Teaching and Learning Computer Programming: Multiple Research Perspectives* (pp. 153–178). Mahwah, NJ: Lawrence Erlbaum.

Phillips, D., & Soltis, J. F. (2015). *Perspectives on Learning*, 5th edn. New York: Teachers College Press.

Piaget, J. (1972). *Psychology and Epistemology: Towards a Theory of Knowledge* (Vol. 105). London, UK: Penguin Books Ltd.

Piccioni, M., Estler, C., & Meyer, B. (2014). SPOC-supported introduction to programming. In *19th Conference on Innovation and Technology in Computer Science Education (ITiCSE '14)* (pp. 3–8). New York: ACM.

Pirker, J., Riffnaller-Schiefer, M., & Gütl, C. (2014). Motivational active learning: engaging university students in computer science education. In *2014 Conference on Innovation and Technology in Computer Science Education (ITiCSE '14)* (pp. 297–302). New York: ACM.

Politz, J. G., Krishnamurthi, S., & Fisler, K. (2014). In-flow peer-review of tests in test-first programming. In *10th Annual Conference on International Computing Education Research (ICER '14)* (pp. 11–18). New York: ACM.

Pollock, L., & Harvey, T. (2011). Combining multiple pedagogies to boost learning and enthusiasm. In *16th Annual Joint Conference on Innovation and Technology in Computer Science Education (ITiCSE '11)* (pp. 258–262). New York: ACM.

Porter, L., & Simon, B. (2013). Retaining nearly one-third more majors with a trio of instructional best practices in CS1. In *44th ACM Technical Symposium on Computer Science Education (SIGCSE '13)* (pp. 165–170). New York: ACM.

Portillo, J. A. P., & Campos, P. G. (2009). The jigsaw technique: Experiences teaching analysis class diagrams. In *Mexican International Conference on Computer Science* (pp. 289–293). New York: IEEE Press.

Pulimood, S. M., & Wolz, U. (2008). Problem solving in community: A necessary shift in cs pedagogy. *ACM SIGCSE Bulletin*, 40(1), 210–214.

Purchase, H. (2000). Learning about interface design through peer assessment. *Assessment & Evaluation in Higher Education*, 24(4), 341–352.

Preston, G., Phillips, R., Gosper, M., McNeill, M., Woo, K., & Green, D. (2010). Web-based lecture technologies: Highlighting the changing nature of teaching and learning. *Australasian Journal of Educational Technology*, 26(6), 717–728.

Prince, M. (2004). Does active learning work? A review of the research. *Journal of Engineering Education*, 93(3), 223–231.

Ragonis, N., & Ben-Ari, M. (2005). A long-term investigation of the comprehension of OOP concepts by novices. *Computational Science Education*, 15(3), 203–221.

Reeves, T. C., & Reeves, P. M. (1997). Effective dimensions of interactive learning on the World Wide Web. In B. H. Khan (Ed.), *Web-Based Instruction* (pp. 59–66). Englewood Cliffs, NJ: Educational Technology Publications.

Reilly, M., Shen, H., Calder, P., & Duh, H. (2014). Towards a collaborative classroom through shared workspaces on mobile devices. In *28th International BCS Human Computer Interaction Conference on HCI 2014 – Sand, Sea and Sky – Holiday HCI (BCS-HCI '14)* (pp. 335–340). London, UK: BCS.

Reza, S., & Baig, M. (2015). A study of inverted classroom pedagogy in computer science teaching. *International Journal of Research Studies in Educational Technology*, 4(2). Retrieved from www.learntechlib.org/p/151048/

Rich, L., Perry, H., & Guzdial, M. (2004). A CS1 course designed to address interests of women. *SIGCSE Bulletin*, 36(1), 190–194.

Rizzardini, R. H., & Amado-Salvatierra, H. R. (2017). Full engagement educational framework: A practical experience for a MicroMaster. In *4th ACM Conference on Learning @ Scale (L@S '17)* (pp. 145–146). New York: ACM.

Rubin, M. J. (2013). The effectiveness of live-coding to teach introductory programming. In *44th ACM Technical Symposium on Computer Science Education (SIGCSE '13)* (pp. 651–656). New York: ACM.

Rubio, M. A., Romero-Zaliz, R., Mañoso, C., & De Madrid, A. P. (2015). Closing the gender gap in an introductory programming course. *Computers & Education*, 82, 409–420.

Rudestam, K., & Schoenholtz-Read, J. (2010). The flourishing of adult online education: an overview. In K. Rudestam & J. Schoenholtz-Read (Eds.), *Handbook of Online Learning*, 2nd edn (pp. 1–28). Thousand Oaks, CA: SAGE.

Rudman, P. (2002). *Investigating Domain Information as Dynamic Support for the Learner During Spoken Conversations* (PhD thesis). University of Birmingham.

Salmon, G. (2004). *E-Tivities: The Key to Active Online Learning*, 2nd edn. Abingdon, UK: Taylor & Francis e-Library.

Sanders, K., Boustedt, J., Eckerdal, A., McCartney, R., & Zander, C. (2017). Folk pedagogy: Nobody doesn't like active learning. In *2017 ACM Conference on International Computing Education Research (ICER '17)* (pp. 145–154). New York: ACM.

Schneider, B., & Blikstein, P. (2016). Flipping the flipped classroom: A study of the effectiveness of video lectures versus constructivist exploration using tangible user interfaces. *IEEE Transactions on Learning Technologies*, 9(1), 5–17.

Sharples, M., de Roock, R., Ferguson, R., Gaved, M., Herodotou, C., Koh, E., Kukulska-Hulme, A., Looi, C-K., McAndrew, P., Rienties, B., Weller, M. & Wong, L. H. (2016). *Innovating Pedagogy 2016: Open University Innovation Report 5*. The Open University.

Shulman, L. (2005). Pedagogies. *Liberal Education*, 91(2), 18–25.

Siemens, G. (2005). Connectivism: A learning theory for the digital age. In *International Journal of Instructional Technology and Distance Learning*, 2(1), 3–10.

Siemens, G. (2012). MOOCs are really a platform. *ELearnspace*. Retrieved from www.elearnspace.org/blog/2012/07/25/moocs-are-really-a-platform/

Simon, B., & Cutts, Q. (2012). Peer instruction: A teaching method to foster deep understanding. *Communications of the ACM*, 55(2), 27–29.

Sirkiä, T. (2016). Combining parson's problems with program visualization in CS1 context. In *16th Koli Calling International Conference on Computing Education Research (Koli Calling '16)* (pp. 155–159). New York: ACM.

Sirkiä, T., & Sorva, J. (2015). Tailoring animations of example programs. In *15th Koli Calling Conference on Computing Education Research (Koli Calling '15)* (pp. 147–151). New York: ACM.

Slavin, R. E. (1991). Synthesis of research on cooperative learning. *Educational Leadership*, 48(5), 71–82.

Slavin, R. E., & Cooper, R. (1999). Improving intergroup relations: Lessons learned from cooperative learning programs. *Journal of Social Issues*, 55, 647–663.

Smith, P. A., & Webb, G. I. (1995). Reinforcing a generic computer model for novice programmers. In *7th Australian Society for Computer in Learning in Tertiary Education Conference* (ASCILITE '95). Retrieved from www.ascilite.org/conferences/melbourne95/smtu_bak/papers/smith.pdf

Smith, J., Tessler, J., Kramer, E., & Lin, C. (2012). Using peer review to teach software testing. In *9th Annual International Conference on International Computing Education Research (ICER '12)* (pp. 93–98). New York: ACM.

Sonnentag, S. (1998). Expertise in professional software design: A process study. *Journal of Applied Psychology*, 83, 703–715.

Sorva. J. (2013). Notional machines and introductory programming education. *Transactions on Computing Education (TOCE)*, 13(2), 8.

Sorva, J., Karavirta, V., & Malmi, L. (2013). A review of generic program visualization systems for introductory programming education. *Transactions on Computing Education (TOCE)*, 13(4), 15.

Sorva, J., & Sirkiä, T. (2010). UUhistle: A software tool for visual program simulation. In *10th Koli Calling International Conference on Computing Education Research (Koli Calling '10)* (pp. 49–54). New York: ACM.

Srinivasan, V., Butler-Purry, K. & Pedersen, S. (2008). Using video games to enhance learning in digital systems. In *2008 Conference on Future Play: Research, Play, Share (Future Play '08)* (pp. 196–199). New York: ACM.

Summet, J., Kumar, D., O'Hara, K., Walker, D., Ni, L., Blank, D., & Balch, T. (2009). Personalizing CS1 with robots. *ACM SIGCSE Bulletin*, 41(1), 433–437.

Swan, K., Day, S., & Bogle, L. (2016). Metaphors for learning and MOOC pedagogies. In *3rd ACM Conference on Learning @ Scale* (pp. 125–128). New York: ACM.

Tarimo, W. T., Deeb, F. A., & Hickey, T. J. (2015). A flipped classroom with and without computers. In *International Conference on Computer Supported Education* (pp. 333–347). New York: Springer International Publishing.

Titterton, N., Lewis, C. M., & Clancy, M. J. (2010). Experiences with lab-centric instruction. *Computer Science Education*, 20(2), 79–102.

Toven-Lindsey, B., Rhoads, R. A., & Lozano, J. B. (2015). Virtually unlimited classrooms: Pedagogical practices in massive open online courses. *The Internet and Higher Education*, 24, 1–12.

Umapathy, K., & Ritzhaupt, A. D. (2017). A meta-analysis of pair-programming in computer programming courses: Implications for educational practice. *ACM Transactions on Computing Education (TOCE)*, 17(4), 16.

Utting, I., Cooper, S., Kölling, M., Maloney, J., & Resnick, M. (2010). Alice, Greenfoot, and Scratch – A discussion. *ACM Transactions on Computing Education (TOCE)*, 10(4), 17.

Vassiliadis, B., Kameas, A., & Sgouropoulou, C. (2016). A closer look at MOOC's adoption from a qualitative perspective. In *20th Pan-Hellenic Conference on Informatics (PCI '16)* (p. 17). New York: ACM.

Vickers, R., Cooper, G., Field, J., Thayne, M., Adams, R., & Lochrie, M. (2014). Social media and collaborative learning: Hello Scholr. In *18th International Academic MindTrek Conference: Media Business, Management, Content & Services (AcademicMindTrek '14)* (pp. 103–109). New York: ACM.

Vozniuk, A., Holzer, A., & Gillet, D. (2014). Peer assessment based on ratings in a social media course. In *4th International Conference on Learning Analytics And Knowledge (LAK '14)* (pp. 133–137). New York: ACM.

Vygotsky, L. S. (1978). *Mind in Society: The Development of Higher Psychological Processes*. Cambridge, MA: Harvard University Press.

Wakeling, D. (2008). A robot in every classroom: Robots and functional programming across the curriculum. In *2008 International Workshop on Functional and Declarative Programming in Education (FDPE '08)* (pp. 51–60). New York: ACM.

Walker, J. D., Brooks, D. C., & Baepler, P. (2011). Pedagogy and space: Empirical research on new learning environments. *EDUCAUSE Quarterly*, 34(4). Retrieved from https://eric.ed.gov/?id=EJ958727

Watson, C., & Li, F. W. B. (2014). Failure rates in introductory programming revisited. In *2014 Conference on Innovation and Technology in Computer Science Education (ITiCSE '14)* (pp. 39–44). New York: ACM.

Wenger, E. (1998). Communities of practice. Learning as a social system. *Systems Thinker*. 9(5). Retrieved from https://thesystemsthinker.com/communities-of-practice-learning-as-a-social-system/

Williams, L. (2000). *The Collaborative Software Process* (PhD dissertation). University of Utah.

Williams, L., & Kessler, R. (2002). *Pair Programming Illuminated*. Boston, MA: Addison-Wesley Longman Publishing Co., Inc.

Williams, L., McCrickard, D. S., Layman, L., & Hussein, K. (2008). Eleven guidelines for implementing pair programming in the classroom. In G. Melnik & M. Poppendieck (Eds.), *Agile Conference* (pp. 445–452). New York: IEEE Press.

16 Equity and Diversity

Colleen M. Lewis, Niral Shah, and Katrina Falkner

16.1 Introduction

It is frequently observed that some groups are underrepresented in computing education and the computing profession. While these patterns of underrepresentation vary by country, in many Western countries, computing is dominated by White and Asian men. For example, in the USA, people who identify as Black, Latinx, Native American, or Hawaiian and/or women are not participating at rates comparable to their portion within the US population (National Science Foundation, National Center for Science and Engineering Statistics, 2017). Perhaps surprisingly, in this chapter, we will not summarize the current state of underrepresentation. These patterns of underrepresentation are not unique to computing and are general patterns that can be seen across most science, technology, engineering, and mathematics (STEM) fields. These patterns can also be seen in non-STEM disciplines and are typically consistent with other systems of inequity (e.g., sexism and racism). Documentation of patterns of underrepresentation may provide motivation for action, but does not point to the necessary actions. We argue that understanding the ways in which systems of inequity produce dominant and marginalized groups is essential to understanding and addressing current patterns of underrepresentation and inequity.

16.1.1 Goals and Structure of the Chapter

In this chapter, we hope to provide readers with resources for understanding the roots of underrepresentation and how these can play out in computing classrooms. Throughout the chapter, we explore the relevance of narratives about computing and computer scientists for issues of equity and diversity. We begin by developing a shared set of terminology as it relates to equity research in computing education (CEd; Section 16.1.2). This includes exploring common arguments for why addressing patterns of underrepresentation in computing is a pressing concern. We next introduce these narratives, their connections to historical patterns of marginalization and injustice, and our use of "narratives" as opposed to the more common term "stereotypes" (Section 16.1.3). We then introduce research related to unconscious or implicit bias in order to identify the ways in which these narratives about computing and computer scientists can produce harm and the patterns of underrepresentation that are frequently observed (Section 16.1.4).

Instead of providing a decontextualized review of the remaining literature, we ground our review within four hypothetical scenarios that we call vignettes (Section 16.2). These vignettes allow us to show how the research helps us understand particular patterns and interactions within computing classrooms. These vignettes also concretely illustrate the relevance of particular interventions used to promote diversity in computing. The chapter closes by expanding this focus and identifies open questions (Section 16.3). These open questions provide pointers to relevant literatures outside the scope of the chapter.

16.1.2 An Overview of Equity Terminology and Rationales for Action

Terms like "equity," "diversity," and "access" have proliferated in computing education to describe and conceptualize issues related to marginalized groups. Indeed, these terms figure prominently in many of the foundational documents in computer science (CS) education (e.g., the K–12 Computer Science Framework, 2016). In using these terms throughout this chapter, we want to provide a common understanding of what these terms mean. Further, we note that there has been a tendency to conflate these terms in problematic ways. For those reasons, we begin by briefly discussing conceptual distinctions between them, as well as their relative affordances and limitations.

"Equity" has been an umbrella term used throughout much of the CEd research (CEdR) literature, which has been conceptualized at multiple grain sizes corresponding to multiple organizing concepts. In everyday use, equity and equality are sometimes used interchangeably, but for our purposes, the differences are important. Equality refers to the state where everyone has or is allocated the same things in the same degree, whereas equity typically refers to having access to what is needed. Equality can be a waypoint toward equity, but they are not the same thing (Reinholz & Shah, 2018). There are situations where everyone might need the same thing in the same degree, in which case equality would also be equitable. In general, though, equity, and not equality, defines fair and just learning opportunities.[1] A limitation of the term is that achieving equity relies on the difficult task of knowing what students need.

Within the umbrella of equity, an organizing concept is "diversity," which refers to which groups are and are not represented or included in various spaces and practices. In computing and CEd, studies have focused on diversity in computing classes and majors (Google Inc. & Gallup Inc., 2016), in Advanced Placement test-taking (College Board, 2017), and the workforce (Information

---

1 The comment "women's groups are unfair" may be an example of conflating equity and equality. If a "women in computing" group is only open to women, then this is not equal for people of all genders. That is, what people are provided is not the same. However, a women's group may be important to help counteract some of the narratives about the inferiority of women as discussed in this chapter. Ultimately, equity and fairness do not necessitate equality.

is Beautiful, 2016), to name a few. The impetus for diversity in computing is manifold.

First, there is a moral concern that the computing community reflect society writ large, particularly with respect to race, gender, dis/ability, sexuality, and other social markers. Rather than be restricted to certain groups or an elite few, many in the field espouse the democratic view that computing be widely available. This perspective is reflected in numerous initiatives advocating "CS for all" (Ladner & Israel, 2016).

Second, some link diversity to the size of the workforce, suggesting that greater inclusion is needed to fill gaps in the computing labor force (National Center for Women & Information Technology, 2017). Expanding diversity in the workforce would require increased participation by people from groups that are currently underrepresented in computing, which could have the result of increasing the total number of workers.[2] Third, there is a related pragmatic and economic argument that diversity in product design teams will lead to better products. One explanation for this benefit is that diverse teams have been shown to produce better results (Hunt et al., 2018). A second explanation for this benefit is that the team may choose to make products that are accessible to a greater portion of consumers in the marketplace (K–12 Computer Science Framework, 2016, p. 29). However, this second explanation may require decision-makers within the organization to see more accessible products as consistent with their financial incentives or moral values, which does not directly relate to the social identities of the product design or engineering team.

Within the umbrella of "equity," another organizing concept is "access," which acknowledges that representation and performance in computing are closely related to students' access to the resources needed for participation in computing. This way of thinking about access also relates to the prevailing metaphor of "participation": opening access to these kinds of structural resources is viewed as a critical lever toward broadening participation to include students from marginalized groups[3] in the computing "pipeline." In computing, studies have attended to the number of schools that offer computing courses (Google Inc. & Gallup Inc., 2015), racial and class disparities in the communities where those computing courses are offered (Margolis et al., 2012), and disparities in access to qualified computing teachers and the physical resources needed to study computing (Google Inc. & Gallup Inc., 2015; Margolis et al., 2008). Importantly, the focus on access shifts attention from performance gaps to *opportunity* gaps between dominant and marginalized groups (Milner, 2012). By measuring disparities in how access has been distributed in society, researchers

---

2 However, when relating diversity to the expansion of the workforce, the term "diverse" is sometimes used to label individual people, as in "a diverse computer scientist." This example does not use diverse to describe variation within a group of people. This non-standard usage may instead represent avoidance of discussing social markers such as race, but these discussions are likely necessary for increasing diversity.

3 In the USA, people who identify as African American, Black, and/or Latinx are typically referred to as members of marginalized groups (Walton & Cohen, 2011), but many social markers can lead to marginalization.

reduce opportunities for people to interpret performance or participation gaps as innate differences in potential, intelligence, or interest.

In addition to structural resources, "access" has also been conceptualized in terms of the content and organization of the learning environment itself. As Margolis et al. (2012) note, "broadening participation goes beyond issues of access to computer science (CS) learning; we also must transform CS classroom culture and teaching" (p. 71). To that end, studies have investigated the affordances of building on students' cultural funds of knowledge[4] (González et al., 2006) and situating computing ideas in real-world problem-solving (Goode, 2008; Kafai et al., 2014; Margolis & Fisher, 2003; Margolis et al., 2014). These pedagogical efforts seek to move beyond traditional lecture formats and narrow views on computing content to make deeper connections to students' lives and backgrounds. Further, there has been research examining equity and inequity in student participation patterns across various classroom interactional contexts, such as pair programming (Lewis & Shah, 2015; Shah & Lewis, in press).

Finally, a term that is receiving increasing attention in this part of the field is "social justice," in which students use computing for the purpose of addressing injustice in their local communities and in society writ large (Bobb, 2016; Toyama, 2015; Vakil, 2014). This perspective challenges widely held assumptions about the very purpose of CEd. Rather than simply enrolling more students of color in computing majors or hiring more women software engineers, computing is conceptualized as a "discipline in service of society, its people, and their needs" (K–12 Computer Science Framework, 2016, p. 26). Importantly, this view acknowledges that CEd is situated within a sociopolitical context. This necessitates a more expansive view of what we mean by "equity" in computing, from considering equity within CEd to considering equity across society.

In summary, various terms organize field-wide discourse about equity and marginalization. A key point, though, is that none of these terms by themselves are adequate – each has its affordances and limitations. In our view, this seems entirely reasonable, as "equity" is a complex, multifaceted idea that cannot and should not be reduced to a single perspective. While a comprehensive analysis is beyond the scope of this chapter, tensions between these various ways of conceptualizing equity issues in computing set the stage for future research in this area. We return to this at the end of the chapter in our discussion of open questions (Section 16.3). Next, we review narratives about computing and computer scientists and explain our use of narratives instead of the related term "stereotypes." We highlight narratives and stereotypes separately from the terms described above because of the importance of narratives in understanding historical patterns of marginalization and injustice.

---

4 Moll et al. (2006) define funds of knowledge as "historically accumulated and culturally developed bodies of knowledge and skills essential for household or individual functioning and well-being (Greenberg, 1989; Tapia, 1991; Vélez-Ibáñez, 1988)" (pp. 72–73).

16.1.3 Narratives about Computing and Computer Scientists

Negative stereotypes of computer scientists are pervasive (Ensmenger, 2010). We argue that the systems of inequity appear to rely on stereotypes about computing and computer scientists. However, instead of referring to these as stereotypes, we will use the term "narrative." We see the terms "stereotypes" and "narratives" as connected, but conceptually distinct. The term "narrative" captures the notion that beliefs about computing and computer scientists are communicated by and between people and therefore can and do change. The stories that people tell about computing and computer scientists form the basis for what we think about the field and its practitioners. By changing the stories (i.e., the narratives), we can (and should) change our thoughts about computing and computer scientists.

A prevailing narrative is that computer scientists are socially inept, non-hygienic, White men (Ensmenger, 2010). These exclusive narratives about computer scientists can discourage participation if they are interpreted as requirements of the field or even just present an unappealing view of the social interactions that a career in computing might involve (Lewis et al., 2016).

In addition to narratives like these about who computer scientists are and how they behave, there are also narratives about the nature of computing ability. For example, there are prevailing beliefs that it requires a "geek gene" (Ensmenger, 2012; Lewis et al., 2011). This connects to other narratives about intelligence – who has it and who doesn't. In particular, there has been a historical pattern of claims that some people have inferior intellects (Kendi, 2016). While reports of biological differences among races continue today (Reich, 2018), this work has long been critiqued as "scientific racism" (Fairchild, 1991). People have attempted to use science to explain why people of African descent are intellectually inferior (Bobo et al., 2012; Kendi, 2016). However, these claims are false and have no empirical basis.

Stepping back, we want to consider some of the staying power of these narratives. If these narratives about innate differences between groups are false, what supports their continued existence? This can be explained by a few things. First and foremost, the narratives are hierarchical and benefit some people. For example, the narrative that Black people are intellectually inferior implies that non-Black people are intellectually superior (Kendi, 2016). In this chapter, we will identify some of the ways in which these hierarchical narratives serve to affect behavior and outcomes that ultimately benefit or harm particular individuals and groups.

16.1.4 Unconscious Bias

As mentioned above, narratives can be discouraging to individuals because they may present a narrow view of who can do computing or the values and characteristics of the community that might be required in order to join. However, this individual-focused explanation of how these narratives discourage participation is only part of the story. Most obviously, these narratives can cause harm through explicit, conscious bias referred to as "prejudice" (Amodio, 2014). That is not the primary focus here because it appears to be more easily identified (although no more easily addressed). Instead, we focus on the less overt forms of bias that can cause disadvantage and marginalization and are fueled by these narratives – "implicit bias" or "unconscious bias" (Greenwald & Banaji, 1995).

Unconscious bias can influence split-second decisions, is fueled by narratives, and causes harm to those who are negatively stereotyped. The evidence of these biases primarily comes from what are referred to as "résumé studies" (Steinpreis et al., 1999). In this line of research, two copies of the same résumé are made and sent to people who might hire someone in the same field as the résumé. One group of people receive a copy of the résumé with one name on it. Others receive a copy of the résumé with a different name on it. Researchers modify the names to see if names that are associated with negative stereotypes about intelligence receive fewer positive responses. In Moss-Racusin et al.'s (2012) study on the influence of gender on application assessment, they found that both male and female science faculty rated male applications significantly higher than female applicants, selecting a higher starting salary and professional development support. Bertrand and Mullainathan (2004) used stereotypically White and African-American names, and applications were found to be more likely to result in an interview request if associated with a stereotypically White name. Pager (2003) explored this in a follow-up study incorporating multiple participants interviewing for positions with a number of set résumés and identical interview training; they found that African-American candidates with no criminal record received a callback at the rate of White candidates with a criminal record.

Another stunning example of unconscious bias comes from studies of hiring (Uhlmann & Cohen, 2005). Research participants were asked to evaluate applicants for a police chief position. One of the provided applicants had significant practical experience while the other had significant academic experience. The researchers found that whichever résumé they put a man's name on (with a woman's name on the other résumé), the participants would offer reasoned arguments about the importance of particular aspects of the male applicant's credentials. In the case where the man's name appeared on the résumé with practical experience, they argued for the importance of practical experience. In the case where the man's name appeared on the résumé with academic experience, they argued for the importance of academic experience. This shows that even when decisions involve a sound rationale, that rationale may be unconsciously shaped by bias.

While these examples may be a bit removed from the context of computing education, letters of recommendation may also demonstrate implicit bias. Studies show that authors tend to use more communal and supportive language when writing letters of recommendation for female candidates and more decisive and direct language when writing for male candidates (Madera et al., 2009; Trix & Psenka, 2003). This influence hits in multiple ways – not only in the way that recommendations are made, but then also in how they are perceived (see Barker, 2010, for a review and recommendations for avoiding such bias).

As additional evidence of bias, studies have found that both parents and teachers tend to overestimate boys' abilities in mathematics and science areas (Lindberg et al., 2010). Research has demonstrated that teachers treat boys and girls differently in their development of mathematical skills, with boys encouraged to pursue independent problem-solving processes, while girls are encouraged to follow fixed, algorithmic approaches (Hyde & Jaffee, 1998). Girls are less likely to be encouraged into CS roles by parents and teachers, with boys being more likely to be told explicitly that they could be good at CS (Google Inc. & Gallup Inc., 2017).

A natural question in the research above is whether the research participants in these examples were demonstrating sexism or racism. The answer depends upon the definitions of these terms. Certainly, the research suggests that people, regardless of their identities, have biases consistent with these cultural narratives that may unconsciously shape their words and behavior. When biases about race are embedded within policies and practices within institutions, it is referred to as structural racism,[5] even though it does not imply racist intent.

16.1.5 Aggregate Harm from Unconscious Bias

While some of these studies described above may seem to lead to small differences, even such small differences can have enormous aggregate impact. In particular, as researchers and educators, we are interested in considering the aggregate impact of unconscious bias and the ways in which it is embedded within policies and practices within institutions (Smith, 2015, p. 35). To consider the potential for aggregate harm, we remind the reader about emergent phenomena in which small behaviors can lead to macroscopic, observable patterns. Similarly, a small magnitude of bias could lead to macroscopic patterns of discrimination, marginalization, or underrepresentation.

Martell et al. (1996) created a simulation of bias against women in a company that was originally populated at every level of the company by 50 percent women and 50 percent men. To simulate bias, men were rated each year with scores of 1–100 and women were rated each year with scores of 0–99. They simulated multiple years, assuming yearly attrition and yearly promotions based upon ratings. The simulation showed a much larger pattern of underrepresentation of women at senior levels (only 35 percent at the top level). This simulation helps us connect our understanding of bias to the larger patterns of emergent phenomena; even small amounts of bias can lead to a substantial aggregate impact.

Additionally, research has also shown that students' perceptions of their abilities can also be impacted by bias, with teachers' perceptions of ability predicting students' own assessments (Keller, 2001; Tiedemann, 2000). This can form a

---

5 Smith (2015) states, "Institutionalized isms are standards, policies, and practices that are embedded in the institution, that have a disparate impact on particular groups, and that are not essential to fulfill the institution's mission" (p. 35).

negative cycle of ability perception, leading students to make critical decisions on capability, career goals, and study directions based on information that does not truly reflect their capability or potential.

16.1.6 Call to Action

This chapter seeks to help connect patterns of underrepresentation to these larger cultural narratives and systems of oppression such as sexism and racism. However, in doing so, it may appear that these problems are too large. These problems are indeed interconnected with these larger systems of oppression, and these problems are unlikely to be completely addressed without dismantling these larger systems. However, just as small amounts of bias can lead to an aggregate effect, so too can work to counteract these narratives and bias lead to an aggregate effect. We hope that our readers can see the historical roots of the problems while also seeing the imperative to act within their sphere of influence to make change and work toward justice.

For example, it is important to consider times when we are making decisions that are subjective because these subjective decisions are likely to be affected by bias. While these processes of bias are unconscious, it requires conscious effort to counteract them (Fiarman, 2016). If grading sometimes requires giving students "the benefit of the doubt," this may unconsciously be unevenly applied to student work (Malouff & Thorsteinsson, 2016). Educators may mitigate this by grading student work anonymously and using rubrics when possible. Research shows that being more aware of the biases that we have can help us reduce their impact on our decision-making (Morewedge et al., 2015). Even in our local decisions about grading we can contribute to addressing these much larger problems.

16.2 Vignettes

The following vignettes present hypothetical scenarios that we expect to resonate with the concerns and experiences of educators. We expect that this computing classroom-focused perspective also aligns with the interests of CEd researchers. Within the analysis of each of the vignettes we hope to provide helpful references to relevant research from CEd and beyond. Across the four vignettes, we draw on unconscious bias and the underlying narratives that fuel this bias, as described above (Sections 16.1.4 and 16.1.3, respectively). Additionally, we hope to use this research to discredit interpretations of the vignettes that simply apply narrow narratives about computing and computer scientists. Our discussion of each vignette ends with a description of relevant interventions.

16.2.1 Ways Structural Barriers and Stereotype Threat Shape Performance

As you are reviewing grades at the end of the semester, you notice that the grades of the only two Black women in your class, Nia and Kiara, were in the bottom quartile.

16.2.1.1 Vignette Analysis

We expect that a common interpretation is that those students who do poorly in the course lack an innate ability to learn computing. There is no evidence that there exists an innate ability for computing (Patitsas et al., 2016; Robins, 2010), and a belief in innate ability can lead students to pursue unproductive learning strategies (Dweck, 2008). To analyze this vignette, we will consider two bodies of literature related to structural barriers to computing and stereotype threat.

This analysis still takes into account the identities of Nia and Kiara, but does not rely on the false narratives described in Section 16.1.3 that women and Black people are generally less capable of success in computing. These are false interpretations. Black students *are* competent and as academically brilliant as any other students (Leonard & Martin, 2013). Although this might seem an obvious statement, we feel it is important to state this clearly and unequivocally, particularly in light of long-standing racist beliefs about Black people as intellectually deficient (Bobo et al., 2012). These false beliefs persist in the background, even though people might not explicitly vocalize them as often as before.

A first question you might ask is whether Nia and Kiara have had similar opportunities to learn computing as their peers. Differential access can have consequential implications for performance (Lewis et al., 2012). Additionally, research shows previous experience is often conflated with potential (Barker et al., 2002). In the USA, unequal access to computing instruction for Black and Latinx students and women has been well documented (College Board, 2017; Google Inc. & Gallup Inc., 2015). In the book *Stuck in the Shallow End: Education, Race, and Computing*, Margolis et al. (2008) described the structures that prevent students of color from having access to a rich computing curriculum. This work by Margolis et al. contributes to the body of work regarding our understanding of structural barriers to accessing advanced coursework for students of color (Mulkey et al., 2005). These structural barriers that disadvantage students of color are typically referred to as structural racism or institutionalized racism.

If Nia and Kiara have had fewer opportunities to learn computing, these broad patterns of structural racism may be a central explanation. However, it is important to remember that descriptions of these broad patterns do not mean that they will apply uniformly to students from a particular group. We should not assume simply based upon their race that Nia and Kiara have had fewer opportunities to learn computing.

Compounding racial disparities in access to CS instruction, women are less likely to have access to CS instruction (College Board, 2017; Google Inc. & Gallup Inc., 2015). While we can connect racial disparities in access to patterns of segregation (Orfield & Eaton, 1996) and structural racism, gender disparities require additional explanation because gender-segregated schooling is much less common. Unconscious bias (Section 16.1.4) can also explain why women would be less likely to be encouraged by adults to participate in

CS learning opportunities. In a US-based survey of 7th through 12th grade students, boys were more likely than girls to be told they would be good at CS by a teacher (39 vs. 26 percent) or a parent (46 vs. 27 percent; Google Inc. & Gallup Inc., 2017). Unconscious bias can also help explain why women might be less likely to choose to participate in CS learning. For students with identities that do not align with current narratives of computer scientists, this fact may lead to them perceiving a lack of fit with computing and depress their interest (Lewis et al., 2016). We know that children start to form gendered views of careers and behaviors at an early age (Miller et al., 2018) and that messages from their community, and specifically key role models, can have a significant impact on the decisions that they make regarding their intended careers and study directions (Google Inc., 2014).

As Black women, Nia and Kiara may be less likely to be encouraged to pursue computing because their race and gender do not match the narratives about computer scientists. Research has documented the barriers faced by women of color as a "double bind" (Malcom et al., 1976; Ong, 2011; Ong et al., 2011; Scott & Martin, 2014; Williams et al., 2014). The double bind captures ways in which gender and race contribute and interact to shape the experiences of women of color.

Psychology research has demonstrated evidence of a pattern referred to as "stereotype threat" (Steele, 2010; Steele & Aronson, 1995). This research argues that negative stereotypes may influence our behavior in ways that lead to behavior more consistent with the stereotype (Steele, 2010; Steele & Aronson, 1995). For example, Shih et al. (1999) investigated the impact of the narratives that women are bad at math and that Asian students are good at math. When a group of Asian women were given a math test and reminded of their gender, their performance was lower. When another group of Asian women were reminded of their race, but not their gender, their performance was higher. Stereotype threat has been demonstrated across domains, with some evidence from computing (Kumar, 2012). There is debate among psychologists regarding the mechanism that produces this depression of performance. Schmader et al. (2008) argue that stereotype threat, through multiple mechanisms, consumes students' executive functioning resources. False narratives about the inferior intellectual potential of Black people and women create an environment where stereotype threat may take place. This helps us to understand the surprising performance of Nia and Kiara.

16.2.1.2 Recommendations

Based upon differential patterns of access, it is important to ask: Can students without secondary school experience with computing be successful in these classrooms and programs of study? The most likely place to look for problems is in your institutions' introductory computing course. Given that students come with varied prior experience in computing, it is important to consider what paths through the institution are privileged. For example, at Harvey Mudd College, students are given the option of three different levels of introductory course (Alvarado et al., 2012). There is one course for students with no prior computing exposure. There is a second course designed for students with some prior computing exposure. Because of their prior exposure, it is likely less effortful for these students to develop fluency with the material. To avoid simply reinforcing initial differences in computing experience, this second course covers CS topics that are unlikely to confer an advantage before students reach upper-division CS courses. That is, the goal is to level the playing field between students who start the program with little or no prior experience. There is a third course for students with a lot of prior computing experience. These students take a single course that covers the content of the first two CS courses. Harvey Mudd College's practice of stratifying the introductory course can be seen as contributing to the high percentage of CS majors who identify as women (Alvarado et al., 2012).

A second recommendation is to attempt to avoid stereotype threat. Stereotype threat appears to be mitigated if students are told that the test does not exhibit any bias between groups or if students are not reminded of the stereotyped dimension of their identity (Steele & Aronson, 1995). Additionally, research has found that it can be helpful to communicate to students that tests are an opportunity to provide feedback about their learning, but are not a way to evaluate their potential (Cohen et al., 1999). Additionally, as discussed above, differential participation sometimes results from differential encouragement. Therefore, it can be helpful to provide explicit encouragement.

In addition to strategies specific to removing structural barriers and reducing stereotype threat, "transparent teaching" (Winkelmes et al., 2016) and "active learning" (Freeman et al., 2014) have been shown to have a differential benefit for students of color and other groups. Winkelmes et al. (2016) argue for making assignments "transparent" by stating explicitly what you want students to learn, what the students should do to accomplish the goals of the assignment, and how you will grade students. They found that when faculty made two of their assignments more "transparent," students' self-report of their academic confidence, sense of belonging, and "mastery of skills that employers value" were higher ($p < 0.05$). The effect sizes were higher for students who are the first in their family to attend college, low-income students, and non-White students.

Another class of strategies is referred to as "active learning," which can include a range of pedagogical strategies that seek to encourage students to engage with the content as they are learning. Active learning is sometimes defined as requiring students to do more than listen to a lecture (Freeman et al., 2014). While active learning describes a range of pedagogical strategies, this more-than-lecture set of approaches has been effective at reducing the rates at which students receive a grade of D or F or withdraw from the course (beyond any early course attrition). In a meta-review of 225 studies of STEM classrooms, Freeman et al. (2014) found that students in lecture-only sections were 1.5 times more likely to fail and had lower exam scores (6 percent lower or 0.64 standard deviations). Similarly, Treisman (1992) introduced a structured problem-solving session to create opportunities for collaboration and the development of social connections among Black and Latinx students in calculus classes at the University of California, Berkeley. This form of active learning was so effective that it has been replicated across many institutions with positive results in calculus (Moreno & Muller, 1999) and computing (Chinn et al., 2007).

Active learning or other pedagogical improvements may have differential benefits for students with less prior access to computing instruction. Because of racial and gendered disparities in access to computing instruction, more effective pedagogy may tend to be more beneficial for women and students of color of all genders. While the aggregate result of active learning is positive, this obscures variation in students' experiences. It may be necessary to respond to unintended consequences of these interventions even if the research suggests that positive results are likely.

16.2.2 Ways Environmental Cues Shape Belonging and Identity

Your advanced computing class for computing majors is racially diverse, but most of the students in the class are White or Asian – only three of your students identify as Black: Malik, Jaylisha, and Christopher. During class discussions, nearly all of your students participate by asking questions or sharing their ideas. However, Malik only contributes to class discussions occasionally, and Jaylisha and Christopher have not spoken at all in class. This bothers you because you feel committed to all of your students' learning.

16.2.2.1 Vignette Analysis

One common interpretation of this scenario is that Black students are inherently less competent than students of other racial backgrounds and that they might avoid participating in class discussions to hide that incompetence. As described in Section 16.2.1.1, this is false and relies only on false narratives about Black students for support.

A second common interpretation is that Black students might be less interested in computing, such that their apathy toward the subject causes them to participate less in class. This is also false. Research shows that Black students actually have higher rates of interest in CS fields relative to their peers of other racial backgrounds (Wang et al., 2017). Further, if Malik, Jaylisha, and Christopher were not interested in computing, then they would not have enrolled in the class or remained in the major. Their interest in computing, as well as their potential to excel in computing, should be taken as given.

Finally, a third interpretation of this scenario is that all three of these students participated less because they just happened to be "more shy" or more quiet than their classmates. Certainly, this is plausible – students will vary in terms of their extroversion and willingness to participate in public. However, it is important that educators do not focus on students' personalities to the point that the potential impact of social forces like racism or sexism are minimized or dismissed altogether. Further, even if Malik, Jaylisha, and Christopher all just happened to be more reticent, it is still incumbent on educators to find ways to support them to make their voices heard in class discussions.

First and foremost, it is important to consider student participation in relation to the *opportunities* to participate being made available to students. That is, teachers must consider the extent to which they make participation opportunities accessible to all of their students, especially those from historically marginalized groups. Were Malik, Jaylisha, and Christopher being called on to participate as frequently as other students? What criteria were used to select students for participation? Were only the fastest students to raise their hands invited to participate, or perhaps only those that volunteered at all? Teachers have tremendous discretion over which students do and do not participate in class discussions, and despite one's best intentions, implicit biases can influence who teachers do and do not call on. In fact, research shows that women and non-Asian students of color tend to be both called on less and asked to perform less cognitively demanding tasks when called on (McAfee, 2014; Sadker et al., 2009).

It is also potentially significant that Malik, Jaylisha, and Christopher are the only Black students in the entire class. Students in this position can feel tremendous pressure from being "spotlit," as if they are constantly being scrutinized and made to represent their entire race (Andrews, 2012). Do they trust that their ideas will be valued and taken up by their peers and teacher? Understandably, the absence of trust might short-circuit student participation. Additionally, imposter syndrome,[6] where an individual questions their belonging and abilities despite evidence to the contrary, can lead to decreased participation.

Over the past two decades, studies have shown that learning and identity are intertwined (Lave & Wenger, 1991; Nasir & Cooks, 2009; Wenger, 1998; Wortham, 2006). As people learn to do something, they begin to see themselves (and potentially are seen by others) as a *doer* of that thing. Conversely, coming to identify more with a given activity also increases the likelihood of productive engagement in the learning process. Do they see themselves as emergent computer scientists? What kinds of messages along these lines might they be receiving – either explicitly or implicitly – from both their classmates and you?

Whether a student comes to feel they belong and builds a robust identity as a learner of computing depends, in part, on how the computing classroom is structured. Using ethnographic methods, Barker et al. (2002) found that the computing learning environments they studied were often impersonal, isolating, and competitive in ways that fostered defensive classroom climates. Researchers have even found that the physical artifacts and layout of a computing classroom can diminish women's sense of belonging in the field (Cheryan et al., 2009).

---

6 Imposter syndrome was originally identified as "imposter phenomenon" (Clance & Imes, 1978), but is colloquially referred to as imposter syndrome.

16.2.2.2 Recommendations

A simple but powerful action that computing instructors can take is to systematically track the participation opportunities they are making available to students from marginalized groups. Instructors can reflect on the extent to which they are actively soliciting these students' participation. In addition to traditional peer observation, tools exist to support instructors in identifying subtle inequities in how participation opportunities are distributed by race, gender, and other social markers (see Reinholz & Shah, 2018). If inequities do exist, then an instructor can think strategically about implementing specific teaching practices to include marginalized students in class discussions. For example, teachers can call on students in a random order so that all students have an equal chance to participate (Shah et al., 2013). We can also try to address more directly students' sense of belonging in our classrooms through encouragement. Additionally, instructors can examine the types of examples we include (e.g., video games) to push back against stereotypical influences that may have impacted our curriculum and our classroom environments.

16.2.3 Ways Biased Statements Cause Harm

Midterm grades have been posted and students are discussing their scores. It turns out that Marcos, a Latinx student, got the highest grade in the class. John, a White classmate, finds out and tells Marcos, "Nice job, Marcos! You must have that Asian gene!" You overhear this and aren't sure if you should say something or what you should do.

16.2.3.1 Vignette Analysis

Instructors that do not recognize the fallacy of these cultural narratives might perceive John's comment to Marcos as harmless. Noticing a disproportionately higher enrollment by Asian students in computing at their institution, they might take John's statement as grounded in some degree of truth – that Asians really are naturally better at computing. Alternatively, they might consider it an innocent joke. Indeed, on a superficial level, the statement seems like a compliment to Asians. In our view, it would be a problematic for a variety of reasons.

In the USA, there is a racial narrative that Asian people are inherently superior in STEM fields, such as math, engineering, and computing. Not only do cultural representations of Asians as "technologically savvy" saturate US media (Paek & Shah, 2003), but there is also evidence that students are aware of such racial narratives (Shah, 2017) and even endorse them as they get older (Cvencek et al., 2015). Importantly, though, racial narratives about Asians being genetically predisposed for technology-related fields like computing are false. No empirical evidence exists to support the notion that some racial groups are better than others at computing. Further, such narratives assume that racial categories are somehow "real," as opposed to sociopolitical constructions intended to produce social hierarchies (Omi & Winant, 2015). Another problematic aspect of the comment is that it reflects the widespread narrative that performance in computing depends on an innate ability for the discipline. This too is a false narrative that imposes barriers to students from marginalized groups.

Racial talk among STEM learners has been documented in a number of studies (Nasir et al., 2009; Schaffer & Skinner, 2009; Shah, 2013). Students sometimes engage in racial talk to make sense of educational phenomena like performance patterns. Because race is widely considered a taboo topic (Pollock, 2004), such talk tends to take place in more private spaces away from a teacher. However, given the way race and racism saturate many societies around the world (Bonilla-Silva, 2003; Essed, 2002; Telles, 2004), educators can presume – even if they have not observed it directly – that their students are participating in racial talk related to computing.

This particular vignette was adapted from data collected in a study of racial discourse among students in mathematics (Nasir & Shah, 2011). There are strong similarities between mathematics and computing with respect to racial patterns in performance, representation, and opportunities to learn. For that reason, although studies of racial discourse specific to computing have yet to be conducted, we might reasonably expect similar forms of racial talk among computing students. To some, John's statement might seem like a harmless joke. However, this kind of superficial interpretation ignores the harm that racial narratives about STEM ability can cause (McGee & Martin, 2011; Shah, 2017). Instead, we can understand John's statement as a *microaggression*. According to psychologist Derald Wing Sue and colleagues (2007), "racial microaggressions are brief and commonplace daily verbal, behavioral, or environmental indignities, whether intentional or unintentional, that communicate hostile, derogatory, or negative racial slights and insults toward people of color" (p. 271). Certainly, microaggressions are not only racial; research has found evidence of microaggressions related to gender, religion, class, and other social markers (Sue et al., 2007).

John's statement functions as a racial microaggression through the deployment of multiple racial narratives about computing ability, including the false notions that Asian people have a natural ability for computing and that Latinx people are less competent in computing. These racial narratives cause harm in a couple of ways. First, they distort and narrow the types of identities available to students of color in computing. For Asians, the "Asians are naturally good at computing" narrative suggests that Asian students can *only* succeed in technical fields. Research shows that awareness of racial narratives about Asians having superior ability in STEM in the US context is widespread (Cvencek et al., 2015; Shah, 2017; Trytten et al., 2012). Further, this can exert undue pressure on Asian students to fulfill the narrative.

For Latinx people, and perhaps for non-Asian people of color more broadly, the narratives undermine the possibility of their success in computing. Instead, certain groups of color are pigeonholed into identities of underperformance. In this vignette, Marcos's Latinx identity is wrongly put in opposition to an identity as a successful computing learner, as if these identities cannot coexist. Whereas associations of Asians as "nerds" seem normal, such cultural representations for people of color cause dissonance and are rare in pop culture (Eglash, 2002). Racial narratives about Asians exacerbate the positioning of non-Asians of color as less capable in computing. In that sense, racial narratives are relationally linked in ways that produce false racial hierarchies of ability in a domain (Shah, 2017).

Second, John's microaggression also causes harm to the discipline of computing itself. By attributing Marcos's success to an "Asian gene," John reproduces the false idea that success in computing depends on an innate capacity for the subject. Given that race itself is often incorrectly viewed as a genetic trait (Gould, 1996), it is perhaps unsurprising that racial talk in STEM and discourses of innate ability often go hand in hand. In doing so, racial talk can perpetuate perceptions of computing as a domain reserved for certain groups and not others.

16.2.3.2 Recommendations

Overall, computing educators need to recognize that CEd exists within a racial context that influences how students perceive their own and their classmates' performance. Computing is not immune or divorced from the influence of race in society writ large. Educators should not ignore deployments of racial talk that further marginalize students of color; they must intervene.

One possible response is to make an immediate and direct verbal intervention that clearly states that race, gender, or any other social marker has no bearing on computing ability. It is important that students hear unequivocal statements about this from their computing instructors, since students see these people as authorities in the field. A private conversation with the students who were involved can signal to them the gravity of such "jokes." Beyond addressing those students, though, it can be impactful to have this discussion with the whole class as well. Other students may have overheard and been influenced by the interaction, and even if they were not, all students – but especially non-Asian students of color – must know for certain that their instructor believes in their capacity to succeed in computing.

Of course, situations like these can be awkward for instructors, and it may be challenging or uncomfortable to intervene in the moment. However, it is not necessary to respond immediately. Just as instructors provide students wait time before responding to a question in a class discussion, it can be productive to reflect on the interaction and revisit the interaction with students later during office hours or during the next class session.

In addition to verbal interventions, instructors can take steps to begin shifting the cultural narratives about who can succeed in computing. For example, research shows that the physical artifacts in a computing classroom (such as a Star Trek poster) can send signals about who belongs in computing (Cheryan et al., 2009). How can a classroom space be organized in ways that signal inclusion? Continual exposure to images of computer scientists from marginalized groups is one way of doing this (see Shah et al., 2013). While we acknowledge that cultural narratives have considerable inertia and are difficult to change, we argue that this is one simple, concrete action missing from many computing classrooms that would foster equity.

16.2.4 Ways We Can Validate and Improve Students' Experiences of Bias

Suzanne, a student in your Data Structures class, has come to your office hours to discuss a concept from that week's lecture. After discussing it with her for a few minutes, Suzanne begins to tell you about her experience in the class: "When I'm in lab and we're working in groups, the men in my group never listen to my ideas. The guys just turn toward each other and never ask me for help or my input. When I say something, they just ignore me."

16.2.4.1 Vignette Analysis

Despite the preponderance of evidence of sexism in computing and in society, some instructors might still feel that Suzanne is exaggerating – that "it's all in her head" – or that the incident was not as significant as Suzanne feels. Others might feel that she is playing the "gender card" to cover for being less competent than her male peers. Further, if one assumes that Suzanne is actually less competent, an instructor might feel that her peers should not be expected to seek out Suzanne's input. Overall, such interpretations reify false gender narratives about computing ability and diminish the continued impact of patriarchy in everyday life, including computing learning contexts. Honoring students' experiences requires educators to ask themselves the following question: Do I have the right to judge the validity of my students' experiences? With respect to gender issues in computing, given that the field is dominated by men, this is a particularly pressing question.

Many computing educators have themselves had positive experiences in learning computing. However, we must acknowledge that some of our students may be having different experiences. Research shows that people from historically marginalized groups in STEM tend to have categorically different experiences from people from dominant groups (Harper & Hurtado, 2007; McGee & Martin, 2011; Stinson, 2008). Computing educators need to both honor students' experiences as learners and also realize that their own positive experiences with computing can obfuscate an appreciation for their students' negative experiences.

In Suzanne's case, her experience of being marginalized by men in her group aligns with research documenting sexism in computing (Cohoon et al., 2009; Margolis & Fisher, 2003). Similar to the previous vignette, the experience of being ignored and having one's ideas dismissed or not solicited in the first place constitutes a microaggression (Sue et al., 2007). The men in Suzanne's group do not make overtly sexist comments, but Suzanne interprets their talking only to each other as a sexist move; this is her experience and must be taken seriously. Of course, these men might not have realized they were ignoring Suzanne. While it is possible that these students were overtly and intentionally sexist, it is also possible that their behavior was the unintentional result of implicit gender biases they held about women in computing and in general. In either case, students need opportunities to learn about how inequity operates in regular classroom interactions and what they can do to mitigate how they contribute to such inequities.

16.2.4.2 Recommendations

Before considering pedagogical responses to Suzanne's story of marginalization, instructors can do something simple but impactful to support students from marginalized groups: believe them. It takes courage for students to share such experiences with their instructors, especially when those instructors belong to dominant groups. Believing in the possibility that students' self-reports of inequity have merit can validate students' subjective experiences. Further, the risk of harm with such inequities is so great that it behooves instructors to take reports of them seriously. One concrete way to show this is to actively listen to students' experiences without evaluating those experiences. Instructors have considerable power in the instructor–student relationship, so listening without judgment is critical to managing students' vulnerability.

Beyond listening without judgment, students may want their instructors to take some kind of action. In our experience, it is okay to tell students that you will think about what they have shared and follow up with them with potential solutions. It also can be empowering to work collaboratively with the student to think of solutions that might work for them. Regardless, following up with students after an initial meeting can assure them that you have not forgotten about what they shared and are taking it seriously. Finally, it is also important to maintain confidentiality (unless the incident falls under mandatory reporting statutes). Explicitly telling students that you will keep what they have told you confidential can be an important step in trust-building. It is particularly helpful to learn about your legal responsibilities for reporting so that you can clearly communicate these to students.

One issue here is that students from marginalized groups often do not feel comfortable sharing experiences of inequity with instructors, perhaps in part because of a fear that they will not be believed or that action will not be taken. Just because students have not shared stories about their negative experiences does not mean they are not happening. Instructors should actively implement ways for students to report such incidents – for instance, an anonymous survey given periodically throughout a course can be a way for students to report their experiences. This can also signal to students that they have an instructor that cares about equity.

Finally, efforts can be taken to educate students about how inequity operates in social interaction. For example, students can be given readings on implicit bias and microaggressions early in the course, coupled with class discussions about how these phenomena might come up in their particular class. Additionally, students might be required to take an Implicit Association Test (IAT) as part of an ungraded assignment – the results of the IAT might also be fodder for class discussion about inequity. Last, an institution might organize a training session around implicit bias for all of their students. This sends the message that the burden for addressing these inequities does not fall on students like Suzanne, but rather on students like her male group members. Companies like Google and Facebook have made their internal training modules on implicit bias available for free to the public (see Google's modules at https://rework.withgoogle.com/subjects/unbiasing and Facebook's modules at https://managingbias.fb.com). Associating learning about implicit bias with these companies may also reinforce the notion that this is important for students' professional training.

16.3 Open Questions

We now expand our focus and identify particular open questions, having already identified relevant terms in equity and diversity (Section 16.1.2) and summarized problematic narratives about computing and computer scientists (Section 16.1.3) and how these narratives cause harm through implicit bias (Sections 16.1.4 and 16.1.5). The vignettes above also introduced research about structural barriers and stereotype threat (Section 16.2.1), belonging and participation (Section 16.2.2), biased statements in the classroom and their impact (Section 16.2.3), and the importance of listening to students (Section 16.2.4).

16.3.1 Computing for What Purposes?

In this chapter, we have made certain assumptions about the goals of CEd in relation to issues of equity and inequity. By focusing on the social-interactional barriers faced by students from particular groups, we have assumed that increasing the number of women computer scientists and computer scientists of color, for example, is a worthy goal. Many educators and scholars within our field are in agreement on this, and we stand by this assumption. At the same time, though, we as a field must also take a critical stance on why people should learn computing in the first place.

There is an economic rationale for learning computing, in that computing can open access to high-paying jobs, which include jobs in the computing field and jobs that involve computing. For groups that have been systematically excluded from opportunities to accumulate wealth and are simultaneously targeted for state-sponsored plunder, the chance to attain financial stability through CEd is nontrivial. Working toward more computer scientists from marginalized groups is also a matter of cultural representation. Instances of bias in software that result in the propagation of White supremacy, patriarchy, and other forms of domination have been well documented (Rose, 2010; Tatman, 2016).

Presumably, greater demographic diversity in computing would mitigate such biases and lead to more inclusive and humane technologies. Overall, these are good reasons for greater equity in computing. And yet, pursuing equity only for the sake of capitalism or cultural representation can perpetuate inequity. We must question what we mean by "computing education" and our motivations for encouraging students to learn computing (Lewis, 2017).

Computing is not inherently good. Like anything else, it matters how we use it. Indeed, computing has been used to commit corporate fraud (Tabuchi & Ewing, 2016) and has also contributed to social injustice (O'Neil, 2016). STEM disciplines more broadly have long since been implicated in militaristic endeavors (Schoenfeld, 2004). What does it mean to push for equity in versions of CEd focused narrowly on producing technology for the sake of profit or that causes harm? Do we want more people of color or women in computing to do this kind of work? To what kinds of computing are we broadening participation?

In thinking about equity in CEd, it is imperative that as a field we expand the forms and goals of computing. Computing can be used for self-expression and to explore identities and cultural experiences (Eglash et al., 2013; Harrell, 2013; Kafai et al., 2014; Scott & White, 2013). Computing can also be used to understand the world better and foster justice in both students' local communities and society writ large (Vakil, 2014). A version of computing oriented toward the pursuit of social justice requires conceptualizations of equity that begin with an understanding of historical patterns of oppression and a deep analysis of sociopolitical values and goals (Martin, 2003; Vossoughi et al., 2016).

We encourage future research on equity and inequity in CEd to embrace and to develop versions of CEd that can lead to humanization and greater justice for people from marginalized groups.

16.3.2 Problematizing "Equity" Terminology

Language matters. As we discussed earlier, the language we use to describe marginalization and efforts to attenuate marginalization comes with various affordances and constraints. "Equity" and "diversity" are among the terms most preferred by the field. However, we must continue to question equity-related terminology in relation to our goals for CEd. In part, this involves pushing for specificity in how we deploy equity discourse. For example, "diversity" is a vague term. In writing and in presentations, it is important to specify what forms of diversity we are referring to at any particular time (e.g., racial diversity, linguistic diversity, gender diversity). Further, terms can become conflated in problematic ways, such as "equity" and "equality," and the use of "culture" and "urban" for "race."

Without specificity and clear intention, equity-related language risks becoming facile slogans devoid of real meaning (Apple, 1992). Scholars in other STEM disciplines have engaged with these issues. In mathematics education, for example, Martin (2003) has critiqued the persistent "mathematics for all" rhetoric as "broad and non-specific" (p. 13). Martin argues that the word "all" allows stakeholders in education to avoid naming social markers like race, which serves to obscure the specific needs and inequities experienced by members of particular marginalized groups. Similar rhetoric abounds in computing – what are the limitations of the "for all" language as a way to frame equity issues?

Future research in this area would be well served in asking: Is the language of "equity" and "diversity" adequately radical? In what ways does it reproduce what Gutiérrez (2008) has called "gap-gazing," which refers to an overemphasis on performance gaps between racial groups or gender gaps in participation along the CEd pipeline? Performance and participation are important foci, but CEd can and should engage with larger issues and questions. What does computing have to do with the murder of Black people at the hands of the police, or how does computing contribute to – and how can it help in pushing back against – global Islamophobia? To what extent does the currently dominant equity-related discourse in computing make it possible to address questions of this kind? In posing these questions to the field, we simultaneously find ourselves asking them of ourselves and reflecting on what they mean for the directions of our own future work.

Language always has its limits. We do not believe that a "perfect" set of terms exist that cover all aspects of the complex problems of inequity and injustice. However, we feel it is important that the field not take terminology for granted – both in definition and in conceptual validity. We argue for an interrogatory stance toward equity-related language, particularly in relation to the goals of equity work in CEd.

16.3.3 Researching Equitable Practices

The pedagogies that we employ and the tools and environments in which they are positioned can have distinct implications for equity and students' opportunities to learn. There remain open questions that may help us build toward a more equitable culture of CEd. Here, we introduce two open questions that highlight some exciting recent work in CEd.

What role does culturally responsive pedagogy play? The Exploring CS curriculum (Goode et al., 2012; Margolis et al., 2015) explores social, creative, and culturally responsive computing contexts. Similarly, the work of Fields et al. (2017) and Kafai et al. (2014) explores ethnocomputing with e-textiles. Brady et al. (2017) use social and diverse computing contexts in addition to physical computing and maker technologies. Rubio et al. (2015) also adopt a physical computing approach, with their study closing the gap in gendered perceptions of the difficulty of computing and the desire to continue with computing learning opportunities. Medel and Pornaghshband (2017) explore the ways that gendered names, imagery, and language lead to gender bias in the curriculum. As these interventions and curricula are refined and evaluated, we look forward to learning how to effectively integrate culturally responsive pedagogies and curricula.

What characteristics of the intervention and context are necessary and sufficient for interventions that have been successful at fostering diversity (Alvarado et al., 2012; Falkner et al., 2016; Guzdial, 2013)? For example, Media Computation is an approach for teaching introductory computing through having students create and manipulate digital media. While this approach increased retention more broadly and girls found the content more motivating, there was no significant difference in learning gain for participants (Guzdial, 2013). In their Media Computation-based massive open online course (MOOC), Falkner et al. (2016) report significantly higher enrollment by female students (34 percent) than typically reported for computing MOOCs. Collaborative and active learning pedagogies have been effective in promoting increased learning outcomes (Prince, 2004). However, collaborative pedagogies have also been shown to lead to marginalization (Lewis & Shah, 2015). There is a lot that remains to be explored in the design of effective and equitable curricula and pedagogies.

16.4 Conclusion

In our use of vignettes, we have focused on a contextualized review of the literature. The work we decided to foreground was intentional, but still we regret not being able to include more context, information, and resources. We hope that our readers will use the chapter as a jumping-off point to continue to explore these important issues and how they can improve their current context in pursuit of equity and justice.

References

Alvarado, C., Dodds, Z., & Libeskind-Hadas, R. (2012). Increasing women's participation in computing at Harvey Mudd College. *ACM Inroads*, 3(4), 55–64.

Amodio, D. M. (2014). The neuroscience of prejudice and stereotyping. *Nature Reviews Neuroscience*, 15(10), 670–682.

Andrews, D. J. (2012). Black achievers' experiences with racial spotlighting and ignoring in a predominantly White high school. In *Teachers College Record*, 114(10), 1–46.

Apple, M. W. (1992). Do the standards go far enough? Power, policy, and practice in mathematics education. *Journal for Research in Mathematics Education*, 23(5), 412–431.

Barker, L. (2010). Avoiding Unintended Gender Bias in Letters of Recommendation (Case Study 1). Reducing Unconscious Bias to Increase Women's Success in IT. *Promising Practices, National Center for Women and Information Technology.* Retrieved from www.ncwit.org/sites/default/files/resources/avoidingunintendedgenderbiaslettersrecommendation.pdf

Barker, L. J. Garvin-Doxas, K., & Jackson, M. (2002). Defensive climate in the computer science classroom. *ACM SIGCSE Bulletin*, 34(1), 43–47.

Bertrand, M., & Mullainathan, S. (2004). Are Emily and Greg more employable than Lakisha and Jamal? A field experiment on labor market discrimination. *American Economic Review*, 94(4), 991–1013.

Bobb, K. (2016). Why teaching computer science to students of color is vital to the future of our nation. *The Root*. Retrieved from www.theroot.com/articles/culture/2016/03/why_teaching_computer_science_to_students_of_color_is_vital_to_the_future/

Bobo, L. D., Charles, C. Z., Krysan, M., Simmons, A. D., & Fredrickson, G. M. (2012). The real record on racial attitudes. In *Social Trends in American Life: Findings from the General Social Survey since 1972* (pp. 38–83). Princeton, NJ: Princeton University Press.

Bonilla-Silva, E. (2003). "New racism," color-blind racism, and the future of whiteness in America. In A. W. Doane & E. Bonlilla-Silva (Eds.), *White Out: The Continuing Significance of Racism* (pp. 271–284). London, UK: Routledge.

Brady, C., Orton, K., Weintrop, D., Anton, G., Rodriguez, S., & Wilensky, U. (2017). All roads lead to computing: Making, participatory simulations, and social computing as pathways to computer science. *IEEE Transactions on Education*, 60(1), 59–66.

Cheryan, S., Plaut, V. C., Davies, P. G., & Steele, C. M. (2009). Ambient belonging: How stereotypical cues impact gender participation in computer science. *Journal of Personality and Social Psychology*, 97(6), 1045–1060.

Chinn, D., Martin, K., & Spencer, C. (2007). Treisman workshops and student performance in CS. *ACM SIGCSE Bulletin*, 39(1), 203–207.

Clance, P. R., & Imes, S. A. (1978). The imposter phenomenon in high achieving women: Dynamics and therapeutic intervention. *Psychotherapy: Theory, Research & Practice*, 15(3), 241–247.

Cohen, G. L., Steele, C. M., & Ross, L. D. (1999). The mentor's dilemma: Providing critical feedback across the racial divide. *Personality and Social Psychology Bulletin*, 25(10), 1302–1318.

Cohoon, J. M., Wu, Z., & Chao, J. (2009). Sexism: Toxic to women's persistence in CSE doctoral programs. *ACM SIGCSE Bulletin*, 41(1), 158–162.

College Board (2017). AP program participation and performance data 2017 [Data file]. Retrieved from https://research.collegeboard.org/programs/ap/data/archived/ap-2017

Cvencek, D., Nasir, N. I. S., O'Connor, K., Wischnia, S., & Meltzoff, A. N. (2015). The development of math–race stereotypes: "They say Chinese people are the best at math". *Journal of Research on Adolescence*, 25(4), 630–637.

Dweck, C. S. (2008). *Mindset: The New Psychology of Success*. New York: Random House.

Eglash, R. (2002). Race, sex, and nerds: From black geeks to Asian American hipsters. *Social Text*, 20(2), 49–64.

Eglash, R., Gilbert, J. E., Taylor, V., & Geier, S. R. (2013). Culturally responsive computing in urban, after-school contexts: Two approaches. *Urban Education*, 48(5), 629–656.

Ensmenger, N. (2010). Making programming masculine. In T. J. Misa (Ed.), *Gender Codes: Why Women Are Leaving Computing* (pp. 115–141). Hoboken, NJ: Wiley.

Ensmenger, N. L. (2012). *The Computer Boys Take Over: Computers, Programmers, and the Politics of Technical Expertise*. Cambridge, MA: MIT Press.

Essed, P. (2002). Cloning cultural homogeneity while talking diversity: Old wine in new bottles in Dutch organizations. *Transforming Anthropology*, 11(1), 2–12.

Fairchild, H. H. (1991). Scientific racism: The cloak of objectivity. *Journal of Social Issues*, 47(3), 101–115.

Falkner, K., Falkner, N., Szabo, C., & Vivian, R. (2016). Applying validated pedagogy to MOOCs: An introductory programming course with media computation. In *Proceedings of the 2016 ACM Conference on Innovation and Technology in Computer Science Education (ITiCSE '16)* (pp. 326–331). New York: ACM.

Fiarman, S. E. (2016). Unconscious bias: When good intentions aren't enough. *Educational Leadership*, 74(3), 10–15.

Fields, D. A., Kafai, Y. B., Nakajima, T., & Goode, J. (2017). Teaching practices for making e-textiles in high school computing classrooms. In *Proceedings of the 7th Annual Conference on Creativity and Fabrication in Education (FabLearn '17)* (p. 5). New York: ACM.

Freeman, S., Eddy, S. L., McDonough, M., Smith, M. K., Okoroafor, N., Jordt, H., & Wenderoth, M. P. (2014). Active learning increases student performance in science, engineering, and mathematics. *Proceedings of the National Academy of Sciences*, 111(23), 8410–8415.

Goode, J. (2008). Increasing diversity in K–12 computer science: Strategies from the field. *ACM SIGCSE Bulletin,* 40(1), 362–366.

Goode, J., Chapman, G., & Margolis, J. (2012). Beyond curriculum: The exploring computer science program. *ACM Inroads*, 3(2), 47–53.

Google Inc. (2014). Women who choose computer science – What really matters: The critical role of exposure and encouragement. Retrieved from https://docs.google.com/file/d/0B-E2rcvhnlQ_a1Q4VUxWQ2dtTHM/edit

Google Inc., & Gallup Inc. (2015). Searching for computer science: Access and barriers in U.S. K–12 education. Retrieved from http://g.co/cseduresearch

Google Inc., & Gallup Inc. (2016). Diversity Gaps in Computer Science: Exploring the Underrepresentation of Girls, Blacks and Hispanics. Retrieved from http://goo.gl/PG34aH

Google Inc., & Gallup Inc. (2017). Encouraging Students Toward Computer Science Learning. Results From the 2015–2016 Google–Gallup Study of Computer Science in U.S. K–12 Schools (Issue Brief No. 5). Retrieved from https://goo.gl/iM5g3A

Gould, S. J. (1996). *The Mismeasure of Man*. New York: WW Norton & Company.

Greenberg, J. B. (1989). Funds of knowledge: Historical constitution, social distribution, and transmission. Presented at *Annual Meeting of the Society for Applied Anthropology*, Santa Fe, NM.

Greenwald, A. G., & Banaji, M. R. (1995). Implicit social cognition: Attitudes, self-esteem, and stereotypes. *Psychological Review*, 102(1), 4.

Gutiérrez, R. (2008). A "gap-gazing" fetish in mathematics education? Problematizing research on the achievement gap. *Journal for Research in Mathematics Education*, 39(4), 357–364.

Guzdial, M. (2013). Exploring hypotheses about media computation. In *Proceedings of the Ninth Annual International ACM Conference on International Computing Education Research* (pp. 19–26). New York: ACM.

Harper, S. R., & Hurtado, S. (2007). Nine themes in campus racial climates and implications for institutional transformation. *New Directions for Student Services*, 2007(120), 7–24.

Harrell, D. F. (2013). *Phantasmal Media: An Approach to Imagination, Computation, and Expression*. Cambridge, MA: MIT Press.

Hunt, V., Yee, L., Prince, S., & Dixon-Fyle, S. (2018). Delivering through Diversity. McKinsey & Company Report. Retrieved from www.mckinsey.com/business-functions/organization/our-insights/delivering-through-diversity

Hyde, J. S., & Jaffee, S. (1998). Perspectives from social and feminist psychology. *Educational Researcher*, 27(5), 14–16.

Information is Beautiful (2016). Diversity in tech: Employee breakdown of key technology companies. Retrieved from www.informationisbeautiful.net/visualizations/diversity-in-tech/

Kafai, Y. B., Lee, E., Searle, K., Fields, D., Kaplan, E., & Lui, D. (2014). A crafts-oriented approach to computing in high school: Introducing computational concepts, practices, and perspectives with electronic textiles. *ACM Transactions on Computing Education (TOCE)*, 14(1), 1–20.

Kafai, Y., Searle, K., Martinez, C., & Brayboy, B. (2014). Ethnocomputing with electronic textiles: Culturally responsive open design to broaden participation in computing in American indian youth and communities. In *Proceedings of the 45th ACM Technical Symposium on Computer Science Education* (pp. 241–246). New York: ACM.

Keller, C. (2001). Effect of teachers' stereotyping on students' stereotyping of mathematics as a male domain. *The Journal of Social Psychology*, 141(2), 165–173.

Kendi, I. X. (2016). *Stamped from the Beginning: The Definitive History of Racist Ideas in America*. New York: Nation Books.

Kumar, A. N. (2012). A study of stereotype threat in computer science. In *Proceedings of the 17th ACM Annual Conference on Innovation and Technology in Computer Science Education* (pp. 273–278). New York: ACM.

Ladner, R., & Israel, M. (2016). "For all" in "computer science for all." *Communications of the ACM*, 59(9), 26–28.

Lave, J., & Wenger, E. (1991). *Situated Learning: Legitimate Peripheral Participation*. Cambridge, UK: Cambridge University Press.

Leonard, J., & Martin, D. B. (Eds.) (2013). *The Brilliance of Black Children in Mathematics*. Charlotte, NC: IAP.

Lewis, C. M., Anderson, R. E., & Yasuhara, K. (2016). I don't code all day: Fitting in computer science when the stereotypes don't fit. In *Proceedings of the 2016 ACM Conference on International Computing Education Research* (pp. 23–32). New York: ACM.

Lewis, C. M., Yasuhara, K., & Anderson, R. E. (2011a). Deciding to major in computer science: A grounded theory of students' self-assessment of ability. In *Proceedings of the Seventh International Workshop on Computing Education Research* (pp. 3–10). New York: ACM.

Lewis, C. M., Titterton, N., & Clancy, M. (2012). Using collaboration to overcome disparities in Java experience. In *Proceedings of the Ninth Annual International Conference on International Computing Education Research* (pp. 79–86). New York: ACM.

Lewis, C. M. (2017). Twelve tips for creating a culture that supports all students in computing. *ACM Inroads*, 8(4), 17–20.

Lewis, C. M., & Shah, N. (2015). How equity and inequity can emerge in pair programming. In *Proceedings of the Eleventh Annual International*

Conference on International Computing Education Research (pp. 41–50). New York: ACM.

Lindberg, S. M., Hyde, J. S., Petersen, J. L., & Linn, M. C. (2010). New trends in gender and mathematics performance: A meta-analysis. *Psychological Bulletin*, 136(6), 1123–1135.

Madera, J. M., Hebl, M. R., & Martin, R. C. (2009). Gender and letters of recommendation for academia: Agentic and communal differences. *Journal of Applied Psychology*, 94(6), 1591–1599.

Malcom, S. M., Hall, P. Q., & Brown, J. W. (1976). *The Double Bind: The Price of Being a Minority Woman in Science*. Washington, DC: American Association for the Advancement of Science.

Malouff, J. M., & Thorsteinsson, E. B. (2016). Bias in grading: A meta-analysis of experimental research findings. *Australian Journal of Education*, 60(3), 245–256.

Margolis, J., Estrella, R., Goode, J., Jellison-Holme, J., & Nao, K. (2008). *Stuck in the Shallow End: Education, Race, and Computing*. Cambridge, MA: MIT Press.

Margolis, J., & Fisher, A. (2003). *Unlocking the Clubhouse: Women in Computing*. Boston, MA: MIT Press.

Margolis, J., Goode, J., & Chapman, G. (2015). An equity lens for scaling: A critical juncture for exploring computer science. *ACM Inroads*, 6(3), 58–66.

Margolis, J., Goode, J., Chapman, G., & Ryoo, J. J. (2014). That classroom "magic". *Communications of the ACM*, 57(7), 31–33.

Margolis, J., Ryoo, J., Sandoval, C., Lee, C., Goode, J., & Chapman, G. (2012). Beyond access: Broadening participation in high school computer science. *ACM Inroads*, 3(4), 72–78.

Martell, R. F., Lane, D. M., & Emrich, C. (1996). Male–female differences: A computer simulation. Retrieved from www.ruf.rice.edu/~lane/papers/male_female.pdf

Martin, D. B. (2003). Hidden assumptions and unaddressed questions in mathematics for all rhetoric. *The Mathematics Educator*, 13(2), 7–21.

McAfee, M. (2014). The kinesiology of race. *Harvard Educational Review*, 84(4), 468–491.

McGee, E. O., & Martin, D. B. (2011). "You would not believe what I have to go through to prove my intellectual value!" Stereotype management among academically successful Black mathematics and engineering students. *American Educational Research Journal*, 48(6), 1347–1389.

Medel, P., & Pournaghshband, V. (2017). Eliminating gender bias in computer science education materials. In *Proceedings of the 2017 ACM SIGCSE Technical Symposium on Computer Science Education* (pp. 411–416). New York: ACM.

Miller, D. I., Nolla, K. M., Eagly, A. H., & Uttal, D. H. (2018). The development of children's gender-science stereotypes: A meta-analysis of 5 decades of US draw-a-scientist studies. *Child Development*, doi:10.1111/cdev.13039.

Milner IV, H. R. (2012). Beyond a test score: Explaining opportunity gaps in educational practice. *Journal of Black Studies*, 43(6), 693–718.

Moll, L., Amanti, C., Neff, D., & González, N. (2006). Funds of knowledge for teaching: Using a qualitative approach to connect homes and classrooms. In N. González, L. Moll, & C. Amanti (Eds.), *Funds of Knowledge: Theorizing Practices in Households, Communities, and Classrooms* (pp. 71–87). New York: Routledge.

Moreno, S. E., & Muller, C. (1999). Success and diversity: The transition through first-year calculus in the university. *American Journal of Education*, 108(1), 30–57.

Morewedge, C. K., Yoon, H., Scopelliti, I., Symborski, C. W., Korris, J. H., & Kassam, K. S. (2015). Debiasing decisions: Improved decision making with a single training intervention. *Policy Insights from the Behavioral and Brain Sciences*, 2(1), 129–140.

Moss-Racusin, C. A., Dovidio, J. F., Brescoll, V. L., Graham, M. J., & Handelsman, J. (2012). Science faculty's subtle gender biases favor male students. *Proceedings of the National Academy of Sciences*, 109(41), 16474–16479.

Mulkey, L. M., Catsambis, S., Steelman, L. C., & Crain, R. L. (2005). The long-term effects of ability grouping in mathematics: A national investigation. *Social Psychology of Education*, 8(2), 137–177.

Nasir, N. I. S., & Cooks, J. (2009). Becoming a hurdler: How learning settings afford identities. *Anthropology & Education Quarterly*, 40(1), 41–61.

Nasir, N. S., Atukpawu, G., O'Connor, K., Davis, M., Wischnia, S., & Tsang, J. (2009). Wrestling with the legacy of stereotypes: Being African American in math class. In D. B. Martin (Ed.), *Mathematics Teaching, Learning, and Liberation in the Lives of Black Children* (pp. 231–248). New York: Routledge.

Nasir, N. S., & Shah, N. (2011). On defense: African American males making sense of racialized narratives in mathematics education. *Journal of African American Males in Education*, 2(1), 24–45.

National Science Foundation, National Center for Science and Engineering Statistics (2017). *Women, Minorities, and Persons with Disabilities in Science and Engineering: 2017*. Special Report NSF 17-310. Arlington, VA. Retrieved from www.nsf.gov/statistics/wmpd/

National Center for Women and Information Technology (2017). By the Numbers. Retrieved from www.ncwit.org/bythenumbers

O'Neil, C. (2016). *Weapons of Math Destruction: How Big Data Increases Inequality and Threatens Democracy*. New York: Crown.

Ong, M. (2011). The status of women of color in computer science. *Communications of the ACM*, 54(7), 32–34.

Ong, M., Wright, C., Espinosa, L., & Orfield, G. (2011). Inside the double bind: A synthesis of empirical research on undergraduate and graduate women of color in science, technology, engineering, and mathematics. *Harvard Educational Review*, 81(2), 172–209.

Omi, M., & Winant, H. (2015). *Racial Formation in the United States*. New York: Routledge.

Orfield, G., & Eaton, S. E. (1996). *Dismantling Desegregation. The Quiet Reversal of Brown v. Board of Education*. New York: The New Press.

Paek, H. J., & Shah, H. (2003). Racial ideology, model minorities, and the "not-so-silent partner": Stereotyping of Asian Americans in US magazine advertising. *Howard Journal of Communication*, 14(4), 225–243.

Pager, D. (2003). The mark of a criminal record. *American Journal of Sociology*, 108(1), 937–975.

Patitsas, E., Berlin, J., Craig, M., & Easterbrook, S. (2016). Evidence that computer science grades are not bimodal. In *Proceedings of the 2016 ACM Conference on International Computing Education Research* (pp. 113–121). New York: ACM.

Pollock, M. (2004). Race wrestling: Struggling strategically with race in educational practice and research. *American Journal of Education*, 111(1), 25–67.

Prince, M. (2004). Does active learning work? A review of the research. *Journal of Engineering Education*, 93, 223–231.

Reich, D. (2018). *Who We Are and How We Got Here: Ancient DNA and the New Science of the Human Past*. Oxford, UK: Oxford University Press.

Reinholz, D., & Shah, N. (2018). Equity analytics: A methodological approach for quantifying participation patterns in mathematics classroom discourse. *Journal for Research in Mathematics Education*, 49(2), 140–177.

Robins, A. (2010). Learning edge momentum: A new account of outcomes in CS1. *Computer Science Education*, 20(1), 37–71.

Rose, A. (2010). Are face-detection cameras racist? *TIME*. Retrieved from http://content.time.com/time/business/article/0,8599,1954643,00.html

Rubio, M. A., Romero-Zaliz, R., Mañoso, C., & Angel, P. (2015). Closing the gender gap in an introductory programming course. *Computers & Education*, 82(1), 409–420.

Sadker, D., Sadker, M., & Zittleman, K. (2009). *Still Failing at Fairness: How Gender Bias Cheats Girls and Boys in School and What We Can Do about It*. New York: Scribner.

Schaffer, R., & Skinner, D. G. (2009). Performing race in four culturally diverse fourth grade classrooms: Silence, race talk, and the negotiation of social boundaries. *Anthropology & Education Quarterly*, 40(3), 277–296.

Schmader, T., Johns, M., & Forbes, C. (2008). An integrated process model of stereotype threat effects on performance. *Psychological Review*, 115(2), 336–356.

Schoenfeld, A. H. (2004). The math wars. *Educational Policy*, 18(1), 253–286.

Scott, K. A., & White, M. A. (2013). COMPUGIRLS' standpoint: Culturally responsive computing and its effect on girls of color. *Urban Education*, 48(5), 657–681.

Scott, A., & Martin, A. (2014). Perceived barriers to higher education in science, technology, engineering, and mathematics. *Journal of Women and Minorities in Science and Engineering*, 20(3), 235–256.

Shah, N., & Lewis, C.M. (in press). Amplifying and attenuating inequity in collaborative learning: Toward an analytical framework. *Cognition and Instruction*.

Shah, N. (2013). *Racial Discourse in Mathematics and its Impact on Student Learning, Identity, and Participation* (PhD thesis). University of California, Berkeley.

Shah, N., Lewis, C. M., Caires, R., Khan, N., Qureshi, A., Ehsanipour, D., & Gupta, N. (2013). Building equitable computer science classrooms: Elements of a teaching approach. In *Proceeding of the 44th ACM Technical Symposium on Computer Science Education* (pp. 263–268). New York: ACM.

Shah, N. (2017). Race, ideology, and academic ability: A relational analysis of racial narratives in mathematics. *Teachers College Record*, 119(7), 1–42.

Shih, M., Pittinsky, T. L., & Ambady, N. (1999). Stereotype susceptibility: Identity salience and shifts in quantitative performance. *Psychological Science*, 10(1), 80–83.

Smith, D. G. (2015). *Diversity's Promise for Higher Education: Making it Work*. Baltimore, MD: JHU Press.

Steele, C. M., & Aronson, J. (1995). Stereotype threat and the intellectual test performance of African Americans. *Journal of Personality and Social Psychology*, 69(5), 797–811.

Steele, C. M. (2010). *Whistling Vivaldi: How Stereotypes Affect Us and What We Can Do*. New York: WW Norton & Co.

Steinpreis, R. E., Anders, K. A., & Ritzke, D. (1999). The impact of gender on the review of the curricula vitae of job applicants and tenure candidates: A national empirical study. *Sex Roles*, 41(7–8), 509–528.

Stinson, D. W. (2008). Negotiating sociocultural discourses: The counter-storytelling of academically (and mathematically) successful African American male students. *American Educational Research Journal*, 45(4), 975–1010.

Sue, D. W., Capodilupo, C. M., Torino, G. C., Bucceri, J. M., Holder, A., Nadal, K. L., & Esquilin, M. (2007). Racial microaggressions in everyday life: Implications for clinical practice. *American Psychologist*, 62(4), 271.

Tabuchi, H., & Ewing, J. (2016). Volkswagen to pay $14.7 billion to settle diesel claims in U.S. *The New York Times*. Retrieved from www.nytimes.com/2016/06/28/business/volkswagen-settlement-diesel-scandal.html

Tapia, J. (1991). *Cultural Reproduction: Funds of Knowledge as Survival Strategies in the Mexican American Community* (doctoral dissertation). University of Arizona.

Tatman, R. (2016). Google's speech recognition has a gender bias. Making noise and hearing things. Retrieved from https://makingnoiseandhearingthings.com/2016/07/12/googles-speech-recognition-has-a-gender-bias/

Telles, E. E. (2004). *Race in Another America: The Significance of Skin Color in Brazil*. Princeton, NJ: Princeton University Press.

Tiedemann, J. (2000). Parents' gender stereotypes and teachers' beliefs as predictors of children's concept of their mathematical ability in elementary school. *Journal of Educational Psychology*, 92(1), 144–151.

Toyama, K. (2015). *Geek Heresy: Rescuing Social Change from the Cult of Technology*. Philadelphia, PA: PublicAffairs.

Treisman, U. (1992). Studying students studying calculus: A look at the lives of minority mathematics students in college. *The College Mathematics Journal*, 23(5), 362–372.

Trix, F., & Psenka, C. (2003). Exploring the color of glass: Letters of recommendation for female and male medical faculty. *Discourse & Society*, 14(2), 191–220.

Trytten, D. A., Lowe, A. W., & Walden, S. E. (2012). "Asians are good at math. What an awful stereotype." The model minority stereotype's impact on asian american engineering students. *Journal of Engineering Education*, 101(3), 439–468.

Uhlmann, E. L., & Cohen, G. L. (2005). Constructed criteria: Redefining merit to justify discrimination. *Psychological Science*, 16(6), 474–480.

Vakil, S. (2014). A critical pedagogy approach for engaging urban youth in mobile app development in an after-school program. *Equity & Excellence in Education*, 47(1), 31–45.

Vélez-Ibáñez, C. G. (1988). Networks of exchange among Mexicans in the U.S. and Mexico: Local level mediating responses to national and international transformations. *Urban Anthropology*, 17, 27–51.

Vossoughi, S., Hooper, P. K., & Escudé, M. (2016). Making through the lens of culture and power: Toward transformative visions for educational equity. *Harvard Educational Review*, 86(2), 206–232.

Walton, G. M., & Cohen, G. L. (2011). A brief social-belonging intervention improves academic and health outcomes of minority students. *Science*, 331(6023), 1447–1451.

Wang, J. Hejazi Moghadam, S., & Tiffany-Morales, J. (2017). Social perceptions in computer science and implications for diverse students. In *Proceedings of the ACM Conference on International Computing Education Research* (pp. 47–55). New York: ACM.

Wenger, E. (1998). *Communities of Practice: Learning, Meaning, and Identity*. Cambridge, UK: Cambridge University Press.

Williams, J. C., Phillips, K. W., & Hall, E. V. (2014). Double Jeopardy: Gender Bias Against Women of Color in Science. Retrieved from https://repository.uchastings.edu/faculty_scholarship/1278

Winkelmes, M. A., Bernacki, M., Butler, J., Zochowski, M., Golanics, J., & Weavil, K. H. (2016). A teaching intervention that increases underserved college students' success. *Peer Review*, 18(1/2), 31.

Wortham, S. (2006). *Learning Identity: The Joint Emergence of Social Identification and Academic Learning*. Cambridge, UK: Cambridge University Press.

New Milieux

17 Computational Thinking

Paul Curzon, Tim Bell, Jane Waite, and Mark Dorling

17.1 Motivational Context

The term "computational thinking" was popularized by Wing (2006) as the form of thinking computer scientists practice. Computational thinking has since been widely accepted and promoted both as the skill set that programmers develop and as the general thinking skills that should be developed by computer scientists as they learn the discipline. Wing also advocated it as a generally useful problem-solving skill set that all should learn. Computational thinking also arguably offers a powerful way of both thinking and doing across a wide range of subject disciplines, transforming the way that they are carried out, such as through the use of computational modeling.

17.1.1 Computation

Computational thinking is not primarily about the development of electronic computer systems. It is about computation and the development of systems based on computation. Computation dates back millennia. The first algorithms were developed thousands of years before digital computers. One of the earliest, and most famous, is Euclid's algorithm (c. 300 BCE; cited in Euclid, 1997) for computing the greatest common divisor of two numbers. The word "algorithm" derives from the name of the Muslim scholar Muḥammad ibn Mūsā al-Khwārizmī and is most closely associated with his work *On the Calculation with Hindu Numerals* (al-Khwārizmī, c. 825). It concerns the algorithms for doing arithmetic with decimal positional numbers. Computation is not just about numeric calculation, however. It concerns symbol processing more generally. Early algorithms, predating electronic computers, include encryption-related algorithms that concern the manipulation of letters and other symbols. Computation does not need to be done by machines, of course. Humans can follow algorithms, and al-Khwārizmī's book was about algorithms for people to follow. Indeed, the first actual "computers" were people, not machines. The term was originally used to describe the people tasked with doing the astronomical calculations needed to develop maritime tables for navigation at sea (OED, 1993). Indeed, Charles Babbage did this job, and it was a motivation for him to develop machines that could do the calculations automatically. The developers of these pre-computer age algorithms were certainly engaged in a form of computational thinking, in the sense of solving computational problems through precise algorithmic solutions.

Turing (1936) famously articulated a formal idea of computation in the thought experiment of a Turing machine, and a variety of other models of computation have been devised that have been proved equivalent. These models define the limits of what computation, and so algorithms, can do. Since computational thinking concerns the design of computational systems, these theories give limits on the possible.

Computation is not restricted to the manipulation of abstract symbols. It can and does happen to physical things in the world that embody information, and not just inside computer chips (which are embodiments of computation in the physical world too). Computation in such a computational system involves information processing through, for example, the movement and transformation of information between different physical objects. This is a core idea behind distributed cognition (Hutchins, 1995), where the brain is seen as an information processing agent and cognition is seen as extending to incorporate such computational systems in the world. Hutchins' core example is analysis of the computational properties of ship navigation, exploring how information is transformed as it passes between different forms, physical and mental. This richer view of computation is actually vital in the development of the modern computer systems that play an increasingly physical role in the world, augmenting human processes in complex ways.

This view of computation as including movement and transformation of physical objects means that "unplugged computing," where physical objects and role play are used to illustrate computing concepts (Bell, Alexander, Freeman, & Grimley, 2009; Bell, Rosamond, & Casey 2012), is not just the use of analogy, but is actually about computation itself. Computational thinking is being done in devising unplugged computational systems, whether inventing a self-working magic trick (an algorithm for a magical effect) as illustrated by Curzon and McOwan (2017) or devising an activity of searching for numbered balls under cups using a binary search algorithm. This mirrors real-world, everyday uses of computational thinking too, such as when a teacher, presented with a pile of 400 paper exam scripts that must be put in sorted order by ten-digit student number, devises a form of radix sorting as an efficient way to do so in preference to using some variation of bubble sorting. A more forward-thinking computational thinker might later redesign the system as a whole, allocating desks to students in the required order, allowing the students to physically sort themselves and so their scripts. Even without turning to digital solutions, algorithmic thinking is useful.

17.1.2 What Is Computational Thinking?

Wing (2006) is clear that computational thinking is about thinking like a computer scientist. It is, however, also a fundamental analytical skill for everyone, not just for computer scientists. She is also clear that the concept she is defining is about computing processes, whether they are executed by a human or by a machine. It is specifically not just the skill of computer programming, but

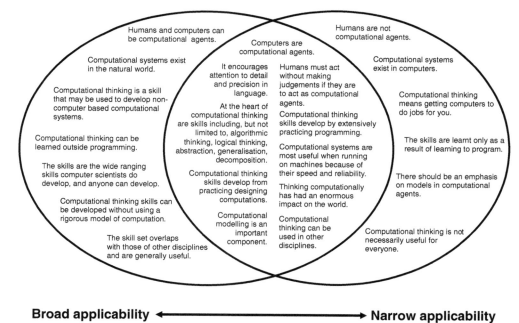

Humans and computers can be computational agents.

Computational systems exist in the natural world.

Computational thinking is a skill that may be used to develop non-computer based computational systems.

Computational thinking can be learned outside programming.

The skills are the wide ranging skills computer scientists do develop, and anyone can develop.

Computational thinking skills can be developed without using a rigorous model of computation.

The skill set overlaps with those of other disciplines and are generally useful.

Computers are computational agents.

It encourages attention to detail and precision in language.

At the heart of computational thinking are skills including, but not limited to, algorithmic thinking, logical thinking, abstraction, generalisation, decomposition.

Computational thinking skills develop from practicing designing computations.

Computational modelling is an important component.

Humans are not computational agents.

Computational systems exist in computers.

Humans must act without making judgements if they are to act as computational agents.

Computational thinking skills develop by extensively practicing programming.

Computational systems are most useful when running on machines because of their speed and reliability.

Thinking computationally has had an enormous impact on the world.

Computational thinking can be used in other disciplines.

Computational thinking means getting computers to do jobs for you.

The skills are learnt only as a result of learning to program.

There should be an emphasis on models in computational agents.

Computational thinking is not necessarily useful for everyone.

Broad applicability ◀————————————————▶ **Narrow applicability**

Figure 17.1 *Agreement and disagreement around two views of what computational thinking should be.*

the much wider way of thinking that computer scientists (not specifically programmers) develop.

There are, unfortunately, now a wide variety of sometimes polarized views over what computational thinking should be (Denning, 2017; Tedre & Denning, 2016; Denning & Tedre, 2019). This has led to problems, not least that research studies use different definitions, often without being clear what they mean by the term. This diversity of views is largely a result of how successful the original definition was, resonating around the world. This success has led to it being incorporated into education systems globally, and this has made its meaning an issue of politics, with different groups using it with their own definition to fit their own priorities and agendas. Views mainly differ on the breadth of applicability and the nature of computational agents (Figure 17.1). Most literature is closer to the middle of this diagram, but the authors have regularly encountered professionals who argue strongly for one of the extreme views.

Despite the different views, it is ultimately more useful as an educator to focus on the agreement, which as Figure 17.1 shows is large, and not worry which end of the spectrum resonates personally. There is general agreement around a large central core (see Section 17.3 for a deeper summary) that computational thinking is the way of thinking used to develop solutions in a form that ultimately allows "information processing" or "computational" agents to execute those solutions. The computational agent should be guaranteed to achieve some specified result without further thought or problem-solving involved, just by blindly and precisely following the solution. Ultimately, solutions are not one-off answers like "the cheapest route is via Hong Kong," but rather are *algorithms* that solve a general case (e.g., "find the cheapest route"). Computational thinking is thus concerned with the development of systems involving information processing, and it is the focus on algorithmic solutions that differentiates it from other problem-solving approaches. There are different views, however, on what can be a computational agent. It could be a machine or human (or possibly even an animal or other biological system if it can follow those instructions precisely and blindly). It could also be a combination of both.

Programming relies directly on this skill set, but computational system design and development is about far more than just coding itself. The development of higher levels of computational systems relies on these skills, as does innovation in computing more generally. As Wing (2006) notes, "Thinking like a computer scientist means more than being able to program a computer. It requires thinking at multiple levels of abstraction."

Although the idea of "computational thinking" has been around for centuries, the term was first used by Papert (1980) as part of his call for a new approach to teaching mathematics based on computational methods (see also Chapters 1, 19, 20, and 22). This original definition is about the idea that computational thinking is a way of doing other subjects differently. He suggested it as part of a teaching methodology for computational environments through the Logo programming language. In this context, it can be seen more as a novel way of gaining understanding rather than narrowly about solving problems. It is this idea that is transforming science and leading to innovation more generally (see Section 17.1.9). However, it was Wing's use of the term, not Papert's, which led to the concept being widely adopted.

17.1.3 A "Traditional" View or Not?

Denning (2017) has brought differing views to a head. He identifies what he calls a "traditional view". Essentially, this boils down to the idea that computational thinking should be based on computational models and algorithms that have definite computational steps. Part of this view is that computational agents must act like machines (or, at least, well-defined models of machines) and therefore are most likely to be encountered by beginners when developing software (i.e., developing instructions in formally defined languages for electronic computers of the kind that currently exist). Denning claims that there is no evidence that developing programming skills alone extends to more general problem-solving, so this justification of computational thinking for all should be dropped, at least until evidence is produced that it has broader benefits. He argues that the ultimate goal of computational thinking is computational design. More widely, its goal is computational *systems* design.

As many of the concepts that have been espoused as fundamental to the term "computational thinking" are well known in other disciplines, Denning (2017) argues that computational thinking should not be given the special status it has as a general problem-solving approach.

Wing (2006), on the other hand, argues that computational thinking is much more than this. It is both a skill that leads to programming ability and a generally useful skill. A consequence of this view is that it can be learned separately from programming. Even if programming does not lead to general problem-solving skill, this wider definition of computational thinking that intersects with other subject views of problem-solving may lead to more general problem-solving skills.

Denning outlines a series of precursors to Wing in discussing the general skill set developed by programmers and advises we stick to Aho's more recent though "historically well-grounded definition":

> Mathematical abstractions called models are at the heart of computation and computational thinking. Computation is a process that is defined in terms of an underlying model of computation and computational thinking is the thought processes involved in formulating problems so their solutions can be represented as computational steps and algorithms.
> (Aho, 2012, pp. 834–835)

Denning grounds the skill set of computer scientists firmly in working throughout with defined models of computation, and rules out calling anything computation that is not based on such a model. It appears to rule out both informal demonstrations (such as the classic sandwich-making exercise where instructions are followed literally) and working at higher levels of abstraction without a specific model targeted. However, a major point of thinking at higher levels of abstraction for a problem means the details (and model) at lower levels are explicitly ignored, and this skill of working at all levels needs to be developed. That is part of the power of computational thinking and is certainly important in creating programs.

17.1.4 What Is a Computational Agent?

A key question is whether only machines should be classed as computational agents. If so, this leads to the position that computational thinking is only concerned with the creation of programs. If so, then arguably there is no need for a new term of "computational thinking" at all, as programming itself is the skill set.

Wing and many others since have argued for a wide definition. At the outset, Wing (2006), for example, stated that computational agents can be humans, not just machines. This wider view puts the emphasis not on machines or programming, but on information processing and the design and understanding of systems that do such information processing. Humans can and do perform such information processing, though they are clearly less capable of following instructions precisely. This is embodied in computing curricula in England and other countries, and it is because of this wide definition that the idea of computational thinking has become so widespread. It is also the foundation of the arguments for computing for all and the basis of the resultant push around the world that it, and not just programming, should be taught in school, not just in higher education. A significant reason for this push is because it makes clear that computational thinking is a useful tool for all to learn, not just programmers. If it is just useful for programmers as a skill, then there is far less justification for teaching it to all from primary upwards.

Denning (2017) argues for a narrower definition: that a computational agent should not involve human judgment. This frames it as a skill for students who are learning to program, since this is the environment in which a beginner might encounter such computational agents. He argues that there is no evidence that this narrow version has any transferable benefits beyond computing itself and therefore such claims should be dropped. Lee (2016) takes a related view, arguing that computational thinking is definitely not about creating algorithms for humans to follow, but that it is more than just programming. She puts the emphasis on it being about taking *real-world problems* and creating abstractions of them and algorithms that solve them, which are then implemented on computers.

17.1.5 An Evolving Definition

Denning, in part, is reacting to the way a range of authors have adapted the meaning of the term. According to Dagienė et al. (2017), authors that have further developed the meaning include Grover and Pea (2013), Kalelioglu et al. (2016), Lu and Fletcher (2009), Selby and Woollard (2013), and Wolz et al. (2011). These authors have argued that there is a place in the progression of learning to think computationally for activities that do not necessarily result in implementing a programmed solution.

For example, Lu and Fletcher (2009), though taking computational thinking to be about solving problems with computers, explicitly argued that it should be split from programming in the early years. They argued that the focus should be on

> establishing vocabularies and symbols that can be used to annotate and
> describe computation and abstraction, suggest information and execution,
> and provide notation around which mental models of processes can be built.
> (Lu & Fletcher, 2009, p. 260)

They posited that doing so would lead to students being in a better position, with such a foundation, to learn both programming and more advanced computing. Their argument is that a computational thinking language (CTL) must permeate the pedagogy. They give wide-ranging examples of how such language and unplugged computational thinking might be developed in an interdisciplinary way from US curricula, all concerning the students doing computation, not writing programs. The focus is on computation and information processing tasks generally, not on how they are specifically implemented in computers. Curzon's practical approach to teaching programming itself, as well as data structure and algorithms concepts (Curzon, 2002), takes a similar explanatory approach, teaching programming ideas divorced from writing programs, using wide-ranging analogies with real-world processes to explain general computing concepts, but getting completely away from the syntax and detailed semantics of a specific language. He advocates the same approach for introducing computational thinking as embodied by the Teaching London Computing website (http://teachinglondoncomputing.org).

Selby and Woollard (2013), in searching for an appropriate definition to use in school education, looked for consensus. They surveyed the literature concerned with computational thinking and came up with a definition based on the most commonly agreed-upon components of computational thinking. Computing at School (CAS) adopted this basic definition to promote computational thinking in England (Csizmadia et al., 2015). This is based on the five top-level categories that were most commonly encountered and so showed the most consensus from the research community: algorithmic thinking, abstraction, decomposition, generalization, and evaluation.

Further evolution of the term may also be needed if "computational thinking" is taken to be the skill set needed to develop computational systems in the future. For example, Chapter 20 argues for the need to include more explicitly the underlying skills needed for new areas such as machine learning, distributed computing, and quantum computing paradigms. This implies that not just logical thinking, but also statistical and probabilistic thinking skills will be needed for the development of computational systems in the future.

17.1.6 Problem-Solving, Expression, Creativity, and Communication

Computational thinking is currently mainly associated with problem-solving, but this may limit the opportunities for getting the most from it, as well as limiting those who might be attracted to using it. Bers (2017) links back to Papert's call for technological fluency as well as computational thinking (Papert, 1980), describing technological fluency as when one can express oneself "creatively, in a fluent way, effortlessly and smoothly as one does with language" (Bers, 2008). She sees computational thinking as too associated with problems and draws out the potential for using it for communication, creativity, and expression beyond science, technology, engineering, and mathematics (STEM). This resonates with classroom practice, where students probably do not see their programs as algorithms that solve a problem, but as instructions that make something happen. Brennan and Resnick's (2012) computational thinking concepts, practices, and perspectives meet Denning's point about the link between computational thinking and programming, but they highlight the importance of expression, connecting, and questioning as a means to "code to learn" rather than just learning to code (Resnick, 2013). Kafai (2016) advocates for "computational participation" rather than just computational thinking. Calling it "participation" allows for more emphasis on community, where code is written to be shared rather than a disposable exercise, where developing software occurs in the context of a community, and where others' work can be remixed.

17.1.7 Pedagogy and Pragmatism

There are two distinct issues in this debate that need to be separated: (1) What is the skill set involved in computational thinking? (2) How does one take children on the journey to gain those skills? Teaching is a pragmatic endeavor. Many subjects are taught using a spiral learning model where "lies to children" (misconceptions) are used to simplify concepts in order to make them accessible at a younger age. Denning and Tedre (2019) highlight that what computational thinking really is varies by necessity as students progress from beginner to professional, and that failing to make this distinction leads to conflict. Whether or not one wishes to take a narrow or wide definition of computational thinking, there is still a great deal of benefit to be gained by looking for a simplified progression and taking a constructivist approach, building on everyday ideas that are already understood. There are good pedagogic reasons for doing this. It involves presenting more accessible versions of computational thinking to younger age groups – ones that fudge the details. A perfectly sensible first step is to work on writing clear instructions with young primary school students (such as telling a friend how to walk the outline of a square, writing recipes, or writing out a dance routine). Later, the limitations of human instructions such as recipes can be explored, and this can motivate the need for the more rigorous, formal treatment found in programs. Foundational concepts can be introduced in this way, then built on and refined as one progresses through the education system.

Even if analogical approaches are rejected, the issue is not whether there is a formal model per se, but whether a computational agent, in principle, could blindly follow the resulting algorithm, and if it did so accurately, whether it would guarantee the same outcome over and over again. Attempts at creating algorithms by younger learners are likely to be incomplete, inaccurate, and clumsy, but as they make progress, precision, completeness, cohesion, and elegance will improve, thereby showing such progression. This will apply whether one is starting to write programs, recipes, or other instructions for humans. Just because the young, novice developer has not provided or worked with a precise model of computation, a mathematical semantic model, or implemented a fully working, complete computational stack all the way down doesn't mean they are not thinking computationally or about computation. Human-centered software development also does not start with algorithms and models, but rather with understanding human and socio-technical needs. It is only later in good development processes that underlying models, precision, and completeness enter the scene.

Despite issues with definitions, pragmatically, the idea of computational thinking has proved immensely useful, especially in putting a focus on the importance of the general skill set of computer scientists, as well as promoting computing for all in education systems worldwide. It has helped improve the standing of computing in schools as a rigorous subject that is more than office IT skills in a variety of countries.

Whichever definition we adopt, it is clear that programming is a key step in teaching computational thinking, but also that learners build upon existing knowledge and skills starting with relevant and familiar contexts. Similarly, we also need to be aware that becoming a programmer is not the goal for all students, in the same way that becoming a professional novelist is not the goal for all those learning to write.

17.1.8 Changes to School Curricula

A consequence of the push arising from Wing's seminal article (Wing, 2006) has been that computational thinking has become a foundation stone of new syllabuses of computing. It has also provided a useful term to articulate changes that were already planned for curricula and enabled curriculum designers to articulate the broader principles intended in revised curricula. This has especially avoided the perception that the changes were only about esoteric topics of interest to programmers or just about developing skills to groom students for work purely in the software development industry. For example, the purpose of study of the English National Curriculum for Computing (Department for Education, 2013), which applies from primary school upwards, starts: "A high-quality computing education equips pupils to use computational thinking and creativity to understand and change the world." A key aim, in line with the Royal Society report (Royal Society, 2012), was that computing should be more than just programming. Computational thinking was placed at its heart in part to emphasize this, following Wing's definition. Explicit aims include the following:

- "can understand and apply the fundamental principles and concepts of computer science, including abstraction, logic, algorithms and data representation"
- "can analyse problems in computational terms"

An outline of skill and knowledge progression is set out. For example, at ages 5–7, pupils should be able to "understand what algorithms are; how they are implemented as programs on digital devices; and that programs execute by following precise and unambiguous instructions." At ages 7–11, pupils should be able to (among other things): "solve problems by decomposing them into smaller parts," and also "use logical reasoning to explain how some simple algorithms work and to detect and correct errors in algorithms and programs." At ages 11–14, pupils should be able to "design, use and evaluate computational abstractions," and "use logical reasoning to compare the utility of alternative algorithms for the same problem." For more on this, see also reference to the US curriculum in Chapter 20 and in other countries in Chapter 18.

Computational thinking is increasingly being made a central framework as countries update their school curricula. A review of computing education in K–12 schools across 12 countries (Hubwieser et al., 2015) revealed that computational thinking or algorithmic concepts were now addressed by curricula in Germany/Bavaria, France, New Zealand, Finland, the USA, Israel, Russia, the UK, Korea, Sweden, and India. New Zealand has even called the core computing part of their proposed curriculum "computational thinking" (NZ Ministry of Education, 2017).

As these ideas are embedded in national curricula from primary school upwards, making sure such interventions now deliver practical benefits to the students involved is a vital and pressing issue.

17.1.9 Practical Benefits

One purported benefit of computational thinking skills is that they are the basis of being able to program. With such thought processes in place, programming becomes easier and better programs are written. However, it is more than just about low-level programming. Many of the same skills apply in designing hardware systems too, and in developing systems at higher levels. Developing maintainable, usable, and used software systems needs more than just coding skills. Modern computer systems are socio-technical systems, and the design of real-world systems requires an understanding of the wider systems, so development of the skills to design such complex computational systems through experience is more than just programming.

The explosion of interest in computational thinking has come about not because of its basis in programming per se, but because of the argument that it is a general problem-solving skill set and mode of thought that is desirable for more than just programmers or even computer scientists to possess. The world is now digital as well as physical, and it is argued that everyone can benefit from being able to think algorithmically and understand deeply how the digital world works, particularly how it is driven by algorithms. This is important as if you understand how something is constructed, whether physical or digital, then you have a stronger basis for understanding its potential uses and its effects on society (Royal Society, 2012, 2017a, 2017b). For example, a policy-maker who understood how GPS algorithms work would be in a better position to see how it would transform the way we do so many things and to see new possibilities for it, including new cyber-threats, such as it potentially being spoofed. A hiker would also better understand the risk of losing that signal when entering a deep, narrow canyon. To take a different real case, the lives of several innocent nurses were blighted due to such a lack of understanding (Thimbleby, 2018). In 2018, a UK court case was brought against these nurses, accusing them of negligence and, in particular, of fabricating paper patient records that differed from automated computer logs of tests administered. At the last minute, the prosecution offered no evidence when expert witnesses showed that hospital administrators, police, and prosecutors had not understood enough about the way the system worked or was used to realize that those computer logs could be inaccurate. Had the hospital administrators understood the algorithms more deeply, they might also have procured a more reliable system. It also matters in the sense of being able to contribute to the development of appropriate algorithmic socio-technical solutions to problems. Participatory design is a powerful way to develop systems that truly work for the people involved.

Thinking about socio-technical systems as computational systems is a new way of thinking about them that is important to anyone who is already operating in, who could be operating in, or who is interacting with the digital world. Note that this is not a point just about using technology or the introduction of the term "computational thinking" per se (the introduction of the term didn't represent the point in time when that way of thinking started to exist), but about the way of thinking it embodies, which long predates the term, as discussed in Section 17.1.4. It matters not just in terms of designing interactive systems or in understanding how digital devices work, but also in making informed decisions as citizens about ethical issues where we may choose (or not) to place limits on how we use computation (such as artificial intelligence in decision-making or self-driving vehicles).

A more general argument still is that even aside from understanding and making the best use of digital technology, thinking of systems explicitly as computational systems and of algorithmic ways of doing things can make us all more effective in everyday life, whether working in a coffee shop, running a factory, or sorting exam scripts. If we think computationally about the things we do, then we can develop more effective ways of working or achieving tasks more generally. Whether we call this "computational thinking" or not is merely a matter of definition of terms.

Thinking computationally is about more than just problem-solving: it provides a whole new way of thinking. Millican and Clark (1996) and Millican (n.d.), for example, argue that new modes of explanation based on the ideas stemming from Turing have had a revolutionary impact on philosophy and the intellectual world more generally, providing a new algorithmic mode of explanation. This is one basis for the idea that computational thinking is of use for all. There is "clear potential for algorithmic explanation in such fields as psychology, politics, sociology, and economics" (Millican, n.d.) as well as the traditional sciences. This is as big a revolution as those of Newton or Einstein on our modes of thought.

These reasons apply whether for scientists, lawyers, artists, or politicians. It provides a new lens through which to look at (and understand) the world and so craft new ways of doing things, new ways of working. Taking law as an example, Susskind (2017) makes the case that lawyers must "start to innovate, to practice law in ways that we could not have done in the past," in part due to computing innovation. Lawyers who can drive this themselves and even directly contribute rather than relying on computer scientists will have a big advantage. "We require a new cadre of self-sufficient legal technologists whose impact on modern society will be profound." He outlines a range of future careers for lawyers with computer science skills, including systems engineering and programming, and suggests a computer science degree will be one future route to becoming a lawyer. Such lawyers of the future will need computational thinking skills as well as legal skills in order to both see and grab opportunities. Similar arguments to Susskind's apply across the spectrum of professions.

The way science is conducted has already changed profoundly. In the past, science was moved forward by theory – rigorous thinking about the possibilities – and empirical experiment in the real world. There is now a third way. Phenomena of interest can be modeled algorithmically: theory is encoded with algorithmic rules. The phenomena can then be explored through simulation or proof. Virtual experiments can be performed on the models created, exploring the consequences of the rules, including emergent properties. This can be compared with the results of experiments. If the results differ, then it suggests the rules, and therefore the underlying understanding, need further refinement. It also leads to prediction for real experiments. It can thus drive both theory and empirical research, and it applies even to massively complex systems such as the climate.

Computational modeling dates back to some of the earliest uses of computers, where complex calculations were needed to understand phenomena. The early EDSAC (Electronic Delay Storage Automatic Calculator) family of computers contributed in this way to the work of three Nobel Prize winners, in Chemistry, Medicine, and Physics. John Kendrew and Max Perutz credited it for the discovery of the structure of myoglobin, Andrew Huxley for work on understanding the way nerves function, and Martin Ryle for work in radio astronomy. All acknowledged EDSAC in their Nobel Prize speeches. The astronomer, Joyce Wheeler, also used EDSAC to investigate the nuclear reactions that keep stars burning. Computational modeling of the weather by Edward Lorenz led to the observations that small changes to inputs led to widely differing results. This ultimately led to the development of chaos theory, showing how computational modeling can contribute to whole new theory. Now, computational modeling is a standard approach across science.

This idea is closely tied to that of Papert (1980) that computational methods could be used as the basis for learning mathematics and other subjects (see Chapter 19). Simulation can be used to explore and understand subjects that are new to the learner. Application of computational thinking by learners in non-computing subjects, such as in mathematics, economics, or physics, to find mathematical solutions to problems at different levels of abstraction (i.e., algorithms and then computer code) is a demonstration of how computational thinking skills can lead to deeper, more meaningful learning. A similar approach can be used in biology (e.g., by coding the behavior of ants laying and following trails, which can lead to a deeper understanding of that behavior as a learner).

17.2 The Elements of Computational Thinking

While there are differing views as to the details, there is a lot of agreement at least as to the core elements that make up computational thinking: algorithmic thinking, logical thinking, abstraction, generalization, and decomposition, for example, are generally agreed to play a part (Selby & Woollard, 2013). A range of other aspects have also been suggested, including recursive thinking, pattern matching, representation, heuristic thinking, scientific thinking, probabilistic and statistical reasoning, understanding people, concurrency and parallelism, and attention to detail. We discuss the core, uncontroversial elements in depth here. Many other aspects are arguably sub-skills of, or closely linked to, these core elements. For example, recursive thinking can be thought of as an advanced form of decomposition. In the examples given below, the skills described draw upon a combination of the core elements – particularly generalization, decomposition, and abstraction. Other definitions (e.g., Google, n.d.; ISTE/CSTA, 2014) are in part different because they group the separate aspects differently, such as pulling out pattern matching as a separate skill from generalization or linking abstraction and decomposition together as a single core element.

17.2.1 Algorithmic Thinking

Algorithmic thinking is the idea that solutions to problems are not limited to one-off answers like, "The vending machine will give a $5 and $10 note as the change," but rather are algorithms that can give answers whenever needed for general cases: instructions that, if followed blindly and precisely, are guaranteed to lead to an answer, such as, "Here's how to work out the notes and coins to give if you buy an item worth x dollars and give the vending machine y dollars." If a person can express the solution to a problem as a general algorithm that will solve it for all cases, then they have shown a deeper understanding of the problem than otherwise. It is possible to be able to do related tasks without that deeper understanding of the algorithm. For example, most people can give correct change, but articulating the process exactly (see if the largest note is too much, if not, give one out, then …) is quite difficult to do. This is akin to the fact that people can catch a ball without being able to explain the laws of gravity. If a student writes an algorithm that another person can follow or implements an algorithm as a program that works correctly for any input (such as giving change for any amount of money), then they have demonstrated that they do deeply understand the process.

An important issue in creating algorithms, and therefore algorithmic thinking, is in trying to get the most efficient algorithm for the job, where this could, for example, mean the fastest or alternatively the least memory-hungry algorithm. Often the best answer involves trade-offs in choosing between algorithms, rather than there being a single right answer.

A key part of algorithmic thinking, given Turing's result on the essence of computation and Turing completeness (Böhm & Jacopini, 1966; Aho, 2012), is that a computational thinker can give instructions making use of all three of sequence, selection, and iteration. Without this basic minimum, one cannot claim to have a true grasp of computation. Because these "big three" define everything that computational devices can do in terms of flow of control, having an understanding of them opens the full power of computation. It also defines the limits of computation and underpins our understanding of what computers *can't* do (Harel, 2003).

Algorithmic thinking is the core part of the computational thinking skill set that makes it different from the thinking skills of other disciplines such as scientific thinking, mathematical thinking, design thinking, and so on where the other building blocks of computational thinking arise. Computing overlaps and draws on many other subjects. The core of computing is centered around algorithms, however. Similarly, computational thinking draws on and overlaps with other problem-solving approaches from those disciplines. In this sense, algorithmic thinking is the defining part that makes it different. However, on its own, algorithmic thinking is not enough to be generally useful as a way of problem-solving (unless one subsumes all of the other aspects into the term "algorithmic thinking").

17.2.2 Logical Thinking

Being able to think logically is a core skill that underpins all versions of computational thinking. Logic underpins the semantics of programming languages, and thinking in a logical way is needed to develop algorithms, to implement these as programs, and to verify whether or not they work correctly, either informally or formally. Computer scientists developing algorithms need to be able to think through a problem, being sure that their solutions cover all possibilities that might arise and that they are guaranteed to always give the correct solution. Of course, with the advent of machine learning approaches, this becomes a question of probabilistic reasoning, rather than pure logical reasoning (see Chapter 20). At one end of the logical thinking spectrum lies simply thinking clearly and precisely, including avoiding errors and with attention to detail. At the other end lies an ability to reason about algorithmic solutions using formal logic. In between lies being able to put together rigorous arguments based on deductive or inductive reasoning. While formal reasoning in logic is a core aspect of computing, few computer scientists learn to do it well, so what usually seems to be meant by commentators in the context of computational thinking is the less rigorous versions. Formal logical reasoning is, however, a sophisticated aspect of computational thinking that is certainly desirable for programmers and can be considered a part of the highest levels of progression in computational thinking skill.

17.2.3 Abstraction

Abstraction is the process of simplifying and hiding detail to get at the essence of something of interest. As part of computational thinking, it provides a way to manage complexity in order to make problem-solving easier and allow truly massive computational systems to be designed. By building in levels of abstraction, the fine details of lower levels can be ignored when working on higher levels. Once you have logic gates, you can ignore the details of transistors. Once you have a computer architecture, you can ignore the details of logic gates, and so on. Once you have a programming language, you can ignore assembly language, which itself allowed you to ignore machine code. This is a core skill underpinning the way that the subject of computing has developed. It is also a core skill of computer scientists because without it, building the immensely large and complex systems that we now rely on is intractable. It is only by building in layers with clean interfaces between them that complex systems can be built, so that the complexity of each new layer is simple once the complexity of the lower layers has been hidden by the interface. A course has even been given where students build all of the layers of abstraction one at a time, starting with logic gates, and ending up with a working program running on an operating system (Schocken & Nisan, 2004). Such an endeavor is made possible by breaking it into 12 levels of abstraction.

Computer scientists make use of a wide variety of forms of abstractions both in programming and in system design more generally. These include control abstraction, which is the core of developing programs based on procedures and functions, and data abstraction, which is the core idea behind building complex data types from simpler ones.

Being able to think at multiple levels of abstraction and move between levels is a key ability. This is needed as one develops solutions, moving back and forth, for example, between the level of the problem, design levels, and programming levels. Linked to this is being able to view systems through different abstractions: the bus map intended for passengers may not, for example, include locations and times where drivers swap as their shifts start and end, whereas the abstract version for drivers would have very different information.

Abstraction is not just important for building systems, but also for the development of theory. For example, O-notation focuses on critical operations rather than all operations or processor cycles. Hiding that detail allows us to reason effectively about the efficiency of algorithms. Abstract models of computation (such as Turing machines, finite-state machines, and random access models) allow us to understand computation itself, including its limits.

17.2.4 Generalization

Generalization involves taking the solution to a problem and creating a more general version that is applicable to a wider set of problems. In a computational thinking context, this is first and foremost applied to algorithms. Having come up with a way to solve a specific problem, can the details be abstracted away to give a more general algorithm that is not just specific to that problem?

At a simple level, a sequence of instructions that are applied repetitively can be generalized to a loop. A more sophisticated generalization is to develop general-purpose functions. For example, if there are several situations where the user enters a date, a function could be developed once and for all that allows the user to do this, verifying that it is valid. A more general version of the function might have parameters that restrict the range of dates (e.g., a booking website would not allow a user to enter a date in the past). Generalization can be applied to both problems and solutions. For example, the problem of listing the top ten scores in a game could be generalized to creating a list of any number of scores. A possible solution – sorting the scores into order – could be generalized to a procedure that will sort any list of values into ascending or descending order.

Generalization is closely related to pattern finding (another idea that is often given as an element of computational thinking). When a pattern is noticed either in a program or in data, there is an opportunity to express it more generally by capturing the pattern rather than the specific case. For example, students might use a programming language to draw a square by giving the sequence of instructions "turn right, forward ten steps, turn right, forward ten steps, turn right, forward ten steps, turn right, forward ten steps." This could be generalized by a loop that repeats the two-instruction pattern four times; and that in turn could be generalized to draw polygons by changing the number of repetitions and the angle of the turn.

Generalization skills do not just apply to programming, but also to problem-solving more generally. Whether or not the ultimate intention is a program, generalizing a problem or situation in the same way can, for example, lead to a deeper understanding of that problem or situation, which may be important in its own right.

17.2.5 Decomposition

Decomposition is the idea that to solve a complex problem, including writing a complex program, it can often be broken into smaller parts that can each be solved separately and much more easily. This is closely connected to control abstraction. The simplest forms are task-based, or procedural, decomposition. For example, if one is creating a robot face that shows "emotions" through expressions, one could break the problem into that of solving each whole task (i.e., how to present each emotion). Program a happy face first, then separately program a sad face, and so on.

A different take on decomposition is to focus on the real-world problem or context, focusing on the real-world objects making up the system to be modeled and splitting the problem into one of modeling each of those aspects separately. This leads to an object-based decomposition. Taking the same example of programming a robot face, one could instead decompose the problem into that of programming a mouth for all emotions, then separately programming an eye, and so on. Object-based decomposition potentially provides a higher level of structuring than a procedural decomposition.

Another focus of decomposition can be on the processing of data structures. Rather than process the whole of a data structure, it can be split into parts and either the same or different algorithms can then be developed for processing those parts.

Decomposition links to generalization in that if we can decompose a problem into subproblems that generalize to ones that we have solved before, then we can just take those sub-solutions and reuse them. Abstraction means we do not have to worry about how those sub-solutions work, just that they solve the given subproblem. This leads to more sophisticated forms of decomposition and, in particular, recursive and divide-and-conquer problem-solving.

17.2.6 Evaluation

Evaluation is a potential element of computational thinking. However, there is no complete consensus on its inclusion. Practically, it is clearly an important part of any problem-solving approach. It is also very clearly a vital part of the skill of programming, where more time is typically spent testing solutions than writing code itself. The contentious issue is simply whether it should be considered as a part of "computational thinking." For example, Berry (2014), who takes computational thinking to be "looking at problems or systems in a way that considers how computers could be used to help solve or model these," omits evaluation from his description of computational thinking for primary schools. Selby and Woollard (2013), however, identified it as one of the more widely claimed terms that are used in relation to computational thinking in a survey of educators and other experts. That in itself does not mean it should be part of a definition, just that it is widely accepted as being so. It was consequently included in the UK Computing at School definition (Csizmadia et al., 2015). This is just one example of the different ways of defining computational thinking.

One argument for its inclusion is that unlike in school mathematics problem-solving, where an answer is right or wrong, in computing there are lots of ways to achieve the same result, some of which are better than others. Importantly, coming up with a solution requires trade-offs to be made (e.g., with respect to speed and memory usage). Evaluation of whether requirements are met (beyond just producing correct answers) matters. Programmed solutions may technically meet a functional specification, but be unfit for purpose because they are too slow or don't scale. This might also be due to usability or user experience issues. Evaluation of whether solutions are fit for purpose therefore has to be a core part of any successful computing-related problem-solving approach. If computational thinking does not include elements of evaluation, it would be only a partial approach for computer scientists.

17.2.7 Computational Modeling

Some of the apparent differences between authors over the definition of computational thinking are really just to do with what one considers to be the top-level skills. For example, we have argued that computational modeling is a key computing approach that has changed research and development in other subjects. As such, modeling is an important aspect of computational thinking. Denning (2017) proposes it is an absolutely central component. Computational modeling can be thought of as a separate topic or as one aspect of algorithmic thinking where it is applied to problems that can be simulated.

On the other hand, computational modeling applies not just to simulation approaches (so programming solutions). At higher levels of abstraction, it can be used with models that are not executable. One can do proof and model checking of appropriately designed computational models too. This leads to similar ends as with programmed simulation models, but allows exhaustive experiments to be conducted. This is an example where computational thinking is potentially about much more than the skill of coding. It leads to the application of verification tools and techniques rather than programming ones, and applying them to the understanding of the world too. These tools require models to be written in formal logical languages with an axiomatic basis (e.g., Peano's axioms) rather than programming languages with a model of computation as their basis, but otherwise the issues are similar – we are just working at a higher level of abstraction. The more sophisticated logical thinking skills mentioned above – working with formal logic – are needed here. The use of such tools and thinking is a part of formal program development for safety-critical systems, so any definition of computational thinking as being about the wider development of programs rather than narrowly as coding should include it.

17.2.8 Expressing Algorithms in Formal Languages

None of the computational thinking concepts above explicitly addresses the step of writing actual code (i.e., expressing the algorithm in a precise syntax that has a detailed, formally defined semantics). A student may have developed a design including algorithms in a loose pseudocode or in a flow chart language, but it is another step – and another skill – to be able to implement this as code in a specific language correctly. This often seems to be implicitly assumed by commentators, rather than explicitly stated. If computational thinking is the skill of developing programs, then expressing an algorithm as code must be part of the computational thinking skill set. This transition from a logical design to a physical implementation is part of the ability to work at multiple levels of abstraction. This is more than just about programming, though – expressing an algorithm precisely needs a level of rigor, and more formal pseudocode- or logic-based specification languages require similar skills in using formal language precisely. Guzdial (2008) explicitly discusses issues around this skill. For example, there are higher-level issues to be explored, such as the way people naturally omit certain steps, like else cases, from formal descriptions. A separate issue again, beyond having mastery of the language constructs, is having mastery over their pragmatic use to best develop readable and maintainable code. Machines must be able to follow code, but humans must be able to understand it.

17.2.9 A Holistic View

In practice, computer scientists use mixtures of these separate skills at different times, and when combined they are much more powerful than alone. For example, thinking in terms of layers of abstraction to decompose a problem and drawing on previous generalized solutions makes it much easier to create algorithmic solutions to problems. Understanding the separate elements is important. However, it is also important that this holistic aspect is understood too, not just the individual skills. Educators need to consider how best to help students develop both of these elements and how to develop the skill of combining the separate parts into computational thinking as a whole. In practice, most lessons and activities will use a range of the skills at the same time.

17.2.10 Links to the Skill Sets of Other Disciplines

Is computational thinking something new and totally different from thinking and problem-solving in other subjects? Computing itself emerged from a range of subjects, including mathematics, engineering, design, and the social sciences. Likewise, computational thinking builds on problem-solving and modes of thinking from other subjects. Generalization, decomposition, abstraction, logical thinking, and other components all play important parts in other disciplines. It draws on design ("the ultimate goal is computational design" [Denning, 2017], and interaction design is also a key part of making usable systems), mathematics, scientific methods (e.g., in evaluation A/B testing, virtual experiments, etc.), engineering methods, and general problem-solving methods.

There is no reason why computational thinking has to be totally unique in order to be an important concept and skill. If it were to be no different from other problem-solving skill sets, then that is an argument for the importance of teaching it to all. However, as argued, from a philosophical point of view, it *has* led to a seismic change in modes of thought. The difference is ultimately in the importance placed on algorithms in the skill set and how the separate skills used in other disciplines apply to algorithmic thinking, not the elements themselves. Algorithmic solutions in turn lead to the possibility of programmed solutions.

17.3 Research: What Is Known

There has been increasing research in how to teach and assess computational thinking explicitly, especially since the 2006 revolution. This has built on earlier work on teaching computer science and programming, given that even without the name, the component skills were still being taught, if implicitly. There has been an explosion of interest on the back of Wing's work, culminating in 2017 with a new international conference series being launched with a sole focus on computational thinking education (CSE, 2017). This bodes well for the future as researchers investigate the best ways to teach different aspects, their actual effects on student learning and skills, and whether there is general benefit to be had or not, divorced from programming skills. However, care has to be taken in that different authors often use their own interpretations of what computational thinking is across the full range of possibilities discussed and more, so results are not necessarily about the same thing. We overview some major themes in the existing research below.

17.3.1 Unplugged Computational Thinking

Unplugged activities (Bell, Rosamond, & Casey, 2012) have long been successfully used at all levels, from primary to master's levels, as well as when teaching adult teachers, as a way to teach programming and computing concepts more generally in constructivist ways. This covers a variety of techniques, including role-playing, puzzles, games, and magic, to illustrate concepts (Curzon & McOwan, 2017). These activities often help develop computational thinking in its widest sense too. Activities can also be used to explicitly illustrate the high-level elements of computational thinking, like decomposition, generalization, and abstraction. Teaching London Computing (http://teachinglondoncomputing. org), the Digital Schoolhouse (www.digitalschoolhouse.org.uk), and the lesson plans on csunplugged.org, for example, make these opportunities explicit across a wide range of cross-curricula activities.

Curzon (2014) argues that the core ideas of computational thinking can be explained in powerfully memorable ways using a combination of contextually rich stories and unplugged activities. He gives example activities embedded in such stories that have successfully been used. Examples given include stories concerned with helping people with locked-in syndrome, using games and role-play, and the design of medical devices using magic trick-based activities. These ideas are expanded upon in Curzon and McOwan (2017). This approach has successfully been used as part of continuous professional development for teachers. A series of workshops given following this approach had shown strongly positive evaluation results (Curzon, 2014; Meagher, 2017).

However, much of the work on unplugged approaches is anecdotal and much more research is needed, including on the important issue of how such approaches are linked to programming itself.

17.3.2 Computational System Design and Programming

Computational system design involves a wider set of activities than programming, and those activities include computational thinking elements. When analyzing the requirements and designing the solution, the task is broken into manageable parts to attend to, and so decomposition is used; at each stage of increasing exploration of the task, abstraction is needed to work at an appropriate level of detail, and so on. Research on effective teaching of overall design processes is therefore relevant. Here, we focus on research where there are links between computational thinking ideas and programming.

McCracken et al. (2001) describe a five-step process for problem-solving that learners should use to aid computational design. These fives step map to the computational thinking core concepts of Selby and Woollard (2013):

1. Abstract the problem from its description (abstraction)
2. Generate subproblems (decomposition)
3. Transform subproblems into subsolutions (generalization and algorithmic thinking)

4. Recompose (algorithmic thinking)
5. Evaluate and iterate (evaluation)

However, McCracken et al. (2001) highlighted that few students were able to use this process and noted that students appeared "clueless." Lister et al. (2004, 2011) and Lopez et al. (2008) highlight the importance of being able to read and trace code as precursors to the problem-solving skills needed to write code, so these may be precursors to any form of programming-based computational thinking. For example, this suggests that before one can do functional abstraction, one needs to be able to read and trace existing code that uses such abstraction. A precursor to that is understanding the basic concepts and their semantics.

Fuller et al. (2007) identified 11 programming skills needed by students, and mapped them to Bloom's taxonomy, presented in a matrix format. For example, the ability to debug requires "application" and "analysis" thinking skills. Each of the 11 skills is underpinned by the computational thinking core elements discussed above. For example, tracing and adapting code develop evaluation and generalization skills. Designing and modeling solutions (as algorithms and/ or programs) develop algorithmic thinking, abstraction, and evaluation skills (Sentance & Csizmadia, 2017). Developing the computational thinking skill appears to provide a foundation for the corresponding programming skill.

Computational thinking skill is not the only thing needed by programmers, of course. They also need to understand the syntax of the language they are using as well as the programming constructs available to them in order to implement the design. This leads back to some of the earlier extensions discussed, as it implies that issues to do with language concepts and terminology are precursors to computational thinking.

17.3.3 Abstraction

Abstraction is a particularly important pillar of computational thinking and has attracted specific attention. An important question now that computational thinking is part of school syllabuses is: How young can you start to learn about abstraction? It is sometimes suggested that Piaget's work implies that children cannot learn about abstraction until they reach a particular age and stage of development – that of formal operational at around the age of 12. The National Research Council report on computational thinking (National Research Council, 2011) asked for a review of this. However, Piaget himself suggested that children use abstraction from before the age of two and that abstraction is used continuously when learning "without end and especially without an absolute beginning" (Piaget, 2001, p. 136).

Armoni (2013) pointed out that abstraction, as part of the process of developing programs from solutions, is hard to teach. She suggested a "level of abstraction" framework and gave guidelines for teaching abstraction. Several authors have argued that programming ability can be developed by explicitly focusing students on abstraction, particularly different levels of abstraction, as part of the process of writing programs. This has been considered both with respect to tertiary institution students (Aharoni, 2000; Cutts et al., 2012; Hazzan, 2003) and school students (Armoni, 2013; Statter & Armoni, 2016; Waite et al., 2016, 2017). Cutts et al. (2012), for example, argued that focusing on a model of three levels of abstraction helps students develop their programming ability. Their levels were: English descriptions, computer science speak (i.e., a halfway house such as pseudocode, where some of the terminology of code, like variable and procedure names, is embedded in English phrasing), and code. Statter and Armoni's (2016) model is similar, but with four levels: the statement of the problem, its description as an algorithm or design level, the program itself, and finally the concrete execution of that program. Grade 7 students who were explicitly taught these different levels did focus more on the algorithm level in their descriptions. Thus, explicitly teaching about abstraction, even with a simple set of levels, can help the development of programming skill.

17.3.4 Assessment

A critical research area is how to assess computational thinking (see also Chapters 10 and 14). Denning (2017) suggests that it should be assessed as a skill, with others focusing on knowledge frameworks such as those of Computing at School (Csizmadia et al., 2015) and K12CS (https://k12cs.org). However, skills and knowledge coexist and, in particular, conceptual computer science knowledge, computational thinking skills, and programming skills can and should coexist. As with programming itself, assessing it as a skill does not preclude the pedagogical importance of assessing understanding of knowledge too. Having a strong conceptual knowledge of a discipline can also support the development of related skills – if you understand how a gearbox works, learning the skill of changing gears in a car can be easier. Similarly, if you have a deep understanding of the concept of abstract data types, then using that form of abstraction in programs is easier. Knowledge helps refine skills as you know more of what you are trying to do and why.

A variety of researchers have explored ways to assess computational thinking as a skill. This could be done by assessing the individual component skills or by assessing computational thinking as a holistic single skill. One approach is to directly assess the skills based on evidence in programs. If programming is seen as the whole point, then the idea is that computational thinking can be assessed by the quality of the programs that a student produces. Another approach is to assess the skills using more general problems at a higher level of abstraction than that of writing programs. We provide an overview of some of the research on these topics below.

17.3.4.1 Assessing Computational Thinking through Programming

Several automated approaches have been suggested to assess computational thinking based on evaluating programs. For example, both Dr. Scratch

(Moreno-León, Robles, & Román-González, 2015) and Seiter and Foreman's (2013) "Progression of Early Computational Thinking" (PECT) model are applied to Scratch programs to assess primary-aged students' development of computational thinking skills. These approaches are based on the idea that computational thinking skills should ultimately be evident in programs written. As such, they may therefore not assess more general application of the skills and are dependent on sub-skills concerned with actually embodying an algorithm in a formal language.

PECT (Seiter & Foreman, 2013) aims to combine direct measures of programs with broad design patterns that are linked to computational thinking concepts. Seiter and Foreman applied PECT to 150 Scratch projects of primary students of differing ages, concluding that it showed that progression in students' skills improved as they got older.

Seiter (2015) has also used the Structure of Observed Learning Outcomes (SOLO) taxonomy (Biggs & Collis, 1982) to give insight into computational thinking ability as embodied in Scratch programming. This was based on how well students could understand the structure of the problem. It focused on such things as their ability to synchronize the costumes and motions of single and multiple sprites. However, the low numeracy and literacy of some students meant that those students could not understand the tasks at all. Seiter concluded that students above this level can understand multiple concerns and incorporate them into a single script. They can also synchronize a single concern between more than one script. However, synchronizing many concerns across many scripts was a challenge.

17.3.4.2 Assessing Computational Thinking through Problem-Solving

An alternative to basing assessment of computational thinking skill on programs is to assess proficiency at more general problem-solving tasks. Several authors have aimed to do this based on Bebras (Dagiene & Futschek, 2008). Bebras is an international competition with questions on both computing concepts and computational thinking skill. Hubwieser and Mühling (2014) suggested that Bebras tasks were suitable as an international benchmark test for computing ability in the style of the Programme for International Student Assessment (PISA) tests. They give a methodology for finding and validating groups of questions that measure specific competencies. Such an approach could be used to identify problems that test specific computational thinking competencies. Dagienė and Sentance (2016) give recommendations on how Bebras tasks can be used to develop and assess children's computational thinking skills specifically. They created an explicit two-dimensional classification scheme for questions (Dagienė et al., 2017). Computational thinking aspects act as one dimension and content knowledge as the other.

Project Quantum (Oates et al., 2016) is a crowdsourced multiple-choice computer science question bank being pioneered in the UK to provide formative assessment. Quality assurance is integral via a feedback loop based on big data that will be generated from its expected widespread use. Questions are machine-markable and algorithms will generate data about the quality of questions. Bebras questions are one of the sources used, and so this could be a way of determining and/or improving the quality of the computational thinking questions, ultimately generating a large, quality-assured set of questions.

Several other specific "computational thinking" tests have been developed. The "Computational Thinking Test" (CTt) (Román-Gonzáles, 2015) is a multiple-choice questionnaire involving 28 questions, such as whether a particular program will lead a character along a given maze path. It tests understanding of programming concepts such as loops and conditionals. Korkmaz, Çakirb, and Özdenc (2017) similarly developed a set of 29 five-point Likert scale questions to assess computational thinking. Tested on over 1,000 students, the authors concluded that it is a valid and reliable tool for measuring computational thinking skills. Brennan and Resnick (2012), however, suggest that assessment requires a combination of approaches. They used an analysis of projects, artifact-based interviews, and pupils completing design scenario challenges. They concluded that this triangulation leads to an understanding of computational thinking concepts and practices, but that these approaches do not effectively reveal changes in expressing, connecting, and questioning perspectives.

17.3.4.3 Determining Progression and Age-Appropriate Curricula

Designing assessment requires both an understanding of what is to be assessed and a methodology for capturing the specific knowledge, skills, and understanding at a point in time. In school, teachers develop lesson activities to teach objectives for learners that help them make progress. What those objectives are and how one might move from one objective to another to provide progression matter as computational thinking is brought into the school curriculum.

Dorling and Walker (2014) interpreted the English curriculum in the form of an easily digestible table. This table presented the learning statements by either topic area taken from the Computing at School Curriculum for Schools document (Computing at School, 2012) or by subject strands: Computer Science, Information Technology, and Digital Literacy. Dorling, Selby, and Woollard (2015) suggested that this interpretation of the curriculum had aligned computational thinking core elements to all of the statements in the table. A later version of the grid was cross-referenced to the computational thinking concepts outlined in Csizmadia et al. (2015). Rich et al. (2017) also consider progression of conceptual ideas and links to computational thinking based on a detailed review of over 100 computing education research articles. They use concept maps to show progress and also propose an alternative model to the spiral curriculum.

Barefoot (2014a, 2014b), which provides material for primary school teaching of computing, suggests ideas for progression in computational thinking for children aged 3–11. However, this is not a complete progression, as it only provides suggestions for a limited set of lessons, some set in programming contexts, others in a cross-curricula scenarios.

Bebras (Dagiene & Futschek, 2008) is also structured by age, using six groupings of questions from ages 5 to 19 with the complexity of the problems increasing. This is a loose organization, and individual countries can choose the questions that they think are appropriate. However, the groups of questions are linked to age, and therefore a progression is implied.

Denning (2017) suggests existing progression frameworks are focused on progression of knowledge and that this is misguided. This is not entirely true – as noted above, several groups have considered skills-based progression. However, he makes the important point that there are two separate issues: knowledge-based progression and skills-based progression. Both should be addressed. Frameworks for progression of both skills and conceptual knowledge within subjects are needed, and arguably integrated versions are needed too. Research about the appropriateness and effectiveness of progression frameworks is needed.

17.3.4.4 Validity

In all approaches to assessment, validation of the underlying models and/or the tools and techniques based on them is needed. Methods might concern computational thinking as a whole, some specific subset of it, or individual foundational skills. Much research is needed in this area. For example, according to Armoni (2013), in 2013, there were no validated methods to assess abstraction ability.

An important issue is whether different approaches produce the same answers – their convergent validity. Román-Gonzáles et al. (2017) explore this for three approaches: Dr. Scratch (Moreno-León & Robles, 2015), Bebras (Dagiene & Futschek, 2008) and CTt (Román-Gonzáles, 2015). Their results suggest that CTt partially converges with the other two. They suggest that the three approaches are complementary, and they use a revised version of Bloom's taxonomy (Krathwohl, 2002) as a way to classify this. They conclude that Dr. Scratch assesses the very top "create" and "evaluate" levels of Bloom's taxonomy, Bebras assesses the "analyze" and "apply" levels, and CTt assesses the "understand" and "remember" levels, as it focuses on the concepts related to computational thinking rather than the practice of it. In essence, this is saying that Dr. Scratch assesses the programming part of computational thinking, Bebras targets more general thinking skills, and CTt targets conceptual knowledge of computational thinking.

17.4 Implications for Practice

17.4.1 Implications Depending on the View Taken

If one takes the view that computational thinking is primarily associated with learning to program, and it doesn't directly support learning in other subjects, then the important focus becomes how to teach programming itself well. Studying the component skills can still enhance insight into how to teach programming. One such insight is that making students explicitly focus on levels of abstraction when programming helps develop programming ability (Cutts et al., 2012; Statter & Armoni, 2016).

If one takes the intermediate view expounded by Lee (2016) that computational thinking is about more than coding itself, but the person concerned must have an aim that the resulting algorithm be carried out on a computer, not by a human, then the focus is different. The key practical point Lee recommends is that repeated practice is needed of working with real-world problems and how they are solved using information processing devices. Practice is needed in taking real-world problems, developing from them statements of the problems in a form that can be solved by computers, designing algorithms that solve those problems, and implementing those algorithms as programs, specialized hardware, or combinations of the two. This involves both understanding and taking into account, from the outset, the actual goals and needs of stakeholders and verifying and validating those solutions in the real world.

If one takes the wide view that computational thinking is a transferable skill for all and that algorithms go beyond computers and may be usefully followed by humans too (as in the original definition of the words "algorithm" and "computer"), the implications are different again. This implies that computational thinking can and should be developed both through programming and through other means. The focus then turns to how to develop the individual skills across a wide range of information processing situations, physical and otherwise, in computing and other subject contexts. Exploring how best to use them together is also critical, so developing the holistic skill matters. Any skill is developed with practice: the more, the better. Therefore, students need to be encouraged to practice as much as possible, in as many contexts as possible, not just programming contexts. In this view, starting to develop general computational thinking skills, not just programming skills, should start early in primary school, as some countries are now doing. Making links from activities such as writing clear instructions to early programming tasks is also important.

Whichever view is taken, intrinsic motivation to practice the skills needs to be developed (see also Chapter 11). Ensuring such practice is fun and engaging is one important element, as is providing realistic context. The educational community also needs to develop appropriate progression pathways for their pupils from primary school upwards that develop and refine the skills over time.

Developing the component skills separately provides a foundation for learning computational thinking as a whole. Knowledge supports the development of skill, and teachers need to understand the barrier concepts and points so that they can help students overcome them.

As with any skill, having an understanding of the underlying concepts and having the vocabulary to express them by themselves can help develop the skills in a reflective way. Therefore, the skills and concepts need to be developed in parallel. Unplugged methods provide a powerful, constructivist way to do this at all levels if used well. The theory of semantic waves (Macnaught et al., 2013; Maton, 2013) provides guidance on how to do this – as suggested by Curzon et al. (2018), one should travel up and down the semantic wave from abstract concepts to concrete examples of them (whether unplugged, real world, or programming) and back to the abstract ones, making clear the links between the levels.

Whichever view one takes of the definition of computational thinking, it is important to be pragmatic regarding developing the best ways to teach it. Whether one considers computational thinking as something that can be developed separately from programming or not, and whether or not it includes physical computation in the world, analogies with real-world ideas *are* powerful ways of teaching concepts and of developing skills. According to the theory of semantic waves (Macnaught et al., 2013; Maton, 2013), good explanation involves moving from technical, abstract concepts to concrete illustration, and then back to technical concepts. This is what good use of analogy and unplugged teaching does. Analogy and simplified explanations are used widely across other subjects as effective ways to teach. This should not be lost to computing because of ideology. Ideas such as unplugged teaching should not be dropped just because one thinks of them as only analogy. Instead, the fact that they are analogy should be made clear. For example, whether or not one believes writing a recipe involves any aspect of computational thinking, a recipe book is still a useful initial way to help students understand concepts including breaking a problem down into parts (procedural abstraction) and the ordering of the parts (how the flow of control involved in procedure call works). Having such understanding about concepts is a critical foundation for learning to program.

It certainly does help to keep the focus on the general value of skills and conceptual understanding, even if very specific examples are being taught; for example, students might be learning the syntax of a Python "for" loop, but the point is to understand iteration in programs; they might be learning a version of binary search, but the wider picture is that it is an example of the power of using divide and conquer to decompose a problem.

Also, whatever view is taken, to develop computational thinking skills fully does, of course, ultimately involve programming too. This is another kind of example that can be used to travel a semantic wave of good explanation (Macnaught et al., 2013; Maton, 2013). Ideally, programming skills should be developed in conjunction with more general computational thinking skills and understanding. For example, the Computing at School Working Group suggests:

> Computer Science is more than programming, but programming is an absolutely central process for Computer Science. In an educational context, programming encourages creativity, logical thought, precision and problem-solving, and helps foster the personal, learning and thinking skills required in the modern school curriculum. Programming gives concrete, tangible form to the idea of "abstraction," and repeatedly shows how useful it is.
> (Computing at School, 2012)

17.4.2 Practical Resources for Teaching

A wide variety of practical resources and tools exist to support the teaching of computational thinking. These include:

- CS Unplugged (http://csunplugged.org)
- Teaching London Computing (http://teachinglondoncomputing.org)
- Barefoot (http://barefootcas.org.uk)
- The International Society for Technology in Education's Computational Thinking Toolkit (Sykora, 2014)
- Google's Exploring Computational Thinking (Google, n.d.)
- Bebras (Bebras, n.d.)
- Dr. Scratch (www.drscratch.org)
- Digital Schoolhouse (www.digitalschoolhouse.org.uk)
- Computational thinking rubric (Dorling & Stephens, 2016)

There are many more such resources and resource collections, with more being developed all the time.

17.5 Open Questions

Computational thinking is still a relatively new idea, and designing curricula that use it is even newer. There are many open questions, making it a very fertile area for future research. The most fundamental open question is just what definition of computational thinking should be adopted and how wide it should stretch. In the absence of agreement about definitions of the term, those doing such research need to be precise about the definition that they are working with.

What definition is appropriate depends to a large extent on the answers to more specific open questions. For example, we need to determine the true extent of the transferability of the skills (see also Chapter 9, which explores transfer of learning). How useful are or can be the skills in practice to learning in other areas if either a narrow or a wide view is taken? Is there a difference in general usefulness if you learn them only as programming versus taking a wider approach to teaching them? Are they useful at all? Is knowledge of computational thinking useful in understanding the digital world and how? Can computational thinking skills be developed effectively outside of programming? How effective are the various unplugged methods for teaching computational thinking? For example, does early practice using logic puzzles to refine logical thinking skills actually lead to better computational thinking skills and so make programming easier to learn? Similar issues apply to the other components of computational thinking. What makes an effective unplugged computational thinking activity in general and what makes them ineffective? How does one best link unplugged and programming techniques? Rigorous evidence is needed of what actually does work and why.

If computational thinking is primarily useful for programmers and can only usefully be taught through programming, then the question becomes how to enhance those skills more effectively through programming. Even if they can be developed in other ways, this is still an important question. Either way, we need to better understand the importance of the conceptual knowledge, programming skills, and computational thinking skills for developing independence and resilience in learners. In particular, we need further consideration of the relationships between programming skills and the core computational thinking concepts. Does a better grasp of computational thinking concepts and subskills lead to better holistic computational thinking and programming skills, and if so, how best do knowledge and skills combine? It is often suggested that math is an important precursor to being able to cope on a tertiary institution computing course. However, it is also often suggested that it is not the math content that matters. What exactly are those mathematical precursor skills? Perhaps it is because math does develop some of the relevant precursor skills, such as attention to detail, logical thinking, or abstraction skills (e.g., in algebra). This might suggest that teaching the subskills of computational thinking in other contexts does help.

Validated progression frameworks are needed for both skills and knowledge. What do you teach at different levels from primary upwards to achieve the best learning? And how best do you then teach at each level of progression and each topic? The questions are not just about how to teach. We need to know what the effective means of both formative and summative assessment are too. There are very big unanswered questions as to how to assess both programming and computational thinking skills. How are each of the progression levels best assessed both formatively and summatively? This applies both to computational thinking overall and to the separate subskills, such as abstraction and generalization.

At the moment, arguments are being made and policy implemented based on opinion and early results, as there is a lack of evidence. Experiments need to be founded in rigorous theories of the mechanisms involved. For many of the research areas outlined, some work has been done, though often on a small scale and in uncontrolled ways. What is needed is really rigorous evidence around all of these issues that is more than just action research suggesting an intervention was a positive experience in a single context. Research needs to be replicated, including situating the studies in real classrooms, with real teachers, over longer periods of time, and on larger scales. We need large-scale, longitudinal comparison of teaching, learning, and assessment of computational thinking across schools, cultures, and age groups. We then need continuous professional development for teachers and resources to be developed based on the research. This material needs to be organized in a validated progression, affording educators the means to plan lessons and evaluate students' progress, allowing students to show what they know and can do.

References

Aharoni, D. (2000). Cogito, ergo sum! Cognitive processes of students dealing with data structures. *ACM SIGCSE Bulletin*, 32(1), 26–30.

Aho, A. V. (2012). Computation and computational thinking. *The Computer Journal*, 55(7), 832–835.

al-Khwārizmī, M. (c. 825). *On the Calculation with Hindu Numerals*.

Armoni, M. (2013). On teaching abstraction in computer science to novices. *Journal of Computers in Mathematics and Science Teaching*, 32(3) 265–284.

Barefoot (2014a). Barefoot Computing. Retrieved from http://barefootcas.org.uk/

Barefoot (2014b). Computational thinking: What does computational thinking look like in the primary curriculum? Retrieved from https://barefootcas.org.uk/barefoot-primary-computing-resources/concepts/computational-thinking/

Bebras (n.d.). Bebras International Challenge on Informatics and Computational Thinking. Retrieved from www.bebras.org

Bell, T., Alexander, J., Freeman, I., & Grimley, M. (2009). Computer science unplugged: School students doing real computing without computers. *New Zealand Journal of Applied Computing and Information Technology*, 13(1), 20–29.

Bell, T., Rosamond, F., & Casey, N. (2012). Computer Science Unplugged and related projects in math and computer science popularization. In H. L. Bodlaender, R. Downey, F. V Fomin, & D. Marx (Eds.), *The Multivariate Algorithmic Revolution and Beyond: Essays Dedicated to Michael R. Fellows on the Occasion of His 60th Birthday, Lecture Notes in Computer Science* (pp. 398–456). Berlin, Germany: Springer.

Berry, M. (2014). Computational Thinking in Primary Schools. Retrieved from http://milesberry.net/2014/03/computational-thinking-in-primary-schools/

Bers, M. U. (2017). *Coding as a Playground: Programming and Computational Thinking in the Early Childhood Classroom*. New York: Routledge.

Bers, M. U. (2008). *Blocks to Robots: Learning with Technology in the Early Childhood Classroom*. New York: Teachers College Press.

Biggs, J. B., & Collis, K. F. (1982). *Evaluating the Quality of Learning: The SOLO Taxonomy (Structure of the Observed Learning Outcome)*. New York: Academic Press.

Böhm, C., & Jacopini, G. (1966). Flow diagrams, Turing machines and languages with only two formation rules. *Communications of the ACM*, 9(5), 366–371.

Brennan, K., & Resnick, M. (2012). New frameworks for studying and assessing the development of computational thinking. Vancouver, Canada: Educational Research Association. Retrieved from https://scholar.harvard.edu/kbrennan/publications/new-frameworks-studying-and-assessing-development-computational-thinking

Computing at School (2012). Computer science: A curriculum for schools. Computing at School Working Group. Retrieved from www.computingatschool.org.uk/data/uploads/ComputingCurric.pdf

CSE (2017). Proceedings of the 1st International Conference on Computational Thinking Education, July, Hong Kong. Retrieved from www.eduhk.hk/cte2017/

Csizmadia, A., Curzon, P., Dorling, M., Humphreys, S., Ng, T., Selby, C., & Woollard, J. (2015). Computational thinking: A guide for teachers. Retrieved from http://computingatschool.org.uk/computationalthinking

Curzon, P. (2002). Computing without Computers: A Gentle Introduction to Computer Programming, Data Structures and Algorithms. Retrieved from https://teachinglondoncomputing.org/resources/inspiring-computing-stories/computingwithoutcomputers/

Curzon, P. (2014). Unplugged computational thinking for fun. In T. Brinda, N. Reynolds, & R. Romeike (Eds.), *KEYCIT – Key Competencies in Informatics and ICT,*

Commentarii Informaticae Didacticae (pp. 15–28). Potsdam, Germany: Universitätsverlag Potsdam.

Curzon, P., & McOwan, P. W. (2017). *The Power of Computational Thinking: Games, Magic and Puzzles to Help You Become a Computational Thinker.* Hackensack, NJ: World Scientific.

Curzon, P., McOwan, P. W., Donohue, J., Wright, S., & Marsh, D. W. R. (2018). Teaching of concepts. In S. Sentance, E. Barendsen, & C. Schulte (Eds.), *Computer Science Education: Perspectives on Learning and Teaching in School* (pp. 91–108). London, UK: Bloomsbury.

Cutts, Q., Esper, S., Fecho, M., Foster, S., & Simon, B. (2012). The abstraction transition taxonomy: developing desired learning outcomes through the lens of situated cognition. In *Proceedings of the Ninth Annual International Conference on International Computing Education Research* (pp. 63–70). New York: ACM.

Dagienė, V., & Sentance, S. (2016). It's computational thinking! Bebras tasks in the curriculum. In A. Brodnik & F. Tort (Eds.), *Informatics in Schools: Improvement of Informatics Knowledge and Perception (ISSEP 2016). Lecture Notes in Computer Science* (pp 28–39). Berlin, Germany: Springer.

Dagienė, V., Sentance, S., & Stupienė, G. (2017). Developing a two-dimensional categorization system for educational tasks in informatics. *Informatica* 28(1), 23–44.

Dagiene, V., & Futschek, G. (2008). Bebras international contest on informatics and computer literacy: Criteria for good tasks. In R. T. Mittermeir & M. M. Sysło (Eds.), *Informatics Education – Supporting Computational Thinking. ISSEP 2008. Lecture Notes in Computer Science* (pp. 19–30). Berlin, Germany: Springer.

Denning, P. (2017). Remaining trouble spots with computational thinking. *Communications of the ACM*, 60(6), 33–39.

Denning, P., & Tedre, M. (2019). *Computational Thinking*. Cambridge, MA: MIT Press.

Department for Education (2013). National Curriculum in England: Computing programmes of study. Retrieved from www.gov.uk/government/publications/national-curriculum-in-england-computing-programmes-of-study

Dorling, M., Selby, C., & Woollard, J. (2015). Evidence of assessing computational thinking. In A. Brodnik & C. Lewin (Eds.), *IFIP 2015: A New Culture of Learning: Computing and Next Generations* (pp. 1–11). Laxenburg, Austria: IFIP.

Dorling, M., & Walker, M. (2014). Computing Progression Pathways. Retrieved from http://community.computingatschool.org.uk/files/5098/original.xlsx

Dorling, M., & Stephens, T. (2016). Computational Thinking Rubric: Dispositions, Attitudes and Perspectives, Retrieved from https://community.computingatschool.org.uk/resources/4793/

Euclid (1997). *Elements* [c. 300 BCE]. D. E. Joyce (Ed.). Retrieved from http://aleph0.clarku.edu/~djoyce/java/elements/toc.html

Fuller, U., Johnson, C. G., Ahoniemi, T., Cukierman, D., Hernán-Losada, I., Jackova, J., Lahtinen, E., Lewis, T. L., Thompson, D. M., Riedesel, C., & Thompson, E. (2007). Developing a computer science-specific learning taxonomy. In *Proceedings of the ITiCSE-WGR '07 Working Group Reports on Innovation and Technology in Computer Science Education* (pp. 152–170). New York: ACM.

Google (n.d.). Exploring Computational Thinking, Google for Education. Retrieved from https://edu.google.com/resources/programs/exploring-computational-thinking/

Grover, S., & Pea, R. (2013). Using a discourse-intensive pedagogy and Android's App inventor for introducing computational concepts to middle school students. In *Proceedings of the 44th SIGCSE Technical Symposium on Computer Science Education* (pp. 723–728). New York: ACM.

Guzdial, M. (2008). Education: Paving the way for computational thinking. *Communications of the ACM*, 51(8), 25–27.

Harel, D. (2003). *Computers Ltd: What They REALLY Can't Do*. Oxford, UK: Oxford Paperbacks.

Hazzan, O. (2003). How students attempt to reduce abstraction in the learning of mathematics and in the learning of computer science. *Computer Science Education*, 13(2), 95–122.

Hubwieser, P., & Mühling, A. (2014). Playing PISA with Bebras. In *Proceedings of the 9th Workshop in Primary and Secondary Computing Education* (pp. 128–129). New York: ACM.

Hubwieser, P., Giannakos, M. N., Berges, M., Brinda, T., Diethelm, I., Magenheim, J., Pal, J., Jackova, J., & Jasute, E.(2015) A global snapshot of computer science education in K–12 schools. In *Proceedings of the 2015 ITiCSE on Working Group Reports* (pp. 65–83). New York: ACM.

Hutchins, E. (1995). *Cognition in the Wild*. Cambridge, MA: MIT Press.

ISTE/CSTA (2014). Operational Definition of Computational Thinking for K–12 Education. Retrieved from www.iste.org/docs/ct-documents/computational-thinking-operational-definition-flyer.pdf

Kafai, Y. B. (2016). From computational thinking to computational participation in K–12 education, *Communications of the ACM*, 59(8), 26–27.

Kalelioglu, K., Gülbahar, Y., & Kukul, V. (2016). A framework for computational thinking based on a systematic research review. *Baltic Journal of Modern Computing*, 4(3), 583–596.

Korkmaz, Ö., Çakir, R., & Özden, M. Y. (2017). A validity and reliability study of the Computational Thinking Scales (CTS). *Computers in Human Behavior*, 72, 558–569.

Krathwohl, D. R. (2002). A revision of Bloom's taxonomy: An overview. *Theory into Practice*, 41(4), 212–218.

Lee, I. (2016). Reclaiming the roots of CT. *CSTA Voice: The Voice of K–12 Computer Science Education and Its Educators,* 12(1), 3–4.

Lister, R., Adams, E. S., Fitzgerald, S., Fone, W., Hamer, J., Lindholm, M., McCartney, R., Moström, J. E., Sanders, K., Seppälä, O., & Simon, B. (2004). A multinational study of reading and tracing skills in novice programmers. *ACM SIGCSE Bulletin,* 36(4), 119–150.

Lister, R. (2011). Concrete and other neo-Piagetian forms of reasoning in the novice programmer. In *Proceedings of the Thirteenth Australasian Computing Education Conference* (pp. 9–18). Darlinghurst, Australia: Australian Computer Society, Inc.

Lopez, M., Whalley, J., Robbins, P., & Lister, R. (2008). Relationships between reading, tracing and writing skills in introductory programming. In *Proceedings of the Fourth International Workshop on Computing Education Research* (pp. 101–112). New York: ACM.

Lu, J. J., & Fletcher, G. H. (2009). Thinking about computational thinking. *ACM SIGCSE Bulletin*, 41(1), 260–264.

Maton, K. (2013). Making semantic waves: A key to cumulative knowledge-building. *Linguistics and Education*, 24(1), 8–22.

Macnaught, L., Maton, K., Martin, J. R., & Matruglio, E. (2013). Jointly constructing semantic waves: implications for teacher training. *Linguistics and Education*, 24, 50–63.

McCracken, M., Almstrum, V., Diaz, D., Guzdial, M., Hagen, D., Kolikant, Y. B., Laxer, C., Thomas, L., Utting, I., & Wilusz, T. (2001). A Multi-National, Multi-Institutional Study of Assessment of Programming Skills of First-year CS Students. In *Proceedings of the 6th Annual Conference on Innovation and Technology in Computer Science Education, Working Group Reports (ITiCSE-WGR '01)* (pp. 125–180). New York: ACM.

Meagher, L. (2017). Teaching London Computing Follow-up Evaluation through Interviews with Teachers, Technology Development Group, Summer. Retrieved from https://teachinglondoncomputing.org/evaluation/

Millican, P., & Clark, A. (Eds.) (1996). *The Legacy of Alan Turing, Volume 1: Machines and Thought*. Oxford, UK: Oxford University Press.

Millican, P. (n.d.). A New Paradigm of Explanation? Retrieved from www.philocomp.net/home/paradigm.htm

Moreno-León, J., & Robles, G. (2015). Dr. Scratch: A web tool to automatically evaluate Scratch projects. In *Proceedings of the Workshop in Primary and Secondary Computing Education* (pp. 132–133). New York: ACM.

Moreno-León, J., Robles, G., & Román-González, M. (2015). Dr. Scratch: Automatic analysis of scratch projects to assess and foster computational thinking. *RED. Revista de Educación a Distancia*, 46(10), 1–23.

National Research Council (2011). *Committee for the Workshops on Computational Thinking: Report of a Workshop of Pedagogical Aspects of Computational Thinking*, Washington, DC: The National Academies Press.

NZ Ministry of Education (2017). The New Zealand Curriculum Online: Technology: Learning area structure. Retrieved from http://nzcurriculum.tki.org.nz/The-New-Zealand-Curriculum/Technology/Learning-area-structure

Oates, T., Coe, R., Peyton-Jones, S., Scratcherd, T., & Woodhead S. (2016). Quantum: Tests worth teaching. White Paper, March, Computing at School. Retrieved from http://community.computingatschool.org.uk/files/7256/original.pdf

OED (1993). *The New Shorter Oxford English Dictionary*. Oxford, UK: Oxford University Press.

Papert, S. (1980). *Mindstorms: Children, Computers and Powerful Ideas*. New York: Basic Books.

Piaget, J. (2001). *Studies in Reflecting Abstraction*. Edited and translated by R. L. Campbell. Hove, UK: Psychology Press.

Resnick, M. (2013). Learn to Code, Code to Learn. Edsurge, May 8. Retrieved from www.edsurge.com/news/2013-05-08-learn-to-code-code-to-learn

Rich, K. M., Strickland, C., Binkowski, T. A, Moran C., & Franklin, D. (2017). K–8 learning trajectories derived from research literature: Sequence, repetition, conditionals. In *Proceedings of the 2017 ACM Conference on International Computing Education Research (ICER'17)* (pp. 182–190). New York: ACM.

Román-González, M. (2015). Computational thinking test: Design guidelines and content validation. In *Proceedings of the 7th Annual International Conference on Education and New Learning Technologies (EDULEARN 2015)* (pp. 2436–2444). Valencia, Spain: IATED Academy.

Román-Gonzáles, M., Moreno-León, J., & Robles, G. (2017). Complementary tools for computational thinking assessment. In *Proceedings of the International*

Conference on Computational Thinking Education (CTE2017) (pp. 154–159). Ting Kok, Hong Kong: The Education University of Hong Kong.

Royal Society (2012). *Shut Down or Restart? The Way Forward for Computing in UK Schools.* London, UK: The Royal Society.

Royal Society (2017a). *After the Reboot: Computing Education in UK Schools.* London, UK: The Royal Society.

Royal Society (2017b). *Machine Learning: The Power and Promise of Computers That Learn by Example.* London, UK: The Royal Society.

Schocken, S., & Nisan, N. (2004). From NAND to Tetris in 12 easy steps. In *Proceedings of the 34th Annual Conference on Frontiers in Education* (p. 1461). New York: IEEE.

Seiter, L., & Foreman, B. (2013). Modeling the learning progressions of computational thinking of primary grade students. In *Proceedings of the 9th Annual International ACM Conference on International Computing Education Research (ICER'13)* (pp. 59–66). New York: ACM.

Seiter, L. (2015). Using SOLO to classify the programming responses of primary grade students. In *Proceedings of the 46th ACM Technical Symposium on Computer Science Education* (pp. 540–545). New York: ACM.

Selby, C., & Woollard, J. (2013). Computational thinking: The developing definition. Retrieved from http://eprints.soton.ac.uk/356481

Sentance, S., & Csizmadia, A. (2017). Computing in the curriculum: Challenges and strategies from a teacher's perspective. *Education and Information Technologies*, 22(2), 469–495.

Statter, D., & Armoni, M. (2016). Teaching abstract thinking in introduction to computer science for 7th graders. In *Proceedings of the 11th Workshop in Primary and Secondary Computing Education* (pp. 80–83). New York: ACM.

Susskind, R. (2017). *Tomorrow's Lawyers: An Introduction to Your Future*, 2nd edn. Oxford, UK: Oxford University Press.

Sykora, C. (2014). Computational thinking for all. Arlington: ISTE. Retrieved from www.iste.org/explore/articleDetail?articleid=152&category=Solutions&article=Computational-thinking-for-all

Tedre, M., & Denning, P. J. (2016). The long quest for computational thinking. In *Proceedings of the 16th Koli Calling Conference on Computing Education Research* (pp. 120–129). New York, NY: ACM.

Thimbleby, H. (2018). Misunderstanding IT: Hospital cybersecurity and IT problems reach the courts. *Digital Evidence and Electronic Signature Law Review*, 15, 11–32.

Turing, A. M. (1936) (published 1937). On computable numbers, with an application to the Entscheidungs problem. *Proceedings of the London Mathematical Society*, 2(42), 230–265.

Waite, J., Curzon, P., Marsh, D. W., & Sentance, S. (2016). Abstraction and common classroom activities. In *Proceedings of the 11th Workshop in Primary and Secondary Computing Education* (pp. 112–113). New York: ACM.

Waite, J., Curzon, P., Marsh, W., & Sentance, S. (2017). Teachers' uses of levels of abstraction focusing on design. In *Proceedings of the 12th Workshop in Primary and Secondary Computing Education* (pp. 115–116). New York: ACM.

Wing, J. (2006). Computational thinking. *Communications of the ACM*, 49(3), 33–35.

Wolz, U., Stone, M., Pearson, K., Pulimood, S. M., & Switzer, M. (2011). Computational thinking and expository writing in the middle school. *ACM Transactions on Computing Education (TOCE)*, 11(2), 9.

18 Schools (K–12)

Jan Vahrenhold, Quintin Cutts, and Katrina Falkner

In recent years, there has been a growing focus on Computer Science at the K–12 level from both an educational and a research perspective. This chapter briefly surveys some of these developments and describes areas where research, specifically in K–12 classrooms, is being conducted. Note that, as explained at the start of Section 18.2, we use the term "Computer Science," since it is used predominantly in the school sector to describe study beyond learning how to use digital technology.

18.1 (Re-)Introducing Computer Science in Schools

In contrast to other subjects in the area of Science, Technology, Engineering, and Mathematics (STEM), Computer Science has a relatively short history in schools (K–12). While some countries, such as Israel (Gal-Ezer & Stephenson, 2014), Poland (Sysło, 2014), or Germany (Knobelsdorf et al., 2015), have included Computer Science in their curricula for several decades, other countries only recently introduced this subject in schools (Heintz et al., 2015) or executed major revisions of their curricula (Bell et al., 2014; Sysło & Kwiatkowska, 2015). A recent report of a joint working group established by the Association for Computing Machinery Europe (ACM-E) and Informatics Europe presents a comprehensive snapshot of the current situation in Europe (Vahrenhold et al., 2017); see also the overview article by Webb et al. (2017).

An earlier snapshot of the situation in the USA and selected other countries was presented by Wilson et al. (2010). Their widely cited report "Running on Empty: The Failure to Teach K–12 Computer Science in the Digital Age" illustrated a prevailing lack of opportunities to study Computer Science in K–12 for full curriculum credit. In the meantime, the "CS4All" initiative (White House Office of the Press Secretary, 2016) has led to a collection of implementation efforts, including a large investment in teacher training for K–12 Computer Science.

Perhaps the most radical change, however, in K–12 Computer Science occurred in England in the early 2010s. In 2012, the Royal Society described the current situation of K–12 Computer Science in the UK in a report aptly named "Shut Down or Restart – The Way Forward for Computing in UK Schools" (The Royal Society, 2012). The authors pressed for the upcoming review of the national "Computing" curriculum to be "an opportunity to look at a radical overhaul of ICT in schools including rebranding and providing clarity on the different aspects of Computing currently lumped together under this heading" (The Royal Society, 2012, p. 8). They also recommended the provision of better initial teacher education for specialist "Computing" teachers bundled with provision for continuing professional development. Their call for action was supported by representatives from both academia and industry and finally led to a complete overhaul of the "Computing" curriculum and teacher training in England (Brown et al., 2014, Sentance & Czismadia, 2017). The overhaul consisted of a shift from an almost exclusively computer *use* or Digital Literacy curriculum across the K–8 age range to one almost entirely based around Programming and Computer Science.

Another major change that was similar in spirit was initiated in 2007 in New Zealand (Bell et al., 2014). Responding to decreasing enrollment numbers in tertiary computer science courses, curricula that used to include technology-enhanced teaching and learning only were refocused according to "Digital Technology Guidelines." After a brief pilot phase, however, the curricula were reshaped again to include a "Programming and Computer Science" strand. This strand was then implemented subsequently in a bootstrapping process. As the overarching curriculum was in effect already, teaching material for the new strand had to be designed, implemented, and tested almost concurrently with teacher training and instruction in schools; see Bell et al. (2014) for more details.

Within Australia, development of a Computer Science curriculum within the K–10 context began with the release of a draft curriculum statement in early 2013, receiving input across the education sector, in addition to industry and academia, identifying both the importance of such a curriculum, but also the many challenges in implementation. The Technologies curriculum, containing the Digital Technologies learning area, was endorsed for implementation in late 2015 (ACARA, 2015). This learning area introduces students to the fundamentals of Computational Thinking and Programming from Foundation (Kindergarten) to Year 10. The Australian Curriculum influences curricula across all states and territories within Australia, but may be adapted as per local context. Falkner, Vivian, and Falkner (2014) undertook a systematic literature review of Computing research within the K–10 context relevant to the Digital Technologies learning area, identifying the need for considerable further research to support the implementation of related curricula.

18.2 Implications and Challenges for Practice

In the previous section, we outlined several recent developments in K–12 Computer Science around the world. While several of these developments occurred almost concurrently, they happened seemingly in isolation, resulting in independent implementation and case study reports. In this section, we argue why this is unavoidable and discuss the implications and challenges for practice resulting from this.

Given the widespread acceptance of standardized curricula such as the ACM/ Institute of Electrical and Electronics Engineers (IEEE) 2013 Computing Curricula (Sahami et al., 2013) for computer science in a tertiary context, it may come as a surprise that there exists a variety of different approaches to teaching Computer Science on a K–12 level (e.g., see Brinda et al., 2009; Seehorn et al., 2011; Webb et al., 2017). As recent overview studies show, the focus as well as the content of Computer Science classes varies vastly across the world (Hubwieser et al., 2015b; Vahrenhold et al. 2017). At times, even the terminology is different: courses may be referred to as "Computer Science," "Computing," or "Informatics." To complicate matters, the interpretation of these terms can vary depending on the educational context up to the point of referring to the technical skills of how to use a computer or text processing software (Gander et al., 2013; Vahrenhold et al., 2017). In the context of this chapter, we will use the term "Computer Science" to denote the "scientific discipline … covering principles such as algorithms, data structures, systems architecture, design, problem solving etc." (The Royal Society, 2012, p. 17).

Setting aside terminology issues, there is still a broad spectrum of what is being taught in K–12 Computer Science and how. For example, two recent special issues of the *ACM Transactions on Computing Education* (Hubwieser et al., 2014, 2015a) present case studies from 13 countries. In contrast to the more standardized teaching environments in tertiary education, particularly in introductory college courses, this variety hinders the transfer and reproducibility of empirical research studies in different educational contexts.

18.2.1 Varying Educational Systems: The Berlin Model

One explanation of the varying educational contexts in K–12 education stems from the so-called *Berlin model* proposed by Heimann (1962) and further developed together with his students Otto and Schulz. In this work, Heimann did not focus on specific theories of teaching and learning in schools such as Herbart (1841; see Esterhues, 1984), Steiner (1984), or Montessori (1909). To be independent of any such theory, he modeled the planning and analysis of K–12 teaching by (1) preconditions, (2) fields of decision, and (3) consequences; see Heimann (1962) for a discussion of how this model relates to other approaches, including the body of work by Klafki, Haussmann, or Roth. According to Heimann, planning and analyzing teaching involves considering the sociocultural and anthropological–psychological preconditions and implications of all involved parties. Within the context set by these preconditions and implications, the teacher makes his or her decisions regarding goals, topics, methods, and media. These decisions are guided by professional training, experience, and curricula and are highly interrelated: any decision in one of these fields has implications for decisions in all other fields.

What sets apart K–12 education from most of tertiary education is the importance of anthropological–psychological and sociocultural factors both as preconditions and as consequences. Regarding anthropological–psychological factors, it is noteworthy that K–12 education encompasses a wide variety of types of schools including special needs education, vocational education, and precollege education. Also, students are usually not self-selected as is the case in tertiary education, since almost all subjects are mandatory. Hence, successful attempts to advance Computer Science to a subject worth full curriculum credit bring with them significant additional research problems in Computer Science education research, particularly related to diagnostic teaching and individual advancement (Vahrenhold, 2012).

Regarding sociocultural factors, the socioeconomic status of the students' families has been found to strongly influence students' performance (see, e.g., Benner et al., 2016, for a recent study), as well as means of communication between the school and parents (Wong-Villacres et al., 2017). This implies that the in-class settings are likely to depend on the demographics of the school district, as found in Seiter (2015), for example.

However, the sociocultural factor that is most different from tertiary education is the influence of educational policy. Depending on the administrative organization, policy decisions can be made on very different levels ranging from the individual teacher to policy-makers at the national level. For instance, the success of the initiative to redesign the Computing curriculum in England has been partially attributed to the involvement of industry leaders and the executive-level decision of the UK's Secretary of State for Education to "disapply" the existing curriculum while maintaining the status as a mandatory subject (see Brown et al., 2014).

18.2.2 Varying Research Settings: The Darmstadt Model

Hubwieser et al. (2011) extended the Berlin model to describe research conducted in K–12 Computer Science. For this, they introduced two additional dimensions: *range of influence* and *educationally relevant areas*. The first additional dimension describes the range in which the authors of a study can influence policies and implementations related to the subject of their study; this dimension ranges from "zero" (added by Hubwieser, 2013) to "international." The second additional dimension describes issues of direct relevance to educational activities (e.g., policies, teacher qualification, curricular issues, or intentions).

18.2.3 Challenges for Computing Education Research

As mentioned above, the alignment of Computer Science curricula in large parts of tertiary education facilitates the transfer of research results and revalidation studies across different institutions and national contexts. In contrast, the Berlin model explains why great care has to be taken when attempting such transfers and revalidation studies in secondary education: unlike tertiary education, secondary education is very much dependent on the overarching educational system. Combining the findings from the reports by Wilson et al. (2010) and Vahrenhold et al. (2017), we see a spectrum of administrative independence ranging from policies being decided on a classroom level to policies being decided by a central national authority.

Similarly, learners are not the same everywhere. To start with, different educational systems may provide different types of schools, varying even within a single country (see Hubwieser et al., 2011). Depending on the country, schools may also be selective or inclusive; in contrast to tertiary education, such information is usually not available publically. Finally, the question of whether or not Computer Science courses are optional (i.e., not worth curriculum credit), elective, or mandatory directly affects the degree of self-selection of the learners and hence the degree to which results can be expected to generalize. We refer the reader to Chapter 16 for an in-depth discussion of equity and diversity in computer science classrooms.

Whether computer science as a subject is worth full curriculum credit or not also has implications to teacher training. Across most of Europe, for example, provisions are in place to train computer science teachers in the same way as teachers of any other discipline (Vahrenhold et al., 2017). However, in contrast to other subjects such as Mathematics, low-level retraining requirements, if any, for teaching computer science persist, particularly where Computer Science is only an optional subject. Given the bootstrapping efforts in many countries, researchers are advised to also take into account whether or not the teachers involved in a particular study had the chance to have undergone formal training both in the formal subject of Computer Science and in its didactics (see, e.g., Lang et al., 2014).

As a consequence of these issues, most if not all of the existing research is likely to be very context-dependent. Hence, researchers must take great care as they attempt to build on earlier work.

In addition to the general issues related to study design discussed in Chapter 4, the design of studies in K–12 faces additional challenges. By definition, the subjects in these studies are underage, so the consent of parents or legal guardians needs to be secured in writing. Low response rates can jeopardize a study (see, e.g., Woszczynski, 2006). If schools offer only one section of a Computer Science course per age group, access to control groups may be problematic, as external factors such as the ones captured in the Berlin model are outside the control of the researchers. Schanzer et al. (2018) comment on whether or not to prefer a small study with control groups or a large study without control groups. Thies and Vahrenhold (2013) discuss how to set up experimental and control groups within a single class; their follow-up study (Thies & Vahrenhold, 2016) addresses possible influences of school type and teachers. In any case, a transparent description of the research environment and a discussion of factors outside the researchers' control need to be included when writing a research report.

18.3 Current Research

We now present the results of our literature review. For this review, we sought to summarize empirical research studies on K–12 Computer Science that took place *in classrooms as part of a course in Computer Science*, ignoring other contexts. The review broadly aims to lay the boundaries of current research in a number of areas, implicitly suggesting directions for future research.

We aimed to maximize visibility and also geographic coverage, surveying *ACM Transactions on Computing Education* and *Computer Science Education*, the two top journals in the field, and the conferences *ACM Conference on Innovation and Technology in Computer Science Education* (ITiCSE), *ACM Conference on International Computing Education Research* (ICER), *ACM Technical Symposium on Computer Science Education* (SIGCSE), *Australasian Computing Education Conference* (ACE), *International Conference on Informatics in Schools* (ISSEP), and *Workshop in Primary and Secondary Computing Education* (WiPSCE). We have focused on research results published in English, but given the prevalence of localized conferences and workshops, readers are urged to also consult local research outlets to complement the findings summarized below.

In contrast to previous surveys (e.g., the literature review by Waite, 2017), we did not employ a search engine to find relevant keywords. Instead, we manually checked all proceedings present in the DBLP Computer Science Bibliography (https://dblp.org) to see whether any papers matched the inclusion/exclusion criteria. From this search, an interesting pattern emerged: irrespective of the geographic context, papers on in-class research in Computer Science Education hardly appeared in any of the conferences and journals surveyed before 2006. Isolated reports, however, on teacher training (Epstein et al., 1987) or Programming in high school (Schollmeyer, 1996) were published in earlier years. Also, reports on outreach programs and out-of-school experiences, which are beyond the scope of this chapter, emerged in the late 1990s and early 2000s.

As a consequence of the different educational systems and contexts discussed in the previous section, researchers wishing to build upon or reproduce empirical research studies on K–12 Computer Science have to keep in mind that these results may have been obtained under highly localized conditions. Hence, a careful examination of these contexts is in order, regardless of whether or not results can be confirmed.

We have divided the papers we found into a number of sections, each corresponding to a different area of interest, and these are now presented.

18.3.1 Programming

Chapter 12 presents a detailed overview of the teaching of Programming within the context of CS1. Accordingly, here we will present a brief summary of research undertaken in regard to Programming development within the K–12 context.

Gujberova and Kalas (2013) explore the development of Programming pedagogy within the primary space, identifying gradational sequences of tasks designed to promote student learning, while Franklin et al. (2017) conduct an analysis of elementary student work to provide early insight into appropriate concept sequencing within later elementary years. Gordon et al. (2012) explore the idea of scenario-based programming as one that is "natural" within the K–12 context, identifying examples within student work within a non-scenario-oriented programming environment. Tessler et al. (2013) explore differences in learning outcome (in relation to recursion) when employing game-based pedagogy. Shah et al. (2015) and Grover and Basu (2017) both explore the development of misconceptions in K–12 in relation to introductory Programming concepts.

The type and paradigm of programming language used within K–12 contexts is also of relevance to current research. Werner et al. (2012a, 2012b) explore the ability of children to learn advanced Programming concepts within Visual Programming environments and present an assessment instrument. Haberman (2004) explores the development of mental models related to recursion and the relationship with Programming paradigms. The study of Ginat et al. (2013) investigated novices' difficulties with interleaved pattern composition.

Armoni et al. (2015) explore the use of Visual Programming environments and the benefits of prior exposure to Visual Programming environments in transitioning through to general-purpose programming languages. Weintrop and Wilensky (2018) contrast the direct learning outcomes of two cohorts, one exposed to Visual Programming and the other to a general-purpose programming language, finding greater learning gains for the Visual Programming cohort. Franklin et al. (2016) identify the explicit knowledge needed for general-purpose programming languages that is not addressed within Visual Programming, including ideas to assist in transfer, while Tabet et al. (2016) explore the use of "mediated transfer" to aid transition between the two environment mediums.

Ruf et al. (2014) conduct a comparative study of two Visual Programming environments, identifying that the choice of environment is likely not crucial to the development of successful learning outcomes. Merkouris et al. (2017) explore the benefits of adopting Tangible Computing environments, in combination with Visual Programming to motivate and engage students, while Martinez et al. (2015) explore the benefits of Tangible Computing through a variety of programming environments (this topic is also discussed further in Chapter 22). Felleisen et al. (2004) explore the teaching of functional programming within the K–12 context. Cutts et al. (2014) argue against the use of poorly specified pseudocode in Programming assessment, which is of particular relevance when considering the scale of K–12 assessment for Computer Science.

Code tracing has been identified both as a strategy that may be employed when learning programming as well as due to the potential insights it offers into the development of relevant mental models. Within the K–12 context, Dwyer et al. (2015) have explored the concept of tracing applied to Visual Programming languages. Aggarwal et al. (2018) conduct a study on program reasoning, including reading and tracing, within an elementary school context.

There is considerable interest in the impact of exposure to Computer Science courses in student perceptions on computing as a field and students' interests in continued studies. While discussed further below, Duncan and Bell (2015) explore the impact of Programming course components on Programming knowledge, incorporating student self-evaluations on ability. Duncan and Bell explore gender differences within their study, identifying that female students were less successful at correctly assessing their abilities, despite equal perform-ance. Funke and Geldreich (2017) continue this exploration of gender in their study of differences between girls and boys in block selection and programming method. Kaila et al. (2017) explore differences in the maturity of the learning of Programming between a K–12 and a tertiary cohort.

18.3.2 Software Engineering

Compared to Programming, the area of Software Engineering (i.e., pro-gramming in the large) has received only little attention in research in K–12 classrooms. A study surveying students in a Software Engineering curriculum (DeLyser, 2014) will be discussed in the section on course design.

Project-based learning has a long-established place in STEM subjects in sec-ondary schools. Hence, it is not surprising that team-based techniques from Software Engineering have found their way into K–12 classrooms. Meerbaum-Salant and Hazzan (2010) responded to the requirements for teacher support established in a previous study (Meerbaum-Salant & Hazzan, 2009) by pro-viding and evaluating a year-long template for mentoring software projects that was designed based on the so-called *Agile Constructionist Mentoring Methodology*. This concept aligns typical agile programming characteristics with constructivism and Shulman's Teacher Knowledge Base Model (Shulman, 1987). The authors verified that all requirements were addressed by at least one aspect of the proposed methodology. The implementation of this template and the iterative refinement of the approach was conducted in Israeli high schools and followed up using a mixed-methods approach surveying 90 teachers, 20 prospective teachers, and 70 high school students. The main conclusion from the data analysis was that the template facilitated implementing an agile soft-ware development technique in a high school classroom while at the same time helping teachers with appropriate pedagogy and content knowledge.

Fronza et al. (2017) instantiated agile software development practices in an Italian middle school, studying 42 sixth-grade students working on Scratch projects. In particular, one educational goal was to ensure that each team had a working prototype with at least a minimal functionality at the end of each iteration. The assessment took place using interviews, rated according to a three-level rubric, and analysis of artifacts, particularly with respect to the number of linearly independent paths in the program flow as captured by its cyclomatic complexity (McCabe, 1976). The authors found that their approach was well suited to helping the students reach the learning goals of the course. With respect to generalizability, the authors point out the need for replication studies both with a focus on the instructional approach and the validity of the assessment instrument.

Kastl et al. (2016) report on the instantiation of agile practices in four German high schools. During an eight-month Computer Science course implemented using project-based learning, 170 students (aged 14–18) worked on software projects in which teachers acted as moderators where needed, but did not intervene unless asked. This is strictly an experience report, but with findings worth following up. According to the teachers' reports, students appeared to develop a more independent working attitude and experienced formal modeling to be practically relevant. Furthermore, the project-based, long-term nature of instruction appeared to help students with a slower pace of learning to contribute to a project's success.

Summarizing the discussion above, we note that reports of in-class research on Software Engineering topics in K–12 Computer Science is currently limited to investigating the feasibility and effectiveness of using agile software development methods. The few studies we found, however, indicate that these practices can be implemented in K–12 classrooms. More advanced topics in Software Engineering, however, as well as a discourse on whether or not such topics can and should be addressed in K–12 Computer Science, remain the subjects of future studies.

18.3.3 Computational Thinking/Abstraction

Chapter 17 discusses the various views of Computational Thinking in great detail. In this section, we will present a brief summary of research undertaken in classrooms to understand the development of Computational Thinking, particularly abstraction, in more detail. The research mostly explores algorithmic thinking and abstraction, where abstraction is associated with problem-solving and the need to discard or ignore detail from the problem domain in order to identify appropriate abstractions for use in the solution.[1]

Studies range from age 18 right down to age 7. Sakhnini and Hazzan (2008) present one of the earliest studies, exploring problem-solving with abstract data types by Grade 12 students. The work is set in the *reducing abstraction* framework, originating in Mathematics Education (Hazzan, 1999), and shows how learners will attempt to find, either explicitly or implicitly, less abstract forms of their problems to aid their understanding. This reducing of abstraction may help explain other studies, such as Seiter and Foreman (2013), where 150 Scratch projects were analyzed for complexity: the older the author, the more likely they were to make use of the more complex and abstract features of a language (e.g., variables and control flow) compared to simpler constructs such as costume changing and sequential animation. Similarly, Grover et al. (2018) found that

---

1 Compare this to the use of abstraction in which the detail in code is hidden behind, for example, a procedural interface.

middle school students made limited use of variables and repetition more complex than a do-forever loop. Grover et al. (2016a) found when assessing middle school students after an algorithmic thinking course that the combination of variables and repetition was the biggest stumbling block.

Sakhnini and Hazzan (2008) raise another important issue – relevant to the time constraints in typical classroom courses – that students should be exposed to vast numbers of problems of different types, particularly analogous problems, to aid transfer of their developing skills to other contexts. This is further explored in Whitherspoon et al. (2018), where the approach is to use videos and worked examples, with fading, to improve competency. Joentausta and Hellas (2018) find that subgoal labeling (Catrambone, 1998) is required with worked examples when working with third-grade students. Smetsers-Weeds and Smetsers (2017) make extensive use of flowcharts to teach program plans more explicitly, and this focus enables learners to select and apply plans more effectively. In all four cases, success is linked to the number of plans to which the students are exposed. Brackmann et al. (2017) observed a positive connection between using an unplugged approach and development of computational thinking skills.

Smetsers-Weeda and Smetsers' (2017) aim is "think first," not "act first." This approach is also found to be highly successful by Statter and Armoni (2016). Their focus is seven to eight-year-olds, who will tend to reduce abstraction (echoing Sakhnini & Hazzan, 2008) by rushing straight to the machines, because concrete realizations can be crafted so quickly. However, Armoni's four-level approach to algorithmic description enabled the students to write good descriptions first, before going to the machine. Furthermore, in Statter and Armoni (2017), they report the highly positive effect of this approach to teaching abstraction for girls over boys.

Different views on "think first" vs. "act first" are adopted in different studies. Meerbaum-Salant et al. (2013) use a constructionist (e.g., more "act first") approach with Scratch on middle school students and found that some important concepts were learned, although not repeated execution, concurrency, and variables. Grover et al. (2015) adopt a balanced pedagogy between these two extremes, making use of the Exploring CS framework (Goode et al., 2012), as well as scaffolding and cognitive apprenticeship: code reading and tracing are used extensively, thinking and discussion take place before solution modeling, and pseudocode is developed before coding. Their study results in learning gains in Computational Thinking transfer skills, implying a deep level of conceptual understanding has been attained. At the other end of the spectrum, inquiry-based learning is being used, for example in Vaníček (2015) and Chiprianov and Gallon (2016), where the results are less strong. From the investigation of studies for this chapter, it appears that where a sound educational rationale for the studies is provided, the emphasis is on a "think-first" approach, which subsequently leads to successful action on the machine.

The remaining papers do not fall into neat categories. Al Sabbagh et al. (2017) describe a middle school intervention in Qatar involving several hundred students and a program of sixty 45-minute teaching sessions. A broad

Computational Thinking assessment of critical thinking and problem-solving showed a 6–7 percent increase from pre- to post-test between experimental and control groups. Rodriguez et al. (2016) updated CS Unplugged activities for regular classroom use, aiming to achieve educational goals, not just attitude changes. It is hard to determine exactly what was learned. Serafini (2011) describes a Computational Thinking intervention with 8–13-year-olds that was run for six years, involving 176 students across three schools, with positive results reported mainly at the affective level. Kiesmüller (2009) explores the use of tool support to determine the problem-solving strategies of 100 seventh-grade students in Bavaria, Germany. Finally, Seiter (2015), in a study of fourth-grade students in two schools, found significant differences in Computational Thinking skills according to which school the student attended. The less able students were in a school where the Reading and Mathematics comprehension scores were below the state requirements.

18.3.4 Attitudes and Views

If K–12 education is to include mandatory computer science content, then the broad range of learners' backgrounds must be taken into account in order to ensure that the majority of learners are included. Turkle and Papert were among the earliest to raise concerns that the narrow epistemological view of computing within the discipline could lead to exclusivity and the "boys-only" clubhouse (Margolis & Fisher, 2001). The pervasive narrow view of computing education, projected from its optional, tertiary-level-only origins, sets the attitudes of young people. This section reviews studies that shed further light on these issues, on how we want to be seen as a discipline, on the identities we wish to foster in our learners, and on a wide range of successful interventions. These are divided into age, context, and disciplinary appreciation.

Note that it is as important to address the teachers' attitudes as it is those of the students. They are just as much a part of the shift as we move to mandatory Computer Science Education, since in the old, optional world, all teachers were computing specialists. We will increasingly have generalist teachers, particularly in primary schools, whose developing attitudes to Computer Science will be crucial.

Many studies report on the age of the learner. One aspect of age involves considering how early a student is able to pick up complex computing concepts. Frost (2007) presents the impact of a Text-Based Programming course on 58 fourth graders, reporting significant pre- to post-test improvements. But a much larger aspect concerns the age at which learners form their attitudes and beliefs about computing. The developing view is that this takes place at the primary level. Using unplugged activities with 300 Austrian students from primary up to late secondary, Bischof and Sabitzer (2011) report that the largest effects on attitudes are in the primary age range, particularly in relation to gender effects. In a Swiss intervention for 133 students, using Scalable Game Design (Basawapatna et al., 2010), Lamprou et al. (2017) report that perceptions of "having learned something new" and wanting to continue were greatest among the primary students. Buffum et al. (2016) recognize that students are already making career choices by middle school, and so awareness and influencing must be addressed earlier. Backing this up, Carter et al. (2012) used mixed teaching methods in a breadth curriculum with US students from Grades 6–8, finding that improved appreciation and understanding of the subject immediately after the intervention were reduced a year later, hence determining that an earlier start is necessary.

The context in which the subject is taught, from which examples are drawn, has been shown to have a significant effect on attitudes involving both ethnicity and gender. Where example contexts are abstract or set in contexts of little interest, relevance, or social acceptability, learners are less likely to engage in their studies. A learner's identity is an important touchstone in these studies – "Is this relevant to me? Is this something I am able to study?" The founding example of context-aware computing is Guzdial's (2003) Media Computation work, but this has largely been in the tertiary context (although see Arauja et al., 2018). Kafai's work in this area particularly explores the exclusivity of both context and epistemology; her work in, for example, the e-textiles area gives both a new context and a "bricolage" approach to learning, in which top-down, rule-based, divide-and-conquer methods are replaced with more exploratory learning – trying things out, rearrangement, negotiation, and discussion based around meaningful individual projects. In separate studies with 15 and 28 US learners, the creativity afforded to the learners, the physical nature of the artifacts produced, and their authenticity in relation to the outside world are highly valued (Kafai et al., 2014; Searle et al., 2014). Effective contexts reported in other studies are as follows: interactive journalism to encourage whole-school inclusion of Computational Thinking, including middle school arts teachers (Wolz et al., 2011); the use of fractal designs in African artwork with 34 tenth-grade US learners of relevant ethnic backgrounds to develop Computational Thinking skills, showing very significant improvements in understanding in the experimental group (Eglash et al., 2011); music, as a key part of any culture, in a course involving music remixing and production with one-hundred 9th–12th-grade US students, demonstrating significantly improved attitudes toward Computer Science as a general subject of study, particularly among the female participants (Magerko et al., 2016); and chatbots and gamification, used in a major Argentine study involving thousands of participants in a national online competition and around 50 students in a pilot school setting, showing a marked increase in interest from female participants (Benotti et al., 2014). Interestingly, while gamification was valued in Benotti et al.'s study, it is not always effective in influencing attitudes positively: Robertson (2013) found that game making was not liked by girls and did not increase the desire to study Computer Science across both genders in a study of 992 learners across 13 schools in Scotland. Bell et al. (2012a) confirm the importance of authenticity for engaging and motivating students in the study of Programming based on New Zealand studies.

Instead of making the subject more relevant to the learner, another group of studies has attempted to paint a more truthful picture of the discipline. This builds on the recognition that many attitudes are based on false understandings. For example, Corradini et al. (2017), in a survey of 972 Italian primary teachers, determined that only eight teachers gave good definitions of Computational Thinking, with only a further 72 being acceptable. Grover et al. (2016b) asked US students (28 primary, 117 secondary) the question, "What is a computer?" – a discussion question often posed in an introductory computing class. The answers are problematic in that they understandably focus on the technology rather than the skills and understanding at the heart of our subject, suggesting teachers are inadvertently setting incorrect perceptions with such questions. Schulte and Magenheim (2005) surveyed 600 German 11th-grade students for attitudes toward software development. Results differed by gender (e.g., on self-confidence with and motivation for computer use) and prior experience (those having taken a Computer Literacy course at primary, particularly girls, tend to have a better understanding of software development concepts). In a pilot study of 23 US students, Grover et al. (2014b) report the prevalent view that Computer Science is about building and fixing computers and studying the internals.

To provide a more accurate picture of the subject, Grover et al. (2014b) give a good sense of what Computer Science as a career may entail, as well as the broad applicability of the subject in many diverse fields of human endeavor. A key tool in their study is the use of short video vignettes, provided by industry or academics, to give insight into current activities broadly across the discipline. Used with 26 seventh and eighth graders, appreciation of the subject was significantly advanced. Peters and Rick (2014), working on the image of the subject, created a Software Engineering-style setting for nine Swedish students to build a key interactive game section of the school website. Rather than seeing themselves as nerds, the team, whose software was used by over 90 teachers and students in the school, radically adjusted their identity to "I am an expert, I am needed and responsible." Similar realizations were made across the school population. Finally, Hildebrandt and Diethelm (2012) report on a program for Grades 7–9 adopted by 13 schools in northern Germany, the evaluation of which shows increased interest, perception of ability, and vocational orientation for computing, particularly for females. However, Siegel and Zarb (2016) observe in a study with 249 students in secondary schools in Scotland that decisions about whether or not to transition to higher education Computer Science are part of a longer process and thus need to be treated differently at different times of this process.

18.3.5 Physical Computing

Only recently have Physical Computing devices such as robots or programmable boards become available for large-scale deployment in schools. Hence, there is only a very limited number of research reports investigating the use of such devices in K–12 classrooms.

Sentance et al. (2017) present the results of an interview study involving 54 students (aged 11–12) and 15 teachers from 15 English schools; this study took place after the first use in UK schools of BBC micro:bit Physical Computing devices. In their qualitative analysis of interviews, the following themes emerged: students, even those reported to usually struggle in class, found the devices to be easy to use; previous findings from the literature that showed the tangibility of the devices to support learning could be confirmed; collaboration, while in principle encouraged through the curriculum, did not take place, as students had access to individual devices; and creativity appeared to be supported by the fact that modifications to programs and hardware would be visible in the real world.

Even with falling hardware prices, however, providing hardware to K–12 classrooms may not be affordable for all schools. Hence, Wu et al. (2008) performed a study with 151 Taiwanese students (aged 15–16) to compare robotics simulations and physical robots. While they could not find any statistically significant differences in the subject matter knowledge, the students that had worked with physical robots exhibited more positive attitudes toward Computer Science and reported better perceptions of the robot's behavior.

A study very similar in nature was conducted by Liu et al. (2013). Working with three small groups of US high school students, they found no significant performance differences between students working in virtual environment and students working in both virtual and physical environments. They noted that working with physical robots took more time due to occasional mechanical failures. On the other hand, students also working with physical robots showed significantly stronger gains with respect to the authors' measurement of algorithmic thinking.

The work of Ben-Bassat Levry and Ben-Ari (2015) reexamines the folklore knowledge that working with robots is "fun." Using the *Theory of Planned Behavior*, the authors demonstrated in a study with over 700 Israeli middle school students in both extracurricular and regular classes that indeed attitudes engender intentions, which in turn cause behavior – in their case, to further pursue studies in STEM. They also observed that, while initial motivation is high, having a concrete goal to work toward is of particular importance when working with robotics.

Brinkmeyer and Kalbreyer (2016) followed up on this observation. They used robotics in a German vocational grammar school with 15 students (aged 16–20) where an Engineering contextualization was prevalent throughout the whole course. Their analysis of student feedback showed that indeed the motivation had not decreased over the course.

Martinez et al. (2015) conducted a study with 190 Argentine children in four groups covering the age range from three to ten years. While they confirmed folklore knowledge about some algorithmic concepts being difficult to grasp for very young students, they concluded that their curriculum based upon robotics could generally be taught even in preschool. In particular, they make a case for inquiry-based, developmentally appropriate teaching strategies that can be implemented using robotics. A similar study with all students of an elementary school in a small, rural environment in the USA was reported upon by Heiner

(2018); in this case, however, the author concedes that a rigorous evaluation could not be conducted.

18.3.6 Unplugged

CS Unplugged (Bell et al., 2012b) characterizes a class of kinesthetic activities developed to introduce children to concepts in Computer Science without using a computer. Such activities were developed starting in the 1990s and gained widespread attention in the early 2000s when they were referred to in the curricular recommendations of the Computer Science Teachers Association. Initially created as outreach activities, they have attracted significant interest as in-class resources, particularly given their "non-computer" relationship with Computational Thinking. As a result, some studies have been conducted in realistic in-class settings. Localized, Unplugged-like approaches have been developed mainly for outreach to very young children; Gärtig-Daugs et al. (2016) describe a pilot test of such material with German children aged 3–4 in preschool and primary school.

The earliest study of this kind was reported by Nishida et al. (2008). The authors taught lessons using Unplugged material in three different schools in Japan, reaching 112 students in junior high school and 43 students in senior high school. The intervention was evaluated by self-reported proficiency, enjoyment, and free-text comments. The authors found that the students generally enjoyed the activities and reported no severe deficits in understanding the material.

The study by Taub et al. (2012) followed a mixed-methods approach. The authors examined student artifacts and performed an observational study as well as interviews to investigate the influence of a CS Unplugged curriculum on the attitudes and views of students. The student population in this study consisted of 78 students (aged 12–13) in secondary schools in Israel. The main outcome of this study was that the Unplugged approach indeed influenced the students toward a more mathematical view of Computer Science. However, at the same time, the interest in studying Computer Science declined. The authors suggested remedying this latter effect by reviewing the activities for use with older children, such as including more "central concepts" in Computer Science.

Feaster et al. (2011) report on a two-semester study using CS Unplugged in a US high-school. They worked with 29 students in Grades 9–12 to investigate the effects of Unplugged activities in a Programming course on both self-reported content understanding and attitudes. The outcome of this study was that the experimental group (14 students) did not show any statistically significant differences in either of the two factors. Several factors that may have influenced the outcome are reported.

In a different setting of a German secondary school, Thies and Vahrenhold (2013) conducted a controlled study with 25 students (aged 11–12). They compared the effectiveness of using CS Unplugged to introduce a topic in Computer Science against other, more traditional approaches. Using both quantitative and qualitative methods, they found that statistically significant differences in content understanding could be observed neither immediately after instruction nor six weeks later after the course. This study was replicated later (Thies & Vahrenhold, 2016) in order to validate independence of the results from teachers and cohorts; this revalidation study also extended the scope to students into high school (aged 16–17).

Rodriguez et al. (2016, 2017) extended some CS Unplugged activities according to the suggestions of Taub et al. (2012) and piloted these activities in seventh-grade US classrooms with a total of 272 students in the experimental and control groups. The purpose of this study was to develop an assessment for Computational Thinking and – using this instrument – to document the extent to which knowledge was gained and retained from CS Unplugged activities. The authors report positive developments in both aspects; a cross-validation of the development instrument, however, remains a subject of future research.

A study by Hermans and Aivaloglo (2017), conducted with 35 students (aged 8–12) in a Dutch elementary school, aimed at understanding whether an introduction to Programming in Scratch that starts with CS Unplugged material led to different learning outcomes from a Scratch-only introduction. The intervention lasted eight weeks, the first four weeks of which differed by whether or not Unplugged material was used. The authors found that as far as grades were concerned, the level of mastery of the programming language was not influenced in a statistically significant way by the method of instruction. However, students in the group that was taught using the Unplugged material used a wider vocabulary of Scratch blocks and were found to exhibit a higher level of self-efficacy.

Judging from the research settings described above, there does not seem to be a contextual dependence regarding the acceptance of Unplugged material and whether or not it can be implemented in classrooms. However, the question of the extent to which attitudes are influenced is not fully answered yet; in particular, the comparison of Computer Science and Mathematics may depend on the cultural context. As of this writing, two other open questions are: (1) Which learning goals can and should be reached through Unplugged? (2) How can these be assessed using validated instruments? Existing studies have presented first attempts to answer these queries, but a consensus has not yet been reached.

18.3.7 Collaboration

Only a small number of research papers deals with collaboration practices in K–12 classrooms from a computing education perspective, but we refer the reader to the literature on learning sciences in general and computer-supported collaborative learning.

Israel et al. (2017) discuss a qualitative study in a US elementary school with nine students in Grades 3 and 4. Using the Collaborative Computing Observation Instrument (C-COI) to study students during problem-solving tasks, they found the following three prevalent interaction mechanisms: collaborative problem-solving; conversations expressing excitement and curiosity about computing activities; and conversations in which students socialized.

Deitrick et al. (2017) report on a video study with two pairs of students in Statistics and Computing classrooms in a US high school. They discuss how these pairs behaved during the three phases of agreeing on the precise nature of the problem to be solved, agreeing on what knowledge was needed for solving the activity, and acquiring or sharing that knowledge.

A study on Pair Programming in a South African secondary school (Grade 11) was presented by Liebenberg et al. (2012). The study focused on a group of six female students who had experienced Solo Programming in Grade 10. The students self-reported more enjoyment, greater persistence, and more interest in the subject as a result of Pair Programming being used in class.

Tsan et al. (2016, 2018) analyzed the artifacts from Scratch Pair Programming sessions in a US elementary school. In their first study, the authors found evidence of an early gender gap, as pairs in which at least one male student was present produced significantly better solutions than female-only pairs. The second study focused on verbal cues and actions, resulting in three major suggestion types: "proposal," "command," and "next step."

The limited number of in-class collaboration studies can also be attributed to the technical and legal issues related to running a video study. For a detailed account on all aspects of such a study, we refer the reader to Seidel et al. (2005).

18.3.8 Assessment

The Berlin model indicates that educational contexts and thus course-specific learning goals may vary significantly from country to country. Also, many assessment specialists object to the publication of standardized tests to avoid teaching-to-the-test effects. As a consequence, very little research has been published on how to assess Computer Science concepts on a larger scale than just a single classroom. Most of these refer to assessing Computational Thinking concepts; note that the sections on Computational Thinking and Programming discuss papers on assessment within a single classroom.

This Handbook chapter does not cover research in the areas of Information and Communication Technology Education and Media Education; the reader is encouraged to also consider the respective research outlets for assessing students' performance in these areas. In particular, the International Computer and Information Literacy Study (ICILS; https://icils.acer.org) assesses competencies regarding the use of computers and information. The ICILS 2013 results were based upon almost 60,000 students and 35,000 teachers from 21 different educational contexts (Frailon et al., 2014); the ICILS 2018 study, in progress as of this writing, also includes a module on Computational Thinking.

Snow et al. (2017) discuss an instrument they developed for assessing the Exploring Computer Science (ECS) curriculum (Goode et al., 2012), particularly with respect to the instrument's validity. This instrument, available at https://csforallteachers.org/exploring-computer-science, was developed in parallel with the instrument used in the ICILS 2018 study, for which instrument design started in 2015. Another evaluation of the ECS curriculum benchmarked the performance of 755 US students by means of the Mathematics part of the California STAR Test (Lewis et al., 2015). Cateté et al. (2016) present their approach to developing and validating a rubric for a particular assignment from the Beauty and Joy of Computing curriculum.

Grover and Basu (2017) describe a set of assessment items they piloted with 100 US students in Grades 6–8. Their research was driven by the question of how to organize a set of learning outcomes related to Computational Thinking into a technically sound assessment. As part of their iterative refinement, they were able to confirm misconceptions that had been reported in earlier work. Reges (2008) examined over 7,300 exams that were taken during the 1998 Advanced Placement Computer Science courses and found misconceptions related to assignments and recursion. A revalidation study by Lewis et al. (2013) could not replicate Reges' findings regarding the correlation of certain types of items on the 2004 and 2009 data and advances Reges' hypothesis on the importance of the students' mental model of program execution. Kohn (2017) reports that his analysis of artifacts from 100 Swiss high school students collected over a period of four years seemed to imply that a notional machine with algebraic capacities (i.e., the ability to replace a variable by its defining expression) could induce misconceptions regarding variable evaluation; see also Chapter 27.

Grover et al. (2014a) report on their study in a US middle school that used an instrument that had been piloted in Israeli nationwide exams (Zur-Bargury et al., 2013). Except for one item, the results did not differ in a statistically significant way. This study discusses the different educational contexts, but concedes that not enough details about the pilot study are known to fully explain the one data outlier.

Mühling et al. (2015) present an instrument for assessing basic programming abilities; their instrument was developed using Item Response Theory and tested with German students in Grades 7–10. Using this instrument, they were able to detect misconceptions regarding loops with exit conditions and conditional statements. A study on the pre-instructional knowledge of students in elementary school regarding step-by-step instructions and algorithm development was presented by Dwyer et al. (2014); this study serves as a baseline to compare against.

Research on the assessment of factors other than performance has been very limited so far. Cheong et al. (2004) studied motivational factors and academic help-seeking strategies in US K–12 classrooms. They found task goals to be positively correlated with instrumental help-seeking and perceiving the benefits of it, whereas performance-avoiding goals were positively correlated with avoiding help-seeking. The study of Giannakos et al. (2012) focused on high school students from Germany and Greece, as well as Greek first-year tertiary-level students; the authors present preliminary insights on the relationship between Programming self-efficacy and the level of Programming.

In conclusion, a major open research problem is the development of validated research assessments for topics in K–12 Computer Science, particularly as the different educational contexts in the K–12 space pose major obstacles. For a treatment of assessment techniques in higher education and a discussion of how these may be employed in UK schools, see the literature review by Kallia (2017).

18.3.9 Course Design

As Computer Science is a mandatory K–12 subject in only a few countries, instruction and related in-class research often take place in the context of other subjects. However, researchers are occasionally given the opportunity to develop, deploy, and research newly designed curricula in a K–12 context. In this section, we discuss several such approaches that have been documented in research publications. Given the worldwide movements to introduce Computer Science in schools, this section will present the results in somewhat more depth. Wherever possible, we also outline the circumstances under which these courses were piloted and how these can be expected to generalize in other educational contexts. The reader is also referred to the work by Hug et al. (2013), who take a sociocultural point of view to describe and analyze the introduction and growth of Computer Science courses at a US high school.

As part of evaluating the New York City Foundation for Computer Science Education, DeLyser (2014) reports on demographics and pre-/post-surveys regarding attitudes and (growth) mind-sets of 1,800 students in Software Engineering programs in New York City, the largest school district in the USA. These students had taken an introductory and an Advanced Placement Computer Science course. Students reported an interest in Computer Science and Software Engineering topics, the confidence to be able to deepen their knowledge and to solve problems, and the desire to take more courses in these areas. Interestingly, female students reported a much lower influence from their peer group on their decision whether or not to enroll in Computer Science courses.

In contrast, the educational system in North-Rhine Westphalia, Germany, has a 40-year history of Computer Science in secondary schools (Knobelsdorf et al., 2015). However, Computer Science has been at most an elective, predominantly high school subject. In a proof-of-concept study, Pasternak and Vahrenhold (2012) developed and implemented a Computer Science curriculum for Grades 6–10, designed according to Bruner's spiral curriculum (Bruner, 1960), intertwining so-called *strands* focusing on Programming, (Semi-)Structured Data, Typed Systems, Multimedia, and Operating Systems. A long-term evaluation of this project (Pasternak, 2016) with 27 students shows moderate effect sizes in comparison to the control groups. Most notably, students were found to have better knowledge related to topics in Digital Literacy than students in a control group that had enrolled in a Digital Literacy course; this might be used to defuse arguments that favor including Digital Literacy instruction into other subjects over establishing Computer Science courses in high schools.

A study undertaken in a ninth-grade classroom in Brazil (28 students) examined motivational factors and their correlation to learning when using a media-based spiral curriculum. Arauja et al. (2018) followed the contextualized Media Computation approach (Guzdial, 2003). In their study, they found both motivation to study and perceptions of Programming and Computing to significantly increase over the course of instruction. As the report is a case study in which no control groups was used, the authors caution that the results may not generalize well beyond the educational context of their study.

Bootstrap (Schanzer et al., 2015) is a curriculum for K–12 rooted in the *How to Design Programs* philosophy of Felleisen et al. (2000). This 25-hour curriculum uses a functional programming language to embed Computer Science concepts in other classrooms, most notably in Algebra classrooms. Schanzer et al. (2015) conducted studies relating to functional decomposition and word problems with 149 students in six US middle school classrooms. While the experimental group saw a gain from pre- to post-assessment (using a standardized Algebra test), no such gain could be observed for the control group whose Mathematics classes did not include Bootstrap elements. A somewhat surprising outcome was that the scores for word problems in the control group dropped; the teachers conjecture this to be a motivational issue. A follow-up study with 468 students (aged mostly 12–15) from 22 classrooms focused on word problems only (Schanzer et al., 2018). The results of the initial study could be confirmed as far as the study design without a control group allowed. The main instructional insight from this study was that using a step-by-step program design process that leverages multiple representations of functions appeared to aid student skills related to expressing word problems.

With respect to generalization, we note that the Bootstrap project is facilitated by low barriers for individual teachers in the USA to adopt third-party curricula and thus can be expected to generalize well in this context. In other educational systems that have a more centralized structure, a similar approach would need to be approved officially for curricular use. Also, the strong alignment of the research reported so far with the Algebra curriculum certainly strengthens the results related to learning goals specific to the transfer to Algebra. Whether the curriculum can also be used successfully in less focused contexts remains a subject of future research.

Another large-scale project in US K–12 Computer Science Education is the *Middle-years Computer Science* (MyCS) project (Schofield et al., 2014). It differs from *Bootstrap* in the following two significant aspects: first, the curriculum is designed as a stand-alone curriculum as opposed to being integrated into another subject; and second, the instructional goal is "to promote a positive computational identity among its students" (Castro et al., 2016, p. 558). In a large-scale survey, 5,475 students responded to a set of Likert-type items gauging computational identities (Castro et al., 2016). A breakdown by gender showed that a slightly lower percentage of students in the experimental group (613 students taking a full MyCS course; 1,502 students only took some lessons) was female compared to the control group

(3,360 students); the ratio, however, was not too imbalanced (42.9 percent females). Female students were found to respond to the computational identity questions in a statistically significantly more positive way in the experimental group. With respect to broadening participation across different ethnicities, the demographics show that a diverse set of students was enrolled in the MyCS courses. The distribution, however, was not a perfect fit with the demographics of the control group: most notably, more students identifying as "Latina/o" and fewer students identifying as "multiracial" were part of the experimental group. A restriction of this study is that, by design of the intervention, computational knowledge and skill sets were not in the focus of the study and thus not measured. Also, the authors observe a positive development of computational identity in both the control group and the experimental group; this raises repeatability questions regarding possible external factors such as the technology market mentioned by the authors themselves.

A rather different approach to instruction was reported by Woszczynski (2006). In her study, the author examined an online course delivered to US schools with high percentages of students from underrepresented groups and low socioeconomic backgrounds. The course covered History of Computing, Hardware, Software Systems Management, Operating Systems, Data Communication and Networking, the World Wide Web, and Concepts of Programming. The analysis, performed as pre- and post-assessment and attitudinal surveys, showed a learning gain for the 45 respondents and overall satisfaction with the instruction. As no control group was used, it remains unclear how this approach compares to other methods of instruction and to what extent tailoring to the intended audience was successful.

Augmenting an existing Scratch course in a US middle school to also include multiple sessions on writing, Burke and Kafai (2012) worked with 11 students (aged 12–14) on digital storytelling. Their workshop included sessions on planning, drafting, revising, editing, and publishing a (digital) story. The authors used attitudinal pre/post-surveys, field notes, video observations, and interviews and analyzed the resulting Scratch projects. Among other results, the authors found that their approach, as intended, stressed the connections between coding and writing as part of composition. Also, students reported high levels of enjoyment and self-efficacy. However, the authors also observed that the linear structure of the developed stories greatly reduced the use of Boolean logic and conditionals in the resulting projects and thus cautioned the reader to keep this in mind when designing similar workshops.

Other projects have focused on bringing introductory Computer Science courses to high schools; see Poirot (1979) for an early discourse about the challenges of such approaches and possible solutions. Xu et al. (2016) report on their instantiation of a college-level Creative Computing CS1 course in Grades 9–12 of two US high schools. While being mainly descriptive, the paper reports a significant uptake of students and a high percentage of female students, as well as in Advanced Placement Computer Science, indicating that the curriculum was well-received. Details about other instructional goals or the assessments of these need to be provided by follow-up studies.

A very similar curriculum was proposed by Wood et al. (2016). In their study, the authors evaluated an implementation of a college-level Computational Arts curriculum in a US high school. The evaluation of this course, using post-course surveys, found that this course encouraged students to enroll in further Computer Science courses; also, compared to a pre-course survey in which most students identified as either artists or technologists, more students identified as a mixture of both. As for the approach by Xu et al. (2016), we note that the assessment of learning goals is subject to future research. In both cases, the generalizability of the approaches depends on whether or not the educational context allows for the introduction of new interdisciplinary courses in a high school curriculum. Settle et al. (2012) describe how the curricula of several subjects, including Graphic Arts and Latin, in a US Laboratory School (middle and high school) were altered to include Computational Thinking components and in which challenges were faced as part of this process.

Feaster et al. (2014) report on a group of loosely coupled interventions that combine Unplugged ideas and working with "serious toys" hardware. Their program was piloted with over 150 students in a US middle school; as a result of these interventions, students reported an increasing interest in Computer Science and an increased understanding of the content. A similar course, using a web-based programming system for LED display kits, was studied by Chun and Ryoo (2010) in South Korean elementary schools. The authors found that the large majority of students found the course interesting and helpful and intended to further pursue Computer Science.

We finish our discussion of course design by summarizing a study aimed at diversifying an already existing Computer Science curriculum in US high schools. Hansen et al. (2016) report on their analysis, modification, and field testing of a curriculum that was reworked according to the principles of Universal Design for Learning, a design approach fostering inclusive classrooms (see, e.g., King-Sears, 2014, for a brief introduction). The authors modified the existing curriculum to differentiate it for students with limited proficiency in the language of instruction, with varying mathematical skill levels, as well as with varying paces of learning. Also, cultural references were reconsidered. The study was performed in two rounds. The first round involved 500 students (aged 9–12), while the second round expanded the scope to 1,500 students. The authors also report on accommodations in the classroom and modifications to learning objectives. With respect to generalizability, the main points of the study are likely to carry over to other educational contexts; the details of in-classroom modifications, on the other hand, are bound to be very context-specific up to the point of being instructor- and student-specific. As the project is ongoing at the time of this writing, further results are to be expected. For more details on diversification in (tertiary) classrooms, we refer the reader to Chapter 16; best practices for K–12 classrooms have been collected by Lemov (2015) and Lemov et al. (2016).

18.3.10 Other Topics

In many countries, Computer Science courses are accessible to students no earlier than in high school (see, e.g., Vahrenhold et al., 2017). As a consequence of this limited exposure of K–12 students to Computer Science, topics other than those mentioned in the preceding sections are rarely touched upon or even researched in K–12 classrooms.

One example of this is non-determinism as present in concurrent programming. This topic has been researched by Ben-David Kolikant (2001) and Alexandron et al. (2013) in the context of Israeli high schools. In the same context, Ginat and Alankry (2012) report on their work with "advanced high school students" on language concatenation in a Computational Models course.

Carruthers et al. (2011) worked with a small group of students in a Canadian Mathematics classroom on the graph-theoretic ideas of Social Network Analysis, and Gibson (2012) reports on his observations and experiences with teaching graph concepts to French K–12 students in different age groups. How to introduce the concept of finite-state automata, also part of the Computer Science Unplugged activities and covered in some of the studies summarized above, was studied by Isayama et al. (2017). The authors report on a gamification-based approach deployed in Japanese primary and lower secondary schools.

Benacka and Reichel (2013) used a simulation-based approach to introduce programming to students (aged 15–18) in a Slovakian grammar school, and Musicant et al. (2015) augmented the classic "traffic signal" setup used in simulations by video sequences produced by the students as part of the intervention.

An approach to establishing professional norms such as non-tolerance for faulty programs was developed by Ben-David Kolikant and Pollack (2004). The authors describe a short case study with two groups of Israeli high school students. Brinda and Terjung (2017) surveyed 192 German middle and high school students regarding their conceptions of databases and how phenomena occurring during everyday use of smartphones might be related to databases. Finally, Ioannou and Angeli (2014) report on the effects of a short instructional unit in a Cypriot classroom on conceptions and misconceptions regarding the central processing unit of a computer.

18.4 Conclusions

It is hard to draw straightforward conclusions from the complex picture that Section 18.3 has painted. There is such a broad spread of research across many topics and relatively so few studies in each topic that there is little definitive ground to stand on.

Of particular note is that almost no study is a close replication of another. In addition to the variations in educational contexts as discussed in Section 18.2, this is largely because many of the studies involve the introduction of a new curriculum, a new teaching sequence, or a new pedagogical technique. In such an environment, we hazard to give strong advice, but the following observations and suggestions may be of value.

Stakeholders in K–12 Computer Science Education need to be aware of what has gone before. Much has been learned over the decades back to the 1960s and 1970s, but a general (though not universal) lack of undergraduate or master's level Computer Science Education units, modules, or whole programs means that this knowledge is not widely known.

Particularly when considering a new curriculum or pedagogy for a region or a whole country, there are hopefully enough well-structured and reasonably researched existing curricula that we could now pick one of them and adopt it, adjust it, and hopefully improve it, rather than laboriously re-executing a succession of previous developments.

To make this work, our research community has to become more accepting of replication studies of all kinds, particularly including the adoption of an existing curriculum or pedagogy in a new context. The Darmstadt Model tells us how many small or large differences there are likely to be, which is sure to give such studies a unique edge. But maybe the shift needed is in the attitudes of both researchers and research venues toward accepting that we as a community should be *building on*, not *creating from scratch*.

Considering the multi-institutional, multinational studies exemplified by the Scaffolding, Bootstrapping, and Building Research in Australasian Computing Education (BRACE) projects led by Sally Fincher and Marian Petre in the early 2000s, many of the participants of which are authors of this Handbook, we need similar studies for the school sector. However, the original studies, and the many subsequent studies the participants undertook, were relatively simple to organize: autonomous academics in autonomous tertiary institutions able to bend individual courses (rarely, if ever, whole programs) to their researching wills in order to reach equivalences appropriate for the replication needed. We have noted the significantly greater complications involved in the school sector in Section 18.2, but nonetheless, we should aspire to similar studies in schools. This is a grand challenge for Computer Science Education Research.

References

Aggarwal, A., Touretzky, D. S., & Gardner-McCune, C. (2018). Demonstrating the ability of elementary school students to reason about programs. *Proceedings of the 49th ACM Technical Symposium on Computer Science Education (SIGCSE 2018)* (pp. 735–740). New York: ACM Press.

Al Sabbagh, A., Gedawy, H., Alshikhabobakr, H., & Razak, S. (2017). Computing curriculum in middle schools: An experience report. *Proceedings of the 2017 ACM Conference on Innovation and Technology in Computer Science Education (ITiCSE '17)* (pp. 230–235). New York: ACM Press.

Alexandron, G., Armoni M., Gordon, M., & Harel, D. (2013). On teaching programming with nondeterminism. *Proceedings of the 8th Workshop in*

Primary and Secondary Computing Education (WiPSCE 2013) (pp. 71–74). New York: ACM Press.

Araujo, L. G. J., Bittencourt, R. A., & Santos, D. M. B. (2018). An analysis of a media-based approach to teach programming to middle school students. *Proceedings of the 49th ACM Technical Symposium on Computer Science Education (SIGCSE 2018)* (pp. 1005–1010). New York: ACM Press.

Armoni, M., Meerbaum-Salant, O., & Ben-Ari, M. (2015). From Scratch to "real" programming. *ACM Transactions on Computing Education (TOCE)*, 14(4), 25.1–25.15.

Australian Curriculum, Assessment and Reporting Authority (ACARA) (2015). Australian Curriculum: Digital Technologies. Retrieved from www.australian curriculum.edu.au

Basawapatna, A. R., Koh, K. H., & Repenning, A. (2010). Using scalable game design to teach computer science from middle school to graduate school. *Proceedings of the Fifteenth Annual Conference on Innovation and Technology in Computer Science Education (ITiCSE '10)* (pp. 224–228). New York: ACM Press.

Bell, T., Andreae, P., & Robins, A. (2014). A case study of the introduction of computer science in NZ schools. *ACM Transactions on Computing Education (TOCE)*, 14(2), 10.1–10.31.

Bell, T., Newton, H., Andreae, P., & Robins, A. (2012a). The introduction of computer science to NZ high schools – An analysis of student work. *Proceedings of the 7th Workshop in Primary and Secondary Computing Education (WiPSCE 2012)* (pp. 5–15). New York: ACM Press.

Bell T., Rosamond F., & Casey N. (2012b) Computer science unplugged and related projects in math and computer science popularization. In H. L. Bodlaender, R. Downey, F. V. Fomin, & D. Marx (Eds.), *The Multivariate Algorithmic Revolution and Beyond. Lecture Notes in Computer Science 7370* (pp. 398–456). Berlin, Germany: Springer.

Benacka, J., & Reichel, J. (2013). Computer modeling with Delphi – Constructionism and IBL in practice and motivation for studying STEM. In *Proceedings of the 6th International Conference on Informatics in Schools: Situation, Evolution, and Perspectives (ISSEP 2013), Lecture Notes in Computer Science 7780* (pp. 136–46). Berlin, Germany: Springer.

Ben-Bassat Levry, R., & Ben-Ari, M. (2015). Robotics – Is the investment worthwhile? In *Proceedings of the 8th International Conference on Informatics in Schools: Situation, Evolution, and Perspectives (ISSEP 2015), Lecture Notes in Computer Science 9378* (pp. 22–31). Berlin, Germany: Springer.

Ben-David Kolikant, Y. (2001). Gardeners and cinema tickets: High school students' preconceptions of concurrency. *Computer Science Education*, 11(3), 221–245.

Ben-David Kolikant, Y., & Pollack, S. (2004). Establishing computer science professional norms among high-school students. *Computer Science Education*, 14(1), 21–35.

Benner, A. D., Boyle, A. E., & Sadler, S. (2016). Parental involvement and adolescent's educational success: The roles of prior achievement and socioeconomic status. *Journal of Youth and Adolescence*, 45(6), 1053–1064.

Benotti, L., Martínez, M. C., & Schapachnik, F. (2014). Engaging high school students using chatbots. In *Proceedings of the 2014 Conference on Innovation & Technology in Computer Science Education (ITiCSE '14)* (pp. 63–68). New York: ACM Press.

Bischof, E., & Sabitzer, B. (2011). Computer science in primary schools – Not possible, but necessary?! In *Proceedings of the 5th International Conference on Informatics in Schools: Situation, Evolution, and Perspectives (ISSEP 2011), Lecture Notes in Computer Science 7013* (pp. 95–105). Berlin, Germany: Springer.

Brackmann, C. P., Román-González, M., Robles, G., Moreno-León, J., Casali, A., & Barone, D. (2017). Development of computational thinking skills through unplugged activities in primary school. In *Proceedings of the 12th Workshop in Primary and Secondary Computing Education (WiPSCE 2017)* (pp. 65–72). New York: ACM Press.

Brinda, T., Puhlmann, H., & Schulte, C. (2009). Bridging ICT and CS: Educational standards for computer science in lower secondary education. In *Proceedings of the 14th Annual ACM SIGCSE Conference on Innovation and Technology in Computer Science Education (ITiCSE 2009)* (pp. 289–292). New York: ACM Press.

Brinda, T., & Terjung, Th. (2017). A database is like a dresser with lots of sorted drawers: Secondary school learners' conceptions of relational databases. In *Proceedings of the 12th Workshop in Primary and Secondary Computing Education (WiPSCE 2017)* (pp. 39–48). New York: ACM Press.

Brinkmeier, M., & Kalbreyer, D. (2016). A case study of physical computing in computer science education. In *Proceedings of the 11th Workshop in Primary and Secondary Computing Education (WiPSCE 2016)* (pp. 54–59). New York: ACM Press.

Brown, N. C. C., Sentance, S., Crick, T., & Humphreys, S. (2014). Restart: The resurgence of computer science in UK schools. *ACM Transactions on Computing Education (TOCE)*, 14(2), 9.1–9.22.

Bruner, J. (1960). *The Process of Education.* Cambridge, MA: Harvard University Press.

Buffum, P. S., Frankorsky, M. H., Boyer, K. E., Wiebe, E. N., Mott, B. W., & Lester, J. C. (2016). Empowering all Sstudents: Closing the CS confidence gap with an in-school initiative for middle school students. In *Proceedings of the 47th ACM Technical Symposium on Computer Science Education (SIGCSE 2016)* (pp. 382–387). New York: ACM Press.

Burke, Q., & Kafai, Y. (2012). The writers' workshop for youth programmers: Digital storytelling with scratch in middle school classrooms. In *Proceedings of the 43rd ACM Technical Symposium on Computer Science Education (SIGCSE 2012)* (pp. 433–438). New York: ACM Press.

Carruthers, S., Milford, T., Pelton, T., & Stege, U. (2011). Draw a social network. In *Proceedings of the 16th Annual Joint Conference on Innovation and Technology in Computer Science Education (ITiCSE '11)* (pp. 178–182). New York: ACM Press.

Carter, E., Blank, G., & Walz, J. (2012). Bringing the breadth of computer science to middle schools. In *Proceedings of the 43rd ACM Technical Symposium on Computer Science Education (SIGCSE 2012)* (pp. 203–208). New York: ACM Press.

Castro, B., Diaz, T., Gee, M., Justice, R., Kwan, D., Seshadri, P., & Dodds, Z. (2016). MyCS at 5: Assessing a middle-years CS curriculum. In *Proceedings of the 47th ACM Technical Symposium on Computer Science Education (SIGCSE 2016)* (pp. 558–563). New York: ACM Press.

Cateté, V., Snider, E., & Barnes, T. (2016). Developing a rubric for a creative CS principles lab. In *Proceedings of the 2016 ACM Conference on Innovation and Technology in Computer Science Education (ITiCSE 2016)* (pp. 290–295). New York: ACM Press.

Catrambone, R. (1998). The subgoal learning model: Creating better examples so that students can solve novel problems. *Journal of Experimental Psychology: General*, 127(4), 355–376.

Cheong, Y. F., Pajares, F., & Oberman, P. S. (2004). Motivation and academic help-seeking in high school computer science. *Computer Science Education*, 14(1), 3–19.

Chiprianov, V., & Gallon, L. (2016). Introducing computational thinking to K–5 in a French context. In *Proceedings of the 2016 ACM Conference on Innovation and Technology in Computer Science Education (ITiCSE 2016)* (pp. 112–117). New York: ACM Press.

Chun, S. Y., & Ryoo, J. (2010). Development and application of a web-based programming learning system with LED display kits. In *Proceedings of the 41st ACM Technical Symposium on Computer Science Education (SIGCSE 2010)* (pp. 310–314). New York: ACM Press.

Corradini, I., Lodi, M., & Nardelli, E. (2017). Computational thinking in Italian schools: Quantitative data and teachers' sentiment analysis after two years of "Programma il Futuro". In *Proceedings of the 2017 ACM Conference on Innovation and Technology in Computer Science Education (ITiCSE '17)* (pp. 224–229). New York: ACM Press.

Cutts, Q., Connor, R., Donaldson, P., & Michaelson, G. (2014). Code or (not code) – Separating formal and natural language in CS education. In *Proceedings of the 9th Workshop in Primary and Secondary Computing Education (WiPSCE 2014)* (pp. 20–28). New York: ACM Press.

Deitrick, E., Wilkerson, M., & Simoneau, E. (2017). Understanding student collaboration in interdisciplinary computing activities. In *Proceedings of the 2017 ACM Conference on International Computing Education Research (ICER 2017)* (pp. 118–126). New York: ACM Press.

DeLyser, L. A. (2014). Software engineering students in the city. In *Proceedings of the 9th Workshop in Primary and Secondary Computing Education (WiPSCE 2014)* (pp. 37–42). New York: ACM Press.

Duncan, C., & Bell, T. (2015). A pilot computer science and programming course for primary school students. In *Proceedings of the 10th Workshop in Primary and Secondary Computing Education (WiPSCE 2015)* (pp. 39–48). New York: ACM Press.

Dwyer, H. A., Hill, C., Hansen, A., Iveland, A., Franklin, D., & Harlow, D. (2015). Fourth grade students reading block-based programs: Predictions, visual cues, and affordances. In *Proceedings of the Eleventh International Computing Education Research Conference (ICER 2015)* (pp. 111–119). New York: ACM Press.

Dwyer, H. A., Hill, C., Carpenter, S., Harlow, D., & Franklin, D. (2014). Identifying elementary students' pre-instructional ability to develop algorithms and step-by-step instructions. In *Proceedings of the 45th ACM Technical Symposium on Computer Science Education (SIGCSE 2014)* (pp. 511–516). New York: ACM Press.

Eglash, R., Krishnamoorthy, M., Sanchez, J., & Woodbridge, A. (2011). Fractal simulations of African design in pre-college computing education. *ACM Transactions on Computing Education (TOCE)*, 11(3), 17.1–17.14.

Epstein, R. G., Aiken, R. M., Snelbecker, G., & Potosky, J. (1987). Retraining high school teachers to teach computer science – Observations on the first course. In *Proceedings of the 18th SIGCSE Technical Symposium on Computer Science Education (SIGCSE 1987)* (pp. 136–140). New York: ACM Press.

Esterhues, J. (Ed.) (1984) *Johann Friedrich Herbart. Band I. Umriß pädagogischer Vorlesungen.* Paderborn, Germany: Schöningh. In German.

Falkner, K., Vivian, R., & Falkner, N. (2014). The Australian digital technologies curriculum: Challenge and opportunity. In *Proceedings of the Australasian Computing Education Conference (ACE 2014)* (pp. 3–12). Sydney, Australia: Australian Computer Society.

Feaster, Y., Ali, F., Zhai, J., & Hallstrom, J. O. (2014). Serious toys: Three years of teaching computer science concepts in K–12 classrooms. In *Proceedings of the 2014 Conference on Innovation & Technology in Computer Science Education (ITiCSE '14)* (pp. 69–74). New York: ACM Press.

Feaster, Y., Segars, L., Wahba, S. K., & Hallstrom, J. O. (2011). Teaching CS Unplugged in the high school (with limited success). In *Proceedings of the 16th Annual Joint Conference on Innovation and Technology in Computer Science Education (ITiCSE 2011)* (pp. 248–252). New York: ACM Press.

Felleisen, M., Findler, R. B., Flatt, M., & Krishnamurthi, S. (2000). *How to Design Programs: An Introduction to Programming and Computing.* Cambridge, MA: MIT Press.

Felleisen, M., Findler, R. B., Flatt, M., & Krishnamurthi, S. (2004). The TeachScheme! Project: Computing and programming for every student. *Computer Science Education*, 14(1), 55–77.

Fraillon, J., Ainley, J., Schulz, W., Friedman, T., & Gebhardt, E. (2014). *Preparing for Life in a Digital Age: The IEA International Computer and Information Literacy Study International Report.* Cham, Switzerland: Springer.

Franklin, D., Hill, C., Dwyer, H. A., Hansen, A. K., Iveland, A., & Harlow, D. B. (2016). Initialization in Scratch: Seeking Knowledge transfer. In *Proceedings of the 47th ACM Technical Symposium on Computer Science Education (SIGCSE 2016)* (pp. 217–222). New York: ACM Press.

Franklin, D., Skifstad, G., Rolock, R., Mehrotra, I., Ding, V., Hansen, A., Weintrop, D., & Harlow, D. (2017). Using upper-elementary student performance to understand conceptual sequencing in a blocks-based curriculum. In *Proceedings of the 48th ACM Technical Symposium on Computer Science Education (SIGCSE 2017)* (pp. 231–236). New York: ACM Press.

Fronza, I., El Ioini, N., & Corral L. (2017). Teaching computational thinking using agile software engineering methods: A framework for middle schools. *ACM Transactions on Computing Education (TOCE)*, 17(4), 19.1–19.28.

Frost, D. (2007). Fourth grade computer science. In *Proceedings of the 38th ACM Technical Symposium on Computer Science Education (SIGCSE 2007)* (pp. 302–306). New York: ACM Press.

Funke, A., & Geldreich, K. (2017). Gender differences in Scratch programs of primary school children. In *Proceedings of the 12th Workshop in Primary and Secondary Computing Education (WiPSCE 2017)* (pp. 57–64). New York: ACM Press.

Gal-Ezer, J., & Stephenson, C. (2014). A tale of two countries: Successes and challenges in K–12 computer science education in Israel and the United States. *ACM Transactions on Computing Education (TOCE)*, 14(2), 8.1–8.18.

Gander, W., Petit, A., Berry, G., Demo, B., Vahrenhold, J., McGettrick, A., Boyle, R., Drechsler, M., Stephenson, C., Ghezzi, C., & Meyer, B. (2013). *Informatics Education: Europe Cannot Afford to Miss the Boat.* Informatics Europe & Association for Computing Machinery. Retrieved from www.informatics-europe.org/images/documents/informatics-education-acm-ie.pdf

Gärtig-Daugs, A., Weitz, K., Wolking, M., & Schmid, U. (2016). Computer science experimenter's kit for use in preschool and primary school. In *Proceedings of the 11th Workshop in Primary and Secondary Computing Education (WiPSCE 2016)* (pp. 66–71). New York: ACM Press.

Giannakos, M. N., Hubwieser, P., & Ruf, A. (2012). Is self-efficacy in programming decreasing with the level of programming skills? In *Proceedings of the 7th Workshop in Primary and Secondary Computing Education (WiPSCE 2012)* (pp. 16–21). New York: ACM Press.

Gibson, J. P. (2012). Teaching graph algorithms to children of all ages. In *Proceedings of the 17th ACM Annual Conference on Innovation and Technology in Computer Science Education (ITiCSE '12)* (pp. 34–39). New York: ACM Press.

Ginat, D., & Alankry, R. (2012). Pseudo abstract composition: The case of language concatenation. In *Proceedings of the 17th ACM Annual Conference on Innovation and Technology in Computer Science Education (ITiCSE '12)* (pp. 28–33). New York: ACM Press.

Ginat, D., Menashe, E., & Taya, A. (2013). Novice difficulties with interleaved pattern composition. In *Proceedings of the 6th International Conference on Informatics in Schools: Situation, Evolution, and Perspectives (ISSEP 2013), Lecture Notes in Computer Science 7780* (pp. 56–67). Berlin, Germany: Springer.

Goode, J., Chapman, G., & Margolis, J. (2012). Beyond curriculum: The Exploring Computer Science Program. *ACM Inroads*, 3(2), 47–53.

Gordon, M., Marron, A., & Meerbaum-Salant, O. (2012) Spaghetti for the main course?: Observations on the naturalness of scenario-based programming. In *Proceedings of the 17th ACM Annual Conference on Innovation and Technology in Computer Science Education (ITiCSE '12)* (pp. 198–203). New York: ACM Press.

Grover, S., & Basu, S. (2017). Measuring student learning in introductory block-based programming: Examining misconceptions of loops, variables, and boolean logic. In *Proceedings of the 48th ACM Technical Symposium on Computer Science Education (SIGCSE 2017)* (pp. 267–272). New York: ACM Press.

Grover, S., Basu, S., & Schank, P. (2018) What we can learn about student learning from open-ended programming projects in middle school computer science. In *Proceedings of the 49th ACM Technical Symposium on Computer Science Education (SIGCSE 2018)* (pp. 999–1004). New York: ACM Press.

Grover, S., Cooper, S., & Pea, R. (2014a). Assessing computational learning in K–12. In *Proceedings of the 2014 Conference on Innovation & Technology in Computer Science Education (ITiCSE '14)* (pp. 57–62). New York: ACM Press.

Grover, S., Pea, R., & Cooper, S. (2014b). Remedying misperceptions of computer science among middle school students. In *Proceedings of the 45th ACM Technical Symposium on Computer Science Education (SIGCSE 2014)* (pp. 343–348). New York: ACM Press.

Grover, S., Pea, R., & Cooper, S. (2015). Designing for deeper learning in a blended computer science course for middle school students. *Computer Science Education*, 25(2), 199–237.

Grover, S., Pea, R., & Cooper, S. (2016a). Factors influencing computer science learning in middle school. In *Proceedings of the 47th ACM Technical Symposium on Computer Science Education (SIGCSE 2016)* (pp. 552–557). New York: ACM Press.

Grover, S., Rutstein, D., & Snow, E. (2016b). "What is a computer": What do secondary school students think? In *Proceedings of the 47th ACM Technical*

Symposium on Computer Science Education (SIGCSE 2016) (pp. 564–569). New York: ACM Press.

Gujberova, M., & Kalas, I. (2013). Designing productive gradations of tasks in primary programming education. In *Proceedings of the 8th Workshop in Primary and Secondary Computing Education (WiPSCE 2013)* (pp. 108–117). New York: ACM Press.

Guzdial, M. (2003). A media computation course for non-majors. In *Proceedings of the 8th Annual Conference on Innovation and Technology in Computer Science Education (ITiCSE 2003)* (pp. 104–108). New York: ACM Press.

Haberman, B. (2004). How learning logic programming affects recursion comprehension. *Computer Science Education*, 14(1), 37–53.

Hansen, A. K., Hansen, E. R., Dwyer, H. A., Harlow, D. B., & Franklin, D. (2016). Differentiating for diversity: Using universal design for learning in elementary computer science education. In *Proceedings of the 47th ACM Technical Symposium on Computer Science Education (SIGCSE 2016)* (pp. 376–381). New York: ACM Press.

Hazzan, O. (1999). Reducing abstraction level when learning abstract algebra concepts. *Education Studies in Mathematics*, 44, 71–90.

Heimann, P. (1962). Didaktik als Theorie und Lehre. *Die Deutsche Schule*, 54(9), 407–427. In German.

Heiner, C. (2018). A robotics experience for all the students in an elementary school. In *Proceedings of the 49th ACM Technical Symposium on Computer Science Education (SIGCSE 2018)* (pp. 729–34). New York: ACM Press.

Heintz, F., Mannila, L., Nygårds, K., Parnes, P., & Regnell, B. (2015). Computing at school in Sweden – Experiences from introducing computer science within existing subjects. In *Proceedings of the 8th International Conference on Informatics in Schools: Situation, Evolution, and Perspectives (ISSEP 2015), Lecture Notes in Computer Science 9378* (pp. 118–130). Berlin, Germany: Springer.

Hermans, F., & Aivaloglo, E. (2017). To Scratch or not to Scratch?: A controlled experiment comparing plugged first and unplugged first programming lessons. In *Proceedings of the 12th Workshop in Primary and Secondary Computing Education (WiPSCE 2017)* (pp. 49–56). New York: ACM Press.

Hildebrandt, C., & Diethelm, I. (2012). The school experiment InTech: How to influence interest, self-concept of ability in informatics and vocational orientation. In *Proceedings of the 7th Workshop in Primary and Secondary Computing Education (WiPSCE 2012)* (pp. 30–39). New York: ACM Press.

Hubwieser, P. (2013). The Darmstadt Model: A first step towards a research framework for computer science education in schools. In *Proceedings of the 6th International Conference on Informatics in Schools: Situation, Evolution, and Perspectives (ISSEP 2013), Lecture Notes in Computer Science 7780* (pp. 1–14). Berlin, Germany: Springer.

Hubwieser, P., Armoni, M., Brinda, T., Dagiene, V., Diethelm, I., Giannakos, M. N., Knobelsdorf, M., Magenheim, J., Mittermeir, R. T., & Schubert, S. (2011). Computer science/informatics in secondary schools. In *ITICSE-WGR '11: Proceedings of the 16th Annual Conference Reports on Innovation and Technology in Computer Science Education – Working Group Reports* (pp. 18–38). New York: ACM Press.

Hubwieser, P., Armoni, M., & Giannakos, M. N. (2015a). How to implement rigorous computer science education in K–12 schools? Some answers and many questions. *ACM Transactions on Computing Education (TOCE)*, 15(2), 5.1–5.12.

Hubwieser, P., Armoni, M., Giannakos, M. N., & Mittermeir, R.T. (2014). Perspectives and visions of computer science education in primary and secondary (K–12) schools. *ACM Transactions on Computing Education (TOCE)*, 14(2), 7.1–7.9.

Hubwieser, P., Giannakos, M. N., Berges, M., Brinda, T., Diethelm, I., Magenheim, J., Pal, Y., Jackova, J., & Jasute, E. (2015b). A global snapshot of computer science education in K–12 schools. In *ITICSE-WGR '15: Proceedings of the 2015 ITiCSE Working Group Reports* (pp. 65–83). New York: ACM Press.

Hug, S., Guenther, R., & Wenk, M. (2013). Cultivating a K12 computer science community: A case study. In *Proceedings of the 44th ACM Technical Symposium on Computer Science Education (SIGCSE 2013)* (pp. 275–280). New York: ACM Press.

Ioannou, I., & Angeli, C. (2014). Examining the effects of an instructional intervention on destabilizing learners' misconceptions about the central processing unit. In *Proceedings of the 9th Workshop in Primary and Secondary Computing Education (WiPSCE 2014)* (pp. 93–99). New York: ACM Press.

Isayama, D., Ishiyama, M., Relator, R., & Yamazaki, K. (2017). Computer science education for primary and lower secondary school students: Teaching the concept of automata. *ACM Transactions on Computing Education (TOCE)*, 17(1), 2.1–2.28.

Israel, M., Wherfel, Q. M., Shehab, S., Melvin, O., & Lash, T. (2017). Describing elementary students' interactions in K–5 puzzle-based computer science environments using the Collaborative Computing Observation Instrument (C-COI). In *Proceedings of the 2017 ACM Conference on International Computing Education Research (ICER 2017)* (pp. 110–117). New York: ACM Press.

Joentausta, J., & Hellas, A. (2018). Subgoal labeled worked examples in K–3 education. In *Proceedings of the 49th ACM Technical Symposium on Computer Science Education (SIGCSE 2018)* (pp. 616–621). New York: ACM Press.

Kafai, Y. B., Lee, E., Searle, K., Fields, D., Kaplan, E., & Lui, D. (2014). A crafts-oriented approach to computing in high school: Introducing computational concepts, practices, and perspectives with electronic Textiles. *ACM Transactions on Computing Education (TOCE)*, 14(1), 1.1–1.20.

Kaila, E., Lindén, R., Lokkila, E., & Laakso, M. (2017). About programming maturity in Finnish high schools: A comparison between high school and university students' programming skills. In *Proceedings of the 2017 ACM Conference on Innovation and Technology in Computer Science Education (ITiCSE '17)* (pp. 122–127). New York: ACM Press.

Kallia, M. (2017). *Assessment in Computer Science Courses: A Literature Review*. London, UK: The Royal Society.

Kastl, P., KIesmüller, U., & Romeike, R. (2016). Starting out with projects – Experiences with agile software development in high schools. In *Proceedings of the 11th Workshop in Primary and Secondary Computing Education (WiPSCE 2016)* (pp. 60–65). New York: ACM Press.

Kiesmüller, U. (2009). Diagnosing learners' problem-solving strategies using learning environments with algorithmic problems in secondary education. *ACM Transactions on Computing Education (TOCE)*, 9(3), 17.1–17.26.

King-Sears, P. (2014). Introduction to *Learning Disability Quarterly* special series on universal design for learning: Part one of two. *Learning Disability Quarterly*, 37(2), 68–70.

Knobelsdorf, M., Magenheim, J., Brinda, T., Engbring, D., Humbert, L., Pasternak, A., Schroeder, U., Thomas, M., & Vahrenhold, J. (2015). Computer science education in North-Rhine Westphalia, Germany – A case study. *ACM Transactions on Computing Education (TOCE)*, 15(2), 9.1–9.22.

Kohn, T. (2017). Variable evaluation: An exploration of novice programmers' understanding and common misconceptions. In *Proceedings of the 48th ACM Technical Symposium on Computer Science Education (SIGCSE 2017)* (pp. 345–350). New York: ACM Press.

Lamprou, A., Repenning, A., & Escherle, N. A. (2017). The Solothurn Project: Bringing computer science education to primary schools in Switzerland. In *Proceedings of the 2017 ACM Conference on Innovation and Technology in Computer Science Education (ITiCSE '17)* (pp. 218–223). New York: ACM Press.

Lang, C., Craig, A., & Casey, G. (2014). Unblocking the pipeline by providing a compelling computing experience in secondary schools: Are the teachers ready? In *Proceedings of the Australasian Computing Education Conference (ACE 2014)* (pp. 149–158). Sydney, Australia: Australian Computer Society.

Lemov, D. (2015). *Teach Like a Champion 2.0: 62 Techniques That Put Students on the Path to College*, 2nd edn. San Francisco, CA: Jossey-Bass.

Lemov, D., Hernandez, J., & Kim, J. (2016). *Teach Like a Champion Field Guide 2.0: A Practical Resource to Make the 62 Techniques Your Own*, 2nd edn. San Francisco, CA: Jossey-Bass.

Lewis, C. M., Khayarallah, H., & Tsai, A. (2013). Mining data from the AP CS A exam: Patterns, non-patterns, and replication failure. In *Proceedings of the International Computing Education Research Conference (ICER 2013)* (pp. 115–122). New York: ACM Press.

Lewis, D. W., Kohne, L., Mechlinski, T., & Schmalstig, M. (2015). The exploring computer science course, attendance and math achievement. In *Proceedings of the 2015 ACM Conference on Innovation and Technology in Computer Science Education (ITiCSE '15)* (pp. 147–152). New York: ACM Press.

Liebenberg, J., Mentz, E., & Breed, B. (2012). Pair programming and secondary school girls' enjoyment of programming and the subject information technology (IT). *Computer Science Education*, 22(3), 219–236.

Liu, A., Schunn, C., Flot, J., & Shoop, R. (2013). The role of physicality in rich programming environments. *Computer Science Education*, 23(4), 315–331.

Magerko, B., Freeman, J., McKlin, T., Reilly, M., Livingston, E., McCoid, S., & Crews-Brown, A. (2016). EarSketch: A STEAM-based approach for underrepresented populations in high school computer science education. *ACM Transactions on Computing Education (TOCE)*, 16(4), 14.1–14.25.

Margolis, J., & Fisher, A. (2001). *Unlocking the Clubhouse: Women in Computing*. Cambridge, MA: MIT Press.

Martinez, C., Gomez, M. J., & Benotti, L. (2015). A comparison of preschool and elementary school children learning computer science concepts through a multilanguage robot programming platform. In *Proceedings of the 2015 ACM Conference on Innovation and Technology in Computer Science Education (ITiCSE '15)* (pp. 159–164). New York: ACM Press.

McCabe, T. J. (1976). A complexity measure. *IEEE Transactions on Software Engineering*, SE-2(4), 308–320.

Meerbaum-Salant, O., Armoni, M., & Ben-Ari, M. (2013). Learning computer science concepts with Scratch. *Computer Science Education*, 23(3), 239–264.

Meerbaum-Salant, O., & Hazzan, O. (2010). An agile constructionist mentoring methodology for software projects in the high school. *ACM Transactions on Computing Education (TOCE)*, 9(4), 21.1–21.29.

Meerbaum-Salant, O., & Hazzan, O. (2009). Challenges in mentoring software development projects in the high school: Analysis according to Shulman's teacher knowledge base model. *Journal of Computers in Mathematics and Science Teaching*, 28(1), 23–43.

Merkouris, A., Chorianopoulos, K., & Kameas, A. (2017). Teaching programming in secondary education through embodied computing platforms: Robotics and wearables. *ACM Transactions on Computing Education (TOCE)*, 17(2), 9.1–9.22.

Montessori, M. (1909). *Il Metodo della Pedagogia Scientifica Applicato All'educazione Infantile Nelle Case dei Bambini*. Città di Castello, Italy: S. Lafi.

Mühling, A., Ruf, A., & Hubwieser, P. (2015). Design and first results of a psychometric test for measuring basic programming abilities. In *Proceedings of the 10th Workshop in Primary and Secondary Computing Education (WiPSCE 2015)* (pp. 2–10). New York: ACM Press.

Musicant, D., & Selcen Guzey, S. (2015). Engaging high school students in modeling and simulation through educational media. In *Proceedings of the 46th ACM Technical Symposium on Computer Science Education (SIGCSE 2015)* (pp. 464–469). New York: ACM Press.

Nishida, T., Idosaka, Y., Hofuku, Y., Kanemune, S., & Kuno, Y. (2008). New methodology of information education with "computer science unplugged". In *Proceedings of the 3rd International Conference on Informatics in Schools: Situation, Evolution, and Perspectives (ISSEP 2008), Lecture Notes in Computer Science 5090* (pp. 241–252). Berlin, Germany: Springer.

Pasternak, A. (2016). Contextualized teaching in the lower secondary education: Long-term evaluation of a CS course from Grade 6 to 10. In *Proceedings of the 47th ACM Technical Symposium on Computer Science Education (SIGCSE 2016)* (pp. 657–662). New York: ACM Press.

Pasternak, A., & Vahrenhold, J. (2012). Design and evaluation of a braided teaching course in sixth grade computer science education. In *Proceedings of the 43rd ACM Technical Symposium on Computer Science Education (SIGCSE 2012)* (pp. 45–50). New York: ACM Press.

Peters, A. K., & Rick, D. (2014). Identity development in computing education: Theoretical perspectives and an implementation in the classroom. In *Proceedings of the 9th Workshop in Primary and Secondary Computing Education (WiPSCE 2014)* (pp. 70–79). New York: ACM Press.

Poirot, J. L. (1979). Computer education in the secondary school: Problems and solutions. In *Proceedings of the Tenth SIGCSE Technical Symposium on Computer Science Education (SIGCSE 1979)* (pp. 101–104). New York: ACM Press.

Reges, S. (2008). The mystery of "b:= (b = false)". In *Proceedings of the 39th ACM Technical Symposium on Computer Science Education (SIGCSE 2008)* (pp. 21–25). New York: ACM Press.

Robertson, J. (2013). The influence of a game-making project on male and female learners' attitudes to computing. *Computer Science Education*, 23(1), 58–83.

Rodriguez, B., Kennicutt, S., Rader, C., & Camp, T. (2017). Assessing computational thinking in CS Unplugged activities. In *Proceedings of the 48th ACM Technical Symposium on Computer Science Education (SIGCSE 2017)* (pp. 501–506). New York: ACM Press.

Rodriguez, B., Rader, C., & Camp, T. (2016). Using student performance to assess CS Unplugged activities in a classroom environment. In *Proceedings of the 2016 ACM Conference on Innovation and Technology in Computer Science Education (SIGCSE 2016)* (pp. 95–100). New York: ACM Press.

Ruf, A., Mühling, A., & Hubwieser, P. (2014). Scratch vs. Karel – Impact on learning outcomes and motivation. In *Proceedings of the 9th Workshop in Primary and Secondary Computing Education (WiPSCE 2014)* (pp. 50–59). New York: ACM Press.

Sahami, M., Danyluk, A., Fincher, S., Fisher, K., Grossman, D., Hawthorne, E., Katz, R., LeBlanc R., Reed, D., Roach, S., Cuadros-Vargas, E., Dodge, R., France, R., Kumar, A., Robinson, B., Seker, R., & Thompson A. (2013). *Computer Science Curricula 2013 – Final Report*. Association for Computing Machinery & IEEE-Computer Society. Retrieved from http://dx.doi.org/10.1145/2534860

Sakhnini, V., & Hazzan, O. (2008). Reducing abstraction in high school computer science education: The case of definition, implementation, and use of abstract data types. *Journal of Educational Resources in Computing*, 8(2), 5.

Schanzer, E., Fisler, K., & Krishnamurthi, S. (2018). Assessing Bootstrap: Algebra students on scaffolded and unscaffolded word problems. In *Proceedings of the 49th ACM Technical Symposium on Computer Science Education (SIGCSE 2018)* (pp. 8–13). New York: ACM Press.

Schanzer, E., Fisler, K., Krishnamurthi, S., & Felleisen, M. (2015). Transferring skills at solving word problems from computing to algebra through Bootstrap. In *Proceedings of the 46th ACM Technical Symposium on Computer Science Education (SIGCSE 2015)* (pp. 616–621). New York: ACM Press.

Schofield, E., Erlinger, M., & Dodds, Z. (2014). MyCS: CS for middle-year students and their teachers. In *Proceedings of the 45th ACM Technical Symposium on Computer Science Education (SIGCSE 2014)* (pp. 337–342). New York: ACM Press.

Schollmeyer, M. (1996). Computer programming in high school vs. college. In *Proceedings of the 27th SIGCSE Technical Symposium on Computer Science Education (SIGCSE 1996)* (pp. 378–382). New York: ACM Press.

Schulte, C., & Magenheim, J. (2005). Novices' expectations and prior knowledge of software development: Results of a study with high school students. In *Proceedings of the International Computing Education Research Workshop (ICER 2005)* (pp. 143–153). New York: ACM Press.

Searle, K. A., Fields, D. A., Lui, D. A., & Kafai, Y. (2014). Diversifying high school students' views about computing with electronic textiles. In *Proceedings of the International Computing Education Research Conference (ICER 2014)* (pp. 75–82). New York: ACM Press.

Seehorn, D., Carey, S., Fuschetto, B., Lee, I., Moix, D., O'Grady-Cunniff, D., Boucher Owens, B., Stephenson, C., & Verno, A. (2011). *K–12 Computer Science Standards – Revised 2011*. New York: Computer Science Teachers Association & Association for Computing Machinery.

Seidel, T., Prenzel, M., & Kobarg, M. (Eds.) (2005). *How to Run a Video Study. Technical Report of the IPN Video Study*. Münster, Germany: Waxmann.

Seiter, L. (2015). Using SOLO to classify the programming responses of primary grade students. In *Proceedings of the 46th ACM Technical Symposium on Computer Science Education (SIGCSE 2015)* (pp. 540–545). New York: ACM Press.

Seiter, L., & Foreman B. (2013). Modeling the learning progressions of computational thinking of primary grade students. In *Proceedings of the International Computing Education Research Conference (ICER 2013)* (pp. 59–66). New York: ACM Press.

Sentance, S., & Czismadia, A. (2017). Computing in the curriculum: Challenges and strategies from a teacher's perspective. *Education and Information Technologies*, 22(2), 469–495.

Sentance, S., Waite, J., Hodges, S., MacLeod, E., & Yeomans, L. (2017). "Creating cool stuff": Pupils' experience of the BBC micro:bit. In *Proceedings of the 48th ACM Technical Symposium on Computer Science Education (SIGCSE 2017)* (pp. 531–536). New York: ACM Press.

Serafini, G. (2011). Teaching programming at primary schools: Visions, experiences, and long-term research prospects. In *Proceedings of the 5th International Conference on Informatics in Schools: Situation, Evolution, and Perspectives (ISSEP 2011), Lecture Notes in Computer Science 7013* (pp. 143–154). Berlin, Germany: Springer.

Settle, A., Franke, B., Hansen, R., Spaltro, F., Jurisson, C., Rennert-May, C., & Wildeman, B. (2012). Infusing computational thinking into the middle- and high-school curriculum. In *Proceedings of the 17th ACM Annual Conference on Innovation and Technology in Computer Science Education (ITiCSE '12)* (pp. 22–27). New York: ACM Press.

Siegel, A. A., & Zarb, M. (2016). Student concerns regarding transition into higher education CS. In *Proceedings of the 2016 ACM Conference on Innovation and Technology in Computer Science Education (ITiCSE 2016)* (pp. 23–28). New York: ACM Press.

Shah, P., Capovilla, D., & Hubwieser, P. (2015). Searching for barriers to learning iteration and runtime in computer science. In *Proceedings of the 10th Workshop in Primary and Secondary Computing Education (WiPSCE 2015)* (pp. 73–75). New York: ACM Press.

Shulman, L. E. (1987). Knowledge and teaching: Foundations of the new reform. *Harvard Educational Review*, 57(1), 1–22.

Smetsers-Weeda, R., & Smetsers, S. (2017). Problem solving and algorithmic development with flowcharts. In *Proceedings of the 12th Workshop in Primary and Secondary Computing Education (WiPSCE 2017)* (pp. 25–34). New York: ACM Press.

Snow, E., Rutstein, D., Bienkowski, M., & Xu, Y. (2017). Principled assessment of student learning in high school computer science. In *Proceedings of the 2017 ACM Conference on International Computing Education Research (ICER 2017)* (pp. 209–216). New York: ACM Press.

Statter, D., & Armoni, M. (2016). Teaching abstract thinking in introduction to computer science for 7th graders. In *Proceedings of the 11th Workshop in Primary and Secondary Computing Education (WiPSCE 2016)* (pp. 80–83). New York: ACM Press.

Statter, D., & Armoni, M. (2017). Learning abstraction in computer science: A gender perspective. In *Proceedings of the 12th Workshop in Primary and Secondary Computing Education (WiPSCE 2017)* (pp. 5–14). New York: ACM Press.

Steiner, R. (1984). *Erziehungskunst. Seminarbesprechungen und Lehrplanvorträge.* Dornach, Germany: Rudolf Steiner Verlag. In German.

Sysło, M. M. (2014) The first 25 years of computers in education in Poland: 1965–1990. In A. Tatnall & B. Davey (Eds.), *Reflections on the History of Computers in Education. IFIP Advances in Information and Communication Technology*, Vol. 424 (pp. 266–290). Berlin, Germany: Springer.

Sysło, M. M., & Kwiatkowska, A. B. (2015). Introducing a new computer science curriculum for all school levels in Poland. In *Proceedings of the 8th International Conference on Informatics in Schools: Situation, Evolution, and Perspectives (ISSEP 2015), Lecture Notes in Computer Science 9378* (pp. 141–154). Berlin, Germany: Springer.

Tabet, N., Gedawy, H., Alshikhabobakr, H., & Razak, S. (2016). From Alice to Python. Introducing text-based programming in middle schools. In *Proceedings of the 2016 ACM Conference on Innovation and Technology in Computer Science Education (ITiCSE 2016)* (pp. 124–129). New York: ACM Press.

Taub, R., Armoni, M., & Ben-Ari, M. (2012). CS Unplugged and middle-school students' views, attitudes, and intentions regarding CS. *ACM Transactions on Computing Education (TOCE)*, 12(2), 8.1–8.29.

Tessler, J., Beth, B., & Lin, C. (2013). Using Cargo-Bot to provide contextualized learning of recursion. In *Proceedings of the International Computing Education Research Conference (ICER 2013)* (pp. 161–168). New York: ACM Press.

The Royal Society (2012). *Shut Down or Restart – The Way Forward for Computing in UK Schools*. Retrieved from https://royalsociety.org/~/media/education/computing-in-schools/2012-01-12-computing-in-schools.pdf

Thies, R., & Vahrenhold, J. (2013). On plugging "Unplugged" into CS classes. In *Proceedings of the 44th ACM Technical Symposium on Computer Science Education (SIGCSE 2013)* (pp. 365–370). New York: ACM Press.

Thies, R., & Vahrenhold, J. (2016). Back to school: Computer science unplugged in the wild. In *Proceedings of the 2016 ACM Conference on Innovation and Technology in Computer Science Education (ITiCSE 2016)* (pp. 118–123). New York: ACM Press.

Tsan, J., Boyer, K. E., & Lynch, C. F. (2016). How early does the CS gender gap emerge?: A study of collaborative problem solving in 5th grade computer science. In *Proceedings of the 47th ACM Technical Symposium on Computer Science Education (SIGCSE 2016)* (pp. 288–293). New York: ACM Press.

Tsan, J., Rodriguez, F. J., Boyer, K. E., & Lynch, C. (2018). "I think we should…": Analyzing elementary students' collaborative processes for giving and taking suggestions. In *Proceedings of the 49th ACM Technical Symposium on Computer Science Education (SIGCSE 2018)* (pp. 622–627). New York: ACM Press.

Vahrenhold, J. (2012). On the importance of being earnest: Challenges in computer science education. In *Proceedings of the 7th Workshop in Primary and Secondary Computing Education (WiPSCE 2012)* (pp. 3–4). New York: ACM Press.

Vahrenhold, J., Nardelli, E., Pereira, C., Berry, G., Caspersen, M. E., Gal-Ezer, J., Kölling, M., McGettrick, A., & Westermeier, M. (2017). *Informatics Education in Europe: Are We All in The Same Boat?* Association for Computing Machinery & Informatics Europe. Retrieved from http://dx.doi.org/10.1145/3106077

Vaníček, J. (2015). Programming in Scratch using inquiry-based approach. In *Proceedings of the 8th International Conference on Informatics in Schools: Situation, Evolution, and Perspectives (ISSEP 2015), Lecture Notes in Computer Science 9378* (pp. 82–93). Berlin, Germany: Springer.

Waite, J. (2017). *Pedagogy in Teaching Computer Science in Schools: A Literature Review*. London, UK: The Royal Society.

Webb, M., Davis, N., Bell, T., Katz, Y.J., Reynolds, N., Chambers, D. P., & Sysło, M. M. (2017). Computer science in K–12 school curricula of the 21st century: Why, what and when? *Education and Information Technologies*, 22(2), 445–468.

Weintrop, D., & Wilensky, U. (2018). Comparing block-based and text-based programming in high school computer science classrooms. *ACM Transactions on Computing Education (TOCE)*, 18(1), 3.1–3.20.

Werner, L., Campe, S., & Denner, J. (2012a). Children learning computer science concepts via Alice game-programming. In *Proceedings of the 43rd ACM Technical*

Symposium on Computer Science Education (SIGCSE 2012) (pp. 427–432). New York: ACM Press.

Werner, L., Denner, J., Campe, S., & Kawamoto, D. C. (2012b). The Fairy Performance Assessment: Measuring computational thinking in middle school. In *Proceedings of the 43rd ACM Technical Symposium on Computer Science Education (SIGCSE 2012)* (pp. 215–220). New York: ACM Press.

White House Office of the Press Secretary (2016). *FACT SHEET: President Obama Announces Computer Science For All Initiative.* Retrieved from https://obamawhitehouse.archives.gov/the-press-office/2016/01/30/fact-sheet-president-obama-announces-computer-science-all-initiative-0

Whitherspoon, E. B., Higashi, R. M., Schunn, C. D., Baehr, E. C., & Shoop, R. (2018). Developing computational thinking through a virtual robotics programming curriculum. *ACM Transactions on Computing Education (TOCE)*, 18(1), 4.1–4.20.

Wilson, C., Sudol, L.A., Stephenson, C., & Stehlik, M. (2010). *Running on Empty: The Failure to Teach K–12 Computer Science in the Digital Age.* New York: Association for Computing Machinery & Computer Science Teachers Association.

Wolz, U., Stone, M., Pearson, K., Pulimood, S. M., & Switzer, M. (2011). Computational thinking and expository writing in the middle school. *ACM Transactions on Computing Education (TOCE)*, 11(2), 9.1–9.22.

Wong-Villacres, M., Ehsan, U., Solomon, A., Pozo Buil, M., & DiSalvo, B. (2017). Design guidelines for parent-school technologies to support the ecology of parental engagement. In *Proceedings of the 2017 Conference on Interaction Design and Children* (pp. 73–83). New York: ACM Press.

Woszczynski, A. B. (2006). CyberTech I: Online introduction to computer science course for high school students. In *Proceedings of the 36th ACM Technical Symposium on Computer Science Education (SIGCSE 2006)* (pp. 153–157). New York: ACM Press.

Wood, Z. J., Muhl, P., & Hicks, K. (2016). Computational art: Introducing high school students to computing via art. In *Proceedings of the 47th ACM Technical Symposium on Computer Science Education (SIGCSE 2016)* (pp. 261–266). New York: ACM Press.

Wu, C.-C., Tseng, I.-C., & Huang, S.-L. (2008). Visualization of program behaviors: Physical robots versus robot simulators. In *Proceedings of the 3rd International Conference on Informatics in Schools: Situation, Evolution, and Perspectives (ISSEP 2008), Lecture Notes in Computer Science 5090* (pp. 53–62). Berlin, Germany: Springer.

Xu, D., Cadle, A., Thompson, D., Wolz, U., Greenberg, I., & Kumar, D. (2016). Creative computation in high school. In *Proceedings of the 47th ACM Technical Symposium on Computer Science Education (SIGCSE 2016)* (pp. 273–278). New York: ACM Press.

Zur-Bargury, I., Pârv, B., & Lanzberg, D. (2013). A nationwide exam as a tool for improving a new curriculum. In *Proceedings of the 18th ACM Conference on Innovation and Technology in Computer Science Education (ITiCSE '13)* (pp. 267–272). New York: ACM Press.

19 Computing for Other Disciplines

Mark Guzdial

19.1 Computing for the Rest of Us

When Seymour Papert started teaching computer programming to children in 1967, he was not trying to avert a programmer labor shortage. He was teaching programming because he thought it was a powerful tool to think with (Papert, 1980). If he expected any effect on future careers, he might have predicted that he would create more mathematicians (Papert, 1972).

When Kemeny and Kurtz invented Basic in 1964, they did it to give everyone access to the mainframe computers at Dartmouth (Kemeny & Kurtz, 1985). Kemeny and Kurtz were not concerned about producing software developers either. Since they were mathematicians, they would probably side more with Papert than with latter-day computing education efforts that emphasize the desperate need for more programmers in the labor force. Kemeny and Kurtz wanted to make computers accessible to non-professionals, for whatever purposes the students needed.

Until the efforts to grow computing education in K–12 schools in the last decade, most of computing education research has been undertaken with a focus on improving undergraduate computer science. Undergraduate degrees in computer science were created to prepare and certify software developers (Ensmenger, 2010). The economic impact of software is enormous in our world today, and providing programmers to fuel the software industry is critically important. Understanding how to prepare students to become effective software developers is a critical need. But there are other needs, and there are other purposes for programming.

Motivational Context: Most students will not pursue computing professional careers. They may care to learn computing for other purposes, such as end-user programming. Providing computing education for this cohort is a much larger task than training future software professionals.

This chapter connects current computing education research back to those original purposes for teaching programming: making programming accessible to those who will not become professional software developers. The chapter considers two central reasons for teaching programming to non-professionals that mirror the original purposes of Papert and Kemeny and Kurtz, respectively:

- *Programming as a tool to think with:* The original purpose for teaching programming to children was to help them in their learning, which is closer to computational thinking (Wing, 2006) than software engineering. Andrea diSessa coined the term "computational literacy" to represent the ability to describe and explore ideas in computational terms and thus use the computer as we might use text or numbers (diSessa, 2001) as a tool for aiding our thinking.

- *Programming as a tool for learning and doing*: Programming can be an important medium to support learning or to support the user's disciplinary tasks. Computational scientists and engineers use computing as a new methodology of science (Humphreys, 2004). But it's not just scientists and engineers who use computing. An estimate in 2005 suggested that for every professional software developer in the world, there were at least four and possibly as many as nine *end-user programmers* (Scaffidi et al., 2005). These are users who learn to program because they find programming useful for whatever tasks in which they are engaged. There is a benefit for everyone. Evidence suggests that those who learn to program earn higher wages than comparable workers who do not (Scaffidi, 2017).

The below sections consider these two reasons in three parts: learning programming as a medium to think with; learning programming to support learning (in non-computational domains); and learning programming to support doing. In this chapter, the term "computing" is used as a shorthand to represent *computational literacy* (diSessa, 2001; i.e., the use of computing as a medium to express ideas, to communicate these ideas to others, and to support reflection). We support reflection so that the computer can serve as a tool to think with (Resnick et al., 1998; i.e., as a canvas for the reflective practitioner [Schön, 1987]). Programming is the notation for this medium (Guzdial, 2015). To form and control this medium is what I mean by *programming*. When I use the term "computing" in a learning context, I imply the need to learn programming.

19.2 Learning Programming to Think with

Logo was a programming language explicitly designed for children (see Chapter 22 for more on the design of Logo). It was meant to be a piece of Papert's larger vision for a different kind of education for children (Papert, 1987). He wanted children to be producers of technology, creators of their own knowledge, and thinkers about their own thinking (Papert, 1980). While he wanted students to think like mathematicians (Papert, 1971), he had no particular goal of influencing their career choices.

Papert saw the computer as a unique device for allowing students to explore their own thinking. He theorized that students debugging their programs, as externalizations of their own understanding of how to perform a process, would be debugging their own thinking. Papert's vision for Logo crossed the curriculum, from the earliest work in linguistics, through mathematics, and into the sciences (Papert & Solomon, 1971).

Logo was a technological cog in Papert's vision for the educational machine. Logo was the medium in which students might explore microworlds and live in a MathLand (Papert, 1980). Roy Pea and his colleagues studied students using Logo and found that the student's study of programming did not have a significant effect on their thinking (Pea & Kurland, 1984; Pea et al., 1985; Pea, 1987). Papert critiqued Pea as being *technocentric* (Papert, 1987) because Pea was focusing on the technology rather than the overall goal of a constructionist classroom (Papert, 1991). Constructionism is Papert's approach to education based on his belief that learning (building knowledge structures) "happens especially felicitously in a context where the learner is consciously engaged in constructing a public entity, whether it's a sand castle on the beach or a theory of the universe" (Papert, 1991).

For the purpose of this chapter, we set aside the question of whether we want a constructionist classroom in Papert's vision. Instead, let's consider the design of a programming language whose purpose is to enable students to use programming as a tool to think with. Logo was designed to meet that goal, but in Pea's evaluation, it did not achieve it.

19.2.1 Designing Languages and Environments to Support Programming to Think with

Andrea diSessa designed *Boxer* to be a programming language to support computational literacy (diSessa, 2001; diSessa & Abelson, 1986). Most modern user interfaces are meant to be understood immediately with little instruction or documentation. The goal of Boxer was not to be usable immediately. diSessa believed that literacy requires effort. Boxer had Logo-like semantics, but used visual "boxes" to represent all data and procedures. A change to a variable resulted in a change to a visible (not invisible or abstract) box. diSessa aimed to tap into users' spatial schemata so that program behavior would be more concrete and learnable (diSessa, 1985).

Alan Kay and his group at the Xerox Palo Alto Research Center (PARC) had a similar goal. Kay envisioned a hardware and software device called a *Dynabook* (Kay, 1972) that would be a *meta-medium*. It would represent all other media and include interactivity in order to respond to the reader (Kay & Goldberg, 1977). Kay was inspired by Papert's vision, and like diSessa, aimed to change the user interface as well as create a new programming language, Smalltalk (Kay, 1993). Kay's goal was broader than computational literacy – he aimed to create a new medium in which humans could express ideas, communicate, and problem-solve. In order to achieve this goal, Kay and his group invented the *desktop user interface*, the so-called WIMP interface with overlapping Windows, Icons, Menus, and a mouse Pointer. The desktop user interface has become the dominant form of user interface today, created in order to realize the vision of computation as a tool to think with.

Natural languages are used by both children and adults for a wide variety of purposes. Programming languages might similarly be used to express ideas, explore them, and communicate about them by both adults and children. Modern programming languages designed for pedagogical use, like Scratch (Brennan et al., 2009; Maloney et al., 2008a; Resnick et al., 2009), are designed to support student production, but are rarely used by adults. Modern programming languages for general use, like JavaScript (Flanagan, 2006), are used by professionals in non-technical domains (e.g., Dorn & Guzdial, 2006), but are not designed to be easily learnable by children. We rarely see programming languages being designed for the lofty goal of serving as a medium for expression, communication, and reflection. It is still an open research question as to how to create programming languages and environments that serve as a medium across different ages and purposes.

19.2.2 Programming and Problem-Solving

There is little evidence that programming works as a tool for learning about problem-solving. In a meta-analysis across decades of research, Palumbo found no evidence that learning to program leads to improvements in problem-solving ability (Palumbo, 1990). Where Pea found no evidence in support of the conjecture for Logo, Palumbo found none across any programming languages in several studies.

While we have no evidence that programming *in itself* leads to cognitive or metacognitive benefits, we have ample evidence that programming can be used as a context for learning transferable cognitive and metacognitive skills. Sharon Carver, in her dissertation work, showed that she could teach general debugging skills by teaching students to program in Logo (Carver, 1986; Carver & Klahr, 1986; Klahr & Carver, 1988). Carver developed a model of the debugging skills she wanted students to learn. She then taught those skills using Logo. Later, students demonstrated those debugging skills when fixing flawed directions with the use of a map. Logo turns out to be a good activity for learning problem-solving skills when the goal is teaching problem-solving skills.

Why didn't Pea and Palumbo see those same cognitive benefits? Previous studies expected cognitive benefits from simply the act of programming. Carver was focused in her learning objectives and explicit in how programming could help achieve those objectives. Further, Carver taught only the parts of Logo that she needed to achieve her learning objectives. By limiting what she taught, she was more successful in achieving her goal of teaching some problem-solving skills. Previous studies of Logo aimed to teach programming generally, but that was too large of a learning objective – achieving literacy takes a lot of time and effort (Wolf, 2007). Students did not become as computationally literate as their teachers hoped (Noss & Hoyles, 1996). If students do not actually *learn* programming, it's not surprising if there are no later benefits from receiving instruction in programming (Kurland et al., 1986; Pea et al., 1985).

19.2.3 Computational Thinking

In her 2006 essay, Jeannette Wing described *computational thinking* as a way that programming might influence thinking completely apart from computers

(Wing, 2006). Wing believed that understanding computing would have a positive impact on problem-solving in everyday situations. If you understand prefetching and caching, Wing argued, this will influence how you pack your backpack each morning. If you understand performance modeling for multi-server systems, you can use that when choosing which line to stand in at the supermarket. We do know that people can solve surprisingly complex computational problems without learning about programming or receiving explicit instruction in computational thinking (Simon et al., 2006). Wing claimed that learning about computing will directly impact everyday problem-solving.

We have little evidence that anyone uses computing knowledge and problem-solving in everyday thinking. Wing may, as may other experts in computing, but it likely takes a high level of expertise to see any transfer. Transfer is notoriously difficult to achieve and is facilitated by expertise (Anderson et al., 1993; Olson et al., 1987; and see also Section 19.2.1). If you know a field very well, you are more likely to see ways that your field can be useful in other endeavors. Even then, our strongest theories explaining transfer say that it happens when people see two situations as being similar (Pirolli & Recker, 1994).

If we set aside the "everyday" part of Wing's argument, there is something important about her notion of computational thinking that is well-supported by the literature. Wing is right that computing is critical in many tasks. We know that there are many professionals who use programming in their tasks (*end-user programmers*), but who are not professional software developers (Scaffidi et al., 2005). More recent literature suggests that workers who program and use spreadsheets get a wage benefit over similar workers without those computational skills (Scaffidi, 2017). There is ample evidence that programming can be an important and useful activity for learning, as described in more detail in the next section. We have little evidence that learning computing in itself leads to a different way of thinking about problem-solving in our everyday lives, but significant evidence that learning computing leads to skills in computational problem-solving, and these can be used every day for many people.

Papert's vision is echoed in Wing's calls for computational thinking (Wing, 2006, 2010). With research evidence, we can refine that vision to be about supporting people to use computing in their everyday problem-solving. What does a computational environment look like for everyday problem-solving? diSessa and Kay informed our understanding of how we might design computing environments in order to be useful as a tool for thinking with computing, Palumbo showed us that cognitive benefits do not appear simply from the activity of programming, and Carver showed us that we can design education for more general, transferable cognitive benefits with programming as the medium.

19.3 Learning Programming as a Tool for Learning

While programming does not automatically convey benefits for learning in other disciplines and contexts, we can design effective educational experiences that include programming that lead to learning in non-computing subjects. The goal of the studies described in this section is for students to learn some other discipline through the use of programming. Here, we use programming as a *medium*, rather than as *a learning objective*. The other disciplines are not depicted as a kind of computation. Rather, computing serves as a cognitive tool and an affordance for learning the non-computing domain (Taylor, 1980).

Several of the early computing education efforts were aimed at non-computing students. Marc Eisenstadt's SOLO was a tool for psychology students (Eisenstadt, 1979). Alan Perlis described students learning programming at Carnegie Tech for efforts like building economic simulations (Perlis, 1962). Kemeny and Kurtz developed Basic for the whole campus at Darmouth (Kemeny & Kurtz, 1980). But studies of how much students learned about the non-computing domain did not appear until later.

19.3.1 Students Building Software to Teach

Idit Harel's Instructional Design Software Project had fourth graders learn about mathematics and computation by asking them to design software to teach fractions to third graders (Harel & Papert, 1990). By asking the fourth graders to design instructional software, Harel explicitly engaged students in thinking about another discipline (mathematics, or more specifically, fractions) in terms of computational representations. By asking them to design for third graders, she created social pressure for the fourth graders to engage with the subject matter and the medium. The end result was remarkable, with the fourth graders learning significantly more than a comparison group about both mathematics and programming. Harel found that students integrated their understanding of mathematics into their daily lives, with students reporting that they saw fractions in such everyday objects as traffic lights.

Yasmin Kafai continued Harel's work and explored different possibilities in Harel's scenario. For example, Kafai considered asking students to explicitly design instructional video games (rather than any instructional software) to encourage students to explore with more sophisticated programming and different representations for the domain to be taught (Kafai, 1995, 1998). She explored different models for social engagement, such as asking last year's fourth graders to serve as consultants to the new class of fourth graders building for the third graders (Kafai & Ching, 2001). Kafai found that these richer collaborative structures led to more student discussion about the domain (science, in this study), which led to more reflection and more learning. Kafai, in her later work, explored different computational media, including Scratch (Maloney et al., 2008b) and wearable crafts (Kafai et al., 2014; Searle & Kafai, 2015; Vasudevan et al., 2015).

19.3.2 Representing Physics in Code

Harel and Kafai showed us that coding could be a powerful and rich medium for expressing and learning about ideas in mathematics and science. But why should it work? What's special about reading and writing program code? Bruce Sherin explored that question when he contrasted learning physics with equations versus executable code (in Boxer).

Sherin taught two groups of physics students kinematics. One group of students learned using equations like $x = x_0 + vt + 1/2at^2$. The other group of students learned to compute the velocity and position of a falling object by using a loop for time. Each time through the loop, the object would move based on the velocity, and then the velocity would be changed by the acceleration.

Sherin interviewed the students to learn what they understood about physics (Sherin, 2001). He found that the students using equations were able to solve a wide variety of problems, because the equations described *balance*. Equation-using students could compute x or t if all other variables were given. The code-using students, on the other hand, had a richer sense of temporality and causality. They understood how acceleration influenced velocity, which is not evident in the equation form. The opposite was not true. Students using equations rarely developed a temporal and causal model, and students using program code could not explore balance in the same way as those using equations.

Guzdial replicated Sherin's interviews with similar code, but in a different computational medium. Guzdial had students work in Apple's HyperCard using the HyperTalk programming language. HyperTalk was explicitly designed to draw on computing education research and be accessible for novices and even children (Katz & Porter, 1991; Smith et al., 1996). Guzdial created an environment, Emile, that scaffolded students using HyperTalk in order to create physics simulations like those that Sherin was using in Boxer. Guzdial similarly found that students would mentally simulate the timing loops in order to answer physics questions, rather than manipulate equations (Guzdial, 1995).

19.3.3 Today's Use of Computing in Mathematics and Science Classes

Today, computing appears as a cognitive tool most often in science and mathematics courses. It is still relatively uncommon, as few science and mathematics secondary school teachers are prepared to integrate computing into their practice. Our best research evidence for the value of computing as a tool for learning another domain appears in science and mathematics courses.

The Bootstrap project started from a critical insight – while learning computing is important, learning algebra is a critical step toward post-secondary education (Felleisen & Krishnamurthi, 2009). Bootstrap:Algebra uses the Racket programming language to motivate students to learn algebra. Racket is a descendant of Scheme with similar syntax and semantics, which is an algebraic substitution model. Bootstrap facilitates the learning of algebra by providing an evaluation engine for algebraic statements and a motivating context – students build video games using Racket and algebra. The results are striking, with Bootstrap-using students improving significantly in their algebra skills compared to other students (Schanzer et al., 2015). The effect was significant for both scaffolded and unscaffolded word problems in a larger-scale study (Schanzer et al., 2018).

Uri Wilensky and his colleagues have been developing a series of activities to support science teachers in achieving science learning objectives through programming (Wilensky et al., 2014). Most of Wilensky's projects use NetLogo, a descendant of Papert's Logo designed to support agent-based modeling (Wilensky & Rand, 2015). One can think about agent-based modeling as having thousands of Logo-style turtles, each of which can represent an agent in the world, such as ant, termite, or car (Resnick, 1994). This style of programming is particularly appropriate for representing objects in simulations of natural objects. Since science itself is increasingly relying on computational tools, agent-based modeling in science classes is *authentic* (Shaffer & Resnick, 1999) in the sense that students are engaging in science through computing in the same way as modern scientists (Weintrop et al., 2016).

In a series of studies, Wilensky and his colleagues are identifying how programming as a medium for learning science leads to new kinds of understanding of science. Students modeling individual atoms as agents develop a better understanding of underlying principles and behaviors in how materials behave at the macroscopic level (Blikstein & Wilensky, 2009). A common theme in these studies is that working with agent-based simulations leads students to abstract their understanding differently (Wilkerson-Jerde et al., 2015). Students before learning about programming have a tendency to see programs and simulations as event-based – one thing happens that triggers another thing (Pane et al., 2001). Students using agent-based models to understand science move from thinking about events to identifying general rules and patterns (Guo et al., 2016). Science is about developing a generalized understanding of our world, and programming as a tool based in abstraction may play a role in helping students to develop that more generalized understanding.

Given the benefits of teaching mathematics and science with programming as a medium described in this section, we might wonder why all mathematics and science teachers are not adopting this approach. In part, it's because programming does not necessarily lead to *better* learning than traditional methods, but it is certainly *different* learning. As Sherin pointed out, equations have some real representational benefits over code, such as representing balance. Code has different representational benefits. The code examples that Sherin and Guzdial explored were more causal and temporal and led to a different kind of abstraction. When the mapping works well (as in the mapping from Racket to algebra), code can provide significant motivational benefits, because it can be executed, understood in the domain (algebra terms), and create effects in the world, like video games.

The bigger challenge is dealing with the realities of science and mathematics classrooms. Teachers in science and mathematics are not usually taught to teach with programming. Their learning objectives are rarely described in terms of code. Efforts to teach programming emphasize "real" computer science, which contrasts with the goals of science and mathematics teachers. Without a background in programming and without standards asking for the benefits of code, few teachers might be expected to develop the use of programming in their classes. Programming remains a special subject, locked away in computer science class and even physically in the computer lab. Papert called this part of a "school's defense mechanisms" in his essay, "Why school reform is impossible" (Papert, 1997). He argued that schools, when faced with reform that might change their practices, will instead find a way to change the reform. While "impossible" is too strong, the "defense mechanisms" do make integration of programming into other subjects challenging.

19.4 Learning Programming As a Tool for Doing

Most people who use programming are neither preparing to be software professionals nor are planning to use programming to learn something else. By our best estimates, the majority of people who program are trying to solve problems in their daily tasks (Scaffidi et al., 2005). These problems might include processing data (e.g., computational scientists), building models and running simulations (e.g., computational engineers), batch processing pictures (e.g., graphic designers and web developers), or teaching computing (e.g., secondary school teachers). These kinds of programmers are called *end-user programmers*, and they have different development needs than professional developers (Ko et al., 2011).

Implications for Practice: This section asks the questions of how we design educational tools and experiences to meet the needs of students who will be using programming as a tool within their own discipline.

19.4.1 Design Requirements for Programming As a Tool

Most programming languages are designed to serve professional programmers. Languages may be designed for new features (like object orientation) with backwards compatibility (like C++ or Java). Languages may be designed to facilitate collaboration in a team or may be designed to guarantee type safety.

Programming languages for end users might have a different set of requirements. There are likely overlapping requirements between professional programmers and end-user programmers. For example, end users want their programs to be correct and without errors, too (Antoniu et al., 2004). However, end users are typically less willing to invest time and effort in the programming itself. The software is not their end goal.

There are programming languages that have been developed explicitly for end-user programmers. R for statisticians and MATLAB for engineers are two examples of languages that have been developed for and by end-user programmers explicitly for their communities of practice. These languages have not necessarily been designed to be easy to learn, or even easy to use. They have been designed to solve problems for those practitioners. LabView has a graphical language that has been used for many years by engineers, but empirical studies have shown that text-based languages are easier to understand and to use when debugging than LabView's language (Green & Petre, 1992; Green, Petre, & Bellamy, 1991). We need to learn how to design programming languages that meet the needs of end users and will be accepted by end users, even if the languages are designed by researchers in computing education, programming languages, or learning sciences.

One goal for an end-user programming language is for it to be "natural" (i.e., to build on metaphors and ways of thinking that are already comfortable to the end users; Myers et al., 2004). A series of experiments over several decades has tried to define what is most natural for end-user programmers. Early research asked office workers to write procedures for manipulating files and records as if to be executed by another human (Miller, 1974, 1981). These procedures were then studied as a form of human specification of programs. Later researchers showed undergraduates and young children recordings of video games and asked the participants how they thought programmers specified those programs (Pane et al., 2001).

The results of these studies define languages that are radically different from the ones we use today. Participants rarely used an **else** on a conditional. Object-oriented classes never appeared. Participants often described computational activity as being triggered by events. One surprise was that participants in these studies rarely specified end conditions for loops. Miller wondered if other humans could infer the end condition without specification. He tested whether humans would really know when to stop when given a procedure without loop end conditions, and the readers of condition-less loops executed those procedures flawlessly (Miller, 1981). Pane created a programming language, HANDS, that was inspired by these results and allowed students to specify programs using more natural constructs (Pane et al., 2001).

Designers and researchers have often explored the possibility of using graphical notations instead of textual languages to ease the use of programming. Petre and Green compared visual to textual notations for programming and did not find evidence that visual languages had benefits over textual languages (Green & Petre, 1992, 1996; Green et al., 1991). Their participants were faster and more accurate in using text-based languages than blocks-based languages. However, they noted that the advantages of textual languages may be cultural and not natural. In modern society, we tend to have much more experience with textual notations (i.e., using letters and numbers) than graphical notations (e.g., circles, arcs, boxes, and arrows).

Hundhausen reinvigorated the debate about visual and textual languages when he showed benefits of direct manipulation (e.g., drag and drop) graphical programming languages over traditional text languages (Hundhausen et al., 2006). He and his colleagues showed that the average students learning direct manipulation languages became productive more quickly than those using textual languages and transferred their knowledge to textual programming later. Hundhausen's studies did not explicitly include participants with visual disabilities or challenges using mice, which limit the use of graphical notations (Koushik & Lewis, 2016).

A series of graphical languages have since been produced, and several are widely used around the world (Fincher et al., 2010), with Scratch the most popular of these with over 25 million users (Maloney et al., 2010; Resnick et al., 2009). The current generation of graphical programming languages (like Scratch, Snap!, and Blockly) are typically called *blocks-based languages* because students drag and drop (direct manipulation) graphical blocks, which are constructed to write programs (Weintrop & Wilensky, 2015a, 2015b). Syntactic errors are impossible with blocks-based languages.

The success of blocks-based languages does not necessarily challenge Petre and Green's results. Like in Hundhausen's findings, research into blocks-based languages has shown that students are able to create programs more quickly using these languages than with text-based languages (Weintrop & Wilensky, 2017) and with fewer errors (Weintrop & Wilensky, 2017). However, students using text-based languages recognize the authenticity of what they are doing, seeing that it's more like what professional programmers do (Weintrop & Wilensky, 2017). Students transfer their knowledge from blocks-based programming to text-based programming, and most students move to text-based languages before they try building large or complicated programs. It's not clear whether students can debug blocks-based programs faster or more accurately than text-based programs.

19.4.2 Teaching End-User Programmers

Undergraduate computer science (CS) courses were set up to train future software developers (Ensmenger, 2010). Students who are aiming for other careers are often dissatisfied by the courses set up for CS majors, and this can lead to poor course results (e.g., lower retention and success rates; Forte & Guzdial, 2005; Guzdial, 2009; Rich et al., 2004). End-user programmers often discover an interest in learning to program when they are working professionals, beyond formal education. While it may be hard to teach non-CS undergraduates about the computing that they will need, they are at least on campus and in classrooms. It is harder to serve the educational needs of working professionals.

Greg Wilson has been developing courses explicitly to serve the needs of scientists and engineers who want to use computation in their work (Wilson, 2016). The challenge for him is to rethink the introductory course curriculum. Much of his focus is on tools, not concepts. He is less worried about students understanding hash functions and recursion and more worried about making sure that they can use version control systems and can generate the graphics that they need. His focus is explicitly on the needs of the learners as they determine them – as adults, they control their learning objectives.

Brian Dorn studied graphic designers who programmed (Dorn & Guzdial, 2006). They would write scripts to control tools like Adobe Photoshop or GIMP (e.g., to batch process images). Some would learn programming in order to do graphical design work for the web. Dorn surveyed graphic designer end-user programmers and found that they did not consider themselves to be programmers, even though they wrote some significant programs. All of his participants had written programs of over 100 lines (Dorn & Guzdial, 2010). In fact, they had decidedly negative views of programmers as "boring" and "nerdy." Further, the majority of his participants had art degrees and had no formal education in computing. Teaching them the programming they needed would be challenging, since they were unlikely to take classes or read books whose goals were to teach programming.

He developed a technique for teaching them computing based on examples (Dorn, 2011, 2012). The graphic designer end-user programmers relied on repositories of examples to serve as starting points for their work. Dorn discovered that his graphic designers needed to learn computer science terms, like Boolean variables and exception handling, in order to do the web searches they needed to solve their problems. Dorn inserted these terms into the examples through comments and in narrative explanations of how the programs were written. His results suggest that his designers learned, they found the examples useful, and nobody had to read a book for programmers.

19.4.3 Teaching the Teachers

Secondary school teachers meet the definition of people who learn to program but not to develop software. Teachers learn computing in order to teach computing. Like graphic designers, they may not have any background in computing and may not want to refer to themselves as "programmers."

Preparing enough CS teachers to meet growing needs is a worldwide problem (Diethelm et al., 2012; Ericson et al., 2005, 2007; Hubwieser, 2012; Pasternak & Vahrenhold, 2010; Whitehead et al., 2011). Most of the research into preparing CS teachers focuses on the programs that are being created. There are relatively few studies of how the teachers develop expertise (or do not succeed at developing expertise) in teaching CS over time.

Lijun Ni's dissertation tracked teachers over the course of a year, starting at their first attendance at a professional learning opportunity (Ni, 2009, 2011; Ni & Guzdial, 2011). Ni asked if the teachers developed a sense of identity as computing teachers – did they call themselves "CS teachers?" She found that the factors that influenced the development of identity as a CS teacher rarely had much to do with the learning experiences, materials, curricula, or programming languages. Instead, the issues were mostly social. Did the teachers feel welcomed as CS teachers? Did they have a sense of a community of peers and colleagues who could help them if they needed it? Did they find role models that could give them a goal for what they hoped to become? Examples and repositories were not key to the success of Ni's teachers. They needed a sense of belonging and community.

19.4.4 Teaching for a Future Need

Teaching CS at the undergraduate level but to non-computing majors is challenging. At Georgia Tech, all undergraduate students are required to take a course in CS as part of their general education requirements. Other than the CS majors, the undergraduates are not learning CS in order to become software developers. Many of them (like Dorn's graphic designers) dislike the idea of learning programming (Hewner & Guzdial, 2008). They are not learning CS in order to learn problem-solving skills or to learn in their own major. They are learning CS because their faculty believe it's an important part of being well-educated and that they may need computing one day. Thus, it's an example of learning computing for doing, but before the students have any "doing" to do. During the first four years of the requirement to take a programming course, Georgia Tech students in the liberal arts, architecture, and management programs were failing or withdrawing from the course at a rate of around 50 percent each semester (Guzdial, 2013).

The Media Computation curriculum was developed as an approach to teach programming to liberal arts, architecture, design, business, and management students (Guzdial, 2003; Guzdial & Forte, 2005; Rich et al., 2004). The course is aimed at students for whom computing is more about communication than calculation (Forte & Guzdial, 2004). Students manipulate digital media using Python at the level of pixels, samples, and frames in order to create effects in images, sounds, and videos. Media Computation has a goal of explaining digital media to students who will likely be working with digital media in their careers.

The design of Media Computation meets the challenge of teaching a skill to students who do not yet have a need for that skill. Informed by situated learning (Lave & Wenger, 1991), the goal is create a sense of a community of practice when there is no real community of practice outside the classroom (Guzdial & Tew, 2006). The course succeeds through the creation of a sense of community, hiring alumni of the course as teaching assistants, and generating excitement about the artifacts created in the course.

The measure of success for Media Computation was improvement in retention rates. After the Media Computation course started, the success rate rose to over 85 percent (from 50 percent previously) and has remained there for over a decade (Guzdial, 2013). Media Computation has been part of similar improvements in success rates at other institutions, such as the University of Illinois, Chicago (Sloan & Troy, 2008) and the University of California, San Diego (Simon et al., 2010). The approach has been used by others to develop non-majors classes in other languages (Lee, 2013).

19.5 Open Research Questions on Computing Education for Other Disciplines

The premise for this chapter is that there is value in learning programming other than for professional software development. Explicitly, there is value in programming as a medium for communicating, sharing, and exploring ideas, there is value in programming as a tool for learning, and there is value in using programming to achieve tasks other than professional software development.

Programming for all of these purposes is more like textual literacy than a vocational skill.

Maryanne Wolf's book *Proust and the Squid: The Story and Science of the Reading Brain* (Wolf, 2007) describes the history of how we developed a textually literate society. Egyptians had hieroglyphics, but they did not develop a literate culture because hieroglyphics were too hard to learn. Literate culture depends on many members of the culture being able to read and write. The Ugaritic and Phoenician writing systems led to literate cultures as the direct antecedents of the Greek system. There were several important inventions in these script systems, not the least of which was listing the letters of the script in a fixed order. There is no reason that "A" must precede "B," which precedes "C," and so on. But putting them in a fixed order makes it easier to memorize and learn the letters. The development of mechanisms for *teaching* literacy were critical in the development of a literate culture.

The implication of the analogy is that computing education will likely play an important role in the development of computational literacy. We may not yet have a programming language that can be easily learned and serve as a medium across domains and ages. An important characteristic of a highly learnable programming language is that computing educators will be able to teach it.

19.5.1 Programming for Thinking

Our best evidence suggests that learning programming does not lead to improved generalized problem-solving skills. However, that evidence also suggests that students in these studies did not learn much programming. If students developed significant expertise in programming, would we see some benefits in problem-solving skills? It's unlikely, based on our experience with mathematics and transfer (Sweller et al., 2010), but it is still an open question.

We do have evidence that we can use programming to teach specific problem-solving skills, as seen in Carver's work with debugging. What other problem-solving skills can we teach with programming? Are they transferable to many domains, and is it worth the effort to develop them?

19.5.2 Programming for Learning

We have evidence that programming can be a useful domain for learning in science and mathematics. In what other domains might programming serve as a useful tool?

A critical question is whether there is synergy between learning to program and learning other domains. If learning domain X (e.g., algebra, geometry, physics) takes time T1 and learning to program enough to benefit X takes time T2, does using programming to learn X take time T1 + T2? Is there a synergy to be gained such that it takes less time than the sum? Or is the programming needed in other domains roughly the same, so that the T2 time cost is borne once, but then students can use programming in all domains X?

If students are to learn programming to help with learning, when should that learning take place? One argument is to teach programming as early as possible, so that it can be used to learn in many domains. However, we do not yet know how to teach programming to all children, we do not yet know in what domains programming facilitates programming, and we do not yet know if the programming learned for algebra transfers to physics (as one example). Until we answer these questions, it's an expensive gamble to teach programming to all students.

19.5.3 Programming for Doing

Rather than teach programming as early as possible, another argument is to wait until students are learning or doing in a domain where programming is useful. Then there's a purpose for learning programming, which can be motivating. It might, however, also be expensive in terms of how much time it takes. How much time T2 is needed to learn programming? Should it be borne all at once (e.g., in algebra class) or is it better to space out the learning of programming over many years?

Finally, there is value in learning a programming language that many others know. We have seen in the experiences with teachers that community is critical, and it is also important to provide the repositories that graphic designers draw upon for learning. How important is a critical mass? What size is the critical mass? Is it small enough that each domain might have its own unique domain-specific programming language? That might be expensive in terms of learning costs if students were to work in several domains and so would need to learn several domain-specific languages. Can we develop programming languages that are easy to learn and effective in multiple domains? That would be a wonderful tool, and computing education researchers will likely play a critical role in developing such a language.

References

Anderson, J. R., Conrad, F., Corbett, A. T., Fincham, J. M., Hoffman, D., & Wu, Q. (1993). Computer programming and transfer. In J. R. Anderson (Ed.), *Rules of the Mind* (pp. 205–234). Hillsdale, NJ: Lawrence Erlbaum Associates.

Antoniu, T., Steckler, P. A., Krishnamurthi, S., Neuwirth, E., & Felleisen, M. (2004). Validating the unit correctness of spreadsheet programs. In *Proceedings of the 26th International Conference on Software Engineering* (pp. 439–448). Hoboken, NJ: IEEE Computer Society.

Blikstein, P., & Wilensky, U. (2009). An atom is known by the company it keeps: A constructionist learning environment for materials science using agent-based modeling. *International Journal of Computers for Mathematical Learning*, 14, 81–119.

Brennan, K., Hernández, A. M., & Resnick, M. (2009). Scratch: Creating and sharing interactive media. In *CSCL'09: Proceedings of the 9th International Conference on Computer Supported Collaborative Learning* (p. 217). Boulder, CO: International Society of the Learning Sciences.

Carver, S. M. (1986). *Transfer of LOGO Debugging Skill: Analysis, Instruction, and Assessment* (PhD thesis). Carnegie Mellon University.

Carver, S. M., & Klahr, D. (1986). Assessing children's LOGO debugging skills with a formal model. *Journal of Educational Computing Research*, 2, 487–525.

Diethelm, I., Hubwieser, P., & Klaus, R. (2012). Students, teachers and phenomena: educational reconstruction for computer science education. In *Proceedings of the 12th Koli Calling International Conference on Computing Education Research* (pp. 164–173). New York: ACM.

Disessa, A. (2001). *Changing Minds*. Cambridge, MA: MIT Press.

Disessa, A. A. (1985). A principled design for an integrated computational environment. *Human–Computer Interaction*, 1, 1–47.

Disessa, A. A., & Abelson, H. (1986). Boxer: A reconstructible computational medium. *Communications of the ACM*, 29, 859–868.

Dorn, B. (2011). ScriptABLE: Supporting informal learning with cases. In *ICER '11: Proceedings of the Seventh International Workshop on Computing Education Research* (pp. 69–76). New York: ACM.

Dorn, B., & Guzdial, M. (2006). Graphic designers who program as informal computer science learners. In *ICER '06: Proceedings of the Second International Workshop on Computing Education Research* (pp. 127–134). New York: ACM.

Dorn, B., & Guzdial, M. (2010). Discovering computing: Perspectives of web designers. In *ICER '10: Proceedings of the Sixth International Workshop on Computing Education Research* (pp. 23–30). New York: ACM.

Dorn, B. J. (2012). *A Case-based Approach for Supporting the Informal Computing Education of End-user Programmers* (PhD thesis). College of Computing, Georgia Institute of Technology.

Eisenstadt, M. (1979). A friendly software environment for psychology students. *Communications of the ACM*, 26, 1058–1064.

Ensmenger, N. L. (2010). *The Computer Boys Take Over: Computers, Programmers, and the Politics of Technical Expertise*. Cambridge, MA: MIT Press.

Ericson, B., Guzdial, M., & Biggers, M. (2005). A model for improving secondary CS education. In *SIGCSE '05: Proceedings of the 36th SIGCSE Technical Symposium on Computer Science Education* (pp. 332–336). New York: ACM.

Ericson, B., Guzdial, M., & Biggers, M. (2007). Improving secondary CS education: Progress and problems. *SIGCSE Bulletin*, 39, 298–301.

Felleisen, M., & Krishnamurthi, S. (2009). Viewpoint: Why computer science doesn't matter. *Communications of the ACM*, 52, 37–40.

Fincher, S., Cooper, S., Kölling, M., & Maloney, J. (2010). Comparing Alice, Greenfoot, & Scratch. In *SIGCSE '10: Proceedings of the 41st ACM Technical Symposium on Computer Science Education* (pp. 192–193). New York: ACM.

Flanagan, D. (2006). *JavaScript: The Definitive Guide*. Newton, MA: O'Reilly Media, Inc.

Forte, A., & Guzdial, M. (2004). Computers for communication, not calculation: Media as a motivation and context for learning. In *Proceedings of the Proceedings of the 37th Annual Hawaii International Conference on System Sciences (HICSS'04) – Track 4 – Volume 4* (p. 10) Hoboken, NJ: IEEE Computer Society.

Forte, A., & Guzdial, M. (2005). Motivation and non-majors in computer science: Identifying discrete audiences for introductory courses. *IEEE Transactions on Education*, 48, 248–253.

Green, T. R. G., & Petre, M. 1992. When visual programs are harder to read than textual programs. In G. C. V. D. Veer, M. J. Tauber, S. Bagnarola, & M. Antavolits (Eds.), *Human–Computer Interaction: Tasks and Organisation, Proceedings EECE-6 (6th European Conference on Cognitive Ergonomics)* (pp. 167–180) Rome, Italy: CUD.

Green, T. R. G., & Petre, M. (1996). Usability analysis of visual programming environments: A "cognitive dimensions" framework. *Journal of Visual Languages and Computing*, 7, 131–174.

Green, T. R. G., Petre, M., & Bellamy, R. K. E. 1991. Comprehensibility of visual and textual programs: A test of "superlativism" against the "match–mismatch" conjecture. In J. Koenemann-Belliveau, T. Moher, & S. Robertson (Eds.), *Empirical Studies of Programmers: Fourth Workshop* (pp. 121–146). Norwood, NJ: Ablex.

Guo, Y., Wagh, A., Brady, C., Levy, S. T., Horn, M. S., & Wilensky, U. (2016). Frogs to think with: Improving students' computational thinking and understanding of evolution in a code-first learning environment. In *Proceedings of the 15th International Conference on Interaction Design and Children* (pp. 246–254). New York: ACM.

Guzdial, M. (1995). Software-realized scaffolding to facilitate programming for science learning. *Interactive Learning Environments*, 4, 1–44.

Guzdial, M. (2003). A media computation course for non-majors. *SIGCSE Bulletin*, 35, 104–108.

Guzdial, M. (2009). Education: Teaching computing to everyone. *Communications of the ACM*, 52, 31–33.

Guzdial, M. (2013). Exploring hypotheses about media computation. In *Proceedings of the Ninth Annual International ACM Conference on International Computing Education Research* (pp. 19–26). New York: ACM.

Guzdial, M. (2015). *Learner-Centered Design of Computing Education: Research on Computing for Everyone*. San Rafael, CA: Morgan & Claypool Publishers.

Guzdial, M., & Forte, A. (2005). Design process for a non-majors computing course. *SIGCSE Bulletin*, 37, 361–365.

Guzdial, M., & Tew, A. E. (2006). Imagineering inauthentic legitimate peripheral participation: An instructional design approach for motivating computing education. In *Proceedings of the Second International Workshop on Computing Education Research* (pp. 51–58). New York: ACM.

Harel, I., & Papert, S. (1990). Software design as a learning environment. *Interactive Learning Environments*, 1, 1–32.

Hewner, M., & Guzdial, M. (2008). Attitudes about computing in postsecondary graduates. In *ICER '08: Proceeding of the Fourth International Workshop on Computing Education Research* (pp. 71–78). New York: ACM.

Hubwieser, P. (2012). Computer science education in secondary schools – The introduction of a new compulsory subject. *Transactions on Computing Education*, 12, 16:1–16:41.

Humphreys, P. (2004). *Extending Ourselves: Computational Science, Empiricism, and Scientific Method*. Oxford, UK: Oxford University Press.

Hundhausen, C. D., Farley, S., & Brown, J. L. (2006). Can direct manipulation lower the barriers to programming and promote positive transfer to textual programming? An experimental study. In *Visual Languages and Human-Centric Computing, 2006. VL/HCC 2006* (pp. 157–164). Hoboken, NJ: IEEE.

Kafai, Y. B. (1995). *Minds in Play: Computer Game Design As a Context for Children's Learning*. Abingdon, UK: Routledge.

Kafai, Y. B. (1998). Video game designs by girls and boys: Variability and consistency of gender differences. In *From Barbie to Mortal Kombat: Gender and Computer Games* (pp. 90–114). Cambridge, MA: MIT Press.

Kafai, Y. B., & Ching, C. C. (2001). Affordances of collaborative software design planning for elementary students' science talk. *Journal of the Learning Sciences*, 10, 321–363.

Kafai, Y. B., Lee, E., Searle, K., Fields, D., Kaplan, E., & Lui, D. (2014). A crafts-oriented approach to computing in high school: Introducing computational concepts, practices, and perspectives with electronic textiles. *Transactions on Computing Education*, 14, 1–20.

Katz, E. E., & Porter, H. S. (1991). HyperTalk as an overture to CS1. *SIGCSE Bulletin*, 23, 48–54.

Kay, A., & Goldberg, A. (1977). Personal dynamic media. *Computer*, 10(3), 31–41.

Kay, A. C. (1972). A personal computer for children of all ages. In *Proceedings of the ACM Annual Conference – Volume 1*. New York: ACM.

Kay, A. C. (1993). The early history of Smalltalk. In *The Second ACM SIGPLAN Conference on History of Programming Languages* (pp. 69–95). New York: ACM.

Kemeny, J. G., & Kurtz, T. E. (1980). *Basic Programming*. Hoboken, NJ: John Wiley & Sons, Inc.

Kemeny, J. G., & Kurtz, T. E. (1985). *Back to Basic: The History, Corruption, and Future of the Language*. Boston, MA: Addison-Wesley Longman Publishing Co., Inc.

Klahr, D., & Carver, S. M. (1988). Cognitive objectives in a LOGO debugging curriculum: Instruction, learning, and transfer. *Cognitive Psychology*, 20, 362–404.

Ko, A. J., Abraham, R., Beckwith, L., Blackwell, A., Burnett, M., Erwig, M., Scaffidi, C., Lawrance, J., Lieberman, H., & Myers, B. (2011). The state of the art in end-user software engineering. *ACM Computing Surveys (CSUR)*, 43(3), 21.

Koushik, V., & Lewis, C. (2016). An accessible blocks language: Work in progress. In *Proceedings of the 18th International ACM SIGACCESS Conference on Computers and Accessibility* (pp. 317–318). New York: ACM.

Kurland, D. M., Pea, R. D., Clement, C., & Mawby, R. (1986). A study of the development of programming ability and thinking skills in high school students. *Journal of Educational Computing Research*, 2, 429–458.

Lave, J., & Wenger, E. (1991). *Situated Learning: Legitimate Peripheral Participation*. New York: Cambridge University Press.

Lee, C. B. (2013). Experience report: CS1 in MATLAB for non-majors, with media computation and peer instruction. In *Proceeding of the 44th ACM Technical Symposium on Computer Science Education* (pp. 35–40). New York: ACM.

Maloney, J. H., Peppler, K., Kafai, Y., Resnick, M., & Rusk, N. (2008a). Programming by choice: Urban youth learning programming with Scratch. In *SIGCSE '08: Proceedings of the 39th SIGCSE Technical Symposium on Computer Science Education* (pp. 367–371). New York: ACM.

Maloney, J., Resnick, M., Rusk, N., Peppler, K. A., & Kafai, Y. B. (2008b). Media designs with Scratch: What urban youth can learn about programming in a computer clubhouse. In *ICLS'08: Proceedings of the 8th International Conference for the Learning Sciences* (pp. 81–82). Utrecht, The Netherlands: International Society of the Learning Sciences.

Maloney, J., Resnick, M., Rusk, N., Silverman, B., & Eastmond, E. (2010). The Scratch programming language and environment. *Transactions on Computing Education*, 10, 16:1–16:15.

Miller, L. A. (1974). Programming by non-programmers. *International Journal of Man–Machine Studies*, 6, 237–260.

Miller, L. A. (1981). Natural language programming: Styles, strategies, and contrasts. *IBM Systems Journal*, 29, 184–215.

Myers, B. A., Pane, J. F., & Ko, A. (2004). Natural programming languages and environments. *Communications of the ACM*, 47, 47–52.

Ni, L. (2009). What makes CS teachers change?: Factors influencing CS teachers' adoption of curriculum innovations. In *SIGCSE '09: Proceedings of the 40th ACM Technical Symposium on Computer Science Education* (pp. 544–548). New York: ACM.

Ni, L. (2011). *Building Professional Identity as Computer Science Teachers: Supporting High School Computer Science Teachers Through Reflection and Community Building* (PhD thesis). Georgia Institute of Technology.

Ni, L., & Guzdial, M. (2011). Prepare and support computer science (CS) teachers: Understanding CS teachers' professional identity. In *American Educational Research Association (AERA) Annual Meeting*. New Orleans, LA: AERA.

Noss, R., & Hoyles, C. (1996). *Windows on Mathematical Meanings: Learning Cultures and Computers*. Rotterdam, The Netherlands: Springer Science & Business Media.

Olson, G. M., Catrambone, R., & Soloway, E. (1987). Programming and algebra word problems: a failure to transfer. In *Empirical Studies of Programmers Workshop* (pp. 1–13). Norwood, NJ: Ablex Publishing Corp.

Palumbo, D. J. (1990). Programming language/problem-solving research: A review of relevant issues. *Review of Educational Research*, 60(1), 65–89.

Pane, J. F., Ratanamahatana, C., & Myers, B. (2001). Studying the language and structure in non-programmers' solutions to programming problems. *International Journal of Human–Computer Studies*, 54(2), 237–264.

Papert, S. (1972). Teaching children to be mathematicians versus teaching about mathematics. *International Journal of Mathematical Education in Science and Technology*, 3(3), 249–262.

Papert, S. (1980). *Mindstorms: Children, Computers, and Powerful Ideas*. New York: Basic Books.

Papert, S. (1987). Information technology and education: Computer criticism vs. technocentric thinking. *Educational Researcher*, 16, 22–30.

Papert, S. (1991). Situating constructionism. In I. Harel & S. Papert (Eds.), *Constructionism* (pp. 1–11). Norwood, NJ: Ablex Publishing Corp.

Papert, S. (1997). Why school reform is impossible. *Journal of the Learning Sciences*, 6(4), 417–427.

Papert, S. A., & Solomon, C. (1971). Twenty Things to Do with a Computer. Retrieved from https://dspace.mit.edu/handle/1721.1/5836

Pasternak, A., & Vahrenhold, J. (2010). Braided teaching in secondary CS education: Contexts, continuity, and the role of programming. In *Proceedings of the 41st ACM Technical Symposium on Computer Science Education* (pp. 204–208). New York: ACM.

Pea, R. D. (1987). The aims of software criticism: Reply to Professor Papert. *Educational Researcher*, 16, 4–8.

Pea, R. D., & Kurland, D. M. (1984). On the cognitive effects of learning computer programming. *New Ideas in Psychology*, 2(2), 137–168.

Pea, R. D., Kurland, D. M., & Hawkins, J. (1985). Logo programming and the development of thinking skills. Technical Report 16. Retrieved from https://eric.ed.gov/?id=ED249930

Perlis, A. J. (1962). The computer in the iniversity. In M. Greenberger (Ed.), *Computers and the World of the Future* (pp. 180–217). Cambridge, MA: MIT Press.

Pirolli, P., & Recker, M. (1994). Learning strategies and transfer in the domain of programming. *Cognition and Instruction*, 12, 235–275.

Resnick, M. (1994). *Turtles, Termites, and Traffic Jams: Explorations in Massively Parallel Microworlds*. Cambridge, MA: MIT Press.

Resnick, M., Maloney, J., Monroy-Herández, A., Rusk, N., Eastmond, E., Brennan, K., Millner, A., Rosenbaum, E., Silver, J., Silverman, B., & Kafai, Y. (2009). Scratch: Programming for all. *Communications of the ACM*, 52(11), 60–67.

Resnick, M., Martin, F., Berg, R., Borovoy, R., Colella, V., Kramer, K., & Silverman, B. (1998). Digital manipulatives: new toys to think with. In *CHI '98: Proceedings of the SIGCHI Conference on Human Factors in Computing Systems* (pp. 281–287). Los Angeles, CA: ACM Press/Addison-Wesley Publishing Co.

Rich, L., Perry, H., & Guzdial, M. (2004). A CS1 course designed to address interests of women. In *Proceedings of the 35th SIGCSE Technical Symposium on Computer Science Education* (pp. 190–194). New York: ACM.

Scaffidi, C. (2017). Workers who use spreadsheets and who program earn more than similar works who do neither. In *VL/HCC 2017* (pp. 233–237). Hoboken, NJ: IEEE.

Scaffidi, C., Shaw, M., & Myers, B. (2005). An approach for categorizing end user programmers to guide software engineering research. *SIGSOFT Software Engineering Notes*, 30, 1–5.

Schanzer, E., Fisler, K., Krishnamurthi, S., & Felleisen, M. (2015). Transferring skills at solving word problems from computing to algebra through Bootstrap. In *Proceedings of the 46th ACM Technical Symposium on Computer Science Education* (pp. 616–621). New York: ACM.

Schanzer, E., Fisler, K., & Krishnamurthi, S. (2018). Assessing Bootstrap: Algebra students on scaffolded and unscaffolded word problems. In *Proceedings of the 49th ACM Technical Symposium on Computer Science Education* (pp. 8–13). New York: ACM.

Schon, D. A. (1987). *Educating the Reflective Practitioner*. Hoboken, NJ: Jossey-Bass.

Searle, K. A., & Kafai, Y. B. (2015). Boys' needlework: Understanding gendered and indigenous perspectives on computing and crafting with electronic textiles. In *ICER '15: Proceedings of the Eleventh Annual International Conference on International Computing Education Research* (pp. 31–39). New York: ACM.

Shaffer, D. W., & Resnick, M. (1999). "Thick" authenticity: New media and authentic learning. *Journal of Interactive Learning Research*, 10, 195–215.

Sherin, B. L. (2001). A comparison of programming languages and algebraic notation as expressive languages for physics. *International Journal of Computers for Mathematical Learning*, 6, 1–61.

Simon, B., Chen, T.-Y., Lewandowski, G., McCartney, R., & Sanders, K. (2006). Commonsense computing: What students know before we teach (Episode

1: Sorting). In *Proceedings of the Second International Workshop on Computing Education Research* (pp. 29–40). New York: ACM.

Simon, B., Kinnunen, P., Porter, L., & Zazkis, D. (2010). Experience report: CS1 for majors with media computation. In *Proceedings of the Fifteenth Annual Conference on Innovation and Technology in Computer Science Education* (pp. 214–218). New York: ACM.

Sloan, R. H., & Troy, P. (2008). CS 0.5: A better approach to introductory computer science for majors. In *Proceedings of the 39th SIGCSE Technical Symposium on Computer Science Education* (pp. 271–275). New York: ACM.

Smith, D. C., Cypher, A., & Schmucker, K. (1996). Making programming easier for children. *Interactions*, 3, 58–67.

Sweller, J., Clark, R., & Kirschner, P. (2010). Teaching general problem-solving skills is not a substitute for, or a viable addition to, teaching mathematics. *Notices of the AMS*, 57, 1303–1304.

Taylor, R. (Ed.) (1980). *The Computer in the School: Tutor, Tool, Tutee*. New York: Teachers College Press.

Vasudevan, V., Kafai, Y., & Yang, L. (2015). Make, wear, play: Remix designs of wearable controllers for scratch games by middle school youth. In *IDC '15: Proceedings of the 14th International Conference on Interaction Design and Children* (pp. 339–342). New York: ACM.

Weintrop, D., Beheshti, E., Horn, M., Orton, K., Jona, K., Trouille, L., & Wilensky, U. (2016). Defining computational thinking for mathematics and science classrooms. *Journal of Science Education and Technology*, 25, 127–147.

Weintrop, D., & Wilensky, U. (2015a). Using commutative assessments to compare conceptual understanding in blocks-based and text-based programs. In *Proceedings of the Eleventh Snnual International Conference on International Computing Education Research* (pp. 101–110). New York: ACM.

Weintrop, D., & Wilensky, U. (2015b). To block or not to block, that is the question: Students' perceptions of blocks-based programming. In *Proceedings of the 14th International Conference on Interaction Design and Children* (pp. 199–208). New York: ACM.

Weintrop, D., & Wilensky, U. (2017). Comparing block-based and text-based programming in high school computer science classrooms. *Transactions on Computing Education*, 18(1), 1–25.

Whitehead, C., Ray, L., Khan, S., Summers, W., & Obando, R. (2011). Implementing a computer science endorsement program for secondary school teachers. In *Proceedings of the 42nd ACM Technical Symposium on Computer Science Education* (pp. 547–552). New York: ACM.

Wilensky, U., Brady, C. E., & Horn, M. S. (2014). Fostering computational literacy in science classrooms. *Communications of the ACM*, 57, 24–28.

Wilensky, U., & Rand, W. (2015). *An Introduction to Agent-Based Modeling: Modeling Natural, Social, and Engineered Complex Systems with NetLogo*. Cambridge, MA: MIT Press.

Wilkerson-Jerde, M., Wagh, A., & Wilensky, U. R. I. (2015). Balancing curricular and pedagogical needs in computational construction kits: Lessons From the DeltaTick Project. *Science Education*, 99(3), 465–499.

Wilson, G. (2016). Software Carpentry: Lessons learned. *F1000Research*. Retrieved from www.ncbi.nlm.nih.gov/pmc/articles/PMC3976103/

Wing, J. (2010). Computational Thinking: What and Why. *The Link*. Carnegie Mellon University. Retrieved from www.cs.cmu.edu/link/research-notebook-computational-thinking-what-and-why

Wing, J. M. (2006). Computational thinking. *Communications of the ACM*, 49, 33–35.

Wolf, M. (2007). *Proust and the Squid: The Story and Science of the Reading Brain.* New York: Harper Collins.

20 New Programming Paradigms

R. Benjamin Shapiro and Mike Tissenbaum

20.1 Motivation

20.1.1 A Possible Future

Imagine the following scenario:

> Davina, a seventh-grade girl, lives in a rural community. She loves her dog, Slayer, and wonders what he does all day. Like many other dogs in her area, Slayer doesn't spend a lot of time indoors at home; he goes on adventures during the day, and returns home many nights for food and sleep. Davina's friends have similar curiosities: Where do their dogs go? What other dogs do they hang out with? They decide to work together to build technologies that will get them answers to these questions. With their teacher's help, they use the BBC Micro:bit (a small, low-cost microcontroller with built-in sensors and wireless communication) to create animal wearables that they can use to create a data set about their dogs' social and geo-spatial activities. They assign each dog a unique ID number and program each dog's Micro:bit to broadcast that unique ID every 30 seconds using the built-in short-range wireless radio. They also program each device to listen for broadcasts from other dogs' devices; each device will count up how many times it receives broadcasts from every other device. The next time they see their dogs, they attach the Micro:bits (in waterproof cases) to the dogs' collars, and send them out on their adventures. Then, when they see the dogs again, the students download their dogs' data sets to their laptops. They bring these data to class, and each creates a graph of how much time their dog hangs out with every other dog.

> Their teacher points out that if they combine their data, they could also create a representation of the dogs' social networks, and use that to ask, and answer, deeper questions. For example, are some dogs more popular than others? Are there dog friend groups? The students iterate on their data collection and analysis to dig deeper.

> Once the students investigate these questions, they realize that they still haven't answered one of their original questions: Where do the dogs go? So they plan a second investigation based on some theories they have. Maybe they go to the creek to get water. Maybe they go to the hills where the rabbits are to get food – are those the days they don't come home to eat? They grab a few more Micro:bits and program them like the others, except these won't be put on dogs, but in the places where they hypothesize that the dogs go. By combining dog-wearable data with beacons placed in important places, they'll be able to figure out where the dogs go, and who they go there with.

This scenario is an exciting one because it shows how several emerging computing paradigms could be manifested in K–12 computing education. In addition to responding authentically (Shaffer & Resnick, 1999) to students' interests, this scenario also offers authentic engagement with a number of aspects of contemporary computer science. Davina and her friends investigate their dogs' lives by creating a partition-tolerant, eventually consistent, wireless distributed system that combines low-power cyber-physical systems, used to collect data, with more traditional laptop/desktop computers, which they use for data analysis. By doing so, the students' construction of tools for their own inquiry mirrors the approaches to computing that are increasingly used by academic and industrial computer scientists to build the technological fabric of our daily lives.

Yet these approaches to the design and development of computing systems are largely absent from core computer science (CS) curricula in higher education and are missing altogether in standards, frameworks, and curricula in K–12.

In this chapter, we examine the recent and present evolution of computing paradigms and then their theoretical and practical consequences for the future of computing education.

20.1.2 Shifting Paradigms and Education to Fit Them

Debates about paradigms for computing education often revolve around topics like imperative vs. functional programming, whether to introduce object-oriented programming early, late, or not at all, and the merits of using block-based editors early in computing education and when and how to fade their use.

These debates generally make the following two presuppositions:

1. The theoretical model of computation is Church–Turing equivalent.
2. The essence of computational thinking is the construction of human-comprehensible formalisms for information processing.

While these presuppositions have been appropriate for much of the history of computing education and computing education research, fundamental shifts in our paradigms for computation necessitate revisiting and revising them.

In this chapter, we describe how changes in the field of computer science temper the appropriateness of these assumptions, and then discuss how new paradigms for computing education might embrace these changes in the field. Specifically, we will examine changes in how computer scientists build computing systems, how they use those systems to process large amounts of data in reasonable amounts of time, and how they engineer systems where humans are computational elements.

We will then describe how these advancements in the field require us to reframe discussions about paradigms for computing education to embrace non-determinism, statistical reasoning, and human involvement in contemporary computation. Though they complicate the epistemology of what computing is, we believe these shifts will lead computing education to be a more inclusive field, creating pathways into the field that amplify its apparent relevance to people whose primary interests are not primarily computation-qua-computation. To illustrate the possibilities that we envision, we present two vignettes from hypothetical computing education experiences in art and biology, calling out the ways in which the experiences embrace learning about contemporary computing paradigms and how they might be facilitated by advances in new kinds of programming tools that embrace more diverse frameworks for understanding and defining computational thinking and CS education.

20.2 Classical Paradigms

20.2.1 Theory of Computation

The central theoretical model of computing and computing education has long been the universal Turing machine. The Turing machine is an abstract model of computation that accounts for the practical capabilities of nearly all computers today and serves as the mathematical basis for mainstream approaches to algorithm analysis. The von Neumann architecture is a blueprint for the construction of actual computing hardware, including PCs, mobile phones, and servers that are in widespread use today. The Turing machine and the von Neumann machine are equivalent in the sense that there is a proportional relationship[1] between the number of operations or memory required for an algorithm to be executed by a von Neumann-based computer and the number of operations or memory that a Turing machine would require to execute the same algorithm.

One major way to distinguish between the costs of algorithms is between those that require polynomial vs. exponential amounts of resources to compute solutions. Many common computing problems have algorithmic solutions that require a polynomial amount of resources. For example, a common computing problem is to sort a data set. Even Bubble Sort, the worst non-perverse sorting algorithm (Gruber, Holzer, & Ruepp, 2007), has a cost that is expressible as a fixed polynomial: its typical time cost is n^2, where n is the number of items to be sorted. In comparison, quicksort, one of the most efficient[2] sorting algorithms, averages n log n, though its worst-case performance is n^2. In both cases, their worst-case performance can be expressed using a fixed polynomial, even while their typical performance can be quite different.

However, some problems have algorithmic solutions that demand so much computational work that they have solutions that are exponentials (or worse) of the size of their input. For example, the Traveling Salesperson Problem requires finding the shortest route that connects a number of destinations. All known

1 More formally, the Turing machine and von Neumann machine are theoretically equivalent because polynomial time algorithms exist to transform any program for a von Neumann machine into a program for a Turing machine and vice versa.
2 In general, comparison-based sorting algorithms must take at least n log n (Knuth, 1998).

algorithms for solving Traveling Salesperson require greater than exponential time to compute; they require the computation and evaluation of every possible route, and the number of new routes grows exponentially as additional destinations are added to the search space.

This approach (i.e., of comparing the runtimes of algorithms to reach precise solutions) to analyzing algorithms has several embedded assumptions:

1. That algorithms are specified as sequences of automated steps that the computer executes;
2. That these steps are executed one[3] at a time;
3. That the execution of these steps yields a deterministic result: the same algorithm executed repeatedly with the same input will always yield the same result.

Frameworks for computational thinking (CT; see Chapter 17) and computing education (e.g., Computer Science Teachers Association, 2017; Computing at School Working Group, 2012; K–12 Computer Science Framework, 2016; The College Board, 2017) are tightly tied to these base assumptions, emphasizing skills like sequencing and representing information in binary form. We wish to show how new paradigms for computation undermine these assumptions and necessitate new frameworks for CT and computing education.

20.3 New Paradigms

The field of CS is rapidly changing. Machine learning and distributed computing have fundamentally altered the practical underpinnings of today's CS. Quantum computing is poised to do the same as it transitions from being a theoretical possibility to a field of nascent practicality. All three of these approaches to computing have substantial implications for computing education, including altering our definitions of what CT even is. In this section, we describe these new paradigms for computation and their implications for computing education. We focus especially on the increasing emphasis on probabilistic and statistical methods for computing.

20.3.1 Machine Learning

As discussed in Section 20.2, deterministic and logically verifiable algorithms have been central to the epistemology and practices of CS. Algorithms are often coupled to data structures, which are human-designed, human-comprehensible, and machine-processable representations of problem domain data that are

---

3 Multi-core, high-performance, and distributed computing challenge this assumption by offering architectures for computers to perform many operations simultaneously. However, they do not change the combinatorics of algorithms sufficiently to transform exponentially hard problems into polynomially hard ones. After all, an exponential function divided by a constant is still an exponential function.

suitable for use with the algorithms chosen by system designers. As noted above (Section 20.2.1), computer scientists (e.g., Aho) and CS educators (e.g., Wing) consider the construction of human-comprehensible abstractions and automations (i.e., algorithms) to be the core disciplinary practices of CS.

Computer scientists are increasingly using techniques for computational problem-solving that have remarkable utility, but that challenge the primacy of human-comprehensible abstractions and automations. For example, machine learning is an approach to the construction of software systems that is fundamentally statistical and probabilistic, rather than logical and deterministic. Machine learning now powers a huge range of computational technologies, from speech recognition systems to search engines and prison sentencing systems. Rather than being programmed by humans, these systems *learn* their behaviors from data.

Today's most powerful machine learning techniques involve artificial neural networks, typically just called "neural networks." Neural networks are collections of nodes, called neurons, that are linked together in ways that resemble the connections between neurons in biological brains. A network (of the most common type) can be thought of as a probabilistic function in that it computes a set of outputs given a set of inputs, and the accuracy of this mapping between input and output isn't logically described so much as itself a function of the distribution of associations within the data that are used to create (i.e., *train*) the network. The computation is performed in a distributed manner: each node in the network has an activation function (e.g., a sigmoid ranging 0–1) whose domain is the sum of the weighted inputs from other nodes.

In simpler instantiations, neural networks are feed-forward systems, which means that they are directed acyclic graphs that send activation data in one direction from input nodes (e.g., receiving sensor data) through some number of middle layers of neurons (called *hidden layers*) to output nodes (Figure 20.1). More advanced implementations, known as recurrent neural networks, can include cyclic structures.

Different mechanisms exist for *training* neural networks to produce useful results (i.e., for automating the learning of the networks). Learning with neural networks entails configuring the weights of the links between nodes, as well as sometimes adjusting activation thresholds within nodes, or even pruning nodes from the network. Supervised learning refers to cases where a network is trained using data sets that include desired/labeled output from the network (i.e., where exemplar pairings of desired function domain and range are available). The quality of a trained network can be assessed by comparing the actual output of the network to the desired output.

One approach to supervised learning is called *backpropagation*. Whereas the use of a trained model involves sending information from input nodes through the network toward output nodes, backpropagation proceeds in reverse, from output to input. Backpropagation algorithms compare the output of a network for a given input to the known correct output. The difference between these is the error of the network for that input case. Backpropagation recursively traverses the network in reverse, calculating each node's contribution

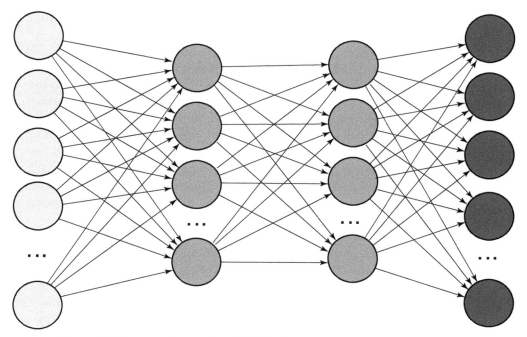

Figure 20.1 *A neural network with hidden layers.*
Source: Wikipedia public domain.

to the observed error and then proportionately adjusting weights (and other parameters) to reduce the amount of the error.

Human participation in neural network development, including the articulation (i.e., design and programming) of abstractions and automations, is often domain unspecific. For example, a neural network for recognizing images of cat faces might be structured identically to one that is used to process other visual data, or even to work with very different information (e.g., mortgage lending data). In particular, the programmers building such systems might use essentially identical abstractions (nodes and edges) and automations (e.g., backpropagation) to construct neural networks across hugely varying domains. The actual representation of domain-specific knowledge is in the configurations of weights (and other tunable network properties) that the algorithms produce. The utility of a trained network is therefore a useful emergent epiphenomenon produced by the interaction of human-constructed algorithms and automations and training data.

The epiphenomenology of neural networks has crucial consequences for the nature of neural networks as functions and for the CT required for their construction and use. First, their correctness is not logically provable,[4] but is instead

4 Neural network algorithms are provable, but the correctness of trained neural networks is not, except through exhaustion in some discrete problem domains. However, in such cases, neural networks may not be needed anyway, since a proof by exhaustion would necessarily indicate that a symbolic articulation of a function is possible.

probabilistic and contingent upon the characteristics of the data used to train and use them.

Second, the internal knowledge of a network is rarely comprehensible to humans. Trained models are useful black boxes, but their internal structure is rarely comprehensible to humans. Few people can discern semantically meaningful structure in collections of millions of floating point values. Research on increasing the human comprehensibility of internal neural network structure is an increasingly active area (e.g., Mahendran & Vedaldi, 2015), but computer scientists employing neural networks do not typically need to understand much about their inner workings. Neural networks and other machine learning systems are potent inversions of Knuth's aphorism: they are useful for problem-solving with computers despite only rarely being understood by humans.

Third, despite trained networks' internal inscrutability, computer scientists can assess the accuracy of the models that they construct; they do so primarily by empirically evaluating the performance of trained networks as black boxes (Arlot & Celisse, 2010) and make changes to network structure (e.g., adding or removing hidden layers), model inputs (e.g., transformations of raw data into features that might provide stronger signals for networks to learn), and other things that they can understand. This work is probabilistic and statistical, rather than logical and deterministic: the accuracy of a neural network (or other machine learning system) is a function of the properties of its training data set and the resemblance of that set to the data that the model will process when it is later used.

Machine learning requires us to reimagine CT and CS education. Machine learning is strongly probabilistic, and so increases the relevance of statistics education and probabilistic reasoning to CS. As such, it is also a strong departure from the provable logic of traditional CS. We discuss the consequences of this in Section 20.4.1.

20.3.2 Distributed Systems

Another critical transition within computing is the emergence of distributed systems as routine computing architectures. In CS, distributed systems (also called distributed computing) refers to models of computation in which some unit of computational work is performed by multiple systems working together, coordinating their activities via communication over a network (Tanenbaum & Van Steen, 2007).

Numerous examples of distributed systems pervade everyday computing. For example, consider the example of a mobile app that displays a weather forecast. It participates in a distributed system that involves its communication with an online service that provides weather data. Likely this service provides an application programming interface (API) that the mobile app, or other pieces of software, can use to query it for weather information. What these two systems can accomplish together exceeds the capabilities of either device alone. The mobile phone[5] and app have few direct means to sense or predict the weather, but can render information on a high-resolution screen and can be carried on a user's person. Large servers lack both of these affordances, but do have reliable power and network connections, as well as the processing power to compute sophisticated weather models.

Crucially, the mobile app and the weather server are two different programs, each executing classical computer programs, with communicative links between their processes yielding more complex functionality through the interactions between the systems. Numerous different structures for organizing communicating sequential processes (Hoare, 1978) exist in CS research and practice (Tanenbaum & Van Steen, 2007), each with different strengths and limitations. The simplicity of the API-based app–server interaction belies significant complexity behind the scenes. How is the weather server able to provide useful information? Likely the many web servers that balance the load of communication with mobile apps are part of a much more complex distributed system involving weather stations, databases, and high-performance computing systems for weather model simulation, all connected via a network. The weather-sensing stations, which likely include a variety of sensors and a small amount of computation, must be geographically distributed in order to capture data about conditions in a variety of locations, and likely even include sensors on satellites. Data flow from these sensors to databases to simulation systems that store computed results in databases that are then queried by the web servers that the mobile app communicates with.

Every one of these connections, and every one of the connected systems, bears some risk of failure. Reasoning about failure is central to the study of distributed systems, and three crucial concepts for doing so are availability, partition tolerance, and consistency. A system is available[6] if it can respond to requests. The system's partition tolerance is its ability to remain available even as some of the elements of the system become disconnected from one another. Consistency refers to the extent to which different nodes in a system have a shared view of the information contained in the system. Strong consistency would mean that all queries to the system – regardless of which web server handles the request and which database servers they query – would return identical results even if the network becomes partitioned. For formal definitions of these terms, see Kleppmann (2015). It is not possible for a distributed system to

---

5 Many phones now include embedded barometric pressure sensors and other hardware that is relevant to weather monitoring, though their primary use is not to monitor weather. For example, barometric pressure sensors are usually used in concert with accelerometers to detect whether the phone's user is climbing stairs.

6 There is some ambiguity about the formal definition of "availability" used by different researchers in the field, with some regarding it as an observable, measurable, continuous property of systems and others treating it as a formal algorithmic property (Kleppmann, 2015).

be strongly consistent while also being partition tolerant and always available (Brewer, 2000; Gilbert & Lynch, 2002).

Different applications have different requirements with respect to these three properties. The designers of a weather information network might prioritize availability and partition tolerance over consistency. A hurricane is the sort of event that is likely to lead to network partitions (by knocking power and communication lines offline), and so the times when the system can be at its most valuable to users are also the times when computer scientists' choices about the properties of the distributed system are most consequential. Users in the path of a hurricane would probably prefer that they get slightly differing information about the current weather from one another (i.e., that the system should remain available) over getting no information at all until everybody is able to get identical information (strong consistency). Consequently, the system should be engineered to remain available even if there are partitions and even if the system might return inconsistent results.

In other domains, it may be preferable to not be available, or to only allow a restricted set of operations, during a partition. For instance, the owner of an automated teller machine (ATM) may not want the machine to dispense cash if a customer's account balance cannot be verified with a bank. In the event of a partition internal to the bank's systems, the bank may not allow withdrawals in order to prevent overdrafts. It might, however, allow deposits because deposits can be tallied after a partition has ended to eventually reach a consistent state.

Consistency, availability, and partition tolerance are properties of distributed systems in their aggregate operation. These properties are the product of the careful design of distributed algorithms, including communication protocols, which are executed by the nodes of the system. Research on distributed systems typically focuses on the design and evaluation (including formal proof) of protocols that meet specific goals for consistency, availability, partition tolerance, as well as performance, including throughput and latency. Notable highly consistent algorithms include Paxos (Lamport, 1998, 2001) and Bitcoin (Nakamoto, 2008), while other approaches offer higher throughput and lower latency in favor of eventual consistency (Vogels, 2009).

The fundamental reason that trade-offs between consistency, availability, partition tolerance, throughput, and latency are required within distributed systems is that the semantics of distributed systems fundamentally differ from classical computers. Whereas classical computer programs and classical computers are fundamentally sequential, distributed systems are not, and many of their most challenging properties do not occur in sequential computation (Aho, 2012). It is not possible to know the total order of operations within a distributed system, though knowledge about local orderings is possible (Lamport, 1978). Whereas it is possible to prove that some algorithms will always terminate on a sequential computer, it is not possible to do so on asynchronously communicating distributed systems that include the possibility of even a single node failing (Fischer, Lynch, & Paterson, 1985); this finding is called "FLP impossibility."

These two properties – the non-linearizability of time and FLP impossibility – fundamentally change how one designs the abstractions and automations of computer programs for distributed computing as compared to classical computing. Inasmuch as the design of abstractions and automations is the essence of CT (Wing, 2008) and distributed computing changes the knowledge necessary to grapple with CT, we must consider how computing education can prepare students for a distributed computing-rich world. We discuss how computing educators might do so in Section 20.4.2.

20.3.3 Computational Complexity and Quantum Computing

In Section 20.2.1, we described the classical approach to describing and comparing algorithms and the assumptions that underlie this approach. Specifically, we noted how traditional approaches to the runtime analysis of algorithms are tightly tied to a Turing-equivalent model of computing and described two major categories of algorithms: those that can be executed in fixed polynomial time and those that require exponential time.

The distinction between polynomial and exponential runtimes of algorithms is fundamental to how computer scientists analyze algorithms and how they decide what sorts of problems are computationally hard or easy. For instance, the security of the RSA encryption algorithm depends upon the fact that all known techniques for factoring large prime numbers require an exponential amount of time. The exponential costs associated with searching for prime factors for the keys typically used are so great that even adding greater numbers of faster computers to such a search would not change the likelihood of such a search taking longer than the likely habitable existence of Earth.

But what if new architectures for computation could change these dynamics? That is, what if new types of computers could transform exponentially hard problems into polynomially hard problems? This is the promise of quantum computing. Richard Feynman (1982, 1986) theorized that the properties of quantum mechanical systems could be used to design new kinds of computers that simultaneously explore all possible paths of a problem solution space, transforming problems that require an exponential number of steps with a Turing-equivalent computer into problems of polynomial or linear difficulty. Since Feynman's purely theoretical speculation, Shor (1994) proved how (then still theoretical) quantum computers would be able to perform prime factorization in polynomial time.

Several primers about quantum computing explain how the quantum approach differs from the classical (universal) computing model (Aaronson, 2002; Metodi, Faruque, & Chong, 2011; Nielsen & Chuang, 2010, chapter 1). While academic and industry researchers have recently succeeded in building the first quantum computers, these do not yet possess all of the properties that Feynman theorized about (Mohseni et al., 2017; Tichy, 2017).

One very critical distinction between the classical and the quantum computational models is that classical computation is deterministic and algorithms' correctness can be assessed logically. An algorithm's correctness has classically been defined as whether the algorithm yields a precisely accurate result under all valid inputs; on a deterministic Turing machine, a correct algorithm will always return a proper result, and the correctness of an algorithm can often be proven logically. However, in quantum computing, correctness is probabilistic: a quantum computer will return a right answer with some probability.

An additional difference is the design of algorithms for quantum computers. Research in this area is at its infancy, and there is much we still do not know about what programming languages and compilers for quantum computers should be like (Chong, Franklin, & Martonosi, 2017; Tichy, 2017) and what the computing problems that quantum computing can be helpful with even are (Harrow & Montanaro, 2017; Nielsen & Chuang, 2010). Even the basic abstractions that should underpin quantum programming are not yet known, but some sharp contrasts with classical computation are known. For example, while it is common for classical computers to copy information (e.g., to pass as function parameters or to send over a network), quantum information cannot be copied (Nielsen & Chuang, 2010). Though currently a subject of great uncertainty, as well as limited in utility, quantum computing is an area of massive research investment. It is possible that true quantum computers will be developed within our lifetimes and will permit the solution of problems that historically have been very hard. This raises a critical question: What does computing education look like for quantum computing? We return to this question in Sections 20.4.1 and 20.4.2.

20.4 Implications for CT and Computing Education

20.4.1 Probabilistic and Statistical Reasoning

Traditional approaches to the study of algorithms and the design of computer programs involve assessment of the efficiency and correctness of algorithms. Within such work, correctness has historically been defined to mean that an algorithm provides an exactly right answer whenever it is run with valid input. This epistemology of correctness is reflected in computing education in manifold ways. At the K–12 level, Advanced Placement (AP) CS A calls for students to be able to analyze program correctness, including defining and assessing algorithms' pre- and post-conditions and other invariants, as well as constructing and using test cases to assess algorithms (The College Board, 2014). AP CS Principles calls for students to "evaluate algorithms analytically and empirically for efficiency, correctness, and clarity" by "reasoning formally or mathematically about [an] algorithm," though it does not require formal proof of correctness; this reasoning is expected to be logical and not an empirical (statistical) evaluation. The joint Association for Computing Machinery (ACM)–Institute of Electrical and Electronics Engineers (IEEE) Computer

Science Curricula 2013 specifies numerous techniques for formal (logical, mathematical) correctness proofs. CS1 curricula implementing these specifications often require students to write test code to accompany the algorithms that they implement, with these tests including examples for common cases and boundary conditions that the algorithms should handle (Felleisen et al., 2014). Algorithm analysis and theory courses and textbooks typically involve students writing proofs about whether algorithms (or other computational objects like state machines) will yield correct results (Cormen et al., 2009; Sipser, 2012).

However, the growing ubiquity of machine learning, the need to work with ever larger data sets, and the coming utility of quantum computing necessitate a broader epistemology of correctness than what is logically provable or exhaustively testable. *Computing education must embrace probabilistic and statistical thinking as a way to reason about the correctness of computational tools.*

As already discussed, machine learning algorithms produce models of training data. These models can do useful work, but do so probabilistically. That is, they produce best guesses of correct results given some algorithmic interpretation of the statistical distributions of information within training data sets. Evaluation approaches that involve assessments of whether such models will always yield correct answers do not fit the machine learning paradigm. Instead, statistically oriented evaluation methods like Bootstrap or k-fold cross-validation are necessary (Kohavi, 1995).

Similarly, many interesting and practically useful computing problems today involve the expensive combination of exponentially hard algorithms and large data sets. This combination is common in bioinformatics and in network analysis (Carrington, Scott, & Wasserman, 2005). Yet many of these problems can be solved for practical purposes by approximation algorithms (e.g., Vandin, Upfal, & Raphael, 2011). Approximation algorithms offer good but not always precisely correct results, with provable upper bounds on how far from correct they can be (Williamson & Shmoys, 2011). As with the assessment of machine learning models, the determination of whether an approximation algorithm is appropriate for a given problem, and then what acceptable error bounds are, is a statistical question, one for which the traditional logical reasoning about algorithms of CS and CS education is insufficient.

Quantum computing is intrinsically probabilistic. In theory, quantum computers can provide precisely correct answers to hard problems, but can only do so probabilistically. Sometimes they give correct answers, and other times they do not. Therefore, reasoning about the results of quantum computation is necessarily probabilistic reasoning. This can involve modeling the propagation of uncertainty through a computation that involves the combination of multiple classical and quantum computations and identifying how to reduce uncertainty to produce useful results. There is a subtle difference between quantum computing and algorithms in this regard: there is a knowable probability that a quantum computer will give a correct answers, while approximation algorithms give answers within a knowable bound from precisely correct. In both cases, just as with machine learning, probabilistic and statistical reasoning is necessary in order to construct, apply, and evaluate new computing systems to solve problems.

The probabilistic and statistical nature of these approaches and the concomitant development of technologies for working with them (e.g., probabilistic programming) indicate a strong need for CS education to embrace probability and statistics as essential to the nature of future CT. Rather than simply testing whether an outcome of a program is correct, students will need to learn how to evaluate whether results are acceptably accurate, given statistical/probabilistic criteria. Logical reasoning will not diminish in importance, but will be joined by probabilistic and statistical reasoning as essential for reasoning about the properties of computing systems. As we discuss below, it is quite plausible that machine learning could begin to migrate from being an advanced topic in CS to one that is included in CS1. The recently released Royal Society Report on Machine Learning (2017) recommends schools introduce key machine learning topics, and further argues for curriculum reform that considers the implications of machine learning in the lives of young people and for their future work. We expect that when this happens, probability and statistics will migrate from optional or late-stage curricular elements to conclusion in the lower-division CS curriculum alongside introductory discrete mathematics.

Achieving this progress will require changes in the standards and frameworks of computing education. Neither the ACM nor the IEEE currently recommend that probability and statistics be core parts of the computing curriculum, and indeed have labeled it "not necessary" (ACM & IEEE, 2013, p. 50). Likewise, these topics are essentially excluded from K–12-focused computing education frameworks, with no mention of probability and statistics in the K12CS Framework or the 2017 Computer Science Teachers Association (CSTA) Standards. This is despite the growing call in education more broadly for students to increase their data and statistical fluencies and their literacies for recognizing and understanding patterns in data (Next Generation Science Standards). In light of the changes that have already happened to CS and are likely to happen soon due to quantum computing, these frameworks, though recently published, run the risk of quickly becoming woefully out of date. Future standards must embrace the probabilistic–statistical nature of contemporary computing.

20.4.2 Heterogeneous Architectures

Most computing systems used today involve some aspect of distributed computing. Mobile phones, laptops, and Internet of Things devices all communicate with the servers that constitute today's so-called "cloud computing." Crafting these applications entails designing programs that perform robustly when running across heterogeneous assemblages of hardware, with wildly varying architectures, processing capabilities, storage capacities, electrical power efficiencies, network connectivities, sizes, weights, and affordances for interaction with the physical world (from rainfall sensors to touch screens and analog circuitry built into self-driving cars to control the amount of gas entering an engine).

Yet distributed computing tends to occupy only elective elements of university-level CS curricula and is typically left out altogether in K–12. The ACM–IEEE Curriculum 2013 relegates distributed computing to an elective topic (p. 153). Some K–12 frameworks include minimal detail about relevant subject matter. The CSTA Standards (2017) includes a category called "Networks and the Internet," but the only concrete learning goal that is actually about networking or the Internet is that students should learn about the idea of packet-switched networking. The K–12 Computer Science Framework (2016) does not specify any related goals. To the best of our knowledge, no frameworks or standards actually recommend that students learn about how to design and implement their own networked or distributed computing systems.

One published curriculum that does embrace some relevant ideas is MobileCSP, an implementation of the AP CS Principles course that revolves around the development of mobile apps, but its coverage is very limited.

The Scratch project has attempted to empower students to create applications with distributed computing-supported functionality while, remarkably, disclaiming the need for students to learn anything new to program such systems. The Cloud Variables functionality of Scratch was created so that beginner programmers could create features like high-score lists and chat rooms. A central design goal within the Cloud Variables project is that "children get the ability to store and retrieve data online, without having to learn new language syntax" (Dasgupta, 2013). To achieve this goal, the Scratch team created a new kind of variable that has an identical interface to ordinary variables (its value can be retrieved or changed), but also has automatic value synchronization between all instances of the same variable in all copies of the same program.

On the one hand, this is a remarkably simple solution to a complex problem: with only a minimal change to the programming paradigm of a very popular introductory computing tool, learners can create distributed programs. On the other hand, this approach is both intellectually and practically limited; it obscures the core computational ideas and practices involved in reasoning about how to design distributed programs (see Section 20.3.2) and also cannot scale[7] (Repenning, Webb, & Ioannidou, 2010) beyond a narrow set of problems and solution structures.

As described in Chapter 17, arguments in favor of computing and CT education typically center upon the ways in which learning computing can empower students to learn to conceptualize and solve problems in new ways. In this worldview, computing education tools should be constructed to support this empowerment. Yet the simplicity of the Cloud Variables approach is intended specifically to avoid the need to learn new skills. Thus, rather than being about computing education for new programming paradigms, Cloud Variables is

---

7 "Scale" here refers not to quantity (of users or data), but to the capacities of ideas or techniques learned to be built upon by users as they progress toward more advanced learning. An approach to programming that is so stripped of its disciplinary authenticity that it must be abandoned wholesale in order to do more advanced work is not scalable.

firmly anchored in old paradigms that cannot rise to meet new challenges and new possibilities for education.

A different approach that allows – and even requires – learners to understand the relationships between the distinct programs that compose distributed systems is called "message passing." In this paradigm, programs communicate with one another by exchanging information according to protocols defined by application developers. This approach is the basis for many of the distributed systems created by researchers and industry. In addition to being identified as an important paradigm for undergraduate (elective) computing education in the ACM–IEEE 2013 Curriculum, it has also been included for decades in novice-friendly programming tools (DiSessa & Abelson, 1986; Kay, 1993), though researchers have only recently empirically described how adolescent programmers can design and think about computing systems using this approach.

The Universe library for the Racket language includes support for building distributed programs. With support from their teachers, students in introductory computing (CS1) courses have used this functionality to build distributed (client–server) multiplayer video games through message passing (Felleisen et al., 2009; Morazán, 2018). Though this prior work describes the structure of the curriculum within which students created these distributed programs, as well as students' and teachers' generally positive impressions of these experiences, no papers describe how students conceptualize these distributed programs and their strategies for designing, implementing, and debugging them. That is, the literature illustrates that it is possible to incorporate distributed systems into university-level CS1, but offers little insight into how the processes of student learning within the paradigm differ from learning about classical programming, or about how students apply this knowledge to new problems (e.g., not client–server video games).

The BlockyTalky project has investigated how designing and implementing distributed systems can be a part of computing education for middle school students (Kelly et al., in press; Shapiro et al., 2017). Much like the Universe work, students using BlockyTalky work together to create interactive distributed systems, where the distinct programs that constitute those systems communicate with each other via message passing.

The early phases of this work involved students creating interactive computer music performance systems, with students writing programs for musical synthesis and for handling user input via sensors. The synthesizers and the input devices were separate computers (typically two to six Raspberry Pis per project) and communicated with one another over a local Wi-Fi network. The research team deliberately engineered the synthesizer system so that each synthesizer could only produce one audio track at a time in order to necessitate students' contention with the challenges of synchronizing multiple synthesizers. Students creating BlockyTalky music projects were responsible for designing the topologies of the distributed program and for creating the message passing protocols that supported their desired model of system–system and human–computer

Figure 20.2 *FitBit for dogs.*

interactions, including handling the synchronization (in time) of multiple synthesizers via mutual subscription to a shared clock and scheduling of real-time sound synthesis. Kelly et al. (under revision) illustrate how students creating BlockyTalky music projects created projects with a variety of topologies, how they debugged their distributed programs through comparisons between logs of message passing traffic and their code, and how they drew upon the networked affordances of these tools over time to continuously rearrange their own group social structures over time during problem-solving.

In subsequent work, Shapiro and students have adapted the BlockyTalky model to work with programmable technologies that are quite popular for K–12 computing education. The BlockyTalkyBLE toolkit (Laboratory for Playful Computation, 2017) is a set of extensions for MIT App Inventor and the BBC Micro:bit that permits the construction of distributed systems (e.g., for wearables or Internet of Things applications) using these tools. In pilot studies, middle school-aged girls have used these tools to create an animal activity tracker (Figure 20.2), robotic vehicles, and interactive props for theatrical performances.

Apart from the BlockyTalky research, we know little about how people learn about distributed computing; there is no other published research about how students conceptualize distributed systems or reason about programming interactions between systems with different architectures. Given the myriad of ways in which heterogeneously constituted computing systems are critical to contemporary computing, such research is dearly needed. Moreover, this research, and then consequent changes in teaching practices, will only become more necessary as quantum computers become ready for widespread use. Researchers are still figuring out what quantum computers can and cannot do well, but it seems virtually certain that quantum computers will not be stand-alone entities.

Rather, they will be combined with classical computation into ever more heterogeneous distributed systems. Future computing education will need to include the design and use of such systems.

This quantum computing-induced increase in architectural heterogeneity also has implications for education about computer architecture. The traditional physical basis of computing is electronic, and it is common for undergraduate CS coursework to include electronics and digital logic. The expansion of maker pedagogy has recently pushed these topics down into K–12. Indeed, many students' first experiences with programming include the design of the very electronic devices that they are programming (Buechley et al., 2013). But what should computer architecture coursework look like in a quantum computing world? Should CS students take quantum physics and quantum chemistry? We do not have answers to this, and likely cannot have them until the building blocks (and usable abstractions) of quantum computing systems solidify. But computing educators should begin to consider how research on physics education could inform future computing curricula.

20.4.3 Epistemology vs. Utilitarianism

Drawing from Chapters 1, 17, and 19, formal definitions of CS and CT have focused heavily on epistemology. That is, computers have been tools for developing new knowledge about the universe, and the programs that run on them have typically been constructed using abstractions that are formal representations of relations between objects in the universe. Within computer science, this epistemological focus is typified by Aho's (2011) claim that "abstractions called computational models are at the heart of computation and computational thinking." Abelson argues that the field of computer science is "not about computers" (Abelson, Sussman & Sussman, 1996) in the same way that physics is not about particle accelerators: both computers and accelerators are tools for doing other knowledge-building work.

CS education has long been anchored in similar beliefs. The computing education literature focuses strongly on the idea of abstraction and of the computer as a scriptable automaton working with those abstractions (Computer Science Teachers Association, 2017; The College Board, 2017; Wing, 2011). Denning (1989, 2017) has extensively reviewed the prominence of the formulation of abstractions within the computing education literature. In Papert's revolutionary treatise *Mindstorms: Children, Computers, and Powerful Ideas* – written while a member of MIT's Epistemology and Learning Group – he argues that "the most powerful idea of all is the idea of powerful ideas" (Papert, 1980, p. 76). Papert claims that the computer is a "protean machine" capable of representing nearly any idea, and that its ability to do so makes it a powerful learning tool because students could use it to build, test, and share their own formalisms (epistemologies). He provides examples of powerful ideas like ratio and recursion; both terms describe abstract relations between objects and, as such, are epistemological tools.

Later, Papert critiqued mainstream schooling's emphasis on "skills and facts" as a bias *against ideas* (Papert, 2000). This construction, which positions learning skills and facts as somehow opposite to the development of ideas, runs contrary to recent transformative developments within the field of CS. As discussed in Section 20.3.1, machine learning has enabled computer scientists to construct effective solutions to problems so challenging that they have defied years of work using more classical techniques. For example, we now have better tools for automated language translation than ever before (Lewis-Kraus, 2016). These breakthroughs have been possible because computer scientists have been willing to somewhat abandon the construction of human-comprehensible, domain-specific abstractions about information in favor of statistical models whose inner structures are often incomprehensible to humans. We can understand this transition as a shift in the values of the field of CS from overwhelmingly valuing abstractions that have strong epistemological bases toward valuing tools that have strong utilitarian value. CS education needs to account for this shift and embrace a utilitarian mindset. For Papert, students learned about geometry through building computer programs that enacted the geometric behaviors they programmed. However, with machine learning, computer scientists can solve many problems without deep knowledge of problem domains. This moves Papert's theories of developing big ideas into a new space – a space in which students can have big ideas and develop solutions to those ideas without having to know how every part of the system supports the solution. For example, Google has built advanced translations systems using machine learning without the engineers who built them needing to know much about the particularities of the languages that they support; rather, the computer learns these particularities from data. This is very different from Papert's early visions of computing and geometry and produces an interesting question of whether it is problematic to produce linguistic (or geometric) products without learning much about linguistics (or geometry).

Interestingly, Turkle and Papert (1992) anticipate this need in their paper "Epistemological Pluralism and the Revaluation of the Concrete." They identify and contrast two styles of computer programming. The first, which they call a "hard" style of computer programming, makes heavy use of abstractions and strives toward efficiency. The second, which they call a "soft" style, emphasizes closeness between the programmer and the concrete detail of their project, often involves few abstractions, and can be computationally inefficient. Turkle and Papert argue that CS and CS education's valuing of the so-called hard style leads to the exclusion of people, especially women, who, they argue, tend more naturally to the soft style.

The emergence of useful machine learning creates an additional reason to reconsider the monopoly of the hard-style in our valuation of what constitutes good computing practice or good computer science pedagogy. Like human-made soft-style programs, machine learning models are tightly tied to concrete details, do not contain abstractions (by any traditional definition), and are inefficient (machine learning has been around for decades but is so computationally expensive that it took the widespread deployment of GPUs to make it practical). The widespread impact of machine learning on computing raises an intriguing question: will computer scientists more easily embrace concrete-first, and even abstraction-free, computation than they did two decades ago?

Extending both Turkle and Papert's notions of soft computing and Abelson's idea that "computing is not about computers" requires us to ask a fundamental question about our goals for CS education: Should the focus be on students developing a deep understanding of how computer programs work (i.e., an epistemological framing), or instead, should CS education aim to empower students to be able to apply computing toward solving problems in their everyday lives (i.e., a utilitarian approach)? We argue that a shift toward utilitarianism – and away from the primacy of strong abstractions as a bedrock foundation of CT – would better align computing education with shifts that are already happening in computing and that are already reflected in some computing education curricula. We have already argued (see Section 20.4.1) for the kinds of changes in computing pedagogy that would enable students to learn the kinds of statistical methods that are necessary for working with machine learning. Further changes will be necessary to shift the values and vocabulary of the field to account for the utilitarian shift that is already happening.

Yet there are already widely used curricula for which this shift is not necessary. Many cases where students are learning CS, either nominally or through the use of computing to support learning in other disciplines, already are highly utilitarian. Consider the case of the Technovation Challenge (http://technovationchallenge.org): this competition encourages girls to develop prosocial mobile applications and business plans to support their sustainable development. The Challenge website offers a complete mobile app and business plan development curriculum, which covers topics like interface design, programmatic interaction with the web, and honing a business plan pitch. Students typically emerge from the Technovation program with working app prototypes. Yet they probably have formulated few – if any – abstractions, and only the briefest of algorithms. Over 15,000 girls have participated in this program. Can we really say that they have not learned CS in an authentic way? We think not. Nor can we say that their focus on skill building over abstract ideas is a poor use of time, as Papert might. Instead, we must develop ways of discussing computing and computing education that value utilitarian value as highly as we they value epistemology.

The rise of mobile computing and other modes of computing such as the Internet of Things that are decoupled from traditional desktop or computer lab approaches to computing education is also supporting this utilitarian shift.

These new modes of computing are allowing computation to move off learners' screens and into their everyday lives. Allowing learners to connect their computing education to real-world applications that meaningfully connect to their own lives can help motivate them and help them develop their computational identities (Tissenbaum et al., 2017). This is in stark contrast to traditional CS education, which focuses on learning the elements of computing (e.g., abstraction, loops, etc.) divorced from personally relevant applications. By sticking to an epistemological approach to CS education, we risk students seeing computation as something that is disconnected from the practical needs of their daily lives (similar to the challenges in math and other sciences; Flegg, Mallet, & Lupton, 2012; Williams et al., 2003).

20.5 Visions of the Future – Implications and Open Questions

We have now described evolutions in the fundamental nature of computing that are already occurring, including shifts toward more distributed, statistical, and even quantum models. We have then argued that these shifts necessitate reimagining CT and computing pedagogies in ways that are more probabilistic–statistical (and less exclusively logical), more architecturally heterogeneous (and less tied to a Turing or von Neumann sequential model of computation), and more utilitarian (and less obsessed with epistemology). But what would computing education be like if computing educators adopted our suggestions?

20.5.1 CT for Distributed Computing

We opened this chapter with a vignette that illustrates the possibility of embracing distributed and architecturally heterogeneous computing early in K–12 CS education. None of the programming involved in the example is necessarily more complex than would be involved in implementing a moderately sophisticated Scratch game. Each animal wearable could execute an identical program and would not require more than 20 lines of code. (The example in Figure 20.3 records the amount of time the dog-wearer is near to each other dog who the dog-wearer encounters.) Yet reasoning about how the interactions between these programs constitute a distributed system requires different concerns within CT from what has typically been embraced by computing educators (except in advanced/elective coursework).

To understand how the system behaves, one must think not only about the computation of the individual programs, but also about the aggregate interactions between those programs. While that kind of thinking has not been well integrated into early pathways into computing, there has been related work in computational modeling for science education. Most notably, Wilensky and Resnick (1999) identify the cognitive phenomenon of thinking in levels as the ability to reason about systems across the scale of individual agents and systems

```
// send out our own serial every second
basic.forever(() => {
    radio.sendNumber(control.deviceSerialNumber())
    basic.pause(1000)
})

// increment our count when we hear from a peer
radio.onDataPacketReceived(({ serial }) => {
    beacon_counter.increment_beacon_count(serial);
})

// write out what we've heard every 10min
basic.forever(() => {
    basic.pause(1000 * 60 * 10); //millis * seconds * minutes
    beacon_counter.save_to_file("peer_counts.csv");
})
```

Figure 20.3 *Dog collar beacon program.*

of interacting agents. They provide examples of young people reasoning about the mechanisms that drive systems like traffic jams or the collective behavior of slime mold cells. In their account, people's naive intuitions about *how* such systems behave involve top-down (centralized) control over the behavior of elements of a system, rather than coordinated-seeming action emerging from bottom-up interactions between system elements. Nearly all of the research that Wilensky and students have conducted since then (Levy & Wilensky, 2009; Sengupta & Wilensky, 2009; Stieff & Wilensky, 2003) has focused on how students can learn to reason about these sorts of complex systems. Most of this work has involved students adjusting the parameters for preprogrammed models, though some of it also involves model construction (Wilkerson-Jerde, Wagh, & Wilensky, 2015). We think it is also worth noting that the runtime behavior of the programming tool used throughout this work, NetLogo, has been engineered to provide guarantees about program behavior that obviate some of the most critical challenges of designing and understanding distributed systems; the individual agents that make up NetLogo models execute their programs sequentially (one agent at a time), synchronously, and without risk of partitions or other sources of invisible failure. Consequently, while this work sheds light on how students can develop understandings of some kinds of emergent interactions, new languages and tools will be needed to offer accessible and authentic entry points into the complexity of distributed computing systems.

Frameworks for CT should grow to embrace the development of understandings of different types of distributed systems. New curricula are needed that offer students opportunities to interact with, construct, and learn about the trade-offs of different models for organizing distributed systems. Davina and friends' dog trackers are much like the objects in Wilensky and Resnick's (1999) traffic jams and slime mold simulations: all of the trackers are equal and at no point is any tracker more privileged than any other. As such, Davina's project shows what one possible entry point to distributed computing, representing one possible system organization model, could be. We eagerly await others' investigations of how other authentic problems can motivate learning about other ways of beginning to construct such systems, and of how student learning can gradually progress from simple beginnings to more robust participation in the disciplinary practices of distributed computing.

20.5.2 Mobile Apps, Communities, and Computational Action

CS researchers originally chided Papert when he stated that one day every learner would have access to a computer lab to think and create with. Now, with mobile computing, most young learners carry computers in their pockets more powerful than the ones used by those early CS researchers. Freeing computing from the confines of the computer lab and out into students' daily lives offers radical new ways for us to think about how youth can learn about and apply computation (Klopfer, 2008). By harnessing the growing ubiquity of mobile computing, we can empower young learners to learn about and design for the potential of distributed computing systems to have meaningful change in their communities.

In Stefanesti, Moldova, one group of young women (14–16 years old) recognized a growing crisis in their community due to the *E. coli*, hepatitis, and heavy water contamination in their drinking water: "In our school we have 67 cases of Hepatitis A, because of the water" (Reader, 2015). This was largely due to the fact that in Stefanesti people need to get their water from wells. In response, they developed an app using MIT's App Inventor called Apa Pura. Apa Pura harnessed the ubiquity of mobile devices to allow citizens to collaboratively test and share the water quality at wells across the region. This information was displayed on a map available to everyone. This project has had a profound effect on the young women's community. Similar to the example of youth programming for their pets, the code for this project doesn't require significantly complex programming knowledge (none of these young women had ever programmed before), but it did require them to consider a wealth of additional information in order for it to be successful: What information did their community need? How could they harness the distributed power of the larger community to collect this information? What was the best way to display this information so that it was usable? How do you deal with reliability or gaps in the information? Each of these factors requires a much broader understanding of the computing system they are designing for and how it all works together.

Given the further proliferation of the Internet of Things, it is not hard to see how these young innovators could extend their work and their CT. Deploying water-quality sensors could provide real-time updates on water quality, rather than relying on individuals to update the information. Implementing this system would require the youth to consider the system's availability, partition tolerance, and consistency: How often would the system need to update in order to be reliable? What would it mean for individual sensors to be down? How accurate do the readings have to be to be "safe?" Understanding how these systems interconnect requires recontextualizing them into personally meaningful contexts.

In order to enable youth to have these kinds of transformational computing opportunities, we need develop learning approaches that not only allow youth to understand how heterogeneous and interconnected system work, but also situate their learning in personally relevant contexts.

We are seeing a natural progression in the vision for computing education. Papert's original vision of intellectual empowerment with computing focused on ways of thinking and understanding concrete ideas (1980); Brennan and Resnick extended this line of thinking to expand computation as a means of empowering youth as empowered designers within the confines of the Scratch environment (2013); now, by extending computation into the real world, youth can be truly empowered to make impactful change. In order to achieve this vision, we need computing education to progress beyond the epistemologically focused lens of current CT to an approach that focuses on *computational action* (Tissenbaum, Sheldon & Abelson, in press), in which learners develop personally meaningful applications that have a real connection to their lived lives.

20.5.3 Machine Learning, Statistics, Art, and Embodiment

We argue above that machine learning should be moved to the core of CS and that we should investigate what machine learning in CS1 could be like. Fortunately, in seeking to do so, we need not start from scratch. Prior work on interactive machine learning (IML) (Fails & Olsen, 2003) for computer music (Fiebrink, Cook, & Trueman, 2011) provides rich examples of how people who have never programmed before (or even studied statistics) can develop nuanced understandings of machine learning. Moreover, this work shows how creative approaches to machine learning education might embrace embodied and artistic knowledge to support interdisciplinary approaches to machine learning-rich introductory computing education. IML refers to a set of techniques for supervised machine learning where humans interactively and iteratively construct training data sets, use generated machine learning models, and then edit the training set in order to adjust the performance of the machine learning model.

One of the most powerful applications of machine learning is the development of computational technologies that support more natural interactions between people and computers. A prime example of this has been the development of more advanced natural language processing tools, from automatic translation to autocomplete. But machine learning also offers computer scientists new ways to develop technologies for rich gestural interactions with computers. Computer music is a compelling domain for such applications, particularly when computer music includes expressive digital instruments that offer the kinds of gestural or embodied interfaces that traditional instruments afford. IML enables musicians to customize the behavior of gestural computer music interfaces by carefully crafting the machine learning models within such instruments to comport with their styles of play, including the nuances of how they use their bodies to do so.

Playing traditional instruments and *learning* to play those instruments are fundamentally embodied experiences. Learning to play a cello, for example, isn't just an abstract, symbolic process of learning mappings between notes and finger positions, but involves extensive amounts of practice learning *how* to put one's fingers in the right places, how to move the bow, when and how to breathe in the flow of different movements of finger, bow, and the rest of body, and how different sequences of musical elements within a piece of music, suggesting different emotional meanings, necessitate different ways of using one's body to do all of these things.

New kinds of computer music instruments can offer this degree of rich, embodied interaction. And, perhaps surprisingly, the construction of hybrid traditional-and-computer instruments through novice-friendly IML tools can lead the musician to simultaneously improve their mastery of the traditional instrument and also learn about statistical modeling and machine learning. Fiebrink, Cook, and Trueman (2011) describe the case of a cellist who uses the Wekinator IML toolkit (Fiebrink, Trueman, & Cook, 2009) in order to create a computer music instrument to accompany her performance using a cello. In this case, the "instrument" was software that responded to inputs from sensors embedded in an electronic bow, including "acceleration along three axes, tilt, horizontal and vertical position of the bow relative to the instrument, hair tension, and grip pressure." The cellist received only a brief overview of machine learning from the researchers, and also worked with the researchers to create a parameterizable computer music program in Max/MSP (a popular sound/music programming environment). Then she used the Wekinator to create rich mappings between the bow data and those program parameters. Over time, she iteratively:

- Created training data indicating relationships between states of the bow and desired musical program input. In some cases, these relationships were mappings whose domains were data values at individual moments in time, and in other cases, these were mappings from temporal data (i.e., sequences of input data, such as different gestures of the bow).
- Fed these training data to machine learning algorithms, with guidance from the researchers about which algorithms were appropriate for modeling moment-in-time data and which were appropriate for temporal modeling.
- Evaluated the correctness of the resulting model by comparing the intended program behavior (i.e., what they thought the system should do) with its actual behavior. She did so by playing her instrument and listening for whether the system accompanied her in the way that she desired.
- Inspected the confidence of the machine learning model as it interpreted her play. She recognized that instances of correct classification with low confidence indicated cases where the system would be most likely to misinterpret her play, indicating a need to either provide additional training data, change the way she performed in order to generate more easily distinguishable input scenarios, or modify her program in order to handle input data differently.
- Used a visualization of the posterior distribution of model labels to identify regions of her gestural input space where the model was especially likely to make mistakes.

- Generated additional training examples in order to improve the accuracy of the model.
- Changed her playing technique in some cases in order to generate better data: "for example, noticing that the bowing articulation model was not discriminating well between riccocet and spiccato strokes, she reexamined her own technique for those strokes and discovered that her spiccato technique actually needed to be improved in order to be less like riccocet. After adjusting her technique, she was able to both train a model that performed better and produce a better cello sound."

Through this iterative process, the cellist used her musical knowledge to create and hone a computer music system that could accompany her as she performed with her cello. She used that knowledge to both generate a data set and evaluate the machine learning system's construction of a predictive model based upon that data set. This knowledge enabled her to envision a kind of performance that would add to her capabilities with the cello and to realize it through a dialogue between herself and the machine learning system, mediated by her movements of the bow. This interaction empowered her to create a new computational technology that was tailored to herself as a musician, and also enabled her to identify areas for improvement in her own expert-level performance with her cello.

It is worth noting that, prior to this episode, the cellist had had only a cursory introduction to machine learning. And yet, the musician was able to do quite sophisticated statistical modeling work (e.g., analysis of posterior distributions to assess the conditional likelihood of erroneous model outputs). What does this case tell us about how computing education could embrace machine learning early in the curriculum?

Curricula could begin by embracing activities in which students already have expertise, and then use machine learning techniques to empower learners to create performance-enhancing technologies. Music, dance, and sports are all obvious domains for doing so. Our cellist's needs and processes need not be so different from a tennis player seeking real-time feedback on his swing and so working with a coach to create training data sets with labeled examples of good and less good swings and then creating a wearable to provide sonified, real-time feedback during a practice match. These artistic and athletic scenarios are quite different from the kinds of projects that early-stage programmers typically work on.

One reason for this is that writing purely symbolic programs (i.e., through code) to handle multidimensional gestural interaction is exceedingly difficult to do well, and so beginner projects, if they involve interaction at all, often focus on simple keyboard-and-mouse-based interactions that are suitable for games, interactive stories, or other traditional kinds of elementary computer programs. New hardware technologies (e.g., for wearable sensing) and interactive machine learning make it possible to rapidly build gesture recognizers that can be embedded into beginner-level programming projects. It is not at all far-fetched to expect that the next generation of tools like Scratch could include multimodal machine learning tools to support the synthesis of new functions (and accompanying blocks) within the construction of hybrid symbolic–statistical interactive programs.

Another reason for the dissimilarity between our sense of the potential of embodied athletic and artistic domains to anchor computing education and the typical beginnings of computational participation today is that CS has long been regarded as a science, technology, engineering, and mathematics (STEM) discipline, and we have, at least in the USA, regarded STEM as a participatory space that is quite distinct from arts and athletics. Basic categorizations like jock, artist, and nerd presuppose a separation between computational practices and athletic or artistic ones. Here again, new kinds of technologies, including the advent of interactive machine learning technologies, offer us the capacity to transcend these barriers, and to do so in introductory computing experiences. There is no good reason why the construction of the aforementioned tennis wearable could not happen in a physical education class. Currently, in the USA, what federal research funding is available to investigate the integration of computing into other disciplines focuses exclusively on the combination of computing with other STEM disciplines, like math or the natural sciences. Machine learning could enable us to explore a much larger space of possible integrations and, furthermore, to motivate the learning of statistics-rich computing through the promise of athletic and artistic enhancement. Students' and teachers' initial motivations in such scenarios may be quite utilitarian: enhancing students' development of a physically demanding skill rather than mastery of algorithms or data structures. We do not see this as problematic, but rather as a motivational and authentic beginning to participation in contemporary computing.

20.5.4 Quantum Educational Futures

The field of quantum computing is too unsettled for us to yet imagine what participation in computing educational spaces could be like.

20.6 Conclusion

As shown throughout this and other chapters in this book (and in Chapters 1 and 17 in particular), what we think of as computing, CT, and computing education have changed significantly over the years. New approaches, such as tangible computing (see Chapter 22) and new tools and environments (see Chapter 21), have and will continue to shape the entire field of computing. As computing researchers, it is imperative for us to acknowledge that this is an ongoing process and that the present state is only a snapshot in time – we should not mistake it for the "natural" or permanent position.

Papert's groundbreaking work on how children can think, create, and learn with computers was originally chided for not being realistic, with prominent computer scientists stating that children would never need to use the "overpowered" computing infrastructures of the time. The advances we are witnessing in distributed computing, machine learning, and tangible and embodied computing are similarly challenging what we think of as thinking and creating computationally. In order for computing educational to serve the needs of the next generation of learners, we need to properly understand how these advances are changing computing broadly and how we need to change our definitions of computing and computing education to keep pace. We need to be mindful of not repeating the mistakes of other disciplines such as math and physics by alienating learners through educational approaches that are not consistent with how computing is increasingly being used and how it connects to students' lived lives.

This chapter, along with the others in this Handbook, is an attempt at casting a critical eye toward understanding what the state of computing is while acknowledging where it might (or should) go. Computing is an extraordinarily dynamic field, and computing innovations (e.g., the invention of the graphical user interface) have had large, though gradual, impacts on computing education (e.g., the advent of blocks-based programming editors). These advances in the field of CS suggest exciting opportunities for the future of computing education, including what and how students will program. Considerable research is needed into what those educational experiences could be like, including how they begin and how they progress over time. We look forward with great eagerness to our field's collective development of new approaches to making new computing paradigms part of computing education. We are also eager to see how advancements in computing education may shape the future of computing in general, whether through the cultivation of new generations of computer scientists who are skilled in working within new computing paradigms or through the development of societies populated by people whose computational literacies enable them to make wise decisions about the computational infrastructure that supports those societies.

Acknowledgments

We thank Kristin Searle for her coauthorship of the Davina scenario. We also thank the National Science Foundation for funding the first author's efforts on the development of contemporary computing education (CNS-1562040).

References

Aaronson, S. (2002). Quantum Computing for High School Students. Retrieved from www.scottaaronson.com/writings/highschool.html

Abelson, H., Sussman, G. J., & Sussman, J. (1996). *Structure and Interpretation of Computer Programs*. Cambridge, MA: MIT Press.

ACM/IEEE–CS Joint Task Force on Computing Curricula (2013). *Computer Science Curricula 2013*. USA: ACM Press and IEEE Computer Society Press.

Aho, A. V. (2011). Ubiquity symposium: Computation and computational thinking. *Ubiquity*, January 2011, Article 1 (8 pages). New York, NY: ACM.

Aho, A. V. (2012). Computation and computational thinking. *The Computer Journal*, 55(7), 832–835.

Arlot, S., & Celisse, A. (2010). A survey of cross-validation procedures for model selection. *Statistics Surveys*, 4, 40–79.

Buechley, L., Peppler, K., Eisenberg, M., & Yasmin, K. (Eds.) (2013). *Textile messages: Dispatches from the world of e-textiles and education*. In New York: Peter Lang Publishing Group.

Brennan, K., & Resnick, M. (2013). Imagining, creating, playing, sharing, reflecting: How online community supports young people as designers of interactive media. In C. Mouza & N. Lavigne (Eds.), *Emerging Technologies for the Classroom* (pp. 253–268). New York: Springer.

Brewer, E. A. (2000). Towards robust distributed systems (abstract). In *Proceedings of the 19th Annual ACM Symposium on Principles of Distributed Computing (PODC '00)* (p. 7). New York, NY: ACM.

Carrington, P. J., Scott, J., & Wasserman, S. (Eds.) (2005). *Models and Methods in Social Network Analysis*. Cambridge: Cambridge University Press.

Chong, F. T., Franklin, D., & Martonosi, M. (2017). Programming languages and compiler design for realistic quantum hardware. *Nature*, 549, 180–187.

Computer Science Teachers Association (2017). K–12 Computer Science Standards. Retrieved from www.csteachers.org/page/standards

Computing at School Working Group (2012). Computer science: A curriculum for schools. sCurric.pdf

Cormen, T. H., Leiserson, C., Rivest, R., & Stein, C. (2009). *Introduction to Algorithms*. Cambridge, MA: MIT press.

Dasgupta, S. (2013). From surveys to collaborative art: Enabling children to program with online data. In *Proceedings of the 12th International Conference on Interaction Design and Children* (pp. 28–35). New York: ACM.

Denning, P. J. (2017). Remaining trouble spots with computational thinking. *Communications of the ACM*, 60(6), 33–39.

Denning, P. J. (1989). A debate on teaching computing science. *Communications of the ACM*, 32(12), 1397–1414.

diSessa, A. A., & Abelson, H. (1986). Boxer: A reconstructible computational medium. *Communications of the ACM*, 29(9), 859–868.

Fails, J. A., & Olsen Jr., D. R. (2003). Interactive machine learning. In *Proceedings of the 8th International Conference on Intelligent User Interfaces* (pp. 39–45). New York: ACM.

Felleisen, M., Findler, R. B., Flatt, M., & Krishnamurthi, S. (2014). How to Design Programs, Second Edition. Retrieved from www.ccs.neu.edu/home/matthias/HtDP2e/

Felleisen, M., Findler, R. B., Flatt, M., & Krishnamurthi, S. (2009). A functional I/O system or, fun for freshman kids. *ACM SIGPLAN Notices*, 44(9), 47–58.

Feynman, R. P. (1982). Simulating physics with computers. *International Journal of Theoretical Physics*, 21(6), 467–488.

Feynman, R. P. (1986). Quantum mechanical computers. *Foundations of Physics*, 16(6), 507–531.

Fiebrink, R., Trueman, D., & Cook, P. R. (2009). A meta-instrument for interactive, on-the-fly machine learning. In *Proceedings of NIME 2009* (pp. 280–285). International: NIME.

Fiebrink, R., Cook, P. R., & Trueman, D. (2011). Human model evaluation in interactive supervised learning. In *Proceedings of the SIGCHI Conference on Human Factors in Computing Systems* (pp. 147–156). New York: ACM.

Fischer, M. J., Lynch, N. A., & Paterson, M. S. (1985). Impossibility of distributed consensus with one faulty process. *Journal of the ACM*, 32(2), 374–382.

Flegg, J., Mallet, D., & Lupton, M. (2012). Students' perceptions of the relevance of mathematics in engineering. *International Journal of Mathematical Education in Science and Technology*, 43(6), 717–732.

Gilbert, S. & Lynch, N. (2002). Brewer's conjecture and the feasibility of consistent, available, partition-tolerant web services. *ACM SIGACT News*, 33(2), 51–59.

Gruber, H., Holzer, M., & Ruepp, O. (2007). Sorting the slow way: An analysis of perversely awful randomized sorting algorithms. In *International Conference on Fun with Algorithms* (pp. 183–197). Berlin, Germany: Springer.

Harrow, A. W., & Montanaro, A. (2017). Quantum computational supremacy. *Nature*, 549, 203–209.

Hoare, C. A. R. (1978). Communicating sequential processes. In P. B. Hansen (Ed.), *The Origin of Concurrent Programming* (pp. 413–443). New York: Springer.

K–12 Computer Science Framework (2016). K–12 Computer Science Framework. Retrieved from https://k12cs.org

Kay, A. (1993). The early history of smalltalk. *ACM SIGPLAN Notices*, 28(3), 511–598.

Kelly, A., Finch, L., Bolles, M. & Shapiro, R. B. (in press). BlockyTalky: New programmable tools to enable students' learning networks. *International Journal of Child-Computer Interaction*. https://doi.org/10.1016/j.ijcci.2018.03.004

Kleppmann, M. (2015). A Critique of the CAP Theorem. Computing Research Repository. Retrieved from https://arxiv.org/pdf/1509.05393.pdf

Klopfer, E. (2008) *Augmented Learning: Research and Design of Mobile Educational Games*. Cambridge, MA: MIT Press.

Knuth, D. E. (1998). *The Art of Computer Programming: Sorting and Searching* (Vol. 3). London, UK: Pearson Education.

Kohavi, R. (1995). A study of cross-validation and bootstrap for accuracy estimation and model selection. *IJCAI*, 14(2), 1137–1145.

Laboratory for Playful Computation (2017). BlockyTalkyBLE. Retrieved from www.playfulcomputation.group/blockytalkyble.html

Lamport, L. (1978). Time, clocks, and the ordering of events in a distributed system. *Communications of the ACM*, 21(7), 558–565.

Lamport, L. (1998). The part-time parliament. *ACM Transactions on Computer Systems*, 16(2), 133–169.

Lamport, L. (2001). Paxos made simple. *ACM SIGACT News*, 32(4), 18–25.

Lewis-Kraus, G. (2016). The great AI awakening. *The New York Times Magazine*, December 14, 2016. Retrieved from www.nytimes.com/2016/12/14/magazine/the-great-ai-awakening.html

Levy, S. T., & Wilensky, U. (2009). Students' learning with the Connected Chemistry (CC1) curriculum: Navigating the complexities of the particulate world. *Journal of Science Education and Technology*, 18(3), 243–254.

Mahendran, A., & Vedaldi, A. (2015). Understanding deep image representations by inverting them. In *Proceedings of the IEEE Conference on Computer Vision and Pattern Recognition* (pp. 5188–5196). New York: IEEE.

Metodi, T. S., Faruque, A. I., & Chong, F. T. (2011). Quantum computing for computer architects, second edition. In M. D. Hill (Ed.), *Synthesis Lectures on Computer Architecture* (pp. 1–203). San Rafael, CA: Morgan & Claypool Publishers.

Mohseni, M., Read, P., Neven, H., Boixo, S., Denchev, V., Babbush, R., Fowler, A., Smelyanskiy, V., & Martinis, J. (2017). Commercialize quantum technologies in five years. *Nature News*, 543(7644), 171–175.

Morazán, M. (2018). Infusing an HtDP-based CS1 with distributed programming using functional video games. *Journal of Functional Programming*, 28, e5.

Nakamoto, S. (2008). Bitcoin: A Peer-to-Peer Electronic Cash System. Retrieved from https://bitcoin.org/bitcoin.pdf

Nielsen, M. A., & Chuang, I. (2010). *Quantum Computation and Quantum Information: 10th Anniversary Edition*. Cambridge, UK: Cambridge University Press.

Papert, S. (1980). *Mindstorms: Children, Computers, and Powerful Ideas*. New York: Basic Books, Inc.

Papert, S. (2000). What's the big idea? Toward a pedagogy of idea power. *IBM Systems Journal*, 39(3–4), 720–729.

Repenning, A., Webb, D., & Ioannidou, A. (2010). Scalable game design and the development of a checklist for getting computational thinking into public schools. In *Proceedings of the 41st ACM Technical Symposium on Computer Science Education* (pp. 265–269). New York, NY: ACM.

Sengupta, P., & Wilensky, U. (2009). Learning electricity with NIELS: Thinking with electrons and thinking in levels. *International Journal of Computers for Mathematical Learning*, 14(1), 21–50.

Shaffer, D. W., & Resnick, M. (1999). "Thick" authenticity: New media and authentic learning. *Journal of Interactive Learning Research*, 10(2), 195–216.

Shapiro, R. B., Kelly, A., Ahrens, M., Johnson, B., Politi, H., & Fiebrink, R. (2017). Tangible distributed computer music for youth. *The Computer Music Journal*, 41(2), 52–68.

Shor, P. W. (1994). Algorithms for quantum computation: Discrete logarithms and factoring. In *Foundations of Computer Science, 1994 Proceedings* (pp. 124–134). Chicago, IL: IEEE.

Sipser, M. (2012). *Introduction to the Theory of Computation*. Boston, MA: Cengage Learning.

Stieff, M., & Wilensky, U. (2003). Connected chemistry – Incorporating interactive simulations into the chemistry classroom. *Journal of Science Education and Technology*, 12(3), 285–302.

Tanenbaum, A. S., & Van Steen, M. (2007). *Distributed Systems: Principles and Paradigms*. Upper Saddle River, NJ: Prentice-Hall.

The College Board (2014). *Computer Science A: Course Description*. New York: The College Board.

The College Board (2017). *AP Computer Science Principles*. New York: The College Board.

The Royal Society (2017). Machine learning: The power and promise of computers that learn by example. Retrieved from http://royalsociety.org/machine-learning

Tichy, W. (2017). Is quantum computing for real? An interview with Catherine McGeoch of D-Wave Systems. *Ubiquity*, 2007, 2.

Tissenbaum, M., Sheldon, J., Seop, L., Lee, C. H., & Lao, N. (2017). Critical computational empowerment: Engaging youth as shapers of the digital future. In *Global Engineering Education Conference (EDUCON), 2017 IEEE* (pp. 1705–1708). New York: IEEE.

Tissenbaum, M., Sheldon, J., & Abelson, H. (in press). From Computational Thinking to Computational Action. To appear in *Communications of the ACM*.

Turkle, S., & Papert, S. (1992). Epistemological pluralism and the revaluation of the concrete. *Journal of Mathematical Behavior*, 11(1), 3–33.

Reader, R. (2015). Code Girl documentary perfectly sums up why more girls don't code. VentureBeat. Retrieved from https://venturebeat.com/2015/11/04/code-girl-documentary-perfectly-sums-up-why-more-girls-dont-code/

Vandin, F., Upfal, E., & Raphael, B. J. (2011). Algorithms for detecting significantly mutated pathways in cancer. *Journal of Computational Biology*, 18(3), 507–522.

Vogels, W. (2009). Eventually consistent. *Communications of the ACM*, 52(1), 40–44.

Wilensky, U., & Resnick, M. (1999). Thinking in levels: A dynamic systems approach to making sense of the world. *Journal of Science Education and Technology*, 8(1), 3–19.

Wilkerson-Jerde, M., Wagh, A., & Wilensky, U. (2015). Balancing curricular and pedagogical needs in computational construction kits: Lessons from the DeltaTick project. *Science Education*, 99(3), 465–499.

Williams, C., Stanisstreet, M., Spall, K., Boyes, E., & Dickson, D. (2003). Why aren't secondary students interested in physics? *Physics Education*, 38(4), 324.

Williamson, D. P., & Shmoys, D. B. (2011). *The Design of Approximation Algorithms*. Cambridge, UK: Cambridge University Press.

Wing, J. M. (2006). Computational thinking. *Communications of the ACM*, 49(3), 33–35.

Wing, J. M. (2008). Computational thinking and thinking about computing. *Philosophical Transactions of the Royal Society of London A: Mathematical, Physical and Engineering Sciences*, 366(1881), 3717–3725.

Wing, J. (2011). Research notebook: Computational thinking—What and why? *The Link Magazine*, Spring. Retrieved from www.cs.cmu.edu/link/research-notebook-computational-thinking-what-and-why.

Systems Software and Technology

21 Tools and Environments

Lauri Malmi, Ian Utting, and Andrew J. Ko

21.1 Introduction

The roots of computing as a discipline stem from the need to present and manipulate data automatically. Building software tools has therefore always been an important activity in the field, both in professional practice and in academic work. Correspondingly, learning to use the tools needed for professional programming has been one of the core elements in computing education. Languages have, of course, changed and developed over the decades, but the basic skills in using compilers, interpreters, editors, and debuggers have always been necessary to learn. In current computing education, similar learning goals persist even though modern integrated development environments (IDEs), like Eclipse, have reduced (but not excluded) the need to learn to use separate tools.

There is a large diversity of types of tools that contribute to the learning of computing. Some programming languages and environments have been developed primarily as tools for education. Early examples of these included BASIC (Kemeny & Kurtz, 1964) and Pascal (Wirth, 1973). More recent cases include, for example, Scratch (Resnick et al., 2009) and Alice (Cooper et al., 2000). The basic idea behind these languages has been to provide a simplified environment for learning programming and to hide many of the complexities in the world of professional programming. The more recent graphical programming environments also aim at reaching the younger population (e.g., Meerbaum-Salant et al., 2013), from preschool onward, instead of tertiary-level students only, though some institutions also use these environments as a gentle introduction to programming (Cooper et al., 2003).

Other attempts at simplifying tools and environments for beginners have looked at ameliorating the complexity of elements of the professional tools that tend to be more complex and general than is needed in education. Areas of concern have been input/output (I/O) and graphics libraries (Bruce et al., 2001; Wolz & Koffman, 1999), and even the language itself, revealing more complete subsets of the language as beginners develop their skills (Felleisen et al., 1998)

Learning programming has always been challenging for a large number of students. Therefore, it is natural that computing educators have started to develop educational tools that focus on supporting various aspects of students' learning process. A notable early example was the BALSA algorithm animation tool (Brown & Sedgewick, 1984), which provided visualizations of algorithm execution. Such tools were initially stand-alone applications and were often platform-dependent, limiting access to them. With the widespread availability of network access to resources that came with the Internet, dissemination of tools became much easier. Moreover, due to the rapid expansion in the number and diversity of web development tools and with the dramatic increase in the bandwidth available to students (at least in some countries), most current educational tools are either wholly browser-based or have a browser interface that interacts with server-side applications.

In this chapter, we seek to survey these various categories of tools and the research on them. We start by discussing the motivation for such research, what forms of tools exist, and for whom they have been developed. Then, we present overviews of several important application areas. Finally, we discuss some generic challenges in tools research.

21.2 Why Are Tools Important for Computing Education?

Computing is partly a practical field, and so most computer science education focuses on teaching students to design and implement complex systems to solve problems. Tools are usually a central part of the learning, but only implicitly, as technical implementations needed to reach a desired goal. It is therefore natural that computing educators have been highly active in developing and evaluating tools to support learning, as well as their own work as teachers. Tools can often be considered pedagogical support mechanisms, and compared with many other fields, computer scientists have the privilege that they (and their students) are much more often capable of designing and building the tools themselves.

It is thus not surprising that a significant share of computing education research concern tools. Valentine (2004) surveyed 444 papers addressing CS1/CS2-level education published in 1983–2004 in Special Interest Group on Computer Science Education (SIGCSE) Symposium proceedings and identified that in 99 of them (22%) the main topic was some form of tool. Simon (2007) analyzed four years of Australasian Computing Education (ACE) and National Advisory Committee on Computing Qualifications (NACCQ) conferences (2004–2007) and identified that in 16 percent of the papers the topic was teaching/learning/assessment tools. In a further analysis, Simon (2009) showed that 26 percent of conference papers in the first seven years (2001–2007) of the Koli Calling conference concerned tools, as did 17 percent of Innovation and Technology in Computer Science (ITiCSE) papers in the years 2005–2008 (Sheard et al., 2009).

21.3 What Is a Tool?

Educational tools in computing take many forms. An obvious case is a *software application*, which one can download and install, such as the BlueJ (www.bluej.org) environment for learning object-oriented programming in Java. A tool could also be a *web application providing some service*, like Problets (www.problets.org), which are "problem solving software assistants for learning, reinforcement and assessment of programming concepts," and PeerWise (http://peerwise.cs.auckland.ac.nz), which supports student-generated multiple-choice questions as a pedagogical method. On the other hand, there are hundreds or thousands of small interactive applications available via the web that demonstrate the operation of individual concepts, like particular data structures or sorting algorithms. Often these have been developed as student projects and published "as is," sometimes collected and curated, and possibly incorporating other non-tool resources such as YouTube videos.

Another class of tools includes *software frameworks* that can be used to build new educational applications. For example, Tango (Stasko, 1990) was a software library for building algorithm animations. The increase in availability of rich interactive content, also called smart learning content (Brusilovsky et al., 2014), is often the result of the availability of such frameworks, because the same technological framework can been used to generate multiple different instances of examples or exercises. For instance, the jsVEE framework (Sirkiä, 2016) has been developed to enable building visualizations of Scala and Python programs, and jsParsons (Helminen et al., 2012) is a tool for building Parsons' problems. Instances of these visualizations and problems have been made available at the ACOS content server (Sirkiä & Haaranen, 2017; acos.cs.hut.fi), which is a software architecture supporting dissemination of smart learning content into different learning management systems. All of these frameworks and servers can be considered tools for teachers to create and disseminate smart learning content for students.

However, a tool can also be a *definition language*. Initially, the Pascal language was designed as an educational programming language. While there had to be Pascal compilers to build executable programs, these were separate tools generating code for different platforms.

Another example of language tools is that some algorithm visualization systems, like JAWAA (www.cs.duke.edu/csed/jawaa2), are built on using a scripting language, which can be processed into a visualization (Rodger, 2002).

Of course, there are many tools used in computing education that are not specific to the discipline, as well as many tools that are specific to the discipline but are not in essence educational. In the rest of this chapter, we will leave aside discussion of generic educational tools and platforms such as learning management and support systems like Moodle or PeerWise and general interactive tutorial systems. Professional tools like Eclipse or general-purpose programming languages and corresponding systems software are frequently used in computing education, and learning to use them is an important goal of learning in computing curricula. While these may be complex for novices, it is then possible for teachers to focus on using only a core set of operations, and even to provide a simplified user interface for students. Later on, actual professional tools can be adopted. We do not discuss professional tools explicitly in this chapter.

Finally, we restrict our discussions to software tools, leaving out tools for physical computing or CS Unplugged (www.csunplugged.org) (Chapters 18 and 22 focus on these topics).

21.4 Stakeholders

Tools can be considered from several stakeholders' points of view. Many educational tools and applications focus on supporting *students'* work, including, for example, tools for visualizing and concretizing program execution (program visualization, algorithm visualization), intelligent tutoring systems, automatic feedback tools, etc. But some tools have primarily been developed for *teachers*, such as plagiarism detection tools (e.g., Lancaster & Culwin, 2004; Rosales et al., 2008) or frameworks (see above) that allow teachers to build new learning content or assist in assessment. These tools can, of course, also be used by students, such as in project work where the task is to delve into some topic and prepare a learning resource as the outcome.

Teachers can act both as *producers* and *consumers*. Firstly, teachers can build new learning content using some tool and use it in their own education, while also providing other teachers with the possibility of accessing and adopting the material. Then the other teachers act as consumers. They might use the available resources as such, but they might also wish to tune them, for example, by adding annotations to the material. Kelmu (Sirkiä, 2016) is such a tool for consumers, which has been used to annotate program visualizations, but could be used to annotate other types of animations, too.

Finally, there are *developers*, who implement and maintain tools. Of course, teachers could act as developers, too, and often do. However, it is useful to differentiate between these roles, because the needs for tools are quite different from the points of view of various roles. For teachers and students, easy access, a low learning curve and high usability are important, while for developers, maintainability, code quality, choice of technologies, architecture, and available documentation are more important.

21.5 Classification of Tools

The range of tools in computing education is broad, and it is impossible to discuss thoroughly all tools research in this chapter. It is, however, useful to provide some structure for the area. A good resource here is the paper by Kelleher and Pausch (2005), who presented a taxonomy of educational tools for programming, identifying several dozen different tools designed for novice programmers to learn to code. While the paper focuses narrowly on programming, and not on all topics in computing, it actually covers a great majority of the tools relevant to this chapter.

Kelleher and Pausch split tools into two major categories. *Teaching systems* attempt to teach programming for its own sake and have goals, such as simplifying the creation of code, finding alternatives to typing programs, providing new ways of structuring programs, supporting better understanding of program execution, supporting social learning, and providing a motivating context. The second major category they called *empowering systems*. They argued that "the designers of these [latter] systems are not concerned with how well users can translate knowledge ... to a standard programming language. Instead, they focus on trying to create languages and methods of programming that allow people to build as much as possible." Here, they identify systems that support new methods of specifying the program logic, improvements in programming languages, and applications in entertainment and education in other domains of knowledge.

Another, more narrow survey of tools supporting programming education, published at roughly same time, is the work of Gómez-Albarrán (2005). It focuses on 20 important tools operating in the following four different domains: reducing the complexity of the development environment; providing examples (to guide/of) programming; visualizing program/algorithm execution; and providing a simulated world where the programmer can control activities. These fall in the domain of teaching systems in the categorization of Kelleher and Pausch.

While this top-level categorization is helpful for comparing the goals of the system, it does not provide much granularity about the instructional and learning properties in prior work. Moreover, there has been more than a decade of additional work since its publication. The rest of this chapter will attempt to provide some of this increased granularity, with sections discussing some of the most important types of tools that have been designed to support different aspects of learning computing.

A broad area could be described as tools for *scaffolding learning*. First, there are tools and environments that support *planning, designing, analyzing and constructing programs* (Section 21.5.1). These tools provide a simplified environment that hides some of the complexity of programming concepts and processes as compared to working directly with professional tools. For example, block-based programming languages and environments, like Scratch or Blockly (http://developers.google.com/blockly), efficiently remove the requirement for students to engage with fine details of syntax.

A second category of scaffolding tools covers different types of *feedback* for students on their work. As an example, *automatic assessment tools* (Section 21.5.4) can provide feedback on students' programs in terms of their correctness, style, structure, and efficiency. There are also tools for analyzing formal design specifications. Such tools are naturally valuable for teachers, too, because they can reduce their workload by analyzing and grading student work automatically. Teachers can then use their time more for guidance and giving feedback on such aspects of student work that are hard to analyze automatically, such as design choices or use of algorithms.

Third, computing concepts are frequently abstract and invisible. Therefore, scaffolding student learning with *visualization* and *animation* (Section 21.5.5) is a broadly explored area of tools research. Some such tools provide opportunities for various types of interaction with the visualization, such as responding to questions, browsing or zooming in and out in the dynamic presentation, or providing input values and thus *simulating* a system or operation.

In all of the above categories, one important aspect of tool-based scaffolding is the pace: getting immediate feedback on one's solution or work is valuable because it supports personal reflection on learning much better than getting teacher feedback several days or even weeks later. Many tools also allow students to resubmit a revised solution or explore interactively how a particular system or concept works, although some impose a delay to avoid very fine-grained interaction.

The fourth area of scaffolding concerns support for students' motivation. This is an area where various forms of *educational games* and *gamified approaches* work (Section 21.5.2). Finally, there is research carried out on *e-books*, which form comprehensive interactive resources for learning programming (Section 21.5.3).

We discuss each of these areas in more depth below.

21.5.1 Supporting the Writing of Programs

Since educational programming languages and environments first came into existence, there has always been a tension between providing specific tools to decrease barriers to entry and engaging learners with professional tools as their abilities grow.

Languages designed or adapted for use in education have long been integrated with development environments tailored to that purpose, from BASIC in the 1960s through to Turbo Pascal in the 1980s and on to graphical IDEs (e.g., Scratch) in the twenty-first century.

In the early stages of their development, although these IDEs were designed to be used by professional software developers, they were simple enough to be used by beginners without significant learning overheads, but as they matured beyond the simple edit–compile–run cycle to include the rapidly expanding software development tool chain, they became less and less accessible. For their target professional audience, this is not a major problem, as they are expected to use the tools every day and be prepared to invest in learning their increasingly complex interfaces, but for beginners, the barrier to entry became increasingly high. This led to a number of attempts from around 2000 to subset existing and emerging IDEs (Eclipse for Education, Visual Studio Express) or provide plugins specific to educational settings (the NetBeans BlueJ plugin). These efforts have largely been abandoned due to the cost of maintenance, or subsumed into a more general "freemium" licensing model where they have lost any specific educational focus.

A more successful approach has focused on the creation of IDEs specifically targeting learners and existing languages: DrScheme for Scheme (Findler et al., 2002), which later became DrRacket, BlueJ for Java (Kölling, 2003), and DrJava (Allen et al., 2002). As well as providing features for learners (such as BlueJ's direct object manipulation and DrScheme's read–evaluate–print loop), these tools typically included a subset of the functionality of professional IDEs, which over time expanded to include access to other components of the modern software development tool chain such as static code analysis (Cardell-Oliver & Wu, 2011) and revision control systems (Fisker et al., 2008). The latter has particularly opened up research opportunities using students' commits of evolving source code as a research tool (Spacco et al., 2006)

Despite the existence of this wide variety of IDEs for education, the use of command line tools alone for teaching introductory programming is remarkably persistent, with Davies et al. (2011) reporting that 15 percent of their sample of 367 US institutions used the command line alone in their CS1 course. A similar proportion was reported for Australian institutions in 2010 by Mason et al. (2012), although they report a decline from 45 percent in the previous ten years, citing as the major reason a change of perception from IDEs representing an increase in cognitive load ("learning to use the IDE") to a reduction ("reducing the amount that the students had to learn"). With a few exceptions (e.g., Uysal, 2016), these perceptions remain largely untested by research, with such work as has been done largely subsidiary to comparisons of programming languages (e.g., McIver, 2002).

21.5.2 Games and Learning Programming

Whereas many of the tools discussed above have played the role of being supportive of learning by simplifying programming languages or providing more supportive code editors or programming environments (Kelleher & Pausch, 2005), some tools have tried to explicitly structure, scaffold, and guide the entire learning experience. These environments are much more than tools, often offering whole curricula for a set of learning objectives. These environments fall roughly into the following two categories: *interactive games* and *e-books* (which are similar to tutorials and tutors). Both types of environments offer learning materials, curricula, and some form of sequencing to guide learning, but differ in how they motivate and reinforce learning.

Game-based learning environments motivate learning by creating extrinsic motivation (Gee, 2014) and applying game mechanics and instructional principles to achieve particular learning objectives (Aleven et al., 2010). There have been numerous games that teach aspects of programming. Among the earliest were the Rocky's Boots and Robot Odyssey games (Robinett & Grimm, 1982), which offered a series of increasingly difficult puzzles in which players connected logic gates to achieve particular program outputs. This puzzle-based paradigm is followed in numerous other commercial games, including Lightbot (lightbot.com), CodeCombat (http://codecombat.com), and Human Resource Machine (tomorrowcorporation.com/humanresourcemachine). These tend to offer their own simplified programming language, with game-specific commands and operations to manipulate a game world of some kind. Some other games focus on low-level programming and/or building hardware, such as Shenzhen I/O (www.zachtronics.com/shenzhen-io), Silicon Zeroes (http://store.steampowered.com/app/684270/Silicon_Zeroes), and TIS-100 (www.zachtronics.com/tis-100). It is also worth noting that while all of these games focus on programming or computing concepts, there is variation over whether the focus of the game is mainly educational or entertainment.

Some researchers have explored the paradigm of puzzle-based programming games in more depth. For example, Gidget (Lee et al., 2014) explores a collaborative (rather than competitive) framing of a player's relationship with the computer, framing the computer as a reliable but fallible collaborator incapable of problem-solving; it also focuses players on fixing defective programs rather than expecting players to write programs from scratch. Others have explored how to use games to teach more advanced topics, such as concrete debugging strategies (Miljanovic & Bradbury, 2017), SQL queries (Soflano et al., 2015), test case generation (Tillmann & Bishop, 2014), and software engineering requirements gathering (Connolly & Stansfield, 2006). There is some evidence that programming games are well-liked (Ibrahim et al., 2010), quickly shift attitudes about programming to positive (Charters et al., 2014), and can lead to better learning outcomes than environments with similar interactive features that are not framed as games (Lee & Ko, 2015). However, there is little evidence that playing these games leads to transferable knowledge to other programming contexts. Moreover, even if they do, there is some evidence that most players play only a few levels of these games before abandoning them once they encounter difficulties and cannot find help (Yan et al., 2017).

While the focus of the previous tools was teaching programming or some aspects of it, there are also other game-related approaches that support building motivation for learning programming. There are many games that allow the user to enhance their capabilities through programming. Kerbal Space Program (www.kerbalspaceprogram.com/en) is a game where the player designs and flies spaceships and rockets to explore the planetary system in the game. There is an additional component called kOS (ksp-kos.github.io/KOS) that adds a custom programming language to the game, enabling players to control the rockets programmatically. Another example is the popular game Minecraft (https://minecraft.net) and its "redstone" mechanism to create logical operations. Interestingly, Minecraft has been used to create some very complex artifacts, like a Basic interpreter (www.youtube.com/watch?v=t4e7PjRygt0) or Atari 2600 emulator (www.youtube.com/watch?v=jPRkjNDmTlc). While these examples can be considered as their authors' heroic achievements in using such frameworks, there is more to it than this. In gaming communities, a highly popular activity is game streaming, where a game player streams the game play with oral comments on the working. The above videos of Minecraft belong to this category. Another category is live streaming, for example in Twitch (www.twitch.tv), where the audience can also interact with the author through chat discussion. Streaming playing an educational game like Shenzhen I/O has a clear educational perspective and can act as a method of attracting followers to learn more about programming (Haaranen & Duran, 2017). Such streaming has also extended to live programming (Haaranen, 2017). There is very little research currently on these novel approaches to demonstrating computer science concepts and programming in this context.

21.5.3 E-Books

Whereas programming games offer extrinsic motivations to learn, interactive e-book environments lack any game-specific premise or extrinsic motive, expecting learners to bring their own motivations to reading and completing the book. Unlike games, however, e-books often provide more explicit instruction and feedback on learning objectives. For example, commercial coding tutorials such as Codecademy (www.codecademy.com) and Khan Academy (www.khanacademy.org) offer structured curricula for programming language basics, OpenDSA (Fouh et al., 2014; https://opendsa-server.cs.vt.edu) is an e-book on data structures and algorithms, and CS Principles (Ericson et al., 2016) is an interactive book on Python programming (www.interactivepython.org/runestone/static/StudentCSP/index.html). All three of these are essentially content, expecting learners to be in a motivating context.

Research environments have focused on providing more detailed, interactive explanations of concepts. For example, some offer interactive program visualizations that supplement natural language explanations of concepts (Fouh et al., 2014; Miller & Ranum, 2012; Rossling & Vellaramkalayil, 2009), providing learners with opportunities to see programs execute. Some of these, such as the PLTutor environment, place program visualizations at the center of the experience, focusing learner attention on the specific effects of a programming language's semantics on a program's control flow and state, using natural language explanations to supplement the visualization (Nelson et al., 2017). Several studies of e-books have shown that use of e-book features varies wildly between different students (Alvarado et al., 2012) and different populations of users such as students and teachers (Ericson et al., 2015; Parker et al., 2017), but that deeper engagement with an e-book's interactive features is generally associated with better learning outcomes (Alvarado et al., 2012). One of the only studies of the causal effect of integrated program visualizations on learning showed that, at least with highly granular visualizations of program behavior, learning outcomes are significantly higher than with no program visualizations at all (Nelson et al., 2017).

While games, e-books, tutorials, and tutors offer promising opportunities for learning, the body of evidence of their efficacy is still quite shallow, with only a few studies evaluating learning outcomes. Moreover, pedagogical analyses of these genres of learning technology show that all but the most carefully designed research environments fail to meet even basic learning principles, such as adapting instruction to prior knowledge, providing personalized feedback on practice, and promoting self-regulated learning (Kim & Ko, 2017). There is considerable room for future work to personalize learning while sustainably engaging learners in the use of these learning environments.

21.5.4 Supporting Assessment and Feedback

Assessment and feedback have always been a fundamental part of programming education, and grading student work in large introductory programming courses is very labor-intensive. It is therefore no wonder that developing tools for automatic assessment of students' exercises has always received considerable interest among computing educators. Hollingsworth (1960) reported an early implementation of a mainframe tool for running submitted work against a set of tests and producing a grade from the results. This paper already notes the advantages in terms of cost (although here it's the cost of machine time),

Later work includes systems like ASSESS and AUTOMARK (Redish & Smyth, 1986), ASSYST (Jackson & Usher, 1997), Ceilidh (Benford et al., 1994), and PASS (Thorburn & Rowe, 1997). These systems analyze various aspects of programming assignments, such as program correctness, programming style, efficiency, and code complexity. ASSYST also evaluated students' test coverage, and PASS compared students' submissions with the teacher's solution plan and thus also focused on code design. Later important tools include BOSS (Joy et al., 2005), CourseMaster (Higgins et al., 2002), and Web-CAT (Edwards, 2003; www.web-cat.org). For more information, there are several survey papers that cover the area well, except for the most recent work (Ala-Mutka, 2005; Douce et al., 2005; Ihantola et al., 2010).

Most work on automatic assessment tools has focused on analyzing programming submissions, where several different aspects can be assessed. *Program correctness* is the most widely analyzed feature, which, in most cases, is implemented by running a student's program in a safe sandbox against teacher-defined test cases and comparing the results against teachers' model results. Text-based comparison of output is the most common approach, but is fraught with difficulty in detecting semantically uninteresting variations in formatting, and is gradually being replaced by the use of automated testing frameworks such as JUnit (https://junit.org). *Programming style* is also a frequent measure, covering aspects like code indentation, function lengths, variable names, etc., and may include analyzing *code complexity* using well-known software metrics. More recent work with Web-CAT (Edwards et al., 2017) reports using commercial static analysis programs to perform this function, but cautions that their comprehensive nature can result in overemphasis on superficial "faults." Some more pedagogically focused systems trace whether certain *syntactic structures* have been used, either because they were requested in the assignment or because their use was denied. For example, Scheme-robo (Saikkonen et al., 2001) compared the actual list structures that students' programs used against a model solution. *Code efficiency* can be measured by running the programs against test cases with different runtime expectations. Some tools also analyze *program design/structure* by analyzing the functional structure (Saikkonen et al., 2001; Thorburn & Rowe, 1997).

ASSYST, and more recently Web-CAT, also analyze students' *test cases*. The rationale here is that many students start using automatic systems as kinds of debugging tools, focusing only on passing teachers' test cases, when the focus should be on their own testing. Edwards (2003) emphasizes test-driven development by analyzing how well students' own test cases have covered the source code (and that the code passes them), and additionally how well the program passes teachers' test cases. The results are combined, and it is impossible for students to get high marks with only poor code coverage from their own tests.

While mainstream research has focused on programming submissions, there are also other applications areas. CourseMaster (Higgins et al., 2002) provides tools to analyze flowcharts, OO diagrams, and even electrical circuits. Ali et al. (2007) present a tool for analyzing UML diagrams. Shukur et al. (1999) present a tool for automatic analysis of formal specifications written in the Z language. Dekeyser et al. (2007) describe a tool for analyzing students' skills in SQL queries. Malmi et al. (2004) developed an algorithm simulation system called TRAKLA2 that allowed students to simulate, in terms of graphical user interface manipulation operations, how an algorithm changes a given data structure (e.g., sorting an array of keys). The simulation sequence log is compared with the sequence generated by a correct implementation of the algorithm to provide feedback for the students. Students can view the model execution as an algorithm animation and restart the exercise with new randomized data; thus, they can rehearse and refine their solution with no limitations until their final submission.

Automatic assessment tools can be used in different ways. Firstly, they can provide highly valuable *formative feedback* for students because they can allow students to *resubmit* their work after considering the feedback and refining their solution. Secondly, they can act as prefilters for incomplete student submissions (Ala-Mutka et al., 2004; Joy et al., 2005) by checking, for example, that the program passes a number of tests, satisfies code quality requirements, etc., before the submission is forwarded for teacher evaluation. The final marking is carried out by the teacher, who has access to the automatic analysis results of the submission. Plagiarism detection may also be included in this filtering phase. Finally, the tools can also be used for *summative assessment*, where the results are automatically recorded as (part of) the grade awarded. In this kind of approach, it is important that the student gets information about how the marking was carried out and, if in doubt, can contact the teacher to clarify issues with the grading.

There are many challenges with automatic assessment, such as:

- What is the appropriate level and specificity of feedback? Mitrovic et al. (2002) analyzed the impacts of five different detail levels of feedback by SQL-tutor, ranging from a simple report of success/failure to providing complete model solution, and explored the role of feedback level and student success. Best results were reported when students were given relevant hints on where to focus when correcting the erroneous solution, but challenges remain in identifying the "relevant" feedback and delivering it in a timely fashion.

- In tools that allow students to revise their solution and resubmit it to the system, what is the appropriate number of allowed submissions and what kind of policy in general is good to use? As reported above, one problem is that students use the system as a testing tool instead of testing their programs themselves. Edwards (2003) provided one solution to this. Other solutions, if test case evaluation is not available, include limiting the number of submissions, imposing a penalty for excessive submissions, or slowing the process of providing feedback. Karavirta et al. (2006) and Malmi et al. (2005) have analyzed the impacts of various resubmission policies in students work in the context of TRAKLA2 algorithm simulation exercises.

- How can students be discouraged from "working to the test" by iteratively creating programs that only pass the tests applied to them on submission? This can be addressed by randomizing either the choice of tests or the details of the tests applied, but such randomization is not always trivial, as some cases are more likely to trigger test failures than others.

Chapter 14 elaborates on more on challenges in assessment.

21.5.5 Concretizing the Virtual/Revealing the Hidden

Software is a complex artifact. Its structure is in principle visible in program code, but the length and complexity of the code can obscure the structure and make it difficult to capture even for professionals. The dynamic execution of a program is invisible. We can see only the effect (output) of the program, which could be correct or incorrect, or that the execution ends in an error. While error messages may give information about the proximate cause of the problem, the initial causes of the problem are generally not accessible by looking at the error messages or incorrect results only (Eisenstadt, 1997, called this the "Cause/Effect Chasm"). Therefore, both program code and the actual execution process need to be considered. *Software visualization* is an area of research that seeks to address these challenges. It covers both educational and professional applications in order to understand software, its development, and its execution. Good overviews of the field include Diehl (2007) and Stasko (1998).

For educational purposes, there are two main areas of software visualization: *program visualization* (PV) and *algorithm visualization* (AV). PV is "the visualization of actual program code or data structures in either static or dynamic form" (Stasko, 1998). It is a field that aims to make the code-level execution of a program visible for a programmer. Some well-known examples are Jeliot (Ben-Ari et al., 2011), jGrasp (www.jgrasp.org), and Online Python tutor (Guo et al., 2013). Sorva et al. (2013) presented a fairly recent survey of the whole field. Most PVs are targeted to novices and are restricted to small, illustrative programs, since step-by-step execution of large software systems in order to investigate their logic is beyond the scope of reasonable work.

One way to view the goal of PV is to help learners understand a *notional machine* (du Boulay, 1986), which is an abstract, most often simplified model of what happens in program memory. Most PV systems aim to help with understanding of program execution on a notional machine level by showing how the program execution proceeds statement by statement and visualizing variable values, simple data structures, stack frames, and heap structures. Visualization is not popular at the hardware (processor) level, because modern computers and processors are so complex that exact understanding of all details is frequently beyond the scope of even advanced practitioners. However, moderate understanding of, for example, what happens during the execution of Java or C programs is essential for becoming a competent programmer.

It is worth emphasizing that a notional machine is not a strictly defined concept; the level of abstraction can vary depending on what level of detail is relevant for the stage and goals of education. The PLTutor system (Nelson et al., 2017) targeted a precise and comprehensive level of understanding about JavaScript, providing detailed pedagogy about each individual operation at the instruction level, rather than the line or sub-expression level of a program. The system was based on a theory of programming language semantics knowledge that argues that learning a language involves learning a mapping between syntax and the causal effects of syntax defined by the language's semantics. To teach this mapping, the tutor interleaves conceptual instruction about language semantics with explanations of the side effects of individual components or language constructs. In one of the few studies of PV effects on learning outcomes, this low level of semantic granularity led to significantly better learning outcomes than coding tutorials that involve writing simple programs with these constructs.

AV is a genre of learning technologies that aim at visualizing programs and data at a more abstract level, focusing more on data structures (typically depicted as graphical entities) and how a program manipulates those structures. While algorithm code is frequently included, the visualization focuses on what happens with data and not so much on code-level details. The boundary between program and algorithm visualization is not strict, and many systems include features on both levels. Some famous systems include Sorting-out-sorting video (Baecker & Sherman, 1983), Tango (Stasko, 1990), jHAVÉ (Naps et al., 2000), TRAKLA2 (Malmi et al., 2004), ALVIE (Crescenzi, 2010), Animal (Rößling & Freisleben, 2002), and jFLAP (Rodger, 2006). A somewhat dated but useful survey of the field can be found in Shaffer et al. (2010).

Most PV and AV systems focus on *animation* of the execution, where the user can browse the dynamic execution stepwise, possibly choosing the granularity of steps, while executions are carried out by the computer. An alternative approach is *program simulation* or *algorithm simulation*, where the user acts as the processor and executes the program or algorithm using available graphical interaction tools. The system can evaluate the correctness of the steps and provide feedback for the student. An example of a program simulation system is UUhistle (Sorva and Sirkiä, 2010) and examples of algorithm simulation systems include TRAKLA2 (Malmi et al., 2004) and jSAV (Karavirta & Shaffer, 2013).

The literature in this area also uses other terms. *Code visualization* and *code animation* overlap with PV, but focus solely on code-level details. *Program animation* is sometimes used as a synonym of PV. *Static program visualization* refers to (static) visualization of program structures rather than (dynamic) execution. *Visual debugging* refers to debuggers that include visualizations of program and data structures instead of textual program code only. *Visual programming* is, on the other hand, an entirely separate genre of programming languages and environments that focus on constructing programs using visual rather than textual entities. These visual languages have nothing to do with visualization tools.

There has been considerably empirical research on PV and AV systems, especially the latter. Research has mainly focused on engagement and presentation. A milestone in the research was the meta-study of empirical evaluations of AV systems by Hundhausen et al. (2002). The results indicated that the main difference between studies where better learning results following using AV systems in education were reported or not reported was *student engagement.* That is, if students were actively working with the visualizations vs. merely viewing them, they learned better. An important follow-up work was carried out in an ITiCSE working group (Naps et al., 2002) that defined the *engagement taxonomy* for differentiating between various forms of engaging activities while using AV systems. This widely cited framework has guided much of the consequent research. In its original form, it identified six different modes. *No viewing* (nothing) and *viewing* were the lowest levels with no engaging activity involved. In *responding* mode, learners are presented with questions related to the visualization. The *changing* level allows them to modify the visualization, such as by varying the input data set. In *construction* mode, they can create their own visualization of a program or an algorithm. And finally, in *presenting* mode, they present visualizations to others for feedback and discussion.

Many studies have been carried out to evaluate whether the assumption holds that higher engagement levels would lead to higher learning results. While many positive results have been found, there is also critique that the taxonomy is insufficient and should be revised or augmented. Myller et al. (2009) extended the taxonomy with finer variations in the interactions with visualization tools and used it to analyze collaborative learning processes. Sorva et al. (2013) presented another extension by adding a second dimension concerning the ownership of the task at hand. That is, the engagement is also related to whether learners only manipulate given content or provide their own input cases, modify the visualization software, or even create their own software. Furthermore, few studies actually investigate whether program visualization tools cause better learning. The most recent evaluation of PLTutor (Nelson et al., 2017) involved a controlled experiment that holistically demonstrated improved learning outcomes, but this study did not separate the effect of the visualization from other aspects of its surrounding instruction.

While the engagement taxonomy has had a significant impact on research, there are no compelling results to confirm that the original taxonomy or its extensions accurately reflect the relation of engagement and learning outcomes.

These remain open questions. Moreover, the taxonomy also does not consider the role of how information is presented in the visualization and what kind of textual or audio information supports the visualization.

21.6 Discussion

21.6.1 Incentives for Tools Research

Tool contributions in computing education research are likely to be of continued importance. First, digitalization and massification are transforming education at all levels. While the emergence of massive open online courses (MOOCs) a few years ago did not cause the revolution many teachers in computing education feared (Eckerdal et al., 2014; Sheard et al., 2014), they have become a part of mainstream education and have a significant role both in tertiary education and, particularly, continuing professional development. Due to the sheer number of participants – often many thousands – MOOCs cannot be operated without software tools. With the increased number of students pursuing computing in higher education, many of these same challenges of teaching at scale have reached traditional institutions of education, thus creating an incentive for the development and deployment of automatic assessment and feedback tools. Moreover, because MOOCs cannot generally build on pedagogical foundations that require student–teacher interaction, there is an obvious need for tools supporting self-study of computing topics. Peer review and group work are also widely used in MOOCs, and so there is also an incentive to develop more computing-specific tools supporting these methods.

The influence of MOOCs is also apparent in *blended learning*, which has become a mainstream method for organizing and managing traditional face-to-face teaching and learning in the face of rising enrollments, providing similar incentives for tool development and use. Furthermore, pedagogical practices are moving toward student-centered approaches that generally activate students more compared with the teacher-centered tradition. While practical exercises using either professional or educational tools have always been a central part of computing education, the shift toward even more active methods further drives efforts on tool development and research.

The second important factor promoting tools is the demographic change in students. This is visible in two ways. First, students of this generation have used digital tools for their whole lives and often expect digital tools to be a natural part of their studying. To keep students motivated, learning environments have to develop to include more (appropriate) digital content and opportunities for student interaction. Secondly, institutions have a large and growing number of non-traditional students who study from distance either temporarily or permanently and who thus need more digital content and services than traditional students. They are blended learners by necessity.

The use of learning analytics (see Chapter 25) is a third factor. They are increasingly being applied in education at all levels to analyze student behavior. Compared with traditional methods, digital content and tools can log student activities in great detail and provide huge opportunities to monitor students' progress either at the course or at the program level. The gathered data can also be used to generate feedback for students themselves (e.g., on their study practices; Auvinen et al., 2015) and feedback for curriculum developers about hot and cold spots in their instructional design, as well as cohort-level feedback about difficulties. For example, Code.org iterates on its curriculum based on qualitative feedback, but also through instrumentation of the use of its online tools. However, applying these logging facilities needs careful ethical consideration in research. For example, the granularity of logging (e.g., submission-level logging, key-level logging, even accessing information about other activities students are doing while working on their tasks) should be treated with care in order to avoid ethical conflicts.

21.6.2 Challenges in Computing Education Tools Research

Conducting research on learning technologies for computing education poses some unique challenges.

In many cases, tool development requires significant effort. Usability and efficiency considerations are crucial if the tool is to be used at scale in real course environments, possibly with large numbers of students. This is even true for running carefully controlled laboratory studies, as there are a range of confounding factors in tool design that can mask the benefits of the tool. Ko et al. (2015) present a detailed guide for evaluating programming tools.

Publishing details of the functionality of new tools, supported only by small single-cohort satisfaction analyses, is becoming increasingly difficult, with many conferences and journals requiring more rigorous evaluation studies. Thus, the time (and effort) between deployment of a new tool and dissemination of its features and advantages has increased significantly. Papers describing such systems per se may be publishable in other venues (e.g., software engineering, programming, or CHI conferences and workshops), but for that they often need to make a significant, novel, technical contribution in the domain of the publication, which is not always clearly the case. A similar problem arises when an existing tool is reimplemented for use in a different programming language, such as DrJava (Allen et al., 2002), derived from DrScheme, which was itself originally reported in a symposium on programming languages (Findler et al., 1997).

Sustaining tool research is another challenge. Tools are often designed and implemented as a part of a fixed-term research project or a PhD student's work, and there is no one to continue maintenance and development after the project funding finishes or the thesis is submitted and the student has moved on. Numerous tools have suffered such a fate and are therefore inaccessible to a wider audience or for continuing research. Obviously, for any teacher or institution, adopting a tool that has unclear prospects of long-term support is a significant risk. Bugs might not get fixed, hosted services might terminate at short notice, and support may not be available. Some tools lack features that are required for widespread use, such as comprehensive support for internationalization (e.g., character set and interface translations) or accessibility features for students with disabilities. The latter is a particular issue for tools with custom graphical interfaces, which take them beyond the reach of the facilities provided as standard by the underlying platform. Although it's not often considered in an educational setting, there may also be issues around ownership or licensing of intellectual property in work created using a tool, especially in cases where the tool is inextricably linked with students' work, e.g., Scratch (scratch.mit.edu) or Greenfoot (www.greenfoot.org).

A problem for tool sustainability is that technologies evolve rapidly. This applies both to the technologies the tools use and to those they teach. While ten years ago many tools were delivered as Java applets or Flash applications, current web browsers no longer support these technologies, and so these tools are inaccessible. The same problems apply to tools implemented as plugins for professional tools (e.g., Eclipse or NetBeans) with rapidly changing APIs. Old versions may simply cease working when platforms change, and therefore constant updating or even reimplementations are needed. This is work that has little scientific value, even though from a practical point of view it may be essential. Tools that aim to teach rapidly evolving topics or languages such as Java or Python, or libraries like JUnit, are also at the mercy of changes in their infrastructure.

Only a few tools have been able to reach a state where there is an established research group, dedicated individual, or external funding that can ensure their long-term future. Examples include BlueJ, Web-CAT, jGRASP, DrRacket, Scratch, and Alice. Sometimes the development team has been able to build a business that develops and supports the tool by, for example, charging for enhanced support or back-end services. Sometimes a large enough developer community has emerged, providing the resources to maintain and further develop the tool. Some tools have also formed successful user communities that provide valuable feedback for developers, as well as showcases and discussion forums that can serve as peer and developer support for users (Roque et al., 2012).

Finally, research on tools often possesses some common weaknesses. Many papers motivate tool development through a teacher's observations, and these observations may or may not reflect the students' actual learning problems. It would be valuable to demonstrate evidence of learning or studying problems, generate a hypothesis as to how the problem can be addressed, and build the tool as a test machine for the hypothesis. Secondly, another related aspect is that tools research is frequently disconnected from any educational or psychological theories about students' learning or behavior. Such theories could direct future research by providing more explicit arguments for the observed learning problems, generated hypotheses, and interpretation of empirical results. The field needs theories specific to programming and computing to help build a more robust understanding of how tools mediate learning.

References

Allen, E., Cartwright, R., & Stoler, B. (2002). DrJava: A lightweight pedagogic environment for Java. *ACM SIGCSE Bulletin*, 34(1), 137–141.

Ala-Mutka, K. M. (2005). A survey of automated assessment approaches for programming assignments. *Computer Science Education*, 15(2), 83–102.

Ala-Mutka, K., & Jarvinen, H. M. (2004). Assessment process for programming assignments. In *Proceedings. IEEE International Conference on Advanced Learning Technologies, 2004* (pp. 181–185). New York: IEEE.

Aleven, V., Myers, E., Easterday, M., & Ogan, A. (2010). Toward a framework for the analysis and design of educational games. In *Digital Game and Intelligent Toy Enhanced Learning (DIGITEL)* (pp. 69–76). New York: IEEE.

Ali, N. H., Shukur, Z., & Idris, S. (2007). Assessment system for UML class diagram using notations extraction. *International Journal on Computer Science Network Security*, 7, 181–187.

Alvarado, C., Morrison, B., Ericson, B., Guzdial, M., Miller, B., & Ranum, D. (2012). Performance and use evaluation of an electronic book for introductory Python programming. *Computer Science Faculty Publications. 62.* University of Nebraska at Omaha. Retrieved from https://digitalcommons.unomaha.edu/compscifacpub/62

Auvinen, T., Hakulinen, L., & Malmi, L. (2015). Increasing students' awareness of their behavior in online learning environments with visualizations and achievement badges. *IEEE Transactions on Learning Technologies*, 8(3), 261–273.

Baecker, R. M., & Sherman, D. (1983). Sorting Out Sorting: Narrated colour videotape, 30 minutes, presented at ACM SIGGRAPH '81 and excerpted in ACM SIGGRAPH Video Review #7.

Benford, S., Burke, E., Foxley, E., Gutteridge, N., & Zin, A. M. (1994). Ceilidh as a course management support system. *Journal of Educational Technology Systems*, 22(3), 235–250.

Ben-Ari, M., Bednarik, R., Levy, R. B. B., Ebel, G., Moreno, A., Myller, N., & Sutinen, E. (2011). A decade of research and development on program animation: The Jeliot experience. *Journal of Visual Languages & Computing*, 22(5), 375–384.

Brown, M. H., & Sedgewick, R. (1984). A system for algorithm animation. *SIGGRAPH Computer Graphics*, 18(3), 177–186.

Bruce, K. B., Danyluk, A., & Murtagh, T. (2001). A library to support a graphics-based object-first approach to CS 1. *ACM SIGCSE Bulletin,* 33(1), 6–10.

Brusilovsky, P., Edwards, S., Kumar, A., Malmi, L., Benotti, L., Buck, D., Ihantola, P., Prince, R., Sirkiä, T., Sosnovsky, S., & Urquiza, J. (2014). Increasing adoption of smart learning content for computer science education. In *Proceedings of the Working Group Reports of the 2014 on Innovation & Technology in Computer Science Education Conference* (pp. 31–57). New York: ACM.

Cardell-Oliver, R., & Doran Wu, P. (2011). UWA Java tools: Harnessing software metrics to support novice programmers. In *Proceedings of the 16th Annual*

Joint Conference on Innovation & Technology in Computer Science Education (pp. 341–341). New York: ACM.

Charters, P., Lee, M. J., Ko, A. J., & Loksa, D. (2014). Challenging stereotypes and changing attitudes: the effect of a brief programming encounter on adults' attitudes toward programming. In *Proceedings of the 45th ACM Technical Symposium on Computer Science Education* (pp. 653–658). New York: ACM.

Connolly, T. M., & Stansfield, M. H. (2006). Enhancing eLearning: Using computer games to teach requirements collection and analysis. Presented at *Second Symposium of the Working Group on Human-Computer Interaction and Usability Engineering of the Austrian Computer Society*, Vienna, Austria.

Cooper, S., Dann, W., & Pausch, R. (2000). Alice: A 3-D tool for introductory programming concepts. *Journal of Computing Sciences in Colleges*, 15(5), 107–116.

Cooper, S., Dann, W., & Pausch, R. (2003). Teaching objects-first in introductory computer science. *ACM SIGCSE Bulletin*, 35(1), 191–195.

Crescenzi, P. (2010). AlViE 3.0. Retrieved from https://sites.google.com/site/alviehomepage/alvie3

Davies, S., Polack-Wahl, J. A., & Anewalt, K. (2011). A snapshot of current practices in teaching the introductory programming sequence. In *Proceedings of the 42nd ACM Technical Symposium on Computer Science Education* (pp. 625–630). New York: ACM.

Dekeyser, S., de Raadt, M., & Lee, T. Y. (2007). Computer assisted assessment of SQL query skills. In *Proceedings of the Eighteenth Conference on Australasian Database – Volume 63* (pp. 53–62). Sydney, Australia: Australian Computer Society, Inc.

Diehl, S. (2007). *Software Visualization: Visualizing the Structure, Behaviour, and Evolution of Software*. Berlin, Germany: Springer Science & Business Media.

Douce, C., Livingstone, D., & Orwell, J. (2005). Automatic test-based assessment of programming: A review. *Journal on Educational Resources in Computing (JERIC)*, 5(3), 4.

du Boulay, B. (1986). Some difficulties of learning to program. *Journal of Educational Computing Research*, 2(1), 57–73.

Eckerdal, A., Kinnunen, P., Thota, N., Nylén, A., Sheard, J., & Malmi, L. (2014). Teaching and learning with MOOCs: Computing academics' perspectives and engagement. In *Proceedings of the 2014 Conference on Innovation & Technology in Computer Science Education* (pp. 9–14). New York: ACM.

Edwards, S. H. (2003). Rethinking computer science education from a test-first perspective. In *Companion of the 18th Annual ACM SIGPLAN Conference on Object-Oriented Programming, Systems, Languages, and Applications* (pp. 148–155). New York: ACM.

Edwards, S. H., Kandru, N., & Rajagopal, M. (2017). Investigating static analysis errors in student Java programs. In *Proceedings of the 2017 ACM Conference on International Computing Education Research* (pp. 65–73). New York: ACM.

Eisenstadt, M. (1997). My hairiest bug war stories. *Communications of the ACM*, 40(4), 30–37.

Ericson, B. J., Guzdial, M. J., & Morrison, B. B. (2015). Analysis of interactive features designed to enhance learning in an ebook. In *Proceedings of the Eleventh Annual International Conference on International Computing Education Research* (pp. 169–178). New York: ACM.

Ericson, B. J., Rogers, K., Parker, M., Morrison, B., & Guzdial, M. (2016). Identifying design principles for CS teacher ebooks through design-based research. In *Proceedings of the 2016 ACM Conference on International Computing Education Research* (pp. 191–200). New York: ACM.

Felleisen, M., Findler, R. B., Flatt, M., & Krishnamurthi, S. (1998). The DrScheme project: An overview. *ACM Sigplan Notices*, 33(6), 17–23.

Findler, R. B., Flanagan, C., Flatt, M., Krishnamurthi, S., & Felleisen, M. (1997). DrScheme: A pedagogic programming environment for Scheme. In *International Symposium on Programming Language Implementation and Logic Programming* (pp. 369–388). Berlin, Germany: Springer.

Findler, R. B., Clements, J., Flanagan, C., Flatt, M., Krishnamurthi, S., Steckler, P., & Felleisen, M. (2002). DrScheme: A programming environment for Scheme. *Journal of Functional Programming*, 12(2), 159–182.

Fisker, K., McCall, D., Kölling, M., & Quig, B. (2008). Group work support for the BlueJ IDE. *ACM SIGCSE Bulletin*, 40(3), 163–168.

Fouh, E., Karavirta, V., Breakiron, D. A., Hamouda, S., Hall, S., Naps, T. L., & Shaffer, C. A. (2014). Design and architecture of an interactive eTextbook – The OpenDSA system. *Science of Computer Programming*, 88, 22–40.

Gee, J. P. (2014). *What Video Games Have to Teach Us about Learning and Literacy*. Basingstoke, UK: Macmillan.

Gómez-Albarrán, M. (2005). The teaching and learning of programming: A survey of supporting software tools. *The Computer Journal*, 48(2), 130–144.

Guo, P. J. (2013). Online Python tutor: Embeddable web-based program visualization for CS education. In *Proceeding of the 44th ACM Technical Symposium on Computer Science Education* (pp. 579–584). New York: ACM.

Haaranen, L. (2017). Programming as a performance: Live-streaming and its implications for computer science education. In *Proceedings of the 2017 ACM Conference on Innovation and Technology in Computer Science Education* (pp. 353–358). New York: ACM.

Haaranen, L., & Duran, R. (2017). Link between gaming communities in YouTube and computer science. In *Proceedings of the 9th International Conference on Computer Supported Education* (pp. 17–24). Setúbal, Portugal: ScitePress.

Helminen, J., Ihantola, P., Karavirta, V., & Malmi, L. (2012). How do students solve parsons programming problems?: An analysis of interaction traces. In *Proceedings of the Ninth Annual International Conference on International Computing Education Research* (pp. 119–126). New York: ACM.

Higgins, C., Symeonidis, P., & Tsintsifas, A. (2002). The marking system for CourseMaster. *ACM SIGCSE Bulletin*, 34(3), 46–50.

Hollingsworth, J. (1960). Automatic graders for programming classes. *Communications of the ACM*, 3(10), 528–529.

Hundhausen, C. D., Douglas, S. A., & Stasko, J. T. (2002). A meta-study of algorithm visualization effectiveness. *Journal of Visual Languages & Computing*, 13(3), 259–290.

Ibrahim, R., Yusoff, R. C. M., Omar, H. M., & Jaafar, A. (2010). Students perceptions of using educational games to learn introductory programming. *Computer and Information Science*, 4(1), 205.

Ihantola, P., Ahoniemi, T., Karavirta, V., & Seppälä, O. (2010). Review of recent systems for automatic assessment of programming assignments. In *Proceedings of the*

10th Koli Calling International Conference on Computing Education Research (pp. 86–93). New York: ACM.

Jackson, D., & Usher, M. (1997). Grading student programs using ASSYST. *ACM SIGCSE Bulletin*, 29(1), 335–339.

Joy, M., Griffiths, N., & Boyatt, R. (2005). The BOSS online submission and assessment system. *Journal on Educational Resources in Computing (JERIC)*, 5(3), 2.

Karavirta, V., Korhonen, A., & Malmi, L. (2006). On the use of resubmissions in automatic assessment systems. *Computer Science Education*, 16(3), 229–240.

Karavirta, V., & Shaffer, C. A. (2013). JSAV: The JavaScript algorithm visualization library. In *Proceedings of the 18th ACM Conference on Innovation and Technology in Computer Science Education* (pp. 159–164). New York: ACM.

Kelleher, C., & Pausch, R. (2005). Lowering the barriers to programming: A taxonomy of programming environments and languages for novice programmers. *ACM Computing Surveys (CSUR)*, 37(2), 83–137.

Kemeny, J. G., & Kurtz, T. E. (1964). *BASIC: A Manual for BASIC, the Elementary Algebraic Language Designed for Use with the Dartmouth Time Sharing System*, 1st edn. Hanover, NH: Dartmouth College Computation Center.

Kim, A. S., & Ko, A. J. (2017). A pedagogical analysis of online coding tutorials. In *Proceedings of the 2017 ACM SIGCSE Technical Symposium on Computer Science Education* (pp. 321–326). New York: ACM.

Ko, A. J., Latoza, T. D., & Burnett, M. M. (2015). A practical guide to controlled experiments of software engineering tools with human participants. *Empirical Software Engineering*, 20(1), 110–141.

Kölling, M., Quig, B., Patterson, A., & Rosenberg, J. (2003). The BlueJ system and its pedagogy. *Computer Science Education*, 13(4), 249–268.

Lancaster, T., & Culwin, F. (2004). A comparison of source code plagiarism detection engines. *Computer Science Education*, 14(2), 101–112.

Lee, M. J., Bahmani, F., Kwan, I., LaFerte, J., Charters, P., Horvath, A., Luor, F., Cao, J., Law, C., Beswetherick, M., & Long, S. (2014). Principles of a debugging-first puzzle game for computing education. In *2014 IEEE Symposium on Visual Languages and Human-Centric Computing (VL/HCC)* (pp. 57–64). New York: IEEE.

Lee, M. J., & Ko, A. J. (2015). Comparing the effectiveness of online learning approaches on CS1 learning outcomes. In *Proceedings of the Eleventh Annual International Conference on International Computing Education Research* (pp. 237–246). New York: ACM.

Malmi, L., Karavirta, V., Korhonen, A., Nikander, J., Seppälä, O., & Silvasti, P. (2004). Visual algorithm simulation exercise system with automatic assessment: TRAKLA2. *Informatics in Education*, 3(2), 267.

Malmi, L., Karavirta, V., Korhonen, A., & Nikander, J. (2005). Experiences on automatically assessed algorithm simulation exercises with different resubmission policies. *Journal on Educational Resources in Computing (JERIC)*, 5(3), 7.

Mason, R., Cooper, G., & de Raadt, M. (2012). Trends in introductory programming courses in Australian universities: Languages, environments and pedagogy. In *Proceedings of the Fourteenth Australasian Computing Education Conference – Volume 123* (pp. 33–42). Sydney, Australia: Australian Computer Society, Inc.

McIver, L. (2002). Evaluating languages and environments for novice programmers. In *Fourteenth Annual Workshop of the Psychology of Programming Interest Group (PPIG 2002)* (pp. 100–110). London, UK: Brunel University.

Meerbaum-Salant, O., Armoni, M., & Ben-Ari, M. (2013). Learning computer science concepts with Scratch. *Computer Science Education*, 23(3), 239–264.

Miller, B. N., & Ranum, D. L. (2012). Beyond PDF and ePub: Toward an interactive textbook. In *Proceedings of the 17th ACM Annual Conference on Innovation and Technology in Computer Science Education* (pp. 150–155). New York: ACM.

Miljanovic, M. A., & Bradbury, J. S. (2017). RoboBUG: A serious game for learning debugging techniques. In *Proceedings of the 2017 ACM Conference on International Computing Education Research* (pp. 93–100). New York: ACM.

Mitrovic, A., Martin, B., & Mayo, M. (2002). Using evaluation to shape ITS design: Results and experiences with SQL-Tutor. *User Modeling and User-Adapted Interaction*, 12(2), 243–279.

Myller, N., Bednarik, R., Sutinen, E., & Ben-Ari, M. (2009). Extending the engagement taxonomy: Software visualization and collaborative learning. *ACM Transactions on Computing Education (TOCE)*, 9(1), 7.

Naps, T. L., Eagan, J. R., & Norton, L. L. (2000). JHAVÉ – An environment to actively engage students in web-based algorithm visualizations. *ACM SIGCSE Bulletin*, 32(1), 109–113.

Naps, T. L., Rößling, G., Almstrum, V., Dann, W., Fleischer, R., Hundhausen, C., Korhonen, A., Malmi, L., McNally, M., Rodger, S., & Velázquez-Iturbide, J. Á. (2002). Exploring the role of visualization and engagement in computer science education. *ACM Sigcse Bulletin,* 35(2), 131–152.

Nelson, G. L., Xie, B., & Ko, A. J. (2017). Comprehension first: Evaluating a novel pedagogy and tutoring system for program tracing in CS1. In *Proceedings of the 2017 ACM Conference on International Computing Education Research* (pp. 2–11). New York: ACM.

Parker, M. C., Rogers, K., Ericson, B. J., & Guzdial, M. (2017). Students and teachers use an online AP CS principles ebook differently: Teacher behavior consistent with expert learners. In *Proceedings of the 2017 ACM Conference on International Computing Education Research* (pp. 101–109). New York: ACM.

Resnick, M., Maloney, J., Monroy-Hernández, A., Rusk, N., Eastmond, E., Brennan, K., Millner, A., Rosenbaum, E., Silver, J., Silverman, B., & Kafai, Y. (2009). Scratch: Programming for all. *Communications of the ACM*, 52(11), 60–67.

Redish, K. A., & Smyth, W. F. (1986). Program style analysis: A natural by-product of program compilation. *Communications of the ACM*, 29(2), 126–133.

Robinett, W., & Grimm, L. (1982). *Rocky's Boots/Robot Odyssey*. San Francisco, CA: The Learning Company.

Rodger, S. H. (2002). Using hands-on visualizations to teach computer science from beginning courses to advanced courses. Presented at Second Program Visualization Workshop. Retrieved from www2.cs.duke.edu/csed/rodger/papers/pviswk02.pdf

Rodger, S. H., & Finley, T. W. (2006). *JFLAP: An Interactive Formal Languages and Automata Package*. Burlington, MA: Jones & Bartlett Learning.

Rosales, F., García, A., Rodríguez, S., Pedraza, J. L., Méndez, R., & Nieto, M. M. (2008). Detection of plagiarism in programming assignments. *IEEE Transactions on Education*, 51(2), 174–183.

Rößling, G., & Vellaramkalayil, T. (2009). A visualization-based computer science hypertextbook prototype. *ACM Transactions on Computing Education (TOCE)*, 9(2), 11.

Rößling, G., & Freisleben, B. (2002). ANIMAL: A system for supporting multiple roles in algorithm animation. *Journal of Visual Languages & Computing*, 13(3), 341–354.

Roque, R., Kafai, Y., & Fields, D. (2012). From tools to communities: Designs to support online creative collaboration in Scratch. In *Proceedings of the 11th International Conference on Interaction Design and Children* (pp. 220–223). New York: ACM.

Saikkonen, R., Malmi, L., & Korhonen, A. (2001). Fully automatic assessment of programming exercises. *ACM SIGCSE Bulletin*, 33(3), 133–136.

Shaffer, C. A., Cooper, M. L., Alon, A. J. D., Akbar, M., Stewart, M., Ponce, S., & Edwards, S. H. (2010). Algorithm visualization: The state of the field. *ACM Transactions on Computing Education (TOCE)*, 10(3), 9.

Sheard, J., Eckerdal, A., Kinnunen, P., Malmi, L., Nylén, A., & Thota, N. (2014). MOOCs and their impact on academics. In *Proceedings of the 14th Koli Calling International Conference on Computing Education Research* (pp. 137–145). New York: ACM.

Sheard, J., Simon, S., Hamilton, M., & Lönnberg, J. (2009). Analysis of research into the teaching and learning of programming. In *Proceedings of the Fifth International Workshop on Computing Education Research* (pp. 93–104). New York: ACM.

Shukur, Z., Burke, E., & Foxley, E. (1999). The automatic assessment of formal specification coursework. *Journal of Computing in Higher Education*, 11(1), 86–119.

Simon, A. (2007). classification of recent Australasian computing education publications. *Computer Science Education*, 17(3), 155–169.

Simon, S. (2009). Informatics in education and Koli Calling: A comparative analysis. *Informatics in Education*, 8(1), 101.

Sirkiä, T. (2016). Jsvee & Kelmu: Creating and tailoring program animations for computing education. In *2016 IEEE Working Conference on Software Visualization (VISSOFT)* (pp. 36–45). New York: IEEE.

Sirkiä, T., & Haaranen, L. (2017). Improving online learning activity interoperability with ACOS server. *Software: Practice and Experience*, 47(11), 1657–1676.

Soflano, M., Connolly, T. M., & Hainey, T. (2015). An application of adaptive games-based learning based on learning style to teach SQL. *Computers & Education*, 86, 192–211.

Sorva, J., & Sirkiä, T. (2010). UUhistle: A software tool for visual program simulation. In *Proceedings of the 10th Koli Calling International Conference on Computing Education Research* (pp. 49–54). New York: ACM.

Sorva, J., Karavirta, V., & Malmi, L. (2013). A review of generic program visualization systems for introductory programming education. *ACM Transactions on Computing Education (TOCE)*, 13(4), 15.

Spacco, J., Hovemeyer, D., Pugh, W., Emad, F., Hollingsworth, J. K., & Padua-Perez, N. (2006). Experiences with Marmoset: Designing and using an advanced submission and testing system for programming courses. *ACM SIGCSE Bulletin*, 38(3), 13–17.

Stasko, J. T. (1990). Tango: A framework and system for algorithm animation. *Computer*, 23(9), 27–39.

Stasko, J. (Ed.) (1998). *Software Visualization: Programming as a Multimedia Experience*. Cambridge, MA: MIT Press.

Thorburn, G., & Rowe, G. (1997). PASS: An automated system for program assessment. *Computers & Education*, 29(4), 195–206.

Tillmann, N., Bishop, J., Horspool, N., Perelman, D., & Xie, T. (2014). Code hunt: Searching for secret code for fun. In *Proceedings of the 7th International Workshop on Search-Based Software Testing* (pp. 23–26). New York: ACM.

Uysal, M. P. (2016). Evaluation of learning environments for object-oriented programming: Measuring cognitive load with a novel measurement technique. *Interactive Learning Environments*, 24(7), 1590–1609.

Valentine, D. W. (2004). CS educational research: A meta-analysis of SIGCSE technical symposium proceedings. *ACM SIGCSE Bulletin*, 36(1), 255–259.

Wirth, N. (1973). The Programming Language Pascal (Revised Report). ETH Zürich. Retrieved from https://doi.org/10.3929/ethz-a-000814158

Wolz, U., & Koffman, E. (1999). simpleIO: A Java package for novice interactive and graphics programming. *ACM SIGCSE Bulletin*, 31(3), 139–142.

Yan, A., Lee, M. J., & Ko, A. J. (2017). Predicting abandonment in online coding tutorials. In *IEEE Symposium on Visual Languages and Human-Centered Computing (VL/HCC)* (pp. 191–199). New York: IEEE.

22 Tangible Computing

Michael Horn and Marina Bers

22.1 Introduction

Seymour Papert's book, *Mindstorms: Children, Computers, and Powerful Ideas* (1980), featured a startling photograph for the time – a large dome-like robot, a floor turtle, which could be programmed by children to draw geometric forms on paper sheets. This was Logo – not just the turtle on the screen that spread throughout the world on the floppy disks of the 1980s, but a physical–digital hybrid system, an embodied configuration of metal, glass, plastic, and bits. The spirit of physicality in Logo, and many other educational languages of the time (see Kelleher & Pausch, 2005), became mostly metaphorical – the turtle moved in the physical space of a virtual world of abstracted geometry. But, metaphor though it was, the creators of these languages saw physicality as an essential link between children's embodied experiences in the world and the new universe of computer code.

This chapter is about *tangibility* in computer science education. And, even though the term "tangible" didn't gain widespread use in human–computer interaction until the turn of this century, the history of computing education is clearly anchored in tangible roots that have grown and blossomed over the last 30 years. We see these roots in early educational programming language paradigms. diSessa and Abelson spoke of "spatial metaphor" and "naive realism" in their design of Boxer (diSessa & Abelson, 1986); Papert evoked the concept of "body syntonic" reasoning in children's use of Logo (1980); and with Karel the Robot (1981), Richard Pattis sought to introduce computer science to learners in terms of navigating a grid world. We see other echoes of tangibility in the panoply of visual programming languages that rely heavily on physical and spatial metaphors to represent concepts such as encapsulation, scope, flow of control, and syntax (diSessa & Abelson, 1986; Erwin, Cyr, & Rogers, 2000; Kelleher & Pausch, 2005; Repenning, 1993; Resnick et al., 2009). And, remarkably, in the 1970s, researchers were thinking about physical computer *languages* that they imagined could open the door to programming for children who were still learning how to read and write (see McNerney, 2004). In all of this work was the democratizing idea that anyone, regardless of age or background, could engage in computational literacy (diSessa, 2001) experiences. Tangibility, whether real or metaphorical, was central to this vision. We'll talk a little about this history in this chapter, but our main focus will be on why tangible computing matters now and how we see it shaping the future land-scape of computing education. The chapter will touch on physical computing and robotics, but our main emphasis will be on the use of tangible technologies to support computer programming in and with the physical world. We express cautious optimism about this future. Despite the progress we've made, it's clear that tangible computing as an educational endeavor is still very much in its infancy. This field has potential to invite a diverse new generation into computing and to advance computer science education, but there is still work to be done to fully realize this vision.

22.2 A Brief History of Tangible Computing Education

In the years leading up to the turn of the century, the physicality of computing education experienced something of a resurgence through both technological advances as well as the sustained efforts of researchers to advance human interaction with computers beyond the computer screen and into the real world. Ishii and Ullmer (1997) coined the term "tangible" to describe a class of computer interfaces that employ physical objects and surfaces as a means to both manipulate and represent digital information. Their use of the term was meant to capture the idea that much of the richness of human interaction with the physical world through the use of tools has been replaced by uniform interaction with narrow-bandwidth input devices such as mice, keyboards, and touchscreens. They were also considering a much older history of computation anchored in physical materials (such as the abacus). The incorporation of a variety of physical objects and multisensory feedback was seen as a way to recapture some of this richness to *humanize* human–computer interaction. Later definitions such as Dourish's notion of *embodied interaction* (Dourish, 2004) and Hornecker and Buur's (2006) *tangible interaction* emphasized the degree to which interactive systems could be meaningfully embedded in physical, social, and cultural contexts. In this sense, tangibility became less about the physical nature of the interface and more about the idea that interaction with digital systems could be entangled within material and social realities beyond that of an individual sitting in front of a computer screen. All of these ideas have roots in the *ubiquitous computing* movement of the late 1980s and early 1990s that imagined a world in which machines would increasingly conform to human dimensions, capabilities, and activity structures rather than the other way around (Weiser, Gold, & Brown, 1999).

Perhaps not surprisingly, much of the research involving tangible interaction has emphasized education and learning (Bers, 2008; O'Malley & Fraser, 2004; Shaer & Hornecker, 2010). For example, the work of Resnick and collaborators at the MIT Media Lab is notable for its focus on *digital manipulatives*, computationally enhanced versions of traditional children's toys that created new opportunities for learners to engage with complex concepts. For example, Digital Beads (Resnick et al., 1998) allowed children to create simple programs in a language of one-dimensional cellular automata by stringing together small capsules with embedded LEDs that could transmit, absorb, or destroy light passed from adjacent beads. The System Blocks project (Zuckerman, Arida, & Resnick, 2005) provided a similar interface for simulating dynamic systems. Wooden blocks with embedded electronics expressed behaviors of complex systems, such as stocks, flows, and feedback loops. The work of this group also helped to open physical computing and robotics to a broader (and younger) audience. Their LEGO/Logo project made it possible for children to write computer programs to control animated LEGO constructions incorporating sensors and motors (Resnick, Ocko, & Papert, 1988). This work was followed by other influential projects like LEGO Mindstorms and the MIT Cricket (Resnick et al., 1998; see also Blikstein, 2013). Blikstein's review of physical computing kits (2013) describes four waves of innovation in physical computing education, starting with systems such as LEGO/Logo (Resnick, Ocko, & Papert, 1988) in the 1980s and leading to systems such as the Arduino (Mellis, Banzi, Cuartielles, & Igoe, 2007), PICO Cricket (Rusk et al., 2008), Cubelets (Schweikardt & Gross, 2006), and the LilyPad Arduino (Buechley & Eisenberg, 2008).

In addition to physical computing systems programmed with graphical or text-based languages, researchers have also explored the idea that computer code itself can be represented using physical objects. With a text-based language, programmers use words like BEGIN, IF, and REPEAT to instruct a computer. This code must be written according to strict, and often frustrating, syntactic rules. With a visual or graphical language (see Chapters 13 and 21), words are replaced by pictures, and programs are expressed by arranging and connecting icons on the computer screen. Syntactic rules can be conveyed to the programmer through a rich set of visual cues based on cultural and diagrammatic conventions. Visual languages can be less intimidating for beginners and have become popular in educational settings (Chapter 13). Tangible languages go a step further. Instead of relying on pictures and words on a computer screen, tangible languages use physical objects in the real world to represent various programming elements, data abstractions, and flow-of-control structures. Users manipulate, arrange, and connect these physical elements to construct runnable programs. Rather than relying on implied rules, spatial metaphors, and user interface conventions, tangible languages can exploit the physical properties of objects such as size, shape, and material to express and enforce syntax.

Researchers began exploring the idea of tangible languages as early as the 1970s. Radia Perlman, then a researcher at the MIT Logo Lab, believed that the syntax rules of text-based computer languages represented a serious barrier to learning for young children. To address this issue, she developed an interface called Slot Machines (see McNerney, 2004) that allowed young children to insert cards representing various Logo commands into three colored racks, which in turn represented subroutines.

Almost two decades later, projects such as Suzuki and Kato's AlgoBlocks (Suzuki & Kato, 1995) began to revisit these ideas. Since that time, a wide variety of tangible languages have been developed and explored, including projects that blend movement and action and physical space with digital programming (Fernaeus & Tholander, 2006; Sherman et al., 2001), robots that are also embodied algorithmic structures (Schweikardt & Gross, 2006; Wyeth, 2008), the incorporation of found or crafted materials into algorithmic expressions (Smith & Kotzé, 2010), and the integration of physical activity and play with programming (Smith, 2007). Increasingly, tangible languages are making their way out of research labs and into the public sphere in the form of offerings such as museum exhibits, educational tools, and commercial products (Horn, Crouser, & Bers, 2012; Hu, Zekelman, Horn, & Judd, 2015; Sullivan, Bers, & Mihm, 2017).[1] As these ideas have gained a commercial foothold, researchers have started to consider the learning affordances of tangible vs. screen-based interfaces (Horn et al., 2012; Pugnali et al., 2017; Strawhacker & Bers, 2015; Strawhacker et al., 2013; Sullivan & Bers, 2018).

In this chapter, we broadly classify tangible languages into the following three categories: smart block languages, demonstration languages, and externally compiled languages.

Smart Block Languages: Smart block programming languages feature interlocking physical blocks that can be stacked or connected to form a program. In all cases, the blocks themselves contain electronic components or microprocessors, which, when connected, form structures that are more than just abstract representations of algorithms; they form working, specialized computers that can execute code through the sequential interaction of the blocks. Their physical structures embody both the program and the means for its execution. For example, McNerney's Tangible Computation Bricks (2004) embedded Cricket microprocessors into LEGO bricks that could be stacked to form physical algorithmic structures. The bricks also accepted a single-parameter card that could interchangeably be a constant, a timer, a sensor, or some user-adjustable value. Along similar lines, Wyeth (2008) created a smart block language for younger children (ages four to eight) also using stackable LEGO-like blocks to describe simple programs. This language consisted of sensor blocks, logic blocks, and action blocks for generating light, sound, and motion. Schweikard and Gross (2006) developed a distributed construction kit system consisting of interlocking cubes that encouraged users to combine sensors, logic elements, and actuators, exposing them to a variety of advanced concepts including kinematics, feedback, and distributed control.

Tangible Demonstration Languages: A second class of tangible language allows users to program physical systems or environments by demonstrating a set of rules or actions that can be kinetic, audible, or digital. The computer then repeats these steps to act out a program. Researchers at the University of Maryland have explored approaches for controlling ubiquitous computing environments for storytelling (Sherman et al., 2001). Working with children,

---

1 See also www.primotoys.com, www.bee-bot.us/bluebot.html, www.playosmo.com/en/coding.

the researchers developed and evaluated demonstration-based programming systems called StoryKits. Using a "magic wand," young children (ages four to six) were able to program the various props and physical icons that made up their story worlds. In a slightly different direction, Frei, Su, Mikhak, and Ishii designed an educational toy called Curlybot (Frei, Su, Mikhak, & Ishii, 2000) that could record and play back its motion on a flat surface. Children could program the robot by dragging the robot to demonstrate motion. Taking this idea of kinetic memory further, Raffle, Parkes, and Ishii created Topobo (2004), a system that allows children to construct imaginative creatures composed of passive and active building components. The active components have the ability to record and play back physical motion, helping children learn about animal movement and their own bodies in the process.

Externally Compiled Languages: Unlike smart block languages, programs created with an externally compiled tangible language are only symbolic representations of actual algorithms – much in the way that Java or C++ programs are only collections of text files. An additional piece of technology (a compiler or interpreter) must be used to translate the abstract representations of the program into a machine language that will be executed on some computer system. Ideally, the tangible elements of a compiled language contain little or no electronic components, affording the language designers more freedom in the choice of objects and materials to work with. For instance, paper or flat cards with attached RFID tags become realistic options. Early examples of such languages come from Horn and colleagues with projects like Quetzal and Tern (Horn & Jacob, 2007). These languages use passive tangible objects encoded with computer vision fiducials that allow a camera to translate blocks into working programs. Researchers at the DevTech research group at Tufts University developed KIBO (Bers, 2018a; Sullivan, Bers, & Mihm, 2017), a robot that can be programmed with wooden blocks with barcodes. Children assemble the robot by incorporating its sensors, motors, and art platforms, and then utilize the embedded barcode scanner to compile their programs, block by block, creating a direct link between the robot and the program it executes. Newer systems have made use of augmented reality and video-based object tracking (Hu et al., 2015) to combine some of the real-time interaction of smart block languages with the practical advantages of passive tangible objects.

Each of the three classifications of tangible languages – smart block languages, demonstration languages, and externally compiled languages – present their own challenges and affordances and can better serve different populations of learners with their own unique needs and developmental capabilities.

22.3 Why Tangibility Matters (Four Themes)

Given the history and accelerating interest in tangible and physical computing for education, a reasonable question to ask is: Why does it all matter?

Creating tangible materials comes with associated costs that simply aren't a factor for pure software systems. While software can be deployed online, physical materials have to be designed, manufactured, and distributed. These costs will decrease given advances in 3D printing, homemade electronics, and the increasing availability of maker spaces, but it is still worth asking what we gain from tangibility that makes added costs worthwhile. A tempting answer is that physicality confers a certain degree of cognitive leverage in learning situations, especially for younger children. Variants of this argument, usually anchored in notions of sensorimotor engagement with the material world, have been around for decades.[2] For example, research based on *conceptual metaphor theory* (Lakoff & Johnson, 2008) has argued that learning experiences that make use of physical properties of materials, movement through space, and relationships between objects and people might more successfully reference sensorimotor schema that form the foundation for much of abstract thought (e.g., Hurtienne & Israel, 2007; Macaranas et al., 2012). While we agree that it is appealing to consider the cognitive benefits of tangibles for learning, here we propose four other broad themes that have perhaps received less attention in the literature, but nonetheless illustrate what we see as important future directions of tangibility in computer science education research. These themes have to do with broadening the access to and appeal of computational literacy experiences, in part by making them more universal and visible. For each theme, we highlight example projects that illustrate the potential of tangibles in the future of computer science education.

22.3.1 Theme 1: Early Childhood Learning

The world of early childhood education often privileges children's engagement in rich sensorimotor experiences with both the natural world and physical materials, while remaining cautious about "exposure" to digital media and screen time (American Academy of Pediatrics, 2016). In this context, the development of programming languages that make it possible for children to code with objects such as wooden blocks, tiles, beads, or even craft materials has helped reimagine computational thinking as a developmentally appropriate activity that can be integrated with other classroom experiences in a natural way (Bers, 2008, 2018a; Bers & Horn, 2010). Using programming and robotics systems, children can program, debug, and play with concepts like sequences, patterns, logic, loops, sensors, and actuators, often without ever interacting with screen-based media (Figures 22.1 and 22.2).

One of the earliest examples is KIBO, a robotics and tangible programming kit for children aged four to seven years old. KIBO started as a research project at the DevTech research group at Tufts University and became a commercially available product in 2014 (Bers, 2018a). KIBO lets children build their own

---

2 Literature on manipulative materials in early mathematics education is an interesting case that has had mixed results (see Uttal, Scudder, & DeLoache, 1997).

Figure 22.1 *A prototype tangible programming language based on computer vision technology.*
Image credit: Felix Hu.

Figure 22.2 *KIBO robot and its blocks.*
Reproduced with permission from Bers (2018b).

robots, decorate them with art supplies, and program them, without requiring PCs, tablets, or smartphones. To program their robotic creations, children put together sequences of instructions (programs) using the wooden KIBO blocks that they can then scan with a barcode reader built into the body of the robot (see Figure 22.2). The language syntax in KIBO (i.e., a sequential connection of blocks) is designed to support and reinforce sequencing skills in young children (Bers, 2018a; Horn, Crouser, & Bers, 2012).

Research with KIBO in early childhood classrooms has shown that children as young as preschool age were able to create sequential programs as well as more sophisticated algorithms that utilize control structures with number and sensor parameters (Sullivan & Bers, 2016, 2017). Research also shows statistically significant improvement of kindergarten children in sequencing skills, which are predictors of later numeracy and literacy (Kazakoff & Bers, 2012).

Beyond classrooms, researchers are using similar approaches to introduce foundational computational literacy experiences for young children through culturally relevant artifacts. For example, Horn et al. (2013) explored the use of coding "stickers" embedded in a children's storybook as a way to engage parents and children together in playful computer programming activities. The technology combined a paper storybook with computer programming activities that children complete by adhering stickers to the pages of the book. The programs then controlled an interactive digital character that appeared on the screen of a smartphone or tablet computer. The researchers argued that children's storybooks are powerful *cultural forms* of literacy that support subtle but powerful parent–child reading practices that scaffold parental involvement in children's early *computational* literacy activities.

The designers of these and similar systems are intentionally shaping materials to better speak the language of early childhood. In this context, educators can start to blend computational artifacts within a broader child-driven inquiry model. Tangible materials and technologies will continue to create opportunities to support learning with younger children, enabling designers to think about what emerging computational literacy might look like. However, the accelerated availability of commercial products claiming that they can engage young children in learning about computer science, while most of them only provide a limited "playpen" as opposed to an open-ended "playground" (Bers, 2012; 2018a), might invite researchers and policy-makers to examine what are the minimal design features of such environments to claim that they support learning the sequential, algorithmic, and problem-solving skills associated with programming, as well as afford expressiveness of ideas through projects that are personally meaningful to children.

22.3.2 Theme 2: Appealing to a Broader Audience

The inability of computer science education to attract and retain diverse learner participation, both in schools and beyond, is a persistent and discouraging trend that has been taken up multiple times in this book already (Chapters 16 and 24). It is possible that we are now at a turning point with new and more inclusive learning environments and programs that are connecting with learners from backgrounds previously underrepresented in computer science and related fields. However, the weight of evidence from post-secondary degree programs suggests that we still have much work to do (Zweben & Bizot, 2016). One of the most appealing aspects of tangible computing is its potential to connect with a broader audience, representing a more diverse range of cultural traditions, practices, and value systems.

In the realm of physical computing, projects like LilyPad Arduino (Buechley & Eisenberg, 2008; Kafai et al., 2014; Searle et al., 2014) and e-textiles are using innovative designs to integrate computational and electronic materials with craft traditions such as sewing, scrapbooking, drawing, music, and fashion. Such craft traditions have rich cultural roots characterized by multigenerational communities of practice. The transformation here, although perhaps not fully realized, is subtle. It's not that computation is being superficially dressed up in new clothes so as to become more palatable to a diverse audience; rather, these tool kits and materials are ideally appropriated by existing communities as a new medium of expression, grounded in evolving communities and practices. These new systems help illustrate the potential relevance of computer science education in a much broader array of activities and endeavors (including craft traditions, music, dance, fashion, visual arts, storytelling, and so on).

Another example of this potential comes from the work of Horn and colleagues on a tangible programming and robotics exhibit that was installed at the Museum of Science, Boston. The exhibit allowed visitors to control the movement of a robot on a platform by constructing programs from chains of wooden blocks shaped like jigsaw puzzle pieces. Compared to a version of the exhibit in which visitors used a computer mouse to program in the same robot, children (and girls in particular) were significantly more likely to try the exhibit in the tangible condition (Horn et al., 2012). And, although visitors created similar programs in the two conditions, they were also more likely to engage in collaborative exploration with other family members in the tangible condition.

Tangible approaches have also shown potential for children with a range of cognitive and physical abilities. KIBO was used with children with autism spectrum disorder, and preliminary results from a pilot study in Panama show that children were not only able to successfully program their robots and understand their code in order to debug it, but also to engage in social interactions through the activity of arranging blocks in a sequence (Albo-Canals et al., 2018). Other researchers have explored affordances of tangible programming languages for children with visual impairments (Thieme et al., 2017).

22.3.3 Theme 3: Increasing the Visibility of Digital Artifacts in Learning Spaces

Robotics activities in educational settings are characterized by the creative chaos of building, testing, failure, rebuilding, and refining. Children move back and forth between programming stations (such as laptop computers) where they build and refine simple computer programs that provide the logical glue between sensors (touch, light, etc.) and actuators (motors, sounds, lights). One wonderful aspect of this kind of work is that robots and the construction process have a physical presence that is highly visible. But this visibility also highlights the relatively little attention that software (the programs that students construct to control the robots) receives compared to hardware. Robots are colorful, physical creatures that come alive with light, sounds, and motion. Computer code, on the other hand, often lives a transient and anonymous life on a computer display. It's much harder to see, it gets covered up by other windows of digital content, and it is often forgotten altogether. After the lights turn off and the children go home, the robots are often still displayed in the classroom, while the code that made the robots run is nowhere to be seen. This can happen across a variety of computer science education activities, including animation, graphics, video games, e-textiles, and robotics competitions. In the landscape of computational artifacts, code can become a forgotten, second-class citizen.

One appealing aspect of tangible programming languages is that they give "code" a persistent, physical life in the learning space. Code has the potential to become a structure that can be literally held on to as a robot executes its program, and something that is persistently visible and available for the same level of tinkering, refinement, and debugging as the robot itself. This tangibility also facilitates debugging in a social context. Children can see what doesn't work and they can help fix it. Depending on the system, the programs might take a variety of forms: stickers on a piece of paper, interlocking wooden blocks, magnetic tiles on a whiteboard, or even Lego bricks that piggyback on the robot itself. The added visibility of code might bring attention to previously neglected properties and concepts such as elegance, the importance of debugging, and testing for edge cases and other unusual situations. In other words, code has the potential to become an object of conversation and attention in a way that it might not have been before.

22.3.4 Theme 4: Beyond Toys and Games

Although we see much promise in tangible computing, most of the existing work focuses on younger children, with relatively less attention directed toward older learners. The reasons for this are varied. The push away from predominantly screen-based media is a move that resonates with early childhood education, and for young children with developing literacy and fine motor skills, physical materials offer an appealing and perhaps more accessible entry point into computational literacy. However, another reason for this has to do with current technical limitations of tangible interfaces and their fit for more advanced educational, professional, and real-world settings. While touch-sensitive devices and computer displays have made tremendous strides in the past 20 years, tangible interfaces still predominantly rely on computer vision techniques or embedded electronic components. Computer vision suffers from usability problems when a camera can't clearly see target objects. On the other hand, objects with embedded electronics are relatively difficult and expensive to manufacture and depend on pieces having power and electrical connections. This contrasts with the needs of even moderately sophisticated visual languages that provide learners with dozens of distinct programming elements that must be organized through a menu system. Saving and restoring programs is also difficult, at least with today's technology, because physical structures are hard to automatically rebuild. For the same reasons, the clipboard functions (e.g., copy, cut, paste, and delete) of text-based and visual programming languages would be difficult to implement with most tangible languages, making programming tedious for more advanced programmers who want to quickly copy and modify existing pieces of code.

Along with these barriers is the perception that *real* coding is done in text-based languages, preferably on editors with a dark background and candy-colored syntax highlighting. This perception has shifted as visual languages have grown in popularity and now appear in high school and even college-level curricula. But there is still a dominant view that the authentic programming of engineers and other practitioners is done in text.

And yet, even with this laundry list of limitations, technology will continue to advance, making the tedious, flaky, or impossible of today much more appealing, practical, and reliable tomorrow. As an obvious example, dramatic improvements in augmented reality will open many new possibilities for learners to collaboratively build and debug programs created with low-cost and generic physical objects. These advancements will expand the role for tangible programming languages in the areas of education and non-professional programming situations, and not just for younger children, or even children at all.

One obvious area for innovation is in end-user programming systems. In the age of smart technology (smart homes, smart thermostats, smart cars, the Internet of Things, and ecosystems of connected devices), the opportunities and need for end-user programming environments will proliferate (see Blackwell & Hague, 2001; Myers, Ko, & Burnett, 2006). While the control of an individual device may be limited to simple configurations of input options and settings ("When it's after 8 p.m. on a Wednesday, turn the heat down by 10 degrees"), in an increasingly ubiquitous world, the complexity of simple interconnected devices will multiply. This complexity will manifest itself in multiple spheres, including (and perhaps especially) in social spheres that play out between family members, coworkers, neighbors, and citizens. The ability for end users to write programs – even programs consisting of simple interdependent conditions and outcomes – might be necessary to manage the myriad unanticipated situations that arise when such systems are deployed on a large scale. As we're seeing in the current debate around the role of algorithms in society (see Mittelstadt et al., 2016), we need to think carefully about issues of power and accessibility when it comes to end-user programming systems.

While the algorithms that control social media news feeds impact millions of users, end-user programming might intersect with the social dynamics of a family, school, or work space. This "programming" might look quite different from languages used in introductory computer science classes, but there are also certainly rich opportunities for computational thinking. For example, imagine a family argument over conflicting rules given to a programmable thermostat. How are these rules resolved by the system, and what rules *should* take precedent to make family members happy and comfortable? More to the point, who has the power to make decisions on behalf of the family, and how visible are these decisions? Family members might have different opinions about temperature and time settings (when is bedtime, and how much should we adjust the temperature?). But, going beyond the case of household heating and cooling systems, there are many examples of potential end-user programming systems that we could imagine becoming tangible. Beyond smart homes, there are many other domains where tangible programming might make sense in professional and creative settings. For example, musicians, DJs, and visual performance artists often write live code (see Blackwell, McLean, Noble, & Rohrhuber, 2014, for an extensive overview) that becomes an integral part of the performance itself. We've already seen tangible systems in this space (e.g., Xambó, 2017), and the area seems ripe for exploration.

22.4 Conclusion

Advancements in technology will continue to drive new forms of human interaction with computational systems. With these changes will come new opportunities for computer science education to reach broader audiences and engage learners in new ways. In the past several years, we have already seen the outpouring of new tangible programming products marketed to young children and their parents. There is a wealth of research opportunity in this space, as well as a need for thoughtful reflection and study on understanding both the benefits and limitations of tangible technologies. In this chapter, we have reviewed the following four potential themes that suggest the relevance of tangible computing for the computer science education research community: thinking about computer science education in early childhood; reaching and engaging more diverse learners; increasing the visibility of computer code in educational practice; and engaging broader audiences beyond traditional education settings. This is not an exhaustive list, but it hints at the broad array of research questions yet to be addressed.

Acknowledgments

Much of this work was made possible through funding from the National Science Foundation (grants DRL-1451762, IIS-0414389, DRL-0735657,

DRL-1118897, DRL-0735657). Any opinions, findings, and conclusions or recommendations expressed in this material are those of the authors and do not necessarily reflect the views of the National Science Foundation.

References

Albo-Canals, J., Barco, A., Relkin, E., Hannon, D., Heerink, M., Heinemann, M., Leidl, K., & Bers, M. (2018). The use case of KIBO robot to positively impact social and emotional development in children with ASD. *International Journal of Social Robots*, 10, 371–383.

American Academy of Pediatrics (2016). Media and young minds. *Pediatrics*, 138(5), e20162591.

Bers, M. (2008). *Blocks to Robots: Learning with Technology in the Early Childhood Classroom*. New York: Teachers College Press.

Bers, M. U. (2012). *Designing Digital Experiences for Positive Youth Development: From Playpen to Playground*. Cary, NC: Oxford University Press.

Bers, M. U. (2018a). *Coding as a Playground: Programming and Computational Thinking in the Early Childhood Classroom*. New York: Routledge Press.

Bers, M. U. (2018b). Coding, playgrounds and literacy in early childhood education: The development of KIBO robotics and ScratchJr. In *Global Engineering Education Conference (EDUCON)* (pp. 2094–2102). New York: IEEE.

Bers, M. U., & Horn, M. S. (2010). Tangible programming in early childhood. In I. R. Berson & M. J. Berson (Eds.), *HighTech Tots: Childhood in a Digital World* (pp. 49–70). Charlotte, NC: IAP.

Blackwell, A. F., & Hague, R. (2001). AutoHAN: An architecture for programming the home. In *Proceedings of the IEEE Symposia on Human-Centric Computing Languages and Environments, 2001* (pp. 150–157). New York: IEEE.

Blackwell, A., McLean, A., Noble, J., & Rohrhuber, J. (2014). Collaboration and learning through live coding (Dagstuhl Seminar 13382). In *Dagstuhl Reports* (Vol. 3, No. 9). Wadern, Germany: Schloss Dagstuhl-Leibniz-Zentrum fuer Informatik.

Blikstein, P. (2013). Gears of our childhood: Constructionist toolkits, robotics, and physical computing, past and future. In *Proceedings of Interaction Design and Children* (pp. 173–182). New York: ACM Press.

Buechley, L., & Eisenberg, M. (2008). The LilyPad Arduino: Toward wearable engineering for everyone. *IEEE Pervasive Computing*, 7(2), 12–15.

diSessa, A. A. (2001). *Changing Minds: Computers, Learning, and Literacy*. Cambridge, MA: MIT Press.

diSessa, A. A., & Abelson, H. (1986). Boxer: A reconstructible computational medium. *Communications of the ACM*, 29(9), 859–868.

Dourish, P. (2004). *Where the Action Is: The Foundations of Embodied Interaction*. Cambridge, MA: MIT press.

Erwin, B., Cyr, M., & Rogers, C. (2000). Lego engineer and robolab: Teaching engineering with labview from kindergarten to graduate school. *International Journal of Engineering Education*, 16(3), 181–192.

Fernaeus, Y., & Tholander, J. (2006). Finding design qualities in a tangible programming space. In *Proceedings of the SIGCHI Conference on Human Factors in Computing Systems* (pp. 447–456). New York: ACM Press.

Frei, P., Su, V., Mikhak, B., & Ishii, H. (2000). Curlybot: Designing a new class of computational toys. In *Proceedings of the SIGCHI Conference on Human Factors in Computing Systems* (pp. 129–136). New York: ACM Press.

Horn, M. S., AlSulaiman, S., & Koh, J. (2013). Translating Roberto to Omar: Computational literacy, stickerbooks, and cultural forms. In *Proceedings of Interaction Design and Children* (pp. 120–127). New York: ACM Press.

Horn, M. S., Crouser, R. J., & Bers, M. U. (2012). Tangible interaction and learning: The case for a hybrid approach. *Personal and Ubiquitous Computing*, 16(4), 379–389.

Horn, M. S., & Jacob, R. J. (2007). Designing tangible programming languages for classroom use. In *Proceedings of Tangible and Embedded Interaction* (pp. 159–162). New York: ACM Press.

Hornecker, E., & Buur, J. (2006). Getting a grip on tangible interaction: A framework on physical space and social interaction. In *Proceedings of the SIGCHI Conference on Human Factors in Computing Systems* (pp. 437–446). New York: ACM Press.

Hu, F., Zekelman, A., Horn, M., & Judd, F. (2015). Strawbies: Explorations in tangible programming. In *Proceedings of Interaction Design and Children* (pp. 410–413). New York: ACM Press.

Hurtienne, J., & Israel, J. H. (2007). Image schemas and their metaphorical extensions: intuitive patterns for tangible interaction. In *1st International Conference on Tangible and Embedded Interaction* (pp. 127–134). New York: ACM Press.

Ishii, H., & Ullmer, B. (1997). Tangible bits: Towards seamless interfaces between people, bits and atoms. In *Proceedings of the SIGCHI Conference on Human Factors in Computing Systems* (pp. 234–241). New York: ACM Press.

Kafai, Y., Searle, K., Martinez, C., & Brayboy, B. (2014). Ethnocomputing with electronic textiles: Culturally responsive open design to broaden participation in computing in American indian youth and communities. In *Proceedings of the ACM Technical Symposium on Computer Science Education* (pp. 241–246). New York: ACM Press.

Kazakoff, E., & Bers, M. (2012). Programming in a robotics context in the kindergarten classroom: The impact on sequencing skills. *Journal of Educational Multimedia and Hypermedia*, 21(4), 371–391.

Kelleher, C., & Pausch, R. (2005). Lowering the barriers to programming: A taxonomy of programming environments and languages for novice programmers. *ACM Computing Surveys (CSUR)*, 37(2), 83–137.

Lakoff, G., & Johnson, M. (2008). *Metaphors We Live By*. Chicago, IL: University of Chicago Press.

Macaranas, A., Antle, A. N., & Riecke, B. E. (2012). Bridging the gap: Attribute and spatial metaphors for tangible interface design. In *Sixth International Conference on Tangible, Embedded and Embodied Interaction* (pp. 161–168). New York: ACM Press.

McNerney, T. S. (2004). From turtles to tangible programming bricks: Explorations in physical language design. *Personal and Ubiquitous Computing*, 8(5), 326–337.

Mellis, D., Banzi, M., Cuartielles, D., & Igoe, T. (2007). Arduino: An open electronic prototyping platform. In *Proceedings SIGCHI Conference on Human Factors in Computing Systems (Extended Abstracts)*. New York: ACM Press.

Mittelstadt, B. D., Allo, P., Taddeo, M., Wachter, S., & Floridi, L. (2016). The ethics of algorithms: Mapping the debate. *Big Data & Society*, 3(2), 1–21.

Myers, B. A., Ko, A. J., & Burnett, M. M. (2006). Invited research overview: end-user programming. In *Proceedings SIGCHI Conference on Human Factors in Computing Systems (Extended Abstracts)*. New York: ACM Press.

O'Malley, C., & Fraser, D. S. (2004). *Literature Review in Learning with Tangible Technologies. A NESTA Futurelab Research report – Report 12*. Bristol, UK: FutureLab.

Papert, S. (1980). *Mindstorms: Children, Computers, and Powerful Ideas*. New York: Basic Books.

Pugnali, A., Sullivan, A., & Bers, M. U. (2017) The impact of user interface on young children's computational thinking. *Journal of Information Technology Education: Innovations in Practice*, 16, 172–193.

Pattis, R. E. (1981). *Karel the Robot: A Gentle Introduction to the Art of Programming*. Hoboken, NJ: John Wiley & Sons, Inc.

Raffle, H. S., Parkes, A. J., & Ishii, H. (2004). Topobo: A constructive assembly system with kinetic memory. In *Proceedings of the SIGCHI Conference on Human Factors in Computing Systems* (pp. 647–654). New York: ACM Press.

Repenning, A. (1993). Agentsheets: A tool for building domain-oriented visual programming environments. In *Proceedings of the INTERACT'93 and CHI'93 Conference on Human Factors in Computing Systems* (pp. 142–143). New York: ACM Press.

Resnick, M., Maloney, J., Monroy-Hernández, A., Rusk, N., Eastmond, E., Brennan, K., & Kafai, Y. (2009). Scratch: Programming for all. *Communications of the ACM*, 52(11), 60–67.

Resnick, M., Martin, F., Berg, R., Borovoy, R., Colella, V., Kramer, K., & Silverman, B. (1998). Digital manipulatives: New toys to think with. In *Proceedings of the SIGCHI Conference on Human Factors in Computing Systems* (pp. 281–287). New York: ACM Press.

Resnick, M., Ocko, S., & Papert, S. (1988). LEGO, Logo, and design. *Children's Environments Quarterly*, 5(4), 14–18.

Rusk, N., Resnick, M., Berg, R., & Pezalla-Granlund, M. (2008). New pathways into robotics: Strategies for broadening participation. *Journal of Science Education and Technology*, 17(1), 59–69.

Schweikardt, E., & Gross, M. D. (2006). roBlocks: A robotic construction kit for mathematics and science education. In *Proceedings of Multimodal Interfaces* (pp. 72–75). New York: ACM Press.

Searle, K. A., Fields, D. A., Lui, D. A., & Kafai, Y. B. (2014). Diversifying high school students' views about computing with electronic textiles. In *Proceedings of International Computing Education Research* (pp. 75–82). New York: ACM Press.

Shaer, O., & Hornecker, E. (2010). Tangible user interfaces: Past, present, and future directions. *Foundations and Trends in Human–Computer Interaction*, 3(1–2), 1–137.

Sherman, L., Druin, A., Montemayor, J., Farber, A., Platner, M., Simms, S., …, Kruskal, A. (2001). StoryKit: Tools for children to build room-sized interactive experiences. In *SIGCHI Conferene on Human Factors in Computing Systems* (pp. 197–198). New York: ACM Press.

Smith, A. C. (2007). Using magnets in physical blocks that behave as programming objects. In *Proceedings of the 1st International Conference on Tangible and Embedded Interaction* (pp. 147–150). New York: ACM Press.

Smith, A. C., & Kotzé, P. (2010). Indigenous African artefacts: Can they serve as tangible programming objects? In *IST-Africa, 2010* (pp. 1–11). New York: IEEE.

Strawhacker, A. L., & Bers, M. U. (2015). "I want my robot to look for food": Comparing children's programming comprehension using tangible, graphical, and hybrid user interfaces. *International Journal of Technology and Design Education*, 25(3), 293–319.

Strawhacker, A., Sullivan, A., & Bers, M. U. (2013). TUI, GUI, HUI: Is a bimodal interface truly worth the sum of its parts? In *Proceedings of Interaction Design and Children* (pp. 309–312). New York: ACM Press.

Sullivan, A., & Bers, M. U. (2016). Robotics in the early childhood classroom: Learning outcomes from an 8-week robotics curriculum in pre-kindergarten through second grade. *International Journal of Technology and Design Education*, 26(1), 3–20.

Sullivan, A., & Bers, M. U. (2017). Computational thinking and young children: Understanding the potential of tangible and graphical interfaces. In H. Ozcinar, G. Wong, & T. Ozturk (Eds.), *Teaching Computational Thinking in Primary Education* (pp. 123–137). Hershey, PA: IGI Global.

Sullivan, A., & Bers, M. U. (2018). Dancing robots: Integrating art, music, and robotics in Singapore's early childhood centers. *International Journal of Technology and Design Education*, 28(2), 325–346.

Sullivan, A. A., Bers, M. U., & Mihm, C. (2017). Imagining, playing, and coding with KIBO: Using robotics to foster computational thinking in young children. In *Proceedings of the International Conference on Computational Thinking Education* (pp. 110–115). Ting Kok, Hong Kong: The Education University of Hong Kong.

Suzuki, H., & Kato, H. (1995). Interaction-level support for collaborative learning: AlgoBlock – An open programming language. In *The First International Conference on Computer Support for Collaborative Learning* (pp. 349–355). Hillsdale, NJ: Lawrence Erlbaum Associates.

Thieme, A., Morrison, C., Villar, N., Grayson, M., & Lindley, S. (2017). Enabling collaboration in learning computer programing inclusive of children with vision impairments. In *Proceedings of the 2017 Conference on Designing Interactive Systems* (pp. 739–752). New York: ACM Press.

Uttal, D. H., Scudder, K. V., & DeLoache, J. S. (1997). Manipulatives as symbols: A new perspective on the use of concrete objects to teach mathematics. *Journal of Applied Developmental Psychology*, 18(1), 37–54.

Weiser, M., Gold, R., & Brown, J. S. (1999). The origins of ubiquitous computing research at PARC in the late 1980s. *IBM Systems Journal*, 38(4), 693–696.

Wyeth, P. (2008). How young children learn to program with sensor, action, and logic blocks. *Journal of the Learning Sciences*, 17(4), 517–550.

Xambó, A., Drozda, B., Weisling, A., Magerko, B., Huet, M., Gasque, T., & Freeman, J. (2017). Experience and ownership with a tangible computational music installation for informal learning. In *Tangible and Embedded Interaction* (pp. 351–360), New York: ACM Press.

Zuckerman, O., Arida, S., & Resnick, M. (2005). Extending tangible interfaces for education: Digital montessori-inspired manipulatives. In *Proceedings of the SIGCHI Conference on Human Factors in Computing Systems* (pp. 859–868). New York: ACM Press.

Zweben, S., & Bizot, B. (2016). Taulbee survey. *Computing Research News*, 29(5), 3–51.

23 Leveraging the Integrated Development Environment for Learning Analytics

Adam Carter, Christopher Hundhausen, and Daniel Olivares

23.1 Motivational Context

In recent years, learning process data have become increasingly easy to collect through computer-based learning environments. Moreover, the availability of low-cost, high-power machines has made it increasingly easy to store and process such data. These developments have led to the creation of two distinct but mutually complementary fields of educational data mining (EDM) and learning analytics (Siemens & Baker, 2012). Whereas EDM tends to emphasize the process of identifying significant patterns in large data sets, learning analytics tends to emphasize the process of making sense of a learner's behaviors with the ultimate aim of improving instruction and pedagogy (Baker & Siemens, 2014). Because of this difference, learning analytics tend to have preconceived notions of what *virtuous* learning looks like, whereas EDM tends to use data to discover *virtuous* learning. However, the lines between the two are often blurred. Indeed, our own prior work both attempts to discover patterns in large data sets (e.g., Carter & Hundhausen, 2016, 2017) and applies these results in ways that can better inform pedagogy (e.g., Olivares, 2015). While this chapter approaches data collection in service of improving learning analytics research, the ideas discussed are of interest to both research groups.

23.1.1 Approaching Learning Analytics Research

Verbert and Duval (2012) define the following two approaches to learning analytics research: (1) identify patterns of behavior based on the learning process data collected; and (2) derive interventions aimed at improving the learning process. Below, we briefly review computing education research that has taken each of these approaches.

23.1.1.1 Identify Patterns of Behavior

Computing educators' interest in studying programming behavior dates back at least to the mid-1970s (Shneiderman, 1976). Many of the studies of novice programming that occurred in the 1980s relied on think-aloud protocols (Ericsson &

Simon, 1984). The first studies to collect and analyze log data on learners' programming processes can be traced to the mid-1980s, when Soloway et al. (1983) studied novice Pascal programmers by collecting code snapshots submitted to the compiler. Another early effort to collect and analyze programming log data was that of Guzdial (1994). Building on the software-logging techniques used by Card, Moran, and Newell (1983) in their seminal studies of human–computer interaction, Guzdial (1994) investigated novice programming practices at a finer level of granularity by collecting keystroke-level data.

Since the early 2000s, computing educators' interest in leveraging integrated development environment (IDE) log data to study and understand programming behavior has gradually increased. In an influential line of work, Jadud (2006) studied novice programming behavior based on log data automatically collected through the BlueJ novice programming environment (Kölling et al., 2003). This research led to one of the first predictive models of novice programming performance. A number of efforts to understand and predict novice performance and outcomes based on automatically collected IDE log data have followed (see Ahadi et al., 2015; Carter et al., 2015; Watson et al., 2013).

Ihantola et al. (2015) present the most comprehensive review of this growing body of research to date. Drawing on 76 research studies published in ten different computing education venues between 2005 and 2015, their review classifies the studies along eight different dimensions, ranging from research goals, to data collection methods, to research quality. In addition, they present case studies that highlight the difficulties of replicating the methods and results of previously published research and identify grand challenges for future learning analytics research in computing education. The review presented here differs from the Ihantola et al. (2015) review in the following two key ways: (1) by presenting a principled process model for organizing the IDE-based learning analytics literature; and (2) by expanding the focus of learning analytics to include in-IDE intervention design.

23.1.1.2 Deriving Interventions

As previously illustrated, a large body of computing education research has used programming process log data to study computer programming. A markedly smaller body of research has actually used such data as a basis for designing IDE interventions. Examples of interventions developed in this body of research include the following:

- Dynamically tailoring feedback (Buffardi & Edwards, 2013) and providing incentive mechanisms (Buffardi & Edwards, 2013; Spacco et al., 2013) in order to improve students' testing behaviors;
- Enhancing syntax error messages to make them more understandable (Denny et al., 2014);
- Dynamically generating hints based on patterns mined from the programming data of previous and current users of an IDE (Dominguez et al., 2010; Hartmann et al., 2010; Piech et al., 2015);

- Awarding badges to students who meet certain time management and learning goals in computer programming exercises (Haaranen et al., 2014);
- Scaffolding the programming process by providing intermediate goals (Guzdial, 1994; Vihavainen et al., 2013)

23.1.2 Collecting Learner Data within the IDE

Data in the service of learning analytics can be collected from a variety of sources. For example, we may gain additional insights related to learning processes in computing education by collecting data from interactive online textbooks (e.g., Parker et al., 2017), assignment submission platforms (e.g., Braught & Midkiff, 2016), Q&A forums (e.g., Robinson, 2017), software engineering and collaborative development tools (e.g., Feliciano et al., 2016), or students' problem-solving environments (i.e., IDEs; see Carter & Hundhausen, 2017; Feliciano et al., 2016). While each data source has its own constraints as to what can be collected (e.g., it would be difficult to collect programming process data from a Q&A forum), we believe that the IDE provides researchers with the broadest spectrum of learner process data, as this is where students spend a large majority of their time problem-solving.

While their primary purpose is to support the development of computer programs, several IDEs have been instrumented to collect data on students' programming processes, including their edits, compilation errors, and runtime exceptions (e.g., see Brown et al., 2014). IDEs can also be augmented with additional features that collect assessment data while potentially enhancing student learning. For example, in our own research, we have augmented an IDE with a social networking-style activity stream, which automatically collects data on students' online conversations about their programming activities – conversations that take place in the same context as those programming activities (Carter & Hundhausen, 2015). Moreover, one can imagine augmenting an IDE with additional data collection mechanisms that provide a basis for delivering enhanced learning experiences. For example, survey or quiz questions (e.g., Bosch & D'Mello, 2013; Rodrigo et al., 2009; Rodrigo & Baker, 2009) could be administered through the IDE during the programming process in order to collect data on students' understanding of concepts or on students' attitudes during the programming process. Likewise, as has already been done through specialized research tools, one could collect eye-tracking data (e.g., Busjahn et al., 2014) or physiological data (e.g., galvanic skin response; see Shi et al., 2007) as students work within an IDE. These data could be used to interpret or augment traditional data on students' programming processes.

Just as an IDE can be used to collect learning process data, so too might it be used as a mechanism for delivering learning interventions designed to enhance students' learning processes and outcomes. For example, suppose that, based on programming process data, an IDE detects that a student is engaged in programming behaviors that, according to a predictive model (e.g., Carter et al., 2015; Jadud, 2006; Watson et al., 2013), are negatively correlated with course success. The IDE could then present the learner with an intervention – for example, a pop-up message that nudged the learner toward a more productive behavior. Likewise, imagine an IDE that presents computing students with a continuously updated visual analytics dashboard (e.g., Verbert et al., 2014) of their progress toward established learning goals. Alternatively, a dashboard could provide visualizations that situate a given student relative to his or her peers. Research demonstrates that such visualizations can have a positive impact on certain students (Auvinen et al., 2015). Students could use such a dashboard to guide them toward virtuous learning activities.

23.1.3 Privacy Concerns

The automatic collection of the kinds of learning data described in this chapter raises obvious ethical concerns with respect to data privacy and security. Indeed, just as consumers may not be comfortable with the automatic collection of their online activity by search engines and websites, so too may computing students be uncomfortable with the automatic collection of their in-IDE activities. What data should be collected? How should the data be stored? Who will have access to the data? For what purposes will the data be used? Can data collection be terminated at any point? Per standard ethical practices, IDEs that automatically collect data should provide, in a clear policy statement, answers to questions like these. Moreover, in any research endeavor involving the automatic collection of IDE data, an IDE should automatically collect data on a given student only if that student explicitly grants informed consent.

As studies that use automatically collected IDE data become more common in computing education, researchers will need to gain a better understanding of the increasingly stringent laws governing educational data collection (e.g., see Herold, 2014), as well as the specific privacy concerns and limits of those they are studying. Addressing questions like the following will thus become increasingly important:

- What level of privacy do students expect to maintain as they work on programming assignments, potentially in collaboration with others?
- To what degree should students be able to customize the amount and type of their own learning data that they share with their classmates, instructors, and researchers? What customizations are most important?
- Should students be able to share their data *anonymously* with others? Will such sharing have the same educational value as it would if students' identities were associated with their data?
- Might students and instructors be willing to participate in learning communities that go beyond local classes, in which the sharing and discussion of learning data across courses are central community activities?

For additional considerations related to privacy and ethical considerations, we refer the reader to Chapter 4, which discusses study design in computing education research.

23.1.4 Learning Analytics versus Intelligent Tutoring Systems

Within computing education, there has been a long tradition of research into intelligent tutoring systems (ITSs), which aim to provide individually tailored feedback and assistance to learners as they perform programming tasks (e.g., see Anderson et al., 1989; Anderson & Skwarecki, 1986; Barr et al., 1976; Corbett & Anderson, 1992). ITSs are based on expert models of how a given programming task should be performed. As a learner programs, the learner's trajectory is compared against the expert's trajectory, and individualized hints and assistance are dynamically generated in order to keep the learner on track. While ITS research has much in common with learning analytics research, the two research areas are different in at least two important respects, as discussed below.

A key goal of ITSs is to automate the learning and teaching process by augmenting individual instruction through homework and practice drills. To that end, ITSs furnish a curriculum (a series of programming problems) and instruction (individually tailored hints as learners work on those problems). In contrast, learning analytics tends to enhance classroom instruction by collecting and analyzing learner process data across entire cohorts of students. Thus, in contrast to ITSs, such wider-scale data collection and analysis enable a learning analytics infrastructure to provide teachers with the information and resources to teach better and/or help learners to connect with others in their cohort who can provide support and assistance.

Because they are based on expert models of problem-solving, ITSs rely on knowledge of the specific programming problems being solved by learners. Individualized feedback is generated by comparing the learner's solution path against the expert's solution path for a given problem. More recently, research in the EDM community has explored ITSs that automatically generate hints and feedback based on learning process data (Jin et al., 2012; Rivers & Koedinger, 2013; Stamper et al., 2013). In contrast to much of the ITS research, IDE-based learning analytics environments assume no knowledge of the specific problems being solved. In addition, in the learning analytics design space assumed in this chapter, individual programming problems are assigned by course instructors, not by an ITS. Thus, the kinds of expert and learner models typically employed by ITSs cannot be leveraged by a learning analytics environment, which must instead provide feedback based on more general information on learners' programming processes, outcomes, and attitudes.

23.1.5 Chapter Outline

The possibility of using the IDE both to collect learning process data and to intervene in the learning process suggests an interesting design space for computing education researchers to explore. As researchers explore this design space of *IDE-based learning analytics* within the context of computing education, at least three key questions must be addressed:

- What learning data should be collected within an IDE in order to provide a foundation for improving student learning?

- How should the learning data be analyzed in order to provide useful information on student learning?
- Based on the learning data, what interventions should be delivered through an IDE in order to benefit student learning?

This chapter proposes a process model for IDE-based learning analytics that can help researchers to explore these research questions systematically. Within the context of computer programming activities, our process model decomposes the cyclical learning analytics process into five key activities. For each activity in this process, we identify the key design dimensions and review the relevant computing education literature. Lastly, we propose an agenda for future research that can advance the field.

23.2 Implications When Conducting Research in Learning Analytics

In software engineering, process models have traditionally been used as abstractions for a given software development process (Scacchi, 2002). Such models identify and parameterize the key activities of the given process, providing a basis for discussing, reasoning about, and simulating those activities without actually performing them. In this spirit, we propose a cyclical process model for IDE-based learning analytics that distills the learning analytics process into the following five essential activities (see Figure 23.1): (1) operationalizing observable behaviors; (2) collecting data; (3) analyzing data; (4) designing interventions; and (5) delivering interventions. Below, we use this model to explore the design space of IDE-based learning analytics. For each activity, we identify key design dimensions and review relevant research.

23.2.1 Operationalizing Observable Behaviors

The foundational step in learning analytics research should be to first consider how a learner's observable behaviors and outcomes might manifest themselves in data. Skipping this operationalization step may result in the inability of researchers to use learning analytics data to address their desired research outcomes. For example, we examined video logs of students programming at a recent workshop on learning analytics (Hundhausen & Adesope, 2017). Our intention was to connect specific problem-solving activities (e.g., debugging, writing new code, fixing existing code, etc.) with observable log traces. In performing this analysis, we discovered that even though the log data collected were extensive, they still lacked sufficient detail to answer our research questions. Had we instead skipped the preliminary step of operationalizing behaviors, we would have spent countless hours collecting and analyzing data only to discover that our questions could not be answered. This example illustrates a key point: *prior to collecting data, first consider what information might need to be*

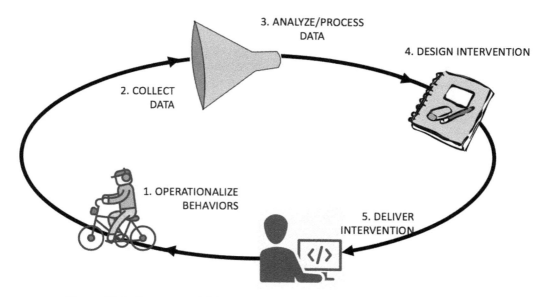

Figure 23.1 *Process model for IDE-based learning analytics in computing education.*

collected and how such information can ultimately be used to answer specific research questions.

We see the process of connecting learner-produced data to observable behaviors and outcomes as falling under the umbrella of human activity recognition (HAR), which attempts to "provide information on a user's behavior that allows computing systems to proactively assist users with their tasks" (Bulling et al., 2014). A key difference between HAR and other areas of recognition (e.g., vision, natural language processing, etc.) is that HAR tends to be less well-defined. People tend to perform the same task in different manners (Bulling et al., 2014), and often human activities tend to overlap (Kim et al., 2010). Whereas HAR often relies on multiple sensor inputs, some of which are worn by participants (e.g., Nguyen et al., 2015), learning analytics researchers are often restricted to the use of a single sensor (i.e., the computer) measuring a single source of activity (e.g., the IDE). While it is possible to employ multiple sensors in learning analytics research (see Begel, 2016; Busjahn et al., 2014), using such setups on a massive scale, as is the case with Blackbox data (e.g., Brown et al., 2014), is often infeasible.

Bulling et al. (2014) provide a comprehensive overview of HAR as well as the principle challenges faced by researchers. Challenges of particular interest to those in computing education are the notions of intraclass variability, interclass similarity, diversity of activities, ground truth annotation, and data collection and experimental design.

Intraclass variability occurs when the same task is performed differently by different individuals. In the context of learning analytics, it is likely that certain activities (e.g., debugging) are likely to differ greatly between students. Indeed, prior research already demonstrates that editing activities do indeed vary greatly between students (Leinonen et al., 2016). Thus, researchers must consider how to best collect sufficiently detailed data from a sufficient number of different individuals so as to be resilient against intraclass variability.

Interclass similarity occurs when disparate activities manifest themselves in similar manners within log data. As discussed in the opening paragraph of this section, interclass similarities prevented our research group from connecting log data to specific activities because the log data similarity between activities was too high. A potential solution to this problem is to collect a greater amount of data at a greater level of detail. We discuss specific data collection strategies in greater detail in Section 23.2.2.

Unlike intraclass variability, which denotes how activities differ between individuals, *diversity of activity* denotes how an activity might differ within a single individual. Difficulties encountered when diversity of activity exists are further compounded when the behaviors of interest are *routine* (Banovic et al., 2016). Routine behaviors tend to exhibit greater variability for a given task. For example, under the general category of "debugging" we might see marked differences in activity when a learner is attempting to debug a logic error versus attempting to debug a memory exception. Compounding this problem is the fact that learners progress: it is unlikely that a learner attempting to debug a memory exception at the start of a CS1 course will address the same debugging issue near the end of that same course.

Ground truth annotation is the process of having an expert label streams of log data so that systems can better connect log data to activity. Such annotations frequently occur within a controlled lab setting. We not aware of any attempt by learning analytics researchers to produce such a rigorously labeled stream of log data. However, as our past research demonstrates, beginning with ground truth-labeled training data will likely allow researchers to make stronger inferences from log data with respect to student learning (Carter & Hundhausen, 2017).

Data collection and experimental design issues stem from the fact that data are often collected by individual research groups and are analyzed by proprietary tools that do not lend themselves to data sharing or repeat analysis. This issue is shared equally by learning analytics researchers and is discussed Section 23.3.1.

23.2.2 Collecting Data

As described in the review of Ihantola et al. (2015), a variety of mechanisms have been used to collect students' programming data, including automated grading systems (e.g., Edwards & Perez-Quinones, 2008) and version control systems. However, the learning analytics process considered in this chapter focuses on data collected directly through the IDE – what Ihantola et al. (2015) call *IDE instrumentation*.

23.2.1.1 Standard Data

The most obvious learning data to collect through an IDE are *programming* data generated by students as they engage in programming tasks within an IDE. Figure 23.2 presents a taxonomy of standard programming data that can be automatically collected by instrumenting a traditional IDE.

Commercial IDEs such as Eclipse and NetBeans typically support the automatic collection of programming data (e.g., Eclipse.org, 2016; Netbeans.org, 2016). However, in order to support product improvements, such data collection is directed more toward understanding feature usage than understanding programming processes. In contrast, within computing education, there is a clear focus on better understanding how students learn to program. In the 1990s, some research prototype IDEs, including Emile (Guzdial, 1994) and GPCEdit (Guzdial et al., 1998), supported automatic data collection in order to explore related research questions. More recently, automatic data collection facilities have been increasingly integrated into IDEs that are more widely distributed, including stand-alone IDEs such as BlueJ (Brown et al., 2014; Norris et al., 2008), Eclipse (Spacco et al., 2004), and NetBeans (Vihavainen et al., 2013), as well as web-based IDEs such as CloudCoder (Papancea et al., 2013). Hackystat (P. Johnson, 2010) is unique in that it is IDE-agnostic; it can be attached to any IDE through a web services application programming interface (API).

23.2.1.2 Augmented Data

The interface and functionality of many IDEs can be extended through a plugin architecture. This opens up the possibility of augmenting an IDE to facilitate the collection of a broader range of data that might provide additional insight into the learning process. Figure 23.3 presents a taxonomy of additional data that can be collected through an IDE augmented with additional features and functionality. By augmenting an IDE with a social networking activity feed, as we have done in our own research (Carter & Hundhausen, 2015), one can collect social data: asynchronous class discussions (posts and replies) that take place within the IDE as students work on programming assignments, as well as the helpful marks (or "likes") that participants give to posts and replies. It is also possible to support one-on-one and group conversations through a personal messaging system and to support badges or reputation points, as are used in some question-answering systems such as Stack Overflow (Stack Overflow, 2012).

Automated testing tools enable a computer program to be automatically tested against a set of test cases (e.g., Edwards & Perez-Quinones, 2008). When incorporated into an IDE, they can be used as a basis for collecting testing data on students' testing practices and performance. For example, IDE plugins have been developed to interface Eclipse with automated testing tools such as Web-CAT (Luke, 2015).

Empirical studies within computing education have been interested in identifying relationships between student attitudes and outcomes (e.g., see Hundhausen et al., 2010; Rosson et al., 2011). In a similar vein, computing

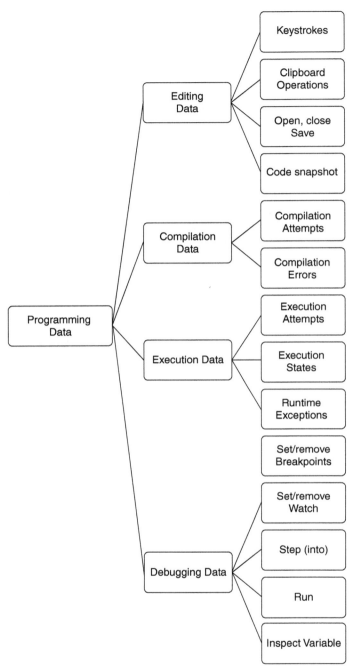

Figure 23.2 *Programming process data that can be automatically collected through a standard IDE.*

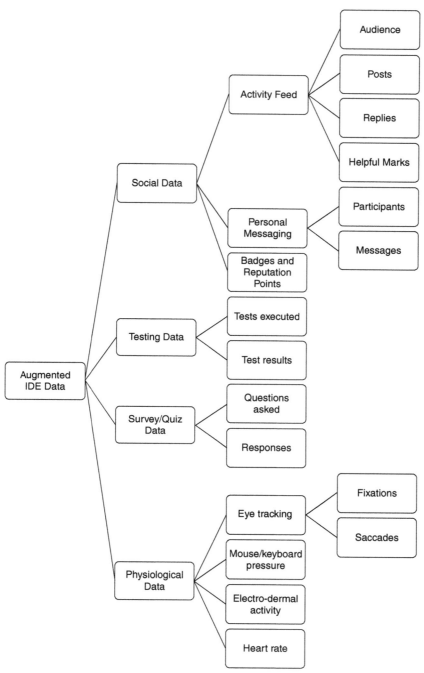

Figure 23.3 *Data that can be automatically collected through an IDE augmented with additional features and functionality.*

educators often administer quizzes or tests intermittently throughout an academic term – most often for the purpose of evaluating student knowledge and performance. While computing educators typically administer both surveys and quizzes/tests relatively infrequently, the ability to collect survey/quiz data more frequently in the context of programming tasks could provide additional insight into students' programming knowledge, including their misconceptions. Survey and quiz questions could, for example, be dynamically tailored to the situation in order to better understand students' attitudes about and conceptual understanding of the tasks and concepts immediately before them. Perhaps the only example of an IDE with such a facility is TestMyCode (Ihantola et al., 2014), a NetBeans plugin that supports a dynamic quiz facility.

Finally, a relatively new research area within computing education is the collection and analysis of the physiological data of programmers as they perform programming tasks. The best-known examples are studies that collect the eye-tracking data of programmers (e.g., see Bednarik & Tukiainen, 2004; Busjahn et al., 2014; Kevic et al., 2015). In addition, within the context of computer programming, there has been some interest in collecting and analyzing mouse and keyboard pressure (Begel, 2016), electro-dermal activity (Ahonen et al., 2016; Müller, 2015), and heart rate (Begel, 2016; Müller, 2015; Müller & Fritz, 2016). Even though, to our knowledge, none of the hardware devices required to collect these kinds of data have been directly integrated with an IDE, such integration would enable a broader range of data to be brought to bear on the IDE-based learning analytics process.

Tables 23.1 and 23.2 presents a comparison of seven publicly available IDE tools used in computing education with respect to their support for automatic data collection, using the data taxonomies presented in Figures 23.2 and 23.3 as a basis for the comparison. Two of these work in conjunction with the BlueJ novice IDE: the built-in Blackbox data collection facility (Brown et al., 2014) and the Clock-It plugin for BlueJ (Norris et al., 2008). The next three of these work with the Eclipse IDE: the DevEventTracker plugin that interfaces Eclipse with Web-CAT (Luke, 2015); the Marmoset plugin to Eclipse (Spacco et al., 2006); and the open-source HackyStat data collection and analysis framework, which interfaces with Eclipse through a web API (P. Johnson, 2010). The final two of these are plugins to Visual Studio (Carter, 2013) and NetBeans (Vihavainen et al., 2013).

While by no means exhaustive, the set of IDE tools compared in Tables 23.1 and 23.2 represents a majority of the publicly available tools. As such, it provides a reasonable foundation for making at least two general observations regarding the state of the art with respect to IDE data collection tools. First, notice that relative to the basic programming data they collect, the seven tools vary widely. In fact, although not shown in Tables 23.1 and 23.2, the seven tools even vary with respect to the manner in which they collect individual data points. For example, the tools employ a variety of techniques for collecting editing operations: some collect all keystrokes, while others collect the addition and deletion of lines or known programming constructs. Second, notice that while four of the seven

Table 23.1 *Comparison of five IDEs used in computing education based on the data they collect for the programming category.*

Category (from Figures 23.2 and 23.3)	BlueJ + Blackbox	BlueJ + ClockIt	Eclipse + Web-CAT	Eclipse + Marmoset	Eclipse + HackyStat	Visual Studio + OSBIDE	NetBeans + TMC
Editing							
Editing actions	✓	✓	✓		✓	✓	✓
Clipboard operations						✓	✓
File/project actions		✓	✓		✓	✓	✓
Code snapshot	✓		✓	✓	✓	✓	✓
Compilation							
Compile attempt		✓	✓		✓	✓	
Compile errors	✓	✓	✓		✓	✓	
Execution							
Execution attempts	✓					✓	
Package/object invocation	✓	✓					
Runtime errors	✓					✓	
Execution state							
Debugging							
Set/remove break	✓				✓	✓	
Set/remove watch						✓	
Step/run	✓					✓	
Inspect variable						✓	
Assignment							
View assignment							✓
Submit final solution			✓	✓		✓	✓

tools collect *augmented* data beyond the basic programming data, only a limited range of augmented data are collected. Three of the seven tools collect testing data, with one tool collecting some social data and another tool collecting some survey/quiz data. This suggests that existing publicly available IDE tools collect only a limited subset of the range of data that could be collected.

Table 23.2 *Comparison of five IDEs used in computing education based on the data they collect for the social, testing, survey/quiz, and physiological categories.*

Category (from Figures 23.2 and 23.3)	BlueJ + Blackbox	BlueJ + ClockIt	Eclipse + Web-CAT	Eclipse + Marmoset	Eclipse + HackyStat	Visual Studio + OSBIDE	NetBeans + TMC
Social (activity feed/ Q&A forum)							
Audience							
Posts and replies						✓	
Likes/helpful marks						✓	
Badges/reputation							
Social (personal messaging)							
Recipient(s)							
Message content							
Testing							
Tests executed	✓		✓				✓
Test results	✓		✓				✓
Survey/quiz							
Questions asked							✓
Responses							✓
Physiological							
Eye tracking							
Mouse/keyboard pressure							
Electro-dermal activity							
Heart rate							

23.2.3 Analyzing Data

In the third step of the process model, data automatically collected through the IDE are further processed and analyzed. In this step, a fundamental task is to transform the data into *useful information* that sheds further light on students' learning processes, attitudes, and outcomes, and therefore can serve as a suitable foundation for educationally effective interventions. Table 23.3 proposes a taxonomy of useful information. In order to generate this taxonomy, we began by creating a list of information that would be potentially derivable from the raw data presented in Figures 23.2 and 23.3. Then, in collaboration with a team of computing education researchers and practitioners who attended a learning analytics workshop held in conjunction with the 2015 Association for Computing Machinery (ACM) International Computing Education Research (ICER) Conference, we narrowed down the list to those items that we believed would be of potential value to computing education researchers and practitioners interested in intervening in the learning process. While we make no claim that

Table 23.3 *A taxonomy of useful information derivable from IDE data.*
NPSM = normalized programming state model.

Measure/metric	Analysis type
Programming behavior	
Time management	
Time spent on task (non-idle time)	Count
Time-idle distribution over time (timeline of work vs. idle time during a programming assignment work period)	Count
Procrastination (time between first edit and assignment deadline)	Count
Programming process	
Amount of code added/changed between builds	Count
Number of executions between builds	Math
Percentage of executions in debug mode vs. non-debug mode	Math
Number of unit tests written	Count
Quality and coverage of unit tests written	Algo
Error Quotient Score (Jadud, 2006)	Algo
WatWin Score (Watson et al., 2013)	Algo
NPSM State and Score (Carter et al., 2015)	Algo
Stuckness (Carter & Dewan, 2010)	ML
Program content, correctness, and efficiency	
Program size (non-comment lines of code, number of methods, etc.)	Count
Presence of target keywords or constructs	Algo
Goodness of comments and style	Algo
Closeness of match with canonical solution	ML
Presence of pasted code whose size meets given threshold	Algo
Similarity of code with other solutions	ML
Test case results (pass, fail, error)	Count
Program efficiency (time to execute test cases)	Count
Physiological response information	
Mood (e.g., anxious, frustrated, relaxed)	Algo
Stuck vs. in the flow (e.g., Müller & Fritz, 2015)	Algo
Social behavior	
Participation level	
Number of posts made	Count
Number of questions asked	Count
Number of questions answered	Count
Number of answers marked helpful	Count
Badges or reputation points earned	Count
Participation content and quality	
Post content	Algo
Goodness of questions	Algo
Goodness of answers	Algo
Knowledge	
Number of questions answered correctly and incorrectly	Math
Extent to which correct questions cover target knowledge	Algo
Extent to which correct answers cover target knowledge	Math

(continued)

Table 23.3 (*continued*)

Measure/metric	Analysis type
Attitudes	
Self-efficacy (e.g., Askar & Davenport, 2009)	Algo
Sense of community (e.g., Rovai, 2002)	Algo
Motivation (e.g., Pintrich et al., 1991)	Algo
Self-reported emotions (e.g., Shaw, 2004)	Count
Eye movement information	
Heat map (highlight "hot" zones where users focused gaze)	Vis
Animation of screen fixations and saccades over time	Vis
Static map of screen fixations and saccades	Vis
Extent to which learners gaze on given screen target (an intervention, their code, compile error messages, etc.)	Math

the taxonomy includes *all* information that is derivable from IDE data and is potentially valuable to the design of interventions, we believe it serves as a reasonable starting point for researchers in the field to build on.

The taxonomy includes seven top-level information categories that correspond with the range of learning behaviors, attitudes, and physiological responses that might be captured through automatically collected data. In order to provide further organization, the taxonomy partitions some of the top-level categories into logical subcategories. The leaf nodes are the actual informational *measures* (i.e., quantifications of data) or *metrics* (i.e., derivatives of one or more measures) that can be extracted through further processing or analysis of the data. Some of these were inspired by Cardell-Oliver's (2011) description of software metrics for novice programmers.

The right-hand column of the taxonomy indicates the analysis technique used to derive each informational measure or metric. As can be seen, at least six different techniques can be used:

Count: Useful information can be obtained by simply *counting* raw data points. In order to do so, one needs to select the data points to be counted – for example, based on a timespan within which they occurred, based on the type of data, or based on the person to whom the data correspond.

Math: A slightly more sophisticated analysis technique is a *mathematical formula* that computes information from data. Common examples of this are to take the average of a set of data over time or to compute the percentage of data points that meet a certain criterion.

Algo: One often needs to apply some sort of *algorithm* to the data in order to transform the data into useful information. For example, judgments of quality or content may require the algorithmic application of a set of heuristics. Likewise, predictive measures are typically computed through some sort of algorithm that processes relevant data and outputs a number corresponding to the prediction.

Vis: *Visualizations* of data can often furnish valuable insights that could not be gained by simply analyzing raw data points.

ML: *Machine learning* represents a special class of algorithms that aim to learn from, identify patterns in, and make predictions about data.

It is important to underscore that the information items identified in the taxonomy serve as (potentially crude) proxies for the kinds of information described by the top-level categories. For example, while the time between a student's first edit and the assignment deadline can be suggestive of the extent to which the student has procrastinated, it is by no means always suggestive of procrastination. Indeed, it may well generate a false positive due to the limits of in-IDE data collection: a student may have worked on the assignment outside of the IDE well before that first edit. Likewise, the number of executions between compilation attempts may provide useful information regarding a student's reliance on execution to test code, but is not sensitive to any mental simulation of the code that the student may be doing – an activity that could also be potentially valuable to the programming process. Clearly, any effort to pursue learning analytics based on automatically collected IDE data needs to be sensitive to this limitation.

23.2.4 Designing Interventions

In this step of the process, one leverages the data analysis performed in the previous step to design in-IDE interventions. Here, we use the term "intervention" to denote an event in which some combination of information, guidance, and feedback is shared with learners for the purpose of positively influencing the learner's behavior, attitudes, or physiological state. Figure 23.4 presents a taxonomy of design dimensions for in-IDE interventions. The taxonomy is organized around three fundamental high-level questions that any intervention designer must address:

- *Content: What* information will the intervention contain?
- *Presentation*: *How* will the intervention be presented to the learner?
- *Timing*: *When* will the intervention be delivered?

Below, we describe these dimensions in further detail.

23.2.4.1 Content

Perhaps the most basic choice an intervention designer must make is *what* to present to the learner. One option is simply to update learners on their processes and progress by presenting the types of data and information described in Figure 23.3 and Table 23.3. Such data and information can provide a basis for providing a critique of learners' processes or progress. In order to encourage learners to improve, one could also present a concrete suggestion, or even provide encouragement not to give up or to keep up the good work.

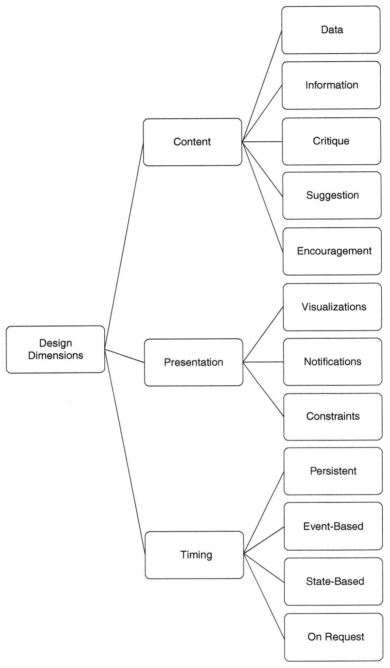

Figure 23.4 *Taxonomy of design dimensions for IDE-based interventions.*

23.2.4.2 Presentation

A second fundamental design choice concerns the manner in which the intervention is presented to the learner. A computer-based learning environment such as an IDE offers at least three distinct mechanisms for presenting interventions, as discussed below.

Visualizations: In the spirit of *learning dashboards* – a popular means of presenting visual analytics in a learning environment (e.g., Verbert et al., 2014) – an IDE could present interventions in the form of visualizations (e.g., graphs and charts) that enable learners to visually explore their learning process and progress. An important design consideration for visualizations is that they are most effective in promoting learning if they *actively engage* the learner (Hundhausen et al., 2002). This implies the need to provide some level of *interactivity* in the visualizations that are used as interventions – by, for example, allowing learners to perform what-if analyses. Basic principles of human perception and human–computer interaction can also improve the effectiveness of visualizations. For example, visualizations should be designed so as present information *relevant* to learners' immediate tasks, with the relevant information easily recognizable and within the learner's foveal view (J. Johnson, 2010; Norman, 2013).

Notifications: The notification presentation mechanism differs from the visualization delivery mechanism in two key ways. First, it is a *textual* message as opposed to a *visual* representation. Second, whereas a visualization intervention is presented to the learner in a non-obtrusive way (the learner must potentially seek it out by navigating to it and clicking on it), a notification may be, but is not necessarily, delivered *obtrusively*, in the form of a *modal* pop-up message that interrupts the learner within the IDE. For example, a modal dialogue box could pop up within an IDE in order to help the learner get back on track at points at which the learner appears to be struggling.

Constraints: In user interface design, constraints prevent illegal or undesirable user interface actions, thereby guiding the user toward legal or desirable user interface actions (Norman, 2013). Constraints typically manifest themselves as user interface controls that limit the actions that can be taken – for example, menu items that contain only allowable actions or selection sliders that are capable of moving over only a legal range. In the context of IDE interventions, constraints could be used to prevent the learner from taking actions that are seen as incompatible with desirable trajectories, thus guiding the learner toward desirable trajectories. For instance, if the learner has not compiled his or her program in a long time, the IDE could disable editing (a constraint) and present a pop-up a message (a notification) informing the user that compilation might be a good idea. Note that constraints are an *extreme* form of intervention; they prevent the user from performing further actions. Therefore, they should be used with care – only in situations that warrant them, such as when other, less extreme forms of interventions have been tried repeatedly and failed (J. Johnson, 2010).

23.2.4.3 Timing

The timing dimension relates to *when* a given intervention should be presented to the learner. One option is for an intervention to be persistent – that is, continuously available in the IDE. A persistent intervention could be part of a tab or area within the IDE to which users navigate when they want to access the intervention. An example of this would be a *learner dashboard* (e.g., Verbert et al., 2014) that shows the learner's current goals and progress. A second option is a triggered intervention – an intervention that is dynamically delivered to the learner in response to the immediate actions the learner is taking. For example, if the learner performs an action that is recognized as generally unproductive with respect to the learner's goals, then that action could trigger a notification that suggests an alternative course of action. Conversely, if a learner performs an action that is recognized as educationally beneficial, then that action could trigger a notification that provides encouragement to keep up the good work.

In a similar vein, another option is a state-based intervention that is triggered when the user is recognized as transitioning into or remaining within a state that is believed to be educationally unproductive. For example, the NPSM model described by Carter et al. (2015) characterizes programming behavior based on the current semantic and syntactic correctness of the program being edited. If a learner remains for long periods of time in a syntactically unknown state (i.e., the learner has not compiled the program), such behavior negatively correlates with programming success. Hence, a state-based intervention could remind the learner to compile his or her program.

A final timing option is to deliver an intervention on demand (i.e., only when the user explicitly requests it). For example, an IDE could provide a "Get Hint" button that, when clicked, would deliver a suggestion or critique to the learner (e.g., Dominguez et al., 2010; Piech et al., 2015). This type of timing differs somewhat from the persistent timing option in that, although it is always available, it is not actually visible to the learner unless the learner explicitly requests it.

23.2.5 Delivering Interventions

In the final step of the process, an intervention designed in the previous step is delivered to learners through the IDE. This is the culmination of the learning analytics process. If designed effectively, an intervention should produce some sort of change in the learner. For example, the learner may be prompted to act differently, or the learner may experience some sort of attitudinal or physiological shift. Ideally, such changes will lead to improved learning processes and outcomes – improvements that manifest themselves in the "collect data" step and that can be recognized in the "analyze data" step.

It is important to recognize that changes in response to interventions often happen *gradually*, not immediately. This is because the learning analytics process is inherently *cyclical*: learning data lead to interventions, which lead to new learning data and additional interventions. Hence, even if initial interventions lead to no detectable changes in learner behavior or attitudes, detectable changes may well occur over a longer period of time through an iterative process of progressive refinement.

23.3 Directions for Future Research

In this chapter, we have presented a review of IDE-based learning analytics structured around a process model with the following five activities: (1) operationalizing observable behaviors; (2) collect data; (3) analyze data; (4) design interventions; and (5) deliver interventions. Based on the foregoing review, we conclude by presenting potential future directions in IDE-based learning analytics research.

23.3.1 Develop a More Unified Research Infrastructure

Our review indicated that, while numerous IDEs now support automatic data collection, IDEs vary widely with respect to both the data they collect and the manner in which they collect the same types of data (see Tables 23.1 and 23.2). For instance, we saw that, while many IDEs collect editing data, some do so at the keystroke level, while others log snapshots of the code when the code is compiled or saved.

Because the data collection approaches of IDEs differ widely, it is difficult to perform empirical comparisons across IDEs. We believe this is unfortunate: as the field of IDE-based learning analytics matures, it will be increasingly important to study learning differences promoted by different IDEs. Therefore, we think it is in the best interests of researchers who collect and analyze IDE log data to work collaboratively toward a *standardized* format for IDE log data.

Learning analytics researchers working in this space could go even further by building a universal repository of anonymized IDE log data. In the spirit of BlueJ's Blackbox project (Brown et al., 2014), we envision a publicly accessible, web-based repository of large, anonymized corpora of data collected through numerous IDEs, in many different computing courses, and at many different institutions. Such a repository would make it possible for more researchers – even those who do not collect their own data – to conduct the kinds of cross-IDE, cross-language studies that are conspicuously lacking in computing education research.

We believe that the non-standard nature of the plugin architectures supported by IDEs also poses a barrier to conducting cross-IDE, cross-language research. While plugin architectures make it increasingly easy to augment IDEs with facilities both to automatically collect data and to deliver dynamic interventions, building such facilities remains a specialized craft. In order to do so, one needs to become intimately familiar with the plugin architecture of a specific IDE. Unfortunately, implementation skills do not readily transfer between different IDEs, as each plugin architecture has its own peculiar standards and libraries.

We believe that this barrier could be reduced through the development of a standard API for implementing IDE plugins. Of course, teams of programmers would need to write, for each IDE, the specialized code to support the API. However, if such an API could be ultimately supported by a broad range of IDEs, data collection and intervention design could be more easily replicated across IDEs. This, in turn, would increase the likelihood that studies of student programming processes, and the impact of in-IDE interventions, could be replicated across a broad range of IDEs, and ultimately that there would be an increase in the kinds of cross-IDE, cross-language empirical studies that we believe are important to advancing the field.

23.3.2 Develop IDE Facilities to Collect and Analyze a Broader Range of Data

Our review revealed that IDE-based learning analytics research presently collects and analyzes only a fraction of the possible data that could be automatically collected (see Tables 23.1 and 23.2). The present focus is squarely on programming process data related to editing, compiling, running, and testing programs. This focus neglects many of the *augmented* data we identified, including social data, survey/quiz data, and physiological data. Our own research suggests that we can develop better predictive models of performance and gain greater insight into the learning process by studying the *interplay* of multiple types of IDE data (Carter & Hundhausen, 2016). We also suspect that, with a broader array of IDE data, interventions can be designed so as to be not only more helpful to learners, but also more responsive to their needs. Therefore, we think it will be important, in future research, to develop IDE facilities that support the collection and analysis of more diverse sets of data, including the augmented data described in Figure 23.3.

23.3.3 Design and Evaluate Interventions Based on Theory

In Section 23.1.2, we identified only a couple of lines of past research into intervention design that were actually driven by learning theory: Guzdial (1994) and Carter and Hundhausen (2015). In computing education research in general and IDE-based learning analytics research in particular, our observation has been that research frequently proceeds in an ad hoc fashion. Key research decisions are often dictated by the particular courses and educational technologies to which a researcher has access, rather than by a theoretical account of what might actually be effective. We certainly sympathize with this state of affairs: research must inevitably proceed within the messy confines of real courses and institutions. At the same time, our review suggests that learning theory could have a lot to say about how to design educationally effective interventions, including what they should include (*content*), what they should look like (*presentation*), and when they should be delivered (*timing*). We argue that, in order to have the best chance to systematically advance the field, researchers need to proceed from explicit theoretical orientations. We hope that future research pivots toward more theoretically driven research into IDE-based learning analytics.

23.4 Acknowledgments

This work is supported by the National Science Foundation under grant no. IIS-1321045. It has been excerpted and adapted with permission from: Hundhausen, C., Carter, A. & Olivares, D. IDE-based learning analytics for computing education: a process model, critical review, and research agenda. *ACM Transactions on Computing Education (TOCE)*, 17(3), 11, © 2017 ACM, Inc. DOI: https://doi.org/10.1145/3105759.

References

Ahadi, A., Lister, R., Haapala, H., & Vihavainen, A. (2015). Exploring machine learning methods to automatically identify students in need of assistance. In *Proceedings of the Eleventh Annual International Conference on International Computing Education Research* (pp. 121–130). New York: ACM.

Ahonen, L., Cowley, B., Torniainen, J., Ukkonen, A., Vihavainen, A., & Puolamaki, K. (2016). *S1: Analysis of Electrodermal Activity Recordings in Pair Programming from 2 Dyads*, PLoS One. Retrieved from http://journals.plos.org/plosone/article/asset?unique&id=info:doi/10.1371/journal.pone.0159178.s001

Anderson, J. R., Conrad, F. G., & Corbett, A. T. (1989). Skill acquisition and the LISP tutor. *Cognitive Science*, 13(1), 467–506.

Anderson, J. R., & Skwarecki, E. (1986). The automated tutoring of introductory computer programming. *Communications of the ACM*, 29(9), 842–849.

Askar, P., & Davenport, D. (2009). An investigation of factors related to self efficacy for Java programming among engineering students. *Turkish Journal of Educational Technology*, 8(1), 26–32.

Auvinen, T., Hakulinen, L., & Malmi, L. (2015). Increasing students' awareness of their behavior in online learning environments with visualizations and achievement badges. *IEEE Transactions on Learning Technologies*, 8(3), 261–273.

Baker, R. S. J., & Siemens, G. (2014). Educational data mining and learning analytics. In R. K. Sawyer (Ed.), *The Cambridge Handbook of the Learning Sciences*, 2nd edn. (pp. 253–274). Cambridge, UK: Cambridge University Press.

Banovic, N., Buzali, T., Chevalier, F., Mankoff, J., & Dey, A. K. (2016). Modeling and understanding human routine behavior. In *Proceedings of the 2016 CHI Conference on Human Factors in Computing Systems* (pp. 248–260). New York: ACM.

Barr, A., Beard, M., & Atkinson, R. C. (1976). The computer as a tutorial laboratory: The Stanford BIP Project. *International Journal of Man–Machine Studies*, 8(1), 567–596.

Bednarik, R., & Tukiainen, M. (2004). Visual attention tracking during program debugging. In *Proceedings of the Third Nordic Conference on Human-computer Interaction* (pp. 331–334). New York: ACM.

Begel, A. (2016). Fun with software developers and biometrics: Invited talk. In *Proceedings of the 1st International Workshop on Emotion Awareness in Software Engineering* (pp. 1–2). New York: ACM.

Braught, G., & Midkiff, J. (2016). Tool design and student testing behavior in an introductory Java course. In *Proceedings of the 47th ACM Technical Symposium on Computing Science Education* (pp. 449–454). New York: ACM.

Bosch, N., & D'Mello, S. K. (2013). Sequential patterns of affective states of novice programmers. Presented at *The First Workshop on AI-Supported Education for Computer Science (AIEDCS 2013)*, Memphis, TN.

Brown, N. C. C., Kölling, M., McCall, D., & Utting, I. (2014). Blackbox: A large scale repository of novice programmers' activity. In *Proceedings of the 45th ACM Technical Symposium on Computer Science Education* (pp. 223–228). New York: ACM.

Buffardi, K., & Edwards, S. H. (2013). Impacts of adaptive feedback on teaching test-driven development. In *Proceeding of the 44th ACM Technical Symposium on Computer Science Education* (pp. 293–298). New York: ACM.

Bulling, A., Blanke, U., & Schiele, B. (2014). A tutorial on human activity recognition using body-worn inertial sensors. *ACM Computing Surveys*, 46(3), 33:1–33:33.

Busjahn, T., Schulte, C., Sharif, B., & Antropova, M. (2014). Eye tracking in computing education. In *Proceedings of the Tenth Annual Conference on International Computing Education Research, Glasgow* (pp. 3–10). New York: ACM.

Card, S. K., Moran, T. P., & Newell, A. (1983). *The Psychology of Human–Computer Interaction*. Hillsdale, NJ: Lawrence Erlbaum Associates.

Cardell-Oliver, R. (2011). How can software metrics help novice programmers? In *Proceedings of the Thirteenth Australasian Computing Education Conference – Volume 114* (pp. 55–62). Darlinghurst, Australia: Australian Computer Society, Inc.

Carter, A. S. (2013). OSBIDE. Retrieved from http://osbide.codeplex.com

Carter, A. S., & Hundhausen, C. D. (2015). The design of a programming environment to support greater social awareness and participation in early computing courses. *Journal of Computing Sciences in Colleges*, 31(1), 143–153.

Carter, A. S., & Hundhausen, C. D. (2016). With a little help from my friends: An empirical study of the interplay of students' social activities, programming activities, and course success. In *Proceedings of the 2016 ACM Conference on International Computing Education Research* (pp. 201–209), New York: ACM.

Carter, A. S., & Hundhausen, C. D. (2017). Using programming process data to detect differences in students' patterns of programming. In *Proceedings of the 48th ACM Technical Symposium on Computer Science Education* (pp. 105–110), New York: ACM.

Carter, A. S., Hundhausen, C. D., & Adesope, O. (2015). The normalized programming state model: Predicting student performance in computing courses based on programming behavior. In *Proceedings of the Eleventh Annual International Conference on International Computing Education Research* (pp. 141–150), New York: ACM.

Carter, J., & Dewan, P. (2010). Are you having difficulty? In *Proceedings of the 2010 ACM Conference on Computer Supported Cooperative Work* (pp. 211–214). New York: ACM.

Corbett, A. T., & Anderson, J. R. (1992). The LISP intelligent tutoring system: Research in skill acquisition. In J. Larkin, R. Chabay & C. Scheftic (Eds.), *Computer Assisted Instruction and Intelligent Tutoring Systems: Establishing Communication and Collaboration* (pp. 73–110), Hillsdale, NJ: Erlbaum.

Denny, P., Luxton-Reilly, A., & Carpenter, D. (2014). Enhancing syntax error messages appears ineffectual. In *Proceedings of the 2014 Conference on Innovation & Technology in Computer Science Education* (pp. 273–278), New York: ACM.

Dominguez, A. K., Yacef, K., & Curran, J. R. (2010). Data mining for individualized hints in e-learning. In *Proceedings of International Conference on Educational Data Mining* (pp. 91–100). International: International Educational Data Mining Society.

Eclipse.org (2016). Usage Data Collector User Guide. Retrieved from https://eclipse.org/org/usagedata/userguide.php

Edwards, S. H., & Perez-Quinones, M. A. (2008). Web-CAT: Automatically grading programming assignments. In *Proceedings of the 13th Annual Conference on Innovation and Technology in Computer Science Education* (pp. 328–328), New York: ACM.

Ericsson, K. A., & Simon, H. A. (1984). *Protocol Analysis: Verbal Reports as Data.* Cambridge, MA: MIT Press.

Feliciano, J., Storey, M., & Zagalsky, A. (2016). Student experiences using GitHub in software engineering courses: A case study. In *Proceedings of the 38th International Conference on Software Engineering Companion* (pp. 422–431), New York: ACM.

Guzdial, M. (1994). Software-realized scaffolding to facilitate programming for science learning. *Interactive Learning Environments*, 4(1), 1–44.

Guzdial, M., Hohmann, L., Konneman, M., Walton, C., & Soloway, E. (1998). Supporting programming and learning-to-program with an integrated CAD and scaffolding workbench. *Interactive Learning Environments*, 6(1–2), 143–179.

Haaranen, L., Ihantola, P., Hakulinen, L., & Korhonen, A. (2014). How (not) to introduce badges to online exercises. In *Proceedings of the 45th ACM Technical Symposium on Computer Science Education* (pp. 33–38), New York: ACM.

Hartmann, B., MacDougall, D., Brandt, J., & Klemmer, S. R. (2010). What would other programmers do: Suggesting solutions to error messages. In *Proceedings of the 28th Conference on Human Factors in Computing Systems* (pp. 1019–1028), New York: ACM.

Herold, B. (2014). "Landmark" student-data-privacy law enacted in California. *Education Week*. Retrieved from http://blogs.edweek.org/edweek/DigitalEducation/2014/09/_landmark_student-data-privacy.html

Hundhausen, C. D., & Adesope, O. (2017). Leveraging Programming and Social Analytics to Improve Computing Education Workshop, Tacoma, WA. Retrieved from https://icer.acm.org/icer-2017/leveraging-programming-and-social-analytics-to-improve-computing-education/

Hundhausen, C. D., Agrawal, A., Fairbrother, D., & Trevisan, M. (2010). Does studio-based instruction work in CS 1?: An empirical comparison with a traditional approach. In *Proceedings of the 41st ACM Technical Symposium on Computer Science Education* (pp. 500–504), New York: ACM.

Hundhausen, C. D., Douglas, S. A., & Stasko, J. T. (2002). A meta-study of algorithm visualization effectiveness. *Journal of Visual Languages and Computing*, 13(3), 259–290.

Ihantola, P., Sorva, J., & Vihavainen, A. (2014). Automatically detectable indicators of programming assignment difficulty. In *Proceedings of the 15th Annual Conference on Information Technology Education* (pp. 33–38), New York: ACM.

Ihantola, P., Vihavainen, A., Ahadi, A., & Toll, D. (2015). Educational data mining and learning analytics in programming: literature review and case studies. In *Proceedings of the 2015 ITiCSE on Working Group Reports* (pp. 41–63), New York: ACM.

Jadud, M. C. (2006). Methods and tools for exploring novice compilation behaviour. In *Proceedings of the Second International Workshop on Computing Education Research* (pp. 73–84), New York: ACM.

Jin, W., Barnes, T., Eagle, M., Johnson, M. W., & Lehmann, L. (2012). Program representation for automatic hint generation for a data-driven novice programming tutor. In *International Conference on Intelligent Tutoring Systems* (pp. 304–309), Berlin, Germany: Springer Verlag.

Johnson, J. (2010). *Designing with the Mind in Mind: Simple Guide to Understanding User Interface Design Rules.* San Francisco, CA: Morgan Kaufmann Publishers, Inc.

Johnson, P. (2010). Hackystat – A framework for collection, analysis, visualization, interpretation, annotation, and dissemination of software development process and product data. Retrieved from https://code.google.com/p/hackystat/

Kevic, K., Walters, B. M., Shaffer, T. R., Sharif, B., Shepherd, D. C., & Fritz, T. (2015). Tracing software developers' eyes and interactions for change tasks. In *Proceedings of the 2015 10th Joint Meeting on Foundations of Software Engineering* (pp. 202–213), New York: ACM.

Kim, E., Helal, S., & Cook, D. (2010). Human activity recognition and pattern discovery. *Pervasive Computing, 9*(1), 48–53.

Kölling, M., Quig, B., Patterson, A., & Rosenberg, J. (2003). The BlueJ system and its pedagogy. *Journal of Computer Science Education, 13*(4), 249–268.

Leinonen, J., Longi, K., Klami, A., & Vihavainen, A. (2016). Automatic inference of programming performance and experience from typing patterns. In *Proceedings of the 47th ACM Technical Symposium on Computing Science Education* (pp. 132–137), New York: ACM.

Luke, J. A. (2015). *Continuously Collecting Software Development Event Data As Students Program* (MSc thesis). Virginia Tech, Blacksburg, VA.

Müller, S. C. (2015). Measuring software developers' perceived difficulty with biometric sensors. In *Proceedings of the 37th International Conference on Software Engineering – Volume 2* (pp. 887–890). New York: IEEE Press.

Müller, S. C., & Fritz, T. (2015). Stuck and Frustrated or in Flow and Happy: Sensing Developers' Emotions and Progress. In *Proceedings of the 37th International Conference on Software Engineering – Volume 1* (pp. 688–699). Piscataway, NJ: IEEE Press.

Müller, S. C., & Fritz, T. (2016). Using (bio)metrics to predict code quality online. In *Proceedings of the 38th International Conference on Software Engineering* (pp. 452–463), New York: ACM.

NetBeans.org (2016). NetBeans Usage Data Tracking. Retrieved from http://netbeans.org/about/usage-tracking.html

Nguyen, L. N. N., Rodriguez-Martin, D., Catala, A., Perez-Lopez, C., Sama, A., & Cavallaro, A. (2015). Basketball activity recognition using wearable inertial measurement units. In *Proceedings of the XVI International Conference on Human Computer Interaction* (pp. 60:1–60:6). Berlin, Germany: Springer.

Norman, D. A. (2013). *The Design of Everyday Things: Revised and Expanded Edition.* New York: Basic Books.

Norris, C., Barry, F., Fenwick Jr., J. B., Reid, K., & Rountree, J. (2008). ClockIt: Collecting quantitative data on how beginning software developers really work. *SIGCSE Bulletin*, 40(3), 37–41.

Olivares, D. (2015). Exploring learning analytics for computing education. In *Proceedings of the Eleventh Annual International Conference on International Computing Education Research* (pp. 271–272), New York: ACM.

Papancea, A., Spacco, J., & Hovemeyer, D. (2013). An open platform for managing short programming exercises. In *Proceedings of the Ninth Annual International ACM Conference on International Computing Education Research* (pp. 47–52), New York: ACM.

Parker, M. C., Rogers, K., Ericson, B. J., & Guzdial, M. (2017). Students and Teachers use an online AP CS Principles eBook differently: Teacher behavior consistent with expert learners. In *Proceedings of the 2017 ACM Conference on International Computing Education Research* (pp. 101–109), New York: ACM.

Piech, C., Sahami, M., Huang, J., & Guibas, L. (2015). Autonomously generating hints by inferring problem solving policies. In *Proceedings of the Second ACM Conference on Learning @ Scale* (pp. 195–204), New York: ACM.

Pintrich, D., Smith, D., Garcia, T., & McKeachie, W. (1991). A manual for the use of the motivated strategies for learning questionnaire (Technical report No. NCRIPTAL-91-B-004). Ann Arbor, MI: National Center for Research to Improve Postsecondary Teaching and Learning. Retrieved from http://eric.ed.gov/ERICDocs/data/ericdocs2sql/content_storage_01/0000019b/80/23/3c/44.pdf

Rivers, K., & Koedinger, K. R. (2013). Automatic generation of programming feedback: A data-driven approach. Presented at *The First Workshop on AI-Supported Education for Computer Science (AIEDCS 2013)*, Memphis, TN.

Robinson, D. (2017). How Do Students Use Stack Overflow? Retrieved from https://stackoverflow.blog/2017/02/15/how-do-students-use-stack-overflow/

Rodrigo, M. M. T., & Baker, R. S. J. D. (2009). Coarse-grained detection of student frustration in an introductory programming course. In *Proceedings of the Fifth International Workshop on Computing Education Research Workshop* (pp. 75–80), New York: ACM.

Rodrigo, M. M. T., Baker, R. S., Jadud, M. C., & Tabanao, E. S. (2009). Affective and behavioral predictors of novice programmer achievement. *SIGCSE Bulletin*, 41(3), 156–160.

Rosson, M. B., Carroll, J. M., & Sinha, H. (2011). Orientation of undergraduates toward careers in the computer and information sciences: Gender, self-efficacy and social support. *ACM Transactions on Computing Education (TOCE)*, 11(3), 1–23.

Rovai, A. P. (2002). Development of an instrument to measure classroom community. *Internet and Higher Education*, 5, 197–211.

Scacchi, W. (2002). Process models in software engineering. In *Encyclopedia of Software Engineering*, John Wiley & Sons, Inc. Retrieved from http://dx.doi.org/10.1002/0471028959.sof250

Shaw, T. (2004). The emotions of systems developers: An empirical study of affective events theory. In *Proceedings of the 2004 SIGMIS Conference on Computer*

Personnel Research: Careers, Culture, and Ethics in a Networked Environment (pp. 124–126). New York: ACM.

Shi, Y., Ruiz, N., Taib, R., Choi, E., & Chen, F. (2007). Galvanic skin response (GSR) as an index of cognitive load. In *CHI '07 Extended Abstracts on Human Factors in Computing Systems* (pp. 2651–2656), New York: ACM.

Shneiderman, B. (1976). Exploratory experiments in programmer behavior. *International Journal of Man–Machine Studies*, 5(2), 123–143.

Siemens, G., & Baker, R. S. J. (2012). Learning analytics and educational data mining: towards communication and collaboration. In *Proceedings of the 2nd International Conference on Learning Analytics and Knowledge* (pp. 252–254), New York: ACM.

Soloway, E., Bonar, J., & Ehrlich, K. (1983). Cognitive strategies and looping constructs: an empirical study. *Communications of the ACM*, 26, 853–860.

Spacco, J., Fossati, D., Stamper, J., & Rivers, K. (2013). Towards improving programming habits to create better computer science course outcomes. In *Proceedings of the 18th ACM Conference on Innovation and Technology in Computer Science Education* (pp. 243–248), New York: ACM.

Spacco, J., Hovemeyer, D., & Pugh, W. (2004). An Eclipse-based course project snapshot and submission system. In *Proceedings of the 2004 OOPSLA Workshop on Eclipse Technology eXchange* (pp. 52–56), New York: ACM.

Spacco, J., Hovemeyer, D., Pugh, W., Emad, F., Hollingsworth, J. K., & Padua-Perez, N. (2006). Experiences with Marmoset: Designing and using an advanced submission and testing system for programming courses. *SIGCSE Bulletin*, 38(3), 13–17.

Stack Overflow (2012). Stack Overflow. Retrieved from http://stackoverflow.com

Stamper, J., Eagle, M., Barnes, T., & Croy, M. (2013). Experimental evaluation of automatic hint generation for a logic tutor. *International Journal of Artificial Intelligence in Education*, 22(1–2), 3–17.

Verbert, K., & Duval, E. (2012). Learning analytics. *Learning and Education*, 1(8), Retrieved from http://nbn-resolving.de/urn:nbn:de:0009-5-33367

Verbert, K., Govaerts, S., Duval, E., & Klerkx, J. (2014). Learning dashboards: An overview and future research opportunities. *Personal and Ubiquitous Computing*, 18(6), 1499–1514.

Vihavainen, A., Vikberg, T., Luukkainen, M., & Pärtel, M. (2013). Scaffolding students' learning using test my code. In *Proceedings of the 18th ACM Conference on Innovation and Technology in Computer Science Education* (pp. 117–122), New York: ACM.

Watson, C., Li, F. W. B., & Godwin, J. L. (2013). Predicting performance in an introductory programming course by logging and analyzing student programming behavior. In *Proceedings of the 2013 IEEE 13th International Conference on Advanced Learning Technologies* (pp. 319–323). Washington, DC: IEEE Computer Society.

Teacher and Student Knowledge

24 Teacher Knowledge for Inclusive Computing Learning

Joanna Goode and Jean J. Ryoo

24.1 Introduction

This Handbook chapter provides a synthesis of the teacher knowledge literature, situated within a sociocultural understanding of how students learn. Because research on teaching and learning spans disciplinary boundaries, this chapter begins with an overview of basic knowledge on theories of learning that have been established over several decades. After reviewing sociocultural theories of learning that establish the motivational context, this chapter describes the implications for practice related to the following: (1) teacher knowledge of computing content as "specialized content knowledge" – or the domain knowledge *and* skills unique to teaching; (2) pedagogical practices that lead to impactful student learning; (3) pedagogical practices that use an additive approach to building off of students' cultural knowledge; and (4) understanding how school systems and policies shape students' educational pathways. We explain why these ideas matter in practice, building on an example from computing education literature. After this, the chapter explores two open questions for the field that reinforce the need for additional empirical research in computing classrooms and an articulation of the disciplinary connection between computational thinking and computing teacher knowledge.

24.2 Motivational Context

Nations worldwide have taken up the call to ensure all students have the opportunity to learn computing. In the USA, President Obama introduced the CS For All initiative that focuses on empowering new generations of Americans to gain computing (computer science) skills that will allow them to thrive in an increasingly digital economy. The UK has introduced a new computing curriculum that forms part of the National Curriculum, and New Zealand recently infused computing as a subject into schools. Other countries and regions worldwide are expressing enthusiasm for teaching computing education in schools (see Chapter 18).

As computing becomes institutionalized as a subject area that students must learn in primary and secondary education, an important question arises about how to prepare educators to teach computing. How can educators take on this task of welcoming all students into a new and ever-changing field? More specifically: What do computing teachers need to know?

In the current computing education landscape in countries like the USA, both state and federal computing teaching certification pathways are still few and far between. As a result, in various US states at the secondary level, for example, computing teachers are being pulled from different content areas (e.g., mathematics, social studies, science, etc.) to teach one or two computing courses. These teachers seek various computing professional development opportunities or lean on previous career experiences or personal interests in computing that can bolster their teaching efforts. And in some schools where there is a lack of teachers available to teach computing, schools and corporations have been coming together to bring industry computer scientists into the classroom based on their knowledge of content (Granor, DeLyser, & Wang, 2016).

Of course, as we seek to fill computing classrooms with teachers, people often assume that computer scientists and individuals with strong computing content knowledge would make the best computing teachers. Yet, while computing content knowledge is essential to effective computing teaching, we have all had experiences in our own schooling trajectories with educators who were amazing scientists, historians, artists, etc., but not necessarily the best teachers of those subject areas.

This is because teacher knowledge requires more than just content knowledge. Teacher knowledge must be rooted, first, in an understanding of *how* people learn that motivates student engagement, interest, and persistence with new subject learning.

Computing teachers need to know how people come to understand, know, and imagine various ideas, skills, and practices regarding computing. Educational theories that make sense of how people learn provide the essential compass that computing teachers need for navigating ways to organize activities, design learning environments, and convey computing content/skills/practices for their students. And, more specifically, educational theories that provide educators with the knowledge of how to engage *all*, and not just a privileged few, are needed.

Sociocultural theories of learning serve as a useful lens to such ends, elucidating how people learn, specifically in contexts involving computers (Cole, 2006). Building on the ideas of Vygotsky (1929, 1960), Luria (1928, 1932), and Leont'ev (1932), sociocultural theories emphasize how culture mediates all human life and activity. Culture is not limited to the food, clothing, and customs most often associated with various ethnic groups' "cultures" across the world, but also encompasses the social practices, languages, signs, tools, institutions, architectural organizations of space, etc., in which all humans engage beyond ethnic lines (Cole & Engestrom, 2007).

Secondly, such culture – in the form of both material and ideal artifacts – impacts not only our conditions of existence, but also our psychic condition or human cognition (Luria, 1928). In the context of computing classrooms, one can see what this looks like in relation to the cultural tool of the computer that has obvious physical and psychological impacts on human users, yet is simultaneously shaped by its human users. Furthermore, attention must be paid to the actual activity of individuals (what people are focused on doing both alone and with others while using the world of objects around us) that reflects the "system" within the "larger system of social relations" (Leont'ev, 1981, p. 47). In other words, when we take into account what leading activities are guiding a learner's trajectory (e.g., at birth, the leading activity is connecting with the group into which one is born, but early childhood and "preschool" are often focused on play, etc.), then we can gain a clearer grasp of the sociocultural group's value systems regarding what should be most important and enacted at various ages or experience levels (or the social expectations) in a learning context (Cole & Engestrom, 2007; Leont'ev, 1981). Thus, keeping activity in relation to cultural practices/values in mind results in a deeper understanding of what drives learning within the larger institution, the teacher, and the student.

Relatedly, these principles recognize that human cognition is not limited to individual minds, but involves structures and processes that can be understood as distributed across people, material and ideal artifacts, the environment, and time (Zhang & Patel, 2006). When considering student thinking and learning in the context of working with computers, it becomes useful to turn to Hutchins' (1995) description of what distributed cognition looks like when working with a machine. In the example of successful completion of a flight, Hutchins describes the way a system is produced that involves human cognition distributed across at least two pilots interacting with one another, the technology used to fly, technology on the ground, and the information as represented and transformed through the tools and tasks at hand (Hutchins, 1995). Similarly, in the computer-based classroom, students are engaged with one another, computers, and information (signs, tools, etc.) as represented and transformed through computing in ways that show how cognition is not located within a single student or teacher, but distributed across the learning environment. For example, when attempting to program a robot to physically react to sound, students will engage with one another and the educator(s), the physical technology of the computer, the signs and information communicated by that technology, as well as the technology of the robot itself in order to make the robot sense sound and move. Thinking and cognition are not limited to a single student's actions in this situation, but move across various actors and objects through various cultural practices within the space.

Thirdly, human psychological functions cannot be understood divorced of their historically accumulated forms of human activity (Cole & Engestrom, 2007). In order to understand how human psychological functions work in the present, you must take a "genetic" perspective or, in other words, study its history and how it came to be in its present form. Teacher knowledge requires efforts to understand what students understand and can do in relation to their historical contexts, with an eye toward the future as well.

Finally, sociocultural theories of learning emphasize that learning does not happen in a vacuum. Learning is a social phenomenon. Psychological processes develop through interactions between people within varying cultural contexts.

As Vygotsky (1978) explains, "learning awakens a variety of internal developmental processes that are able to operate only when the child is interacting with people in his environment and in cooperation with his peers. Once these processes are internalized, they become part of the child's independent developmental achievement" (p. 90).

From this theoretical standpoint (also discussed in the Chapter 9), sociocultural theories of learning emphasize that learning is not the same thing as development and development is not the gradual accumulation of separate changes (Cole & Engestrom, 2007). Yet learning and development are interrelated from our very first days of life as we engage in social interaction with others (Vygotsky, 1978). In order to tease apart the difference between a student's developmental stage and new learning, teachers find use in exploring their students' zones of proximal development (ZPDs). The ZPD defines the space between a person's developmental level (determined by what that individual can do alone) and that person's future developmental state (determined by what that person can do in collaboration with or guidance from more expert others). As such, development lags behind learning, but becomes visible through the ZPD that shows the "buds" of that potential development (Vygotsky, 1978, p. 86).

Thus, teachers must know how to create conditions to make their students' ZPDs visible, so that they can better understand their students' developmental and learning states and organize for future learning. This requires that teachers understand how to organize and support social interactions in ways that allow students to draw upon prior knowledge while engaging with peers (prior knowledge that educators must seek to know and understand by considering the cultural–historical origins of such student knowledge) – illuminating what they can do without and with help – toward designing future learning experiences that allow students to acquire new understandings that they can consciously control.

Sociocultural theories of learning thus serve as a valuable foundation for teachers upon which to build opportunities for students to learn computing content and skills that seek to meet students where they are and evolve from that point forward.

24.3 Implications for Practice

Given that the purpose of teaching is to facilitate student learning, teacher knowledge must build on these theories of learning to develop an instructional approach that is effective and inclusive for all classroom students. More specifically, beyond computing content knowledge, teachers must consider the following: (1) how cultural practices that students experience at home, in school, outside of school, etc., impact the ways we engage in the world and thus learn; (2) that learning and student cognition are not limited to the individual alone, but occur across interactions that individuals have with others, material and ideal artifacts, the environment, and time; (3) that to understand how students think and learn, teachers must understand students' historical

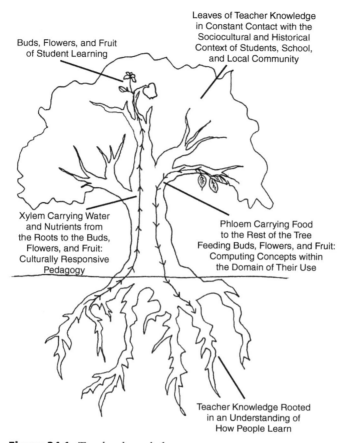

Leaves of Teacher Knowledge
in Constant Contact with the
Sociocultural and Historical
Context of Students, School,
and Local Community

Buds, Flowers, and Fruit
of Student Learning

Xylem Carrying Water
and Nutrients from
the Roots to the Buds,
Flowers, and Fruit:
Culturally Responsive
Pedagogy

Phloem Carrying Food
to the Rest of the Tree
Feeding Buds, Flowers, and Fruit:
Computing Concepts within
the Domain of Their Use

Teacher Knowledge Rooted
in an Understanding of
How People Learn

Figure 24.1 *Teacher knowledge.*

contexts and experiences impacting the way they are and how they learn in the present toward how they could be and could learn in the future; (4) that learning is a social process that becomes visible through students' interactions with peers, teachers, etc.; and thus (5) creating opportunities to make past, present, and future learning visible through educational and social interactions that draw on students' prior knowledge while engaging both independently and with others.

So, for teachers to effectively teach computing to students, there are multiple and overlapping areas of knowledge that educators must possess in order to effectively teach students and to accurately represent and engage students in the field of computing. In addition to an appreciation of the sociocultural tenets of student learning, teachers need to have knowledge of the daily computing activities, instructional practices, and student characteristics that lead to learning in computing classrooms. This section will contextualize teacher knowledge in computing within a review of the literature that has explored and empirically studied teacher knowledge across primary and secondary domain areas.

Figure 24.1 shows a diagram illustrating computing teacher knowledge that reflects the multiple and overlapping areas of knowledge that educators must possess. The teacher's knowledge (or the tree) must be rooted in an understanding of how people learn (sociocultural theories of learning as the earth). This teacher knowledge (the tree) can then feed the buds, flowers, and fruit of student computing learning through systems that bring computing content to students by way of culturally responsive pedagogy that supports teaching for understanding and teaching computing concepts *within* the domain of their use (and not divorced from it) toward the development of computational practices across computing topics. Yet the tree cannot bring nutrients to its buds, flowers, and fruit without maintaining contact between its leaves and an understanding of the sociocultural/historical context of students, schooling structures, and the local community (or the sun, air, and water).

In computing, there is often a primary focus on growing computing teaching expertise through a singular focus on increasing teachers' content knowledge. Yet research shows the limitations of content knowledge alone (Ferguson & Womack, 1993), suggesting that teachers must also hold a knowledge base for how to effectively teach computing in ways that lead to conceptual understanding for a range of students. And because of the importance of connecting learning with student's interests, experiences, and identities, a culturally responsive computing pedagogy is an essential skill for teaching in computing classrooms. Lastly, having a repertoire of how schools function and how to help students navigate pathways in computing acknowledges the important advising and advocating roles teachers play in schools. In the rest of this section, each of these areas is discussed in terms of its importance for defining the set of knowledge for successful computing teachers.

24.3.1 Teaching Computing

To activate student learning and effectively teach computing, what must teachers know about the subject of computing? Though there is scarce research in the field of computing, the scholarship of teaching proposed by Shulman (1986) and further developed by other scholars provides a conceptual orientation and a set of analytical distinctions that are useful for focusing research and policy on the types of knowledge needed to teach computing.

There is a great deal of support for the importance of teachers holding content knowledge in the areas they are teaching in the classroom. Understanding what should be taught, why is it taught, and what mastery looks like are important capacities of teachers (National Research Council, 2005). One clear point from the literature is that adequate content knowledge does not just involve a familiarity with facts and concepts, but also an understanding of how the knowledge is organized that underlies the ability to understand and solve problems. As pioneering learning scientist Bruner (1977) asserted: "The curriculum of a subject should be determined by the most fundamental understanding that can be achieved of the underlying principles that give structure to a subject. Teaching specific topics or skills without making clear their context in the broader fundamental structure of a field of knowledge is uneconomical" (p. 33). Ball (1990) provides useful phrasing to illustrate this point. She suggests that teachers not only need to have "knowledge in" a domain, but also "knowledge of" the domain so they can highlight the nature of knowledge in that subject area.

Shulman's (1986) research on the scholarship of teaching highlights the importance of the content knowledge paradigm of teacher understanding, arguing that teachers are charged with establishing norms and principles for the content area that accurately represent the rules for what is legitimate to say or do in a particular domain area. In more recent work, Ball, Thames, and Phelps (2008) draw on their empirical mathematics education research to expand on the scholarship of teaching. They suggest using the construct of "common content knowledge" to denote the essential knowledge and skills of a discipline that teachers need to accurately depict in the classroom. By "common," they explain that this domain understanding is not unique to teaching, but is conventional knowledge used in a wide range of settings. The research literature also postulates that teachers require "horizon knowledge" of the domain area (Ball, 1993; Ball, Thames, & Phelps, 2008); that is, an awareness of how computing topics are related over the span of a computing learning pathway in the curriculum to understand how a student will encounter a particular concept over time.

Notably, many scholars have argued that, for teaching, having deep subject matter knowledge in an area related to the instructional content is markedly distinct from having advanced content preparation in the field unrelated to the targeted learning area. In fact, a synthesis of studies has shown no relationship between teachers' scores on subject areas tests of the National Teacher Examinations' (NTE) as measured by student performance or performance evaluations (Darling-Hammond, 2000) or as measured by mathematics teaching practice (Smith, Desimone, & Ueno, 2005). A study using another large-scale data set found evidence that teachers' content knowledge, as measured by course taking, is positively related to student achievement in science and mathematics courses (Monk, 1994). Yet this study showed that above a threshold level of five courses for mathematics, there were diminishing returns on student achievement. This finding suggests that knowledge of the material to be taught is crucial to classroom teaching, but that returns on subject matter expertise grow smaller beyond a minimal essential level that exceeds the demands of the curriculum (Darling-Hammond, 2000).

To help explain this content knowledge threshold, Ball and colleagues draw from their study of practicing teachers and suggest that it is the "specialized content knowledge" – or the domain knowledge and skills unique to teaching – that is essential for teaching effectively in a subject area (Ball, Thames, & Phelps, 2008). Because specialized content knowledge of a subject area is unique to teaching, an unpacking of the discipline is not needed or desired in other settings. For instance, in computing, understanding how students' confuse assignment and equal operators informs teacher instruction of the lesson (Brown & Altadmri, 2017; Hristova, Misra, Rutter, & Mercuri, 2003); for practicing computer scientists, however, simply using the correct operator is appropriate without having this specialized content knowledge of how to teach the concept. This type of educator understanding captures the computing domain demands of teaching that bridge the academic knowledge with the knowing of students and pedagogy.

Computing education has experienced many international, regional, and organizational attempts at codifying appropriate computing topics and skills for teaching students in recent years. Efforts have been made to develop sets of Computer Science Learning Standards (CSTA, 2017), a K–12 Computer Science Framework (2016), and national curriculum frameworks and courses. While each of these ways of organizing the targeted knowledge for students varies in scope and sequence, what is conspicuous is the move away from a coding-centric approach to computing. Rather, topics such as human–computer interaction, computing and data, networks and the Internet, and working with sensors and tangible forms of computers now have a prominent place in computing learning standards alongside more traditionally taught topics centered on programming. Still, while these frameworks and standards provide lists of topics and skills teachers are charged with teaching, they are not intended to provide teachers with a conceptual understanding of the underlying principles of how computing knowledge is structured or organized.

Further, nationally scaled secondary computing courses purposefully incorporate building students' computational practices in the classroom, highlighting the importance of the skills and behaviors of computer scientists, such as creating computational artifacts, analyzing problems, connecting computing topics and real-world problems, abstracting, collaborating, and communicating about computing activities (Astrachan & Briggs, 2012; Margolis et al., 2014). These practices mirror the USA's move to reform science education through a framework of domain knowledge using the terms of concepts and practices (National Research Council, 2013). Teachers must be prepared not only to help students learn about computing, but also to facilitate the development of these computational practices in students across computing content topics.

This dynamic nature of the field of computing presents a unique need to computing teachers – the skills and knowledge acquired to teach a particular programming language no longer represent sufficient disciplinary knowledge to teach a more comprehensive version of computing topics.

24.3.2 Teaching for Understanding

In their edited book *How Students Learn* (2005), Bransford and Donovan assert that "instruction must begin with close attention to students' ideas, knowledge, skills, and attitudes, which provide the new foundation on which new learning builds" (p. 14). They note that an important feature of teaching for understanding is presenting students with "just-manageable difficulties" that are challenging enough to maintain motivation and engagement. As we know from sociocultural learning theories, teaching to students' ZPDs is an essential ingredient for effective learning.

The importance of pedagogy is evident when examining the research literature for how teacher preparation contributes to student performance in the classroom. Studies have shown positive relationships between teacher education program participation and teacher performance in the classroom (Denton & Lacina, 1984; Guyton & Farokhi, 1987). But what do teachers need to know in order to create computing instructional activities that lead to impactful student learning?

Numerous large-scale studies have concluded that teacher education coursework, as opposed to subject matter courses, is the most influential teacher preparation when measuring student performance (Begle, 1979; Monk, 1994; Perkes, 1967). In fact, in a study of graduates from a teacher education program, researchers found that the number of education courses completed by teachers explained more than four times the variance in their performance than indicators of content knowledge in the subject area, as measured by grade point average and test scores (Ferguson & Womack, 1993).

This dyad of subject matter knowledge and pedagogical skill is a construct that exists only in theoretical discussions, as in practice pedagogy either illuminates or shades the content area understanding of the teacher (Darling-Hammond, 2000). That is, without preparation of the pedagogical knowledge that ignites and supports student learning, extensive computing content knowledge is inadequate for the task of teaching. As Darling-Hammond highlights, Byrne (1983) discussed the following:

> It is surely plausible to suggest that insofar as a teacher's knowledge provides the basis for his or her effectiveness, the most relevant knowledge will be that which concerns the particular topic being taught and the relevant pedagogical strategies for teaching it to the particular types of pupils to whom it will be taught. If the teacher is to teach fractions, then it is knowledge of fractions and perhaps of closely associated topics which is of major importance … Similarly, knowledge of teaching strategies relevant to teaching fractions will be important. (p. 14)

Given this review of the literature on teachers' instructional preparation, holding pedagogical knowledge and instructional skills is critical for computing teachers to effectively engage students in classroom learning. Emerging scholarship in computing education verifies the importance of teacher's knowledge of teaching. Our recent study of a long-term professional development program demonstrated that teachers place a higher value on pedagogical preparation and developing a professional learning community than on learning content area material (Ryoo, Goode, & Margolis, 2016).

24.3.3 Teaching Diverse Students

In education, there is a historical legacy of opportunity gaps, education debts, and discrepancies in achievement across subject areas and marked by gender, race, ability, and socioeconomic class. As discussed in Chapter 16, in computing classes, these inequities are exacerbated due to long-term patterns of access to the technology needed to engage in computing-related learning. An important component of broadening participation in computing is the enactment of a culturally responsive pedagogy in computing learning spaces. Indeed, it is important to remember that the primary task of computing teachers is not to teach computing, but to teach people who bring their own interests, knowledge, and life experiences with them into the learning space.

There is much evidence that ignoring race, gender, and other defining characteristics of a student is an ineffective approach to teaching all students in the classroom. Instead, as Cochran-Smith (1995) suggests, a rejection of a color-blind pedagogy allows for an understanding of the values and practices of diverse families and cultures and permits teachers to construct pedagogy that considers these issues in design. Indeed, a culturally responsive approach to pedagogy presupposes that all student learning is increased when teachers use an additive approach to building off of the possibilities and promises of students, rather than focusing on perceived deficits or deficiencies (Gay, 2010; Ladson-Billings, 1995).

Building off of the theoretical constructs of culturally responsive pedagogy, scholars examining how culturally relevant computing education incorporates the experiences and perspectives of diverse groups of students have found positive results in engaging historically underrepresented populations (Kafai et al., 2014; Scott, Sheridan, & Clark, 2015). Findings from culturally relevant computing studies reveal how this pedagogical approach connects computing to student identity and encourages a critique of inequity in computing (Eglash, Gilbert, & Foster, 2013; Eglash, Gilbert, Taylor, & Grier, 2013). These principles underlie pedagogical strategies for broadening participation in computing, including addressing issues of access and structural barriers (Margolis et al., 2008; Martin, McAlear, & Scott, 2015), and give students a wider perspective on the field and potential pathways in computing education.

24.3.4 Teaching in schools

We have outlined so far that computing teachers must know the following: (1) how students learn; (2) key computing content and its sociohistorical impacts; and (3) the pedagogical practices necessary to best engage all learners (through culturally responsive computing). But there is yet a fourth key area that computing teacher knowledge must also include: an understanding of school structures and how they impact students' computing education and career pathways. Educators must ask themselves: Who decides what courses are available in a school? How are students enrolled in those courses? Are students able to choose what courses they take? What school-based supports and barriers exist to students being able to pursue an area of personal interest? And how are students' interests – personal, academic, and career – fostered through schooling contexts? Are youth given access to mentors both within and beyond school walls who can connect them to future opportunities related to those interests?

To answer these questions with regard to computing education specifically, we can turn to research exploring the state of computing education in public high schools. While more recent efforts have begun both in the USA and internationally to ensure that youth learn computing across all grade levels (e.g., President Obama's CS for All initiative; the UK's national school curriculum), access to quality computing education in many schools remains an issue. As described by Margolis et al. (2008): (1) there is a dearth of computing course options for most youth due to a lack of curricula, resulting in many schools offering only typing or simple computer applications-based classes; (2) this is exacerbated by a need for computing teachers due to a lack of computing teacher education and certification pathways, such that many computing educators are pulled away from teaching math, science, or other topic areas in order to teach computing classes; (3) when computing courses *do* exist in a school, they are often only at the most advanced level, limiting success to youth who were given access to computing learning outside of school through the preparatory privilege of summer camps or technological tools at home; and (4) school counselors serve as gatekeepers to computing learning because they make the final decisions about who can enroll in which classes, and such decisions are, unfortunately, subject to counselors' stereotypes and biases about who can and should excel with technology.

Computing teacher knowledge must, therefore, include not only an awareness of how youth get tracked in and out of computing classes, but also how best to advocate for *all* youth to be given equal opportunities to learn computing across grade levels (Milner, 2015). Computing educators must advocate to school counselors and administration for students' rights to learn computing. Also, in order to prepare youth for the computing courses that exist in one's school, computing teachers must have a knowledge of learning opportunities beyond school hours and walls that might supplement what may be missing during schooltime. This includes connecting youth to community college courses, after-school programs, summer opportunities, internships, and peer or adult mentors. Relatedly, when youth show an interest in computing, computing teachers must know how to foster that interest by showing how it may grow into various new skill sets, passions, and careers. Computing teachers must know the strengths and resources already present in the local community, while also drawing on her/his/their own educational network, to help students understand not only what computing interest can lead to, but also *how* to get to such a place. Connecting youth with experts who have experienced computing education and career-related pathways is important for computing teachers to do, so that youth can learn about the joys, challenges, and strategies for success one may need to know when pursuing computing learning in school and beyond.

24.4 Engaging Knowledge in Practice

Reflecting on the key areas of teacher knowledge that we have outlined thus far, what does it actually look like to engage such knowledge in practice? Turning to well-known literature in computing education allows us to better understand applications of teacher knowledge to practice.

Consider, for example, Turkle and Papert's (1990) description of the brico-leur computing student. Through a description of the ways a bricoleur com-puter scientist approaches computer programming compared to the structured "planner's" approach (an approach that is treated preferentially by both industry and academia) one begins to recognize exactly why it is of crucial importance for teachers to know not only computing content, but also how to recognize, acknowledge, and support the diverse ways people learn and engage with the world, as impacted by varying sociocultural and historical perspectives and experiences. Turkle and Papert (1990) describe that the structured "planner's" approach is often treated as the "right way" to solve a program-ming problem: by separating the problem into parts and designing solutions that fit each part toward solving the entire issue in a "top-down, divide-and-conquer way." However, the bricoleur constructs understanding in a way that is very different: by arranging and rearranging, playing with various program elements, and moving them around as if they were "material elements ... elem-ents of a collage." For example, Turkle and Papert (1990) share the case of Anne, a fourth grader who was learning to program by using the knowledge and skills she gained from her favorite hobby: painting. In her program, she wanted a flock of birds of varying colors to appear and disappear in the sky on the computer screen, at varying places and times. Since the birds were all different colors, Anne had to use algebraic thinking to figure out how to make each one be recognized by the computer, then made invisible, then made visible again when desired. However, rather than use this traditional approach to pro-gramming her birds (in which a programmer might store each bird's color as a variable, change those colors to invisible, then have the program show the spe-cific variable for each color at different points), Anne used her painting cultural practices to inform how she solved this programming challenge. Recognizing that when you want something to disappear on a canvas, you literally paint on top of it, Anne programmed her computer to place sky-colored screens over each bird when she wanted them to disappear while maintaining each bird's color without a specific variable. She incorporated her understanding of com-pound objects in the programming language to grow beyond simply additively making a picture bigger into, instead, covering one another in ways that allowed her bird sprites to appear and disappear. As a bricoleur, she experimented with the materials and created the effects she wanted, rather than following a single, structured pathway to achieving her goal.

Anne's bricolage approach to computing, while not normally valued in trad-itional computing learning and industry contexts, is not unique. However, one can imagine how critical a teacher's response to her approach could be to either elevating her engagement with and learning of computing or stalling her interest and growth with computing. If an educator doesn't understand why or how Anne chose an alternative route to programming that purposefully moved away from developing variables for bird color or fails to understand the reasoning behind Anne building on her personal knowledge of painting and engaging with the world by layering sky screens over the colored birds, then various things might occur that could negatively impact Anne and her computing learning: (1) Anne's approach might be shut down as simply "wrong" by the teacher, making Anne feel like her creative problem-solving approaches are neither recognized nor valued; (2) Anne might be forced by the teacher to approach programming in a different way that does not build on her previous knowledge and thus may feel either alien or unnatural; and (3) this, in turn, may result in Anne disengaging completely with the task at hand (such that Anne thinks she doesn't "like" computers or computing) or in coming to the conclusion that she simply isn't "good" at programming. However, if a teacher sees the depth of thinking, creativity, and personal knowledge that Anne is bringing to her programming practice – in the ways that Turkle and Papert (1990) have recognized – then Anne may gain opportunities to feel valued, to identify as someone who is interested in and skilled with computers, to connect learning across different contexts of her life (from painting to programming), and to grow her interest in and pursuit of further computing learning. This is why teacher knowledge that takes into account the diverse ways learners engage with the world, through their own sociocultural perspectives and unique historical contexts, is so critical beyond content knowledge alone.

24.5 Open Questions for Future Research

24.5.1 Particulars of Computing Teacher Knowledge

Most of the literature and sociocultural theories on teaching and learning described above come from a rich legacy of research in other subject matter domains, particular mathematics and science. Though science, technology, engineering, and mathematics (STEM) education is often discussed as a homogenous set of knowledge, the subject area domain shapes both the types and areas of inquiry when studying teaching and learning. For instance, a rich and growing area of mathematics education is cognitively guided instruction, which focuses on appreciating students' diverse processes for solving mathematical problems. The research on cognitively guided instruction is uniquely situated within discrete mathematical tasks and activities common to classrooms, such as addition and subtraction (Fennema et al., 1996).

In computing education, most studies examining student misconceptions and mistakes have so far focused exclusively on students' experiences of learning programming languages. For instance, a research study examined which programming mistakes students make and identified the typical syntax, semantic, and logic errors that students make when learning Java (Hristova et al., 2003). Yet empirical research has concluded that there is little association between educators' predictions of students' Java programming errors and their years of teaching experience (Brown & Altadmri, 2017), suggesting either that educator experience does not matter in predicting programming errors or that forecasting such errors is not important to the skill set of programming teachers – a notable divergence from research findings in physics education (Sadler et al., 2013). More computing-specific domain studies are needed to dig deeper into how teacher knowledge is related to identifying and correcting student misconceptions across multiple topics in computing education.

What is unique about computing education, as President Obama pointed out when introducing "CS for All," is that students should have "opportunities to be producers, not just consumers, in the digital economy, and to be active citizens in our technology-driven world." Now that curricular standards and nationally scaled courses encourage students to design and create original artifacts much like art, what is the unique knowledge of teachers needed to simultaneously support student learning of concepts while also engaging in the process of producing and refining new digital artifacts? How can educators make sense of student learning as distributed across people and artifacts, especially with computing tools that are able to digitally record and store students' in-process thinking? And what knowledge is necessary to support collaborative work between youth with varying ability and understanding to enhance students' ZPDs in ways that move away from isolating students from each other with the introduction of computers? Capturing the teacher knowledge and pedagogy that effectively activates this tangible design and production through student learning is an area ripe for future computing educational research.

So while we cautiously draw from the empirical studies in other disciplines to point to our current understanding of teacher knowledge, we simultaneously note the need for future research purposefully located in computing teaching and learning. As courses with common curricular guidelines grow internationally, increased opportunities to study computing learning in context will certainly bolster our understanding of computing teacher knowledge beyond single studies on programming competencies and toward contextualized studies of teaching and learning in computing classrooms.

24.5.2 Is Computational Thinking Computing?

In discussions of what teachers should know about computing, often the concept of "computational thinking" is used interchangeably with "computing" when referencing the domain knowledge educators should hold to be effective teachers. Because of the popularity of policies pointed toward infusing "computational thinking" into the curriculum and its prevalence in conversations about preparing teachers to bring this knowledge to classrooms, it is important to address what the implications of this are for teacher knowledge. We find that introducing the terminology of computational thinking to the discussion of teacher knowledge, as something ill-defined and yet supposedly distinct from doing computing, adds little clarity or empirical knowledge for understanding computing teacher knowledge.

The concept of "computational thinking" – or the philosophy of thinking about computing – has been growing in popularity, especially in primary classrooms where teachers are generalists, yet there is often little connection between discrete activities and computing learning trajectories. While some scholars suggest computational thinking is a valued approach used in other disciplines to infuse computing (Barr & Stephenson, 2011), the recent K–12 Computer Science Framework (2016) related computational thinking to a subset of defined computing practices. They argue, "The most effective context and approach for developing computational thinking is learning computer science; they are intrinsically connected. Computational thinking is at the heart of the computer science practices." As research syntheses have pointed out (National Research Council, 2010, 2011; Grover & Pea, 2013) and as is discussed at length in Chapter 17, there is little consensus on the scope and nature of computational thinking in the educational arena.

In computing education in the primary grades, many published studies that examine teacher knowledge take place within a framework of computational thinking (Angeli et al., 2016; Voogt et al., 2015). For the secondary level, there is a focus on the dynamics between computing subject area concepts and practices. This perhaps indicates a broader trend in preparing non-computing teachers to teach computing – to infuse "computational thinking" into the primary curriculum and teach "computing" in later grades. Yet if computational thinking is conceptually synonymous with the implementation of practices associated with computing, how do we reconcile the need to connect computing instruction with cohesive learning pathways appropriate for the disciplinary knowledge of computing? Is teacher competence at integrating computational thinking in the curriculum, divorced from computing scope and sequence of learning content, sufficient knowledge for introducing young children to the field of computing? Though there are no apparent answers to these questions, we believe they are critical to address as we continue to develop understanding of what teachers should know and be able to do in order to be effective instructors of computing.

24.6 Conclusion

This chapter's focus on teacher knowledge forwarded a sociocultural perspective to examining teacher knowledge needed for educators to effectively teach all students. As computing education moves from the periphery of an enrichment subject and toward a core and compulsory topic in schools, it is critical to ensure that teachers are skilled not only with the content knowledge needed to teach the curriculum, but also with a deep and nuanced understanding of how students learn and how to teach for understanding and with a commitment to inclusion.

References

Angeli, C., Voogt, J., Fluck, A., Webb, M., Cox, M., Malyn-Smith, J., & Zagami, J. (2016). A K–6 computational thinking curriculum framework: Implications for teacher knowledge. *Journal of Educational Technology & Society*, 19(3), 47–57.

Astrachan, O., & Briggs, A. (2012). The CS principles project. *ACM Inroads*, 3(2), 38–42.

Ball, D. L. (1990). The mathematical understandings that prospective teachers bring to teacher education. *The Elementary School Journal*, 90(4), 449–466.

Ball, D. L. (1993). With an eye on the mathematical horizon: Dilemmas of teaching elementary school mathematics. *The Elementary School Journal*, 93(4), 373–397.

Ball, D. L., Thames, M. H., & Phelps, G. (2008). Content knowledge for teaching: What makes it special? *Journal of Teacher Education*, 59(5), 389–407.

Barr, V., & Stephenson, C. (2011). Bringing computational thinking to K–12: What is Involved and what is the role of the computer science education community? *ACM Inroads*, 2(1), 48–54.

Begle, E. G. (1979). *Critical Variables in Mathematics Education: Findings from a Survey of the Empirical Literature*. Washington, DC: Mathematical Association of America.

Bransford, J. D., & Donovan, M. S. (2005). Scientific inquiry and how people learn. In M. S. Donovan & J. D. Bransford (Eds.), *How Students Learn: History, Mathematics, and Science in the Classroom* (pp. 397–420). Washington, DC: National Academies Press.

Brown, N. C., & Altadmri, A. (2017). Novice Java programming mistakes: Large-scale data vs. educator beliefs. *ACM Transactions on Computing Education (TOCE)*, 17(2), 7.

Bruner, J. S. (1977). *The Process of Education* (rev. ed.). Cambridge, MA: Harvard University Press.

Byrne, C. J. (1983). Teacher knowledge and teacher effectiveness: A literature review, theoretical analysis and discussion of research strategy. Paper presented at the meeting of the Northwestern Educational Research Association, Ellenville, NY.

Cochran-Smith, M. (1995). Color blindness and basket making are not the answers: Confronting the dilemmas of race, culture, and language diversity in teacher education. *American Educational Research Journal*, 32(3), 493–522.

Cole, M. (2006). *The Fifth Dimension: An After-School Program Built on Diversity*. New York: Russell Sage Foundation.

Cole, M., & Engestrom, Y. (2007). Cultural–historical approaches to designing for development. In J. Valsiner & A. Rosa (Eds.), *The Cambridge Handbook of Sociocultural Psychology* (pp. 484–506). New York: Cambridge University Press.

Computer Science Teachers Association (2017). K–12 Computer Science Standards. Retrieved from www.csteachers.org/page/standards

Darling-Hammond, L. (2000). Teacher quality and student achievement. *Education Policy Analysis Archives*, 8(1), 1–42.

Denton, J. J., & Lacina, L. J. (1984). Quantity of professional education coursework linked with process measures of student teaching. *Teacher Education and Practice*, 1, 39–64.

Eglash, R., Gilbert, J. E., & Foster, E. (2013). Toward culturally responsive computing education. *Communications of the ACM*, 56(7), 33–36.

Eglash, R., Gilbert, J. E., Taylor, V., & Geier, S. R. (2013). Culturally responsive computing in urban, after-school contexts: Two approaches. *Urban Education*, 48(5), 629–656.

Fennema, E., Carpenter, T. P., Franke, M. L., Levi, L., Jacobs, V. R., & Empson, S. B. (1996). A longitudinal study of learning to use children's thinking in mathematics instruction. *Journal for Research in Mathematics Education*, 27(4), 403–434.

Ferguson, P., & Womack, S. T. (1993). The impact of subject matter and on teaching performance. *Journal of Teacher Education*, 44(1), 55–63.

Gay, G. (2010). *Culturally Responsive Teaching: Theory, Research, and Practice.* New York: Teachers College Press.

Granor, N., DeLyser, L. A., & Wang, K. (2016). Teals: Teacher professional development using industry volunteers. In *Proceedings of the 47th ACM Technical Symposium on Computing Science Education* (pp. 60–65). New York: ACM.

Grover, S., & Pea, R. (2013). Computational thinking in K–12: A review of the state of the field. *Educational Researcher*, 42(1), 38–43.

Guyton, E., & Farokhi, E. (1987). Relationships among academic performance, basic skills, subject matter knowledge, and teaching skills of teacher education graduates. *Journal of Teacher Education*, 38(5), 37–42.

Hristova, M., Misra, A., Rutter, M., & Mercuri, R. (2003). Identifying and correcting Java programming errors for introductory computer science students. *ACM SIGCSE Bulletin*, 35(1), 153–156.

Hutchins, E. (1995). How a cockpit remembers its speeds. *Cognitive Science*, 19, 265–288.

K–12 Computer Science Framework (2016). K–12 Computer Science Framework. Retrieved from www.k12cs.org

Kafai, Y., Searle, K., Martinez, C., & Brayboy, B. (2014). Ethnocomputing with electronic textiles: Culturally responsive open design to broaden participation in computing in American Indian youth and communities. In *Proceedings of the 45th ACM Technical Symposium on Computer Science Education* (pp. 241–246). New York: ACM.

Ladson-Billings, G. (1995). But that's just good teaching! The case for culturally relevant pedagogy. *Theory into Practice*, 34(3), 159–165.

Leont'ev, A. N. (1932). Studies in the cultural development of the child, 3: The development of voluntary attention in the child. *Journal of Genetic Psychology*, 37, 52–81.

Leont'ev, A. N. (1981). The problem of activity in psychology. In J. V. Wertsch (Ed.), *The Concept of Activity in Soviet Psychology* (pp. 37–71). White Plains, NY: Sharpe.

Luria, A. R. (1928). The problem of the cultural development of the child. *Journal of Genetic Psychology*, 35, 506.

Luria, A. R. (1932). *The Nature of Human Conflicts.* New York: Liveright.

Margolis, J., Estrella, R., Goode, J., Jellison Holme, J., & Nao, K. (2008). *Stuck in the Shallow end: Education, Race, and Computing.* Boston, MA: MIT Press.

Margolis, J., Goode, J., Chapman, G., & Ryoo, J. J. (2014). That classroom "magic". *Communications of the ACM*, 57(7), 31–33.

Martin, A., McAlear, F., & Scott, A. (2015). Path Not Found: Disparities in Access to Computer Science Courses in California High Schools. Retrieved from https://files.eric.ed.gov/fulltext/ED561181.pdf

Milner IV, H. R. (2015). *Rac(e)ing to Class: Confronting Poverty and Race in Schools and Classrooms.* Cambridge, MA: Harvard Education Press.

Monk, D. H. (1994). Subject area preparation of secondary mathematics and science teachers and student achievement. *Economics of Education Review*, 13(2), 125–145.

National Research Council (2005). *How Students Learn: Science in the Classroom.* Washington, DC: Committee on How People Learn.

National Research Council (2010). *Report of a Workshop on the Scope and Nature of Computational Thinking*. Washington, DC: National Academies Press.

National Research Council (2011). *Report of a Workshop on the Pedagogical Aspects of Computational Thinking*. Washington, DC: National Academies Press.

National Research Council (2013). *Next Generation Science Standards: For States, by States*. Washington, DC: National Academies Press.

Perkes, V. A. (1967). Junior high school science teacher preparation, teaching behavior, and student achievement. *Journal of Research in Science Teaching*, 5(2), 121–126.

Ryoo, J., Goode, J., & Margolis, J. (2015). It takes a village: Supporting inquiry- and equity-oriented computer science pedagogy through a professional learning community. *Computer Science Education*, 25(4), 351–370.

Sadler, P. M., Sonnert, G., Coyle, H. P., Cook-Smith, N., & Miller, J. L. (2013). The influence of teachers' knowledge on student learning in middle school physical science classrooms. *American Educational Research Journal*, 50(5), 1020–1049.

Scott, K. A., Sheridan, K. M., & Clark, K. (2015). Culturally responsive computing: A theory revisited. *Learning, Media and Technology*, 40(4), 412–436.

Shulman, L. S. (1986). Those who understand: Knowledge growth in teaching. *Educational Researcher*, 15(2), 4–14.

Smith, T. M., Desimone, L. M., & Ueno, K. (2005). "Highly qualified" to do what? The relationship between NCLB teacher quality mandates and the use of reform-oriented instruction in middle school mathematics. *Educational Evaluation and Policy Analysis*, 27(1), 75–109.

Turkle, S., & Papert, S. (1990). Epistemological pluralism: Styles and voices within the computer culture. *Signs: Journal of Women in Culture and Society*, 16(1), 128–157.

Voogt, J., Fisser, P., Good, J., Mishra, P., & Yadav, A. (2015). Computational thinking in compulsory education: Towards an agenda for research and practice. *Education and Information Technologies*, 20(4), 715–728.

Vygotsky, L. S. (1929). The problem of the cultural development of the child, II. *Journal of Genetic Psychology*, 36, 415–34.

Vygotksy, L. S. (1960). *The Development of Higher Psychological Functions*. Moscow, Russia: Izdael'stov Akademii Pedagogicheskikh Nauk, in Russian.

Vygotsky, L. S. (1978). *Mind in Society*. Cambridge, MA: Harvard University Press.

Zhang, J., & Patel, V. L. (2006). Distributed cognition, representation, and affordance. *Pragmatics & Cognition*, 14(2), 333–341.

25 Teacher Learning and Professional Development

Sally A. Fincher, Yifat Ben-David Kolikant, and Katrina Falkner

25.1 Introduction

In this chapter, we explore some of the theory that underpins approaches to the professional development of teachers and explore in more depth three models that have been used in computing education. This chapter is not concerned with initial teacher education, but with the continuing professional development (CPD) of staff, and we draw from both school and university settings.

Teacher learning and development is an important area of research, both in the practice of education and in educational policy. As Darling-Hammond (2017) observes, "Teacher effectiveness has rapidly risen to the top of the education policy agenda, as many nations become convinced that teaching is one of the most important school-related factors in student achievements." While nations pay attention to teacher development, they do not do so equally. In surveying educationally high-performing countries (i.e., those whose students come at the top of the annual Programme for International Student Assessment [PISA] test), Lucy Crehan identifies five high-level "principles" that contribute to those countries' success. One of these principles, drawing on the emphasis that Finland puts on teacher professionalism, is "treat teachers as professionals," and she identifies ongoing development and support as a crucial element to achieving this (Crehan, 2016).

For computing, the importance of teacher learning and development is particularly acute. Within schools, computing is a very recently introduced subject. Teachers were (and are) not recruited with the expectation that they would be teaching computing and have little existing subject knowledge to draw on (there are, for instance, few school teachers with degrees in computing). As computing is encouraged as a subject ever earlier in the curriculum, this problem increases. In the UK, the Royal Society noted in their 2017 report "After the Reboot: Computing Education in UK Schools" that "Inspirational teaching begins with 'teachers who know and love their subject'. For pupils to thrive, knowledgeable, highly skilled teachers need support from the school community," and the report goes on to recognize that this must involve "more opportunities for training, dedicated time for CPD, and specialist expert advice to assist teachers with subject knowledge" (The Royal Society, 2017). So one imperative for computing education research is to devise, identify, and evaluate successful CPD approaches.

In the rest of this chapter, we situate professional development in the acquisition and development of pedagogic content knowledge (PCK). We explore this concept first, and then turn to computing-specific activities in the following three areas: using PCK as a framework; developing PCK via lead teachers; and developing PCK within communities of peers.

25.1.1 Components of Teacher Knowledge

Investigating and supporting teachers' professional growth are not trivial.

Firstly, it is hard to classify exactly what "teacherly knowledge" consists of. Researchers agree that it is a complex of characteristics, although they do not agree on how these are divided or ordered. Anderson and Page (1995) usefully observe that it combines knowledge at various levels. They define the following four distinct areas:

- *Technical knowledge* ("academic knowledge is technical knowledge")
- *Local knowledge* ("includes the narratives that are idiosyncratic to a local school or community setting ... included within this domain is knowledge of local politics, and local cultures and sub-cultures")
- *Craft knowledge* ("consists of the repertoire of examples, images, understandings and actions that practitioners build up over time")
- *Personal knowledge.*

Secondly, teacher expertise is largely professional, embodied, situated, and contingent: a teacher may know five or six or ten ways to teach recursion and to exemplify it to students, but they will not use them all every time they teach the topic. They will draw on their expertise and select what is appropriate to the circumstances of the particular students on a particular day. The contingent nature of this knowledge – that it is called into use by the nuance of circumstance Ạ is typical of Schön's notion of "reflection in action" that characterizes professional performance (Schön, 1983) and the classroom expertise that van Manen calls "noncognitive, nondiscursive confidence" (van Manen, 1995). However, teaching as an expert practice differs from other professions (such as hospital medicine or the law courts) in that it is largely private, conducted for the most part solely in front of students and not in the presence of a community of peers.

By far the most significant definition in terms of teacher knowledge has been the characterization of PCK, which was first proposed by Lee Shulman (1986, 1987) in his investigation of the constituents of teachers' expertise. In conducting this work, he found the need for "a more coherent theoretical framework" and created the following seven categories to describe teacher knowledge:

- *Content knowledge.*
- *General pedagogical knowledge*, with special reference to those broad principles and strategies of classroom management and organization that appear to transcend subject matter.

- *Curriculum knowledge*, with particular grasp of the materials and programs that serve as "tools of the trade" for teachers.
- *PCK*, that special amalgam of content and pedagogy that is uniquely the province of teachers – their own special form of professional understanding.
- *Knowledge of learners* and their characteristics.
- *Knowledge of educational contexts*, ranging from the workings of the group or classroom and the governance and financing of school districts to the character of communities and cultures.
- *Knowledge of educational ends, purposes, and values* and their philosophical and historical grounds.

From this framing, PCK has been taken up far beyond the rest of the classification as a unique and distinguishing indicator of teaching expertise (in fact, the rest of the taxonomy has effectively been discarded or ignored). The importance of the concept of PCK, and perhaps the reason why this concept appeals to many, is because it highlights that teachers have specific knowledge that experts in the domain who are not teachers lack.

Shulman's initial definition refers mostly to *repertoire*: "ways of representing and formulating the subject that make it comprehensible for others," which he describes thus: "Since there are no single most powerful forms of representation, the teacher must have at hand a veritable armamentarium of alternative forms of representation, some of which derive from research whereas others originate in the wisdom of practice" (Shulman, 1986, p. 9). In addition to multiple representations, repertoire also includes understanding the development of students' conceptions within a subject area, as well as the commonly held preconceptions and misconceptions students exhibit.

Shulman's definition of PCK has been vastly studied, revisited, and extended throughout the years; see Gess-Newsome et al. (1999) and Berry et al. (2015) for substantial research explorations and Bullough (2001) for an examination of the history and evolution of the idea. One extension of this concept was suggested by Lee Shulman's protégé, Pamela Grossman (Howey & Grossman, 1989), who defines PCK using three questions that govern a teacher's pedagogical decisions: *Why teach? What to teach? What about the students?* Another of Shulman's PhD students, Sigrun Gudmundsdottir (1990, 1991), explored a narrative construction of PCK in the way teachers construct "curriculum stories" to lay out learning opportunities for their students. A "curriculum story" encompasses the choices teachers make about what parts of a syllabus are important, which have similarities, in what order they are to be taught, and what connections may be emphasized between parts. There are also useful reviews on the concept in the context of mathematics education research by Depaepe, Verschaffel, and Kelchtermans (2013), as well as a literature review on more general components of teacher knowledge by Ben-Peretz (2011).

There have also been criticisms of the concept. Loewenberg Ball and her colleagues, in the context of mathematics education, claim that PCK "has lacked definition and empirical foundation, limiting its usefulness" (Loewenberg Ball,

Thomas, & Phelps, 2008, p. 389; see also Hill et al., 2008). They highlight the importance of in-action knowledge, of asking "[w]hat do teachers need to know and be able to do in order to teach effectively? Or, what does effective teaching require in terms of content understanding? This places the emphasis on the use of knowledge in and for teaching rather than on teachers themselves." Depaepe et al. (2013), in their comprehensive literature review, criticize some researchers as failing to adequately define PCK: "the difficulty to distinguish PCK from other knowledge categories has often led to an elusive description of what PCK entails." However, these criticisms have not (to date) been strongly influential, and within computing education at least no alternative to PCK has been proposed that has gained such traction in the literature.

Teachers may have high content knowledge, but with low pedagogic knowledge they will be but poor teachers; conversely, teachers with high pedagogic knowledge may use this to mask their lack of content knowledge. Neither is PCK a fixed commodity. For example, Liberman, Ben-David Kolikant, and Beeri (2012) examined in-service computer science teachers at the time of a dramatic curricular change (when the curriculum shifted from procedural programming to object-oriented programming). They defined the term "regressed experts" to denote the new state of expert teachers dealing with significant curricular changes. Despite their fragile subject knowledge, the teachers did not behave as novices in the classroom. They could not function as flexibly as experts, so instead they employed pedagogic tactics that masked their limited content knowledge. The teachers did not stay in that state, though, but returned to their expert status within two years of teaching.

Teachers who are able to draw on a repertoire of approaches to respond to student needs, to present and explain material in a wide variety of ways, to draw disparate areas of the curriculum together, and to show how the material being learned is linked to more advanced concepts (or to concepts already well-known) are characterized as having high PCK.

	Low pedagogic knowledge	High pedagogic knowledge
High content knowledge	Expert non-teacher Subject matter expert	Expert teacher "Adaptive expert"
Low content knowledge	–	Experienced teacher "Regressed expert"

In 2015, addressing the so-called "PCK Summit," Shulman expanded on his original definition: "PCK is an attribute that teachers develop, and it cannot be found among mere subject matter experts or among those who are 'good with kids'" (Shulman, 2015).

Development of PCK, however – moving from low to high – is not a given. Drawing on Patricia Benner's work with nurses, some teachers may be described as "experienced but not expert" (Benner, 1996); that is, those teachers who have been teaching for a long time but who have not improved in their practice nor developed their material nor updated their approaches. David Berliner, in his examination of the distinct characteristics of *good* teachers and *successful* teachers, observes, "Although inexperience is equated perfectly with novice status in a field, the acquisition of experience does not automatically denote expertise" (Berliner, 2001).

25.1.2 The Nature of Pedagogic Change

There is a second issue with investigating professional development in that it must rest on ideas of how, when, and on what evidence teachers actually change their practice. It is often naively assumed that a teacher will change their practice (e.g., approach a new subject or adopt a new method or novel type of assessment) either because they are given new materials or because someone makes a policy decision that they should do so – that pedagogic change is a straightforward identification-and-adoption task. This ignores the reality of situated practice, where change is always enacted by a teacher within a specific context. Teachers will draw on their own complex of knowledge (subject, personal, professional) in working out a change that will fit. Neither does the naive view take into account the fact that change is not laid onto a blank canvas. Teachers are already doing *something*, and to take on a new practice means they must alter their old practice. They must stop doing something familiar and take on something initially alien. The possibilities for things "going wrong" in such a process are obvious, and this may explain both the reluctance of practitioners in the face of new initiatives and also the observation that when teachers do initiate changes, these tend to be fragmentary. As House observes, "The teacher will reject or adopt a piece of [a proposed innovation], depending on who sponsors it, what is said about it, personal values, and the existential situation. Almost never will it be adopted in its entirety" (House, 1974).

Content-based CPD "professional development" interventions, when someone comes into the school (or other learning environment) to present a new method, are disliked by staff. As Mike Rose notes in his authoritative examination of public education in America:

> The topic of in-service workshops came up several times, and the young teachers made it clear they were *not* talking about the typical one-day presentation, usually given by an outside consultant. What they had in mind was an on-going series … where teachers could come, learn some things, try them, and come back, discuss the results, fine-tune, modify, or abandon what they tried, and learn more.
> (Rose, 1995, p. 86)

And indeed short CPD offerings, focused on content knowledge and associated pedagogy, have been recognized as of limited effectiveness (Bell & Gilbert, 1996; Cordingley et al., 2015; Sentance, Humphreys, & Dorling, 2014).

The point of CPD is to effect positive change in teachers. But change is difficult – difficult to instantiate and difficult to sustain. The problems of promulgating and disseminating change initiatives are experienced at many levels, from the individual teacher, to the district, even (in the current situation of needing thousands of computing teachers) to the nation. And ineffective approaches to supporting teacher development are not restricted to primary and secondary education. In reviewing 191 papers detailing change strategies in STEM higher education, Henderson and his colleagues concluded:

> Two commonly used change strategies are clearly not effective: developing and testing "best practice" curricular materials and then making these materials available to other faculty, and "top-down" policy-making meant to influence instructional practices. Effective change strategies: are aligned with or seek to change the beliefs of the individuals involved; involve long-term interventions, lasting at least one semester; require understanding a college or university as a complex system and designing a strategy that is compatible with this system. (Henderson et al., 2011)

In this, they recognize that change in practice cannot be imposed by "transferring" materials or dictating through policy, but must be developed with the teachers and in their context. In secondary education, too, effective CPD is respectful of change as a process. Successful approaches are sustained (of long duration) and focused on aspirations for students. They are based on classroom evidence and they enable and encourage teachers to collaborate with each other (Cordingley et al., 2015; Darling-Hammond, 2017; Park & Sung, 2013; Sentance, Humphreys, & Dorling, 2014; Wei, Darling-Hammond, & Adamson, 2010).

In this section, we have proposed that teacher expertise is rooted in the concept of PCK and outlined the associated literature. We have reviewed ideas of pedagogic change and have noted that the idea of change as "adopting innovations" leads to common but ineffective models of teacher development. We have proposed that understanding pedagogic change as a process characterizes effective CPD models. In the next section, we will look at how these ideas have been developed and researched within computing education.

25.2 Ways of Researching PCK

Researchers have broadly taken one of three approaches to developing PCK in teachers, which we examine in this section. One approach is to articulate it as an "objective" framework, against which teachers – and their knowledge – can be measured, assessed, and compared (Section 25.2.1, content representation; Section 25.2.2, TPACK); a second is to put inexperienced teachers in contact with experienced ones to lead them to new knowledge (Section 25.2.3, lead teachers and master teachers); and a third is to put peers together in situations that facilitate sharing of practical knowledge (Section 25.2.4, lesson study and disciplinary commons). We consider each of these approaches in turn.

25.2.1 PCK As a Framework

Some researchers take the view that PCK can be defined abstractly and objectively (i.e., without reference to embodied expertise), or that it can be considered to be the property of a *group* of teachers, rather than an attribute of an individual. In this space, researchers take it as axiomatic that PCK can be collected, compared, and transferred. One popular tool for collecting PCK is a "content representation" (CoRe) for pedagogic content knowledge, developed by Jack Loughran and his colleagues (Loughran et al., 2006). A CoRe is a two-dimensional grid that captures ideas concerning a single important disciplinary concept in a specific pedagogic context (i.e., high school, first-year university, etc.). Along the vertical axis of the grid is a series of questions or prompts intended to elicit teachers' pedagogic knowledge of the concept under consideration:

- What do you intend the students to learn about this idea?
- Why is it important for students to know this?
- What else do you know about this idea (that you do not intend students to know yet)?
- Difficulties or limitations connected with teaching this idea.
- Knowledge about the students' thinking that influences your teaching of this idea.
- Other factors that influence your teaching of this idea.
- Teaching procedures (and particular reasons for using these to engage with this idea).
- Specific ways of ascertaining students' understanding or confusion around this idea (include likely range of responses).

Along the horizontal axis, the teacher captures their subject knowledge of the concept under consideration by listing what they consider to be the "big ideas" associated with it. There is no restriction on the number of ideas; teachers can include as many as they wish. At the intersection of each row and column, the teacher makes an entry documenting their response to the row prompt for the big idea in the column.

A CoRe is an effective tool to capture and represent the PCK of an individual (Shinners-Kennedy & Fincher, 2015). However, it has most often been used in group settings or to try and define an abstract level of achievement. In computing education, this approach has been spearheaded by researchers such as Saeli et al. (2011, 2012a, 2012b) and Hubwieser et al. (2013). Additionally, Buchholz, Saeli, and Schulte (2013) use the CoRe approach in the context of initial teacher training of computing teachers. For a more general overview of studies using a CoRe approach, see Lehane and Bertram (2016).

25.2.2 Technological, Pedagogical, and Content Knowledge: TPACK

Another "objective" approach to PCK is the TPACK model (Koehler & Mishra, 2009), which expands on Shulman's model of PCK to include the knowledge base a teacher needs to effectively teach with technology and within a domain. The model characterizes individual components of technological, pedagogical, and content knowledge that teachers require (see Table 25.1), as well as an understanding that emerges from interactions between the components.

Table 25.1 *Knowledge in the TPACK model.*

Technological knowledge	Knowledge of the different ways digital technology (tools, applications, or software) can be used and the advantages and disadvantages of tools and software (technology-focused, not pedagogical considerations)
Pedagogical knowledge	Knowledge of how to teach, including professional beliefs and visions, theory, teaching, and learning strategies, knowledge about how learners learn best, reflection on practice, and the advantages and disadvantages of pedagogical approaches
Content knowledge	Knowledge of the central topics, concepts, and areas of the subject matter that can be and are taught to students, as well as curricula knowledge

Conceptualizations of TPACK are contested in the literature (Voogt et al., 2013), suggesting that the model is not fully developed; however, it can provide a framework for assessing teachers' various professional knowledge bases.

At this time, there is not a great awareness of TPACK as a concept within the computing education research community, although computer science teachers certainly do use technology for their teaching. Moreover, they also (unlike many other teachers) can and do design and develop educational technology (e.g., PeerWise BlueJ). It is also probable that computer science teachers have qualitatively different TPACK because of their domain knowledge: they simply know more about the technology than teachers of other subjects do. There may be future work in capturing these teachers' TPACK and associated epistemological knowledge in regard to technology use for learning and teaching.

The use of PCK in this way, as a measuring tool, is not unique to computing. Depaepe et al. (2013) call this a "cognitive" approach and note a "paradigmatic disagreement" in math education research, with two strands of PCK work that take either "a more cognitive or more enacted perspective on PCK." In the following sections, we will look at such situated, enacted studies within computing.

25.2.3 Lead Teachers

Some researchers, and some policy-makers, take the view that PCK is an embodied construct that belongs to an individual teacher (i.e., I cannot give you my PCK nor take yours) and that it is expressed in a context (i.e., it is exists only in the presence of learners, in the practice of teaching). In this it shares much with the idea of "personal practical knowledge" identified by Carl Bereiter (2014), a concept he defines loosely as "know-how" combined with "know-why," and more precisely as "explanatorily coherent practical knowledge." For those taking this view, PCK has to be – can only be – nurtured and developed in individuals.

Here, CPD is often thought to be best delivered by teachers who have done it before; that is, near-peers who are "one step ahead." In an interview with Tami Lapidot, the director of the Israeli National Teaching Centre for computing, she asserted, "There is nothing like the knowledge the teachers themselves hold and therefore we must take the advantage of this resource. No professional or academic course will be equivalent in terms of impact and helping teachers in the field as the information transmitted by good teachers to their colleagues." Frequently, these approaches are rooted in existing communities (schools or universities) with the expectation that teachers with high PCK can be identified and will be willing to share their expertise in the development of others. In schools, such people are often referred to as "lead teachers," and in this section we examine some of the ways in which these have been used, drawing on examples from Israel and the UK. Israel is an interesting case study because of its considerable experience in large-scale computing education at post-primary level. The UK makes an interesting case study because of the Computing at School (CAS) network, a "community of teachers, academics and industry supporters" that offers professional development opportunities to teachers locally, regionally, and nationally (CAS, 2018).

25.2.3.1 What Defines a Lead Teacher?

There is a confusing variety of terms used in this area. *Expert teachers* or *master teachers* are defined as excellent teachers, namely those that have a high influence on their students' learning. Their sophisticated PCK allows the expert teachers flexibility to connect curricular and pedagogical knowledge with the needs and abilities of their students in real time, thereby addressing students' difficulties quickly and effectively (Berliner, 2001; Michaeli & Sommer, 2014). The term "adaptive expert teacher" (Bransford, Darling-Hammond, & Lepage, 2005) is often used to describe the strengths of expert teachers in times of significant curricular changes that force them to deal with a significant withdrawal in both their content knowledge and PCK. Not only do adaptive expert teachers adapt quickly to change, but they are also characterized by viewing the need to change and renew themselves not as a threat or burden, but rather as an opportunity to specialize and further develop.

In the UK, the CAS organization, which exists to promote computer science education in schools and support computer science teachers, selects "master teachers" for excellent subject matter pedagogy as well as experience in interacting with peers professionally (e.g., mentoring colleagues) (Sentance, Humphreys, & Dorling, 2014). The term "master teachers" intersects with but differs from two other concepts used in the literature: "expert teachers" and "teacher educators" (TEs) (European Commission – Education and Training, 2013; Even, 1999; Loughran, 2014).

The term TEs, as well as the similar terms *teacher trainers*, *mentors*, and *teachers' teachers*, relates to those who deal with professional development of in-service teachers. Their specialty is the combination of professional knowledge and in-class teaching abilities (Abell et al., 2009; Smith, 2005), although teaching experience is not a requirement for being a TE.

In contrast, lead teachers are expected to *be* teachers and to be able to influence other teachers. Some of the definitions of lead teachers focus on knowledge and abilities. A report of a steering committee in Israel, headed by Ben-Peretz and Shulman, defines lead teachers as those who can be leaders of excellence in teaching and education. Lead teachers have rich content knowledge and diverse pedagogical and didactical expertise. They possess skills of leadership and have an interest in working to foster the professional competence of colleagues (Michaeli & Sommer, 2014). Another definitional issue refers to the roles lead teachers take and the expectation that they contribute to professional communities. Their roles involve being in-house experts (Feiler, Heritage, & Gallimore, 2000) and in creating "pedagogic conversations" between teachers, which connects experience in the field, theory, and research. Often, they are expected to serve as a leadership layer in order to help reforms take place in schools and classrooms (Hofstein, Carmi, & Ben-Zvi, 2003, Lapidot, 2007; Lapidot & Aharoni, 2007).

Although it is widely agreed in the literature that "lead teacher" and similar terms are ambiguous (Cranston & Kusanovich, 2015; Hairon, Goh, & Chua, 2015), the commonality across the many definitions and uses of this term is the expectation that lead teachers will interact with and influence other teachers. However, the purpose of this interaction, the community within which they act, and the experience of lead teachers are all imprecisely defined. Thus, "teacher leadership" is sometimes used to refer to dutiful enactments of top-down policy (e.g., Poekert, 2012), while at other times it stands for a grassroots-level shift in power and leverage in schools. Sometimes it refers to solo endeavors and at other times to the collective. Sometimes the community within which teacher leaders are expected to act is their school and sometimes it is the community of other teachers in the same subject domain (e.g., all computer science teachers).

25.2.3.2 Lead Teachers in Computing

The concept of lead teachers with respect to computing has received increased attention in recent years due to curricular changes in many countries, especially the tendency to include computational thinking and programming in K–12. One such example is President Obama's Computer Science for All initiative, aimed at ensuring all American students from kindergarten through to high school learn computer science and be equipped with computational thinking skills. The aim is for these students to be creators in the digital economy, not just consumers, and to be active citizens in our technology-driven world. This educational change is challenging as most teachers are not familiar with computer science and do not have the relevant subject knowledge. Another example is in the UK – in 2012, after the Royal Society report *Shut Down or Restart? The Way Forward for Computing in UK schools* found computing studies in schools to be unsatisfactory, the government changed the national curriculum to include computing in the school curriculum and removed the preceding ICT program. This meant that many teachers had to quite suddenly develop the subject knowledge and pedagogic skills to deliver computing in their classrooms.

Sentance et al. (2012) describe several models in which computing lead teachers lead their peers: (a) training – that is, teaching new content (e.g., Python) in 25-hour CPD (either spread over ten weekly meetings or focused in five consecutive days); (b) in professional learning communities (called "hubs") where, in hub meetings, they discuss issues related to teaching computing in school; and (c) serving in the CAS Network of Excellence, a funded initiative (2015–2018) in which ten specified universities supported schools in their computing teaching.

In Israel, there are at least five subject domains in which the concept of lead teachers is used in relation to in-service teachers' CPD: physics, chemistry, biology, computer science, and science and technology for junior high school. The Israeli Education System establishes National Teachers' Centers (NTCs) within the science disciplines. Among other responsibilities, they are charged with cultivating a leadership layer (i.e., a layer of teacher leaders that influence a wider population of teachers in order to disseminate curricular change and to improve teaching practices). Although education is centralized in Israel, the Ministry of Education does not provide a clear picture of the desired characteristics of such teachers, nor the criteria upon which they will be chosen. In practice, every NTC has a different interpretation of the roles this leadership layer should play, and accordingly different criteria and populations have participated in those courses, as well as there being different structures to these courses.

The Israeli, the practical interpretation of lead teachers in computer science NTCs relies on the belief that an organized group of in-service teachers can influence peers and help them to deal with new content and topics (Lapidot, 2007). Each year the computer science NTC runs a CPD course, the content of which changes according to the current needs of the field. New lead teachers are recruited annually, and integrated with teachers from previous cohorts. The lead teacher courses are aimed at achieving the following three main goals (Lapidot, 2007): (1) deepening participants' subject knowledge and their understanding of new contents, advanced topics, and professional problems; (2) strengthening the group of participants as a professional community; and (3) encouraging the growth of professional leadership in the field of computer science.

25.2.4 Community of Peers

Rather than design a situation to put together teachers at different stages of experience, other models for teacher learning and development have been based around peers meeting to mutually examine their teaching practice. CPD interventions that take a community of peers approach are based on different assumptions about how teachers develop their professional knowledge, in that they do not need to be instructed by others, but can develop expertise within their own communities. These approaches that put teachers in contact with each other draw on a construction of development broadly known as *professional learning communities* (PLCs). A PLC is "an intentionally developed community that exists to promote and maximize the individual and shared learning of its members. There is ongoing interaction, interplay, and collaboration among the community's members" (Lenning et al., 2013). Research in this area was active in the late 1990s, with later, more mature work appearing around 2004–2007. DuFour (2004) puts the following three "big ideas" at the heart of a PLC: (1) ensuring that students learn; (2) a culture of collaboration; and (3) a focus on results. In their substantial literature review, Stoll et al. (2006) list the following five characteristics by which one can distinguish a PLC: shared values and vision; collective responsibility; reflective professional enquiry; collaboration; and the promotion of group as well as individual learning.

In practice, however, in computing education at least, these definitions are rarely rigorously followed, and specific initiatives will involve permutations and combinations of these characteristics. Nevertheless, there is evidence that such communities can be effective. Based on a review of empirical work on PLCs of science teachers, Dogan, Pringle, and Mesa (2016) claim that PLCs can help teachers increase their PCK as well as their content knowledge, which in turn may facilitate desired change in their practice. Studies have explored the characteristics that make learning communities successful. These include a focus on joint, concrete tasks such as curriculum development (Little, 1990), supportive leadership, and empowerment of teachers as decision-makers and cocreators (Louis, Marks, & Kruse, 1996). Structuring opportunities for collaboration can assist in establishing group norms and provide a task focus (Hollins, McIntyre, DeBose, Hollins, & Towner, 2004), while a focus on authentic tasks within the professional context aids engagement (Darling-Hammond & Richardson, 2009). Cameron's work (2016) cautions that for a PLC to be effective, leadership is critical, and teachers must be given adequate time to engage if there is to be an impact on practice.

25.2.4.1 Lesson Study

Probably the most formalized and well-known of these community approaches is "Lesson Study." Lesson Study is a practice of sharing and reflecting on (and so improving) teaching that originated in Japanese schools, where it is called *jugyokenkyu*: *jugyo* means "lesson" and *kenkyu* means "study" or "research" (Fernandez & Yoshida, 2004).

In Japan, Lesson Study is conducted by a group of four to six teachers within a school. They select a topic or area they are interested in examining or improving. Often these areas are chosen because they are part the school's mission statement, and correspondingly, a school's mission is often explored and expressed through Lesson Study. In its originating context, Lesson Study has a precise form: the group of teachers comes together and collectively plans a lesson – "This planning is of a meticulous and collaborative nature." One of the group then teaches the lesson with the other teachers observing. The group comes together to reflect on the lesson, and they may revise it and teach it again.

The iterated version will not be taught by the same teacher, as "varying the teacher and the students provides the group a broader base of experiences to learn from" (Fernandez & Yoshida, 2004, p. 8). Finally, the results of a cycle of Lesson Study may be shared via an "open house," where teachers from outside the school are invited to come and observe the new lessons and/or take away written reports.

Lesson Study has been influential far beyond Japan, particularly since the publication of *The Teaching Gap* (Stigler & Herbert, 1999), which brought the idea to the USA (see Perry & Lewis, 2009, for an overview). True to the originating context, it has been instantiated in schools, often in mathematics, but the differing national contexts have meant differences in instantiation. If teachers are brought together from different schools, then even if they are from the same district, they lack the coherence of a single context with a single mission.

25.2.4.2 Disciplinary Commons

Community models of CPD and their importance are not limited to schools. In a synthesis of 1,200 meta-analyses, John Hattie extracted 196 influences on university students' learning and ranked them according to the size of their effect. *Collective teacher efficacy* was ranked second. Hattie says that "it is very difficult … to see each teacher as an island," and that universities "need to legitimize the debates about impact in their departments, create a trusting and fair environment for this to occur, and provide the resources (e.g., time) for collective collaborations in the pursuit of the highest possible impact on students" (Hattie, 2015).

The Disciplinary Commons is one model for CPD to enhance collective teacher efficacy that was initiated in university-level teaching of computing. A Commons is constituted of 10–20 educators sharing the same disciplinary background, teaching the same subject matter – sometimes the same course – in different institutions. In this it differs from Lesson Study, in that educators are drawn from different institutional contexts. However, it is important that the educators are teaching the same subject matter, as this is a rare situation in higher education where subject matter tends to be specialized, and often only taught by a single person. As quoted from the Sharing Practice project (Fincher, 2008):

> Actually, I don't know how others teach sorting, you, or my colleagues. That is a bit shocking. I don't know how other people teach something as fundamental as sorting. I know what the algorithm is. And the textbooks. But how do others get students through that?

Members of a Commons come together in a series of meetings over the course of a year to share their knowledge about teaching and student learning. Participants in a Commons also produce a record of the practice they examine. This has taken several forms, from portfolios to structured posters, making previously private practice public, peer reviewed, and amenable for future use and development by other educators, thereby creating a teaching-appropriate document of practice equivalent to the research-appropriate journal paper.

The design of a Commons privileges long-term engagement and is highly respectful of context, and so escapes simplistic notions of "transfer of best practice" that Henderson et al. identify as ineffective (Section 25.1.2). As House cautions, to encourage effective change:

> Avoid the primary pursuit of transferable innovations. Distributed problems cannot be solved by a single innovation that will work in all local settings, for those settings are not only different and unpredictable in specifics, but they are also constantly changing … Different innovations will be more or less useful under widely different specific circumstances of their application. There is no Golden Fleece.
> (House, 1974)

The combination of critical self-examination and peer review helps participants understand their own practice, identify places where innovation and change are desirable, share what works, borrow from others, and see their own work in the context of a broad range of possibilities. In this way, local knowledge is extended by understanding "what works" elsewhere and by expanding the repertoire of possible responses.

The Commons model has been used in university-level computing education (Fincher & Tenenberg, 2005, 2007; Tenenberg & Fincher, 2007) and with high school teachers of computing in the USA (Morrison, Ni, & Guzdial, 2012; Ni et al., 2011). In the UK, the model was adapted to a professional development program for existing computing teachers in Scottish secondary schools, called "PLAN C" (Cutts et al., 2017).

25.2.4.3 Cross-Context Issues

Community approaches take educators out of their home institutions. There are two features of these approaches that are important in facilitating participants' examination of their own practice in new ways: the use of *boundary objects and the artifactual literacy* they afford (Fincher, 2012).

Boundary Objects. An element of these approaches is that participants share specified artefacts – a course description, a textbook, some graded student work – brought from their own classroom. Individual pieces of "home" practice are thus represented in a "foreign" context, but discussions are anchored and materials can be compared. In this way, the material artefacts mediate communities. As originally observed in the identification of the "boundary object" phenomenon (where fur trappers traded animal skins with museum curators) meanings are made clear as they are embodied in the object that is shared, and the meaning it has for both communities (Star & Griesemer, 1989). In community approaches, objects (e.g. syllabi, student assessments) cross the boundaries of one community (a School) into another (this professional community) and in their journey institutional constraints are made apparent (class sizes, QA and other documentary conventions etc.), disciplinary interpretation (e. g. "objects-first") and pedagogic understanding (e.g. "pair-programming") may be read.

Artifactual Literacy. Within a professional community part of the "work" of a boundary object is to afford "artifactual literacy". This is a concept developed by Pahl and Roswell in the context of schoolchildren and immigrant families, where the telling of important narratives (of family, home, tradition) is facilitated by being associated with a physical object (Pahl & Rowsell, 2010). So, in their terms, "within everyday lives [a meaningful object] symbolises and represents relationships and events that matter". People can tell a story about an object that they may not have been able to express without it. Artefacts afford the expression of complex realities of a world not present. Children who may be inarticulate in a "school" context can tell a powerful story when it is anchored by a meaningful artefact, the object liberates their literacy. In similar fashion, disciplinary academics who may be daunted by the language of educational development and professional reflection (often disparagingly referred to as "eduspeak") may yet talk fluently and compellingly about their teaching (and its rationale, aims and framing) when the discussion is associated with an object that arises from their practice. It is not so much a case of "every picture tells a story" but "every object allows a story to emerge".

25.2.5 Online Opportunities

It has been shown that teachers find it hard to engage with professional communities in an online environment (see Chapter 26). However, learning spaces as afforded by online professional communities have been shown to increase the accessibility of professional learning communities, to provide support for continuous development, and can adapt flexibly to participant needs (Trust, Krutka, & Carpenter, 2016).

Lloyd and Cochrane (2006), in the context of technology adoption, provide a framework for understanding the key principles of professional learning. Falkner et al. (2017) adapt this model to the online space, including its characteristics for successful professional learning:

- Context: Learning must be associated with a context immediately relevant to that of the learner, be authentic, and be practical in application (i.e., not requiring translation).
- Time (Sustained and timely): Learning must be available just in time, while also being available over an extended period of time.
- Community: Learning must be supported by an authentic, professional community.
- Personal growth: Learning must add to personal knowledge, take into account the current knowledge and skill of the learner, and support reflection.

The Computer Science Education Research Group (CSER), based at the University of Adelaide in Australia, offers the CSER Digital Technologies massive open online course (MOOC) program (Falkner et al., 2017). This provides professional development support for teachers across Australia, supporting the implementation of the national digital technologies learning area (representing computer science). This program is constructed around a joint context of course content and community, following Lloyd and Cochrane (2006). Course content is provided through a traditional MOOC structure, while community context is supported through a separate medium (Google+) to assist in sustained community engagement and is in contrast with media more typically used, such as discussion forums. There are activities within the formal course structure designed to explicitly establish this joint context.

The MOOC structure is primarily self-paced, enabling participants to access course and community resources as needed. All resources are accessible outside of official course cohort offerings. Participants take the concepts and examples from the course structure and develop either a professional learning activity for their peers or a classroom activity for their teaching context. The community task development model has been influenced by that of Salmon (2002) through the adoption of scaffolded task development, moving from navigational tasks through to active thinking tasks and the application of new concepts in their professional environment.

Programs such as CSER's Digital Technologies MOOCs, the ScratchED community (Harvard, 2015), and CAS's online platform (Humphreys, 2017) have adopted community-centric models for the professional development of teachers, supporting ongoing teacher engagement and professional learning outcomes in an online environment.

There is some limited evidence that online communities work for teacher development. Go and Dorn analyzed data from two online communities: a forum of the US Computer Science Teacher Association (CSTA) and CS Teaching Tips. They found that matters pertaining to PCK were discussed. However, as their analysis was limited to online interactions they could not say whether these discussions were acted on to actually increase a teacher's effectiveness (Go & Dorn, 2016).

25.3 Discussion/Conclusion

This chapter has grounded teacher development as the acquisition and development of PCK. We have surveyed the following three ways in which PCK has been used in computing education research: as an objective framework in order to measure and gauge the quantity of PCK a teacher may possess; as a situated expertise to be developed by putting more experienced "lead teachers" into an educational environment; and as embodied expertise to be developed by putting teachers together in communities of peers, either face-to-face or online.

Although it is important in all disciplines, in computing, understanding teacher professional development and pursuing ways to support it are particularly pressing for a number of reasons: firstly, because of the lack of computing subject knowledge in teachers in primary and secondary schools; secondly, because of the immense – and increasing – demand for graduates (of schools or tertiary institutions) with computational competence; and thirdly, because ever-changing technology (and associated software) means that teachers have to regularly learn – and then teach – new material, often in new ways.

In examining teacher learning and development, we have identified two dominant research strands. One is to look at the construct of PCK itself in order to identify its constituents and find reliable ways of locating and identifying them; another is to support its development in teachers throughout their careers. Open questions remain in both areas.

If, as has been suggested (Berliner, 2001; Downes et al., 2001), PCK is contextually dependent, then there is much work to be attempted both in defining and characterizing indicators of PCK within the context of computing and in identifying the development of PCK in differing CPD contexts.

There is some evidence to support the use of online platforms in guiding professional development (Falkner et al., 2017; Goode, Margolis, & Chapman, 2014; Humphreys, 2017; Trust et al., 2016), but little work has been done on exploring the longer-term impacts of these informal professional learning opportunities and on the development of teachers' PCK. Trust et al. (2016) identify a specific need for further research to substantiate the long-term impact on practice of online learning communities. In their study of online communities, Macià and García (2016) identify both that the understanding of these communities is still at a relatively early stage and that there are numerous instantiations and social configurations that can occur in such environments, leading to open questions as to how to structure such communities in order to be effective.

While there is empirical work on computing teachers' PCK (as surveyed in this chapter), more work is needed. Teaching computational thinking to 7-year-old pupils and 16-year-old students requires different PCK. Additionally, computing and consequently computing curricula are characterized by great instability (Roberts, 2004), which poses a lifelong learning challenge for teachers, who may experience fragile knowledge several times in the course of their career (Liberman, Ben-David Kolikant, & Beeri, 2012). To exacerbate this complexity, computer science teachers with fragile knowledge have to cope in laboratory sessions where students' receive immediate feedback from the computer and expect their teachers to support them in interpreting and understanding this. Understanding how computer science teachers' knowledge evolves, the support that these teachers value, and the roles technology can play in their professional development would be of benefit for us and for the broader community of education research.

References

Abell, S. K., Rogers, M., Park, A., Hanuscin, D. L., Lee, M. H., & Gagnon, M. J. (2009). Preparing the next generation of science teacher educators: A model for developing PCK for teaching science teachers. *Journal of Science Teacher Education*, 20(1), 77–93.

Anderson, G. L., & Page, B. (1995). Narrative knowledge and educational adminstration: The stories that guide our practice. In R. Donmoyer, M. Imber & J. J. Scheurich (Eds.), *The Knowledge Base in Educational Administration: Multiple Perspectives* (pp. 124–135). Albany, NY: State University of New York Press.

Bell, B., & Gilbert, J. (1996). *Teacher Development: A Model from Science Education*. London, UK: Falmer Press.

Benner, P. A. (1996). Impediments to the development of clinical knowledge and ethical judgement in critical nursing care. In C. A. Tanner & C. A. Chesla (Eds.), *Expertise in Nursing Practice: Caring, Clinical Judgement, and Ethics* (pp. 171–198). New York: Springer Publishing Co.

Ben-Peretz, M. (2011). Teacher knowledge: What is it? how do we uncover it? what are its implications for schooling? *Teaching and Teacher Education*, 27(1), 3–9.

Bereiter, C. (2014). Principled practical knowledge: Not a bridge but a ladder. *Journal of the Learning Sciences*, 23(1), 4–17.

Berliner, D. C. (2001). Learning about and learning from expert teachers. *International Journal of Educational Research*, 35(5), 463–482.

Berry, A., Friedrichsen, P. J., & Loughran, J. (Eds.) (2015). *Re-Examining Pedagogical Content Knowledge in Science Education*. Abingdon, UK: Routledge.

Bransford, J., Darling-Hammond, L., & LePage, P. (2005). Introduction. In L. Darling-Hammond & J. Bransford (Eds.), *Preparing Teachers for a Changing World: What Teachers Should Learn and Be Able to Do*, 1st edn. (pp. 1–39). San Francisco, CA: Jossey-Bass.

Buchholz, M., Saeli, M., & Schulte, C. (2013). PCK and reflection in computer science teacher education. In *Proceedings of the 8th Workshop in Primary and Secondary Computing Education* (pp. 8–16). New York: ACM.

Bullough, R. V. (2001). Pedagogical content knowledge circa 1907 and 1987: A study in the history of an idea. *Teaching and Teacher Education*, 17(6), 655–666.

Cameron, D. J. (2016). *The Effectiveness of a Learning Community in Bringing About Changes to Instructional Practices in the Area of Assessment for Learning* (PhD thesis). University of Calgary.

CAS (2018). Computing at school. Retrieved from www.computingatschool.org.uk

Cordingley, P., Higgins, S., Greany, T., Buckler, N., Coles-Jordan, D., Crisp, B., … Coe, R. (2015). *Developing Great Teaching: Lessons from the International Reviews into Effective Professional Development*. London, UK: Teacher Development Trust.

Cranston, J., & Kusanovich, K. (2015). Learning to lead against the grain: Dramatizing the emotional toll of teacher leadership. *Issues in Teacher Education*, 24(2), 63–78.

Crehan, L. (2016). *Cleverlands: The Secrets Behind the Success of the World's Most Celebrated Education Systems*. New York: Unbound/Random House.

Cutts, Q., Robertson, J., Donaldson, P., & O'Donnell, L. (2017). An evaluation of a professional learning network for computer science teachers. *Computer Science Education*, 27(1), 30–53.

Darling-Hammond, L. (2017). Teacher education around the world: What can we learn from international practice? *European Journal of Teacher Education*, 40(3), 291–309.

Darling-Hammond, L., & Richardson, N. (2009). Teacher learning: What matters? *Educational Leadership*, 66(5), 46–53.

Depaepe, F., Verschaffel, L., & Kelchtermans, G. (2013). Pedagogical content knowledge: A systematic review of the way in which the concept has pervaded mathematics educational research. *Teaching and Teacher Education*, 34, 12–25.

Dogan, S., Pringle, R., & Mesa, J. (2016). The impacts of professional learning communities on science teachers' knowledge, practice and student learning: A review. *Professional Development in Education*, 42(4), 569–588.

Downes, T., Fluck, A., Gibbons, P., Leonard, R., Matthews, C., Oliver, R., … Department of Education, Science and Training (2001). *Making Better Connections: Models of Teacher Professional Development for the Integration of Information and Communication Technology into Classroom Practice*. Canberra, Australia: Australian Curriculum Studies Association, Australian Council for Computers in Education, Technology Education Federation of Australia, University of Western Sydney.

DuFour, R. (2004). What is a professional learning community? *Educational Leadership*, 61(8), 6–11.

European Commission – Education and Training (2013). *Education and Training Monitor*. Retrieved from http://ec.europa.eu/assets/eac/education/library/publications/monitor13_en.pdf

Even, R. (1999). The development of teacher leaders and inservice teacher educators. *Journal of Mathematics Teacher Education*, 2(1), 3–24.

Falkner, K., Vivian, R., Falkner, N., & Williams, S. (2017). Reflecting on three offerings of a community-centric MOOC for K–6 computer science teachers. In *Proceedings of the 2017 ACM SIGCSE Technical Symposium on Computer Science Education* (pp. 195–200). New York: ACM.

Feiler, R., Heritage, M., & Gallimore, R. (2000). Teachers leading teachers. *Educational Leadership*, 57(7), 66–69.

Fernandez, C., & Yoshida, M. (2004). *Lesson Study: A Japanese Approach to Improving Mathematics Teaching and Learning*. Mahwah, NJ; London, UK: Lawrence Erlbaum.

Fincher, S. (2008). Sharing practice. Retrieved from www.sharingpractice.ac.uk

Fincher, S. (2012). *Using narrative methodology*. University of Kent at Canterbury. Retrieved from https://kar.kent.ac.uk/32059/

Fincher, S., & Tenenberg, J. (2005). Disciplinary commons, overview page. Retrieved from www.disciplinarycommons.org

Fincher, S., & Tenenberg, J. (2007). Warren's question. In *Proceedings of the Third International Workshop on Computing Education Research* (pp. 51–60). New York: ACM.

Gess-Newsome, J., & Lederman, N. G. (Eds.) (1999). *Examining Pedagogical Content Knowledge: The Construct and Its Implications for Science Education*. Dordrecht, The Netherlands; London, UK: Kluwer Academic.

Go, S., & Dorn, B. (2016). Thanks for sharing: CS pedagogical content knowledge sharing in online environments. In *Proceedings of the 11th Workshop in Primary and Secondary Computing Education* (pp. 27–36). New York: ACM.

Goode, J., Margolis, J., & Chapman, G. (2014). Curriculum is not enough: The educational theory and research foundation of the exploring computer science professional development model. In *Proceedings of the 45th ACM Technical Symposium on Computer Science Education* (pp. 493–498). New York: ACM.

Gudmundsdottir, S. (1990). Curriculum stories. In C. Day, M. L. Pope, & P. Denicolo (Eds.), *Insights into Teachers' Thinking and Practice* (pp. 107–118). London, UK: Falmer.

Gudmundsdottir, S. (1991). Story-maker, story-teller: Narrative structures in curriculum. *Journal of Curriculum Studies*, 23(3), 207–218.

Hairon, S., Goh, J. W. P., & Chua, C. S. K. (2015). Teacher leadership enactment in professional learning community contexts: Towards a better understanding of the phenomenon. *School Leadership & Management*, 35(2), 163–182.

Harvard (2015). ScratchEd. Retrieved from http://scratched.gse.harvard.edu

Hattie, J. (2015). The applicability of visible learning to higher education. *Scholarship of Teaching and Learning in Psychology*, 1(1), 79–91.

Henderson, C., Beach, A., & Finkelstein, N. (2011). Facilitating change in undergraduate STEM instructional practices: An analytic review of the literature. *Journal of Research in Science Teaching*, 48(8), 952–984.

Hill, H. C., Loewenberg Ball, D., & Schilling, S. G. (2008). Unpacking pedagogical content knowledge: Conceptualizing and measuring teachers' topic-specific knowledge of students. *Journal for Research in Mathematics Education*, 39(4), 372–400.

Hofstein, A., Carmi, M., & Ben-Zvi, R. (2003). The development of leadership among chemistry teachers in israel. *International Journal of Science and Mathematics Education*, 1(1), 39–65.

Hollins, E. R., McIntyre, L. R., DeBose, C., Hollins, K. S., & Towner, A. (2004). Promoting a self-sustaining learning community: Investigating an internal model for teacher development. *International Journal of Qualitative Studies in Education*, 17(2), 247–264.

House, E. R. (1974). *The Politics of Educational Innovation*. Richmond, CA: McCutchan.

Howey, K. R., & Grossman, P. L. (1989). A study in contrast: Sources of pedagogical content knowledge for secondary english. *Journal of Teacher Education*, 40(5), 24–31.

Hubwieser, P., Magenheim, J., Mühling, A., & Ruf, A. (2013). Towards a conceptualization of pedagogical content knowledge for computer science. In *Proceedings of the Ninth Annual International ACM Conference on International Computing Education Research* (pp. 1–8). New York: ACM.

Humphreys, S. (2017). Computing at school: 10 years on. In *Proceedings of the 12th Workshop on Primary and Secondary Computing Education* (p. 3). New York: ACM.

Koehler, M. J., & Mishra, P. (2009). What is technological pedagogical content knowledge (TPACK)? *Contemporary Issues in Technology and Teacher Education*, 9(1), 60–70.

Lapidot, T. (2007). Supporting the growth of CS leading teachers. In *Proceedings of the 12th Annual SIGCSE Conference on Innovation and Technology in Computer Science Education* (p. 327). New York: ACM.

Lapidot, T., & Aharoni, D. (2007). The Israeli summer seminars for CS leading teachers. In *Proceedings of the 12th Annual SIGCSE Conference on Innovation and Technology in Computer Science Education* (p. 318). New York: ACM.

Lehane, L., & Bertram, A. (2016). Getting to the CoRe of it: A review of a specific PCK conceptual lens in science educational research. *Educación Química*, 27(1), 52–58.

Lenning, O. T., Hill, D. M., Saunders, K. P., Solan, A., & Stokes, A. (2013). *Powerful Learning Communities: A Guide to Developing Student, Faculty, and Professional Learning Communities to Improve Student Success and Organizational Effectiveness*. Sterling, VA: Stylus.

Liberman, N., Kolikant, Y. B., & Beeri, C. (2012). "Regressed experts" as a new state in teachers' professional development: Lessons from computer science teachers' adjustments to substantial changes in the curriculum. *Computer Science Education*, 22(3), 257–283.

Little, J. W. (1990). The persistence of privacy: Autonomy and initiative in teachers' professional relations. *Teachers College Record*, 91(4), 509–536.

Lloyd, M., & Cochrane, J. (2006). Celtic knots: Interweaving the elements of effective teacher professional development in ICT. *Australian Educational Computing*, 21(2), 16–19.

Loewenberg Ball, D., Thames, M. H., & Phelps, G. (2008). Content knowledge for teaching: What makes it special? *Journal of Teacher Education*, 59(5), 389–407.

Loughran, J. (2014). Professionally developing as a teacher educator. *Journal of Teacher Education*, 65(4), 271–283.

Loughran, J., Berry, A., & Mulhall, P. (2006). *Understanding and Developing Science Teachers' Pedagogical Content Knowledge*. Rotterdam, The Netherlands: Sense Publishers.

Louis, K. S., Marks, H. M., & Kruse, S. (1996). Teachers' professional community in restructuring schools. *American Educational Research Journal*, 33(4), 757–798.

Macià, M., & García, I. (2016). Informal online communities and networks as a source of teacher professional development: A review. *Teaching and Teacher Education*, 55, 291–307.

Michaeli, N., & Sommer, O. (Eds.) (2014). *Activity Report by the Steering Committee Chaired by Prof. Miriam Ben-Peretz and Prof. Lee Shulman: Leading Teachers As Agents of Improvement in the Education System*. Jerusalem: The Israel Academy of Sciences and Humanities.

Morrison, B., Ni, L., & Guzdial, M. (2012). Adapting the disciplinary commons model for high school teachers: Improving recruitment, creating community. In *Proceedings of the Ninth Annual International Conference on International Computing Education Research* (pp. 47–54). New York: ACM.

Ni, L., Guzdial, M., Tew, A. E., Morrison, B., & Galanos, R. (2011). Building a community to support HS CS teachers: The disciplinary commons for computing educators. In *Proceedings of the 42nd ACM Technical Symposium on Computer Science Education* (pp. 553–558). New York: ACM.

Pahl, K., & Rowsell, J. (2010). *Artifactual literacies: Every object tells a story*. New York, NY: Teachers' College Press.

Park, M., & Sung, Y. (2013). Teachers' perceptions of the recent curriculum reforms and their implementation: What can we learn from the case of korean elementary teachers? *Asia Pacific Journal of Education*, 33(1), 15–33.

Perry, R. R., & Lewis, C. C. (2009). What is successful adaptation of lesson study in the US? *Journal of Educational Change*, 10(4), 365–391.

Poekert, P. E. (2012). Teacher leadership and professional development: Examining links between two concepts central to school improvement. *Professional Development in Education*, 38(2), 169–188.

Roberts, E. (2004). The dream of a common language: The search for simplicity and stability in computer science education. In *Proceedings of the 35th SIGCSE Technical Symposium on Computer Science Education* (pp. 115–119). New York: ACM.

Rose, M. (1995). *Possible Lives: The Promise of Public Education in America*. Boston, MA: Houghton Mifflin Company.

Saeli, M., Perrenet, J., Wim, M. G. J., & Zwaneveld, B. (2011). Teaching programming in secondary school: A pedagogical content knowledge perspective. *Informatics in Education*, 10(1), 73–88.

Saeli, M., Perrenet, J., Wim, M. G. J., & Zwaneveld, B. (2012a). Pedagogical content knowledge in teaching material. *Journal of Educational Computing Research*, 46(3), 267–293.

Saeli, M., Perrenet, J., Wim, M. G. J., & Zwaneveld, B. (2012b). Programming: Teachers and pedagogical content knowledge in The Netherlands. *Informatics in Education*, 11(1), 81–114.

Salmon, G. (2002). *E-Tivities: The Key to Active Online Learning*. London, UK: Kogan Page.

Schön, D. (1983). *The Reflective Practitioner: How Professionals Think in Action*. London, UK: Temple Smith.

Sentance, S., Dorling, M., McNicol, A., & Crick, T. (2012). Grand challenges for the UK: Upskilling teachers to teach computer science within the secondary curriculum. In *Proceedings of the 7th Workshop in Primary and Secondary Computing Education* (pp. 82–85). New York: ACM.

Sentance, S., Humphreys, S., & Dorling, M. (2014). The network of teaching excellence in computer science and master teachers. In *Proceedings of the 9th Workshop in Primary and Secondary Computing Education* (pp. 80–88). New York: ACM.

Shinners-Kennedy, D., & Fincher, S. (2015). Scaffolded autoethnography: A method for examining practice-to-research. In *6th Research in Engineering Education Symposium* (pp. 504–512). Melbourne, Australia: Curran Associates.

Shulman, L. S. (1986). Those who understand: Knowledge growth in teaching. *Educational Researcher*, 15(2), 4–14.

Shulman, L. S. (1987). Knowledge and teaching: Foundations of the new reform. *Harvard Educational Review*, 57(1), 1–23.

Shulman, L. S. (2015). PCK: Its genesis and exodus. In A. Berry, P. J. Friedrichsen, & J. Loughran (Eds.), *Re-Examining Pedagogical Content Knowledge in Science Education* (p. 3). Abingdon, UK: Routledge.

Smith, K. (2005). Teacher educators' expertise: What do novice teachers and teacher educators say? *Teaching and Teacher Education*, 21(2), 177–192.

Star, S. L., & Griesemer, J. R. (1989). Institutional ecology, 'translations' and boundary objects: Amateurs and professionals in Berkeley's museum of vertebrate zoology, 1907–39. *Social Studies of Science, 19*(3), 387–420.

Stigler, J. W., & Hiebert, J. (1999). *The Teaching Gap: Best Ideas from the World's Teachers for Improving Education in the Classroom*. New York: Free Press.

Stoll, L., Bolam, R., McMahon, A., Wallace, M., & Thomas, S. (2006). Professional learning communities: A review of the literature. *Journal of Educational Change*, 7(4), 221–258.

Tenenberg, J., & Fincher, S. (2007). Opening the door of the computer science classroom: The disciplinary commons. In *Proceedings of the 38th SIGCSE Technical Symposium on Computer Science Education* (pp. 514–518). New York: ACM.

The Royal Society (2017). *After the Reboot – Computing Education in UK Schools*. London, UK: The Royal Society.

Trust, T., Krutka, D. G., & Carpenter, J. P. (2016). "Together we are better": Professional learning networks for teachers. *Computers & Education*, 102, 15–34.

van Manen, M. (1995). On the epistemology of reflective practice. *Teachers and Teaching*, 1(1), 33–50.

Voogt, J., Fisser, P., Pareja, R. N., Tondeur, J., & van Braak, J. (2013). Technological pedagogical content knowledge – A review of the literature. *Journal of Computer Assisted Learning*, 29(2), 109–121.

Wei, R. C., Darling-Hammond, L., & Adamson, F. (2010). *Professional Development in the United States: Trends and Challenges*. Dallas, TX: National Staff Development Council.

26 Learning Outside the Classroom

Andrew Begel and Andrew J. Ko

The history of computing education research is replete with studies about learning in *formal* contexts (i.e., students learning from teachers in school classrooms). In this chapter, we explore other contexts in which learning about computing occurs (e.g., through reading books, working through online tutorials, competing in hackathons, or asking and answering computing questions on a Q&A website). These activities are all examples of *informal learning* – learning that is opportunistic, rather than planned; unstructured, rather than pedagogically created; self-directed, rather than teacher-centric; and integrated authentically into life activities (Marsick & Watkins, 2001), rather than taking place in a classroom environment. We collect and synthesize research about informal learning of computing and discuss open questions around where and how it occurs and how to best support it.

26.1.1 Background

Since the 1970s, many education and learning science researchers have studied and described informal learning. However, all research in informal learning implicitly recognizes the centrality of the individual's learning context: the learner is in control of what is to be learned and when. This contrasts with most school-based and teacher-driven scenarios, where such decisions define the role, purpose, and authority imbued in teachers. In the settings we focus on in this chapter, learning is a central act of life, taking place in the most individual of circumstances on topics that may only be meaningful to the learner (e.g., as Papert describes his beloved gears in *Mindstorms*; Papert, 1980).

Definitions of informal learning vary. A literature review by Marsick and Volpe finds the following six characteristics are intrinsic to informal learning: (1) integrates with life activities; (2) occurs when triggered; (3) is not always conscious; (4) can be haphazard; (5) involves repeated reflection and action; and (6) links to the learning of other people (Marsick & Volpe, 1999). Many of these characteristics have long been studied, most notably by Knowles (1975). Knowles described and prescribed *self-directed learning*, "a process in which individuals take the initiative without the help of others in diagnosing their learning needs, formulating goals, identifying human and material resources, and evaluating learning outcomes." Some studies have investigated the "triggered" aspect of informal learning by investigating learning that occurred after unexpected events, such as nurses having to learn on the job while at war (Menard, 1993). Whereas these viewed informal learning as a mostly solitary activity, more recent views have considered the integration with life and other people, leveraging social learning perspectives. For example, some argue that with the proliferation of information on the Internet, having knowledge is not as important as the process of discovering knowledge, which makes information resources such as people and technology more important than anything a learner already knows (Siemens, 2005). Other recent views of informal learning argue that the divide between formal and informal learning is blurring, challenging the notion of the classroom as a "container" for learning (Leander et al., 2010). Within this view, the emergence of virtual spaces online has amplified the capacity for learning throughout one's physical and social spaces, not just the classroom.

The only thing that makes a course "online" is the medium a student uses to access resources and feedback from a teacher. The only thing that makes "remote" learning remote is that a student is physically distant from a teacher. If you remove the teacher from the learning or you view the teacher as just one of many resources for knowledge and feedback, then the lines between formal, school-centered learning and other types of learning become blurred. From this perspective, informal learning can occur anywhere, including work, play, and on the side, but also at school (e.g., in extracurricular activities) or in service of school goals, such as consulting a programming tutorial to prepare for a challenging course.

In this chapter, we view informal learning from Papert's perspective, where the learner is in control instead of the teacher (Papert, 1980). This learner-centered view reshapes what it means to be motivated and to stay motivated to learn. In a classroom-centric view of learning, a teacher is charged with motivating and engaging a student. A learner-centered view focuses on learners' motivations and acknowledges that learners' motivation are likely to be more heterogeneous outside of a traditional educational institution. For example, a recent study of motivations to learn in massive open online courses (MOOCs) found that students had several distinct reasons for accessing MOOC content: fulfilling a knowledge gap relevant to their life, preparing for their future, satisfying a curiosity, or connecting with people (Zheng et al., 2015). This diversity of motivations means that "completing" a course cannot be viewed as the only notion of success: many learners may never have intended to complete it.

Since informal learning is so learner-centric, to an educator, it can appear quite haphazard. How, then, can informal learning be facilitated at all? Marsick and Watkins propose the following three conditions to enhance one's informal learning: (1) encouraging critical reflection on what one already knows; (2) encouraging the learner to proactively identify missing skills and learn new strategies to facilitate learning; and (3) stimulating creativity to enable the learner to explore a wide range of resources (Marsick & Watkins, 2001). One notable idea that attempts to support all three is the notion of a personal learning environment (PLE), which is any constellation of tools, communities, and services that learners use to direct their learning and pursue education goals (Dabbagh & Kitsantas, 2012). Recent studies have found that when students have the self-regulation skills needed to reflect on what they do and do not know, they create more socially enriched PLEs and experience a greater sense of learning (Cho et al., 2010). Few works, however, have examined how to promote these self-regulation skills or experimentally demonstrate that they are the cause of these richer experiences and learning outcomes.

In computing education, research has focused on numerous kinds of informal learning, but without the depth that one finds in the learning science research literature. Instead, research has largely explored the vast range of opportunities for informal learning and the systems needed to support it. This area is therefore full of open research questions that could bridge these literatures.

26.2 Environments for Informal Learning

In this section, we explore several contexts for informal learning. We begin with the primary modern informal learning environment – online learning – which is enabled by the ubiquity of the Internet. Online, learners must discover and use materials and resources, as well as learn to engage the online community. Recently, learners have been able to take advantage of digital textbooks while attending MOOCs. Finally, we take a look at summer camps for coding, which expose learners to programming and computing concepts outside the structure afforded in a school environment. Note that we do *not* discuss other forms of informal learning that have not yet been studied, such as the use of books, magazines, and other media for self-study.

26.2.1 Online Learning

Some of the first efforts to investigate informal learning in computing were in the form of *distance learning*. This phrase, which we now more commonly refer to as *online learning*, emerged from the goal of increasing access to computing education. The teaching and research community viewed this shift as one of essentially *translating* classroom activities to computer-based media.

The earliest research on distance learning coincided with the proliferation of access to the Internet in the 1990s. This made it possible for students to attend class remotely. As with most new technologies, teachers attempted to translate existing teaching material such as lectures into new media on the web. Instructors teaching entirely online quickly found that teaching at a distance was not a simple matter of translating content (Gersting, 2000). Instructors wrote about the challenges in translating written classroom notes into recorded lectures that students watched on PCs (Gal-Ezer et al., 2009). Others investigated the challenges of translating synchronous in-person lectures into synchronous online lectures, discovering that engaging students at a distance was more challenging (Koppelman & Vranken, 2008). Some experimented with office hours through instant messaging and phone calls (Malan, 2009). Many instructors built robust, scalable courseware for packaging lecture content as web content (Dankell & Hearn, 1997), created custom tutorials and tool support for writing and submitting programs online (Hitz & Kögeler, 1997), and developed generic tool kits for synchronous chat and lectures (Pullen, 2006). Some experimented with hybrid online courses that included both classroom and online activities, under the assumption that "independent learning" was an inherent part of learning computer science (Rosbottom, 2001); such work continues, investigating blended online and in-person learning in MOOCs (Grover et al., 2015).

Throughout all of these efforts, attempts to evaluate effects on student learning were almost completely absent, with most evaluations simply reporting informally solicited, positive attitudes toward the new media. One of the only rigorous evaluations of learning computing online was performed by Carswell at the Open University in the UK, who found that communicating over the Internet via email had no significant effect on learning outcomes relative to other communication media such as phones (Carswell, 1997).

Researchers were more experimental with the web, arguing that the medium had new affordances that needed to be understood (Carswell, 1998), such as new opportunities for observation and experimentation on learning that classrooms do not have (Howard et al., 2010). Instructors experimented with coding live in front of students, where students used instant messaging to provide a shared display of feedback and guidance on the instructor's programming decisions (Bower, 2008). Some instructors experimented with platforms like Second Life, a virtual environment that supported avatars and chat, embedding development environments and collaboration (Crellin et al., 2009). Others tried using video-conferencing to facilitate large-scale, object-oriented design sessions in which a teacher and a student group developed and discussed solutions to systems design problems (von Wright, 2000). As online courses increased in size with the proliferation of MOOCs, it became possible to experiment longitudinally and at scale with new techniques. For example, one study ran a nine-year experiment and found that gamification techniques caused a significant increase in engagement with online class activities (Lehtonen et al., 2015). Few of these studies investigated the informal learning skills required to support online learning in formal coursework.

While all of this work nominally occurred in formal learning environments, research throughout this period of experimentation revealed online learning required many of the same strategies found in informal learning environments. For example, a study of help-seeking in a web development course found that nearly all students sought help in unstructured discussion forums, from both instructors and peers, and that they often relied on the Internet to learn independently (Park & Wiedenbeck, 2011). A study of help-seeking in a user interface development course found that online documentation of application programming interfaces (APIs) and development platforms were fundamental learning resources (Ko & Myers, 2004). These studies show that whatever materials a class provides, when there are more robust materials online, course materials have trouble rivaling the scope, scale, or relevance of content on the entire web. This has the effect of shifting a lot of the learning online, even when students are learning in collocated classroom settings.

26.2.2 Finding and Using Online Resources

Another opportunity for learning occurs when informal learners struggle to find, assess, and use online information resources. Learners employ a variety of resources, including online Q&A websites like Stack Overflow, code search, digitals textbooks, MOOCs, and videos.

Online Q&A communities are key resources for developers seeking answers to programming questions about languages and APIs (Jones & Churchill, 2009). Not only do peers help diagnose programming bugs, they can also help learners avoid starting from scratch by enabling building projects based on one another's shared code (and introducing challenges around plagiarism, which are discussed in Chapter 14). Chambers et al. found that students depend on this online information; they frequently used code examples to overcome compilation errors and rarely referenced information sources that could have given them better success rates (Chambers et al., 2012). Other developers use code search to discover this kind of information. Sadowski et al. studied professional developers at Google and found that when they searched for code, they wanted to answer questions about how to use an API, for examples on how the code operates, and to learn why it might be failing (Sadowski et al., 2015). Dorn and Guzdial found that graphic designers also engage with Q&A forums and other documentation sites in order to learn how to automate their work by programming scripts (Dorn & Guzdial, 2006). From the perspective of Q&A site owners, it requires substantial design investment and community leadership to make forum designs effective at nurturing inviting, helpful discussions (Begel et al., 2013; Mamykina et al., 2011).

Several studies have found that there are critical information retrieval skills necessary to successfully using online resources about computing. For example, the use of Q&A sites and code search requires people to learn search and query reformulation skills, which are non-obvious to novices (Dorn et al., 2013). DiSalvo discovered that parents looking for computer science educational resources for their children had trouble obtaining good results from what they thought were reasonable search queries (DiSalvo, 2014). Many researchers have found that novice searchers have trouble writing effective queries and recognizing good sources because they focus shallowly on the surface of a website and lack confidence in their awareness of appropriate online resources (Moraveji et al., 2011).

Other types of online resources can provide useful orientations for students who need a first place to look. Hao et al. found that students who face difficult problems first look online, but as the difficulty level rises, they would rather seek out help from peers or other resources (Hao et al., 2016). One problem with online resources is that because learners often have very specific personal goals and resources are rarely tailored to those goals, learners struggle to assess the quality and relevance of those resources (Dorn & Guzdial, 2010). Studies of professional software developers' use of API documentation have found that while they use documentation to learn, over time, they continue to rely on them as a form of external memory, stalling recall and deeper learning until just before they are needed (Brandt et al., 2009).

26.2.3 MOOCs

Informal learners often engage with content developed for formal instruction, such as digital textbooks, but doing so without the structure of a formal learning context can have benefits and drawbacks. For example, Warner et al. found that informal learners who accessed digital textbooks made extensive use of interactive components, such as executing code and answering multiple-choice questions, but rarely viewed textbook sections out of order (Warner et al., 2015). Guo and Reinecke also found that it was easy for learners to become disengaged with materials, as evidenced by a large-scale study of MOOC students' navigation history with course materials, showing that learners frequently skipped materials, read them out of order, and read shallowly (Guo & Reinecke, 2014).

There are also many tensions between the formats used in online media and the need to discuss code. For example, Zhu et al. noticed that text-based discussion forums were inefficient for teaching programming; in order to increase engagement, forums should integrate interactive and visual programming features (Zhu et al., 2015). Guo et al. found that engagement increases when MOOC videos are short, display talking heads, and use handmade tablet-based drawings (Guo et al., 2014).

Research about the quality of online materials is still scarce. Researchers have partly tried to measure quality by measuring engagement, but measuring engagement can be complex because of underlying factors of attitudes and motivation (Chapter 28). For example, in evaluating videos in MOOCs, people engage more by pausing or rewatching the same MOOC video segment; this can actually mean either that they are interested or that they are simply confused (Kim et al., 2014). Kim and Ko conducted an evaluation of dozens of coding tutorials using a more principled, analytical method, finding that coding tutorials lack most of the key requirements for successful learning (Kim & Ko, 2017), such as personalized feedback about problem-solving, explanations about why concepts are important to larger problem-solving guidance, guidance on common errors, and adaptation to learners' prior knowledge. Similarly, in a reflection on five years of MOOC education at Stanford, Cooper and Sahami felt that the lack of personalized instruction and feedback limits positive learning outcomes (Cooper & Sahami, 2013).

26.2.4 Camps

Another widely studied, semi-informal learning context is camps. These can come in the form of after-school programs, weekend programs, or week or multi-week summer programs. Camps are formal in that there are often multiple instructors guiding learners' experiences and creative efforts. They are informal, however, in that learners, rather than teachers, are ultimately the ones in charge of what they learn, how engaged they are, and even whether they attend regularly. After all, since camps are not compulsory, but often voluntary, supplemental activities to formal learning, learners view them as a chance to explore their interests rather than satisfy a school requirement. This reduces the teachers' authority, which shifts them slightly (but not fully) from formal to informal learning

Computing camps are now ubiquitous in some countries. Some are run for profit, while others are nonprofits. Some are supported by local colleges and universities and others are run as research projects. And because they often occur outside of the context of a formal education institution, they can be structured in richly diverse ways. One computing camp followed a weeklong summer curriculum for middle school girls aiming to convey future careers by connecting students with invited speakers and using programming environments like Alice to tell stories by writing simple computer programs (Webb & Rosson, 2011). Others used the App Inventor platform to scaffold the creation of mobile application development through daily support and guidance (Wagner et al., 2013). The Georgia Computes! project was perhaps one of the most extensive efforts at informal learning of computing, as it spanned the entire state of Georgia. It offered camps that leveraged a variety of platforms, including PicoCrickets, Scratch, LEGO NXT Kits, Alice, LEGO Textrix kits, LEGO WeDo Kits, and Pleo robots, which engaged a broad range of learner interests (Ericson & McKlin, 2012). Beyond these camps offered by researchers, there are countless nonacademic organizations that offer camps as a way of engaging youth in computing. This variety of offerings and content is essential, as learners' interests are very diverse – without diverse content to serve those interests, many learners would lack the motivation to engage.

As a context for research on informal learning, camps are compelling because they offer more control than purely informal settings without teachers. Researchers can devise exactly the experience they want to test or probe into experience in precise and systematic ways not usually possible in more constrained classroom environments. However, because they lack the compulsory nature of formal learning environments, they can be more dominated by learners' interests and motivations. This has meant that much research on camps focuses on changes in interest, motivation, and identity, rather than learning.

Research on camps has often lacked rigor. One analysis of published studies found that only 8 percent of them offered longitudinal evidence of impact of any kind. Most focused instead on measuring attitudes, interest, or programming skills, and reported positive or neutral findings (Decker et al., 2016). Another survey found that camps designed by researchers were significantly different from camps designed by practitioners. The research camps used different approaches, framed alternative outreach goals, and used more rigorous methods to analyze learners' experiences (DeWitt et al., 2017). Part of the challenge of conducting rigorous analyses of camps is their unstructured nature – learners in the same camp may do substantially different things based on their interests, making it difficult to systematically observe outcomes. The result is that many studies rely on short-term, self-reported changes in self-efficacy, learning, and other outcomes (e.g., Aritajati et al., 2015; McGill et al., 2015).

Some studies devised creative ways of observing impact without relying on self-reports. For example, Kelleher et al. wanted to measure how a version of Alice that was designed for storytelling mediated middle school learners' motivation to create Alice programs (Kelleher et al., 2007). Rather than asking learners to self-report their motivation to learn, the researchers structured the camp to hold numerous breaks with highly desirable treats like cookies. Researchers then measured how long learners continued to work after the breaks started, getting a continuous measure of in situ motivation relative to desire for snacks and food. Loksa et al. used another powerful idea – giving high school students in a web development camp a list of requirements for a personal website they were to create, but also encouraging them to devise self-defined requirements (Loksa et al., 2016). The researchers assessed the complexity and volume of self-defined requirements and analyzed the degree to which students implemented those requirements, and they used these to measure productivity over an entire week.

Some research on camps has gone beyond the unit of analysis of a single camp, or even a constellation of camps, investigating entire systems and pipelines of informal learning opportunities. Most notably, the Georgia Computes! project investigated the role of state policy, the interaction between formal and informal learning, and the longitudinal effects of a pipeline of informal learning opportunities on identity and engagement (Guzdial et al., 2014). This type of policy research has led to recommendations about requirements for success, suggesting the importance of the support of policy stakeholders and partners, of high-quality portable resources, of an explicit goal to replicate success across outreach activities, and of multiple levels of details about the system.

26.3 Strategies for Informal Learning

In this section, we discuss several strategies that learners engage in when learning informally. We start off with self-directed learning, add a social component with peer learning, and move onto large-scale community-based involvement in a learner's progression. We end by looking at how teachers can also be informal learners and can take advantage of the same environments and strategies that other learners enjoy.

26.3.1 Self-Directed Learning

Only a few works have considered truly self-directed, independent learning of computing. McCartney et al., for example, investigated how computer science undergraduate students approach informal, self-directed learning to supplement their formal education (McCartney et al., 2010). They found that students were inspired to learn in order to complete personally meaningful projects, employing a variety of programming languages and technologies. These students chose to work on these projects because they would be relevant to their work, their home lives, or their careers (e.g., to prepare for future coursework or to help out friends and family). Boustedt et al. built upon these findings, reporting that while students in school enjoy informal learning because they gain agency over the process, they believe that they miss important aspects of a topic, have difficulty assessing their learning, and miss the structure of school (Boustedt et al., 2011).

Zander et al. studied self-directed learning by focusing on computing professionals (Zander et al., 2012). They found that professionals were implicitly expected to learn on their own, and used a range of resources (e.g., Internet search), strategies (e.g., getting help from others, learning by trial and error, breaking problems into subproblems, etc.), and collaborators (for information gathering) to help them in the process. Professionals found their work-related learning to be enjoyable and expressed a sense of confidence and pride. Yet they often found informal, self-directed learning to be stressful, describing it as a never-ending process.

Many studies of informal learning concern adults. For example, many of the studies by Lee et al. (e.g., Lee & Ko, 2011, 2015) involved adults seeking opportunities to learn online through coding tutorials. Guo investigated the motivations behind this adult learning, finding that many people over 60 years of age want to learn to code, but get frustrated by their declining cognitive faculties, their lack of opportunities to interact socially with tutors, peers, and teachers, and their difficulties with constantly changing software technologies (Guo, 2017). Adults can also shift their attitudes about computing quickly. For example, a pre/post-attitudinal survey of adults playing the Gidget game rapidly shifted their beliefs about the difficulty of programming from negative to positive after just 15 minutes of play (Charters et al., 2014). Few studies, however, have explored these issues longitudinally.

26.3.2 Peer Learning

As Vygotsky proposed, a lot of learning happens in the company of and due to one's peers. Many studies have reinforced this theoretical claim. For example, while social interactions occur face-to-face and virtually, they all take place in contextually linked places, such in tutoring centers, at whiteboards, in Facebook groups, or even at home where people can work on projects together (Knox & Fincher, 2013). Klomsri et al. found that South African youths took advantage of the ubiquity of Facebook's social networking to learn about one another's viewpoints, support one another, share their own content with an audience of their design, and effectively achieve their own goals without significant overheads caused by any formal pedagogy or structure (Klomsri et al., 2013). Studies of mentoring around computing have found that many adolescents' interest in computing comes from informal peer mentors and not from classes (Ko & Davis, 2017).

Hackathons – large events where people gather to complete projects in collaborative programming teams – offer a significant amount of peer learning. Mentors from tertiary institutions and industry can provide round-the-clock, hands-on support, troubleshooting, and advice. Nandi and Mandernach found that undergraduate students participating in hackathons spent quality time practicing the art of working together in teams (Nandi & Mandernach, 2016). Students are motivated to participate in these hackathons primarily for the social appeal of working in a fun environment with new people and new technology (Warner & Guo, 2017). After interviewing six hackathon participants, Warner and Guo found that hackathons were perceived by the students to be more authentic, intense, and democratic than classroom learning experiences. Hackathon activities motivate students to learn new skills because of their practical applicability, not their academic value. Working on hackathon projects helps reinforce students' communication skills while catalyzing their personal motivations and self-confidence to work on personally relevant projects.

26.3.3 Engaging with Communities of Practice

As we have discussed, a lot of informal learning is social. There is some evidence, however, that effective informal learning requires social engagement with not just peers, tutors, or strangers online, but whole communities (Lave & Wenger, 1991). Learners often engage with community members in the "real world" at work, during academically sponsored service learning opportunities, co-ops, and internships (Fincher & Knox, 2013). Non-work-based contexts occur in many kinds of authentic communities, such as those that spring up around particular application domains, open-source projects, and capstone course projects. The popularity and success of the Scratch programming environment (Resnick et al., 2009) has created and supported a community of young learners who "remix" one another's projects to build their own. Dasgupta et al. found that learners who remix more often have larger repertoires of programming commands, even after controlling for the numbers of projects and amount of code shared. They also found that exposure to computational thinking concepts through remixing was associated with an increased likelihood of using those concepts (Dasgupta et al., 2016). Another study found that while building off one another's projects helps learners get started, it does not correlate to them using more complex concepts in their Scratch projects (Fields et al., 2014).

Engaging in authentic communities of practice can have both positive and negative effects on learners. For instance, Ellis et al. found that students working on humanitarian-oriented open-source projects increased their interest in computing, as they gained experience in developing software in a distributed environment (Ellis et al., 2015). Students also improved their performance in attendant skills, such as communication and distributed teamwork. However, Hislop et al. found that while engaging in open-source projects made students feel more comfortable interacting with professionals, it also made them feel that they knew much less than they thought they did before (Hislop et al., 2015).

Many institutions offer a capstone course, in which a team of senior undergraduate students works with an outside for-profit or not-for-profit company (e.g., Cicirello, 2013, Stone et al., 2011, 2012). While project specifications come from the outside, students engage in authentic work experiences in the safe, monitored environment of tertiary institutions. The outside partners simultaneously monitor the students' progress as they anticipate and eventually receive delivery of the final product. In a report by Bloomfield et al. about the service learning-oriented capstone at the University of Virginia, students connected with local nonprofits to work on meaningful projects with real impact to the community while learning teamwork, customer management, and organizational skills (Bloomfield et al., 2014). Working with outside partners takes real effort and administrative capabilities from tertiary institutions, however. Venkatagiri found that implementing a service-oriented capstone in India required the instructor to negotiate appropriate contracts with outside partners to ensure appropriate expectations were communicated along the way. Instructors also had to train students in soft skills, such as effective brainstorming, presenting progress reports, and engaging with customers (Venkatagiri, 2006).

26.3.4 Teachers As Informal Learners

Teachers are learners too, of course, and because of the demands on their time, much of the learning they do to teach computing is informal. For example, researchers have created online communities with the goal of supporting informal learning of teachers struggling to master new concepts to deploy in their classrooms. These communities can also be used to share knowledge and support one another's pedagogy development. Research in this area focuses on building effective communities of practice (Schlager & Fusco, 2003). Booth and Kellogg studied online communities for teachers and found that fostering a diverse population of members with various perspectives and levels of expertise helped one another co-construct new forms of meaning and understanding in ways that were individually and collectively valuable (Booth & Kellogg, 2015).

Designing online communities for promoting teacher learning is not easy. Fincher et al. studied the Nifty Assignments online resource and found that while *acquiring* contributions was effective (because they come from a special session at the yearly Special Interest Group on Computer Science Education [SIGCSE] computer science education conference), teachers navigating the site had difficulty finding appropriate assignments to use because they preferred to find resources via general web search, rather than browsing through a forum organized by contribution year (Fincher et al., 2010). Teachers found it difficult to identify the pedagogical concepts taught in each assignment and also had to spend time adapting assignments to their own classrooms. For an online community for the Greenfoot environment, Brown and Kölling compared their new site's use with three different populations of educators, and they found that each population behaved very differently (Brown & Kölling, 2013). Some shared information or announcements much more than others, and some asked domain-specific questions when others did not. Even the kinds of contributions and feedback varied among the populations in ways that the designers of the site could only identify, not influence. Leake and Lewis found similar differences in needs between novice and experienced secondary school computer science instructors (Leake & Lewis, 2017). Novice teachers wanted the ability to build off lessons and resources created by more experienced teachers, but simultaneously reported difficulty in adapting those resources to their particular pedagogical contexts.

As Chapter 27 notes, engaging high school teachers in online communities is challenging. Howard and McKeown found that site designers found it difficult to engage communities of teachers because their teachers did not perceive the online community as an integral part of their normal work practice (Howard & McKeown, 2011). Leake and Lewis noted that informal learners who are teachers have a difficult time finding appropriate information resources and do not contribute to them because it takes too much time away from what they perceive as their real job of teaching (Leake & Lewis, 2016). Mitchell and Lutters studied university professors in computer science and found similar results. While most were aware of repositories of instructional materials, only about half had ever used one, and of those who had, most expressed disappointment that the repositories did not meet their needs (Mitchell & Lutters, 2006). Clements et al. classified many different kinds of learning object repositories and suggested that teacher-generated, collaborative, quality instruments are the most sustainable (Clements et al., 2015). Beyond this work, however, there is little design guidance on creating useful informal learning repositories for teachers.

26.4 Supporting Informal Learning of Computing

As we have discussed, prior work shows that people engage in a wide range of informal learning activities to learn computing, but that many struggle to learn independently. Consequently, much of the research on informal computing education has focused on designing tools, resources, and experiences that promote longer engagement and better learning.

One form of improvement is offering *new genres* of instructional content. For example, early research, driven by the advent of the Internet, explored new web-based multimedia tutoring environments that would provide richer explanations of computers, compilers, and circuits than were possible in a classroom, while also offering automated assessments that would allow learners to be self-paced and independent (Connelly et al., 1996). More recently, researchers have focused on a wide range of new experiences. Some have investigated case-based learning aids that embed instruction in tasks, contextualizing learning to the goals that an independent learner might be trying to achieve (Dorn 2011). Others have explored more interactive tools like PythonTutor that provide deeper visibility into notional machines (e.g., Guo, 2013), allowing students to independently explore the behavior of their own programs. Researchers have also explored a range of programming games that translate tasks in programming and debugging into interactive games that promote learning (Bishop et al., 2015; Lee et al., 2014; Miljanovic & Bradbury, 2017; Tillmann et al., 2012). Others have focused on developing interactive e-books, including those with embedded program visualizations to contextualize program behavior with other instruction (Sirkia & Sorva, 2015), worked examples that support self-assessment (Ericson et al., 2015, 2016), and granular interactive explanations of programming language semantics (Nelson et al., 2017). While teachers can use all of these novel genres of interactive instructional content to support formal learning, none of them *require* teachers in order to be used.

Some research is less focused on inventing new genres of instructional content and more on improving existing genres. For example, a series of studies on the Gidget programming game explored how different design decisions affect discretionary engagement in learning. For example, one study found that by visually representing the robot in the game with an anthropomorphic face and by rewriting error messages to use more collaborative personal pronouns such as "I," "you," and "we," learners were more likely to attend to error messages, learn from them, and therefore master programming language concepts more quickly than learners who interacted with more conventional error messages and a robot with no face (Lee & Ko, 2011). This work was one of the first to frame error messages as instructional content. A follow-up study found that by making the objects in the game vertebrate objects like cats and mice instead of inanimate objects like rocks, students spend more time learning and complete more exercises in the game (Lee & Ko, 2012). A third study found that incorporating formative assessments in the game led players to voluntarily play for longer and complete levels more quickly, suggesting more efficient learning (Lee et al., 2013). In MOOCs, some researchers have studied the effect of video, tutorial, and quizzes on dropout rates (Kim et al., 2014), finding that learners are deterred by long videos, abrupt transitions, and learning challenges without resources. These studies show that seemingly small factors in the design of materials can greatly impact the quality and duration of discretionary learning.

Because creating and designing effective instructional material for the wide range of concepts in computing can be challenging and slow, researchers have increasingly investigated techniques for automatically generating instruction using intelligent tutoring systems. For example, some have explored ways of semiautomatically generating API tutorials composed of code examples from open-source projects on the web (Dahotre et al., 2011; Harms et al., 2013).

Preliminary studies of these systems show that they can successfully promote learning, especially relative to fixed media such as textbooks. Others have explored end-user programmers who need to learn a little about programming to help automate a task, embedding end-user software engineering tools that generate context and task-relevant instruction on design, reuse, integration, testing, and debugging (Ko et al., 2011). There are hundreds of such systems, each with the primary goal of helping people automate work, but with the secondary effect of promoting some learning. For example, the Idea Garden concept explored opportunities to generate contextual problem-solving instruction, helping people trying to write simple programs learn problem-solving skills that helped them get unstuck on a programming task (Cao et al., 2011).

While some systems have explored generating instruction, others have focused on generating feedback about learners' skills. Cognitive tutors have focused on providing step-by-step feedback and guidance on problem-solving (Jin & Corbett, 2011). Environments that gamify programming, inspired by how well video games promote skill mastery through feedback, show stronger learning outcomes than environments with no feedback or guidance (Lee & Ko, 2015). For decades, researchers have explored automated feedback in the context of online courses (Fitzpatrick et al., 2017; Truong, 2005). Unless learners can explain to themselves where this feedback comes from, many learners find automatically generated feedback to be untrustworthy (Kulkarni et al., 2014).

Rather than automate feedback, some researchers have explored ways of scaling peer feedback in informal settings. These include structured peer assessment in basic online forums (Warren et al., 2014), but also a range of new media. For example, Codeopticon lets learners simultaneously chat with dozens of other learners, scaling peer feedback (Guo, 2015). Codechella lets multiple people write code, visualize runtime state, debug, and chat in real time (Guo et al., 2015), creating a shared visual display of learning dialogue. Codepourri lets anonymous learners create and share step-by-step coding tutorials for other learners (Gordon & Guo, 2015). These systems explore new ways to help learners support each other in their informal learning, without the aid or guidance of teachers or automatic feedback systems.

26.5 Open Questions

As we noted before, research on informal learning of computing is broad, but not deep. Researchers have explored many novel ways to support informal learning of computing, but only a few projects have deeply explored their impact on learning, and few have deeply leveraged theories of learning to inform design. There are also not yet clear best practices for doing research on these topics: the field still lacks robust, valid measures of many of the constructs it seeks to improve, such as learning, interest, and engagement.

Despite this lack of research infrastructure, there are still many urgent open questions about how informal learning unfolds and how to support it. Because of the inherently learner-centric nature of informal learning, many of the most important questions concern how to support learners if not through a relationship with a teacher in a formal institution of education. For example, should learning technologies structure learning for learners or should learners be taught how to structure their own independent learning? What role can librarians play in helping learners navigate their informal learning? Since learners are often seeking online resources to learn to code, how can they be supported in searching, selecting, and effectively leveraging resources? These questions are important in every setting, whether after school, in a camp, in an online course, or completely separate from a formal learning setting.

Equally important are questions about informal learning resources themselves. How can we know whether a resource is effective? Is it possible to automatically personalize resources so they meet the goals of a specific learner? Is it possible to automatically generate resources to meet the wide range of things that people want to learn about computing, such as new APIs and platforms? How do informal learning materials need to be different from those used in formal education settings? How should resources be maintained and organized? Do they need to provide the same support as a teacher? Can they? Because so much about learning computing involves formal notations, it may be more amenable to automation than many other kinds of learning, but some things, such as a relationship with a trusted, supporting teacher, probably cannot.

Finally, as we have noted throughout the chapter, much informal learning *does* involve teachers, framing them more as facilitators and resources than authority figures. In these learner-driven settings such as camps and online, is the kind of guidance and support that teachers need to provide different from those of formal classrooms, more akin to mentoring than instructing? And given the scarcity of people with expertise in teaching computing, how can we scale the guidance that teachers provide in formal learning?

Finally, we still know very little about the broader impacts of informal learning of computing. For example, widespread efforts such as Code.org's Hour of Code and dozens of online coding tutorials are engaging hundreds of millions of people, but we still know very little about what anyone learns. Is this knowledge robust? Is it comparable to what is learned in formal settings? And is this informal learning more or less equitable than in formal settings?

We are just at the beginning of understanding how people learn computing outside of school. With further research, we may not only find ways of supporting learners in their self-directed learning more effectively, but also how to better integrate learning across formal and informal settings for those in school.

References

Aritajati, C., Rosson, M. B., Pena, J., Cinque, D., & Segura, A. (2015). A socio-cognitive analysis of summer camp outcomes and experiences. In *Proceedings of the 46th*

ACM Technical Symposium on Computer Science Education (SIGCSE '15) (pp. 581–586). New York: ACM.

Begel, A., Bosch, J., & Storey, M. A. (2013). Social networking meets software development: Perspectives from GitHub, MSDN, Stack Exchange, and TopCoder. *IEEE Software*, 30(1) 52–66.

Bishop, J., Horspool, R. N., Xie, T., Tillmann, N. & de Halleux, J. (2015). Code Hunt: Experience with coding contests at scale. In *Proceedings of the 37th IEEE International Conference on Software Engineering* (pp. 398–407). New York: IEEE.

Bloomfield, A., Sherriff, M., & Williams, K. (2014). A service learning practicum capstone. In *Proceedings of the 45th ACM Technical Symposium on Computer Science Education (SIGCSE '14)* (pp. 265–270). New York: ACM.

Booth, S. E., & Kellogg, S. B. (2015). Value creation in online communities for educators. *British Journal of Educational Technology*, 46(4), 684–698.

Boustedt, J., Eckerdal, A., McCartney, R., Sanders, K., Thomas, L., & Zander, C. (2011). Students' perceptions of the differences between formal and informal learning. In *Proceedings of the Seventh International Workshop on Computing Education Research (ICER '11)* (pp. 61–68). New York: ACM.

Bower, M. (2008). The "instructed-teacher": A computer science online learning pedagogical pattern. In *Proceedings of the 13th Annual Conference on Innovation and Technology in Computer Science Education (ITiCSE '08)* (pp. 189–193). New York: ACM.

Brandt, J., Guo, P. J., Lewenstein, J., Dontcheva, M., & Klemmer, S. R. (2009). Two studies of opportunistic programming: interleaving web foraging, learning, and writing code. In *Proceedings of the SIGCHI Conference on Human Factors in Computing Systems (CHI '09)* (pp. 1589–1598). New York, NY: ACM.

Brown, N. C. C., & Kölling, M. (2013). A tale of three sites: Resource and knowledge sharing amongst computer science educators. In *Proceedings of the Ninth Annual International ACM Conference on International Computing Education Research (ICER '13)* (pp. 27–34). New York: ACM.

Cao, J., Fleming, S. D., & Burnett, M. (2011). An exploration of design opportunities for "gardening" end-user programmers' ideas. In *Proceedings of IEEE Symposium on Visual Languages and Human-Centric Computing (VL/HCC)* (pp. 35–42). New York: IEEE.

Carswell, L. (1997). Teaching via the Internet: The impact of the Internet as a communication medium on distance learning introductory computing students. In *Proceedings of the 2nd Conference on Integrating Technology into Computer Science Education (ITiCSE '97)* (pp. 1–5). New York: ACM.

Carswell, L. (1998). The "Virtual University": Toward an Internet paradigm? In *Proceedings of the 6th Annual Conference on the Teaching of Computing and the 3rd Annual Conference on Integrating Technology into Computer Science Education: Changing the Delivery of Computer Science Education (ITiCSE '98)* (pp. 46–50). New York: ACM.

Chambers, C., Chen, S., Le, D., & Scaffidi, C. (2012). The function, and dysfunction, of information sources in learning functional programming. *Journal of Computing Sciences in College*, 28(1), 220–226.

Charters, P., Lee, M. J., Ko, A. J., & Loksa, D. (2014). Challenging stereotypes and changing attitudes: The effect of a brief programming encounter on adults' attitudes toward programming. In *Proceedings of the 45th ACM Technical Symposium on Computer Science Education* (pp. 653–658). New York: ACM.

Cho, M. H., Demei, S., & Laffey, J. (2010). Relationships between self-regulation and social experiences in asynchronous online learning environments. *Journal of Interactive Learning Research*, 21(3), 297–316.

Cicirello, V. A. (2013). Experiences with a real projects for real clients course on software engineering at a liberal arts institution. *Journal of Computing Sciences in College*, 28(6), 50–56.

Clements, K., Pawlowski, J., & Manouselis, N. (2015). Open educational resources repositories literature review – Towards a comprehensive quality approaches framework. *Computers in Human Behavior*, 51(B), 1098–1106.

Connelly, C., Biermann, A. W., Pennock, D., & Wu, P. (1996). Home study software: Complementary systems for computer science courses. *Computer Science Education*, 7(1), 53–71.

Cooper, S., & Sahami, M. (2013). Reflections on Stanford's MOOCs. *Communications of the ACM*, 56(2), 28–30.

Crellin, J., Duke-Williams, E., Chandler, J., & Collinson, T. (2009). Virtual worlds in computing education. *Computer Science Education*, 19(4), 315–334.

Dabbagh, N., & Kitsantas, A. (2012). Personal learning environments, social media, and self-regulated learning: A natural formula for connecting formal and informal learning. *The Internet and Higher Education*, 15(1), 3–8.

Dahotre, A., Krishnamoorthy, V., Corley, M., & Scaffidi, C. (2011). Using intelligent tutors to enhance student learning of application programming interfaces. *Journal of Computing Sciences in College*, 27(1). 195–201.

Dankell, II, D. D., & Hearn, J. (1997). The use of the WWW to support distance learning through NTU. In *Proceedings of the 2nd Conference on Integrating Technology into Computer Science Education (ITiCSE '97)* (pp. 8–10). New York: ACM.

Dasgupta, S., Hale, W., Monroy-Hernández, A., & Hill, B. M. (2016). Remixing as a pathway to computational thinking. In *Proceedings of the 19th ACM Conference on Computer-Supported Cooperative Work & Social Computing* (pp. 1438–1449). New York: ACM.

Decker, A., McGill, M. M., & Settle, A. (2016). Towards a common framework for evaluating computing outreach activities. In *Proceedings of the 47th ACM Technical Symposium on Computing Science Education (SIGCSE '16)* (pp. 627–632). New York: ACM.

DeWitt, A., Fay, J., Goldman, M., Nicolson, E., Oyolu, L., Resch, L., Saldaña, J. M., Sounalath, S., Williams, T., Yetter, K., Zak, E., Brown, N., & Rebelsky, S. A. (2017). What we say vs. what they do: A comparison of middle-school coding camps in the cs education literature and mainstream coding camps (abstract only). In *Proceedings of the 2017 ACM SIGCSE Technical Symposium on Computer Science Education (SIGCSE '17)* (p. 707). New York: ACM.

DiSalvo, B., Reid, C., & Roshan, P. K. (2014). They can't find us: The search for informal CS education. In *Proceedings of the 45th ACM Technical Symposium on Computer Science Education (SIGCSE '14)* (pp. 487–492). New York: ACM.

Dorn, B. (2011). ScriptABLE: Supporting informal learning with cases. In *Proceedings of the Seventh International Workshop on Computing Education Research (ICER '11)* (pp. 69–76). New York: ACM.

Dorn, B., & Guzdial, M. (2006). Graphic designers who program as informal computer science learners. In *Proceedings of the Second International Workshop on Computing Education Research (ICER '06)* (pp. 127–134). New York: ACM.

Dorn, B., & Guzdial, M. (2010). Learning on the job: Characterizing the programming knowledge and learning strategies of web designers. In *Proceedings of the SIGCHI Conference on Human Factors in Computing Systems (CHI '10)* (pp. 703–712). New York: ACM.

Dorn, B., Stankiewicz, A., & Roggi, C. (2013). Lost while searching: Difficulties in information seeking among end-user programmers. In *Proceedings of the 76th ASIS&T Annual Meeting: Beyond the Cloud: Rethinking Information Boundaries (ASIST '13)* (pp. 21:1–21:11). Silver Springs, MD: Association for Information Science and Technology.

Ellis, H. J. C., Hislop, G. W., Jackson, S., & Postner, L. (2015). Team project experiences in humanitarian free and open source software (HFOSS). *Transactions on Computing Education.* 15(4), 1–23.

Ericson, B. J., & McKlin, T. (2012). Effective and sustainable computing summer camps. In *Proceedings of the 43rd ACM Technical Symposium on Computer Science Education (SIGCSE '12)* (pp. 289–294). New York: ACM.

Ericson, B. J., Guzdial, M. J., & Morrison, B. B. (2015). Analysis of interactive features designed to enhance learning in an ebook. In *Proceedings of the Eleventh Annual International Conference on International Computing Education Research (ICER '15)* (pp. 169–178). New York: ACM.

Ericson, B. J., Rogers, K., Parker, M. Morrison, B., & Guzdial, M. (2016). Identifying design principles for CS teacher ebooks through design-based research. In *Proceedings of the 2016 ACM Conference on International Computing Education Research (ICER '16)* (pp. 191–200). New York: ACM.

Fields, D. A., Giang, M., & Kafai, Y. (2014). Programming in the wild: Trends in youth computational participation in the online Scratch community. In *Proceedings of the 9th Workshop in Primary and Secondary Computing Education (WiPSCE '14)* (pp. 2–11). New York: ACM.

Fincher, S., & Knox, D. (2013). The porous classroom: Professional practices in the computing curriculum. *Computer*, 46(9), 44–51.

Fincher, S., Kölling, M., Utting, I., Brown, N., & Stevens, P. (2010). Repositories of teaching material and communities of use: nifty assignments and the greenroom. In *Proceedings of the Sixth International Workshop on Computing Education Research (ICER '10)* (pp. 107–114). New York: ACM.

Fitzpatrick, J. M., Lédeczi, Á., Narasimham, G., Lafferty, L., Labrie, R., Mielke, P. T., Kumar, A., & Brady, K. A. (2017). Lessons learned in the design and delivery of an introductory programming MOOC. In *Proceedings of the 2017 ACM SIGCSE Technical Symposium on Computer Science Education (SIGCSE '17)* (pp. 219–224). New York: ACM.

Gal-Ezer, J., Vilner, T., & Zur, E. (2009). The professor on your PC: A virtual CS1 course. In *Proceedings of the 14th Annual ACM SIGCSE Conference on Innovation and Technology in Computer Science Education (ITiCSE '09)* (pp. 191–195). New York: ACM.

Gersting, J. L. (2000). Computer science distance education experience in Hawaii. *Computer Science Education*, 10(1), 95–106.

Gordon, M. & Guo, P. J. (2015). Codepourri: Creating visual coding tutorials using a volunteer crowd of learners. In *2015 IEEE Symposium on Visual Languages and Human-Centric Computing (VL/HCC)* (pp. 13–21). New York: IEEE.

Grover, S., Pea, R., & Cooper, S. (2015). Designing for deeper learning in a blended computer science course for middle school students. *Computer Science Education*, 25(2), 199–237.

Guo, P. J. (2013). Online Python tutor: Embeddable web-based program visualization for CS education. In *Proceedings of the 44th ACM Technical Symposium on Computer Science Education* (pp. 579–584). New York: ACM.

Guo, P. J. (2015). Codeopticon: Real-time, one-to-many human tutoring for computer programming. In *Proceedings of the 28th Annual ACM Symposium on User Interface Software & Technology.* (pp. 13–21). New York: ACM.

Guo, P. J. (2017). Older adults learning computer programming: Motivations, frustrations, and design opportunities. In *ACM Conference on Human Factors in Computing Systems (CHI)* (pp. 7070–7083). New York: ACM.

Guo, P. J., & Reinecke, K. (2014). Demographic differences in how students navigate through MOOCs. In *Proceedings of the First ACM Conference on Learning @ Scale* (pp. 21–30). New York: ACM.

Guo, P. J., Kim, J., & Rubin, R. (2014). How video production affects student engagement: An empirical study of mooc videos. In *Proceedings of the first ACM Conference on Learning @ Scale* (pp. 41–50). New York: ACM.

Guo, P. J., White, J., & Zanelatto, R. (2015). Codechella: Multi-user program visualizations for real-time tutoring and collaborative learning. In *2015 IEEE Symposium on Visual Languages and Human-Centric Computing (VL/HCC)* (pp. 79–87). New York: IEEE.

Guzdial, M., Ericson, B., Mcklin, T., & Engelman, S. (2014). Georgia Computes! An intervention in a US State, with formal and informal education in a policy context. *Transactions on Computing Education*, 14(2), 13.

Hao, Q., Wright, E., Barnes, B., & Branch, R. M. (2016). What are the most important predictors of computer science students' online help-seeking behaviors? *Computers in Human Behavior*, 62(C), 467–474.

Harms, K. J., Cosgrove, D., Gray, S., & Kelleher, C. (2013). Automatically generating tutorials to enable middle school children to learn programming independently. In *Proceedings of the 12th International Conference on Interaction Design and Children (IDC '13)* (pp. 11–19). New York: ACM.

Hislop, G. W., Ellis, H. J. C., Pulimood, S. M., Morgan, B., Mello-Stark, S., Coleman, B., & Macdonell, C. (2015). A multi-institutional study of learning via student involvement in humanitarian free and open source software projects. In *Proceedings of the Eleventh Annual International Conference on International Computing Education Research (ICER '15)* (pp. 199–206). New York: ACM.

Hitz, M., & Kögeler, S. (1997). Teaching C++ on the WWW. In *Proceedings of the 2nd Conference on Integrating Technology into Computer Science Education (ITiCSE '97)* (pp. 11–13). New York: ACM.

Howard, L., Johnson, J., & Neitzel, C. (2010). Reflecting on online learning designs using observed behavior. In *Proceedings of the Fifteenth Annual Conference on Innovation and Technology in Computer Science Education (ITiCSE '10)* (pp. 179–183). New York: ACM.

Howard, S., & McKeown, J. (2011). *Online Practice & Offline Roles: A Cultural View of Teachers' Low Engagement in Online Communities*. Washington, DC: American Educational Research Association.

Jin, W., & Corbett, A. (2011). Effectiveness of cognitive apprenticeship learning (CAL) and cognitive tutors (CT) for problem solving using fundamental programming concepts. In *Proceedings of the 42nd ACM Technical Symposium on Computer Science Education (SIGCSE '11)* (pp. 305–310). New York: ACM.

Jones, M. C., & Churchill, E. F. (2009). Conversations in developer communities: a preliminary analysis of the yahoo! pipes community. In *Proceedings of the Fourth International Conference on Communities and technologies (C&T '09)* (pp. 195–204). New York: ACM.

Kelleher, C., Pausch, R., & Kiesler, S. (2007). Storytelling Alice motivates middle school girls to learn computer programming. In *Proceedings of the SIGCHI Conference on Human Factors in Computing Systems (CHI '07)* (pp. 1455–1464). New York: ACM.

Kim, A. S., & Ko, A. J. (2017). A pedagogical analysis of online coding tutorials. In *Proceedings of the 2017 ACM SIGCSE Technical Symposium on Computer Science Education (SIGCSE '17)* (pp. 321–326). New York: ACM.

Kim, J., Guo, P. J., Seaton, D. T., Mitros, P., Gajos, K. Z., & Miller, R. C. (2014). Understanding in-video dropouts and interaction peaks in online lecture videos. In *Proceedings of the First ACM Conference on Learning @ Scale* (pp. 31–40). New York: ACM.

Klomsri, T., Grebäck, L., & Tedre, M. (2013). Social media in everyday learning: How Facebook supports informal learning among young adults in South Africa. In *Proceedings of the 13th Koli Calling International Conference on Computing Education Research (Koli Calling '13)* (pp. 135–144). New York: ACM.

Knox, D., & Fincher, S. (2013). Where students go for knowledge and what they find there. In *Proceedings of the Ninth Annual International ACM Conference on International Computing Education Research (ICER '13)* (pp. 35–40). New York: ACM.

Knowles, M. S. (1975). *Self-Directed Learning: A Guide for Learners and Teachers.* New York: Associated Press.

Ko, A. J., Myers, B. A., & Aung, H. H. (2004). Six learning barriers in end-user programming systems. In *2004 IEEE Symposium on Visual Languages and Human Centric Computing* (pp. 199–206). New York: IEEE.

Ko, A. J., Abraham, R., Beckwith, L., Blackwell, A., Burnett, M., Erwig, M., Scaffidi, C., Lawrance, J., Lieberman, H., Myers, B., Rosson, M. B., Rothermel, G., Shaw, M., & Wiedenbeck, S. (2011). The state of the art in end-user software engineering. *ACM Computing Surveys*, 43(3), 21.

Ko, A. J. & Davis, K. (2017). Computing mentorship in a software boomtown: Relationships to adolescent interest and beliefs. In *Proceedings of the 2017 ACM Conference on International Computing Education Research (ICER '17)* (pp. 236–244). New York: ACM.

Koppelman, H., & Vranken, H. (2008). Experiences with a synchronous virtual classroom in distance education. In *Proceedings of the 13th Annual Conference on Innovation and Technology in Computer Science Education (ITiCSE '08)* (pp. 194–198). New York: ACM.

Kulkarni, C. E., Socher, R., Bernstein, M.S., & Klemmer, S.R. (2014). Scaling short-answer grading by combining peer assessment with algorithmic scoring. In *Proceedings of the First ACM Conference on Learning @ Scale* (pp. 99–108). New York: ACM.

Lave, J., & Wenger, E. (1991). *Situated Learning: Legitimate Peripheral Participation.* Cambridge, UK: Cambridge University Press.

Leake, M., & Lewis, C. (2016). Designing a new system for sharing computer science teaching resources. In *Proceedings of the 19th ACM Conference on Computer Supported Cooperative Work and Social Computing Companion (CSCW '16 Companion)* (pp. 321–324). New York: ACM.

Leake, M., & Lewis, C. M. (2017). Recommendations for designing CS resource sharing sites for all teachers. In *Proceedings of the 2017 ACM SIGCSE Technical Symposium on Computer Science Education (SIGCSE '17)* (pp. 357–362). New York: ACM.

Leander, K. M., Phillips, N. C., & Taylor, K. H. (2010). The changing social spaces of learning: Mapping new mobilities. *Review of Research in Education*, 34(1), 329–394.

Lee, M. J., Bahmani, F., Kwan, I., LaFerte, J., Charters, P., Horvath, A., Luor, F., Cao, J., Law, C., Beswetherick, M., Long, S., Burnett, M., & Ko, A. J. (2014). Principles of a debugging-first puzzle game for computing education. In *2014 IEEE Symposium on Visual Languages and Human-Centric Computing (VL/HCC)* (pp. 57–64). New York: IEEE.

Lee, M. J., & Ko, A. J. (2011). Personifying programming tool feedback improves novice programmers' learning. In *International Computing Education Research Workshop (ICER)* (pp. 109–116). New York: ACM.

Lee, M. J., & Ko, A. J. (2012). Investigating the role of purposeful goals on novices' engagement in a programming game. In *IEEE Symposium on Visual Languages and Human-Centric Computing (VL/HCC)* (pp. 163–166). New York: IEEE.

Lee, M. J., Ko, A. J., & Kwan, I. (2013). In-game assessments increase novice programmers' engagement and level completion speed. In *Proceedings of the Ninth Annual International ACM Conference on International Computing Education Research* (pp. 153–160). New York: ACM.

Lee, M. J., & Ko, A. J. (2015). Comparing the effectiveness of online learning approaches on CS1 learning outcomes. In *Proceedings of the Eleventh Annual International Conference on International Computing Education Research* (pp. 237–246). New York: ACM.

Lehtonen, T., Aho, T., Isohanni, E., & Mikkonen, T. (2015). On the role of gamification and localization in an open online learning environment: Javala experiences. In *Proceedings of the 15th Koli Calling Conference on Computing Education Research (Koli Calling '15)* (pp. 50–59). New York: ACM.

Loksa, D., Ko, A. J., Jernigan, W., Oleson, A., Mendez, C. J., & Burnett, M. M. (2016). Programming, problem solving, and self-awareness: Effects of explicit guidance. In *Proceedings of the 2016 CHI Conference on Human Factors in Computing Systems (CHI '16)* (pp. 1449–1461). New York: ACM.

Malan, D. J. (2009). Virtualizing office hours in CS 50. In *Proceedings of the 14th annual ACM SIGCSE Conference on Innovation and Technology in Computer Science Education (ITiCSE '09)* (pp. 303–307). New York: ACM.

Mamykina, L., Manoim, B., Mittal, M., Hripcsak, G., & Hartmann, B. (2011). Design lessons from the fastest Q&A site in the west. In *Proceedings of the SIGCHI Conference on Human Factors in Computing Systems* (pp. 2857–2866). New York: ACM.

Marsick, V. J., & Watkins, K. E. (2001). Informal and incidental learning. *New Directions for Adult and Continuing Education*, 2001(89), 25–34.

Marsick, V. J., & Volpe, M. (1999). The nature of and need for informal learning. In V. J. Marsick & M. Volpe (Eds.), *Informal Learning on the Job, Advances in*

Developing Human Resources, No. 3 (pp. 1–9). San Francisco, CA: Berrett Koehler.

McCartney, R., Eckerdal, A., Moström, J. E., Sanders, K., Thomas, L., & Zander, C. (2010). Computing students learning computing informally. In *Proceedings of the 10th Koli Calling International Conference on Computing Education Research (Koli Calling '10)* (pp. 43–48). New York: ACM.

McGill, M. M., Decker, A., & Settle, A. (2015). Does outreach impact choices of major for underrepresented undergraduate students? In *Proceedings of the Eleventh Annual International Conference on International Computing Education Research (ICER '15)* (pp. 71–80). New York: ACM.

Menard, S. A. W. (1993). *Critical Learning Incidents of Female Army Nurse Vietnam Veterans and Their Perceptions of Organizational Culture in a Combat Area. (Women Vetersans, Nurses)* (PhD dissertation). University of Texas, Austin.

Miljanovic, M. A., & Bradbury, J. S. (2017). RoboBUG: A serious game for learning debugging techniques. In *Proceedings of the 2017 ACM Conference on International Computing Education Research (ICER '17)* (pp. 93–100). New York: ACM.

Mitchell, S. M., & Lutters, W. G. (2006). Assessing the value of computer science course material repositories. In *Proceedings of the 19th Conference on Software Engineering Education and Training Workshops (CSEETW '06)* (p. 2). New York: IEEE.

Moraveji, N., Morris, M., Morris, D., Czerwinski, M., & Riche, N. H. (2011). ClassSearch: Facilitating the development of web search skills through social learning. In *Proceedings of the SIGCHI Conference on Human Factors in Computing Systems (CHI '11)* (pp. 1797–1806). New York: ACM.

Nandi, A., & Mandernach, M. (2016). Hackathons as an informal learning platform. In *Proceedings of the 47th ACM Technical Symposium on Computing Science Education (SIGCSE '16)* (pp. 346–351). New York: ACM.

Nelson, G. L., Xie, B., & Ko, A. J. (2017). Comprehension first: Evaluating a novel pedagogy and tutoring system for program tracing in CS1. In *Proceedings of the 2017 ACM Conference on International Computing Education Research* (pp. 2–11). New York: ACM.

Papert, S. (1980). *Mindstorms: Children, Computers, and Powerful Ideas.* New York: Basic Books, Inc.

Park, T. H., & Wiedenbeck, S. (2011). Learning web development: Challenges at an earlier stage of computing education. In *Proceedings of the Seventh International Workshop on Computing Education Research (ICER '11)* (pp. 125–132). New York: ACM.

Pullen, J. M. (2006). Scaling up a distance education program in computer science. In *Proceedings of the 11th Annual SIGCSE Conference on Innovation and Technology in Computer Science Education (ITICSE '06)* (pp. 33–37). New York: ACM.

Resnick, M., Maloney, J., Monroy-Hernández, A., Rusk, N., Eastmond, E., Brennan, K., Milner, A., Rosenbaum, E., Silver, J., Silverman, B., & Kafai, Y. (2009). Scratch: programming for all. *Communications of the ACM*, 52(11), 60–67.

Rosbottom, J. (2001). Hybrid learning – A safe route into web-based open and distance learning for the computer science teacher. In *Proceedings of the 6th Annual Conference on Innovation and Technology in Computer Science Education (ITiCSE '01)* (pp. 89–92). New York: ACM.

Sadowski, C., Stolee, K. T., & Elbaum, S. (2015). How developers search for code: a case study. In *Proceedings of the 2015 10th Joint Meeting on Foundations of Software Engineering (ESEC/FSE 2015)* (pp. 191–201). New York: ACM.

Schlager, M. S., & Fusco, J. (2003). Teacher professional development, technology, and communities of practice: Are we putting the cart before the horse? *The Information Society*, 19(3), 203–220.

Siemens, G. (2005). Connectivism: A learning theory for the digital age. *International Journal of Instructional Technology and Distance Learning*, 2(1), 3–10.

Sirkiä, T., & Sorva, J. (2015). How do students use program visualizations within an interactive ebook? In *Proceedings of the Eleventh Annual International Conference on International Computing Education Research (ICER '15)* (pp. 179–188). New York: ACM.

Stone, J. A., & Madigan, E. (2011). Experiences with community-based projects for computing majors. *Journal of Computing Sciences in Colleges*, 26(6), 64–70.

Stone, J. A., MacKellar, B., Madigan, E. M., & Pearce, J. L. (2012). Community-based projects for computing majors: opportunities, challenges and best practices. In *Proceedings of the 43rd ACM Technical Symposium on Computer Science Education (SIGCSE '12)* (pp. 85–86). New York: ACM.

Tillmann, N., De Halleux, J., Xie, T., & Bishop, J. (2012). Pex4Fun: Teaching and learning computer science via social gaming. In *Proceedings of the 2012 IEEE 25th Conference on Software Engineering Education and Training (CSEET '12)* (pp. 90–91). Washington, DC: IEEE Computer Society.

Truong, N., Bancroft, P., & Roe, P. (2005). Learning to program through the web. In *Proceedings of the 10th Annual SIGCSE Conference on Innovation and Technology in Computer Science Education (ITiCSE '05)* (pp. 9–13). New York: ACM.

Venkatagiri, S. (2006). Engineering the software requirements of nonprofits: A service-learning approach. In *Proceedings of the 28th International Conference on Software engineering (ICSE '06)* (pp. 643–648). New York: ACM.

von Wright, J. (2000). Distance tutorials in a systems design course. In *Proceedings of the 5th Annual SIGCSE/SIGCUE ITiCSE Conference on Innovation and Technology in Computer Science Education (ITiCSE '00)* (pp. 105–107). New York: ACM.

Wagner, A., Gray, J., Corley, J., & Wolber, D. 2013. Using App Inventor in a K–12 summer camp. In *Proceedings of the 44th ACM Technical Symposium on Computer Science Education (SIGCSE '13)* (pp. 621–626). New York: ACM.

Warner, J., Doorenbos, J., Miller, B., & Guo, P. J. (2015). How high school, college, and online students differentially engage with an interactive digital textbook. In *Proceedings of the 8th International Conference on Educational Data Mining* (pp. 528–531). International: International Educational Data Mining Society.

Warner, J., & Guo, P. J. (2017). Hack.edu: Examining how college hackathons are perceived by student attendees and non-attendees. In *Proceedings of the 2017 ACM Conference on International Computing Education Research (ICER '17)* (pp. 254–262). New York: ACM.

Warren, J., Rixner, S., Greiner, J., & Wong, S. (2014). Facilitating human interaction in an online programming course. In *Proceedings of the 45th ACM Technical Symposium on Computer Science Education (SIGCSE '14)* (pp. 665–670). New York: ACM.

Webb, H. C., & Rosson, M. B. (2011). Exploring careers while learning Alice 3D: A summer camp for middle school girls. In *Proceedings of the 42nd ACM Technical*

Symposium on Computer Science Education (SIGCSE '11) (pp. 377–382). New York: ACM.

Zander, C., Boustedt, J., Eckerdal, A., McCartney, R., Sanders, K., Moström, J. E., & Thomas, L. (2012). Self-directed learning: Stories from industry. In *Proceedings of the 12th Koli Calling International Conference on Computing Education Research (Koli Calling '12)* (pp. 111–117). New York: ACM.

Zheng, S., Rosson, M. B., Shih, P. C., & Carroll, J. M. (2015). Understanding student motivation, behaviors and perceptions in MOOCs. In *Proceedings of the 18th ACM Conference on Computer Supported Cooperative Work & Social Computing (CSCW '15)* (pp. 1882–1895). New York: ACM.

Zhu, J., Warner, J., Gordon, M., White, J., Zanelatto, R., & Guo, P. J. (2015). Toward a domain-specific visual discussion forum for learning computer programming: An empirical study of a popular MOOC forum. In *IEEE Symposium on Visual Languages and Human-Centric Computing (VL/HCC)* (pp. 101–109). New York: IEEE.

27 Student Knowledge and Misconceptions

Colleen M. Lewis, Michael J. Clancy,
and Jan Vahrenhold

27.1 Introduction

Students' knowledge is at the center of computing education (CEd). Research relating to this knowledge has frequently focused on the difficulties experienced by students when learning, which are often referred to as "misconceptions."

Awareness of the misconceptions commonly encountered by students has several benefits for teachers. For example, as teachers gain experience, they are believed to gain knowledge of typical student misconceptions (Sadler et al., 2013). This can partially explain improved learning outcomes for students with more experienced instructors (Ladd & Sorensen, 2017). Moreover, understanding these potential difficulties can help counteract our "expert blindspot" (Guzdial, 2015; Nathan & Petrosino, 2003) where, as relative experts in the domain, we have difficulty anticipating the difficulties that will be experienced by novices.

There is a considerable body of literature on misconceptions in computing. A book chapter (Clancy, 2004) enumerated patterns of misconceptions in computer science (CS). A current summary and review of misconceptions research within introductory CS was published in 2017 by Qian and Lehman. Section 27.2 reviews the literature in order to demonstrate that documentation of misconceptions in computing extends beyond introductory topics.

There has been, however, some controversy in this area. For example, research on misconceptions has been critiqued as being preoccupied with what students cannot do rather than what students can do or can learn to do (Smith et al., 1993). A research paradigm referred to as "expert-novice" research catalogs the ways in which novices demonstrate different knowledge and skills from experts (Bransford et al., 1999). For example, a popular finding from expert-novice research in physics education is that experts classify physics mechanics problems based upon the physics principle that could be used to solve them; perhaps unsurprisingly, novices do not do this (Chi et al., 1981). Instead, they attempt to classify problems using features of the problem, such as grouping all problems that involve an inclined plane. While the characterization of the skills of experts may be helpful in establishing learning goals, simply cataloging the fact that novices do not yet have this expertise can be done in ways that are not illuminating and are dismissive of students. Instead, students' prior knowledge can be seen as a resource for learning, which might enable more effective pedagogy.

We are sympathetic to the argument that misconceptions research may point out trivial differences between experts and novices and may distract from the goal of helping students learn. Despite that, our experience as educators speaks to the value of accumulating an understanding of where students have difficulty. Rather than pointing out deficiencies in students, we can see this research as helping educators recognize their likely weaknesses caused by the expert blindspot (Guzdial, 2015; Nathan & Petrosino, 2003) in not anticipating and understanding students' learning difficulties.

Beyond identifying *what* students have difficulty with, in this chapter, we hope to be able to provide perspectives from outside of science, technology, engineering, and mathematics (STEM) about *why* students experience particular types of difficulties. These perspectives on the difficulties of learning computing are essentially hypotheses based upon education research outside of CEd. In many cases, we also draw on CEd research (CEdR) to affirm these connections. Other chapters provide a more comprehensive review of the cognitive science literature (see Chapter 9). Here, we have selected literature that we believe provides a particular perspective that is helpful for considering students' knowledge and misconceptions. These perspectives are not exhaustive and are overlapping in many cases.

For researchers, we hope that this chapter charts potential directions for future research that connects CEdR with education research outside of computing. For educators, we hope that this chapter provides resources for understanding students' difficulties and that this may ultimately help them improve their teaching practice.

27.2 (Some) Misconceptions in CS

Qian and Lehmann (2017) provided an extensive literature review on programming-related misconceptions encompassing more than three decades of research. However, their scope did not extend beyond introductory programming classes. In this section, we highlight selected research results to illustrate the breadth of topics covered in computing misconceptions research. In our choice of papers discussed, we also aimed at presenting results that are representative of issues instructors may face in class. Given that some of the results presented are very recent at the time of this writing, not all observations have led to documented interventions yet; instead, they should be considered as the basis for additional research projects.

27.2.1 Theory of Computation: Reduction

Gal-Ezer and Trakhtenbrot (2016) report on a five-year exploratory study involving the written work of roughly 650 students from offerings of a theory of computation class. The focus of this study was on misconceptions related to reductions, an abstraction technique that transforms ("reduces") any input for some type of problem into an input for another, sometimes seemingly unrelated type of problem. The goal of such a reduction is usually to show that complexity bounds carry over from one problem to the other. The best-known use of reductions is to establish that any input to one problem that is known to be undecidable or NP-complete can be transformed in time polynomial in the input size to an input to another problem. In such a case, the transformation establishes the undecidability or, if the second problem is in NP as well, NP-completeness of the second problem.

Through their analysis, the authors identified misconceptions related to a "bigger is harder" mental model. Students were found to assume that any problem from a class included in a larger class of problems was reducible to any problem from that larger class. In particular, a corollary of this general misconception was that every problem A in the complexity class P should be polynomially reducible to every problem B in the complexity class NP (which contains P). Variations of this general misconception were that the mapping reduction from a decidable (or recursively enumerable) set A to a set B would be possible if and only if A was a subset of B ("B is bigger than A") or, since the class of enumerable problems contains the class of decidable problems, that any decidable problem C could be reduced to any enumerable problem D.

The authors conjecture that the effect of the "bigger is harder" mental model is strengthened by the typographically similar notations for inclusion and reduction. They suggest to actively address these issues by first presenting a "proof" based upon one of the misconceptions and then discussing its shortcomings using both intuitive and formal lines of reasoning followed by a correct proof or a proof that the sought reduction does not hold.

27.2.2 Algorithms and Data Structures: Heapsort

Danielsiek et al. (2012) investigated misconceptions related to algorithms and data structures by analyzing 400 written exams from offerings of a first-year CS course. Here, we focus on a heapsort test item (given a set of elements, sort it using the heapsort algorithm and show the steps), an item for which both the attempt rate and the average score were lowest across the exams for an introductory course taught by a third party. This was despite the fact that heapsort was discussed in class and was covered in programming assignments. Forty percent of the students did not attempt to solve the heapsort test item. In addition, the average score awarded for completed items was 43 percent.

Several written exams showed margin notes in which students had transformed the input given for the test item (an array of numbers) into a tree structure. From these notes, the authors could observe the following two points: (1) several students had transformed the input into a binary search tree and then (unsuccessfully) tried to run the heapsort algorithm on this structure; and (2) several students appeared to use a (correct) tree-based representation and then inferred the result for the array-based representation. Issues like the ones discussed in the work of Seppälä et al. (2006) (e.g., not executing recursive calls or including spurious swaps) could not be observed.

The authors established and tested hypotheses during weekly recital sessions and conducted think-aloud interviews to follow up on the above observations. The analysis suggested that students might have problems with associating the array-based implementation of a heap (usually discussed in the context of the heapsort algorithm) with the pointer-based tree model (usually discussed when introducing heaps). A closer look at the syllabus showed that the heapsort algorithm was taught in the first part of the course, which focused on algorithms. The heap data structure was taught in the second part of the course, which was immediately after binary search trees were discussed in class. Interestingly, not every student was comfortable with the tree-based heap representation. In a study with 155 students who were given both representations, 20 percent of the students could work with a tree-based representation but not with an array-based representation, whereas 14 percent could work with an array-based representation but not with a tree-based representation; 34 percent of the students could work well with either representation and the remaining 30 percent had problems with both representations.

In a follow-up study (Vahrenhold & Paul, 2014), the authors taught these topics in a different order: binary search trees were taught before heaps or heapsort. Afterwards the focus was on graph algorithms, which raised the need for an efficient implementation of the abstract data type PriorityQueue. For this, heaps were introduced and heapsort was presented as an example of a data structure-based sorting algorithm. On the exam, students were asked to show the intermediate steps on the array- and tree-based representations for the heap construction phase and two iterations of heapsort, working in parallel with both representations. The number of non-attempts dropped to 27 percent and the average score increased to 61 percent. While this change may have been due to other instructional effects as well (demographics were comparable), a follow-up study by Karpierz and Wolfman (2014) in which the topic order also avoided the problematic sequence was also unable to reproduce the misconceptions seen in Danielsiek et al. (2012).

27.2.3 Programming Languages: Scope, Mutation, and Aliasing

With a focus on upper-division programming language courses, Fisler et al. (2017) targeted misconceptions in the areas of scope, mutation, and aliasing in Java and Scheme; these languages have identical semantics with respect to the focus of the study, despite very different syntax and surface-level concepts. Working with two languages was one key feature of the research. Their intent was not only to determine whether students understood those topics, but also to see if advanced students transferred knowledge between languages.

The authors used three instruments. Two were multiple-choice: a pre-test at the start of the course and a post-test after scope, mutation, and parameter passing had been covered. Each contained 12 Scheme-based items and 6 Java-based items. The third instrument, which makes this study stand out from other work, consisted of several activities intended to enrich students' understanding of the topics; these activities included implementing a problematic language feature, writing a test suite, peer reviewing each other's test suite, and answering clicker questions during the lectures.

Preliminary results indicate that the students (n = 66) did poorly on the pre-test and much better on the post-test. Most of the improvement was in Scheme rather than Java, and improvements were not uniform across topics. Though the results were not rich enough to determine the effects of the instructional activities on learning, this work, and in particular the instruments used, is likely to provide a solid basis for future research.

27.2.4 Operating Systems: Indirections

Webb and Taylor (2014) report on their first steps toward developing a *concept inventory* to test operating systems concepts. A concept inventory is an instrument that belongs to the class of so-called formative assessments of instruction (Adams & Wieman, 2011). It consists of multiple-choice questions in which the incorrect answers ("distractors") are designed to indicate a particular form of students' misunderstanding. For more detail on the design process of such questions, see Adams and Wieman (2011) and Almstrum et al. (2006).

The paper by Webb and Taylor explores the following three operating systems concepts: indirection, input/output, and synchronization. Here, we focus on their discussion of indirection in a file system block map. During class, the authors asked a peer instruction question focused on the space requirements given either direct or indirect pointers. Forty-four percent of the students' initial, individual answers were correct. However, after students discussed the question in their groups, only 39 percent of the students' answers were correct. This drop, which is in contrast with general results regarding the effects of peer group discussions on performance, suggests that students have an incorrect but intuitive idea that is competing with the correct reasoning. The authors argue that indirection is difficult for students because "systems often use indirection as an optimization as opposed to it being necessary for correctness … We believe that the challenge of indirection may stem from the fact that a solution using only direct pointers seems to be attractive to students because it would be relatively straightforward" (Webb & Taylor, 2014, p. 106).

They also examined two indirection-related questions on the final exam. One of the questions presented a scenario in which students were asked to determine the numerical properties of a hypothetical page table and then explain (as free-response text) whether or not they would recommend using multiple levels of page tables (indirection) in this scenario. The second question presented a similar hypothetical scenario of a file system block map and eventually asked students to justify the complexity of using indirect pointers. Unsurprisingly, students performed better on the second question, where they were implicitly told that the complexity was useful, as opposed to the former, in which students had to make that decision themselves. This further supports their hypothesis that students' difficulty comes from students' preference for the more straightforward implementation and that "students are more than capable of memorizing the details" (Webb & Taylor, 2014, p. 103).

To summarize, indirection is a difficult concept, and this difficulty may come from a lack of motivation for indirection rather than just a lack of understanding of the details. The authors suggest that students who are learning these concepts may benefit from instructors initially introducing an abstract form of indirection, perhaps by relating it to C memory pointers, which students are likely to find familiar. Discussing indirection abstractly by mapping it to a more comfortable topic may enable students to construct a mental model of indirection prior to adding the confounding details of memory management or file systems.

27.3 Perspectives from Outside CEd and How They Relate to CEd

There is a long history of education literature outside of CEdR, but often few connections are made across disciplines (Confrey, 1990). In the following sections, we seek to highlight particular strands of education research outside of CEdR and how they might apply within computing. When feasible, we summarize CEdR that we believe exemplifies this connection. While this is not an exhaustive list of potential connections outside of CEdR, we seek to encourage the development of additional connections and expect that some of the connections we describe could fuel promising future work in CEdR.

27.3.1 The Role of Intuition in Learning

Conceptual change research outside of CEd often focuses on the role of students' intuitions, particularly the ways in which these intuitions lead to misconceptions (see diSessa, 2014a, for a review). Similarly, CEd has focused on how students' interactions with programming languages are shaped by their experience conversing with a human (Pea, 1986). In both cases, understanding the ways in which students' intuitions lead them astray is seen as essential to effective teaching.

27.3.1.1 Evidence from Outside of Computing

Conceptual change involves understanding learning and has been particularly focused on exploring students' understanding of school-taught scientific content. Generally, conceptual change research rejects the idea that humans begin as a blank slate, and researchers wrestle with the complexity of learning as it is shaped by instruction and students' existing knowledge (Sawyer, 2014). Of particular focus is students' intuitions about particular scientific phenomena. For example, in their study of conceptual change in childhood, Vosniadou and Brewer (1992) found that in learning about the shape of the earth, some students came to believe that the earth was the shape of a pancake, both round and flat. Their study revealed that changing from an initial model of the earth based upon everyday experiences, such as walking on a seemingly flat surface, to the scientifically accepted model of a spherical earth "is slow and gradual" (Vosniadou & Brewer, 1992, p. 582).

As we discussed in the introduction, misconceptions research has been critiqued for focusing only on how prior knowledge fuels intuitions that inhibit learning processes (Smith, diSessa, & Roschelle, 1993). While anticipating students' misconceptions can be pedagogically valuable, an exclusive focus on the negative role played by prior knowledge misses an opportunity to identify the productive role that prior knowledge can play. This is an important critique to keep in mind when producing and reading research about students' understanding or lack thereof.

27.3.1.2 Connections to CS: Observations and Hypotheses

Previous research in CEd has focused on the role of prior knowledge in shaping students' intuitions. For example, CEdR has identified ways in which students' prior knowledge from math and English interfere with their understanding of particular programming constructs (Clancy, 2004). A common example of a misconception in computing that is tied to intuition is the intuition that the computer "knows" more than it does (Pea, 1986). This was originally referred to as a "superbug": "The superbug may be described as an idea that there is a *hidden mind* somewhere in the programming language that has intelligent, interpretive powers" (Pea, 1986, pp. 32–33, emphasis in original). Understanding students' intuitions is practically important for educators who could benefit from anticipating the difficulties students may experience. Pea's early claim is still true: "mapping conventions for natural language instructions onto programming results in error-ridden performances" (Pea, 1986, p. 33).

However, given that computer systems are designed by humans, students' intuitions can be seen as wrong only insofar as the designers of the system did not select the particular behavior that a student expects. For example, students sometimes incorrectly expect that a while loop will exit once the condition stops being met (Bonar & Soloway, 1989; Spohrer & Soloway, 1986). This is incorrect because the condition is only checked before beginning the loop body. However, it would be feasible for a loop to be designed such that the condition is checked after every expression in the loop body, which then would align with students' intuitions. That is, the relevance of students' intuitions is dependent on the programming language.

Understanding students' intuitions is incredibly important, but caution is needed because these intuitions may be incorrect for one programming language and correct for another. Because humans have designed these systems, there may be fewer truly counterintuitive things for students to learn in CS. Because of this, students' incorrect intuitions in computing may respond to instruction differently than intuitions about phenomena not within the complete control of humans.

27.3.2 Chunking

In CEd, we frequently want students to abstract from individual keywords or lines of code to understand the steps in an algorithm. This type of abstraction relates to the idea of chunking (Miller, 1956). The ability to chunk information is a well-established difference between experts and novices in a domain (Bransford et al., 1999). While Chapter 9 provides additional elaboration on chunking (Miller, 1956) and other information regarding working memory (Baddeley & Hitch, 1974), here we focus on the high-level overview so as to connect it to research in education and CEd.

27.3.2.1 Evidence from Outside of Computing

The idea of working memory (Baddeley & Hitch, 1974) gives rise to the common – and likely familiar – idea that people can typically remember seven things, or seven things plus or minus two. The idea of chunking is that, while working memory is finite (Baddeley & Hitch, 1974), the things that are stored in working memory can be "chunks" with a high density of information. This idea of chunking explains the otherwise perplexing result that people can remember approximately seven things, regardless of whether those things were numbers, letters, or monosyllabic words (Miller, 1956). As further elaboration, Miller (1956, p. 15) describes a study where researcher Sydney Smith was able to recall a sequence of 40 binary digits, far greater than the previously reported average of 9 (Pollack, 1953). Smith did this by converting sequences of binary digits into decimal digits, requiring extensive practice to automate this process. While this example related to binary digits might be the most relevant for CEd researchers, the canonical example of chunking comes from studies of chess players (Chase & Simon, 1973). Expert chess players were able to recall the locations of chess pieces with fewer errors than novice chess players. However, for chess board configurations that were not typical of chess game play, expert chess players were no better at recalling the locations of pieces. This is described as *domain-specific* chunking; the expert chess players had chunks to recall particular components of game board configurations. Contrary to conventional wisdom, the expert chess players did not have a greater ability to recall information, only a greater ability to recall particular domain-specific chunks (Bransford et al., 1999).

Chunking has been applied to understanding learning across domains (Baxter & Glaser, 1998; Gobet et al., 2001). For example, how humans process collections of letters into words can be explained as chunking (Gobet et al., 2001). Lane et al. (2000) also used chunking to explain how physics students construct diagrams of electric circuits. The idea of chunking appears to be broadly applicable to understanding learning and problem-solving (Gobet et al., 2001).

27.3.2.2 Connections to CS: Observations and Hypotheses

Ideas about chunking have also appeared within CEdR. Winslow summarizes that there is a "large number of studies concluding that novice programmers know the syntax and semantics of individual statements but they do not know how to combine these features into valid programs" (Winslow, 1996, p. 17). Robins et al. connect this idea to chunking and summarize Winslow as making the claim that novices "approach programming 'line by line' rather than using meaningful program 'chunks' or structures" (Robins et al., 2003, p. 140).

There are multiple examples from computing where educators attempt to make these chunks a learning goal in and of themselves. For example, Sajaniemi and Kuittinen (2005) argue for teaching students about the different roles that variables play in introductory programming tasks. They argue that just ten different roles account for 99 percent of all uses of variables in introductory programming instruction. Educators also use "Parsons' problems" (Denny et al., 2008; Parsons & Haden, 2006) that require students to order and indent complete lines of code to accomplish a particular goal. In providing these complete lines, they attempt to direct student attention to semantics rather than the details of the syntax. At a larger grain size, Gamma et al. (1995) published a set of 23 design patterns for software engineering, which has been used in helping students recognize and apply these larger patterns to solving problems.

A possible reason for teaching Big-O in introductory courses is that it forces the 10,000-foot view that is characteristic of chunking. Rather than seeing a for-loop as a sequence of steps, it can be seen as a more general pattern of repeating something a certain number of times. Similarly, a line of research has found correlations between students' ability to write code and to explain code "in plain English" (Murphy et al., 2012). This may be another example of domain-specific chunking that enables both improved coding performance and improved explanations of code.

27.3.3 Examining Cases

Introductory programming frequently begins with introducing basic operations such as conditionals (Rich et al., 2017). However, there are some long-documented weaknesses that humans demonstrate when reasoning about conditionals. This non-computing research appears to be consistent with CEdR of students' writing or evaluating Boolean expressions (Herman et al., 2012). From these findings we argue that providing a meaningful context for reasoning about conditionals promotes success. Additionally, people are prone to not enumerating all of the relevant cases, and they are much more successful at tasks when they are encouraged to enumerate and consider all of the relevant cases.

27.3.3.1 Evidence from Outside of Computing

Wason (1968) developed a test of human reasoning, referred to as the Wason selection task, which spurred an areas of research into people's reasoning about

Table 27.1 *Truth table for modus ponens, P → Q.*

Configuration	P (has an A on one side)	Q (has a 3 on one side)	P → Q
1	T	T	T
2	T	F	F
3	F	T	T
4	F	F	T

conditional logic. In an original version of the selection task, a person is told that each of four cards in front of them has a letter on one side and a number on the other side. Then the person is asked to determine which of the cards should be flipped to check if an additional rule is violated. For example, consider four cards showing, A, D, 3, and 7 and the rule: "If there is an A on one side of the card, then there is a 3 on the other side of the card." (Wason, 1968). We can think of this rule as using the general modus ponens form $P \rightarrow Q$. That is, P (has an A on one side) implies Q (has a 3 on one side). Based upon this abstraction, the cards can be labeled as P (the A), ¬P (the D), Q (the 3), and ¬Q (the 7), as shown in the truth table in Table 27.1.

To check if the rule is violated by any of the cards, it is necessary to flip over the A and the 7. While this is likely not necessary for most readers, the following bullets explain the logic for each possibility (P, ¬P, Q, ¬Q).

- P (the A): Most people recognize that you need to flip over the A to ensure that there is a 3 on the other side. That is, it is necessary to distinguish between configurations 1 and 2 of the truth table in Table 27.1.
- ¬P (the D): It is not necessary to flip over the D because there are no rules related to letters other than A, and we know that the other side does not have an A, because we were guaranteed that every card has a letter on one side and a number on the other. That is, it is not necessary to distinguish between configurations 3 and 4 of the truth table in Table 27.1.
- Q (the 3): It is not necessary to flip over the 3 because regardless of the other side, it cannot violate the rule. That is, it is not necessary to distinguish between configurations 1 and 3 of the truth table in Table 27.1.
- ¬Q (the 7): Many people do not recognize that it is necessary to flip the 7 because having an A on the other side would violate the rule. That is, it is necessary to distinguish between configurations 2 and 4 of the truth table in Table 27.1.

Many variations of this task exist, and performance can vary greatly on the task when it is worded in different ways. The resulting body of research generally seeks to develop hypotheses about the cognitive mechanisms that explain this variation in task performance. This is an ongoing debate (von Sydow, 2006), but at this time we can abstract away three central points of relevance to computing teaching and learning.

First, this poor performance on the Wason selection task does not appear to be caused by a lack of understanding of the logical operator. In the original work (Wason, 1968), when people were asked to consider each card independently, they were generally able to do so. Additionally, O'Brien et al. (1998) showed that three- and four-year-olds were able to evaluate if a rule such as "If a boy is playing basketball, he is wearing red sneakers" was violated in pictures representing each of the configurations of the modus ponens truth table.

Second, changes in the context of the rule and instructions for the person can change average task performance significantly (Wason & Johnson-Laird, 1972). For example, people are more successful when asked which cards they should flip to determine if people are violating drinking age restrictions. Imagine cards that show a person's age on one side and whether they are drinking soda or alcohol on the other side. Consider the rule, "If someone is under 18, they cannot drink alcohol," and the following cards: P [age = 10], ¬P [age = 30], Q [drinking water], and ¬Q [drinking alcohol]. In this case, people tend to find it more intuitive to flip the cards with the person who is not old enough to drink alcohol and the card with the person who is drinking alcohol. Placing the problem in a more familiar context appears to improve task performance, as does, when appropriate, asking the person to assume the role of a checking authority (O'Brien et al., 2004, p. 101).

From the research described above, we should expect that students will make mistakes when reasoning about logical operators. As stated above, this is true even when they can demonstrate evidence of understanding the logical operator in other contexts.

27.3.3.2 Connections to Computing: Observations and Hypotheses

Consistent with the findings above, Herman et al. (2012) found that students often failed to enumerate or consider all of the cases when writing or evaluating Boolean expressions. However, when students were asked to enumerate all of the cases, they were able to correctly solve the problems. Herman et al. (2012) observed that there are many Boolean operators that are equivalent for a subset of the cases (see Table 27.2, gray cells). They found that students tended to substitute for the "easier" operator in the cases where the cases that they enumerated matched the "easier" operator. Table 27.2 shows some of the overlap between the operators AND, if-then, and if-and-only-if. It appears that when students work with less familiar Boolean operators, they fall back onto using familiar ones such as AND.

Herman et al. (2012) also found that students perform worst when they are answering the question in an unfamiliar context and best if it is a familiar context.

We hypothesize that this may help us understand why human-readable variable names are seen as important. Familiar context may make people more effective at reasoning, as was demonstrated in people's improved performance when enforcing drinking restrictions (O'Brien et al., 2004). Ultimately, human-readable variable names may help connect the code with the domain of the problem that they are trying to solve.

Table 27.2 *Overlap between logical operators AND, if-then, and if-and-only-if.*

A	B	AND	if-then	if-and-only-if
0	0	0	1	1
0	1	0	1	0
1	0	0	0	0
1	1	1	1	1

Additionally, we hypothesize that this may help us understand the importance of *test-driven development* (Beck, 2003). In test-driven development, programmers write test cases *before* writing the code. This allows them to focus on the behavior that is expected from the code and may support individuals in considering all of the relevant cases, which, as we see from the research above, frequently requires scaffolding.

27.3.4 Learning to Reason with Abstraction Symbols

Abstraction is frequently mentioned as a core skill developed when learning programming (Ginat & Blau, 2017). This is similar to the ways in which the learning of algebra is described (Sfard, 1995). Research about practices for helping students adapt to the abstraction involved in algebra may be helpful for identifying pedagogical strategies that could be applicable to CS. In particular, here we will focus on a sequence of instruction called concrete-to-representational-to-abstract, or CRA (Witzel et al., 2008), which we argue might be applicable to computing instruction.

27.3.4.1 Evidence from Outside of Computing

To introduce the basics of CRA we will use the example of a classroom where young students are learning addition. CRA begins by introducing a physical (i.e., *concrete*) object. For example, this could be physical blocks that could be counted to add them together. Once students are comfortable adding together sets of physical blocks, the class could advance to solving the same problems given only a picture (i.e., *representation*) of the blocks, but not the physical blocks. Once students are comfortable using only the pictures, the class could advance to solving the same problems using only numbers (i.e., *abstraction*). If a student has trouble adding together only numbers (i.e., working at the abstract level), they could be encouraged to draw pictures (i.e., returning to the representation level). If a student has trouble adding together numbers using a drawing, they could be encouraged to work with the physical blocks (i.e., returning to the concrete level).

As shown in this example, the concrete, representational, and abstract forms of the problem can be used to "promote overall conceptual understanding and procedural accuracy and fluency" (Witzel et al., 2008, p. 271). Witzel et al. (2008, pp. 271–272) argue that CRA instructional sequences provide the following benefits:

- Providing a connection between abstract content and students' understanding of the steps and definitions used in the concrete version;
- Making the content more memorable, which aids memory;
- Increasing engagement, which can increase students' enjoyment;
- Making the content relevant and personal;
- Enabling students to draw a picture of a concrete object rather than requiring them to manipulate that object directly.

While this particular sequence for teaching addition is likely pervasive across elementary school classrooms, the more general CRA sequence of instruction has been formalized and researched within special education. In their article, "A Meta-Analysis of Algebra Interventions for Learners with Disabilities and Struggling Learners," Hughes et al. (2014) found that the "concrete-representational–abstract sequence had the largest effect sizes" (Hughes et al., 2014, p. 36). Similar results exist within the broad mathematics education literature. Within mathematics education, the use of concrete objects is referred to as "manipulatives" because the student can interact directly with the concrete object. In a meta-analysis of 55 studies of mathematics instruction, there were small to moderate effect sizes "in favor of the use of manipulatives when compared with instruction that only used abstract math symbols" (Carbonneau et al., 2013, p. 380). Also from mathematics education, an earlier meta-analysis had found:

> The use of manipulative devices and drawings also emerged as an effective practice for teaching both computation and word problems. Manipulative devices with and without subsequent drawings were effective. Findings related to the use of drawings without manipulative devices, however, were mixed. (Miller et al., 1998, p. 21)

Despite the positive results referenced above, applying CRA and related pedagogies can be complex. While the meta-analyses show results that tend to be positive, studies comparing math instruction with and without manipulatives have shown null results, positive results, and negative results (Carbonneau et al., 2013, pp. 380–381). Witzel et al. (2008) provide practical advice for teachers who are designing CRA sequences within their math classrooms, which may be of practical value in CEd. They explain that "[w]ithout explicit awareness of how each stage connects with the next interconnected stage, the students may feel as though they are memorizing separate and arbitrary procedures to solve the same mathematical skill" (Witzel et al., 2008, p. 271).

27.3.4.2 Connections to CS: Observations and Hypotheses

Practices of demonstrating concrete instantiations of programming concepts may be much less common than concrete instantiations of mathematical concepts. Unlike the example of adding blocks, in CS, there are infrequently obvious real-world mappings for the abstractions. However, a few examples of common pedagogy in computing bear hallmarks of aligning with the CRA instructional sequence (Pollard & Duvall, 2006). For example, many instructors introduce a variable by showing it as a cup (i.e., the variable) that can hold a particular value or introduce an array of integers by showing a line of objects that each has a number written on it.

An experience from the first author further aligns with the findings described above. She had been struggling to teach students common summations such as $1 + 2 + 4 + \cdots + N / 2 + N$, and $1 + 2 + 3 + \cdots + N - 1 + N$. She had developed visual representations to try to help students build on their understanding of measurement and area, respectively. However, students were frequently unable to recalculate the sums. In the past year, she bought blocks like those that might be used in an elementary school classroom. These blocks could connect together, and she created a set of blocks for each of the terms in the sums. Then, under a document camera, she showed how they could be combined to add up to $2N - 1$ and $N(N + 1) / 2$, respectively. Only then did she show a representation of the same information in a slide. Through the remaining classes, the students appeared to be more capable of recreating the sums for the two sequences described above.

The use of concrete manipulatives as a bridge toward more abstract reasoning seems to be a promising direction for CEd. However, the mix of results as described above (Carbonneau et al., 2013) show some of the complexity of the pedagogical sequence. In particular, the focus on concrete manipulatives should not be mistaken for advocacy of learning styles (Willingham et al., 2015). Some might incorrectly argue that kinesthetic students need opportunities to physically move in order to be able to learn the content. Learning styles research that would make this incorrect claim has been debunked and rejected by the education community (Willingham et al., 2015). Instead, learning should be kinesthetic if the learning goal is kinesthetic. For example, you would teach a child to tie their shoelaces by having them practice the kinesthetic act of tying their shoelaces. If a concept can be practiced using multiple modalities, that additional exposure can be helpful, but the central principle is connecting the content to appropriate modalities and not matching modalities to students' learning styles (Willingham et al., 2015).

27.3.5 Learning Rule-Based Systems

Across domains, education often seeks to help people understand and apply rule systems. For example, when learning algorithms for arithmetic, students learn a set of rules and apply those rules to solve problems. There is a body of work looking at students' "bugs" in learning and applying these algorithms (Young & O'Shea, 1981). We can see connections between students' learning of these algorithms and their understanding of the notional machine (see Chapter 1). Also, there are common goals across CEdR and mathematics education research of documenting and exploring mistakes or "bugs" in students' application of algorithms.

27.3.5.1 Evidence from Outside of Computing

There is a long history of research into the learning of arithmetic. By 1930, Buswell published a series of articles that reviewed 584 articles and books that "report investigations of the methods and results of teaching arithmetic" (p. 766). A common refrain across studies is that students' understanding of algorithms for arithmetic should be rooted in their conceptual understanding of numbers and place value (Chan et al., 2014). Carpenter et al. (1988) argue that "there is general consensus about how children solve different problems" (p. 387). For example, they describe progressions of students' strategies from counting to using a set of number facts to derive other answers (e.g., using $4 + 4 = 8$ to solve $4 + 5 = 9$).

Students' learning of long division might best connect with students' understanding of the notional machine. The algorithm for long division specifies a set of steps, but the actual execution of the algorithm depends upon the numbers in the problem. The algorithm for tracing code for a particular notional machine specifies the behavior of particular lines of code, but the tracing of the code depends upon the lines of code to be traced. These similarities may mean that teaching practices for long division could be helpful for teaching students to trace code. One seemingly common strategy for teaching long division is to use mnemonics to help students remember the steps (Rivera & Smith, 1988). The effectiveness of the use of mnemonics has been demonstrated outside of mathematics (Levin et al., 1992). However, clear recommendations do not appear to have developed from this body of work on teaching long division. Rivera and Smith, in describing a variety of pedagogical approaches for teaching long division, summarize that "research findings to support the efficacy of these strategies are limited" (Rivera & Smith, 1988, p. 77). Similarly, Chan et al. (2014) critique a common developmental model developed by Fuson and colleagues (see Fuson, 1998) for being "built upon informal observations of how children solved additional and subtraction problems" (p. 79) and that the "conceptual structures and developmental sequence remain untested empirically" (p. 79).

27.3.5.2 Connections to CS: Observations and Hypotheses

Understanding recursive code can be seen as an example of a rule-based system, not unlike arithmetic. In CEdR, students' understanding of recursion is a popular area in which to identify "bugs" in students' mental models. McCauley et al. (2015) surveyed over 35 research publications involving comprehension, evaluation, and construction of recursive programs across different programming languages and paradigms. The publications collectively used both quantitative and qualitative methods. Learner populations ranged from elementary school children through to university-level students. In one correct model, recursive procedures are seen to generate new instantiations of themselves, passing control and possibly data forward to successive instantiations and back from terminated ones. Kahney (1989) referred to this as a *copies* model.

An example of an incorrect model is a *looping* model (Kahney, 1989), which repeats the intended recursive code and stops the procedure when a base case is encountered, thus using it as a termination condition rather than a return condition. This may be partly due to a feature of the Logo language used in Kahney's work in which "STOP" means "return." However, the same difficulty was documented in college students more recently (Lewis, 2012).

Similarly, understanding object-oriented programming languages can be seen as an example of a rule-based system, and research has sought to document "bugs" in students' understanding and application of their knowledge. For example, Ragonis and Ben-Ari (2005) identified a total of 58 types of difficulties. They argued that these difficulties could be separated into the following four categories: "objects vs. class," "instantiation and constructors," "simple vs. composed classes," and "program flow." Roughly two-thirds of the difficulties were categorized as misconceptions, since they could be traced back to a specific misunderstanding (e.g., "an object cannot be the value of an attribute" or "attribute values are updated automatically according to a logical context").

In the light of the current interest in functional (see Section 27.4.5) and multiparadigmatic languages (e.g., Scala), we revisit early research on misconceptions related to functional programming and discuss the work of Davis et al. (1993). Consistent with our framing of the notional machine as based on a set of rules, the authors investigated *student-formed* rules in Common Lisp. They investigated the process of learning how Lisp evaluates expressions. The project extended over two semesters: the first to gather data and the second to test an intervention. In the first semester, a predicted list of incorrect rules was constructed, along with an assessment whose questions attempted to detect applications of the rules. Students' performance on the assessment was used to revise the list of incorrect rules. Each student's incorrect answers were then examined to determine what rule(s) could explain each result. In the second semester, several pre-lab activities were added to two of the lab assignments:

- Critique code and fix buggy rules;
- Invent function definitions and calls;
- Predict and explain the result or error message produced by given code.

The results revealed that the number of completely correct calls and the number of errors (incorrect rules used) on the assessment significantly improved in the intervention semester (Davis, 1995).

A more direct example of our framing of rules is a *rule-based* programming environment that has the following two components: a *knowledge* base and a set of *rules*. Each rule contains a *condition* that is checked against the knowledge base and one or more *actions*, which update the knowledge base. *Execution* of a program involves repeatedly identifying rules whose condition is true, then using the actions to update the knowledge base. Rule-based programming is popular in artificial intelligence applications, specifically *expert systems* that imitate the decision-making ability of a human expert. The Prolog language, created in 1972, is most commonly associated with the rule-based approach to programming. Prolog has been taught in introductory programming courses, mostly in Europe, since the early 1980s. It is perceived to be a difficult language to learn and use. As a result, a significant body of CEd work is based on Prolog. (See, for example, two special issues of *Instructional Science*: volume 16, issue 4–5, July 1990, pp. 247–416; and volume 20, issue 2–3, March 1991, pp. 81–266.)

27.3.6 Reading Literature

Programming is frequently compared to the learning of languages. For example, CEd researchers suggest that programming instruction should mimic reading instruction by having students read code as important preparation for learning to write code (Murphy et al., 2012). This and other connections to reading pedagogy seem to be a fruitful direction for consideration as there is a long-standing interest in understanding how humans learn to read. While there are many potential connections between the reading literature and computing, we focus on the pedagogical practice of rereading and close by highlighting a few additional potential connections to CEd.

27.3.6.1 Evidence from Outside of Computing

Reading education has identified that rereading is an effective practice for learners (Dowhower, 1994; Kuhn & Stahl, 2003; Samuels, 1979; Smagorinsky & Mayer, 2014). The pedagogical innovation is to have children reread the same text until they are able to read it relatively quickly with a low error rate. However, reading interventions have been difficult to study because of the ethical implications of having a control group (Kuhn & Stahl, 2003). For example, Stahl and Heubach (2005) report that "the results of the first year were so unexpectedly strong that we felt that denying treatment to a control set of classes was unethical" (p. 38). While repeated reading is praised as an effective practice (Smagorinsky & Mayer, 2014), Kuhn and Stahl (2003) warn that some of the positive results of the technique may be primarily attributed to additional time reading (p. 28).

27.3.6.2 Connections to CS: Observations and Hypotheses

The rereading literature described above presents the idea that repeating a particular task may be advantageous. Resources exist for students to practice specific skills in a programming language (e.g., https://codingbat.com, https://practiceit.cs.washington.edu, www.codestepbystep.com). These websites offer many isomorphic problems so that students can practice particular skills. However, based upon the rereading research, perhaps it is best for a student to solve a single problem multiple times before moving on. At a minimum, the reading literature suggests that achieving a level of fluency may require extended, deliberate practice (Kuhn & Stahl, 2003). Additionally, strategies for helping students make inferences when reading (Hansen & Pearson, 1983) may also be applicable. These connections between reading and programming may be a productive line of inquiry.

Another possible connection relates to two pedagogical phases of reading instruction. The reading literature talks about students' experiences as they transition from "learning to read" to the later stage of "reading to learn" in which students use their skills of reading to acquire new content knowledge (Smagorinsky & Mayer, 2014). In computing instruction, we often have a similar transition in which introductory courses focus on *learning to program*, and then later courses use programming as a way of illustrating particular algorithms, which we could similarly call *programming to learn*.

Lastly, we expect that most educators encourage students to plan their programs before starting to write code. Computing educators may also wish to mention to students that creating an outline improves the quality of a resulting essay (Kellogg, 1994, 2008), and the same may be true for programs. Again, this may be a fruitful direction for research.

27.3.7 Importance of Identity to Learning

There exists a large body of research about the importance of belonging and motivation for student learning. In particular, this work focuses on processes of identity development. Similarly, CEdR focused on equity and diversity frequently addresses students' feelings of belonging in computing (see Chapter 16). Identity development, and the underlying need for motivation and belonging, can further our understanding of the processes of learning in CS.

27.3.7.1 Evidence from Outside of Computing

To understand students' thinking and learning, many have proposed that it is insufficient to consider only the cognitive processes involved in learning (Lave & Wenger, 1991; Nasir & Hand, 2008; Nasir & Shah, 2011; Shah, 2017; Wortham, 2006). Instead, from a sociocultural perspective, it is important to consider students' motivations and other contextual aspects of their experience. An original emphasis on this comes from Lave and Wenger in their discussion of *situated learning*: "Rather than asking what kinds of cognitive processes and conceptual structures are involved, they ask what kinds of social engagements provide the proper context for learning to take place" (Lave & Wenger, 1991, p. 14).

Applying ideas from Lave and Wenger (1991), Stevens et al. (2008) focus on the experiences of individuals in engineering programs, and they propose a framework for engineering education to include disciplinary knowledge, navigation, and identification. Disciplinary knowledge focuses on students' achieving traditional learning outcomes, which may vary drastically as they progress from introductory to advanced courses. Navigation focuses on students' paths through engineering programs. Identification focuses on "[h]ow a person identifies with engineering and is identified by others as an engineer" (Stevens et al., 2008, p. 356). This framework may serve as a model for CEd, particularly in how it challenges the more common narrative about an engineering "pipeline." Stevens et al. explain: "[t]he problem with the pipeline metaphor is that the metaphor's component parts seem to commit its users to a homogeneous view of people/fluids passing through the pipeline" (Stevens et al., 2008, p. 365).

27.3.7.2 Connections to CS: Observations and Hypotheses

Like in other disciplines, identity is related to learning. At a minimum, identity development within computing appears relevant to learning in computing if only because identity development relates to students' decisions to pursue or leave computing. We can see ample connections to the processes of identity development, much of which is reviewed in Chapter 16. For example, Barker et al. (2002) described ways in which computing classrooms can reinforce the ideas that some students belong and others do not. Sapna Cheryan and colleagues have focused on how students' sense of belonging is shaped by environmental cues (Cheryan et al., 2009), interacting with computer scientists who confirm or challenge typical stereotypes (Cheryan et al., 2011), and reading reports that discredit the validity of typical stereotypes of computer scientists (Cheryan et al., 2013).

27.4 Open Questions

27.4.1 How Do Misconceptions Related to Intuition Relate to Misconceptions in Other Domains?

Above, we argued that intuition in introductory programming is different from that in other domains because programming languages could (and are) designed to align with human intuition. At a minimum, this can help us to see students' reasoning as relevant and a productive resource for educators. However, this difference in the nature of the domain leaves open the question of whether the processes of learning and the nature of the resulting knowledge are similar to or different from those in other disciplines. These questions are a central emphasis within the learning sciences and studies of conceptual change, which focus on beliefs that are deeply held and difficult to change (diSessa, 2014a). Are the misconceptions that we observe in computing similar in this respect?

27.4.2 How Should Teachers and Instruction Respond to Misconceptions from Intuition?

There is not a consensus among conceptual change researchers about the best response to misconceptions (diSessa, 2014a). Additionally, responses to misconceptions should likely take into account the nature of the processes of learning and the resulting knowledge. However, as we described in the previous section, these remain open questions. diSessa argues that this "[c]onfront and replace is an implausible instructional strategy" (diSessa, 2014a, p. 102) for conceptual change because of the sheer number of ideas that constitute conceptual understanding. Instead, diSessa argues for building upon students' existing ideas (diSessa, 2014b). However, this returns us to the focus on the nature of the knowledge to be learned. For example, a "confront and replace" strategy might be appropriate for helping students learn to recognize letters in an alphabet. For this type of declarative knowledge, we might find different instructional strategies effective.

27.4.3 How Should Information about Misconceptions be Disseminated among Teachers?

The question of how teachers should respond to misconceptions is interrelated with how information about misconceptions should be disseminated among teachers. Page Keeley and colleagues have published a set of books (e.g., Keeley et al., 2005) to guide teachers' formative assessment to be aligned with possible misconceptions. This format likely provides clearer paths to implementation than literature reviews about misconceptions (Qian & Lehman, 2017) or lists of teacher-identified misconceptions as can be found on CSTeachingTips.org.

27.4.4 What Evidence Should Be Required to Document a Misconception?

To date, multiple methods have been used to identify student misconceptions. For example, Qian and Lehman (2017) summarize misconceptions research that described misconceptions observed in a single student's response. In contrast, Stephens-Martinez et al. (2017) found that a small set of wrong answers (approximately 5 percent of all distinct wrong answers) accounted for approximately 60 percent of the wrong answers that students submitted. However, these wrong answers could include not distinguishing between whether the string X is printed as "x", 'x', or x. This type of common mistake might be valuable for educators, but might not match the typical definition of a misconception. Evidence from single cases might be valuable when it formalizes or explains patterns of student responses that are recognizable to educators. For example, Chung et al. (2017) draw on data from two students to argue that students may develop the misconception that data structures can only store strings or integers. This may simply be the result of a narrow set of examples presented to students, but this reliance on "simple" examples such as storing strings or integers is likely common. Documenting misconceptions might have practical relevance and/or help address the broader questions about the nature of students' knowledge. In the case of practical relevance, the question of what documentation is required may be inseparable from how teachers should integrate this information and how this information will be disseminated to teachers.

27.4.5 Which Curricular Factors Influence the Manifestation of Misconceptions and How?

As discussed in Section 27.2.2, even minor changes in how topics are presented can prevent the formation of misconceptions (Karpierz & Wolfman, 2014; Vahrenhold & Paul, 2014). A prominent example of how much more significant curricular decisions influence which misconceptions may or may not manifest themselves is recursion. As demonstrated by recent surveys (McCauley et al., 2015; Rinderknecht, 2014), a large number of research papers have dealt with issues related to teaching and understanding recursion.

Hamouda et al. (2017) present the development and validation of a basic recursion concept inventory. Based upon a literature review and advice from an expert panel, the authors developed test items focused on the following: (1) passive control flow after reaching the base case; (2) active control flow until reaching the base case; (3) how to formulate the recursive call; (4) how to formulate the stopping condition and when it will be triggered; (5) infinite recursion; (6) confusion with loop structures; and (7) unawareness of how variables are updated on every recursion (Hamouda et al., 2017, pp. 126–127).

As can be seen from the above list, all topics except for the last two are independent of whether the programming language used during instruction was functional, imperative, or object-oriented. In fact, the literature review about recursion by McCauley et al. reports on courses using "LISP, LOGO, BASIC, C, Python, SIMPLE, Scheme, Miranda, SOLO, Pascal, and pseudo-code" (McCauley et al., 2015, p. 38).

McCauley et al. (2015) cite one of the reasons why students may have issues with recursion as that it is difficult to find real-world examples and that students thus do not develop intuition about recursion. However, a curriculum focused on recursive data structures naturally lends itself to algorithms on these using (structural) recursion. One such curriculum is the How to Design Programs curriculum (Felleisen et al., 2000). A study by Fisler (2014) showed that students taught according to this curriculum performed better on a standard programming benchmark, the so-called Rainfall Problem (Soloway, 1986). However, Fisler concedes that one could argue that "Rainfall is biased in favor of functional programming, because [the components used for the solution] are standard, heavily exercised problems in functional CS1 courses" (Fisler, 2014, p. 42). As a consequence, while a functional, decomposition-based approach is promising with respect to understanding recursion, more research is needed to understand at which expenses, if any, this advantage comes.

In a curriculum that starts with object orientation (see Chapter 13 for more details), several types of misconceptions have been found to emerge. In particular, the high interconnectedness of concepts needed to understand object orientation (Pedroni & Meyer, 2010) provides challenges that have been observed and investigated in a number of studies.

Ragonis and Ben-Ari (2005) present the results of two yearlong studies with a total of 47 students in Grade 10. The students were novices with respect to concepts in object-oriented programming and were taught using BlueJ and Java. While the primary focus of the study was on which concepts in object orientation could be taught to students at that age, a second research focus was on which concepts students developed during the course. For the purpose of this, observations were recorded by taking field notes while attending the lectures. In addition, homework assignments, lab exercises, tests, and projects were analyzed as well.

Ragonis and Ben-Ari provide an encyclopedic description that shows the breadth of misconceptions and difficulties related to both object orientation in general and object orientation in Java in particular that can be encountered in class. They note, however, that most of these misconceptions and difficulties "appeared with low frequency and characterized a particular period of learning" (Ragonis & Ben-Ari, 2005, p. 218). Ragonis and Ben-Ari note that, at least in the course monitored, several difficulties disappeared as the course progressed, and they present a set of best-practice recommendations for teaching object orientation; see also similar discussions by Kölling and Rosenberg (2001) and Sanders and Thomas (2007).

In a revalidation study of multiple previous studies, Sanders and Thomas (2007) investigated whether previously reported misconceptions could be detected among a small group of students that were taught in an objects-first course designed by the first author and a colleague. They analyzed 71 artifacts (programs) submitted by the students at various points during the course. The authors were able to confirm students' difficulties with linking classes of a design such that objects of these classes could interact properly; in addition, hierarchies of classes and abstractions were found to be problematic. Furthermore, students were found to occasionally conflate objects and classes as well as classes and collections. Some students seemed to treat objects as nothing more than pieces of code, others created objects that would function within the program but did not correspond to the modeled domain. All of these behaviors confirm results from a previous study by Eckerdal and Thune (2005). On the other hand, Sanders and Thomas were unable to reconfirm a small set of misconceptions, including the conflation of attributes and identity that had been discussed by other authors (e.g., Holland et al., 1997). Even given a small sample size, these observations, or rather the lack thereof, seem to imply that at least some of the misconceptions reported in earlier work can be avoided by carefully selecting examples used when teaching; see Holland et al. (1997) or Kölling and Rosenberg (2001). To aid practitioners, Sanders and Thomas present two checklists containing indicators for students' understanding of concepts in object orientation and indicators for the presence of misconceptions.

In summary, this section demonstrates that a curricular decision may have a significant impact on the formation or avoidance of misconceptions. Educators and researchers thus need to take into account the curricular context when addressing a particular misconception.

27.5 Conclusion

We see the continued exploration of students' learning of computing as fruitful for both improving CEd and expanding our understanding of more general processes of learning. One important lesson from the education research we have surveyed is that learning takes time. In CEd, we often lament the difficulty students have in learning foundational content. The literature we have surveyed leads us to argue that this should be seen as part of the natural learning processes or possibly as evidence of deficiencies in current teaching methods. That mind-set may best drive us to better understand how to help students build a robust knowledge base in computing.

References

Adams, W. K., & Wieman, C. E. (2011). Development and validation of instruments to measure learning of expert-like thinking. *International Journal of Science Education*, 33(9), 1289–1312.

Almstrum, V. L., Henderson, P. B., Harvey, V. J., Heeren, C., Marion, W. A., Riedesel, C., Soh, K.-L., & Tew, A. E. (2006). Concept inventories in computer science for the topic discrete mathematics. *SIGCSE Bulletin*, 38(4), 132–145.

Barker, L. J., Garvin-Doxas, K., & Jackson, M. (2002). Defensive climate in the computer science classroom. In *Proceedings of the 33rd ACM Technical Symposium on Computer Science Education (SIGCSE 2002)* (pp. 43–47). New York: ACM Press.

Baddeley, A. D., & Hitch, G. (1974). Working memory. *Psychology of Learning and Motivation*, 8, 47–89.

Baxter, G. P., & Glaser, R. (1998). Investigating the cognitive complexity of science assessments. *Educational Measurement: Issues and Practice*, 17(3), 37–45.

Beck, K. (2003). *Test-Driven Development by Example*. Boston, MA: Addison-Wesley.

Buswell, G. T. (1930). Summary of arithmetic investigations (1929). *The Elementary School Journal*, 30(10), 766–775.

Bonar, J., & Soloway, E. (1989). Preprogramming knowledge: A major source of misconceptions in novice programmers. *Human–Computer Interaction*, 1(2), 133–161.

Bransford, J. D., Brown, A., & Cocking, R. (1999). *How People Learn: Mind, Brain, Experience, and School*. Washington, DC: National Research Council.

Carbonneau, K. J., Marley, S. C., & Selig, J. P. (2013). A meta-analysis of the efficacy of teaching mathematics with concrete manipulatives. *Journal of Educational Psychology*, 105(2), 380–400.

Carpenter, T. P., Fennema, E., Peterson, P. L., & Carey, D. A. (1988). Teachers' pedagogical content knowledge of students' problem solving in elementary arithmetic. *Journal for Research in Mathematics Education*, 19(5), 385–401.

Chan, W. W. L., Au, T. K., & Tang, J. (2014). Strategic counting: A novel assessment of place-value understanding. *Learning and Instruction*, 29, 78–94.

Cheryan, S., Plaut, V. C., Davies, P. G., & Steele, C. M. (2009). Ambient belonging: How stereotypical cues impact gender participation in computer science. *Journal of Personality and Social Psychology*, 97(6), 1045–1060.

Chase, W. G., & Simon, H. A. (1973). Perception in chess. *Cognitive Psychology*, 4(1), 55–81.

Cheryan, S., Plaut, V. C., Handron, C., & Hudson, L. (2013). The stereotypical computer scientist: Gendered media representations as a barrier to inclusion for women. *Sex Roles*, 69(1–2), 58–71.

Cheryan, S., Siy, J. O., Vichayapai, M., Drury, B. J., & Kim, S. (2011). Do female and male role models who embody STEM stereotypes hinder women's anticipated success in STEM? *Social Psychological and Personality Science*, 2(6), 656–664.

Chi, M. T., Feltovich, P. J., & Glaser, R. (1981). Categorization and representation of physics problems by experts and novices. *Cognitive Science*, 5(2), 121–52.

Chung, A., Shao, P., & Vasquez, A. (2017). Students' misconceptions about the types of values data structures can store. *Journal of Computing Sciences in Colleges*, 32(4), 72–78.

Clancy, M. (2004). Misconceptions and attitudes that interfere with learning to program. In S. Fincher & M. Petre (Eds.), *Computer Science Education Research* (pp. 85–100). Abingdon, UK: Taylor and Francis.

Confrey, J. (1990). A review of the research on student conceptions in mathematics, science, and programming. *Review of Research in Education*, 16, 3–56.

Danielsiek, H., Paul, W., & Vahrenhold, J. (2012). Detecting and understanding students' misconceptions related to algorithms and data structures. In *Proceedings of the 44th ACM Technical Symposium on Computer Science Education (SIGCSE 2012)* (pp. 21–26). New York: ACM Press.

Davis, E. A., Linn, M. C., Mann, L. M., & Clancy, M. J. (1993). Mind your P's and Q's: Using parentheses and quotes in LISP. In C. R. Cook, J. C. Scholtz, & J. C. Spohrer (Eds.), *Empirical Studies of Programmers: Fifth Workshop* (pp. 63–85). Norwood, NJ: Ablex.

Davis, E. A., Linn, M. C., & Clancy, M. J. (1995). Learning to use parentheses and quotes in LISP. *Computer Science Education*, 6(1), 15–31.

Denny, P., Luxton-Reilly, A., & Simon, B. (2008). Evaluating a new exam question: Parsons' problems. In *Proceedings of the Fourth International Workshop on Computing Education Research (ICER '08)* (pp. 113–124). New York: ACM Press.

diSessa, A. A. (2014a). A history of conceptual change research: Threads and fault lines. In R. K. Sawyer (Ed.), *The Cambridge Handbook of the Learning Sciences*, 2nd edn. (pp. 88–108). New York: Cambridge University Press.

diSessa, A. A. (2014b). The construction of causal schemes: Learning mechanisms at the knowledge level. *Cognitive Science*, 38(5), 795–850.

Dowhower, S. L. (1994). Repeated reading revisited: Research into practice. *Reading & Writing Quarterly: Overcoming Learning Difficulties*, 10(4), 343–358.

Eckerdal, A., & Thuné, M. (2005). Novice Java programmers' conceptions of "object" and "class", and variation theory. In *Proceedings of the 10th Annual SIGCSE Conference on Innovation and Technology in Computer Science Education (ITiCSE '05)* (pp. 89–93). New York: ACM Press.

Felleisen, M., Findler, R. B., Flatt, M., & Krishnamurthi, S. (2000). *How to Design Programs: An Introduction to Programming and Computing*. Cambridge, MA: MIT Press.

Fisler, K. (2014). The Recurring Rainfall Problem. In *Proceedings of the International Computing Education Research Conference (ICER 2014)* (pp. 35–42). New York: ACM Press.

Fisler, K., Krishnamurthi, S., & Tunnell Wilson, P. (2017). Assessing and teaching scope, mutation, and aliasing in upper-level undergraduates. In *Proceedings of the 2017 ACM SIGCSE Technical Symposium on Computer Science Education (SIGCSE 2017)* (pp. 21–26). New York: ACM Press.

Fuson, K. C. (1998). Pedagogical, mathematical, and real-world conceptual-support nets: A model for building children's multidigit domain knowledge. *Mathematical Cognition*, 4(2), 147–186.

Gal-Ezer, J., & Trakhtenbrot, M. (2016). Identification and addressing reduction-related misconceptions. *Computer Science Education*, 26(2–3), 89–103.

Gamma, E., Helm, R., Johnson, R., & Vlissides, J. (1995). *Design Patterns: Elements of Reusable Object-Oriented Software*. Boston, MA: Addison-Wesley.

Ginat, D., & Blau, Y. (2017). Multiple levels of abstraction in algorithmic problem solving. In *Proceedings of the 48th ACM Technical Symposium on Computer Science Education (SIGCSE 2017)* (pp. 237–242). New York: ACM Press.

Gobet, F., Lane, P. C. R., Croker, S., Cheng, P. C.-H., Jones, G., Oliver, I., & Pine, J. M. (2001). Chunking mechanisms in human learning. *Trends in Cognitive Sciences*, 5(6), 236–243.

Guzdial, M. (2015). Learner-centered design of computing education: Research on computing for everyone. *Synthesis Lectures on Human-Centered Informatics*, 8(6), 1–165.

Hamouda, S., Edwards, S. H., Elmongui, H. G., Ernst, J. V., & Shaffer, C. A. (2017). A basic recursion concept inventory. *Computer Science Education*, 27(2), 121–148.

Hansen, J., & Pearson, P. D. (1983). An instructional study: Improving the inferential comprehension of good and poor fourth-grade readers. *Journal of Educational Psychology*, 75(6), 821–829.

Herman, G. L., Loui, M. C., Kaczmarczyk, L. C., & Zilles, C. B. (2012). Describing the what and why of students' difficulties in Boolean logic. *ACM Transactions on Computing Education (TOCE)*, 12(1), Article 3, 28 pages.

Holland, S., Griffiths, R., & Woodman, M. (1997). Avoiding object misconceptions. In *Proceedings of the 28th SIGCSE Technical Symposium on Computer Science Education (SIGSCE 1997)* (pp. 131–134). New York: ACM Press.

Hughes, E. M., Witzel, B. S., Riccomini, P. J., Fries, K. M., & Kanyongo, G. Y. (2014). A meta-analysis of algebra interventions for learners with disabilities and struggling learners. *Journal of the International Association of Special Education*, 15(1), 36–47.

Kahney, H. (1989). What do novice programmers know about recursion? In E. Soloway & J. C. Spohrer (Eds.), *Studying the Novice Programmer* (pp. 209–228). Hillsdale, NJ: Lawrence Erlbaum Associates, Inc.

Karpierz, K., & Wolfman, S. A. (2014). Misconceptions and concept inventory questions for binary search trees and hash tables. In *Proceedings of the 45th ACM Technical Symposium on Computer Science Education (SIGCSE '13)* (pp. 109–114). New York: ACM Press.

Keeley, P., Eberle, F., & Farrin, L. (2005). *Uncovering Student Ideas in Science, Vol. 1: 25 Formative Assessment Probes*. Arlington, VA: National Science Teacher Association Press.

Kellogg, R. T. (2008). Training writing skills: A cognitive developmental perspective. *Journal of Writing Research*, 1(1), 1–26.

Kellogg, R. T. (1994). *The Psychology of Writing*. New York: Oxford University Press.

Kölling, M., & Rosenberg, J. (2001). Guidelines for teaching object orientation with Java. In *Proceedings of the 6th Annual SIGCSE Conference on Innovation and Technology in Computer Science Education (ITiCSE '01)* (pp. 33–36). New York: ACM Press.

Kuhn, M. R., & Stahl, S. A. (2003). Fluency: A review of developmental and remedial practices. *Journal of Educational Psychology*, 95(1), 3–21.

Ladd, H. F., & Sorensen, L. C. (2017). Returns to teacher experience: Student achievement and motivation in middle school. *Education Finance and Policy*, 12(2), 241–279.

Lane, P. C., Cheng, P. C. H., & Gobet, F. (2000). CHREST+: A simulation of how humans learn to solve problems using diagrams. *AISB Quarterly*, 103, 24–30.

Lave, J., & Wenger, E. (1991). *Situated Learning: Legitimate Peripheral Participation*. Cambridge, UK: Cambridge University Press.

Levin, J. R., Levin, M. E., Glasman, L. D., & Nordwall, M. B. (1992). Mnemonic vocabulary instruction: Additional effectiveness evidence. *Contemporary Educational Psychology*, 17(2), 156–174.

Lewis, C. M. (2012). *Applications of Out-of-Domain Knowledge in Students' Reasoning about Computer Program State* (PhD dissertation). University of California, Berkeley.

McCauley, R., Grissom, S., Fitzgerald, S., & Murphy, L. (2015). Teaching and learning recursive programming: A review of the research literature. *Computer Science Education*, 25(1), 37–66.

Miller, G. A. (1956). The magical number seven, plus or minus two: Some limits on our capacity for processing information. *Psychological Review*, 63(2), 81–97.

Miller, S. P., Butler, F. M., & Lee, K.-H. (1998). Validated practices for teaching mathematics to students with learning disabilities: A review of literature. *Focus on Exceptional Children*, 31(1), 1–24.

Murphy, L., Fitzgerald, S., Lister, R., & McCauley, R. (2012). Ability to "explain in plain English" linked to proficiency in computer-based programming. In *Proceedings of the International Computing Education Research Conference (ICER '12)* (pp. 111–118). New York: ACM Press.

Nasir, N. S., & Hand, V. (2008). From the court to the classroom: Opportunities for engagement, learning, and identity in basketball and classroom mathematics. *Journal of the Learning Sciences*, 17(2), 143–179.

Nasir, N. S., & Shah, N. (2011). On defense: African American males making sense of racialized narratives in mathematics education. *Journal of African American Males in Education*, 2(1), 24–45.

Nathan, M. J., & Petrosino, A. (2003). Expert blind spot among preservice teachers. *American Educational Research Journal*, 40(4), 905–928.

O'Brien, D., Dias, M. G., Roazzi, A., & Cantor, J. B. (1998). Pinocchio's nose knows: Preschool children recognize that a pragmatic rule can be violated, an indicative conditional can be falsified, and that a broken promise is a false promise. In M. D. S. Braine & D. P. O'Brien (Eds.), *Mental Logic* (pp. 447–457). Hillsdale, NJ: Lawrence Erlbaum Associates.

O'Brien, D. P., Roazzi, A., Dias, M. G., Cantor, J. B., & Brooks, P. J. (2004). Violations, lies, broken promises, and just plain mistakes: The pragmatics of counterexamples, logical semantics, and the evaluation of conditional assertions, regulations, and promises in variants of Wason's selection task. In K. Manktelow & M. C. Chung (Eds.), *Psychology of Reasoning: Theoretical and Historical Perspectives* (pp. 95–126). Hove, UK: Psychology Press.

Parsons, D., & Haden, P. (2006). Parson's programming puzzles: A fun and effective learning tool for first programming courses. In *Proceedings of the 8th*

Australasian Conference on Computing Education (pp. 157–163). Darlinghurst, Australia: Australian Computer Society.

Pea, R. D. (1986). Language-independent conceptual "bugs" in novice programming. *Journal of Educational Computing Research*, 2(1), 25–36.

Pedroni, M. & Meyer, B. (2010). Object-oriented modeling of object-oriented concepts: A case study in structuring an educational domain. In *Proceedings of the 4th International Conference on Informatics in Schools: Situation, Evolution, and Perspectives (ISSEP 2010), Lecture Notes in Computer Science 5941* (pp. 155–169). Berlin, Germany: Springer.

Pollack, I. (1953). Assimilation of sequentially encoded information. *The American Journal of Psychology*, 66(3), 421–435.

Pollard, S., & Duvall, R. C. (2006). Everything I needed to know about teaching I learned in kindergarten: Bringing elementary education techniques to undergraduate computer science classes. In *Proceedings of the 37th ACM Technical Symposium on Computer Science Education (SIGCSE 2006)* (pp. 224–228). New York: ACM Press.

Qian, Y. & Lehman, J. (2017). Students' misconceptions and other difficulties in introductory programming: A literature review. *ACM Transactions on Computing Education (TOCE)*, 18(1), Article 1, 24 pages.

Ragonis, N., & Ben-Ari, M. (2005). A long-term investigation of the comprehension of OOP concepts by novices. *Computer Science Education*, 15(3), 203–221.

Rich, K. M., Strickland, C., Binkowski, T. A., Moran, C., & Franklin, D. (2017). K–8 learning trajectories derived from research literature: Sequence, repetition, conditionals. In *Proceedings of the 2017 ACM Conference on International Computing Education Research (ICER '17)* (pp. 182–190). New York: ACM Press.

Rivera, D., & Smith, D. D. (1988). Using a demonstration strategy to teach midschool students with learning disabilities how to compute long division. *Journal of Learning Disabilities*, 21(2), 77–81.

Rinderknecht, C. (2014). A survey on teaching and learning recursive programming. *Informatics in Education*, 13(1), 87–119.

Robins, A., Rountree, J., & Rountree, N. (2003). Learning and teaching programming: A review and discussion. *Computer Science Education*, 13(2), 137–172.

Sadler, P. M., Sonnert, G., Coyle, H. P., Cook-Smith, N., & Miller, J. L. (2013). The influence of teachers' knowledge on student learning in middle school physical science classrooms. *American Educational Research Journal*, 50(5), 1020–1049.

Sajaniemi, J., & Kuittinen, M. (2005). An experiment on using roles of variables in teaching introductory programming. *Computer Science Education,* 15(1), 59–82.

Samuels, S. J. (1979). The method of repeated readings. *The Reading Teacher*, 32(4), 403–408.

Sanders, K., & Thomas, L. (2007). Checklists for grading object-oriented CS1 programs: Concepts and misconceptions. In *Proceedings of the 12th Annual SIGCSE Conference on Innovation and Technology in Computer Science Education (ITiCSE '07)* (pp. 166–170). New York: ACM Press.

Sawyer, R. K. (2014). Introduction: The new science of learning. In R. K. Sawyer (Ed.), *The Cambridge Handbook of the Learning Sciences*, 2nd edn. (pp. 1–18). New York: Cambridge University Press.

Seppälä, O., Malmi, L., & Korhonen, A. (2006). Observations on student misconceptions – A case study of the build-heap algorithm. *Computer Science Education*, 16(3), 241–255.

Sfard, A. (1995). The development of algebra: Confronting historical and psychological perspectives. *The Journal of Mathematical Behavior*, 14(1), 15–39.

Shah, N. (2017). Race, ideology, and academic ability: A relational analysis of racial narratives in mathematics. *Teachers College Record*, 119(7), 1–42.

Smagorinsky, P., & Mayer, R. E. (2014). Learning to be literate. In R. K. Sawyer (Ed.), *The Cambridge Handbook of the Learning Sciences*, 2nd edn. (pp. 605–625). New York: Cambridge University Press.

Smith, III, J. P., diSessa, A. A., & Roschelle, J. (1993). Misconceptions reconceived: A constructivist analysis of knowledge in transition. *Journal of the Learning Sciences*, 3(2), 115–163.

Soloway, E. (1986). Learning to program = learning to construct mechanisms and explanations. *Communications of the ACM*, 29(9), 850–858.

Spohrer, J. G., & Soloway, E. (1986). Analyzing the high frequency bugs in novice programs. In *Papers Presented at the First Workshop on Empirical Studies of Programmers* (pp. 230–251). Norwood, NJ: Ablex.

Stahl, S. A., & Heubach, K. M. (2005). Fluency-oriented reading instruction. *Journal of Literacy Research*, 37(1), 25–60.

Stephens-Martinez, K., Ju, A., Parashar, K., Ongowarsito, R., Jain, N., Venkat, S., & Fox, A. (2017). Taking advantage of scale by analyzing frequent constructed-response, code tracing wrong answers. In *Proceedings of the 2017 ACM Conference on International Computing Education Research* (pp. 56–64). New York: ACM Press.

Stevens, R., O'Connor, K., Garrison, L., Jocuns, A., & Amos, D. M. (2008). Becoming an engineer: Toward a three dimensional view of engineering learning. *Journal of Engineering Education*, 97(3), 355–368.

Vahrenhold, J., & Paul, W. (2014). Developing and validating test items for first-year computer science courses. *Computer Science Education*, 24(4), 304–333.

von Sydow, M. (2006). *Towards a Flexible Bayesian and Deontic Logic of Testing Descriptive and Prescriptive Rules: Explaining Content Effects in the Wason Selection Task* (PhD dissertation). University of Göttingen.

Vosniadou, S., & Brewer, W. F. (1992). Mental models of the earth: A study of conceptual change in childhood. *Cognitive Psychology*, 24(4), 535–585.

Wason, P. C. (1968). Reasoning about a rule. *The Quarterly Journal of Experimental Psychology*, 20(3), 273–281.

Wason, P. C., & Johnson-Laird, P. N. (1972). *Psychology of Reasoning: Structure and Content*. Cambridge, UK: Harvard University Press.

Webb, K. C., & Taylor, C. (2014). Developing a pre- and post-course concept inventory to gauge operating systems learning. In *Proceedings of the 46th ACM Technical Symposium on Computer Science Education (SIGCSE 2014)* (pp. 103–108). New York: ACM Press.

Willingham, D. T., Hughes, E. M., & Dobolyi, D. G. (2015). The scientific status of learning styles theories. *Teaching of Psychology*, 42(3), 266–271.

Winslow, L. E. (1996). Programming pedagogy – A psychological overview. *ACM SIGCSE Bulletin*, 28(3), 17–22.

Witzel, B. S., Riccomini, P. J., & Schneider, E. (2008). Implementing CRA with secondary students with learning disabilities in mathematics. *Intervention in School and Clinic*, 43(5), 270–276.

Wortham, S. (2006). *Learning Identity: The Joint Emergence of Social Identification and Academic Learning*. Cambridge, UK: Cambridge University Press.

Young, R. M., & O'Shea, T. (1981). Errors in children's subtraction. *Cognitive Science*, 5(2), 153–177.

28 Motivation, Attitudes, and Dispositions

Alex Lishinski and Aman Yadav

28.1 Introduction

The purpose of this chapter is to discuss a wide range of noncognitive factors that influence students' learning outcomes in computing. Specifically, the goal is to inform computing education researchers about constructs related to students' motivation, attitudes, and dispositions that have been found to be important for student success. This chapter discusses what we know about how these factors influence student success, both in computing courses and in general. We use motivation, attitudes, and dispositions as broader umbrellas under which research on a broad range of related constructs is discussed.

Computing education research is focused on how to teach students to work with a computer. More than that, it is about teaching students to understand how a computer works and how to leverage that understanding to use the computer to accomplish their goals. The computer itself is an inflexible and remorseless entity. It does not understand intent or implications, it responds to the explicit inputs that are given to it and it returns predictable outputs. That is the property that makes it powerful, but also difficult for humans to learn to use. Humans operate differently from computers. We have consciousness. We are each unique. We behave the way we do for reasons that are not always rational. We respond to inputs based on our own internal mental states that are not related to the inputs.

Computing educators and computing education researchers occasionally seem to forget that our central concern is the human being that we are trying to teach, not the abstract concepts that we are trying to teach them. It is an understandable mistake, particularly for people who are used to thinking in the mode of computing, to think of the problem of computing education as similar to any other computing problem. Put in the correct curricular inputs and you will get the correct learning outputs. So we focus on ways to organize the curriculum, ways to explain ideas, and tools to facilitate students' work, while neglecting the things that make humans human. Teaching is not like solving a computing problem because students are humans with complex sets of drives and desires that guide their behavior and that do not always contribute to better learning outcomes.

Most computing educators would presumably be very confident in their ability to produce learning outcomes in their students if they had complete control over their students' behaviors. This is not the case, of course, and the antecedents of their behaviors are complex indeed, including motivational states, dispositions, and emotions, among others. But the task of education is to produce learning outcomes in students, who are humans, and so these behavioral antecedents are not unnecessary complexities that can be abstracted away. The task is to produce learning given the behavioral realities of the human beings that you are trying to teach.

Of course, the need to understand the student as a human is not just true of computer science (CS). The question then is: What does the content of computing education – the computer itself – add to the equation? A simplified answer might be: the difficulty. Computing is widely understood to have a steep learning curve, so perhaps the sheer difficulty of the subject creates a need for more motivational and emotional support of students. But it may be more than the mere difficulty – perhaps computing is challenging in a unique way because of the stark differences between the way that a computer operates and the way the human mind operates. Perhaps the underlying reason for the steep learning curve is that students have to acclimatize to a new way of thinking in order to be able to speak to the computer in terms it understands. Perhaps the uniqueness of this task turns the merely challenging into the threatening, which could turn content-related difficulties into emotional or motivational ones. Regardless of the reason, it seems plausible that computing students need more emotional and motivational support, both relative to students in other subjects and relative to the amount they are currently getting.

This is all to say that the **motivating context** of this chapter is to communicate to computing education researchers the central importance of the *noncognitive* portions of their students – the motivational parts, the dispositional parts, the emotional parts. These are contrasted with the *cognitive* parts of their students, which can be roughly understood to mean the parts of the student that do operate similarly to a computer – those concerned with thinking, reasoning, remembering, and the like.

To accomplish this purpose, this chapter presents the results of research from educational psychology and computing education on how noncognitive factors impact learning outcomes. The details of what specific factors are discussed is less important than the overall point that such factors have a central importance – they cannot be ignored when thinking about computing pedagogy. In that same spirit, this chapter does not purport to cover all of the noncognitive factors that may be of interest, but rather it focuses on those factors that have already been the subject of some interest in computing education. This chapter also has limited advice about the **implications for practice** of the research discussed, as there are many **open questions** about how noncognitive factors can be addressed in computing classrooms. Nevertheless, it is our hope to impress upon the reader the absolutely essential need to think beyond the cognitive aspects of the computing education enterprise.

28.1.1 Computing Education Research

Computing education research has historically focused on understanding the cognitive demands of the subject matter on students and the pedagogical demands of the subject matter on teachers. This prior research has investigated various cognitive factors, such as problem-solving, critical thinking, and mathematical ability. Some of these factors have been found to be associated with learning outcomes in computing students. For example, abstract reasoning ability has been found to be associated with programming learning outcomes (Barker & Unger, 1983; Kurtz, 1980). Likewise, some studies have found mathematical ability to be a significant predictor of student outcomes in programming (Bennedsen & Caspersen, 2005; Bergin & Reilly, 2005). Generic problem-solving has also been found to be associated with increased success in learning programming; for example, a study by Hostetler (1983) found a significant relationship between programming course outcomes and generic problem-solving skills, such as formalizing a problem statement with abstract notation and choosing a correct series of steps to reach a solution. See Chapter 12 of this handbook for a much more extensive discussion of the factors that predict success in learning to program.

Noncognitive factors, such as motivation and attitudes, have been given less research attention in computing education than cognitive and pedagogical factors. These are factors that are separate from the content in computing courses, but which are crucially important to student success. Given the well-documented importance of noncognitive factors in predicting students' academic (and general life) success outcomes in other disciplines, even relative to cognitive factors (e.g., see Brunello & Schlotter, 2011; Kappe et al., 2012a; Weber et al., 2013), it is important to study whether and how noncognitive factors influence computing student outcomes. Other computing education researchers have noted the lack of attention to the noncognitive precursors of student outcomes in computing. In a 2005 Special Interest Group on Computer Science Education (SIGCSE) panel, Mark Guzdial claimed that "Too much of the research in computing education ignores the hundreds of years of education, cognitive science, and learning sciences research that have gone before us" (Almstrum et al., 2005). In a 2015 special issue of *Computer Science Education*, Anthony Robins echoed Guzdial's assessment, arguing that this state of affairs remained true ten years later (Robins, 2015).

Additionally, noncognitive factors have been found to be particularly important for traditionally underrepresented groups such as women and minorities (Jacob, 2002; Nasim et al., 2005; Tracey & Sedlacek, 1984). For example, a study by Jacob (2002) found that noncognitive skills, such as the ability to follow directions, work in groups, pay attention in class, and be organized, influenced postsecondary enrollment even after controlling for high school achievement, which could explain gender gaps in enrollment patterns. Thus, considering their broad importance for student success outcomes generally as well as for disadvantaged groups that are participating in computing at lower rates, the importance of these noncognitive factors generally remains underappreciated in computing education research. We need to do further research in order to better understand how noncognitive factors affect computing students, particularly those from underrepresented groups.

For the purposes of this chapter, we have operationalized motivation, attitudes, and dispositions as follows. *Motivation* refers, very broadly, to the underlying psychological mechanisms that cause people to engage and persist in behaviors. The literature from psychology on motivation does not carve out motivation as a conceptually singular entity, but rather as a family of related but diverse theoretical models that are based on different central constructs (Murphy & Alexander, 2000). These constructs include self-efficacy, goal orientation, and self-regulation, which are all discussed in detail below.

Attitudes refers to an individual's beliefs, emotions, and judgments related to some external entity, which in the education context is typically the subject or content being learned (Perloff, 2017). Like motivation, the term "attitudes" does not denote a conceptually singular theoretical entity, but rather a family of related theoretical constructs (such as interest and perceptions). Engagement is discussed under this umbrella as well, which can be thought of as the ways in which a person behaves when they have positive attitudes toward an academic subject matter, such as continuing to study it.

Finally, *dispositions* refers to the enduring behavior patterns that vary between individuals, which can be used to explain why they act in specific ways in specific types of situations (Katz, 1993). In the education context, dispositions have typically been studied in the form of personality traits, which attempt to measure the degree to which an individual possesses a particular underlying characteristic that is manifested as a tendency to engage in a particular set of consistent behaviors (Mischel, 2013).

28.1.2 Computing Gender Participation Gap and the Role of Noncognitive Factors

The gender participation gap is a well-known problem in computing education, as rates of participation are far lower for female students in the Western world. To give a sense of the scale of the problem, in the USA, women earn approximately 57 percent of all bachelor's degrees while earning only approximately 22 percent of computing bachelor's degrees as of 2014–2015. The computing gender participation gap has been paid a lot of attention in recent years, but we still have surprisingly little empirical knowledge about what factors may influence computing participation by gender. However, the existing research has tended to point to the sorts of noncognitive factors discussed in this chapter. See Chapter 16 of this Handbook for a detailed discussion of equity issues in CS education.

The previous research on the gender gap in computing has identified a number of systematic differences between the experiences of male and female students. Female students have been observed to have lower levels of self-efficacy and comfort in computing classes (Beyer, 2008; Busch, 1995). Attributions of success have been found to differ by gender, as female students are significantly more likely to attribute their successes to luck over ability (Cohoon, 2003; Wilson, 2010). Furthermore, the factors that impact success differ systematically by gender as well. Research has shown that comfort level and perceptions of gender equity significantly impact computing course outcomes for female students, but not for male students (Bernstein, 1991; Beyer, 2008).

This discussion of the computing gender participation gap is included in this chapter to provide a context for the sections to come. Issues of motivation, attitudes, and dispositions may seem rather abstract and unnecessary to many computing education researchers, for whom research serves the purpose of improving pedagogical practice through the rigorous empirical investigation of learning outcomes. This is especially likely to be the case given that this chapter opens more research questions than it resolves. By positioning the gender participation gap as an exemplar of the influence of noncognitive/affective factors, it is our hope to make apparent the **motivational context** of this abstract discussion to the endeavor of improving computing education.

28.2 Motivation

The term "motivation" covers a wide range of theories and models that have to do broadly with the affective determinants of behaviors, which include things such as goals, desires, and beliefs. This theoretical breadth is characteristic of many topics in psychology, but motivation has been noted for its conceptual diffuseness (Murphy & Alexander, 2000). Researchers have noted that the terminology used by motivation researchers can be very difficult for the uninitiated to understand because of the ways that specific terms for constructs become shorthand for entire programs of inquiry. Furthermore, these meanings are often specific to small subcommunities of motivation researchers and the meanings may not be consistent or mutually exclusive across these groups. Murphy and Alexander (2000) cataloged dozens of constructs studied by motivation researchers, under broad headings such Goals, Interest, Motivation (intrinsic vs. extrinsic), and Self-Schema, virtually all of which included synonymous (or very similar) terms being used across different subfields. These constructs also tend to have fuzzy boundaries between them. Such breadth (and conceptual vagueness) makes an exhaustive discussion of motivational constructs virtually impossible, but the significance of motivation can be thoroughly discussed and made apparent by focusing on some particularly prominent constructs from the literature.

One prominent body of motivation research is self-regulated learning theory (SRL). SRL consists of a number of different belief, goal, and behavior constructs having to do with the ways that learners manage their learning processes using strategies and behaviors as a way of responding to feedback, as well as the ways learners maintain their beliefs that they can succeed and make plans for how to do so. Motivation constructs connected to SRL have been researched extensively in educational psychology, and a substantial number of computing education studies have examined them as well. The following sections go in-depth into three SRL constructs – self-efficacy, goal orientation, and metacognitive self-regulation.

28.2.1 Self-Efficacy

The concept of self-efficacy originated in Bandura's social-cognitive theory (Bandura, 1977, 1986). The concept is defined as one's belief that one can achieve a desired outcome by successfully executing the necessary behaviors. The effort people are willing to expend to achieve their goals and their coping abilities in the face of difficulties are associated with self-efficacy beliefs (Bandura, 1977). By virtue of its connection with effort regulation and persistence, self-efficacy explains why prior experience and ability is sometimes not enough to predict future achievement (Bandura, 1986). For example, Pajares and Miller (1994) found that math self-efficacy had a stronger impact on math performance than did the amount of prior experience in math courses. Empirical studies have also borne out the notion that greater self-efficacy beliefs for complex or difficult tasks are related to increased resiliency (Schunk, 1995). The theory behind self-efficacy suggests that self-efficacy impacts achievement by inducing students to pursue more adaptive behaviors, such as opportunities for practice and feedback, and empirical research has supported this notion (Pintrich & DeGroot, 1990).

According to Bandura (1977), there are four primary sources of self-efficacy: performance accomplishments, vicarious experience, verbal persuasion, and emotional arousal. *Performance accomplishments* refers to previous experiences of success in activities closely related to the activity that the self-efficacy belief refers to (Bandura, 1977). Bandura considered this to be a particularly influential source of self-efficacy beliefs. *Vicarious experience* refers to prior instances where the individual has observed others successfully (or at least without adverse consequences) engage in the activity (Bandura, 1977). Bandura considered the indirect information provided by vicarious experience to be less potentially influential on self-efficacy beliefs than an individual's own experiences. *Verbal persuasion* refers to attempts by others to convince an individual that they can successfully cope with an activity (Bandura, 1977). Bandura considered verbal persuasion to be a source of weak self-efficacy beliefs, inasmuch as self-efficacy beliefs induced in this manner could be easily overridden by failure experiences that provide contradictory information. *Emotional arousal* refers to the way in which individuals can use their physiological response to an activity as a proxy for how well they will be able to cope with that activity (Bandura, 1977). Bandura noted that diminishing emotional arousal can reduce the chance that individuals will choose to pursue avoidance behavior.

Since Bandura's (1977) original presentation of self-efficacy, the construct has had a large influence on educational research, with many studies finding robust connections between self-efficacy and academic outcomes (e.g., see Andrew, 1998; Bandura, 1995, 1997; Britner & Pajares, 2006; Locke & Latham, 1990; Maddux, 1995; Pajares & Miller, 1994; Pajares & Valiante, 1997; Pintrich & Schunk, 1995; Schwarzer & Katz, 1995; Zimmerman & Schunk, 1989). Furthermore, self-efficacy has been shown to predict academic outcomes across many different subject areas, such as mathematics (Pajares & Miller, 1994), science (Britner & Pajares, 2006), and language arts (Pajares & Valiante, 1997).

For example, a study by Pajares and Graham (1999) found that middle school math students' self-efficacy predicted their performance in a mathematics class at the beginning and end of the school year. This held true while controlling for gender, gifted/regular education status, multiple indicators of prior mathematics performance and ability, and motivational and affective constructs, including anxiety and self-concept. Their models showed that, controlling for all of these other factors, students' math self-efficacy was a significant predictor of math performance over the course of the whole school year.

Self-efficacy has an especially strong influence on students' persistence in difficult classes. For example, mathematics self-efficacy has been found to be more strongly associated with persistence than prior math achievement (Pajares & Miller, 1994). Of particular relevance to computing education, self-efficacy has been found to be significantly related to the choice of mathematics and science careers (Lent & Hackett, 1994). The results of a meta-analysis have shown that the effects of self-efficacy on achievement outcomes are robust across subject areas when controlling for prior achievement (Valentine et al., 2004). For example, a study by Miller (2015) used the NELS:88 longitudinal data set (including over 10,000 students) to show that student self-beliefs, including self-efficacy, are significantly related to students' persistence in science, technology, engineering, and mathematics (STEM) at the undergraduate level. A self-belief scale that included STEM-specific self-efficacy measures was a significant predictor of whether or not students pursued a STEM major in college when controlling for participation in STEM activities outside the classroom and parental aspirations for pursuing STEM (Miller, 2015).

Self-efficacy may also have reciprocal effects on students' academic performance, with self-efficacy and performance affecting one another over time. This is significant because it would suggest that self-efficacy has an even more significant impact, influencing academic outcomes both directly and indirectly through these reciprocal effects. A multinational study using Programme for International Student Assessment (PISA) data by Williams and Williams (2010) found evidence for reciprocal effects between self-efficacy and mathematics performance. Using structural equation modeling, they specified a model including reciprocal effects using cross-sectional data and fit it to the PISA data for 33 different countries. The model tested whether a domain-specific mathematics self-efficacy score was reciprocally related to the PISA mathematics achievement construct from the 2003 version of the PISA, which was termed "mathematics literacy." The model was an overall good fit to the data in 30 of the 33 countries, and all of the reciprocal effects were significant in 24 of these 30 countries, which suggests that the PISA data provide strong, if not overwhelming evidence for reciprocal effects of self-efficacy on achievement. However, some previous research has also suggested that students' self-efficacy can be stabilized, and a negative self-efficacy feedback loop prevented, by having students engage in a self-evaluation task (Schunk & Ertmer, 2000). This intervention is purported to work because the self-evaluation task induces students to use self-monitoring and reflection strategies that lead to academic success.

In summary, self-efficacy is a construct that provides a way to understand how beliefs can bridge the gap between goals and behaviors, because self-efficacy increases the adaptive patterns of behaviors that enable students to achieve their goals. Below, we discuss how self-efficacy plays a role in computing classes, especially when students are first learning to program.

28.2.1.1 Self-Efficacy and Computing Education

Of self-regulated learning constructs, self-efficacy has been among the most studied in CS education, and this prior research has mostly found that higher levels of self-efficacy predict greater student performance in computing, analogous to findings in other STEM fields. For example, Ramalingam et al. (2004) examined the self-efficacy beliefs of 75 students in an undergraduate CS1 course, including students from both computing majors and a wide variety of other majors. The authors found that previous programming experience (including courses taken, programming languages learned, and number and length of programs written) was positively associated with self-efficacy, which was also positively associated with students' final course grades at the end of the semester. In another study, Wiedenbeck (2005) found a positive association between self-efficacy and two different programming course outcomes: overall course grade and performance on a debugging task.

A more comprehensive study examined many different predictors of success in CS1, including a number of so-called "traditional predictors," such as self-efficacy, math background, science background, learning style, attribution of success, and learning strategies, as well as a number of so-called "dynamic" predictors of success, which were derived using data-driven algorithms that identified patterns of behavior from students' log data (e.g., patterns of compiler errors and time spent resolving errors) (Watson & Godwin, 2014). Examining a total of 41 predictors (29 traditional and 12 dynamic), self-efficacy was found to be the second-strongest predictor overall, and one of only two traditional predictors in the top ten (the other being attribution of success to ability).

Another study examined the relationship between self-efficacy beliefs and belongingness for first-generation female students pursuing academic and career pathways in computing (Blaney & Stout, 2017). The results of this study showed that first-generation women had significantly lower self-efficacy and belongingness than other groups of students. The study also found that perceptions of inclusivity were most closely connected to self-efficacy for the female first-generation students. In a smaller qualitative study, Kinnunen and Simon (2011) found that students' self-efficacy beliefs are subject to frequent revision over the length of a computing course and that the emotional reactions caused by the work done in the course can influence how self-efficacy beliefs are revised. Furthermore, they found that task difficulty and achievement goal orientation may moderate these changes in self-efficacy. Overall, the existing research on self-efficacy in computing education has found that it is a significant predictor of student outcomes.

In recognition of the importance of self-efficacy, a few computing educa-tion researchers have attempted to develop self-efficacy instruments specific to computing contexts. Ramalingam and Wiedenbeck (1999) developed a 32-item self-efficacy survey to capture different dimensions of self-efficacy, including magnitude, strength, and generality. More recently, Danielsiek et al. (2017) have built on this original instrument to develop a new instrument for an algorithms course. The purpose of this study was largely to develop and pilot the instrument and test its factor structure, but they also investigated hypothesized differences in self-efficacy levels, such as before and after an exam, and gender differences. They found that there were no significant differences between male and female students, nor for individual students before and after a midterm exam (Danielsiek et al., 2017). They also investigated the correlations between their self-efficacy scale and that of Ramalingam and Wiedenbeck (1999), finding a large correlation between the two scales. Bhardwaj (2017) took a different approach to developing a computing self-efficacy instrument, focusing on the context-specific nature of the construct of self-efficacy (Bandura, 1986), because the existing generic self-efficacy measures were not seen as fully informative of students' self-beliefs in the computing context. Further research on the impact of self-efficacy on students' performance in computing should use and refine these instruments to further develop the theory behind a computing-specific notion of self-efficacy.

Previous work in computing education has also examined the possibility of a self-efficacy feedback loop in introductory programming students. Lishinski et al. (2016) collected student programming project scores at multiple points of time during the semester and had students complete self-efficacy items from the Motivated Strategies for Learning Questionnaire (Pintrich et al., 1993). Using path analysis, the authors found evidence of reciprocal relationships between self-efficacy and course outcomes over the course of the semester, meaning that students' initial self-efficacy beliefs influenced initial course outcomes, which then influenced later self-efficacy beliefs, which then influenced later course outcomes. The path analysis also showed that self-efficacy mediates the asso-ciation between metacognitive self-regulation and course outcomes, meaning that self-regulation is related to outcomes by virtue of the fact that it is related to self-efficacy (Lishinski et al., 2016). These path analysis findings further uncovered evidence that the self-efficacy feedback loop operates differently for male and female students, suggesting that female students are quicker to revise their self-efficacy beliefs in response to feedback than male students (Lishinski et al., 2016). These findings are useful for understanding how self-efficacy impacts novice programming students' outcomes, and perhaps also for gaining a better understanding of the computing gender participation gap, which may be in part related to different self-efficacy profiles of male and female students.

28.2.2 Goal Orientation

Goal orientation is another important component of self-regulated learning theory. In this context, goals are the academic outcomes that students desire for themselves, whereas *goal orientation* refers to an individual's tendency to prefer certain types of goals. Goals and goal orientation are central to self-regulated learning theory because any possible model of self-regulated learning requires that there be some sort of criterion or standard against which one's learning progress can be judged, which in turn provides a basis for determining what sort of course correction may be necessary (Pintrich, 2000).

A student's goal orientation is important because it determines how students judge themselves when they monitor their own progress or performance (Locke & Latham, 2012). Students' goal orientations have traditionally been described along two primary dimensions: intrinsic/mastery goal orientation and extrinsic/performance goal orientation. Intrinsic goal orientation is the degree to which a student values learning for the sake of personal growth, whereas extrinsic goal orientation is the degree to which a student values learning for the sake of social demonstration of success (Pintrich & Schunk, 1995). More recent research on goal orientations has added additional dimensions to the performance goal category – performance approach and performance avoidance – although much research has neglected this distinction (Pekrun et al., 2014; Tuominen-Soini et al., 2012). Performance-approach goals have to do with affirmatively demonstrating competence, whereas performance-avoidance goals have to do with avoiding the demonstration of incompetence (Elliot & Harackiewicz, 1996).

Generally speaking, previous research has shown that higher intrinsic goal orientation is associated with greater success in academic situations, whereas higher extrinsic goal orientation is associated with more difficulties (Wolters & Yu, 1996). Previous work on goal orientation has suggested that its importance may be related to self-efficacy. A study by Phillips and Gully (1997) showed that a performance goal orientation is negatively related to self-efficacy and that a mastery goal orientation is positively related to self-efficacy for undergraduate students. Other research has suggested a connection between goal orientation and self-regulation. A study by Bouffard et al. (1995) found that mastery goal orientation was associated with more use of self-regulatory strategies for undergraduate students. Furthermore, this study found evidence of a gender difference in this relationship, as mastery goal orientation was associated with a greater increase in self-regulatory strategy use for female students than for male students.

Previous computing education research on the impact of goal orientations has found a positive association with course grades. Studies of CS1 students have found positive relationships between intrinsic goal orientation and interest in computing, as well as course outcomes. Bergin and Reilly (2005) examined motivation and comfort level constructs that may influence performance in an introductory programming course with 110 undergraduate students. They found the strongest association with course performance in self-efficacy and intrinsic goal orientation. Zingaro and Porter (2016) examined the association between intrinsic goal orientation and two different outcomes: course exam grade and interest in computing. They found significant positive associations between intrinsic goal orientation and both of those outcomes.

28.2.3 Metacognitive Self-Regulation

Metacognitive self-regulation is another important component of self-regulated learning theory that consists of self-monitoring behaviors and strategies that students implement in order to overcome academic challenges (Corno, 1986). These behaviors include setting goals for oneself while learning and checking one's comprehension as one studies. Metacognitive strategies can be distinguished from cognitive strategies, which have more to do with the specific content of a learning task, whereas metacognitive strategies have more to do with managing one's behaviors and approach to the learning process. These strategies have been shown empirically to mediate the link between cognitive strategies and academic performance (Ford et al., 1998; Winne, 1996).

Self-regulation has been often studied, and its role and importance in academic settings are well established. A study by Shell and Husman (2008) linked high use of self-regulation strategies to a number of important noncognitive variables in a group of 397 undergraduate students. The authors examined the connection between strategic self-regulation and factors like goal orientation, self-efficacy, affect, outcome expectancy, control beliefs, and causal attributions. The results of this study showed that higher use of self-regulation strategies was associated with several positive noncognitive characteristics, including higher self-efficacy, positive affect, effort causal attribution, and mastery goal orientation (Shell & Husman, 2008). A study by Graham and Harris (2000) showed the importance of self-regulation for developing specific sets of academic skills – in this case, writing. Their model of writing skill development hypothesized a combination of self-regulatory and transcription skills to be necessary for the development of writing competency. The study looked at the available evidence from previous studies, finding that the evidence supported the hypothesis that the development of writing competence requires good self-regulatory skills and that individual differences in self-regulatory skills predict individual differences in writing competency.

Previous research has also found a positive association between metacognitive self-regulation and student outcomes in computing courses. A study by Bergin et al. (2005) examined the connection between metacognitive strategy use and programming performance with undergraduate students in an introductory object-oriented programming course. They found that the use of metacognitive resource management strategies was significantly associated with higher programming ability. A qualitative study by Havenga (2015) involved interviewing four senior undergraduate computing students about their experiences working through programming projects and tracking the degree to which they were succeeding at their task at various stages of the process. The study found common threads in all students' lack of metacognitive skills and their failures to solve the programming problems. A qualitative study by Falkner et al. (2014) examined the types of metacognitive strategies that were used by successful introductory programming students. They found that these students used many metacognitive strategies, including appropriate assessment of task difficulty, effective problem decomposition, and diligent time management and planning.

28.2.4 Conclusions

The previous discussion of motivational constructs suggests that self-efficacy, goal orientation, and metacognitive self-regulation are important for computing students and are good predictors of success in learning to program. While research is starting to emerge on the role of motivational constructs in computing education, we still don't have a complete picture of how these constructs interact to predict student learning in computing. We also know little about the influence of motivation in predicting success for students from traditionally underrepresented groups, including women and minorities. Researchers should further examine how we can develop pedagogical approaches and curricula to support computing students with respect to the motivational variables discussed above. For example, while we have a number of studies that identify the importance of self-efficacy for success in computing, we have no studies about how to help students develop and maintain their self-efficacy in computing. The ever-increasing interest in motivation constructs in computing education research is an encouraging sign, and as it becomes more mainstream for issues of motivation to hold equal importance to issues of computing content for researchers, we should see more research that provides evidence of how we can address the issue of motivation through pedagogy, and thereby increase the percentage of computing students that have successful outcomes.

28.3 Attitudes

Attitudes are defined in psychology simply as evaluative judgments about something (Maio & Haddock, 2009). In other words, an individual holds an attitude toward something when they have an enduring feeling toward something. Attitudes differ in valence, which is to say that attitudes can be positive or negative. They also differ in strength, which refers to their stability and resistance to change over time, as well as to their ability to guide our behavior and to influence how we process information (Maio & Haddock, 2009). A person can hold an attitude toward anything that is subject to evaluative judgment; people can have attitudes toward themselves as well as external things. Attitudes can be formed on the basis of thoughts (which are pieces of information that we believe to be true about the object), feelings (which are our subjective affective experiences of the object), and past behaviors (Maio & Haddock, 2009). The goal of this section is to discuss research on students attitudes toward computing (e.g., computing interest), precursors of attitude formation (e.g., emotional responses), and behavioral proxies for attitudes (e.g., engagement). The following sections provide a broad overview of the different ways that attitudes can influence students' success and persistence in computing.

28.3.1 Interest and Engagement

Interest and engagement are two aspects of attitudes that have been studied with computing students. To directly address students' attitudes toward computing, researchers have typically investigated students' interest in and perceptions of computing, whereas measures of student engagement are more concerned with observable behaviors. This section gives a brief overview of the concepts of interest and engagement in education, followed by a review of the studies in computing education that have addressed these constructs.

Student interest has been discussed in educational research going back at least to Dewey (1913), who defined interest as being engaged or engrossed in an activity because it is recognized as worthy (Dewey, 1913). Empirical research outside of computing has identified interest as an important affective factor influencing success in academic settings. A study by Singh et al. (2002) examined the connections between motivation, attitudes, and engagement and achievement in math and science using a nationally representative sample of eighth graders from the NELS:88 data set. Math and science attitudes/interest were assessed using survey instruments asking students to indicate the degree to which they thought math/science would be useful for their future and whether they looked forward to math/science class. Using structural equation modeling, they tested the relationships between the affective factors and math and science achievement, finding that attitudes/interest toward math had a significant direct effect on math achievement, stronger even than math motivation, and that attitudes/interest toward science had a significant indirect effect on science achievement, mediated by time spent studying (Singh et al., 2002). A study by Ackerman and Heggestad (1997) investigated the connections between interests and intellectual abilities. The results of this study found significant connections between math, spatial, and mechanical aptitude scores and interest in science and engineering fields.

Much of the research on interest in computing has focused on the gender participation gap and the finding that female students have lower levels of interest in computing than male students. This research has attempted to identify reasons why this is the case and has posited a number of possible contributing factors, such as female students' conceptualization of computing as a male-dominated field (Schulte & Knobelsdorf, 2007) and female students' sense of the limited relevance of computing (Goode et al., 2006). There have been few studies that have examined interest in computing outside the context of the gender gap. A study by Carter (2006) explored the reasons why high school students who we would expect to have a strong aptitude for computing have a lack of interest in computing and choose not to pursue it. This study found that the biggest reason for lack of interest in computing among high school students is an incorrect perception of what computing is, with the vast majority of students surveyed having no idea what computing is, a small minority associating computing with programming, and a much smaller minority identifying computing with the target definition that included writing programs, designing hardware, problem-solving, and interdisciplinary connections between computing and other fields (Carter, 2006).

Some prior research has examined the problem of how to influence students' interest in computing. Hildebrandt and Diethelm (2012) identified several important factors based on previous research on the topic: relevance of the material, quality of instruction, enthusiasm of the instructor, social integration, support of competence, and support of autonomy. An even more foundational factor is exposure. Prior research has found that students' perceived importance of computing significantly increased after completing a CS1 course (Edwards, Back, & Woods, 2011). Pedagogical factors may also influence student interest in computing. A study by Zingaro (2015) examined the influence of different instructional models on student interest in an undergraduate CS1 course. They compared a traditional lecture-based course to one based on peer instruction and they found that the peer instruction students enjoyed their CS1 course more than traditional lecture students, although interest in computing between the two groups was no different. However, they did find that students with a performance goal orientation had lower interest in computing, but only in the traditional lecture class (Zingaro, 2015). These findings are interesting and suggest that instructional models like peer instruction, although they do not boost interest in computing generally, may have a positive effect in terms of keeping some students (those with a performance goal orientation) from losing interest in computing at the initial stage. These findings on interest in computing suggest that getting students into the field requires developing their interest in the field by ensuring that they get exposure to computing and gain an understanding of what the field is about. Furthermore, once students are in the door, sustaining their interest (and persistence) in computing requires quality instruction and support.

Engagement is another area of research in education that has been shown to be important in academic settings, particularly in higher education, and for addressing the needs of underrepresented groups (Quaye & Harper, 2014). Engagement has been used in educational research to broadly examine how involved and connected students are with their classes, institutions, and peers (Axelson & Flick, 2011). Whereas interest can be thought of more as a purely attitude-based construct, concerned only with students' perceptions and evaluative judgments, engagement has more to do with students' behaviors that are caused by their underlying attitudes.

Studies on engagement have typically looked at pedagogical factors that might influence students' engagement levels. A study by Shapka and Keating (2003) examined the effects of girls-only math and science classrooms on a group of ninth- and tenth-grade students, comparing them to girls in coeducational classes. They investigated group differences between the girls-only and coed students on a number of outcomes, including math and science achievement, perceived math competence, math anxiety, and engagement, in the form of math and science course enrollment as well as survey items asking students about their level of effort expended in math and science. The results of this study showed that, while controlling for previous achievement and background in math and science as well as psychological characteristics, the girls in the girls-only classes had higher math and science achievement, as well as higher self-reported effort expended and higher enrollment in further math and science courses for the rest of their high school careers (Shapka & Keating, 2003). A qualitative study by Rowan-Kenyon et al. (2012) examined factors that influence middle school students' engagement in math classes and how these factors influence these students' later math engagement and interest. The authors found that small-group cooperative learning and teacher encouragement were particularly beneficial in boosting students' math engagement. Disruptive behavior from peers, on the other hand, was found to detract from students' math engagement. These results are important because they show that engagement can be influenced by factors that educators have the ability to change.

Engagement has been an important area to study in computing education in order to understand whether students are engaged as well as how to positively influence engagement. One thing that has been found to influence computing students' engagement is self-efficacy. A study by Miura (1987) investigated the connection between self-efficacy and interest in computing and engineering among 368 undergraduate students. The study found significant correlations between a self-efficacy composite score and interest in computing, perceptions of the relevance of computing, and plans to take a computing course. The study also found that male students had a significantly higher level of self-efficacy and interest in computing. However, when controlling for self-efficacy, these differences in interest were not significant (Miura, 1987). A study by Kanaparan et al. (2017) investigated the connection between self-efficacy and behavioral engagement in a group of 433 undergraduate introductory programming students. Their model hypothesized that self-efficacy, measured using the programming self-efficacy survey (Ramalingam & Wiedenbeck, 1999), would influence three indicators of behavioral engagement (help-seeking, effort, and persistence) as measured by a survey instrument. Using structural equation modeling, they found that programming self-efficacy was indeed significantly related to the three behavioral engagement measures, being positively related to persistence and effort and negatively related to help-seeking. Of the three engagement indicators, two were significantly related to the programming course grade outcome: help-seeking being negatively related and effort being positively related (Kanaparan et al., 2017). The results of these studies show the important influence of self-efficacy on interest and engagement in computing.

Engagement has also been studied by examining students' feelings of belongingness. A study by Cheryan et al. (2009) examined the effects of computing classroom environments and computing stereotypes on belongingness and participation of female students. They found that merely changing the objects in a computing classroom from stereotypical ones (Star Trek posters, video games, etc.) to non-stereotypical ones (nature posters) was enough to completely level out the disparity in computing interest between male and female students (Cheryan et al., 2009).

In many ways, attitudes and motivation are two sides of the same coin. Students who hold a positive attitude toward computing are more likely to be motivated to participate and succeed in computing (Cheryan et al., 2009; Miura, 1987). Likewise, motivated students are more likely to be engaged in the behaviors that lead to success in computing. In this way, attitudes can be seen as a necessary precursor to motivation. As in the case of the studies of computing interest discussed previously, students who would likely be motivated to succeed in computing are unlikely to do so when they have no interest in the field, which may be simply due to having an insufficient understanding of the field. Exactly how we connect attitudes to motivation is less important than understanding the significance of both, particularly with respect to the goals of broadening computing participation and increasing persistence. Nevertheless, more research is needed on how to build and maintain students' interest and engagement in computing.

28.3.2 Emotional Responses

Another important component of students' affective experiences in computing courses are the emotions that they experience in response to the coursework. Emotional experiences are an important source of information in the formation of attitudes, so emotional responses could have the effect of pushing students in a positive or negative direction with regard to interest and engagement in computing, above and beyond their actual performance in computing courses. This makes emotional reactions an important area of study for computing education researchers who are interested in increasing not just participation in computing, but persistence in computing. This section first gives an introduction to research on emotions in education, followed by an overview of the most relevant prior research examining student emotions in computing courses.

The topic of emotions in academic settings has been studied a fair bit, with research finding that they are related to more global affective characteristics (such as academic engagement), as well as students' academic outcomes (Linnenbrink-Garcia, 2011). Other research has found distinct differences between the emotions experienced in response to homework assignments and those experienced in the classroom (Goetz et al., 2012). Homework assignments have been found to have the potential to create unpleasant emotions in students by virtue of the perceived quality of the assignment, and these unpleasant emotions can then lead to decreases in both effort and achievement (Dettmers et al., 2011). To connect to the importance of self-regulation detailed in the previous section, research has also found that emotions that students experience while problem-solving can significantly influence their self-regulation (Hannula, 2015).

In the context of computing and in particular learning to program, emotional reactions have not been given much attention. One study examined programming students' emotional responses to learning threshold concepts (Eckerdal,

2007). Eckerdal (2007) defined threshold concepts as core concepts in a discipline that structure the curriculum, which are characterized as being both essential to the discipline and troublesome and difficult for students to understand. The results of this study showed that learning a threshold concept was associated with an emotional trajectory that began with negative emotions like frustration and depression, but that then led to confidence when students were able to grasp the concept (Eckerdal, 2007).

Kinnunen and Simon (2010, 2011, 2012) conducted a series of in-depth qualitative studies on students' emotional responses when learning to program. In the first of these studies, Kinnunen and Simon conducted five in-depth interviews over a ten-week period with nine freshman computing major students at the end of their first year. Students were asked about their experiences completing a programming assignment, and the interviews were transcribed and coded for salient and interesting episodes. The data analysis identified the typical emotional responses that students had while working on programming projects and put them into the following five overarching categories: Proud/ Accomplished, Frustrated/Annoyed, Inadequate/Disappointed, Relaxed/ Relief, and Apprehensive/Reluctant. They also noted commonly experienced emotional response events, such as the "struck by lightning" experience, when students are caught off guard by a failure in their code, which causes a strong emotional response for most students.

A more recent study built upon the qualitative results from Kinnunen and Simon (2010), conducting a broader quantitative investigation of students' emotional responses to programming assignments in a CS1 course. The results of this study found significant connections between emotional responses early in the course and outcomes later in the course (Lishinski et al., 2017). Students' feelings of frustration early in the course were significantly related to lower outcomes near the end of the course, whereas students' confidence that they would do well early in the course was positively associated with later course outcomes. Furthermore, this study found evidence of significant indirect effects of emotional responses, suggesting that there is a reciprocal feedback loop process occurring (Lishinski et al., 2017).

28.4 Dispositions

Dispositions are enduring characteristics that vary between individuals. One type of disposition commonly studied in psychology is personality traits. Conceptually, personality traits are associated with enduring patterns of behavior that are consistent and unique within an individual (Mischel, 2013). Research on academic achievement has long since recognized the association between individuals' personality traits and their academic achievement (Komarraju, 2009), particularly at the postsecondary level (O'Connor & Paunonen, 2007), with empirical results suggesting that personality traits explain variation in academic achievement above and beyond the influence of intelligence (Kappe, 2012a).

Personality traits, as discrete factors that make up distinct components of one's overall "personality," have been used in models since the 1940s, but the most prominent model used in psychology today is the Big Five model of personality. The Big Five model originates from work by Goldberg (1990), who proposed a model of personality based on five orthogonal factors. The five factors were labeled *Surgency* (now called Extraversion), *Agreeableness*, *Conscientiousness*, *Emotional Stability* (now called Neuroticism), and *Intellect* (now called Openness to Experience). Extraversion/Surgency is the tendency to be sociable and seek stimulation through social interaction. Agreeableness is the tendency to be trusting, to cooperate, and to help others. Conscientiousness is the tendency to be organized, disciplined, and dependable. Neuroticism/ Emotional Stability is the tendency to experience negative emotions such as anxiety and depression. Intellect/Openness to Experience is the tendency to be willing to try new things and to be intellectually curious.

Prior research has found that Big Five personality traits are significantly related to academic outcomes, especially at the postsecondary level (Connor, 2007; Kappe, 2012; Komarraju, 2009). For example, Komarraju (2009) examined the relationship between the Big Five personality traits, an academic motivation survey instrument containing four intrinsic motivation scales and four extrinsic motivation scales, and college grade point average (GPA) for a group of 308 undergraduates. The results suggested that personality traits explained substantial variance in intrinsic and extrinsic motivation, as well as GPA. In particular, Agreeableness and Conscientiousness were correlated with GPA, and Conscientiousness was significantly correlated with all of the intrinsic and extrinsic motivation subscales.

Of the Big Five traits, Conscientiousness and Openness to Experience have been found to have the largest correlations with academic outcomes. Research has found that Conscientiousness explains the most variance in both high school and college GPAs, whereas Openness to Experience correlates most strongly with standardized test scores (Noftle & Robins, 2007). The Big Five personality traits are often found to compare favorably to other predictors of academic success as well. For example, one study found that Conscientiousness explains five times more variance in college GPA than intelligence (Kappe, 2012). A meta-analysis of the relationships between the Big Five traits and academic outcomes had similar results, finding that Conscientiousness is related to academic performance when controlling for intelligence, and that Conscientiousness, Openness to Experience, and Agreeableness were significantly correlated with academic outcomes (Poropat, 2009). Some research has suggested that the Big Five traits that impact academic outcomes do so by influencing intrinsic motivation. For example, multiple studies have found that Conscientiousness is interrelated with intrinsic motivation (Kappe, 2012; Komarraju, 2009). Other studies have pointed to factors such as academic effort and perceived ability as the mediators between Conscientiousness and academic outcomes.

Overall, personality traits have largely been studied in the computing education context in relation to pair programming. A number of researchers have sought to investigate whether personality traits and, more importantly, the interaction of the different personality traits of two people could influence how successful pair programming was for student learning. The available studies using the Big Five model have found that the traits did not impact (or only modestly impacted) the effectiveness of pair programming in increasing student outcomes (Hannay et al., 2010; Salleh et al., 2009). Studies of pair programming and personality using the Myers-Briggs model of personality, by contrast, have found evidence that heterogeneous personality pairings lead to significantly greater satisfaction and knowledge acquisition (Choi et al., 2008; Sfetsos et al., 2009). These inconsistent results suggest that perhaps the different models of personality and their associated measures are not tapping into the same underlying constructs. Nevertheless, beyond the context of pair programming, the influence of the Big Five traits on overall programming outcomes has not been sufficiently researched given the known importance of these factors in other academic settings. Further research is needed to investigate this question, not just to identify whether personality traits are related to outcomes, but also to investigate whether traits are related to outcomes because they impact aspects of students' affective experiences that are potentially more malleable than personality traits, such as self-efficacy.

28.5 Conclusions

It is our hope that this chapter has been a useful introduction to some of the uniquely human parts of computing students. This chapter intends to also serve as a reminder of how important these parts are. Let us not forget that the students are at the center of computing education, and that the motivational and emotional parts of them are not complications to be abstracted away, but are endemic to the task of education. This chapter has covered a broad range of noncognitive factors that have a significant impact on computing students, and it is our hope that the reader of this chapter has a better understanding of these factors themselves, their significance, and what we know currently about how they affect computing students. This chapter has admittedly opened more questions than it has resolved about the **implications for practice** of the research on noncognitive factors. There remain many **open questions** to be answered about how we can apply our knowledge of these factors to increase student success in computing classes. However, it is our hope that computing education researchers who read this chapter give greater consideration to these types of factors when devising research studies, given how important they are with respect to student outcomes, as well as the goal of increasing and broadening participation.

There is still much to discover about how the aspects of students' experiences that we have the power to influence may be affected by pedagogical interventions. For example, we know much about the importance of self-efficacy, but very little about how to positively influence students' self-efficacy, particularly in the computing context. Future research should look into ways that we can alter pedagogy in computing with an eye toward improving things like self-efficacy, engagement, and interest, while also being mindful about the factors like personality traits that might make particular instructional models effective for some students while not for others.

References

Ackerman, P. L., & Heggestad, E. D. (1997). Intelligence, personality, and interests: Evidence for overlapping traits. *Psychological Bulletin*, 121(2), 219–245.

Almstrum, V. L. et al. (2005). Challenges to computer science education research. In *Proceedings of the 36th SIGCSE technical symposium on Computer science education (SIGCSE '05)* (pp. 191–192). New York: ACM.

Andrew, S. (1998). Self-efficacy as a predictor of academic performance in science. *Journal of Advanced Nursing*, 27(3), 596–603.

Axelson, R. D., & Flick, A. (2011). Defining student engagement. *Change* (January/February), 38–43.

Bandura, A. (Ed.) (1995). *Self-Efficacy in Changing Societies*. Cambridge, UK: Cambridge University Press.

Bandura, A. (1997). *Self-Efficacy: The Exercise of Control*. New York: Macmillan.

Bandura, A. (1986). *Social Foundations of Thought and Action: A Social Cognitive Theory*. Englewood Cliffs, NJ: Prentice-Hall.

Bandura, A. (1977). Self-efficacy: Toward a unifying theory of behavioral change. *Psychological Review*, 84(2), 191–215.

Barker, R. J., & Unger, E. A. (1983). A predictor for success in an introductory programming class based upon abstract reasoning development. *ACM SIGCSE Bulletin*, 15(1), 154–8.

Bennedsen, J., & Caspersen, M. E. (2005). An investigation of potential success factors for an introductory model-driven programming course. In *Proceedings of the First International Workshop on Computing Education Research (ICER '05)* (pp. 155–163). New York: ACM.

Bergin, S., & Reilly, R. (2005). Programming: Factors that influence success. *ACM SIGCSE Bulletin*, 37(1), 411–5.

Bernstein, D. R. (1991). Comfort and experience with computing: Are they the same for women and men? *ACM SIGCSE Bulletin*, 23(3), 57–61.

Beyer, S. (2008). Predictors of female and male computer science students' grades. *Journal of Women and Minorities in Science and Engineering*, 14(4), 377–409.

Bhardwaj, J. (2017). In search of self-efficacy: Development of a new instrument for first year Computer Science students. *Computer Science Education*, 27(2), 79–99.

Blaney, J. M., Hall, M., Plaza, P., & Stout, J. G. (2017). Examining the relationship between introductory computing course experiences, self-efficacy, and belonging among first-generation college women. In *Proceedings of the 2017 ACM SIGCSE Technical Symposium on Computer Science Education (SIGCSE '17)* (pp. 69–74). New York: ACM.

Bouffard, T., Boisvert, J., Vezeau, C., & Larouche, C. (1995). The impact of goal orientation on self-regulation and performance among college students. *British Journal of Educational Psychology*, 65, 317–329.

Britner, S. L., & Pajares, F. (2006). Sources of science self-efficacy beliefs of middle school students. *Journal of Research in Science Teaching*, 43(5), 485–499.

Brunello, G., & Schlotter, M. (2011). *Non Cognitive Skills and Personality Traits: Labour Market Relevance and their Development in Education and Training Systems. IZA Discussion paper 5743*. Bonn, Germany: The Institute for the Study of Labor (IZA).

Busch, T. (1995). Gender differences in self-efficacy and attitudes toward computers. *Journal of Educational Computing Research*, 12(2), 147–158.

Carter, L. (2006). Why students with an apparent aptitude for computer science don't choose to major in computer science. *ACM SIGCSE Bulletin*, 38(1), 27–31.

Cheryan, S., Plaut, V. C., Davies, P. G., & Steele, C. M. (2009). Ambient belonging: How stereotypical cues impact gender participation in computer science. *Journal of Personality and Social Psychology*, 97(6), 1045–1060.

Choi, K. S., Deek, F. P., & Im, I. (2008). Exploring the underlying aspects of pair programming: The impact of personality. *Information and Software Technology*, 50(11), 1114–1126.

Cohoon, J. M. (2003). Must there be so few? Including women in CS. In *Proceedings of the 25th International Conference on Software Engineering* (pp. 668–674). New York: IEEE.

Corno, L. (1986). The metacognitive control components of self-regulated learning. *Contemporary Educational Psychology*, 11(4), 333–346.

Danielsiek, H., Toma, L., & Vahrenhold, J. (2017). An instrument to assess self-efficacy in introductory algorithms courses. In *Proceedings of the 2017 ACM Conference on International Computing Education Research (ICER '17)* (pp. 217–225). New York: ACM.

Dettmers, S., Trautwein, U., Lüdtke, O., Goetz, T., Frenzel, A. C., & Pekrun, R. (2011). Students' emotions during homework in mathematics: Testing a theoretical model of antecedents and achievement outcomes. *Contemporary Educational Psychology*, 36(1), 25–35.

Dewey, J. (1913). *Interest and Effort in Education*. Boston, MA: Houghton Mifflin.

Eckerdal, A., McCartney, R., Moström, J. E., Sanders, K., Thomas, L., & Zander, C. (2007). From limen to lumen: Computing students in liminal spaces. In *Proceedings of the Third International Workshop on Computing Education Research (ICER '07)* (pp. 123–132). New York: ACM.

Edwards, S. H., Back, G. V., & Woods, M. J. (2011). Experiences evaluating student attitudes in an introductory programming course. In *Proceedings of the 2011 International Conference on Frontiers in Education: Computer Science and Computer Engineering* (pp. 477–482). New York: IEEE.

Elliot, A. J., & Harackiewicz, J. M. (1996). Approach and avoidance achievement goals and intrinsic motivation: A mediational analysis. *Journal of Personality and Social Psychology*, 70(3), 461–475.

Falkner, K., Vivian, R., & Falkner, N. (2014). Identifying computer science self-regulated learning strategies. In *Proceedings of the 2014 Conference on Innovation & Technology in Computer Science Education (ITiCSE '14)* (pp. 291–296). New York: ACM.

Ford, J. K., Smith, E. M., Weissbein, D. A., Gully, S. M., & Salas, E. (1998). Relationships of goal orientation, metacognitive activity, and practice strategies with learning outcomes and transfer. *Journal of Applied Psychology*, 83(2), 218–233.

Goetz, T., Nett, U. E., Martiny, S. E., Hall, N. C., Pekrun, R., Dettmers, S., & Trautwein, U. (2012). Students' emotions during homework: Structures, self-concept antecedents, and achievement outcomes. *Learning and Individual Differences*, 22(2), 225–34.

Goldberg, L. R. (1990). An alternative "description of personality": The Big-Five factor structure. *Journal of Personality and Social Psychology*, 59(6), 1216–1229.

Goode, J., Estrella, R., & Margolis, J. (2006). Lost in translation: Gender and High School Computer Science. In J. Cohoon & W. Aspray (Eds.), *Women and Information Technology: Research on Underrepresentation* (pp. 89–114). Cambridge, MA: MIT Press.

Graham, S., & Harris, K. R. (2000). The role of self-regulation and transcription skills in writing and writing development. *Educational Psychologist*, 35(1), 3–12.

Hannay, J. E., Arisholm, E., Engvik, H., & Sjøberg, D. I. K. (2010). Effects of personality on pair programming. *IEEE Transactions on Software Engineering*, 36(1), 61–80.

Hannula, M. S. (2015). Emotions in problem solving. In S. J. Cho (Ed.), *Selected Regular Lectures from the 12th International Congress on Mathematical Education* (pp. 269–288). Berlin, Germany: Springer International Publishing.

Havenga, M. (2015). The role of metacognitive skills in solving object-oriented programming problems: A case study. *Journal for Transdisciplinary Research in Southern Africa*, 11(1), 133–147.

Hildebrandt, C., & Diethelm, I. (2012). The school experiment InTech – How to influence interest, self-concept of ability in Informatics and vocational orientation. In *Proceedings of the 7th Workshop in Primary and Secondary Computing Education (WIPCSE '12)* (pp. 30–39). New York: ACM.

Hostetler, T. R. (1983). Predicting student success in an introductory programming course. *SIGCSE Bulletin*, 15(3), 40–44.

Jacob, B. A. (2002). Where the boys aren't: Non-cognitive skills, returns to school and the gender gap in higher education. *Economics of Education Review*, 21, 589–598.

Kanaparan, G., Cullen, R., & Mason, D. D. M. (2017). Self-efficacy and behavioural engagement in introductory programming courses self-efficacy and behavioural engagement. In *PACIS 2017 Proceedings* (p. 209). Atlanta, GA: AIS.

Kappe, R., & Van Der Flier, H. (2012). Predicting academic success in higher education: What's more important than being smart? *European Journal of Psychology of Education*, 27(4), 605–619.

Katz, L. G. (1993). Dispositions as Educational Goals. ERIC Digest. Retrieved from https://files.eric.ed.gov/fulltext/ED363454.pdf

Kinnunen, P., & Simon, B. (2011). CS majors' self-efficacy perceptions in CS1: Results in light of social cognitive theory. In *Proceedings of the Seventh International Workshop on Computing Education Research (ICER '11)* (pp. 19–26). New York: ACM.

Kinnunen, P., & Simon, B. (2010). Experiencing programming assignments in CS: The emotional toll. In *Proceedings of the Sixth International Workshop on Computing Education Research (ICER '10)* (pp. 77–85). New York: ACM.

Kinnunen, P., & Simon, B. (2012). My program is ok – Am I? Computing freshmen's experiences of doing programming assignments. *Computer Science Education*, 22(1), 1–28.

Komarraju, M., Karau, S. J., & Schmeck, R. R. (2009). Role of the Big Five personality traits in predicting college students' academic motivation and achievement. *Learning and Individual Differences*, 19(1), 47–52.

Kurtz, B. L. (1980). Investigating the relationship between the development of abstract reasoning and performance in an introductory programming class. *ACM SIGCSE Bulletin*, 12(1), 110–117.

Lent, R. W., & Hackett, G. (1994). Sociocognitive mechanisms of personal agency in career development: Pantheoretical prospects. In M. L. Savikas & R. W. Lent (Eds.), *Convergence in Career Development Theories: Implications for Science and Practice* (pp. 77–101). Palo Alto, CA: CPP Books.

Linnenbrink-Garcia, L., & Pekrun, R. (2011). Students' emotions and academic engagement: Introduction to the special issue. *Contemporary Educational Psychology*, 36(1), 1–3.

Lishinski, A., Yadav, A., & Enbody, R. (2017). Students' emotional reactions to programming projects in introduction to programming: Measurement approach and influence on learning outcomes. In *Proceedings of the 2017 ACM Conference on International Computing Education Research (ICER '17)* (pp. 30–38). New York: ACM.

Lishinski, A., Yadav, A., Good, J., & Enbody, R. (2016). Learning to program: Gender differences and interactive effects of students' motivation, goals and self-efficacy on performance. In *Proceedings of the 12th Annual International ACM Conference on International Computing Education Research (ICER '16)* (pp. 211–220). New York: ACM.

Locke, E. A., & Latham, G. P. (1990). *A Theory of Goal Setting and Task Performance*. Englewood Cliffs, NJ: Prentice-Hall.

Locke, E. A., & Latham, G. P. (2012). *New Developments in Goal Setting and Task Performance*. New York, NY: Routledge.

Maddux, J. E. (1995). Self-efficacy theory. In J. Maddux (Ed.), *Self-Efficacy, Adaptation, and Adjustment* (pp. 3–33). Boston, MA: Springer.

Maio, G., & Haddock, G. (2009). *The Psychology of Attitudes and Attitude Change*. London, UK: Sage.

Miller, J. (2015). *Predictors of Student Persistence in the STEM Pipeline: Activities Outside the Classroom, Parent Aspirations, and Student Self-beliefs Using NELS:88 Data* (doctoral dissertation). Notre Dame of Maryland University.

Mischel, W. (2013). *Personality and Assessment*. London, UK: Psychology Press.

Miura, I. T. (1987). The relationship of computer self-efficacy expectations to computer interest and course enrollment in college. *Sex Roles*, 16(5/6), 303–311.

Murphy, P. K., & Alexander, P. A. (2000). A motivated exploration of motivation terminology. *Contemporary Educational Psychology*, 25, 3–53.

Nasim, A., Roberts, A., Harrell, J. P., Young, H., Roberts, A., & Harrell, J. P. (2005). Non-cognitive predictors of academic achievement for African Americans across cultural contexts. *Journal of Negro Education*, 74(4), 344–358.

Noftle, E. E., & Robins, R. W. (2007). Personality predictors of academic outcomes: Big Five Correlates of GPA and SAT scores. *Journal of Personality and Social Psychology*, 93(1), 116–130.

O'Connor, M. C., & Paunonen, S. V. (2007). Big Five personality predictors of post-secondary academic performance. *Personality and Individual Differences*, 43, 971–990.

Pajares, F., & Graham, L. (1999). Self-efficacy, motivation constructs, and mathematics performance of entering middle school students. *Contemporary Educational Psychology*, 24(2), 124–139.

Pajares, F., & Miller, M. D. (1994). Role of self-efficacy and self-concept beliefs in mathematical problem solving: A path analysis. *Journal of Educational Psychology*, 86(2), 193–203.

Pajares, F., & Valiante, G. (1997). Influence of self-efficacy on elementary students' writing. *Journal of Educational Research*, 90(6), 353–360.

Pekrun, R., Cusack, A., Murayama, K., Elliot, A. J., & Thomas, K. (2014). The power of anticipated feedback: Effects on students' achievement goals and achievement emotions. *Learning and Instruction*, 29, 115–24.

Perloff, R. M. (2017). *The Dynamics of Persuasion: Communication and Attitudes in the Twenty-First Century*, 6th edn. London, UK: Routledge.

Phillips, J. M., & Gully, S. M. (1997). Role of goal orientation, ability, need for achievement, and locus of control in the self-efficacy and goal-setting process. *Journal of Applied Psychology*, 82(5), 792–802.

Pintrich, P. R., Smith, D. A. F., Garcia, T., & McKeachie, W. J. (1993). Reliability and predictive validity of the Motivated Strategies for Learning Questionnaire (MSLQ). *Educational and Psychological Measurement*, 53(3), 801–813.

Pintrich, P. R. (2000). The role of goal orientation in self-regulated learning. In M. Boekaerts, P. R. Pintrich, & M. Zeidner (Eds.), *Handbook of Self-Regulation* (pp. 451–529). Amsterdam, The Netherlands: Elsevier Science & Technology.

Pintrich, P. R., & De Groot, E. V. (1990). Motivational and self-regulated learning components of classroom academic performance. *Journal of Educational Psychology*, 82(1), 33–40.

Pintrich, P. R., & Schunk, D. H. (1995). *Motivation in Education: Theory, Research, and Applications*. Englewood Cliffs, NJ: Prentice-Hall.

Poropat, A. E. (2009). A meta-analysis of the five-factor model of personality and academic performance. *Psychological Bulletin*, 135(2), 322–38.

Quaye, S. J., & Harper, S. R. (Eds.) (2014). *Student Engagement in Higher Education: Theoretical Perspectives and Practical Approaches for Diverse Populations*. London, UK: Routledge.

Ramalingam, V., LaBelle, D., & Wiedenbeck, S. (2004). Self-efficacy and mental models in learning to program. In *Proceedings of the 9th Annual SIGCSE Conference on Innovation and Technology in Computer Science Education (ITiCSE '04)* (pp. 171–175). New York: ACM.

Ramalingam, V., & Wiedenbeck, S. (1999). Development and validation of scores on a computer programming self-efficacy scale and group analyses of novice programmer self-efficacy. *Journal of Educational Computing Research*, 19(4), 367–381.

Robins, A. (2015). The ongoing challenges of computer science education research. *Computer Science Education*, 25(2), 115–119.

Rowan-Kenyon, H. T., Swan, A. K., & Creager, M. F. (2012). Social cognitive factors, support, and engagement: Early adolescents' math interests as precursors to choice of career. *The Career Development Quarterly*, 60, 2–15.

Salleh, N., Mendes, E., Grundy, J., & Burch, G. (2009). An empirical study of the effects of personality in pair programming using the five-factor model. In *Third International Symposium on Empirical Software Engineering and Measurement (ESEM 2009)* (pp. 214–225). New York: ACM.

Schulte, C., & Knobelsdorf, M. (2007). Attitudes towards computer science–computing experiences as a starting point and barrier to computer science. In *Proceedings of the Third International Workshop on Computing Education Research (ICER '07)* (pp. 27–38). New York: ACM.

Schunk, D. H. (1995). Self-efficacy and education and instruction. In J. Maddux (Ed.), *Self-Efficacy, Adaptation, and Adjustment: Theory Research and Application* (pp. 281–303). New York: Springer US.

Schunk, D. H., & Ertmer, P. A. (2000). Self-regulation and academic learning: Self-efficacy enhancing interventions. In M. Boekaerts, P. R. Pintrich, & M. Zeidner (Eds.), *Handbook of Self-Regulation* (pp. 631–649). Amsterdam, The Netherlands: Elsevier Science & Technology.

Schwarzer, R., & Fuchs, R. (1995). Changing risk behaviors and adopting health behaviors: The role of self-efficacy beliefs. In A. Bandura (Ed.), *Self-Efficacy in Changing Societies* (pp. 259–288). Cambridge, UK: Cambridge University Press.

Sfetsos, P., Stamelos, I., Angelis, L., & Deligiannis, I. (2009). An experimental investigation of personality types impact on pair effectiveness in pair programming. *Empirical Software Engineering*, 14(2), 187–226.

Shapka, J. D., & Keating, D. P. (2003). Effects of a girls-only curriculum during adolescence: Performance, persistence, and engagement in mathematics and science. *American Educational Research Journal*, 40(4), 929–960.

Shell, D. F., & Husman, J. (2008). Control, motivation, affect, and strategic self-regulation in the college classroom: A multidimensional phenomenon. *Journal of Educational Psychology*, 100(2), 443–459.

Singh, K., Granville, M., & Dika, S. (2002). Mathematics and science achievement: Effects of motivation, interest, and academic engagement. *The Journal of Educational Research*, 95(6), 323–332.

Tracey, T. J., & Sedlacek, W. E. (1984). Noncognitive variables in predicting academic success by race. *Measurement and Evaluation in Guidance*, 16, 171–178.

Tuominen-Soini, H., Salmela-Aro, K., & Niemivirta, M. (2012). Achievement goal orientations and academic well-being across the transition to upper secondary education. *Learning and Individual Differences*, 22(3), 290–305.

Valentine, J. C., Dubois, D. L., & Cooper, H. (2004). The relation between self-beliefs and academic achievement: A meta-analytic review. *Educational Psychologist*, 39(2), 111–133.

Watson, C., Li, F. W. B., & Godwin, J. L. (2014). No tests required: Comparing traditional and dynamic predictors of programming success. In *Proceedings of the 45th ACM Technical Symposium on Computer Science Education (SIGCSE '14)* (pp. 469–474). New York: ACM.

Weber, H. S., Lu, L., Shi, J., & Spinath, F. M. (2013). The roles of cognitive and motivational predictors in explaining school achievement in elementary school. *Learning and Individual Differences*, 25, 85–92.

Wiedenbeck, S. (2005). Factors affecting the success of non-majors in learning to program. In *Proceedings of the 2005 International Workshop on Computing Education Research (ICER '05)* (pp. 13–24). New York: ACM.

Williams, T., & Williams, K. (2010). Self-efficacy and performance in mathematics: Reciprocal determinism in 33 nations. *Journal of Educational Psychology*, 102(2), 453–66.

Wilson, B. C. (2010). A study of factors promoting success in computer science including gender differences. *Computer Science Education*, 12(1–2), 141–164.

Winne, P. H. (1996). A metacognitive view of individual differences in self-regulated learning. *Learning and Individual Differences*, 8(4), 327–353.

Wolters, C., & Yu, S. (1996). The relation between goal orientation and students' motivational beliefs and self-regulated learning. *Learning & Individual Differences*, 8(3), 211–238.

Zimmerman, B. J., & Schunk, D. H. (1989). *Self-Regulated Learning and Academic Achievement: Theory, Research, and Practice*. New York: Springer-Verlag.

Zingaro, D. (2015). Examining interest and grades in Computer Science 1. *ACM Transactions on Computing Education (TOCE)*, 15(3), 1–18.

Zingaro, D., & Porter, L. (2016). Impact of student achievement goals on CS1 outcomes. In *Proceedings of the 47th ACM Technical Symposium on Computer Science Education (SIGCSE '16)* (pp. 279–284). New York: ACM.

29 Students As Teachers and Communicators

Beth Simon, Christopher Hundhausen, Charlie McDowell, Linda Werner, Helen Hu, and Clif Kussmaul

29.1 Introduction

Students as teachers? For most of us who experienced a transmissionist model of computing education (i.e., teacher tells/explains information to students), this sounds ludicrous. How can two novices teach each other the material they are both learning? However, for those who believe that learning is more than the passing of information from one brain to another, engaging students in teaching and learning together holds a lot of promise.

In this chapter, we start from a theoretical foundation of social constructivism. Though we won't adhere to any one specific definition, in general this work stems from the theory that human knowledge or development is both socially situated and constructed through the interaction of people. While such interaction in the settings we propose is often mediated by an instructor, the majority of the learning occurs when students interact with and, yes, "teach" each other. We present four practices that leverage the power of socially constructed learning among students: pair programming, peer instruction, studio-based learning, and process-oriented guided-inquiry learning (POGIL). The first pair of these we present as recommended practices, as there is extensive and replicated research showing beneficial impacts of these on learning in computing. The second two we present as promising practices, where some evidence for improving outcomes has been shown, but work is actively continuing to strengthen those findings and replicate them in multiple computing education settings.

29.2 Recommended Practice: Pair Programming

In four questions, we provide an overview of the practice before our in-depth description.

What Is It? It is a variation on an industry-standard practice. In education settings, students work synchronously in teams of two to create a program. Students take turns in one of two roles: the driver, who has their hands on the computing device, and the navigator, who provides instructions and guidance to the driver. Students constantly engage in communication and switch roles regularly.

What Beneficial Impacts Have Been Shown? For students in beginning programming courses (e.g., CS1) where pair programming was required for all programming assignments, students were more likely to pass the course and more likely to pass the next course where pair programming was not required.

In What Settings Does It Work? Introductory programming courses have undergone the most rigorous study of their impact on retention and success in the follow-on course. However, pair programming is and can be used in many courses, including software engineering or other "programming project-heavy" courses.

What Are the Limitations on What We Know? Very little comparative research exists on the impact of pair programming on learning or outcomes beyond the first programming course or with K–12 students. Current research focuses on how to best pair up students, but lacks definite advice.

29.2.1 What Is It?

The phrase "pair programming" was first applied to one practice within the agile software development methodology called "extreme programming" (XP). It was first studied in the university classroom by Williams and Kessler (2000a). Pair programming refers to a two-person team working together at a single computing device to accomplish some programming-related task. The two people typically take on two roles: that of a driver and a navigator. The driver is the one with their hands on the computing device (e.g., keyboard, mouse, or trackpad) and the navigator is looking on, making suggestions, watching for errors, and otherwise providing guidance to the driver. The partners constantly engage in conversation and frequently switch roles. In practice, as discussed below, these roles can become blurred. Pair programming was later adopted as a promising practice in higher education settings because of the benefits of increased retention of students continuing their study of computing, increases in programming confidence in students, and reductions in the "confidence gap" between female and male students.

There are a number of factors to consider when implementing pair programming in an educational setting. It is simplest, and probably most effective, when applied in a closed lab situation. In a closed lab, the students complete the entire programming activity while being supervised in a lab or classroom setting. In this setting, it is possible to enforce good pair programming techniques such as switching roles regularly and making sure both members of the pair are actively engaged in the process, including verbal and nonverbal behaviors. At the other extreme is the use of pair programming in an open lab situation, where all or most of the programming assignments are completed in an unsupervised setting at a time and location of the students' choosing. The trade-offs of using pair programming in an open lab situation are also discussed below.

A second key element in the implementation of pair programming is how to form the pairs. The two main decisions are in relation to the role that student preference plays in pair formation and the duration of a partnership. From an implementation point of view, the simplest approach for pair formation is to let the students choose their own partners. Other options are random assignments, assignments based upon some measure of compatibility (e.g., skill level, friendship), or some combination (e.g., the students provide short lists of preferred partners and pairs are formed from those lists, taking into account some prior measure of skill level). How best to assign partners may also depend upon how often partners are changed. Partners can be changed for each assignment, assigned for the entire length of the course, or anything in between.

A constant and lingering criticism of pair programming is that it will allow some students to skate through without doing the work and thus not learn the material. This is less of a problem in the closed lab setting as engagement and role switching can be closely monitored. In the open lab setting, it is reasonable to assume that some students will indeed "get credit" for some programming assignments that they would not be able to reproduce on their own and to which they may have contributed very little. We believe this should not be a reason to abandon pair programming in open labs for the following two reasons: first, even if not allowed to work with a partner, some students will get help that results in assignments they could not reproduce on their own. That help could come from a classmate, a well-intentioned but overly helpful teaching assistant, an online resource, or a family member. A simple approach to minimize the impact of such freeloading is to base a relatively small percentage of the grade on the programming assignments. One option could be to have lab-based tutors administer a couple of simple questions to each partner orally and individually (e.g., "What does this part of your code do?" or "If you wanted to change this part of the code to do Y instead of X, what would you change?"). Second, after numerous studies (McDowell et al., 2006; Salleh et al., 2011), most evidence indicates that individual exam performance in pair programming situations is as good as or better than that in comparable scenarios where all programming assignments were mandated to be completed individually.

29.2.1.1 What Theoretical Background Aligns with This Practice?

Cooperative or collaborative learning models involve two or more individuals taking turns helping one another learn information (Horn, Collier, Oxford, Bond, & Dansereau, 1998). Building on the research of Vygotsky (1978), socio-constructivists have studied how discussion and reflection on a specific task can help children construct an understanding that goes beyond what they can achieve on their own. For example, working with a partner encourages students to summarize and explain what they know, respond to immediate partner feedback, and work through by questions and discussion what they do not understand – all considered high-level thinking skills that improve performance (Palincsar & Brown, 1984). The consensus from numerous investigations is that academic achievement is enhanced when a student learns information with others as opposed to when they learn alone (O'Donnell & Dansereu, 1992; Slavin, 1996; Totten, Digby, & Russ 1991).

Within information technology fields, computer programming has traditionally been taught and practiced as a solitary activity (Cockburn & Williams, 2000). Collaborative activities have been taught and practiced for other software system development tasks, but not for programming (Basili, Green, Laitenberger, Lanubile, Shull, Sørumgård, & Zelkowitz, 1996; Fagan, 1986; Sauer, Jeffery, Land, & Yetton, 2000; Schlimmer, Fletcher, & Hermens, 1994). However, advocates of collaborative programming have independently emerged over the last decade (Williams & Kessler, 2000a). In 1991, Nick Flor, a cognitive scientist, observed and recorded verbal and nonverbal exchanges between two programmers working collaboratively on a software maintenance task. Flor and Hutchins (1991) found that collaboration allowed each member to contribute their unique prior experiences, task-relevant knowledge, and perspectives to the problem, resulting in a greater potential for the generation of more diverse plans and ultimately a greater capacity to solve the problem. These observations emphasize the effectiveness of collaborative programming and provide evidence for the theory of distributed cognition. According to the theory of distributed cognition, "knowledge is commonly socially constructed, through collaborative efforts toward shared objectives or by dialogues and challenges brought about by differences in persons' perspectives" (Pea, 1993).

29.2.2 What Does Research Say It Does?

Two 2011 systematic literature reviews (SLRs) of papers of studies of pair programming in higher education published between 1999 and 2010 (Hanks, Fitzgerald, McCauley, & Zander, 2011; Salleh, Mendes, & Grundy, 2011) report on a wide range of measures of effectiveness, including technical productivity, program/design quality, academic performance, satisfaction persistence, and retention and factors possibly impacting that effectiveness such as compatibility of partners, academic background, prior experience, physical configuration of environment, self-report of confidence, enjoyment, skill level, gender, ethnicity, and satisfaction.

The key findings are as follows:

- Almost all studies from the SLRs claim evidence that pair programming leads to success in beginning programming courses.
- Almost all studies from the SLRs reported similar findings, with students presenting greater satisfaction and enjoyment when using pair programming.
- The consensus from the SLRs is that pair programming works best when the partners have similar skill levels. The evidence is less clear about the role of personality type.
- A meta-analysis of six studies (Salleh et al., 2011) that reported their data in a manner allowing for meta-analysis found that students' individual performance in final exams is similar whether students are learning to program using pair programming or using solo programming. This seems to strongly refute any concern about significantly larger numbers of students sliding by without learning the material when working with a partner versus solo.

So if pair programming does not usually significantly improve exam performance for tertiary institution students, why use it? There are numerous reasons. At a very practical level, it means there are fewer programs to grade and fewer questions for the instructor or teaching assistant to answer (partners provide the answers). In at least one study (McDowell et al., 2006), although the final exam scores did not go up (or down), more students persisted to the end of the quarter, so in fact, more learning was taking place. Students also gain practice with teamwork and communication. Finally, there is evidence that the widely reported increase in satisfaction leads to greater retention, with more students completing the course and more students continuing on into more advanced courses.

29.2.3 What to Keep in Mind When Implementing

It is important that students be given some instruction about pair programming at the beginning of the course. Students need to understand that pair programming is not a "divide-and-conquer" team strategy where each partner works on a separate piece and then the parts are assembled in the end. They should also be given some explanation of the benefits to them of pair programming. Those benefits include the following:

- Having a classmate with whom you can freely discuss the problems without running afoul of cheating guidelines.
- Getting some questions answered more quickly without having to wait for the instructor or teaching assistant.
- Developing the vocabulary and discussion patterns they will use in industry.
- Having someone to celebrate with who understands the effort you have put in.
- Being less likely to procrastinate in an open lab because you need to preschedule time to work with your partner.

Options to help educate students and faculty about pair programming include the following:

- For high school or tertiary institution students, ask students to read "All I Really Need to Know about Pair Programming I Learned in Kindergarten" (Williams & Kessler, 2000b).
- For elementary and middle school students, view "Pair Programming" from Code.org (2014) featuring Fiona and Semira from Generation Code.
- For faculty, see NCWIT (2009) for a case study about pair programming (Barker & Cohoon, 2017) and "in-a-box" materials.

Appropriate space for two students to sit together at a single computing device is needed for pair programming when using the co-location, single-computing device model. Other configurations have been studied, such as two computing devices where an adjacent computer is used for documentation, and even distributed, where students do not work in the same physical location. Experimental findings are similar to those of co-location studies (Hanks et al., 2011).

Enforce an instructor-defined coding standard that reduces arguments about trivial coding issues.

In an open lab setting, it is important that students not be penalized or have a sense of being penalized for a pairing that didn't work. Scheduling times during which partners can work can be difficult. This is not a problem for students working in closed labs, since attending labs at predetermined times is part of the course enrollment process. Specifically, there should be a way for a student to make an individual submission rather than be forced to give an uncooperative partner credit for work they did not do. How you implement this depends upon the mechanism you use for collecting program submissions. One simple approach is to ask every student to submit their program along with a brief statement about how their pair worked. For successful pairings, both will submit the exact same program and indicate – possibly in the opening block comment of the program – that they completed the program using pair programming. For an unsuccessful pairing, the partners will each submit different programs that may share substantial code because they completed at least some of it together. This second group of programs will include a statement that they worked with so-and-so, but that they ended up completing the program on their own. The inclusion of the partner's name, even in a failed pairing, is important in order to avoid accusations of copying when portions of the submissions are found to match. In our experience of more than 15 years of using pair programming in the classroom, only a very small fraction of pairings dissolve with the result of each partner submitting different completions of the same initial effort.

There is some tension between having pairs remain together for more than a single session in order to allow them to "gel" and switching pairs frequently to avoid having one student be "stuck" with a particularly uncooperative partner for the entire term. Having most pairs stay together for the entire term can be effective provided there is a mechanism for dissolving and reforming pairs that are not working effectively.

In a closed lab situation, changing partners for each lab session minimizes the impact of an uncooperative partner or partners with drastically different skill levels. Changing partners can help individual learners be exposed to a broader range of communication and thinking styles and can help with building a community, which could be a reason for greater retention in the major.

One of the authors (CM) has evolved a system in which students are assigned a different partner for each programming assignment in an open lab setting. Each assignment extends over one or two weeks. Some effort is made to create pairs with similar skill levels. At the start of the quarter, this is based on either their grade in the prerequisite course if there was one or, in some cases, their major or level in school. Later in the quarter, an estimate of their course grade is used. More importantly, in addition to the default of getting an assigned partner, students may request a specific partner. For small classes, asking the students to justify the request can help avoid some problematic pairs in which friends with widely varying skill levels ask to work together. For larger classes where evaluating the requests is too costly timewise, at the minimum having a request mechanism that requires some explicit action from both partners is advisable. For example, simply requiring an email from both partners requesting the other will avoid one person asking for a partnership that is not desired by the other person.

29.2.4 Next Steps

Since pair programming has been identified as a best practice (in various venues, including multiple articles in the *Communications of the ACM* and by organizations such as the National Center on Women in Information Technology [NCWIT] and Code.org), more recent research seems to be focused on pair compatibility and equity rather than experiments of solo versus pair programming. The recent research of tertiary institution students using pair programming looked at code quality and learning gains and found higher code quality and learning gains were positively correlated with more contributions by both partners, partner feedback (either positive or non-positive), meta-comments (such as thinking out loud), and the expressivity of the student driver (Rodríguez, Price, & Boyer 2017). Pair compatibility is a hard problem and needs more work.

We have begun to see research of middle school students using pair programming. One study's results show that computing confidence determines who influences whom and therefore affects what is learned (Werner, Denner, Campe, Ortiz, DeLay, Hartl, & Laursen, 2013). Friendship status of the partners moderated the findings, such that the less confident partner influenced the more confident partner only if partners were also friends. The greatest increases in programming knowledge occurred among confident partners who were paired with a friend who had relatively greater initial programming knowledge. Other research with middle school students found that students who each worked on programming problems on their own computers but intermittently stopped to discuss problems with a nearby neighbor (called intermittent collaboration) completed programming exercises more quickly than students using pair programming. These two groups did not differ significantly in their performance on daily quizzes or responses to attitudinal survey questions (Lewis, 2011). Other results for middle school students looked at conversational equity or lack of it, as well as the kinds of talk (whether questions or commands). This research found that less equitable pairs wanted to complete tasks quickly, which the researchers hypothesized may have led to patterns of marginalization and domination. A focus on speed was not seen in the more equitable pairs (Lewis & Shah, 2015).

Future research needs to focus on studies that look at the reasons for *why* and *how* pair programming is beneficial. Since pair programming does not help all students, perhaps qualitative studies can be used to provide insight for educators and suggest areas of future research. Simon and Hanks (2008) used a qualitative, "student-focused" study to investigate introductory programming students' impressions of their pair programming experiences based on semi-structured interviews. Their study reinforced the results found in most quantitative studies;

however, they did observe results that we have not seen elsewhere in pair programming studies and that we feel need further study. One of these is that students using pair programming reported that they did not understand their program code as much as when they were solo programming. Another is that pair programming students reported a sense of reduced satisfaction when a program worked compared to when they were solo programming.

Can distributed pair programming be used to improve retention rates for students of introductory programming massive online open courses (MOOCs)?

Campaigns such as CS For All and organizations such as CSTA and Code.org are working toward computing standards, curricula for K–12 students, and training computer science (CS) K–12 teachers. There is little research of pair programming with K–12 students.

29.3 Recommended Practice: Peer Instruction

In four questions, we provide an overview of the practice before our in-depth description.

What Is It? Peer instruction (PI) is a specific protocol by which students in a classroom setting are engaged with challenging questions designed to confront misconceptions or push their zone of proximal development (see below). Students are presented with a multiple-choice question that they answer on their own (often with a clicker – a handheld voting device), discuss with peers in small groups, and then answer again. The instructor leads a final class-wide discussion and/or provides additional instruction to bring the topic to a close.

What Beneficial Impacts Have Been Shown? A range of positive student outcomes have been shown, including reduced course fail rates, increased student performance on exams, and positive student valuation. Studies using isomorphic questions show immediate learning from the discussion of PI questions.

In What Settings Does It Work? Studies have spanned both lower- and upper-division computing tertiary institution courses, including theory-focused and programming-focused courses. Studies span a range of class sizes from very small (10–20) to very large (>250) and private and public institutions. Most studies have been conducted in the USA and Canada.

What Are the Limitations of What We Know? In courses that require students to get questions correct in order to get credit (instead of giving credit primarily for participating), PI is far less valued by students, with <75 percent recommending other instructors use PI. Studies on student performance gains on exams are generally from lower-division courses. Work has begun to explore the potential of PI data from the first few weeks of the course in predicting students at risk of failing the course.

29.3.1 What Is It?

PI is a specific protocol by which students in a classroom setting are engaged with challenging questions designed to confront misconceptions or push their "zone of proximal development" (ZPD). (Vygotsky's ZPD is the space between what a learner can do independently and what they can with assistance; i.e., the space where learning can occur; e.g., see Chaiklin, 2003, and discussion in Chapters 8, 9, and 24 of this Handbook). Specifically, students are asked to individually consider and answer a multiple-choice question, usually recording their answer with a clicker. Then, with no additional information being given, students discuss the question in small teams. After this discussion, all students are asked to re-answer the question again with their clicker. Finally, the instructor may show the results of either or both polls and lead a class-wide discussion in which students share their thinking and, as needed, the instructor models their thinking or otherwise brings the discussion to an end.

PI is often implemented in conjunction with a flipped classroom model. Because so much time in the classroom is devoted to students discussing and answering challenging questions, students are often asked to learn some of the more basic material before class, often by reading the textbook. This learning is incentivized and checked through basic "reading quizzes," which can be administered before class online or at the beginning of the class, often using clickers. In this way, "easier" material can be learned by students independently, and student–instructor face-to-face interaction time can be focused on the more challenging concepts and applications.

PI was developed by Harvard physicist, Eric Mazur, in the context of introductory physics courses, though it has since been used and studied in upper-division and graduate physics courses, as well as in tertiary institution mathematics, chemistry, biology, and other science, technology, engineering, and mathematics (STEM) courses. In particular, Dr. Mazur was inspired to this approach when he found that his students, who could generally fare well on his typical "plug-and-chug" problem-solving-based exams, scored very low on the Force Concept Inventory (Hestenes & Halloun, 1995) featuring questions requiring the higher-level application of concepts. In tertiary institution STEM course settings, PI questions are sometimes described as "Concept Test" questions and may be described as questions that address common student misconceptions in a field (e.g., that a larger truck impacting a smaller car will impart a larger force on the car than the car will on the truck – a conception that contradicts Newton's third law of motion).

There has been less discussion of specific "types" of computing questions, and in general there is less focus on "misconceptions" in computing (see Chapter 27), as the challenges are generally not as aligned with preexisting misconceptions from the natural world (as is common for the natural sciences). Questions may focus on things students commonly misunderstand or get wrong (e.g., in code, in a proof, or given a bug) or involve students in evaluation of trade-offs (e.g., in operating systems or architecture). However, based on anecdotal advice from Mazur, a question that only 25–75 percent of students get right on the initial vote is considered "good" – although many students are not clear on the answer, they can engage with it in a productive manner in discussion. It is not uncommon for >90 percent of students to get a question correct after discussing it with their peers.

29.3.1.1 What Theoretical Background Aligns with This Practice?

PI shares much with the theoretical background of pair programming. Both are fundamentally grounded in socio-constructivist theory (Vygotsky, 1978), in that a small group of learners at the same level are collaboratively constructing knowledge through synchronous engagement with a problem in the discipline.

Another view of PI is as a form of peripheral participation. Legitimate peripheral participation "describes how newcomers become experienced members and eventually old timers of a community of practice" (Lave & Wenger, 1999). Obviously, in no professional setting are computer scientists sitting around considering multiple-choice questions. In this sense, PI is not a form of legitimate peripheral participation. However, as multiple-choice questions are designed around common mistakes and problems to be solved in computing, these can be seen as a way to engage students in having the discussions and performing the analyses that they will be called upon to do in professional settings. Both the small-group and the class-wide discussions can give students exposure to ways of framing and organizing an argument or explanation for a technical problem or scenario. Discussing in small groups allows each student to practice and develop their own verbal analysis skills.

Though no specific research has documented it, practitioners have often commented on the value of PI in encouraging a growth mind-set in students of computing – perhaps most notably influencing beginning students who may be learning computing (usually through programming) for the first time (Cutts, Cutts, Draper, O'Donnell, & Saffrey, 2010; Dweck, 2006). Programming as experienced by tertiary institution students (who often have a range of backgrounds with the practice) can be very intimidating. Students are not used to failing so many times (e.g., getting compiler and runtime errors) in solving problems for other topics – and having the computer available to tell them so quickly and repeatedly that they have failed. When the lecture time is composed of a series of PI questions, students can get repeated exposure to not knowing something (e.g., initially answering a multiple-choice question incorrectly), then putting in effort through small-group discussion to better puzzle out and understand the problem. The post-discussion vote histogram, which instructors sometimes explicitly compare to the initial vote histogram, can serve as a very explicit reinforcement that it isn't that one either "is good at computing" or isn't, but that we all can work to increase our intelligence or abilities in computing challenges. This is also reflected in statements heard in class-wide discussion that regularly can take the form of, "Well, at first our group thought it was A because [some rationale], but then we realized it is C because [an analysis]."

The design of valuable versus less valuable PI questions is also a research area that has been little studied. However, anecdotal advice from practitioners suggests that good questions lie in a learner's ZPD. In the case of PI, one would consider the expertly designed multiple-choice question to be the "help" that an instructor provides in terms of focusing and drawing out common misunderstandings that supports a learner in moving beyond what they can know and do on their own.

29.3.2 What Does Research Say It Does?

Much of the original research on the efficacy of PI utilized disciplinary pre- and post-concept test inventories to measure the impacts PI has on student learning. These concept tests focus on high-level understanding of real-world concepts, not detailed problem-solving, and as such are accessible to students at the beginning of a course before they have formally "learned" this material. Most initial studies of the impact of PI compare the gains of students between the pre- and post-concept inventory tests, finding that students in PI classes have higher gains in their learning from pre-test to post-test than students in traditional classrooms. A ten-year overview of Dr. Mazur's experiences found an approximately two-fold increase in learning gains (Crouch & Mazur, 2001), while a more general comparison of active learning approaches in the classroom (only some of which are explicitly PI approaches) reported a range of benefits across different disciplines (Freeman, Eddy, McDonough, Smith, Okoroafor, Jordt, & Wenderoth, 2014).

29.3.2.1 Improved Outcomes

A range of improved outcomes for students have been shown in tertiary institution computing courses.

Learning Gains
Computing doesn't (commonly) have the kinds of concept inventories that could be applied before and after to compare course instances (e.g., an offering of a course with a specific professor, using a specific classroom pedagogy). Moreover, one could argue that course objectives, learning outcomes, and exams vary more in the field of computing than in other disciplines, since it is relatively new and/ or changes at a rapid rate, but this is not documented.

In the realm of computing, two reports have compared student performance on a final exam in a course where one instance of the course was taught using PI and one was taught "traditionally." In Simon, Parris, and Spacco (2013), two sections of a CS0 course were taught by the same instructor in the same term. All grading, activities, and exams in the course were the same – except for what happened in the classroom. In this case, students in the PI section of the course scored 4.7 percent better on the final exam – a result that was statistically significant. In a quasi-replication study in a CS1 course where the instructors differed

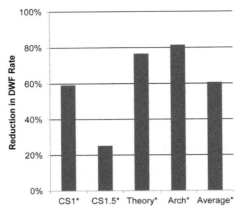

Figure 29.1 *Reduction in course fail rates (DWF is "D" or "F" grades, or withdraw) by course. Arch = architecture.*
Adapted from Porter, Bailey-Lee, and Simon (2013).

for the different sections, similar results were seen for the final exam score, although they were not statistically significant in this study (Zingaro, 2014).

Retention

A metric one can compare across courses (and disciplines) is how many students taking a course fail to pass it. Although this metric likely reflects many student outcome components (e.g., self-efficacy, growth mind-set, attendance, self-regulation), it is also a highly practical one in that it impacts time to (and likely cost to) degree, choice to stay in the major, and student satisfaction with both courses and, more broadly, educational experiences.

In a post hoc, in situ study at one large, public, research-oriented institution, course failure rates over a period of ten years were compared in four computing courses (Porter, Bailey-Lee, & Simon, 2013). On average, course failure rates were reduced by 60 percent when PI was used as the primary mode of instruction in the course (see Figure 29.1, changes marked with an asterisk are statistically significant). This held true for both lower-division (CS1, CS1.5) and upper-division (theory of computation and computer architecture) courses.

Additionally, four of the seven instructors who taught using PI in this study also had at least one instance where they taught the same course without using PI. When comparing the fail rates of each of those instructors, we see the same reduction in fail rate – indicating that it was the method of instruction causing this difference, rather than the personality or other type of difference in the instructor (see Figure 29.2, changes marked with an asterisk are statistically significant).

Student Valuation

The most commonly reported metric around student outcomes has reported the student self-valuation of PI. In very early work on PI in CS classes, one author, Simon, put together a fairly comprehensive end-of-term student survey asking

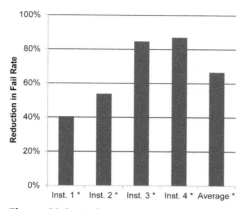

Figure 29.2 *Reduction in course fail rates for instructors teaching the same course with and without PI.*
Adapted from Porter, Bailey-Lee, and Simon (2013).

students to report and reflect on various aspects of the PI experience. While some of these data ask students to share their conformance with and beliefs about the PI protocol (e.g., "most of the time my group actually discusses the clicker questions," "thinking about clicker questions, on my own, before discussing with people around me helped me learn the material," "immediate feedback from clickers helped me focus on weaknesses in my understanding"), the most commonly reported valuation comes from the following two statements:

• "Clickers with discussions is valuable for my learning"
• "I recommend that other instructors use this approach"

In a multi-institutional study spanning seven instructors, seven courses, and five institutions, students agreed with these statements generally at a level of 90 percent or more – with one notable outlier (Porter et al., 2016). Similar reports can be found in Porter et al. (2016). Lee, Garcia, and Porter (2013), Porter, Bailey-Lee, Simon, Cutts, and Zingaro (2011), and Simon, Kohanfars, Lee, Tamayo, and Cutts (2010).

29.3.2.2 Do Students Really Learn from Discussion?

Other work has sought to explore more about how the in-class portion of the PI protocol works. In particular, novice instructors are sometimes loath to "waste time" with a group discussion, figuring that once the students have voted and seen that they didn't get the answer correct, the best thing is for the instructor to dive into an explanation.

Some of the first studies in this area came from biology, where how much a student learned from the small-group discussion was explored by the use of "isomorphic" questions (Smith, Wood, Adams, Wieman, Knight, Guild, & Su, 2009). Students would individually answer a question, discuss it in small groups, and answer it a second time – as normal with PI. However, without being shown

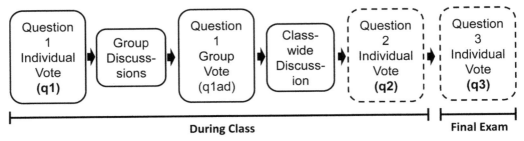

Figure 29.3 *Two locations of isomorphic, multiple-choice questions to test learning gain (q2) and retention (q3).*
Adapted from Zingaro and Porter (2015).

the results or engaging in class-wide discussion, the students would be shown a second question "isomorphic" with the first – defined as covering the same knowledge and skills, but with a different "cover story." The results showed that "peer discussion can be effective for understanding difficult concepts even when no one in the group initially knows the correct answer" (Smith et al., 2009), supporting the constructivist learning value of PI.

In computing, a variety of related studies have explored this in greater variation. Zingaro and Porter (2015) looked at immediate learning with isomorphic questions (in this case, after the class-wide discussion of the first question) and then followed up with isomorphic questions on the final exam (see Figure 29.3). While the first step looks at immediate, in-class learning from the whole PI process, the second step confirms longer-term learning – whether that persisted from in-class learning or whether the experience provided feedback to the students, which may have led them to further study or focus on the topic. Overall, the authors showed that learning that occurred in the classroom was sustained on the final exam.

29.3.2.3 Using PI Voting Data to Predict Student Success

Recently, researchers have been looking to leverage the naturally occurring data generated by student votes on PI questions to identify students at risk of failing or performing poorly in a course (Porter, Zingaro, & Lister, 2014). Using course data from a previous term, researchers have been able to create a machine learning model to support identification of at-risk CS1 students within the first three weeks of the term (Liao, Zingaro, Laurenzano, Griswold, & Porter, 2016) This work has not been replicated in other disciplines to our knowledge.

29.3.3 What to Keep in Mind When Implementing

Students, perhaps especially at tertiary institutions, are often socialized to expect to learn from expert and distinguished professors. Adopting PI in the classroom makes it very clear to students that they should spend as much or more time talking as the instructor does. As was reported in one professor's student evaluations: "I really wish Professor X had spent more time lecturing. With clickers, I had to learn the material myself." If we take a constructivist view of learning then, yes, this is correct – the professor cannot do the learning for the student. But this issue lies at the heart of much of the advice for implementing PI in computing – tell, remind, and reinforce with students the theory, the research results, and (positive) quotes from other students to help them come to internalize why PI is valuable for their learning.

On the PeerInstruction4CS website (www.peerinstruction4cs.org), leading researchers on PI in computing have compiled a variety of materials to support instructors looking to adopt PI. Some of the items that can be found there include the following:

- A step-by-step guide to getting started, spanning a time frame "long before class starts," to what to do during the term, to how to document the impacts of PI.
- Instructor classroom cheat sheets.
- Materials/slides for guiding instructors in speaking to students about the value of PI.
- A set of things "not to do."
- Clicker/PI questions for a range of common lower- and upper-division computing courses (often aligned with popular textbooks).

Additionally, through the Porter et al. (2016) study, student valuation of PI was shown to be somewhat resilient to the novice-ness of the instructors implementing it. The key finding reported there was that requiring students to get (all) of the questions correct in order to get points (which are usually recommended for participation only) seemed to align with lower student valuation of PI.

PI has been studied in a relatively large range of tertiary institution computing settings, from small, primarily undergraduate institutions with small courses sizes (Porter et al., 2013) to larger public institutions with larger class sizes. The benefits of PI have been shown across lower- and upper-division courses. A common question is whether there are any particular computing classes that PI would not be suited for. While this has not be formally studied, any class that requires more analysis and evaluation, in contrast with memorization, should be able to find computing PI questions to use a model.

29.3.4 Next Steps

There is still much to be done in terms of accurately documenting learning that stems from PI question discussion in the classroom. Traditional final exams, especially in lower-division courses, still focus primarily on reading, tracing, and writing code for correctness. A student's ability to analyze or evaluate may be only implicitly measured in these types of questions. A simple way to begin work in this area is to assign similar or "isomorphic" PI questions on a final exam but, in addition to having students select the correct answer, also requiring a written analysis of the type one would like to hear in classroom small-group discussions.

A very exciting area for study, given the relatively robust research results, is how to gain wider adoption on PI in computing courses. Work at the Center for Research on Educational Change in Postsecondary Education (http://wmich.edu/changeresearch) and the Increase the Impact project (www.increasetheimpact.com) should be leveraged in pursuing this goal.

There is much promising work yet to be done in surfacing, analyzing, and presenting ongoing clicker data in ways to meaningfully support both instructors and students to make proactive change in learning challenges earlier. However, once clicker data can identify a problem, what opportunities do we have as instructors or learners to encourage and guide improvement?

Finally, there likely remain opportunities to optimize student learning by providing better-scoped or better-targeted pre-class preparation. The more we can create materials segmented out to "things you should be capable of learning through self-preparation," the better we can direct student time and attention in pre-class preparation work. One such example is an interactive and collaborative textbook reading system – Perusall (perusall.com). In this system, readings can be assigned at a very fine-grained level and a specific number of comments or questions can be "required" of each student for a given reading. A machine learning approach is used to automatically grade the quality of the questions and/or comments.

29.4 Promising Practice: Studio-Based Learning

In four questions, we provide an overview of the practice before our in-depth description.

What Is It? Studio-based learning (SBL) is a socially oriented instructional model that has been the centerpiece of architecture and fine arts education for over a century. SBL can be conceptualized as an iterative process in which learners refine their individual solutions to disciplinary problems through two key activities. In the *design studio*, students build camaraderie by working on solutions in a common physical space. In *design crits* (design critiques), students present their evolving solutions for feedback and discussion (Moog & Spencer, 2008).

What Beneficial Impacts Have Been Shown? In computing education, SBL design crits have promoted significant gains in two attitudinal variables – *self-efficacy* and *peer learning* – that are hypothesized to be positively correlated with student persistence (Hundhausen et al., 2010). Additional attitudinal variables have also been positively affected, including motivation, perceived learning, and perceived problem-solving ability.

In What Settings Does It Work? SBL *design crits* have been shown to be widely adaptable to a variety of computing courses. However, SBL design crits are particularly appropriate for courses that emphasize software and user interface design because they are good at highlighting design and implementation trade-offs and tacit design knowledge.

What Are the Limitations of What We Know? There have been multi-institutional studies of the effectiveness of SBL design crits in a variety of computing courses. While several of these studies indicate that SBL design crits can promote positive attitudinal shifts in learners, none of the studies has shown that SBL design crits promote significant learning gains. Moreover, since the SBL design studio is difficult to implement with the constraints of conventional computing curricula, the effectiveness of the SBL design studio has not been studied within the context of computing education.

29.4.1 What Is It?

While many educators have used the term "studio-based learning" to denote hands-on learning activities in a common social space (e.g., see Faro & Swann, 2006), we use the term here to denote the *signature pedagogy* of architectural and design education (Crowther, 2013), which is rooted in the master–apprentice educational system used in the guilds of the Middle Ages (Lackney, 1999). The architectural schools of Europe and North America adopted this system in the form of the *design studio*: a place where students set up their own work spaces – drafting tables, books, drawing and modeling materials – and spend much of their time working individually on common design tasks (Schon, 1983). As students spend long hours working on these tasks, they build camaraderie, looking to each other for support and feedback as they work toward a common purpose (Lackney, 1999).

The SBL curriculum encompasses a series of design problems, which may be either progressively more challenging or different components of the same overall design project. The cornerstone of the curriculum is a series of *design crits*: review sessions at which students present their evolving solutions to these problems for feedback and discussion. In addition to producing specific comments about design, these presentation sessions typically generate educationally valuable discussions about the general design principles, trade-offs, and methods being explored in the course.

In their comprehensive review of architecture education, Boyer and Mitgang (1996) concluded that "the core elements of architectural education – learning to design within constraints, collaborative learning, and the refining of knowledge through the reflective act of design – have relevance and power far beyond the training of future architects" (p. iv). Given that many courses in computing education focus on the design and analysis of software, the studio-based approach would appear to have tremendous potential to enhance computing education.

While the physical and temporal constraints of undergraduate computing curricula make it difficult to implement a pure SBL curriculum in the way it is implemented in architecture and fine arts education (but see Docherty, Sutton, Brereton, & Kaplan, 2001), one aspect of SBL – the *design crit* – proves more readily implementable. Several adaptations of SBL design crits have been explored in computing education. These include the following: *pedagogical code review* (Hundhausen, Agrawal, & Agarwal, 2013), an SBL adaptation modeled after the formal code inspection process used in the software industry (e.g., see Gilb & Graham, 1993; Wiegers, 1995); *peer code reviews*, in which student teams present algorithm designs to the class for feedback and discussion (Hendrix, Myneni, Naryanan, & Ross, 2010; Hundhausen & Brown, 2008); and *user interface design crits*, in which students present prototype user interface designs for feedback and discussion within the context of human–computer interaction courses (Hundhausen, Fairbrother, & Petre, 2012; Kehoe, 2001; Reimer & Douglas, 2003).

29.4.1.1 What Theoretical Background Aligns with This Practice?

Two theoretical perspectives are useful in accounting for the potential educational benefits of SBL design crits. First, according to *social constructivist learning theory* (Lave & Wenger, 1991), the design crit activity facilitates learning by providing students with opportunities to participate, in increasingly central ways, in the practices of a disciplinary community: as solution designers, as observers in the critical review process, as designer participants in the critical review process, and ultimately as reviewers in the critical review process. From this view, learning comes about through *changes in identity* facilitated by such participation, which, because it is mediated by learner-constructed artifacts (students' solutions), is seen as especially valuable in bridging the gap between expert and novice perspectives (Lave, 1993). Second, the design crit activity provides students with opportunities to assess themselves relative to others. According to *self-efficacy theory* (Bandura, 1997), such opportunities are crucial to forming accurate perceptions of one's own abilities. Without them, students are more likely to leave the discipline (Bandura, Barbaranelli, Caprara, & Pastorelli, 2001).

29.4.2 What Does Research Say It Does?

From 2010 through to 2013, one of the authors (CH) was involved in a multi-institutional, quasi-experimental study of SBL design crits in undergraduate computing education. The study included over 1,000 students enrolled in computing courses at 15 undergraduate institutions in seven US states (Narayanan et al., 2018). The study compared versions of these courses in which SBL design crits were implemented against similar ("traditional") versions of the courses that were implemented without SBL design crits. Overall, the results showed that learning outcomes did not differ significantly between students in SBL and traditional treatments. However, data collected on pre-/post-attitudinal surveys revealed numerous statistically significant differences between the SBL and traditional treatments. For example, 87 percent of students in the SBL treatments reported motivation to take more computing courses, versus 57 percent in

Table 29.1 *Key findings of a study of PCRs. An adaptation of SBL for early computing courses (Hundhausen, Agrawal, & Agarwal, 2013).*

Pedagogical goal	Relevant findings
1. Improve code quality	• No significant differences in pre- to post-test improvement between the courses with and without PCRs • No pre- to post-PCR improvement in solution grades
2. Consider and discuss coding practices and issues at multiple levels	• PCRs prompted students to consider a broad range of programming issues • Types of issues identified in PCRs shifted over the course of the semester from lower-level formatting issues to higher-level design and implementation issues
3. Develop skills in critical review, communication, and teamwork	• Analyses of video footage and exit surveys indicate that face-to-face PCRs promoted skills in critical review, communication, and teamwork • Qualitative analysis of PCR exit surveys suggests that online PCRs largely failed to promote such skills
4. Develop positive self-efficacy	• In the course with face-to-face PCRs, students' self-efficacy did not significantly change from pre- to post-survey • In the course with no PCRs and the course with online PCRs, students' self-efficacy decreased significantly
5. Develop positive sense of community and peer learning	• In all courses, students' sense of community did not change significantly from pre- to post-survey • In the course with face-to-face PCRs, students' attitudes toward peer learning increased at a level that approached significance, as compared to the control course and the course with online PCRs

traditional treatments. Likewise, 92 percent of students in SBL courses reported improved comfort levels in working with others, compared with just 48 percent in traditional courses. Whereas 98 percent of students in SBL courses felt that SBL design crits benefited their learning, just 83 percent of students in traditional courses felt that traditional lab activities done in place of SBL design crits benefited their learning.

A study of pedagogical code reviews (PCRs), a form of SBL design crit implemented in the CS1 course at Washington State University, provides a richer account of the benefits of SBL (Hundhausen, Agrawal, & Agarwal, 2013). Table 29.1, an adaptation of SBL for early computing courses, summarizes the key findings of the study relative to the pedagogical goals of PCRs.

Finally, a content analysis of the students' and instructor's conversations within design crits of user interface prototypes in a human–computer interaction course (Hundhausen, Fairbrother, & Petre, 2012) showed that those conversations focused squarely on issues central to the course. Some 53 percent of all talk focused on issues related to user interface design and content. Moreover, some 60 percent of students' critiques of user interface designs were directly supported by one or more justifications, with 30 percent of those justifications resting on an empirical or theoretical basis. This suggests that the design crits provided valuable opportunities for students to apply key course concepts to the analysis of each other's work.

29.4.3 What to Keep in Mind When Implementing

The research on SBL design crits described above suggests a number of best practices for implementing SBL design crits in computing courses:

- *Establish ground rules.* It is unlikely that undergraduate computing students have ever engaged in anything like design crits, which require them both to subject their own work to the scrutiny of their peers and to review their peers' work with a critical eye. We have observed that, for many students, just thinking about this process conjures up feelings of fear and discomfort. To counteract these common perceptions of the critical review process and to foster a positive "culture of review," we have found that it is essential to establish clear ground rules for participating in the activity. These include (a) the need for critiques to emphasize the strengths of a solution and improvements that could be made, rather than focusing on its flaws, and (b) the importance of having a *skilled moderator* lead design crits in order to facilitate higher-level discussions of design issues, strategies, and trade-offs.
- *Model the activity.* Since computing students are unlikely to have experience with the critical review process, it is essential to model the activity for students – that is, to have them view, and possibly participate in, a demonstration of a "mock" design crit prior to their participation in a "real" design crit.
- *Require both independent and team review.* A study of the code inspection process in the software industry (Gilb & Graham, 1993) found that significantly more issues were identified when individual, independent reviews of code artifacts were performed before team reviews. Likewise, in their study of PCRs, Hundhausen, Agrawal, and Agarwal (2013) found that requiring individuals to review peers' code artifacts prior to team reviews had pedagogical benefits, because it invested students more fully in the team review process. Moreover, the team review process offered pedagogical benefits by providing opportunities for students to practice key communication, collaboration, and teamwork skills.
- *Avoid redundancy in reviewing.* Having students review multiple solutions to the same problem can become tedious in practice, especially when the assigned problem does not lend itself to an interesting variety of alternative solution paths. Rather than prompting students to consider design trade-offs and higher-level design issues, the review of multiple solutions can devolve into busywork, raising students' resentment and lowering their level of

satisfaction with the activity. Thus, it is important that design crits be set up such that solutions to a variety of different problems are considered. If that is not possible, then different components of solutions should be strategically selected for each individual design crit.

- *Require resubmission.* The SBL model is iterative by nature; solutions are successively improved through feedback. So that learners actually implement the changes suggested in design crits, it is important to require them to resubmit their work for credit. If grading resources are limited, only the final submission should be graded. Experience shows that students are sufficiently motivated to put effort into their initial solutions because they know they will be reviewed in a public forum.

- *Use online tools to support design crits.* Implementing design crits can present computing instructors with numerous logistical challenges. These include forming review teams, training students in the review process, distributing student solutions to teams for review, and tracking issues that are raised within the design crits. Many of these logistical hurdles can be eased through the use of an online course management tool such as Moodle (Dougimas & Taylor, 2003) or OSBLE (Olivares & Hundhausen, 2016).

29.4.4 Next Steps

Past research into SBL design crits indicates that it has promise as a pedagogical approach in computing education. As a socially oriented pedagogy, SBL design crits provide students with valuable opportunities to learn not only computing content knowledge, but also soft skills (e.g., communication, collaboration, and teamwork) through critical design dialogues focused on students' own solutions. The activity appears to promote both positive shifts in students' perceptions of their learning and motivation, as well as conversations squarely focused on relevant computing issues and concepts. Future work should further explore the extent to which SBL design crits facilitate both positive learning outcomes and conceptual change in learners.

Design crits are just one of the two core activities of the SBL pedagogy. In future work, computing educators should explore adaptations of the *design studio*, which is regarded in architecture and fine arts education as equally important to the SBL process. Because of the logistical barriers to implementing design studios within the constraints of conventional computing degree programs, adaptations of the design studio for computing education will likely need to promote online, asynchronous interactions among students. To that end, Carter and Hundhausen (2015) have explored the potential for a computer programming environment augmented with a social networking-style activity feed to facilitate the kind of social learning community present in a traditional design studio. Additional studies of this and other adaptations of the design studio are needed in order to adapt and evaluate the efficacy of SBL design studios in computing education.

29.5 Promising Practice: POGIL

In four questions, we provide an overview of the practice before our in-depth description.

What Is It? Process-oriented guided-inquiry learning (POGIL) is a student-centered pedagogy that focuses on the simultaneous development of both content knowledge and process skills (e.g., problem-solving, teamwork, and written/oral communication). Students work in teams to complete inquiry-based activities that guide them to discover key concepts for themselves.

What Beneficial Impacts Have Been Shown? Students in chemistry POGIL classrooms have been shown to have decreased attrition, greater content mastery over longer periods of time, and more positive attitudes about the course and instructors than students in traditional classrooms (Hanson, 2006). Across multiple institutions, chemistry POGIL classes had half the percentage of students earning failing grades (Ds or Fs) or withdrawing from the course compared to traditional chemistry classes (Straumanis & Simons, 2008).

In What Settings Does It Work? POGIL has been implemented for high school and college class sizes ranging from 10 to 100. Instructors in other STEM fields have successfully adopted POGIL in large lecture halls with the help of teaching assistants.

What Are the Limitations of What We Know? As POGIL was originally developed and used by chemistry college instructors in the mid-1990s, most studies have been completed in chemistry classrooms. Its effectiveness in computing classrooms has not been extensively studied.

29.5.1 What Is It?

A typical POGIL classroom will involve the following:

- Students working collaboratively in self-managed **learning teams**, where each student is assigned a unique role and set of responsibilities for the class period, The instructor acts as a facilitator to help these learning teams work, rather than as the presenter of information.
- The assignment of **guided inquiry** materials that use a learning cycle approach (explore–invent–apply) to help students construct their own understanding of the course content.
- A focus on **process skills** development in the POGIL activities and by the instructor, who is acting as a facilitator in the classroom.

The **learning teams** usually consist of three to four students working together for multiple weeks, which allows students to rotate at least once through each of the four roles. Different POGIL instructors prefer different role names and responsibilities, but a typical set of roles would include a manager, a spokesperson, a recorder, and a reflector. Distributing role cards can help remind students of their responsibilities; a variety of role cards can be found online.

The most defining element of the POGIL methodology is the **guided inquiry materials**, which guide students through a series of "models" and questions to construct their own understanding, rather than providing an explanation of the material in lecture or written format. Superficially, these POGIL activities resemble worksheets, but they are written to follow a learning cycle approach of *exploration*, *concept invention*, and *application*. Each POGIL activity will usually consist of three or four models, where new information is provided to serve as a basis of the new understanding that will be constructed. Each model is followed by a series of five to ten questions. The first few questions are typically exploration questions, where the student is guided to consider various aspects of the model. Concept invention questions follow, prompting students to discover patterns and develop concepts, typically before the standard terms for these ideas are introduced. Finally, the concept is reinforced and extended in the application phase with exercises and problems. Ideally, at least some of these questions are too difficult to be answered individually and will require the learning team to collaborate in order to reach satisfactory answers.

For example, one POGIL activity on complexity analysis begins with a model with instructions for a two-player game, where Player A picks a number from 0 to 100 and then answers "too high" or "too low" in response to Player B's guesses. Questions prompt the student teams to play the game (explore) and then to identify a set of strategies for Player B, such as "guess at random," "count up by 1s," or "split the range in half." As the teams work, the instructor circulates through the classroom, listening to team discussions, answering questions, and prompting teams to improve their descriptions. After a few minutes, the instructor has each team describe a strategy to the class, which ensures that every team has a variety of strategies. Next, teams rank their strategies by number of guesses and how hard they are to describe and compare the rankings to discover the common trade-off between speed and difficulty (invent). Teams then identify other situations with similar trade-offs and share them with the class (apply). In the next cycle, the strategies are the model, which teams explore to find the maximum (worst case) and average number of guesses for each strategy, leading them to invent O()-style complexity analysis.

Because these POGIL activities have been specially designed to lead students through this learning cycle, they are intended to be the students' first introduction to this content. Students should not have worked on any of the POGIL activity prior to class, and they are generally expected to complete all of the questions during the class period, with possible application questions or exercises to be completed later. The instructor's role during most of the class period is to circulate the classroom and serve as a facilitator to student learning rather than as a lecturer.

At the end of a POGIL session, team members are prompted to reflect on their group dynamics and how the group might improve on the process next time. The seven process skills that are targeted by POGIL activities are teamwork, oral and written communication, management, information processing, critical thinking, problem-solving, and assessment. Several examples of reflection prompts are provided in appendices A and B of the "Instructor's Guide to Process-Oriented Guided-Inquiry Learning" (Hanson, 2006).

A typical day in a POGIL classroom will begin with the students gathering with their teammates and assigning new roles, so that each team member has new responsibilities compared with the last POGIL activity. The instructor introduces the POGIL activity by reminding students of prior course content that will connect to this new material and explaining the relevance of the new material. Students then work in teams to read the model and answer the learning cycle questions while the instructor circulates around the room, monitoring students' progress and intervening with guidance (but not answers) to teams that are struggling or are answering questions incorrectly. Periodically (generally after all teams have completed each model), the instructor should stop the class to poll them on answers to the most difficult key questions in the activity. Where appropriate, these class discussions may lead to a mini-lecture where the instructor emphasizes key concepts, provides context for the new material, and brings closure to the lesson. The end of the POGIL activity should include some element of individual accountability, such as requiring students to individually answer questions at the end of this class period or the beginning of the next one.

Most instructors do not grade every question in a POGIL activity, but rather they assign some points for participating in the POGIL activity, reflecting on the process skills, and completing the individual portion of the assignment. Ideally, grading policies should reward learning of course content by *all* team members. To motivate positive interdependence, some instructors award bonus points to teams where all team members score above a threshold on weekly quizzes.

29.5.1.1 What Theoretical Background Aligns with This Practice?

Like the other student-centered learning approaches described in this chapter, POGIL is based on socio-constructivist principles (Vygotsky, 1986) that students learn by constructing their understanding of new material based on their prior knowledge and experiences through discussion with other students. In particular, POGIL activities rely on the three phases of Karplus and Thier's learning cycle: exploration, concept attainment, and application (Karplus & Thier, 1967). The formalized roles and responsibilities in POGIL teams are based on effective practices for cooperative learning (Johnson et al., 1991; Slavin, 1990).

29.5.2 What Does Research Say It Does?

Because POGIL was first developed in the 1990s by chemistry instructors, most studies on POGIL's effectiveness have examined general chemistry and organic chemistry students. Many of these studies have relied on the American Chemistry Society standardized exams for general chemistry and organic chemistry to demonstrate that students in POGIL classrooms learn and retain more information than their peers in traditional classrooms. Other studies of student performance in a POGIL classroom have found a decrease in the number of students who did not pass the course (whether by withdrawing or receiving a D or F grade) (Straumanis & Simons, 2008). A multi-institutional study found POGIL students self-reported significantly more growth in process skills development (Straumanis & Simons, 2008). Another study across two semesters found POGIL students retained the material learned in the first-semester course much better than students who took a traditional first-semester course; the majority of the lecture students scored below 50 percent on an unannounced quiz on the first day of the second semester, whereas more than 20 percent of the POGIL students scored above 90 percent and fewer than 25 percent of the POGIL students scored below 50 percent (Ruder & Hunnicutt, 2008).

Computing education researchers have conducted a small number of studies of POGIL in CS classrooms. In a survey of 26 CS POGIL instructors, instructors reported that their POGIL students were more engaged in class, had a deeper understanding of concepts, and were more effective at working in small groups. A survey of 32 CS instructors who had attended a POGIL workshop found that the three greatest obstacles to adopting POGIL were a lack of preparation time, a lack of POGIL activities, and pressure to cover more content (Hu, Kussmaul, Knaeble, Mayfield, & Yadav, 2016). In a study of CS0 courses for non-majors, students who experienced POGIL pedagogy at two different institutions became significantly more comfortable with computers and technology compared to students taking the same course without POGIL one year earlier from the same instructors. By the end of these POGIL classes for non-majors, students at four institutions became significantly more interested in taking computing classes, with gender differences decreasing significantly over the semester (Hu & Campbell, 2017).

29.5.3 What to Keep in Mind When Implementing

Instructors interested in adopting POGIL should either attend a POGIL workshop or observe an experienced POGIL instructor in order to better understand how instructors should facilitate learning in a POGIL classroom. While students are working through the POGIL activities, the instructor should be encouraging students to think deeper about their answers to the questions and to reflect on their learning process. Instructors should be alert to problematic group dynamics, some of which can be mitigated by emphasizing student roles. If multiple groups are struggling with the same concept, the instructor should consider discussing the concept with the entire class sooner, either immediately or after most groups have completed that model.

Usually, instructors will stop the class one to three times to review answers to key questions in the activity. These key questions are either questions identified by the instructor prior to the start of class or questions about which the instructor has overheard more student discussion. Students will appreciate not reviewing answers to *all* of the questions in the POGIL activity; reviewing fewer answers is generally better than reviewing more answers, as students will lose interest. Instructors can better keep students' attention by using a variety of methods for students to share answers with the class. Besides asking group to verbally report their answers, instructors can having groups write their answers on the board to shorten the time it takes to review answers as a class. An effective method for encouraging a deeper discussion between groups is to send a representative from each team to share with other teams ("jigsaw") or to ask the class to collaboratively develop a definition on the board out of their individual team answers.

New POGIL instructors are advised to adopt a minimum of three to four POGIL activities within a month, because it takes a few class periods to familiarize students with working in POGIL teams and to see the benefits of POGIL instruction. Because completing the activities generally requires more work on the part of the student than listening to a lecture, instructors sometimes encounter student resistance to POGIL, which they can counter by discussing the value of developing process skills, such as teamwork and management. Some POGIL instructors include one model on process skills each week in the first few weeks of the semester; others show some of the 42 videos of both positive and negative student interactions for classroom discussions on appropriate behaviors and responses (all 42 are listed and linked in the POGIL Project's Implementation Guide (The POGIL Project, 2018)). Other strategies for promoting positive and respectful student collaborations are provided in the second half of the "Instructor's Guide to Process-Oriented Guided-Inquiry Learning" (Hanson, 2006).

The greatest obstacle to implementing POGIL in a class is finding or developing appropriate POGIL activities. POGIL activities exist for CS0, CS1, and CS2 classes. A growing number of additional POGIL activities (cspogil. org) have been authored for more advanced CS courses, although not a sufficient number to implement POGIL throughout entire courses.

29.5.4 Next Steps

The National Science Foundation (NSF) has recently funded a project to study POGIL's effectiveness in introductory computing classrooms (http://cspogil.org/IntroCS%20POGIL%20Project) to see if POGIL is as effective in computing as it has been found to be in chemistry. A second NSF project (elipss.com) has developed assessments to measure students' process skills development in POGIL classrooms.

Instructors interested in learning more about POGIL should attend a POGIL workshop, because experiencing a POGIL classroom is the best way to understand its key principles and implementation. A three-hour POGIL workshop provides attendees with a good understanding of how POGIL differs from other forms of active learning, whereas longer workshops prepare attendees for implementing POGIL in their classes. The POGIL Project maintains a list of upcoming workshops on their website (http://pogil.org). Other helpful resources include the "Instructor's Guide to Process-Oriented Guided-Inquiry Learning" (Hanson, 2006), the POGIL Project's Implementation Guide (www.pogil.org/educators/additional-resources), and the CS POGIL website, which inventories available CS POGIL activities (cspogil.org).

Acknowledgments

The research reported in Section 29.4 was supported by the NSF, most recently under grant no. IIS-1321045. Portions of the section were excerpted and adapted from a journal article that originally appeared in the *ACM Transactions on Computing Education Research* (Hundhausen, Agrawal, & Agarwal, 2013).

References

Bandura, A. (1997). *Self-Efficacy: The Exercise of Control*. New York: Macmillan.

Bandura, A., Barbaranelli, C., Caprara, G. V., & Pastorelli, C. (2001). Self-efficacy beliefs as shapers of children's aspirations and career trajectories. *Child Development*, 72(1), 187–206.

Barker, L., & Cohoon, J. M. (2017). Pair Programming (Case Study 1). Retrieved from: www.ncwit.org/resources/how-do-you-retain-women-through-collaborative-learning/pair-programming-case-study-1

Basili, V. R., Green, S., Laitenberger, O., Lanubile, F., Shull, F., Sørumgård, S., & Zelkowitz, M. V. (1996). The empirical investigation of perspective-based reading. *Empirical Software Engineering*, 1(2), 133–164.

Boyer, E. L., & Mitgang, L. D. (1996). *Building Community: A New Future for Architecture Education and Practice: A Special Report*. Princeton, NJ: The Carnegie Foundation for the Advancement of Teaching.

Carter, A. S., & Hundhausen, C. D. (2015). The design of a programming environment to support greater social awareness and participation in early computing courses. *Journal of Computing Sciences in Colleges*, 31(1), 143–153.

Chaiklin, S. (2003). The zone of proximal development in Vygotsky's analysis of learning and instruction. In A. Kozulin, B. Gindis, V. Ageyev, & S. Miller (Eds.), *Vygotsky's Educational Theory in Cultural Context, 1* (pp. 39–64). Cambridge, UK: Cambridge University Press.

Cockburn, A., & Williams, L. (2000). The costs and benefits of pair programming. *Extreme Programming Examined*, 8, 223–247.

Code.org (2014). Pair Programming. Retrieved from www.youtube.com/watch?v=vgkahOzFH2Q

Crouch, C. H., & Mazur, E. (2001). Peer instruction: Ten years of experience and results. *American Journal of Physics*, 69(9), 970–977.

Crowther, P. (2013). Understanding the signature pedagogy of the design studio and the opportunities for its technological enhancement. *Journal of Learning Design*, 6(3), 18–28.

Cutts, Q., Cutts, E., Draper, S., O'Donnell, P., & Saffrey, P. (2010). Manipulating mindset to positively influence introductory programming performance. In *Proceedings of the 41st ACM Technical Symposium on Computer Science Education* (pp. 431–435). New York: ACM.

Docherty, M., Sutton, P., Brereton, M., & Kaplan, S. (2001). An innovative design and studio-based CS degree. *ACM SIGCSE Bulletin*, 33(1), 233–237.

Dougiamas, M., & Taylor, P. (2003). Moodle: Using learning communities to create an open source course management system. In *World Conference on Educational Multimedia, Hypermedia and Telecommunications (EDMEDIA)* (pp. 171–178). Waynesville, NC: Association for the Advancement of Computing in Education.

Dweck, C. S. (2006). *Mindset: The New Psychology of Success*. New York: Random House.

Fagan, M. E. (1986). Advances in Software Inspections. *IEEE Transactions on Software Engineering*, 12(7): 744–751.

Faro, S., & Swan, K. (2006). An investigation into the efficacy of the studio model at the high school level. *Journal of Educational Computing Research*, 35(1), 45–59.

Flor, N. V., & Hutchins, E. L. (1991). A case study of team programming during perfective software maintenance. In J. Koenemann-Belliveau, T. G. Moher, & S. P. Robertson (Eds.), *Empirical Studies of Programmers: Fourth Workshop* (pp. 36–59). Norwood, NJ: Ablex Publishing.

Freeman, S., Eddy, S. L., McDonough, M., Smith, M. K., Okoroafor, N., Jordt, H., & Wenderoth, M. P. (2014). Active learning increases student performance in science, engineering, and mathematics. *Proceedings of the National Academy of Sciences*, 111(23), 8410–8415.

Gilb, T., & Graham, D. (1993). *Software Inspection*. Menlo Park, CA: Addison-Wesley.

Hanks, B., Fitzgerald, S., McCauley, R., Murphy, L., & Zander, C. (2011). Pair programming in education: A literature review. *Computer Science Education*, 21(2), 135–173.

Hanson, D. M. (2006). *Instructor's Guide to Process-Oriented Guided-Inquiry Learning*. Lisle, IL: Pacific Crest.

Hendrix, D., Myneni, L., Narayanan, H., & Ross, M. (2010). Implementing studio-based learning in CS2. In *Proceedings of the 41st ACM Technical Symposium on Computer Science Education* (pp. 505–509). New York: ACM.

Hestenes, D., & Halloun, I. (1995). Interpreting the force concept inventory. *The Physics Teacher*, 33(8), 502–506.

Horn, E. M., Collier, W. G., Oxford, J. A., Bond Jr., C. F., & Dansereau, D. F. (1998). Individual differences in dyadic cooperative learning. *Journal of Educational Psychology*, 90(1), 153–161.

Hu, H. H., & Campbell, P. B. (2017). A framework for Levels of student participation and stages of relevant curriculum. *Computing in Science & Engineering*, 19(3), 20–29.

Hu, H. H., Kussmaul, C., Knaeble, B., Mayfield, C., & Yadav, A. (2016). Results from a survey of faculty adoption of process oriented guided inquiry learning (POGIL) in computer science. In *Proceedings of the 2016 ACM Conference on Innovation and Technology in Computer Science Education* (pp. 186–191). New York: ACM.

Hundhausen, C. D., Agrawal, A., & Agarwal, P. (2013). Talking about code: Integrating pedagogical code reviews into early computing courses. *ACM Transactions on Computing Education (TOCE)*, 13(3), 14.

Hundhausen, C. D., & Brown, J. L. (2008). Designing, visualizing, and discussing algorithms within a CS 1 studio experience: An empirical study. *Computers & Education*, 50(1), 301–326.

Hundhausen, C., Agrawal, A., Fairbrother, D., & Trevisan, M. (2010). Does studio-based instruction work in CS 1?: An empirical comparison with a traditional approach. In *Proceedings of the 41st ACM Technical Symposium on Computer Science Education* (pp. 500–504). New York: ACM.

Hundhausen, C. D., Fairbrother, D., & Petre, M. (2012). An empirical study of the "prototype walkthrough": A studio-based activity for HCI education. *ACM Transactions on Computer-Human Interaction (TOCHI)*, 19(4), 26.

Johnson, D. W., Johnson, R. T., & Smith, K. A. (1991). *Active Learning: Cooperation in the College Classroom*. Edina, MN: Interaction Book Company.

Karplus, R., & Thier, H. D. (1967). *A New Look at Elementary School Science: Science Curriculum Improvement Study*. Chicago, IL, and New York: Rand McNally.

Kehoe, C. M. (2001). Bringing design dialog to HCI education. In *CHI'01 Extended Abstracts on Human Factors in Computing Systems* (pp. 473–474). New York: ACM.

Lackney, J. (1999). A history of the studio-based learning model. Retrieved from: http://edi.msstate.edu/work/pdf/history_studio_based_learning.pdf

Lave, J. (1993). The practice of learning. In S. Chaiklin & J. Lave (Eds.), *Understanding Practice: Perspectives on Activity and Context* (pp. 3–32). Cambridge, UK: Cambridge University Press.

Lave, J., & Wenger, E. (1991). *Situated Learning: Legitimate Peripheral Participation*. Cambridge, UK: Cambridge University Press.

Lave, J., & Wenger, E. (1999). Legitimate peripheral participation. In P. Murphy, (Ed.), *Learners, Learning and Assessment* (pp. 83–89), London: Paul Chapman Publishing Ltd.

Lee, C. B., Garcia, S., & Porter, L. (2013). Can peer instruction be effective in upper-division computer science courses? *ACM Transactions on Computing Education (TOCE)*, 13(3), 12.

Lewis, C. M. (2011). Is pair programming more effective than other forms of collaboration for young students? *Computer Science Education*, 21(2), 105–134.

Lewis, C. M., & Shah, N. (2015). How equity and inequity can emerge in pair programming. In *Proceedings of the Eleventh Annual International Conference on International Computing Education Research* (pp. 41–50). New York: ACM.

Liao, S. N., Zingaro, D., Laurenzano, M. A., Griswold, W. G., & Porter, L. (2016). Lightweight, early identification of at-risk CS1 students. In *Proceedings of the 2016 ACM Conference on International Computing Education Research* (pp. 123–131). New York: ACM.

Moog, R. S., & Spencer, J. N. (2008). POGIL: An overview. In R. S. Moog & J. N. Spencer (Eds.), *Process-Oriented Guided Inquiry Learning: ACS Symposium Series 994* (pp. 1–13). Washington, DC: American Chemical Society.

McDowell, C., Werner, L., Bullock, H. E., & Fernald, J. (2006). Pair programming improves student retention, confidence, and program quality. *Communications of the ACM*, 49(8), 90–95.

Narayanan, N. H., Hendrix, D., Ross, M., Hundhausen, C., & Crosby, M. (2018). *Broadening Studio-Based Learning in Computing Education: Final Report to NSF 2015. Technical Report CSSE18-01*. Auburn, AL: Department of Computer Science & Software Engineering, Auburn University.

NCWIT (2009). Pair Programming-in-a-Box: The Power of Collaborative Learning. Retrieved from www.ncwit.org/pairprogramming

O'Donnell, A. M., & Dansereau, D. F. (1992). Scripted cooperation in student dyads: A method for analyzing and enhancing academic learning and performance. In R. Hertz-Lazarowitz & M. Norman (Eds.), *Interaction in Cooperative Groups: The Theoretical Anatomy of Group Learning* (pp. 120–141). Cambridge, UK: Cambridge University Press.

Olivares, D. M., & Hundhausen, C. D. (2016). OSBLE+: A next-generation learning management and analytics environment for computing education. In *Proceedings of the 47th ACM Technical Symposium on Computing Science Education* (p. 5-5). New York: ACM.

Palinscar, A. S., & Brown, A. L. (1984). Reciprocal teaching of comprehension-fostering and comprehension-monitoring activities. *Cognition and Instruction*, 1(2), 117–175.

Pea, R. D. (1993). Practices of distributed intelligence and designs for education. In G. Salomon (Eds.), *Distributed Cognitions: Psychological and Educational Considerations* (pp. 47–87). Cambridge: Cambridge University Press.

Porter, L., Bailey-Lee, C., & Simon, B. (2013). Halving fail rates using peer instruction: A study of four computer science courses. In *Proceeding of the 44th ACM Technical Symposium on Computer Science Education* (pp. 177–182). New York: ACM.

Porter, L., Bailey-Lee, C., Simon, B., Cutts, Q., & Zingaro, D. (2011). Experience report: A multi-classroom report on the value of peer instruction. In *Proceedings of the 16th Annual Joint Conference on Innovation and Technology in Computer Science Education* (pp. 138–142). New York: ACM.

Porter, L., Bouvier, D., Cutts, Q., Grissom, S., Lee, C., McCartney, R., Zingaro, D., & Simon, B. (2016). A multi-institutional study of peer instruction in introductory computing. *ACM Inroads*, 7(2), 76–81.

Porter, L., Garcia, S., Glick, J., Matusiewicz, A., & Taylor, C. (2013). Peer instruction in computer science at small liberal arts colleges. In *Proceedings of the 18th ACM Conference on Innovation and Technology in Computer Science Education* (pp. 129–134). New York: ACM.

Porter, L., Zingaro, D., & Lister, R. (2014). Predicting student success using fine grain clicker data. In *Proceedings of the Tenth Annual Conference on International Computing Education Research* (pp. 51–58). New York: ACM.

Reimer, Y. J., & Douglas, S. A. (2003). Teaching HCI design with the studio approach. *Computer Science Education*, 13(3), 191–205.

Rodríguez, F. J., Price, K. M., & Boyer, K.E. (2017). Exploring the pair programming process: characteristics of effective collaboration. In *Proceedings of the 2017 ACM SIGCSE Technical Symposium on Computer Science Education* (pp. 507–512). New York: ACM.

Ruder, S. M., & Hunnicutt, S. S. (2008). POGIL in chemistry courses at a large urban university: A case study. In *ACS Symposium Series* (Vol. 994, pp. 133–147). Oxford: Oxford University Press.

Salleh, N., Mendes, E., & Grundy, J. (2011). Empirical studies of pair programming for CS/SE teaching in higher education: A systematic literature review. *IEEE Transactions on Software Engineering*, 37(4), 509–525.

Sauer, C., Jeffery, D. R., Land, L., & Yetton, P. (2000). The effectiveness of software development technical reviews: A behaviorally motivated program of research. *IEEE Transactions on Software Engineering*, 26(1), 1–14.

Schlimmer, J. C., Fletcher, J. B., & Hermens, L. A. (1994). Team-oriented software practicum. *IEEE Transactions on Education*, 37(2), 212–220.

Schon, D. A. (1983). *The Reflective Practitioner: How Professionals Think in Action*. New York: Basic Books.

Simon, B., & Hanks, B. (2008). First-year students' impressions of pair programming in CS1. *Journal on Educational Resources in Computing (JERIC)*, 7(4), 5.

Simon, B., Kohanfars, M., Lee, J., Tamayo, K., & Cutts, Q. (2010). Experience report: Peer instruction in introductory computing. In *Proceedings of the 41st ACM Technical Symposium on Computer Science Education* (pp. 341–345). New York: ACM.

Simon, B., Parris, J., & Spacco, J. (2013). How we teach impacts student learning: Peer instruction vs. lecture in CS0. In *Proceeding of the 44th ACM Technical Symposium on Computer Science Education* (pp. 41–46). New York: ACM.

Slavin, R. E. (1996). Research on cooperative learning and achievement: What we know, what we need to know. *Contemporary Educational Psychology*, 21(1), 43–69.

Slavin, R. E. (1990). *Cooperative Learning: Theory, Research, and Practice*. Englewood Cliffs, NJ: Prentice Hall.

Smith, M. K., Wood, W. B., Adams, W. K., Wieman, C., Knight, J. K., Guild, N., & Su, T. T. (2009). Why peer discussion improves student performance on in-class concept questions. *Science*, 323(5910), 122–124.

Straumanis, A., & Simons, E. (2008). A multi-institutional assessment of the use of POGIL in organic chemistry. In R. S. Moog & J. N. Spencer (Eds.), *Process-Oriented Guided Inquiry Learning: ACS Symposium Series 994* (pp. 226–239). Washington, DC: American Chemical Society.

The POGIL Project (2018). POGIL Implementation Guide. Retrieved from www.pogil. org/educators/additional-resources

Totten, S. S., Digby, T. A., & Russ, P. (1991). *Cooperative Learning: A Guide to Research*. New York: Garland.

Vygotsky, L. S. (1978). *Mind in Society*. Cambridge, MA: Harvard University Press.

Vygotsky, L. S. (1986). *Thought and Language – Revised Edition*. Cambridge, MA: MIT Press.

Werner, L., Denner, J., Campe, S., Ortiz, E., DeLay, D., Hartl, A. C., & Laursen, B. (2013). Pair programming for middle school students: Does friendship influence academic outcomes? In *Proceeding of the 44th ACM Technical Symposium on Computer Science Education* (pp. 421–426). New York: ACM.

Wiegers, K. E. (1995). Improving quality through software inspections. *Software Development*, 3(4), 1–15.

Williams, L. A., & Kessler, R. R. (2000a). The effects of "pair-pressure" and "pair-learning" on software engineering education. In *Proceedings of the 13th Conference on Software Engineering Education & Training* (pp. 59–65). New York: IEEE.

Williams, L. A., & Kessler, R. R. (2000b). All I Really Need to Know About Pair Programming I Learned in Kindergarten. *Communications of the ACM*, 43(5), 108–114.

Zingaro, D. (2014). Peer instruction contributes to self-efficacy in CS1. In *Proceedings of the 45th ACM Technical Symposium on Computer Science Education* (pp. 373–378). New York: ACM.

Zingaro, D., & Porter, L. (2015). Tracking student learning from class to exam using isomorphic questions. In *Proceedings of the 46th ACM Technical Symposium on Computer Science Education* (pp. 356–361). New York: ACM.

Case Studies

30 A Case Study of Peer Instruction

From University of California, San Diego to the Computer Science Community

Leo Porter and Beth Simon

30.1 Why Look at Peer Instruction?

In a span of about ten years, peer instruction (PI) has gone from a pedagogy almost unexplored in computing to one of our best-understood teaching methods in terms of both research and faculty adoption. This is a story of how an idea with strong research roots in other disciplines came to be adopted, studied, adapted, and spread in computing. This chapter examines what happened in particular and provides reflections from those heavily involved as to why it has been so successful.

There are a number of successful practices in computing (e.g., computing in context and pair programming, among others). We focus on PI because: (1) it was successfully applied in other science, technology, engineering, and mathematics (STEM) disciplines prior to adoption in computing; (2) its adoption in computer science (CS) was possible, in part, because of a clear mandate for curricular change; (3) we collected data on its efficacy from the very beginning, which led to research results and publications; and (4) it became adopted in a wide variety of schools and courses by a number of instructors.

30.1.1 Overview of PI

PI and the research on PI in computing is described in depth in Chapter 29; however, we wish here to briefly summarize the practice itself.

Before Class: Students engage with the material so that they are introduced to the concepts that will be discussed in class. The pre-class material often takes the form of reading assignments or videos. Students are then typically asked to complete a pre-class quiz on the assigned material.

In Class: The instructor structures the material around a series of questions. These questions typically address core conceptual understanding or common misconceptions, or are used to motivate the material. Each question then follows the same algorithm as follows:

1. The instructor poses a question for students to consider.
2. Students then vote individually (often using clickers) on their answer to the question. This is often called the "individual vote."

3. Students discuss the question in small groups. The instructor often teaches students early in the term to focus not just on which answer is correct, but why incorrect answers are incorrect.
4. Students vote individually again, perhaps having changed their answer based on discussion. This is often called the "group vote."
5. The instructor leads a class-wide discussion about the question, soliciting student thinking from the audience. Depending on student success on the individual and group votes, the instructor may move quickly through the discussion or pause to spend more time as appropriate.

30.1.2 Why Explore PI in Computing: Because of Research Results in Other STEM Disciplines

PI is a pedagogy or instructional approach originally designed for use in introductory university physics at Harvard. The seminal ten-year report on the success at Harvard reports on the years 1990–2000, with PI first being implemented in 1991 (Crouch & Mazur, 2001). In that report, learning gains were approximately two-fold greater than with lectures as measured by pre- and post-tests on the Force Concept Inventory (Hestenes et al., 1992). Since then, many other reports of the efficacy of PI measured on a range of student outcomes have been produced (see Chapter 29). These reports span multiple STEM disciplines including physics, biology, chemistry, and math.

As for implementation and adoption in computing, references in the Association for Computing Machinery (ACM) Digital Library to PI can be difficult to track, in part because of a more generic use of the term "peer instruction" to refer to a variety of settings and manners in which peers instruct and learn with each other. Nonetheless, by as early as 2006, we can find clear reference to Mazur's definition of PI, often in conjunction with the discussion of "clickers" or "audience response systems" (Murphy, 2008; Pargas & Shah, 2006). That said, the majority of PI-related publications in computing stem from an initial implementation at University of California (UC), San Diego in 2008. How this came about is outlined in the rest of this chapter.

30.1.2.1 Implementing Evidence-Based Practices: The Impact of the Carl Wieman Science Education Initiative at the University of British Columbia

Starting in 2006, the Carl Wieman Science Education Initiative (CWSEI) was formed with the goal of "achieving the most effective, evidence-based science education (effective science education, backed by evidence)" (Wieman, 2018). More specifically, the CWSEI sought to engage a majority of STEM faculty at the University of British Columbia (UBC) in adopting evidence-based practices in their teaching. To support these efforts, CWSEI hired multiple Science Teaching and Learning Fellows as postdocs or visiting scholars within departments to support faculty in adopting various practices to improve student learning. In the 2007–2008 academic year, Beth Simon, an Assistant Teaching Professor at UC San Diego with a history of studying and implementing affordances for improved computing classroom learning, accepted a position as a fellow in the CWSEI.

During Beth's tenure at the CWSEI, she was given the opportunity to learn about and engage deeply with the research on teaching practices that improve student learning outcomes in STEM. Among those practices, the one that most resonated with her was PI. Not only did PI have some of the strongest and most widely replicated evidence for its efficacy, but also it could be implemented in the traditionally designed lecture halls common at large campuses. Moreover, PI engages students in "deep analysis" by having students solve problems, and she felt that this type of analysis would be valuable in a variety of computing courses (particularly introductory programming).

While all computing faculty are trained first and foremost as scientists, it is not uncommon to hear faculty speaking of their students and their classrooms in very anecdotal manners. Instructors often try to gauge student comprehension through "looks of confusion" on student faces. They sometimes wonder if there's a bimodal distribution of student scores in classes – wondering if some students can succeed in computing and others simply can't (see Chapter 12 for more details). But studies, especially quantitative ones, on the impacts of pedagogical approaches in CS education had been scant. What Beth found compelling about PI was the rigorously measured evidence for its success in other STEM fields. Although those successes alone could not guarantee its efficacy in the computing classroom, taken together with the kinds of thinking and analysis that PI questions in those fields supported, there was enough commonality to lead Beth to think that a similar experience could be had in computing courses.

Finally, an important aspect of the CWSEI was the opportunity not just to read research about PI, but also to talk with faculty who had implemented it (albeit in other disciplines), to observe it in real classroom settings, and to learn about the PI questions themselves. By analyzing and discussing actual PI questions, Beth was able to better understand how they were developed, which features were critical to their design, and how students interacted with them to reach greater understanding. Research papers often do not provide this depth of detail regarding critical issues of successful classroom implementation, though some of this is now available as advice for faculty on various websites (Lee et al., 2018; Wieman, 2018).

30.1.3 Overview of How PI Was Adopted in Computing

The remainder of this chapter discusses the events related to PI in considerably more detail. To begin, we provide a brief summary of the timeline.

After returning to UC San Diego from the CWSEI in 2008, Beth was part of a departmental discussion on how to substantially revise the introductory programming course. Given this opportunity to implement change, Beth piloted

PI (along with pair programming and media computation) in UC San Diego's CSE8A course. CSE8A is the introductory course for students without any prior programming experience. Leo Porter, then a graduate student, was Beth's Teaching Assistant (TA) and designed the programming assignments for the course.

The new version of CSE8A spread to other faculty teaching the course, and, by adopting this new version, these faculty also adopted PI. At the same time, Leo and other graduate students and former graduate students began adopting PI in their courses. These initial runs of PI came to be well studied and formed the basis of much of the initial research on PI in computing. PI was also adopted outside UC San Diego by a variety of institutions, with the University of Toronto as one of the first adopters. PI then spread in the CS education community through a combination of graduate students graduating and taking on teaching careers outside of UC San Diego, educators adopting PI based on the research evidence or the publicly available course materials, and direct outreach efforts in the form of workshops and personal mentoring by those already using PI.

30.2 The Inaugural Computing Course at UC San Diego

In this and the following section, we examine the introduction of PI at UC San Diego and the subsequent adoption by other instructors and at other institutions. We begin by looking at the particular story of the adoption of PI at UC San Diego. First, we outline the story of how this course came to be and was offered. Next, we reflect on the specific factors we believe, in hindsight, contributed to the success of the implementation of that course. Of necessity, this reflection includes components that may be more or less prevalent or impactful in differing educational settings (e.g., outside the USA or outside of a large, research-focused public US institution).

30.2.1 Creating the First PI Course at UC San Diego

Upon planning her return to UC San Diego after working at the CWSEI, Beth was in communication with a departmental colleague who had been leading the CS education undergraduate curriculum committee. He had brought an analysis to the department suggesting we needed to improve retention and attraction of majors – particularly those from diverse backgrounds. Collaborating in a review of research on increasing interest and success in introductory programming courses, a proposal was made to the faculty to support the redesign of the first course to implement three best practices: PI, Computing in context with media computation, and pair programming. A month of summer salary was authorized to support the development of the course. An important impact of the background supporting the redesign (and the summer salary allocation) was that it was expected that some sort of analysis and evaluation of the course would be conducted to understand the impact of the changes.

Beth Simon, the instructor, served as the primary lead in designing the course, especially the PI questions. Beth used the general complaint from physics that "students could plug and chug but not really understand," even after reading the textbook or attending lecture. To develop questions, she read through the course textbook using media computation (Guzdial & Ericson, 2007) and used her teaching experience to identify places students might not "get" the deeper implications of the explanations or examples.

Other factors in the design of the course were supported by Leo Porter, a TA who had a specific interest in CS education. Leo supported the development of the new course by spending a significant amount of time discussing the course design, attending, observing, and providing feedback on class sessions, and collaborating in the design of programming assignments and managing the logistics of pair programming for homeworks.

30.2.2 Factors Contributing to the Success of the Course

Although instructors can generally adopt a pedagogical approach like PI in their courses at their own discretion, in hindsight, there were specific aspects of the case of CS1 at UC San Diego that we believe shed light on how PI came to be studied and adopted by others in CS.

30.2.2.1 Authorization to Make Evidence-Based Curricular Change

Most of us teach a common set of courses and generally have a relatively large amount of control over what happens in those courses. Perhaps there is a commonly accepted textbook, especially in introductory programming course sequences, which drives some of our course design. But ultimately, control over assignments, labs, and exams is often left up to the instructor in most countries. What is often not discussed is how instructors "use" lecture time.

However, as previously described, the implementation of PI in this course was, in a sense, authorized through a departmental-level decision to redesign the introductory course. A process of evaluation of options and selection of specific aspects, including PI, had been completed. That is, this was less an instance of a professor "trying something new" in her course as it was a "pilot" of an intentional set of changes with a specific goal in mind: increased success as measured by retention in the major. *This explicit mandate to find, evaluate, and make decisions as a formal "course redesign" based on evidence-based research papers in the computing education field was critical and, perhaps, somewhat unusual.*

30.2.2.2 Looking to Best Practices in Related Disciplines: Active Learning

Simultaneously, the national discussion around "active learning" was starting to gain momentum. As described earlier, given the compelling learning gains measured in physics and the similarities in learning concerns between physics and introductory programming, Beth decided to draw on an evidence-based practice from another field to shape the redesign of the course. We believe that *identifying an already vetted pedagogical approach that addresses a concern about learning is better than reinventing the wheel.*

30.2.2.3 Adapting with a Principled Approach

Prior work on PI had mostly been in physics, which meant that the exemplar materials for PI were largely about getting students to think like a physicist. Reviewing these materials was valuable in gaining insight into PI, but did not provide clear recommendations for how to design questions in CS. Instead, the concept of pedagogical content knowledge (Shulman, 1986) was used to drive initial CS PI questions and to guide developers of subsequent CS PI question sets. Pedagogical content knowledge constitutes the teacher's thoughts and experiences of the common challenges students face in learning a specific topic. This knowledge of common student difficulties was used to design PI questions that would engage students in solving problems for which there were common misunderstandings. By addressing these early, the goal was to promote learning and engender thinking like a computer scientist. In practice, this led to a more broad range of PI activities, including analyzing code segments with common errors and explaining the overall purpose of code segments. This made for a compelling argument to those considering adopting PI: "PI has students doing the easier things before class, with class time spent on the 'hard stuff'." Lastly, not all questions were successful at first, and iteration was necessary to find questions that were appropriately difficult, conceptually focused, and fostered discussion. *When using evidence-based approaches from other fields, adaptation is necessary, and we recommend that such adaptations be explored through a principled approach.*

30.2.2.4 Support from Educationally Minded TAs and Staff

As the original course restructuring was starting, Beth selected two people from the department to help support the change. The first was Leo Porter, a PhD student who had been a TA for Beth in the past, who was asked to be the TA for the course. In addition to standard TA duties, Beth asked him to design all of the course assignments utilizing other best practices: media computation and pair programming. The second person was Sarah (Esper) Guthals, an undergraduate student who had previously tutored for Beth. She was similarly asked to redesign all of the course labs to incorporate media computation and pair programming. In addition to helping redesign the course, Leo and Sarah would later help with the initial data gathering related to the course described in the next section.

As with many institutions with large (>100-student) classes, course success and experience at UC San Diego are heavily impacted by teaching staff. Although the course redesign was fundamentally led by Beth, *the presence of capable instructional staff support helped make the design a success, especially in creating quality materials and documentation that would support another instructor to "pick up" and offer this course.* Later in this chapter, we will discuss the role of mentoring in more detail, but we note here that both Leo and Sarah would go on to be involved heavily in CS education, largely in part from Beth's mentoring and the positive experience in the redesign.

30.3 PI Gains Momentum

Similar to the last section, we will start by discussing the timeline of initial results, data gathering, publications, and our view of how PI spread. Then we will reflect on the factors that we believe led to PI's external success.

30.3.1 Timeline of PI After the First UC San Diego Course

Given how far PI has come in the past decade, it is sometimes hard to remember how novel this approach felt to our students on campus and how generally excited they, and we (the authors and adopters), were about the change back in 2008. Back in that first course, we were intensely curious about how students would perceive the change and were unsure how things would turn out. To that end, Beth, Leo, and Sarah designed a survey instrument for students to measure the success of PI and to gauge student impressions on this new teaching practice.

When the feedback came back as overwhelmingly positive, we were excited to see that things had gone well. But when we read an open-ended question we had posed about their "role" in the new class structure, we heard things that were frankly surprising at the time. Students reported feeling responsible for their own learning, worrying that not coming to class might let their discussion group down, and that they felt what they learned in class prepared them well for exams, sometimes with substantially less studying outside class. Those comments heartened us that the hard work of course redesign was worth it, but that we needed to try it in more classes.

While Beth wrote up her experiences with her introductory programming class in a Special Interest Group on Computer Science Education (SIGCSE) paper published in 2010 (Simon et al., 2010), Leo and Cynthia Lee (a former UC San Diego graduate student and UC San Diego lecturer) both adopted PI in upper-division courses as lead instructors of computer architecture and theory of computation, respectively. Other faculty in the department also began teaching the redesigned introductory programming course and using PI, with Beth mentoring them.

In 2010, a number of us also collaborated together on a study replicating Michelle Smith and colleagues' (2009) article in *Science* about PI in biology classes. We measured student learning from discussion using isomorphic questions. As with the finding in biology, we documented measurable learning from the peer discussions. We published these results in the International Computing Education Research (ICER) 2011 meeting proceedings (Porter et al., 2011). This was also the year we received National Science Foundation (NSF) funding to continue the work of studying PI and developing new course materials.

In 2011, we also began researching Beth's original goal: to improve the retention of students in computing. As part of the retention study, we also looked at course failure rates in PI versus lecture classes. In both studies, we were simply astounded. Failure rates were down by 67 percent (from 20 to 7 percent on average) across four computing courses (Porter et al., 2013b). One-year major retention from the redesigned introductory computing course was up from 51 to 80 percent (Porter & Simon, 2013). Both papers on these studies appeared in SIGCSE 2013, with the retention study earning Best Paper (Porter et al., 2013b; Porter & Simon, 2013). There were three other PI papers at SIGCSE that year: Beth and collaborators showed that students in a PI section of a course outperformed the lecture section on a final exam (Simon et al., 2013); Dan Zingaro and collaborators showed the value of reading quizzes (Zingaro et al., 2013); and Cynthia Lee reported on how to use PI in an introductory programming course in MATLAB (Lee, 2013).

At this point, the project had clearly moved from its infancy to a somewhat acknowledged success. Beth, along with Quintin Cutts and Sarah (Esper) Guthals, created a new CS Principles course at UC San Diego using PI. Leo, Beth, Dan Zingaro, and Cynthia Lee began hosting a number of workshops at a variety of conferences. At UC San Diego, more faculty adopted PI both inside and outside computing as Beth advised them from her new role as the Director of the Center for Teaching Development. Outside UC San Diego, other faculty had adopted PI and developed materials for others to use (notably John Glick at the University of San Diego, Jaime Spacco at Knox College, Cynthia Taylor at Oberlin College, Hung-Wei Tseng at North Carolina State University, Kevin Webb at Swarthmore College, and Dan Zingaro at the University of Toronto). To be clear, though, there were a number of instructors adopting PI around the country, and we weren't privy to many of these adoptions and would only later learn of some adopters.

This isn't to say that everything went swimmingly. As success spread, so did the number of detractors. Faculty at various institutions would call PI a "gimmick" and would challenge if students were *really* learning anything more, and some would dismiss the change as obvious – saying that their occasional use of worksheets and asking students questions in class offhand were the same thing. These detractors still exist today, though their numbers may be fewer. We like to think this is partly because a number of researchers have done the work to answer many of these challenges through research studies at other institutions and partly because more faculty are using PI and observing its value.

At this point, we know of a number of universities and colleges who have embraced PI. At UC San Diego, the use of PI has widened and, as a result, students are now likely to encounter PI in many classes before graduating. Studies continue to examine the efficacy of PI, and new work seeks to explore how to use the data that are naturally gathered by using clickers when teaching with PI. Lastly, Beth, Leo, Cynthia Lee, and Mark Guzdial (also a PI adopter) now work on faculty adoption of PI by hosting an annual, NSF-funded, New Computer Science Faculty Teaching Workshop. In the remainder of the chapter, we examine factors that we believe led to PI's success.

30.3.2 Factors Contributing to the Success of PI in the CS Education Community

A novice to the world of educational change might think that an effective peda-gogy would automatically gain widespread adoption and attention. Those more versed in educational change know it takes much more than that. In the pre-vious section, we looked at factors associated with the initial development and adoption of PI in CS. In this section, we reflect on the factors that made it successful in growing the number of faculty adopting PI and the variety of CS courses in which it is used.

Often faculty trying to create change in courses are met with numerous barriers. There are faculty who wish to protect the status quo, there are other courses in the curriculum that can be impacted by changes, there is the time and overhead of creating the new course, there are concerns that creating a new course might result in poor student evaluations, etc. Despite this, we have seen PI use in CS grow substantially beyond the initial efforts of those studying PI – both at UC San Diego and in other institutions. While we have not been able to conduct a comprehensive survey of PI use in CS nor a detailed study of why different instructors adopted it, we draw on what we do know to highlight some aspects we believe were valuable in contributing to the adoption and success of PI in the CS community.

30.3.2.1 Expectation of Documentation Leads to Research Publications

Back when Beth adopted PI in introductory computing, the departmental authorization to design a best-practices curriculum came with a matching and very important factor: the expectation of documenting the impact of the change. Perhaps surprisingly, there were no preset metrics of evaluation, no common assessments of student learning, nor any clear timeline on how the evaluation should be conducted. Although some of this falls on the annual change in lead-ership in the undergraduate curriculum committee, there are broader issues at play in academia and in computing. Computing at many institutions lacks a culture of quantitative or qualitative evaluation of teaching or student learning beyond basic student satisfaction surveys. Again, the course redesigner's (Beth's) influence at the CWSEI helped lead the identification of important data. This began with the aforementioned carefully constructed student survey that solicited student feedback on the fidelity of the instructor's implementation of the components of PI (e.g., how often did students discuss questions in their group?) along with overall views of the course. This survey was run in the initial course offerings and it allowed the instructor to adapt to concerns identified by students. Although this survey was later used by multiple instructors at various institutions, other metrics of student success were explored shortly thereafter, including course failure rates, retention of majors, student learning on final exams, and student learning on individual questions. Ultimately, the impetus to design a common *student evaluation survey benefited research across multiple instructors, courses, and institutions and was a core element of early PI research.*

30.3.2.2 Presence of Eager Early Adopters: The Benefits of Working with Graduate Students

As previously mentioned, after Beth's adoption of PI, the next two adopters at UC San Diego were Cynthia Lee and Leo Porter. Cynthia had recently received her PhD in High-Performance Computing, had a mentoring relationship with Beth around teaching generally, and was teaching for the department. She'd heard of Beth's use of PI in classes and wanted to try it herself. Cynthia first adopted it in the summer of 2010, developing the course materials for the department's Theory of Computation course. Leo was still a PhD student in the department researching computer architecture, but having taught a course as an adjunct at the University of San Diego and having seen PI firsthand in Beth's classes, he was eager to try PI in a summer course. He also adopted PI in the summer of 2010, developing course materials for a Computer Architecture course.

Although Leo and Cynthia would go on to mentor and help other faculty adopt PI themselves, Beth's teaching of the department's TA training course led to more PhD students teaching summer classes using PI. These students included Cynthia Taylor (now at Oberlin College), Kevin Webb (now at Swarthmore College), and Hung-Wei Tseng (now at North Carolina State University). Cynthia Lee is now a lecturer at Stanford University.

Additionally, because the graduate students often taught upper-division electives in the major (sometimes in summer), this supported the creation of high-quality PI questions (as they were mentored by Beth) that were specifically designed for UC San Diego versions of these courses. *Both the specific "match" to UC San Diego's version of the course and regular faculty trust in their own graduate students supported the adoption of these materials by other professors at UC San Diego.*

Because many of the first adopters were graduate students who went on to be professors at other universities and colleges after graduation, PI spread more quickly through personal connections and direct mentoring at other schools.

30.3.2.3 Parallel Adoption of PI at Other Institutions

Very early on, Dan Zingaro adopted PI for the remedial CS1 course at the University of Toronto having heard of Beth's work at UC San Diego. Shortly thereafter, Dan, Beth, Cynthia, and Leo joined efforts to study PI and to teach workshops at various venues (Consortium for Computing Sciences in Colleges [CCSC], SIGCSE). (In fact, Dan's PhD thesis in education ultimately focused on PI in computing.) Ultimately, the combined team was able to produce PI materials for a wide variety of classes quickly (all had teaching-focused positions), and because all members of the team were CS education researchers, they were able (and willing) to conduct research in their classes.

Through personal and professional connections at other institutions, this group studying PI grew quickly. With individuals using PI at different schools, some were able to effect change within their own departments and, in some cases, help other faculty adopt PI.

A variety of other faculty have adopted PI in CS courses. Exactly what encouraged or enabled them to do so is rarely a subject of discussion, but rationales are sometimes made evident through discussion at conferences. Some have mentioned reading research about PI and/or having heard the presentation of that research at CS education conferences. In addition, a number of workshops led by Beth, Dan, Cynthia, Leo, John Glick, and Jaime Spacco at conferences had success. Some of the participants adopted PI when they returned to their home institutions and word spread.

In some cases, institutions had multiple faculty adopt PI for different reasons. For example, the University of Illinois, Chicago hired UC San Diego graduate Chris Kanich as an Assistant Professor. Given his background at UC San Diego working with Beth, he adopted PI in his courses. Joe Hummel, teaching faculty at the University of Illinois, Chicago, adopted PI after attending a summer workshop led by Leo, Cynthia, and Beth. Cynthia Taylor first adopted PI at UC San Diego and continued to use PI when she joined Oberlin and the University of Illinois, Chicago as teaching faculty. (We note that Cynthia Taylor and Joe Hummel now lead workshops on PI themselves.) There are many others who have worked with us in workshops, asked for our materials, or led discussions on PI at their own schools. We would attempt to list everyone, but would inevitably miss someone out, so instead we just wish to briefly thank our many collaborators and colleagues.

Ultimately, we believe PI spread most successfully via one-on-one mentoring. This began with personally mentoring a group of graduate students at UC San Diego. After graduation, many of them became faculty at new institutions throughout the country where they, in turn, mentored their new colleagues.

30.3.2.4 Research Showed PI to Be Effective in CS: Did It Matter?

One question that we often ask ourselves is whether the fairly extensive research on PI – replicated in multiple institutions and varying courses – had any impact on the adoption of PI. Did those reporting that replication research originally adopt PI because of the initial research? Or did they adopt because of personal connections with other instructors using PI? Or was it both? We know of examples for each of these scenarios. But we have not (nor possibly have the adopting instructors themselves) sat down and thoroughly considered or documented the rationales for adopting PI.

This would be a worthy subject for study and has been done in other fields (Dancy & Henderson, 2010; Froyd et al., 2013; Prince et al., 2013). More generally, work on instructor change and the adoption of evidence-based practices in higher education can be found in the research by Charles Henderson (Beach & Henderson, 2018; Henderson, 2018a) and the Center for Research on Instructional Change in Postsecondary Education (CRCPE) at Western Michigan University. This work generally finds that research reports alone are not enough to engage faculty in changing their instructional habits. The Increase the Impact project seeks to help "innovators in undergraduate

STEM education learn strategies for effectively sharing their work with others" (Henderson, 2018b).

However, we can state some facts about how PI-related research engagement in the CS education community happened.

With studying PI a first priority from the start, the early group of PI adopters went on to publish a wide variety of studies showing its value in computing (see Chapter 29 for full details). These publications appeared in common venues for both CS education researchers and CS education practitioners (SIGCSE, Innovation and Technology in Computer Science Education [ITiCSE], ICER, and *ACM Transactions on Computing Education* [TOCE]), as well as general education venues (*Computers & Education* and American Educational Research Association [AERA]). These publications may have made other faculty aware of its potential value. More accessible overviews in *Communications of the ACM* (Porter et al., 2013a; Simon & Cults, 2012), Mark Guzdial's Computing Education Blog (Guzdial, 2018), and Mark Guzdial's book with some discussion of PI (Guzdial, 2015) may have also helped reach additional instructors. Recently, through an NSF-funded project, an annual teaching workshop helps educate newly hired tenure track faculty at institutions in the USA about the benefits and use of PI, among other evidence-based approaches and teaching advice.

30.4 Suggestions for Future Adopters

In 2012, Cynthia Lee, Leo Porter, Dan Zingaro, and Beth Simon started a website for potential adopters of PI in computing (www.peerinstruction4cs.org). At that website, practical advice is provided on how to adopt PI, how to explain it to students, and how to handle logistical concerns (e.g., clickers). As developing good PI questions is often the largest hurdle to adoption, the website also provides course materials (questions, reading quizzes, mini-lectures) for a variety of courses including (as of 2018): CS Principles, CS1-Python, CS1-MATLAB, CS1-Java, CS2-Java, CS2-C++, Discrete Mathematics, Operating Systems, Programming Languages, Computer Architecture, and Theory of Computation. These materials can be particularly valuable to new adopters of PI as they provide example questions that have worked well in past classes, and they are valuable to new course instructors as the questions themselves, being heavily focused on common student misconceptions, provide a form of pedagogical content knowledge. Lastly, if anyone is interested in adopting PI, they are encouraged to reach out to other instructors on campus who use PI, attend a workshop, or reach out to us directly.

30.5 Summary

PI started as a new pedagogy in physics, designed to foster better conceptual understanding of physics in students. Given its success, we brought PI to our computing courses at UC San Diego and found that the courses were highly successful, with high student satisfaction, lower failure rates, higher retention, and higher student performance. A number of us saw the success of that initial course at UC San Diego and brought PI to our own courses. In turn, the corpus of teaching materials available for PI in computing grew quickly, as did the number of adopters. Although PI has become firmly entrenched in computing, we suspect that we are many years from it becoming more common than lectures. For those reading this who may be encouraged by this chapter to try PI, please see www.peerinstruction4cs.org for course materials or please join us at one of the many workshops on the topic hosted at conferences annually.

Acknowledgments

In addition to the many reviewers who provided us with feedback on this chapter who are acknowledged at the beginning of the book, we wish to personally thank Dan Zingaro and Minhtuyen Mai for their helpful suggestions. We also wish to thank our many colleagues who have contributed so much to PI in computing by aiding in research studies, adopting PI in their classes, mentoring new faculty in PI adoption, and helping PI gain traction in numerous institutions worldwide. Lastly, this material is based upon work supported by the NSF under grant no. DUE-1140731.

References

Beach, A., & Henderson, C. (2018). Research on Instructional Change in Postsecondary Education. Retrieved from http://wmich.edu/changeresearch

Crouch, C. H., & Mazur, E. (2001). Peer instruction: Ten years of experience and results. *American Journal of Physics*, 69(9), 970–977.

Dancy, M., & Henderson, C. (2010). Pedagogical practices and instructional change of physics faculty. *American Journal of Physics*, 78(10), 1056–1063.

Froyd, J. E., Borrego, M., Cutler, S., Henderson, C., & Prince, M. J. (2013). Estimates of use of research-based instructional strategies in core electrical or computer engineering courses. *IEEE Transactions on Education*, 56(4), 393–399.

Guzdial, M. (2018). Computing Education Research Blog. Retrieved from https://computinged.wordpress.com (Various posts: search for "peer instruction.")

Guzdial, M. (2015). Learner-centered design of computing education: Research on computing for everyone. *Synthesis Lectures on Human-Centered Informatics*, 8(6), 1–165.

Guzdial, M., & Ericson, B. (2007). *Introduction to Computing and Programming in Java: A Multimedia Approach*. London, UK: Pearson.

Henderson, C. (2018a). Charles Henderson Publications. Retrieved from http://homepages.wmich.edu/~chenders/Publications/Publications.htm

Henderson, C. (2018b). Increase the Impact. Retrieved from www.increasetheimpact.com

Hestenes, D., Wells, M., & Swackhamer, G. (1992). Force concept inventory. *The Physics Teacher*, 30(3), 141–158.

Lee, C. B. (2013). Experience report: CS1 in MATLAB for non-majors, with media computation and peer instruction. In *Proceedings of the 44th ACM Technical Symposium on Computer Science Education* (pp. 35–40). New York: ACM.

Lee, C. B., Porter L., Zingaro, D., & Simon B. (2018). Peer Instruction for CS. Retrieved from www.peerinstruction4cs.org

Murphy, T. (2008). Success and failure of audience response systems in the classroom. In *Proceedings of the 36th Annual ACM SIGUCCS Fall Conference: Moving Mountains, Blazing Trails* (pp. 33–38). New York: ACM.

Pargas, R. P., & Shah, D. M. (2006). Things are clicking in computer science courses. *ACM SIGCSE Bulletin*, 38(1), 474–478.

Porter, L., Guzdial, M., McDowell, C., & Simon, B. (2013a). Success in introductory programming: What works? *Communications of the ACM*, 56(8), 34–36.

Porter, L., Lee, C. B., & Simon, B. (2013b). Halving fail rates using peer instruction: A study of four computer science courses. In *Proceedings of the 44th ACM Technical Symposium on Computer Science Education* (pp. 177–182). New York: ACM.

Porter, L., Lee, C. B., Simon, B., & Zingaro, D. (2011). Peer instruction: Do students really learn from peer discussion in computing? *In Proceedings of the Seventh International Workshop on Computing Education Research* (pp. 45–52). New York: ACM.

Porter, L., & Simon, B. (2013). Retaining nearly one-third more majors with a trio of instructional best practices in CS1. In *Proceedings of the 44th ACM Technical Symposium on Computer Science Education* (pp. 165–170). New York: ACM.

Prince, M., Borrego, M., Henderson, C., Cutler, S., & Froyd, J. (2013). Use of research-based instructional strategies in core chemical engineering courses. *Chemical Engineering Education*, 47(1), 27–37.

Shulman, L. S. (1986). Those who understand: Knowledge growth in teaching. *Educational Researcher,* 15, 4–14.

Simon, B., & Cutts, Q. (2012). Peer instruction: A teaching method to foster deep understanding. *Communications of the ACM*, 55(2), 27–29.

Simon, B., Kohanfars, M., Lee, J., Tamayo, K., & Cutts, Q. (2010). Experience report: Peer instruction in introductory computing. In *Proceedings of the 41st ACM Technical Symposium on Computer Science Education* (pp. 341–345). New York: ACM.

Simon, B., Parris, J., & Spacco, J. (2013). How we teach impacts student learning: Peer instruction vs. lecture in CS0. In *Proceedings of the 44th ACM Technical Symposium on Computer Science Education* (pp. 41–46). New York: ACM.

Smith, M. K., Wood, W. B., Adams, W. K., Wieman, C., Knight, J. K., Guild, N., & Su, T. T. (2009). Why peer discussion improves student performance on in-class concept questions. *Science*, 323(5910), 122–124.

Wieman, C. (2018). The Carl Wieman Science Initiative. Retrieved from www.cwsei.ubc.ca

Zingaro, D., Lee, C. B., & Porter, L. (2013). Peer instruction in computing: The role of reading quizzes. In *Proceedings of the 44th ACM Technical Symposium on Computer Science Education* (pp. 47–52). New York: ACM.

31 A Case Study of Qualitative Methods

Colleen M. Lewis

31.1 Introduction

In research – and many parts of life – we only see the finished product, a snapshot of calm and certainty even when the reality is chaotic. When people meet me, they might learn that I am a computer science (CS) professor. I assume they would never guess that I nearly failed my data structures course in college and still struggled in my second attempt. They would never imagine how many interviews I bombed and graduate schools I did not get into. They don't see the inevitable paper and grant rejections or poor teaching evaluations. Those things aren't on my CV, but reflecting back, I see these as some of the most influential elements for my learning.

This chapter is a narrative of the actual doing of a research study, what Roth (2006) calls a *praxis narrative*. I hope to give you a "feel for the game" (Bourdieu, 1992) of doing one type of qualitative research. Ideally, you will gain some insights into qualitative methods, or at least recognition that if it feels chaotic, it is not necessarily wrong. Textbooks about qualitative methods have a burden of providing clarity to the methods. This chapter instead seeks to show all of the mess and ambiguity. In our current context, where computing knowledge is often perceived as only available to the intellectual elite or people with a "geek gene," it is our responsibility to challenge these notions and help others see our humanness. I will attempt to do that while telling the backstory of this paper.

In this chapter, I will share some of what I learned through writing, revising, and now reflecting on a paper that traversed a particularly rocky path. My qualitative analysis was eventually published in a paper at the Association for Computing Machinery (ACM) Special Interest Group on Computer Science Education (SIGCSE) International Computing Education Research (ICER) conference (Lewis, 2012a), but the path there was a bit bumpy. The analysis came from my master's thesis (submitted December 2009), abbreviated to submit to ICER in April of 2010. It was rejected from ICER in 2010 and again in 2011. Despite my suspicion that the manuscript was doomed, I decided to revise and resubmit it again in 2012. Only in this third submission to ICER was it accepted. I received incredibly thoughtful – and harsh – reviews of my first submission to ICER in 2010. At that time, my work was described as preliminary and that the contribution was fairly minimal.

When it was finally accepted in 2012, it was awarded the inaugural Chair's Award at the 2012 ICER conference, "given to the paper that, in the judgment of the organizing committee, best illustrates the highest standards of empirical computing education research, taking into account the quality of its questions asked, methodology, analysis, writing, and contribution to the field." As an eternal imposter, I am distrustful of this characterization, but I can confidently claim that my work got much better and that the story of this growth captures important parts of my learning about qualitative methods.

The feedback I received at each point, even when it seemed unnecessarily harsh, was thoughtful and ultimately helpful. In terms of the volume of new and edited text, each new ICER submission was a significant revision. However, the changes themselves were never burdensome. The ideas were there, I just did not know how to put them into words, or even that I *should* put them into words. The key learning was subtle and led to reframing, restructuring, and ultimately much better analysis.

The following sections will chronicle my insights within the process distilled into *tips*. The tips are sequenced to roughly align with the broad categories of data collection, analysis, and writing. Each tip tells part of the story of the work of qualitative research. In recounting a part of the story, I attempt to capture something I think I learned about these broad, often interwoven categories of doing qualitative research. I have written each tip as a declarative statement, but these statements serve only as labels for the messiness that the real work of qualitative methods involves. Given that messiness, these declarative tips might be improved by adding "when possible" to the end of each. Now that I have written these tips, they seem obvious; they might even appear in qualitative methods textbooks. Perhaps I had even read them with them in one of the two qualitative methods courses I took en route to my PhD in science and mathematics education. However, qualitative methods require juggling multiple goals, and I simply had not developed fluency and consistency in applying these ideas and strategies.

Data Collection

- Check and organize your data as you go (Section 31.2.1).
- Don't plan to collect data when you are developing a new curriculum (Section 31.2.2).
- Adapt your data collection as you go (Section 31.2.3).

Data Analysis

- Keep detailed notes as your analysis evolves (Section 31.3.1).
- Follow your instincts (Section 31.3.2).
- Try to cherry-pick some interesting data (Section 31.3.3).
- Invent terms (i.e., constructs) so that you can work toward more precise analysis (Section 31.3.4).
- It would be easier if it were systematic (Section 31.3.5).
- When your analysis is good, it will seem obvious (Section 31.3.6).

- Acknowledge that your epistemological assumptions will shape the analysis (Section 31.3.7).

Writing

- Provide structure to help your reader understand your data (Section 31.4.1).
- Distinguish description and interpretation (Section 31.4.2).
- Present enough data so that someone could disagree with your interpretation (Section 31.4.3).
- Explain why you chose qualitative methods (Section 31.4.4).
- Explain the limitations of the work (Section 31.4.5).
- Explain how your analysis fits into the ongoing conversation (Section 31.4.6).
- Tie the motivation to the analysis (Section 31.4.7).
- Make the implications for teaching explicit (Section 31.4.8).

I encourage you to read the paper. It reveals how much of the real work is invisible in the final product. However, I will assume you haven't read it and will provide the relevant context as necessary. The paper describes a student that I gave the pseudonym Kevin as he debugs a Scratch program over the course of less than five minutes. Kevin was one of fifty 11–12-year-old students enrolled in a summer enrichment program for academically advanced students. I taught the enrichment course with the help of two other adults. The students were divided between a morning and afternoon section, each with 36 hours of instruction. One class used Scratch and the other used Logo. Each day, students in each class did isomorphic tasks using their given programming language. In this design, I was also generating quantitative data from surveys and daily quizzes to see how students' attitudes and performance differed between the two sections. This quantitative data was described in another paper (Lewis, 2010). Kevin was technically pair programming at the time, but his partner, Rachel, did not say anything during the episodes I analyzed, and from the video of the classroom she appears to not be looking at their computer screen or Kevin. With that context, you are ready for the tips!

31.2 Data Collection

In preparation for my data collection, I frequently received advice that I was collecting too much data. With student assent and parental consent, I recorded students' screens during each of the 36 hours of instruction in the summer enrichment program. My students, 11–12-year-olds, worked in a total of 25 pairs, with 12 pairs in the first offering and 13 pairs in the second offering. Every hour of instruction was also recorded on three video cameras. Therefore, I had over 900 hours or over 38 days of video recordings. "Too much data" seems like a reasonable critique and an understatement. I am nearly certain that I will deserve this critique again on future projects. However, the following three tips attempt to capture what I have learned and hope to apply in data collection for future projects.

31.2.1 Tip – Check and Organize Your Data As You Go

I am dismissive of the "too much data" critique, but it is not wrong. As my mentors and peers predicted, I was totally overwhelmed during data collection, and as a result I did not sufficiently check and organize the data during the course. That is a mistake I hope to avoid repeating. I had done plenty in advance of the summer course, but it was still insufficient.

In preparation for the data collection, I had collected and analyzed data from a one-hour pilot study with four students. This short intervention did not pilot the whole curriculum, but I began the summer having written a paper using the same type of data.

That summer, I had prepared by installing the screen recording software on all of the computers in my classroom and confirmed that it recorded using each of the external microphones that were required. I determined that the battery in the external microphones would need to be replaced daily to ensure audio recordings were made. I had developed a labeling system for the physical tapes recorded by each of the three video cameras in the room. I made elaborate checklists that we used to ensure we collected and stored the data. I owe a huge debt of gratitude to my co-teachers Brittany Murlas and Christa Henderson because they did not know what they had signed up for! We had very little data lost during the summer; given the complexity of the data collection, I think this was impressive.

There was just one catch. In longer screen recordings, the audio and the video got out of sync. When I opened the file with video editing software, the audio component was about two-thirds of the length of the video. Only when the audio component was stretched to match the length of the video did the audio appear to sync up with the video. This easily could have been detected before the end of the summer if I had been checking the data throughout. Instead, it required that I use a computer in my research lab to stretch the audio, which took more time to process than the length of the original video. It seems likely that if I had caught this earlier I could have avoided this additional step. Will this same problem repeat itself? No, but surely something else will go wrong, and I might as well set aside the time during data collection to figure that out.

31.2.2 Tip – Don't Plan to Collect Data When You Are Developing a New Curriculum

The course in which I collected data was a course I had never taught before. I had prepared all of the curriculum in advance, but students completed the content I had planned for the three-week course within the first week. I spent the remaining two weeks sleep-deprived as I tried to keep up with the students and generate more activities for them. How were my results changed because the curriculum was far from perfect? Recall that I taught computing using Scratch and Logo to address quantitative questions related to the strengths and weaknesses of each. The curriculum was likely equally bad between the Scratch and Logo offerings of the course, and I hope did not affect my results comparing Scratch and Logo (Lewis, 2010).

From that experience, I now strongly believe that you should not collect data in the first offering of a course. This seems like another tip that I will ignore sooner than is wise, but the flaws in a first offering of a course most likely will reduce the interpretability of results. Perhaps only collecting data with polished curricula is unrealistic, but describing the weaknesses of the curriculum is necessary. If I could go back and revise that publication (Lewis, 2010), I would include more information about the ways in which the class was rocky. I think I owe that to my readers and the research community generally.

31.2.3 Tip – Adapt Your Data Collection As You Go

One of my reviewers in 2010 argued that I should standardize my data collection and appeared to imply that qualitative work requires that all participants be given the same set of problems. While I reject the larger argument that the participants need a consistent experience, there are definitely practical considerations that would justify this. First, qualitative research requires a lot of space to explain the methods and analysis. If participants are each answering different questions, a lot of real estate could be lost to the description of the relevant problems that appear in the analyses. Second, asking the same question multiple times may provide the opportunity to follow up on hypotheses that are developed from an earlier participant's answer. This was helpful in my dissertation (Lewis, 2012b), which involved one-on-one interviews with students solving programming problems during a clinical interview. Often a student's answers puzzled me, and their responses to my follow-up questions provided no illumination. If another student expressed a similar idea, follow-up questions with that second student might be more fruitful. This opportunity was only available because I asked all students a common set of questions. However, these follow-up questions are examples where each student may be asked different questions. These unplanned follow-up questions allowed me to explore topics I did not know to plan interview questions for.

31.3 Data Analysis

I have frequently received the advice to be more systematic in my analysis. I think an assumption in the word "systematic" is that there are prescriptive steps that should be followed to ensure that qualitative methods are done correctly. That has not been my experience. I will concede in the first tip below that I should be more systematic in keeping detailed notes of my analysis decisions. However, the remaining tips embrace the openness of qualitative methods. Qualitative methods do not guarantee that another researcher would find the same result. My paper focused on less than five minutes of Kevin's interaction with Scratch. With over 900 hours of video recordings, there is seemingly no chance that another researcher would have identified this same five-minute excerpt! The first analysis task I had was to narrow the focus of the research and data analysis. This task feels anything but systematic, and I have gotten more and more comfortable with that. Section 31.4 describes the ways I try to build trust with my reader when I am not following a predetermined set of steps.

31.3.1 Tip – Keep Detailed Notes As Your Analysis Evolves

One way to be systematic is to document the analysis process as you go. In qualitative methods, this documentation is typically referred to as "memos." I think about it as a lab notebook or journal describing the analysis. I have good systems for implementing this on my collaborative projects, but not my individual ones.

In all of my collaborative projects, we coedit a shared Google doc during each meeting, and those notes nearly form a transcript of the meeting. In one project that spanned multiple years (Lewis, Anderson, & Yasuhara, 2016; Lewis, Yasuhara, & Anderson, 2011), we made it easier to refer back to these meeting notes by labeling each document with a title and including a one-sentence summary of the discussion at the top of the document. This was invaluable when we later wrote up our methods, and it helped us during the analysis to avoid inadvertently backtracking.

A weakness of the methods in my individual analysis efforts is that I do not have comprehensive notes about the path of my analysis. When I watch video data, I take notes in what is often called a "content log." This helps me document my observations and initial hypotheses, but it does not capture the continual snapshots of my analysis process like I have done in my collaborative projects. In my future individual analyses, I need to learn to incorporate the generation of this type of artifact. For this aspect of being systematic, I see only advantages.

31.3.2 Tip – Follow Your Instincts

To sift through 900 hours of video, I began my analysis focused on a particular piece of the curriculum: where students draw a brick wall, as shown in Figure 31.1. For those not familiar with Scratch, characters, like the cat shown in Figure 31.1, can draw lines as they move around the screen. The task of drawing the brick wall, which was designed by Guy Haas (n.d.), involves a relatively complex set of movements of the character that involve alternating whether the character is drawing a line (i.e., to draw a brick) or is not drawing a line (i.e., to create a space). It is pretty tricky to pick lengths for the bricks, partial bricks, and spaces that allow each row of bricks to line up. Additionally, it is tricky to navigate the character between these lines. If you are dying to see the code, you might try it directly in Scratch or read the published paper (Lewis, 2012a).

Figure 31.1 *Completed drawing of a brick wall in Scratch.*

I started with the brick wall activity based upon my experience of students completing the activity in class. Students often appeared to productively engage with the activity for between one and two hours.[1] Students hit predictable bugs, which appeared to be conceptually rich. Best of all, these bugs were immediately recognizable to me from what was drawn on the screen. For example, students often hit a point where the rows were skewed like a staircase. From having taught the class in which data were collected, my gut instinct was to focus on this problem in order to observe debugging behavior.

Perhaps my description of why I picked the brick wall sounds systematic. I certainly had reasons to pick the brick wall task. However, these reasons evolved as I started the analysis, and I could have picked another task and generated compelling reasons for focusing on that task instead. Narrowing the focus of the analysis is fundamentally open, and I have begun to come to grips with the fact that my plan is to trust my instincts. Luckily, as a CS instructor, I am constantly able to refine and test my instincts about how people learn CS, which increases my confidence in my instincts. However, focusing on one thing means there is less time to focus on other things, and there is nothing other than my fallible instincts on which to rely.

31.3.3 Tip – Try to Cherry-Pick Some Interesting Data

Once I had picked the task and I had started watching videos, one might describe my process of picking specific video excerpts as cherry-picking. While cherry-picking is used as a critique, I now think about this work as choosing the *right* cherries to pick! In other projects, I have cherry-picked quotes to illustrate a point in the completed analysis (e.g., Lewis, Yasuhara, & Anderson, 2011), but in this project, cherry-picking was an early step in the analysis.

---

1 This difficult a task might have been risky in a classroom with only a single teacher, but we had three adult instructors with class sizes of 24 and 26.

As I recall, I had watched hours of video before finding Kevin's excerpt. I was looking for times where I could reasonably claim that the students were debugging. There were plenty of things that might be debugging. The video showed the students' screens, which meant in watching the videos I could observe a bug in their code and then could observe them making changes to their code. However, it was not clear that the students and I were seeing the same thing. Had they noticed the bug? Did they think that the changes they made to the code would fix the bug? This was a pretty deep rabbit hole.

I eventually stumbled upon the video of Kevin and Rachel. Kevin and Rachel's statements were unique in that they made their debugging explicit. Sometimes this was from Kevin and Rachel's dialogue and sometimes this was when Kevin seemed to be talking to himself or perhaps to the computer. The episode in the ICER paper began with Kevin stating, "What? Wait." It seemed clear that Kevin had recognized a bug.

Stumbling upon these data was like finding a gold mine! The ambiguity in every other video I had watched was disambiguated here by their statements. In the explicitness of their debugging, they were unlike other pairs. However, they did not seem to be outliers in other ways. In focusing on a single pair, I was not going to be sure of the exact extent to which the patterns I observed would generalize. Finding examples where I could observe the things I was interested in for my research (i.e., finding some cherries to pick) was the most important thing at this stage.

31.3.4 Tip – Invent Terms (i.e., Constructs) So That You Can Work toward More Precise Analysis

My analysis revolves around Kevin's understanding of program state. This idea of "state" is my primary *construct*. Methods books may provide a more comprehensive definition of construct, but I think of it is as a term that I use in my research for which I provide a specific definition. Across my projects, I have developed constructs that help me think about the analysis. Often I will develop constructs that do not appear in the final paper, but the process of iteratively refining my definition for the construct helps me refine my ideas and analysis.

Unfortunately, my construct of state is imperfect. The following definition of state from my paper has at least two *big* problems:

> State represents the idea, present in all programming environments, of a set of temporary or permanent variables that completely describe the current environment on which a program can act. This includes programmer-defined variables as well as other aspects of the runtime environment such as the current stack frame. Program commands change aspects of the computer program's state and the process of writing programs involves developing sequences of state change operations to achieve a particular goal.
> (Lewis, 2012a, p. 127)

First, my definition is inconsistent with a way that computer scientists talk about state. Specifically, computer scientists talk about functional programming languages as being stateless. This relies on the idea that a function, from the mathematical definition, has a single output for each input. That is, if you pass a function the same input multiple times, you are guaranteed to get the same output. They describe functions as "stateless" because the output only depends on the input. This contrasts with imperative programming where a function that adds two to the variable x will each time result in a different value of x; that is, it is stateful.

Second, based on my definition, absolutely everything in programming is state – everything. What is not state? Nothing. This is not good. Hopefully, in the future, I will be able to narrow in on something well-defined and more specific. With a construct too broadly defined, it seems less likely to be helpful.

The first big problem with my construct tends to make some computer scientists mad, but I think the "everything is state" problem is much worse. A similar critique could likely be made of the notional machine construct (see Chapter 1), which encompasses all of how programs are executed by computers. This is not a new revelation that my construct of state has big problems. I have spent a lot of time thinking about it, and I have decided that the construct is still useful. In particular, I knew that my use of state was inconsistent with another usage, but – for people without that context – "state" seemed intuitive to them, and for people with that context, it was never difficult to clarify my meaning.

31.3.5 Tip – It Would Be Easier if It Were Systematic

I think a jigsaw puzzle analogy is helpful for qualitative research. There appear to be endless puzzle pieces to choose from and I am trying to pick out and connect enough pieces to provide a clear, even if small, picture. Unfortunately, there is no box lid to guide the process and no edges of the puzzle to help me pick a place to start. There are just puzzle pieces, and I have to continually convince myself that I will be able to put some of them together if I spend time considering the possible connections.

In my experience, qualitative analysis takes a long time before it seems like the pieces fit together. Along the way, I will often figure out that the pieces do not fit in the way I had believed or that a piece I had barely noticed is probably more important than some of the other connections I had made. Sometimes hours, weeks, and months can go by with seemingly no measurable progress. Qualitative analysis takes time, and it does not follow a recipe of steps where it is possible to make continual forward progress.

Each of my qualitative projects has involved multiple and sometimes prolonged periods of doubt about the direction and content of the analysis. Without a set of steps to follow, this openness can be overwhelming. Two things have been helpful for me in managing this doubt and uncertainty. First, I track my time and I give myself a sticker for every 45 minutes of work.[2] There might

---

2 I am not kidding: see https://medium.com/@colleenlewis/intrinsic-motivation-is-overrated-dc1cbd4a7b7c

not be measurable progress, but there are no shortcuts for this work, and I need to get myself to put in the time. Second, I frequently share my analysis with colleagues. In graduate school, we had faculty-run research groups where one or two students would sign up to present their work and lean on the group to help them chart their next steps. As a faculty member, I no longer had access to these groups, and in 2014, I started hosting the Work in Progress workshop at ICER in order to provide a similar venue of support. Many times, new perspectives can help us to find a path forward.

31.3.6 Tip – When Your Analysis Is Good, It Will Seem Obvious

My greatest frustration in doing qualitative research is that when I think I'm done, it all seems obvious. Why had that taken me so long? I have put some puzzle pieces together and now there is a clear picture. I think that this feeling of obviousness is a feature of well-done qualitative work, but I think this leads me (and others) to underestimate it. Consider the key finding in my paper:

> I hypothesize that a key competence in debugging is learning to identify what elements of program state are important to pay attention to and that this attention, and not only domain knowledge, mediates the debugging process. (Lewis, 2012a, p. 127)

Of course it is important for students to pay attention to the right elements of program state. However, even if the finding seems obvious, I think there is something important here. In the paper, I argue that once students pay attention to the right element of state, the bug feels like a simple mistake. By eventually dismissing many – or potentially most – bugs as simple mistakes, students may miss that part of learning to program is learning what elements of state they should pay attention to. The connection between qualitative results being obvious and students discounting bugs as obvious is just a coincidence, but one I appreciate.

I might not convince readers of this chapter that my key finding in my paper is meaningful, but I hope to share my experience of frustration when the final result seems obvious because the pieces have come together so well. While I find this deeply frustrating, I now see obviousness as the goal for my analysis and perhaps as something I can help my readers value.

31.3.7 Tip – Acknowledge That Your Epistemological Assumptions Will Shape the Analysis

In the end, my analysis connected directly to the theoretical work of my advisor, Andrea (Andy) diSessa. Is that a coincidence? No. My advisor works in the general area of epistemology. He focuses on physics, but his theories have been applied to other domains. By the time I started working on this analysis, I had – consistent with my advisor's work – started to think of learning as a process of developing the ability to solve problems across contexts. In Andy's work, he talks about how students learn to pay attention to the right things in order to solve problems in physics (e.g., diSessa & Sherin, 1998). In my dissertation, I argued that students' thinking and learning about state are consistent with his model, which was developed around students' thinking and learning about force in physics. Building upon his work, in my dissertation, I proposed changes to his theory. I argued why CS content motivated these changes and that these changes were also applicable to physics.

Connections to existing theories can be important for moving the field forward. These epistemological connections were helpful in connecting my work to the broader body of literature about education or, more specifically, "conceptual change."

While these connections to my advisor's work can be seen as biases, I think they are, to some extent, unavoidable. In educational research, our epistemological assumptions are necessarily going to shape how we make sense of students' thinking and learning. Like our instincts, these shape how we navigate the openness of qualitative research. Again, qualitative methods don't guarantee us that different researchers would find the same thing. The point is to focus on phenomena where prescriptive steps would be insufficient, and we can attempt to make these assumptions that guide our work explicit.

31.4 Writing

I have frequently received the advice to "write clearly." Probably nothing could be less helpful. I certainly have had mixed results in my writing. Even from my accepted 2012 submission, I received a disparaging comment about my writing and a suggestion to do a "careful revision." I had certainly engaged in "careful revision," but that does not mean that my careful revision is sufficient to produce clear writing. Instead, I have settled on the following tips, which I hope steer me toward writing clearly.

31.4.1 Tip – Provide Structure to Help Your Reader Understand Your Data

After years of working with this data set, I found the lines of transcript, and Kevin's accompanying actions, crystal clear. This was not the case for my formal and informal readers. In early drafts, I was surprised by the things that my readers found opaque, and their feedback forced me to be explicit and structured in my writing.

I believe that the most consequential change that I made across the revisions to improve clarity was breaking the analysis up into short, sequential excerpts that each included subsections titled "Summary," "Data," and "Analysis." However, this structure was present in my 2011 submission, which notably was still rejected. Even if this structure did not unlock the elusive acceptance, it was foundational in how I now think about describing my analyses.

Each excerpt began with a "Summary," which provided a brief overview of what happened in the excerpt to follow. I tried to write this in a way that no one would dispute and that would prepare my readers to read the transcript that followed. For example, beginning in 2011 and present in the published version, I wrote, "In excerpt three, Kevin executes the program to draw the first two rows and retraces the first and second row before accidentally tracing over the first row with a copy of the second row." I think it would be reasonable to quibble with my use of "accidentally," which I think implies an interpretation of Kevin's actions. However, the rest seems a cut-and-dried description.

The next subsection, "Data," provided the transcript for that portion and would likely be nearly impossible for a reader to read without having first read the summary. Parentheticals within the transcript described Kevin's actions of executing or modifying code. I used sequential line numbers between excerpts to show that the content progressed sequentially. I think that helping the reader to understand the overall chronology is important, and therefore I never use ellipses to indicate pauses because they can be misinterpreted as removed text. Instead, I note pauses as a parenthetical note, as in "(pause)." Realistically, using ellipses is probably fine provided that the convention is stated.

Section 31.3, "Analysis," walked through the episode chronologically, alternating description and interpretation. The structure of these subsections is likely less important for the reader than in drawing my attention, as I am writing and revising, to the fact that I am engaged in interpretation. This might seem rather simplistic, but analysis tasks are difficult enough that this metacognition is still difficult and relevant for me. The next tip is dedicated to this difficulty.

31.4.2 Tip – Distinguish Description and Interpretation

In this work, I want to understand Kevin's thinking. Unfortunately, I can only make inferences or assumptions about his thinking based upon his statements and actions. Therefore, whenever I make a statement about Kevin's thinking, I need to include a hedging term such as "appears" or "I hypothesize."

For example, the first subsection of analysis began: "Kevin retraced the top row three times and appeared unsure why a third line was not drawn." The first half of the sentence constitutes my description of the events and the second half constitutes an interpretation. Another example appears in the second episode's analysis: "From Kevin's statement 'why isn't this working?' (line 10) I assume that he identified a problem, but had not identified the cause" (Lewis, 2012a, p. 131). The content of my interpretation and its source are explicit.

As an author, I might describe my task as "describing what I think happened." However, this includes relatively distinct elements such as: (1) the events that are part of the overall sequence of events and context; (2) the specific events that shape my opinion; (3) my interpretation based upon those events; and (4) any technical content knowledge a reader might not have. Again, I find this challenging. Exploring the following two sentences in the final paper can capture some of this challenge:

> By experimenting with the rotation of the character, he appeared to be appropriately attending to the direction of the character. However, for a complete

understanding of the bug he also needed to attend to the position of the character.
(Lewis, 2012a, p. 131)

The first phrase presents my description: "By experimenting with the rotation of the character." Unfortunately, even in this simple phrase, the line between description and interpretation is blurry. Specifically, my use of "experimenting with" is not purely descriptive. Instead, "experimenting with" likely evokes a goal-driven action, and I do not provide support for this interpretation. This description could likely be improved by removing "experimenting with" and replacing it with "modifying," which better fits the goal of description rather than interpretation.

Moving on from this imperfection, the second phrase presents my interpretation: "he appeared to be appropriately attending to the direction of the character." With the hedging phrase "appeared to," I signal the claim as interpretive. The third phrase presents technical content: "However, for a complete understanding of the bug he also needed to attend to the position of the character." Here, I attempt to treat the technical details of the bug objectively, without hedging, to clearly communicate an aspect of the episode that relies on content knowledge that a reader might not have. Again, there is a lot to think about in writing and analysis.

31.4.3 Tip – Present Enough Data That Someone Could Disagree with Your Interpretation

In each submission, my reviewers have provided alternative interpretations of the data. Their sometimes forceful presentation of alternative interpretations made me question my work and my interpretations. While initially frustrating, these were sometimes some of the most helpful comments that I received because they helped me identify specific strengths and weaknesses of my analysis.

First and foremost, providing enough data that someone could form an alternative hypothesis is helpful for ensuring that you can get feedback that will help improve the work. This can be challenging because of page limits, but earlier stages of formative feedback can provide the opportunity to expose more of the data to alternative hypotheses. Additionally, I could expose to them how I had chosen to select particular data (see Section 31.3.2). Before my first ICER submission, I had received multiple rounds of feedback, most notably from peers and advisors at the University of California, Berkeley. Second, transparency in the analysis is important because other researchers might not have focused on the same thing if they analyzed your data. I figure it cannot be stated too many times: qualitative methods do not provide a set of prescriptive steps that will produce a particular analysis. As discussed above, the knowledge and perspectives of the researcher are naturally embedded within qualitative analysis. By providing enough data that someone could disagree with you, your reader has the opportunity to critique your interpretations.

Developing alternative interpretations (or "rival hypotheses"; Yin, 2013) has become an essential part of my process of analysis, and I believe it is helpful if this can be made visible to my readers. In a more recent ICER paper (Lewis & Shah, 2015), my collaborator and I compiled a list of alternative hypotheses and discussed the strengths and weaknesses of each in the paper.

31.4.4 Tip – Explain Why You Chose Qualitative Methods

In the process of writing this chapter, I can now see how comments that I had dismissed from my 2010 reviewers may have actually been a symptom of not explaining why I chose qualitative methods. Across my reviews, I think that reviewers' comments requesting more standard data collection and analysis suggest that I had not done the work of explaining why qualitative data collection and analysis were appropriate. My 2010 submission did little more than describe the work as "a fine grain analysis." The "Data Collection" section in my 2011 submission said:

> The data collection was designed to capture students engaged in programming and debugging … Rather than gathering information such as performance on quizzes, we attempted to capture students' process of solving problems.

This specified what data were collected, but not why. The text removed between the two sentences above further described the content of that data. However, my study design had reasons for the data collection and analysis. Only in the final draft, after the 2012 submission, did I explain the reason for my use of qualitative data analysis within the methods section:

> There are a number of challenges in studying students' debugging behavior. Observing students debugging their own buggy code does not provide any consistency across research participants because the bugs they identify and fix will be unique. However, observing students debugging uniform bugs in code they did not write may be an unfamiliar experience for students and not representative of their behavior debugging their own code. The methods used in this study prioritized observing natural debugging behavior rather than documenting behavior that could easily be compared across research participants.
> (Lewis, 2012a, p. 128)

Here, I situate my goal of "observing natural debugging behavior" as central to the research question of understanding students' debugging behavior. I try to make the point that no other methods would be sensible, and I remind the reader of these points in the conclusion.

31.4.5 Tip – Explain the Limitations of the Work

In the CS education community, much of the research is quantitative. At times, it seems that reviewers are critiquing my work for not being quantitative or are implicitly critiquing the fact that I am not making quantitative claims. I am sympathetic to slipping into the dominant, quantitative frame. In the CS education research course that I teach, some students initially propose a quantitative research question for their qualitative research project. Quantitative studies are so common that warning students about this pitfall does not seem to particularly help. Instead, I have found that the prompt, "Would this question be better answered with thousands of research participants?" can help students evaluate their research question once it is written. A quantitative research question might motivate the study, but the selection of qualitative methods implies that we are not yet able to conduct a quantitative study about the topic.

I believe that in addition to motivating the use of qualitative methods, it is necessary to specify what the analysis does not claim. It is not sufficient merely not to include unsupported quantitative claims. It is necessary to draw the reader's attention to this. For example, in the final version, I included an explanation of these bounds: "The case study is intended to illustrate details of this model, but is not intended to establish the prevalence of this pattern" (Lewis, 2012a, p. 127). Additionally, before presenting the body of the analysis, I reminded the reader about what the analysis does not show: "Case studies like this one are not intended to prove that a particular pattern of behavior exists within a population. Instead, the data serve to inform and exemplify hypotheses regarding features of learning within a domain" (Lewis, 2012a, p. 129). I think these reminders are helpful even if, in principle, they should not be required.

31.4.6 Tip – Explain How Your Analysis Fits into the Ongoing Conversation

I have had a difficult time situating the work within the existing literature. Reviewer 2 in 2010 critiqued my submission for not referencing relevant papers and particularly pressed me to reference relevant papers that had appeared at ICER. My initial response to this comment was righteous indignation; perhaps the reviewer was upset that I had not referenced one of their publications. After years, I have a better understanding of this comment, and I feel a bit of sheepishness for my initial response. In submitting my paper to ICER, I was attempting to join an ongoing conversation. However, by omitting relevant work published at ICER, I appeared ill informed about the current state of the conversation. This was not a self-centered reviewer – this was a reviewer helping me to understand the norms of academic research, and I now appreciate it if reviewers point me to relevant work even if I had made the conscious decision to exclude it.

Beyond including relevant references, the paper's "Previous Research" section should highlight the gap in the extant literature that I am attempting to address and should summarize the extant literature in order to contextualize that gap and bring my reader into the conversation. I have had trouble applying this idea when I think I have a novel insight about the literature or when the literature that inspired me to conduct the study does not actually relate to the contribution I am trying to make in the paper. For example, in my 2010 submission, I thought I was particularly clever for sharing how state was central across different bodies of research:

> This section reviews a diverse set of work that helps emphasize the importance of state. The first category focuses on a reframing of prior misconceptions research with an emphasis on state. The second category

focuses on researchers who either explicitly or implicitly argue for the importance of state. The third category focuses on programming environments that make state visible for novice programmers. (Lewis, 2010)

However, it probably is not that difficult to convince a reader that state is interesting. And these connections did not relate to my analysis beyond the fact that they were about state. In later versions, I cut these connections entirely. If I had kept them, they would probably be best placed in a discussion section. They could possibly fit into a previous research section if I did not repeat the mistake of omitting how the previous research actually motivates the current analysis.

Similarly, in my master's thesis, I foolishly included literature that motivated me in pursuing this line of work. Unrelated to the analysis or results, the abstract of my master's thesis began, "The paper presents a critique of a line of computer science education research that focuses on identifying predictors of programming aptitude and assumes a static view of intelligence." My master's thesis included basically all of the content from the paper I have been describing, but also included a diatribe about arguments claiming that some students could never learn CS. This frame from my master's thesis still provides the underlying motivation for my work, but is utterly disconnected from the analytic work and research questions that I address. It seems silly now, but this previous research was connected for me, and it seemed intuitive that it should be included. I assume that I will continue to make this mistake and hope that I can remember to remove it in later drafts.

31.4.7 Tip – Tie the Motivation to the Analysis

Similar to my instinct to include irrelevant previous literature, I have had difficulty describing the gap in the literature that I am attempting to address. Since qualitative methods do not progress along a prescriptive path, it is not possible to target a narrow gap in the research. Instead, the contribution of the work is emergent. The work forms a picture with many possible connections to the existing literature. Now I see the need to more narrowly motivate the work. Excerpts from the abstracts of each of my ICER submissions show how I was attempting to motivate or otherwise frame the work.

I began with an absurdly huge framing, and in each submission refined the focus. The abstract for my first submission to ICER started to narrow in on the construct of state: "State is a technical computer science term for the current environment of a computer program. I argue that the concept of state is as difficult to learn and central to programming as the concept of force within physics education." This is unrelated to the analysis, and the second sentence ends with a bold and unsupported claim. What support do I have for it? None. It is a manifestation of the connections I was starting to make between CS and physics learning. However, that theoretical connection did not come close to providing support for the bold claim I made. The absurdity of this unsupported claim did not appear to be lost on my reviewers. I only mentioned the argument about force in the abstract, which I do not recommend, but because of the absurdity of this claim that probably mitigated some of the damage.

The abstract for my second submission to ICER continued to narrow my focus, and I wisely opted to not lead with an unsupported claim: "To better understand the challenges in learning to program, we conducted a qualitative analysis of young students engaged in debugging computer programs they had written in Scratch." This goal of "understand[ing] the challenges in learning to program" is certainly central to the work. However, this is still far removed from the analytic work of the paper. This likely motivates the majority of CS education research, but is not specific to my project or work.

The abstract for my third submission to ICER further narrowed in on debugging: "To develop a model of students' debugging processes, we conducted a qualitative analysis of young students engaged in debugging computer programs they had written in Scratch." This is almost identical to the previous submission, except that my goal "To better understand the challenges in learning to program" became "To develop a model of students' debugging processes." My analysis is about understanding Kevin's debugging behavior. That is certainly a component of his learning to program, but the narrower focus seems to connect directly to the analysis, and yet is still broad enough to be perceived as generally important. In the future, I will probably only refine my understanding of my primary contribution at the end, but hope to remember to move it to the beginning of the paper.

31.4.8 Tip – Make the Implications for Teaching Explicit

I think that a strength and a weakness of the CS education research community is that many of us are also computing educators. This is a strength because computing educators can readily evaluate claims based upon their own experience, and my reviewers frequently noted that the importance of state was clear to them from their teaching. This is a weakness because, as computing educators, we need to make decisions about what and how to teach, and we might devalue the incremental work of education research. Education research is frequently incremental and may sometimes require years or decades to mature to the point of having clear educational implications. For those of us who are also CS educators, this may be exceptionally frustrating, but it is likely important to accept this in order to make progress in the field.

While I value the incremental work of computing education, in response to the audience of computing educators, of which I am a member, I try to explicitly connect to educators' intuitions and provide concrete recommendations. Without providing recommendations, readers might believe that the research simply documents a deficiency of students. I believe that documenting students' difficulties is productive for improving pedagogy. However, I believe that the responsibility for change rests with the educators and educational institutions.

It is far too tempting to write students off as "bad students" without finding ways that we can change the structures in small and large ways to support their success. The recommendations from my research are essentially always tentative, but by making my tentative recommendations explicit, I can hopefully prevent some misunderstandings that we can let ourselves off the hook by blaming our students. As an educator, I am frequently making small tweaks to my teaching, and if they are really just small tweaks, the risk of doing so before there is research support is probably low.

31.5 Conclusion

Your mileage with these tips may vary. Some of them are very general and may be applicable for qualitative, quantitative, and mixed-methods studies. It seems like "check and organize your data as you go" might be universally necessary. However, these tips came from particular challenges that I have faced in using and writing about qualitative methods. I hope that this will motivate me to return to these tips as a checklist throughout my later projects. I imagine that I might be the person who benefits most from the existence of this chapter, but I hope that it provides some benefit for others.

Beyond the content of the tips, I hope that this chapter helps you see how much is hidden in the unpublished backstories of research papers. Because these stories are unpublished, many people – particularly while pursuing a PhD – come to falsely believe that they are alone in wrestling with the messiness of research and the disappointment of rejection.

Acknowledgments

This chapter was originally a joint venture between myself and Josh Tenenberg. Josh provided the encouragement and coaching to help me recognize and articulate these tips. I honestly couldn't have done it without that support! Thanks, Josh! In addition to the helpful comments of the editors, I appreciate that Michael Clancy, Michael Loui, Mark Guzdial, Sebastian Dziallas, Shriram Krishnamurthi, Kathi Fisler, and Andy Ko provided helpful comments and feedback!

References

Bourdieu, P. (1992). The practice of reflexive sociology (The Paris Workshop). In P. Bourdieu & L. J. D. Wacquant (Eds.), *An Invitation to Reflexive Sociology* (pp. 216–260). Chicago, IL: Chicago University Press.

diSessa, A. A., & Sherin, B. L. (1998). What changes in conceptual change? *International Journal of Science Education*, 20(10), 1155–1191.

Haas, G. (n.d.) BFOIT Introduction to Computer Programming. Retrieved from http://guyhaas.com/bfoit/itp/Iteration.html#more_projects

Lewis, C. M. (2010). How programming environment shapes perception, learning and goals: Logo vs. Scratch. In *Proceedings of the 41st ACM Technical Symposium on Computer Science Education* (pp. 346–350). New York: ACM Press.

Lewis, C. M. (2012a). The importance of students' attention to program state: A case study of debugging behavior. In *Proceedings of the International Computing Education Research Conference (ICER 2012)* (pp. 127–134). New York: ACM Press.

Lewis, C. M. (2012b). *Applications of Out-of-Domain Knowledge in Students' Reasoning about Computer Program State* (PhD dissertation). University of California, Berkeley.

Lewis, C. M., Anderson, R. E., & Yasuhara, K. (2016). I don't code all day: Fitting in computer science when the stereotypes don't fit. In *Proceedings of the 2016 ACM Conference on International Computing Education Research (ICER '16)* (pp. 23–32). New York: ACM Press.

Lewis, C. M., & Shah, N. (2015). How equity and inequity can emerge in pair programming. In *Proceedings of the International Computing Education Research Conference (ICER 2015)* (pp. 41–50). New York: ACM Press.

Lewis, C. M., Yasuhara, K., & Anderson, R. E. (2011). Deciding to major in computer science: A grounded theory of students' self-assessment of ability. In *Proceedings of the Seventh International Workshop on Computing Education Research* (pp. 3–10). New York: ACM Press.

Roth, W.-M. (2006). Textbooks on qualitative research and method/methodology: Toward a praxis of method. *Forum: Qualitative Social Research*, 7(1), 11.

Yin, R. K. (2013). *Case Study Research: Design and Methods*, 5th edn. Thousand Oaks, CA: Sage Publications.

Index

Abelson, H., 19, 384, 622, 624, 663
abstraction, 524, 526–527, 531, 533–534,
    555–557, 622, 784
    CRA, 784–786
academic development, 282–283
academic integrity, 421, 429, 430, 431, 434–435
academic misconduct, 415, 421, 428–429, 434,
    435
access, 482, 483–484, 489
accounts, 183
ACM (Association for Computing
    Machinery), 293, 327, 328, 329
active learning, 304–305, 448–449, 451–452,
    491–492, 502
activities, 182–183, 456–457
activity theory, 217
Adaptive Control of Thought (ACT / ACT-R)
    model, 246
Advanced Placement (AP) exams, 425
Ahadi, A., 680, 686
Aivaloglo, E., 562
algorithm animations, 28–29
algorithm visualization (AV), 650, 651–652
algorithmic thinking, 524, 525–526, 531
algorithms, 29, 256, 380, 513–514, 520, 525–526,
    530, 615–617, 786
    approximation, 617
aliasing, 379, 388
Alice programming environment, 394, 756
Almstrum, V., 532–533
alpha bloat, 168–169
AlSulaiman, S., 670, 671
Amos, D. M., 790–791
analogical encoding, 253
Anderson, G. L., 728
Anderson, J. R., 22, 23, 210, 342
Anderson, R., 26
Angel, P., 464, 501
Angotti, J. A. P., 462
animated representations, 28–29
ANOVA (analysis of variance), 144, 147, 150–157
Anton, G., 464, 501
Apa Pura, 627
APIs (Application Programming Interfaces),
    612–613, 700

approximation algorithms, 617
Armoni, M., 390, 533, 537, 553, 556, 561, 562
artifacts, 183
assessment, 284–286, 358, 414, 415, 416, 421–423,
    425–426, 431–433, 435
    automated, 427, 433, 643, 648–650
    computational thinking, 534–537
    K–12 education, 563
    learning outcomes, 416–417
    plagiarism, 416
assessment design, 414, 415, 418, 429–430
assessment literacy, 424–425
assessment repositories, 426
assurance of learning, 284, 288
ASSYST, 648, 649
attention, 234–235
attitudes, 804, 812
    emotions, 816–817
    engagement, 814–816
    interest, 813–814
automated assessment, 427, 433, 643, 648–650

Ball, D. L., 715, 729
Bandura, A., 299, 806
Barnett, S. M., 250
BASIC, 11, 15, 21, 343
Basso, K. H., 197–198
batch programs, 382
Batista, A. L. F., 462
Bayesian analysis, 133–134
beacons, 22
Bebras (international competition), 535, 537
Beck, L., 454–455
behavioral psychology, 446–447
behaviorism, 244–245, 278–279, 447
Ben-Ari, M., 390, 553, 556, 560, 561, 562, 788,
    793–794
Ben-Bassat Levry, R., 560
Bennedsen, J., 71, 249, 260, 330, 331, 341–342,
    345, 347, 354, 355, 357
Benotti, L., 560
Berland, M., 66, 67, 68, 337
Berlin Model, 549–550, 551, 563
Berliner, D. C., 730
Berry, M., 341, 529

Bers, M. U., 519
biased statements, 494–496
Biggs, J., 280, 282
Black, P., 416–417
black students, 489, 492
blended learning, 449, 457, 458–459
Blikstein, P., 665
blocks-based languages, 19–20, 28, 382, 388, 389–391, 594
BlockyTalky project, 223–224, 620–621
Bodner, G. M., 299–300
Bonferroni correction, 169
Boolean operators, 783
Booth, S. E., 23, 24, 759
Bootstrap project, 26, 244, 566, 590
Boustedt, J., 198–199, 449, 451, 757
Boxer programming language, 19–20, 586, 663
Boyer, E. L., 276–277, 563
Boys' Needlework, 174–178, 179, 181, 186, 194–196, 201
Brady, C. E., 464, 501, 591
Brennan, K., 519, 536, 628
Brooks, F. P., 329
Brooks, R. E., 14, 17, 22, 337, 357
Brown, M. H., 28
Brown, N., 426, 430, 759
Bruner, J. S., 212, 278
Buechley, L., 64, 66, 67–68, 71–72
Burke, Q., 567
Butler, M., 434–435

Campos, P. G., 454
camps, 755–756
Cannara, A. B., 16, 17
Carbone, A., 418, 424, 453
Carroll, J., 431
Carver, S., 21, 587, 588
case comparison, 196, 200–201
Caspersen, M. E., 249, 260, 330, 331, 345, 347, 357
Catrambone, R., 348
Ceci, S. J., 250
childhood education, early, 668–670
chi-squared test, 144, 159
Chizhik, A., 454–455
Christopher (vignette), 492, 493
chunking, 236, 344, 780–781
Clancy, M. J., 27, 66, 73, 344, 788
CLT (cognitive load theory), 84, 257, 258–259, 298–299, 344–345
COBOL, 11, 17
Cochrane, J., 741, 742
code reuse, 419, 433–434
coding, 14–15, 72
cognition, 711
cognitive apprenticeship, 211, 213–215
cognitive constructivism, 448
cognitive development, 242–244, 346–347

cognitive factors, 802–803
cognitive load, 242, 256–259, 261, 343–344, 391
    notional machines, 388
    Parsons' problems, 261
    subgoal labels, 253, 260–261
    worked examples, 259–260
cognitive processes, 279, 790–791
    Adaptive Control of Thought model, 246
    Soar Cognitive Architecture, 246
cognitive psychology, 446, 447–449
cognitive science, 12, 20, 22, 209–210, 231, 232
cognitivism, 246–247, 279, 298, 423
Cohen's d, 130–131
coherence, study design, 98–99
collaborative learning, 452–454, 502, 562–563, 829–830
collusion, 419
Common Lisp, 788
community engagement, 758–759
comparison groups, 128
computation, 513–514, 517, 608–609
computational agents, 515, 516, 517–518, 520, 591
computational design, 532–533
computational literacy, 19, 27, 61–63, 585, 587, 597, 670
computational literacy rationale, 2, 59, 61–63
computational modelling, 513, 524, 529–530
computational systems, 514, 516, 627–628
computational thinking (CT), 61, 211, 513, 514–517, 518–519, 522–525, 530–531, 537–539, 540–541, 587–588, 625, 626–627, 631–632, 722–723
    abstraction, 524, 526–527, 533–534
    algorithmic thinking, 524, 525–526
    assessment, 534–537
    computational agents, 515, 516, 517–518, 520
    computational design, 532–533
    computational literacy, 62–63
    computational modelling, 529–530
    decomposition, 524, 528–529
    evaluation, 529
    generalization, 524, 527–528
    K–12 education, 555–557
    logical thinking, 524, 526
    Papert, 30, 516
    programming, 532–533, 585
    unplugged activities, 532
    Wing, 60–61, 513, 516, 520–521, 587–588
computational thinking rationale, 2, 59, 60–61
Computational Thinking Test (CTt), 536, 537
computer education, 209–211, 216, 557–559, 588–589
computer music, 628–630
computer science (CS), 59–60, 64, 65, 66–68, 70, 72–73, 208, 547–549, 550–551, 594–596, 622–625, 631–632, 670–671
    K–12 education, 569–570

computer science teachers, 72–74, 595
computing, 11, 12, 292, 590, 625, 631–632, 640
Computing at School (CAS) UK, 426, 519, 539, 735
computing devices, 559–561
computing education (CEd), 1–2, 29–30, 31, 56–57, 59–60, 65–66, 67, 68–69, 74–76, 104, 249, 499–500, 584, 622–625, 631–632, 709–710, 718–719, 794–795, 801–802
computing education research (CEdR), 1, 2–4, 11–13, 27, 30, 52–54, 102–103, 225, 231, 246, 360–362, 749, 778, 801
computing paradigms, 607–608
computing pedagogies, 625
computing systems, 607
computing teacher knowledge, 709, 710, 712–716, 719–722
computing technology, 1, 11, 12
concept inventories (CIs), 426
conceptual change, 778–779, 791
confidence interval (CI), 157–158
confounding variable, 129–130
Connolly, T., 462
construct validity, study design, 94
constructionism, 213, 586
constructive alignment, 280, 281, 284, 416
constructivism, 211–213, 218, 278, 423, 447–449
constructivist pedagogies, 212–213, 222, 254–255, 447
content creation, 456, 457
contract cheating, 421, 428, 434
control groups, 128
Cook, P. R., 629–630
Cooper, G., 261, 345
Cooper, S., 394, 460, 559
cooperative learning, 454–455, 829–830
CoRe (content representation), 732–733
Corral, L., 554–555
correctness, 355, 427, 611, 615–618, 648
correlation, 118–125, 159–160
correlation studies, 146
    p-values, 144
CORT (code restructuring tool), 260
cost models, 400–401
course design, 358–359
    K–12 education, 565–568
CPD (continuing professional development), 727–728, 731–732, 734–735, 742–743
    Disciplinary Commons, 739–740
    informal learning, 759–760
    lead teachers, 734–737
    online communities, 759–760
    online professional communities, 741–742
    professional development of teachers, 727–728
    professional learning community, 737–741
        Craig, M., 418, 422, 424
critical thinking, 289, 290

Crosby, M. E., 453
CS1 (Computer Science 1), 328, 330–333, 356–358, 359–360, 617
Csizmadia, A. P., 422, 426
CSP (contributing student pedagogy), 455–457
CSTA (Computer Science Teachers Association), 56, 57
Cullen, R., 815
cultural narratives, 494–497
cultural–historical activity theory (CHAT), 217
curricula, 70–72, 394, 521–522, 547–548, 550, 709
curricular materials, 70
Curzon, P., 518–519, 532
CWSEI (Carl Wieman Science Education Initiative), 862–863

Dalbey, J., 354
Darmstadt Model, 550, 570
data analysis, 97, 187, 193–194, 196–197, 201
    Boys' Needlework, 186, 201
    case comparison, 192–193, 196, 200–201
    ethnographic adequacy, 192, 199–200, 201
    inductive categorization, 191–192, 196, 198–199, 201
    thick description, 190–191, 196, 197–198, 201
data collection, 97, 182–186, 201
    Boys' Needlework, 181, 195
    IDE, 686–695, 699–700
data scales, 106–107
Davis, E. A., 337, 788
Davis, M., 431
de Croock, M. B. M., 344
de Raadt, M., 261
debugging, 12, 14, 21, 22, 391, 399
declarative (explicit) memory, 239–240
decomposition, 524, 528–529, 531
DeLyser, L. A., 565
demonstration languages, 666–667
Denning, P. J., 516, 517, 518, 529, 534, 537
dependent variable (DV), 104–106
descriptive statistical techniques, 107, 131, 133
    graphical, 107–112
    numerical, 113–118
design thinking, 469
design-based research (DBR), 219–222
Dewey, J., 279
Diaz, D., 532–533
Digital Beads, 664
direct instruction, 212–213, 254
DiSalvo, B. J., 223, 391
discipline-based education research (DBER), 292, 295
diSessa, A. A., 19, 27, 61–62, 63, 72, 384, 585, 663
    Boxer programming language, 586
    student misconceptions, 792
dispositions, 289, 804, 817–819

distributed computing, 609, 612–615, 618–622, 625–627
diversity, 463–464, 482–483, 500, 501
diversity of activity, 686
DLCI (Digital Logic Concept Inventory), 308
Doorenbos, J., 754
Dorn, B., 345, 594–595, 742, 753
Driscoll, M. P., 279
Druin, A., 20
du Boulay, J. B. H., 13, 26, 341, 355
Duval, E., 679
Dwyer, H. A., 553, 568
Dynabook, 586

e-books, 645, 647–648, 761
Eckerdal, A., 449, 451, 757, 817
EDM (educational data mining), 679
educational research, 20, 21, 276–277, 297
Ehrlich, K., 22, 23, 337, 386
El Ioini, N., 554–555
embedded programming, 402
emotions, 816–817
Emrich, C., 487
Enbody, R., 809
engagement, 814–816
Engeström, Y., 217
engineering assessment, 303, 308–309
engineering design, 305
engineering education, 292, 293–295, 299–301, 303, 307–308
engineering education research, 292–293, 295–297, 301–303, 309–312
    engineering assessment, 303, 308–309
    engineering epistemologies, 303–304
    engineering learning mechanisms, 303, 304–305
    engineering learning systems, 303, 305–306
    learning theories, 298–299, 301
    mixed methods, 302
    qualitative methods, 302
    systematic literature reviews, 302
engineering epistemologies, 303–304
engineering identity, 297–298, 307–308
engineering learning mechanisms, 303, 304–305
engineering learning systems, 303, 305–306
episodic memory, 239–240
epistemological pluralism, 70
equity, 482, 484, 500–502
equity of participation rationale, 2, 59, 63–65
error messages, 399–400, 650
Esmail, A., 451
ESP (empirical studies of programmers), 24–25
ethical study design, 96
ethnographic adequacy, 192, 199–200, 201
evaluation, 284, 286–288, 529
Evans, C., 424–425
event-driven programs, 382

expectancy-value theory (EVT), 211, 217–218, 219, 300
experimental hypothesis (H_1), 139, 140, 146
experts, 299
Exploring Computer Science (ECS) curriculum, 563–564
external validity, study design, 95–96
externally compiled languages, 666, 667
extraneous cognitive load, 84, 257, 258, 298, 343

Facione, P. A., 289
factorial design, 128
factorial plots, 109–112
Falkner, K., 434–435, 460, 502, 741
Falkner, N., 460, 502, 741
FCI (Force Concept Inventory), 308
feasibility, study design, 92–94
Feaster, Y., 561, 568
feedback, 255, 283–284, 286, 287, 416, 643
    informal learning, 762
Felleisen, M., 566
Fenwick, J. B., 451
Feynman, R. P., 615
Fiebrink, R., 629–630
file drawer problem, 169–170
Fincher, S. A., 26, 68, 84, 97, 338, 339, 354, 415, 422, 426, 759
Fisher, A., 463
Fisler, K., 355, 396, 566, 776, 793
Fitzgerald, S., 787, 793
Fletcher, G. H., 518
flipped classrooms, 304, 449, 457, 458–459
Flot, J., 560
Follman, D. K., 299–300
Foreman, B., 535
formative analytics, 469, 470
formative assessments, 286, 358, 416–417, 432
FORTRAN, 11, 15, 17
Franklin, D., 553, 568
frequencies, 158–159
frequency distributions (FDs), 107–109, 113, 115
Friend, J., 14, 16
Fronza, I., 554–555
functional (FP) paradigms, 380, 381, 382
functional context transfer, 251
functional languages, 383
fundamental ideas, 338

Galison, P., 3
Garrison, L., 790–791
Gasson, J., 118
Geertz, C., 190
Gellenbeck, E., 386
gender narratives, 497–498
gender participation gap, 803, 804–805
generalizability, 223
generalization, 224, 524, 527–528, 531

Georgia Computes! project, 755, 756
germane cognitive load, 257, 258, 298, 343
Gick, M. L., 252
Gidget programming game, 84, 399, 646, 761
Giordano, D., 422, 426
Glitch Game Testers, 223, 391
Go, S., 742
goal orientation, 809–810
Gomez, M. J., 560
Good, J., 809
Goodwin, C., 199, 200
Gordon, M., 754
graduate attributes, 288–289
graphical descriptive statistics, 107–112
graphical languages, 592, 593–594, 665
Green, T. R. G., 13, 14, 28, 334–336, 593
Grissom, S., 787, 793
Grossman, P. L., 729
ground truth annotation, 686
Grover, S., 60, 61, 63, 65, 68–69, 70, 72, 389,
    460, 553, 555, 556, 559, 564
Guo, P. J., 754, 757
Guzdial, M., 26, 61, 63, 67, 69, 71, 73, 345,
    425, 463, 530, 532–533, 558, 590, 591,
    680, 753

hackathons, 758
Haden, P., 118, 422, 452
Hagan, H., 532–533
Hallstrom, J. O., 561, 568
Hancock, C., 336–337
Hansen, A. K., 553, 568
Hansen, E. R., 568
HAR (human activity recognition), 685
Hardin, G., 200
Harel, I., 589
Harlow, D. B., 553, 568
Hattie, J., 283, 739
Hazzan, O., 424, 554
heapsort, 775–776
Heimann, P., 549
Herman, G. L., 783
Hermans, F., 562
hierarchical linear modelling, 167
Hobbs, R., 336–337
Hodges, S., 559–560
Holyoak, K. J., 247, 252
Horn, M. S., 60, 62, 63, 591, 670, 671
House, E. R., 731, 740
Huang, S.-L., 560
human languages, 27
Hundhausen, C. D., 28, 392, 453, 593
Hutchins, E., 514, 711
Hutchison-Green, M. A., 299–300
hypothesis testing, 134–135, 136, 139,
    141–143
  morning coffee, 135, 139, 140
  pair programming, 136–137, 138–139, 140

identity development, 790, 791
IDEs (integrated development environments),
    391, 392, 644–645
  data collection, 686–695, 699–700
  interventions, 680–682, 695–699
  learning analytics, 683–690, 700–701
Ihantola, P., 680, 686
importance, research questions, 86–87
indirection, 777–778
inductive categorization, 195, 196, 198–199,
    201
inferential hypothesis
  morning coffee, 135
  pair programming, 136–137
inferential statistical techniques, 107, 113, 115,
    131, 133–134, 137, 143–145, 146
  ANOVA, 150–157
  chi-squared test, 159
  confidence interval, 157–158
  correlation, 159–160
  frequencies, 158–159
  hypothesis testing, 136
  predictions, 146, 160–163
  t-tests, 144, 146, 147–150
informal learning, 749–751, 756, 760–763
  camps, 755–756
  community engagement, 758–759
  CPD, 759–760
  feedback, 762
  MOOCs, 754, 761
  online communities, 759–760
  online learning, 751–754
  peer learning, 757–758
  self-directed learning, 757
innate ability, 489, 495
Instructional Design Software Project, 589
intelligence, 248, 300–301, 350
intended learning outcome (ILO), 280–281,
    285–286
interactive games, 645–647, 761
interactive machine learning (IML), 628, 630–631
interclass similarity, 686
interest, 813–814
internal validity, study design, 94–95
International Computing Education Research
    (ICER) Conference (2005), 11, 26
International Computing Education Research
    (ICER) Conference (2017), 40–54
Internet, 27
interventions, 358–359
  IDEs, 680–682, 695–699
interviews, 57–59
intraclass variability, 685
intrinsic cognitive load, 257, 258, 298, 343, 344
intrinsic motivation, 300, 538
introductory computing course, 490–491
introductory programming, 12, 260, 327, 353–356
intuition, 778–780, 791

IQ (intelligence quotient), 243, 248, 350
Ishii, H., 664
Israel, M., 562–563
iteration, 394–396
ITSs (intelligent tutoring systems), 683
IVs (independent variables), 109, 125–128
  multiple, 128

Jadud, M., 84, 680
Java, 17, 213, 341, 381, 388, 390, 392, 403
Jaylisha (vignette), 492, 493
Jocuns, A., 790–791
John (vignette), 494, 495, 496

K–10 education, 548
K–12 education, 218, 547–550, 551, 552,
    569–570, 616
  assessment, 563
  Berlin Model, 549–550, 551, 563
  collaborative learning, 562–563
  computational thinking, 555–557
  computing devices, 559–561
  course design, 565–568
  Darmstadt Model, 550, 570
  distributed computing, 619
  programming, 552–554
  software engineering, 554–555
Kaczmarczyk, L. C., 783
Kafai, Y. B., 174, 175, 181, 186, 194–196, 501,
    519, 558, 567, 589
Kahney, H., 16, 787–788
Kanaparan, G., 815
Kastl, P., 555
Kay, A., 18, 19, 586, 588
Keating, D. P., 814–815
Kelleher, C., 356, 643, 756
Kellogg, S. B., 759
Kemeny, J. G., 584, 589
Khayarallah, H., 564
Kiara (vignette), 488–489, 490
KIBO, 667, 668–670, 671
Kiesler, S., 756
KIesmüller, U., 555
Kim, A. S., 754
Kim, J., 754
Kinnunen, P., 808, 817
knowledge domain transfer, 250–251
Ko, A. J., 83–84, 96, 97, 383, 399, 754
Koh, J., 670, 671
Kolikant, Y. B., 532–533, 730
Kölling, M., 335, 341, 426, 759, 760
Krishnamurthi, S., 566, 776
Kurland, D. M., 20–21
Kurtz, B. L., 451
Kurtz, T. E., 584, 589

labor market rationale, 2, 59, 60
Lane, D. M., 487

language acquisition, 244, 403
language design, 13, 14–15
language tools, 639, 641
Lash, T., 562–563
Lave, J., 216, 278, 790
Laxer, C., 532–533
lead teachers, 734–737
Leake, M., 760
learning analytics, 449, 469–470, 654, 679–682,
    683
  IDE, 683–690, 700–701
learning communities, 448
learning outcomes, 352–353, 416–417, 801–802
learning programming, 11, 12–13, 20–23, 584,
    639–640
learning sciences, 208–211, 218–219, 222–223,
    224–225
  cognitive apprenticeship, 211, 213–215
  constructivism, 211–213, 218
  expectancy-value theory, 211, 217–218
  sociocultural theory, 211, 216–217, 219
learning sciences research, 209, 219
  design-based research, 219–222
learning theories, 246, 277–280, 423, 700–701,
    709
  engineering education research, 298–299,
    301
  sociocultural theory, 211, 216–217, 219,
    710–712
Lee, I., 501, 518, 538
Lee, M. J., 83–84, 399
LEM (learning edge momentum), 351–352,
    359–360
lesson study, 738–741
levels of analysis, 232–234, 262–263
Lewis, C. M., 389, 564, 760
Likert scales, 114, 115
linear regression, 161, 162–166
  hierarchical linear modeling, 167
  logistic regression, 167
  multiple linear regression, 167
Linn, M. C., 27, 344, 354, 788
Lishinski, A., 809
LISP, 22, 23
literacy, 597
Liu, A., 560
Lloyd, M., 741, 742
logic paradigms, 380
logical thinking, 524, 526, 531
logistic regression, 167
Logo programming language, 13, 15–16, 17,
    18, 20, 21, 56, 210, 585–586, 587, 663,
    787–788
Logo turtle, 15, 18, 20, 663
long-term memory (LTM), 237–240, 251
Loui, M. C., 783
Lu, J. J., 518
Luria, A. R., 189–190

machine learning (ML), 609–612, 617, 618, 623–624, 628, 630–631
MacLeod, E., 559–560
Maiorana, F., 422, 426
Malik (vignette), 492, 493
Mann, L. M., 788
Mañoso, C., 464, 501
Marcos (vignette), 494, 495, 496
marginalization, 484, 486, 494, 497–499, 500
Margolis, J., 66, 67, 68, 73–74, 463
Margulieux, L. E., 225, 260–261, 348
Marr, D., 232
Marsden, S., 422, 426
Martell, R. F., 487
Martin, F., 336–337
Martinez, C., 560
Mason, D. D. M., 815
Mason, R., 261, 345
Mayer, R. E., 15, 17, 341, 343, 355, 357
Mazur, E., 835, 836
McCartney, R., 449, 451, 455, 757, 787, 793
McCracken Working Group, 25–26, 331, 417–418, 425, 432
McCracken, M., 532–533
Mead, J., 345
measures of central tendency (MCT), 113–115
measures of effect size, 130–131
Medel, P., 464, 501
media computation, 451, 463, 502
Media Computation curriculum, 596
Meerbaum-Salant, O., 390, 424, 553, 554, 556
Melvin, O., 562–563
memory, 232, 235, 240–242, 246, 279
    long-term memory, 237–240, 251
    sensory memory, 235–236, 237
    short-term memory, 236, 237
    working memory, 236–237, 344
memory categories, 240–241
mental models, 22, 26–27, 248, 340–341, 342–343, 358, 403
    notional machines, 341–342, 387, 465, 466–467
message passing, 620
metacognitive self-regulation, 811
microaggressions, 495, 496
Middle-years Computer Science (MyCS) project, 566–567
Miller, B., 754
Miller, L. A., 13–14, 387, 593, 807
MIMN (multi-institutional, multinational), 25–26
Mishra, S., 422, 426
Miura, I. T., 815
mixed-methods research, 302
modality transfer, 251
MOOCs (massive open online courses), 449, 457, 459–461, 502, 653, 741–742, 750, 751, 754, 761

Morgan, M., 434–435
morning coffee (hypothesis testing), 135, 139, 140
Morrison, B. B., 225, 247, 261, 345
Moström, J. E., 757
motivation, 299–301, 644, 804, 805, 812
    expectancy-value theory, 217–218, 219
multinational, multi-institutional (MNMI) studies, 82, 96, 97
multiple independent variables, 128
multiple linear regression, 167
multi-way ANOVA, 150–151
Murphy, L., 787, 793

Narayanan, N. H., 453
narratives, 481, 485, 488
    unconscious bias, 485–488
National Teachers' Centers (NTCs), Israel, 737
NCTM (National Council of Teachers of Mathematics), 57
Nelson, G. L., 383
neo-Piagetian theories, 243, 347, 350
NetLogo, 591, 626
neural networks, 610–612
NHST (null hypothesis significance testing), 133–134
Ni, L., 595
Nia (vignette), 488–489, 490
noncognitive factors, 802, 803, 819–820
    attitudes, 804, 812
    dispositions, 804, 817–819
    gender participation gap, 803, 804–805
    motivation, 804, 805, 812
nonparametric tests, 168
normalization, 115–118
notional machines, 12, 15, 17, 26–27, 248, 358, 382–384, 385–386, 387–388, 651, 786
    mental models, 341–342, 387, 465, 466–467
    object-oriented (OO) languages, 383, 393
    pedagogic practices, 464–467
    programming languages, 383, 398
novelty, research questions, 87–89
novice programmers, 23, 29, 217, 247, 251–252, 327, 335–337, 348–352, 356
    engineering education research, 299
    language design, 14–15
    notional machines, 383
    programming difficulties, 13–14, 18, 242, 334–336
    programming knowledge, 337–339
    programming strategies, 339–340
NSTA (National Science Teachers Association), 57
null hypothesis (H_0), 139, 140, 141, 142–143, 144–145, 146
numerical descriptive statistics, 113–118

O'Connor, K., 790–791
Obama, B., 1, 709, 722, 736

object-oriented (OO) languages, 380–381,
    392–394
    notional machines, 383, 393
object-oriented (OO) paradigms, 380–381, 382
object-oriented (OO) programming, 18–19,
    788, 793–794
one-tailed t-tests, 149
one-way ANOVA, 150, 154
online communities, 759–760
online learning, 751–754
online professional communities, 741–742
online Q&A communities, 753
operational definition (OD), 104, 105
order effects, 126–127
Orton, K., 464, 501
Ostrom, E., 200–201
outcomes-based education (OBE), 280, 281
outliers, 121

Page, B., 728
pair programming (PP), 160, 422, 451, 455,
    827–829, 830–834
    hypothesis testing, 136–137, 138–139, 140
Palumbo, D. J., 21, 71, 354, 587, 588
Pane, J. F., 387, 593
Papert, S., 18, 21, 30, 56, 70, 557, 622–623, 624,
    627, 628, 631, 720–721
    computational thinking, 30, 516
    constructionism, 213
    learning programming, 12, 584, 623
    Logo programming language, 13, 15, 56,
        210, 585–586, 663
paradigms, 377, 379–382, 386, 402–403
parametric tests, 168
Parsons' problems, 261, 355, 422, 452, 781
Parsons, D., 118, 422, 452
Pascal, 11, 15, 16–17, 22, 23, 401
Pasternak, A., 565
Pausch, R., 356, 394, 643, 756
PCK (pedagogical content knowledge), 728–731,
    732, 734–735, 742–743
    CoRe, 732–733
    TPACK model, 733–734
Pea, R., 17, 20–21, 26, 30, 386, 460, 559, 586,
    587
Pearson product moment correlation (r), 119–121,
    159–160
pedagogic practices, 446, 449–451, 461–464,
    467–470, 716–718
    active learning, 304–305, 448–449, 451–452,
        491–492, 502
    blended learning, 449, 457, 458–459
    collaborative learning, 452–454, 502, 562–
        563, 829–830
    cooperative learning, 454–455, 829–830
    CSP, 455–457
    notional machines, 464–467
pedagogical code reviews (PCRs), 845

pedagogy, 445–446, 461, 501–502
    behavioral psychology, 446–447
    cognitive psychology, 446, 447–449
peer assessment, 455–456
peer instruction (PI), 451, 453, 827, 834–842,
    861–864, 869, 870–873
    UC San Diego, 863–868, 869–870
peer learning, 757–758
peer review, 456
PeerWise system, 457
perception, 234
Perkins, D. N., 336–337
Perlis, A. J., 27, 29, 589
Perlman, R., 20, 665
personal learning environment (PLE), 751
personality traits, 804, 817–819
Petersen, A., 418, 422, 424
Petre, M., 26, 28, 422, 593
p-hacking, 170–171
Phelps, G., 715, 729
phenomenography, 23–24, 198–199, 281
physical context transfer, 251
Piaget, J., 212, 243, 346–347, 350, 533
plagiarism, 414, 416, 418–421, 427–428,
    430–431, 433–434, 435
    contract cheating, 421, 428, 434
plugin IDE, 687, 699–700
Portillo, J. A. P., 454
Pournaghshband, V., 464, 501
PPIG (Psychology of Programming Interest
    Group), 24
predictions, 146, 160–163
predictor variables, 161
probabilistic thinking, 617–618
problem-solving, 71, 247, 248–249, 354
    analogical encoding, 253
    schemata, 22, 253–254
    worked examples, 252–253
problem-based learning (PBL), 282,
    305, 451
procedural (implicit) memory, 239
process-oriented guided inquiry learning
    (POGIL), 827, 848–853
productive failure, 215–216, 468
professional communities, 216
professional learning community (PLC),
    737–742
program visualization (PV), 28–29, 642, 647,
    650–652
programmer aptitude tests (PATs), 328–329
programming, 12–13, 27–29, 327–330, 333–334,
    352, 360–362, 377, 584–585, 587, 588–589,
    591–592, 596–598, 623, 625, 790
    computational thinking, 532–533, 585
    difficulties, 13–14, 18, 242, 334–336
programming knowledge, 337–339
programming languages, 11, 17, 20–23, 28,
    71–72, 327, 334, 352, 355–356, 377–378,

386–387, 391–392, 397–398, 586–587, 592–594, 597, 598, 639, 644–645
error messages, 399–400, 650
notional machines, 383, 398
paradigms, 377, 379–382, 386, 402–403
problem-solving, 396–397
syntax, 378–379
types, 401
programming models, 402
programming paradigms, 12
programming plans, 22
programming processes, 27
programming strategies, 339–340
Project Quantum, 426, 535
Prolog language, 22, 788–789
property of interest (PI), 103–105
prospective memory, 240
public education, 180
Pulimood, S. M., 463–464
p-values, 144, 145

qualitative research, 4, 201–202, 302, 875–877, 885–886, 888–892
data analysis, 879–888
data collection, 877–879
qualitative research studies, 173–174, 187–190
Boys' Needlework, 174–178, 179, 181, 186, 187–188, 194–196
case comparison, 192–193
ethnographic adequacy, 192
inductive categorization, 191–192
sampling, 180–181
thick description, 190–191
quantitative methods, 188, 301–302
quantum computing, 609, 615–616, 617–618, 621–622, 631

racial narratives, 494–496
Racket language, 620
radiation problem (Duncker), 252
Ragonis, N., 788, 793–794
Rainfall Problem (Soloway, 1986), 249, 396–397, 793
reading pedagogy, 789–790
reasoning, 189, 232, 247–249, 781–784, 791
recursion, 394–396
recursive thinking, 525
reductions, 774–775
regression, 161–162
hierarchical linear modelling, 167
linear regression, 161, 162–166
logistic regression, 167
multiple linear regression, 167
Reinecke, K., 754
Reiser, B. J., 23
repetition, 394–396
research questions, 83–91, 173, 178–179

Resnick, M., 20, 26, 62, 63, 70, 72, 519, 536, 625–626, 628, 664
retrospective memories, 240
Riedesel, C., 422, 426, 455, 533
Rist, R. S., 246, 338, 340, 354
Robins, A., 247, 351
robots, 463, 528, 560, 671–672
KIBO, 667, 670, 671
Logo turtle, 15, 18, 20, 663
Rodriguez, S., 464, 501, 563
Romeike, R., 555
Romero-Zaliz, R., 464, 501
Rubin, R., 754
Rubio, M. A., 464, 501
rule systems, 786–789

sampling, 180–181
Sanders, K., 449, 451, 455, 757, 794
scaffolding, 214, 215, 219, 243, 393
scaffolding tools, 643–644
scatter plots (scattergrams), 112, 119, 121
SCCT (Social Cognitive Career Theory), 298
Schaeffer, L. M., 348
Schanzer, E., 566
schemata, 22, 253–254, 298
schemata, memory, 241–242
Schneider, G. M., 354
Schulte, C., 341–342
Schunn, C., 560
Scratch projects, 554, 555, 567, 619
Searle, K., 174, 175, 181, 186, 194–196, 501
Segars, L., 561
Seiter, L., 535, 557
Selby, C., 519, 529, 532
self-determination theory (SDT), 300
self-directed learning, 757
self-efficacy, 298, 299–300, 308, 806–809, 812, 819
self-regulated learning theory (SRL), 89–90, 805
goal orientation, 809–810
metacognitive self-regulation, 811
self-efficacy, 806–809, 812, 819
semantic memory, 239–240
semantic waves, theory of, 539
sensory memory (SM), 235–236, 237
Sentance, S., 62–63, 65, 66, 559–560, 737
Shapiro, R. B., 67, 69, 223–224, 621
Shapka, J. D., 814–815
Sheard, J., 418, 424, 434–435, 453, 455
Shehab, S., 562–563
Sherin, B. L., 590, 591
Shoop, R., 560
short-term memory (STM), 236, 237
Shulman, L. S., 277, 715, 728–729, 730
Siebert, S., 386
SIGCSE (Special Interest Group in Computer Science Education, ACM), 25, 26, 231, 329

Sime, M. E., 14
Simmons, R., 336–337
Simon, B., 423, 424, 434–435, 808, 817
Simon, H. A., 209, 640
Sirkiä, T., 452, 466
Sleeman, D., 17, 27
Smalltalk, 18–19, 586
smart block languages, 666, 667
Smetsers, S., 556
Smetsers-Weeda, R., 556
Snow, E., 29, 563
Soar Cognitive Architecture, 246
social constructivism, 278, 827
social context transfer, 251
social justice, 484, 500
social media, 449, 468
sociocultural constructivism, 448
sociocultural theory, 211, 216–217, 219,
    710–712
software engineering, 554–555, 684
software tools, 639–641, 650
SOLO taxonomy, 16, 347–348, 350, 422, 423–424,
    535, 589
Soloway, E., 22, 23, 336, 337, 342, 355, 356,
    386, 396
Sorva, J., 28, 29, 341, 343, 344, 346, 389, 466,
    652
    notional machines, 387
    SOLO taxonomy, 424
SOTL (Scholarship of Teaching and
    Learning), 222, 294–295
soundness, research questions, 86
spaced practice, 255
Spohrer, J. C., 336, 355, 356
spontaneous transfer, 250, 256
Stager, G., 69
standard deviation, 115
Stasko, J. T., 28
state, 384–385
statistical errors, 168, 171
    alpha bloat, 168–169
    file drawer problem, 169–170
    p-hacking, 170–171
statistical techniques, 103, 106, 107, 121, 171
    descriptive statistical techniques, 131, 133
    descriptive statistics, graphical, 107–112
    descriptive statistics, numerical, 113–118
    inferential statistical techniques, 107, 113,
        131, 133–134
statistical thinking, 617–618
Stefik, A., 386, 392
STEM (science, technology, engineering, and
    mathematics), 56, 500, 631, 721
stereotype threat, 490, 491
Stevens, P., 426, 759
Stevens, R., 790–791
structural racism, 487, 489
student feedback, 287

student misconceptions, 303–304, 388, 773–774,
    776–777, 779, 791–794
    heapsort, 775–776
    indirection, 777–778
    reductions, 774–775
student participation, 492–493, 494
student-centered teaching, 281–282
students of color, 489
studio-based learning (SBL), 451, 453–454,
    827, 842–847
study design, 81–82, 85, 90–92, 96–100, 187
    ethical, 96
    feasibility, 92–94
    research questions, 83–91
    validity, 94–96
subgoal labels, 225, 253, 260–261, 348
sublanguages, 398
summative assessments, 286
superbug, 17, 26
Suzanne (vignette), 497
syntax, 378–379
System Blocks project, 665
systematic literature reviews, 302

tangibility, 663–664, 667–668, 671
tangible computing, 672–674
tangible languages, 665–666, 671, 672
    demonstration languages, 666–667
    externally compiled languages, 666, 667
    smart block languages, 666, 667
Tashakkori, R., 451
Tate, S. R., 451
Taub, R., 561, 562
taxonomy of learning objectives, Bloom, 346,
    348, 422, 423, 424
Teachback, 468
teacher knowledge, 72–74, 595, 714–717, 723,
    728
    computing teachers, 709, 710, 712–716,
        719–722
    PCK, 728–731, 742–743
teaching methods, 17–18
technology, 449
temporal context transfer, 251
Tenenberg, J., 26
text-based languages, 28, 389, 390, 592, 593,
    594, 665
Thames, M. H., 715, 729
thick description, 196, 197–198, 201
Thies, R., 551, 561–562
Thomas, L., 532–533, 757, 794
three-way ANOVA, 153–154
threshold concepts, 338–339
Timperley, H., 283
Toll, D., 680, 686
tools, 11, 29, 639–644, 645–647, 653–656
    assessment, 648–650
    e-books, 645, 647–648, 761

feedback, 648–650
interactive games, 645–647, 761
software tools, 639–641, 650
TPACK (Technological, Pedagogical and
    Content Knowledge) model, 733–734
trading zones, 3
transfer in learning, 71, 254–256, 355, 385–386,
    403, 588
    analogical encoding, 253
    schemata, 253–254
    worked examples, 252–253
translation, 13–14
transparent teaching, 491
Trueman, D., 629–630
Tsai, A., 564
Tseng, I.-C., 560
t-tests, 144, 146, 147–150
Turing machine, 514, 608, 615
Turkle, S., 70, 557, 623, 624, 720–721
turtles, 27
    Logo turtle, 15, 18, 20, 663
two-way ANOVA, 151–153, 154–156
types, 401

UC San Diego (UCSD), 863–868, 869–870
Ullmer, B., 664
unconscious bias, 485–488, 489–490, 493,
    498–499
underrepresentation, 177, 481–482, 487, 803
units of analysis, 193–194
unplugged activities, 532, 561–562
user interface technologies, 19, 20
Utting, I., 426, 532–533, 759

Vahrenhold, J., 551, 561–562, 565, 809
validity, 92–94, 187, 537
van Merriënboer, J. J. G., 260, 344
variability, 115
Verbert, K., 679
video games, 223, 469
Vihavainen, A., 680, 686
Vinikiene, L., 422, 426
visual languages, 388–389, 665
visualization, 465–467, 644, 652–653
Vivian, R., 460, 502, 741
von Neumann machine, 608
Vygotsky, L. S., 189, 212, 214, 243, 278, 448

Wahba, S. K., 561
Waite, J., 559–560
Warner, J., 754
Wason selection test, 781, 782–783
Web-CAT, 648, 649
Weerasinghe, A., 434–435
Weinberg, G. M., 13, 14, 329, 336
Weintrop, D., 28, 389, 390, 391, 464, 501, 553
Wenger, E., 216, 278, 448, 790
Western Apache, 197–198
Weyer, S. A., 17
Wherfel, Q. M., 562–563
White, J., 754
Wiedenbeck, S., 22, 342, 393, 808, 809
Wilensky, U., 28, 389, 390, 391, 464, 501, 553,
    591, 625–626
Wiliam, D., 416–417
Williams, S., 460, 741
Wilson, G., 594
Wilusz, T., 532–533
Wing, J., 60–61, 517
    computational thinking, 60–61, 513, 516,
        520–521, 587–588
Winslow, L. E., 331, 336, 354
Wolz, U., 463–464, 567, 568
Wood, K., 118, 568
Woollard, J., 519, 529, 532
worked examples, 252–253
    subgoal labels, 225, 253
working memory, 236–237, 344
Woszczynski, A. B., 567
Wu, C.-C., 560

Xie, B., 383

Yadav, A., 809
Yeomans, L., 559–560
Yongpradit, P., 61, 66, 67, 69, 72, 73

Zander, C., 449, 451, 757
Zanelatto, R., 754
Zhu, J., 754
Zilles, C. B., 783
Zingaro, D., 418, 422, 424, 840
zone of proximal development (ZPD), 214,
    243–244, 448, 712, 716
z-scores (normal scores), 117–118

Lightning Source UK Ltd.
Milton Keynes UK
UKHW051242080419
340595UK00014B/59/P